D1550519

OPERANT BEHAVIOR

THE CENTURY PSYCHOLOGY SERIES

Richard M. Elliott, Gardner Lindzey & Kenneth MacCorquodale

Editors

OPERANT BEHAVIOR

Areas of Research and Application

edited by
WERNER K. HONIG
Dalhousie University, Canada

NEW YORK

APPLETON-CENTURY-CROFTS

DIVISION OF MEREDITH PUBLISHING COMPANY

Acknowledgments

The following publishers and journals have kindly granted permission to reproduce or adapt previously published figures to which they hold the copyright:

American Association for the Advancement of Science, seven figures from *Science*.

American Physiological Society, two figures from the *American Journal of Physiology*.

American Psychological Association, one figure from the *Journal of Abnormal and Social Psychology*; 18 figures from the *Journal of Comparative and Physiological Psychology*; and 14 figures from the *Journal of Experimental Psychology*.

Canadian Journal of Psychology, one figure.

Child Development Publications, seven figures from *Child Development*.

Federation of American Societies for Experimental Biology, one figure from *Federation Proceedings*.

Journal of Chronic Diseases, one figure.

Journal of the Experimental Analysis of Behavior, 45 figures.

Journal Press, one figure from *Genetic Psychology Monographs* and one figure from the *Journal of Psychology*.

J. B. Lippincott Co., one figure from *Endocrinology*.

New York Academy of Sciences, one figure from the *Annals of the New York Academy of Sciences*.

Optical Society of America, one figure from the *Journal of the Optical Society of America*.

Psychological Reports, 1957, 3, 243-250; one figure, reproduced with permission of author and publisher.

Scientific American, two figures.

Stanford University Press, one figure from *Stimulus Generalization*, edited by David Mostofsky.

Williams and Williams Co., two figures from the *Journal of Pharmacology and Experimental Therapeutics*.

From *Conflict and Creativity* edited by Farber and Wilson. Copyright © 1963 McGraw-Hill, Inc. Used by permission of McGraw-Hill Book Company. One figure.

From S. Fisher (Ed.), *Child Research in Psychopharmacology*, 1959. Courtesy of Charles C Thomas, Publisher, Springfield, Illinois. One figure.

Credit for the source of every figure is briefly indicated in the caption of each figure where appropriate, in the style used for referencing in the text of this book. The full source is entered in the reference list at the end of the appropriate chapter.

In any edited book, the contributing authors deserve the credit for its content. So it is with this volume. It has been a pleasure for me to work and to correspond with them, and while any project of this size is subject to delays, frustrations and sometimes disagreements, my contact with the contributors has been on the whole a happy experience. Some contributors would have cause for complaint, either because they completed a manuscript on time and had to wait for its publication, or because they were called on more or less at the last minute and asked to prepare a chapter under pressure of time. It is to their credit that I have heard very few complaints.

I wish to acknowledge the support and encouragement of colleagues at Denison University, particularly Irvin Wolf, Paul Mountjoy, and Edward Hovorka, who urged me to proceed with this project in its difficult early stages. Later on, I valued the cooperation of Kenneth MacCorquodale, series editor for Appleton-Century-Crofts, and of the editorial staff of that publishing house.

I am grateful to Miss Megan Kemp, Miss Valerie Speed, and Miss Linda Nelson for their secretarial services, and to Mrs. Norma Gilgan, who typed the index. I called on them often and at considerable length as this book neared completion.

In all phases of the planning and preparation of this volume, the support and help of my wife Cecily have been invaluable. Several years ago she typed the first letters to the contributors, asking whether they would be willing to contribute to a volume of this kind. Since then, she has typed numerous editorial comments, read manuscripts, checked references, read proof and more proof, and finished up compiling a name index containing close to a thousand entries. Without her help on these tasks, the publication of this volume would have been delayed; in fact, it might never have come about at all.

Halifax, Nova Scotia   W.K.H.

Contents

Introductory Remarks [1]

Werner K. Honig

SCOPE AND PURPOSE

Each chapter in this book describes an area of thought and research in psychology where operant methods are used. Some areas, such as the study of schedules (Chapter 3) and of fully programmed environments (Chapter 19) have grown directly out of the development of operant methodology. Other areas, such as physiological psychology (Chapter 13) and the behavior of children (Chapter 17) have a longer history; in these, operant methods have been applied to traditional problems, often with remarkable success. While the various chapters vary a good deal in organization and coverage, most of them provide a description of the methods employed and a survey of the major findings in the area with which the chapter is concerned. Implications of the findings for current empirical and theoretical problems are also discussed. While this book would ideally provide a complete survey of the use of operant methods, this is almost impossible to accomplish in an edited volume. Their use is expanding so rapidly that certain areas have developed even since this book was planned. Furthermore, the delays which inevitably arise in the writing and editing of nineteen chapters by different authors, have prevented coverage of the most recent material in some of them. Regrettable as these gaps are, they do illustrate the lively interest in operant methods and the expansion of their use. The material contained in this book thus portrays an active aspect of current psychology, and even if the portrait is not quite complete, at least its subject is very much alive.

The integration of operant methods into modern psychology is a recent development as well as an important one. Skinner's earliest papers date back only three decades, and even much more recently, the use of operant meth-

[1] John Boren, Roger Kelleher, and John McNulty read the original draft of these remarks and made many valuable suggestions. Chapter 12 by John Boren originally contained a section on the general characteristics of operant methods; at my request, he eliminated it from his chapter and very kindly permitted me to incorporate portions of the material in these introductory remarks.

ods was considered by many to be odd and rather fruitless. One professor of mine was of the opinion that putting an organism into a "Skinner box" taught us a lot about the workings of the box, and very little about the workings of the organism. While this attitude has certainly become less frequent within the last decade, some psychologists still think that with a restricted environment and a limited opportunity for a variety of responses, operant methods are more suitable for the study of simple processes rather than more complex, higher-level behaviors. Much of the material in this book will counteract such an impression, if it is still current. Furthermore, operant methods provide efficient ways of investigating those basic psychological functions of which the more complex performances may well be composed.

Operant methods provide one approach to the study of instrumental behavior in general. The distinction between operant and instrumental behavior is almost entirely methodological: the study of operant behavior involves the repeated emission of the same response, while the study of instrumental behaviors also includes those situations where the response of interest occurs only once per trial, or where a complex sequence of different responses is involved. As a result, the primary dependent variable in operant studies tends to be response rate; in other instrumental studies, topography, latency, amplitude, or probability are often measured. These distinctions are not always clearcut: concurrent operants of widely differing topographies may be studied together (Chapter 6); interresponse times (the latencies of repeated responses) are used in data analysis (Chapter 3); there is a new emphasis on operant response topography, particularly in discrimination learning (Chapter 7); and discrete trials terminated by an operant response are used in some areas such as discriminated avoidance (Chapter 11). Nevertheless, the distinction that I have suggested is valid in a general sense, and it may be useful to review the general characteristics of operant methods and of the conceptual developments for which they are responsible. Such a general review is not presented in any one of the chapters that follow, and the material for this introduction is distilled largely from their more specific contents.

CHARACTERISTICS OF OPERANT METHODS

The discovery of order within the subject matter of a science is an essential ingredient of the scientific enterprise. It requires precision not only of the method of investigation, but also of the identification of the events that are observed and the relationships between them. In psychology, the subject matter consists of evanescent events rather than an array of permanently available objects, and the repeatability of findings in a given situation is therefore essential. Operant methods facilitate precision in research in a number of ways.

The Intensive Study of Individual Subjects

Typically, a small number of subjects is used in an experiment. With close observation and firm experimental control, the individual subject will behave predictably from session to session and even from minute to minute. This provides a stable "baseline" condition upon which the independent variable of interest is imposed. Thus, when an effective drug is injected in the middle of a session, or when the nature of the reinforcement or the characteristics of a discriminative stimulus are changed, the deviation from baseline behavior should be apparent even in the individual subject.

One of the most intractable methodological problems in traditional psychology has been inter-subject variability, which often results in between-group differences caused by factors other than the independent variable whose effects are being studied. With operant methods, the same subjects can often be run under all conditions of the independent variable, thus eliminating these differences. In some experiments, order effects among different treatments make it difficult to carry out this strategy; but this problem can often be resolved at least in part by counterbalancing or randomizing the order of treatments, or by letting the behavior reach a steady state under each condition, when it is reasonable to suppose that the effects of the previous condition will not be permanent. Furthermore, order effects may be small compared to the inter-subject differences described above. Even when independent groups are necessary, good experimental control is not wasted, since it will reduce inter- as well as intra-subject variability.

Control of the Experimental Environment

With animal subjects, the basic apparatus is often a closed box inside a sound-resistant, light-proof shell. In its simple form, the box contains little more than an operandum, a few stimulus sources for light and sound, and a reinforcement mechanism. The purposes of the isolation are two-fold: to eliminate unwanted external influences and to provide an environment where the experimenter can precisely control the critical variables. Thus, if there is a sudden change in response rate, this can be attributed to a condition wilfully imposed, rather than an accidental extraneous stimulus.

Environmental control permits the use of the powerful "yoked box" (or "yoked chair") technique when independent groups of subjects have to be used in an experiment. In this method, two (or more) subjects are run concurrently, and all conditions are identical in both boxes except for some critical difference, such as the relationship between the subject's response and the consequence of the response. Thus, one subject may avoid shocks by pressing a lever, while the lever presses of the second subject are ineffective, but both receive shocks at the same time when the first subject fails to avoid them (see Chapter 14).

Use of a Repetitive Response That Has Little Immediate Effect upon the Environment

Environmental constancy as well as environmental control are necessary for behavioral stability. The stability of rate as a dependent variable is partly due, no doubt, to the fact that individual responses such as lever pressing and key pecking produce little change in the organism's environment as a direct result of their execution. The feedback that they do produce is consistent, so that rapid adaptation can take place. In a maze or a runway, the behavior of interest—locomotion—changes the subject's environment, and is likely to cause changes in the performance. In operant situations, the occurrence of programmed consequences (as distinguished from response-produced feedback) usually removes the subject from the relevant discriminative stimuli only temporarily. When punishment occurs, for example, changes in behavior are not caused by the subject's running away from the place where he is punished and thus removing himself from the situation. When long-term stimulus changes are programmed as a consequence of a response, as in a chained reinforcement schedule, this change is usually the only one that occurs while the rest of the environment stays constant. If the effect of immediate response-produced changes are minimized, the effects of programmed consequences will be maximized.

Effective Means of Controlling the Subject's Behavior

In operant studies, the experimenter imposes stimuli upon an organism which is often in a state of deprivation. The most important stimulus events are the reinforcers, which are contingent upon the behavior under study and strengthen or maintain it. Reinforcers are applied according to certain rules or contingencies called *schedules of reinforcement* (Chapters 3 and 5). These exert powerful control over the temporal patterning of responses, and response rates can be made to vary over a wide range. Since most schedules provide intermittent reinforcement, extinction takes place slowly, and this permits experimenters to apply various stimulus conditions or contingencies when it is undesirable to combine these with the occurrence of reinforcers. It is, of course, only with a repetitive response that schedules can be generated, and that their control over behavior can be examined.

Stimuli which are normally presented independently of responses are called *discriminative stimuli,* and can be combined with schedules of reinforcement to exert powerful control over behavior. Discriminative stimuli are usually maintained over a period of time during which a given schedule (which may be extinction) is in effect, or in which responses with some specified characteristic are reinforced. Discriminations consist of the development of the behavior appropriate to each stimulus (see Chapters 7 and 15).

Powerful control over behavior can also be exerted by stimuli which strengthen behavior when they are terminated or avoided; these are called *aversive stimuli* (Chapters 10 and 11). Such stimuli will usually reduce the rate of a response if their presentation is made contingent upon it; this effect is known as *punishment* (Chapter 9). If aversive or punishing stimuli are presented independently of responding and cannot be avoided or terminated by a response, they will tend to depress an ongoing operant. If such stimuli are consistently paired with some neutral stimulus, this depressing effect is restricted to the presentation of the latter, and conditioned suppression is thereby established (see Chapter 11).

These are the basic tools for exerting control over the behavior of individual organisms in an operant situation. The laws governing their effects have been studied extensively for their own sake. On the other hand, the behavioral control that these stimuli and contingencies make possible provides the means by which the effects of other kinds of treatments can be examined.

Continuous Observation and Recording of Behavior

A simple, readily repeatable response is usually selected, one which can be objectively and automatically recorded, which the subject can execute over long periods without fatigue, and which can be performed at a wide range of response rates. With such responses, effects like drug action can be followed over long periods of time, and with the use of proper schedules of reinforcement, satiation effects can be avoided. Experiments can be carried out in one continuous session where the subject lives in the experimental chamber (Chapter 19) or has continuous access to it (Chapter 15).

Automatic Recording and Programming

Relays, timers, and predetermining counters often program experimental procedures, while cumulative recorders, magnetic counters, and time meters record the behavioral output. Automatic equipment is not essential to valid experimentation, as many a laboratory course in psychology has demonstrated, but the advantages growing out of its use are substantial. The more obvious of these are (1) precision of control (response contingencies and other stimulus events are carefully programmed in advance), (2) objective recording (magnetic counters are unbiased observers), (3) reliability (relay circuits work reliably and without error), and (4) convenience (the experimenter can go to lunch while the experiment is running). Not so well recognized is the fact that automatic equipment makes certain difficult experiments feasible. An experimenter can readily investigate a complex discrimination which requires 200 hours of equipment time, not experimenter time. Or he can follow the course of a slow-acting drug in an individual subject over 48 hours. And the contingencies may be so complex that they would tax the capacity of a human being, where a complex circuit can be programmed to handle them easily.

CHARACTERISTICS OF DATA AND CONCEPTS BASED ON OPERANT BEHAVIOR

Precise methods in a science are a necessary though not a sufficient condition for significant advances, and they are likely to influence not only the direction taken by research, but also the nature of the concepts based on the data. In experimental psychology, where the methods determine the production as well as the observation of the phenomena of interest, this influence is likely to be especially marked. While the characteristics of "operant data" and "operant concepts" are harder to specify than the characteristics of operant methods, there are again some general features that are suggested by the material in this book.

Response Rate as a Dependent Variable

The fact that rate is based on the number of events in a span of time has more than one important consequence. For one thing, it is meaningful to talk about the *amount* of responding; twice as many responses mean twice as much behavior, while it is much less certain that twice the amplitude, half the latency, etc., of a response have the same kind of direct numerical implication. It simplifies analysis and interpretation of data when the dependent variable is the frequency of occurrence of events of a certain class, rather than some aspect of each individual event which must be averaged over each member of the class. Measures that are descriptive of individual responses often involve problems like the identification of a "typical" response, and the division of the continuum of measurement into classes for analysis.

But the use of a rate measure also has a statistical advantage. By definition, rate is derived from the observation of a number of more fundamental events—responses—in a span of time. The variability inherent in the individual interresponse times is "averaged out" when the rate measure is obtained. While it makes sense to refer to the latency or amplitude of a discrete response, one cannot talk about the "rate" of a single, discrete event. The characteristics applicable to discrete responses usually require explicit statistical treatment; but this is unnecessary for response rates, where the averaging process is inherent in obtaining the measure. Naturally, there

may be large, unsystematic fluctuations in rate, but these can often be reduced through the characteristics of operant methods discussed above.

A parallel may be drawn between response rate and many other scientific measures which involve the average of a large number of more "fundamental" events. Very reliable measurements of gas temperature or pressure
are based on the random activity of an enormous sample of molecules.
Observations in genetics, bacteriology, etc., are also based on large samples,
although the individual events, like the motion of an individual molecule,
will be unpredictable. Similarly, if rate is analyzed in terms of the interresponse times of the individual events, variability will generally be observed, and distributions of interresponse times can provide valuable information (Chapters 3, 5, and 10). Variability is inherent to some degree
in behavior, as it is in all physical and biological systems; it is advantageous,
therefore, to make use of a measure that reduces it in relation to the effects
of the independent variables.

Concentration upon Independent Variables in Psychological Research

The use of a set of dependent variables based on the rate of a selected
response may appear to impoverish psychology, and certainly it does so in
the obvious sense that only one kind of behavior is studied where other
kinds are also occurring. But science is analytic, and any scientific treatment
will focus upon a class of events. This restriction is observed in other experimental approaches to psychology. The behaviors of interest in perceptual studies and verbal learning, for example, are a very selected portion of
the subject's repertoire. In these areas, the limitation on behavior is imposed through instructions; in operant work, control of the environment
facilitates the concentration upon one kind of response by removing the
opportunity for strong competing behaviors. While psychology is the science
of behavior, it is naive to believe that "all" the behaviors in a situation must
be observed and recorded, any more than the digestion of all possible substances is observed at one time in physiology, or the inheritance of all possible characteristics in genetics. The relationships between different kinds of
concurrent behavior in an experimental situation may be of great interest,
but this study is usually fruitful when the experimental analysis of at least
one of the behaviors is well advanced.

When observation is restricted to responses of a single class, the research emphasis quite naturally shifts from description to analysis, which
involves the study of the effects of experimental treatments upon response
rate. In other words, research concentrates upon the application of the independent variables available to the experimenter. With the use of appropriate
procedures, variables can be isolated in order to analyze their effects. To
determine whether the response-shock contingency is important for the response reduction found in punishment, one can compare this procedure

with the effect of non-contingent shocks in a yoked-box situation (see Chapter 9). Does the "behavioral contrast" occurring in discrimination learning result from the extinction of responses in the negative stimulus, or is it due to a change in the prediscrimination reinforcement schedule? This question can again be answered with suitable designs (see Chapter 7).

In this connection, it is important to note that the application of independent variables is useful in comparing and even in identifying psychological processes. When similar changes in behavior are brought about by different means, the question often arises whether the same process or different processes are involved. For example, increased responding for water can be brought about by hypothalamic lesions, intracranial injections of minute amounts of saline, and water deprivation. To what extent do the similar changes in behavior resulting from these treatments represent the "same" process? A meaningful answer to this kind of question can be provided by applying some independent treatment known to affect thirst-motivated behavior, like a drug, or pre-experimental satiation procedures, to see whether its effect is similar under all conditions. Naturally, one cannot for this purpose use treatments that raise or lower all response levels indiscriminately; one must have variables available that are known to have selective effects. If the behavioral phenomena in question react similarly to the application of these independent variables, we say that they reflect the same process; if they react differently, different processes are presumably involved.

The identification of a behavioral process often involves a similar strategy. Many operant concepts are functionally defined, involving both behavioral and procedural factors in the definition, and the identification of the process may therefore involve the manipulation of a condition or variable which is one of its defining characteristics. For example, a superstition (Chapter 2) is the accidental strengthening or maintenance of a behavior through the application of a reinforcer. In a discrimination where two stimuli are concurrently presented, responses to the negative stimulus may persist in spite of the fact that no reinforcement is programmed for that particular behavior. This may be due to superstitious chaining, if responding to the negative stimulus is sometimes followed by reinforced responses to the positive. A superstition of this kind can be identified by altering one of the conditions in terms of which the process is defined: a change-over delay procedure may be introduced, so that errors cannot be followed by reinforcement for a certain length of time. If this eliminates errors, the process is identified as a superstition; if not, some other factor, such as a failure to discriminate the physical characteristics of the stimuli, must be responsible.

Emphasis on External, Observable Causes of Behavior

The atheoretical or even antitheoretical attitude adopted by many psychologists working with operant behavior is often described as a simple bias based on Skinner's influential writings. The reasons for this attitude are probably more subtle than this, and can be understood without an appeal to authority. There is no reason why operant methods cannot be used to study theoretical issues, and this has often been done (see, for example, the discussion of response chaining and secondary reinforcement in Chapter 3). But the emphasis tends to shift away from the description of unobservable processes and intervening states, because the conditions controlling behavior—its causes, in short—can be manipulated. Much of traditional behavior theory has been encouraged by the inexact and often complex relationships between stimulus and response variables. When these relationships are made more precise, the need for terms referring to unobservable states or responses diminishes. In Chapter 7 it is pointed out that the concept of "attention" is based on the variability in the relationships between discriminative stimuli and responding; at times the discriminative stimulus controls behavior and at times it does not. We may postulate an "attentional" process to "account" for this variation, but when the independent variables which determine this variability are discovered, the need to postulate an unobservable process will disappear. The emphasis is passing from theory construction to an explanation in terms of necessary and sufficient conditions or underlying physiological processes. Such analyses do not involve the postulation of unobservable states or events, although they are theoretical in the sense that they involve general principles and laws.

The Emergence of Functionally Defined Terms and Concepts

Consider the following three definitions of punishment:

1. Punishment occurs when a response is immediately and consistently followed by a painful or unpleasant stimulus.

2. Punishment occurs when bar presses made by a white rat in a Model 7690B operant behavior apparatus are followed by a foot shock of at least 0.75 ma lasting not less than 0.5 sec.

3. Punishment is a reduction of the future probability or rate of a specific response as a result of the immediate delivery of a stimulus contingent upon that response.

The last of these is slightly modified from Chapter 9 on punishment. While the first two are creations of the writer, they are certainly similar to many other definitions of psychological concepts which actually occur in the literature. Most psychologists would reject the first because of subjective terms like "painful" or "unpleasant." The second definition looks more respectable, since it adheres to the criteria of operationism, an influential doctrine in modern psychology. But it demonstrates the major pitfalls of a purely procedural description, namely that a different definition of punishment may be required for every different set of circumstances; if similar operations are grouped together to provide a common concept, it is due to the apparent similarity of the procedures rather than the similarity of the effects of the punishing stimulus on behavior. Strictly speaking, the *effect* of the foot shock is an empirical question, and has no bearing on the concept of punishment defined in this way.

The third definition (and most of those based on operant situations) has the advantage that its content is not so much physical as functional. Stimuli and responses can be identified in many experimental situations; rate, probability, immediate delivery, contingency, and the other terms in the definition are also not hard to define. In the resulting definition of punishment, the relationship between a set of determining conditions and their effects is specified as a part of the definition.

The third definition is typical of many that are based on operant situations in that it is functional in content, rather than merely procedural or subjective. The relationship between a set of determining conditions and their effects on behavior is central to the definition. Since different specific procedures may be used to produce the same (or very similar) effects, the class of instances which can be identified as falling under the definition can be quite broad. Functional definitions therefore have the advantage of being general without being ambiguous; in the example, it is possible to identify the process of punishment as long as stimulus, response, immediate delivery, probability, etc., can reliably be identified. While such functional definitions gain their power and usefulness from the causal relationship that they specify, this does not mean that they describe the mechanism underlying the behavioral process which they define or that they provide a complete explanation for it.[2]

Functional definitions are not the exclusive domain of operant behavior, nor should they be. But they will be useful only in areas of psychology where the methods of experimental analysis are precise enough to determine whether the causal relationships specified in the definition are actually observed. For this reason, the reliability and stability of operant behavior will facilitate the formulation and use of functional definitions, both in the original observation of the phenomenon which is encompassed by the definition, and in the later identification of a behavioral effect as belonging to the class in question.

This discussion has therefore come full circle: it began with the characteristics of operant methods and proceeded to various conceptual problems, ending with a discussion of the definition of terms, which in turn is

---

[2] Functionally defined terms are sometimes used to refer to the application of a procedure even when it does not result in the specified effect. Thus, one may read, "Even the application of repeated punishment had no effect upon the rate of response." In a case like this, "punishment" refers to a procedure which is *normally* effective, and a distinction should indeed be made between a "procedural usage" and a "functional usage" in cases of this sort. I would contend that the functionally defined concept is the more fundamental, and that the strictly procedural usage is derived from it.

facilitated by the use of precise and reliable experimental methods. It should be apparent that experimental methods, empirical findings, and conceptual developments in psychology cannot be considered separately; these phases are so closely related that significant advances in psychology require contributions from all three. As their central theme, the various chapters in this book stress the role played by operant behavior in all three of these phases of thought and research in psychology.

1

Operant Behavior

B. F. Skinner

PURPOSE AND BEHAVIOR

We are interested in the behavior of an organism because of its effects on the environment. (One effect on the social environment is, of course, the arousal of our interest.) Some effects seem to throw light on the behavior which produces them, but their explanatory role has been clouded by the fact that they follow the behavior and therefore raise the specter of teleology.

An attempt has been made to solve the problem by creating a prior surrogate of a given effect. A quality or property of purpose is assigned to behavior to bring "what the organism is behaving for" into the effective present; or the organism is said to behave in a given way because it intends to achieve, or expects to have, a given effect; or its behavior is characterized as possessing utility to the extent that it maximizes or minimizes certain effects. The teleological problem is, of course, not solved until we have answered certain questions: what gives an action its purpose, what leads an organism to expect to have an effect, how is utility represented in behavior?

The answers to such questions are eventually to be found in past instances in which similar behavior has been effective. The original problem can be solved directly in the same way. Thorndike's Law of Effect was a step in that direction: the approximately simultaneous occurrence of a response and certain environmental events (usually generated by it) changes the responding organism, increasing the probability that responses of the same sort will occur again. The response itself has passed into history and is not altered.

By emphasizing a change in the organism, Thorndike's principle made it possible to include the effects of action among the causes of future action without using concepts like purpose, intention, expectancy, or utility. Up to that time, the only demonstrable causes of behavior had been antecedent stimuli. The range of the eliciting stimulus was later to be extended by

Pavlovian conditioning, and the concept could be broadened to include the releasers of the ethologists, but only a small part of behavior can be predicted or controlled simply by identifying or manipulating stimuli. The Law of Effect added an important new class of variables of which behavior could be shown to be a function.

Thorndike's solution was probably suggested by Darwin's treatment of phylogenetic purpose. Before Darwin, the purpose of a well-developed eye might have been said to be to permit the organism to see better. The principle of natural selection moved "seeing better" from the future into the past: organisms with well-developed eyes were descended from those which had been able to see better and had therefore produced more descendants. Thorndike was closer to the principle of natural selection than the above statement of his law. He did not need to say that a response which had been followed by a certain kind of consequence was more likely to occur again but simply that it was not less likely. It eventually held the field because responses which failed to have such effects tended, like less favored species, to disappear.

Thorndike was concerned with how animals solved problems rather than with the concept of purpose, and his Law of Effect did not end purposive formulations. The devices used for the study of behavior during the next quarter of a century continued to emphasize an intentional relation between behavior and its consequences. The relation was represented spatially. In mazes, runways, and open fields, for example, organisms ran *toward* their goals. In discrimination apparatuses they chose the door which led *to* food. They escaped *from* the dangerous side of shuttle-boxes or pulled *away from* sources of dangerous stimulation. They drew objects *toward* them with rakes or strings. The experimenter could see the purpose of an action in the spatial relation of the organism and the objects toward which it was moving or from which it was withdrawing. It was even asserted that the organism itself should see a purposive relationship in some such form in order to behave effectively. Köhler, for example, criticized Thorndike on just this score.

The spatial representation of purpose, expectancy, or intention obscured one of the most important features of the relation emphasized by Thorndike. The process he identified remained unexplored for 30 years and during that time was confused with rote habit formation and with various formulations of Pavlovian conditioning. In the late 1920's, however, the consequences of behavior began to be studied with devices of another sort. Pavlov's technique for the study of conditioned reflexes contributed to their development, even though Pavlov himself was not primarily concerned with consequences as such. In his basic studies, indeed, it might be said that the organism did not receive food *for* doing anything; the salivation elicited by the conditioned stimulus did not produce the food which followed. The experimental design, however, called for food to be introduced at a given moment automatically. Once the procedure was familiar, it was no great step to arrange devices in which a response "produced" food in a similar fashion. Ivanov-Smolensky (1927), one of Pavlov's associates, studied an experimental arrangement, close to Thorndike, in which a child squeezed a rubber bulb and delivered candy into his mouth. Miller and Konorski (1928) devised an apparatus in which a shock to the foot of a dog elicited flexion of the leg, and the resulting movement was followed by the presentation of food; the leg eventually flexed even when the foot was not shocked. In America D. K. Adams (1927) used a similar arrangement with cats, and in England Grindley (1932) with guinea pigs. The essential features may be seen in an apparatus in which depression of a lever operates a food-dispenser (Skinner, 1932). Pressing a lever is not a natural or unconditioned way of getting food. The response produces food only in the sense that food follows it—a Humean version of causality. Behavior is nevertheless altered. The consequences of action change the organism regardless of how or why they follow. The connection need not be functional or organic—as, indeed, it was not in Thorndike's experiment.

PRACTICAL ADVANTAGES

These early devices were not designed to eliminate spatial representations of purpose; but they all did so, and the fact had far-reaching consequences. Some of these were practical. The experimenter could choose a response which was conveniently recorded; or one which the organism could execute rapidly and without fatigue for long periods of time; or one which minimized the peculiarities of a species and thus furthered a comparison between species with respect to properties not primarily related to the topography of behavior. In particular, it was possible to choose a response which was relatively free of extraneous variables and not likely to be confused with responses elicited or evoked by them. When a shuttle-box, for example, is used to study the effect of the postponement or termination of a shock, the behavior affected (running or jumping from one side to the other) is topographically similar to unconditioned responses to the shock, such as startle or jumping into the air, and to more elaborate patterns of escape from a space in which shocks have been received. It may also resemble responses of both these sorts conditioned in the Pavlovian manner and elicited by the warning stimuli. The inevitable confusion can be avoided by making the postponement or termination of a shock contingent on an arbitrary response, such as pressing a lever in the Sidman arrangement, which is not otherwise related to the variables at issue.

A response which is only temporally related to its consequences could also be conveniently studied with automatic equipment. Instruments were developed which permitted the investigator to conduct many experiments simultaneously, particularly when unskilled technical help was available. It is true that automatic mazes and discrimination-boxes had been or were soon to be built, but most modern programming and recording equipment can be traced to research on responses with arbitrarily arranged consequences for the very good reason that the conditions are easily instrumented. The availability of automatic equipment has helped to standardize experiments and has facilitated the study of relations between responses and consequences too complex to be arranged by hand or followed by eye.

Anther practical result was terminological. The concept of the reflex made no reference to the consequences of a response. Reflexes were often obviously "adaptive," but this was primarily a phylogenetic effect. The term "operant" was introduced to distinguish between reflexes and responses operating directly on the environment (Skinner, 1937). The alternative term, *instrumental,* suggests the use of tools. To say that a rat "uses a lever to obtain food" has purposive overtones, and where nothing can be identified as an instrument, it is often said that the organism "uses a response" to gain an effect. For example, verbal behavior is interpreted as "the use of words," although the implication that words exist as things apart from behavior unnecessarily complicates an analysis (Skinner, 1957). Another change was from *reward* to *reinforcement.* Reward suggests compensation *for* behaving in a given way, often in some sort of contractual arrangement. Reinforcement in its etymological sense designates simply the strengthening of a response. It refers to similar events in Pavlovian conditioning, where reward is inappropriate. These changes in terminology have not automatically eliminated purposive expressions (such as "The pigeon was reinforced *for* pecking the key"), but a given instance can usually be rephrased. Comparable teleological expressions are common in other sciences, as Bernatowicz (1958) has pointed out.

RATE OF RESPONDING AS A DATUM

A more important result of studying an arbitrary connection between a response and its consequences, together with the simplified procedures which then become available, has been to emphasize rate of responding as a property of behavior. Earlier devices were almost always used to study responses from trial to trial, where rate of responding was controlled by the experimenter and hence obscured as a datum. When the organism can respond at any time, its rate of responding varies in many subtle ways over a wide range. Changes in rate comprise a vast and largely unsuspected subject matter. (The changes are made conspicuous with a cumulative recorder, the ubiquity of which in the study of operant behavior is no accident. In a cumulative record, rate and changes in rate are visible at a glance over substantial periods of time. The "on-line" record permits the experimenter to note changes as they occur and take appropriate steps.)

Rate of responding is important because it is especially relevant to the principal task of a scientific analysis. Behavior is often interesting because of what might be called its *character*. Animals court their mates, build living quarters, care for their young, forage for food, defend territories, and so on, in many fascinating ways. These are worth studying, but the inherent drama can divert attention from another task. Even when reduced to general principles, a narrative account of *how* animals behave must be supplemented by a consideration of *why*. What is required is an analysis of the conditions which govern the probability that a given response will occur at a given time. Rate of responding is by no means to be equated with probability of responding, as frequency theories of probability and comparable problems in physics have shown. Many investigators prefer to treat rate of responding as a datum in its own right. Eventually, however, the prediction and control of behavior call for an evaluation of the probability that a response will be emitted. The study of rate of responding is a step in that direction.

Rate of responding is one of those aspects of a subject matter which do not attract attention for their own sake and which undergo intensive study only when their usefulness as a dependent variable has been discovered. Other sciences have passed through comparable stages. The elements and compounds studied by the chemist also have fascinating characters— they exist in many colors, textures, and states of aggregation and undergo surprising transmutations when heated, dissolved, combined, and so on. These are the characteristics which naturally first attract attention. They were, for example, the principal concern of the alchemists. In contrast, the mere weight of a given quantity of a substance is of little interest in its own right. Yet it was only when the weights of substances entering into reactions were found to obey certain laws that chemistry moved into its modern phase. Combining weight became important because of what could be done with it. Rate of responding has emerged as a basic datum in a science of behavior for similar reasons—and, hopefully, with comparable results.

Rate of responding differs from the measures derived from earlier devices and procedures, such as the time required to complete a task or the effort expended or the number of errors made in doing so, and the two kinds of data have led to different conceptions of behavior as a scientific subject matter. We like to believe that basic processes are orderly, continuous, and significant, but the data obtained from mazes, memory-drums, shuttle-boxes, and so on, vary "noisily" from trial to trial and depend for their dimensions on particular tasks and apparatuses. Orderly and significant processes are therefore sought elsewhere—in some mental, physiological, or merely conceptual inner system which by its nature is neither directly observed in, nor accurately represented on any given occasion by, the performance of an organism. There is no comparable inner system in an operant analysis. Changes in rate of responding are directly observed, they have dimensions appropriate to a scientific formulation, and under skillful experimental control they show the uniformity expected of biological proc-

esses in general. Those accustomed to the older formulation have nevertheless found difficulties in accepting changes in rate as an alternative subject
for analysis.

BEHAVIORAL PROCESSES

One difficulty is that changes in rate do not closely resemble the behavioral processes inferred from earlier measures. A few examples may be
cited from the field of learning. By arranging a reinforcing consequence, we
increase the rate at which a response occurs; by eliminating the consequence, we decrease the rate. These are the processes of operant conditioning and extinction. Topographical properties of the response depend on the
contingencies. The force with which a lever is pressed, for example, is related to the force required to operate the food-dispenser. An initial, moderate force can be increased indefinitely, within physiological limits, by progressively requiring greater forces. A complex topography can be "shaped"
with a series of changing contingencies, called a *program,* each stage of
which evokes a response and also prepares the organism to respond at a
later stage. A shaping program can be mechanically prescribed in advance,
but the process is most easily demonstrated when the experimenter impro-
vises contingencies as he goes.

The behaviors evoked by mazes, puzzle-boxes, memory-drums, and so
on, are also shaped but almost always without specific programming of
contingencies. The organism is usually exposed at once to a set of *terminal*
contingencies, for which it possesses no adequate behavior. Responses occur, however—the rat explores the maze, the subject guesses at the next
nonsense syllable—and some of these may be reinforced in ways which lead
at last to a terminal performance. What can we conclude from the series of
stages through which this comes about?

Such data are usually plotted by trials in so-called *learning curves*
showing, let us say, the times required to complete a task or the number of errors made in doing so. These are facts and in some sense quantifiable. From
such a curve we may predict within limits how another organism will behave in similar circumstances. But the shape of the curve tells us little or
nothing about the processes of conditioning and extinction revealed in an
operant analysis. It merely describes the rather crude overall effects of
adventitious contingencies, and it often tells us more about the apparatus
or procedure than about the organism.

Similar discrepancies appear in the analysis of stimuli. In so-called
stimulus-response theories, a stimulus is broadly defined as something
which regularly precedes a response—the eliciting stimulus in a conditioned
reflex, the "cue" to more complex behavior, or even an internal "drive
state." The term is little more than a synonym for cause, and various relations between cause and effect are usually not distinguished. The stimulus

control of an operant, on the other hand, has been carefully analyzed. Although we can shape the topography of a response without identifying or manipulating any anterior stimulus, stimuli enter into a more complex type of contingency in which a response is reinforced in the presence of a stimulus and is therefore more likely to be emitted in its presence. The relations among the three terms in this contingency—stimulus, response, and reinforcement—comprise a substantial field for investigation.

One property of the control acquired by a stimulus when a response is reinforced in its presence is shown in the so-called stimulus generalization gradient. Hypothetical gradients in mental, neurological, or conceptual inner systems have been discussed for years, but thanks to the work of Guttman and his students (Guttman, 1963), and others, behavioral gradients are now directly observed. A pigeon, reinforced when it pecks a circular key of a given color and size, will peck keys of other shapes, colors, or sizes at lower rates depending upon the differences in the properties. When the response is reinforced in the presence of one property and extinguished in the presence of others—the well-known process of *discrimination*—a very sensitive and powerful control is established. In a classroom demonstration a response is brought under the control of a red as against a green key. So long as the key is green, no response is made; when it turns red, the pigeon pecks it immediately. The power of the stimulus can be dramatically shown by changing from red to green just as the pigeon's beak moves toward the key. The pecking response will be interrupted in mid-air, even though stopping probably requires more energy than following through. Stimulus control can also be shaped by changing relevant stimuli in a program which leads the organism into subtle discriminations, often without "errors," as Terrace (1963) has recently shown. Very little of this is seen in traditional studies of sensory learning, however. In using a classic multiple-choice apparatus, for example, the organism is exposed at once to a set of terminal contingencies. Its progress toward an appropriate performance is represented in a curve showing, say, the number of errors made or the times required to reach a criterion, over a series of trials, but the dimensions of these measures are again arbitrary, and the behavior is obviously the product of shifting, largely adventitious contingencies.

Classic studies of learning have emphasized the process of *acquisition,* presumably because one can easily see that an organism is doing something new or is responding to a new stimulus, but reinforcement is also responsible for the fact that an organism goes on responding long after its behavior has been acquired. The fact has usually been attributed to motivational variables, but an experimental analysis has shown that various schedules of intermittent reinforcement are usually involved. The nature or quantity of reinforcement is often much less important than the schedule on which it is received. Programming is again important, for many schedules can take effect only when the organism has passed through intervening contingencies.

To take a very simple example, an apparatus which reinforces every hundredth response will have no effect at all if a hundred responses are never emitted, but by reinforcing every second, then every fifth, then every tenth response, and so on, waiting until the behavior is well developed at each stage, we can bring the organism under the control of the more demanding schedule. The pathological gambler and the dedicated scientist both show terminal behavior resulting from a special history of reinforcement on a related ("variable ratio") schedule—a history which society attempts to prevent in the former case and encourage in the latter.

The history which brings a complex terminal schedule into control is not, of course, visible in the terminal performance. A scientist once borrowed an apparatus to demonstrate the use of a multiple fixed interval, fixed ratio schedule in assessing the effects of certain drugs. When one of the pigeons lent with the apparatus was accidentally killed, he purchased another, put it into the apparatus, and was surprised to find that nothing happened. We make the same mistake when we attempt to explain conspicuous effects of reinforcement on human behavior by examining only *current* schedules.

Complex terminal contingencies involving multiple stimuli and responses, in sequential or concurrent arrangements, are often called *problems*. An organism is said to have solved such a problem when it comes under the control of the terminal contingencies. Its capacity to respond appropriately under such contingencies must, however, be distinguished from its capacity to reach them through a given series of intervening stages. Whether an organism can solve a problem in this sense is as much a question of the program through which it passes—and the skill of the programmer who constructed it—as of any so-called problem-solving ability. Whether an organism can solve a problem without the help of a prepared program depends on the behavior initially available and the more or less accidental contingencies which follow from it. Apparent differences in problem-solving ability among species or among organisms of different ages or other properties within a species must be interpreted accordingly. Solving a problem, like learning, is again often attributed to an inner system, although the supposed inner processes, like the facts they explain, are more complex. Those committed to sequestered faculties and thought processes are not likely to feel at home in an analysis of the behavior itself and may, therefore, find it inacceptable as an alternative enterprise.

STATISTICS

Changes in rate of responding are studied with methods which also may seem strange to the student of the learning processes said to take place in some inner system. The latter can usually be investigated only with "statistics." If learning is never accurately represented in one performance, performances must be averaged. If statements about the inner system cannot be directly confirmed, hypotheses must be set up, and theorems deduced and tested, following established practices in logic and scientific method. If some properties of the inner system are meaningful only with respect to larger sets of facts, a procedure such as factor analysis may be needed. It is not surprising that research on this pattern has come to be judged by the sophistication of its statistical and logical techniques. Confidence in an experiment is proportional to the number of subjects studied, an experiment is good only if properly "designed," and results are significant only at a level determined by special tests.

Much of this is lacking in the experimental analysis of behavior, where experiments are usually performed on a few subjects, curves representing behavioral processes are seldom averaged, the behavior attributed to complex mental activity is analyzed directly, and so on. The simpler procedure is possible because rate of responding and changes in rate can be directly observed, especially when represented in cumulative records. The effect is similar to increasing the resolving power of a microscope: a new subject matter is suddenly open to direct inspection. Statistical methods are unnecessary. When an organism is showing a stable or slowly changing performance, it is for most purposes idle to stop to evaluate the confidence with which the next stage can be predicted. When a variable is changed and the effect on performance observed, it is for most purposes idle to prove statistically that a change has indeed occurred. (It is sometimes said in such a case that the organism is "used as its own control," but the expression, borrowed from a basically different methodology, is potentially troublesome.) Much can be done in the study of behavior with methods of observation no more sophisticated than those available, say, to Faraday, with his magnets, wires, and cells. Eventually the investigator may move on to peripheral areas where indirect methods become necessary, but until then he must forego the prestige which attaches to traditional statistical methods.

Some traditional uses must also be questioned. Learning curves remain inadequate no matter how smooth they are made by averaging cases. Statistical techniques may eliminate noise, but the dimensions are still faulty. A curve which enables us to predict the performance of another organism does not therefore represent a basic process. Moreover, curves which report changes in variables having satisfactory dimensions can often not be averaged. The idiosyncrasies in a cumulative record do not necessarily show caprice on the part of the organism or faulty technique on the part of the experimenter. The complex system we call an organism has an elaborate and largely unknown history which endows it with a certain individuality. No two organisms embark upon an experiment in precisely the same condition nor are they affected in the same way by the contingencies in an experimental space. (It is characteristic of most contingencies that they are not precisely controlled, and in any case they are effective only in combination with the behavior which the organism brings to the experiment.) Statistical techniques cannot eliminate this kind of individuality; they can only obscure and falsify it. An averaged curve seldom correctly represents any of the cases contributing to it (Sidman, 1960).

An analysis which recognizes the individuality of the organism is particularly valuable when contact is made with other disciplines such as neurology, psychopharmacology, and psychotherapy, where idiosyncratic sets of variables must also be considered. The rigor of the analysis is not necessarily threatened. Operant methods make their own use of Grand Numbers: instead of studying a thousand rats for one hour each, or a hundred rats for ten hours each, the investigator is likely to study one rat for a thousand hours. The procedure is not only appropriate to an enterprise which recognizes individuality, it is at least equally efficient in its use of equipment and of the investigator's time and energy. The ultimate test of uniformity or reproducibility is not to be found in the methods used but in the degree of control achieved, a test which the experimental analysis of behavior usually passes easily.

The study of operant behavior also seldom follows the "design of experiments" prescribed by statisticians. A prior design in which variables are distributed, for example, in a Latin square, may be a severe handicap. When effects on behavior can be immediately observed, it is most efficient to explore relevant variables by manipulating them in an improvised and rapidly changing design. Similar practices have been responsible for the greater part of modern science. This is not, however, the tenor of R. A. Fisher's *Design of Experiments,* which, as Lancelot Hogben (1957) has said, gives the reader

> . . . the impression that recourse to statistical methods is prerequisite to the design of experiments of any sort whatever. In that event, the whole creation of experimental scientists from Gilbert and Hooke to J. J. Thomson and Morgan has been groaning and travailing in fruitless pain together; and the biologist of today has nothing to learn from well-tried methods which had led to the spectacular advances of the several branches of experimental science during the last three centuries (p. 29).

Statistics, like logic and scientific methodology in general, emphasizes the verbal behavior of the scientist: how reliable are his measures, how significant are the differences he reports, how confident can we be that what he says is true? His non-verbal behavior is much less easily codified and analyzed. In such considerations what the scientist *does* takes second place to what he *says*. Yet the *a priori* manipulation of variables, guided by directly observed effects, is superior to the *a posteriori* analysis of co-variation in many ways. It leads more rapidly to prediction and control and to practical recombinations of variables in the study of complex cases. Eventually, of course, the experimenter must behave verbally. He must describe what he has done and what he has seen, and he must conduct his research with this obligation in mind. But a compulsive preoccupation with validity or significance may be inimical to other, equally important obligations.

A non-statistical strategy may also be recommended for its effect on the behavior of the investigator, who is perhaps as strongly reinforced during a successful experiment as the organism he studies. The contingencies to which he is submitted largely determine whether he will continue in similar work. Statistical techniques often inject a destructive delay between the conduct of an experiment and the discovery of the significance of the data—a fatal violation of a fundamental principle of reinforcement. The exceptional zeal which has often been noted in students of operant behavior is possibly attributable to the immediacy of their results.

THE CIRCUMVENTION OF AN OPERANT ANALYSIS

By accepting changes in rate of responding as basic behavioral processes and by emphasizing environmental variables which can be manipulated with the help of automatic equipment, research on operant behavior has been greatly simplified. But it has not been made easy. Technical advances have been offset by the demand for increasing rigor, by the problems which arise in studying one organism at a time, and by the attack on more and more complex arrangements of interrelated operants. Behavior—human or otherwise—remains an extremely difficult subject matter. It is not surprising that practices which seem to circumvent or simplify an operant analysis are common. In particular, verbal communication between subject and experimenter is widely used in lieu of the explicit arrangement of contingencies of reinforcement and the objective recording of behavior. The practice goes back to the study of mental life and is still favored by psychologists who formulate their subject matter in mental terms, but it survives as if it were a labor-saving device in many essentially behavioristic formulations.

The manipulation of independent variables appears to be circumvented when, instead of exposing an organism to a set of contingencies, the contingencies are simply described in "instructions." Instead of shaping a response, the subject is told to respond in a given way. A history of reinforcement or punishment is replaced by a promise or threat: "Movement of the lever will sometimes operate a coin dispenser" or ". . . deliver a shock to your leg." A schedule of positive or negative reinforcement is described rather than imposed: "Every response to the right lever postpones the shock but increases the number of responses to the left lever required to operate the coin dispenser." Instead of bringing the behavior under the control of a stimulus, the subject is told to behave as if a discrimination had been established: "Start when the light goes on, stop when it goes off." Thus instructed, the subject is asked either to behave appropriately or to describe behavior he might emit under such circumstances. The scope of the verbal substitute can be estimated by considering how a non-verbal organism, human or otherwise, could be similarly "instructed."

Descriptions of contingencies are, of course, often effective. Hypothetical consequences are commonly used for practical purposes ("Will you do the job if I pay you $50?" or "How would you feel about going if I told you that X would be there?"), and the subject is worth studying. Verbal instructions may be defended when the resulting behavior is not the primary object of interest; for example, the experimenter may show a subject how to operate a piece of equipment rather than shape his behavior through reinforcement so long as he is not concerned with the acquisition of the response but with what happens to it later. Verbal communication is not, however, a substitute for the arrangement and manipulation of variables.

There is no reason why a description of contingencies of reinforcement should have the same effect as exposure to the contingencies. A subject can seldom accurately describe the way in which he has actually been reinforced. Even when he has been trained to identify a few simple contingencies, he cannot then describe a new contingency, particularly when it is complex. We can scarcely expect him, therefore, to react appropriately to descriptions by the experimenter. Moreover, the verbal contingencies between subject and experimenter must be taken into account. Instructions must in some way promise or threaten consequences not germane to the experiment if the subject is to follow them.

The other major task in an operant analysis may seem to be circumvented when, instead of recording behavior so that rate or probability of response can be observed or inferred, the experimenter simply asks the subject to evaluate his tendency to respond or to express his preference for responding in one way rather than another. The subject may do so by describing his "intentions" or "plans" or by reporting "expectations" regarding the consequences of an action. Such behavior may be worth investigating, but it is not a substitute for the behavior observed in an operant analysis. Only in the simplest cases can a person correctly describe his ongoing behavior. The difficulty is not linguistic; the subject could be given an operandum and permitted to "model" the behavior—for example, to generate a cumulative record. It is highly unlikely that he would construct a curve closely resembling the curve he would generate if actually exposed to a specific set of contingencies, or even a curve he had already generated when so exposed. Changes in rate of responding are never easy to describe. They necessarily take place in time, and even a second observer cannot "see" them until they have been reduced to graphic form. The subject's own behavior presents other difficulties. If we ask him to say simply whether he will be more or less likely to respond, or will respond more or less rapidly, we have increased his chances of being right only by asking him to say less. Any report, no matter how specific, is subject to the verbal contingencies which induce a person to describe his behavior and possibly to similar contingencies elsewhere which may classify his behavior, for examaple, as right or wrong.

Verbal substitutes for arranged or observed variables may be used at different points in an investigation: contingencies may be described to the subject and his behavior then actually observed; he may be exposed to a set of contingencies and then asked to evaluate the nature or probability of his responses; and so on. Similar practices are used to evaluate the reinforcing or aversive properties of a given event or procedure, to predict the outcome of several variables operating at once, and so on, and are subject to the same criticism.

To those interested primarily in mental processes, verbal communication may not be an attempted circumvention or shortcut. On the contrary, an operant analysis may seem to be the long way around. The position is sometimes defended by insisting that the student of behavior always begin with an interest in mental life—possibly his own—and design his experiments essentially to test hypotheses about it. Whatever the case may once have been, operant research has long since passed the point at which the experimenter can be guided by considering possible effects of variables on himself. The introspective vocabulary used in circumventing an experimental analysis is hopelessly inadequate for the kinds of facts currently under investigation. If one field is to borrow from the other, the debt will henceforth almost certainly be in the other direction: from the study of the behavior of other organisms, the experimenter is most likely to come to understand himself. In some theories of knowledge, introspective observations may be regarded as primary data, but in an analysis of behavior they are a form of theorizing which is not required or necessarily helpful (Skinner, 1963).

FORMAL ANALYSES OF CONTINGENCIES OF REINFORCEMENT

The consequences of action and their effects on behavior also enter into theories of probability, decision making, conflict, and games. The classical urn containing a given proportion of black and white balls, like other sample spaces, may be analyzed without reference to behavior, but it would be of little interest if the consequences of drawing either a black or white ball were not in some way reinforcing. (There has always been a close connection between probability theory and gambling, where every play is punished to the extent of its cost and some plays are also reinforced.) Probability theory also often takes into account the fact that this reinforcement will occur on an intermittent schedule and that as a consequence the drawer will experience a given subjective or felt probability, or exhibit a given probability of drawing again.

The probability that the drawer will draw again is usually assumed to be related to the probability function of the sample space. A relation is implied when it is said that a subject who has sufficient knowledge about a given system, possibly inferred from his experience with it, can behave "rationally," A relation is also implied when it is argued that irrational behavior requires explanation. For example, the fact that intermittent reinforcement raises the probability of responding above the value generated when all responses are reinforced has recently occasioned surprise (Lawrence & Festinger, 1962). Any such relation is, of course, an empirical fact, to be determined experimentally. Standard operant equipment can be used to set up contingencies of reinforcement which have the effect of classical sample spaces. A schedule could, if necessary, be programmed by actually drawing balls from an urn. An organism can then be exposed to the schedule and the effect on its behavior observed.

In such a procedure the status of the probability function of the sample space (the schedule of reinforcement arranged by the programming equipment) is clear. The probability that the organism will respond at a given time is inferred from its rate. The relation between these two probabilities is complicated by the fact that rate of responding under a given schedule depends, as we have seen, on previous exposure to the schedule. When introduced into an experimental space for the first time, an organism may be said to show a certain "prior probability" of responding—the so-called operant level. A first response is or is not reinforced, and the rate rises or falls accordingly. This brief history contributes to what is now a different situation. When the organism responds again and is again possibly reinforced, the situation changes still more substantially. A given set of contingencies yields a performance which combines with the programming equipment to generate other contingencies which in turn generate other performances, and so on.

Many of these interactions between behavior and programming equipment have been carefully studied. Under a variable interval schedule of reinforcement, for example, the organism often responds at a nearly constant rate for long periods of time. All reinforcements therefore occur when it is responding at that rate, *although this condition is not specified by the equipment.* The rate becomes a discriminative and, in turn, a reinforcing stimulus, which opposes any change to a different rate—such as would otherwise be induced by, say, a psychopharmacological agent. As another example, when only the first response after the passage of a fixed interval of time is reinforced, the organism comes to exhibit a fairly stable performance in which the number of responses emitted during an interval approaches constancy. The organism is then being reinforced not only after a constant interval of time but after emitting a constant number of responses. The latter condition, *which is not specified by the equipment,* is characteristic of a fixed ratio schedule, and it generates a much higher rate of responding. As rapid responding breaks through, the stability of the fixed interval performance is destroyed, the number of responses per reinforcement is no longer constant, and a stable interval performance is restored as another cycle begins (Ferster & Skinner, 1957).

A third example is closer to probability theory. A schedule in which a response is reinforced upon completion of an appreciable fixed or variable number of responses must often be reached through a program, as we have seen. The number must first be small, but the schedule favors reinforcement when the organism is responding at a high rate, and it is soon possible to "stretch" the requirement. When a hungry rat is reinforced with food for running in a wheel, the required distance can be increased until more energy is consumed than is available in the food received (Skinner, 1938). The behavior of the gambler, which almost always shows a similar "negative utility," is the result of the same kind of stretching. The variable ratio schedules inherent in gambling systems maintain behavior only after a history of reinforcement in which behavior has combined with the programming equipment to generate certain powerful terminal contingencies.

In summary, a scheduling system has no effect until an organism is exposed to it, and then it no longer fully determines the contingencies. Still other interactions between equipment and performance arise when a second response is introduced in order to study choice or decision making. Suppose, for example, that a subject may press either of two keys, *A* and *B,* on which reinforcements are independently scheduled. The performance on either key can be accounted for only by examining the combined action of equipment and earlier performances *on both keys.* For example, if reinforcements are programmed on interval schedules, responding to *A* after *B* is more likely to be reinforced than responding to *B* after *B,* since the equipment may have set up a reinforcement on *A* while a response was being made to *B.* The behavior of changing from *A* to *B* or from *B* to *A* may be favored to the point at which the performance becomes a simple alternation (Skinner, 1950). This yields the same rate on both keys, even though the schedules may be substantially different. The interaction may be corrected with a *change-over delay* in which, for example, a response to *B* is not reinforced if a response to *A* has been made during the preceding second, or in which the first response to either key after changing over is never reinforced (Herrnstein, 1961; see also Chapter 6). The contingencies on the two levers are nevertheless still subject to the other interactions mentioned previously. (By manipulating the change-over delay and other characteristics of the schedules, it may be possible to generate rates of responding on the two keys which would be predicted from some hypothesis of rationality or utility, but it would be a mistake to regard these as optimal conditions and possibly to stop the search when they have been found.)

Interactions between performance and programming system are still more complex if the performance changes the system, as in the so-called *adjusting* and *interlocking* schedules (Ferster & Skinner, 1957). Many examples are to be found in the theory of games and conflict, where the behavior of one organism alters the contingencies affecting another, and vice versa. The rules of any game can be represented by programming equipment which is subject to modification by the performances of the players, but the actual contingencies of reinforcement are still more complex, for they include conditions not specified by the equipment but generated by the earlier performances of all parties.

That there is a limitation inherent in formal analyses is suggested by the fact that mathematical inquiries into probability, decision making, conflict, and games confine themselves almost exclusively to ratio schedules. The contingencies defined in sample spaces and rules practically always specify reinforcement as a function of a number of responses, a restraint traceable perhaps to practical issues involving winning, losing, and ultimate utility. Yet the interactions between equipment and performance are the same when reinforcement is scheduled by clocks or speedometers rather than by counters, and the same processes are involved, as an experimental analysis has abundantly shown.

The formal properties of sample spaces, like the various conditions under which choices are made, games played, or conflicts resolved, may be analyzed without taking behavior into account or, at most, by assuming selected performances. Those interested primarily in a formal analysis are likely to approach behavior, if at all, by setting up hypotheses. The research which follows has the nature of hypothesis testing and is wasteful if the data collected lose their value when a hypothesis has been disproved or abandoned for any reason. An experimental analysis of the behavior generated by the contingencies in sample spaces may be conducted without guessing at the results.

THE USE OF FORMAL ANALYSES

Formal analyses of contingencies of reinforcement are related to behavior in another way when they are used as guides. The behavior of a person who has calculated his chances, compared alternatives, or considered the consequences of a move is different from, and usually more effective than, the behavior of one who has merely been exposed to the unanalyzed contingencies. The formal analysis functions as a discriminative stimulus. When such a stimulus is perfectly correlated with reinforcement, the behavior under its control is maximally reinforced. On an interval schedule and in the absence of related stimuli, an organism emits unreinforced or "wasted" responses, but if the apparatus presents a conspicuous stimulus whenever a reinforcement becomes available, the organism eventually responds only in the presence of that stimulus and no responses are wasted. Clocks provide stimuli of this sort in connection with events occurring on interval schedules and are built and used for just that reason. Stimuli less closely correlated with reinforcement yield lesser improvements in efficiency. If a given setting on a clock cannot be sharply discriminated, for example, some responses will be emitted prior to "the time to respond" and some potentially effective responses may be delayed, but performance is nevertheless improved. A speedometer serves a similar function when reinforcement depends on a given rate of responding.

Formal analyses of sample spaces serve the same function as imprecise clocks and speedometers. Not every response under their control is reinforced, but there is still a net gain. When a man learns to play poker under the contingencies arranged by the cards and rules, his sampling of the possible contingencies is necessarily limited, even in prolonged play. He will play a more successful game, and after a much shorter history, if he consults a table showing his chances of success in making given plays. The contingencies in poker also depend upon the behavior of other players, and prior stimuli correlated with that behavior are therefore also useful. They are particularly important in a game such as chess. Chess playing may be shaped by the unanalyzed contingencies generated by the rules of the game and by the performances of opponents, but a player will play a better game, after a shorter history, if he can consult standard gambits, defenses, endgames, and so on, which show some of the likely consequences of given moves.

A stimulus commonly correlated with reinforcement and hence useful in improving efficiency is the record left by previous behavior. When a man finds his way from one place to another, he may leave traces which prove useful when he goes that way again. He wears a path which supplements the change taking place in his behavior and may even be useful to others who have not gone that way before. A path need not be constructed because it serves this function, but the advantages gained may reinforce the explicit leaving of traces. A trail is "blazed," for example, precisely because it is more easily followed. Comparable reinforcing advantages have led men to construct pictures and verbal descriptions of paths.

Many proverbs and maxims are crude descriptions of contingencies of social or non-social reinforcement, and those who observe them come under a more effective control of their environment. Rules of grammar and spelling bring certain verbal contingencies of reinforcement more forcefully into play. Society codifies its ethical, legal, and religious practices so that by following a code the individual may emit behavior appropriate to social contingencies without having been directly exposed to them. Scientific laws serve a similar function in guiding the behavior of scientists.

A person could, of course, construct rules of grammer and spelling, maxims for effective personal conduct, tables of probabilities in the games he plays, and scientific laws for his own use, but society usually analyzes the predictable contingencies for him. He constructs comparable stimuli for himself when he makes resolutions, announces intentions, states expectations, and formulates plans. The stimuli thus generated control his behavior most effectively when they are external, conspicuous, and durable—when the resolution is posted or the plan actually drafted in visible form—but they are also useful when created upon occasion, as by recalling the resolution or reviewing the plan. The gain from any such discriminative stimulus depends upon the extent to which it correctly represents the contingencies which led to its construction.

Discriminative stimuli which improve the efficiency of behavior under given contingencies of reinforcement are important, but they must not be confused with the contingencies themselves, nor their effects with the effects of those contingencies. The behavior of the poker player who evaluates his chances before making a given play merely resembles that of the player whose behavior has been shaped by prolonged exposure to the game. The behavior of one who speaks correctly by applying the rules of a grammar merely resembles the behavior of one who speaks correctly from long experience in a verbal community. The efficiency may be the same, but the controlling variables are different and the behaviors are therefore different. Nothing which could be called following a plan or applying a rule is observed when behavior is a product of the contingencies alone. To say that "the child who learns a language has in some sense constructed the grammar for himself" (Chomsky, 1959) is as misleading as to say that a dog which has learned to catch a ball has in some sense constructed the relevant part of the science of mechanics. Rules can be extracted from the reinforcing contingencies in both cases, and once in existence they may be used as guides. The direct effect of the contingencies is of a different nature.

The distinction bears on two points already made. In the first place, the instructions used in circumventing an operant analysis also have the status of prior stimuli associated with hypothetical or real contingencies of reinforcement, but behavior in response to them is not the behavior generated by exposure to the contingencies themselves even when, on rare occasions, the two are similar. When subjects report that they "understand instructions" and hence "know what to expect," it does not follow that comparable reportable states of understanding or knowledge are generated by the contingencies themselves. In the second place—to return at last to the point with which this paper began—when a man explicitly states his purpose in acting in a given way he may, indeed, be constructing a "contemporary surrogate of future consequences" which will affect subsequent behavior, possibly in useful ways. It does not follow, however, that the behavior generated by the consequences in the absence of any statement of purpose is under the control of any comparable prior stimulus, such as a felt purpose or intention.

THE CONTINGENCIES OF REINFORCEMENT

The Law of Effect specifies a simple temporal order of response and consequence—the relation implied by the term "operant." The contingencies of reinforcement currently under investigation are much more complex. Reinforcement may be contingent not only on the occurrence of a response, but on special features of its topography, on the presence of prior stimuli, and on scheduling systems. An adequate analysis must also reach into the traditional fields of motivation and emotion to determine what is reinforcing and under what conditions. Interrelated systems of operants raise other problems.

The techniques of an experimental analysis have fortunately remained commensurate with the increasing complexity of the subject. Rate of responding has come to be examined over a much wider range and in much greater detail. Cumulative records have been supplemented by distributions of interresponse times and, very recently, by "on-line" computer processing. Improved measures of topographical properties are available. Independent variables have been effectively controlled over a wider range and in increasingly complex patterns. Arrangements of operants resembling many of the behaviors attributed to higher mental processes have been successfully constructed and studied.

The experimental space has been improved. Brief, daily experimental periods have given way to continuous observation for many hours, days, weeks, or even months. More of the behavior exhibited in the experimental space has been controlled, recorded, and analyzed. Total control of the environment from birth is within range. As in the study of animal behavior in general, the hundreds of thousands of extant species are still far from adequately sampled, but problems of instrumentation have been solved for a fairly wide range of anatomical and behavioral differences.

The contingencies of reinforcement which define operant behavior are important in the analysis of variables of other sorts. The stimulus control of behavior is central to a kind of non-verbal psychophysics, where interest may be primarily in the action of receptor mechanisms. Operant techniques are important in defining the behavioral effects of physiological variables— surgical, electrical, and chemical—in specifying what aspects of behavior are to be attributed to hereditary endowment, in tracing features of mature behavior to early environment, and so on. They are important in clarifying the nature of defective, retarded, or psychotic behavior. As Lindsley (1963) has pointed out, the important thing about a psychotic is often not what he is doing but what he is not doing, and in such a case it is important to be able to predict normal performances under standard conditions.

Contingencies of reinforcement are also valuable in interpreting behavior not easily submitted to a laboratory analysis. Verbal behavior, for example, can be defined just in terms of its contingencies: its special characteristics are derived from the fact that reinforcement is mediated by other organisms. In education, the instructional programming of reinforcement is the *raison d'être* of teaching machines, the future of which is much brighter than current activities may suggest. It is too early to predict the effect of comparable analyses in other branches of the social sciences, for example, economics and government; but if the history of physical technology is any guide, the knowledge and skills derived from an experimental analysis will become increasingly important.

In short, in the field of human behavior as a whole, the contingencies of reinforcement which define operant behavior are widespread if not ubiquitous. Those who are sensitive to this fact are sometimes embarrassed by the frequency with which they see reinforcement everywhere, as Marxists see class struggle or Freudians the Oedipus relation. Yet the fact is that reinforcement *is* extraordinarily important. That is why it is reassuring to recall that its place was once taken by the concept of purpose; no one is likely to object to a search for purpose in every human act. The difference is that we are now in a position to search effectively. In its very brief history, the study of operant behavior has clarified the nature of the relation between behavior and its consequences and has devised techniques which apply the methods of a natural science to its investigation.

REFERENCES

ADAMS, D. K. (1927) Experimental studies of adaptive behavior in cats. *Comp. Psychol. Monogr., 6,* 1-168.

BERNATOWICZ, A. I. (1958) Teleology in science teaching. *Science, 128,* 1402-1405.

CHOMSKY, N. (1959) Review of Skinner's *Verbal behavior. Language, 35,* 26-58.

FERSTER, C. B., and SKINNER, B. F. (1957) *Schedules of reinforcement.* New York: Appleton-Century-Crofts.

GRINDLEY, G. C. (1932) The formation of a simple habit in guinea pigs. *Brit. J. Psychol., 23,* 127-147.

GUTTMAN, N. (1963) Laws of behavior and facts of perception. In S. Koch (Ed.), *Psychology: A study of a science,* Vol. 5. New York: McGraw-Hill. Pp. 114-178.

HERRNSTEIN, R. J. (1961) Relative and absolute strength of response as a function of frequency of reinforcement. *J. exp. Anal. Behav., 4,* 267-272.

HOGBEN, L. (1957) *Statistical theory.* London: Norton. P. 29.

IVANOV-SMOLENSKY, A. G. (1927) On methods of examining conditioned food reflexes in children and in mental disorders. *Brain, 50,* 138-141.

LAWRENCE, D. H., and FESTINGER, L. (1962) *Deterrents and reinforcement.* Stanford: Stanford Univ. Press.

LINDSLEY, O. R. (1963) Direct measurement and functional definition of vocal hallucinatory symptoms. *J. nerv. ment. Dis., 136,* 293-297.

MILLER, S., and KONORSKI, J. (1928) Sur une forme particulière des réflexes conditionnels. *C. R. Soc. Biol., 99,* 1155-1157.

SIDMAN, M. (1953) Avoidance conditioning with brief shock and no exteroceptive warning signal. *Science, 118,* 157-158.

SIDMAN, M. (1960) *Tactics of scientific research.* New York: Basic Books.

SKINNER, B. F. (1932) Drive and reflex strength: II. *J. gen. Psychol., 6,* 38-48.

SKINNER, B. F. (1937) Two types of conditioned reflex: A reply to Konorski and Miller. *J. gen. Psychol., 16,* 272-279.

SKINNER, B. F. (1938) *The behavior of organisms.* New York: Appleton-Century-Crofts.

SKINNER, B. F. (1950) Are theories of learning necessary? *Psychol. Rev., 57,* 193-216.

SKINNER, B. F. (1957) *Verbal behavior.* New York: Appleton-Century-Crofts.

SKINNER, B. F. (1963) Behaviorism at fifty. *Science, 140,* 951-958.

TERRACE, H. S. (1963) Discrimination learning with and without "errors." *J. exp. Anal. Behav., 6,* 1-27.

2

Superstition: A Corollary of the Principles of Operant Conditioning[1]

R. J. Herrnstein

INTRODUCTION

When we say that the behavior of an animal has been positively reinforced, we are referring both to a procedure and to an effect of the procedure. The procedure requires a particular form of an animal's behavior
to be succeeded by a particular environmental event. The effect of the procedure is an increase in the rate of the particular form of behavior. The
events are called reinforcers and the forms of behavior are called responses.
There has been much controversy about the concept of reinforcement, often
centering on whether all reinforcers share some fundamental characteristic,
such as the reduction of physiological needs. But research has not favored
this powerful hypothesis; rather, it has suggested several different classes of
reinforcers. And it may be that reinforcers have in common only their capacity to increase the rate of instrumental behavior. One may question the
ultimate value of the concept of reinforcement, but at a descriptive level it
is appropriate to any situation in which the procedure has the stipulated
effect. The present article does not attempt, however, to deal with the nature of reinforcement itself, but with the nature of the correlation between
response and reinforcer. This correlation is purely temporal, since the required procedure for positive reinforcement stipulates only that the response
should be followed by the reinforcer. The existence of such purely temporal
processes entails a number of implications about behavior, both animal and
human.

[1] The cost of preparation of this paper was paid for by funds from a National
Science Foundation grant to Harvard University.

SUPERSTITION AND PRIMARY REINFORCEMENT

Suppose a hungry animal is given periodic access to food. If the food is given regardless of what the animal is doing, then we might not readily think of the procedure as positive reinforcement, even though we know that food is an effective reinforcer for hungry animals. But since the animal must have been doing something at the moment the food was presented, it seems reasonable to extend the notion of positive reinforcement to this procedure. Some act or response, albeit unknown, may have been contiguous in time with the reinforcer, and the effect may well be an increase in its rate. If food is not presented again, then we may expect the unknown response to disappear gradually in accordance with the process of extinction, or, if not to disappear, at least to return to its original frequency of occurrence. If, however, the food is presented repeatedly at intervals that are shorter than the duration of complete extinction, then there may be a progressive increase in the rate of the unknown response. We may, in fact, be able to identify this unknown response, if its frequency increases sufficiently.

A procedure consisting of repeated presentations of food, occurring at short intervals of time and independently of behavior, has been described by Skinner (1948). He found that hungry pigeons given brief, periodic access to food developed idiosyncratic, repetitive actions. The precise form of the behavior varied from pigeon to pigeon, but was in all cases highly stereotyped. He referred to the phenomenon as *superstition* through a plausible analogy with certain forms of human behavior. What happened to these pigeons is easily described in terms of positive reinforcement. The delivery of food increased the rate of whatever form of behavior it happened to follow. Food was then presented again, before the effects of the previous presentation had dissipated. Because the reinforced behavior was by then occurring at an increased rate, it was more likely to be reinforced again. The second reinforcement caused a further increase in rate, which further improved its chances of being reinforced, and so on. We need not assume that the course of events was actually this simple. The delivery of food may have strengthened various different forms of behavior before any one form became dominant. The food, on occasion, may have failed to strengthen any form at all, since it may eventually prove to be true that only certain forms of behavior are susceptible to the action of reinforcement. In order for this account to be plausible, reinforcement need only have an effect on some appreciable fraction of an animal's behavior and need only occasionally show its effects after a single temporal contiguity. And these two minimal requirements are well enough established to need no further documentation.

If an observer were permitted only to watch experimental animals, he might initially find it difficult to distinguish between an animal that was explicitly trained to engage in a certain form of behavior and one whose behavior was *superstitious*. In each case, the observer would see an animal engaging in a repetitive, stereotyped act, which was temporally contiguous with the reinforcer. For one animal, this contiguity is explicitly arranged by the experimenter; for the other, it is both a cause and an effect of the high rate of the stereotyped act. The explicit program of reinforcement rigorously guarantees certain physical properties of the response, such as its force and location. Because the other procedure guarantees nothing, the physical properties of the response of this animal may "drift" over a period of time. On the basis of these differences, the observer might eventually distinguish between the animals.

SUPERSTITION AND RESPONSE-DOMINANCE

Skinner's superstitious pigeons received no explicit training for any particular form of behavior. Each of them probably engaged in a large number of different, and potentially conditionable, forms of response at first, and each of them eventually settled on a fairly restricted and stereotyped act. If, however, Skinner had used animals whose behavior was stereotyped to begin with, then his procedure would probably have served merely to emphasize the existing stereotype. Actually, since the sorts of acts that Skinner reported, such as head bobbing and pecking, are distinctly pigeon-like, his procedure may have simply accentuated the very forms of response that were initially dominant among the pigeons. In more systematic experimentation, it may sometimes be useful to know beforehand precisely which response will be dominant, for then the experimenter could observe not only the fate of this dominant response, but he could also observe more than one animal under comparable conditions. One way to make a particular form of behavior dominant is to train the animal explicitly to engage in this behavior. Later, when the reinforcers are presented independently of behavior, the dominant response will tend to be the one that is contiguous with the reinforcer.

A demonstration of this technique is summarized in Figure 1.[2] A pigeon was trained to peck at an illuminated disk. Pecking produced food for the pigeon on an FI 11 sec. schedule. Sessions were terminated after the fortieth reinforcement. The first nine sessions of the figure show the rate of responding obtained with this schedule of reinforcement. Following session nine, the pigeon was no longer reinforced for pecking, but received brief access to food every 11 seconds irrespective of its behavior. The second portion of the figure (sessions 10-31) shows that though the rate of pecking declined, it remained at a substantial level. On session 32, the fixed interval schedule, on which a peck actually produces the food, was reinstated, and it can be seen that the result was an increase in the rate of

[2] This experiment was done in collaboration with W. H. Morse.

responding. During the final portion of the figure (sessions 50-65), the food was not delivered at all and pecking did, in fact, cease. The final portion of the figure demonstrates that pecking does not occur spontaneously in this situation.

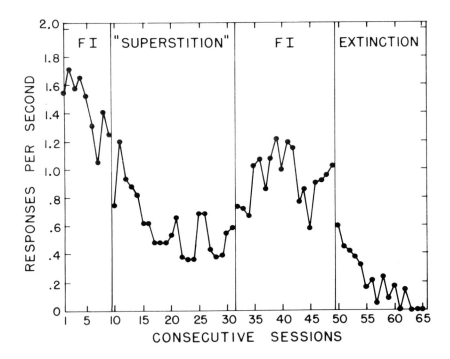

Figure 1. A pigeon's rate of pecking at a key over the course of 65 daily experimental sessions. During the first portion of the experiment (sessions 1-9), the pigeon received food for the first peck that occurred at least 11 seconds after the preceding delivery of food. During the second portion (sessions 10-31), food was delivered every 11 seconds, independent of the pigeon's behavior. During the third portion (sessions 32-49), the conditions of the first portion were duplicated. During the last portion (sessions 50-65), food was no longer delivered.

It is not possible to prove that the superstitious pecking (sessions 10-31) would have gone on indefinitely. It might eventually have disappeared, had this procedure been continued longer. The disappearance would, however, have been gradual, judging from the apparent stability of the rate of responding during the second portion of Figure 1. If pecking were to disappear with this procedure, it would not necessarily be because the food had lost its control over the pigeon's behavior, but because the form of the behavior had "drifted" away from pecking so much that the apparatus was no longer picking up the activity of the pigeon. Pecking may be an unusually tenacious form of behavior for the pigeon, and the technique used in this demonstration provides a means of comparing various forms of behavior with respect to their tenacity.

In both of the demonstrations of superstition mentioned thus far, at least three characteristics of conditioning are involved. Without any one of these factors, it is unlikely that we would ever observe superstitious responding. The first is the purely temporal nature of reinforcement, which allows the necessary and sufficient relation of conditioning—temporal contiguity—to take place even when behavior and reinforcer are mutually independent. The second is the slowness of extinction, relative to conditioning. Because of this slowness, responses may be reinforced only intermittently and still be dominant. The third is that reinforcement does not require an exact, but only an approximate, temporal contiguity between behavior and reinforcer. A form of response may increase in rate even when it has been followed by a reinforcer after an interval of a few seconds. These three factors are well known; each has been studied in its own right.

There may, however, be a fourth characteristic that favors the development of superstitious behavior: less reinforcement may be required to maintain behavior than to cause its acquisition. Several kinds of anecdotal evidence suggest this principle. For example, in teaching an animal a new form of behavior, the experimenter must reinforce virtually every occurrence of the response; but once the response is learned he can reinforce it only infrequently without causing a decrease in its rate. Another example of the same principle may be implicit in the common laboratory practice, when food is the reinforcer, of making the animal extremely hungry during initial training and then reducing the severity of the hunger as the animal's performance develops. If already-conditioned behavior can tolerate more intermittency and less deprivation of the reinforcer than unconditioned behavior, we may presume, by analogy, that already-conditioned behavior can also tolerate longer delays of reinforcement. This last presumption bears on the demonstration summarized in Figure 1 because here pecking was conditioned, whereas the other forms of behavior in the situation were not; and we might, therefore, expect the food to strengthen pecking selectively, even on occasions when some other form of behavior was in closer temporal contiguity with the food. The first three characteristics of conditioning that were mentioned appear adequate to explain the phenomenon of superstitious behavior, but the fourth characteristic may play a significant role when already-conditioned behavior is present.

SUPERSTITION AND THE NON-INSTRUMENTAL ASPECTS OF AN INSTRUMENTAL RESPONSE

In experiments that use primary reinforcers, like food or water, there is usually a precise correlation between the behavior and the reinforcer. Because the reinforcer is presented to the animal as a consequence of a specified form of response, there would seem to be little or no opportunity for other forms of response to be temporally contiguous with the reinforcer, hence no superstitious behavior would be expected. However, the specified correlation between behavior and reinforcer usually involves only some of the properties of the response. In the apparatus used with pigeons, pecks must occur in a given location and with at least a minimum force. But, ordinarily, nothing is specified about the duration of the response, the rate at which it occurs, or the manner in which it is executed. If the duration, rate, and manner of execution of the response are potentially conditionable, then it is possible that they will be as much influenced by their temporal proximity to the reinforcement as are the location and force. Since the whole response, and not just its criterial aspects, are temporally contiguous with the reinforcer, all of its conditionable properties may be affected. However, force and location are properties that are affected in accordance with particular criteria for reinforcement, while the others are affected, at least in part, by chance. Pigeons might therefore locate their responses similarly and peck with roughly equal forces, but they are likely to differ from each other markedly with respect to such things as duration, rate, or topography of response. Although differing from each other, each pigeon ought to be self-consistent in these properties of response. The stereotypy of an animal's responding which in the past has been used as evidence against the notion of reinforcement (Guthrie & Horton, 1946) is actually one of the direct implications of the concept.

The accidental correlation between reinforcement and non-criterial properties of response may not be the only factor determining the fate of these properties. For a pigeon, the duration of a peck is probably, to some extent, built in, as is its topography; and the rate of pecking almost certainly depends in part upon factors like the frequency of reinforcement and the quality of the reinforcer. It is within the limits imposed by these other factors that the accidental correlations of behavior and reinforcer have their effects. We may expect that with regard to any of these non-criterial properties of behavior, a group of animals will show variation within a predictable range, but that each animal within the group will tend to become progressively more stereotyped with training.

SUPERSTITION AND CONDITIONED REINFORCEMENT

Thus far, only primary reinforcers have been discussed, but it seems reasonable to assume that conditioned reinforcers function in essentially the same way. The conditioned reinforcers, however, warrant additional consideration here because of the special ways in which they are used in experiments. For example, a common procedure for studying the process of stimulus discrimination is to alternate a stimulus in whose presence some form of response is reinforced (the positive stimulus) with a stimulus in whose presence no reinforcers are forthcoming (the negative stimulus). Ordinarily, one would say that this procedure involves a primary reinforcer, which is correlated with behavior during the positive stimulus, and two stimuli which are to be discriminated by the animal. However, these two stimuli may have properties in addition to their discriminability, even though they are selected for their "neutrality," since the procedure itself may make them either reinforcing or punishing. An originally neutral stimulus in whose presence behavior is positively reinforced is known to become a stimulus which can itself reinforce other behavior, i.e., a conditioned reinforcer. Since the positive stimulus is, by definition, present when the animal emits the reinforced response, it is likely to become a conditioned reinforcer. Moreover, it is presented to the animal regardless of its behavior. As a reinforcer that is being presented to an animal independently of its behavior, it may produce superstitious responding. Any superstitious responding would occur during the negative stimulus periods because it is only during these periods that a response can be contiguous in time with the onset of the positive stimulus.

The stimulus discrimination procedure is, therefore, like a multiple schedule (Ferster & Skinner, 1957). There are two stimuli: in the presence of one of them (the positive stimulus) a specified form of behavior is maintained by a primary reinforcer, and in the presence of the other (the negative stimulus) some unspecified form of behavior is maintained adventitiously by the onset of the positive stimulus. The unspecified form is likely to be the same sort of responding (for example, pecking) that is reinforced during the positive stimulus periods, especially if the two stimuli are physically similar or if the experiment started with a procedure in which this form of responding was reinforced in the presence of both stimuli. If the experimenter wishes to discover how long it takes for an animal to learn to discriminate between the two stimuli, and if he is using as his measure of discrimination the presence of responding during positive stimulus periods and the absence of responding during negative stimulus periods, this procedure may be highly misleading. Responding during negative stimulus periods may continue long after the animal has discriminated between the two stimuli; the responding may go on indefinitely or at least until the form of the response "drifts" away from that being recorded by the experimenter (Morse, 1955).

The stimulus discrimination procedure is easily remedied. If an adequate delay is interposed between positive and negative stimuli, then the behavior during the negative stimulus periods will not come under the control of the positive stimulus and the problem is solved, assuming that the delay itself is not acting in some way on behavior. The principle exemplified by the stimulus discrimination procedure is that in any procedure in which stimuli occur independently of behavior, there is the possibility that some unknown response is being adventitiously influenced. The opening of the start-box of a maze or runway may come to influence the behavior of the animal as it waits in the start-box. Some experimenters have learned that this is true, and adopt some rule for when the box may be opened. If the experimenter is recording the time it takes the animal to traverse the maze or runway, then the rule he adopts for opening the start-box may have an effect on the data he obtains. Although the effect may be small, it may be a source of inter-subject and inter-experimenter variability. In general, whenever stimuli are presented independently of behavior, the possibility exists not only that superstitious responding will be produced, but that the responding will interact with the experiment's dependent variable.

SUPERSTITION AND STIMULUS CONTROL

Positive reinforcement is not the only behavioral process based on a correlation of events in time. For example, it was mentioned earlier that a stimulus in whose presence a response is reinforced may become a conditioned reinforcer. This process, too, is purely temporal, and the adventitious creation of a conditioned reinforcer has already been described in the discussion of the stimulus discrimination experiment. That experiment contains still another purely temporal process: the rule of *stimulus control*. By reinforcing behavior in the presence of one stimulus and extinguishing it in the presence of another, the experiment exploits the fact that behavior tends to be governed solely by the stimulus in whose presence it is occurring; in this example, the two processes of conditioning and extinction would be associated with the two stimuli. There are interactions between the two processes (Herrnstein & Brady, 1958; Reynolds, 1961), but independence, rather than interaction, is the rule. The rule of stimulus control is, then, a principle of behavior stating that a stimulus gains power over behavior by virtue of its presence when behavior is reinforced or extinguished. Sometimes, several different stimuli are associated with several different schedules of reinforcement and we find that the behavior in the presence of each stimulus is in general appropriate to the correlated schedule (Ferster & Skinner, 1957).

The rule of stimulus control can become the basis of a phenomenon very like superstitious behavior. Morse and Skinner (1957) reported an experiment in which pigeons were reinforced for pecking on a VI schedule. Occasionally, a light was turned on briefly. Although the light was not correlated with any change in conditions, one of the pigeons came to respond rapidly in its presence and another came to respond slowly. We may surmise what happened. On a VI schedule, reinforcements will occasionally be separated by relatively short times, and occasionally by relatively long times. Because the procedure presents the incidental light without regard to the schedule of reinforcement, it is possible that for one pigeon it first came on when reinforcements were relatively infrequent and for the other pigeon when reinforcements were relatively frequent. However, since the light was actually in a random relation to the scheduling of reinforcements, the frequency of reinforcement in the presence of the light must eventually have averaged out to the same value as in the schedule as a whole. But by this time, the superstitious discrimination could have exerted its effect.

Let us suppose that at first the light was, in fact, correlated with a high frequency of reinforcement for one pigeon and a low frequency for the other. By the rule of stimulus control, we would expect the rates in the presence of the stimuli to change in the appropriate, and opposite, directions for these two pigeons. For one pigeon, the light seemed to signal a better schedule than was programmed in its absence, and this pigeon's rate of responding therefore increased when the light came on; for the other pigeon, whose rate of responding decreased, the light seemed to signal a poorer schedule of reinforcement. As the account now stands, these alterations in the rate of responding should have been transient, for as the frequency of reinforcement in the presence of the light gradually averaged out to the same value as in the absence of the light, the rate should have returned to the original level. Morse and Skinner do, in fact, report such transience.

The effect need not, however, be transient in order to conform to the paradigm of superstitious behavior. The rate of responding is elevated or depressed by the higher or lower frequency of reinforcement in the presence of the incidental stimulus. But then, since the rate of responding is itself a conditionable characteristic of behavior (Anger, 1956), the animal may continue to respond at the elevated or depressed rate even after the frequency of reinforcement is no longer differentially correlated with the incidental stimulus. It may seem paradoxical to say that the rate of responding will vary with the frequency of reinforcement and also to say that it may be directly conditioned by adventitious correlation with the reinforcer. The paradox is, however, only apparent. It may be, for example, that a given frequency of reinforcement determines a range of possible rates of responding and that within this range superstitious effects will occur. A similar point was made earlier: the accidental correlation between a characteristic of behavior and reinforcement tends to have its effect within the normal range of variation for the characteristic in question.

The significance of superstitious control by stimuli is limited by a number of factors. If stimuli are precisely and consistently correlated with reinforcement, then there is little opportunity for accidental stimulus control. Furthermore, stimuli may ostensibly fail to gain control over behavior even in the absence of precise and consistent correlations, if the experimenter's measure of behavior is very narrowly specified by the procedure. For example, in an experiment in which only the rate of responding is measured, and only a particular rate of responding is reinforced, a procedure of the type employed by Morse and Skinner would probably have no observed effect.

SUPERSTITION AND AVERSIVE STIMULI

In the case of aversive stimuli, the experimenter once again arranges correlations in time between behavior and environment. An animal learns to escape in the sense that behavior becomes more frequent if it results in (that is to say, is followed in time by) the removal of an aversive stimulus. We would expect superstitious behavior to develop if we exposed an animal to a painful electric shock which was periodically terminated independently of the animal's actions. Like Skinner's superstitious pigeons, these animals should also develop ritualized behaviors as a result of correlations in time between their activities and the occurrence of the reinforcer. This experiment has not been done, but if it were to fail it would be necessary to revise our view of escape conditioning. In studies of punishment, an aversive stimulus is made directly contingent upon behavior, and the result is a diminution in the frequency of the response most immediately contiguous in time with the punisher. Once again, we would expect accidental temporal correlations to have predictable effects in situations that permit such correlations. It seems unnecessary to go into any further detail, since according to our present knowledge, these superstitions should not in principle differ from those already described in connection with the positive reinforcers.

SUPERSTITION AVERTED

Is it possible that the accidental correlations in time among responses, stimuli, and reinforcers do not exert control over behavior? It is instructive to ask this question because the possible inadequacies of the present analysis are limited in number and point in specific directions of investigation. The limitation arises because much of the analysis is based on empirical fact: we know that reinforcement and the various other processes operate through temporal contiguity; we know that the process of conditioning is more rapid than the process of extinction; and we know that behavior can be affected by an event even when the event is slightly delayed.

The present analysis would be wrong if animals could detect causation as such. Such insight, which would certainly protect animals from being misled by accidental correlations of various sorts, is unlikely on the purely rational grounds that causation is nothing more than invariable correlation. Nevertheless, the issue deserves mention because psychologists occasionally imply some other concept of causation. For example, some people (e.g., Adams, 1929) object to the usual procedure for demonstrating positive reinforcement because it does not enable the animal to "understand" the connection between behavior and its consequence. If "understanding" means anything at all here, it must mean a recognition of something more than mere correlation, and this something more must be causation.

There are more plausible ways in which the present analysis could fall short. One of the characteristics of accidental correlations between behavior and environmental events is *variability*. Every aspect of behavior may vary and yet be contiguous with a reinforcer that is independent of the behavior. In contrast, behavior that is instrumental must have at least one aspect that has a more or less fixed correlation with the reinforcer. Were animals sensitive to this difference, they could detect those events over which their behavior has no real control. To prevent superstition, this mechanism would have to cause the animal to cease engaging in any behavior whose aspects were contiguous with a reinforcer, but were at the same time highly variable. Superstition would be prevented only imperfectly by this mechanism, for it becomes irrelevant in a given situation as soon as reinforcement has had the effect of sufficiently narrowing the range of variation in the behavior. Only an imperfect mechanism, however, is plausible, since superstitions do occur at least sometimes.

The variability of superstitious responding could be the basis of yet another mechanism to limit the effectiveness of events that are independent of behavior. If we assume that behavior obeys a principle of least effort, then superstitious responding should always "drift" in the direction of minimal forms. Because the reinforcer is actually independent of the response, there is an opportunity for increasingly minimal forms of the response to occur and still be in temporal contiguity with the reinforcer. We would expect that the behavior would eventually become so minimal in form and effort as to become altogether unobservable.

AN EXTRAPOLATION TO HUMAN BEHAVIOR

This has been a discussion of behavior under the influence of events that are independent of it. The influences appear to be predictable from a knowledge of the effect of these same events when they are in a specified relation to behavior. The discussion is not based on any new principles; instead, it has been an attempt to apply only well-established principles. Is there, then, any value in this discussion—either theoretical or practical? In experiments on animal behavior, important stimuli ordinarily do not occur in uncontrolled association with behavior. And even when this precise control is lacking, there is a reasonable chance that the behavior under observation will be unaffected by accidental coincidences. If experimenters took further special pains to control the temporal relations among responses, stimuli, and reinforcers, there would probably be an overall decrease in the variability from animal to animal, but the decrease might not justify the extra pains. But to say that superstitions are relatively unimportant in well-controlled experiments implies a reciprocal relation between the degree to which the experimenter regulates the various relations among events and the degree to which accidental correlations do so. It is in this reciprocity that the importance of superstition is to be found, for as one leaves the experimental setting and approaches the natural environment, one ought to find progressively more influence of adventitious events. Most of the happenings in the animal's natural world take place independently of its behavior, and, depending upon the various other factors that have been described, its behavior will be affected by them. To the extent that an animal is capable of learning, it will be the victim of events over which it has no real control.

To find superstition at its maximum we are naturally led to a consideration of the most teachable animal, man, in his natural environment. That men are superstitious, there can be no question, since in the past it has been their behavior that this word describes, and only very recently, the behavior of animals. There may, however, be a question whether the superstitions of men and those of animals really arise from the same fundamental processes. Certainly, the traditional view of human superstition, one in which a predominantly rational creature occasionally holds an irrational belief, seems different from the view outlined here in the description of animal behavior. Yet some psychologists (e.g., Skinner, 1953) have argued that the traditional view, when translated into an acceptable scientific language, becomes a description of accidental coincidences between behavior and events in the environment. Although this argument has been generally stated, and widely accepted by those who are disposed toward a behavioristic account of human behavior, it has not yet been examined in detail.

Consider, then, some human superstitions to see if they are plausibly handled by the model of the pigeon engaging in a stereotyped act that has only an accidental relation to a reinforcer. Here are two familiar human superstitions, convenient for our purposes because they appear to be based on negative and positive reinforcement, respectively, and because they are relatively simple, as human behavior goes. Some people refuse to allow three cigarettes to be lit by a single match; others carry a rabbit's foot for "good luck." In order for the pigeon-model to apply, we should be able to say that each of these acts has been generated in a person's own experience by accidental correlations with punishing or reinforcing events. The man who carries a rabbit's foot would be like the pigeon that futilely turns a figure eight, each one showing how an irrelevant act may be selected by an incidental reinforcer. But there seems to be something wrong here. Men happen to carry rabbits' feet, refuse three on a match; they do not happen to carry squirrels' ears nor do they refrain from three in an automobile. If, however, there is actually something special about rabbits' feet and cigarette lighting, then these acts are no longer accidental in the way the pigeon's turning is.

We could go on with the other well-known human superstitions. Walking under ladders, black cats, Friday the thirteenth, and so on are each a well-known superstition, hence not arbitrary, and not nearly as infrequent as, let us say, superstitions about fire escapes, yellow dogs, Wednesday the eleventh. Or, suppose we wish to argue that religion is superstitious. The rituals are, again, not arbitrary in any particular social community. Given that a boy is Jewish, it is no accident that he is confirmed at age thirteen, nor is it an accident that a particular Catholic believes in transubstantiation. In fact, some students of human superstition, operating within the framework of classical anthropology and not behavioristic psychology, have found the uniformity in these patterns of behavior so impressive that they have been led to theories that talk of underlying archetypes, only slightly modified from locality to locality.

Even if the notion of archetypes is not supported by the evidence, there is no doubt that human superstitions fail to show the quality of arbitrariness that is the essence of superstition in the pigeon, as described by Skinner (1948). This does not mean, however, that the attempt to relate human and animal superstition must be abandoned. It means only that the relationship is not the simple one that comes first to mind. Human superstition, unlike that of animals, arises in a social context. The process of acculturation—the extensive education of new members of a culture by older members—seems to include indoctrination in superstition. One is told, or one overhears, that a rabbit's foot is good luck, three-on-a-match bad luck, and so on. That men are influenced by what they hear is self-evident, if not easily explained, and no explanation will be attempted here. Thus, each member of a particular culture gets his start in the conventional superstitions of his culture.

These conventional superstitions provide the baseline upon which individual experience operates. We hear about rabbits' feet, we can even buy one, but then accident determines whether carrying it become reinforced. Of the many who take the first steps toward this superstition only a few become addicted to it. Yet even these few are many, in comparison with the number we would expect if rabbits' feet were not a conventional superstition. Similarly, we may be born into a family of Presbyterians and therefore behave like one at first, but again accident must settle whether we come to believe in the acts associated with this sect. The born Presbyterian, given his start in this direction, rarely grows up to be a religious Moslem, and vice versa.

The example of religion is instructive—in addition to being controversial—because it reveals the snares that await anyone who would analyze human superstition. Religion is superstitious only if its theological doctrines are essentially false. One may be willing to make this assumption, but should recognize it as such. The falsity of the doctrines is, however, not sufficient proof that the religious activities of an individual person are properly called superstitious. A person may practice the rituals of a church because he lives in a social community that reinforces religious conformity and punishes transgressions. Behavior such as this, that is under the control of genuine contingencies of reinforcement and punishment, is not superstitious. But even if one could exclude the social pressure for conformity, as well as reject the theological doctrines, there may still be genuine sources of reinforcement in religion. The value of its code of morality, the beauty of its art and music, the comforting intimacy with other people that it provides, may all contribute to its potency. Religion, then, is complex, and any honest and complete account should mirror this complexity. In the present analysis, however, only that part of religion is explained that is legitimately termed superstitious.

The sort of process involved in the conventional human superstitions was outlined early in this paper in the discussion of superstition as response-dominance. A hungry pigeon had been trained to peck at a disk for reinforcement by food (see Figure 1). When food was later delivered intermittently, but independently of behavior, the pigeon nevertheless continued to peck. Pecking was now superstitious, maintained only by the accidental correlations with the reinforcer. Although superstitious, pecking had not arisen by chance, but had been established as the dominant response by the preliminary training. Similarly, the individual person is predisposed toward the conventional superstition by his social surroundings.

Each of the well-known human superstitions can be viewed as the strengthening of an already-available act by accidental coincidences between behavior and environment. Just as the experimenter decides which response would be initially favored in the pigeon experiment, the culture decides in the case of human superstition. As far as superstition alone is concerned, the analysis could stop here, with the culture establishing in people a response-dominance whose fate is governed by accident. But since culture itself is merely a shorthand way of speaking about behavior, we may venture some guesses about the origin of these particular cultural practices. It may be that most human superstitions originated not as superstitions, but as acts that were genuinely effective in some different environment, just as pecking was during preliminary training. The case of three-on-a-match appears to be of this type, having originated in the trenches of World War I when each moment of illumination risked detection by the enemy. Other superstitions may have started out as genuine accidents in the lives of exceptionally powerful members of social groups, who could then inflict their personal superstitions on lesser members. Either mode of origination is plausible. Beyond the question of how a superstition originated, there is the question how it is carried forth from generation to generation. It may be that it owes its continued existence to the few individuals in whose lives accident has confirmed the superstition. Or it may be that human conventions can survive for many generations without requiring this kind of accidental support.

We may presume that at least some superstitions originate as genuinely effective acts. They cease being effective when the environment changes, but they may then begin their history as ritual. The injunction against three-on-a-match has been cited as an example of this process, but an even more typical example is the dietary practices of some religious groups. Some Jews, to pick an example, will not eat pork. It could reasonably be argued that at the time this practice became a convention, the eating of pork was literally dangerous because of the preponderance of contaminated swine. Today, swine are no longer so likely to be contaminated with disease, but the practice of abstinence, supported by the scripture, has been maintained. The change from dangerous to harmless swine has probably been very gradual, extending over centuries, unlike the rapid change from the genuinely dangerous to the utterly harmless lighting of three cigarettes on a match. Most of the changes in the environment are likely to be relatively slow, as measured by human lifetimes, and in this gradualness there is almost a guarantee that a once-effective act will be preserved in ritual. For as the once-effective act gradually loses its effectiveness, it is maintained by an ever more intermittent schedule of reinforcement, a situation that has been shown (Ferster & Skinner, 1957) to be ideal for generating high levels of unreinforced behavior. This behavior may then serve as the dominant response to be maintained indefinitely by accidental contingencies.

This conversion of effective acts into ritual may help to explain why anthropologists find uniformity in the rituals of widely scattered cultures. Dietary laws, for example, exist in numerous religions, even where no mutual influence can be found. As a matter of fact, a dietary law may be superstition in one part of the world, but good sense in another, given the diversity of sanitary sophistication. At some time in the future, we may hopefully predict, such laws will be superstitious wherever found, and their existence will be based not on archetypes, but on the natural process just described.

Some rituals do not seem to allow this simple derivation from once-effective acts. For example, it is hard to construct a plausible account in these terms for rituals concerned with death, or weather, or other events over which man may never have had any significant degree of control. Some anthropologists would have us believe that these sorts of ritual also turn up in unrelated cultures. In explaining these uniformities, the present analysis can only point out that ritual is to be expected especially in connection with those reinforcers and punishers over which man has little control. If man can produce rain, he will not pray for it. The analogy with animal experimentation is implicit in the reciprocal relation between the degree to which the experimenter controls the occurrences of important events and the degree to which superstition is likely to occur. It may be, then, that anthropologists have observed the tendencies of certain important events to become the foci of rituals, and not real uniformities in the rituals themselves.

The well-known human superstitions have been likened to superstition as response-dominance in animals. Simple superstition in animals, as first described by Skinner, is also relevant to human behavior; but the word "superstition" may not be appropriate. The paradigm of simple superstition in animals requires that an act be selected or suppressed by a chance association with a reinforcer or punisher. In the case of human beings, we may speak of such irrational and idiosyncratic acts as compulsions, obsessions, and tics. The person who is plagued by more than the usual number of these acts is spoken of as "neurotic," not superstitious. But probably everyone has experienced the compulsion to engage in some accidentally reinforced act or to avoid some accidentally punished one. Whether these commonplace experiences are on the same continuum with the massive and debilitating compulsions of the seriously neurotic person cannot be asserted positively as yet. However, since we know how to make the simple superstition of the pigeon more or less powerful just by varying simple parameters, there seem to be safe grounds for considering this a genuine continuum.

Human superstitions tend to be based on convention; compulsions, on the other hand, are intrinsically idiosyncratic. The pigeons described by Skinner were dramatically idiosyncratic. Idiosyncrasy is found in pigeons in connection also with the non-instrumental aspects of instrumental acts. It was pointed out earlier that pigeons may become markedly stereotyped in the execution of a learned response because of the contiguity between each conditionable feature of the response and the reinforcer. Thus, in an experiment in which the pigeon is reinforced for a peck of a given force at a particular location, we may find that the rate, duration, and topography of the peck also become conditioned. Among a group of pigeons, it is likely that each will have an idiosyncratic rate, duration, and topography.

In human behavior, the accidental conditioning of non-instrumental aspects of instrumental behavior is not ordinarily termed *superstition*. Consider, for example, the matter of handwriting. The letter "a" in script is defined by certain criterial features: the upright, asymmetrical loop and the stroke to the right. However, a considerable range of variation is permissible: the loop may tilt in either direction from the vertical, it may be left unclosed, it may vary in the ratio of the horizontal to the vertical dimension, the stroke may start at various points in the loop, and so on. Given a large enough sample of writers, virtually all permissible variations would be seen. Yet, each one of the writers would be stereotyped in regard to the non-criterial features of the letter. Just as the pigeon is explicitly taught only the criterial aspects of the response—the location and the force of the peck—so the writer is explicitly taught only the asymmetrical loop and the stroke to the right. In both cases, however, non-instrumental properties are inadvertently "taught," merely by being contiguous with the reinforcer.

A man's idiosyncratic handwriting is known as his writing *style*. Other applications of the word *style* seem also to be based on the conditioning of non-instrumental aspects of instrumental behavior. The difference in style that distinguishes the gaits of two men are differences that do not involve success in walking, since both succeed in getting around. The different batting styles of two great baseball players, let us say Ted Williams and Mickey Mantle, may not be related to performance in any essential way since both are high performers. It is presumably what they have in common, and not their idiosyncratic styles, that makes them great.

Style, taste and *preference* are words we use to describe the distinctive non-instrumental aspects of instrumental human behavior. We can recognize a man by his style (handwriting, walking, speaking, and so on) just because the non-instrumental aspects of behavior will vary from man to man, but be distinctively each man's own. Precisely the same state of affairs was encountered earlier with respect to the pecking of pigeons. It was then pointed out that the accidents of reinforcement may not be the only factor influencing the non-instrumental aspects of the response. So it is with man. The conformation of his arm may have something to do with handwriting, that of the body as a whole with walking, and so on. But the conformation of the body, as well as any other factor, will merely establish a range of possible variation for the response in question, a range from which accidental reinforcement selects the distinctive style.

Some appreciable fraction of psychology is devoted to an analysis of men from their styles (handwriting and otherwise). The present argument may seem, at first, to be inimical to this part of psychology. But this is not so. As has been pointed out before, in any situation in which accidental contingencies are operating, the net result may be simply an accentuation of a response already dominant. Thus, the person whose handwriting is distinguished by unusually firm pressure on the pencil or pen may be one who responds vigorously in many contexts. To discover this about him from so minute a sample of his behavior as a line of writing is impressive economy of observation. However, the conditioning of these non-instrumental aspects of behavior is fundamentally a statistical process. There is no guarantee that the vigorous responder will happen to be reinforced for vigorous penmanship; there is only a good chance that he will. The users of such diagnostic techniques as graphology may have to content themselves with only moderate and statistical success.

SUMMARY

Given certain features of the process of operant conditioning—that it takes place when response and reinforcer are in temporal contiguity, that the contiguity need only be approximate, and that conditioning is fast relative to extinction—we can predict, on purely deductive grounds, that responses may occasionally be conditioned by reinforcers that are actually occurring at random. This phenomenon, termed *superstition,* has been demonstrated empirically in animals. If a hungry animal is intermittently given food, independently of what it is doing, it will nevertheless come to engage in some stereotyped act. In the original demonstration of animal superstition, the experimenter left to chance which act would be accidently reinforced. In a subsequent demonstration, however, it was shown that by first training an animal to engage in some act and then giving food randomly, the experimenter could select a particular form for the superstition. The presentation of food to an animal possessing a dominant form of response served simply to augment and maintain the dominance. It was further pointed out that when particular aspects of a response are explicitly reinforced, other, non-instrumental aspects are likely to be inadvertently reinforced as well. For example, a pigeon that is explicitly taught to peck a disk at a certain location and with a certain minimal force, also learns incidentally to peck at a particular rate and with a narrowly defined topography. As long as these non-instrumental aspects of the behavior are in temporal contiguity with the reinforcer and are conditionable dimensions of behavior, they will become just as stereotyped as the essential aspects of the behavior.

In extrapolating these ideas to human behavior, we find, first of all, that human superstitions are most closely paralleled by accidentally reinforced response-dominances. Because most human superstitions are conventional modes of responding—modes that are, by one means or another, taught to new members of a culture by the older members—people in a particular culture will share predispositions toward particular superstitions rather than toward others. Secondly, although there is a human parallel to the simple superstitions of animals, it is probably not what we usually call *superstition.* The superstitions of an animal are intrinsically idiosyncratic and entirely dependent upon the personal history of that animal. In human behavior, such idiosyncratic forms of responding are usually termed *compulsive* or *obsessive.* Finally, the so-called *style* evident in some kinds of human behavior seems to be based in part on the accidental reinforcement of non-instrumental aspects of instrumental behavior. For example, the distinctiveness of an individual person's handwriting involves the non-essential features of penmanship and is probably influenced by accidents of reinforcement.

REFERENCES

ADAMS, D. K. (1929) Experimental studies of adaptive behavior in cats. *Comp. Psychol. Monogr., 6,* No. 1 (Whole No. 27).

ANGER, D. (1956) The dependence of interresponse times upon the relative reinforcement of different interresponse times. *J. exp. Psychol., 53,* 145-161.

FERSTER, C. B., and SKINNER, B. F. (1957) *Schedules of reinforcement.* New York: Appleton-Century-Crofts.

GUTHRIE, E. R., and HORTON, G. P. (1946) *Cats in a puzzle box.* New York: Holt, Rinehart & Winston.

HERRNSTEIN, R. J., and BRADY, J. V. (1958) Interaction among components of a multiple schedule. *J. exp. Anal. Behav., 1,* 293-300.

MORSE, W. H. (1955) An analysis of responding in the presence of a stimulus correlated with periods of non-reinforcement. Unpublished doctoral dissertation, Harvard University.

MORSE, W. H., and SKINNER, B. F. (1957) A second type of superstition in the pigeon. *Amer. J. Psychol., 70,* 308-311.

REYNOLDS, G. S. (1961) An analysis of interactions in a multiple schedule. *J. exp. Anal. Behav., 4,* 107-117.

SKINNER, B. F. (1948) "Superstition" in the pigeon. *J. exp. Psychol., 38,* 168-172.

SKINNER, B. F. (1953) *Science and human behavior.* New York: Macmillan.

3

Intermittent Reinforcement [1]

W. H. Morse

INTRODUCTION

The outstanding characteristic of operant behavior is that it can be differentiated in form and in temporal patterning by consequent events. Conditioned operant behavior emerges out of undifferentiated behavior through successive approximations to new and more complex forms by the process of successive differential reinforcement (shaping). Behavior that has become highly differentiated can be understood and accounted for only in terms of the history of reinforcement of that behavior—when, and how, and under what stimulus conditions reinforcers acted to shape the behavior. Except for trivial cases, this history of reinforcement will have been intermittent. Because the genesis and modulation of operant behavior depend primarily on a history of intermittent reinforcement, the effects of intermittent reinforcement are involved in all the phenomena of operant behavior.

Intermittency of reinforcement in the development of complex behavior is inevitable. Ferster and Skinner (1957) point out that even casual observation of the normal environment of an organism will show that the conditions in the traditional study of learning, where "right" responses are always rewarded and "wrong" responses are always allowed to go unrewarded, are atypical, Verplanck (1957) also notes that regular reinforcement has almost no analogue in the behavior of animals in a free environment. It is indeed curious that the more natural condition of intermittent reinforcement has been subsumed under the more limited and artificial laboratory condition of regular reinforcement to such an extent that most psychologists have placed the burden of explaining all of the phenomena of

(margin handwritten note: How ?! about .. univevo Rs)

[1] The preparation of this chapter was supported by Research Grants MH-02094 and MH-07658 from the Institute of Mental Health of the National Institutes of Health, and by a Public Health Service research career program award, 5-K3-GM-15,530, from the Institute of Mental Health. I wish to thank Drs. P. B. Dews and R. T. Kelleher for their helpful comments and Mrs. Suzanne Ledecky-Janecek and Miss Eleanor Bates for help in preparation of the manuscript.

partial reinforcement on interpretations of regular reinforcement. But intermittent reinforcement is much more than a mere falling-short of the ideal of regular reinforcement. Only under intermittent reinforcement can the effects of reinforcement be fully manifested, and many characteristics of learned behavior are directly attributable to the dynamic interactions of variables which are necessarily in effect under intermittent reinforcement.

The Concept of Reinforcement

A clear understanding of the concept of reinforcement is fundamental for an appreciation of the scope and importance of intermittent reinforcement. A reinforcer (reinforcing stimulus) is an event which changes subsequent behavior when it follows behavior in time. Operationally, an event is identified as a positive reinforcer if the frequency of responses of a given class (operant) increases when the presentation of the event is made contingent upon a response of that class. Reinforcement is the presentation of a reinforcer in a specified temporal relation to an operant.[2]

The primary effect of reinforcement is to strengthen and intensify certain aspects of ensuing behavior. This alteration in behavior usually occurs immediately, persists in time, becomes weaker, and gradually declines in the absence of further reinforcement. It is customary to divide this effect of reinforcement into conditioning and extinction. Conditioning refers to the strengthening of behavior by reinforcement; extinction refers to its subsequent decline after reinforcement is discontinued. The concepts of conditioning and extinction are unquestionably useful in analyzing the effects of intermittent reinforcement and will be used in this chapter. They are largely restrictive concepts that describe behavior in particular situations; but because experiments have been arranged to study the pure cases of conditioning or extinction, we know many details about the strengthening and decline of behavior that can be applied to the study of intermittent reinforcement. For example, many findings about intermittent reinforcement can be predicted because conditioning is rapid and extinction is slow. But it should be noted that these are only different aspects of a unitary effect of reinforcement. An important characteristic of reinforcement is that conditioned behavior is rapidly acquired; an equally important characteristic is that conditioned behavior persists in time and is slowly lost.

Reinforcement generates a reproducible behavioral process in time (see Zimmerman, 1963). The action of reinforcement in time is emphasized when a single instance of reinforcement changes subsequent behavior. A response occurs, is followed by a reinforcer, and further responses occur

---

[2] Strictly speaking, this chapter is about intermittent positive reinforcement, although many of the general relations discussed also apply to intermittent negative reinforcement. The topics of negative reinforcement and punishment are considered in other chapters of this book.

with a characteristic temporal patterning. Conventional experiments on reinforcement obscure this orderly temporal process by dichotomizing it into
a conditioning phase and an extinction phase. To emphasize the fact that
the weakening of conditioned behavior normally requires the occurrence
of behavior, extinction is said to occur because responses are unreinforced.
But conditioning also depends upon the occurrence of behavior. A response
that does not occur following reinforcement is not extinguished; similarly
a response that does not occur preceding reinforcement is not conditioned.
Responses normally do occur after reinforcement, of course, and the temporal patterning of these responses is an effect of reinforcement. Reinforcement strengthens and determines the temporal pattern of ensuing behavior;
additional reinforcement further strengthens and patterns the already altered
behavior. New forms of behavior develop because successive reinforcements act on changing behavior, and for this to happen reinforcement must
occur when the effects of previous reinforcement are still manifest. Most
temporal patterns of behavior will develop only when reinforcement is
intermittent. Viewing the occurrence of behavior following reinforcement
simply as the weakening of conditioned behavior in extinction obscures the
potential of reinforcement for generating and changing temporal patterns of
responding. The concepts of conditioning and extinction can be powerful
analytic tools, but they can also emphasize trivial relations and make simple phenomena seem complex.

The Effects of Reinforcement

Specifically, what changes in behavior are engendered by presenting a
reinforcer? It is important to distinguish between the simple defining operations customarily employed to establish a reinforcer, and other possible
effects of following some identifiable bit of behavior with a known reinforcer. The defining characteristics of a reinforcer do not encompass all
its effects on behavior. For example, the operational definition of a reinforcer specifies its temporal relation to an identified class of responses, yet
adventitious reinforcement, the presentation of reinforcers without reference to behavior, has characteristic effects on behavior (Herrnstein &
Morse, 1957; Skinner, 1948). (See also Chapter 2 by Herrnstein.)

Usually when a response is reinforced it subsequently occurs more frequently than before it was reinforced. Under optimum circumstances the
increase in frequency may be demonstrated with only a single reinforcement (Skinner, 1938, p. 88). Other aspects of the response, e.g., its force,
duration, and topography, also change as a result of reinforcement. All
these changes characteristically appear to be enhancements; yet there are
exceptions. For certain classes of responses, presenting a known reinforcer
may decrease the frequency of the reinforced response class. Skinner and
Morse (1958) found that making a known reinforcer (food) contingent

upon wheel turning (running) in the rat, decreased rather than increased the rate of running under conditions in which a high rate of running normally occurred. The effects of reinforcement seemed to depend upon the ongoing level of the behavior reinforced. Unfortunately relatively little is known about the effects of reinforcement on quantitative properties of behavior other than its rate of occurrence. Skinner (1953) has emphasized that behavior has a continuity into which the effects of reinforcement blend. Consequently the effects of reinforcement may be different or even opposite with different behaviors. Reinforcement may be assumed to have a characteristic and reproducible effect on a particular behavior, and usually it will enhance and intensify that behavior.

Properties of behavior intensified by reinforcement are revealed in exaggerated form when reinforcement (either regular or intermittent) is discontinued (extinction). Since the effect of a single reinforcement is to intensify subsequent behavior, it is natural that a series of reinforcements also intensifies subsequent behavior. The most carefully studied example of this intensification has been the increase in rate of responding during extinction, but similar observations have been made for other aspects of conditioned behavior (force—Skinner, 1938; stereotypy—Antonitis, 1951; Herrnstein, 1961b; duration—Skinner, 1938). This intensification of conditioned behavior when reinforcement is withheld should be considered as a dynamic temporal effect of reinforcement itself rather than as a separate effect of extinction.

Because conditioned operant behavior is intensified in extinction before it subsequently declines, one can give a general formula for shaping operant behavior: select a response with properties that can be designated quantitatively, follow the occurrence of a particular magnitude of this response with a reinforcer one or more times, then withhold reinforcement until the response magnitude exceeds the values previously reinforced, and reinforce this greater magnitude. When a particular property of behavior is reinforced, the quantitative values of that property subsequently become more variable and values exceeding the one reinforced almost inevitably occur. Thus, by making reinforcements intermittent and contingent upon some progressively changing property of behavior (by differential and intermittent reinforcement), one can shape behavior toward an ultimate specification through successive approximations.

While conditioned operant behavior becomes exaggerated in extinction, this does not imply that extinction is a necessary part of differentiated operant behavior. A skillful experimenter can shape a complex behavior pattern, in which successively longer and longer sequences of behavior are reinforced and blended into the new pattern, without appearing to withhold reinforcement. To arrange conditions so that, at every step, the effect of reinforcement is to engender only the desired behavior may possibly be the optimum technique of shaping. This principle has been used with success in developing complex discriminative control over behavior (Hively, 1962; Holland, 1962; Terrace, 1963).

A brief explanation of the shaping of behavior can enable one to develop new forms of behavior that could not exist without an explicit history of differential reinforcement. Nevertheless, important aspects of the shaping process are still unknown. Different responses vary in stereotypy, rate of occurrence, the extent to which they are changed by reinforcement, and discreteness of identification. The effects of reinforcement interact with the quantitative properties of behavior so that different responses are modified differently. The defining property of reinforcement, the increase in frequency of the operant specified by the contingencies of reinforcement, is easier to demonstrate in an operant with a low than with a high frequency of occurrence. Because the presentation of a positive reinforcer tends to enhance behavior, it is far easier to shape a response involving some discrete activity than a response involving sustained immobility. In fact, it is usually difficult to use a reinforcer to decrease the level of responding, or to shape an operant involving little or no movement, such as "holding" or "standing still" (Blough, 1958). Yet operants come under the *schedule control* of reinforcement even when their average rate is refractory to the usual effects of reinforcement. In Skinner and Morse's (1958) experiment on running in the rat, the presentation of the known reinforcer on an FI schedule produced a pattern of responding characteristic of FI, even though the reinforcer decreased the average rate.

In shaping a new pattern of behavior, intricate interactions between quantitative properties of behavior and the effects of reinforcement will determine what scheduling of reinforcements is most desirable. When behavior is shaped toward a final form according to slightly different general prescriptions, the resulting behavior will inevitably show idiosyncratic features dependent upon the particular schedule of reinforcement employed. Although the importance of the history of reinforcement in determining the changing complex of operant behavior may be clear even in demonstrations of shaping, quantitative information about the scheduling of reinforcements in shaping behavior is limited. Precise specifications of the criteria for presenting reinforcers are lacking when the programming of reinforcers is determined by an experimenter who is intuitively applying a general formula.

The Definition and Importance of Schedules

The effects of presenting reinforcers according to precise specifications have been studied systematically only for discrete responses, and the use of *schedule of reinforcement* will be restricted to such cases. In situations which permit the identification of discrete, unitary responses, a schedule of reinforcement is the prescription for initiating and terminating stimuli, either discriminative or reinforcing, in time and in relation to responses.

Schedules of this type have been studied extensively for two reasons. The first is the theoretical and historical importance of the frequency of occurrence of a response in time as a fundamental unit of analysis in the study of operant behavior. A change in the frequency of emission of behavior is generally accepted as the definition of operant conditioning. The concept of frequency of emission can be applied with equal generality to radically different kinds of behaviors, and many behavioral problems have been clarified by reformulations in these terms. It is therefore natural that the scheduling of reinforcements should have been studied extensively in situations involving the emission of a repetitive response.

A second reason for the study of schedules of reinforcement of discrete responses in time is the ease of studying the frequency of occurrence of a convenient, arbitrary response compared to the difficulty of objectively studying changing patterns of topography, force, location, etc. Skinner's (1938, Chapter 8) interesting experiments on differential reinforcements with respect to the intensity and duration of responses showed that it was possible to schedule reinforcement with respect to properties of behavior other than rate of occurrence. Today, many experimenters are studying the effects of reinforcement on particular quantitative properties of behavior and on forms of responding other than the repetitive occurrence of a discrete response (for example, see Blough, 1958; Hefferline & Keenan, 1963; Herrnstein, 1961b; Notterman & Mintz, 1962; Skinner & Morse, 1958). Sufficient experimental evidence has accumulated to indicate that the concept of a schedule, as a prescription for a history of reinforcement, can be generalized to situations other than those involving only the repetitive occurrence of a unitary response. For example, complex behavior can be shaped through the careful programming of the stimulus control of responding (Hively, 1962; Holland, 1962; Terrace, 1963). Such programs have general pertinence to the topic of schedules. The behavior engendered by a program depends critically upon the specification of the program. Different programs are like different schedules in producing characteristically different effects (Hively, 1962; Terrace, 1963).

Apart from the special theoretical importance of frequency of responding in time, schedules of reinforcement of discrete responses are important because they represent the most intensively studied and best understood body of information on the generation and maintenance of operant behavior. The experiments pertaining to schedules have additional general significance in showing the tremendous range of behaviors that can be produced by schedules, the power of behavioral control induced by schedules, and the intricate relations that exist among the variables controlling behavior.

The range and the complexity of behaviors that can be produced by intermittently reinforcing responses in time is incredible. That these scheduling procedures are the most powerful techniques known for generating behavior is, of course, of fundamental significance; it emphasizes that histories of reinforcement are the primary determinants of behavior. It is also relatively easy to use schedules to generate behavior. Even persons with a minimum of training can follow simple, specified procedures for producing stable, standard behavior patterns of various types in any individual of a variety of different species. Schedules of reinforcement can be used to produce practically any conceivable pattern of responding. A strong claim can be made that schedules are not merely useful but crucial in psychological investigations. Dews (1963) makes the point with an analogy:

> This emphasis on the importance of schedules is not intended to imply that all of psychology should be reduced to a study of them. An influence can be all-pervading without being all-embracing. No one would maintain that all mechanisms of physiology can be reduced to the laws of osmosis; yet osmotic phenomena are ubiquitous in physiology; wherever they can operate, they do; and the student of any physiological mechanism ignores osmosis at his peril. Similarly, it is suggested that schedule influences operate generally in psychology; that when these influences can operate, they will; and that a student of any problem in psychology—motivation, generalization, discrimination or the functions of the frontal lobes—ignores the consequences of the precise scheduling arrangements of his experiments at his peril (p. 148).

Schedules are therefore important for the study of traditional problems of psychology even for those people who do not take the next step of reformulating or discarding the traditional problems, and recasting them within the context of patterns of behavior controlled by histories of differential reinforcement.

A specific example will show how the wealth of phenomena that can be developed using different schedules has encroached upon the domain of motivation. Consider a demonstration in which the presentation of an effective reinforcer is programmed to appear intermittently according to two different schedules, each of which is designated by a correlated stimulus. In this way the performance appropriate to either of the two schedules can be produced merely by presenting the appropriate discriminative stimulus, and one performance can be changed to the other by changing the discriminative stimuli. An untrained observer watching a subject responding under either of these schedule conditions would ordinarily describe the performance in language implying an overall motivational state. If one of the conditions is fixed ratio reinforcement (FR), the predominance of key-directed behavior to the exclusion of all other behavior is likely to be described as highly motivated, forceful, and persistent, and the subject as being energetic and industrious. If the second condition is a variable interval schedule with a low-rate contingency (VI drl), these adjectives will not fit the other performance. Now the emission of responses will occur at a lower rate and will be interspersed with movements away from the key. The different histories of reinforcement under the two schedules produce different patterns of responding, different average rates of responding, and different demeanors.

Many psychologists find the apparent motivational qualities of schedule-controlled performances surprising, but reinforcement, as the primary determinant of behavior, engenders a great deal of what traditionally has been called motivation. An observer who describes a schedule-controlled performance using traditional motivational traits is likely to be astonished when he watches a subject responding on a multiple FI, VI drl schedule and sees that schedule-controlled behavior patterns come under transient stimulus control and are not enduring characteristics of behavior. Radically different patterns of responding and associated general demeanor can be made to appear, change, and disappear in the same subject over brief periods of time. Furthermore, any member of most species will give a similar performance on the same schedules.

The control exerted by schedules often alters the effects of many independent variables as forcefully as it alters the grossly observable patterns of behavior. Schedule performances, especially multiple-schedule performances, have been used extensively as dependent variables in investigating other variables of behavioral interest. It has been found repeatedly that the effects of deprivation, of punishment, of discriminative stimuli, and of drugs all depend upon the controlling schedule and have different effects with different schedules. In other words, schedule-controlled behavior is so powerful that it overshadows the effects of traditional psychological variables.[3] When schedule performances are used as tools, the concepts of schedule-controlled behavior gradually come to replace traditional formulations. This phase of development has proceeded farthest in the field of behavioral pharmacology. Initial use of schedules as "baselines" for assessing how drugs affect other variables has now given way to the explicit study of how drugs affect schedule-controlled patterns and rates of responding. (For a fuller treatment of this topic see Chapter 12 in this book; also Dews, 1963; 1964; Dews & Morse, 1961; Morse, 1962.) The usefulness of schedules, both technically and conceptually, in studying other phenomena will be amply documented in many chapters of this book.

It is noteworthy that complex behavior can be produced merely by reinforcing discrete responses in time. It might be thought necessary to

[3] The view that schedule-controlled performances are usually more powerful than traditional psychological variables is strongly supported by experimental evidence. A broader view is that powerful control of behavior by discriminative stimuli and by reinforcers such as food and water actually develops because they are favorably scheduled events. The effectiveness of reinforcers depends as much on proper scheduling as on their quality. Falk (1961) has shown that certain scheduling of drinking can result in an intake of water far exceeding that caused by conventional deprivation regimens. The chapter by Kelleher in this book shows that conditioned reinforcers can, when appropriately scheduled, be incredibly effective or quite ineffective in maintaining behavior.

create a rich stimulus environment and to control explicitly many relations between the subject and his environment; in actuality these schedule performances are produced by procedures that may appear at first to be ridiculously simple. In fact, many writers have commented on the barrenness and the sterility of the general situation in which the only events are the inputs of reinforcers and the outputs of responses in time, in contrast with the richness of the real world. These events are studied because they are isolated conditions amenable to analysis. Yet the situation has a richness in providing the subject with the opportunity for a precise history of differential and intermittent reinforcement, the essential ingredient of conditioned operant behavior. That such a range of behavior can be produced by such limited means should be particularly revealing to people who consider the schedule situation bare and limited.

These situations are bare and limited in the sense that they reduce the number of extraneous factors which obscure understanding in our everyday familiarity with behavior. Complex patterns of behavior can be generated in seemingly simple situations (the "box") with seemingly simple subjects (the pigeon). It is unnecessary to invoke complex hypotheses worthy only of application to humans to explain differences in the output level, the persistence, and the genesis of behaviors of the sort that can arise from differences in the schedule histories in animals. This approach of describing the richness of everyday human behavior in terms of histories of reinforcement has been fully developed by Skinner (1953; 1961).

The primary interest in schedules has been in their technical usefulness for the study of other phenomena and in the understanding of the operation of schedule influences in everyday affairs. But the study of schedules, particularly the intricate relations obtaining under basic schedules of reinforcement, is of intrinsic scientific interest. Behavior is like other biological phenomena in that complex forms and functions are developed out of simple interrelations of mechanisms existing at lower levels of complexity. The operations involved in the generation of complex schedule-controlled performances are fundamental, significant, and can be specified quantitatively. The detailed study of the relations existing in these situations would appear to offer excellent opportunities for theoretical and experimental analysis of the basic nature of the dynamic interactions among the factors determining behavior. The remainder of this chapter will consider how complex behavior develops from the selective histories of reinforcement produced by basic schedules of reinforcement.

SCHEDULES OF REINFORCEMENT

A schedule of reinforcement is a prescription for initiating and terminating stimuli, either discriminative or reinforcing, in time and in relation to some behavior. This chapter will be primarily concerned with schedules in which the only stimulus changes programmed into the subject's environmental space during the experimental session are events of one type (the presentations of reinforcers), and the outputs from the experimental space are all events of another type (responses). The schedule is the formal specification of the relations between responses and reinforcers (i.e., outputs and inputs). Note that it is the dependence of input upon output which is formally and explicitly stated: the relation of responses (outputs) to reinforcers (inputs) is determined by the effects of reinforcement on behavior.[4]

Schedules in which reinforcers are presented contingent upon responses in time are specified by combinations of two terms: n (number of responses) and t (time since some event, which can be either a response or reinforcement). The classification of schedules proposed by Skinner (1938), and extended by Ferster and Skinner (1957), distinguishes between schedules that reinforce a response on the basis of time (interval) and on the basis of responses (ratio). This chapter will consider the basic differences between ratio and interval schedules: the formal differences between these types of schedules, the major differences in behavior which occur under these schedules, and how these differences in behavior depend upon both the direct and the indirect contingencies existing under these schedules. Most of the schedules described by Ferster and Skinner (1957) can be considered as variations or combinations of simple ratio and interval schedules; consequently a full discussion of the fundamental distinctions between these schedules and the characteristics of behavior they engender will relate to much of the literature on schedules in general.

The primary aim of this chapter is to give an appreciation of how a schedule of intermittent reinforcement operates upon behavior to engender characteristic patterns of responding. It is believed that this objective can be accomplished best by considering the intricate relations between controlling variables existing under intermittent reinforcement on ratio and interval schedules. No attempt will be made to describe and to analyze inclusively all the empirical results from ratio and interval schedules. The interested reader can find many published accounts of detailed descriptions of performances on these and other schedules (e.g., Ferster & Skinner, 1957). The purpose of this chapter is rather to show how reinforcement enhances the level of responding and selectively shapes responding; these effects combine to produce the patterns of responding typifying performances on ratio and interval schedules.

----

[4] This analysis of schedule performances assumes an appreciable tendency for the subject to emit responses in time. The occurrence of responses is ordinarily guaranteed by conditioning the desired response according to a highly standardized procedure described by Ferster (1953), Ferster and Skinner (1957), and Skinner (1938).

Definitions

A notational system and terminology are essential for the study of schedules. The unambiguous specification of schedules is merely a necessary requirement of a notational system; ideal systems could be used to generate experimental procedures of behavioral interest and would explicate the analysis of behavior under a given schedule. There are advantages to all of the various notational systems that have been used in describing schedules (Ferster & Skinner, 1957; Findley, 1962; Mechner, 1959; Schoenfeld, Cumming, & Hearst, 1956). The designations of schedules by Ferster and Skinner furnish a set of terms that have connotations to those already familiar with the literature on schedules and will be followed in this chapter.

In a *ratio schedule* a response is reinforced after the emission of some designated number of responses since the last reinforced response or some other specified event. The number required may be fixed or variable, giving rise to *fixed ratio* (FR) and *variable ratio* (VR) reinforcement. In an *interval schedule,* a response is reinforced after some designated period of time since some event (usually the last reinforcement). In *fixed interval* reinforcement (FI) the time between the onset of the interval and the availability of reinforcement is fixed, and the next response after the end of the time period is reinforced. *Variable interval* reinforcement (VI) is similar except that the designated time periods are variable in duration.[5] The event initiating the time period may be reinforcement, the end of a previous time period (*limited hold*), changes in discriminative stimuli, or a response (*tandem* schedules). An essential feature of interval schedules is that no explicit specifications are made about responses between the initiation of the interval and the availability of reinforcement. A temporal schedule in which reinforcement is made available after a fixed time since the immediately preceding response (DRL) is not, strictly speaking, an interval schedule.

The availability of reinforcement on ratio and interval schedules can be further restricted by imposing additional specifications which set limits to the time periods during which a response can be reinforced. For example, under an interval schedule, instead of reinforcing the first response which occurs after the end of the interval, the period of availability may be limited to a specific duration. Ferster and Skinner designate interval schedules so qualified as *limited hold* (see also time-correlated schedules, p. 96ff). Similarly, another restriction on the availability of reinforcement described by Ferster and Skinner is that the time between a designated response and the succeeding response (or series of responses) must be less than some specified duration (drh) or exceed some specified duration (drl).

[5] The terms FI, FR, VI, and VR are those of Ferster and Skinner (1957), who define VR and VI in terms of a random series of particular parameter values. By usage, *variable* has come to mean that the parameter is not constant.

Still other procedures useful in the analysis of the effects of ratio and interval schedules are combinations of these schedules. In a *tandem* schedule the availability of reinforcement is determined by a particular ordered sequence of component schedules in which, except for the last component, the only consequence of the response which terminates a component is that it initiates the next component. In *concurrent* schedules either of two independent schedules programmed simultaneously determines the availability of reinforcement, while in *compound* schedules the availability of reinforcement is jointly determined by interactions between number and time requirements. For example, in a *conjunctive* fixed ratio, fixed interval schedule the availability of reinforcement is dependent upon both the emission of a given number of responses and the passage of a minimum period of time since the last reinforcement. In an *interlocking* fixed ratio, fixed interval schedule the availability of reinforcement is dependent upon the emission of a number of responses that changes as a function of time since the last reinforcement. Some of these relations are shown schematically in Figure 1. In these diagrams the ordinate represents responses, the abscissa represents time, and the line on the diagram indicates the availability of reinforcement. On FR a response is reinforced after the emission of n

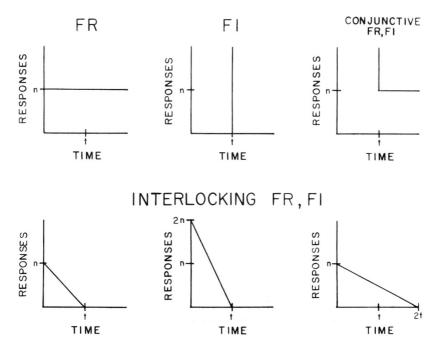

Figure 1. Diagrams of number-time plots for different schedules. (After Herrnstein & Morse, 1958; Skinner, 1958.)

responses; on FI a response is reinforced after time *t*. On a conjunctive FR FI schedule, a response is reinforced after both *n* responses and time *t*. On interlocking FR FI schedules, the availability of reinforcement is determined by the sloping line. As the value of *n* increases the schedule approaches FI; as the value of *t* increases, the schedule approaches FR.

Ferster and Skinner define other schedules which are sequences of simple schedules. *Multiple schedules* combine two or more schedules, each schedule being accompanied by a different stimulus. *Mixed schedules* are similar to multiple schedules except that no differential stimuli are correlated with the different schedules. *Chained schedules* are similar to tandem schedules in that availability of reinforcement depends upon an ordered sequence of component schedules, but in chained schedules the component schedules (or the change in components) are correlated with stimuli (see Chapter 5).

Intrinsic Properties of Schedules

Before undertaking to show how behavior is maintained by a given schedule, we need to consider further the implications of specifying a schedule of reinforcement in terms such as those used above. A great deal follows from the specification of a schedule of reinforcement of responses in time. What in fact are we specifying when we designate a schedule, and how do these specifications enter into the control of behavior? The complexity of interacting variables controlling the performance on the simplest sorts of schedules cannot be overemphasized. Certain of these relations between reinforcements and responses in time will be exactly determined, while others will be only indirectly and approximately determined. For example, when we say that the thirtieth response since the previous reinforcement is to be reinforced (FR 30), or that the first response occurring 5 minutes after the previous reinforcement is to be reinforced (FI 5), certain conditions will necessarily obtain in each schedule cycle and they will be different for the two schedules. To consider the most obvious, in the case of FR, the number of responses emitted when the reinforcer is presented is always the same, whereas on FI the number can and will vary. The time between successive reinforcements depends directly upon the subject's rate of responding in the case of FR 30, and is limited at the lower end only by the minimum time to emit 30 responses; whereas on FI 5 the time between successive reinforcements has a fixed lower limit at five minutes and is essentially independent of the subject's moderately high rate of responding under usual circumstances.

The extent to which consistent and recurrent features of a schedule, such as the constancy in the number of responses emitted on FR or the approximate constancy in the interreinforcement time on FI, are factors in determining performances must be determined experimentally. It is likely that at some parameter values most, if not all, of these properties of a schedule will produce some behavioral consequence; but certain of the characteristics are more important than others. In some instances the lack of exact specification, such as the time between reinforcements on FR, or the number of responses per reinforcement on FI, may be of behavioral importance.

The temporal relation between the response which is reinforced and the immediately preceding response is a subtle but exceedingly important feature inherently determined by specifying either FR 30 or FI 5. The relation is different for ratio and interval schedules, and this difference constitutes one of the major distinctions between these schedules. On FR, the probability of the next response, R_N, being reinforced is independent of the time between it and the preceding response (the interresponse time), whereas on an interval schedule, the probability of the next response being reinforced increases with the time elapsed since the last response.

Constant and Fluctuating Influences

It is difficult to determine how a schedule acts to control responding because the characteristic and stable behavioral performances produced by schedules are jointly determined both by relations between responding and reinforcement which necessarily follow when one specifies a schedule, and by other relations which may follow depending upon the nature of the subject's responding. Certain consequences of specifying a schedule, such as the number required on FR, or the minimum time of the interval on FI, will be true for all variations in patterns of responding. But the actual contingencies at reinforcement arise both from features of the schedule and from the subject's behavior, and some of the consequences of specifying a schedule will vary depending upon the performance brought into the situation. We may distinguish therefore between constant influences and fluctuating influences. *Constant* schedule influences depend upon responding but are independently constant as the pattern of responding varies. By *fluctuating* influences we mean that certain patterns of responding may interact with the schedule contingencies so as to produce an equilibrium having consistent features which in turn controls subsequent responding. Such behavior-dependent characteristics of schedules will result for most, if not all, subjects exposed to a particular schedule. When each of several subjects brings into the experiment a tendency to respond in a particular way, the behavior-dependent contingencies may well be quite similar. Therefore even the characteristic performances generated by schedules of reinforcement may result from steady-state conditions which do not necessarily follow from any static properties of a schedule, but rather depend upon the sequential and developmental interactions between features of the schedule and the subject's responding.

Schedule-controlled Operant Behavior

Primary emphasis will be given to the behavioral process of reinforcement in identifying and analyzing how the inherent features of ratio and interval schedules operate to determine the response patterns characteristic of these procedures. As described in the introductory section, reinforcement both enhances behavior and differentiates or shapes behavior. The joint operation of these two aspects of reinforcement appears to be sufficient to account for many characteristics of schedule performances. The effect of reinforcement in differentiating behavior is shown by an increase in the occurrence of specifiable aspects of behavior that immediately precede reinforcement. The effect of reinforcement in strengthening behavior is shown by quantitative relations between parameters of reinforcement and rate of responding.

In recent years the overwhelming emphasis in the study of schedules has been on the identification of consistent relationships prevailing at the moment of reinforcement. This point of view is well illustrated by the introductory chapter in Ferster and Skinner (1957):

> Under a given schedule of reinforcement, it can be shown that at the moment of reinforcement a given set of stimuli will usually prevail. A schedule is simply a convenient way of arranging this. Reinforcement occurs in the presence of such stimuli, and the future behavior of the organism is in part controlled by them or by similar stimuli according to a well-established principle of operant discrimination (p. 3).

> When a more-or-less stable performance has been well-established under a given schedule, the organism is being reinforced under certain stimulus conditions. The experimenter arranges some of these, such as the details of the experimental chamber and special stimuli added for explicit purposes. But among the physical events occurring in the experimental chamber are the activities of the organism itself. These enter into the contingencies and must be specified as part of the animal's environment.

> In certain cases the topography of behavior can serve as a discriminative stimulus controlling other behavior. In general, however, the important properties of such stimuli are precisely those of our dependent variable; namely, the rate. A given rate of responding may be both a dependent variable (a description of the bird's behavior at the moment of reinforcement) and an independent variable (a stimulus upon which reinforcement is contingent). This distinction may be the source of considerable confusion. We deal with a response both as an activity of the organism and as part of a series of events affecting the organism as a stimulus (p. 10).

In many respects the general conception of the effects of schedules represented in this chapter follows Ferster and Skinner. It emphasizes the importance of the prevailing conditions at the moment of reinforcement, the importance of the subject's own behavior to the development of a stable performance, and especially that rates of responding interact with schedules to control subsequent rates of responding. In keeping with the general emphasis on intermittently reinforced behavior as shaped or differentiated operant behavior, however, the conditions which prevail on a schedule at the moment of reinforcement will be considered as differential reinforcing contingencies of patterns of responses in time rather than as discriminative stimuli. This distinction is discussed in detail by Skinner (1938, Chapter 8) with respect to the differentiation of force and response duration. It is assumed that the time preceding the emission of a response (its latency or interresponse time) is a measurable and conditionable aspect of that response. Patterns of responding are assumed to be similarly conditioned and can be thought of as complex, differentiated responses (see Keller & Schoenfeld, 1950, p. 187; Logan, 1960, Chapter 6). Conditions prevailing under a schedule are emphasized here as factors shaping behavior directly and positively, but this does not rule out the momentary stimulation that is presumably occurring when a subject responds, or the possibility that the stimulation arising from a subject's own behavior might come to control its future behavior as a discriminative or eliciting stimulus. On the other hand, one important aspect of the general conception of operant behavior is that we need not and should not be burdened with the postulation of stimulus control over behavior in situations where the stimuli are unknown and not independently manipulable.

ANALYSES OF SCHEDULES IN TERMS OF INTERRESPONSE TIME

Whether the time between successive responses is considered as a stimulus which controls responding or as a conditionable property of behavior itself, the importance of the interresponse time (IRT) in the analysis of schedule performances is generally accepted. In this chapter Anger's (1954; 1956) term, *interresponse time* (IRT), will be used with the following modification. The elapsed time between the initiation of the response (R_{N-1}) and the next response (R_N) will be considered as a measurable property of the response R_N and called its interresponse time. Thus, reinforcement can be made contingent upon a response having an IRT exceeding some given duration, just as reinforcement can be made contingent upon the topography or intensity of a response. The conception of an IRT as a property of behavior differs from Anger's (1956) definition of an IRT as a time interval between responses (a stimulus), but it differs only slightly from Anger's (1956) usage, since he refers to the reinforcement of particular IRTs as an abbreviation for the reinforcement of the response terminating that IRT (p. 145).

The generality of the concept of IRT is extended by allowing the initiation of an IRT to begin with events other than the previous response, such as the end of a reinforcement cycle or the presentation of a discriminative stimulus. In this chapter the first response made after reinforcement will be considered to have an IRT that began at the termination of the reinforcer.

Relation between Terminal IRT and Reinforcement on Ratio and Interval Schedules

In *The Behavior of Organisms* Skinner made a formal distinction between ratio and interval schedules which is important in explaining the performances generated by these schedules. The distinction, which Skinner called "the temporal discrimination of the preceding response" (Skinner, 1938, pp. 274-284), is concerned with the probability that IRTs of different durations will be reinforced under ratio and interval schedules. The distinction can be made along several lines of reasoning, and, with certain assumptions and restrictions, can be rigorously stated as the probability that a response R_N will be reinforced as a function of the IRT of that response. Ratio schedules, as ordinarily programmed, reinforce a response after the completion of n responses, the parameter n being either fixed or variable. The probability that the next response will be reinforced is not dependent upon the IRT of the response. If one response in ten is reinforced (FR or VR 10), then under the assumption of a random sampling of responses, the probability that any single response R_N will be reinforced will be 0.1, and this will be independent of the IRT value. This relation is shown diagrammatically in Figure 2 by the line FR or VR.

In contrast to ratio schedules, the likelihood that the next response R_N will be reinforced on interval schedules is dependent upon the IRT of R_N. In a fixed interval of 100 seconds duration, an IRT exceeding 100 seconds is certain to be reinforced; an IRT of 50 seconds will be reinforced only if it begins after 50 seconds since the start of the interval; and an IRT of 10 seconds will be reinforced only if it begins after 90 seconds. Under the assumption that the initiation of an IRT is equally likely to occur throughout the interval, on FI 100 sec. the probability of an IRT of t seconds being reinforced is 0.05 for a 5-second IRT, 0.1 for a 10-second IRT, and 0.5 for a 50-second IRT (see Figure 2). The dashed line in Figure 2 shows the function for VI 100 sec. comprised of one interval each of 50, 100, and 150 seconds. The probability of an IRT of 50 seconds being reinforced is 0.611, which is the sum of the probabilities of this IRT being reinforced on each of the separate intervals constituting the VI schedule. The probability of an IRT of 50 seconds being reinforced is 1.0 if the 50-second interval is in effect, 0.5 if the 100-second interval is in effect, and 0.33 if the 150-second interval is in effect. Since each of these intervals will be in effect one-third of the time, the probability of a 50-second IRT being reinforced is ⅓(1 + 0.5 + 0.33) = 0.611. The curvature of the function for VI depends upon the distribution of intervals constituting the VI schedule, and the smoothness of the curve depends upon the number of different intervals in the schedule. The function reaches unity only after an IRT equals or exceeds the maximum interval in the series (150 seconds in Figure 2).

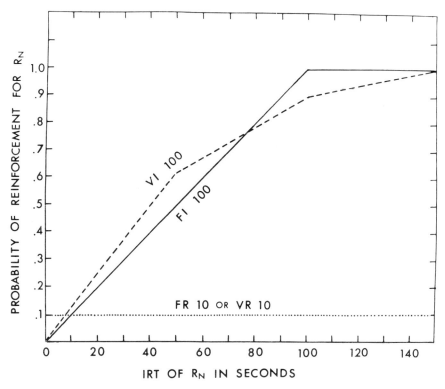

Figure 2. Curves showing probability of reinforcement of a response on ratio and interval schedules as a function of the IRT of that response. (After Anger, 1956.)

The function for FI changes when sequences of responses are considered (Morse & Herrnstein, 1955). Figure 3 shows how the probability of reinforcement for the next response R_N changes when the IRT of the previous response R_{N-1} is specified. On FI 100 sec., if the IRT of R_{N-1} was 50 seconds, and under the assumption of an equal likelihood that the response R_{N-1} terminated between 50 and 100 seconds, then a 25-second IRT of R_N has a 0.5 probability of being reinforced. The same relations

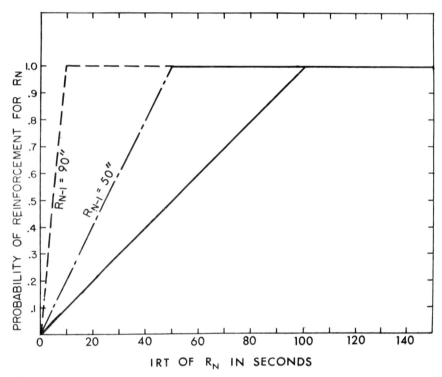

Figure 3. Curves showing the probability of reinforcement of a response on FI as a function of the IRT of that response and IRTs of previous responses. The solid curve is the function when only the IRT of R_N is known. The other curves show how the cumulative durations of a sequence of IRTs change the function for the IRT of R_N.

would also hold for any sequence of unreinforced responses terminating with R_{N-1} that had a total IRT duration of 50 seconds. If the sequence of IRTs terminating with R_{N-1} had a total duration of 90 seconds, then a 5-second IRT of R_N has a 0.5 probability of being reinforced. Figure 4 shows how increasing durations of the sequence of IRTs terminated by R_{N-1} change the probability that a constant duration IRT of response R_N will be reinforced. This curve was obtained by plotting the values of sequence durations (Figure 3) that correspond to two different IRTs of R_N (10 seconds and 50 seconds).[6]

[6] While the relation of these curves to patterns of responding on FI is at present still a highly speculative matter, a fixed interval schedule can be rigorously defined as a schedule in which reinforcement occurs when the sum of the IRTs since the last reinforcement exceeds the value of the interval. Defining FI as a schedule reinforcing a minimum cumulative sum of IRTs emphasizes the sequential patterning of IRTs that characterize FI performance, and, in addition, tends to obvert concern over why responding occurs during the interval.

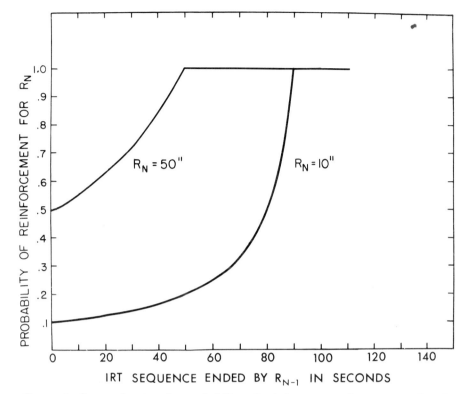

Figure 4. Curves showing the probability of reinforcement of a response R_N of constant IRT duration on FI as a function of the cumulative durations of the sequence of IRTs preceding R_N.

Limitations of Theoretical Probability Relations

Although IRT probability models show certain formal relations of schedules, there are limitations on their usefulness in accounting for the patterning of responding under ratio and interval schedules. First and most important, other factors besides the probability of reinforcement of IRTs are operating to control schedule performances. Second, distinctions of the sort shown in Figures 3 and 4 are of behavioral importance only if the subject can be controlled by slight differences in the likelihood of reinforcement of particular IRTs. Experimenters have studied situations in which IRTs greater or less than some value are reinforced (Anger, 1956; Ferster & Skinner, 1957; Kelleher, Fry, & Cook, 1959; Wilson & Keller, 1953), but continuous variations in the differential reinforcement of IRTs have not been studied explicitly. Therefore we have only indirect evidence that responding is actually controlled by the differential reinforcement functions indicated in the formal probability models of statistical populations of IRTs on ratio and interval schedules. Third, the predictive usefulness of these probability functions depends greatly on the assumption that the initiation of an IRT is equally likely to occur during any portion of the schedule. There is some evidence that IRTs occur in time independently of the reinforcement schedule under initial exposure to certain schedules (Anger, 1956; Mueller, 1950; Sidman, 1960). For example, Anger (1956) has presented evidence that after 26 to 38 days of exposure to VI 5, the number of reinforcements of each IRT class interval approximated the theoretical probability values for VI multiplied by the number of IRTs of that class (p. 153). But with continued exposure to a schedule, an unqualified assumption that the initiation of IRTs is independent of the schedule becomes less and less tenable.

Finally, what should be predicted about behavior from probability functions such as arc shown in Figures 2-4? These probability plots show formal properties of ratio and interval schedules; they show how these schedules selectively reinforce different IRTs; but they do not indicate the behavioral effect of this selective reinforcement. The differential reinforcement of long IRTs will tend to increase the frequency of long IRTs, and the differential reinforcement of short IRTs will tend to increase the frequency of short IRTs. The question now is what specific predictions about performances on ratio and interval schedules follow most naturally from the general notion of selective reinforcement of IRTs.

The need to be specific about the behavioral effect of differential reinforcement under a schedule can be illustrated by considering hypothetical examples of how differential reinforcement of IRTs might act. One possibility, which fits best with a conception of an IRT as a stimulus which occasions a response, is that a response will occur whenever the likelihood that it will be reinforced exceeds some minimum value. For example, a particular subject on FI 100 sec. might respond whenever the probability of an IRT being reinforced exceeded 0.1. The first response would occur after a 10-second pause. Given a 10-second IRT, then a 9-second IRT has a 0.1 probability of reinforcement (see Figure 3), so a second response would occur after 19 seconds. Given an IRT sequence duration of 19 seconds, an IRT of 8.1 seconds has a 0.1 probability of reinforcement; given an IRT sequence duration of 27.1 seconds, an IRT of 7.3 seconds has a 0.1 probability of reinforcement. Empirical attempts by the author to determine a minimum probability constant from the terminal rate of responding on FI, and then reproduce fixed interval performances by this method have been unsatisfactory, even when an allowance is made for a post-reinforcement pause. The notion of a minimum probability constant lacks validity when applied rigorously, but it does emphasize the quantitative effects of schedule parameters on schedule performances. Average rates of responding are high when the parameters of the schedule set a high reinforcement frequency and low when the schedule sets a low reinforcement frequency.

Another possibility, and one which seems to enjoy a wide appeal despite severe limitations in predicting schedule phenomena, is that IRTs with the greatest likelihood of reinforcement will tend to occur. From this hypothesis one would erroneously predict that the "differential reinforcement of low rates" provided by interval schedules would produce lower and lower rates, which, of course, does not happen. Likewise one might erroneously conclude that the equal likelihood of reinforcement of all IRT durations provided by ratio schedules would make the selective reinforcement of particular IRTs of no significance on ratio schedules.

That the likelihood of reinforcement is independent of the IRT does not mean that reinforcement has no effect on the IRT that is reinforced. We know from experiments in which stimuli and reinforcers are presented independently of behavior (Herrnstein & Morse, 1957; Morse & Skinner, 1957; Skinner, 1948) that it is the actual conditions prevailing at reinforcement which shape behavior, and not the conditions, either better or worse, that might exist. The most reasonable prediction from probability functions from a behavioral point of view is that responding will be shaped by the IRTs which are actually reinforced. This view will be developed in detail in the next section.

Control of Behavior on VI by Reinforcement of IRTs

From the general notions of differential reinforcement developed in the introduction it follows that subsequent IRTs should tend to conform to the IRTs recently reinforced. Often this sequential history of reinforcement of IRTs appears to be adequately represented by the relative frequency of reinforcement of different IRTs. The experimental work supporting this general point of view is primarily that of Anger (1954; 1956), who studied the dependence of IRTs upon the relative frequency of reinforcement of different IRTs on VI. He summarizes his first experiments on VI as follows:

> At first after conditioning the probability of response was about equal at different times after the last response, but continued exposure to the variable-interval schedule produced a higher probability soon after the last response and a lower probability at longer times after the last response. Analysis of the reinforcements given different interresponse times by the schedule showed that the Reinforcements/Interresponse Time are greatest for long interresponse times, but that the Reinforcements/Hr. are greatest for short interresponse times. The agreement between the greater Reinforcements/Hr. for short interresponse times and the development of a higher probability of response soon after the last response suggests that the relative Reinforcements/Hr., not the relative Reinforcements/Interresponse Time, determines the response probability. Control by Reinforcements/Hr. is surprising since it indicates that the occurrence of far more unreinforced short interresponse times has little influence on the animal's relative probability of response at different times after the last response.

Since the Reinforcements/Hr. for different interresponse times are partially dependent on the responding as well as vice versa, there seems to be a circular relation between reinforcements and responding during variable-interval reinforcement (p. 161).

In brief, the distribution of IRTs on VI is controlled by the relative frequency of actual reinforcements received by different IRTs. The distribution of *reinforced* IRTs depends jointly upon the way the schedule itself allows for the reinforcement of different IRTs and on the subject's actual IRT distribution. The relative rate of reinforcement of different IRTs will in turn have an effect upon the subject so that he tends to produce a distribution of total IRTs approximating the distribution of *reinforced* IRTs.[7] This change in the total distribution of IRTs will produce a subsequent change in the distribution of *reinforced* IRTs, which will have the behavioral effect of shifting the total IRT distribution. The succession of changes may result in a pair of distributions that tend to maintain each other in equilibrium, or as Anger says, "a semi-stable pair." Anger assumes that the form of the distribution of IRTs at equilibrium and the rate at which equilibrium is obtained will depend upon the subject's initial IRT distribution. In his experiments the stable IRT distribution on VI 5 after initial conditioning was different from the stable IRT distribution on VI 5 obtained after an intervening treatment differentially reinforcing IRTs exceeding 40 seconds on VI 5. This problem of the partial determination of responding by the subject's past history of responding is discussed by Anger (1956), Cumming and Schoenfeld (1959), Ferster and Skinner (1957), Schoenfeld and Cumming (1957), and Sidman (1960).

Control of Behavior on FR by Reinforcement of IRTs

Anger's experiments on VI show that a major factor determining responding on VI is the frequency of reinforcement of different classes of IRTs, which in turn is determined by the subject's total distribution of IRTs and the schedule. In generalizing this result to FR, Anger reasons that "compared with FI, FR provides more Reinfs./IRT for short IRTs . . . , and so for similar responding, the Reinfs./Hr. curves would have a much more pronounced peak at shorter IRTs" (p. 155). All IRTs are equally likely to be reinforced on FR, but the relative frequency of reinforcement of different IRTs in time (Reinfs./Hr.) is greater for short IRTs than for long IRTs. Figure 5 compares the relative rate of reinforcement of different IRTs on FR 100 and FI 100 sec. The curves show the maximum number of responses and of reinforced responses that could occur on FR and FI at each IRT in 1000 seconds. In this example, availability of reinforcement

---

[7] Anger suggests that it is the distribution of IRTs/opportunity, a statistic estimating the probability of a response given a certain duration of pause, and not the distribution of IRTs that tends to approximate the distribution of reinforced IRTs, but the results obtained in his experiments do not really permit a choice between these alternatives.

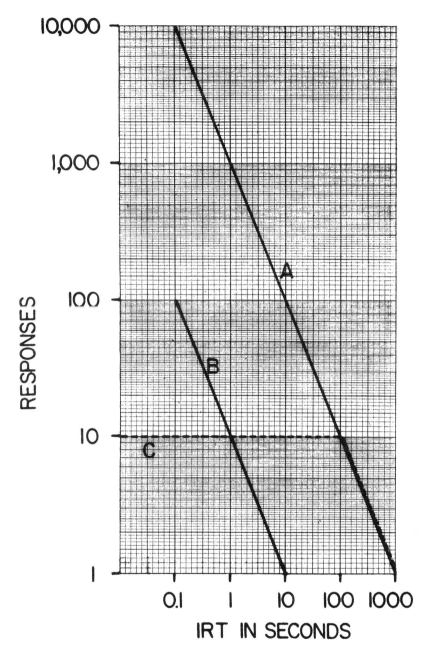

Figure 5. Relative rates of reinforcement of different IRTs on FR 100 and FI 100 sec. Curve A shows the maximum number of responses that could occur in 1000 seconds at each IRT. Curve B shows the maximum number of these responses that would be reinforced on FR. Curve C shows the maximum number that would be reinforced on FI.

on FI occurs every 100 seconds. Computations and comparisons are made easier by considering 1000-second periods in which all IRTs have the same duration, and by plotting responses of different IRT durations as a continuous variable. The special assumptions of this example are that all IRTs in a 1000-second period have the same duration, and that fractional values of responses are possible (e.g., 11.2 90-second IRTs in 1000 seconds). The validity of the relations in Figure 5 in no way depends upon these special assumptions.

Curve A in Figure 5 shows the maximum number of responses that could be made at each IRT. This curve of number of IRTs/1000 sec. is multiplied by the Reinfs./IRT curves for FR and FI (Figure 2) to produce the Reinfs./1000 sec. curves for FR and FI. The curve for maximum number of reinforced responses on FR (Curve B) is parallel to the curve for maximum total responses. In this example one response in 100 is reinforced (FR 100). Therefore 10,000 responses with 0.1-second IRT could be made in 1000 seconds and 100 responses would be reinforced; 100 responses with 10-second IRT could be made and 1 response would be reinforced. The maximum number of reinforced responses on FI (Curve C) is constant for all rates of responding greater than 1 response/interval. In this example 10 Reinfs./1000 sec. will be obtained on FI 100 sec. for all IRTs up to 100 seconds, and thereafter the rate of reinforced responses equals the rate of responding. In a real sample, except for IRTs occurring exactly at the end of each 100-second period, the maximum number of reinforced responses on FI will be 9 instead of 10. This detail of Curve C pertains to this example and is relatively unimportant; the essential point is that the rate of reinforcement on FI is constant and independent of the rate of responding over a wide range. Comparing Curves B and C shows that when IRTs are less than one second, the rate of reinforcement will be higher on FR than on FI; when IRTs exceed one second, the rate of reinforcement will be lower on FR than FI.

Since most schedule-maintained responding tends to produce distributions of IRTs with a high frequency of short IRTs, it will generally be true that on FR more short IRTs are reinforced than on FI. It is of theoretical interest whether a high rate would develop on FR as a result of this selective reinforcement of short IRTs independently of changes in average frequency of reinforcement with changes in rate. Unfortunately, there is no evidence on this point. According to the principle that the *total* IRT distribution eventually tends to match the *reinforced* IRT distribution, one might argue that within the errors of sampling variations, the distribution of reinforced IRTs on FR always matches the total distribution; consequently no change in the total distribution of IRTs should take place because of a "shaping" effect on the reinforced IRT. It is probably more reasonable to assume that a high rate of reinforcement of short IRTs *will* have a shaping effect to increase further the number of short IRTs.

All operant behavior is not equally amenable to being shaped by re-inforcement, and this undoubtedly holds for the selective reinforcement of different IRTs. Reinforcing a short IRT appears to be more effective in changing patterns of responding than reinforcing a long IRT (Anger, 1956; Dews, 1962; see also p. 93f). Also, as described by Anger, the circular re-lations that produce the semi-stable pairs of approximate matching of the total and reinforced IRT distributions are equilibrium conditions that are achieved slowly and by approximations. Local features in the distribution of reinforced IRTs may be of special importance. Anger suggests that sub-jects may be controlled by the major trend rather than the exact shape of the distribution of reinforced IRTs. In his experiments on VI, the rein-forced IRT distribution jointly determined by these initial distributions of IRTs and the VI schedule had a peak relative frequency between four and eight seconds, but the eventual behavioral outcome of exposure to VI was a distribution of IRTs (both total and reinforced) with the modal peak under four seconds. It is reasonable to suppose that the effect of a distribu-tion of reinforced IRTs in determining subsequent responding depends upon its shape, and that when it is flat or slowly changing it is likely to modify behavior differently from when it is peaked. Unfortunately there is not enough quantitative information about how reinforcement of IRT's changes subsequent IRT distributions to be more specific.

One reason why the role of many variables influencing schedule-con-trolled behavior remains unclear is that multiple factors are interrelated in a complex fashion even under the simple schedules most frequently studied. A simple schedule is one that is simple to specify and program rather than one that has a simple relation to behavior. To show that a particular factor is important in the control exerted by a schedule, an attempt is made to hold other variables constant. But all too often when a variable is held con-stant it is forgotten; parameter values of schedules are frequently omitted in the discussions of experimental papers. There appears to be tacit belief on the part of many writers interested in schedules that those variables that can change as a function of behavior exert the major control on a schedule, and variables that are held constant are either less important or have no effect. As an example of this special interest in variables over which the subject has partial control, i.e., an interest in fluctuating behavior-dependent influences rather than constant influences, Ferster and Skinner (1957) mention the frequency of reinforcement in time as a factor that must be evaluated on FR, but they do not discuss the operation of this factor on FI, even though in *The Behavior of Organisms* it was shown that rate of re-sponding was directly related to frequency of reinforcement on FI.

The average frequency of reinforcement enters into the control of re-sponding on both ratio and interval schedules. The actual frequency of reinforcement on interval schedules closely approximates the maximum possible frequency permitted by the value of the schedule. When the distribution of IRTs changes, it in turn changes the distribution of *reinforced* IRTs by changing the relative frequency of reinforcement of different IRTs; but the total reinforcements/time remains constant. In the case of FR, another circular relation exists, because the average frequency of reinforcement depends upon the mean of the distribution of IRTs, while, in turn, the average frequency of reinforcement determines an approximate rate of responding. If for some reason the rate of responding increases slightly on FR, it will result in an increase in the frequency of reinforcement which may act on the subject to cause an increase in rate of responding. Conversely, if the rate falls, the frequency of reinforcement falls, and this may result in a further drop in rate of responding. Before we can evaluate the possible effect of this and other relations between rate of responding and frequency of reinforcement on FR and FI, we need a great deal more quantitative information about the relation between rate of responding and frequency of reinforcement.

REINFORCEMENT AND RESPONSE STRENGTH

The persistence in time of behavior altered and intensified by reinforcement implies that a high frequency of reinforcement will have cumulative effects and will strengthen behavior more than a low frequency of reinforcement. The "shaping" function of reinforcement, its effect in changing certain properties of behavior that are correlated with reinforcement, has been emphasized in the previous sections more than the "quantitative" effects of a reinforcer upon behavior. In this section empirical evidence relating generalized strength of responding to quantitative properties of reinforcers will be considered. Particular emphasis will be given to the relation between frequency of reinforcement and rate of responding.

The notion of reinforcement creating a "reserve" of responses was an important integrating concept in Skinner's early work. In the subsequent 20 years almost no research on schedules was directed toward general quantitative relations between rate of responding and reinforcement. In *Schedules of Reinforcement,* for example, little emphasis is placed on functional relations between rate and the parameters of intermittent schedules. In recent years an active interest in the topic has developed again, but only a small part of the current work on response strength will be discussed in this chapter (see Chapter 6 by Catania in this book).

Many experiments have shown that rate of responding is directly related to the frequency of reinforcement on interval schedules; in fact, a proportional relation is often found (Herrnstein, 1961a; Skinner, 1938). Yet in other experiments this relation is not clearly seen (Herrnstein, 1955). As Herrnstein (1961a) notes, this insensitivity of rate of responding to frequency of reinforcement probably weakens our interest in the concept of strength of responding. In general it appears that rate of responding is not very sensitive to frequency of reinforcement in situations involving a single schedule programmed on a single response key; direct relations between rate of responding and frequency of reinforcement are more often obtained in situations involving concurrently programmed schedules, certain chained schedules, and multiple schedules. Recent experiments, most of them involving responding on concurrently programmed schedules on simultaneously present response keys, indicate that under certain conditions it is possible to devise experimental situations in which frequency of reinforcement is the most significant factor determining a subject's responding (Autor, 1960; Catania, 1963a; Herrnstein, 1961a; Reynolds, 1961; see also Chapter 6). These results may be looked upon, in part, as a confirmation and extension of Anger's (1956) conclusion that the relative frequency of IRTs on VI is controlled by the relative frequency of reinforcement of different IRTs. Simple dependencies of rate upon frequency of reinforcement are obtained most often in situations in which the relative rate of responding under two or more conditions can be related to the relative frequency of reinforcement under those conditions.

The relation of rate of responding to frequency of reinforcement is an excellent example of the way in which different aspects of intermittent reinforcement jointly determine a performance. According to Herrnstein (1961a), the orderly relations between relative rates of responding and frequencies of reinforcements on concurrent VI, VI schedules actually depend upon the separate relations between responding and frequency of reinforcement on the two response keys. His analysis implies that frequency of reinforcement must be operating to control rate in single-key situations. In single-key situations, however, rate of responding on VI is often not related to frequency of reinforcement in a direct way, presumably because the selective effect of reinforcement on particular IRTs becomes overwhelmingly dominant. The effects of reinforcement seem also to interact with and mask the effects of deprivation on rate of responding. Under some conditions, rate of responding is related to degree of deprivation in a lawful way (Clark, 1958), yet an orderly relation between rate of responding and deprivation is not obtained in many experiments involving intermittent reinforcement (Ferster & Skinner, 1957). Deprivation is most important during the early stages of conditioning when strong conditioned behavior is not yet developed. A prolonged history of intermittent reinforcement attenuates the effects of deprivation so that it becomes less important for the maintenance of schedule-controlled behavior. (See p. 59, n. 3.)

The relation of rate of responding to magnitude of reinforcement is even more obscure than its relations to frequency of reinforcement or deprivation level. Changes in reinforcement magnitude may or may not change rate of responding (e.g., Ferster & Skinner, 1957; Guttman, 1953; Keesey & Kling, 1961). There is some indication that the types of situation which yield sensitive relations between rate and frequency of reinforcement also show orderly relations between rate and magnitude of reinforcement (Catania, 1963b). In addition, changing the magnitude of the reinforcer has been found to have an effect in situations in which the rate of responding is low, but it has little effect in situations in which the rate of responding is high. When an animal is already conditioned, a reinforcer of small magnitude, presented fairly frequently, can sustain an enormous amount of behavior; greater magnitudes of the reinforcer may not have a proportionally

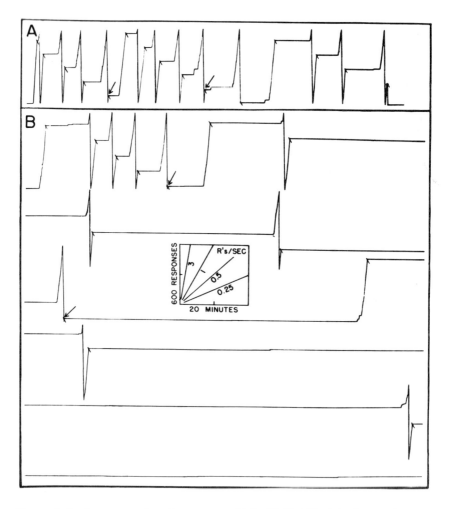

Figure 6. Performance of a pigeon on multiple FR 600 FR 600. The reinforcer in component A was a ten-second duration of access to a hopper of grain; the reinforcer in component B was a five-second duration of access to grain. The session began with component A present and alternated every five reinforcements as indicated by the arrows.

greater effect. This lack of correlation with rate has led to a neglect of magnitude of reinforcement as a factor in schedule-controlled responding, and has fostered the erroneous tendency to regard reinforcement as a constant effect with magnitudes below some threshold value not being reinforcers, and all magnitudes above that value being equally effective reinforcers.

A direct relation between the magnitude of a reinforcer and response output can be obtained in a situation in which responding is not steadily maintained. In an unpublished experiment performed by the author in collaboration with B. F. Skinner, responses were reinforced at the same parameter value of FR in the presence of two different discriminative stimuli, each of which was correlated with a different duration of access to the reinforcer. For values of FR up to 300, there was little difference in the average rate of responding under the two conditions, but at FR 600 the rate in the condition correlated with the ten-second duration of the reinforcer was much higher than the rate in the presence of the stimulus correlated with the five-second duration of the reinforcer. Figure 6 shows the performance on the multiple FR 600, FR 600 schedule. Component A shows responding on FR 600 (in the presence of a blue stimulus) maintained by a ten-second duration of access to a hopper of grain; component B shows responding on FR 600 (in the presence of a green stimulus) maintained by a five-second access to the grain. The session began with component A present and alternated to component B after five reinforcements (at the first arrow). After five reinforcements on component B, component A was again in effect, and the sequence continued alternating every five reinforcements for a total of three presentations of each component. The average rate of responding maintained by the ten-second reinforcer (component A) was more than five times greater than that maintained by the five-second reinforcer (component B). The difference between the two conditions was more pronounced later in the session than at the beginning, which suggests that reinforcement magnitude interacts with other variables controlling behavior.

The Joint Operation of Differential Reinforcement and Response Strength

It is the thesis of this chapter that most schedule-controlled responding results from the joint operation of the differential reinforcement of IRTs and the generalized effects of reinforcement to strengthen responding. Schedules of reinforcement selectively reinforce different IRTs. A given magnitude and frequency of reinforcement have a quantitative relation to rate of responding. Different strengths of responding engendered by reinforcement will result in different distributions of IRTs, and thus will interact with the selective reinforcement of IRTs by the schedule. Although considerable progress has been made in identifying the effects of reinforcement on IRTs and on average rate of responding considered separately, it is still unclear how these factors are interrelated even in simple schedules.

Unfortunately there have been few experiments concerned with interactions between the selective reinforcement of different IRTs and the distribution of IRTs determined by a particular frequency of reinforcement. Experiments on the analysis of IRTs usually do not add additional complications by deliberately changing the frequency of reinforcement, and when it is changed, the effect is not large. Conversely, experiments on response strength are usually done in situations in which little emphasis is given to analysis in terms of IRTs. It is simply not known how differences in average rate of responding resulting from different rates of reinforcement change the form of IRT distributions. More information is necessary to integrate the effects of reinforcement in strengthening responding with its effects in shaping behavior, and at present, conclusions from experiments primarily concerned with one or the other of these effects of reinforcement are often conflicting.

Examples will be given of experiments that emphasize the dependence of rate of responding on one or the other of these alternative aspects of reinforcement. Reynolds (1961c) has shown that the proportionality between relative frequency of reinforcement and relative rate of responding can apply to multiple schedules comprising VI and FR components. When the frequency of reinforcement was varied for either component while the reinforcement parameter for the other component was held constant, the relative rates of responding in the two components changed in such a way as to be proportional to the relative frequency of reinforcement. In this experiment the effect of frequency of reinforcement effectively masked any tendency for these schedules to generate different average rates of responding through the differential reinforcement of IRTs.

In contrast to Reynolds' result, Ferster and Skinner (1957) and Clark (1959) found that different schedules produced different rates of responding even when the average frequency of reinforcement was made identical by using a yoked-experiment procedure (Clark's experiment will be described in the section on "Limited Availability Experiments," p. 99). Ferster and Skinner established matched performances on VI in pairs of birds prior to changing the schedule for one member of the pair to VR. For the other member of the pair the VI was changed so that reinforcement availability was programmed by the delivery of food to the bird on VR. While it is difficult to tell from their report just how the frequency of reinforcement changed, it was the same for the two birds. Yet the rates of responding of the VR bird were higher than that of the yoked VI bird. This experiment shows that a ratio reinforcement contingency can override the effects of frequency of reinforcement. A change in frequency of reinforcement alone cannot account for the greater increase in rate for the bird switched from

VI to VR, since the control bird on yoked VI was reinforced with the same frequency and did not develop as high a rate. On the other hand, the experiment does not show that a change in frequency of reinforcement is unimportant for the increase in rate. The effect of changing the frequency of reinforcement may interact with the effects of a ratio contingency to produce a result that is different from that of changing the frequency of reinforcement on interval schedules.

The Effect of Frequency of Reinforcement on FR

Aside from any general effects of frequency of reinforcement on response strength, there is some suggestive evidence that the direct relation between rate of responding and frequency of reinforcement on ratio schedules is an important factor determining response rate on FR or VR. On interval schedules the frequency of reinforcement can be closely specified and has a maximum value; on ratio schedules the frequency of reinforcement depends entirely on rate and cannot be precisely specified. Although it is generally true that decreasing the average frequency of reinforcement decreases the average rate of responding, local decrements in the rate of reinforcement can increase rate of responding. Rate of responding increases during the initial phase of extinction. Ferster (1958a), Jenkins (1961), Reynolds (1961a; 1961b), and Terrace (1963) have recently described in detail how periods of non-reinforcement and reinforcement designated by stimuli interact to produce an increased rate of responding in reinforced periods. Also, local decrements in rate of responding may be correlated with subsequent increases in rate of responding. Skinner (1938) has reported many instances in which periods of low rate of responding (or high rate) are followed by periods of higher rate (or lower rate), and has discussed these compensatory effects in relation to a "reserve of responding" whereby some steady rate is maintained over time.

Quite commonly in the initial development of performance on FR, decrements in responding (and in reinforcement frequency) are followed by increases in rate. In the majority of the transitions from crf to FR illustrated by Ferster and Skinner (1957, Chapter 4), increased rates of responding follow after a period of deceleration in rate of responding and in reinforcements received. For example, see the stylized plot of their Figure 12, and the actual cumulative records of their Figures 13, 14, 16, and 17. Ferster and Skinner comment on this by saying that:

> The special contingencies imposed by a fixed ratio begin to operate during the first decline in rate; in particular, the pauses during the low rate are not likely to be followed by reinforcement as in interval schedules. Reinforcements tend to occur after responses which are members of small groups (p. 43).

Still other results bear on the relation between rate of responding and frequency of reinforcement on FR. There is diverse evidence that local rate of responding may increase as the value of FR increases. Figure 7 shows the relation between rate of responding and ratio size obtained in the rat by Boren (1953). Note that the rate of responding increases with increases in ratio size up to FR 25. Ferster and Skinner report that the rate is

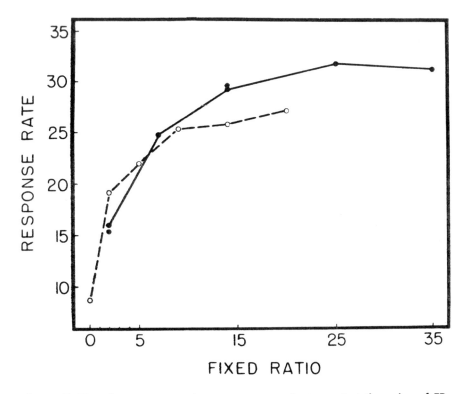

Figure 7. Plot of response rate in responses per minute against the value of FR. The two curves show results from two experiments. Redetermined points are indicated. (From Boren, 1953.)

higher on moderate-valued ratios (100 ± 50) than on small-valued ratios (30 ± 10). Hutchinson and Azrin (1961) have recently reported increases in rate of responding with increases in the size of the ratio in psychotic humans. It is difficult to tell from these experiments whether the frequency of reinforcement in time decreases as the value of FR is increased, but it is reasonable to suppose that the increase in rate with increases in value of FR may be related to the increase in rate following decrements in reinforcement frequency. These increases in rate might depend upon special contrast or compensatory phenomena, or they might simply result from the greater intermittency in the same way as rate and force of responding increase in extinction. Whatever the cause may be, a decrement in rate of responding (and frequency of reinforcement) on FR is likely to be followed subsequently by a transitory higher rate of responding. When this happens, the higher rate may be sustained because of an increased frequency of reinforcement for short IRTs and a higher average frequency of reinforcement. The likelihood of this "contrast" factor being important in the development of high rates of responding on FR rests more upon the empirical findings on transitions from crf to FR, and from one FR value to another, than upon the intrinsic logic of the argument, which assumes that rate of responding can increase both after decreases and after increases in the frequency of reinforcement (see also "Limited Availability Experiments," p. 96ff).

Additional evidence suggesting an interaction between rate of responding and frequency of reinforcement on FR comes from experiments on interlocking and conjunctive schedules. These schedules combine the schedule requirements of FR and FI. In an interlocking FR FI schedule, the number of responses required for reinforcement changes with time since the previous reinforcement. In the case in which the response requirement decreases as a linear function of time, the schedule is defined by two parameters, the ratio requirement immediately after reinforcement, and the time at which reinforcement is potentially available for the next response when no responses have occurred. This interlocking schedule is shown in Figure 1; the availability of reinforcement is determined by the sloping line. As the ratio requirement is increased the sloping line becomes more vertical and the schedule approaches FI; as the time requirement is increased the line becomes more horizontal and the schedule approaches FR.

Berryman and Nevin (1962) studied several values of an interlocking FI FR schedule in a group of four rats. A careful study of their Table I (p. 217) permits many interesting comparisons. One consistent result was that the rate of responding increased when the time requirement was increased (i.e., the schedule became more like FR). Changing the interlocking schedule from FR 72, FI 2, to FR 72, FI 4 and from FR 36, FI 4 to FR 36 (i.e., making the time requirement infinite) increased the average rate in all animals. In about half of these instances the rate increases were accompanied by slight decreases in the average frequency of reinforcement.

In a conjunctive FR FI schedule a ratio contingency is introduced in such a way that the average frequency of reinforcement has a maximum limit as in interval schedules. Reinforcement is made available when both n responses and t seconds have elapsed since the preceding reinforcement (see Figure 1). Herrnstein and Morse (1958) studied a conjunctive schedule in which the FI component was always constant (15 minutes) and the FR component was systematically changed (0 to 240 responses). They found that introducing an FR component into an FI 15 schedule had no tendency to increase the rate in either of the two pigeons studied; in fact, the rate of responding decreased as the parameter value of the FR component increased. When no ratio requirement was present, the number of responses per 15-minute period was about 300; this number decreased proportionally as the value of the FR requirement was increased. At FR values of 120 and 240 the response output fell so low that the average frequency of reinforcement was reduced below the maximum of four per hour set by the FI schedule. This result suggests that the rate-enhancing effects of a ratio contingency are partially dependent upon the direct relation between rate and frequency of reinforcement on FR.

The increases in rate described above, which accompany decreases in frequency of reinforcement on FR, probably occur over only a very narrow range of reinforcement frequencies and tend to be transient phenomena. On FR, as on FI or VI, decrease in frequency of reinforcement generally decreases the rate of responding. Also, the discussion in this chapter has been almost exclusively concerned with performances on ratio and interval schedules which are well maintained. When these schedules are compared at extreme values, there are further differences between them. Fixed ratio schedules may generate higher rates of responding than FI or VI at high frequencies of reinforcement, but the reverse is true at extremely low frequencies of reinforcement. Excluding situations involving control by stimuli, ratio contingencies are involved in most experiments in which behavior is weak and poorly maintained. Unfortunately experiments at large parameter values of ratio and interval schedules are difficult to compare, as other procedural differences such as length of session, conditions of deprivation, and past history become important. Experiments involving both ratio and interval contingencies, such as the conjunctive and interlocking procedures (Figure 1), and experiments employing yoked conditions will be especially useful for comparing ratio and interval performances over a wide range of parameter values.

Response Patterning and Temporal Discriminations

Aside from the complexity of the interactions, our understanding of schedule performances is fettered by the tendency of many authors to ignore the dynamic equilibrium conditions inherent in responding under a schedule and to explain schedule performances instead as discriminations of subtle differences in inferred stimulus conditions. Explanations of schedule-controlled patterns of responding in terms of temporal discriminations neglect the multiple sources of control of schedule peformances. The implication is that the rate of responding is controlled by the durations of the prevailing stimuli in a manner analogous to the control exerted by a gradually changing external discriminative stimulus correlated with reinforcement at some physical value. The dangers in evoking unknown stimulus events have already been discussed and apply equally to the temporal durations of stimuli; in addition still other considerations apply to the use of time durations as controlling discriminative stimuli.

Skinner notes in *The Behavior of Organisms* (pp. 263-264) that certain instances in which time enters into the control of behavior may seem to involve "discriminations" based upon time durations but actually do not. By altering the temporal conditions of dynamic processes it is possible to change the resulting state of the behavior and hence demonstrate what might be called a "differential response to time." Two examples given by Skinner of such dynamic relations are the relation between rate of responding and frequency of reinforcement, and the effect of a time delay between a response and the presentation of a reinforcer. A change in the average interval of reinforcement on FI from five to six minutes decreases the rate of responding, which shows that subjects are controlled by the difference between interreinforcement times of five and six minutes. But this control is exerted through the inherent input-output relation between rate of responding and frequency of reinforcement rather than through time durations acting as controlling discriminative stimuli. Similarly, when a response is followed immediately by a reinforcer, the rate of responding is higher than when a response is followed by a reinforcer after a two-second delay, and the rate is lower still when reinforcement follows after an eight-second delay. In a situation involving two concurrently present response keys, responses on one reinforced after a two-second delay and responses on the other after an eight-second delay, a difference in rate of responding on the two keys would be properly considered as the dynamic effect of reinforcement in strengthening behavior, and not the result of a temporal discrimination.

According to Skinner, "temporal discriminations" are different from the above sorts of correlations between responding and the temporal parameter values of schedules. "When we establish a coincidental relation between a second event and some point in the course of a prolonged stimulus, the organism may begin to distinguish between the stimulus momentarily at that point and the same stimulus momentarily at some other point by reacting differently to the two" (Skinner, 1938, p. 265). In commenting on the analogy of reinforcement at a point in time with reinforcement in the presence of an external discriminative stimulus, Skinner notes that temporal discriminations necessarily involve gradual stimulus changes and emphasizes the multiple control of responding in situations involving temporal discriminations. He goes on to discuss two kinds of temporal discriminations: (1) discriminations based on the preceding reinforcement, and (2) discriminations based on the preceding response. Many of the schedule-controlled patterns associated with FI and FR are analyzed in terms of interactions between these two discriminations.[8]

That experimental subjects can respond to the duration of a stimulus as a discriminative stimulus has been clearly shown by Reynolds and Catania (1962). Brief periods in the presence of a light followed dark periods that varied from 3 to 30 seconds in duration. Responding during the light period was reinforced on VI only after one particular duration of the dark period (either the shortest or the longest duration). Three of the four pigeons used as subjects responded most frequently in the light period after the duration correlated with reinforcement and responded progressively less after durations that differed more and more from the one correlated with reinforcement. It seems reasonable to suppose that discriminations of the quality obtained by Reynolds and Catania enter into the control of responding on a schedule, but these temporal discriminations are not like discriminations involving external stimuli of the ordinary sort. The discriminable temporal properties of a prolonged stimulus necessarily interact with the dynamic effects of reinforcement. For example, Skinner (1938, pp. 296-297) describes the pause after reinforcement on FR as being jointly determined by the temporal discrimination that responses are never reinforced soon after a previous reinforcement and the temporary effect of emitting the responses required for the previous reinforcement (strain on the reserve). When the value of the FR is low enough to sustain responding, there may be no pauses after reinforcement, but at higher values of FR, responding is not maintained and "the preceding run which occurs under reinforcement at a fixed ratio places the reserve in a state of strain which acts with the temporal discrimination of reinforcement to produce a pause of some length" (p. 298).

A primary objection to the use of the concept of "temporal discriminations" is that it tends to obscure the interactions between multiple controlling factors, particularly the dynamic effects of reinforcement. A striking effect of delayed reinforcement on distributions of IRTs is seen in an experiment by Dews (1963). The basic schedule was that the third response with an IRT exceeding ten seconds was reinforced. This schedule can be designated as a fixed ratio of minimum IRTs, or as a tandem IRT, IRT, IRT (Dews & Morse, 1958). Performance on this schedule was compared with performance on a modified schedule that was identical, except that after the completion of the second IRT exceeding ten seconds, the reinforcer was presented when ten seconds had elapsed *without* a response. Thus, the minimum pause requirements of the schedule and the minimum time between presentations of the reinforcer were the same for the basic schedule and the modified schedule. If the basic schedule is viewed as one

---

[8] It is interesting to compare this formulation in Chapter 7 of *The Behavior of Organisms* with Anger's (1963) recent analysis of avoidance responding in terms of stimuli correlated with the last response and with the last shock.

requiring a ten-second pause and a response in sequence, then the modified schedule is identical except that the terminal response (but not the terminal minimum pause) is omitted.

Figure 8 shows relative frequency distributions of different IRTs for one pigeon on these two schedules. Row A is the average IRT distribution for ten complete 50-minute sessions on the schedule reinforcing a sequence of three ten-second IRTs. Row G is the comparable IRT distribution for ten complete 50-minute sessions on the delayed reinforcement schedule. Reinforcing a sequence of three ten-second IRTs produced a higher level of responding than reinforcing a sequence of two ten-second IRTs after a delay of ten seconds. The immediate reinforcement of a response engendered far more than three responses in 30 seconds, and relatively few IRTs exceeded 10 seconds (Figure 8, Row A). Presenting the reinforcer following a ten-second delay after the second ten-second IRT reduced the output of responses. Lowering the rate shifted the IRT distribution toward longer IRTs, and in this instance increased the frequency of reinforcement (Figure 8, Row G). The shift in the IRT distribution occurred presumably because of the weaker effect of delayed reinforcement in strengthening responding; the resulting distribution clearly depends upon both the rate-enhancing effect and the shaping effect of reinforcement.

The distribution of IRTs shifted after a single instance of delayed reinforcement. Rows B through F of Figure 8 show consecutive segments of the session in which the schedule was changed. Row B shows the distribution of IRTs on the schedule reinforcing a sequence of three ten-second IRTs from the beginning of the session until the thirteenth reinforcement; Row C shows the distribution of IRTs between the thirteenth and fourteenth reinforcements. At this time the change to the delayed reinforcement schedule was made. Row D shows the distribution of IRTs between the fourteenth and fifteenth reinforcements. Until the reinforcer was presented following a ten-second pause after the second ten-second IRT, there was no way the change in schedule could have been detected; the only change was omitting the requirement of the terminal response. Consequently this distribution is similar to the preceding ones. Row E shows the distribution of IRTs between the fifteenth and sixteenth reinforcements. The single presentation of delayed reinforcement changed the subsequent distribution of responding, even though the pigeon had received more than 1400 reinforcements and had emitted more than a quarter of a million responses on the schedule requiring the terminal response. The common practice of referring to IRT distributions obtained from schedules reinforcing minimum IRT durations as temporal discriminations conceals the dynamic balancing of multiple controlling factors that always exist in this situation.

Recently, Holz and Azrin (1962) have shown that the delivery of electric shocks can control rate of responding as a discriminative stimulus, but because the electric shock has punishing properties also, it cannot be

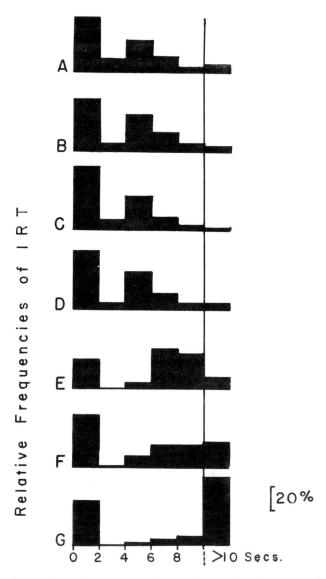

Figure 8. Change in performance on change in schedule from immediate to delayed reinforcement. The rows show relative frequency distributions of IRTs between 0-2 seconds, 2-4 seconds, etc. In Rows A, B, and C, a sequence of three ten-second IRTs was reinforced. In Rows D, E, and F a sequence of two ten-second IRTs was reinforced after a ten-second delay with no response. The first presentation of the delayed reinforcement (Row D) immediately changed the distribution of IRTs (Row E). See text for a fuller explanation. (From Dews, 1963.)

considered merely as a discriminative stimulus. Similarly, the temporal correlation of a response with a reinforcer has inherent effects that will necessarily be operating in any situation in which temporal discriminations may be operating.[9] Since these inherent dynamic factors control patterns of responding in time, the continued appeal to temporal discriminations and timing as "pure" stimulus events obverts progress in the analysis of temporally patterned responding.

Not all gradual developments of correlations between responding and events in time are called *temporal discriminations;* the term is reserved for those cases in which the rate of responding is highest at times when reinforcement occurs and lowest at times when reinforcement never occurs. Even in these cases the control of responding by discriminative stimuli is inferred and not explicitly shown, and other formulations are equally capable of explaining the observed behavior. For example, Dews (1962) has suggested that an important factor determining the curvature within FI is the declining, retroactive, rate-enhancing effect of the reinforcing stimulus as the delay between responses and reinforcement is increased (see also Boren, 1953). The immediate presentation of a reinforcer has a greater effect in engendering behavior than the delayed presentation, but delayed presentations do strengthen behavior somewhat, and responding already conditioned can be maintained by reinforcement delayed up to at least 100 seconds (Dews, 1960). Therefore, when reinforcement is presented on FI (or FR), its effect to strengthen responding will be greatest on the terminal response, less on the penultimate response, and even less on responses more remote in time from reinforcement. Dews' notion of a temporal gradient of reinforcement gives a plausible account of the temporal patterning on FI without appealing to a temporal discrimination. In mentioning this possibility and in cautioning against the uncritical use of the concept of temporal discrimination, there is no intention to question that the duration of a stimulus can develop some discriminative control over behavior. Quite possibly the interreinforcement duration, as a discriminative stimulus, enters into the control of responding on FI. The important point is that schedule-controlled patterns of responding are dynamic, steady-state conditions that are jointly determined by interacting environmental conditions. A single ubiquitous explanation of schedule performances is unlikely to be adequate.

---

[9] Even ordinary discriminative stimuli can have additional properties. There is some evidence that the intensity of a stimulus partially controls rate of responding (Blough, 1959; Green, 1953; Terrace, 1963). The development of control by a discriminative stimulus depends also upon the type and the parameter value of schedule with which it is correlated.

EXPERIMENTS ON THE SELECTIVE REINFORCEMENT
OF IRTs

This section will summarize evidence from experiments in which direct manipulations were used to change the relation between the terminal IRT and reinforcement on ratio and interval schedules. Ferster and Skinner (1957) describe three procedures for changing the terminal contingencies of a schedule at the moment of reinforcement: the direct manipulation of the reinforced IRT, the use of limited availability of reinforcement on interval schedules (limited hold), and the use of tandem schedules in which a ratio or interval schedule is added as a terminal component to another schedule. These procedures produce steady-state performances that have been especially useful in the analysis of ratio and interval schedules.

The Explicit Differential Reinforcement of Particular IRTs

drl

The most direct way to show that the reinforcement of particular IRTs can control a temporal pattern of responding is to reinforce IRTs directly in a more controlled and manipulable way than do ordinary ratio and interval schedules. That reinforcing an IRT does affect subsequent rate was established by Skinner (1938), who showed that reinforcing (on FI) only IRTs greater than 15 seconds lowered rate of responding (p. 306). Skinner (1946) also found that reinforcing short response latencies reduced latencies. Ferster and Skinner (1957) reported a number of experiments in which rate specifications were added as special conditions to ratio and interval schedules. They used the terms *differential reinforcement of low rates* (drl) to designate the added requirement of a long IRT and *differential reinforcement of high rates* (drh) to designate the added requirement of a series of short IRTs. Such added contingencies may be viewed either as the modification of schedule conditions prevailing at reinforcement, or as further defining properties of the reinforced response class analogous to specifications of force or location. Adding a drl contingency to the reinforced response on interval schedules is not different from reinforcing a response of the class defined by a minimum IRT, but on ratio schedules the addition of a drl contingency to the reinforced response is very different from reinforcing the nth response exceeding a minimum IRT. In recent years the case in which every response exceeding some minimum IRT is reinforced (the DRL schedule) has been extensively studied as a separate schedule.

All relevant experiments indicate that imposing a rate contingency on the reinforced IRT produces dramatic effects on ratio and interval schedule performances. Ferster and Skinner studied the addition of a drl contingency (up to 12 seconds) on FI, VI, and FR, and Anger studied a VI schedule in which only IRTs of greater than 40 seconds were reinforced. In all cases the performances changed appreciably in the direction of generally lower rates of responding. Inspection of the cumulative records presented by Ferster and Skinner (1957, Chapter 9) indicates that the general features of VI drl resemble simple VI to a greater extent than performances on FI drl resemble FI, or those on FR drl resemble FR. For example, in the FI drl records it appears that requiring a minimum IRT for reinforcement on FI reduced the pause after reinforcement and tended to produce fairly steady responding throughout the interval. Probably other factors interact with the differential reinforcement of IRTs more on FI and on FR than on VI.

The patterns of responding produced by FR drl (Ferster and Skinner, 1957, pp. 477-493; 500-502) are excellent illustrations of the dynamic interactions engendered by schedule contingencies. Figure 9 shows records of the performance of one pigeon on FR 60 drl 6 sec. over a series of days. This schedule clearly generated fluctuating contingencies. There are both accelerations and decelerations in response patterning, and both gradual and abrupt shifts from one pattern to another.

Besides the general effect of producing a low rate of responding, one other effect of imposing a drl contingency is so frequently observed that it deserves special comment. Though poorly understood, it is extremely well documented that reinforcing only long IRTs may result in a high frequency of short IRTs. The effect is clearly seen in the VI drl and FR drl records shown by Ferster and Skinner (1957), and is usually seen on the DRL procedure too. The effect is probably a direct result of the differential reinforcement of a long IRT, but a high percentage of short IRTs does not always occur on DRL (Kelleher, Fry, & Cook, 1959).

A comment on the terminology *differential reinforcement of low rates* seems appropriate. The term *drl* refers to a schedule procedure, and to the extent that it implies a behavioral effect, it is likely to be misleading. Skinner (1938) noted that fixed interval reinforcement differentially reinforced low rates of responding (i.e., a long IRT). Although the operation of the contingency may cause the rate on FI to be lower than it would be if the contingency were not operating, the result is not that FI produces especially low rates of responding. The DRL schedule, which reinforces each IRT exceeding some value, produces a low rate, but another effect of this schedule is that it often produces a high percentage of extremely short IRTs. It would be better to specify this schedule simply as IRT $> t$ sec. In view of the complexity of the behavior produced by schedules, it is probably an advantage for schedule names not to designate the expected behavioral result.

drh

Although the experiments on drh are more limited than those on drl, the conclusion is justified that reinforcing a long IRT has a more reliable effect in increasing the average IRT than reinforcing a short IRT does in

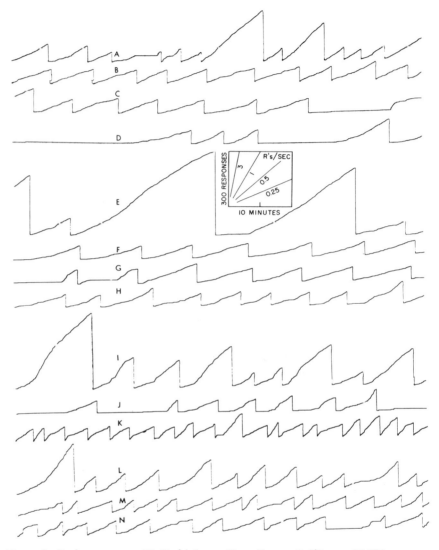

Figure 9. Performance on FR 60 drl 6 sec. (From Ferster & Skinner, 1957.)

decreasing the average IRT. Reinforcing a short IRT will tend to increase rate, but it is likely to have other unusual effects. Ferster and Skinner (1957, p. 33) discuss the desirability of integrating a sequence of IRTs within some short time period rather than reinforcing a single, short IRT, which tends to produce an unusual topography. For other reasons Anger (1956) also concludes that reinforcing a sequence of short IRTs will be more effective in increasing rate than reinforcing a single short IRT. In his experiments on VI he found that reinforcing only $<$ 28-second IRTs on VI 5 made short IRTs ($<$ 16-second) more likely to follow long IRTs ($>$ 16-

second), whereas before the procedure was introduced, short IRTs were more likely to follow short IRTs. His explanation of this result emphasizes the need for careful analysis of schedule specifications and suggests the operation of a temporal gradient of the effect of reinforcement on preceding IRTs:

> These observations correspond to the fact that during reinforcement of < 28-sec. IRTs on a VI schedule the reinforcement of > 16-sec. IRTs is greater following long IRTs than following short. This can be seen from the following: (a) During VI the probability of assignment of a reinforcement during an IRT is greater the longer the IRT until the probability reaches one. . . . (b) But when *only* < 28-sec. IRTs are reinforced, then reinforcements assigned during > 28-sec. IRTs are not delivered until the next < 28-sec. IRT occurs. (c) Hence a < 16-sec. IRT following a long IRT receives the Reinfs./IRT of an IRT as long as the sum of the long and short IRT. This is far greater than the Reinfs./IRT of a < 16-sec. IRT following another < 16-sec. IRT which is just the low Reinfs./IRT of < 16-sec. IRTs. . . . Consequently during reinforcement of only short IRTs on a VI schedule, Ss made two or three responses in succession where before they had made one. The short IRTs increased, but the long IRTs were little affected. Apparently responding is affected not only by the length of the IRT preceding reinforcement, but also by the length of the "second-back" IRT, at least when the immediately preceding IRT is short. To raise the frequency of short IRTs when many long IRTs are present, it seems necessary to reinforce sequences of short IRTs as often or more often than long-short sequences (pp. 160-161).

Synthetic Schedules

Many variables operate under schedules that are simple to program, such as FR or FI. In order to show the effect of a particular variable, such as the differential reinforcement of particular IRTs, it is desirable to manipulate the control of this variable directly, and to see how behavioral performances are modified by it. The demonstration that a variable *is* modifying behavior under certain circumstances is conclusive evidence that it *can* operate under these conditions, but it is only presumptive evidence that it *will* modify behavior in other situations. In understanding behavior, it is not sufficient simply to analyze complex behavior into component factors; a full explanation requires that the behavior be synthesized by explicit manipulations of the component factors. While there is no doubt that reinforcing only IRTs of some given class on FR or FI produces dramatic behavioral effects, that such pronounced changes occur when this contingency is added to a schedule is clear evidence that some aspect of the schedule has also been changed. Therefore, results from experiments involving the direct reinforcement of particular IRTs on interval and ratio schedules can furnish only suggestive evidence that the relative reinforcement of different IRTs is normally operating to control behavior under the basic schedule.

In one series of experiments, Anger (1954) attempted to demonstrate that the relative rate of reinforcement of different IRTs was actually controlling responding on VI. He showed that direct manipulations producing slight changes in the number of reinforcements per hour for different IRTs could result in changes in responding, and that synthetically produced reinforcements per hour for different IRTs which duplicated VI did not significantly change VI performance. Normally on VI, relative frequency of reinforcement of different IRTs depends upon the subject's distribution of IRTs and on the fixed relation between the probability of reinforcement and duration of IRT arranged by the schedule. Anger constructed synthetic VI schedules based upon and providing direct control over the relative frequency of reinforcement of different IRTs. He controlled separately the relative rate of reinforcement of different class intervals of IRTs (0-4 seconds, 4-8 seconds, etc.) with a separate schedule (FI or tandem FI FR or VI FR) for each IRT class to give the same average reinforcements per hour for different IRT classes as did a VI 4 at a particular period in time for individual subjects. Three rats were exposed to VI 4 until their response distributions were stable. Each subject was then shifted from VI to the "synthetic VI" which duplicated the relative reinforcements per hour for different IRT classes occurring at that time for that subject. This shift did not produce significant changes in the patterning of responding over a ten-day period. In the subsequent phases of this experiment, 3.3 reinforcements per hour were eliminated from those received in the 0-4 second IRT class and shifted to longer IRT classes; later the original synthetic VI conditions were reinstated. These changes tended to shift the subjects's IRT distributions in the appropriate direction, although the magnitude of the effect was not great.

Anger (1954, p. 40) discusses some of the factors which might distort the control of responding by the relative frequency of reinforcement of different IRTs. Although the data from this experiment are limited, it is obviously a powerful technique for the analysis of schedule performances to develop "synthetic schedules" that engender precisely some of the characteristics of other schedules. By directly controlling the relative frequency of reinforcement of different IRTs, Anger's synthetic VI schedule eliminated certain interactions between responding and reinforcement on VI. Complex schedule procedures that simplify and eliminate variables operating in easily programmed schedules would thus produce performances that are simple from a behavioral point of view.

Limited Availability Experiments (Time-correlated Schedules)

Limited availability of reinforcement on interval schedules (limited hold) is another powerful procedure for showing the dependence of responding upon the probability of reinforcement of terminal IRTs arranged by ratio and interval schedules. This procedure changes the conditions existing on simple interval schedules in two ways. Limited availability of reinforcement on interval schedules greatly reduces the greater probability of reinforcement of long IRTs over short IRTs. In addition, the average frequency of reinforcement is also likely to decline under this procedure, particularly when the period of availability is progressively shortened.

Figure 2 showed that on FI 100 sec., the probability of an IRT of t seconds being reinforced is 0.05 for a 5-second IRT, 0.1 for a 10-second IRT, 0.5 for a 50-second IRT, and 1.0 for a 100-second IRT. The curve relating probability of reinforcement to IRT duration does not increase to a probability of 1.0, however, if the availability of reinforcement is limited to a ten-second period after the end of the interval. Instead, it has a maximum at 0.1. An IRT of five seconds still has a probability of reinforcement of 0.05, since it will be reinforced if it begins between 95 and 100 seconds since the start of the interval; similarly an IRT of ten seconds has a probability of reinforcement of 0.1, since it will be reinforced if it begins between 90 and 100 seconds. But unlike the situation on ordinary FI 100 sec., IRTs of all class intervals greater than ten seconds have a probability of reinforcement of 0.1, since they must be initiated during a particular ten seconds of the 100-second interval in order to be reinforced. For example, on FI 100 sec. with a limited availability of ten seconds, a reinforced IRT of 50 seconds must be initiated between 50 and 60 seconds since the start of the interval.

Some experiments on "limited hold" were performed by Ferster and Skinner (1957), who found that limited availability (0.24 to 0.75 seconds) increased the average rate of responding on VI 1 to VI 1.5. Schoenfeld, Cumming, and Hearst (1956) initiated a series of systematic investigations of the time parameters involved in interval schedules with limited availability of reinforcement (Brandauer, 1958; Clark, 1959; Cumming & Schoenfeld, 1959; 1960; Hearst, 1958; Millenson, 1959; Schoenfeld & Cumming, 1957; Snapper, 1962; and others). In these investigations the conditions of reinforcement are specified according to the general classification developed by Schoenfeld, Cumming, and Hearst (1956), in which the terms t^D and t^Δ refer, respectively, to time periods during which a response may be reinforced, and time periods during which a response is never reinforced. When t^D and t^Δ are held constant and alternated, and only the first response in a t^D period is reinforced, the schedule corresponds to FI limited hold. The series of experiments on this time-correlated schedule report systematic variations in the total cycle length ($t^D + t^\Delta$), and in the proportion of the cycle during which a response may be reinforced ($t^D/t^\Delta + t^\Delta$ or T) over a wide range of values. Brandauer (1958) studied cycle lengths as short as 1 to 50 milliseconds with t^D periods as short as 50 microseconds; Clark studied cycle lengths up to 10 minutes with t^D periods as short as 1 second.

All these experiments indicate that the average rate of responding increases by several-fold when the availability of reinforcement is limited to brief durations. Pauses followed by abrupt shifts to high rates of responding are more common on this schedule than on ordinary interval schedules, and responding in extinction after limited availability of reinforcement tends to be characterized by abrupt changes from no responding to a high steady rate. These results are strong evidence of the importance of the relative probability of reinforcement of IRTs in determining schedule performance. The function for the probability of reinforcement of the terminal IRT for interval schedules becomes similar to the function for ratio schedules by introducing limited availability of reinforcement, and, in a general way, the resulting behavior becomes more like behavior on ratio schedules.

The effect of limited availability in changing the differential reinforcement of particular IRTs is undoubtedly the major factor responsible for the change in behavior, but changes in the average frequency of reinforcement may also play some role. Short-term decreases in the average frequency of reinforcement are probably related to the increased rate in limited availability experiments. Previously it was shown that increased rates of responding sometimes followed decrements in reinforcement frequency on FR (p. 84). Similar observations of increased rate following decrements in reinforcement have been reported regularly in experiments on limited availability. Schoenfeld and Cumming (1957) comment that "on occasions when a reinforcement was 'missed' by low temporally discriminated responding, there would suddenly emerge a high rate which was generally sustained until the next reinforcement was procured and which sometimes persevered for a while thereafter" (pp. 351-352). Hearst (1958) reported that the "sharp increases in rate take place in the range of Ts where the most sudden drops in number of reinforcements occur" (p. 45). Clark (1959) also suggests that the increased rate is related to missed reinforcements, but not in a simple way. Even in Ferster and Skinner's experiments on limited availability in which they attempt to hold frequency of reinforcement fairly constant by changing the mean value of the VI, there is some indication that higher rates of responding follow periods of lower reinforcement. Ferster and Skinner also report that the limited hold contingency was especially effective for a subject with a previous history of a low rate of responding on a VI drl schedule "by providing maximum contrast between occasions for reinforcement and non-reinforcement while sustaining the behavior at the overall level required if reinforcements are to occur to maintain the behavior" (pp. 463-464).

Ratio schedules and limited availability schedules differ from interval schedules in the relation between rate of responding and frequency of reinforcement. A decrease in rate of responding accompanies a decrease in the frequency of reinforcement on interval schedules (Ferster & Skinner, 1957; Findley, 1958; Herrnstein, 1961a; Reynolds, 1961c; Wilson, 1954). This is generally true for ratio schedules too, but over a limited range, decreases in frequency of reinforcement brought about by increasing ratio size may result in increases in rate of responding (Boren, 1953; Ferster & Skinner, 1957). Introducing a limited availability contingency makes behavior more "ratio-like" in that the rate of responding goes up as the rate of reinforcement goes down. The most satisfactory data on this topic are from the experiments of Clark (1959) who found that the rate more than doubled for a bird on a time-correlated schedule as the frequency of reinforcements per 30-minute session decreased from 15 to 9.3. The delivery of reinforcements for this subject programmed the availability of reinforcements on VI for a "yoked" control subject, and for this subject the rate of responding decreased as the frequency of reinforcement decreased. This result is an example of the multiple causation of responding in a schedule. Probably the sudden decreases in the frequency of reinforcement cause temporary increases in responding on both schedules. On VI the differential reinforcement for longer IRTs will tend to attenuate the rate increase, while on the limited-availability schedule the reinforcements actually obtained at short IRTs together with the lack of any differential reinforcement for long IRTs will tend to sustain the rate increase. Further experiments are needed to determine whether this transitory effect of higher rates following missed reinforcements is always involved in the increased rate of responding obtained in experiments limiting the availability of reinforcements on interval schedules. Clark's (1959) yoked experiments show that "missed" reinforcements on VI alone do not produce a sustained increase in rate, and certainly the major factor responsible for the increase in rate in limited availability experiments is the elimination of differential reinforcement for long IRTs.

The behavior of subjects on interval schedules with limited availability of reinforcement becomes more "ratio-like" in that the average rate increases, intermediate rates between no responding and steady responding occur less frequently, and greater intermittency of reinforcement does not result in lower rates. Although these results strongly support the importance of the selective reinforcement of the terminal IRT in generating performances on ratio and interval schedules, it is not possible to say that all of the effects of limited availability are due entirely to the change in the selective reinforcement of the terminal IRT. Neither is it possible to assess with any quantitative certainty the degree to which performances on interval schedules with limited availability match performances on FR or VR. The stated purpose of the series of experiments beginning with Schoenfeld, Cumming, and Hearst (1956) was to integrate the phenomena of ratio and interval schedules into one conceptual framework. This commendable effort has yielded valuable empirical data on performances on time-correlated schedules. Because many characteristics of behavior generated by ratio and interval schedules can be produced by quantitative changes in the parameters of temporally defined schedules, these procedures offer promise both for the systematic study of schedule-controlled behavior and as useful dependent conditions for studying independent variables other than reinforcement. Nevertheless, the conclusion that time-correlated schedules of certain parameter values are essentially the same as ratio schedules is not justified; there is simply not enough quantitative information available about performances on either type of schedule to permit a definite statement concerning their possible identity.

In the whole series of papers, only Clark (1959) made a direct comparison between a time-correlated schedule and a VR schedule. One pigeon exposed to a time-correlated schedule with a two-minute cycle length and an availability period of 0.4 seconds (T = 0.003) was shifted for seven days to a VR schedule in which the mean value of the VR matched the mean responses/reinforcement occurring on the time-correlated schedule. Although Clark showed no data, he reported that:

> A comparison of the response rates and the pauses after reinforcement indicated no significant differences between the .003 T schedule and the VR schedule. Cumulative response records obtained under both conditions were indistinguishable. It is not possible to say whether further running at the VR schedule would have generated different effects on behavior, but the data do suggest that the same variables are involved in the control of behavior during both the T and the corresponding VR schedule (pp. 13-14).

A more detailed discussion of both the theoretical and empirical relations between ratio schedules and time-correlated schedules has been given by Brandauer (1958), who studied time-correlated schedules with cycle lengths of 1 to 50 milliseconds and T values from 1.0 to .00167. Brandauer called these schedules *random ratios* in distinction to conventionally programmed VR. Under the assumption that the responding of the subject is independent of the generation of pulses, the average number of responses per reinforcement would be given by the relative durations of the periods of availability to the total time periods. The T values studied by Brandauer would correspond to ratio values of 1 to 600 responses per reinforcement. He presented data indicating that this assumption was tenable at a T value of 0.1 for a sample based on 195 reinforcements. A more recent experiment by Snapper (1962), in which the cycle length was 20 milliseconds, gave similar data for T values of 0.02 and 0.04. It is unfortunate that these studies on time-correlated schedules have not given more information on the consistency and stability of responses per reinforcement at different T values. Brandauer noted that the experiments of Schoenfeld and Cumming (1957) with a T of 0.05 more closely approximated the value of 20 responses per reinforcement at short cycle lengths (0.94, 1.88, and 3.75 seconds) than did Hearst's experiments with 30-second cycle lengths and successively smaller T values. He suggested that the independence of responses and reinforcement schedules is more likely to be obtained in experiments with short cycle lengths than in experiments with low T values.

Brandauer also noted the similarities and dissimilarities between his experiments on *random ratio* and the VR experiments of Ferster and Skinner (1957). In these experiments, pauses up to a minute, alternating with periods of responding at a high rate, commonly occurred; in addition, one example of an extremely abrupt shift in total response output from one day to the next is reported (see their Figures 475 and 476). Brandauer reported that he did not find marked day-to-day variability and that pauses were rarely longer than three seconds in birds that responded through the entire session on the random-ratio procedure. On the other hand, Ferster and Skinner (1957) reported "warm-ups" on VI limited hold (p. 360), and Hearst (1958) found high day-to-day variability on a time-correlated schedule with a 30-second cycle length at low T values (0.02 or less). Hearst noted that one bird with a previous history of responding at a high rate went almost 20 minutes without a response. He attributed the day-to-day variability in response rate to the number of reinforcements received during the first few minutes of each daily session. When a bird received almost no reinforcements in the first ten minutes, its rate was likely to decrease radically in the latter half of the session. In contrast, Brandauer reported that a large number of responses per reinforcement at the beginning of the session did not produce a decline in rate as much as a large number of responses per reinforcement later in the session, and that the decline in rate during the session became less with increasing exposure to the schedule. The nature of the correspondence between performances on time-correlated and ratio schedules is clearly far from settled.

Time-correlated schedules are similar to ratio schedules in that the resulting performance on the schedule depends critically upon the history of reinforcement and the sequential development of the current performance. According to general opinion, an average rate of responding under one condition is less likely to depend upon past conditions, and is more likely to be recoverable at a later time, under interval schedules than under ratio schedules (see Cumming & Schoenfeld, 1959; Schoenfeld & Cumming, 1957; Sidman, 1960). The sequential history of reinforcement thus becomes another factor to consider in comparing time-correlated and ratio schedules. Practically all experiments on limited availability begin with an established interval performance; and then the period of availability is gradually reduced to lower and lower values. In one experiment in which Cumming and Schoenfeld (1959) initiated a limited availability schedule after crf, and rapidly changed the cycle length, the change in average rate of responding was less than in a previous experiment in which the change had been made more gradually. Comparisons of limited availability and ratio schedules under comparable past histories and at different parameter values would furnish much valuable information concerning the similarity of these procedures. These schedules should also be studied under extreme degrees of intermittency which only poorly maintain responding; almost all of the experiments described above were performed under conditions which did maintain a high rate of responding.

Tandem Schedules

A third procedure for showing the dependence of responding upon the probability of reinforcement of terminal IRTs on ratio and interval schedules is the use of tandem FI FR and tandem FR FI schedules. Ferster and Skinner (1957) studied two sorts of tandem schedules: FI schedules with a small FR added in tandem and FR schedules with a small FI added in tandem. On a tandem schedule the relation of the terminal IRT to reinforcement is that prevailing on the final component of the tandem schedule.

The few results reported by Ferster and Skinner for tandem FI FR are dramatic. The rate of responding of two pigeons increased greatly when a tandem FR 10 was added to an FI 45 schedule. The performance of the pigeons on FI differed markedly; consequently it is unlikely that the rate-increasing effect of the added tandem FR contingency depended upon any special history. The increased responding almost certainly resulted from the elimination of the selective reinforcement of longer IRTs on the interval schedule.

Ferster and Skinner found that after the rate increase occurred on tandem FI 45 FR 10, responding was still maintained when the tandem FR parameter value was increased quite substantially (up to FR 400). Also, the effect of adding the tandem FR persisted in the subsequent performances on simple FI and FR. In neither the experiments on FI 45, nor those on FI 10 after tandem FI 10 FR 3, did the removal of the tandem FR requirement cause the rate to decrease to its former level. Thus the tandem FI FR procedure appears to be one of the best ways to generate a high output of responses per reinforcement. With a small tandem FR, the schedule produces a high average response output while still retaining an important feature of interval schedules, i.e., that reinforcement can follow after only a few responses (Herrnstein & Morse, 1958). In Ferster and Skinner's experiments, the tandem FR introduced into an existing FI schedule produced a larger number of responses per reinforcement than would ordinarily be obtained with sustained responding on VR or FR schedules.

In contrast to the dramatic effects of tandem FI FR, the results of the tandem FR FI and tandem VR FI experiments described by Ferster and Skinner are more difficult to characterize. Tandem FR FI schedules with fairly large values of FR and fairly small values of FI were studied in transition from crf. For example, in one experiment two birds were exposed to tandem FR 240 FI 7 sec. after crf. One of the birds developed a sustained pattern of responding at these values but the other bird did not, probably because of the high ratio value. Tandem FR FI with lower ratio values (80,

140) did sustain responding. In general the rates were not exceptionally high, but several instances of high rates on tandem FR FI schedules were obtained. There was some indication that fairly high rates eventually developed in all those experiments in which the performance was maintained.

Several interesting observations came from these experiments on tandem FR FI. There were some examples of a decline in rate and frequency of reinforcement being followed shortly by the appearance of high rates. The changes in rate of responding were more gradual on tandem FR FI than the abrupt shifts in responding typically obtained on ratio schedules. Ferster and Skinner show many scalloped records, and there is some suggestion that higher ratio values were possible on tandem FR FI without developing prolonged pauses than on FR alone. These same results also were obtained with tandem VR FI. Birds on tandem VR FI eventually developed a high rate of responding somewhat characteristic of performances on ratio schedules. Removing the FI contingency sometimes, but not always, increased the rate still further. Adding a tandem FI contingency to an already existing ratio performance had a clear effect in decreasing the rate, according to Ferster and Skinner.

The development of high rates on tandem FR FI and VR FI schedules indicates that aspects of ratio performances develop even when FI contingencies are prevailing at the moment of reinforcement. Adding the tandem FI does not rule out the possibility that the increase in rate might be due to the selective effect of reinforcement on IRTs. We have discussed the selective reinforcement only of terminal IRTs on FR and FI schedules, but penultimate and more remote IRTs are also reinforced. The effect is greatest on those IRTs closest in time to reinforcement, but characteristic properties of responding remote in time from reinforcement can still be maintained by reinforcement (Morse & Herrnstein, 1956).

HIGHER-ORDER OPERANTS

Rapid advances in the study of schedule-controlled behavior are being made through the use of complex operants and second-order schedules. A *complex* operant is one in which the presentation of a reinforcer is made contingent upon sequences of responses as a unit. A *second-order* schedule is one in which the behavior specified by a schedule contingency is treated as a unitary response that is itself reinforced according to some schedule. (Second-order schedules in which some exteroceptive stimulus change is produced according to a schedule, and the exteroceptive stimulus is associated with reinforcement according to another schedule, will be discussed in detail in Chapter 5.) While these terms *complex operants* and *second-order schedules* are particularly applicable to certain recent experiments by Ferster (1958b; 1960), Findley (1962), and Kelleher (Chapter 5), it should be clear that many simple schedules can be analyzed in terms of complex responses. Thus FR requires a sequence of responses and certain authors have discussed the merits of treating FR in terms of groups of responses with a functional unity (Boren, 1961; Keller & Schoenfeld, 1951; Skinner, 1938). Tandem schedules such as tandem FI, FI, FI or tandem IRT, IRT, IRT can be viewed as second-order FR schedules in which the response is the completion of the interval or IRT requirement. Beyond mere heuristic speculation, the recent work of Findley (1962) and of Kelleher (Chapter 5) clearly establishes the functional unity of sequences and patterns of responding as operants.

These experiments on higher-order operants are important for the study of intermittent reinforcement in three respects:

1. Complex responses have additional properties which may contribute information not easily obtained from situations involving single discrete responses. For example, Ferster (1958b) found that the stereotypy of an ordered sequence of responding on two response keys was increased by intermittent reinforcement. A chimpanzee was studied in an experiment in which the only reinforced sequence was three responses on one key and one response on the other key. When this sequence was reinforced with food on crf, the percentage of sequences that did not conform to the reinforcement contingency was about 20 percent. When this sequence was followed by a conditioned reinforcer, and only one in every 33 sequences was reinforced with food (a second-order schedule), the percentage of other sequences was about 2 percent. In another experiment Ferster (1960) studied the complex response of *matching to sample* in two pigeons. In a situation involving three response keys, a response on the illuminated sample key (randomly either red or white) illuminated the matching keys. A response on the matching key illuminated with the same color as the sample was reinforced intermittently with food. Ferster found that the percentage of matching responses depended upon the parameter value and the type of schedule of reinforcement; the percentage of matches was higher on FR 10 than on FI 10. The possibility of reinforcement changing aspects of behavior such as "accuracy" or "quality" offers great promise for the study of both the selective shaping and strengthening effects of reinforcement.

2. The range of behaviors that it is possible to produce by second-order schedules appears to stand in relation to ordinary intermittent reinforcement as intermittent reinforcement does to regular reinforcement. The work of Findley (1962) and Kelleher (Chapter 5) indicates that it is possible to produce enormous outputs of behavior using higher-order scheduling of reinforcement.

3. The ability to generate unitary properties in sequences of responses controlled by schedule contingencies offers great technical advantages for detailed analysis of operant behavior. For example, Kelleher, Fry, and Cook (1964) found that an initial pause was followed by a sustained high rate of responding on a schedule in which the completion of an FR com-

ponent was reinforced whenever the first response in the ratio exceeded a minimum IRT. This procedure can be considered simply as a schedule reinforcing each minimum IRT which initiates an operant comprising *n* responses. Both the pause and the high rate appeared to have a functional unity derived from the schedule.

The creation of complex operants with specific functional properties is an exciting development. The analysis of intermittent reinforcement described in this chapter is primarily a fractionation of patterns of responding into sub-units, such as IRTs; now it is possible to identify and manipulate a particular property of behavior by expanding it into a complex but unitary pattern. The relation of these complex patterns to the selective and strengthening effects of reinforcement will pose many questions and provide many answers.

REFERENCES

ANGER, D. (1954) The effect upon simple animal behavior of different frequencies of reinforcement. Final report of Contract DA-49-007-MD-408, Medical Research and Development Board, Office of the Surgeon General, Department of the Army, Washington, D. C.

ANGER, D. (1956) The dependence of interresponse times upon the relative reinforcement of different interresponse times. *J. exp. Psychol., 52,* 145-161.

ANGER, D. (1963) The role of temporal discriminations in the reinforcement of Sidman avoidance behavior. *J. exp. Anal. Behav., 6,* 477-506.

ANTONITIS, J. J. (1951) Response variability in the white rat during conditioning, extinction, and reconditioning. *J. exp. Psychol., 42,* 273-281.

AUTOR, S. M. (1960) The strength of conditioned reinforcers as a function of frequency and probability of reinforcement. Unpublished doctoral dissertation, Harvard University.

BERRYMAN, R., and NEVIN, J. A. (1962) Interlocking schedules of reinforcement. *J. exp. Anal. Behav., 5,* 213-223.

BLOUGH, D. S. (1958) New test for tranquilizers. *Science, 127,* 586-587.

BLOUGH, D. S. (1959) Generalization and preference on a stimulus-intensity continuum. *J. exp. Anal. Behav., 2,* 307-317.

BOREN, J. J. (1953) Response rate and resistance to extinction as functions of the fixed ratio. Unpublished doctoral dissertation, Columbia University.

BOREN, J. J. (1961) Resistance to extinction as a function of the fixed ratio. *J. exp. Psychol., 61,* 304-308.

BRANDAUER, C. M. (1958) The effects of uniform probabilities of reinforcement upon the response rate of the pigeon. Unpublished doctoral dissertation, Columbia University.

CATANIA, A. C. (1963) Concurrent performances: Reinforcement interaction and response independence. *J. exp. Anal. Behav., 6,* 253-263. (a)

CATANIA, A. C. (1963) Concurrent responding: A baseline for the study of reinforcement magnitude. *J. exp. Anal. Behav., 6,* 299-300. (b)

CLARK, F. C. (1958) The effect of deprivation and frequency of reinforcement on variable-interval responding. *J. exp. Anal. Behav., 1,* 221-227.

CLARK, R. (1959) Some time-correlated reinforcement schedules and their effects on behavior. *J. exp. Anal. Behav., 2,* 1-22.

CUMMING, W. W., and SCHOENFELD, W. N. (1959) Some data on behavior reversibility in a steady state experiment. *J. exp. Anal. Behav.*, 2, 87-90.

CUMMING, W. W., and SCHOENFELD, W. N. (1960) Behavior stability under extended exposure to a time-correlated reinforcement contingency. *J. exp. Anal. Behav.*, 3, 71-82.

DEWS, P. B. (1960) Free-operant behavior under conditions of delayed reinforcement. I. CRF-type schedules. *J. exp. Anal. Behav.*, 3, 221-234.

DEWS, P. B. (1962) The effect of multiple S^Δ periods on responding on a fixed-interval schedule. *J. exp. Anal. Behav.*, 5, 369-374.

DEWS, P. B. (1963) Behavioral effects of drugs. In S. M. Farber and R. H. L. Wilson (Eds.), *Conflict and creativity*. New York: McGraw-Hill. Pp. 138-153.

DEWS, P. B. (1964) *Schedules of reinforcement*. Ciba Foundation Symposium. Pp. 191-201.

DEWS, P. B., and MORSE, W. H. (1958) Some observations on an operant in human subjects and its modification by dextro amphetamine. *J. exp. Anal. Behav.*, 1, 359-364.

DEWS, P. B., and MORSE, W. H. (1961) Behavioral pharmacology. *Annu. Rev. Pharmacol.*, 1, 145-174.

FALK, J. L. (1961) The behavioral regulation of water-electrolyte balance. In *Nebraska symposium on motivation*. Lincoln: Univ. of Nebraska Press.

FERSTER, C. B. (1953) The use of the free operant in the analysis of behavior. *Psychol. Bull.*, 50, 263-274.

FERSTER, C. B. (1958) Control of behavior in chimpanzees and pigeons by time out from positive reinforcement. *Psychol. Monogr.*, 72, 1-38. (a)

FERSTER, C. B. (1958) Intermittent reinforcement of a complex response in a chimpanzee. *J. exp. Anal. Behav.*, 1, 163-165. (b)

FERSTER, C. B. (1960) Intermittent reinforcement of matching to sample in the pigeon. *J. exp. Anal. Behav.*, 3, 259-272.

FERSTER, C. B., and SKINNER, B. F. (1957) *Schedules of reinforcement*. New York: Appleton-Century-Crofts.

FINDLEY, J. D. (1958) Preference and switching under concurrent scheduling. *J. exp. Anal. Behav.*, 1, 123-144.

FINDLEY, J. D. (1962) An experimental outline for building and exploring multi-operant behavior repertoires. *J. exp. Anal. Behav.*, suppl. 5, 113-166.

GREEN, E. J. (1953) Stimulus control of operant responding in the pigeon. *Amer. J. Psychol.*, 66, 311-312.

GUTTMAN, N. (1953) Operant conditioning, extinction, and periodic reinforcement in relation to concentration of sucrose used as reinforcing agent. *J. exp. Psychol.*, 46, 213-224.

HEARST, E. (1958) The behavioral effects of some temporally defined schedules of reinforcement. *J. exp. Anal. Behav.*, 1, 45-55.

HEFFERLINE, R. F., and KEENAN, B. (1963) Amplitude-induction gradient of a small human operant in an escape-avoidance situation. *J. exp. Anal. Behav.*, 4, 41-43.

HERRNSTEIN, R. J. (1955) Behavioral consequences of the removal of a discriminative stimulus associated with variable-interval reinforcement. Unpublished doctoral dissertation, Harvard University.

HERRNSTEIN, R. J. (1961) Relative and absolute strength of response as a function of frequency of reinforcement. *J. exp. Anal. Behav.*, 4, 267-272. (a)

HERRNSTEIN, R. J. (1961) Stereotypy and intermittent reinforcement. *Science*, 133, 2067-2069. (b)

HERRNSTEIN, R. J., and MORSE, W. H. (1957) Some effects of response-independent positive reinforcement on maintained operant behavior. *J. comp. physiol. Psychol., 50,* 461-467.

HERRNSTEIN, R. J., and MORSE, W. H. (1958) A conjunctive schedule of reinforcement. *J. exp. Anal. Behav., 1,* 15-24.

HIVELY, W. (1962) Programming stimuli in matching to sample. *J. exp. Anal. Behav., 5,* 279-298.

HOLLAND, J. G. (1962) New directions in teaching machine research. In J. E. Coulson (Ed.), *Programmed learning and computer based instruction.* New York: John Wiley. Pp. 46-57.

HOLZ, W. C., and AZRIN, N. H. (1962) Interactions between the discriminative and aversive properties of punishment. *J. exp. Anal. Behav., 5,* 229-234.

HUTCHINSON, R. R., and AZRIN, N. H. (1961) Conditioning of mental-hospital patients to fixed-ratio schedules of reinforcement. *J. exp. Anal. Behav., 4,* 87-95.

JENKINS, H. M. (1961) The effect of discrimination training on extinction. *J. exp. Psychol., 61,* 111-121.

KEESEY, R. E., and KLING, J. W. (1961) Amount of reinforcement and free-operant responding. *J. exp. Anal. Behav., 4,* 125-132.

KELLEHER, R. T., FRY, W., and COOK, L. (1959) Inter-response time distribution as a function of differential reinforcement of temporally spaced resonses. *J. exp. Anal. Behav., 2,* 91-106.

KELLEHER, R. T., FRY, W., and COOK, L. (1964) Adjusting fixed-ratio schedules in the squirrel monkey. *J. exp. Anal. Behav., 7,* 69-77.

KELLER, F. S., and SCHOENFELD, W. N. (1950) *Principles of psychology.* New York: Appleton-Century-Crofts.

LOGAN, F. A. (1960) *Incentive: How the conditions of reinforcement affect the performance of rats.* New Haven: Yale Univ. Press.

MECHNER, F. (1959) A notation system for the description of behavioral procedures. *J. exp. Anal. Behav., 2,* 133-150.

MILLENSON, J. R. (1959) Some behavioral effects of a two-valued, temporally defined reinforcement schedule. *J. exp. Anal. Behav., 2,* 191-202.

MORSE, W. H. (1962) Use of operant conditioning techniques for evaluating the effects of barbiturates on behavior. In J. H. Nodine and J. H. Moyer (Eds.), *First Hahnemann symposium on psychosomatic medicine.* Philadelphia: Lea & Febiger. Pp. 275-281.

MORSE, W. H., and HERRNSTEIN, R. J. (1955) An analysis of responding under three different forms of fixed interval reinforcement. Paper presented at Eastern Psychol. Ass. meetings, Philadelphia.

MORSE, W. H., and HERRNSTEIN, R. J. (1956) Effects of drugs on characteristics of behavior maintained by complex schedules of intermittent positive reinforcement. *Ann. N. Y. Acad. Sci., 65,* 303-317.

MORSE, W. H., and SKINNER, B. F. (1957) A second type of superstition in the pigeon. *Amer. J. Psychol., 70,* 308-311.

MUELLER, C. G. (1950) Theoretical relationships among some measures of conditioning. *Proc. National Academy of Sciences, 36,* 123-130.

NOTTERMAN, J. M., and MINTZ, D. E. (1962) Exteroceptive cueing of response force. *Science, 135,* 1070-1071.

REYNOLDS, G. S. (1961) An analysis of interactions in a multiple schedule. *J. exp. Anal. Behav., 4,* 107-117. (a)

REYNOLDS, G. S. (1961) Behavioral contrast. *J. exp. Anal. Behav., 4,* 57-71. (b)

REYNOLDS, G. S. (1961) Relativity of response rate and reinforcement frequency in a multiple schedule. *J. exp. Anal. Behav., 4,* 179-184. (c)

REYNOLDS, G. S., and CATANIA, A. C. (1962) Temporal discrimination in pigeons. *Science, 135,* 314-315.

SCHOENFELD, W. N., and CUMMING, W. W. (1957) Some effects of alternation rate in a time-correlated reinforcement contingency. *Proc. National Acad. of Sciences, 43,* 349-354.

SCHOENFELD, W. N., CUMMING, W. W., and Hearst, E. (1956) On the classification of reinforcement schedules. *Proc. National Acad. of Sciences, 42,* 563-570.

SIDMAN, M. (1960) *Tactics of scientific research.* New York: Basic Books.

SKINNER, B. F. (1938) *The behavior of organisms.* New York: Appleton-Century-Crofts.

SKINNER, B. F. (1946) Differential reinforcement with respect to time. *Amer. Psychologist, 1,* 274-275.

SKINNER, B. F. (1948) "Superstition" in the pigeon. *J. exp. Psychol., 38,* 168-172.

SKINNER, B. F. (1953) *Science and human behavior.* New York: Macmillan.

SKINNER, B. F. (1958) Diagramming schedules of reinforcement. *J. exp. Anal. Behav., 1,* 67-68.

SKINNER, B. F. (1961, Summer) The design of cultures. *Daedalus,* (Proc. of the Amer. Acad. of Arts and Sciences), *91,* 534-546.

SKINNER, B. F., and MORSE, W. H. (1958) Fixed-interval reinforcement of running in a wheel. *J. exp. Anal. Behav., 1,* 371-379.

SNAPPER, A. G. (1962) Properties of behavior under response-independent temporally defined reinforcement schedules. Unpublished doctoral dissertation, Columbia University.

TERRACE, H. S. (1963) Discrimination learning with and without "errors." *J. exp. Anal. Behav., 6,* 1-27.

VERPLANCK, W. S. (1957) A glossary of some terms used in the objective science of behavior. *Psychol. Rev., 64,* Suppl. Pp. i-viii, 1-42.

WILSON, M. P. (1954) Periodic reinforcement interval and number of periodic reinforcements as parameters of response strength. *J. comp. physiol. Psychol., 47,* 51-56.

WILSON, M. P., and KELLER, F. S. (1953) On the selective reinforcement of spaced responses. *J. comp. physiol. Psychol., 46,* 190-193.

ZIMMERMAN, D. W. (1963) Functional laws and reproducible processes in behavior. *Psychol. Rec., 13,* 163-173.

4

Studies of
Sensory Reinforcement [1]

G. B. Kish

INTRODUCTION

Within the past decade, a considerable body of literature has accumulated demonstrating that stimuli apparently unrelated to such organic drive states as hunger and thirst are reinforcing. The primary purpose of the present chapter is to review selectively the findings and the experimental techniques of studies concerned with these reinforcers.

The chapter is organized into five sections. The first section briefly introduces the central concept of the chapter, sensory reinforcement. The second section introduces the various methodological approaches to the study of sensory reinforcement by presenting a representative experiment in each research area. The third section presents the evidence bearing upon several theoretical questions concerning sensory reinforcement, such as: (1) the generality of the phenomenon, (2) the question of learning vs. performance, and (3) evidence concerning some competing interpretations. The fourth section reviews the findings concerning a number of variables which have been found to affect the process of sensory reinforcement. Finally, the fifth section presents summary generalizations concerning the properties of sensory reinforcement as revealed by the findings to date.

Although the present volume is concerned primarily with the uses of the free operant technique in the analysis of behavior, this chapter will also include studies using more restricted operant techniques in order to provide a more complete picture of the findings in a given area of investigation.

[1] The author is greatly indebted to Dr. Alan Baron who participated in many discussions which considerably influenced the author's thinking about the sensory reinforcement phenomenon.

SENSORY REINFORCEMENT

The concept of reinforcement holds a key position in several contemporary analyses of behavior (e.g., Hull, 1952; Skinner, 1938). Although there is some theoretical disagreement concerning the basic nature of the reinforcement process (for example, whether or not drive reduction is involved), there appears to be substantial agreement concerning the reality of the phenomenon and the nature of its behavioral effects. The term *reinforcement* is usually applied when a stimulus: (1) is response-contingent, (2) produces some relatively permanent behavioral changes (learning), and (3) is related to some relevant motivational state.

Until recently, the major classes of events capable of producing reinforcing effects could be categorized as follows: (1) presentation of a substance, such as food, which is related to some organic need condition (*primary positive* or *"organic" reinforcement*); (2) removal of such aversive stimulation as bright light, loud sound, and electric shock (*primary negative reinforcement*); (3) presentation of a stimulus which has had prior association with the conditions of category 1 (*secondary positive reinforcement*); and (4) removal of a stimulus which has had prior association with the conditions in category 2 (*secondary negative reinforcement*).

The studies reported in this chapter appear to demonstrate behavioral effects resulting from the response-contingent presentation of stimuli, which do not conform to any of these four types of reinforcement but nevertheless conform to the three criteria for reinforcement presented above. These findings, therefore, have considerably enlarged the class of reinforcing stimuli.

It seems reasonable to add tentatively a fifth category to the above group which we shall call *sensory reinforcement*. Sensory reinforcement will be used to refer to a primary reinforcement process resulting from the response-contingent presentation or removal of stimuli of moderate intensity which cannot be subsumed under classes 1, 2, 3, and 4. It is unlikely that such a category of reinforcers reflects a basic process difference from the more traditional reinforcers. The term is used in this chapter primarily to facilitate differentiation between this group of reinforcers and those recognized above.

RESEARCH METHODS

While studies of sensory reinforcement have involved several rather diverse experimental situations, procedures, and dependent variables, they have had a common concern, namely the reinforcing effects of the sensory consequences of behavior. The following section presents a metholological review of the following research approaches to the study of sensory reinforcement: (1) light-onset reinforcement, (2) manipulation, (3) visual and auditory exploration, (4) locomotor exploration, (5) curiosity, (6) unconditioned operant behavior, and (7) group operant behavior.

For each research area, a representative experiment has been chosen and presented in sufficient detail to illuminate the nature of the technique and to provide the basis for critical evaluation of the contributions of the method to our understanding of sensorily reinforced behavior. The specific research areas were chosen because to some extent they utilize the free operant technique or a variant thereof and have proved to be productive approaches to the general understanding of this phenomenon.

Light-onset Reinforcement

In 1951, John B. Girdner, a graduate student at Duke University, was attempting to devise a situation for the study of exploratory behavior. In exploratory behavior, Girdner reasoned, an animal performs locomotor and orienting responses which successively expose it to "novel" stimulation from the surrounding environment. By analogy with exploration, Girdner devised a situation in which the organism could perform an operationally definable, measurable response which produced a "novel" environmental change. Essentially, Girdner's test situation consisted of a Skinner-type compartment with a fixed brass lever protruding from one wall of the compartment. The floor and lever constituted different sides of an electronic circuit such that closure of this circuit, when the rat contacted the lever, activated a contact relay (Pilgrim, 1948) which operated recording equipment and illuminated a circular milk glass screen directly above the rat. Girdner found that such response-contingent illumination increased the rate of emission of the lever-contact response (Girdner, 1953a; 1953b). At about the same time, other investigators, using similar techniques, also demonstrated the reinforcing effects of response-contingent visual stimulation (Kish, 1955; Marx, Henderson, & Roberts, 1955; Sharpe, 1951). The free operant has proved particularly valuable in the study of light-onset reinforcement. Only a few studies have utilized the more restricted operant situation in which the response-reinforcement sequence terminates the trial.

Since it is becoming increasingly apparent that a large variety of stimuli have reinforcing effects if they are response-contingent (see p. 119 ff.), the optimal test situation for the study of sensory reinforcement would seem to be a homogeneous stimulus environment with the number of other response-contingent stimulus changes held to a minimum. It seems reasonable to suppose that the larger the number of response-correlated stimulus changes the less sensitive will that response be to the stimulus change specifically being studied. For example, if a movable lever is used to define and record the response, each depression of the lever produces a microswitch click, movement-produced stimulation, and tactual stimulation. If such response-contingent stimulation is reinforcing, this would inflate the operant level response rate which is the base from which the reinforcing effects of the independent variable are assessed, thus making the response measure less sensitive to that variable.

Such considerations suggest that the test situation used by Girdner (1953) and Kish (1955) would provide the most sensitive test of sensory reinforcement. Specifically, this includes using a rigid lever with contact recording to eliminate the click and reduce the kinesthetic feedback resulting from response performance. Furthermore, Kish ran his subjects in complete darkness to control visual exploration and tested his subjects in sound-proof boxes to control response-contingent apparatus noises. Review of the studies in this area indicates that, in practice, much of this extraneous stimulation has *not* been controlled and that this factor may be responsible for some of the contradictory results obtained, as well as the rather weak effect obtained in some experiments.

In perhaps 10 percent of the experiments performed by the author, the light-reinforcement effect has not been found. The variables reducing this effect have rarely been specified (but see Kish & Baron, 1962), although this would seem to be a fruitful direction for research. Attempts have been made to maximize the effect by manipulation of several variables. Pre-adaptation to the test environment of at least three sessions appears to enhance the light-reinforcement effect (Girdner, 1953). Food- or water-deprived rather than satiated subjects have been used in a majority of investigations of light reinforcement. This procedure appears to enhance the number of responses produced but whether or not it actually enhances the reinforcement effect or merely raises the general response level cannot be stated with certainty at present (see p. 145). Light intensity has also been found to be a crucial variable with moderate intensities found to be most effective (see p. 142ff).

In summary, the investigator entering this area for the first time should endeavor to devise a homogeneous test situation with a minimum number of extraneous response-correlated stimuli. He should, as a matter of course, include in his experimental designs a pre-adaptation period without the to-be-tested sensory reinforcer. Careful choice of light intensity is recommended to avoid aversive complications.

Visual and Auditory Exploration

An area of investigation which is closely related to the studies of light-onset reinforcement is the study of visual and auditory exploration pioneered by Butler (1953). Previous work at the Wisconsin Laboratory had indicated that monkeys would manipulate complex puzzles without apparent external reinforcers (Harlow, 1950) and would also solve discrimination problems when opportunity to manipulate was the sole reinforcer (Harlow & McClearn, 1954). Observation of monkeys also suggested that they engage in considerable amounts of visual inspection of puzzles and other objects in their environments. Butler, therefore, devised a situation in which complex visual stimulation could be made response-contingent and the functions of such stimulation could be determined. This technique was later extended to the study of auditory incentives (Butler, 1957b).

In general, Butler's technique utilizes a light-proof or sound-proof test cage in which the subjects are provided with the opportunity to perform some response which opens an aperture or closes a loudspeaker connection, thus rewarding the response by providing an increase in stimulation. Approximately half of the studies performed in this area have utilized a free operant procedure while the remainder have used a discrete trial procedure.

In the initial study (Butler, 1953), rhesus monkeys were placed in a light-tight test cage which was illuminated from within. The apparatus wall contained two small doors which could be opened by pushing against them. Each door contained a different-colored card. Pushing against the door with the correctly colored card opened that door for a 30-sec. period. The other door was latched. The 30-sec. view of the laboratory environment terminated the trial. The view of the laboratory included other monkeys in their cages, people walking about, other experiments in progress, etc. A screen was then lowered, the cards were randomly switched, the screen was raised, and the next trial began. Over 20 days of testing, the percentage of correct choices progressively increased above chance level indicating the formation of a color discrimination when the sole reinforcer was the stimulation provided by the 30-sec. view of the laboratory. This result was later confirmed by Butler and Harlow (1954; 1957).

Although the initial study utilized a restricted operant test situation, the similarity of this study to the studies of light reinforcement is clear. Both groups of studies presented increments in stimulation as consequences of a response and observed changes in some measure of response. The basic differences between these groups of studies are: (1) the complexity and consequent difficulty of specification of the stimulation used in the visual exploration situation, and (2) the possibility that some proportion of the reinforcing effects of the visual and auditory incentives derives from the subjects' past conditioning history (i.e., is the result of secondary reinforcement).

The results of two studies by Butler strongly suggest the importance of the subjects' prior conditioning history. Butler (1954) found the following order of reinforcing efficacy (from most to least reinforcing): (1) monkey in a cage, (2) a moving electric train, (3) an array of food, and (4) an empty table top surrounded by black cloth screening. Auditory stimuli were also found to differ in efficacy in the following order: (1) monkey feeding sounds, (2) single monkey sounds, (3) white noise, (4) monkey sounds of rage, and (5) dog sounds (Butler, 1958a).

The general control considerations discussed in connection with light reinforcement, such as the exclusion of extraneous stimulation, also apply in this situation. In some of the studies reported by Butler, the subjects in the visual exploration condition could hear what was going on in the laboratory and, in fact, door openings to view the laboratory environment were correlated with such events as whether someone had just entered the laboratory and slammed the door (Butler & Alexander, 1955). Such uncontrolled stimulation makes interpretation of the results of these studies, except in the most general sense, somewhat difficult.

Manipulatory Behavior

Another form of primate behavior which appears to be learned and maintained by sensory reinforcement is manipulation. H. F. Harlow, M. K. Harlow, and Meyer (1950), in a study designed to test the latent learning hypothesis using a non-maze situation, utilized a puzzle manipulation problem. A mechanical puzzle was presented on a perch outside of the monkey's cage. The puzzle consisted of a hasp which was locked into the closed position by a latch which was held in the closed position by a pin. To disassemble the puzzle, the pin must be removed first, allowing the latch to open which then released the hasp. One group of subjects was exposed to the assembled puzzle for 12 days during which time the puzzle was periodically checked and reassembled if needed. The other group was exposed to the unassembled puzzle for an equal length of time. On the thirteenth and fourteenth days of the experiment, both groups were exposed to the assembled puzzle with a raisin placed under the hasp. Puzzle solutions were rewarded, therefore, by procurement of the raisin. Several interesting findings resulted: (1) Subjects exposed to the assembled puzzle during the initial 12 days manipulated and disassembled the puzzle without apparent reward. (2) Introduction of food reward disrupted puzzle performance during the initial trials with raisin present. An increase in the number of parts of the puzzle touched in the incorrect order was noted. (3) No subjects in the control group were observed to assemble the unassembled puzzle. (4) The performance of subjects with prior experience with the assembled puzzle was considerably superior to the performance of the subjects whose initial experience had been with the unassembled puzzle. The results were interpreted as showing that manipulation of the puzzle without external reward led to the learning of the mode of solution which could be later utilized to obtain food reinforcement. More important, the results led to the study of manipulatory behavior for its own sake and to the important possibility that the act of manipulation is self-reinforcing.

This type of test situation, while clearly demonstrating the learning and maintenance of manipulatory behavior without organic reward, poses problems concerning the precise specification of the reinforcing stimulus. Presumably, the sensory consequences of manipulatory behavior include visual, auditory, kinesthetic, and tactual stimulation occurring in some complex interrelationship. Somewhat better control of the stimulating circumstances would allow more precise specification of the reinforcing stimulus with opportunity to specify the relative contributions of the stimuli in the different sense modalities.

Besides complexity and lack of specifiability of the reinforcing stimulation, further difficulties of interpretation arise since some aspects of the goal object are present before the response is made. It is difficult, therefore, to specify the function of the stimulation. Whether such stimulation is reinforcing, drive arousing, or both, is presently the object of some theoretical controversy. More clear-cut conclusions can be drawn when exposure to stimulation is made response-contingent as in the light-reinforcement and visual exploration studies previously discussed.

Locomotor Exploration

The term *locomotor exploration* is used here to refer to those studies in which an organism's movements are observed in some novel test environment. The test situations used in these studies have been extremely diverse, including: open fields, multiple alley mazes of the Dashiell type, Y mazes, runways, novel compartments attached to the living cage, the Columbia Obstruction apparatus, etc. In general, these studies utilize a modified free operant procedure. During a given test period, the organism's unrestricted locomotor behavior is recorded.

As studies of sensory reinforcement, these situations suffer from several basic difficulties. First of all, the presumed sensorily reinforcing stimuli are exceedingly complex, including simultaneously, visual, tactual, olfactory, kinesthetic, and auditory stimulation. The precise reinforcing stimuli, as a consequence, are exceedingly difficult to specify. Secondly, as in the manipulation situation, the precise functions of the stimulation are difficult to specify since the stimuli are often present prior to as well as consequent upon the activity of the organism. A third difficulty arises from the use of the locomotor response as the dependent variable. This rather large and ill-defined class of responses reflects many variables, including the activity level of the organism. Frequently, as in the studies of the effects of drive upon exploratory behavior, it is difficult to judge whether the changes in locomotor behavior reflect changes in sensitivity to novel stimulation or whether the changes reflect only changes in activity level.

Despite the above difficulties, the locomotor exploratory situation has proved to be a popular and productive approach to the study of sensory reinforcement. Although, as noted above, the situations used have not been homogeneous, we shall take as illustrative of the approach a study by Montgomery (1953a) of the effects of hunger and thirst upon exploratory behavior. Montgomery used an enclosed Y maze without goal boxes into which rats were placed for five or ten minutes of exploration. The dependent variable in this and other studies by Montgomery was the number of 12-inch maze units traversed during some arbitrary portion of the test period (in this case, two-minute intervals) and the order in which the three arms of the maze were successively entered. The number of units traversed is presumed to be a measure of the amount of exploratory drive aroused by the maze situation. The order of unit entries ("orderliness") is a measure of the satiation of exploratory drive as a function of exposure to the stimulation in a given area and the consequent increase in relative novelty and recovery from satiation of stimulation in the arms not yet traversed or traversed at a more remote time.

In general, Montgomery finds that maze activity rapidly falls off during a ten-minute exploration period and recovers during a 24-hour interval of non-exposure. Similarly, measures of "orderliness" conform to the above analysis, the subjects being least disposed to enter alleys most recently explored.

Curiosity

A refinement of the locomotor exploration technique has been reported in several papers by Berlyne (1950; 1955; Berlyne & Slater, 1957). Essentially, this technique involves exposing animal subjects to such stimuli as cubes and spheres, patterned cards, and such novel objects as electric wall plugs. Instead of measuring the animals' locomotor behavior about the test compartment, however, the dependent variable is contact with the stimulus object expressed in the form of nosing, sniffing, and close visual contact.

A major advantage of this technique over the locomotor exploration technique is that it minimizes the contaminating factor of activity level. Although the level of activity may be a factor in determining the frequency with which the subject contacts the stimulus object, the specific stimulus-oriented behavior of the subjects being measured is less likely to reflect this activity than would a locomotor response. A further advantage is somewhat better control over and specification of the stimulation being tested for its reinforcing properties. The stimuli used, however, are still exceedingly complex and probably involve several sense modalities compounded in some complex fashion. In this respect this method suffers from the same difficulties as the locomotor exploration, visual exploration, and manipulation methods discussed above.

Berlyne has used a diversity of test situations in his work on curiosity and novelty, making a choice of a representative study quite difficult. In the later discussions of specific variables affecting sensory reinforcement, those of Berlyne's experiments which depart from the general technique presented above will be discussed in somewhat greater detail.

Unconditioned Operant Behavior

This research area has not been specifically utilized in the study of sensory reinforcement. Recent studies, however, indicate that a considerable proportion of this responding is best understood as being learned and maintained by its own sensory consequences (e.g., Baron, Antonitis, & Clark, 1963; Kish & Antonitis, 1956; Kish & Barnes, 1961).

In their classic paper on unconditioned lever pressing in rats, Schoenfeld, Antonitis, and Bersh (1950) indulged in considerable speculation concerning the determinants of this behavior. They suggested, among other things, that the initial burst of responding which occurs when the lever is inserted into the rat's living cage may be due to the arousal of "excitement" or "exploratory activity." Although the techniques for studying unconditioned operant behavior have varied in the type of manipulandum used and the test situation (i.e., novel apparatus or home cage), the experiment by Schoenfeld *et al.* may be considered as representative of this research area.

These investigators inserted a U-shaped lever into the cages of hungry or thirsty rats and observed the characteristics of the lever depression responses emitted with no organic reward. They found that the rats made a considerable number of responses to the lever which were distributed through the session in an extinction-like fashion. This extinction-like curve reoccurred with a progressive diminution of overall response level on successive test days. They interpreted their findings in several ways. The extinction curves may have expressed the extinction of generalized bar-press-like responses previously learned through rearing up to obtain food from a food cup. On the other hand, the extinction curves may have reflected a gradual reduction of the reinforcing effects of the stimuli arising from the bar-press response (i.e., "satiation"). The within-session decrement in responding bears a remarkable resemblance to the decrements found later in the locomotor exploration studies of Montgomery (1952b) and the "curiosity" studies of Berlyne (1955). Further studies bearing upon a sensory reinforcement interpretation of unconditioned operant behavior will be discussed later in this chapter.

That this method provides unique opportunities for the controlled study of the effects of sensory reinforcers is indicated by the number of studies concerned with light reinforcement which derive essentially from this technique. Unfortunately, the sensory feedback from the bar-press response in the Schoenfeld *et al.* study is somewhat complex, consisting of a microswitch click, recording noises, kinesthetic and tactual stimulation. The relative contributions of these different stimuli to the overall reinforcing effects is difficult to determine. How the method may be refined to minimize interaction of sensory modalities and allow for assessment of the contributions of these various stimuli has been described in the section concerned with light reinforcement.

Group Operant Behavior with Sensory Reinforcement

This interesting variation of the free operant technique which has been applied to the study of sensory reinforcement was recently developed by Antonitis (Antonitis & Barnes, 1961). In the usual operant study, groups of subjects are *individually* exposed to some condition while measures are taken of some aspect of performance. In the group operant technique, a *group* of subjects is tested simultaneously by measuring the rate of performance of some response that all members of the group have the opportunity to perform. In the Antonitis and Barnes study, a lever-pressing apparatus was made available to preschool children. The apparatus was a large cabinet with a straight three-inch lever protruding about two feet above the floor. A screen, which could be illuminated by a light bulb from behind, was placed at about the eye level of the four-year-old child. This cabinet was placed in the nursery schoolroom and was simultaneously available to all the children. Rate of manipulation of the lever was studied under the following conditions: (1) no response-contingent visual stimulation, (2) response-contingent illumination of the screen, (3) response-contingent termination of screen illumination, and (4) response-contingent illumination of silhouettes of cartoon characters. Qualitative observations were also made of the children's reactions to the apparatus and stimuli. In general, the study indicated large increases in response rate over the operant level condition when both light onset and light termination were used as reinforcers. The reinforcing powers of these stimuli diminished with repeated testing. However, the introduction of cartoon cutouts raised the response rate anew with a subsequent drop in rate until a new silhouette was presented.

The technique has certain advantages. Children can be tested without their knowledge and without the necessity of disturbing the children or the nursery school routine by removing a child to a separate test room. The apparatus is merely presented as a new toy in the already familiar nursery school environment.

Several disadvantages may also be noted. Unless the investigator has several nursery schools with comparable children, testing the effects of different variables must be done in a serial fashion. The findings will then be complicated by possible interactions between the different conditions. Another difficulty is the inapplicability of conventional statistical techniques in assessing the reliability of the results. The investigator must completely replicate the results on a new group of subjects before he is able to assess the degree of confidence which may be placed in the data. A further difficulty is the social interaction possible among the subjects which results in non-independence of the behavior of any one subject. Similarly, when sensory reinforcers are used, as in the above study, subjects who are not presently responding are nonetheless exposed to the reinforcing stimulus. With these considerations in mind, one might conclude that the results of the group responding should be different from that of the combined results of a number of subjects tested individually. Unfortunately, no direct test of the comparability of group and individual results has yet been made. It appears, however, that in a gross fashion, the results are comparable. For example, the data on the effects of light onset and termination are comparable to the results of animal studies of these variables using the individual technique. Also, a recent study of the behavior of nursery school children (Hayes, 1958) using reinforcers and responses similar to those of the Antonitis and Barnes study, found comparable results even though the subjects were individually tested.

A recent experiment by Frey (1960) has used this technique to study the effects of auditory reinforcers. Frey used (1) garbled sound ("That's good" played backwards on a tape recorder), (2) "That's good," and (3) "That's bad." The three types of stimuli used were shown to have strong reinforcing effects, with "That's bad" and "That's good" showing approximately equivalent effects upon the bar-pressing rate of nursery school children.

THEORETICAL QUESTIONS

Generality of Sensory Reinforcement

This section reviews the evidence with respect to the reinforcing properties of stimulation in the various sense modalities. In general, the evidence is rather spotty but suggests that stimuli in many modalities may function in a reinforcing capacity.

Vision

A large number of the references included in the bibliography have successfully utilized light onset as the reinforcing stimulus (e.g., Girdner, 1953; Kish, 1955; Marx, Henderson, & Roberts, 1955). Studies using more complex visual stimuli have also yielded results favoring a reinforcement interpretation (e.g., Barnes & Baron, 1961; Berlyne & Slater, 1957; Butler, 1953). Barnes and Baron, for example, found that for mice a complex stimulus pattern in the shape of an illuminated cross was more reinforcing than an illuminated circle, which, in turn, was more reinforcing than the absence of any illumination change.

Audition

Experimentation designed to test the effects of response-contingent auditory stimulation has yielded conflicting results. Symmes and Leaton

(1962) failed to demonstrate any reinforcing properties with rats for either white noise, a 2 kc tone, or a warbling tone all of which were presented with a 70 db intensity. Andronico and Forgays (1962), on the other hand, found weak reinforcing properties for a 6 kc tone presented at 86-98 db.

Barnes and Kish (1961) used mice in a factorial study involving ten frequencies ranging from 700 to 16,000 cps, five intensities ranging from 45-95 db, and two contingencies of pure tone. They found that response-contingent pure tones at the lower frequencies and intensities did tend to maintain response rates over that of non-contingent controls. Higher frequencies and intensities tended, however, to have a depressive effect upon responding. The reinforcing effect was nevertheless extremely weak when compared with light-onset reinforcement. Barnes and Kish suggested that the weakness of the reinforcement effect may have been a function of the simplicity of the tones, and that a more complex tone would prove to be more reinforcing. This was tested by Baron and Kish (1962) with mice, with the response-contingent presentation of a continuous pure tone, an intermittent pure tone, and a patterned tone consisting of three pure tones presented in rapid succession. They found, as did Baron (1959) with rats, that pure tones *depressed* lever responding and, furthermore, that the degree of aversiveness varied directly with complexity, the pattern tone being the most depressive and the continuous tone the least. They suggest, along with Barnes and Kish (1961), that species factors may be the paramount determiners of reactions to sound, the rodents used in these studies tending to find sound aversive.

This conclusion is consistent with reports by Frey (1960) and Butler (1957b; 1958a) demonstrating positively reinforcing effects of auditory stimulation for primates. Frey (1960), using the recently devised group operant technique, found that a response-contingent garbled sound ("That's bad" tape recorded and played backwards) increased the bar-pressing rate of a group of preschool children. Butler (1957b) demonstrated that monkeys would learn to discriminate between two levers when one produced sounds of a monkey colony and the other lever produced no sound. In these experiments, however, the possibility of secondary reinforcement cannot be discounted. Further work is obviously necessary to clarify the factors affecting auditory sensory reinforcement, particularly with respect to species differences.

Kinesthesis

Kinesthetic feedback may be implicated in a reinforcing capacity in several of the experimental situations previously reviewed. For example, it does not seem unreasonable to suppose that in studies of unconditioned lever pressing, the lever-pressing response produces reinforcing kinesthetic feedback. This supposition was tested in a controlled situation by Kish and

Barnes (1961). Using number of contacts and duration of contact with a U-shaped lever as the dependent variables, these researchers compared the responses to a rigid and movable lever. Duration of contact with the lever markedly increased when the lever was made movable, which led to the conclusion that the kinesthetic consequences of bar pressing are reinforcing.

Supporting evidence for such a conclusion comes from somewhat less well-controlled studies by Harlow *et al.* and by Kegan and Berkun (1954). The latter found that rats would learn if the opportunity to run in a running wheel was the reinforcer. H. F. Harlow (1950) and H. F. Harlow, M. K. Harlow, and Meyer (1950) have shown that monkeys would manipulate complex puzzles with the only reinforcement provided by performance of the activity itself. Although the feedback stimuli in these experiments may have been quite complex, the importance of kinesthetic feedback is suggested. This suggestion is supported by the study of Harlow and McClearn (1954) which demonstrated that monkeys would learn to discriminate between different-colored movable and immovable screw eyes.

Gustation

Some evidence is available implying that gustatory stimulation per se may be reinforcing. Studies utilizing food reinforcement may be so interpreted. Unfortunately, these studies are complicated by the organic drive reduction accompanying consummatory activity. The drive reduction hypothesis is only one possible interpretation of the action of reinforcement, however. It is also possible that this basic reinforcing mechanism involves increments in stimulation coincident with or arising from performance of the consummatory response. This is essentially the conclusion drawn by Sheffield, Roby, and Campbell (1954) on the basis of their comparison of the reinforcing properties of dextrose and saccharine. Previously Sheffield and Roby (1950) had demonstrated that saccharine, though of no nutritive value, could act as a reinforcing stimulus. Furthermore, they found that prolonged exposure to saccharine solutions did not result in extinction of the reinforcing effect as might have been expected if these reinforcing properties derived from prior association of sweetness and nourishment. These findings appear to support a sensory reinforcement interpretation.

Further evidence for gustatory sensory reinforcement may be adduced from the similarity between the obtained preference functions for different concentrations of gustatory stimulation and the obtained relationship between light intensity and reinforcing potential. For example, the curves relating sodium chloride concentration and preference begin at a neutral preference level, rise to maximum preference at some intermediate concentration, and rapidly fall off toward the aversive range with further increments in concentration (e.g., Pfaffman, 1958). Curves relating light reinforcement and light intensity show a similar inverted U-shaped function (see p.142ff). (See also Pfaffman, 1960, for a similar analysis of the effects of gustatory stimulation.)

Olfaction

The author is not aware of any studies specifically concerned with the determination of the reinforcing properties of olfactory stimulation. Such reinforcing properties are suggested, however, by several observations. Berlyne's rats (1955) normally spent considerable amounts of time sniffing at the novel stimulus objects presented for test. Similarly, casual observations of the behavior of dogs would appear to suggest that these animals engage in considerable amounts of olfactory exploration. Humans also seem to derive considerable enjoyment from sniffing flowers and spices as well as certain volatile liquids.

Touch

Some observations may be cited suggesting that certain forms of tactual stimulation may be reinforcing. In an interesting experiment, Wenzel (1959) trained kittens to contact a lever in a Skinner box by reinforcing each contact with five seconds of petting. This effect was found despite considerable effort to raise subjects in such a fashion that any association between the experimenter and primary reinforcement was minimal. Wenzel concluded that stroking has primary reinforcing properties distinct from its acquired reinforcing properties, though the latter are contributing factors in normally reared cats. However, Wenzel neglected to note the fact that kittens reared by their mothers receive considerable tactual stimulation in the form of licking and that the mothers also provide primary reinforcement. The obtained reinforcing effects may have occurred by generalization from this early experience with the mother.

Richards and Leslie (1962) presented hungry and thirsty rats with tactually novel arms paired with a familiar arm in a T maze. Motivated subjects tended to choose the tactually novel arms with a greater frequency than would have been expected by chance.

Another study implicating tactual stimulation was performed by Sheffield, Wulff, and Backer (1951). They found that coital activity without ejaculation was reinforcing for male rats. It seems likely that an important source of reinforcing stimulation resulting from such copulatory activity was tactual.

Harlow (1960) demonstrated that the responses of young monkeys were significantly affected by the tactual qualities of the "surrogate" mothers with whom the infants were reared, soft terry cloth being preferred over wire mothers even when the latter provided the infant's sole nourishment.

Everyday observation similarly indicates that children derive considerable pleasure from stroking and fingering such smooth materials as fur and satin. These observations suggest that tactual stimulation of some types, at least, is reinforcing.

Electrical Stimulation

A recent study by Harrington and Linder (1962) suggests the interesting possibility that electrical stimulation may function as a sensory reinforcer. Using an electronic contact relay to record contacts with a lever, rats were given a five-session operant level period followed by two sessions of regular light-onset reinforcement. Thereafter, four groups of three subjects each were tested with 0, 1.2, 4.0, and 12 volts respectively of electric shock administered through the floor and contingent upon each bar-contact response. They found that electric shock had positive reinforcing properties which were a positively accelerated function of shock intensity. Although only three subjects per group were used, the results achieved statistical significance. The authors felt that this effect would be positive up to the point where the aversive threshold for shock was exceeded. They made no attempt, however, to determine the value of this aversive threshold.

Although further experimentation appears necessary to explore the limits of this phenomenon as well as some alternative explanations, the results are consistent with a generalized sensory reinforcement principle.

Conclusions

The evidence presented above suggests that the sensory reinforcement principle may have considerable general applicability. Many questions, however, remain to be answered. Most important of these is the specification of the precise characteristics of those stimuli in a given sensory modality which are reinforcing. Obviously, all stimuli in a given modality do *not* possess reinforcing properties (e.g., compare light onset and termination; also, the differences in preference for salt and bitter substances). Evidence is available concerning the differentiating characteristics of reinforcers and non-reinforcers and is presented in the remainder of the chapter.

Species limitations upon the general applicability of the sensory reinforcement principle also await empirical determination. To date, sensory reinforcement has been demonstrated with mice, rats, monkeys, chimpanzees, human children, and human adults, suggesting some degree of general applicability. It may be expected, however, that species differences would occur and perhaps be most marked in determining the sensory modality to which the organism is most sensitive. For example, although mice show strong reactions to a light-onset reinforcer (Kish, 1955), their reactions to sound reinforcers appear to be minimal (Barnes & Kish, 1961). On the other hand, Butler (1957b) finds strong auditory exploratory tendencies in monkeys. Some evidence is available concerning species and strain variables and is presented below (p. 138f).

Response Contingency

By definition, a reinforcing stimulus must be contingent upon or be temporally closely associated with the performance of a response in order to have an effect upon that response. Studies concerned with the problem find that sensory events must be contingent upon behavior in order to function as reinforcers.

Kish (1955) introduced 150 half-second light flashes uncorrelated with the lever responses of mice in a Skinner box. No significant change in response rate resulted from this procedure. Kling, Horowitz, and Delhagen (1956) worked with rats, and used a yoked control group which received exactly the same pattern of light onset as did the experimental group, but not contingent upon the responses of the subjects. They concluded that lever-light contingency is an important condition for the occurrence of sensory reinforcement.

In another technique which has been used to investigate this problem, two levers are simultaneously available to the subject. One lever produces light onset while the other does not. These studies have uniformly found that subjects accurately discriminated between the two levers indicating that sensory reinforcement is specific to the behavior with which it is correlated (Barnes & Kish, 1958; Butler, 1957b; Forgays & Levin, 1959; Girdner, 1953).

Also relevant is the finding of Levin and Forgays (1960) that delayed light reinforcement was not as reinforcing as immediate light reinforcement.

Learning vs. Performance

The most important defining characteristic of a reinforcer is that it produces learning rather than merely a temporary change in behavior. The most acceptable evidence for learning in a free operant situation is a residual elevation of response rate after removal of the reinforcing stimulus. Several studies of light reinforcement have shown such an extinction effect (Barnes & Baron, 1961a; 1961b; Forgays & Levin, 1958; Hurwitz, 1956; Kish, 1955; Kling, Horowitz, & Delhagen, 1956).

Other acceptable evidence for learning is in the acquisition of discriminations. This has been reported when one lever produces light onset while the other does not (Barnes & Kish, 1958; Forgays & Levin, 1959; Girdner, 1953). Similarly, Butler (1957b) trained monkeys to discriminate between two levers using monkey colony sounds as reinforcement and to discriminate between two colors using a 30-second look at the laboratory environment as reinforcer (Butler, 1953).

Other studies have demonstrated the learning of T mazes when the opportunity to explore a complex Dashiell maze was made contingent upon correct responding (Montgomery, 1954). Harlow and his co-workers demonstrated the learning of complex puzzle solution (Harlow, 1950) and a color discrimination (Harlow & McClearn, 1954) when opportunity to manipulate was the sole reinforcer. Other studies also demonstrate learning, but the above seem sufficient to indicate that learning can occur under conditions of sensory reinforcement.

Drive

The inference of an intermediary mechanism, such as drive, underlying the various phenomena which we have called sensory reinforcement requires that some of the operations affecting such a drive be specified. Two commonly accepted characteristics of a motivational state which enter into its definition are: (1) increments in performance strength as a function of some antecedent operation such as deprivation; and (2) decrements in performance strength resulting from prolonged exposure to the reinforcing stimulus (satiation).

Deprivation

Some evidence is now available indicating that visual reinforcers are affected by deprivation operations. For example, Butler (1957a) found, with monkeys, that confinement in the visual exploration test apparatus for up to eight hours without the opportunity to see out produced increments in later visual exploratory behavior.

In a more recent study, Fox (1962) tested monkeys' light-reinforced lever pressing after 0, 1, 2, 3, 4, and 8 hours of confinement in the dark test apparatus. Rate of lever pressing for light was found to be a positive function of number of hours of deprivation. As in the Butler experiment, eight hours of deprivation was no more effective than four hours in enhancing the reinforcement effect.

Fox also tested the effects of confinement under different levels of illumination. He found a negative relationship between degree of illumination during confinement and rate of subsequent bar pressing for light.

Similar findings relative to deprivation have been reported by Isaac (1962) and Premack, Collier, and Roberts (1957). The latter, in a follow-up study, however, found that bar pressing for light was even further enhanced by various periods of confinement in a *lighted* confinement situation (Premack & Collier, unpublished manuscript). In line with this finding, Robinson (unpublished manuscript) found that three hours of light deprivation *reduced* responding for light in a later tilt-box test situation in which crossings were reinforced by a one-second light flash.

The conflicting results of these studies provide some knotty problems for future research. Since most of the positive findings were obtained using monkeys, and the negative with rats, a plausible explanation of these discrepant findings lies in the relative importance of visual stimulation to these different species. Clearly, monkeys are more visually-oriented organisms than are rats and may, therefore, be expected to react more strongly to confinement in darkness than would rats.

Satiation

In a recent study, Kish and Baron (1962) exposed subjects to blinking or continuous light for a half-hour period immediately prior to a test of light-reinforced responding. Pre-exposure to blinking light eliminated the light-reinforcement effect, while pre-exposure to continuous light significantly decreased but did not eliminate the effect.

The finding that pre-exposure to a continuously lighted environment decreases the light-reinforcement effect is at variance with results reported by Robinson (1959) and by Kish and Barnes in an unpublished study. These studies found that the effect upon light reinforcement of several daily sessions of habituation to a lighted environment was not different from several days of habituation to a totally dark apparatus environment. In the Kish and Barnes and the Robinson studies, testing was carried out on successive test days, while in the Kish and Baron study, tests for light reinforcement were conducted immediately following the pre-exposure period. This suggests that recovery from the satiation induced by exposure to the lighted environment occurred during the 24 hours intervening between pre-exposure and test, thus eliminating the effects of such exposure.

In line with this, Rabedeau and Miles (1959) found a significant recovery of visual exploration after a two-day rest away from the test situation. A similar effect, with light reinforcement, was found by Stewart and Hurwitz (1959).

Taking another tack, Forgays and Levin (1961) studied the effect of distributed versus massed trials upon sensorily reinforced behavior. With a 12-minute test period of lever pressing, groups of subjects were tested for 14 consecutive sessions with a 48-minute or a 24-hour inter-test interval. They found that the 24-hour group maintained a consistently higher rate of light-reinforced responding than did the 48-minute group. Apparently, during the intervening 24-hour period, recovery from the satiation induced by the exposure to light during the test session occurred to a greater extent for the 24-hour group than for the 48-minute group.

Berlyne (1955) also tested the effect of massed and distributed test trials upon the reactivity of rats to a novel cube. The nosing behavior of the subjects was tested during four successive three-minute test periods separated by either ten minutes in the massed condition or 24 hours in the distributed condition. Animals tested under the massed condition showed a decline in investigatory behavior on successive trials while those under the distributed condition did not show any decline. Clearly, prolonged exposure to a sensory reinforcer leads to a weakening of its reinforcing powers while subsequent absence of the reinforcer promotes recovery of its reinforcing powers.

Evidence for a gradual satiation within a given test period can be found in each of the research areas concerned with sensory reinforcement. Responding for light is highest at the beginning of a test session and later falls off (e.g., Kish & Baron, 1962; Roberts, Marx, & Collier, 1958). Locomotor exploratory activity in a Y maze (Montgomery, 1952) as well as non-locomotor investigatory behavior (Berlyne, 1955) also show this intrasession drop-off in responding.

On the other hand, Harlow and his co-workers have indicated that *manipulatory* behavior is extremely resistant to satiation, continuing for many hours with few signs of satiation (Harlow, 1950; Harlow, Blazek, & McClearn, 1956). This behavior can be satiated, however, if testing is continued for a sufficiently extended session (Harlow, 1950), although the tendency does recover after a period of no testing (Welker, 1956c).

The data presented above concerning deprivation and satiation indicate that prior exposure or lack of exposure to stimulation affect the organism's responsiveness to sensorily reinforcing stimuli and are consistent with the postulation of a motive state underlying the sensory reinforcement phenomenon. The precise nature of the motive is still a point of considerable conjecture. Also, whether these studies may best be interpreted as reflecting the operation of a single drive for stimulation or as reflecting the operation of several drives, such as manipulation, exploration, or curiosity, remains for future research and interpretation. Parsimony, however, argues for an analysis in terms of a single "stimulus hunger" or drive for stimulation rather than a series of drives specific to different test situations, or sensory modalities, or perhaps both.

Secondary Reinforcement

A rather persistent interpretation of sensory reinforcement postulates that the reinforcing properties of such stimulation derive from their previous association with primary reinforcement.

The strongest argument in support of this hypothesis is based upon the findings concerning the effects of hunger and thirst. The effectiveness of a *secondary reinforcer* has been found to be a function of the amount of the original or of a related drive which is present during the test for reinforcement (Kimble, 1961, pp. 188-190). Since hunger or thirst enhances sensory reinforcing effects, it may be argued that a history of association with food or water reinforcement is involved in producing them. A number of studies find that deprivation does enhance sensorily reinforced responding. However, the findings are by no means consistent, and where enhancing effects of drive are found, other interpretations appear equally plausible (see pp. 145-148 for a review of these studies). This evidence does not, therefore, appear to be particularly convincing.

Evidence contrary to this interpretation comes from several sources. Secondary reinforcement, as it occurs in the laboratory, is a transient phenomenon, the secondary reinforcer rapidly losing its effectiveness when primary reinforcement is no longer forthcoming. But Harlow and his co-workers (e.g., Harlow & McClearn, 1954; Harlow, 1950) in the manipulatory area, Butler and his co-workers (e.g., Butler & Alexander, 1955; Butler & Harlow, 1954) in the visual exploratory area, and others (e.g., Forgays & Levin, 1958; Hurwitz, 1956) in the light-reinforcement area have reported that such sensorily reinforced behavior is remarkably persistent. In fact, sensorily reinforced behavior has been observed to *increase* in strength as a function of successive test sessions rather than to show the decline in strength expected if secondary reinforcement were involved (e.g., Hurwitz, 1956).

Several investigators have attempted to enhance the reinforcing effects of light onset through association of light with food reinforcement. Roberts, Marx, and Collier (1958) associated feeding with either dark or light conditions. Later tests of light onset and termination as reinforcers did *not* show any effect which could be attributed to this feeding experience.

Hurwitz and Appel (1959) kept rats on a 12-hour darkness and 12-hour light cycle and associated feeding with the later portions of each cycle for different subjects. They found that light onset was reinforcing for both groups, although more reinforcing for the group fed in the light. Interestingly, however, this enhancement of the reinforcing effect was apparent only during the first half-hour session. Subsequently, the advantage of the group fed in light disappeared. Apparently the reinforcing strength attributable to secondary reinforcement rapidly dissipated while the strength attributable to sensory reinforcement persisted.

Anxiety and Sensory Reinforcement

According to several theorists, anxiety may play an important role in sensorily reinforced behavior. Mowrer (1960), for example, feels that light-reinforced behavior may be motivated by anxiety generated by the totally dark, novel environment usually used as the baseline in these studies. Similarly, locomotor exploration may reflect the organism's efforts to escape from fear-inducing novel stimulation. In Butler's visual exploration studies, the opaque test compartment may generate anxiety which is reduced by opening the door and viewing the familiar laboratory environment.

The studies reviewed below suggest that anxiety may play a role in reactions to novel stimulation but that an analysis solely in these terms is probably inaccurate. (See pp. 133-135 for an analysis of the role of novelty in sensory reinforcement.) The evidence appears to indicate that novel stimuli evoke both approach and avoidance tendencies to some degree and that exploratory behavior can best be understood as a reflection of the balance and interplay of these two tendencies.

That novel stimuli do indeed arouse anxiety and avoidance tendencies may be inferred from the cautious, vacillatory behavior observed in many organisms when confronted with novel stimulation. Urination and defecation generally increase when an organism is placed in a novel environment, suggesting the arousal of anxiety.

The observations of Barnett (1958b) indicate that wild rats react with *neophobia* to novel stimulation (see also p. 138). The fear reaction in these animals was particularly noticeable as a depression of eating behavior resulting from introduction of a novel stimulus into the home cage environment.

An unfortunate theoretical problem is posed by the above analysis. The novel stimulus situation which is considered to arouse anxiety is identical with the situation which arouses exploratory behavior. In terms of antecedent conditions, therefore, *anxiety* and *exploratory drive* may be considered to be identical, at least in novel situations. On the other hand, the behavioral consequences of anxiety (movement away from the source of noxious stimulation) and the behavioral consequences of exploratory drive (movement toward the source of stimulation) are different. However, it is extremely difficult to test in any direct fashion the proposition that novel stimuli arouse anxiety in situations in which approach and avoidance behavior cannot be clearly distinguished. In the locomotor exploration situation, for example, the organism is surrounded by novel stimuli and its behavior may be interpreted as either avoidance or approach.

Where a localized sensory reinforcer is used, the demonstration that anxiety diminishes exploratory behavior would provide evidence contrary to the strict anxiety interpretation of exploratory behavior. Such evidence is provided by several studies. Barnett's (1958b) study, mentioned above, suggests that for wild rats, at least, novel stimulation arouses more fear than exploratory tendencies. Butler (1954) notes that the monkeys showing the greatest number of anxiety signs (freezing, crouching in corner, trembling) were the least likely to explore visually and required considerable habituation to the test compartment before visual exploration began.

Kish and Baron (1962) note that if subjects in the light-reinforcement situation respond because of fear of the dark, then prior habituation in a lighted test environment should reduce anxiety and consequently the amount of light-reinforced responding. Although such habituation did reduce responding, it was not nearly as effective a satiator as was a blinking light which allowed relatively little visual familiarization with the test environment and presumably less anxiety reduction. Kish and Baron felt that this finding was not consistent with a fear-of-the-dark interpretation of light reinforcement such as that proposed by Mowrer (1960).

Menzel (1962) observed the reactions of rhesus monkeys to novel stimuli differing in size and proximity to the subject. He found that avoidance of these novel stimuli increased as a function of size and proximity. As the subjects became familiar with the objects, however, avoidance reactions disappeared and the subjects began to make playful contacts with them.

Welker (1956b) noted that young chimpanzees showed some fear in the presence of novel stimuli as indicated by the delay between presentation of the novel stimuli and initial tactual contact. In older chimpanzees this initial contact was relatively prompt. The observation of cautious visual exploration prior to tactual contact is in agreement with an interpretation that stresses the arousal of both fear and exploration by novel stimuli. In young chimpanzees, as contrasted with older animals, the stimuli were relatively more novel (i.e., for the older, more experienced subjects, the stimuli were more likely to resemble stimuli experienced previously) and consequently, the younger subjects displayed greater fear as well as greater curiosity. Once the initial hesitancy was overcome, the younger subjects spent more time in contact with the novel stimulation than did the older subjects, suggesting the arousal of a greater degree of curiosity in the younger chimpanzees.

In the locomotor exploratory situation, the role of fear can be more easily assessed when subjects are given the option either to explore or remain in the familiar home environment. Welker (1957) compared the activity of subjects forced to remain in an open field test situation with the activity of subjects that were allowed access to, but were not forced into, the open field test situation. Forced subjects were found to be significantly more active in the open field than the free subjects. The forced subjects also showed the usual falling curve of activity while the free subjects showed an inverted U-shaped activity curve in time. Welker concluded that the fear aroused by novel stimulation inhibited initial entry into the test box, but as fear dissipated, exploratory tendencies were manifested and the subjects ventured forth from the familiar start-box. Welker suggests that the free exploration technique used in his study provides a purer measure of exploratory tendencies than does the usual forced technique used by Montgomery and others.

Hayes (1960), using a similar technique, compared the behavior of rats under free and forced conditions and found that the most timid rats in the free condition (those that were least likely to move out of the home cage into the novel environment) were also the least active under forced conditions. He concluded that an interpretation of exploratory behavior as fear motivated, with the animal trying to find a way out of the fear-producing environment, did not fit his findings. Similar conclusions were drawn by Montgomery (1955) using a free technique.

In another experiment, Montgomery and Monkman (1955) attempted to enhance fear in the exploratory situation by applying buzzer noises and electric shocks both prior to and during tests of exploratory behavior in a

Y maze. In both instances, either no effect was observed or the fear-inducing stimulus retarded exploratory behavior.

The data presented above seem to support the interpretation that novel stimulation arouses both fear and exploratory tendencies. In general, the fear aroused by novel stimulation inhibits rather than facilitates exploratory behavior. This fear dissipates upon contact with the novel stimulus leading to a relative increase in exploratory activity.

Activity and Sensory Reinforcement

Some of the forms of behavior which have been interpreted in sensory reinforcement terms in this chapter (e.g., locomotor exploration and *unconditioned* operant behavior) may be interpreted as resulting from the operation of a general activity drive. This interpretation involves the assumption that there is such an activity drive which is independent of an exploratory or stimulus-directed motive. That these motives are somewhat independent is essentially the conclusion drawn by Montgomery (1953b).

Montgomery tested the Y-maze exploratory behavior of two groups of rats which were confined in small cages prior to the Y-maze test. During confinement, one group had access to an activity wheel while the other did not. No differences were found in Y-maze exploration between subjects allowed activity and those not allowed activity in the wheel. Length of activity deprivation up to 192 hours was not found to be a significant variable either. There was, however, a high positive rank order correlation ($\rho = +.80$) between amount of wheel turning during the initial days of contact with the activity wheel and exploratory activity in the Y maze. Later wheel activity, however, was not correlated with exploratory behavior. On the basis of these findings, Montgomery concluded that the activity wheel measures a form of exploratory behavior initially and activity tendencies later, after the novelty of the wheel stimuli has worn off, but that the two tendencies are essentially independent.

Although running in an activity wheel produces complex stimulation, it is likely that an important component of this pattern involves kinesthetic stimulation. Montgomery's correlations suggest that activity might partially, at least, be interpreted as kinesthetic exploration or kinesthetic sensorily reinforced behavior, and that the crudity of the Y-maze technique, which involves a complex pattern of visual, olfactory, and tactual as well as kinesthetic stimulation, is responsible for the apparent lack of relationship between activity deprivation and Y-maze exploration. It is also possible that Montgomery's situation was inadequately restrictive of the subject's locomotor behavior.

A more refined technique with more severe restriction of the subject's pretest locomotor behavior should, therefore, show a positive relationship between activity deprivation and kinesthetic sensorily reinforced behavior. Baron, Antonitis, and Beale (1961) tested the effect of various degrees of confinement upon unconditioned operant lever pressing by mice. They found that confinement enhanced bar pressing while an equal degree of exposure to a non-confining novel environment tended to reduce bar-pressing behavior. Although this result could be interpreted as indicating that bar pressing reflects general activity and that this general activity is enhanced by confinement, the authors chose to interpret their findings in terms of sensory reinforcement. They argue that confinement deprives the organism of kinesthetic stimulation. This arouses a motive state which increases the reinforcing strength of the kinesthetic stimulation provided by bar pressing. (See p. 120f for a discussion of kinesthetic sensory reinforcement.)

That unconditioned operant behavior is *not* primarily a reflection of an independent general activity drive is the conclusion drawn by several investigators. Kish and Antonitis (1956) found that the obtained operant level of platform depression was considerably greater than the rate predicted from the area or the perimeter of the test apparatus plus the assumption that activity will be homogeneously distributed throughout the test compartment or about its perimeter.

Similarly, Baron, Antonitis, and Clark (1963) tested the effects of increasing the size of the Skinner box upon unconditioned lever pressing. If activity were the major determinant of unconditioned lever pressing, then the rate of response would be expected to fall in proportion to the increase in the area or circumference of the test box. Although the number of responses emitted during a standard time period did fall as the size of the box was increased, the decline was not as great as predicted from the above considerations. An interesting further finding was that the intrasession response rates increased from the beginning to the end of the test session for the larger test compartments, but not for the smaller compartments. According to Baron *et al.*, the larger boxes provided a greater number of novel stimuli which competed with the lever stimuli in arousing exploratory behavior. This accounted for the reduction of the number of responses with increased box size. Furthermore, as the box stimuli lost their novelty during the test session, the lever stimuli which were more complex became relatively more effective and the bar-pressing activity increased. In either the large or small box, the lever provided comparatively greater and more complex stimulation than the rest of the box, thus arousing a greater amount of lever contact than would be predicted from an activity hypothesis alone.

The relationship between activity and sensory reinforcement still remains to be clarified. The few studies presented above suggest that at least some of the behavior which has been considered to be general activity is possibly sensorily reinforced behavior. The operation of activity deprivation also involves deprivation from stimulation, particularly kinesthetic stimulation. Such deprivation from kinesthetic stimulation may be expected to enhance the reinforcing properties of kinesthetic stimulation. It does not seem unreasonable, therefore, to hypothesize that the activity drive is in reality a stimulus-directed drive similar to exploration except that, in the case of activity, the reinforcing stimuli are intrinsic rather than extrinsic in origin.

VARIABLES AFFECTING SENSORY REINFORCEMENT

Novelty

A basic problem concerning our understanding of the process of sensory reinforcement is the specification of the characteristics of sensorily reinforcing stimuli which distinguish this class of events from stimulation which is not reinforcing. Berlyne (1960) proposes that such stimuli may be characterized as: (1) novel, (2) complex, (3) arousing or relieving uncertainty, and (4) arousing or relieving conflict. With respect to novelty, Berlyne points out the difficulties of definition since many types of novelty can be discriminated. He speaks of: (1) "complete novelty," in relationship to the total life history of the organism, (2) "short term novelty," in relationship to the time since last exposure to the stimulus, (3) "absolute novelty," aroused by stimulation containing elements never before perceived by the organism, and (4) "relative novelty," which is aroused by familiar elements in unfamiliar combination. Novelty, therefore, is a relationship between the perceiving organism and stimulation which must be assessed in terms of the long-term and short-term experiences of the organism with that stimulation.

Experimentation concerned with the factor of novelty has been primarily concerned with short-term novelty. The experiments discussed below confirm the general contention that novelty is an important factor determining reactivity to stimulation.

The experiments concerned with satiation demonstrate that decreased novelty is associated with diminished reinforcing potential. These studies have been thoroughly reviewed (see pp. 126-127) and, in general, show that continued exposure to reinforcing stimulation leads to a gradual diminution of the reinforcing effectiveness of that stimulation. The studies also indicate recovery (more or less complete) during a period of non-exposure to the sensory reinforcer.

Other experiments have directly concerned themselves with a manipulation of this novelty variable essentially by pre-exposing subjects to the stimulus or a similar stimulus and later testing for its reinforcing effects. Most of this work has been performed by Berlyne and his collaborators (Berlyne, 1950; 1951; 1955; 1957; Berlyne & Slater, 1957a). For example, Berlyne (1955), using a free operant nosing response, measured the amount which rats nosed an empty display compartment, a compartment containing a completely novel wooden cube, and a compartment containing a cube to which the subjects had been pre-exposed. The amount of nosing was greatest with respect to the novel object, next with respect to the familiar cube, and least in response to an empty display compartment. In addition, Berlyne (1950) exposed rats to three stimuli prior to test. During a test period a novel stimulus (one not included during the pre-exposure period) replaced one of the three pre-exposure stimuli. The subjects were observed to spend more time near to and sniffing the changed stimulus.

In a recent study with young chimpanzee subjects, Menzel, Davenport, and Rogers (1961) habituated their subjects to a single stimulus object and then exposed them to objects varying from this stimulus in several dimensions. They found that the more different the new objects were from the habituated object, the more contact was elicited.

This general method is further illustrated by an experiment by Dember (1956). Rats were allowed 15 minutes in the stem of a T maze, one arm of which was white and the other black. Access to these arms was prevented by glass partitions. Two minutes after this exposure period, the rats were reintroduced into the maze with the glass partitions removed and both arms now either black or white. A significantly large percentage of the rats were found to make their initial entry into the *changed* alley. The results were interpreted in terms of arousal of exploratory tendencies by the changed (novel) stimulation.

Taking a somewhat different tack, Montgomery (1953c) tested rats for locomotor exploratory tendencies successively in several mazes. He found that the more similiar the succeeding mazes were to the first in the series, the less exploratory behavior was manifested. Conversely, the greater the difference, the more exploration occurred. Apparently, the relative novelty of the succeeding mazes determined to some degree the exploratory tendencies which were manifested.

Antonitis and Barnes (1961), testing the bar-pressing behavior of preschool children in the group operant situation, presented various cartoon silhouettes as reinforcement for bar pressing. Results indicated that initial introduction of a given cartoon character resulted in increases in bar pressing which dropped off with continued exposure. Each introduction of a new cartoon character resulted in similar increases with subsequent diminution of responding.

In a recent study, Welker and King (1962) found that novelty was an important determiner of both the rate of eating and the rate of gnawing of edible and inedible materials by rats. In both instances response rate fell off with continued exposure to the novel stimulus material.

Clearly, previous contact with a given stimulus affects the reinforcing properties of that stimulus. To this extent, at least, the concept of novelty may be subsumed under the concept of stimulus satiation. This would not,

however, account for the *drive-arousing* properties of novel stimulation unless it were hypothesized that stimulation per se is capable of arousing
curiosity or stimulus hunger and that the concept, *novelty,* is merely ex-
pressing the degree to which an organism has become satiated with respect
to that stimulus.

At the present time, however, novelty appears to be a useful construct
for specifying one important characteristic of sensory reinforcers. Further
research to clarify the relationships between novelty and more basic constructs is needed.

Complexity

Complexity is closely related to novelty. The more complex a stimulus
pattern is, the longer it should take for such a pattern to become familiar
and for satiation to manifest itself. This is borne out by some of the experimental evidence presented below.

Berlyne (1960), in his analysis of complexity, notes the following attributes of a stimulus which contribute to its complexity. (1) Complexity
tends to increase with the number of distinguishable elements composing
the pattern and with (2) the dissimilarity between the elements of a pattern.
On the other hand, (3) the greater the possibility of integrating the pattern
into a unitary percept (Gestalt), the less will be the complexity.

Several studies have explored these variables and have generally found
that the greater the complexity of the stimulus pattern, the greater is its atten-
tion-holding value, its exploratory-arousing value and, presumably, its sen-
sory-reinforcing value.

A series of studies by Welker (1956a; 1956b; 1956c) presents evidence concerning the effects of complexity, as well as novelty, upon manipulatory exploration of objects presented to chimpanzees. For example,
Welker (1956a) presented a number of objects attached to a presentation
board to chimpanzee subjects in their home cages and noted the amount of
manipulation of these objects and the number of shifts from one object to
another. The results indicated that the more heterogeneous array of objects
aroused more manipulatory responsiveness and more numerous shifts between arrays. This responsiveness diminished with prolonged contact but
recovered from day to day, to some extent, with the same stimulus array,
and to a considerable extent when the array of stimuli was changed in the
direction of greater complexity. Interestingly, merely changing the color of
the presentation board without changing the array of stimulus objects elicited renewed responsiveness.

In a more rigidly controlled experiment, Barnes and Baron (1961a)
compared the reinforcing effectiveness of different response-contingent light
patterns. Different groups of mice could, by bar contact, produce either an
illuminated cross, circle, square, or a multiple pattern. In the multiple pat-

tern, one of these patterns was available for one minute, after which another pattern became available for one minute. Thus, each minute the subject was reinforced by a different pattern, the cycle repeating itself every three minutes. In all cases, the stimulus only appeared upon bar contact and persisted only as long as bar contact was maintained. Barnes and Baron found that the reinforcing effectiveness of the onset of these patterns was positively related to complexity, the cross and multiple pattern being most reinforcing with the square and circle following in that order. Some evidence for the role of novelty in light reinforcement was also suggested by the results of the multiple pattern group which maintained a high response rate when a new pattern was presented every minute.

Mason and Harlow (1959) found that the initial reactions of infant monkeys to solid foods was a function of the complexity of the food stimuli presented. Complex combinations of colors, textures, etc. produced by combinations of orange pieces, nuts, breads, etc. and banana cubes dyed different colors aroused more manipulation than did plain banana cubes.

Berlyne (1958b) studied the effect of stimulus complexity upon visual fixations in human infants. The more complex stimuli (in terms of amount of contour) aroused the greatest number of fixations. Differences in albedo of the stimulus cards, however, were not reflected in the behavior of the infants.

A study in the area of visual exploration by Rabedeau and Miles (1959) also provides presumptive support for the role of complexity. These investigators found that the view of the darkened laboratory was considerably less reinforcing than the view of a lighted laboratory. A darkened laboratory with little activity is a considerably less complex stimulus than a lighted, busy laboratory.

The literature may be summarized as indicating that a characteristic of stimulation which contributes significantly to its reinforcing effects is its complexity. Other studies supporting this conclusion have been reported by Berlyne (1960). Presumably, all studies using complex stimuli such as the studies of locomotor exploration, manipulation, and visual and auditory exploration support such a view although specific comparisons with simpler forms of stimulation have not been made.

Termination or Reduction of Light

A simple *change hypothesis* such as that proposed by Kish and Antonitis (1956) would predict that the onset and termination of light would be equally effective as sensory reinforcers. Barnes and Kish (1957) tested this hypothesis and found that light termination had no demonstrable reinforcing properties. This finding was also reported by Hurwitz (1956) and Robinson (1959).

On the other hand, Leaton, Symmes, and Barry (1963) and Roberts,

Marx, and Collier (1958) reported positive reinforcing effects for light termination, although the effect was considerably weaker than was the light-onset effect. Furthermore, Barry and Symmes (1963) reported that light onset and light termination were equally effective as sensory reinforcers.

The reasons for these conflicting results are not clear at the present time. One possibility, however, is suggested by the findings concerning re-duction of light to a non-zero level of intensity. Studies show that reductions of light intensity and increments in light intensity, both with a non-zero back-ground illumination, are equally effective as sensory reinforcers (Antonitis & Barnes, 1961; Moon & Lodahl, 1956; Robinson, personal communication). These data suggest that the complexity variable counteracts the effects at-tributable to change when illumination is interrupted. Even if change is an important factor, the change from an illuminated-box environment to a totally dark-box environment is tantamount to reducing stimulus complexity to a zero value. When change in light intensity occurs, but the test environment remains illuminated as in the light reduction studies, positive and negative light intensity changes are found to be equally reinforcing.

Apparatus Habituation

This variable is appropriate only where the reinforcing stimulus is in-dependently manipulated and is introduced into a constant test environ-ment. Thus, it has not been specifically studied in other than the light-rein-forcement situation, although it appears appropriate to other studies, espe-cially of visual and auditory exploration.

The light-reinforcement studies suggest that the effect of light onset is enhanced by several periods of apparatus habituation. Girdner (1953b), using several groups of rats, introduced the light reinforcers after 0, 1, 3, and 6 days of operant level testing. He found the reinforcer to be most ef-fective after three days of habituation, six days having no greater effect than three. Similar findings have been reported by Appel and Hurwitz (1959), by Crowder (1961), and by Leaton, Symmes, and Barry (1963). Other studies have not directly tested this variable but suggest similar results (Hurwitz, 1956; Marx, Henderson, & Roberts, 1955).

These findings may be interpreted in several ways. Berlyne (1960) suggests that habituation affects the "surprisingness" of the light. The greater the surprisingness, the greater is the reinforcing value of the stimulus. In a related manner, this effect might also be conceptualized as a change in the relative novelty of light onset produced by the greater contrast between the now familiar apparatus environment and the novel light. In other words, the reinforcing effects of competing stimuli have become reduced through satiation. Another interpretation might suggest that novel environments pro-duce fear and that apparatus habituation reduced the general inhibiting ef-fects of that fear state. In this respect, Butler (1954) noted that his monkeys required a habituation period before they began to explore visually (see p. 112ff). These interpretations do not conflict in any important ways and it may be possible that all of these factors may be operative in producing the obtained results.

Genetic Factors

That species and strain factors might enter into the determination of the reinforcing properties of stimulation is suggested by what is known of the differences in sensory capacities of various animal species, as well as experimental evidence relating to such characteristics as fearfulness and general responsiveness, which seem to differ among different species and strains.

Experiments specifically manipulating genetic variables in relationship to sensory reinforcement are rare. As noted above, sensory reinforcement has been demonstrated in a variety of species. Specific comparisons have not been made, however, in any of the experiments dealing with light reinforcement, auditory and visual exploration, or curiosity.

An experimental comparison of the unconditioned rate of platform depression by two species of mice has been reported by Kish and Antonitis (1956). C57 Black 6 and C Scott albino mice were tested in an open field test situation with a recording platform in one corner. During six daily test sessions the C57 mice showed higher rates of platform depression than did the C Scott mice. As a function of successive periods, however, the difference between the groups became progressively less until by the fourth test-day the groups were statistically indistinguishable. Kish and Antonitis interpreted their results as indicating greater initial responsiveness to novel stimulation and more rapid satiation of responsiveness on the part of the C57 mice.

Some interesting observations by Barnett (1958b) indicate striking differences in the reactions of wild, hooded, and albino rats to novel stimulation. Barnett placed a novel tin can in the middle of the home cage and noted the resulting behavior. Albino rats immediately began to explore the can while the hooded rats showed greater hesitancy and the wild rats showed considerable signs of fear. In fact, a certain percentage of the wild rats did not eat for a day or two after introduction of the novel stimulus. As might be expected, greater individual differences in reaction were found in the wild strain than in the more inbred laboratory strains.

Carr and Williams (1957) compared the Y-maze exploration of black, white, and hooded rats. The black and the white rats did not differ significantly in number of maze units entered, but both differed significantly from the more active hooded rats. On the other hand, the hooded rats were less orderly in their exploratory behavior. (See p. 116 for consideration of the meaning of orderliness in exploratory behavior.) This finding suggests that the obtained differences may best be interpreted as reflecting a somewhat higher general activity level for the hooded rats.

McClearn (1959), using a variety of exploratory test situations, tested six strains of mice. He found marked strain differences in exploratory activity in most measures, with several sublines of the C57 strain (a pigmented strain) tending to be most reactive while several albino strains were least reactive. Crossbreeding produced F1 generations falling somewhere in between the two parent strains. McClearn felt that several possible inheritable characteristics may be responsible for his findings, including differences in susceptibility to fear, spontaneous activity, sensory acuity, or even intelligence. Interestingly, Thompson (1953), testing the exploratory activity of maze-bright and maze-dull rats, found no significant differences attributable to this factor.

Glickman, Sroges, and Hoff (1961) studied the responsiveness of various species of animals (ranging from reptiles through the primates) to novel stimulus objects placed in their cages. They found that general responsiveness to novel stimulation increased as a function of the subject's position in the evolutionary series. Other studies demonstrating the effect of genetic variables are those of Lockard (1962) and Williams, Zerof, and Carr (1962).

Although more study is needed to determine the inheritable determinants of the differences found, there seems little doubt that a full analysis of sensorily reinforced behavior must include statements concerning the characteristics of the species and strains tested.

Maturation

One proposed explanation of the genesis of exploratory and manipulatory behavior postulates that these are generalized responses which were initially learned in a food-getting or other primary drive-reduction context. The evidence actually supports the contrary proposition that the discovery and discrimination of food from non-food objects is dependent upon the development of the kinds of exploratory activity shown by infant organisms (i.e., sniffing, touching, looking, and mouthing) and that exploratory tendencies antedate the development of solid food-eating behavior.

Harlow, Blazek, and McClearn (1956) found manipulatory behavior in infant rhesus monkeys as early as the twentieth day of life, *before* the infants had eaten solid food. Welker (1959b), similarly, found evidence of play behavior in infant raccoons that began as soon as the eyes opened and before the organisms had had any experience with solid foods. Furthermore, Welker could find no observable relationship between degree of hunger and thirst and amount of play activity.

In another study, Mason and Harlow (1959) found that the initial responses of infant rhesus monkeys to solid food were determined by the stimulus characteristics of the food objects. Colored banana cubes and a varied array containing pieces of orange, bread, grapes, etc. aroused more investigation, manipulation, and mouthing than did cubes of uncolored banana.

Evidence concerning the effects of aging upon sensory reinforcement is somewhat difficult to interpret because of the variety of species tested and the different age ranges used. Mason, Harlow, and Rueping (1959), testing monkeys from 1 to 90 days of age in a variety of situations, found generally increased responsiveness during the first half and a drop-off in responsiveness in the second half of the 90-day age range. Some functions such as knob manipulation, however, showed progressive increases up to at least 90 days of age.

Levin and Forgays (1959) found that the light-reinforced lever pressing of 110-day-old rats was consistently higher than that of 70-day-old animals. Wechkin, Furchtgott, and Dees (1960), using a broader age range (from 35 to 365 days of age), found that older rats explored an open field to a lesser extent than did younger rats. A similar result was reported by Werboff and Havlena (1962) using an open field test with rats between 90 and 540 days of age.

Welker (1956b) tested young chimpanzees and found that, although the older subjects showed a greater initial contact rate with novel stimuli, they satiated more rapidly than did the younger subjects. He also found that younger chimpanzees showed considerable hesitancy and conflict when presented with novel stimuli. Apparently, novel stimuli aroused more fear as well as more curiosity in the younger than in the older subjects.

These findings suggest that a curvilinear relationship exists between age and reactivity to sensory reinforcers, with responsiveness increasing with maturational status to some maximal value and falling off with further increments in age. Welker's data suggest that increasing curiosity in the earlier age ranges may be a function of gradually diminishing timidity on the part of the young animals, although other factors are most certainly involved. The drop-off in responsiveness in the later age ranges may be a function of increased experience with a variety of stimuli, which consequently tends to reduce the related novelty of the stimulus objects presented to those subjects in the test situation.

Rearing Conditions

A number of studies have been concerned with the determination of the effects of prior history of stimulation upon sensory reinforcement. Tests for the effects of rearing conditions have been conducted in the light-reinforcement situation and variations of the locomotor exploration situation and have yielded rather conflicting results.

Roberts, Marx, and Collier (1958) raised rats from weaning until 90 days of age, in total darkness for some groups and in a continuously lighted environment for others. Later, hungry subjects were tested in a bar-press situation with light onset or light termination as the reinforcers. Highest bar-pressing rates were found when the subjects were procuring the light conditions under which they had been reared. Dark-reared subjects found light termination most reinforcing while light-reared subjects found light onset most reinforcing. Interestingly, light onset was reinforcing even for subjects raised in the dark, although it was not as reinforcing as light termination.

In a variant of the locomotor exploration situation, Walk (1960) found that dark- and light-reared rats did not respond differently to stimulus change. In this experiment, 15 minutes of pre-exposure to the stem of a T maze, with a glass partition preventing entry into the arms, was followed by a test run in which the partitions were removed and one arm of the T maze was changed. Response to change was indicated by initial entry of the rat into the changed rather than the unchanged alley. All groups, whether dark- or light-reared, responded significantly to the changed arm.

Zimbardo and Montgomery (1957b) reared rats in normal cages and in enriched cage environments containing blocks, marbles, a trapeze, a tunnel, and other objects for different lengths of time before exposing them to tests of exploratory behavior. The results indicated that females raised in normal cages showed the greatest amount of Y-maze exploration, while normal males and enriched environment males and females showed essentially the same degree of exploratory activity, which was considerably less than that of the normally-reared females. Rearing conditions were, therefore, significant only in interaction with sex of subject.

Menzel, Davenport, and Rogers (1963) compared two-year-old wild-born chimpanzees with similarly aged subjects which had been raised in a restricted environment. The restricted subjects were found to be more timid of novel objects, contacted them rarely, and spent most of their time in stereotyped self-directed activity. These effects were reversed after one year of outdoor colony-living. Basically, the effect of restricted environment rearing seemed to be to enhance the fear reaction to novel stimulation, thus severely inhibiting exploratory behavior.

Meyers (1962) apparently found a critical period for the facilitation of exploratory behavior by early experience. He stimulated rats once each day by removing the brood cage containing the mother and pups, carrying the cage for approximately 40 feet, and then returning the cage to its rack. For different groups of subjects, this procedure was carried out for different five-day periods within the first 20 days of life. The control group was not stimulated in this fashion. Meyers found that stimulation during days 6-10 led to greater exploratory behavior at 61 days of age than did stimulation during any other five-day period. The 11-15 day group also showed some facilitation of exploration, but not as much as the 6-10 day group.

A recent study by Baron, Antonitis, and Schell (1962) reported positive effects attributable to rearing conditions. Mice were reared in cages with low glass ceilings, allowing only one inch of head room, from the twelfth day of life to the seventeenth week of life. The mice were tested in an open field situation in which one wall was made of wire mesh (as was the floor) allowing the mice to climb. Mice reared in low-ceiling environments engaged in significantly less vertical exploration than mice reared in a high-ceiling environment. The mice were then placed permanently into normal high-ceiling environments and tested at 24 weeks and at 31 weeks of life. The depression of vertical exploration was less, but still significant, on the second test and was no longer apparent on the third test. With another group, an attempt to enhance vertical exploration by rearing in cages in which the mice had to climb to get to food was not successful.

Studies by Woods (1959) and Woods, Fiske, and Ruckelshaus (1961) have an indirect bearing upon the present question. These investigators tested the effects of enriched and restricted environments upon maze learning by rats. In general, they found that restricted environment rearing produced poorer maze learning than enriched environment rearing. An interpretation of this finding suggested by these authors is that the poorer performance of the restricted subjects in the maze is a function of increased exploratory tendencies which interfere with goal-directed behavior and produce increased error scores during maze learning.

The conflicting results reported above suggest the need for further work to determine precisely what aspects of the rearing environments are important and what specific behaviors are learned or not learned in such environments which may affect later exploratory behavior. That the effects of early restriction may be very specific is suggested by the experiment of Baron et al. Low-ceiling rearing was found to affect only vertical exploratory behavior but not horizontal exploration. This further suggests that more refined theoretical analysis of the components of exploratory behavior would seem to be prerequisite to experimental clarification of this question.

Intensity of the Reinforcing Stimulus

Studies of the effects of stimulus intensity can be carried out only under circumstances in which the reinforcing stimulus can be rigidly specified and controlled. As a consequence, most of the studies of this variable have been conducted using light as the reinforcing stimulus, although there is some evidence available from studies of audition and gustatory preferences.

Evidence is available indicating that intense stimulation tends to be aversive. Keller (1941) and Barnes and Kish (1957), for example, have demonstrated the aversive qualities of bright light for the white rat, and of intense white noise for the mouse, respectively. Since sufficient evidence is also available to indicate that a variety of stimuli of moderate intensity function as reinforcers, it might be predicted that a curvilinear relationship would be found between intensity of stimulation and its reinforcing powers.[2] With a few exceptions, the studies reviewed in the following pages bear out this analysis.

In the light-reinforcement situation, Henderson (1957), Marx, Henderson, and Roberts (1955), Barnes, Kish, and Wood (1959), and Lockard (1962) have found indications of such a curvilinear relationship.[3] For example, Henderson tested the effect of a one-second, bar-contingent light flash upon the bar-pressing rate of rats. He found an increasing reinforcing effect up to 16.67 ml with subsequent drop-off in reinforcing power with further increases in intensity. This peak figure was also reported by Marx *et al.* Interestingly, Levin and Forgays (1959) found such a curvilinear function for 80-day-old rats but not for rats 110 days of age. It may be presumed, however, that for the older rats the peak intensity value may be higher and was not reached in this study.

The above studies all used a regular reinforcement procedure. Stewart (1960) failed to find intensity effects using regular reinforcement but did find an interaction between intensity and ratio of reinforcement when using a fixed ratio schedule. Increasing light intensity led to higher response rates at high response-reinforcement ratios but not at low response-reinforcement ratios. This latter finding is comparable to that of Guttman with sucrose reinforcement (Guttman, 1953). Stewart's failure to find a relationship between intensity and reinforcing effects under regular reinforcement is difficult to assess. Comparison of intensities used by different investigators is difficult, since the forms of presentation of light and specification of intensity differ considerably between studies.

Barnes and Kish (1961) found an interaction between the frequency of a pure tone used as a reinforcer and the intensity of that tone. They found no evidence to indicate that the magnitude of reinforcement increased with sound intensity. They did, however, note that at frequencies above 12,000 cps, increases in sound pressure to a maximum of 85 db produced a depression in bar-contact rate. It should be noted also, that in this study with mice, pure tone was found to be an extremely weak sensory reinforcer when compared to light onset.

As noted previously (p. 121f), studies of gustatory preferences generally indicate a curvilinear relationship between concentration of the stimulating substance and preference. For example, Pfaffman (1960) presents a number of preference curves for various substances. Some of these are curvilinear, such as those for sodium chloride, sucrose, and alcohol, showing a maximally preferred concentration with subsequent development of aversion at higher concentrations. On the other hand, some substances seem to

---

[2] Leuba's (1962) concept of *optimal stimulation* would also predict such a curvilinear relationship.

[3] A variable which apparently does not affect the degree of sensory reinforcement is the duration of the light flash (Girdner, 1953; Crowder & Crowder, 1961).

be uniformly aversive such as quinine and hydrochloric acid, the aversion increasing with concentration. It is difficult, at this stage of our knowledge, to specify the characteristics which distinguish the reinforcing from the non-reinforcing tastes. Those stimuli which do have rewarding properties, however, show the curvilinear relationship found for other sensory reinforcers.

Berlyne (1960) points out that the studies of the intensity variable confound the possible effects of differing amounts of stimulus change and differing intensities of stimulation. He cites a study by Thompson (1955) which allowed an assessment of the two possible effects independently of each other. Thompson found no effect which could be attributed to amount of change per se, but did find that reinforcing effects increased with intensity. Berlyne notes further that efforts to disentangle these effects should be made before firm conclusions can be drawn concerning the mode of operation of the intensity variable.

Intermittent Sensory Reinforcement

A few experiments have studied the effects of intermittent sensory reinforcements. Hayes (1958) found that children would press buttons to see a cutout of a cat at a greater rate under intermittent reinforcement than under regular reinforcement. Kegan and Berkun (1954) studied the reinforcing properties of the opportunity to run in a running wheel. The amount of bar pressing leading to such activity significantly increased under intermittent reinforcement but not under regular reinforcement. Apparently, with the amount of reinforcement given satiation occurred rapidly; and, consequently, under regular reinforcement the reinforcer rapidly lost its efficacy. Under intermittent reinforcement conditions, on the other hand, satiation occurred more slowly, thus allowing the reinforcing effects to be demonstrated in behavior.

A similar analysis with respect to light reinforcement was suggested by Stewart and Hurwitz (1958) and specifically tested by Stewart (1960). Stewart studied the interrelationship between light intensity and ratio of reinforcement. She found that light intensity significantly interacted with ratio of reinforcement, the higher light intensities producing higher response rates and resistance to extinction at the higher reinforcement ratios.

Stewart notes that Guttman (1953) has reported a similar interaction between concentration of sucrose and schedule of reinforcement. Stewart concluded that the amount of stimulation per unit time is the important factor in explaining the results of her study and those of Guttman. Low intensities of light at high ratios fall below the optimal level while higher intensities at high ratios more closely approximate the optimal amount of stimulation per unit time. It seems reasonable to suppose that there are at least two factors operating to produce these results. With low-efficacy reinforcers such as dim light, the reinforcing effects may not be great enough to counteract the extinction occurring during the non-reinforced trials. On the other hand, with a large amount of reinforcement under a regular reinforcement schedule, the organism rapidly becomes satiated for the reinforcer and it loses its efficacy. An optimal balance between these two processes is achieved by increasing the reinforcement ratio as the amount of reinforcement is increased.

Food and Water Deprivation

A number of studies in the areas of light reinforcement, locomotor exploration, and unconditioned operant behavior have been concerned with determining the effects of organic drive states upon sensorily reinforced behavior. Four possible effects may be envisaged and have been found by various investigators:

1. Drive may enhance the sensory reinforcement effect by sensitizing the organism to the reinforcing stimulus. Such a finding would be consistent with several theoretical positions, the most prominent being the notion that sensory reinforcers derive their reinforcing powers from prior association with organic reinforcement (secondary reinforcement).

2. Drive may raise the general activity level of the organism, thus appearing to enhance sensorily reinforced responding. This would occur even if drive effects and sensory reinforcement effects were independent of each other if increases in general activity affected the measured response in the same direction as sensory reinforcement (as, for example, in the bar-pressing situation).

3. Drive may have no demonstrable effect upon sensorily reinforced behavior.

4. Drive may attenuate sensorily reinforced responding. This would be consistent with an analysis which considers hunger and thirst as irrelevant drives which tend to arouse behavior in conflict with sensorily reinforced behavior.

Four studies are available in the light-reinforcement literature showing that lever responding is greater under organic drive conditions than under satiated conditions (Clayton, 1958; Davis, 1958; Forgays & Levin, 1958; Segal, 1959b). A question raised by these studies concerns the mode of operation of the drive variable. Does drive merely raise overall response levels or does drive sensitize the organism to the light reinforcer? The answer to this question requires an experimental design which permits assessment of the mode of interaction of the drive and the sensory reinforcement variables. A statistically significant interaction between the reinforcement and the drive variables would tend to confirm a sensitization interpretation, while no interaction would indicate an additive process consisting of an increase in overall level of responding upon which the effects of the sensory reinforcer are superimposed.

Forgays and Levin (1958), using a 2 X 2 factorial design in which light reinforcement and no light reinforcement and zero hours and 24 hours of food deprivation were the independent variables, found no significant interaction between light and drive. In fact, the drive effects alone fell somewhat short of statistical significance.

Clayton (1958), using water deprivation, did find such an interaction between drive and light effects. Her finding, however, is due to the fact that drive elevated the operant level during the first six days of testing while it depressed the operant level during the final three days of testing during which the light-reinforcement test was conducted. This study could bear replication to determine the reliability of this reversal of the effects of drive on operant level responding.

Several other studies suggest an interactive effect though statistical assessment is difficult. Davis (1958) used only three groups of rats at 0, 2, and 23½ hours of food deprivation. After three consecutive daily determinations of unconditioned lever pressing, the light reinforcer was introduced for three further daily sessions. The resulting *increments* in response rate were greatest for the 23½-hour group, somewhat less for the 2-hour group, and least for the 0-hour group, suggesting an interaction between the drive and sensory reinforcement variables. This study, incidentally, found that the unconditioned bar-press rate was increased by the presence of organic drive. This interaction of sensory reinforcement and drive was confirmed by Segal (1959b) who, however, found that the unconditioned bar-press rate was decreased by the presence of drive.

In general, the results of these light-reinforcement studies are consistent with the proposition that organic drive sensitizes the organism to sensory reinforcing stimulation.

Most of the studies of unconditioned operant behavior find that organic drive enhances operant level responding (Brandauer, 1953; Clayton, 1958; Davis, 1958; Forgays & Levin, 1958; Murray, 1953). As noted above, however, Clayton (1958) found that during the early periods of testing, drive enhanced operant level responding, while during later test periods drive depressed the operant level. Somewhat in line with this, Segal (1959a), testing the operant level of lever pressing over a 30-day period, found that drive had a slight depressive effect upon responding. Murray (1953) found enhancement of unconditioned behavior by hunger only in interaction with the type of manipulandum used. The more stimulating long bar plus hunger and chain plus hunger aroused more responding than a short bar plus hunger.

It is clear that degree of organic drive has an effect upon unconditioned behavior. The direction of this effect, however, seems to be a function of other variables which have not, as yet, been fully explored. One such variable appears to be the stimulating qualities of the manipulandum. This finding is consistent with the findings from the light-reinforcement situation which appear to indicate that drive sensitizes the organism to sensory reinforcement.

The findings from the locomotor exploration situation cannot be easily summarized. Although the conditions cannot be specified with certainty, it is clear that under some conditions hunger enhances exploratory behavior (Adlerstein & Fehrer, 1955; Dashiell, 1925; Fehrer, 1956; Glickman & Jensen, 1961), under other conditions hunger and thirst have no effect on exploratory behavior (Hall, Low, & Hanford, 1960; Welker, 1959a), while under yet other conditions hunger and thirst depress exploratory behavior (Montgomery, 1953a; Zimbardo & Montgomery, 1957a).

To add further complications to this picture, Glickman and Jensen (1961) report that hunger and thirst had somewhat different effects, with hunger enhancing exploratory behavior at 46 hours of deprivation but having no effect at 22 hours of deprivation. Thirst, on the other hand, had no significant effect on exploratory behavior at either level of strength.

Other studies have given some indication of the conditions which determine the direction of the effects of drive. Zimbardo and Miller (1958) found an interaction between hunger and a period of delay before subjects were admitted to a novel stimulus compartment. Hungry subjects which were delayed for two minutes prior to being given access to a novel stimulus ran faster to this compartment than did the subjects in three other groups: (1) satiated-not delayed, (2) satiated-delayed, and (3) hungry-not delayed. Thompson (1953) found a sex-by-hunger interaction which was later confirmed by Chapman and Levy (1957). Both of the latter investigations found that males responded to increased hunger with increased activity while females responded with decreased activity.

Other variables, interacting with drive to produce the differences in results, have been hypothesized by several investigators. Hall, Low, and Hanford (1960) suggest that drive enhances exploration only if the stimuli in the test situation have previously been associated with food reinforcement. Glickman and Jensen (1961) feel that such a relationship would tend to develop if subjects were placed on a feeding schedule prior to the exploratory test. When they tested this prediction by comparing the exploratory behavior of subjects on a feeding schedule with subjects who had been deprived from an ad lib baseline, however, they found no differences in amount of exploration between the two groups.

Zimbardo and Montgomery (1957a) and Welker (1959) have attacked the problem from a somewhat different angle. They tested exploratory behavior in hungry and thirsty subjects when food and water were present in the test environment. If exploratory activity is controlled independently of the primary drives of hunger and thirst, the hungry and thirsty subjects would be exposed to a conflict situation which should be reflected in the eating and exploring behavior of the subjects.

Zimbardo and Montgomery found that the presence of the food and water incentives in the test situation reduced exploration below that of the groups with drive but no incentive. However, all subjects were observed to engage in considerable amounts of exploration before eating or drinking. Even the 72-hour deprived subjects explored for about one minute before commencing to eat.

Welker (1959) found essentially similar results in a somewhat different situation. He concluded that an interpretation of exploration as food-seeking behavior was not in accord with the facts, since hunger did not facilitate exploration, and the more novel the environment into which the hungry subjects were placed with food, the longer before the subjects commenced eating. Barnett's (1958b) observation of the inhibition of eating in wild rats when in the presence of novel stimulation is consistent with this interpretation (see p. 138).

In summary, organic drive appears to enhance sensorily reinforced responding by sensitizing the organism to the effects of the novel stimulation. This conclusion is supported by the findings from the light-reinforcement and unconditioned behavior situations. The interpretation that responding to novel stimulation is essentially food- or water-seeking behavior or that the sensory reinforcers are, in fact, secondary reinforcers is not consistent with the findings from the exploratory situation. Apparently, the function of organic drive in sensory reinforced behavior is more complex than meets the eye. No doubt in some test situations, food- and water-seeking tendencies and exploratory tendencies complement each other while in other situations, they tend to negate each other's effects. Precise specification of these conditions is a pressing problem for future research.

SUMMARY AND CONCLUSIONS

The sensory reinforcement hypothesis postulates that response-contingent stimulation in any modality is reinforcing. The hypothesis, as stated by Kish (1955), was extremely general and was tentatively presented for the primary purpose of indicating a direction for further research. Evidence concerned with the validity of this hypothesis was almost nonexistent before 1950. Since that time, however, enough data have been gathered to allow the presentation of some tentative generalizations concerning the limits of the sensory reinforcement phenomenon.

The original hypothesis had placed no limitations upon the sensory modalities in which stimulation would be found to be reinforcing. The evidence presented on pages 119-123 is still inadequate with respect to this question, but generally seems to indicate that reinforcing forms of stimulation may be found in many sensory modalities. There is also a suggestion that the stimulus modalities in which sensory reinforcers will be found will vary from species to species. This suggestion is supported by the findings which indicate wide variations in the sensory capacities of different species, for example, the almost total absence of gustatory and olfactory sensitivity in birds. From a functional-evolutionary point of view, stimulation in different sense modalities may have different functions for the organism. For example, for the mouse or rat, auditory stimulation probably functions primarily to alert the organism to danger. Its positive functions may relate only to the discovery of sex objects, but not to the discovery of food and water. For the cat, on the other hand, auditory stimulation may have more important food discovery functions. One might suspect, therefore, that auditory stimulation would tend to arouse relatively more fear than curiosity in rodents and other organisms which fit the above description. The evidence for such an analysis remains to be gathered.

An important problem awaiting clarification is the specification of the characteristics which distinguish the reinforcing from the non-reinforcing stimuli in a given sense modality. For example, in the gustatory modality sodium chloride and saccharine solutions are found to have reinforcing properties up to certain concentrations, while acid and bitter substances are found to be either neutral or aversive, depending upon concentration (Pfaffman, 1958). In this case one might appeal to the existence of physiological sub-hungers for salt and sweet or to secondary reinforcement as factors determining reinforcing properties. The aversiveness of bitter and acid solutions, on the other hand, cannot be handled from this point of view. A functional-evolutionary analysis of the type presented above may also be of value in this instance. Such an analysis would stress the survival value of positive reactions to sweet-tasting substances and negative reactions to bitter and sour substances. Obviously, even if such an analysis were valid, description of the underlying mechanisms would be necessary.

The evidence presented in this chapter allows further conclusions concerning the factors which are involved in determining the amount of reinforcing potential exhibited by a given stimulus pattern. Apparently, increasing the complexity, the changing qualities, and the novelty (within limits) of a sensory reinforcer increases its reinforcing potential (pp. 133-136). Increasing the intensity of stimulation up to an optimal level similarly increases its reinforcing potential. Beyond this optimal point, however, reinforcing potential falls as the aversive properties of the stimulus become more prominent (pp. 142-144).

Other variables which have been found to affect the sensory reinforcement process are:

1. The amount of prior contact with the reinforcers, extensive recent prior contact tending to reduce the reinforcing protential. This may be interpreted as resulting from either satiation for the stimulus or as a loss of novelty (pp. 126-127).

2. Although more evidence is needed, deprivation from the reinforcer appears to enhance its reinforcing potential (p. 125f).

3. Rearing conditions appear to affect sensory reinforcement, although the effects found in the various areas of investigation differ (pp. 140-142).

4. Similarly, degree of hunger and thirst appear to be positively related to sensory reinforcing potential, although contradictory results are frequent (pp. 145-148).

Explanations of sensory reinforcement in terms of activity level or secondary reinforcement do not appear to account adequately for the phenomenon. It is clear, however, that these factors may be important contributors to the sensory reinforcement effect in specific instances.

Similarly, an anxiety explanation does not seem able to handle all of the data in this area. Anxiety, however, does appear to be a contributor to the behavior of organisms faced with novel stimulation, in some cases facilitating and in other cases attenuating the sensory reinforcement effect. Clearly, anxiety is one of the reactions aroused by novel stimulation, and its effects must be taken into account before an analysis of sensorily reinforced behavior can be considered adequate.

Keeping the above qualifications in mind, we may conclude that various forms of stimulation may function as reinforcers even though unrelated to the usual organic drive conditions. Complete description of the factors involved in this sensory reinforcement effect and the mechanism underlying it await further empirical and theoretical efforts.

For other analyses of the research in this area approached from several different theoretical points of view, the reader is referred to works by Berlyne (1960), Butler (1958b), Barnett (1958a), Glanzer (1958), and Lana (1960).

REFERENCES[4]

ADLERSTEIN, A., and FEHRER, E. (1955) The effect of food deprivation on exploratory behavior in a complex maze. *J. comp. physiol. Psychol., 48,* 250-253.

ANDRONICO, M. P., and FORGAYS, D. G. (1962) Sensory stimulation and secondary reinforcement. *J. Psychol., 54,* 209-219.

ANTONITIS, J. J., and BARNES, G. W. (1961) Group operant behavior: An extension of individual methodology to a real life situation. *J. genet. Psychol., 98,* 95-111.

ANTONITIS, J. J., and BARON, A. (1961) A test of the hypothesis of an unconditioned operant reserve. *J. comp. physiol. Psychol., 54,* 457-460.

APPEL, J. B., and HURWITZ, H. M. B. (1959) Studies of light-reinforced behavior: IV. Effects of apparatus familiarization. *Psychol. Rep., 5,* 355-356.

BARNES, G. W., and BARON, A. (1961) Stimulus complexity and sensory reinforcement. *J. comp. physiol. Psychol., 54,* 466-469. (a)

[4] This bibliography represents a compilation of articles published in the English language through May of 1963.

BARNES, G. W., and BARON, A. (1961) Effects of sensory reinforcement on extinction behavior. *J. comp. physiol. Psychol., 54*, 461-465. (b)

BARNES, G. W., and KISH, G. B. (1957) Reinforcing properties of the termination of intense auditory stimulation. *J. comp. physiol. Psychol., 50*, 40-43. (a)

BARNES, G. W., and KISH, G. B. (1957) Behavioral effects of the cessation of weak light energy. *Amer. Psychologist, 12*, 411 (abstract). (b)

BARNES, G. W., and KISH, G. B. (1958) On some properties of visual reinforcement. *Amer. Psychologist, 13*, 417 (abstract).

BARNES, G. W., and KISH, G. B. (1961) Reinforcing properties of the onset of auditory stimulation. *J. exp. Psychol., 62*, 164-170.

BARNES, G. W., KISH, G. B., and WOOD, W. O. (1959) The effect of light intensity when onset or termination of illumination is used as reinforcing stimulus. *Psychol. Rec., 9*, 53-60.

BARNETT, S. A. (1956) Behavior components in the feeding of wild and laboratory rats. *Behaviour, IX*, 24-43.

BARNETT, S. A. (1958) Exploratory behavior. *Brit. J. Psychol., 49*, 289-310. (a)

BARNETT, S. A. (1958) Experiments on "neophobia" in wild and laboratory rats. *Brit. J. Psychol., 49*, 195-201. (b)

BARNETT, S. A. (1958) The nature and significance of exploratory behavior. *Proc. Roy. Physical Soc. of Edinburgh, 27*, 41-45. (c)

BARON, A. (1959) Functions of CS and US in fear conditioning. *J. comp. physiol. Psychol., 52*, 591-593.

BARON, A., ANTONITIS, J. J., and BEALE, R. H. (1961) Effects of activity deprivation upon bar pressing. *J. comp. physiol. Psychol., 54*, 291-293.

BARON, A., ANTONITIS, J. J., and CLARK, A. H. (1963) Bar pressing as a function of test environment area. *J. genet. Psychol., 102*, 159-165.

BARON, A., ANTONITIS, J. J., and SCHELL, S. (1962) Effects of early restriction and facilitation of climbing on later climbing behavior of mice. *J. comp. physiol. Psychol., 55*, 808-812.

BARON, A., and KISH, G. B. (1962) Low-intensity auditory and visual stimuli as reinforcers for the mouse. *J. comp. physiol. Psychol., 55*, 1011-1013.

BARRY, H., and SYMMES, D. (1963) Reinforcing effects of illumination change in different phases of the rat's diurnal cycle. *J. comp. physiol. Psychol., 56*, 117-119.

BERLYNE, D. E. (1950) Novelty and curiosity as determinants of exploratory behavior. *Brit. J. Psychol., 41*, 68-80.

BERLYNE, D. E. (1951) Attention to change. *Brit. J. Psychol., 42*, 269-278.

BERLYNE, D. E. (1954) A theory of human curiosity. *Brit. J. Psychol., 45*, 180-191. (a)

BERLYNE, D. E. (1954) An experimental study of human curiosity. *Brit. J. Psychol., 45*, 256-265. (b)

BERLYNE, D. E. (1955) The arousal and satiation of perceptual curiosity in the rat. *J. comp. physiol. Psychol., 48*, 238-246.

BERLYNE, D. E. (1957) Attention to change, conditioned inhibition (sIr) and stimulus satiation. *Brit. J. Psychol., 48*, 138-140. (a)

BERLYNE, D. E. (1957) Conflict and information theory variables as determinants of human perceptual curiosity. *J. exp. Psychol., 53*, 399-404. (b)

BERLYNE, D. E. (1957) Uncertainty and conflict: A point of contact between information-theory and behavior-theory concepts. *Psychol. Rev., 64*, 329-339. (c)

BERLYNE, D. E. (1958) The influence of the albedo and complexity of stimuli on visual fixation in the human infant. *Brit. J. Psychol., 49,* 315-317. (a)

BERLYNE, D. E. (1958) The influence of complexity and novelty in visual figures on orienting responses. *J. exp. Psychol., 55,* 289-296. (b)

BERLYNE, D. E. (1960) *Conflict, arousal, and curiosity.* New York: McGraw-Hill.

BERLYNE, D. E., and SLATER, J. (1957) Perceptual curiosity, exploratory behavior, and maze learning. *J. comp. physiol. Psychol., 50,* 228-232.

BEXTON, W. A., HERON, W., and SCOTT, T. H. (1954) Effects of decreased variation in the sensory environment. *Can. J. Psychol., 8,* 70-76.

BOLLES, R. C., and DeLORGE, J. (1962) Effect of hunger on exploration in a familiar locale. *Psychol. Rep., 10,* 54.

BRANDAUER, C. M. (1953) A confirmation of Webb's data concerning the action of irrelevant drives. *J. exp. Psychol., 45,* 150-152.

BUTLER, R. A. (1953) Discrimination learning by rhesus monkeys to visual exploration motivation. *J. comp. physiol. Psychol., 46,* 95-98.

BUTLER, R. A. (1954) Incentive conditions which influence visual exploration. *J. exp. Psychol., 48,* 19-23.

BUTLER, R. A. (1957) The effect of deprivation of visual incentives on visual exploration motivation in monkeys. *J. comp. physiol. Psychol., 50,* 177-179. (a)

BUTLER, R. A. (1957) Discrimination learning by rhesus monkeys to auditory incentives. *J. comp. physiol. Psychol., 50,* 239-241. (b)

BUTLER, R. A. (1958) The differential effect of visual and auditory incentives on the performance of monkeys. *Amer. J. Psychol., 71,* 591-593. (a)

BUTLER, R. A. (1958) Exploration and related behavior: A new trend in animal research. *J. indiv. Psychol., 14,* 111-120. (b)

BUTLER, R. A. (1961) The responsiveness of rhesus monkeys to motion pictures. *J. genet. Psychol., 98,* 239-245.

BUTLER, R. A., and ALEXANDER, H. M. (1955) Daily patterns of visual exploratory behavior in monkeys. *J. comp. physiol. Psychol., 48,* 247-249.

BUTLER, R. A., and HARLOW, H. F. (1954) Persistence of visual exploration in monkeys. *J. comp. physiol. Psychol., 47,* 258-263.

BUTLER, R. A., and HARLOW, H. F. (1957) Discrimination learning and learning sets to visual exploratory incentives. *J. gen. Psychol., 57,* 257-264.

BUTLER, R. A., and WOOLPY, J. H. (1963) Visual attention in the rhesus monkey. *J. comp. physiol. Psychol., 56,* 324-328.

CAMPBELL, B. A., and SHEFFIELD, F. D. (1953) Relation of random activity to food deprivation. *J. comp. physiol. Psychol., 46,* 320-322.

CARR, R. M., and WILLIAMS, C. D. (1957) Exploratory behavior of three strains of rats. *J. comp. physiol. Psychol., 50,* 621-623.

CHAPMAN, R. M., and LEVY, N. (1957) Hunger drive and reinforcing effect of novel stimuli. *J. comp. physiol. Psychol., 50,* 233-238.

CHARLESWORTH, W. R., and THOMPSON, W. R. (1957) Effect of lack of visual stimulation on exploratory behavior in the adult white rat. *Psychol. Rep., 3,* 509-512.

CLAYTON, F. L. (1958) Light reinforcement as a function of water deprivation. *Psychol. Rep., 4,* 63-66.

CROWDER, W. F. (1961) Weak light reinforcement and flash distribution. *J. Psychol., 51,* 439-442.

CROWDER, W. F., and CROWDER, T. H. (1961) Duration of weak light reinforcement. *Psychol. Rep., 8,* 130.

CROWDER, W. F., MORRIS, J. B., DYER, W. R., and ROBINSON, J. V. (1961) Resistance to extinction and number of weak light reinforcements. *J. Psychol.,* *51,* 361-364.

CROWDER, W. F., WILKES, W. P., and CROWDER, T. H. (1960) Weak light reinforcement with and without control for response facilitation. *J. Psychol.,* *49,* 181-184.

DASHIELL, J. F. (1925) A quantitative demonstration of animal drive. *J. comp. Psychol., 5,* 205-208.

DAVIS, J. D. (1958) The reinforcing effect of weak light onset as a function of amount of food deprivation. *J. comp. physiol. Psychol., 51,* 496-498.

DAVIS, R. T., SETTLAGE, H., and HARLOW, H. F. (1955) Performance of normal and brain-operated monkeys on mechanical puzzles with and without food incentives. *J. genet. Psychol., 77,* 305-311.

DELORGE, J., and BOLLES, R. C. (1961) Effects of food deprivation on exploratory behavior in a novel situation. *Psychol. Rep., 9,* 599-606.

DEMBER, W. N. (1956) Response by the rat to environmental change. *J. comp. physiol. Psychol., 49,* 93-95.

DOYLE, G. A. (1961) Effects of dl-, d-, and l-amphetamine and hunger on exploratory behavior and latent learning in rats. *Amer. Psychol., 16,* 453 (abstract).

FEHRER, ELIZABETH (1956) Effects of hunger and familiarity of locale on exploration. *J. comp. physiol. Psychol., 49,* 549-552.

FORGAYS, D. G., and LEVIN, H. (1958) Learning as a function of change of sensory stimulation in food-deprived and food-satiated animals. *J. comp. physiol. Psychol., 51,* 50-54.

FORGAYS, D. G., and LEVIN, H. (1959) Discrimination and reversal learning as a function of change of sensory stimulation. *J. comp. physiol. Psychol., 52,* 191-194.

FORGAYS, D. G., and LEVIN, H. (1961) Learning as a function of change of sensory stimulation: Distributed vs. massed trials. *J. comp. physiol. Psychol., 54,* 59-62.

Fox, S. S. (1962) Self-maintained sensory input and sensory deprivation in monkeys. *J. comp. physiol. Psychol., 55,* 438-444.

FREY, R. B. (1960) The effects of verbal reinforcers on group operant behavior. Unpublished MA thesis, University of Maine.

FURCHTGOTT, E., WECHKIN, S., and DEES, J. W. (1961) Open field exploration as a function of age. *J. comp. physiol. Psychol., 54,* 386-388.

GIRDNER, J. B. (1953) An experimental analysis of the behavioral effects of a perceptual consequence unrelated to organic drive states. *Amer. Psychologist, 8,* 354-355 (abstract). (a)

GIRDNER, J. B. (1953) An experimental analysis of the behavioral effects of a perceptual consequence unrelated to organic drive states. Unpublished doctoral thesis, Duke University. (b)

GLANZER, M. (1958) Curiosity, exploratory drive and stimulus satiation. *Psychol. Bull., 55,* 302-315.

GLANZER, M. (1961) Changes and interrelations in exploratory behavior. *J. comp. physiol. Psychol., 54,* 433-438.

GLICKMAN, S. E., and JENSEN, G. D. (1961) The effects of hunger and thirst on Y-maze exploration. *J. comp. physiol. Psychol., 54,* 83-85.

GLICKMAN, S. E., SROGES, R., and HOFF, W. (1961) The evolution of response to novel objects. *Amer. Psychologist, 16,* 445 (abstract).

GUTTMAN, N. (1953) Operant conditioning, extinction, and periodic reinforcement in relation to concentration of sucrose used as reinforcing agent. *J. exp. Psychol., 46,* 213-224.

HALL, J. F., Low, LORRAINE, and HANFORD, P. (1960) A comparison of the activity of hungry, thirsty, and satiated rats in the Dashiell maze. *J. comp. physiol. Psychol., 53,* 155-158.

HARLOW, H. F. (1950) Learning and satiation of response in intrinsically motivated complex puzzle performance by monkeys. *J. comp. physiol. Psychol., 43,* 289-294.

HARLOW, H. F. (1960) Of love in infants. *Nat. Hist., 69,* 18-23.

HARLOW, H. F., BLAZEK, N. C., and McCLEARN, G. E. (1956) Manipulatory motivation of infant rhesus monkeys. *J. comp. physiol. Psychol., 49,* 444-448.

HARLOW, H. F., HARLOW, M. K., and MEYER, D. R. (1950) Learning motivated by a manipulation drive. *J. exp. Psychol., 40,* 228-234.

HARLOW, H. F., and McCLEARN, G. E. (1954) Object discrimination by monkeys on the basis of manipulation motives. *J. comp. physiol. Psychol., 47,* 73-76.

HARRINGTON, G. M., and LINDER, W. K. (1962) A positive reinforcing effect of electrical stimulation. *J. comp. physiol. Psychol., 55,* 1014-1015.

HAYES, J. R. (1958) The maintenance of play in young children. *J. comp. physiol. Psychol., 51,* 788-794.

HAYES, K. J. (1960) Exploration and fear. *Psychol. Rep., 6,* 91-93.

HEFFERLINE, R. F. (1950) An experimental study of avoidance. *Genet. Psychol. Monogr., 42,* 231-334.

HENDERSON, R. L. (1957) Stimulus intensity dynamism and secondary reinforcement. *J. comp. physiol. Psychol., 50,* 339-344.

HENDRY, D. P., and RASCHE, R. H. (1961) Analysis of a new nonnutritive positive reinforcer based on thirst. *J. comp. physiol. Psychol., 54,* 477-483.

HESS, E. H. (1956) Natural preferences of chicks and ducklings for objects of different colors. *Psychol. Rep., 2,* 477-483.

HOWARTH, E. (1962) Activity decrement and recovery during repeated day to day exposure to the same environment. *J. comp. physiol. Psychol., 55,* 1102-1104.

HULL, C. L. (1952) *A behavior system: An introduction to behavior theory concerning the individual organism.* New Haven: Yale Univ. Press.

HURWITZ, H. M. B. (1956) Conditioned responses in rats reinforced by light. *Brit. J. anim. Behav., 4,* 31-33.

HURWITZ, H. M. B., and APPEL, J. B. (1959) Light-onset reinforcement as a function of light-dark maintenance schedule for the hooded rat. *J. comp. physiol. Psychol., 52,* 710-712.

HURWITZ, H. M. B., and DE, S. C. (1958) Studies in light-reinforced behavior: II. Effects of food deprivation and stress. *Psychol. Rep., 4,* 71-77.

ISAAC, W. (1962) Evidence for a sensory drive in monkeys. *Psychol. Rep., 11,* 175-181.

JAMES, W. T. (1961) Preliminary observations of play behavior in puppies. *J. genet. Psychol., 98,* 273-277.

KEGAN, J., and BERKUN, M. (1954) The reward value of running activity. *J. comp. physiol. Psychol., 47,* 108.

KELLER, F. S. (1941) Light aversion in the white rat. *Psychol. Rec., 4,* 235-250.

KIMBLE, G. A. (1961) *Hilgard and Marquis' conditioning and learning.* New York: Appleton-Century-Crofts.

KISH, G. B. (1955) Learning when the onset of illumination is used as reinforcing stimulus. *J. comp. physiol. Psychol., 48,* 261-264.

KISH, G. B., and ANTONITIS, J. J. (1956) Unconditioned operant behavior in two homozygous strains of mice. *J. genet. Psychol., 88,* 121-129.

KISH, G. B., and BARON, A. (1962) Satiation of sensory reinforcement. *J. comp. physiol. Psychol., 55,* 1007-1010.

KISH, G. B., and BARNES, G. W. (1961) Reinforcing effects of manipulation in mice. *J. comp. physiol. Psychol., 54,* 713-715.

KLING, J. W., HOROWITZ, L., and DELHAGEN, J. E. (1956) Light as a positive reinforcer for rat responding. *Psychol. Rep., 2,* 337-340.

LANA, R. E. (1960) Manipulation-exploration drives and the drive reduction hypothesis. *J. gen. Psychol., 63,* 3-27.

LEATON, R. N., SYMMES, D., and BARRY, H. (1961) Habituation to the situation as a factor in the reinforcing effect of change in illumination. *Amer. Psychologist, 16,* 414 (abstract).

LEATON, R. N., SYMMES, D., and BARRY, H. (1963) Familiarization with the test apparatus as a factor in the reinforcing effect of change in illumination. *J. Psychol., 55,* 145-151.

LEUBA, C. (1962) Relation of stimulation intensities to learning and development. *Psychol. Rep., 11,* 55-65.

LEVIN, H., and FORGAYS, D. G. (1959) Learning as a function of sensory stimulation of various intensities. *J. comp. physiol. Psychol., 52,* 195-201.

LEVIN, H., and FORGAYS, D. G. (1960) Sensory change as immediate and delayed reinforcement for maze learning. *J. comp. physiol. Psychol., 53,* 194-196.

LOCKARD, R. B. (1961) Self-regulation of luminance by albino rats. *Psychol. Rep., 9,* 345-346.

LOCKARD, R. B. (1962) Self-regulated light exposure of albino rats. *J. comp. physiol. Psychol., 55,* 641-645. (a)

LOCKARD, R. B. (1962) Some effects of maintenance luminance and strain differences upon self-exposure to light by rats. *J. comp. physiol. Psychol., 55,* 1118-1123. (b)

MARX, M. H., HENDERSON, R. L., and ROBERTS, C. L. (1955) Positive reinforcement of the bar pressing response by a light stimulus following dark operant pretests with no aftereffect. *J. comp. physiol. Psychol., 48,* 73-76.

MASON, W. A., and HARLOW, H. F. (1959) Initial responses of infant rhesus monkeys to solid foods. *Psychol. Rep., 5,* 193-199.

MASON, W. A., HARLOW, H. F., and RUEPING, R. R. (1959) The development of manipulatory responsiveness in infant rhesus monkeys. *J. comp. physiol. Psychol., 52,* 555-558.

McCLEARN, G. E. (1959) Genetics of mouse behavior in novel situations. *J. comp. physiol. Psychol., 52,* 62-67.

McCLEARN, G. E. (1961) Genotype and mouse activity. *J. comp. physiol. Psychol., 54,* 647-676.

MEEHL, P. E. (1950) On the circularity of the law of effect. *Psychol. Bull., 47,* 52-75.

MENZEL, E. W. (1962) The effects of stimulus size and proximity upon avoidance of complex objects in rhesus monkeys. *J. comp. physiol. Psychol., 55,* 1044-1046.

MENZEL, E. W., DAVENPORT, R. K., and ROGERS, C. M. (1961) Some aspects of the behavior toward novelty in young chimpanzees. *J. comp. physiol. Psychol., 54,* 16-19.

MENZEL, E. W., DAVENPORT, R. K., and ROGERS, C. M. (1963) The effects of environmental restriction upon the chimpanzee's responsiveness to objects. *J. comp. physiol. Psychol.*, *56*, 78-85. (a)

MENZEL, E. W., DAVENPORT, R. K., and ROGERS, C. M. (1963) Effects of environmental restriction upon the chimpanzee's responsiveness in novel situations. *J. comp. physiol. Psychol.*, *56*, 329-334. (b)

MEYERS, A. K., and MILLER, N. E. (1954) Failure to find a learned drive based on hunger; evidence for learning motivated by exploration. *J. comp. physiol. Psychol.*, *47*, 428-436.

MEYERS, W. J. (1962) Critical period for the facilitation of exploratory behavior by infantile experience. *J. comp. physiol. Psychol.*, *55*, 1099-1101.

MILES, R. C. (1958) Learning in kittens with manipulatory, exploratory, and food incentives. *J. comp. physiol. Psychol.*, *51*, 39-42.

MILES, R. C. (1962) Effect of food deprivation on manipulatory reactions in cats. *J. comp. physiol. Psychol.*, *55*, 358-362.

MONTGOMERY, K. C. (1951) Relation between exploratory behavior and spontaneous alternation in the white rat. *J. comp. physiol. Psychol.*, *44*, 582-589.

MONTGOMERY, K. C. (1952) A test of two explanations of spontaneous alternation. *J. comp. physiol. Psychol.*, *45*, 287-293. (a)

MONTGOMERY, K. C. (1952) Exploratory behavior and its relation to spontaneous alternation in a series of maze exposures. *J. comp. physiol. Psychol.*, *45*, 50-57. (b)

MONTGOMERY, K. C. (1953) Effect of hunger and thirst upon exploratory behavior. *J. comp. physiol. Psychol.*, *46*, 315-319. (a)

MONTGOMERY, K. C. (1953) Effect of activity deprivation upon exploratory behavior. *J. comp. physiol. Psychol.*, *46*, 438-441. (b)

MONTGOMERY, K. C. (1953) Exploratory behavior as a function of similarity of stimulus situations. *J. comp. physiol. Psychol.*, *46*, 129-133. (c)

MONTGOMERY, K. C. (1954) The role of exploratory drive in learning. *J. comp. physiol. Psychol.*, *47*, 60-64.

MONTGOMERY, K. C. (1955) The relation between fear induced by novel stimulation and exploratory behavior. *J. comp. physiol. Psychol.*, *48*, 254-260.

MONTGOMERY, K. C., and MONKMAN, J. A. (1955) Relation between fear and exploratory behavior. *J. comp. physiol. Psychol.*, *48*, 132-136.

MONTGOMERY, K. C., and SEGALL, M. (1955) Discrimination learning based upon the exploratory drive. *J. comp. physiol. Psychol.*, *48*, 225-228.

MONTGOMERY, K. C., and ZIMBARDO, P. G. (1957) The effect of sensory and behavioral deprivation upon exploratory behavior in the rat. *Percept. mot. Skills*, *7*, 223-229.

MOON, L. E., and LODAHL, T. M. (1956) The reinforcing effect of changes in illumination on lever-pressing in the monkey. *Amer. J. Psychol.*, *69*, 288-290.

MORRIS, J. B., CROWDER, W. F., and CROWDER, T. H. (1961) Stimulus variation and weak-light reinforcement. *Psychol. Rep.*, *8*, 290.

MOWRER, O. H. (1960) *Learning theory and behavior.* New York: Wiley.

MURRAY, E. J. (1953) The effects of hunger and type of manipulandum on spontaneous instrumental responding. *J. comp. physiol. Psychol.*, *46*, 182-183.

NASH, F. A., and CROWDER, W. F. A further study of weak-light reinforcement and response facilitation. *J. Psychol.*, *50*, 287-290.

NISSEN, H. W. (1930) A study of exploratory behavior in the white rat by means of the obstruction method. *J. genet. Psychol., 37,* 361-376.

PFAFFMAN, C. (1958) *Flavor research and food acceptance.* New York: Reinhold.

PFAFFMAN, C. (1960) The pleasures of sensation. *Psychol. Rev., 67,* 253-268.

PILGRIM, F. J. (1948) A simple electronic relay for counting, timing, or automatic control. *J. Psychol., 26,* 537-540.

PREMACK, D., COLLIER, G., and ROBERTS, C. L. (1957) Frequency of light-contingent bar pressing as a function of the amount of deprivation for light. *Amer. Psychol., 12,* 411 (abstract).

RABEDEAU, R., and MILES, R. C. (1959) Response decrement in visual exploratory behavior. *J. comp. physiol. Psychol., 52,* 364-367.

RICHARDS, W. J., and LESLIE, G. R. (1962) Food and water deprivation as influences on exploration. *J. comp. physiol. Psychol., 55,* 834-837.

ROBERTS, C. L. (1962) Stimulus and stimulus-change factors governing the free operant rate. *J. comp. physiol. Psychol., 55,* 375-380.

ROBERTS, C. L., LEBOW, K. E., and YODER, R. M. (1961) Secondary reinforcement based on stimulus change primary reinforcement. *J. exp. Psychol., 61,* 339-344.

ROBERTS, C. L., MARX, M. H., and COLLIER, G. (1958) Light onset and light offset as reinforcers for the albino rat. *J. comp. physiol. Psychol., 51,* 575-579.

ROBINSON, J. S. (1959) Light onset and termination as reinforcers for rats living under normal light conditions. *Psychol. Rep., 5,* 793-796.

SCHOENFELD, W. N., ANTONITIS, J. J., and BERSH, P. J. (1950) Unconditioned response rate of the white rat in a bar pressing apparatus. *J. comp. physiol. Psychol., 43,* 41-48.

SEGAL, E. F. (1959) The stability of operant level and its relation to deprivation. *J. comp. physiol. Psychol., 52,* 713-716. (a)

SEGAL, E. F. (1959) Confirmation of a positive relation between deprivation and number of responses emitted for light reinforcement. *J. exp. Anal. Behav., 2,* 165-169. (b)

SHARPE, P. B. (1951) The effect of delayed introduction of a novel stimulus on rate of responding in children. Unpublished MA thesis, University of Maine.

SHEFFIELD, F. D., and CAMPBELL, B. A. (1954) The role of experience in the "spontaneous" activity of hungry rats. *J. comp. physiol. Psychol., 47,* 97-100.

SHEFFIELD, F. D., and ROBY, T. B. (1950) Reward value of a non-nutritive sweet taste. *J. comp. physiol. Psychol., 43,* 471-481.

SHEFFIELD, F. D., ROBY, T. B., and CAMPBELL, B. A. (1954) Drive reduction vs. consummatory behavior as determinants of reinforcement. *J. comp. physiol. Psychol., 48,* 349-354.

SHEFFIELD, F. D., WULFF, J. J., and BACKER, R. (1951) Reward value of copulation without sex drive reduction. *J. comp. physiol. Psychol., 44,* 3-8.

SIMMEL, E. C. (1962) Social facilitation of exploratory behavior in rats. *J. comp. physiol. Psychol., 55,* 831-833.

SKINNER, B. F. (1938) *The behavior of organisms.* New York: Appleton-Century-Crofts.

STACKHOUSE, S. P., BURNS, N. M., and WOHLFORD, J. (1960) Note on exploratory behavior. *Psychol. Rep., 6,* 455-457.

STEWART, J. (1960) Reinforcing effects of light as a function of intensity and reinforcement schedule. *J. comp. physiol. Psychol., 53,* 187-193.

STEWART, J., and HURWITZ, H. M. B. (1958) Studies in light-reinforced behavior: III. The effect of continuous, zero, and fixed-ratio reinforcement. *Quart. J. exp. Psychol., 10,* 56-61.

SYMMES, D., and LEATON, R. N. (1962) Failure to observe reinforcing properties of sound onset in rats. *Psychol. Rep., 10,* 458.

THIESSEN, D. D. (1961) Mouse exploration and body weight. *Psychol. Rec., 11,* 299-304.

THOMAS, D. G., APPEL, J. B., and HURWITZ, H. M. B. (1958) Studies in light-reinforced behavior. V: Effects of lever size, shift in lever size, and light position. *Psychol. Rep., 4,* 411-413.

THOMPSON, R. H. (1955) The reward value for the rat of changes in illumination. Unpublished MA thesis, University of Aberdeen, Scotland.

THOMPSON, W. R. (1953) Exploratory behavior as a function of hunger in bright and dull rats. *J. comp. physiol. Psychol., 46,* 323-326.

THOMPSON, W. R., and HERON, W. (1954) The effect of early restriction on activity in dogs. *J. comp. physiol. Psychol., 47,* 77-82.

THOMPSON, W. R., and SOLOMON, L. M. (1954) Spontaneous pattern discrimination in the rat. *J. comp. physiol. Psychol., 47,* 104-107.

WALK, R. D. (1960) Response of dark and light reared rats to stimulus change. *J. comp. physiol. Psychol., 53,* 609-611.

WALK, R. D., OWENS, J. W. M., and DAVIDSON, B. J. (1961) Influence of reserpine on avoidance conditioning, exploratory behavior, and discrimination learning. *Psychol. Rep., 8,* 251-258.

WECHKIN, S., FURCHTGOTT, E., and DEES, J. W. (1960) Locomotion and exploration in rats as a function of age. *Amer. Psychologist, 15,* 408 (abstract).

WELKER, W. I. (1956) Variability of play and exploration in chimpanzees. *J. comp. physiol. Psychol., 49,* 181-185. (a)

WELKER, W. I. (1956) Effects of age and experience on play and exploration of young chimpanzees. *J. comp. physiol. Psychol., 49,* 223-226. (b)

WELKER, W. I. (1956) Some determinants of play and exploration in chimpanzees. *J. comp. physiol. Psychol., 49,* 84-89. (c)

WELKER, W. I. (1957) Free vs. forced exploration of a novel situation by rats. *Psychol. Rep., 3,* 95-108.

WELKER, W. I. (1959) Escape, exploratory, and food seeking responses of rats in a novel situation. *J. comp. physiol. Psychol., 52,* 106-111. (a)

WELKER, W. I. (1959) Genesis of exploratory and play behavior in infant raccoons. *Psychol. Rep., 5,* 764. (b)

WELKER, W. I., and KING, W. A. (1962) Effects of stimulus novelty on gnawing and eating by rats. *J. comp. physiol. Psychol., 55,* 838-842.

WENZEL, B. (1959) Tactile stimulation as reinforcement for cats and its relation to early feeding experience. *Psychol. Rep., 5,* 297-300.

WERBOFF, J., and HAVLENA, J. (1962) Effects of ageing on open field behavior. *Psychol. Rep., 10,* 395-398.

WHALEN, R. E. (1961) Effects of mounting without intromission and intromission without ejaculation on sexual behavior and maze learning. *J. comp. physiol. Psychol., 54,* 409-415.

WILLIAMS, C. D., and KUCHTA, J. C. (1957) Exploratory behavior in two mazes with dissimilar alternatives. *J. comp. physiol. Psychol., 50,* 509-513.

WILLIAMS, C. D., ZEROF, S. A., and CARR, R. M. (1962) Exploratory behavior of the crosses of three strains of rats. *J. comp. physiol. Psychol., 55*, 121-122.

WILSON, J. J. (1962) Photic reinforcement as a function of optimal level of stimulation. *Psychol. Rec., 12*, 17-23.

WOODS, P. J. (1959) The effects of free and restricted environment experience on problem solving behavior in the rat. *J. comp. physiol. Psychol., 52*, 399-402.

WOODS, P. J., FISKE, A. S., and RUCKELSHAUS, S. E. (1961) The effects of drives conflicting with exploration on the problem-solving behavior of rats reared in free and restricted environments. *J. comp. physiol. Psychol., 54*, 167-169.

ZIMBARDO, P. G., and MILLER, N. E. (1958) Facilitation of exploration by hunger in rats. *J. comp. physiol. Psychol., 51*, 43-46.

ZIMBARDO, P. G., and MONTGOMERY, K. C. (1957) The relative strengths of consummatory responses in hunger, thirst, and exploratory drive. *J. comp. physiol. Psychol., 50*, 504-508. (a)

ZIMBARDO, P. G., and MONTGOMERY, K. C. (1957) Effects of "free environment" rearing upon exploratory behavior. *Psychol. Rep., 3*, 589-594. (b)

5

Chaining and
Conditioned Reinforcement[1]

R. T. Kelleher

INTRODUCTION

Psychologists have long been interested in studying the development and maintenance of long and orderly sequences of behavior. Human behavior provides many examples of such sequences. Even relatively simple motor skills, such as throwing a ball, comprise complex response sequences. More advanced skills, such as playing the piano, comprise intricate sequences of stimuli and finely graded responses occurring at almost incredible speeds. This area of study has traditionally been called *chaining,* and the sequences themselves are called *chains.*

The concept of chaining was apparently introduced by physiologists studying reflexes that followed one another in rapid succession (for example, Exner, 1894; Loeb, 1900; Sherrington, 1906). A typical reflex chain has been described by Sherrington:

> The dart reflex of the frog's tongue provoked by the seen fly provides, if successful, the stimulus (contact with the mucosa of the mouth) which provokes closure of the mouth, and this probably insures the stimulus for the ensuing deglutition, and so on (1906, p. 182).

The essential characteristic of this reflex chain is that each of the successive stimuli elicits a response. If the sequence is interrupted at any point, it cannot subsequently be resumed.

As psychologists became interested in conditioned reflexes, they extended the concept of chaining to sequences of learned behavior. These

[1] Preparation of this chapter was supported in part by research Grants MH-2094, MY-2645, MH-07658-01 and by a research career development award K3-MH-22,589-01 from the National Institute of Mental Health of the National Institutes of Health, U. S. Public Health Service. I am indebted to P. B. Dews and W. H. Morse for their helpful comments during the preparation of this chapter.

sequences were described as chains of Pavlovian conditioned reflexes in which the conditioned response of one reflex produced the conditioned stimulus for the next reflex (for example, Holt, 1931; Smith & Guthrie, 1921). The examples of chains presented by these psychologists include, however, some extreme extensions of principles of Pavlovian conditioning. They tried to analyze human skills such as piano playing, typing, writing, and dancing as chains of Pavlovian conditioned reflexes. To account for skill sequences in which no differential exteroceptive stimulus changes were obvious, Smith and Guthrie assumed that the successive conditioned stimuli in a chain could be proprioceptive ("movement-produced stimuli").

> Tying a cravat or lacing a shoe is at first dependent upon visual stimuli, but later each component movement becomes almost wholly conditioned by the kinaesthetic and touch stimuli occasioned by the preceding movement (1921, p. 102).

It is now apparent that these early attempts to apply the concept of chained Pavlovian reflexes to learned behavior were overambitious. As Lashley (1951) has noted, when a skilled pianist executes a cadenza, the complete sequence of responses occurs with such speed that sensory control by tactile or kinesthetic stimuli can be ruled out because neural transmission is not fast enough. Also, it is difficult, if not impossible, to specify the chain of unconditioned reflexes upon which the chain of conditioned reflexes is established. Despite the difficulties involved in assuming that complex behavior is comprised of chains of Pavlovian conditioned reflexes, this notion has remained popular, and hypothetical response-produced stimuli have been incorporated into many theoretical accounts of behavior sequences (Hull, 1943; Keller & Schoenfeld, 1950; Miller & Dollard, 1941; Spence, 1956).

The concept of chaining was markedly modified by Skinner (1938). Skinner's laws of behavior, which were modeled on Sherrington's laws of reflexes, included the following law of chaining: "The response of one reflex may constitute or produce the eliciting or discriminative stimulus of another" (Skinner, 1938, p. 32). The distinction between eliciting and discriminative stimuli reflects Skinner's distinction between respondent (Pavlovian) conditioning and operant conditioning. An *eliciting stimulus* is consistently followed by a correlated response (Skinner, 1938); for example, "food-in-the-mouth" is an eliciting stimulus for salivation. In respondent conditioning, a stimulus that is temporally paired with an eliciting stimulus will also elicit the response; for example, a tone that has been paired with "food-in-the-mouth" will elicit salivation. The tone is called a *conditioned stimulus*. If emitted responses are reinforced only when a light is present, responding will occur only when the light is present. The light is called a *discriminative stimulus;* that is, it is a stimulus in the presence of which an operant response is reinforced. Skinner (1938, p. 242) suggested

! N.B. !

that either a conditioned stimulus or a discriminative stimulus could be a conditioned reinforcing stimulus. Thus, the successive stimuli in a chain could be conditioned stimuli or discriminative stimuli and it would be the conditioned reinforcing function of these stimuli that enables them to develop and maintain a chain.

Before proceeding to experimental analyses of chaining and conditioned reinforcement, it is necessary to consider the concept of reinforcement in more detail. A positive reinforcing stimulus (*reinforcer*) increases the probability of occurrence of that class of responses that precedes its presentation; the presentation of a positive reinforcing stimulus is positive reinforcement (see Chapter 3). A *primary reinforcer* is a stimulus whose reinforcing properties do not depend upon a history of conditioning; it will be a reinforcer for most members of a given species. Food and water, for example, are primary reinforcers. A *conditioned reinforcer* is a stimulus whose reinforcing properties are established by conditioning; it will be a reinforcer for only those members of a species who have been exposed to a specific conditioning procedure.[2] A more detailed consideration of the distinction between primary and conditioned reinforcers has been presented by Kelleher and Gollub (1962).

In the present chapter, a discriminative stimulus (S^D) is one that is correlated with a schedule in which either primary reinforcement or conditioned reinforcement is contingent upon the occurrence of an operant response. A stimulus in the presence of which reinforcement never occurs will be called an S^Δ. It is important to note that while the present definitions of S^D and S^Δ are similar to those of Skinner (1938), Keller and Schoenfeld (1950), and Ferster and Skinner (1957), they do not include all schedules with which a stimulus might be correlated. At the present time, there is no convenient term for a stimulus that is correlated with a schedule in which reinforcement occurs independently of responses, or with a schedule in which reinforcement is contingent upon not responding (see pp. 187-189).

Any analysis of chaining and conditioned reinforcement is necessarily an analysis of the functions of stimuli in temporal sequences of stimuli and responses. The following section of this chapter will consider the possible role of hypothetical stimuli in experiments in which only responses are observed. This section will evaluate the usefulness of the assumption that unobserved stimuli are controlling response sequences. The third section will analyze the role of stimuli as conditioned reinforcers which can either prolong responding or generate responding during experimental extinction. This section will

----

[2] Kelleher and Gollub (1962, p. 545) note that, "The popular use of the term secondary reinforcement is unfortunate because it does not encourage an analysis of the processes involved in developing a stimulus as a reinforcer. The use of the term conditioned reinforcement emphasizes the conditioning process, and makes it unnecessary to use awkward and confusing terms such as tertiary and quaternary reinforcement."

discuss hypotheses offered as alternatives to the concept of conditioned reinforcement as well as hypotheses concerning the necessary and sufficient conditions for establishing a stimulus as a conditioned reinforcer.

The last section will present a detailed analysis of the functions of stimuli in procedures in which primary reinforcement is contingent upon the completion of two or more successive schedules. By using such sequences of schedules, it is possible to hold constant the contingencies of primary reinforcement while varying the ways in which stimuli are presented. The results to be discussed show that seemingly trivial variations in presentation of stimuli can produce dramatic changes in behavior. By magnifying the functions of stimuli in sequences of schedules, these new techniques provide a powerful tool for advancing the understanding of chaining and conditioned reinforcement.

STIMULUS FUNCTIONS IN RESPONSE SEQUENCES

A sequence of responses (or response sequence) is a pattern of changes in response frequency or response topography that regularly recurs in the absence of correlated changes in exteroceptive stimulus conditions. As noted above, many theorists have tried to account for observed characteristics of response sequences by assuming that such sequences are actually response chains. A chain of responses (or response chain) is a response sequence in which each response either functions as a discriminative (or eliciting) stimulus or produces a discriminative (or eliciting) stimulus controlling the response that follows. When it is assumed that a response sequence is a response chain, the stimuli in the chain are hypothetical. Hypothetical response-produced stimuli have enabled theorists to provide plausible accounts of many characteristics of response sequences, but there is no *a priori* reason for assuming that response sequences are response chains. It is important to determine whether the properties imputed to the hypothetical stimuli are carefully specified or whether they are so vague that they could account for any finding. The purpose of the present section is to analyze recent studies of response sequences and to determine whether the results are consistent with the notion that response sequences are response chains.

Effects of Interrupting Response Sequences on
Fixed Interval Schedules of Reinforcement

Numerous investigations have shown that fixed interval (FI) schedules of positive reinforcement generate characteristic sequences of responses.[3] Performance on the FI schedule is characterized by an initial pause fol-

[3] Notations of all basic schedules will be in capitals. The numbers used in notations for time-controlled schedules indicate minutes unless otherwise specified.

lowed by positively accelerated responding. This pattern of responding is commonly called an *FI scallop*. If the sequence of responses constituting an FI scallop is a chain of responses, interrupting the sequence should disrupt the moment-to-moment stimulus control by response-produced stimuli, and should therefore disrupt the pattern of positively accelerated responding.

Ferster and Skinner (1957, p. 213ff.) studied the effects of interpolating 30-sec. S$^\Delta$ periods on the performances of pigeons on FI 1 schedules. During S$^\Delta$ periods, the experimental chamber was completely darkened, and the pigeons did not respond. In one experiment the 30-sec. S$^\Delta$ period was interpolated in the middle of every tenth FI 1; that is, the minimum interval between reinforcements was increased to 90 sec., but S$^\Delta$ was present from the thirtieth to the sixtieth second. In another experiment, the S$^\Delta$ period was interpolated at 45 sec. after the start of FI 1. Both experiments showed that interrupting and prolonging the FI by presenting 30-sec. S$^\Delta$ periods did not disrupt the positively accelerated response patterns that were characteristic of the FI 1 schedule. It was as though the S$^\Delta$ periods were periods of "dead time" that did not influence FI performances.

A similar study by Ferster and Skinner (1957, pp. 638-639) provides additional evidence that FI scallops can survive prolonged interruptions even under conditions in which the scallop could be expected to be particularly susceptible to disruption. In this case, pigeons were studied on a multiple FR 125 primed FI 10 schedule of reinforcement. That is, the response key was transilluminated by a steady green light throughout each FR 125 component and during the last 8 min. of each FI 10 component. During the first 2 min. of each FI 10 component, the green light flashed on and off. Performance on FI 10 was characterized by a prolonged period of low rates of responding followed by a gradual increase to an intermediate rate. As in their study of simple FI schedules, Ferster and Skinner investigated the effects of interrupting and prolonging occasional FI 10 components by an S$^\Delta$ period.

In one experiment, 1-min. S$^\Delta$ periods were interpolated near the middle of an occasional interval. The first two S$^\Delta$ periods produced some disruption; however, subsequent S$^\Delta$ periods had "remarkably little effect." In subsequent experiments the S$^\Delta$ period was increased to 5 min. Figure 1 shows that interrupting occasional FI 10 components by a 5-min. S$^\Delta$ period did not disrupt response sequences; for example, compare the FI component that was interrupted at *c* with the one just above it in the figure. Ferster and Skinner (1957, p. 639) conclude, "Whatever is responsible for interval curvature at this point survives a 5-min. period of TO."

Dews (1962) has investigated the effects of repeated interruptions of the performance of pigeons on FI 500-sec. schedules of reinforcement. Initially, responding was established on an FI 500-sec. schedule; the response key was transilluminated, but the house light was not on. Then, the

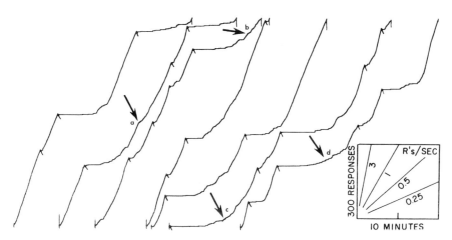

Figure 1. Cumulative response records showing the effects of interpolated 5-min. S$^\Delta$ periods on performance on a mult FR 125 primed FI 10 schedule of reinforcement. Record segments, each including about 900 responses, have been displaced along the abscissa in order to show several hours of performance in a single figure. The small pips on the records indicate reinforcement. The FI components can be distinguished by the time between reinforcements. The arrows at a, b, c, and d indicate the points at which the 5-min. S$^\Delta$ periods were interpolated; the record did not run during S$^\Delta$ periods (from Ferster & Skinner, 1957).

house light was introduced during alternate 50-sec. periods throughout the interval, including the tenth period. The response key was transilluminated throughout each interval; however, reinforcement occurred in the presence of the house light (S^D) but not in its absence (S$^\Delta$). Under this procedure, S$^\Delta$ periods repeatedly interrupted each FI, but did not prolong the minimum interval between reinforcements. Figure 2 compares the patterns of responding in each phase of the experiment. Responding progressively increased throughout the periods in which the house light was on despite the repeated interruptions. Although response rates were relatively low during S$^\Delta$ periods, they tended to increase throughout each FI. Dews (1962, p. 372) concludes, "The general pattern of FI responding is not disrupted by the interposition of repeated S$^\Delta$ periods during the interval. Therefore chaining of responses from moment to moment consecutively through the interval is not necessary for maintenance of the overall scalloped pattern characteristic of FI responding."

To summarize, the chaining concept involves the assumption that each response in a sequence of operant responses either functions as or produces the discriminative stimulus for the response that follows. It is often assumed that the patterns of responding that characterize performance on FI sched-

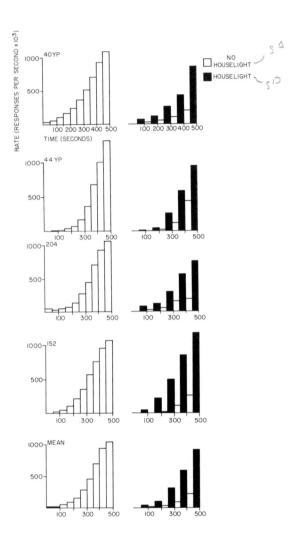

Figure 2. Comparisons of mean rates of responding in successive segments of FI 500-sec. (bar graphs on the left) with rates in comparable segments of FI 500-sec. in which S^Δ periods (no house light) are repeatedly presented (bar graphs on the right). The first four pairs of graphs show comparisons for individual birds; the bottom pairs show comparisons of averaged results for the four birds (from Dews, 1962).

ules of reinforcement are response chains. If this chaining analysis were correct, interrupting the sequence of responding on an FI schedule should interrupt the moment-to-moment control by the stimuli in a response chain and consequently should disrupt the response pattern. Several experiments have shown, however, that various procedures for interrupting FI schedules by interpolating S^Δ periods did not disrupt FI response patterns. These results indicate that response chaining is not necessary for positively accelerated responding on FI, and they suggest that other interpretations of this response pattern may be more useful; for example, Dews (1962) suggests that the FI pattern is maintained by differences in the delay between responses and reinforcement in successive parts of the FI (see also Chapter 3).

Response Sequences in Mixed Schedules of Reinforcement

Mixed schedules of reinforcement provide excellent techniques for the analysis of response sequences that are terminated in the absence of any differential exteroceptive stimulus changes. Under a mixed schedule, two different schedules alternate in an irregular fashion; however, the same discriminative stimulus is correlated with both schedules. Response sequences are most apparent in mixed schedules in which one component schedule has a high frequency of reinforcement while the other has a relatively low frequency of reinforcement.

Ferster and Skinner (1957, Chapter 11) have described a variety of mixed schedules. For example, they studied the performance of pigeons on a mixed schedule in which FR 50 irregularly alternated with 60-min. periods of extinction (mix FR 50 ext 60). A 6-min. S^Δ period followed the completion of each component. Record A of Figure 3 shows representative response patterns in mix FR 50 ext 60. Consistently high response rates of about three responses per second occurred at the start of each component. When FR 50 was in effect, these sequences of rapid responding terminated with reinforcement, as shown at the left of most record segments in Figure 3. When extinction was in effect, each sequence of rapid responding terminated abruptly after 70 to 140 responses. The number of responses comprising such a sequence will be called the sequence length. As shown in Figure 3 A, several discrete sequences ranging in length from about 50 to 275 responses recurred throughout ext 60. Figure 3 B shows later performance with ext 50. After continued training, response sequences were usually confined to the start of each extinction period.

What controls the termination of response sequences in the absence of differential exteroceptive stimulus changes? The response chaining interpretation suggests that sequence length is controlled by response-produced stimuli. Under a mix FR ext schedule, for example, it is assumed that response-produced stimulus conditions change as a function of the number

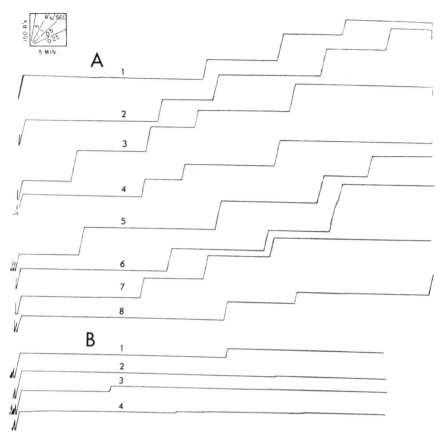

Figure 3. Performance on mixed FR 50 extinction. Occasional FR 50 components are shown at the start of each record. The recording pen resets to the bottom of the record at reinforcement, and the recorder did not run during S^Δ periods. Most of each record segment comprises a complete extinction period. Record A shows the second session with 60-min. extinction periods following training with 30-min. extinction periods. Record B shows well-developed performances with 50-min. extinction periods (from Ferster & Skinner, 1957).

of responses emitted in a sequence. The response-produced stimulus conditions assumed to be present when about 50 responses have been emitted are frequently associated with primary reinforcement; however, the response-produced stimulus conditions assumed to be present when more than 50 responses have been emitted are never associated with primary reinforcement. When more than 50 responses have been emitted in extinction components, it is assumed that response-produced stimulus conditions are discriminably different from those present when about 50 responses have been emitted; therefore, the response sequence is terminated.

Several experiments with the pigeon indicate that the lengths of response sequences in mixed schedules are directly related to the response requirement on the component schedule with a relatively high frequency of reinforcement. For example, response sequences in extinction components under a mix FR 60 ext schedule are longer than response sequences under a mix FR 20 ext schedule (see Ferster & Skinner, 1957). Mechner (1958a; 1958b) studied the performance of the white rat under a general procedure that is similar both to mixed schedules and to the double alternation procedures to be described presently. With Mechner's procedure, as with mixed schedules, two different schedules of primary reinforcement alternate irregularly in the presence of a single exteroceptive discriminative stimulus. Under Schedule A, the nth response on lever A produces primary reinforcement; that is, a simple FR schedule is in effect. Under Schedule B, the first response on lever B following a minimum of n responses on lever A produces primary reinforcement. If a response on lever B occurs before the completion of n responses on lever A, the sequence resets, and a minimum of n responses are still required on lever A. Schedule B is similar to the double alternation procedure in that a response on lever A is sometimes the occasion on which another lever A response will be reinforced and sometimes the occasion on which a lever B response will be reinforced. In this case the number of responses actually occurring on lever A before a response on lever B will be called the *sequence length*. The sequence length can be smaller than n, but reinforcement will occur only when the sequence length is equal to or larger than n.

One experiment by Mechner (1958a), using values of n ranging from 4 to 16 responses, showed that the median sequence length was directly related to the value of n. For example, when four responses were required on lever A ($n = 4$), the median sequence lengths were 5 to 6 for different animals; when n was 16, the median sequence lengths were 19 to 26. The effects of increasing n in Mechner's study were similar to the effects of increasing the FR response requirement on mix FR ext schedules. Interpreting this sequence as a response chain, Mechner suggests that the responses of the sequence are discriminable because even the responses of a single class (pressing lever A) undergo systematic changes in response topography. For example:

> One rat pressed lever A with its right paw while describing a semicircle on the wall with its left paw. Upon reaching the end of this semicircle, it would switch. This pattern was repeated run after run (Mechner, 1958a, p. 118).

There is, however, no evidence to indicate the frequency with which such systematic changes in response topography occur in different animals. Also, as we shall see, several investigators have noted the reliability of response sequences that are completed with extreme rapidity and without observable indications that systematic shifts in response topography were occurring.

Another variable which affects sequence length is the relative frequency of occurrence of the two components in a mixed schedule. Ferster and Skinner (1957) studied the performance of pigeons on a mix FR 60 FR 360 schedule of reinforcement; that is, a response was reinforced on either FR 60 or FR 360. When 67 percent of the reinforcements were programmed on the FR 60 component, a characteristic high rate of responding occurred at the start of each component. If FR 60 was in effect, this high rate terminated in reinforcement; if FR 360 was in effect, the high rate of responding was terminated by a pause and then a resumption of the high rate of responding until reinforcement. The length of the response sequence preceding the pause ranged from about 75 to 150 responses. When 80 percent of the reinforcements were programmed on FR 60, the birds seldom paused at all when FR 360 was in effect. The sequence length was markedly increased by increasing the proportion of FR 60 components.

Using the procedure described previously, Mechner (1958a) studied the performance of rats as a function of the relative frequency of reinforcement on lever A. In this study, n was held constant at 8, while the relative frequency with which Schedule A (FR n on lever A) occurred was varied from 0 to 0.75. For example, when no reinforcements were programmed on lever A, median sequence lengths ranged from about 9 to 11 responses; when 75 percent of the reinforcements were programmed on lever A, sequence lengths ranged from about 12 to 14 responses. The greater the proportion of reinforcements on lever A the longer the sequence length. This result is consistent with those of Ferster and Skinner with mix FR 60 FR 360.

Mechner interpreted his results in terms of two discriminations. The first discrimination is exemplified by the situation in which the animal is reinforced only on lever B. In this case, it is assumed, "as the animal continues responding on lever A, the response-produced stimulus situation becomes increasingly favorable, that is, an even stronger S^D, for switching to lever B" (Mechner, 1958a, p. 117). The second discrimination is assumed to arise when responses on lever A are sometimes directly reinforced. In this case, it is assumed that the subject's having emitted about n responses on lever A acts as an S^D for further responding on lever A.

As an alternative interpretation, one could assume that when a higher proportion of reinforcements occur on lever A (or FR 60), the animal no longer attends to response-produced stimuli because there are relatively few occasions on which it is necessary to terminate the response sequence. On the other hand, if the results had shown that increasing the proportion of reinforcements on lever A (or FR 60) *decreased* sequence lengths, it would also be easy to account for this result in terms of response-produced stimuli. The difficulty with the application of the chaining concept to these response sequences is that one can account for almost any finding. It is only necessary to assume that a hypothetical response-produced stimulus is acting as a discriminative stimulus for the response pattern that is actually obtained.

Response Sequences Terminated by a Response of Different Topography

The procedures considered in this section attempt to develop and maintain a particular response sequence by arranging that reinforcement will occur only when a specified sequence of responses of one topography is terminated by a response (or responses) of another topography. This is a traditional experimental approach to the analysis of response sequences that is exemplified in the literature concerned with the double alternation problem.

The double alternation problem, which was introduced by Hunter (1920), requires that two responses of one topography be followed by two responses of a second topography before primary reinforcement occurs. In a maze, for example, reinforcement would occur when two right turns were followed by two left turns. Hunter deemed it unlikely that proprioceptive or other stimuli arising from a right turn could on one occasion control another right turn and on a subsequent occasion control a left turn. Hunter believed that double alternation behavior in animals was analogous to counting behavior in humans.

Schlosberg and Katz (1943) have presented an interesting account of double alternation lever pressing in the white rat. The apparatus contained a single lever that could be pressed to the right or left. Primary reinforcement occurred whenever the rat pressed the lever twice to the right and then twice to the left (RRLL). The sequence was reinforced even when it included extra responses (for example, RRrLL). Initially, the animals tended to develop a simple alternation (RlRLrL). With further training the rats completed the double alternation sequence without extra responses ("errors") on 50 to 90 percent of the sequences. As many as 35 consecutive sequences without extra responses were observed. Schlosberg and Katz suggest that they established successful double alternation in the white rat because

> . . . in the present situation the behavior sequence is so condensed in time and content that the effects of all stimuli and responses can be fused into a continuous behavior pattern. This would account for the relative ease with which the rat can acquire double-alternation lever pressing (p. 281).

Another characteristic of the procedure used by Schlosberg and Katz may also have been important. Each response of the RRLL sequence produced a distinctive click (the operation of a stepping switch); extra responses did not produce the click. Although this sound could not function as a discriminative stimulus for responses that it followed, it would presumably have been established as a conditioned reinforcer which selectively reinforced each correct response in each sequence. Kelleher and Gollub (1962) suggested that a conditioned reinforcer might be especially useful for reinforcing each of the components of a complex response sequence without disrupting the sequence in the way that a primary reinforcer would.

Hurwitz (1962) compared performances of rats on sequences in which extra responses reset the sequence with performance on sequences that were not reset by extra responses. In Hurwitz's study one response was pressing a lever (lever-responses) while the other response was nuzzling open a plastic door to a food tray (tray-responses). The "counting" schedule (CS) was arranged so that tray-responses produced primary reinforcement following a minimum of three lever-responses. If a tray-response occurred before three lever-responses occurred, the sequence reset, and a minimum of three lever-responses were still required. The FR schedule was arranged so that tray-responses produced primary reinforcement whenever three lever-responses had occurred; tray-responses occurring before three lever-responses had occurred did not reset the sequence.

On schedule CS, the rats averaged more than three lever-responses per reinforcement; on schedule FR, the rats averaged slightly more than three lever-responses per reinforcement. Although Hurwitz did not directly measure each sequence of responses, he inferred that in the CS schedule, 65 percent of the response sequences consisted of three lever-responses followed by a tray-response. On the FR schedule, however, the rats tended to alternate lever-responses and tray-responses. Hurwitz concludes:

> Since suitable exteroceptive stimuli have been deliberately excluded, the control of tray responding—at least for the counting schedule groups of animals—must have passed to movement-produced stimuli (1962, p. 171).

As noted above, Schlosberg and Katz (1943) developed double alternation response sequences in the white rat even though extra responses did not reset the sequence. Noting that Schlosberg and Katz needed many sessions to establish double alternation responding, Hurwitz suggested that prolonged training on his FR schedule might have eliminated simple alternation and engendered sequence lengths of about three responses. Hurwitz's FR schedule did not provide exteroceptive stimulus changes following responses that occurred in the proper sequences. It may be that simple alternation was eliminated in the Schlosberg and Katz study because only responses of the sequence RRLL produced a distinctive click that was intermittently paired with primary reinforcement.

Another type of intermittency was used by Ferster (1958) to study response sequences in a chimpanzee. In this study pressing lever B was reinforced by food only after lever A had been pressed three times. Responses on lever B that occurred after more or fewer than three responses on lever A produced a 10-sec. S^Δ period, and reset the sequence. When a sequence length of exactly three responses was reinforced by food (crf), 80 percent of the sequences were exactly three responses. The schedule was then changed so that each sequence of the required length produced a brief stimulus (buzzing sound and flash of light); sequences that were too long or too short still produced a 10-sec. S^Δ period, and reset the sequence. When primary reinforcement followed every thirty-third presentation of the brief stimulus (FR 33), 98 percent of the sequence lengths were exactly three responses.

Why was an FR 33 schedule more effective than a crf schedule in maintaining the consistency of this complex response sequence? Ferster notes that the brief stimulus was presumably a conditioned reinforcer because it had often been temporally paired with primary reinforcement. This could account for the maintenance of responding, but does not explain the increase in percentage of appropriate sequence lengths. Ferster's results with a complex response sequence may be related to Herrnstein's results with a simple response. Herrnstein (1961) studied changes in the topography (spatial distribution) of the pigeon's pecking response. He found that response topographies were more consistent under a VI 3-min. schedule than under crf (see Chapter 3). It is an intriguing possibility that the stereotypy of complex response sequences, as well as simple responses, can be enhanced by intermittency of reinforcement. Schedules of reinforcement may be as valuable for studying response sequences as they are for studying frequency of individual responses.

The double alternation procedure has been widely used because some psychologists have assumed that it is a good test of comparative "intelligence." However, recent findings emphasize the importance of considering the schedule of reinforcement in making inferences about comparative behavior (see Kelleher, 1965). It might be assumed that the relative frequency with which an animal can execute sequences of exactly three responses is a measure of a higher intellectual process that we might call "counting." The chimpanzee in Ferster's study, however, executed sequences of three responses 80 percent of the time under one schedule (crf) and 98 percent of the time under another schedule (FR 33). Any estimate of the chimpanzee's ability to "count" depends on the schedule of reinforcement. Similarly, it was long assumed that the rat seldom accomplished double alternation sequences because of its position on the phylogenetic scale. However, under appropriate procedures, rats can repeatedly execute double alternation sequences. These findings are surprising only if it is assumed that particular response sequences, such as "counting to three" or double alternation, are unitary processes that are not affected by environmental influences. Such demonstrations of environmental modifications of

i. count R's as f(controlling variables)

complex performances may cause despair in the student of comparative intelligence, but they should have the beneficial effect of encouraging him to develop new conceptions of these complex behavioral processes. In any event, these results open up a fascinating new field of investigation for the student of schedule-controlled behavior.

The analysis of sequences of operants, like the analysis of single operants, does not require the assumption that each response is preceded by a corresponding hypothetical stimulus (Skinner, 1938). It is difficult to evaluate the usefulness of the assumption of response-produced stimuli because there has been no consistent specification of the ways in which such stimuli should function, and because there has been too little study of the variables controlling the development and maintenance of response sequences. The results presented in this section have suggested two interesting ways in which identifiable stimuli may function in response sequences. First, if a brief exteroceptive stimulus is produced by each appropriate response in a sequence (as in the Schlosberg and Katz study), it can function as a conditioned reinforcer which selectively reinforces each appropriate response even though it does not provide a differential discriminative stimulus for the following response. Second, if a brief exteroceptive stimulus is produced by each completion of a sequence (as in the Ferster study), it can function as a conditioned reinforcer which maintains responding despite intermittent primary reinforcement of sequence completions. This is important because of evidence suggesting that sequences may be more consistently executed under conditions of intermittent reinforcement. The following sections of this chapter will be primarily concerned with the analysis of functions of response-produced exteroceptive stimulus changes.

STIMULUS FUNCTIONS IN EXPERIMENTAL EXTINCTION

Psychologists have devoted much attention to the conditioned reinforcing effects of stimuli. Many investigators have attempted to evaluate such effects only after primary reinforcement has been excluded from the experiment. In the present chapter, we will refer to this class of techniques as *extinction procedures*. The popularity of these procedures presumably stems from the assumption that the conditioned reinforcing effects of a stimulus should be measured only when known primary reinforcers have been eliminated from the experimental situation. Thus, the extinction procedures eliminate one source of confounding effects, but at the cost of introducing others. Results obtained with extinction procedures have been previously reviewed (Miller, 1951; Myers, 1958). The purpose of the present section is to describe the extinction procedures, to analyze two studies that used scheduled presentations of stimuli, and to discuss interpretations of conditioned reinforcement (for a more detailed discussion of extinction procedures, see Kelleher & Gollub, 1962).

Extinction Procedures

Two basic extinction procedures have been used, the *new response* procedure and the *established response* procedure. Under the new response procedure, responding is strengthened by having a conditioned reinforcer follow a response in the absence of the primary reinforcer. An experiment by Skinner (1938) illustrates the use of the new response procedure for developing a simple sequence. In the first (training) phase of the experiment, food pellets were delivered to food-deprived rats at irregular time intervals. An audible clicking sound immediately preceded the delivery of each food pellet. As a result of this training, the rats approached the food receptacle only when the click occurred. In the second (extinction) phase, a lever was introduced into the experimental chamber. When the rats pressed the lever, the click occurred, but food pellets were not delivered. Skinner found that lever pressing could be developed even though it produced only the click. He concluded that the click was a conditioned reinforcer.

Under the established response procedure, previously established responding is maintained by having a conditioned reinforcer follow the response during experimental extinction. An experiment by Bugelski (1938) illustrates the established response procedure. In the training phase, food-deprived rats were reinforced by food for pressing a lever. An audible click immediately preceded each primary reinforcement. In the extinction phase, the rats were divided into two groups. For the control group, pressing the lever had no effects. For the experimental group, pressing the lever produced only the click. The results showed that the experimental group responded more than the control group. Bugelski concluded that the click was a "sub-goal" (conditioned reinforcer).

Hypotheses about Stimulus Functions in Extinction

Under the extinction procedures, the effectiveness of the conditioned reinforcing stimulus is being extinguished while it is being measured, and the effects are characteristically small. Several investigators have proposed that these effects can be most parsimoniously interpreted in terms of the other functions a stimulus may have; that is, it may function as an eliciting stimulus, a conditioned stimulus, or a discriminative stimulus. Three hypotheses have been formulated which propose that the results obtained with extinction procedures stem from one or more of these other functions of a stimulus rather than from its effects as a conditioned reinforcer. The *elicitation hypothesis* is that a stimulus (for example, a click) that has been repeatedly paired with a primary reinforcer becomes a conditioned stimulus that elicits lever pressing (Bugelski, 1956). This hypothesis apparently assumes that the primary reinforcer is an eliciting stimulus for lever pressing. The *facilitation hypothesis* is that the click becomes a discriminative stimulus for lever pressing in the established response procedure or for increased activity that tends to increase lever pressing in the new response procedure (Wyckoff, Sidowski, & Chambliss, 1958). According to both of these hypotheses, most responding during extinction should occur during or immediately after the click. The *discrimination hypothesis* is that the amount of responding in extinction is directly related to the similarity between stimulus conditions in training and stimulus conditions in extinction (Bitterman, Fedderson, & Tyler, 1953; Elam, Tyler, & Bitterman, 1954).

Before considering these hypotheses further, it is necessary to specify criteria for determining whether or not a stimulus is a reinforcer. The essential characteristic of a reinforcer is that it increases the probability of occurrence of that class of responses that immediately precedes its presentation (see Chapter 3). In assessing a possible conditioned reinforcing stimulus, however, the demonstration of the development or maintenance of a general level of responding is of little help because it could result from other functions of the stimulus. A convenient resolution of this difficulty is provided by schedules of reinforcement. Numerous studies have shown that patterns of responding can be reliably controlled by scheduled presentations of a primary reinforcer (Ferster & Skinner, 1957). Various schedules can be used to generate relatively high rates of responding, low rates of responding, or recurrently changing rates of responding. An understanding of the ways in which known primary reinforcers develop and maintain patterns of responding provides a valuable tool for assessing the possible reinforcing effects of a stimulus.

In the examples of extinction procedures described above, each response produced the click; that is, the click was presented according to a crf schedule. It is possible, however, to introduce intermittency in the training phase, the extinction phase, or both. For example, in the training phase, the primary reinforcer could be presented after 50 percent of the presentations of the click; in the extinction phase, every tenth response could be followed by the click. The use of intermittency in extinction procedures has two advantages. First, because the reinforcing effectiveness of any stimulus in the sequence is being extinguished while it is being studied, intermittent presentation of the primary reinforcer during training, or of the conditioned reinforcer during extinction, should slow the extinction process. Second, when a stimulus is presented according to a schedule, the pattern of responding that develops can be compared with the pattern that would be established or maintained by a schedule of primary reinforcement. Two experiments that are relevant to the hypotheses presented above will be presented in this section to indicate the usefulness of schedule techniques for analyzing conditioned reinforcing effects in extinction.

Intermittent Presentation of Stimuli in Extinction

In an experiment with the new response procedure, Zimmerman (1957) used intermittency in both training and extinction. In early training, a buzzing tone briefly preceded the delivery of water to water-deprived rats; in later training, the tone was repeatedly presented, but water delivery followed the tone on only one out of ten presentations on the average. Despite the intermittent pairing of tone and water reinforcement, the animals approached the water delivery aperture whenever the tone sounded. In the first session of extinction, a lever was introduced into the experimental space, and each of the first six lever presses (responses) produced the tone. Subsequent responses produced the tone on an FI 1 schedule of reinforcement; that is, the tone was produced by the first response occurring after 1 min. had elapsed since the previous presentation of the tone. Responding developed and was maintained at a rate of about four responses per min. on the FI 1 schedule. After about 15 min. on FI 1, the tone was omitted and responding decreased to near zero within about 10 min. In a second extinction session, responding again produced the tone according to FI 1, and rates increased to about six responses per min. Zimmerman's study demonstrates that responding can be developed in an FI schedule while experimental extinction is in effect. The rates of responding in extinction indicate that the tone was a relatively durable conditioned reinforcer.

In an experiment with the established response procedure, Kelleher (1961) also used intermittency in both training and extinction. During training, two pigeons responded on an FI 5 schedule of food reinforcement; a distinct sound (click) briefly preceded each reinforcement. When the characteristic positively accelerated responding had developed under FI 5, experimental extinction began. During two successive extinction sessions, the click was presented according to two alternating schedules. Representative results from these sessions are shown in Figure 4. At the start of the first extinction session (Frame A), the click was presented whenever the bird had not responded for 10 sec. (DRO 10 sec.); if no responding occurred, the click was presented every 10 sec. During the 75 min. in which DRO 10 sec. was in effect, the average response rate was 14.2 responses per min. Periods during which low rates resulted in frequent presentations of the click are shown at *a* and *b*. Just after the pause at *b,* the schedule was changed to crf, and the next response produced the click. For the remainder of the session, the click was presented on an FR schedule that was increased to FR 25. During the 28 min. in which FR was in effect, the average response rate was 27.9 responses per min. Frame B of Figure 4 shows similar results for the second extinction session. In a subsequent extinction session that followed further training on the FI 5 schedule of food reinforcement, the click was presented according to each of three

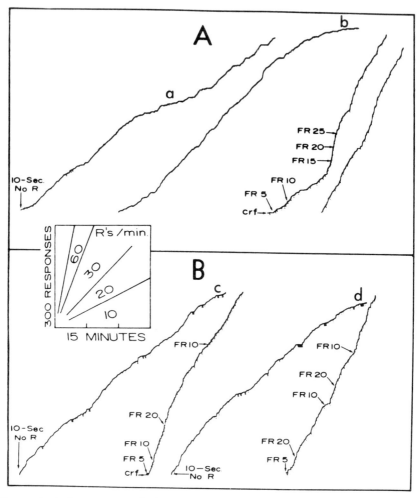

Figure 4. Performances with the presentation of a conditioned reinforcer on dro 10-sec. and various FR values during the first (frame A) and second (frame B) sessions of experimental extinction following training on FI 5 (from Kelleher, 1961).

schedules (FI, FR, and DRO) within the session. Characteristic patterns of responding developed on each schedule.

This experiment shows that a stimulus (the click) might be followed by either a low or a high rate of responding, depending on the schedule of presentation of the stimulus. This finding is opposed to both the elicitation hypothesis and the facilitation hypothesis. Also, as the pigeons had been trained on an FI 5 schedule of food reinforcement, presenting the click on FI 5 in extinction was the condition that was most similar to training. Nevertheless, more responding occurred when the click was presented on an FR schedule than when it was presented on FI 5. This finding is opposed to the discrimination hypothesis.

The experiments of Zimmerman (1957) and Kelleher (1961) have been presented to show the usefulness of scheduling techniques in experimental extinction procedures. Both experiments indicated that patterns of responding can be developed or maintained in extinction by the conditioned reinforcing effects of stimuli that have briefly preceded primary reinforcement.

Establishment of Conditioned Reinforcers

What are the necessary conditions for establishing a stimulus as a conditioned reinforcer? Many studies with the extinction procedures have been concerned with this question. The experimental procedures that have been successfully used are clear, but the appropriate interpretations of the results are not so clear. In both the new response and established response procedures, a stimulus that is not a reinforcer can be established as a conditioned reinforcer if it briefly precedes a primary reinforcing stimulus. This pairing of a stimulus with a primary reinforcing stimulus is obviously similar to the pairing of CS and US in respondent (Pavlovian) conditioning. Thus, one interpretation is that a stimulus becomes a conditioned reinforcer through respondent conditioning. On the other hand, the click is a stimulus in the presence of which approaching the food tray is reinforced by the sight of and ingestion of a food pellet. Thus, a second interpretation is that a stimulus becomes a conditioned reinforcer through becoming a discriminative stimulus (discriminative stimulus hypothesis).

The discriminative stimulus hypothesis has been clearly presented by Keller and Schoenfeld (1950, p. 236ff.). They propose that a stimulus must be a discriminative stimulus for some response in order to become a conditioned reinforcing stimulus; to the extent that a stimulus has been established as a discriminative stimulus it has also acquired conditioned reinforcing effectiveness. Keller and Schoenfeld cite two investigations supporting this hypothesis. First, in an experiment by Schoenfeld, Antonitis, and Bersh (1950), a stimulus light of 1-sec. duration was presented while the animal was eating rather than just before food delivery. After training animals under these special temporal conditions, these investigators were unable to demonstrate that the light was a conditioned reinforcer during extinction. They concluded that the light was not a conditioned reinforcing stimulus. Second, Dinsmoor (1950) compared the discriminative and conditioned reinforcing functions of stimuli. Rats were trained on a crf schedule of food reinforcement in the presence of a light. Three groups were used in extinction. The control group was extinguished with the light off. The first experimental group was extinguished with the light on, but each response turned

it off for 3 sec. The second experimental group was extinguished with the
light off, but each response turned it on for 3 sec. The experimental groups
responded more than the control group, but they did not differ from each
other. Dinsmoor concluded that the discriminative and conditioned reinforcing effects of a stimulus are equal and interchangeable. In summary, the
discriminative stimulus hypothesis states that establishing a stimulus as a
discriminative stimulus is a necessary and a sufficient condition for establishing it as a conditioned reinforcer.

In the experiments described as supporting the discriminative stimulus
hypothesis, one cannot rule out the possibility that respondent conditioning
is playing an important role. The repeated pairing of a click (or other stimulus) and primary reinforcement establishes a complex sequence of responses, including both operant and respondent components. The click is
a discriminative stimulus in the presence of which approaching the food
tray is reinforced by a food pellet, but it is also a stimulus that briefly precedes food-in-the-mouth. Although this pairing of click and food depends
upon what the animal does, it is probable that respondents, such as salivation, are being conditioned at the same time that the click is being established as a discriminative stimulus (Shapiro, 1960). Studies of the intervals
between presentation of stimulus and primary reinforcement are also relevant. For example, Jenkins (1950), using the new response procedure, and
Bersh (1951), using the established response procedure, found that intervals of 0.5 to 1 sec. were optimal for developing effective conditioned reinforcers. It is interesting that these intervals are similar to the optimum
CS-US intervals in respondent conditioning.

It is difficult to test the discriminative stimulus hypothesis with conventional primary reinforcers, such as food or water, because the effective
presentation of the primary reinforcing stimulus depends upon an operant
response. However, this difficulty can be minimized by using a different type
of primary reinforcer, such as intracranial brain stimulation, which can be
conveniently paired with a stimulus independently of operant responding.
One experiment has been reported in which intracranial stimulation was
used as a primary reinforcer to establish a tone as a conditioned reinforcer
in the rat (Stein, 1958). In the first phase of this experiment, responses on
lever A produced a brief tone; responses on lever B had no effects. The
rats responded slightly more on lever B. In the second phase, the levers
were absent, and the tone was frequently presented just before intracranial
stimulation occurred. The pairing of the tone with the primary reinforcer
(intracranial stimulation) in this phase did not require any specific operant
response. In the third phase of the experiment, responses on lever A again
produced only the tone while responses on lever B had no effects. The rats
now responded significantly more on lever A than on lever B. The tone had
been established as a conditioned reinforcer by being paired with intracranial stimulation. Furthermore, these results indicate that it is not necessary

to establish a stimulus as a discriminative stimulus in order to establish it as a conditioned reinforcer.

In summary, the repeated pairing of a stimulus and a primary reinforcer, with the stimulus briefly (0.5 to 1 sec.) preceding the primary reinforcer, is an effective procedure for establishing the stimulus as a conditioned reinforcer. Also, it seems that the stimulus need not be a discriminative stimulus. How does a stimulus that is paired with primary reinforcement become a conditioned reinforcer? At the present time it is not possible to give an exact answer to this question. The available evidence suggests that stimuli become conditioned reinforcers through respondent conditioning, but much more evidence will be required to consolidate this interpretation. Although there is a vast literature on extinction procedures, the present section has been relatively brief because complete reviews of these studies are available for the interested reader (Kelleher & Gollub, 1962; Miller, 1950; Myers, 1958). Also, the techniques presented in the following section are proving to be more valuable than the extinction procedures for studying the conditioned reinforcing functions of stimuli.

STIMULUS FUNCTIONS IN SECOND-ORDER SCHEDULES

In recent years, increasingly complex sequences of schedules and stimuli have been investigated, and the convention of referring to all these sequences as chained schedules is becoming unwieldy (see Findley, 1962). One way to characterize sequences of schedules is as schedules of schedules or *second-order schedules*. A second-order schedule is one in which the behavior specified by a schedule contingency is treated as a unitary response that is itself reinforced according to some schedule of primary reinforcement. The second-order schedule provides a convenient basic specification of the response and primary reinforcement contingencies in a sequence, but it does not specify the exteroceptive stimulus conditions. Standard schedule terminology can be used to describe second-order schedules which are variations of familiar procedures. With new procedures, stimulus conditions can be specified as the need arises. An example of a second-order schedule is the procedure in which primary reinforcement is contingent upon the completion of three successive FI 2 schedules; this will be called FR 3 (FI 2). Note that the schedule contingency that is being treated as a unitary response is enclosed in parentheses; the schedule of primary reinforcement for this unitary response precedes the parentheses. In the most elementary form of FR 3 (FI 2), no exteroceptive stimulus changes occur between the beginning of the sequence and primary reinforcement; this is a *tandem schedule* (tand FI 2 FI 2 FI 2) in the terminology of Ferster and Skinner (1957). Tandem schedules are especially useful as control procedures for evaluating the functions of stimuli in variations of a second-order schedule. If a different exteroceptive stimulus is correlated with each of the component FI 2 schedules, the FR 3 (FI 2) schedule becomes a *chained schedule* (chain FI 2 FI 2 FI 2) in the terminology of Ferster and Skinner (1957). Numerous other procedures for the presentation of stimuli can be arranged with FR 3 (FI 2). For example, a brief exteroceptive stimulus change could occur at the completion of each FI 2 component, or this brief stimulus change could occur only at the completion of the first two FI 2 components. As yet, there is no standard terminology for referring to these variations of the second-order schedule. The purpose of the present section is to describe various second-order schedules and to analyze the functions of stimuli in second-order schedules of reinforcement.

Chained Schedules of Reinforcement

In a chained schedule of reinforcement, responding in the presence of one exteroceptive stimulus produces a second exteroceptive stimulus; responding in the presence of the second stimulus produces a third stimulus, and so forth (Ferster & Skinner, 1957). Each exteroceptive stimulus is correlated with a component of the chained schedule. The topography of the response in each component may or may not be the same. In the present chapter the component stimuli in chained schedules will be numbered sequentially from the last to the first stimulus; that is, in the reverse of the chronological order in which they actually appear. The stimulus that terminates with primary reinforcement is always S1, the penultimate stimulus is S2, and so forth. Two-component chained schedules will be discussed before more extended chained schedules because different types of procedures and problems are emphasized in chained schedules of different lengths.

Two-Component Chained Schedules

In a two-component chained schedule, responding in the presence of S2 is often used as a dependent variable to estimate the effectiveness of S1 as a conditioned reinforcer, and several studies have been concerned with independent variables that might influence this effectiveness. Relevant variables are frequency of reinforcement in the presence of S1 (reinforcements per min.); probability of reinforcement in the presence of S1 (the reciprocal of responses per reinforcement); and the schedule of reinforcement in the presence of S1.

Comparisons of tandem and chained schedules. Gollub (1958) compared the performances of pigeons on tandem and chained schedules under an FR 2 (FI) schedule of primary reinforcement. On an FI schedule a response is reinforced after a specified time has elapsed since some event; responses occurring before the time has elapsed have no specified consequences. Responding is usually positively accelerated between reinforcements (FI scallop). Gollub trained birds on tandem schedules before exposing them to chained schedules. The schedule parameters were FI 30 sec. FI 30 sec., FI 1 FI 1 and FI 3 FI 2. The stimulus that was present throughout the tandem schedule was the stimulus that became S1 in the chained schedule. For example, consider the performance of a bird that was trained on tand FI 1 FI 1 and then on chain FI 1 FI 1. On tand FI 1 FI 1 response rates (responses per minute) were 12.5 in the first component and 99.1 in the second component; the patterns of responding were usually positively accelerated over the entire 2-min. minimum interval between reinforcements. During the transition from the tandem to the chained schedule, response rates in the presence of S2 were 5.9 (compared to 12.5 in the comparable component of the tandem schedule) and 104.5 in the presence of S1. Later, rates in the presence of S2 increased to 16.7 while rates in the presence of S1 decreased to 90.5. Qualitatively similar effects were obtained with the other schedule parameters.

Gollub (1958) found that the transition from the tandem to the chained schedule has three phases. The first phase is probably caused by the introduction of novel stimuli; the magnitude and direction of the changes in rate of responding depend upon the type of stimulus and the bird's experimental history. The second phase, in which response rates decrease in the presence of S2, develops because primary reinforcement occurs in the presence of S1 but not in the presence of S2. In the third phase, response rates again increase in the presence of S2 because S1 is becoming an effective conditioned reinforcer. With prolonged exposure to the chained schedule response rates become higher in the first component of the chained schedule than they had been in the first component of the tandem schedule. This finding supports Gollub's conclusion that S1 is a conditioned reinforcer in this two-component chained schedule.

Ferster and Skinner compared the performances of pigeons on chain FR DRL and on tand FR DRL schedules. Under both chain and tand FR DRL schedules, the completion of an FR response requirement starts a DRL schedule; under a DRL schedule, a response is reinforced only when it follows a preceding response by a specified time interval.[4] The schedule parameters varied from FR 20 and DRL 6 sec. to FR 120 and DRL 6 sec. Figure 5 shows the first session of a pigeon on chain FR 70 DRL 6 sec. following prolonged training on comparable tandem schedules. The performance in the first two record segments is representative of the type of performance that characterized the tandem schedule; the last three records show that response rates in S2 increased markedly on the chained schedule. Figure 6 shows the final performance of each bird on chain FR 95 DRL 6 sec. Response rates in S1 were about five responses per minute, and the frequency of reinforcement

---

[4] In the present notation (cf. Skinner & Morse, 1958), DRL is used in place of the *crf drl* of Ferster and Skinner (1957).

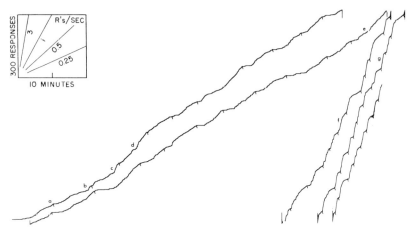

Figure 5. First session on chain FR 70 drl 6-sec. following training on tandem FR 70 drl 6-sec. Changes from the first to the second component are not designated; the small pips on the record indicate food deliveries. Note the rapid change in rate of responding between e and f (from Ferster & Skinner, 1957).

in the presence of S1 was between two and ten reinforcements per minute.[5] Average response rates in the presence of S2 were about 180 responses per minute. Rates and patterns of responding in the presence of S2 resemble those that usually develop on an FR 95 schedule of primary reinforcement. In a subsequent experiment with pigeons on chain FR 120 DRL 6 sec., Ferster and Skinner (1957) varied the discriminability of S2 and S1. When S2 and S1 were similar, response rates in the presence of S2 decreased, approaching the low response rates that prevailed in the presence of S1. When S2 and S1 were easily discriminable, response rates in the presence of S2 increased markedly, while response rates in the presence of S1 remained low.

The results of Ferster and Skinner (1957), like the results of Gollub, show that response rates in S2 are higher on a chained schedule than on a comparable tandem schedule. Inasmuch as the response and primary reinforcement contingencies are identical on the tandem and chained schedules, the differences in performance must be a result of the exteroceptive stimuli in each component of the chained schedules. It is especially interesting that in the Ferster and Skinner study response rates in S1 were markedly lower than response rates in S2. A stimulus that is a discriminative stimulus controlling a low rate of responding can be a conditioned reinforcer for a high rate of responding. Both studies demonstrate that S1 can be a conditioned reinforcer for responding in the first component of a two-component chained schedule. The next section will consider some experiments de-

[5] All response rates from Ferster and Skinner (1957) are estimates from cumulative response records shown in their book.

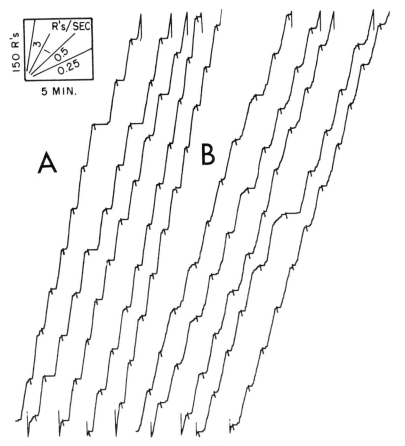

Figure 6. Final performances of two birds on chain FR 95 drl 6-sec. (from Ferster & Skinner, 1957).

signed to investigate conditions that determine the conditioned reinforcing effectiveness of S1.

Effects of varying the probability or frequency of reinforcement correlated with S1. A complete definition of a discriminative stimulus requires a specification of the schedule of reinforcement with which it is correlated. The characteristics of a schedule that would be most likely to influence the conditioned reinforcing effectiveness of its correlated discriminative stimulus would be the probability and frequency of reinforcement that prevailed under the schedule. The probability of reinforcement is the reciprocal of responses per reinforcement; the frequency of reinforcement is reinforcements per minute.

The probability of reinforcement in the presence of S1 can be specified by using fixed ratio (FR) or variable ratio (VR) schedules. For example, Ferster and Skinner trained pigeons on chain VI FR 50, and then studied the effects on decreasing the probability of reinforcement by increasing the response requirement from FR 50 to FR 300. As the FR was increased, performance in the presence of S1 became increasingly strained; that is, relatively long periods of low response rates or pausing occurred before responding started, but once responding started, rates were very high. As the FR requirement was increased, the response rate on VI in the presence of S2 decreased accordingly.

The maximum frequency of reinforcement in the presence of S1 (reinforcements per minute) can be specified by using FI or VI schedules. For example, Findley (1954; 1962) studied the performances of rats on chain VI VI schedules. The schedule in the presence of S2 was held constant at VI 4, while the schedule in the presence of S1 was systematically varied from 30 sec. to 8 min. As the frequency of reinforcement in the presence of S1 decreased, response rates in the presence of S1 decreased slightly, while response rates in the presence of S2 decreased in a negatively accelerated fashion (see Ferster & Skinner, 1957).

Autor (1960) established quantitative relations between conditioned reinforcing effectiveness of S1 and probability and frequency of reinforcement in the presence of S1. He trained pigeons on two concurrently programmed chained schedules. The experimental space contained two response keys, and a two-component chained schedule could be completed on either key. The first components of these chained schedules were identical, but independent, VI 1 schedules. Different stimuli (colored key lights) were correlated with each of these VI schedules. Whenever the stimulus correlated with the second component of the chain was produced on one key, the stimulus associated with the second component of the chain on the other key could not appear, and responses on the other key were ineffective. In studying frequency of reinforcement, Autor held the schedule in the second component on key A constant at VI 15-sec., while systematically varying the schedule in the second component on key B from VI 3.75-sec. to VI 1. When the schedules were chain VI 1 VI 15-sec. on each key, response rates in the first components on keys A and B were about equal. As the frequency of reinforcement in the second component on key B was increased, the relative frequency of responding in the first component on key B increased in a linear fashion.

In studying probability of reinforcement, Autor held the schedule in the second component on key A constant at VR 40, while systematically varying the schedule in the second component on key B from VR 16 to VR 100. When the schedules were chain VI 1 VR 40 on each key, response rates in the first components on keys A and B were about equal. As the probability of reinforcement in the second component on key B was increased, the relative frequency of responding in the first component on key B increased in a linear fashion.

Although a VI schedule specifies a maximum frequency of reinforcement and a VR specifies a probability of reinforcement, frequency and probability are not actually independent under either VI or VR. Under VI the probability of reinforcement, and under VR the frequency of reinforcement, both depend on actual performance. Autor (1960) determined the mean number of responses per reinforcement in S1 and the mean number of reinforcements per minute in S1 for all values of both VI and VR schedules. For either schedule, the conditioned reinforcing effectiveness of S1 was linearly related to both frequency and probability of reinforcement in S1.

Effects of primary reinforcers that are not contingent on responses in S1. Relations between frequency of reinforcement in S1 and performance in S2 can be emphasized by delivering primary reinforcers independently of behavior in S1. Ferster (1953) investigated several variations of a chained schedule in which responding under a VI 1 schedule in S2 produced S1; primary reinforcement occurred independently of responding in S1. In the first experiment, primary reinforcement came after 60 sec. in S1. The use of a blackout as S1 insured that no responding occurred in the presence of S1. Under these conditions, the birds stopped responding in the presence of S2; that is, S1 was not a conditioned reinforcer. In the second experiment, primary reinforcement initially occurred after a delay of 1 sec. in the presence of S1 (blackout); this delay was then gradually increased to 1 min. Under these conditions, the birds continued to respond in the presence of S2. Gradually increasing the delay in reinforcement established S1 as a conditioned reinforcer. In a third experiment, primary reinforcement in the presence of S1 occurred after a delay of 1 min. (S1 consisted of a dark response key, but the house light provided general illumination); however, every response in the presence of S1 postponed reinforcement for 1 min. Under these conditions, the birds responded in S2, but not in S1. Again, S1 was established as a conditioned reinforcer. Observations indicated that the birds had developed "superstitious" unrecorded response patterns in the presence of S1.

Ferster (1953) and Ferster and Skinner (1957, p. 684) trained pigeons on chain VI 1 FI 1 and then changed the schedule so that food was delivered in the presence of S1 after a delay of 1 min. independently of responses in the presence of S1. Response rates in the presence of S1 decreased to near zero, but responding on the VI 1 schedule in S2 was not affected. Ferster and Skinner (1957, p. 685) concluded that "the conditioned reinforcement of the property of the stimulus for the second schedule would appear to derive from its correlation with food, regardless of whether or not the bird is responding in the presence of the second stimulus." They qualified this conclusion, however, by noting that response rate in the presence of S1 did not reach zero.

Using the concurrent chained schedule procedure described above, Autor (1960) also studied the effects of delivering primary reinforcers independently of responses. Again the schedules in the first component were VI 1 on each key. Whenever the stimulus correlated with the second component of the chain was produced on key A, food was delivered every 15 sec. on the average in the presence of this stimulus. Whenever the stimulus correlated with the second component of the chain was produced on key B, food was delivered every t sec. on the average; t was systematically varied from 3.75 sec. to 60 sec. As the birds did not respond in the second component on either key, the probability of reinforcement need not be considered. As the frequency of primary reinforcement in the second component on key B was increased, the relative response rates under the VI 1 schedule in the first component increased in a linear fashion. The results with primary reinforcers delivered independently of responses were the same as those obtained with standard VI schedules of reinforcement. Autor (1960, p. 26) concluded that ". . . the occurrence of the same operant during both parts of the chain was not a necessary condition for the emergence of the relation between relative frequency of reinforcement and relative frequency of response."

A discriminative stimulus was previously defined as one that is correlated with a schedule in which a specified operant response produces a reinforcer. The experiments of Ferster (1953), Ferster and Skinner (1957), and Autor (1960) provide further evidence that it is not necessary to establish a stimulus as a discriminative stimulus in order to establish it as a conditioned reinforcer. Even when a primary reinforcer is delivered independently of responses, however, its delivery will probably be correlated with some behavior (see Ferster, 1953). That is, it has been demonstrated that responses can be "superstitiously" conditioned even when primary reinforcers are delivered independently of recorded responses (see Chapter 2 in this volume). In the experiments of Ferster (1953) and Ferster and Skinner (1957) low response rates were maintained in the second component. These responses might have been superstitiously maintained by food deliveries. In Autor's experiments no responses occurred in the second component; however, the food was delivered at variable intervals, and the presence of some short intervals would favor the development of unrecorded superstitious behavior. Although these possibilities for superstitious responding suggest the need for caution in describing a particular stimulus as a discriminative stimulus, there is no good evidence that superstitious behavior in the presence of a stimulus mediates the conditioned reinforcing effectiveness of that stimulus. In fact, even when a discriminative stimulus is established as a conditioned reinforcer, its conditioned reinforcing effectiveness is not related to the rate of responding with which it is correlated.

Furthermore, even well-maintained superstitious behavior is so variable that it is difficult to understand how it could mediate orderly conditioned reinforcement functions such as those obtained by Autor (1960). The most parsimonious interpretation is that the conditioned reinforcing effectiveness of a stimulus is not related to responding or to the probability of reinforcement in its presence, but is directly related to the frequency of primary reinforcement in its presence.

Effects of S1 when it is not contingent on responses in S2. Skinner (1948) has demonstrated that some identifiable response can be "superstitiously" conditioned when a primary reinforcer is regularly presented at brief intervals independently of responding. Morse (1955) studied the establishment and maintenance of superstitious behavior by means of a conditioned reinforcer. Two groups of pigeons were trained on multiple schedules of food reinforcement. For one group, a green stimulus indicated VI 3 and a red stimulus indicated FR 25 (mult VI 3 FR 25). For the other group, green indicated FR 25 and red indicated FR 25 (mult FR 25 FR 25). When performances were stable, the schedule for both groups was changed to one in which no primary reinforcement occurred in the green stimulus, but FR 25 was still in effect in red. The green stimulus was presented for 2-min. periods, and then the red stimulus appeared independently of responses in green. During the first session, response rates in green decreased rapidly for birds trained on mult FR 25 FR 25, but decreased slowly for birds trained on mult VI 3 FR 25. Because of this slow decrease for the latter group, responses in the presence of the green stimulus were often accidentally correlated with the appearance of the red stimulus, and Morse found that these pigeons developed "FI-like" performances in the presence of green. The pigeons trained on FR 25 responded infrequently in the presence of green. Subsequently, Morse prevented accidental correlations between responding in the presence of the green stimulus and the appearance of the red stimulus by interposing a 2-min. time-out (TO) between them. Response rates in the presence of green were consistently lower when green was followed by TO than when it was followed by red. These experiments, as well as several others that Morse conducted, show that conditioned reinforcers can maintain substantial amounts of behavior when their presentation closely follows a given response.

Such "superstitiously" maintained chained schedules are often developed when investigators attempt to establish discriminations. For example, if one is attempting to establish performance on a mult VI ext schedule by alternating 5-min. periods of VI in the presence of stimulus A with 5-min. periods of extinction in the presence of stimulus B, FI-like behavior may be well maintained in the presence of stimulus B. Although such superstitiously maintained behaviors are interesting to one who is studying chained schedules, they are a source of trouble to one who wishes to establish a zero response rate in the extinction component. As Morse has shown, this behavior can be minimized by interposing a TO between components or by having responses in the extinction component postpone the onset of the VI component.

Extended Chained Schedules

Two important functions of stimuli are emphasized in extended chained schedules. Each component stimulus in a chained schedule may be both a conditioned reinforcer for responses that precede it and a discriminative stimulus in the presence of which a response produces a reinforcing stimulus or another discriminative stimulus. If enough discriminative stimuli are available, the number of components in a chained schedule can conceivably be extended indefinitely. The present section will discuss comparisons of extended chained schedules and tandem schedules.

Comparisons of tandem and chained schedules. The most dramatic difference between performances on extended chained schedules and tandem schedules is the development of prolonged periods without responding in the early components of chained schedules. This phenomenon was first reported in a series of experiments by Gollub (1958). In one experiment, for example, a pigeon was trained on a five-component tandem schedule with FI 1 in each component, and was then changed to the analogous five-component chained schedule. Except for the different stimuli correlated with each component in the chained schedule, the response and primary reinforcement contingencies were identical under the tandem and chained schedules; that is, the basic second-order schedule was held constant at FR 5 (FI 1).

Under the tandem schedule, average pauses of 7 min. and 6 min. developed in the first and second components, respectively, while each of the last three components was completed in about 1 min. Under the chained schedule, prolonged pauses, ranging up to 67 min., developed in the first component. Pauses in the second component lasted about 2 min. on the average, while each of the last three components was completed in about 1 min. The tandem schedule maintained much more responding than the comparable chained schedule.

In an attempt to maintain responding in the early components of extended chained schedules, Gollub established responding on two-component chained schedules, and then added components.

> For all the subjects, a chain of FIs was reached on which responding in the initial components was not maintained. The number of components in the schedule which failed to maintain responding depended upon the duration of the components. Chains with three short (30″) FIs maintained respond-

ing, but 4- and 5-component chains of FI 30″ did not. With longer FIs (1 to 3 min.), responding was not maintained in the initial component of a 3-component chain even when that component was a very short interval. Although other factors are important in maintaining responding on chained schedules, the values of the parameters of the schedule have a great effect (Gollub, 1958, p. 55).

These results show that the initial stimuli in two- or three-component chained FI schedules are discriminative stimuli controlling moderate rates of responding; however, these stimuli are not conditioned reinforcers for responding in a preceding component. Gollub interprets his results as contradicting the hypothesis that a discriminative stimulus is necessarily a conditioned reinforcer.

Gollub's results with extended chained schedules have been confirmed by other investigators. Kelleher and Fry (1962) found that pigeons on three-component chained schedules with FI 60-sec. or FI 90-sec. in each component developed prolonged pausing in the first component, while scallops developed in the second and third components. Neither pauses nor scallops in the component schedules developed on comparable tandem schedules. Similar findings have also been reported by Findley (1962) for extended chained FI schedules, and by Findley (1962) and Ferster and Skinner (1957) for extended chained FR schedules.

The prolonged periods without responding that develop in the early components of chained FI schedules are extremely interesting. On chained FI schedules as on tandem FI schedules, the maximum frequency of reinforcement is determined by the durations of the component FI schedules. For example, under FR 5 (FI 1), the maximum frequency of reinforcement is once in 5 min. When animals are changed from a tandem to a chained schedule, the frequency of reinforcement is initially maintained near the maximum. Nevertheless, pausing in the first component becomes more and more prolonged. Note that in both tandem and chained schedules pauses in each component are additive in decreasing the frequency of reinforcement. The comparison of chained and tandem schedules indicates that it is some characteristic of the stimuli in extended chained FI schedules that suppresses behavior.

As noted above, Gollub's study of two-component chained FI schedules showed that response rates in the presence of S2 were initially lower and subsequently higher than on comparable tandem FI schedules. Gollub attributed the initial decrease in responding to the development of a discrimination; that is, primary reinforcement occurred in the presence of S1 but not in the presence of S2. He attributed the subsequent increase in responding in the presence of S2 to the development of S1 as a conditioned reinforcer. In extended chained FI schedules, however, responding in the initial components decreases but does not recover. The finding indicates that the stimulus correlated with the second component of an extended chained FI schedule does not become established as a conditioned reinforcer.

The conditioned reinforcing effectiveness of a stimulus in an extended chain is determined by two factors. First, a conditioned reinforcer is less effective than the reinforcer (primary or conditioned) used to establish it (Kelleher & Gollub, 1962). In an extended chained schedule, the reinforcing effectiveness of any stimulus depends upon the component with which it is correlated; that is, S3 will be less effective than S2, while S2 will be less effective than S1. Second, the conditioned reinforcing effectiveness of any stimulus is directly related to the frequency of reinforcement occurring in its presence. Although interactions between these two factors have not been established, it is likely that the conditioned reinforcing effectiveness of a stimulus is also related to the frequency of reinforcement in each of the subsequent stimuli in an extended chain. Although responding is poorly maintained on a five-component chained schedule with FI 15-sec. in each component, much longer sequences can maintain responding on comparable tandem schedules and on other second-order schedules in which brief stimulus changes terminate each component (pp. 199-206).

The prolonged periods of no responding (pausing) that develop on extended chained schedules require much further study. This unusual phenomenon is likely to be regarded as a nuisance by experimenters who are eager to identify conditions in which powerful conditioned reinforcing effects can be demonstrated and studied. However, the prolonged pausing is worthy of study in its own right, and two points should be considered. First, the disparities between performance on tandem and chained schedules occur only because the animal sees and comes under the control of the component stimuli of the chained schedule. Attending to environmental stimuli is usually considered an important adaptive characteristic of an organism's behavior. Under some extended chained schedules, however, attention to environmental stimuli works to the severe detriment of the organism. Second, the disparities between tandem and chained schedules develop despite the initial comparability in frequency of reinforcement on the two schedules. These points will be considered again in a later section of this chapter.

Effects of varying sequence of stimuli or chain length. Other investigators, who confirmed Gollub's findings of prolonged pausing in the early components of extended chained schedules, have attempted to specify some of the variables that control this phenomenon. Kelleher and Fry (1962) trained pigeons on a three-component chained schedule with FI 90-sec. in each component and then presented the component stimuli in a variable sequence. That is, no stimulus was consistently correlated with the first component of the chained schedule because the three stimuli appeared in a different order following each primary reinforcement. With this variable stimulus sequence, positively accelerated responding was established and maintained in each component. This pattern of responding may have developed because responses are primarily reinforced in the presence of each stimulus on one out of three times that it appears. On the other hand, the first component always followed primary reinforcement, and the birds were affected by the stimulus changes. Kelleher and Fry (1962) conclude that the stimulus changes were effective conditioned reinforcers, and that they were especially effective because each stimulus was intermittently paired with primary reinforcement. In any event, this study shows that responding can be maintained on a three-component chained FI 90-sec. schedule if the stimuli appear in a variable sequence.

Findley (1962), who had previously found that performance was poorly maintained on a five-component chained FI 15-sec. schedule, studied the effects of varying the chain length; that is, the stimuli appeared in a fixed sequence, but a primary reinforcement (and a return to the start of the sequence) might occur at the end of any component from the first to the fifth. With this type of variable chain, positively accelerated responding was maintained in each component schedule at FI 30-sec. and FI 60-sec.; however, pausing developed at FI 120-sec.

Schedules of Token Reinforcement

Schedules of "token" reinforcement can be considered as variations of extended chained schedules. As in the extended chain, there is a stimulus change at the completion of each component; however, these stimulus changes are more complex. First, the number of stimulus changes in a schedule of token reinforcement is directly related to the number of the primary reinforcers delivered at the completion of the sequence. Second, there is a brief, discrete stimulus change (for example, the sound of the token dispenser) occurring at the completion of each component schedule. Finally, the gradual accumulation of tokens is a continuing stimulus change over the duration of each session.

The "token reward" studies with primates have two phases of training. In the first phase, the animals are "shaped" by food reinforcement to insert tokens (usually poker chips) into a slot; each insertion of the token is reinforced by food delivery. We will refer to such exchanges of tokens for food as *exchange*. In the second phase, the delivery of tokens is made contingent upon some response, such as pressing a lever. The animal may be required to keep the tokens for a specified period of time (the *exchange interval*) before exchange is possible, or to obtain a specified number of tokens (the *exchange ratio*) before exchange is possible. Exchanges may be controlled by physically preventing the insertion of tokens (Wolfe, 1936; Cowles, 1937) or by having token insertions produce food only when a particular stimulus is present (Kelleher, 1957c).

Simple Component Schedules

Fixed interval. Kelleher (1957b) trained chimpanzees on an FI 5 schedule of token reinforcement under which they were required to accumulate groups of tokens before exchange: the basic second-order schedule was FR (FI 5). The exchange ratio (FR value) was gradually increased from two to eight tokens. At ratios of two, three, four, or six tokens, responding was maintained and was positively accelerated in most components; however, pausing developed in the first component as the ratio was increased. At an exchange ratio of six, prolonged pauses, ranging up to 90 min., developed in the first component. At an exchange ratio of eight, responding ceased. The data obtained with chimpanzees on FI schedules of token reinforcement are remarkably similar to those obtained with pigeons on extended chained FI schedules. The basic second-order schedule in both the chimpanzee and the pigeon studies was FR (FI), and the similarity of the results suggests that the stimuli in each type of study were functioning in similar ways. In the chimpanzee study, the number of tokens increases as the exchange period is approached, providing the stimulus changes defining a chained schedule; in the pigeon study, the color of the key-light changes as the end of the chain is approached.[6]

Fixed ratio. In one study, Kelleher (1958) attempted to determine whether the number of tokens in the experimental space controlled performance. Two chimpanzees were trained on an FR 125 schedule of token reinforcement with an exchange ratio of 50 tokens; the basic second-order schedule was FR 50 (FR 125). The animals usually paused for more than two hours at the start of each session. When responding started, it was sporadic until the animal obtained several tokens, and then responding continued at a high rate until the exchange ratio was completed. On extended chained schedules with pigeons, if the order of appearance of stimuli is reversed so that S1 appears at the start of the chain, S1 will continue to control high response rates until a new discrimination develops (for example, Kelleher & Fry, 1962). A similar procedure was used with the chimpanzees that had been trained on the FR 125 schedule of token reinforcement. The animals were given 50 tokens at the start of a session, but still had to obtain another 50 tokens before exchange. A representative result is shown in Figure 7. The long initial periods of pausing (record A) were almost completely abolished when the animal had 50 tokens at the start of the session (record B). This study shows that the number of tokens in the chimpanzee's possession is a powerful controlling stimulus. The prolonged pausing in schedules of token reinforcement with the chimpanzee is

---

[6] Unfortunately, tandem procedures were not studied under FR (FI) with chimpanzees.

controlled in the same way as the prolonged pausing in extended chained schedules with the pigeon.

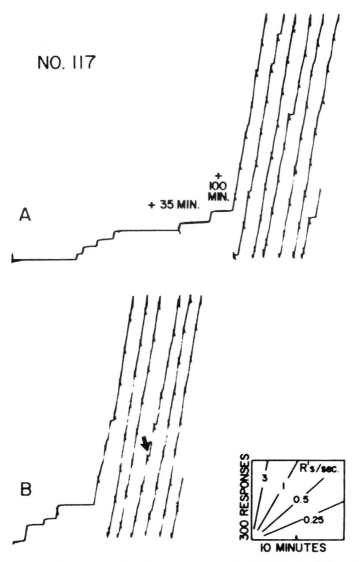

Figure 7. (A) Performance of a chimpanzee on the FR 125 schedule of token reinforcement at an exchange ratio of 50 tokens; periods of no responding have been omitted as indicated. (B) Following session in which the chimpanzee was given 50 poker chips at the start of the session. Insertions of poker chips occurring before the exchange ratio was completed were recorded, but had no specified consequences; the animal inserted one poker chip at the arrow (from Kelleher, 1958).

Variable interval. In studies of token reinforcement schedules, the number of primary reinforcers that could be obtained at the completion of a sequence was directly related to the number of poker chips accumulated. A recent study with the pigeon (Zimmerman & Ferster, 1964) used a procedure that is similar to the token reinforcement schedules used with the chimpanzee. One wall of the experimental chamber contained two transparent response keys, with a voltmeter behind each key. At the start of each session, the keys were transilluminated by a red light. Each time the pigeon completed a component schedule by pecking the left key, the needle of each

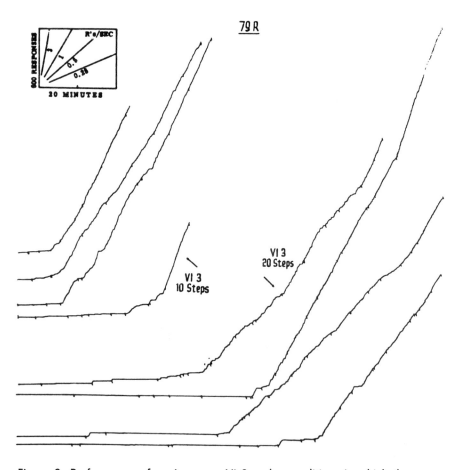

Figure 8. Performance of a pigeon on VI 3 under conditions in which the completion of 10 components (upper record) or 20 components (lower record) were required to produce full deflection. Pips indicate partial deflections of the meter at the completion of each VI 3 component. At the end of each record segment, the meter was fully deflected and food could be obtained on crf (from Zimmerman & Ferster, 1964).

meter moved a fraction of the way toward full deflection. When the meters were fully deflected, responses on the right key were reinforced on a crf schedule of primary reinforcement. When the number of primary reinforcements corresponded to the number of needle deflections that had occurred, the meters reset to zero and the sequence started again.

With responses on the left key producing meter deflections according to a VI 3 schedule, Zimmerman and Ferster (1964) compared performances when 10 or 20 deflections were required to reach full deflection. In this case, the basic second-order schedule was FR 10 (or 20) (VI 3). Responses on the right key prior to full deflection of the meter stopped the VI timer for 10 sec. Figure 8 shows that responding was positively accelerated on this schedule, and that the duration of initial pausing was directly related to the number of components that had to be completed before the meter was fully deflected.

Zimmerman and Ferster (1964) also compared three stimulus conditions using FR 10 (VI 1) as the basic schedule. In the first condition, responding produced deflections of the meter and a brief flash of light according to a VI 1 schedule. The results were similar to those shown in Figure 8. In the second condition, responding produced only a brief flash of light according to the VI 1 schedule. In the third condition (tandem), no exteroceptive stimulus changes occurred at the completion of the successive VI 1 components. Responding occurred at a relatively constant rate throughout the sequence under the second and third conditions. These results show that when the completion of the successive components of a second-order schedule produce successive stimulus changes, the effect may be to weaken performance near the beginning of the sequence. The correlation of the number of stimulus changes with number of primary reinforcements that will occur at the termination of the sequence does not overcome this weakening effect.

Multiple Component Schedules

The studies discussed so far have used a single type of schedule in each component of the second-order schedule. It is possible, however, to use more complex schedules as components. For example, chimpanzees have been trained to respond on multiple FI 5 FR 20 schedules of token reinforcement (Kelleher, 1957a). In the presence of a green stimulus light, responding produced a token according to an FR 20 schedule; in the presence of an orange stimulus light, responding produced a token according to an FI 5 schedule. The exchange ratio was 60 tokens; that is, the basic second-order schedule was FR 60 (mult FI 5 FR 20). Although the average rate of responding in a given type of component generally increased as more tokens were obtained, the response patterns were different in the different components of the multiple schedule. Early in each session the FR performances were severely strained, and FI response rates were low. In the latter part of each session, performances were similar to performances that are characteristic of multiple FI 5 FR 20 schedules of primary reinforcement. Again it is probable that the differences between performances early and late in each session were controlled by the different numbers of tokens in the animal's possession. Nevertheless, in contrast to the FI 5 schedule of token reinforcement, substantial response rates were maintained on the multiple FI 5 FR 20 schedule.

Why was performance maintained on multiple FI 5 FR 20 at an exchange ratio of 60, but not on FI 5 at an exchange ratio of 8? One possibility is that adding an FR 20 component strengthens responding on FI 5 through generalization or induction. High response rates were maintained on FR 20 alone at an exchange ratio of 60. Another possibility is that stimulus changes occurring in the multiple schedule tend to strengthen responding throughout the entire sequence. The stimuli that indicated whether FI 5 or FR 20 was in effect were each associated with the end of half the sequences on the average. Thus, each stimulus was occasionally the discriminative stimulus in the presence of which a response terminated the sequence, and tokens could be exchanged for food. The irregularly alternating stimuli might have effects similar to those obtained by Kelleher and Fry (1962) using three-component chained FI schedules with variable sequences of stimuli. According to this interpretation, responding on either FI 5 or FR 20 components was consistently reinforced by the presentation of a token and occasionally reinforced by the presentation of the discriminative stimulus for the other component schedule.

Once again, the behavior of the pigeon has been studied on a procedure that is similar to the multiple FI 5 FR 20 schedule of token reinforcement with the chimpanzee. In this study (Kelleher, 1963), responding in the presence of a green light produced a brief (0.5 sec.) white light according to an FI 5 schedule of reinforcement; responding in the presence of a red light produced the brief white light according to an FR 20 schedule. These two schedules alternated irregularly with the restriction that the same schedule would occur no more than five times in succession. Primary reinforcement occurred following the fortieth presentation of the white light; responses in the presence of the white light had no programmed consequences. This is an FR 40 (mult FI 5 FR 20) schedule of reinforcement. In the FI 5 components, responding was positively accelerated, and the average rate for the three pigeons was 24 responses per minute. In the FR 20 components, continuous responding occurred, and the average rate was 90 responses per minute. Performances in each component of this second-order multiple schedule were qualitatively similar to performances that usually develop on a comparable multiple schedule of primary reinforcement.

When the same subjects were run with the white light omitted, while all other conditions remained the same, the average FI 5 rate was 26 responses per minute, and the average FR 20 rate was 36 responses per minute. Patterns of responding were irregular, especially when the same component schedule was repeated. Again it is probable that the irregularly alternating red and green stimuli were functioning as both discriminative stimuli and conditioned reinforcers (cf. Kelleher & Fry, 1962). Although this dual function of the red and green stimuli make it difficult to analyze the effectiveness of the white light, it is apparent that the briefly presented white light was necessary to maintain performances similar to those that are maintained on comparable multiple schedules of primary reinforcement.

In the chimpanzee experiments the animal obtains more and more poker chips as it works through the sequence, while in the pigeon experiments there is only a brief exteroceptive stimulus change at the termination of each component schedule. It is interesting that pausing frequently occurred in the early components of the token reinforcement schedule with the chimpanzee, while the performance of the pigeon was maintained throughout the sequence. As noted above, responding tends to be suppressed in the early components of a sequence of schedules when different exteroceptive stimuli, such as the number of tokens, are correlated with early and late components. The pigeon results suggest that the brief stimulus change at the completion of each component was an effective conditioned reinforcer. Because the same stimuli were correlated with early and late components of the sequence, the effectiveness of the brief stimulus change in maintaining responding in early components was not attenuated. As noted above, however, these second-order multiple schedules are difficult to analyze because the stimuli correlated with the FI and FR components may have two functions. They are discriminative stimuli for their respective schedules, and they are probably conditioned reinforcers because they are each associated with primary reinforcement at the termination of half of the sequences. In any event, both types of FR (mult FI 5 FR 20) schedules developed and maintained characteristic multiple schedule control even in components that were temporally remote from primary reinforcement.

Brief Exteroceptive Stimulus Changes

This section will discuss the functions of briefly presented exteroceptive stimuli in second-order schedules of reinforcement. As noted previously, in a second-order schedule the behavior specified by a schedule contingency is treated as a unitary response. A briefly presented stimulus occurring at the termination of component schedules could help to maintain the unity of the scheduled behavior because of its discriminative function; that is, the brief stimulus could function simply to indicate the completion of each component. In addition, if the briefly presented stimulus immediately precedes primary reinforcement, it could help to maintain responding in each component by functioning as a conditioned reinforcer. The results in this section suggest that briefly presented stimuli can have marked effects on behavior maintained by second-order schedules.

Fixed Ratio Components Maintained under Fixed Interval Schedules of Primary Reinforcement

In one study with the pigeon (Kelleher, unpublished data), the basic second-order schedule was FI 10 (FR 20); that is, the occurrence of 20 responses (key pecks) was considered as a unitary response (FR 20) that was reinforced according to an FI 10 schedule of primary reinforcement. Each FR 20 completed during the 10-min. interval produced a brief (0.5 sec.) white stimulus light, but had no other programmed consequences; the first FR 20 completed after the 10-min. interval had elapsed produced the brief white stimulus followed immediately by primary reinforcement. Responses in the presence of the white light had no programmed consequences.

The cumulative response records at the top of Figure 9 show representative performance on this schedule. The pips indicate the presentation of the white light at the completion of each FR 20. Pauses (periods of no responding) after each presentation of the white light were followed by abrupt changes to a high response rate that was maintained until the white light appeared again. In general, the pauses were longest at the start of each fixed interval and became progressively shorter as time elapsed in the interval; that is, the number of FR 20 components completed was positively accelerated over the 10-min. interval. Scheduling complex responses (20 key pecks) on FI 10 has effects that are similar to scheduling simple responses (single key pecks) on FI 10.

Key-pecking patterns within each FR 20 component of one 10-min. interval are shown in the lower part of Figure 9. Although the first FR 20 component was interrupted by a pause of more than 21 sec., the remaining components show relatively uniform patterns of responding. Figure 10 shows interresponse time distributions for the entire session from which the data in Figure 9 were taken. The similarity of the relative frequency distributions from the first and second halves of all the 10-min. intervals confirms the data sample in Figure 9 in showing that the integrity of the complex response is maintained throughout each interval. About 5 percent of the interresponse times were longer than 1.8 sec. because the latencies of the initial responses in each component were included. The distributions are almost identical with modal interresponse times at 0.3 seconds.

Under the FI 10 (FR 20) schedule of reinforcement just described, the briefly presented white light maintained high stable rates of responding within each FR 20 component that are comparable to the patterns of responding maintained on FR schedules of primary reinforcement (Waller & Morse, 1966). Presumably the intermittent temporal pairing of

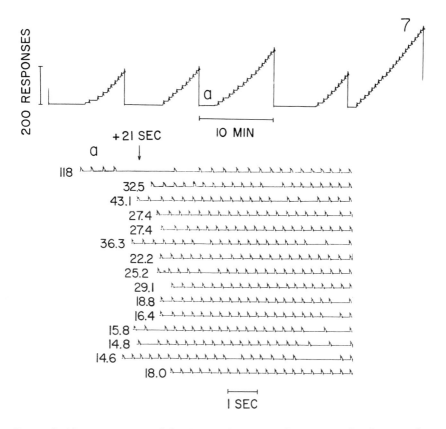

Figure 9. The upper part of the figure shows cumulative records of responding of a pigeon on FI 10 (FR 20). The pips indicate the completion of each FR component; the recording pen reset to the bottom of the record at primary reinforcement. The lower part of the figure shows detailed patterns of key pecking within each FR 20 component of the FI designated a. Each key peck produced a brief upward deflection of the recording pen. The numbers at the left of each record segment indicate the latencies (in seconds) of the initial key peck in each component (Kelleher, unpublished data).

the white light and primary reinforcement established the white light as a conditioned reinforcer; however, these results do not distinguish between the possible discriminative and conditioned reinforcing functions of the stimulus. The results do suggest that the factors controlling the durations of the pauses on the FI 10 (FR 20) schedule are similar to the factors that control interresponse times on a simple FI 10 schedule of primary reinforcement.

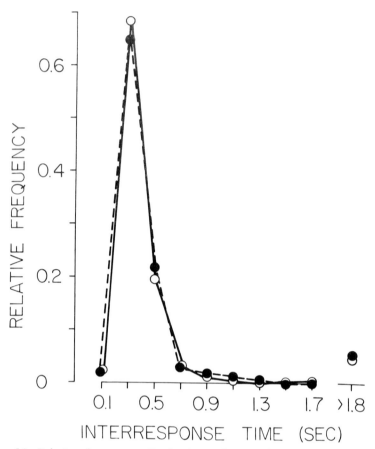

Figure 10. Relative frequency distributions of times between successive key pecks (interresponse times) from an entire session on FI 10 (FR 20). The solid circles and open circles indicate interresponse times from the first and second 5 min., respectively, of each FI. The lines connect the midpoints of the 0.2-sec. class intervals. The points at the right of the graph show interreponse times of more than 1.8 sec. (Kelleher, unpublished data).

Fixed Interval Components Maintained under Fixed Ratio Schedules of Primary Reinforcement

In another study with the pigeon (Kelleher, 1963), the basic second-order schedule was FR 15 (FI 4); each completion of an FI 4 schedule was considered as a complex response that was reinforced according to an FR 15 schedule of primary reinforcement. Each completion of FI 4 produced a brief (0.7 sec.) white stimulus light; in addition, the fifteenth FI 4 was terminated by the brief white stimulus followed immediately by primary reinforcement.

The cumulative response records in Records A and C of Figure 11 show the performance of one pigeon on this schedule. The pips indicate presentations of the white light at the completion of each FI 4 component. Positively accelerated responding, which is a common characteristic of FI schedules of primary reinforcement, occurs in most FI 4 components. Although response rates tended to be lowest in the early components, there is not a consistent increase in rates of responding in each successive component of the FR 15 (FI 4) schedule; components with relatively high response rates are often followed by components with relatively low response rates. Similar results have been observed under simple FI schedules of primary reinforcement.

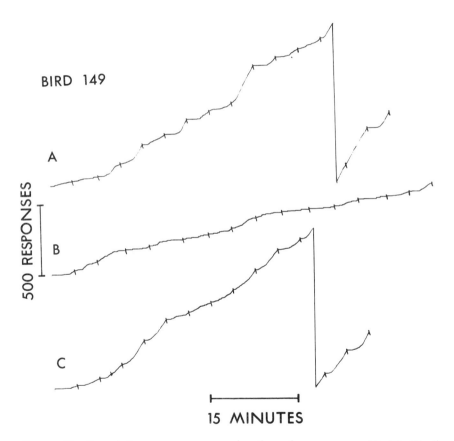

Figure 11. Cumulative response records of performance on FR 15 (FI 4). In Records A and C, the pips indicate 0.7-sec. presentations of a white stimulus light. In Record B, pips indicate completion of each component; however, no exteroceptive stimulus changes occurred until primary reinforcement. Primary reinforcement occurred at the end of each record (from Kelleher, 1963).

Comparison of brief stimulus change and tandem procedures. Using FR 15 (FI 4) and FR 30 (FI 2) as basic second-order schedules, Kelleher (1963) compared procedures involving brief stimulus changes at the completion of each component (brief-stimulus procedure) with tandem procedures. Record B of Figure 11 shows performance on the 15-component tandem FI 4 schedule. The most striking difference between the results obtained with the brief-stimulus and tandem procedures is revealed in the patterns of responding in each FI 4 component. When the brief stimulus is presented according to FI 4, responding is positively accelerated in each component; on the tandem procedure, there is no consistent response pattern and overall response rates are lower.

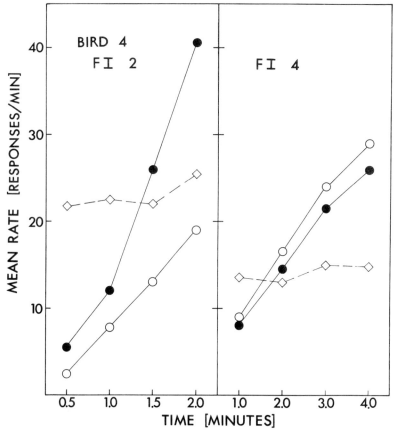

Figure 12. Mean response rates in successive quarters of FI components averaged over the last five sessions on each procedure. The diamonds indicate response rates on the tandem procedure. The circles indicate response rates on the brief-stimulus procedure before (closed circles) and after (open circles) training on the tandem procedure.

Quantitative comparisons between the brief-stimulus and tandem procedures with each of the basic schedules are shown in Figure 12. The
rates of responding in each of the early components of the tandem schedule
are less than in the early components of the brief-stimulus procedure. Under
the tandem procedure, responding occurs at a relatively low average rate
throughout each component; under the brief stimulus procedure, however,
rates of responding increase markedly in successive portions of the FI 4
components. The results indicate that the temporal pairing of the brief white
light and primary reinforcement is effective in establishing the white light as a
conditioned reinforcer, and that this conditioned reinforcing effect is well
maintained even though primary reinforcement is presented no more frequently than once per hour.

*Effects of brief stimulus changes that are not correlated with primary re-
inforcement.* Another experiment was conducted with FR 15 (FI 4) to
determine the effectiveness of a brief stimulus change that indicates the
termination of each component FI 4 schedule but that has not been established as a conditioned reinforcer. In this experiment, each completion of
the FI 4 component produced a brief (0.7 sec.) time-out (dark experimental chamber).[7] The fifteenth FI 4 component was terminated by primary reinforcement, which was not preceded by the brief time-out. The
results obtained with this procedure were similar to results obtained with
the tandem procedure (Figures 11 and 12), indicating that the time-out
was having almost no effect. In maintaining the performances shown in
Records A and C of Figure 11, the brief white light was apparently functioning as a conditioned reinforcing stimulus.

One recent study does show that a brief stimulus change, which has
not been established as a conditioned reinforcer, can be used to maintain
the unity of a complex response in a second-order schedule. Kelleher, Fry,
and Cook (1964) investigated DRL (FR) schedules in the squirrel
monkey. For example, in one part of their study the schedule was DRL 1
(FR 200). When the time that had elapsed before the first response of an
FR 200 component (initial pause) was less than 1 min., the completion of
the FR produced a 0.5-sec. time-out period. When the initial pause was
more than 1 min., however, the completion of the FR produced primary
reinforcement (but no time-out). Note that the occurrence of primary reinforcement is dependent upon the time elapsing before the first response
of the FR, but is independent of the times between subsequent responses.
The upper frame of Figure 13 shows the development of performance on
this procedure. The recording pen on the cumulative response recorder
reset to the bottom of the record at the completion of each FR component.
The dots at the top of some record segments indicate primary reinforce-

[7] Note that this procedure is similar to the "percentage reinforcement" schedules
described by Ferster and Skinner (1957).

ments. The histograms at the left of the cumulative records show the relative frequencies of different initial pause times. By Session 7 on DRL 1
(FR 200), more than 80 percent of the initial pauses were longer than
1 min. In Sessions 8 to 17, the schedule was DRL 2 (FR 200). The lower
frame of Figure 13 shows the development of performance on this procedure. Increasing the DRL requirement produced a corresponding increase in initial pausing. In Session 17 about 58 percent of the pauses were

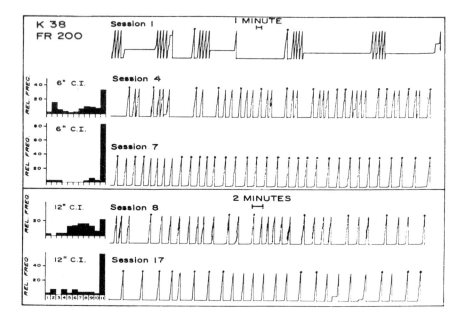

Figure 13. Development of performance of a squirrel monkey on DRL 1-min.
(FR 200) (upper frame) and SO (FR 200) drl 2-min. (lower frame). The dots
indicate FR 200 components that terminated with primary reinforcement; the
remaining FR 200 components terminated with 0.5-sec. time-out. The relative
frequencies of initial pause times are shown in the histograms; the class intervals
are indicated above each histogram (from Kelleher, Fry, & Cook, 1964).

more than 2 min. Although the individual FR components were not analyzed in detail, the cumulative records suggest that the brief time-out functioned to maintain the unity of the complex response. The FR 200 schedule
was considered as a unit of behavior that was itself on a DRL schedule of
primary reinforcement. The effect of increasing the DRL requirement with
FR 200 as the unit of behavior was similar to the effect that is obtained
when a single response is the unit of behavior; that is, the interresponse
time distribution was shifted to the right.

Frequency of Primary Reinforcement in Second-Order Schedules

The experimental results in the present section again show that seemingly minor differences in the ways in which stimuli are presented in second-order schedules can have profound effects upon behavior. In a previous section, we noted that remarkable losses of behavior occur on five-component chained FI 1 schedules. On these chained schedules it was difficult to maintain behavior even with maximum frequencies of primary reinforcement as high as 12 per hour. In the present section, we have considered tandem procedures and brief-stimulus procedures. Behavior was maintained with both procedures even though the maximum frequency of primary reinforcement was one per hour. The programming of the stimuli in second-order schedules seems to exert far more control than variables such as the average frequency of primary reinforcement. The simple second-order schedules of reinforcement with briefly presented stimuli are especially interesting because they not only maintain long sequences of behavior but also provide control over the patterns of responding in each component of the sequence.

Although the results show that average frequency of primary reinforcement can be a relatively weak determinant of behavior in second-order schedules, the frequency of primary reinforcement that is correlated with each stimulus in a second-order schedule may be of the utmost importance. The results obtained with two-component chained schedules indicated that the frequency of primary reinforcement in S1 was a critical determinant of the conditioned reinforcing effectiveness of S1. In these chained schedules, primary reinforcement occurred each time the stimulus was presented, and the frequency of primary reinforcement was varied by changing the minimum duration of S1. In the second-order schedules with brief stimulus changes, the frequency of reinforcement in the presence of the brief white stimulus light that was intermittently paired with primary reinforcement was relatively high. For example, on the FR 15 (FI 4) schedule with the white stimulus presented for 0.7 sec. at the termination of each component, primary reinforcement occurs after a total of 10.5 sec. of presentation of the white stimulus. The results with two-component chained schedules indicate that this is a relatively high frequency of primary reinforcement, which would establish the white stimulus as an effective conditioned reinforcement.

On the other hand, it is misleading to assume that frequency of reinforcement in the white stimulus, which is intermittently paired with primary reinforcement in a second-order schedule, is comparable to frequency of reinforcement in S1 in a chained schedule, which is always paired with primary reinforcement. For example, on FR (FI) schedules there is a specified probability that each presentation of the white stimulus will terminate with primary reinforcement, while on FI (FR) schedules there is a specified maximum frequency with which the white stimulus will terminate with primary reinforcement. The few experiments that have been conducted with second-order schedules have used brief durations (0.5 or 0.7 sec.) of the white stimulus. Under these conditions, the schedule according to which the white stimulus is paired with primary reinforcement seems to affect the conditioned reinforcing effectiveness of the white stimulus in the same way that schedules of primary reinforcement affect the frequency of responding. For example, on a simple FI 10 schedule of reinforcement, times between responses decrease as the interval elapses. On an FI 10 (FR 20) schedule, key pecking occurs at a stable rate in sequences of 20, but the duration of pauses between sequences of responding decreases as the interval elapses. The resulting performance might be considered as a composite of the schedule of presentation of the white stimulus, which maintains the sequences of 20 at a high rate, and changes in the effectiveness of the white stimulus as a conditioned reinforcer.

This type of analysis is even more important in accounting for behavior patterns on the FR 40 (mult FI 5 FR 20) schedules of reinforcement described previously. In this type of schedule, the probability of primary reinforcement being correlated with the white stimulus is low during the initial components, and this low probability presumably attenuates the conditioned reinforcing effectiveness of the white stimulus. In spite of this attenuation, response rates on initial FR 20 components characteristically exceed those on FI 5 components that are closer to primary reinforcement. This difference in response rates indicates the difficulties involved in attempting to compare the effectiveness of reinforcers presented according to different schedules. A relatively weak reinforcer may maintain high response rates on an FR 20 schedule but not on an FI 5 schedule. This difference between the FR and FI response patterns demonstrated that the white stimulus was a conditioned reinforcer but told little about the magnitude of the conditioned reinforcing effectiveness of S1. The changes in the conditioned reinforcing effectiveness of the white stimulus can best be considered by comparing FR (or FI) performance during initial components with FR (or FI) performance during terminal components.

SUMMARY

Any analysis of chaining is essentially an analysis of the functions of stimuli in sequences of behavior. The first section of this chapter discusses the historical development of the concept of chaining from its early application to sequences of unconditioned reflexes to its current application to complex sequences of learned behavior.

The second section is primarily concerned with experimental investigations of response sequences. Response sequences are characterized by orderly changes in patterns of responding in the absence of correlated extero- ceptive stimulus changes. It has usually been assumed that response se- quences are actually chains of stimuli and responses, and that the stimuli are hypothetical response-produced kinesthetic or proprioceptive impulses. In- vestigations of response sequences in simple schedules of reinforcement have shown, however, that these sequences are little affected by prolonged in- terruptions. These findings suggest that such response sequences are not controlled by moment-to-moment changes in response-produced stimuli. The patterns of responding in other types of response sequences, such as mixed schedules or double alternation procedures, cannot reasonably be interpreted in terms of response-produced stimuli because there has not been an adequate specification of the ways in which these hypothetical stimuli should function. Some studies of response sequences have shown that brief exteroceptive stimulus changes can function as conditioned re- inforcers which help to maintain response sequences without functioning as differential discriminative stimuli for changes in patterns of responding.

The third section discusses recent evidence on stimuli functioning as conditioned reinforcers which could be used to generate responding, to pro- long responding, or to change patterns of responding during experimental extinction. This section briefly considers hypotheses that have been of- fered as alternatives to the concept of conditioned reinforcement. These hypotheses fail to account for the results of recent experiments showing that patterns of responding were developed and maintained in extinction by scheduled presentations of stimuli that had preceded primary reinforce- ment; these stimuli were effective conditioned reinforcers. This section also considers experimental evidence concerning the necessary and sufficient conditions for establishing a conditioned reinforcer. The available evidence suggests that stimuli are established as conditioned reinforcers by means of respondent conditioning.

The fourth section is a detailed analysis of the functions of stimuli in second-order schedules. In second-order schedules, the behavior specified by a schedule contingency is treated as a unitary response that is itself rein- forced according to a schedule of primary reinforcement; for example, tandem schedules and chained schedules are variations of second-order schedules. Studies of two-component chained schedules and tandem sched- ules showed that the conditioned reinforcing effectiveness of a stimulus is directly related to the frequency of primary reinforcement in its presence, but is independent of the rate or pattern of responding in its presence. Second-order schedules comprising sequences of component fixed interval schedules were used to evaluate different ways of presenting stimuli. On chained fixed interval schedules, characteristic fixed interval patterns of responding (scallops) developed in the later components, but extremely prolonged periods of pausing developed in the early components of each sequence, even when the maximum frequency of primary reinforcement was 12 per hour. On tandem fixed interval schedules, responding was maintained with a maximum frequency of one primary reinforcement per hour, but scallops did not develop in the fixed interval components. Under the same second-order schedule, when a brief exteroceptive stimulus change occurred at the termination of each component schedule, responding was well maintained and scallops developed in each fixed interval component. These results show that discriminative stimuli in chained schedules with several components are not always conditioned reinforcers; however, a brief stimulus that has simply been paired with a primary reinforcer can be a powerful conditioned reinforcer. Such conditioned reinforcers make it possible to maintain long sequences of behavior in the absence of primary reinforcement, while also providing control over the rates and patterns of responding in each part of the sequence.

REFERENCES

AUTOR, S. M. (1960) The strength of conditioned reinforcers as a function of frequency and probability of reinforcement. Unpublished doctoral dissertation, Harvard University.

BERSH, P. J. (1951) The influence of two variables upon the establishment of a secondary reinforcer for operant responses. *J. exp. Psychol., 41*, 62-73.

BITTERMAN, M. E., FEDDERSON, W. R., and TYLER, D. W. (1953) Secondary reinforcement and the discrimination hypothesis. *Amer. J. Psychol., 66*, 456-464.

BUGELSKI, R. (1938) Extinction with and without sub-goal reinforcement. *J. comp. Psychol., 26*, 121-134.

BUGELSKI, R. (1956) *The psychology of learning.* New York: Holt, Rinehart & Winston.

COWLES, J. T. (1937) Food-tokens as incentives for learning by chimpanzees. *Comp. Psychol. Monogr., 14*, 1-96.

DEWS, P. B. (1962) The effect of multiple S$^\Delta$ periods on responding on a fixed-interval schedule. *J. exp. Anal. Behav., 5*, 369-374.

DINSMOOR, J. A. (1950) A quantitative comparison of the discriminative and reinforcing functions of a stimulus. *J. exp. Psychol., 40*, 458-472.

ELAM, C. B., TYLER, D. W., and BITTERMAN, M. E. (1954) A further study of secondary reinforcement and the discrimination hypothesis. *J. comp. physiol. Psychol., 47*, 381-384.

EXNER, S. (1894) *Entwurf zu einer physiologischen Erklärung der psychischen Erscheinungen.* Leipzig: D. Wein.

FERSTER, C. B. (1953) Sustained behavior under delayed reinforcement. *J. exp. Psychol., 48*, 218-224.

FERSTER, C. B. (1958) Intermittent reinforcement of a complex response in a chimpanzee. *J. exp. Anal. Behav., 1*, 163-165.

FERSTER, C. B., and SKINNER, B. F. (1957) *Schedules of reinforcement.* New York: Appleton-Century-Crofts.

FINDLEY, J. D. (1954) Rates of response in a two-member chain as a function of mean variable-interval schedule of reinforcement on the second member. Unpublished doctoral dissertation, Columbia University.

FINDLEY, J. D. (1962) An experimental outline for building and exploring multi-operant behavior repertoires. *J. exp. Anal. Behav.*, *5*, 113-166.

GOLLUB, L. R. (1958) The chaining of fixed-interval schedules. Unpublished doctoral dissertation, Harvard University.

HERRNSTEIN, R. J. (1961) Stereotypy and intermittent reinforcement. *Science*, *133*, 2067-2069.

HOLT, E. B. (1931) *Animal drive and the learning process: An essay toward radical empiricism.* New York: Holt, Rinehart & Winston.

HULL, C. L. (1943) *Principles of behavior.* New York: Appleton-Century-Crofts.

HUNTER, W. S. (1920) The temporal maze and kinaesthetic sensory processes in the white rat. *Psychobiol.*, *2*, 1.

HURWITZ, H. M. B. (1962) Some properties of behavior under fixed ratio and counting schedules. *Brit. J. Psychol.*, *53*, 167-173.

JENKINS, W. O. (1950) A temporal gradient of derived reinforcement. *Amer. J. Psychol.*, *63*, 237-243.

KELLEHER, R. T. (1957) A multiple schedule of conditioned reinforcement with chimpanzees. *Psychol. Rep.*, *3*, 485-491. (a)

KELLEHER, R. T. (1957) Conditioned reinforcement in chimpanzees. *J. comp. physiol. Psychol.*, *49*, 571-575. (b)

KELLEHER, R. T. (1958) Fixed-ratio schedules of conditioned reinforcement with chimpanzees. *J. exp. Anal. Behav.*, *1*, 281-289.

KELLEHER, R. T. (1961) Schedules of conditioned reinforcement in experimental extinction. *J. exp. Anal. Behav.*, *4*, 1-5.

KELLEHER, R. T. (1963) Sequences of responding maintained by second-order schedules of reinforcement. Paper read at Eastern Psychol. Ass., New York (April).

KELLEHER, R. T. (1965) Operant conditioning. In A. M. Schrier, H. F. Harlow, and F. Stollnitz (Eds.), *Behavior of nonhuman primates: Modern research trends.* Vol. 1. New York: Academic Press. Pp. 211-247.

KELLEHER, R. T., and FRY, W. (1962) Stimulus functions in chained fixed-interval schedules. *J. exp. Anal. Behav.*, *5*, 167-173.

KELLEHER, R. T., FRY, W., and COOK, L. (1964) Adjusting fixed-ratio schedules in the squirrel monkey. *J. exp. Anal. Behav.*, *7*, 69-77.

KELLEHER, R. T., and GOLLUB, L. R. (1962) A review of positive conditioned reinforcement. *J. exp. Anal. Behav.*, *5*, 543-597.

KELLER, F. S., and SCHOENFELD, W. N. (1950) *Principles of psychology.* New York: Appleton-Century-Crofts.

LASHLEY, K. S. (1951) The problem of serial order in behavior. In L. A. Jeffries (Ed.), *Cerebral mechanisms in behavior.* New York: Wiley. Pp. 112-136.

LOEB, J. (1900) *Comparative physiology of the brain and comparative psychology.* New York: Putnam.

MECHNER, F. (1958) Probability relations within response sequences under ratio reinforcement. *J. exp. Anal. Behav.*, *1*, 109-121. (a)

MECHNER, F. (1958) Sequential dependencies of the lengths of consecutive response runs. *J. exp. Anal. Behav.*, *1*, 229-233. (b)

MILLER, N. E. (1951) Learnable drives and rewards. In S. S. Stevens (Ed.), *Handbook of experimental psychology.* New York: Wiley. Pp. 435-472.

MILLER, N. E., and DOLLARD, J. (1941) *Social learning and imitation.* New Haven: Yale Univ. Press.

MORSE, W. H. (1955) An analysis of responding in the presence of a stimulus correlated with periods of non-reinforcement. Unpublished doctoral dissertation, Harvard University.

MYERS, J. L. (1958) Secondary reinforcements: A review of recent experimentation. *Psychol. Bull., 55*, 284-301.

SCHOENFELD, W. N., ANTONITIS, J. J., and BERSH, P. J. (1950) A preliminary study of training conditions necessary for secondary reinforcement. *J. exp. Psychol., 40*, 40-45.

SCHLOSBERG, H., and KATZ, A. (1943) Double alternation lever-pressing in the white rat. *Amer. J. Psychol., 56*, 274-282.

SHAPIRO, M. M. (1960) Respondent salivary conditioning during operant lever pressing in dogs. *Science, 132*, 619-620.

SHERRINGTON, C. S. (1906) *The integrative action of the nervous system.* New York: Scribner.

SKINNER, B. F. (1938) *The behavior of organisms.* New York: Appleton-Century-Crofts.

SKINNER, B. F. (1948) "Superstition" in the pigeon. *J. exp. Psychol. 38*, 168-172.

SKINNER, B. F., and MORSE, W. H. (1958) Sustained performance during very long experimental sessions. *J. exp. Anal. Behav., 1*, 235-244.

SMITH, S., and GUTHRIE, E. R. (1921) *General psychology in terms of behavior.* New York: Appleton-Century-Crofts.

SPENCE, K. W. (1956) *Behavior theory and conditioning.* New Haven: Yale Univ. Press.

STEIN, L. (1958) Secondary reinforcement established with subcortical reinforcement. *Science, 127*, 466-467.

WALLER, M. B., and MORSE, W. H. (In press) Characteristics of performance in fixed ratio 30. *J. exp. Anal. Behav.*

WOLFE, J. B. (1936) Effectiveness of token-rewards for chimpanzees. *Comp. Psychol. Monogr., 12*, 1-72, No. 60.

WYCKOFF, L. B., SIDOWSKI, J., and CHAMBLISS, D. J. (1958) An experimental study of the relationship between secondary reinforcing and cue effects of a stimulus. *J. comp. physiol. Psychol., 51*, 103-109.

ZIMMERMAN, D. W. (1957) Durable secondary reinforcement: Method and theory. *Psychol. Rev., 64*, 373-383.

ZIMMERMAN, J., and FERSTER, C. B. Chained VI performance of pigeons maintained with an added stimulus. *J. exp. Anal. Behav., 7*, 83-89.

6

Concurrent Operants [1]

A. Charles Catania

INTRODUCTION

In the development of an experimental analysis of behavior (Skinner, 1938) a substantial concern has been the dynamics of the single operant, for which an essential datum is whether or not, or how often, the operant occurs within a given period of time. The isolated operant is, however, a special case, and attention inevitably must turn also to the interaction of two or more operants.

Ferster and Skinner (1957, p. 724) have defined concurrent operants as: "Two or more responses, of different topography at least with respect to locus, capable of being executed with little mutual interference at the same time or in rapid alternation, under the control of separate programming devices." In the case of concurrent operants, the organism's alternatives are not simply to respond or not to respond, but, given that it responds, to emit one or another of the available operants. In addition, the behaviors of changing over from one to another of these operants (as when a pigeon, pecking at the response keys in a two-key experimental chamber, moves over from one key to the other) are themselves separate operants that are under the control of the programming devices (Skinner, 1950). Thus, the analysis of concurrent operants must consider not only the ab-

[1] Previously unpublished research described in this chapter was conducted at Harvard University (Figures 4, 5, 7, 14-17, and Table 1), under the support of NSF Grants G8621 and G18167 (B. F. Skinner, principal investigator), and at the Smith, Kline and French Laboratories (Figures 2, 8, 10, 18-20), in collaboration with L. Cook. For help in these two groups of experiments, the author owes thanks, respectively, to Mrs. Antoinette C. Papp and Wallace R. Brown, Jr., and to J. F. Deegan, C. A. Gill, and W. C. Riddle. Some costs of the preparation of the manuscript were defrayed by the New York University Arts and Science Research Fund. This preparation was greatly facilitated by the secretarial skills of Mrs. Geraldine Hansen.

The author also would like to acknowledge his indebtedness to L. R. Gollub, R. J. Herrnstein and G. S. Reynolds for many points, raised in discussion and correspondence over the past few years, that have found their way into the present manuscript.

solute rates of the separate operants, but also their relative frequencies and the frequencies of changeovers from one to another. It is for this reason that it is generally agreed that the dynamics of two concurrent operants are considerably more than twice as complicated as the dynamics of the single operant.

The analysis of concurrent operants would present no problems if it turned out that concurrent performances were the same as those maintained when operants are studied in isolation. There is a long history of research, however, indicating that organisms cannot usually "do two things at once" without having one thing interfere with the other (e.g., Jastrow & Cairnes, 1891-1892). Concurrent operants behave differently together from the way in which each operant behaves in isolation. The intent of the present chapter is to distinguish those properties of an operant performance that are independent of concurrent operants and their schedules of reinforcement from those properties that are affected by or interact with other operants and their schedules.

Many interactions are of a local nature, depending on specific characteristics of concurrent schedules of reinforcement and on such factors as the accidental strengthening of one operant by reinforcements produced by another operant. These interactions can often be manipulated by modifications in the programming of concurrent schedules, several examples of which will be discussed in this chapter. Other interactions seem to be of a more general nature. Evidence will be presented that indicates that, over a range of experimental conditions, concurrent operants are independent with respect to their rates of occurrence, in that changes in the rate of one operant do not affect the rate of other operants; but they are not independent with respect to their consequences, in that changes in the consequences of one operant (such as its frequency of reinforcement) affect the rate of other operants.

COMPATIBLE AND INCOMPATIBLE CONCURRENT OPERANTS

It would appear that a necessary condition for the maximal independence of two or more operants is that they be topographically compatible, so that they can occur at the same time as well as in succession. This criterion is satisfied, for example, by a monkey's presses on one lever with the left hand and on a second lever with the right hand. It is not satisfied by a pigeon's pecks at two keys, because the pigeon cannot peck the two keys simultaneously. In practice, however, topographical compatibility often leads to an incompatibility, with respect to separation of the control of concurrent operants by their respective schedules of reinforcement. When two responses occur simultaneously, the consequences of one necessarily have an effect on both. For example, if two lever presses occur at the same time, and one of the presses produces reinforcement, the other press may be strengthened by the temporal contiguity with reinforcement even though the reinforcement was not programmed for a press on that lever. The accidental strengthening or maintenance of one operant by reinforcement programmed for another is a special case of *superstition* (Skinner, 1948; see also Herrnstein's Chapter 2). In this special case, which may be called *concurrent superstition* (Catania & Cutts, 1963), the accidental correlation of the operant is with reinforcement programmed for a second operant rather than with reinforcement that is independent of behavior.

The control of one operant by the reinforcement schedule for another is illustrated in a variety of concurrent schedules that have been programmed for compatible operants. Sidman (1958), for example, attempted to control independently two compatible operants in monkeys, chain pulls maintained by food reinforcement and lever presses maintained by avoidance of shock. He found that the avoidance schedule in fact controlled both operants. Although subsequent changes in the schedule of food reinforcement permitted a temporary demonstration of independence (concurrent suppression of the food-reinforced chain pull and facilitation of the avoidance lever press during the presentation of a preshock stimulus), the changes in the schedule eventually reversed the control, producing a performance in which avoidance responding was partially under the control of the schedule of food reinforcement.

Ferster (1957) demonstrated a degree of independence of compatible concurrent key presses in chimpanzees, one maintained by variable interval reinforcement (VI 10-min.) and the other by fixed ratio reinforcement (FR 120). Although independent rates of key pressing were maintained by the VI and FR schedules, about one third of the presses on the VI key occurred at the same time as presses on the FR key, and the performances deviated from those that would have been maintained if the VI and FR schedules had been programmed separately.

Lane (1961) studied concurrent pecking and chirping in chicks, two operants with no topographical overlap. When pecking that had been maintained by an FR 20 schedule of reinforcement was extinguished, both pecking and chirping declined in rate, although reinforcement had been programmed only for pecking.

Gollub (personal communication) found that when presses on two levers were reinforced by two independent concurrent schedules, rats often came to respond consistently on both levers at the same time, pressing one with each paw. To separate the performances on each lever when this occurred, it was necessary to prevent reinforcement of simultaneously emitted presses. The author has made similar observations in two-lever experiments with squirrel monkeys.

These findings indicate that, in order to maintain the independence of two compatible operants, it is necessary to make them incompatible by programming explicit reinforcement contingencies that separate the two operants in time. Thus, in the study of concurrent operants with pigeons, it may be an advantage that the pigeon does not have two heads.

Even when concurrent operants are incompatible, however, concurrent superstitions may be established if the operants can occur in rapid succession, because the temporal contiguity of one response with subsequent reinforcement for another may be sufficient to strengthen the first. Ferster and Skinner (1957, Chapter 13), for example, programmed concurrent VI and FI schedules for pigeons' pecks on each of two keys. Considerable responding was maintained early in each fixed interval, whereas when FI schedules are programmed singly, low rates of responding usually are maintained early in each interval. The early FI responses probably were maintained partially by accidental correlation with VI reinforcements for pecks on the other key.

Concurrent superstitions may account in part for Hearst's (1961) finding that presses on each of two levers in rats, concurrently maintained by VI schedules of food and of water reinforcement respectively, were similarly affected by doses of d-amphetamine. Cumulative records showed that the two operants tended to vary together.

Schedules that differentially reinforce low rates of responding (drl schedules) are particularly favorable to the establishment of concurrent superstitions, because reinforced responses occur after pauses during which other behaviors are likely to have occurred. Such performances, *collateral behavior* maintained by drl reinforcement, have been studied in cases where this behavior was itself independently reinforced by a concurrent schedule (Segal, 1961), and where no explicit schedule of reinforcement was programmed for this behavior (Bruner & Revusky, 1961; Segal & Holloway, 1963).

Thus, when concurrent operants are incompatible in the first place, it is often necessary to program concurrent schedules in such a way that the operants become even more incompatible, at least with respect to their relationship to their separate schedules of reinforcement. One technique for producing this separation is the changeover delay (COD: Herrnstein, 1961a), a procedure that allows a response to be reinforced only if a certain interval of time has passed since the last changeover from the other response. The COD guarantees a separation in time between one response and the subsequent reinforcement of a concurrent response. For example, if a 1-sec. COD is programmed with concurrent schedules of reinforcement for key pecking in the pigeon, a peck on a given key cannot be reinforced unless at least 1 sec. has passed since the pigeon moved over from one key to the other. The COD is usually timed from the first peck on the key to which the pigeon has switched.

An illustration of the effect of a COD on concurrent superstition is shown in Figure 1 (Catania & Cutts, 1963), which compares the extinction of one of two concurrent operants (key pecks in the pigeon) with and without a COD. In both cases, pecks on each key previously had been maintained by concurrent VI schedules of reinforcement, and the schedule for one key (ext) was then discontinued. With a COD, the rate of pecking on the ext key declined to zero over 12 1-hr. experimental sessions. In the repetition of this procedure without a COD, key pecking was maintained on

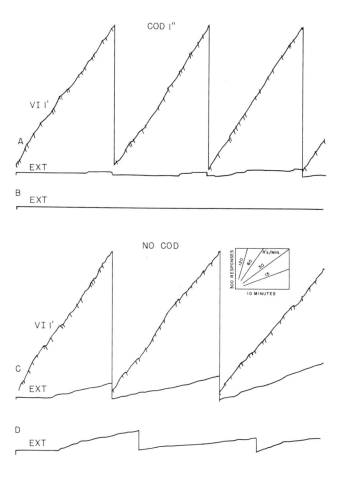

Figure 1. Cumulative records of a pigeon's key pecking maintained by conc VI 1-min. ext schedules, programmed with a 1-sec. COD or with no COD. In each case, a VI 2-min. schedule preceded extinction on the second key. Records a and b show the seventh and twelfth sessions of extinction with COD 1-sec. Records c and d show the seventh and twelfth sessions with no COD. In b and d, the concurrent VI records for the first key are omitted (from Catania & Cutts, 1963).

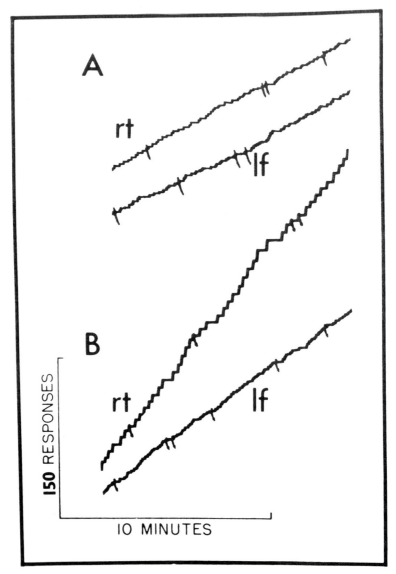

Figure 2. Sample cumulative records of lever pressing in the squirrel monkey maintained by conc VI 2-min. VI 2-min. schedules, programmed with a 2-sec. COD. The upper pair of records (A) illustrate a fairly typical performance: the monkey pressed the right lever with the right hand and the left lever with the left hand. The lower pair (B) illustrate a topographical superstition: this monkey operated the right lever by chewing at it and pressing it with its chin, whereas it pressed the left lever by hand.

the ext key, at a low rate, throughout 12 sessions. The high rate of rein-forcement (VI 1-min. or 60 rft/hr) provided by the key for which rein-forcement was maintained was favorable to the development and mainte-nance of a concurrent superstition when no COD was programmed, because it made likely the accidental correlation of reinforcement with pecks on the ext key.

The usefulness of the COD in maintaining a degree of independence of concurrent performances has been demonstrated in several experiments (Findley, 1958; Herrnstein, 1961a; Sidman, 1962b; Catania, 1962; 1963b). Nevertheless, other types of superstition may develop even with this proce-dure in effect, because the organism spends a given amount of time in re-sponding after changing over from one operant to another before the COD allows a response to be reinforced. The incidental correlation of a given pattern or topography of response with reinforcements that occur after the COD has terminated can generate differences in the concurrent perform-ances maintained by similar schedules of reinforcement. These differences complicate the comparison and analysis of the performances. An example of a topographical superstition from an experiment with squirrel monkeys is shown in Figure 2. Two VI 2-min. schedules were programmed concur-rently, with a 2-sec. COD, for presses on each of two levers. In the typical case (A), monkeys pressed one lever with each hand and the temporal pat-terning of the two responses was similar: several presses on one lever alter-nated with a roughly equal number of presses on the other. In one case (B), however, a monkey pressed the left lever by hand and the right by chewing and chin pressing. The temporal patterning of the performance consisted of short bursts of responses emitted at a high local rate on the right lever (il-lustrated by the steplike grain of the right-lever record in B) alternating with several responses emitted at a much lower local rate on the left lever. Thus, more responses were recorded on the right than on the left lever, de-spite the fact that equal numbers of reinforcements were provided by each schedule. Once this pattern of responding was established, it was inciden-tally maintained by reinforcement and therefore persisted for several weeks.

The occurrence and magnitude of a topographical superstition depends on a number of variables, of which the shaping procedure is probably one of the most important. In any given case, such superstitions can usually be handled by reshaping procedures or by manipulation of the contingencies of reinforcement. Nevertheless, they sometimes present serious difficulties, particularly when they occur in experiments in which it is difficult to dis-tinguish between instances of topographical superstition and other effects.

FORMAL ASPECTS OF CONCURRENT PROGRAMMING

If it is correct that the simultaneity of concurrent operants is incom-patible with the independence of concurrent operants, concurrent procedures must provide that responses occur only in succession. This is in itself a limitation on the independence of concurrent operants, because under such conditions the occurrence of one response at a given moment necessarily implies the non-occurrence of others at the same time.

The limitation on simultaneity also has implications for the relationship of two methods of programming schedules for concurrent operants. In one, the organism switches between two schedules on two operanda by moving back and forth between the operanda; in the other, it switches between two schedules on one operandum, each correlated with a different stimulus, by responding on a second operandum (Findley, 1958). When concurrent responses can only occur successively, the two procedures are equivalent. This is illustrated schematically in Figure 3, using key pecks in

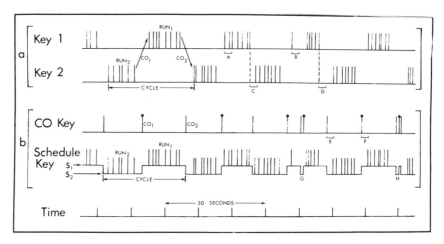

Figure 3. Diagrammatic comparison of two-key (a) and CO-key (b) concurrent procedures. In the two-key procedure, the organism moves back and forth between the two keys. In the CO-key procedure, each schedule is associated with a different stimulus (S_1 and S_2) on the schedule key, and the organism switches from one to the other by pecking the CO-key. For details see text.

the pigeon as the concurrent operants for the purposes of example. In both procedures, each of the concurrent schedules of reinforcement operates continuously. Thus, if a VI schedule is programmed for one operant in these concurrent schedules, the timing of the intervals in this schedule continues even when the organism is emitting the other operant.

The concurrent performance in which a pigeon switches back and forth between two keys, each provided with an independent schedule of reinforcement, is shown in a. Vertical lines indicate pecks. Sequences of pecks on one key (runs) are followed by sequences of pecks on the other. Changeovers (COs), movements from one key to the other, are labelled in terms of the key to which the pigeon switches. The duration of a CO is given by the time from the last peck on one key to the first on the other. This successive performance is generated even with compatible concurrent operants if the programming of the concurrent schedules includes a COD.

In this procedure, a COD may be programmed in two ways: from the first response on a given key after a CO, illustrated for Key 1 at A and B, or from the last response on a key before a CO, illustrated for Key 2 at C and D. With the former COD (Herrnstein, 1961a), at least two responses are required to produce a scheduled reinforcement on a given key: the first response of the run, which initiates the COD, and the first response after the termination of the COD (e.g., the second response of the run at B). With the latter COD (Findley, 1958), the first response on a given key can produce a scheduled reinforcement if the CO is longer than the duration of the COD, as at D. A disadvantage of the latter COD is that it favors long COs that involve superstitious patterns of responding (e.g., after the last peck on one key, the pigeon turns around twice in the chamber before pecking the other key). The former COD (Key 1) favors rapid switching. In most experiments, only one type of COD is programmed, for COs in either direction; subsequent references to two-key CODs in this chapter indicate the former (Key 1) COD.

In the changeover-key or CO-key procedure, each peck on one key changes the schedule and associated stimuli on a second key (Findley, 1958). To illustrate this procedure, Figure 3, in b, shows a performance formally equivalent to that of the two-key procedure: responses on the schedule key correspond in time to those on the two keys in a, and runs of responses in one schedule alternate with runs of responses in the other. The alternation of the two schedules, each correlated with a different stimulus (S_1 and S_2) is shown by the displacements of the schedule-key baseline. The CO-key pecks in b are shown occurring at an arbitrary time between the last peck on one key and the first on the other in the corresponding COs of the two-key performance in a (alternatively, they might have been shown corresponding to the first peck of each run in the two-key performance).

The CODs programmed in CO-key procedures usually are timed from pecks on the CO key, as at E and F. Thus, the first peck in a given schedule may be reinforced, if it occurs sufficiently long after the CO peck. Nevertheless, at least two pecks are required for reinforcement whenever the pigeon moves from one schedule to the other: a peck on the CO key followed by a peck on the schedule key.

An advantage of the CO-key procedure is that it makes the behavior of switching from one schedule to the other explicit. With this arrangement, it is possible to record COs to a given schedule that are not accompanied by pecks in that schedule (e.g., at G, where the pigeon switches from S_1 to S_2 and back again without a peck in the S_2 schedule, and at H, where the pigeon switches from S_1 to S_2 with three successive CO-key pecks).

Another advantage of the procedure is that it reduces the likelihood of topographical superstitions (as in Figure 2) that complicate the comparison of concurrent performances. When two concurrent schedules are programmed on a single operandum, each correlated with a different stimulus, the topographies of responses in the presence of each stimulus are likely to remain more similar than the topographies of responses on two separate operanda. Different stimuli may generate differences in topography, just as, in the "second type of superstition" of Morse and Skinner (1957), they may generate differences in rate. In practice, however, such differences occur less frequently in the CO-key than in the two-key procedure.

One consequence of CO-key programming is that responses on one operandum that occur in the presence of each of two successive stimuli are treated as two different operants (cf. Findley, 1962). Two stimuli are explicitly programmed in the CO-key procedure; in the two-key procedure, the organism is exposed to one complex of stimuli while pecking at one key and to a different complex when pecking at the other key, and thus incidentally changes the complex of stimuli when it moves from one key to the other. Concurrent schedules, therefore, may be considered multiple schedules (schedules presented in alternation, each correlated with a different stimulus) in which the control of the alternation from one schedule to another is in the beak of the organism rather than in the hands of the experimenter.

Because of the explicit nature of the CO response in the CO-key procedure, it is convenient to discuss the components of concurrent performances in the context of this procedure. The observation that concurrent responses must be successive rather than simultaneous (i.e., incompatible rather than compatible) to be independent means that generality is not lost by restricting the discussion to this case. The CO-key procedure separates the two components of the performance maintained by concurrent schedules: multiple schedule or discriminative responding, and changeovers or choice. Each of these components is represented by one of the two keys. Thus, the multiple-schedule component of concurrent performance can be studied in isolation by removing the CO-key and programming the alternation of the schedules and their associated stimuli on the basis of the CO-key responding of either the same organism in preceding sessions or another organism in a second experimental chamber in which a CO-key procedure is programmed. Similarly, the changeover component can be studied in isolation by removing the requirement of responses on the schedule key, and delivering "free" or non-response-contingent reinforcements in the presence of each schedule's stimulus on the basis of the distribution of reinforcements obtained by either the same organism in preceding sessions or another organism in a second experimental chamber.

Taken together, the multiple-schedule and choice components appear to describe the concurrent performance completely. The extent to which the

separated component performances would match the corresponding concurrent performances, however, has yet to be determined experimentally,
because both multiple-schedule and choice performances are in themselves
complex. The rate of responding maintained within a given component of
a multiple schedule, for example, depends on the schedules of reinforcement in each of the components (e.g., Reynolds, 1961b; 1963b) and on
the durations of the components (e.g., Catania, 1961b), and choice behavior, similarly, is affected by a number of variables (e.g., Graf, Bullock,
& Bitterman, 1964). Thus, it is difficult to assess the extent to which concurrent performances represent a simple combination of multiple-schedule
and choice performances, or these performances plus an interaction between them.

One more point to be drawn from this analysis of concurrent performances concerns the continuity of the operation of the separate concurrent
schedules throughout responding in either schedule. This continuity is a
necessary condition for the independent programming of the schedules. If
one schedule stops when responding occurs in the other schedule, then this
schedule may not be independent of the other schedule. In considering the
multiple-schedule component of concurrent performances, however, it is
clear that, at the formal level, this distinction between independent and non-
independent programming is an arbitrary one between multiple schedules
with different distributions of reinforcement within successive components.
Such differences may have different behavioral consequences, and both
conditions may be relevant to an understanding of concurrent performance.
For example, the consequences of timing the intervals in an interval schedule continuously, during responding in either schedule, are different from
those of stopping the timing of these intervals when responding occurs in
the other schedule. In the former case, the longer the organism responds in
one schedule, the more likely it is that a reinforcement has been programmed by the concurrent interval schedule; reinforcement therefore is
likely early in each component, and the procedure favors frequent COs. In
the latter case, the likelihood that a reinforcement has been programmed by
a concurrent interval schedule does not change as the organism responds in
the other schedule, but reinforcement does become more likely in the schedule in which the organism is responding; reinforcement therefore tends to
be uniformly distributed throughout each component, and the procedure
favors infrequent COs (cf. Findley, 1958).

For some schedules, the point is usually irrelevant. In FR schedules,
for example, the schedule advances, and reinforcement becomes more probable, only with FR responses; thus the likelihood of FR reinforcement cannot change as the organism responds in a second concurrently programmed
schedule. It is possible, however, to design interacting FR schedules in
which this is not the case (e.g., Herrnstein, 1958).

A final point concerns data analysis. In the two-key procedure, both keys are always present, and it is customary to present data in terms of the overall rate of responding taken over the entire duration of the session. It is difficult in any case to estimate the rate of responding during the time spent at each key, because such a measure has to discount time spent in COs or arbitrarily assign it to one or the other key (some technical arrangements for recording such data as CO and run durations are discussed in Catania, 1961a). In the CO-key procedure, the durations of the separate stimuli for the two schedules can be more explicitly defined, and thus local rate measures in the presence of each stimulus as well as overall rate measures can be taken (e.g., Findley, 1958). In this chapter, however, rates refer to overall rates over total time rather than local rates over the time spent in a given schedule, unless otherwise indicated. The rationale for this choice is provided by the equivalence of the two-key and CO-key procedures and the fact that, even when the organism is responding in one schedule, the other schedule is always available and can be reached with a CO response. In addition, a surprising outcome of many detailed studies of components of concurrent performances is that local measures of performance often behave in a less orderly way than overall measures. Reynolds (1963a), for example, noted that the relative rates of responding on three keys behaved more consistently than the matrix of CO probabilities among the three keys. Similar observations have been made in two-key experiments (Catania, 1961a; 1962; 1963a). Examples of situations in which overall rate remains invariant while local measures of performance vary will be discussed in greater detail below.

CLASSIFICATION OF CONCURRENT OPERANTS

Within a given experimental situation, responses are reinforced only if they fall within certain limits of force, topography, duration, and so forth. An operant is a class of responses defined by such limits (Skinner, 1938). This implies that concurrent operants need not be distinguished only on the basis of either separate operanda or different stimuli in the presence of which each occurs. Concurrent operants may sometimes be distinguished by other characteristics. For example, one class of responses ranging in force from 10 to 15 grams may be reinforced according to one schedule, whereas, on the same operandum, a second class of responses ranging in force from 20 to 30 grams may be reinforced according to an independent second schedule. In this situation, it may not be meaningful to speak of a changeover from one operant to the other. Nevertheless, the schedules define two response classes that are functionally concurrent operants. These operants are incompatible and thus can occur only in succession.

The possible implications of this formulation for the analysis of schedules of reinforcement can be illustrated by considering Anger's (1954;

1956) studies of interresponse times (IRTs) in VI performances. An IRT is the time separating two successive responses, and, for convenience, an IRT is said to be reinforced when the response that terminates it is reinforced. Anger (1956) showed that the conditional probability of an IRT within a given class interval was related to the rft/hr (number of reinforcements per hour) produced by IRTs within that class interval. For example, if IRTs in the 4- to 8-sec. class interval produced a greater rft/hr than those in the 8- to 12-sec. class interval, the conditional probability of IRTs in the former class was greater than that for those in the latter (the conditional probability, IRTs per opportunity or IRTs/Opp, is the probability of an IRT in a class interval, given that a pause has occurred long enough to permit a response in that class interval; this statistic is computed by dividing the number of IRTs in the class interval by the number of IRTs in that and longer class intervals).

After demonstrating this relationship, Anger (1954) synthesized a VI schedule by concurrently programming different rft/hr for different classes of IRTs. A different VI programmer scheduled reinforcements for IRTs within each class interval. When these separate VI schedules were chosen to provide approximately the same rft/hr for each IRT class as was produced by that class in the preceding single VI schedule, the performance was essentially indistinguishable from that maintained by the single VI schedule. Anger also demonstrated that the conditional probabilities of IRTs in different classes in the synthetic VI schedule could be manipulated by varying the rft/hr. provided by the separate VI schedules making up the synthetic schedule.

It is interesting to note that Anger found it necessary to modify the VI schedule that programmed reinforcement for IRTs in the shortest class intervals (0 to 4 sec.) so that only the last of a sequence of IRTs in this class interval could produce a scheduled reinforcement. Short IRTs that followed long IRTs were more likely to be reinforced than short IRTs that followed short IRTs, because all the VI programmers operated concurrently. Without this procedure, therefore, stereotyped sequences of IRTs might have developed. Thus, this procedure served the same function in the synthetic schedule as does a COD in a two-key or CO-key concurrent schedule.

The synthetic schedule was made up of concurrent VI schedules for which the several concurrent operants were different classes of IRTs. A stochastic reinforcement schedule designed by Weiss and Laties (1964) is another example of a VI schedule arranged by programming different schedules of reinforcement for different IRTs. Other concurrent schedules for different classes of IRTs have been studied by Malott and Cumming (1964). The implication of this interpretation is that, even though a schedule may be arranged for a single operant, differential reinforcement of different properties of the performance may generate different classes of responses that can be treated, in the analysis of the schedule, as concurrent operants. From this point of view, procedures for response differentiation are a special case of concurrent scheduling in which a given class of responses is selected for reinforcement, and extinction is programmed for other classes. In addition to IRTs, a variety of response parameters may be of interest, including among others, locus (Herrnstein, 1961b), magnitude (Hefferline & Keenan, 1963), and force (Notterman & Mintz, 1962). It may be within the context of such procedures that generalization among concurrent operants (Cross & Lane, 1962) can be most fruitfully investigated.

One feature of the schedules that have just been discussed is the apparent absence of a CO response; but a CO, though not recorded, may be implicit whenever a response in one operant class is followed by a response in a concurrent operant class. In addition, in some situations, concurrent operants themselves may be implicit. For example, a stimulus that consistently precedes an aversive stimulus may come to suppress ongoing operant behavior (Estes & Skinner, 1941). Suppression occurs to the extent that the stimulus generates concurrent behavior that competes with or is incompatible with the ongoing behavior (cf. Brady, 1955).

Another procedure that involves unspecified concurrent operants is dro (Reynolds, 1961a: differential reinforcement of zero responding, or "other behavior"). In a multiple VI-dro schedule for key pecking in the pigeon, for example, pecks are reinforced during the VI component according to a VI schedule, and reinforcers are delivered during the dro component whenever no pecks occur for a specified period of time. The key pecking and the "other behavior" define two incompatible concurrent operants, one of which is reinforced in one component of the multiple schedule, and the other in the second component. The dro operant is an extremely broad class of responses, but, because various non-key-pecking responses may be reinforced during dro, topographical and concurrent superstitions presumably are generated in these as in other concurrent schedules, and effectively narrow down the class.

Despite the difficulty of defining CO responses in some of the above schedules, the explicit nature of COs in two-key and CO-key procedures indicates that, at least in these cases, CO responses are also operants that can be defined as a class in terms of their consequences. Because these operants function differently from the concurrent operants that are maintained by separate schedules of reinforcement, their relationship to concurrent performances and to other multi-operant performances must be considered.

Within a concurrent performance, COs do not produce the reinforcements programmed by the concurrent schedules. They do, however, produce or change the stimuli correlated with the respective schedules, and their maintenance may be attributed to the establishment of the respective schedule stimuli as conditioned reinforcers. The CO, therefore, is the first member of a two-member chain, in which the second member consists of the responding within a given concurrent schedule (cf. Kelleher & Gollub, 1962). In some cases, it may be desirable to consider the chains as three-member chains, in which responding in a given schedule is the first member, the CO is the second, and responding in the other schedule is the third; thus, the first member of the chain in one direction is the last of the chain in the other direction.

The formal similarity of COs and chains suggests that the variables that control COs in concurrent performances are similar to those that operate in chained schedules. Some of these variables are discussed in detail in Kelleher and Gollub (1962) and in Kelleher's Chapter 5 in this volume. The complicating feature with two concurrent operants is that two chains are involved, one in each direction. At any given point in a concurrent performance, the organism has the option (cf. Findley, 1962) of maintaining responding within a given schedule, or of initiating the chain leading to the concurrent second schedule. Once the CO has occurred, the option is available in the other direction. This "reversible" characteristic differentiates concurrent schedules from other schedules in which COs are possible only at particular times or only in one direction. In addition to chained schedules, a number of other schedules include COs. In progressive schedules, a schedule parameter changes progressively with time or responses, and a CO returns the schedule to some earlier value of the parameter (Findley, 1958; 1962; Verhave, 1963). Observing-behavior schedules provide a CO that changes the stimuli correlated with different reinforcement contingencies (e.g., the change from mixed- to multiple-schedule programming; Kelleher, Riddle, & Cook, 1962). Schedules that include a response that produces time-out from the experiment may be regarded as concurrent reinforcement and extinction schedules (e.g., Zimmerman & Ferster, 1964), except that the time-out, once produced, is usually maintained for a fixed period of time. Schedules with which COs to time-out have been studied include schedules of positive reinforcement (Azrin, 1961), avoidance (Sidman, 1962b; Verhave, 1962), and reinforcement plus punishment (Hearst & Sidman, 1961).

The reversible character of COs in concurrent performances also distinguishes these performances from those studied in choice experiments. The latter are usually arranged in discrete trials, and it may be that there are important differences between a procedure in which an organism is confronted with two or more alternatives on a given trial, and one in which an organism is engaging in one behavior while the opportunity for a CO to some other behavior is continuously available. This is reflected in the data analysis of choice and concurrent performances. Relative frequencies of responses are often adequate data in the case of discrete trials, whereas the concurrent performance generally requires, in addition, the examination of sequential dependencies among responses (cf. Frick & Miller, 1951) in the treatment of probabilities of COs.

LOCAL INTERACTIONS

An organism tends to change over from one schedule to another when the probability[2] that reinforcement will follow a CO becomes greater than the probability that reinforcement will follow continued responding within a given schedule. Thus, the way in which the probability of reinforcement in each of two concurrent schedules varies with the time spent in responding in either schedule controls when and how often the organism changes over from one schedule to another. These changeovers determine the local characteristics of each performance, or the extent to which the responding maintained by one schedule is interrupted by periods of responding in the other schedule.

Interval Schedules

In interval schedules, the programming of reinforcements is based on the passage of time. Thus, the longer the time spent in responding in one of two concurrent interval schedules, the greater the likelihood that a reinforcement has been programmed by the other schedule. This property of concurrent interval schedules differentially reinforces COs, generating frequent alternation between the two operants (Skinner, 1950).

Consider, for example, a hypothetical pigeon pecking two keys for which two equal VI schedules are concurrently programmed. If initially this pigeon pecks once per second and switches from one key to the other after an average of five pecks, successive runs on a given key last an average of 4 sec. (five pecks at 1-sec. intervals) and are separated by 6 sec. (a 4-sec. run on the other key and a 1-sec. CO in each direction). Given that the programming of reinforcements is independent of the temporal succession of pecks on the two keys, the probability that a reinforcement for a given key will be programmed between runs on the key is 0.6, whereas the probability that it will be programmed during a run on the key is 0.4. The probability that the first peck of a run will produce this reinforcement is therefore 0.6, whereas the probability that a given later peck in the run will do so is 0.4 divided by four pecks, or 0.1. Similar probabilities hold for pecks on the other key, because the schedules and performances are equal for the two keys.

Thus, the probability of reinforcement for a peck following a CO is greater than the probability of reinforcement for a peck following a previous peck on the same key. If the hypothetical pigeon is sensitive to differences in reinforcement probability, COs will become more frequent and runs shorter. Even with average runs of only two pecks the probability of rein-

---

[2] Probabilities here refer to relative frequencies in the organism's previous exposure to an experimental condition.

forcement for a peck following a CO is greater than that for a peck following a peck (successive runs on a key last 1 sec. each and are separated by 3 sec.). The terminal performance to be expected of the pigeon, therefore, is single alternation between the two keys.

Single alternation in fact describes what pigeons do when equal, concurrent interval schedules are programmed with no COD (Skinner, 1950). This alternation presents difficulties for the study of concurrent interval schedules. The primary components of such performances are the COs themselves, rather than the concurrent operants, and such performances are insensitive to changes in the schedule parameters (Herrnstein, 1961a; Catania, 1962). Frequent alternation is maintained, for example, even when the concurrent interval schedules are made unequal. An additional complication is that the frequent alternation is conducive to the development of concurrent superstitions; when pecks on one key are followed frequently by reinforced pecks on the other, each operant comes partially under the control of the schedule for the other operant (the distinction between two phenomena, frequent alternation and concurrent superstition, however, is important: the former is produced by very real contingencies generated in concurrent interval schedules; the latter is an indirect outcome of this concurrent performance and is exhibited when parameters of the schedules are varied and the performance does not change accordingly). It is for these reasons that concurrent interval schedules are most favorably studied when programmed with a COD (Herrnstein, 1961a). The COD reduces the frequency of COs as well as the likelihood of concurrent superstitions.

The effective duration of a COD probably is limited by the interreinforcement intervals making up a given pair of concurrent interval schedules. The COD determines the minimal time interval between a CO and a subsequent reinforcement. Thus, if many of the interreinforcement intervals in a given schedule are shorter than the COD that is imposed after a CO to the other schedule, reinforcement is likely sooner after continued responding in this schedule than after a CO to the other schedule. Under these conditions, responding will probably become restricted to only one schedule. This is seldom a practical problem, however, because CODs longer than 2 or 3 sec. are rarely programmed with interval schedules.

The performance characteristic of concurrent VI schedules programmed with a COD consists of runs maintained by one schedule alternating with runs maintained by the other schedule (cf. Figure 2A). The durations of these runs are, in general, at least as long as the duration of the COD (Catania, 1961a). When unequal VI schedules are programmed concurrently, the duration of the runs maintained by the schedule that provides more frequent reinforcement increases. Nevertheless, even with very disparate VI schedules, responding is maintained by both schedules. With concurrent VI schedules that provide 38 and 2 rft/hr respectively, for example, the latter schedule maintains responding, although at a low rate. As the duration of runs in the former schedule increases, the likelihood that the latter schedule will program a reinforcement during any given run increases. Thus, the less frequent the COs to the latter schedule, the greater the proportion of COs to that schedule that will be followed by reinforcement. The steady-state distribution of responses between the two schedules may be interpreted as an equilibrium between the effects of the relatively low rft/hr provided by the latter schedule and of the increase in the proportion of COs to the latter schedule that are followed by reinforcement when runs in the former schedule increase in duration.

Although no data are available, it may be presumed that similar factors operate within concurrent FI schedules, if the schedules are so chosen that there is no consistent temporal relationship between reinforcements programmed by one schedule and those programmed by the other. Given a consistent temporal relationship (e.g., FI schedules such that one is a simple multiple of the other), the reinforcement programmed by one schedule probably would come to serve as a discriminative stimulus for a CO to the other schedule.

With concurrent VI FI schedules (programmed with a COD), the frequency of COs to the FI schedule and the length of the FI runs increase as the time since the last FI reinforcement increases (Catania, 1962).

Ratio Schedules

Ratio schedules program reinforcement for the last response of a fixed or variable number of responses. Available concurrent data are restricted to fixed ratio (FR) schedules. With these schedules, the longer the time spent in responding in one schedule, the greater the likelihood that a reinforcement will be programmed by that schedule; however, the likelihood that a reinforcement will be programmed by the other schedule does not change. Thus, these schedules generate infrequent COs (which primarily occur after reinforcement), and responding tends to be maintained by only one of the two schedules (Herrnstein, 1958). With equal FR schedules, responding may be maintained by either schedule, with shifts from one schedule to the other occurring from time to time; with unequal FR schedules, responding tends to be maintained only by the schedule with the smaller FR requirement.

Herrnstein (1958) has shown that concurrent key pecks can be maintained in pigeons by FR schedules if the reinforcement of pecks on one key depends on the occurrence of pecks on both keys. Pecks then tend to be distributed between the two keys in proportion to the relative numbers of pecks required on each key.

An important property of the isolated FR performance is that, once responding has begun after a post-reinforcement pause, it continues at a high and roughly constant rate up to the next reinforcement (Ferster & Skinner, 1957). Concurrent scheduling has shown that, despite this uniformity in the rate of isolated FR responding, different tendencies to respond exist at different points in the FR run. Boren (1961), for example, presented a stimulus to rats after varying numbers of FR responses on one lever. In the presence of this stimulus, a single response on a second lever was reinforced. Thus, the stimulus served as a probe of the rat's tendency, at different points in the FR run, to switch away from the FR lever to a concurrent response. The probability of a CO to the second lever decreased as the rat progressed within each FR run.

In a related experiment, Mechner (1958) examined the tendency of rats to switch away from an FR lever when FR reinforcement was occasionally programmed for a terminal response on a second lever rather than on the FR lever. The probability of a CO to the second lever reached a maximum only after the number of responses in the FR run exceeded the FR requirement.

These findings are paralleled by the consequences of programming an FR schedule concurrently with some other continuously operating schedule, such as VI or avoidance. Under these conditions, individual ratios often are characterized by "scalloping," an increasing rate of responding prior to reinforcement that occurs because successive runs within each ratio become longer and more closely spaced as the ratio progresses. The closer the organism is to the end of ratio, the greater the likelihood of COs to the FR schedule and the smaller the likelihood of COs away from the FR schedule. This effect diminishes in magnitude (i.e., the performance becomes more like that in an isolated FR) with decreases in the FR requirement, with decreases in the rft/hr provided by the other schedule, and with continued exposure to the schedules. The effect has been observed with concurrent FI FR schedules in which a fairly constant rate of responding was maintained by FI (Ferster & Skinner, 1957, Chapter 13) and with concurrent avoidance FR schedules in which the FR reinforcement was a period of escape from the avoidance schedule (Sidman, 1962b). A case from concurrent VI FR schedules is illustrated in Figure 5a, discussed below.

Interval and Ratio Schedules

The combination of interval and ratio schedules demonstrates some further properties of local interactions. Figure 4 shows a pigeon's key pecking after about 150 hr. on concurrent FI FR with COD 1-sec. (Catania, 1963c). Both schedules maintained responding. The FR responding tended to occur early within intervals, when FI pecks were never reinforced. At the beginning of the session, for example, the pigeon emitted three ratios in succession on the FR key, with little responding on the FI key. It then switched to the FI key and responded on that key without interruption until the FI reinforcement at *a*. Responding seldom occurred on either key immediately after reinforcement (e.g., after the FI reinforcements at *b* and *g*). The temporal spacing of FR responding is similar to that of wheel running in the rat when wheel running, not explicitly reinforced, is observed concurrently with lever pressing maintained by FI (Skinner & Morse, 1957).

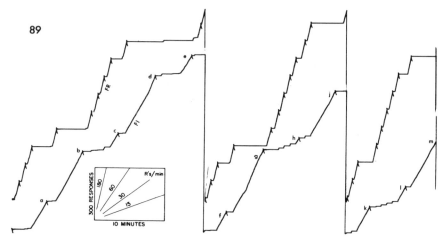

Figure 4. Cumulative record of a full session of a pigeon's key pecking maintained by conc FR 100 FI 5-min. schedules, in a two-key procedure programmed with COD 1-sec. The concurrent records reset to their respective baselines simultaneously. Diagonal strokes indicate reinforcements; FI reinforcements are also lettered. Most changeovers from one key to the other occurred after reinforcement.

With this performance, the COD was irrelevant because, for both keys, once pecking started on the key it usually continued until reinforcement. Thus, on neither key were pecks likely to be followed closely by reinforced pecks on the other key (the COD, however, may have played a role in the development of the performance).

Performances maintained by conc VI FR, programmed with a COD, are illustrated in Figure 5 (Catania, 1963c). After a history of about 15 hr. on conc VI FR (*a*), following a history of various concurrent interval schedules, frequent alternation between the two keys occurred, as shown by the steplike grain of both records. The rate of VI responding fluctuated considerably, and scalloping, discussed above, was evident within most ratios. In the terminal performance, about 75 hr. later (*b*), the rate of VI responding was fairly constant and FR responding occurred less frequently. When FR responding did occur, however, it often continued, without a CO to the VI key, until the FR reinforcement was produced. When the pigeon

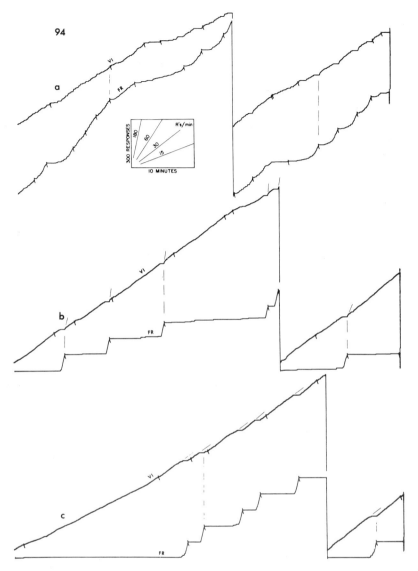

Figure 5. Cumulative records of sessions of a pigeon's key pecking maintained by conc VI 6-min. FR 100 schedules, programmed with a 1-sec. COD. The early performance (a) illustrates acceleration in the rate of FR responding between FR reinforcements. In the stabilized performance (b), long FR pauses preceded FR runs, which often were terminated only after FR reinforcement. During FR runs, no VI responses occurred, but the VI pauses were followed by "compensatory" runs of VI responses at a high local rate. In later sessions, the VI programmer was stopped during FR responding (c), and no VI "compensations" occurred: when the pigeon returned to the VI key after an FR run, it began pecking at the same local rate as had been maintained before the switch away from the VI key.

then returned to the VI key, it pecked at a locally higher rate (indicated by the short strokes above the VI record in *b*) than was usually maintained by VI. The pigeon appeared to make up on the VI key for the time lost in FR responding. This "compensatory" VI pecking, however, can be accounted for in terms of the changes in the probability of VI reinforcement during FR responding: during this responding no pecks occurred on the VI key, but the VI programmer continued to operate and thus the probability of VI reinforcement increased.

During the next 50 hr., the VI programmer was stopped for 0.3 sec. after each FR peck. Because of the high local rate of FR responding, this in effect stopped the VI programmer continuously and thus held the probability of VI reinforcement roughly constant throughout the responding on the FR key. As shown in *c,* this procedure eliminated the high rate of VI responding after the return from the FR key; the VI rate after the return was about equal to that before the CO to the FR key (indicated by the short strokes above the VI record in *c*).

This example indicates that the probability of reinforcement may determine not only the likelihood of COs from one schedule to another, but also the local rate of responding within a schedule once a CO has occurred. It also rules out the possibility that the high rate of VI responding depended on the high rate of the preceding FR responding.

In this particular case, the magnitude of the VI "compensations" may have depended in part on the duration of the COD, but since such "compensations" are observed without a COD after pauses in isolated interval schedules (e.g., Skinner, 1938), the COD is not likely to be the sole determinant of the effect.

Drl Schedules

In a procedure similar to Boren's probe of FR runs, Sidman (1956) studied concurrent lever pressing during drl responding in rats. A press on the drl lever was reinforced if preceded by an IRT of at least 30 sec. In the presence of a stimulus that appeared at various times after drl presses, a press on a second lever was reinforced. The probability of a CO to the second lever was lower the later after the last drl press the stimulus was presented, or, in other words, the closer in time the drl reinforcement.

Segal (1961), studying concurrent VI drl schedules in rats, found that the programming of drl produced long IRTs in the VI as well as the drl responding. A problem in the programming of schedules concurrent with drl is that drl reinforcements are likely to follow closely upon concurrent responses, thus favoring concurrent superstitions. The manner in which CODs may be programmed with a drl schedule, however, has not been determined.

Avoidance Schedules

Some characteristics of concurrent avoidance (AV) schedules are analogous to those of concurrent schedules of positive reinforcement. If, for example, either of two lever presses in rats postpones shock, that lever press tends to be maintained that produces the longer delay of shock (Sidman, 1954). Similarly, if different probabilities of postponing a shock are programmed for the two levers, that press tends to be maintained that has the higher probability of postponing shock (Verhave, 1961). In these cases, the programming of shock is determined by the schedule for the lever that was pressed last; the probability that a shock will be programmed by the schedule for the other lever does not change (i.e., it remains zero). Thus, these concurrent AV schedules generate infrequent COs. If shocks are independently programmed for each of two levers, on the other hand, the longer the time spent in responding on one lever, the greater the probability that a shock will be programmed by the schedule for the other lever. Thus, these concurrent AV schedules generate frequent COs. The latter performances, however, are often difficult to establish and maintain (Sidman, 1962a), perhaps in part because shocks programmed by one AV schedule occasionally follow closely upon COs to the other schedule.

The probability that an AV schedule will program a shock also increases with time spent in responding in a second schedule when the second schedule is a schedule of positive reinforcement. Again, this favors frequent COs to the AV schedule. In addition, because each AV response postpones shock, each AV response is effectively reinforced (cf. Anger, 1963). Thus, schedules concurrent with AV are particularly susceptible to the development of concurrent superstitions. This complication has been discussed in detail by Sidman (1958; 1962b).

QUANTITATIVE RELATIONS AMONG CONCURRENT OPERANTS

In general, the rate of responding maintained by a given schedule is determined not only by the rft/hr provided by that schedule, but also by the rft/hr provided by concurrent schedules for other operants. If, for example, the rft/hr provided by one concurrent interval schedule increases, the rate of responding maintained by the other schedule decreases, while the rate maintained by the first schedule increases. These relationships are illustrated, for concurrent VI schedules, in Figure 6. The figure describes, to a first approximation, data from several two-key and CO-key experiments with pigeons (Findley, 1958; Herrnstein, 1961a; Reynolds, 1963a; Catania, 1963a). The curves are based on the equation: $R_a = \dfrac{k r_a}{(r_a + r_b)^n}$, where R_a

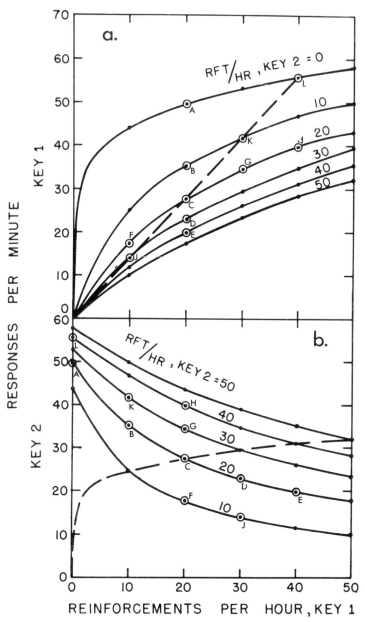

Figure 6. Changes in the rate of emission of an operant as a joint function of the rates of reinforcement (rft/hr) for that operant and for a second operant. In a, the rate on Key 1 is shown as a function of the rft/hr provided by Key 1, with the rft/hr provided by Key 2 as a parameter. In b, the rate on Key 2 is shown as a function of the rft/hr provided by Key 1, with the rft/hr provided by Key 2 as a parameter. Some corresponding points in a and b (corresponding pairs of reinforcement rates) are indicated by letters. The curves are based on equations presented in Catania (1963a).

is the rate of responding (resp/min) for operant a; r_a and r_b are the rates of reinforcement (rft/hr) for operants a and b respectively; and k and n are constants. The units in which rates are expressed determine k (here, $k = 30$), and n is a positive fraction slightly less than 1.0 (here, $n = 5/6$).

The equation was derived from several features of concurrent VI performances: the total output or rate of responding maintained by two schedules is a monotonically increasing, negatively accelerated function of the total rft/hr provided by the two schedules; this total output is independent of the way in which the total rft/hr is distributed between the two operants; and, the proportion of the total output maintained by either schedule matches the proportion of the total rft/hr provided by that schedule.

Figure 6 emphasizes certain implications of the equation. As the rft/hr for a given key increases, the rate of responding on that key increases, given that the rft/hr for the other key remains constant (e.g., Figure 6a, FCGH). Concurrently, the rate of responding on the other key decreases (e.g., Figure 6b, ABCDE). If the two rft/hr for the two keys are so chosen that their sum equals a constant, then the rate of responding on either key is a linear function, passing through the origin, of the rft/hr for that key (e.g., the dashed line JCKL in Figure 6a, representing the following pairs of rft/hr for the two keys: 10,30; 20,20; 30,10; 40,0). The dashed line passing through C in Figure 6b represents the rate of responding on a key when the two rft/hr for the two keys are held equal.

Herrnstein (1964a), in connection with related schedules of conditioned reinforcement discussed below, has proposed an equation similar to that given above, except that the constant n equals 1.0. Herrnstein's equation predicts a total output that remains constant when the total rft/hr provided by two schedules changes. Since actual changes in total output with changes in total rft/hr are in fact usually small, it is perhaps premature to choose between the two functions. Aside from differences in quantitative details, both give a fairly adequate picture of the effects of changes in rft/hr on response rates in concurrent VI schedules.

Qualitatively similar effects are observed with some schedules other than conc VI VI. The rate of VI responding decreases, for example, with the addition of concurrent reinforcement provided by a drl schedule (Segal, 1961). In this case, the relatively low rate of drl responding suggests that the decrease in VI responding depends on either concurrent reinforcement or induction of pausing from the drl to the VI performance, or both, rather than on competition with concurrent responses.

In conc VI FR, similarly, the rate of VI responding decreases with increases in the rft/hr produced in the FR schedule (Catania, 1963c). In addition, the rate of responding maintained by the FR schedule decreases both with increases in the FR requirement and with increases in the rft/hr provided by the VI schedule. This is illustrated in Figure 7, which shows sample records from FR schedules programmed concurrent with 0 rft/hr (no second key), 10 rft/hr (VI 6-min.), and 20 rft/hr (VI 3-min.). A quantitative account of interactions with FR schedules is difficult, however, both because changes in the rate of FR responding produce changes in the rate of FR reinforcement, which in turn may affect the rate of FR responding (cf. Morse's Chapter 3), and because the relationship between the response rate maintained by a schedule and the rft/hr provided by a concurrent schedule probably depends more critically for FR than for VI on the nature of the concurrent schedule (e.g., on whether the concurrent schedule is VI or another FR).

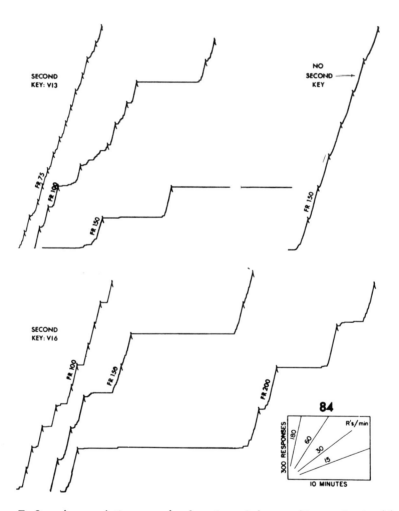

Figure 7. Sample cumulative records of a pigeon's key pecking maintained by various FR schedules of reinforcement programmed alone (no second key) or concurrent with a schedule of reinforcement (VI 3-min. or VI 6-min.) for pecks on a second key.

In the above examples, the same reinforcer was programmed for each concurrent operant. Dissimilar reinforcers may not interact in the same way. Stein (cited in Olds, 1962), for example, used as two reinforcers in rats electrical stimulation of two different brain sites:

> . . . when presented with *lever A* alone to stimulate *electrode A*, one rat regularly maintained a 1,500-rph rate. When offered at the same time *lever B* to stimulate *electrode B*, the rat maintained the 1,500 rph on *A* and by racing back and forth and working twice as hard maintained a similar rate on *lever B* concurrently. Behavior at one pedal was often largely independent of behavior at the other (Olds, 1962, p. 562).

Thus, the addition of reinforcement for one operant did not produce a concurrent decrease in the rate of the other operant. The independence of response rates also suggests that such decreases do not depend on response competition.

In an experiment by Laties and Weiss (1963), the introduction of a concurrent task that did not provide explicit reinforcement produced an increase rather than a decrease in the output maintained by an FI schedule with human subjects.

Another pair of dissimilar reinforcers are food and avoidance of shock. Response rates maintained by FR and AV schedules in squirrel monkeys are shown in Figure 8. The two schedules were programmed either concurrently or separately. The removal of either concurrent schedule did not systematically produce increases in the rate of responding maintained by the other schedule.

This limited evidence that the interactions illustrated in Figures 6 and 7 may depend on similarity of reinforcers indicates the potential interest of concurrent schedules with different reinforcers. Their other possible areas of application include deprivation interactions (e.g., food and water), generalization gradients (Hearst, 1962), and concurrent ratio schedules in which both operants are maintained.

Given concurrent VI schedules with similar reinforcers, the concurrent decrements in responding produced in each schedule by reinforcement in the other schedule are such that the proportion of the total output maintained by each schedule matches the proportion of the total rft/hr that is provided by the schedule, or, in other words, relative rates of responding match relative rates of reinforcement. Mathematically, this matching is expressed by the equation: $\dfrac{R_a}{R_a + R_b} = \dfrac{r_a}{r_a + r_b}$, where R and r are response and reinforcement rates, respectively, for operants a and b.

Matching has been observed by Reynolds (1963a) in an experiment with pigeons in which independent VI 3-min. schedules for three keys programmed either 30-sec. periods of time-out or a stimulus during which pecks on the key were reinforced on FR 25. The rate of reinforcement for

each key was determined by the relative proportions of these two consequences. This extension of the generality of matching to three concurrent
operants provided empirical confirmation for the principle of "independence from irrelevant alternatives" (Luce, 1959), an assumption underlying
mathematical analyses of choice behavior. The principle states that the

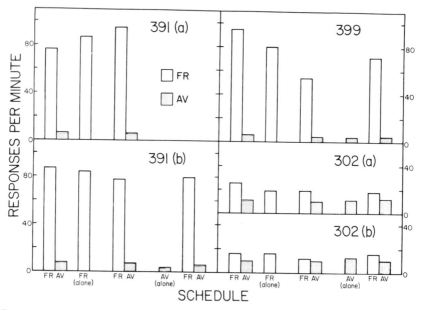

Figure 8. Rates of lever pressing in three squirrel monkeys in FR and AV
schedules programmed either concurrently (FR AV) with no COD, or separately
(FR alone or AV alone) with the lever for the other schedule removed. Presses
on one lever produced food (FR 100). Presses on the second lever, on the opposite wall, avoided 1-sec., 1-ma inescapable shocks (RS = SS = 30 sec.).
Data represents average rates over the last three of about seven daily sessions
(100 reinforcements or 3 hr., whichever came first) in each condition, except for
the second FR AV in Monkey 302's first sequence (a), which represents two
sessions. During AV alone, session durations and supplementary feeding after
sessions were based on average durations and FR reinforcements in the preceding FR AV sessions.

probability that one of two alternatives will be chosen over the other is not
affected by the introduction or elimination of additional alternatives. In one
phase of Reynolds' experiment, one key provided twice the rft/hr of a
second key, while a third key concurrently provided a rate of reinforcement
equal to the sum of the rft/hr for the first two keys. In a later phase, the
third key was covered, and thus provided no reinforcement. Although the

absolute rates of responding increased with the removal of the third key, the first key maintained about twice as much responding as the second in both phases of the experiment.

The phenomenon of matching in concurrent VI schedules has several quantitative implications, of which only two will be mentioned briefly here. The first concerns responses. Revusky (1963) has pointed out that matching implies that each schedule maintains an equal number of responses per reinforcement (resp/rft). If one schedule provides 30 rft/hr and maintains 3000 resp/hr, for example, while a second provides 10 rft/hr and maintains 1000 resp/hr, then in each schedule the organism emits 100 resp/rft. Thus, matching would be a necessary outcome of interval scheduling if it happened that the organism was sensitive to resp/rft, and decreased the relative rate of responding on either key whenever the resp/rft for the key became greater than that for the other key.

The second implication concerns time. The proportion of time spent in the presence of the stimuli for concurrent VI schedules in a CO-key procedure is shown in Figure 9 as a function of the relative rate of reinforcement provided by each schedule. In this experiment, both relative time and relative rate of responding matched relative rate of reinforcement. One interpretation of matching, therefore, is that responses occur at a roughly constant rate in either schedule, and matching is a consequence solely of the relative time spent in each schedule. The argument for this case parallels Revusky's for resp/rft. Although each schedule provides different rft/hr computed over total time, the matching implies that the rates of reinforcement in the presence of each schedule's stimulus are equal. If the organism spends 45 min. of each hour in a schedule that provides 45 rft/hr, for example, and 15 min. of each hour in a concurrent schedule that provides 15 rft/hr, then the average rate of reinforcement in the presence of each schedule's stimulus is 1 rft/min.

In view of the complexity of the local interactions within concurrent VI schedules and the number of variables and their interrelations that must be considered in the analysis of these schedules, the simplicity of the match of various relative measures of behavior to relative rates of reinforcement is remarkable. Nevertheless, this simplicity must be noted with caution, because the extent to which it is determined and potentially manipulable by seemingly trivial aspects of procedure has yet to be determined (cf. Skinner, Chapter 1). The role of the COD is a case in point. If the degree of matching varies with the duration of CODs, matching is only one of a continuum of performances all of which are relevant to the analysis of the variables controlling concurrent operants.

Effects of CODs and their interaction with other contingencies are illustrated in Table 1. In this experiment, the difference between the CODs for each direction of CO was varied. With no other contingencies, the introduction of the differential COD shifted each pigeon's responding slightly

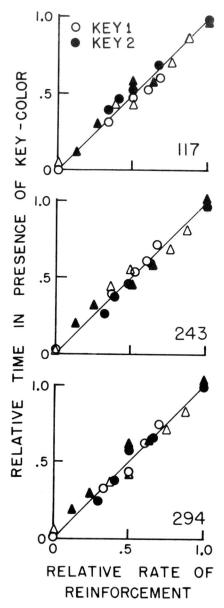

Figure 9. Relative time spent in the presence of a given schedule's stimulus (Key 1 or Key 2) as a function of the relative rate of reinforcement provided by that schedule for three pigeons. Each pair of concurrent VI schedules, programmed in a CO-key procedure with COD 2-sec. (Catania, 1963a), contributed two points to each graph. The diagonal lines represent perfect matching. Circles and triangles represent two different sequences of concurrent schedules.

but consistently to Key 1, for which the shorter COD was programmed. The preference for Key 1 was counterbalanced by the longer period of re-

Table 1

Effects of differential CODs with and without an IRT contingency on two-key responding in concurrent VI 2-min. VI 2-min. schedules. Data show the proportion of total pecks (average for three pigeons) that were emitted on Key 1 over the last 5 of at least 15 sessions in each condition.

COD (sec.)		Proportion of pecks on Key 1	
Key 1	Key 2	No IRT contingency	IRTs longer than 2 sec. not reinforced
0.5	0.5	.48	.54
0.5	1.0	.56	.49
0.5	2.0	.56	.39
2.0	2.0	.53	.56

sponding required for reinforcement on Key 2; thus, the small magnitude of the effect. In a later procedure, IRTs of less than 2 sec. were required for reinforcement, in an attempt to reshape an inadequate topography of key pecking in a fourth pigeon whose data are not included here. Since few IRTs within runs were greater than 2 sec. in the other pigeons, it was anticipated that this contingency would have little effect on their performances. The table shows, however, that the IRT contingency produced a large shift in responding to Key 2 when differential CODs were programmed. For each pigeon, the contingency generated a high rate of pecking maintained for longer periods of time on Key 2 the longer the COD for Key 2. Any preference for Key 1 can be inferred only from the high relative rate on Key 1 compared to the relative duration of the COD for that key. Since this demonstration shows that key preference can be manipulated with CODs, the significance of matching depends on the range of conditions over which matching occurs (cf. Herrnstein, 1961a). Data, however, are not presently available on the way relative responding varies with relative reinforcement as a function of COD, or on the comparison of CODs with other methods of maintaining independence of concurrent operants (e.g., change-over ratios or CORs, which require a minimum number of responses for reinforcement after a CO).

These problems in concurrent schedules are paralleled by those in choice and probability-matching experiments (e.g., Estes & Straughan, 1954), which study concurrent operants in discrete trials in which the reinforcement probabilities for the alternative responses usually sum to 1.0. In these experiments, performances range from matching (of probability of response to probability of reinforcement) to maximizing (or the emission of only the response with the higher probability of reinforcement). Different performances seem to be characteristic of different organisms (e.g., pigeons: Bullock & Bitterman, 1962; rats: Hickson, 1961; and rhesus monkeys: Wilson & Rollin, 1959; Wilson, Oscar, & Bitterman, 1964). Such differences, however, may reflect differences in details of procedure (e.g., intertrial intervals, Herrnstein, 1964a; the extent to which concurrent superstitions are favored, Catania & Cutts, 1963; manner of stimulus presentation; response topography) rather than species differences in the behavioral processes that determine the performances (cf. Graf, Bullock, & Bitterman, 1964).

Some variations in procedure that affect the likelihood of either matching or maximizing are analogous to those in concurrent schedules, in that they generate different probabilities of reinforcement for alternation of responses or for maintenance of a single response. A correction procedure, for example, arranges that a programmed reinforcement is held from trial to trial until the appropriate response occurs. Reinforcement probabilities in one trial therefore depend in part on the consequences of responding in the preceding trial. Without a correction procedure, on the other hand, the probabilities of reinforcement for the alternative responses remain constant over successive trials. The former procedure favors matching, or alternation between responses; the latter favors maximizing, or maintenance of only the response with the higher probability of reinforcement. Thus, the two procedures, respectively, are perhaps distant relatives of concurrent VI schedules with continuously operating programmers, which generally maintain both operants, and those with programmers that operate in alternation, which generally maintain only one of two operants (Findley, 1958).

VARIABLES AFFECTING PREFERENCE

Matching occurs in concurrent VI schedules when reinforcement parameters other than rate of reinforcement are varied. With equal VI schedules, for example, relative rates of responding match relative magnitudes of reinforcement (Catania, 1963b). Differences in reinforcement magnitude that produce large differences in concurrent rates of responding, however, sometimes produce only small changes in the rate of responding when studied in singly programmed VI schedules.

The sensitivity of concurrent performances to variables that have little or no effect when studied with single operants may be attributed to differences in the constraints imposed on performances by concurrent and by singly programmed schedules. Singly programmed schedules impose temporal constraints, such as the differential reinforcement of IRTs, that may override the effects of other variables; the relative measures in concurrent performances, depending on COs as well as on responding within each schedule, are to a large extent free of these constraints (cf. Morse's Chapter 3).

A major application of this property of concurrent performances is the study of conditioned reinforcement (see Kelleher's Chapter 5). In concurrent schedules of conditioned reinforcement, each operant is reinforced by the presentation of a stimulus during which a single schedule of primary reinforcement operates (Autor, 1960; Reynolds, 1963a; Herrnstein, 1964a). One operant, for example, may produce a stimulus in the presence of which a VI schedule provides 60 rft/hr, whereas the concurrent operant may produce a second stimulus in the presence of which a VI schedule provides 30 rft/hr. Such schedules are concurrent chained schedules in which the initial members of each chain operate concurrently and the terminal members operate separately. In the usual procedure with pigeons, the concurrent operants produce conditioned reinforcement (their respective stimuli) according to equal but independent VI schedules, with no COD (an indication, perhaps, that under these circumstances conditioned reinforcement is not sufficient to establish or maintain concurrent superstitions: cf. Kelleher and Gollub, 1962; Kelleher's Chapter 5).

In experiments conducted by Autor (1960) and Herrnstein (1964a), the relative rates of the concurrent responses matched the relative rates of reinforcement in the terminal members of each chain. Herrnstein's experiment also demonstrated, in a comparison of VI and VR schedules in the terminal members of each chain, that this matching did not depend on relative frequencies of reinforcement (rft/resp): equal rates of concurrent responding were maintained by VI and VR schedules in which rft/hr were equal, but not by VI and VR schedules in which rft/resp were equal.

The VI and VR schedules in these terminal members provided an aperiodic distribution of reinforcements in time. A comparison of aperiodic (VI) and periodic (FI) reinforcement (Herrnstein, 1964b) demonstrated a preference for aperiodic over periodic reinforcement. A stimulus correlated with VI reinforcement maintained a higher relative rate of concurrent responding than a stimulus correlated with an equal rate of FI reinforcement.

Concurrent performances are sensitive to punishment as well as to reinforcement. Punishment (e.g., shock) correlated with a given response produces a decrement in the rate of the response. This decrement is accompanied by an increase in the rate of concurrent responses (Reynolds, 1963c), illustrating a facilitating effect of punishment on unpunished behavior (cf. Brethower & Reynolds, 1962). The concurrent comparison of reinforcement plus punishment with reinforcement alone may provide an important baseline for the study of conflict (Miller, 1944; Hearst & Sidman, 1961).

Another area of application of concurrent schedules is the study of drugs, which sometimes have differential effects on each of two concurrent operants (Cook & Catania, 1964). Figure 10 illustrates effects of both drugs and punishment on concurrent responding in the squirrel monkey. In a CO-key procedure, one operant produced reinforcement and a second

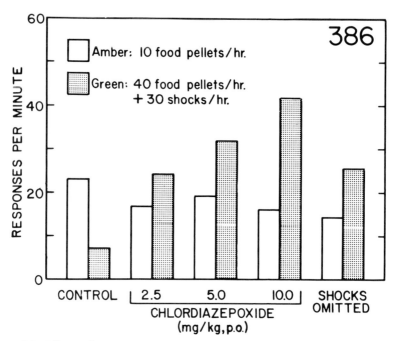

Figure 10. Effects of punishment and drug on a squirrel monkey's lever pressing in a CO-key concurrent procedure. One VI schedule (Amber) provided 10 rft/hr. The concurrent schedule (Green) provided both 40 rft/hr and 30 response-contingent shocks per hour, arranged by separate and independent VI programmers. A 3-sec. COD was programmed for VI reinforcement but not for shocks. Shock duration was 0.5 sec., with its level adjusted to maintain responding at a rate lower than that maintained by the other schedule, which provided fewer rft/hr. Chlordiazepoxide HCl attenuated both effects of punishment: the decrease in the rate of punished Green responding and the concurrent increase in the rate of unpunished Amber responding. Data are from single 2-hr. sessions, except control, which represents an average across the sessions that preceded each dose.

produced both reinforcement and punishment (shock). The level of shock was adjusted so that the punished operant, which provided the higher rate of reinforcement, occurred at a lower rate than the unpunished operant. Chlordiazepoxide HCL produced a dose-related attenuation of the effect of punishment, similar to that produced by omission of shock (the omission of shock produced smaller changes than the drug because the VI programming of shock slowed the effect of its omission).

Effects of drugs often vary with baseline rates of responding (e.g., Cook & Catania, 1964). Supplementary drug experiments with other concurrent VI schedules, however, showed that chlordiazepoxide HCL did not produce increases in baseline rates of responding comparable to those in Figure 10 when no punishment was programmed.

In concurrent schedules designed to study the effects of variables such as those summarized above, the determination of the equivalence of the concurrent operants is important. The definition of response units in singly programmed schedules (Skinner, 1938; Premack, 1959) does not take into account the possible sensitivity of concurrent performances to differences in such other variables as response topography or effort. Chung (1965), for example, in a study using concurrent VI schedules with pigeons, found that the function relating the rate of pecking on one key to the required force of that key peck (over a range from 25 to 300 gms.) was affected by the schedule of reinforcement for the second key, although not by the rate of pecking or the required force on the second key.

Differences between operants also may arise as a result of concurrent superstitions, as in Figure 2. In such cases, an acceptable solution may be to equate the two operants on the basis of their relative rates in concurrent VI schedules that provide equal rft/hr.

Another determinant of preference is stimulus control (see Terrace's Chapter 7), as demonstrated in experiments on generalization and discrimination (e.g., Honig, 1962; Risley, 1964). In a typical experiment on generalization gradients, responding is reinforced in the presence of one value of a stimulus (e.g., wavelength of light), and the extent to which that and other values of the stimulus maintain responding is then tested in extinction. The effects of discrimination training are evaluated by comparing the generalization gradient with post-discrimination gradients, obtained by testing different stimulus values after reinforcement of responding in the presence of one stimulus value and extinction in the presence of a second.

Honig (1962) has shown that the shape of the post-discrimination gradient for wavelength in pigeons depends on whether discrimination training has been successive or simultaneous. In the successive case, the two stimulus values, correlated with VI reinforcement and with extinction respectively, were presented in alternation on a single key (multiple scheduling); in the simultaneous case, they were presented together on each of two keys (concurrent scheduling). In both cases, post-discrimination gradients were obtained under both successive and simultaneous conditions.

Relative to generalization gradients obtained in successive and simultaneous tests after training with reinforcement alone, successive training produced a post-discrimination gradient with lowered rates of responding in the region of and a shift in the peak of the gradient away from the stimulus value correlated with extinction. Simultaneous training, on the other hand, had little effect other than lowering the rate of responding at the stimulus value correlated with extinction.

One account of these findings depends on differences in the responses involved in the two techniques of discrimination training. The simultaneous discrimination presumably affected not only the tendency to peck either key, but also the likelihood of COs between the two keys. The successive discrimination did not involve COs.

Despite the differences in the gradients obtained after the two training techniques, neither gradient was affected by whether it was obtained within a successive or a simultaneous testing procedure. The former provided as data rates of responding to singly presented stimulus values, and the latter preferences when stimulus values were presented on two keys in pairs. After a given type of discrimination training, preferences in the two-key gradient could be predicted directly from relative rates of responding computed for a given pair of stimulus values in the single-key gradient. Local rates of responding to each stimulus value were not affected by simultaneous testing, but the times spent in responding to each were proportional to the relative rates in successive testing. Similar relationships were found for generalization as well as post-discrimination gradients that were obtained both successively and simultaneously. An interpretation of these findings, which may be closely related to the matching observed in concurrent VI schedules, is that the temporal constraints, such as differential reinforcement of IRTs, that operate in singly programmed schedules may have been ineffective in the single-key as well as in the two-key test, because both tests were conducted during extinction.

RESPONSE INDEPENDENCE

One feature of many of the interactions that have been discussed is that increases in the reinforcement of one operant produce decreases in the rate of other concurrent operants. There appear to be two alternative explanations of this effect: the decreases may be attributed directly to the increased reinforcement of the first operant, or they may be attributed to response interference because the increased reinforcement of the first operant produces increases in its rate. The present section reviews several experiments concerned with the separation of the effects of concurrent reinforcement from those of concurrent responses. The evidence indicates that, over a wide range of conditions, interactions in concurrent schedules are produced directly by reinforcement rather than by interference or competition of concurrent responses. Concurrent performances, therefore, may be described as the product of reinforcement interaction, in that the rate of each operant is determined not only by its own rate of reinforcement but also by the concurrent rates of reinforcement of other operants, and response independence, in that the rate of each operant is not determined by the concurrent rates of other operants.

Effects of Concurrent Reinforcement

The dependence of concurrent interactions on reinforcement suggests that the interactions are related to those in multiple schedules. Such a relationship between concurrent and multiple schedules is not unlikely in view of the role of multiple-schedule responding in concurrent performances. Although relative rates of responding in multiple schedules do not match relative rates of reinforcement, increases in the rate of reinforcement in one multiple-schedule component generally produce decreases in the rate of responding in the other component (Reynolds, 1961b; 1963b). It has been shown that this interaction depends on relative rates of reinforcement rather than on characteristics of the distribution of responses in each component (Reynolds, 1961a; Catania, 1961a) and, in any case, the factor of response competition is minimized in multiple schedules by the successive programming of the components.

A separation of the effects of reinforcements and of responses in concurrent performances is shown in Figure 11. In this experiment (Catania, 1963a), concurrent VI schedules in a CO-key procedure with pigeons were programmed in such a way that the rate of responding and the rate of reinforcement for one operant could be varied independently while the rate of reinforcement for the other operant was held constant. The rate of responding for the first operant (Key 1) was manipulated by arranging either a standard VI schedule (A) or a VI schedule of equal value in which a stimulus was presented whenever the schedule programmed a reinforcement (B). A 2-sec. COD was programmed throughout these sessions. In A, a substantial rate of responding was maintained on Key 1; in B, a near-zero rate of responding was maintained on Key 1, because the pigeon switched to Key 1 only after the stimulus was presented and only long enough to obtain the programmed Key-1 reinforcement. The near-zero rate of Key-1 responding in B did not produce a concurrent increase in the rate of Key-2 responding. It is interesting to note that in B it is not appropriate to speak of matching of response and reinforcement rates.

In a third condition (C), reinforcement of Key-1 responding was discontinued. Although the near-zero rate of Key-1 responding was similar to that in B, this procedure produced a substantial increase in the rate of concurrent responding on Key 2. A fourth possible condition, in which Key-1 responding occurred at a high rate but produced no reinforcement, was attainable only transiently, immediately after the change from concurrent VI scheduling to extinction of Key-1 responding. An increase in the rate of Key-2 responding was sometimes observed before the rate of Key-1 responding began to decrease.

Data were obtained in this experiment from three pigeons over a range of rates of Key-1 reinforcement from 10 to 40 rft/hr. Except for one

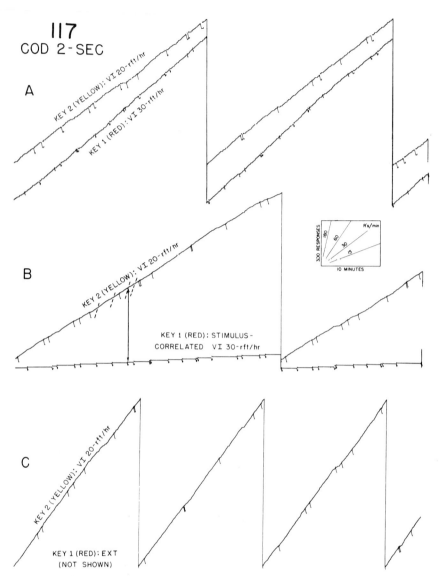

Figure 11. Cumulative records of a pigeon's key pecking during each of three CO-key concurrent procedures. In each, one operant (Key 2: Yellow) provided 20 rft/hr. The other operant (Key 1: Red) provided either 30 rft/hr (A and B) or no reinforcement (C). The rate of Key-2 responding was lower during reinforcement of Key-1 responding (A and B) than during extinction of Key-1 responding (C). During B, however, the CO key was lit and the pigeon had access to Key 1 only when reinforcement had been programmed by the Key-1 schedule. Thus, the rate of Key-1 responding in B was almost as low as in C, when Key-1 responding was not reinforced. The low rate of Key-2 responding during both A and B, relative to that during C, must therefore be attributed to the rft/hr provided by Key-1 responding (A and B) (from Catania, 1963a).

pigeon, there were no consistent differences in the rates of Key-2 responding in conditions A and B. For all pigeons, the rates of Key-2 responding
in A and B were consistently lower than the rates in C. These demonstrations indicate that the interactions may be attributed directly to concurrent
reinforcement rather than to concurrent responses.

Although the low rate of Key-1 responding in B did not produce an
increase in Key-2 responding relative to that in A, the local characteristics
of Key-2 responding changed considerably from those in A. In A, the
Key-2 performance consisted of short runs of responses that were frequently interrupted by periods of Key-1 responding, as indicated by the
steplike grain of the Key-2 record. In B, the Key-2 performance consisted
of relatively continuous responding at a lower rate that was infrequently
interrupted by periods of Key-1 responding, as indicated by the relatively
smooth grain of the Key-2 record.

Rate Constancies

A similar type of change in the local characteristics of performance is
illustrated by the rate constancy shown in Figure 12. In this two-key experiment (Catania, 1962), a pigeon's pecks on one key (VI) were maintained
by a VI 3-min. schedule that operated continuously. Pecks on a second key
(mult) were maintained by a multiple schedule in which 2-min. periods of
VI 3-min. alternated with 2-min. periods of extinction (ext). The concurrent schedules were programmed with COD 0.5-sec. The sample records in
Figure 12 show that the rate of pecking on the VI key remained relatively
constant, despite the change from a substantial rate of pecking to an essentially zero rate of pecking on the mult key. During the VI component of the
multiple schedule, the performance on the VI key consisted of short runs
of responses frequently interrupted by periods of mult-key responding (as
for Key 2 in A, Figure 11); during the extinction component of the multiple
schedule, the performance on the VI key consisted of relatively continuous
responding at a lower rate (as for Key 2 in B and C, Figure 11). Related
observations have been made with conc VI FI: a roughly constant rate of
responding was maintained by the VI schedule throughout the gradual increases in the rate of FI responding that occurred as each fixed interval
progressed (Catania, 1962).

These invariances in the rate of VI responding may be attributed to
the VI *compensations* that occur after pauses in VI responding (Figure
5b). As previously demonstrated (Figure 5c), the increased probability of
VI reinforcement after a VI pause generates a brief run of responding at a
relatively high local rate. With respect to the phenomenon of rate constancy, the term *compensation* is appropriate, in that the high rates make
up for the time spent in pecking a second key in such a way that the overall
rate of responding does not vary with the time lost in concurrent pecking.

The rate constancy illustrated in Figure 12, in which the concurrent schedule alternated between VI reinforcement and extinction, and the reinforcement interaction illustrated in Figure 11, in which the rate of responding on one key increased when the concurrent schedule was changed from VI reinforcement to extinction, are apparently contradictory. The major difference between these two conditions was the length of time the con-

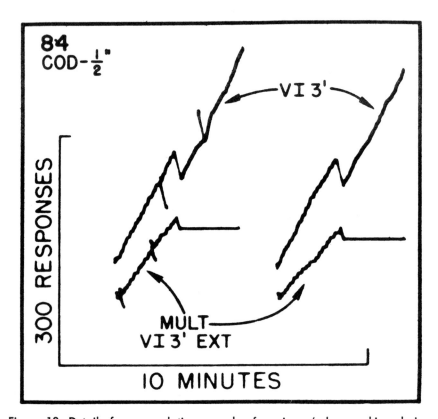

Figure 12. Details from cumulative records of a pigeon's key pecking during a session of VI 3-min. conc with mult VI 3-min. ext, programmed with 0.5-sec. COD and multiple-schedule components of 2 min. Both recording pens were displaced downward during the extinction component of the multiple schedule. When VI schedules operated for both keys (during VI in the multiple schedule), the pigeon switched from one key to the other every few seconds. When the VI schedule for the first key operated alone (during extinction in the multiple schedule), the pigeon pecked this key at a slow but relatively constant rate, infrequently pecking the other key. Despite the differences in the time spent in pecking on the multiple-schedule key during the two multiple-schedule components, the overall rate of pecking on the first key, continuously maintained by its VI schedule, remained roughly constant (from Catania, 1962).

current VI and extinction schedules were in effect. In Figure 12, they alternated every 2 min.; in Figure 11, each was maintained for several sessions. This suggests that the relevant variable in reinforcement interactions is the average rate of reinforcement taken over a period of time longer than the 2 min. that each component of the multiple schedule lasted, and that different rates of responding therefore would have been maintained on the VI key during the two components if the durations of the components had been sufficiently long. An observation in support of this interpretation is that the rate of responding on the VI key was appropriate to the average rate of reinforcement (10 rft/hr) provided by the mult-key schedule; the rate was higher than that maintained in other sessions in which VI alone (20 rft/hr) was programmed continuously on the mult key, and lower than that maintained in other sessions in which extinction alone (0 rft/hr) was programmed continuously on the mult key (Catania, 1962; cf. Figure 6b in this chapter).

The range of component durations over which rate constancies occur, rather than interactions with the separate rft/hr in each multiple-schedule component, has not been determined experimentally, and probably varies with the rft/hr provided by the VI component of the multiple schedule. In an experiment by Ferster (1959), for example, a chimpanzee's presses on one key were reinforced on a VI 10-min. schedule, and presses on a second key were reinforced on a mult FR 475 FI 10-min. schedule. The rate of VI responding was lower during the FR than during the FI component of the multiple schedule, a consequence either of competition with FR responding, which occurred at a high rate, or of the long durations of the multiple-schedule components and the relatively high rate of reinforcement in the FR component. A choice cannot be made between these two alternatives on the basis of the present data, because it is likely that the limits on rate constancy also vary from species to species.

Another case in which response competition and reinforcement interaction are confounded is illustrated in Figure 13 (Catania, 1963c). In this atypical conc VI FR record (cf. Figure 5), a pigeon completed several ratios within an unusually short period of time. A VI compensation occurred after each ratio, but the compensations did not make up for the time lost in FR responding; thus, the overall rate of VI responding was lower than that maintained in the absence of FR responding. The relative contributions of response competition and FR reinforcement to the low rate of VI responding cannot be assessed, because the rapidity of the effect may have depended on the high rate of FR reinforcement (almost 90 rft/hr during the series of ratios) rather than on response competition alone. It may be relevant, however, that the rate of VI responding during FR reinforcement is not inappropriate to the high rate of FR reinforcement (cf. Figure 6b).

In any case, it is likely that at some point the absolute rates of concurrent responses provide a limit on response independence, if for no other reason than that the combined rates eventually must approach the maximum physical capacity of the organism. These physical limits have been explored in single-response experiments (e.g., Ferster & Skinner, 1957); but the extent to which comparably high rates can be maintained effectively within concurrent schedules has not yet been determined.

These examples indicate the rather narrow range of rates of responding and rates of reinforcement over which response independence in concurrent schedules has been studied so far. Nevertheless, the phenomenon

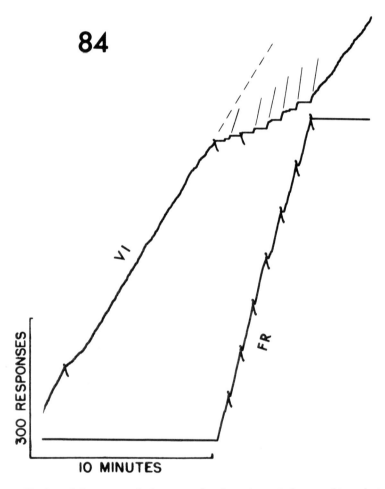

Figure 13. Detail from cumulative records of a pigeon's key pecking during a session of conc VI 6-min. FR 100 schedules, programmed with 1-sec. COD. A high rate of pecking on the FR key was accompanied by a concurrent decrease in the rate of pecking on the VI key.

appears to be of considerable generality. Two experiments discussed here in some detail illustrate this generality, which extends across responses, species, and schedules.

Responses of Dissimilar Topography

The first involves concurrent responses of dissimilar topography in the rat. In the apparatus shown in Figure 14, VI 3-min. and mult VI 3-min. ext schedules were programmed concurrently for lever pressing and for wheel running (Catania, 1964). Figure 15 shows average rates of responding during each multiple-schedule component over full sessions of multiple-schedule reinforcement for wheel running and continuously programmed VI reinforcement for lever pressing. Data for three rats under three experimental conditions are summarized in the figure. As shown in the left column, there were no consistent differences between the rates of lever pressing during VI reinforcement of running and the rates during extinction of running, but for only one of the three rats (R3) was there a consistent difference in the rates of running during the two components. The constancy was not affected, however, when a difference in the rates of running was produced by slowing running with friction on the wheel (middle column). For rat R3, the constancy was maintained throughout a reversal in the difference between the rates of wheel running in the two components: with no friction, the rate of running was lower during VI than during extinction, whereas with friction the rate was higher during VI than during extinction.

The right column shows that, when no COD was programmed, a small but consistent difference developed between the rate of lever pressing during VI reinforcement for running and that during extinction for running, accompanied by an increase in the rate of running during extinction. The COD is similarly important in the maintenance of rate constancies with pigeons (Catania, 1962).

Constancy in the rate of wheel running was examined by reversing the schedules for the two operants, as shown in Figure 16: continuous VI reinforcement was programmed for wheel running, concurrent with multiple-schedule reinforcement for lever pressing. Within these schedules, a high rate of lever pressing during the VI component of the multiple schedule alternated with a considerably lower rate during the extinction component. For only one rat (R2), however, was the rate of running constant across these components (left column). For the other two, the rate of running maintained by continuous VI was lower during the VI than during the extinction component of the multiple schedule for pressing. Two procedures that decreased the overall rate of running, friction on the wheel (middle column) and a decreased level of deprivation (right column), produced constancy in one of the rats (R3) but not in the other (R1). These proce-

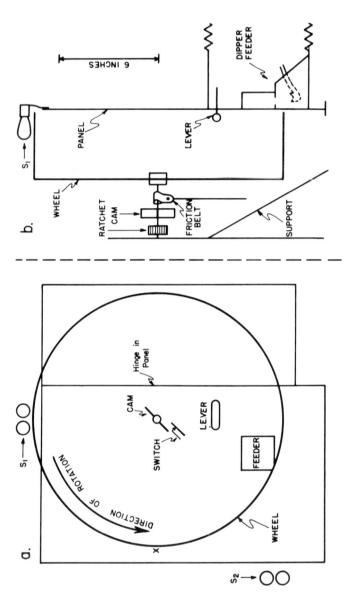

Figure 14. Schematic diagram of apparatus used to study concurrent lever pressing and wheel running in the rat. The cam-operated switch counted half-revolutions of the wheel. Friction on the wheel was adjusted with a spring-loaded belt. Lights (S_1 and S_2) served as multiple-schedule stimuli. The wheel rotated in only one direction, and when the rat ran rapidly and then stopped, the momentum of the wheel carried the rat back past the feeder. Thus, when running was reinforced, the location of the feeder favored slow running, because the rat was able to get to the feeder more quickly after slow than after fast running.

CONC (VI–EXT, wheel) (VI–VI, lever) COD 2-sec

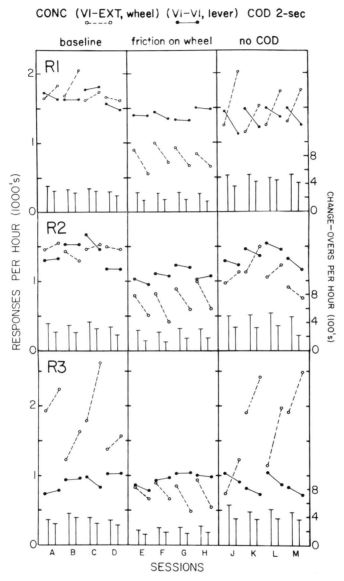

Figure 15. Rates of lever pressing and wheel running in three rats during three conditions programmed with conc VI 3-min. (lever presses) mult VI 3-min. ext (half-revolutions of wheel): COD 2-sec.; COD 2-sec. with friction on the wheel; and no COD. Points represent average rates of responding within each multiple-schedule component over 2-hr. sessions. Components were 5 min. long. Vertical bars indicate rates of changeovers in either direction (scale at right). Data are shown from the last four of at least 21 daily sessions of each condition.

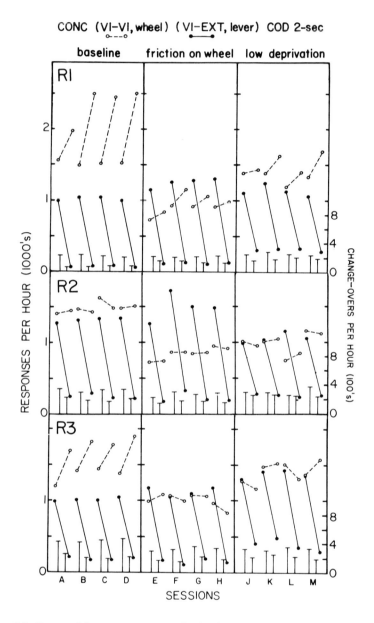

Figure 16. Rates of lever pressing and wheel running maintained by conc VI 3-min. (half-revolutions of wheel) mult VI 3-min. ext (lever presses), programmed with COD 2-sec. The rate of wheel running was manipulated with friction on the wheel and with a decreased level of deprivation that reduced the rate of running without affecting the rate of lever pressing. Details as in Figure 15.

dures did not affect the constancy in the rate of running in the other rat (R2) despite the fact that its rate of running was roughly halved in each case.

In another set of concurrent schedules, shown in Figure 17, one operant was reinforced by a mult VI 3-min. ext schedule while the second operant was not reinforced. When the multiple schedule was programmed for lever pressing, the rate of wheel running was higher during the extinction component of the multiple schedule, in which neither response was reinforced, than during the VI component, thus demonstrating the high operant-level rate of wheel running on which the preceding schedules were superimposed. When the multiple schedule was programmed for wheel running, the rate of running was again higher during the extinction component than during the VI component, thus demonstrating that VI reinforcement for wheel running produced a decrease rather than an increase in the rate of running. This unusual effect of reinforcement can be accounted for by the location of the feeder in the wheel, which favored slow running when running was reinforced because the rat was able to get to the feeder more quickly after slow than after fast running (see Figure 14).

One significant feature of these findings is the implication that response independence is a property of reinforced behavior but not of behavior that is maintained at operant level (cf. Skinner & Morse, 1957), in that the rate of running varied with the schedule of reinforcement for lever pressing when running was not explicitly reinforced. Another is its demonstration that the responses recorded during a given performance do not necessarily reflect the operant classes established by a procedure. In the present case, wheel running consisted of two separate operants: one, the high rate of running maintained because of the intrinsic reinforcement involved in the running response (cf. Premack, 1962; 1963), and the other, the low rate of running maintained because of the interaction of the behavior and the apparatus with the extrinsic reinforcement programmed by the VI schedule. The recording system, a cam-operated switch that counted every half-revolution of the wheel, did not discriminate between these two operants. Thus, the function of the several procedures represented in Figures 16 and 17 was the separation of the two wheel-running operants. Similar experimental separations of different operants must be made when two different concurrent schedules (e.g. FR and AV; Kelleher & Cook, 1959) are programmed on a single operandum.

Concurrent VI and Avoidance Schedules

In another experiment, with squirrel monkeys, response independence was examined in complex multiple and concurrent VI and AV (avoidance) schedules for lever pressing and chain pulling. The development of the performance in one monkey is shown in Figure 18. In initial training, the

schedules for the two operants were programmed separately. Lever presses
were reinforced according to a mult VI 2-min. ext schedule in which the VI

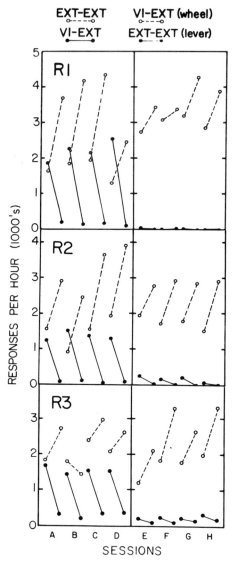

Figure 17. Concurrent lever pressing and wheel running in the rat, with COD
2-sec. The performance maintained by a mult VI 3-min. ext schedule for lever
pressing, with no explicit reinforcement for running, is shown on the left. That
maintained by a multiple schedule for running, with no reinforcement for lever
pressing, is shown on the right. Details as in Figure 15, except that rates of
changeover are omitted.

component, correlated with a white light above the lever, lasted 7.5 min. and the extinction component lasted 2.5 min. (A). In alternate sessions, chain pulls delayed the onset of shock according to a mult AV ext schedule in which the AV component, correlated with diffuse red illumination of the chamber, lasted 7.5 min. and the extinction (no shock) component lasted 2.5 min. (B). After both multiple-schedule performances were well established, the two schedules were combined concurrently but out of phase with each other, so that the extinction component of each schedule occurred while concurrent responding was maintained by the other schedule. A COD of 0.2 sec. programmed during the early concurrent sessions (C) was later increased to 1.0 sec. (D). This resulted in a high frequency of shocks during VI responding, because the first AV chain pull after a VI lever press initiated the COD interval rather than avoiding shock. Nevertheless, a roughly constant rate of VI responding was maintained during the AV and the extinction components of the schedule for chain pulling. The rate of VI responding increased about two fold during these sessions, but in both C and D the average rates of VI responding during the AV and the extinction components differed by less than three percent.

For this monkey, the rate of VI responding was independent of shocks as well as of AV responses. This was not the case for a second monkey, whose performance is illustrated in Figure 19. This monkey's sensitivity to shock was such that VI responding was almost completely restricted to the extinction component of the mult AV ext schedule, despite the fact that VI reinforcements programmed during the AV component were no longer available after component changes (A). When the schedules were modified by decreasing the COD from 2 sec. to 1 sec. so that shock became less frequent during the AV component, VI responding recovered and was maintained at a roughly constant rate during both components (B). The effect on VI responding in A cannot be attributed to competing AV responses, because the rate constancy in B was maintained concurrently with a higher rate of AV responding than that in A. It must therefore be attributed to the stimulus for the AV component of the mult AV ext schedule, which was occasionally paired with shock. This is, in other words, an example within concurrent schedules of suppression of responding by a conditioned aversive stimulus, similar to that demonstrated by Estes and Skinner (1944). The fact that shocks depend on pauses in AV responding supports the generalization that responses are independent of concurrent responding but are not independent of the consequences of that responding. The effect is to be distinguished from the effects of superimposing punishment on a reinforced operant, which generally produces increases rather than decreases in the rate of concurrent operants (e.g., Reynolds, 1963c).

Data from a third monkey, in Figure 20, illustrate that although rate constancy was maintained in the VI schedule, it was not concurrently main-

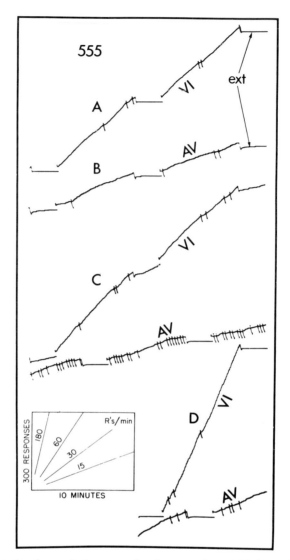

Figure 18. Details of cumulative records of a complex multiple and concurrent VI and AV performance in the squirrel monkey. A mult VI 2-min. ext schedule of food reinforcement was programmed for lever presses (A). In alternate 3-hr. sessions, a mult AV ext schedule was programmed for pulls on a chain on the opposite wall; chain pulls avoided 1-sec., 1-ma inescapable shocks (RS = SS = 15 sec). Separate stimuli controlled the two multiple-schedule performances. Schedule components lasted 7.5 min.; extinction components (recording pen displaced downward) lasted 2.5 min. Combined concurrently (C and D), the multiple schedules were programmed out of phase with each other: conc (mult VI-ext-VI-VI) (mult AV-AV-AV-ext). During both C (third concurrent session, COD 0.2 sec.) and D (two weeks later, COD 1.0-sec.), VI reinforcements not collected at the time of a component change in either multiple schedule were cancelled, and chain pulls during the extinction component of the VI multiple schedule avoided shock on an FR 2 schedule.

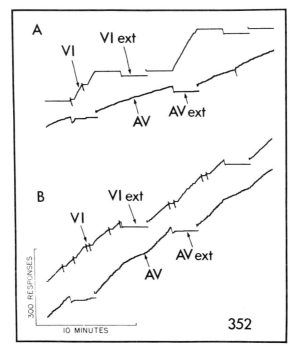

Figure 19. Complex multiple and concurrent VI and AV responding for a second squirrel monkey. In A, with COD 2-sec., the monkey received about 20 shocks per session. In B, with COD 1-sec., the monkey received about ten shocks per session. No FR contingency was programmed for AV responding during the extinction component of the VI multiple schedule. Other details as in Figure 18.

tained in the AV schedule. The rate of AV responding was higher during VI than during extinction in the multiple schedule for lever pressing (A). This failure to obtain constancy may be attributed to the fact that, unlike VI responses, every AV response ordinarily has a consequence. When a COD is programmed, however, at least two successive AV responses are necessary to delay shock after VI responding. Because VI responding generally occurs only during the VI component, the contingencies for the AV response are therefore different during VI and during extinction.

To compensate for this difference, the schedules were modified so that AV responses avoided shock on an FR 2 schedule during the extinction component for the other responses, i.e., only every other AV response avoided shock. This procedure reduced the difference between the rates of AV responding during VI and during extinction increasing the rate during extinction (B). Nevertheless, AV responding during VI was maintained fairly consistently at a rate about 10 percent higher than that during ex-

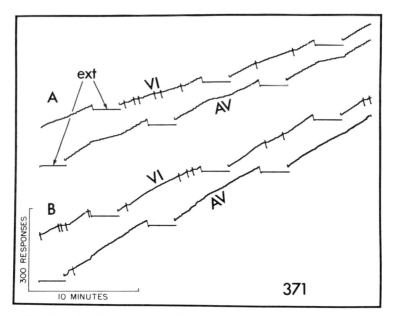

Figure 20. Complex VI and AV performance for a third squirrel monkey, with COD 2-sec. In A, no FR contingency was programmed for AV responses during the extinction component of the VI multiple schedule. In B, chain pulls during the extinction component of the VI multiple schedule avoided shock on an FR 2 schedule. Other details as in Figure 18.

tinction. This demonstration that rate constancy may be restricted to VI responding suggests that comparable differences in rate might be observed with other schedules, such as drl, concurrently programmed with a mult VI ext schedule.

A final observation in these schedules deserves mention. The design of the schedules included a maintained control for the development of concurrent superstitions. If either response came under the accidental control of the other's schedule, then this response would have occurred during its own extinction component. When the COD was removed for 16 consecutive 3-hr. sessions, however, no superstitions developed and the constancy in the rate of VI responding was not affected. Thus, these schedules, in which each response occurred separately, during extinction in the other schedule, as well as concurrently, may provide a technique more powerful than the COD for the maintenance of the independence of concurrent responses.

These examples indicate the generality of the phenomenon of response independence. It occurs in pigeons, rats, and squirrel monkeys, with two-key and CO-key procedures, with a variety of responses of similar and dissimilar topographies, and concurrent with responding maintained by VI, FI, AV, and operant level. The rate of responding maintained by a given schedule of reinforcement is determined by the context of concurrent schedules within which it is programmed, but not by changes in the rates of responding maintained by the concurrent schedules.

CONCLUSION

The present chapter has surveyed the formal properties of concurrent procedures and concurrent performances, the extent to which local interactions in concurrent performances are determined by changes in the probabilities of reinforcement in each of two concurrent schedules, and the quantitative relations among concurrent operants and their controlling variables. Despite the complexity of these relationships, certain generalizations are possible. First, it is necessary that concurrent schedules be programmed in such a way that concurrent operants are in fact independent with respect to their separate schedules of reinforcement; without appropriate programming (e.g., a COD in VI schedules), either operant may come partially under the control of the schedule for the other. Given that the independence of schedules has been established, the concurrent operants also are independent in that, over a range of conditions, changes in the rate of one operant do not affect the rate of other operants. The rate of an operant, however, may be affected by the consequences of other operants. At least three types of effects can be distinguished. When similar reinforcers are programmed for each of two concurrent operants, increases in the rate of reinforcement for one operant produce decreases in the rate of the other operant. When one of the operants is punished, increases in the rate of punishment of that operant produce increases in the rate of the other operant. Finally, when reinforcement is programmed for one operant while a concurrent operant avoids an aversive stimulus, the aversive stimulus or other stimuli with which it is paired may produce decreases in the rate of the first operant.

Among relevant areas of application of these relationships is the technical problem of the elimination of behavior (e.g., Holz & Azrin, 1963). The desirability of eliminating behavior by means of reinforcement for a competing response rather than by extinction, punishment, or physical restraint has been pointed out by Skinner (1953). This technique is exemplified by the concurrent reinforcement of competing operants in dro (differential reinforcement of other behavior: Reynolds, 1961a), a procedure that may be of particular usefulness in the establishment of discriminative performances with a minimum of "errors" (Terrace, 1963).

The decrease in the rate of one operant with increases in the rate of reinforcement for a concurrent operant suggests an analogy with inhibitory interactions in physiological systems (Catania & Gill, 1964). Concurrent operants may be conceived of as reciprocally inhibitory systems in which increases in the stimulation (reinforcement) of one system produce decrements in the activity (rate) of others. In this connection, the polarity of reinforcement and punishment is worth noting: the effect of punishment of one operant on the rate of concurrent operants is in the same direction as that of a decrease in the reinforcement of the operant.

The demonstration of response independence may have significance for the analysis of singly programmed schedules of reinforcement. Although the rate of responding maintained by a given schedule is determined by the context of concurrent schedules within which it is programmed, this rate remains invariant, within limits, with changes in time spent in responding in other schedules. In other words, a given rate of reinforcement tends to maintain a constant total output over time that is independent of the local temporal constraints on this output. To paraphrase Parkinson's Law (1957): the total output will expand to fill the time available for its completion. This formulation is reminiscent of Skinner's (1938) reflex reserve, with the difference that the emphasis is on maintained behavior rather than on behavior in acquisition and extinction. It appears to be an adequate description of rate constancies in concurrent schedules; it also may serve to characterize the processes that generate single operants.

REFERENCES

ANGER, D. (1954) The effect upon simple animal behavior of different frequencies of reinforcement. Report PLR-33, Office of the Surgeon General.[3]

ANGER, D. (1956) The dependence of interresponse times upon the relative reinforcement of different interresponse times. *J. exp. Psychol., 52,* 145-161.

ANGER, D. (1963) The role of temporal discriminations in the reinforcement of Sidman avoidance behavior. *J. exp. Anal. Behav., 6,* 477-506.

AUTOR, S. M. (1960) The strength of conditioned reinforcers as a function of frequency and probability of reinforcement. Unpublished doctoral dissertation, Harvard University.

AZRIN, N. H. (1961) Time-out from positive reinforcement. *Science, 133,* 382-383.

BOREN, J. J. (1961) Stimulus probes of the fixed ratio run. Paper delivered at Eastern Psychol. Ass., Philadelphia, Pa.

BRADY, J. V. (1955) Extinction of a conditioned "fear" response as a function of reinforcement schedules for competing behavior. *J. Psychol., 40,* 25-34.

BRETHOWER, D. M., and REYNOLDS, G. S. (1962) A facilitative effect of punishment on unpunished behavior. *J. exp. Anal. Behav., 5,* 191-199.

[3] This report has been deposited as Document number 7779 with the ADI Auxiliary Publications Project, Photoduplication Service, Library of Congress, Washington 25, D. C. A copy may be secured by citing the document number and by remitting $6.25 for photoprints or $2.50 for 35 mm microfilm. Advance payment is required. Make checks or money orders payable to: Chief, Photoduplication Service, Library of Congress. An abstract of the report appears in *Amer. Psychologist,* 1954, *9,* 321-322.

BRUNER, A., and REVUSKY, S. H. (1961) Collateral behavior in humans. *J. exp. Anal. Behav., 4*, 349-350.

BULLOCK, D. D., and BITTERMAN, M. E. (1962) Probability matching in the pigeon. *Amer. J. Psychol., 75*, 634-639.

CATANIA, A. C. (1961) Behavioral contrast in a multiple and concurrent schedule of reinforcement. *J. exp. Anal. Behav., 4*, 335-342. (a)

CATANIA, A. C. (1961) Effects of component duration on multiple schedule performance. *Amer. Psychologist, 16*, 414 (abstract). (b)

CATANIA, A. C. (1962) Independence of concurrent responding maintained by interval schedules of reinforcement. *J. exp. Anal. Behav., 5*, 175-184.

CATANIA, A. C. (1963) Concurrent performances: Reinforcement interaction and response independence. *J. exp. Anal. Behav., 6*, 253-263. (a)

CATANIA, A. C. (1963) Concurrent performances: A baseline for the study of reinforcement magnitude. *J. exp. Anal. Behav., 6*, 299-300. (b)

CATANIA, A. C. (1963) Concurrent performances: An analysis of ratio and interval schedules of reinforcement. *Amer. Psychologist, 18*, 421 (abstract). (c)

CATANIA, A. C. (1964) Independence of concurrent responding in the rat: Lever-pressing and wheel running. Paper delivered at Eastern Psychol. Ass., Philadelphia, Pa.

CATANIA, A. C., and CUTTS, D. (1963) Experimental control of superstitious responding in humans. *J. exp. Anal. Behav., 6*, 203-208.

CATANIA, A. C. and GILL, C. A. (1964) Inhibition and behavioral contrast. *Psychonom. Science, 1*, 257-258.

CHUNG, S.-H. (1965) Effects of effort on response rate. *J. exp. Anal. Behav., 8*, 1-7.

COOK, L., and CATANIA, A. C. (1964) Effects of drugs on avoidance and escape behavior. *Fed. Proc., 23*, 818-835.

CROSS, D. V., and LANE, H. L. (1962) On the discriminative control of concurrent responses: The relations among response frequency, latency, and topography in auditory generalization. *J. exp. Anal. Behav., 5*, 487-496.

ESTES, W. K., and SKINNER, B. F. (1941) Some quantitative properties of anxiety. *J. exp. Psychol., 29*, 390-400.

ESTES, W. K., and STRAUGHAN, J. H. (1954) Analysis of a verbal conditioning situation in terms of statistical learning theory. *J. exp. Psychol., 47*, 225-234.

FERSTER, C. B. (1957) Concurrent schedules of reinforcement in the chimpanzee. *Science, 125*, 1090-1091.

FERSTER, C. B. (1959) A complex concurrent schedule of reinforcement. *J. exp. Anal. Behav., 2*, 65-80.

FERSTER, C. B., and SKINNER, B. F. (1957) *Schedules of reinforcement.* New York: Appleton-Century-Crofts.

FINDLEY, J. D. (1958) Preference and switching under concurrent scheduling. *J. exp. Anal. Behav., 1*, 123-144.

FINDLEY, J. D. (1962) An experimental outline for building and exploring multi-operant repertoires. *J. exp. Anal. Behav., 5*, 113-166.

FRICK, F. C., and MILLER, G. A. (1951) A statistical description of operant conditioning. *Amer. J. Psychol., 64*, 20-36.

GRAF, V., BULLOCK, D. H., and BITTERMAN, M. E. (1964) Further experiments on probability matching in the pigeon. *J. exp. Anal. Behav., 7*, 151-157.

HEARST, E. (1961) Effects of d-amphetamine on behavior reinforced by food and water. *Psychol. Rep., 8*, 301-309.

HEARST, E. (1962) Concurrent generalization gradients for food-controlled and shock-controlled behavior. *J. exp. Anal. Behav., 5,* 19-31.

HEARST, E., and SIDMAN, M. (1961) Some behavioral effects of a concurrently positive and negative stimulus. *J. exp. Anal. Behav., 4,* 251-265.

HEFFERLINE, R. F., and KEENAN, B. (1963) Amplitude-induction gradient of a small-scale (covert) operant. *J. exp. Anal. Behav., 6,* 307-315.

HERRNSTEIN, R. J. (1958) Some factors influencing behavior in a two-response situation. *Trans. N. Y. Acad. Sci., 21,* 35-45.

HERRNSTEIN, R. J. (1961) Relative and absolute strength of response as a function of frequency of reinforcement. *J. exp. Anal. Behav., 4,* 267-272. (a)

HERRNSTEIN, R. J. (1961) Stereotypy and intermittent reinforcement. *Science, 133,* 2067-2069. (b)

HERRNSTEIN, R. J. (1964) Secondary reinforcement and rate of primary reinforcement. *J. exp. Anal. Behav., 7,* 27-36. (a)

HERRNSTEIN, R. J. (1964) Aperiodicity as a factor in choice. *J. exp. Anal. Behav., 7,* 179-182. (b)

HICKSON, R. H. (1961) Response probability in a two-choice learning situation with varying probability of reinforcement. *J. exp. Psychol., 62,* 138-144.

HOLZ, W. C., and AZRIN, N. H. (1963) A comparison of several procedures for eliminating behavior. *J. exp. Anal. Behav., 6,* 399-406.

HONIG, W. K. (1962) Prediction of preference, transposition, and transposition-reversal from the generalization gradient. *J. exp. Psychol., 4,* 239-248.

JASTROW, J., and CAIRNES, W. B. (1891-1892) The interference of mental processes—A preliminary survey. *Amer. J. Psychol., 4,* 219-223.

KELLEHER, R. T., and COOK, L. (1959) An analysis of the behavior of rats and monkeys on concurrent fixed-ratio avoidance schedules. *J. exp. Anal. Behav., 2,* 203-211.

KELLEHER, R. T., and GOLLUB, L. R. (1962) A review of positive conditioned reinforcement. *J. exp. Anal. Behav., 5,* 543-597.

KELLEHER, R. T., RIDDLE, W. C., and COOK, L. (1962) Observing responses in pigeons. *J. exp. Anal. Behav., 5,* 3-13.

LANE, H. (1961) Operant control of vocalizing in the chicken. *J. exp. Anal. Behav., 4,* 171-177.

LATIES, V. G., and WEISS, B. (1963) Effects of a concurrent task on fixed-interval responding in humans. *J. exp. Anal. Behav., 6,* 431-436.

LUCE, R. D. (1959) *Individual choice behavior: A theoretical analysis.* New York: Wiley.

MALOTT, R. W., and CUMMING, W. W. (1964) Schedules of interresponse time reinforcement. *Psychol. Rec., 14,* 211-252.

MECHNER, F. (1958) Probability relations within response sequences under ratio reinforcement. *J. exp. Anal. Behav., 1,* 109-121.

MILLER, N. E. (1944) Experimental studies of conflict. In J. McV. Hunt (Ed.), *Personality and the behavior disorders. Vol. 1.* New York: Ronald. Pp. 431-465.

MORSE, W. H., and SKINNER, B. F. (1957) A second type of "superstition" in the pigeon. *Amer. J. Psychol., 70,* 308-311.

NOTTERMAN, J. M., and MINTZ, D. E. (1962) Exteroceptive cueing of response force. *Science, 135,* 1070-1071.

OLDS, J. (1962) Hypothalamic substrates of reward. *Physiol. Rev., 42,* 554-604.

PARKINSON, C. N. (1957) *Parkinson's Law.* Boston: Houghton Mifflin.

PREMACK, D. (1959) Toward empirical behavior laws: I. Positive reinforcement. *Psychol. Rev., 66,* 219-233.

PREMACK, D. (1962) Reversibility of the reinforcement relation. *Science, 136,* 255-257.

PREMACK, D. (1963) Prediction of the comparative reinforcement values of running and drinking. *Science, 139,* 1062-1063.

REVUSKY, S. H. (1963) A relationship between responses per reinforcement and preference during concurrent VI VI. *J. exp. Anal. Behav., 6,* 518.

REYNOLDS, G. S. (1961) Behavioral contrast. *J. exp. Anal. Behav., 4,* 57-71. (a)

REYNOLDS, G. S. (1961) Relativity of response rate and reinforcement frequency in a multiple schedule. *J. exp. Anal. Behav., 4,* 179-184. (b)

REYNOLDS, G. S. (1963) On some determinants of choice in pigeons. *J. exp. Anal. Behav., 6,* 53-59. (a)

REYNOLDS, G. S. (1963) Some limitations on behavioral contrast and induction during successive discrimination. *J. exp. Anal. Behav., 6,* 131-139. (b)

REYNOLDS, G. S. (1963) Potency of conditioned reinforcers based on food and on food and punishment. *Science, 139,* 838-839. (c)

RISLEY, T. (1964) Generalization gradients following two-response discrimination training. *J. exp. Anal. Behav., 7,* 199-204.

SEGAL, EVALYN F. (1961) Behavioral interaction under concurrent spaced-responding variable-interval schedules of reinforcement. *J. exp. Anal. Behav., 4,* 263-266.

SEGAL, EVALYN F., and HOLLOWAY, S. M. (1963) Timing behavior in rats with water drinking as a mediator. *Science, 140,* 888-889.

SIDMAN, M. (1954) Delayed-punishment effects mediated by competing behavior. *J. comp. physiol. Psychol., 47,* 145-147.

SIDMAN, M. (1956) Time discrimination and behavioral interaction in a free operant situation. *J. comp. physiol. Psychol., 49,* 469-473.

SIDMAN, M. (1958) By-products of aversive control. *J. exp. Anal. Behav., 1,* 265-280.

SIDMAN, M. (1962) Reduction of shock frequency as a reinforcement for avoidance behavior. *J. exp. Anal. Behav., 5,* 247-257. (a)

SIDMAN, M. (1962) Time out from avoidance as a reinforcer: A study of response interaction. *J. exp. Anal. Behav., 5,* 423-434. (b)

SKINNER, B. F. (1938) *The behavior of organisms.* New York: Appleton-Century-Crofts.

SKINNER, B. F. (1948) "Superstition" in the pigeon. *J. exp. Psychol., 38,* 168-172.

SKINNER, B. F. (1950) Are theories of learning necessary? *Psychol. Rev., 57,* 193-216.

SKINNER, B. F. (1953) *Science and human behavior.* New York: Macmillan.

SKINNER, B. F., and MORSE, W. H. (1957) Concurrent activity under fixed-interval reinforcement. *J. comp. physiol. Psychol., 50,* 279-281.

TERRACE, H. S. (1963) Discrimination learning with and without errors. *J. exp. Anal. Behav., 6,* 1-27.

VERHAVE, T. (1961) Some observations concerning prepotency and probability of postponing shock with a two-lever avoidance procedure. *J. exp. Anal. Behav., 4,* 187-192.

VERHAVE, T. (1962) The functional properties of a time out from an avoidance schedule. *J. exp. Anal. Behav., 5,* 391-422.

VERHAVE, T. (1963) Toward an empirical calculus of reinforcement value. *J. exp. Anal. Behav., 6,* 525-536.

WEISS, B., and LATIES, V. G. (1964) Drug effects on the temporal patterning of behavior. *Fed. Proc., 23,* 801-807.

WILSON, W. A., JR., OSCAR, MARLENE, and BITTERMAN, M. E. (1964) Prob-
ability-learning in the monkey. *Quart. J. exp. Psychol., 16,* 163-165.
WILSON, W. A., JR., and ROLLIN, A. R. (1959) Two-choice behavior of Rhesus
monkeys in a non-contingent situation. *J. exp. Psychol., 58,* 174-179.
ZIMMERMAN, J., and FERSTER, C. B. (1964) Some notes on time out from reinforcement. *J. exp. Anal. Behav., 7,* 13-19.

7

Stimulus Control[1]

H. S. Terrace

INTRODUCTION

Stimulus control refers to the extent to which the value of an antecedent stimulus determines the probability of occurrence of a conditioned response. It is measured as a change in response probability that results from a change in stimulus value. The greater the change in response probability, the greater the degree of stimulus control *with respect to the continuum being studied.*

The function relating stimulus value to response probability is, of course, identical to what we traditionally refer to as a generalization gradient. By our definition of stimulus control, a generalization gradient whose slope is zero indicates no stimulus control along that continuum. As the slope of the gradient increases we say that stimulus control increases.

But why, a parsimonious reader might well ask, should a new term be introduced into an area in which the terms *generalization* and *discrimination* have been traditionally used? A detailed reply to this question cannot be presented without recourse to much of the material that is to be presented in this chapter. Briefly, the basic rationale for favoring the concept of stimulus control over the traditional concepts of generalization and discrimination, stems from the practice of using the terms *generalization* and *discrimination* to describe (processes) rather than empirical (functions) (cf., Brown, 1965; Prokasy & Hall, 1963). It is one thing to say that an organism who has been conditioned to respond to a 1000 cps tone will respond, to a lesser extent, to tones of other frequencies, and another thing to state that response strength generalizes from the 1000 cps tone to other tones. Additional reasons which would make the relatively neutral concept of stimulus control preferable to generalization and discrimination will become apparent throughout the chapter and will receive explicit attention in the conclusion. Our initial task will be to define the scope of our dis-

[1] Preparation of this chapter and some of the author's experiments reported therein were partially supported by NSF grant GB1629 and USPHS grant HD-00930.

cussion of stimulus control, and then to turn to the questions of how stimulus control is established and sharpened.

The proposed definition of stimulus control in terms of the effect of the value of an antecedent conditioned stimulus upon response probability, embraces too broad a range of topics to be comfortably treated in one chapter. Many topics such as perception, psychophysics, thinking, and psycholinguistics, which are directly suggested by this definition, and numerous other topics that are not as directly relevant, would require too much space to be discussed adequately. A number of considerations, however, enable us to reduce our task in a meaningful way to a more manageable size.

The examples of stimulus control that will be discussed in this chapter are mainly concerned with positive reinforcement. Many of the principles will in fact apply to stimulus control based on either positive or negative reinforcement. Certain factors that are specifically relevant to stimulus control established by negative reinforcement are discussed in Hoffman's Chapter 11 in this book.

Another restriction of our treatment of stimulus control will come from considering only one of the functional relationships that may exist between a stimulus and a response. This is the *discriminative* function. A stimulus functions as a discriminative stimulus if it "sets the occasion" for the occurrence of a conditioned operant (Skinner, 1938; Keller & Schoenfeld, 1950). The discriminative function may be distinguished, for example, from the eliciting function, and the primary and secondary reinforcing functions that a stimulus may also assume (Skinner, 1938; Keller & Schoenfeld, 1950). Only the eliciting and the discriminative functions, however, are suggested by the concept of stimulus control, as it is only in these instances that the stimulus precedes a response.

The restriction of the concept of stimulus control in this chapter to the discriminative function will undoubtedly appear somewhat mysterious, especially since one can easily cite many parallel instances where the value of *either* an eliciting or a discriminative stimulus may affect the probability of occurrence of a conditioned response. Since this chapter is concerned with the *acquisition* of stimulus control, it would seem appropriate to keep in mind the different methods used to condition an operant and a respondent (cf. Skinner, 1938).

A respondent becomes conditioned to a new stimulus as a result of its elicitation by a reinforcing stimulus, immediately following the presentation of the new stimulus. A tone, for example, which did not originally elicit salivation will do so after it has been paired with food. In this procedure food is presented after the tone, whether or not the tone evoked any salivation. An operant, on the other hand, is conditioned as a result of its being followed by the occurrence of a reinforcing stimulus. Food, for example, is not presented unless the desired response occurs. By definition, no known stimulus was used to elicit the operant. There is no prior stimulus to refer to as an eliciting stimulus.

In both the respondent and the operant paradigms the occurrence of the reinforcing stimulus can be made conditional upon the prior occurrence of a specific stimulus. This procedure is called *discrimination training*. As Skinner (1935) has pointed out, discrimination training necessarily occurs during the conditioning of the respondent, because the presence of one conditioned stimulus is always contrasted with its absence. In an operant discrimination, however, the stimulus that must be present for a response to be reinforced can be added after the response has been conditioned. Responses are then followed by reinforcement only in the presence of one stimulus and never in the presence of a different stimulus. The function of a discriminative stimulus is merely to indicate to the organism whether or not reinforcement will follow a response, or, (in the more general case, *NB. Judd'r* what schedule of reinforcement is currently in effect) (See, for example, *broad use of* Chapter 5 on chaining and conditioned reinforcement.) *'Schedule'*

Following discrimination training where responding occurs only in the presence of a certain stimulus, one could see a parallel between the onset of the stimulus and the occurrence of a conditioned response in both the operant and respondent cases. The similarity breaks down when one considers the continued emission of responses in the *free-operant* case in which responding is reinforced according to a certain schedule of reinforcement. Since the prevailing stimulus is not removed following the occurrence of a response, more than one response is free to occur in the presence of that stimulus. So long as the stimulus is present responses will be emitted either at some steady rate or in a temporal pattern that is characteristic of the schedule of reinforcement in effect. Thus, barring satiation, the appearance of a discriminative stimulus may be followed by an indefinite number of responses, limited only by the removal of the discriminative stimulus. In the respondent case the conditioned response is usually phasic and quickly diminishes in strength even if the conditioned stimulus is allowed to continue. It is, therefore, only in the respondent case, where we have a typically one-response-to-one-stimulus situation, that we speak of the CS as eliciting the CR.

Having distinguished between the eliciting and the discriminative functions of a conditioned stimulus, and having somewhat arbitrarily restricted our discussion of stimulus control only to those situations that involve discriminative stimuli and positive reinforcement, we may now turn to the systematic questions that will be discussed in this chapter. The first of these is whether differential reinforcement is necessary for the establishment of stimulus control. This question raises the issue of whether stimulus control can be established simply by repeatedly reinforcing an operant in the presence of one stimulus. Those who believe that this is not a sufficient condition for establishing stimulus control argue that it is also necessary to introduce a second stimulus which is either never correlated with reinforcement, or which is correlated with a different schedule of reinforcement. Both positions have undergone extensive theoretical and experimental analysis. As we shall later see, the experimental data on hand indicate that differential reinforcement is necessary to establish stimulus control.

Once stimulus control has been established we are faced with a second question: How can stimulus control be further sharpened? This is typically accomplished by a rigorous differential reinforcement procedure. In the simplest case an attempt is made to insure a higher probability of responding in the presence of a stimulus that is correlated with reinforcement (S+) than in the presence of a stimulus that is not correlated with reinforcement (S—). In many procedures an attempt is made to reduce the probability of responding to S— to zero or to a near zero value. This raises two additional issues: How does the manner in which the physical difference between S+ and S— is reduced affect the number of responses that occur to S—; and, to what extent is the concept of inhibition relevant in describing the elimination of responding to S—?

THE ACQUISITION OF STIMULUS CONTROL

Differential Reinforcement

The role of differential reinforcement in establishing stimulus control has assumed a prominent position in the theoretical writings of Hull, Spence, and Lashley. All of these men were seeking to account for the empirical finding that, following the reinforcement of a response in the presence of one stimulus, other stimuli which have never been associated with reinforcement will also evoke that response. In many cases stimulus control was demonstrated by the fact that the probability of a response to a test stimulus seemed to be a function of the physical difference between S+ and the test stimulus.

In discussing the Hull-Spence position on stimulus generalization it should be noted that in the initial formulation of their theories, neither Hull nor Spence acknowledged the operant-respondent distinction. Accordingly, the examples used to illustrate their theories were drawn from both operant and respondent experiments.

The main assumptions underlying Hull's position on the acquisition of stimulus control, which has been characterized by Lashley (1942, p. 242) as a "continuity theory," are as follows:

1. Whenever a response is followed by the reduction of a need there results an increment in the tendency of all stimuli associated with the response to evoke that response:

> . . . all elements of a stimulus complex playing upon a sensorium of an
> organism at or near the time that a response is evoked, tend themselves in-

dependently and indiscriminately to acquire the capacity to evoke substantially the same response. For our present purposes the indiscriminateness of the tendency is particularly to be noted (Hull, 1929, p. 498).

2. Response strength ($_sH_R$) increases with the number of reinforcements and approaches an asymptote according to a negatively accelerated growth function (Hull, 1943, Postulate 4, p. 178).

3. The increase in response strength occurs with respect not only to the stimuli associated with reinforcement, but also to "adjacent" stimuli (Hull, 1943, p. 143). Hull further assumes that the continua on which new stimuli can be said to be "adjacent" to the conditioned stimulus are innate properties of the afferent nervous system: ". . . with few exceptions the receptors of normal higher organisms appear to yield afferent generalization continua for all the physical stimulus dimensions to which they respond at all" (Hull, 1943, p. 188).

4. The degree of spread of habit strength depends on the difference between the test stimulus and the unconditioned stimulus in difference threshold units (jnds) (Hull, 1943, Postulate 5, p. 199).

5. The manner in which habit strength spreads may be mathematically specified. The nature of the "true shape" of this function was the subject of much discussion by Hull and by other psychologists interested in this question. It seems clear, however, that basic to all attempts to describe the "true shape" of a generalization gradient, was the assumption that response strength did generalize as a result of non-differential reinforcement in the presence of one stimulus.

The assumptions postulated by Hull regarding the process of primary stimulus generalization were elaborated by Spence (1936; 1937) into a more general theory of discrimination in which he made extensive use of generalization gradients of both excitation and inhibition around stimuli that were associated with reinforcement and extinction respectively. Each gradient was given an arbitrary shape, and the gradients of reinforcement and extinction were successfully combined to approximate certain empirical findings in discrimination learning experiments, notably the phenomenon of transposition. Our concern, however, must remain focused upon the basic tenet of the Hull-Spence theory of discrimination learning which maintains that the repeated non-differential reinforcement of the response in the presence of a stimulus is a sufficient condition for all aspects of that stimulus to gain control over the response.

The Hull-Spence theory was subjected to sharp criticism by Lashley and Wade (1946) who called it a thinly disguised modern version of Pavlov's irradiation theory (1928). Lashley and Wade argued that the empirical demonstration that a conditioned response may be evoked by a wide range of stimuli, which have never been paired with reinforcement and which have properties in common with the CS, does not require the postulation of a process whereby response strength or associative tendencies generalized to these new stimuli. The main assumptions of Lashley and Wade's position may be summarized as follows:

1. The phenomenon of stimulus generalization represents a "failure of association" (Lashley & Wade, 1946, p. 74).

2. The "dimensions" of a stimulus are determined by comparison of two or more stimuli and *do not exist for the organism until established by differential training* (Lashley & Wade, 1946, p. 74. Italics added).

In arguing that the phenomenon of generalization represents a "failure of association," Lashley and Wade were saying that the organism failed to discriminate between a test stimulus and the training stimulus. They further argued that a generalization gradient whose slope is greater than zero, in which organisms responded differently to the CS and the test stimuli, was simply the result of prior experience of the organism. This experience presumably allowed the organism to abstract the dimensions of the stimulus before he became an experimental subject. Evidence indicating that stimulus control can be obtained by simply reinforcing a response in the presence of a certain stimulus would therefore be an artifact of pre-experimental differential reinforcement.

Experimental attempts to substantiate the assumptions of the Hull-Spence and the Lashley theories of stimulus control took the form of studies of discrimination reversal and of "continuous" and "non-continuous" discrimination learning (Blum & Blum, 1949). In neither type of experiment were consistent results obtained across individual subjects or across averaged data from different experiments. Most of these experimenters also took stimulus control, with respect to the stimuli being studied, for granted, and therefore contributed little in the way of isolating the conditions necessary for establishing stimulus control.

A more profitable line of research resulted from a procedure that was devised by Skinner (1950, p. 201) and later refined by Guttman and Kalish (1956) in a classical study of stimulus generalization. The basic feature of this procedure was the use of an intermittent schedule of reinforcement to reinforce responding in the presence of S+. This insured a high resistance to extinction of responding in the presence of both S+ and the test stimuli. In the Guttman and Kalish experiment, pigeons were conditioned to peck for food reinforcement at a translucent plastic key which could be transilluminated by monochromatic lights of different wavelengths. A different wavelength was used for training each of four experimental groups. Following conditioning all responses were reinforced on the average of once every minute. Both the response key and the experimental chamber were darkened every 60 sec. for 10 sec. No responses were reinforced during the 10-sec. time-out (TO) periods. During the generalization test the TO periods were used to change the wavelength of the light that was projected on the response key. These periods were inserted during the training sessions to minimize the possibility of their serving as a cue for discriminating between the training and the generalization sessions. Eleven different stimuli were presented in the generalization test, including the stimulus previously correlated with reinforcement. The stimuli were presented in 12 different randomized sequences. Each stimulus period was 30 sec. long, and no responses were reinforced.

The resulting gradients are shown in the upper portion of Figure 1. For each group the peak of the gradient occurred at the value of the training stimulus for that group. The extent to which a test stimulus controlled responding decreased as the distance between the test and the training stimuli increased. It is important to note that the averaged gradients shown in Figure 1 were representative of most of the individual subjects. Thus, these gradients were able to overcome earlier objections (e.g., Razran, 1949) that the shape of the gradient was the result of averaging across many heterogeneous gradients.

The results of the Guttman and Kalish experiment would, at first glance, seem to support Hull's position that stimulus control can be established simply by reinforcing responding in the presence of a certain stimulus. A number of factors, however, prevent us from ruling out the possibility of uncontrolled differential reinforcement that could have arisen from any one of three sources:

1. Differential reinforcement with respect to wavelength could have taken place prior to experimental training. During the course of foraging for food or finding his way in his environment, it is possible and probable that the pigeon learned discriminations based on wavelength.

2. In learning to peck the key a pigeon usually pecks first around it and only gradually learns to peck exclusively at the key. The physical difference between the key and its surround (texture, brightness, wavelength, etc.) permits an easy discrimination between the key and its surround. The resulting tendency to "pay attention" to the key could provide a basis for forming a discrimination between the training stimulus and the subsequently presented test stimuli.

3. Explicit differential reinforcement with respect to the presence and absence of the monochromatic stimuli on the response key could have been established by the TO procedure. This procedure is hard to evaluate because a pigeon rarely responds in the dark without special training to do so. Thus, the TO procedure may have been more analogous to removing the bird from the box or to some other means of physical restraint that would have prevented him from responding than to a differential reinforcement procedure which allows the pigeon the same "opportunity" to respond to S— as it does to respond to S+.

The contribution of the first two types of differential reinforcement in establishing stimulus control have been clarified by subsequent experiments performed by Peterson (1962), Ganz and Riesen (1962), Jenkins and

Harrison (1960), and by Heinemann and Rudolph (1963). The results of
Peterson's experiment suggested that a pre-experimental differential rein-

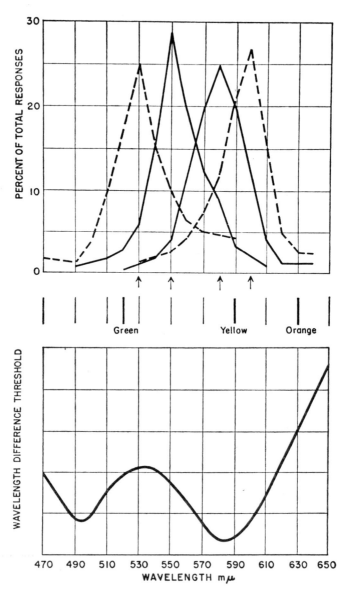

Figure 1. Upper figure: Generalization gradients of wavelength obtained from
pigeons trained at different wavelengths. Lower figure: Sensitivity of the pigeon
to differences in wavelength. The arrows indicate training stimuli for four different groups. (From Guttman & Kalish, 1956).

forcement history with respect to wavelength did in fact contribute to the stimulus control demonstrated in the Guttman and Kalish experiment. Peterson reared ducklings in a monochromatic light of 589 mμ (sodium-arc lamp with appropriate filters) from the moment of hatching. They were trained to peck at a key that was also transilluminated by a light of 589 mμ in the experimental chamber in which they were raised. After 15 days of training on a variable interval (VI) 3' schedule of reinforcement, a generalization test was given in extinction in which the original training stimulus (589 mμ) was presented in an irregular series with test stimuli of other wavelengths. The new stimuli represented the first instance in which the ducklings were exposed to stimuli of a wavelength other than 589 mμ. The results are shown in Figure 2. No evidence of stimulus control was obtained from any of the four subjects. The ducklings responded to the test stimuli to the same extent to which they responded to 589 mμ. Stimulus control was established in a second group of control ducklings who were raised in white light and who had the same history of reinforcement as the experimental group. The gradients for the group reared in white light are shown in the bottom portion of Figure 2. It is clear that a necessary condition for obtaining a generalization gradient of wavelength whose slope is greater than zero is prior exposure to white light. White light presumably allowed differential reinforcement with respect to different wavelengths to occur prior to the generalization test. It should be noted, however, that Peterson's experiment does not shed light on just what types of differential reinforcement are needed for the establishment of stimulus control. It may be possible, for example, to establish stimulus control with respect to all wavelengths following differential reinforcement with only two wavelengths.

Peterson's results are similar to the findings of an experiment by Ganz and Riesen (1962) which showed that macaque monkeys who were reared in darkness later yielded a flat generalization gradient of wavelength. In the Ganz and Riesen study, infant monkeys were separated from their mothers immediately after birth and were reared in total darkness for ten weeks. A second group was reared in normal illumination. Both groups were then trained to press a key for sucrose reinforcement. The dark-reared group was brought to the training apparatus in a light-tight box. The conditioning procedure used for both groups was identical. A plastic cup was fitted over both eyes of each monkey. The cup over the right eye allowed approximately 10 percent of the incident light to be transmitted to the eye. The cup over the left eye was opaque. Light to the right eye was projected through a monochromatic filter. In the presence of a monochromatic light (S+) pressing the key was reinforced on a VI schedule of reinforcement. During the time when no light was projected onto the right eye (S—) no responses were reinforced. Following two to three months of discrimination training between the presence and the absence of the monochromatic

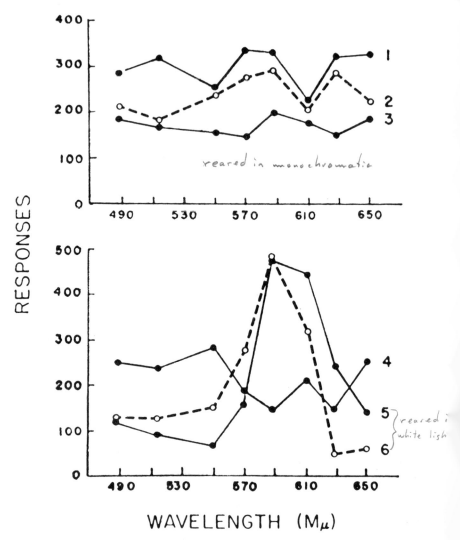

Figure 2. Generalization gradients of wavelength for individual ducklings. Functions 1-4 were obtained from ducklings raised in a monochromatic environment (589mμ). Functions 5 and 6 were obtained from ducklings reared in white light (from Peterson, 1962).

light, a generalization test was performed in which other monochromatic stimuli were presented in a random sequence. The test was carried out for seven successive days during which responding to S+ continued to be reinforced. During the first day of testing the dark-reared group responded almost equally to all of the test wavelengths. On their first test, however, the light-reared group showed a steep generalization gradient. During the ensuing generalization tests the gradients obtained from the dark-reared group became steeper, indicating that the initially flat gradient could not be attributed to atrophied receptors.

An earlier experiment, performed by Jenkins and Harrison (1960), demonstrated that in certain instances differential reinforcement with respect to a certain stimulus is necessary to establish stimulus control even when the organism has been exposed to stimuli on the relevant dimension prior to experimental training. In the first part of their experiment, Jenkins and Harrison used a procedure very similar to that used by Guttman and Kalish (1956). Jenkins and Harrison, however, failed to obtain any evidence for stimulus control along the auditory frequency dimension. Pigeons were reinforced in the presence of a 1000 cps tone on a VI 20″ schedule of reinforcement. Subsequently obtained generalization gradients of tonal frequency (lower portion of Figure 3) were flat across all stimuli and also under the condition in which no stimulus was presented.

Generalization gradients following differential reinforcement were also obtained from a second group of pigeons. The 1000 cps tone was correlated with the same VI 20″ schedule of reinforcement, and the absence of the tone was correlated with extinction. The gradients obtained from the second group appear in the upper portion of Figure 3. It is clear that stimulus control was established only in those pigeons which had a history of differential reinforcement with respect to the presence and absence of the 1000 cps tone.

The Jenkins and Harrison experiment, which was among the first to demonstrate that differential reinforcement was necessary to establish stimulus control, also raised certain questions concerning the interpretation of the Guttman and Kalish procedure. When the training stimulus was a spatially localized patch of monochromatic light, Guttman and Kalish obtained stimulus control with respect to wavelength following non-differential training. When the training stimulus was a diffuse pure tone, Jenkins and Harrison were unable to obtain stimulus control with respect to tonal frequency following a similar non-differential training procedure. Why the same training procedure should yield opposite results with respect to different stimulus continua is not an easy question to answer.

One possible explanation comes from an experiment by Heinemann and Rudolph (1963) on intensity generalization. These experimenters varied the size of a spatially localized stimulus display around the response key in a pigeon apparatus. Three experimental groups were used. For the first group, the stimulus display was the whole front panel of the experimental chamber except for the one-inch circular hole for the response key and the two-inch square opening for the food magazine. For the remaining two groups, the diameters of the stimuli surrounding the response key were 5.25 and 1.75 inches respectively, and the remainder of the front panel

was black cardboard. The luminance of the training stimulus that was correlated with a VI 1′ schedule of reinforcement was 10.1 ft.-l. (The key

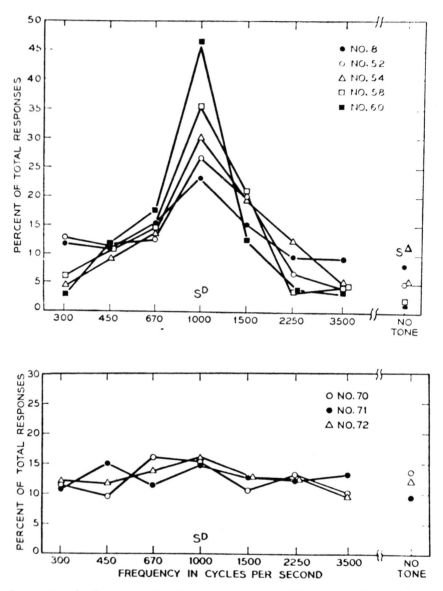

Figure 3. Individual generalization gradients of tonal frequency obtained from
pigeons following two training conditions. Lower figure: Training tone (1000 cps)
was continuously present. Upper figure: These functions were obtained following discrimination training in which S+ was 1000 cps and S— was no tone
(from Jenkins & Harrison, 1960).

had a luminance of 9 ft.-l.) In a subsequent generalization test the luminance of the stimulus was either 15.4, 10.1, or 1.5 ft.-l. The results, shown in Figure 4, indicate that the size of the stimulus sharply affected the slope of the generalization gradient. The clear effect of stimulus size on the

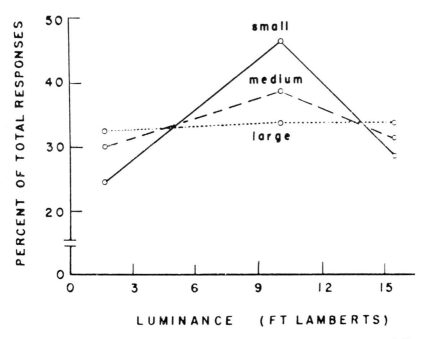

Figure 4. Generalization gradients of luminance obtained from pigeons following non-differential training with either a large, medium, or small stimulus of 10.1 ft.-l. (from Heinemann & Rudolph, 1963).

amount of S+ stimulus control that was obtained following "non-differential" training in the presence of S+ led Heinemann and Rudolph to conclude that:

> . . . it would appear that some discriminative training must inevitably occur in any situation in which the stimulus is a fairly small visual area and the required response is a movement that is directed with respect to this stimulus, such as pecking at the stimulus, or walking or jumping through a door upon which the stimulus appears or turning at a choice point marked by the stimulus. It seems likely that the results of previous experiments which appeared to show that a stimulus does acquire some control over a response in the absence of differential training reflect some unintended differential training (Heinemann & Rudolph, 1963, pp. 657-658).

Heinemann and Rudolph's interpretation of their data emphasizes the role that stimulus size plays in the acquisition of a discrimination between the stimulus and the remaining portions of the experimental chamber. The larger the stimulus the more "immersed" the pigeon is in the stimulus. This would presumably make it relatively difficult to discriminate the stimulus from the remainder of the experimental chamber. As the stimulus size decreases, however, the stimulus patch becomes more "prominent." This would presumably faciliate "paying attention" to the stimulus on hand. The role of attention in this and in other experiments will be treated in greater detail in the next section of this chapter.

The schedule and the nature of reinforcement are other variables which have been shown to affect the slope of the generalization gradient that is obtained with the Guttman and Kalish procedure. Hearst, Koresko, and Poppen (1964) demonstrated that the slope of the gradient depended on the type and the value of the schedule of reinforcement that was correlated with S+. In this experiment, S+ was either a vertical or a horizontal white line on a black background. In one procedure S+ was correlated with either a VI 1′ or with a differential reinforcement of low rate (drl 6″) schedule of reinforcement. The gradients obtained, with various orientions of the white line, after VI training were much steeper than the gradients obtained following drl training. The averaged gradients from each group are shown in Figure 5(a). In another procedure generalization gradients of tilt were obtained following training with VI schedules where the mean interval was either 30 sec., 1 min., 2 min., 3 min., or 4 min. A different group of subjects was used for each VI schedule. The steepest gradients were obtained from the VI 30″ and 1′ groups. For the remaining groups the slope of the gradient varied inversely with the value of the VI schedule. The averaged gradients from each group are shown in Figure 5(b). Similar results have been reported by Haber and Kalish (1963) who demonstrated that the slope of a generalization gradient of wavelength was steeper after VI 15″ or VI 1′ training than following training on a VI 4′ schedule of reinforcement.

Positive and negative reinforcement can also have differential effects upon the slope of a generalization gradient. Hearst (1962) reported differences in the slopes of gradients of light intensity that were related to the use of food-reinforcement and shock-avoidance schedules. In this experiment monkeys were trained to pull a chain for food reinforcement on a VI 2′ schedule and to press a lever to avoid shock on a Sidman avoidance schedule (Sidman, 1953) in which each response postponed the occurrence of a shock by 10 sec. Both responses were trained in the presence of a bright light. In a generalization test, in which food could not be obtained, and shock was not presented, the intensity of the light was randomly varied. The gradients based upon the response that previously obtained food (chain pulling) were steeper than the gradients based on responses that previously

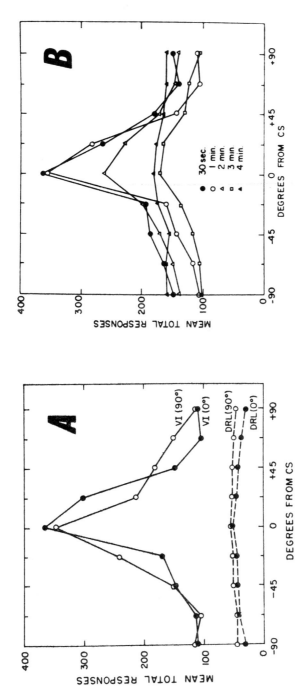

Figure 5 (A). Generalization gradients of tilt following training on a VI or a drl schedule of reinforcement. Each group was composed of two sub-groups, one trained with a vertical line as S+ (0°) and the other with a horizontal line as S+ (90°). (B) Gradients of generalization of tilt for five different VI groups. S+ was a vertical line (0°) for all subjects (from Hearst, Koresko, & Poppen, 1964).

postponed shocks. The gradients of each of Hearst's three subjects are shown in Figure 6(a). Similar results were also obtained in an earlier study in which rats served as subjects (Hearst, 1960).

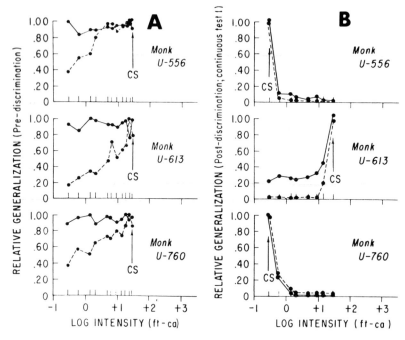

Figure 6 (B). Three individual pre-discrimination generalization gradients of intensity obtained from monkeys. The solid functions are based on avoidance responses; the dotted functions are based on food-rewarded responses. All subjects were trained in the presence of the brightest test intensity (indicated as "CS"). (B). Post-discrimination generalization gradients for subjects shown in Figure 6 (A) for avoidance (solid functions) and food-rewarded (dotted functions) responses. For two subjects S+ was the dimmest test intensity, whereas for the third subject S+ was the brightest test intensity. In all cases S— was at the opposite end of the intensity continuum (from Hearst, 1962).

Hearst et al. have interpreted the relatively poor exteroceptive stimulus control following training on a drl schedule in terms of competing stimulus control resulting from movement-produced and other internal stimuli:

This explanation postulates that the stimulus control of key pecking in the DRL situation is primarily proprioceptive in nature; if this is true, then variations in an exteroceptive dimension like line-tilt ought to be more or less irrelevant for the key-pecking DRL response. In contrast, in the VI situation there appear to be fewer different kinds of stimuli (especially internal-proprioceptive) associated with the key-pecking response; therefore, the visual properties of the key may constitute a proportionally larger part of the conditioned stimulus compound than is the case in the DRL situation—and thus lead to steeper visual gradients for VI (Hearst *et al.*, 1964, p. 375).

A similar explanation was offered for the poor control obtained by the longer VI schedules: "One would expect less control by the exteroceptive properties of the response key on longer VI schedules and therefore flatter generalization gradients" (Hearst *et al.*, 1964, p. 379). Hearst's (1962) explanation of the flatter gradients of avoidance responding cited internal cues that exerted a larger degree of control over an avoidance response than over a response that was reinforced by food.

Blough (1963; 1965) has presented a similar argument in an analysis of the relative amounts of control exerted upon a response by the value of the exteroceptive stimulus and the value of the preceding interresponse time. In a generalization test Blough states that ". . . the occurrence of previous responses may almost completely determine the subsequent emission of responses after short interresponse times (IRTs). Thus, these short IRT responses may only be indirectly controlled by the stimulus. . . ." (Blough, 1965, p. 33). It would seem that one way of eliminating the effect of a previous response in the original Guttman and Kalish procedure would be to allow no more than one response to occur for each presentation of a test stimulus in a generalization test. This would be accomplished by using a trial rather than a free-operant procedure during training and generalization. Each trial would be terminated by the first response or the passage of a short period of time. A high resistance to extinction could be insured by reinforcing only a small fraction of the responses to S+.

Attention

We have previously mentioned the concept of attention in discussing the results of the Heinemann and Rudolph experiment. Numerous other studies have also cited attention, or, more specifically, the lack of attention, to explain instances in which stimulus control was not obtained. In the first portion of Jenkins and Harrison's experiment, for example, in which nondifferential reinforcement in the presence of a 1000 cps tone yielded a flat generalization gradient, one could postulate that the pigeon was not "paying attention" to the 1000 cps tone. One could similarly assume in the Hearst *et al.* study that the pigeons were not paying attention to the stimulus under the drl condition.

Other situations in which the concept of attention has been used reveal the same practice. Attention is typically used in those situations in which a stimulus or some element of a stimulus does *not* reliably control a response. Thus, *attention* seems to be synonymous with *stimulus control* to the extent that failures to establish stimulus control are referred to as failures of attention. Before we evaluate other experiments on attention it would be helpful to see how attention enters into various theoretical accounts of learning. We will then review the types of situations in which incomplete stimulus control has been obtained and see how stimulus control might possibly have been increased.

Theoretical Analyses of Attention

The problem of attention has been specifically discussed by most modern learning theorists. For example, Hull, Spence, Guthrie, and Skinner, each starting with a different set of assumptions, have eventually found that the problem of attention was a major stumbling block in the analysis of many experimental results. In each case there was a growing appreciation of the fact that the occurrence of a given stimulus was, in many instances, an unreliable predictor of a certain response.

We have previously noted that Hull's contention that "all elements of a stimulus complex . . . tend themselves independently and indiscriminately to acquire a capacity to [evoke] substantially the same response" (Hull, 1929, p. 498) was a basic assumption of this theory of discrimination learning. While he never formally repudiated this statement, Hull later postulated two mechanisms whereby, in fact, only certain elements of a stimulus will evoke a response. The first of these was the "pure stimulus act" which constituted modifications and transformations in the stimulus reception processes that resulted from previous learning. Pure stimulus acts facilitated discrimination performance because of the added sensory exposure to the relevant stimulus. Another construct that Hull used to handle imprecise correlations between a stimulus and a response was behavioral oscillation. Reaction potential ($_{s}E_{R}$) rarely occurred at full value prior to the evocation of a certain response. Instead, reaction potential was thought to oscillate randomly around some central value according to a normally distributed function. Thus, given a constant stimulus, the probability of a response varied, within certain limits, according to the normal probability function. According to Hull behavioral oscillation "presumably is responsible for many of the phenomena grouped by the classical psychologists under the head of 'attention'" (1943), p. 393).

In a qualification of his original theory of discrimination learning, Spence suggested that certain mediating responses must occur before a stimulus element will control a response:

> . . . the animal learns many other responses in addition to the final, selective approaching reaction. Prominent and important among these are what has been termed, for want of a better name, "preparatory responses." These latter consist of the responses which lead to the reception of the appro-

priate aspects of the total environmental complex on the animal's sensorium, e.g., the orientation and fixation of the head and eyes toward the critical stimuli. That is, the animal learns to "look at" one aspect of the situation rather than another because of the fact that this response has always been followed within a short temporal interval by the final goal response. Responses providing other sensory receptions are not similarly reinforced in a systematic fashion and hence tend to disappear (Spence, 1937, p. 437).

In a more recent statement of his discrimination theory Spence (1956, p. 100) appealed to "receptor-exposure acts" which intervene between a given stimulus and a given response. Here again, contrary to his original assertion, all elements of a stimulus which impinge upon a given receptor do not necessarily acquire associative strength by virtue of their being paired with reinforcement. Spence postulated that receptor-exposure acts must also occur if the stimulus is to acquire control over the response.

The failure of a given stimulus to reliably evoke a response led Guthrie, a non-reinforcement S-R theorist, to revise his original "law" of conditioning. In 1935 Guthrie (p. 23) stated that "a combination of stimuli which has accompanied a movement will on its recurrence tend to be followed by that movement." More recently he wrote that: "What is being noticed becomes a signal for what is being done" (Guthrie, 1959, p. 186). "What is being noticed," according to Guthrie, "conveys . . . the active part of the organism's own activity in the selection of the physical stimuli through attention" (Guthrie, 1959, p. 186).

Skinner has consistently (defined) the stimulus in terms of its ability to control a given response (Skinner, 1938). The concept of attention has entered the *description* of those situations in which a certain element of a stimulus that is correlated with reinforcement does not reliably control the response in question.

> The control exerted by a discriminative stimulus is traditionally dealt with under the heading of attention. . . . Attention is a controlling *relation*— the relation between a response and a discriminative stimulus. When someone is paying attention he is under special control of a stimulus. We detect the relation most readily when receptors are conspicuously oriented, but this is not essential. An organism is attending to a detail of a stimulus, whether or not its receptors are oriented to produce the most clear-cut reception, if its behavior is predominantly under the control of that detail (Skinner, 1953, pp. 122-124). *SHB*

It should be especially noted that *describing* an unreliable relationship between the controlling properties of a stimulus and a response as attention is a different matter from *explaining* the complete or partial absence of stimulus control. The use of attention as an explanatory principle in these instances is begging the question, and seems to be nothing more than a mask for our ignorance concerning the establishment of stimulus control.

One is still left with the problem of the necessary conditions for getting an organism to pay attention to a particular attribute of a stimulus. One answer to this question was offered by Wyckoff (1954) who postulated an intervening response called an "observing response" as a necessary condition for a stimulus, or a given aspect of a stimulus, to acquire control over a response. These observing responses were analogous in function to the VTEs (vicarious trial and error) postulated by Tolman (1939) and Muenzinger (1956) and also to the receptor-exposure acts postulated by Spence (1956). Their function was to bring the organism in direct contact with exteroceptive stimuli which had discriminative functions.

Experimental studies of observing responses have been performed by Wyckoff (1954), Kelleher (1958), and Zeigler and Wyckoff (1961). The consequence of the observing response in these experiments was to produce exteroceptive discriminative stimuli in a situation in which they were previously absent. In these experiments it was also demonstrated that observing responses could be extinguished once the discriminative functions of the stimuli, produced by the observing response, were abolished. This was done by eliminating any consistent relationship between the stimuli and the prevailing contingencies of reinforcement. It should, however, be noted that in these studies the observing response was in all cases *overt*. Thus, Wyckoff's observing response, the VTE response of Tolman and Muenzinger, and Spence's receptor-exposure act, do not necessarily apply to those situations in which the term *attention* has traditionally applied. Experimental demonstrations of observing responses do indicate that an organism can be reinforced by the presentation of discriminative stimuli. They fail to indicate how an observing response (or an "attentional response") is established in a situation in which no attempt is made to condition an overt response that produces a discriminative stimulus. More specifically, what Wyckoff has labelled as an "observing response" might more appropriately be called a "discriminanda-producing response." It is one thing to show that such responses can in fact be conditioned; it is another to assume that what have been called attentional responses do, in fact, result from a similar conditioning procedure.

Experimental Studies of Attention

The experiments to be discussed in this section all used a composite stimulus in which the experimentally defined elements came from at least two different continua. The problem in each case was to determine to what extent each element acquired control over responding and what variables affected the acquisition of control by that element. The extent to which a change in a complex stimulus will result in a response decrement cannot, at present, be accurately predicted in most situations. Reynolds (1961c) demonstrated that different aspects of a complex S+ acquire control over responding in different subjects. In this experiment two pigeons were trained on a successive discrimination in which S+ was a white triangle on a red background and S— was a white circle on a green background. After responding to S— had been almost completely extinguished, the components of S+ and S— were presented separately during an extinction session. The results are shown in Figure 7. Neither pigeon responded either to the green background or to the white circle. Thus, both aspects of S— acquired control over *not* responding. This was not, however, true of S+. One bird responded only when the red background was presented, whereas the other

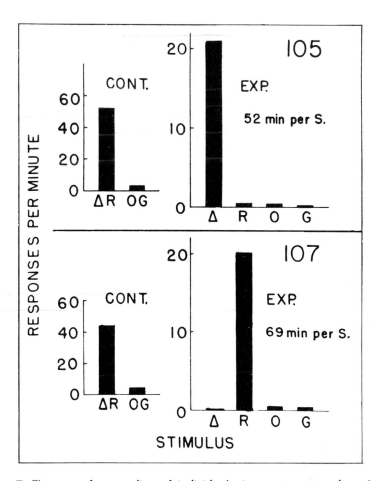

Figure 7. The rate of responding of individual pigeons to a complex stimulus and to the components of the complex stimulus. During discrimination training (cont.) S+ was a white triangle on a red background and S— was a white circle on a green background. During extinction (exp.) the separate components of S+ and S— (triangle, circle, red and green backgrounds) were presented individually in random alternation (from Reynolds, 1961b).

bird responded only when the white triangle was presented. Only one aspect of S+ controlled responding and it did so in an unpredictable manner. Here again the concept of attention was used to explain the unpredictable manner in which the components of S+ controlled responding. In earlier studies in which more complicated stimuli were used, Lashley (1938; 1942) also showed that, in a simultaneous discrimination, different aspects of S+ and S— gained control over responding and not-responding among different rats. For some rats the size of the triangle was crucial, for others the fact that it was a white stimulus on a dark background was crucial, etc.

Fortunately, the conditioning of an organism in the presence of a complex stimulus does not always yield such unpredictable results. Butter (1963), for example, reinforced pigeons for responding to a band of light whose wavelength and orientation could be simultaneously varied. During training the light was 550 mμ and in a vertical position. In a subsequent generalization test the wavelength and the orientation of the training stimulus were varied. Butter found that varying the stimulus along two dimensions resulted in a sharper decrement in responding than did varying the stimulus along only one dimension. That is, the generalization gradients were steepest when changes occurred along two dimensions. Fink and Patton (1953) obtained similar results following conditioning in an apparatus in which the experimenter could vary the stimulus correlated with reinforcement along three dimensions (intensity of light, intensity of sound, and roughness of floor). The decrement in responding that resulted from a change in the value of the stimuli that held during conditioning was a function of the number of dimensions along which the stimulus had been changed.

The Butter and the Fink and Patton studies indicate that a complex stimulus can reliably acquire control over responding along more than one dimension. Unfortunately these studies do not shed any light on the nature of the conditions that are necessary for establishing control along several dimensions. In our earlier evaluation of the conditions necessary for stimulus control to be established along a single dimension, we noted the importance of differential reinforcement. A similar state of affairs seems to hold for the establishment of multi-dimensional stimulus control. As we shall later see, specific differential reinforcement with respect to one of the numerous dimensions along which a stimulus may be specified, makes that dimension more "distinctive" than a dimension which does not enter into the differential reinforcement procedure.

It is not always clear that differential reinforcement per se is necessary for a stimulus from one dimension to control a response to a greater degree than do stimuli from other dimensions. Certain dimensions may be prepotent because of various innate factors (e.g., Guttman, 1963). A pigeon may come to be controlled more readily by visual than by auditory stimuli because, as a result of his environmental needs, the visual system has evolved as the more sensitive system. In other situations Gestalt psychologists have pointed out that certain organizations of complex stimuli are innately more prepotent than others (e.g., Köhler, 1929). It will therefore be useful for us to also examine hierarchies of stimulus control which do not appear to have been established by differential reinforcement. Afterwards we will see how these hierarchies may be modified.

One of the first studies that concerned itself with the dimensions along which a discrimination is learned showed that over an assortment of stimuli varying in color, form, and size, monkeys learned simultaneous discriminations between different pairs of these stimuli mainly on the basis of color (Warren, 1953). A more extensive experiment, reported by Baron (1965), studied the elements of a compound stimulus that gained control of a pigeon's key-pecking response in a successive discrimination. S+ was always a white vertical line on a green background, but a different S— was used for each of three experimental groups. S— was either (1) a green background with no line, (2) a red background with no line, or (3) a red background with a line. The first group had to learn the discrimination on the basis of the presence or the absence of the line. The second group could learn the discrimination on the basis of either color or the presence or absence of the line, while the third group had to learn the discrimination on the basis of color. The discrimination performance of groups 2 and 3 was much better than the performance of group 1.

Another group received non-differential training in the presence of S+. The four groups were then given a generalization test in which the line was presented in various orientations on a green background. The results are shown in Figure 8. Evidence that the line had acquired stimulus control was obtained only from the first group which had to learn the discrimination on the basis of the presence or the absence of the vertical line. The generalization gradients of the other three groups were flat across the different orientations of the line. This study demonstrated that when pigeons are given an opportunity to learn a discrimination on the basis of color, as opposed to the presence or absence of a line, they will learn the discrimination on the basis of color. Stimulus control with respect to the orientation of the line is established only when the presence or the absence of the line is the only stimulus element that can be used to learn the discrimination. Thus, a "non-distinctive" stimulus element may be made "distinctive" by requiring that an organism learn a discrimination with respect to the presence and absence of that element.

A similar situation appears to hold in the previously cited study by Hearst (1962) on the nature of stimulus control under food-reinforcement and shock-avoidance schedules. After obtaining a steep gradient for the food-obtaining response and a flat gradient for the shock-avoidance response, Hearst trained a discrimination in which the food and the shock-avoidance schedules were in effect only at one intensity value. A subsequent

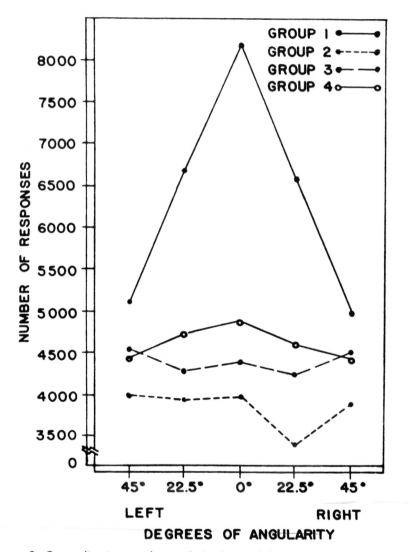

Figure 8. Generalization gradients of tilt obtained from pigeons following different training conditions. See text for identification of each group (from Baron, 1965).

generalization test showed that the intensity of the stimulus light controlled the shock-avoidance response as well as the food-obtaining response. Differential reinforcement appeared to produce exteroceptive control of the avoidance response where none had previously existed. The post-discrimination gradients are shown in Figure 6 (b).

Another technique for changing the hierarchies of stimulus distinctiveness comes from an instructive study performed by Honig (1965), who trained a group of pigeons on a successive discrimination in which S+ and S— were white and pink lights respectively. A second group was given "pseudo-discrimination" training in which the pink and the white lights were randomly correlated with reinforcement. Both groups were then given non-differential training in the presence of the white light on which three parallel vertical black lines were superimposed. In a subsequent generalization test, a steep gradient was obtained from the group which had previously received differential training with respect to the white and pink lights. The second group, which had no prior history of differential training with respect to the stimuli projected on the response key, yielded a relatively shallow gradient. Thus, differential reinforcement on a *prior* and independent discrimination in the same apparatus sufficed to establish stimulus control with respect to a stimulus which other studies (e.g., Baron, 1965) have shown does not normally control a response without specific differential reinforcement. These results also have important implications for experiments which investigate the acquisition of a "new" discrimination in subjects who have had a history of differential reinforcement in the same apparatus with similar discriminanda. While it may be cumbersome to control for the relevant differential reinforcement of the organism prior to his *experimental* history it would seem foolhardy to use subjects in a stimulus control study who have had a history of differential reinforcement, in the same or in a similar apparatus, unless one is specifically interested in transfer between the two discriminations.

Other types of transfer studies have also shown that differential reinforcement in one situation makes the discriminative stimuli more distinctive in a new situation than would have been the case without the earlier differential reinforcement. Two basic paradigms have been used. In the first, the response that is reinforced is the same in both situations; in the second, a different response is required in the second situation.

Studies of the first type have used a classical conditioning paradigm to train a discrimination and have then determined whether or not this training facilitated the discriminative function of the conditioned stimulus in an operant situation. In one of the original studies of this type, performed by Estes (1943), rats were first reinforced with food for bar pressing. The bar was then removed and food was presented at the offset of a 60-sec. tone. Following three sessions during which the tone was paired with the presentation of food, the bar was reinserted and bar pressing was extinguished during a 60-min. extinction session, in which the tone was presented twice, each time for ten minutes. The rate of bar pressing was higher in the presence of the tone than in its absence even though bar pressing had never been reinforced in the presence of the tone. In a second experiment

Estes (1948) obtained similar results even when the tone and food pairings occurred prior to the conditioning of the bar press.

Morse and Skinner (1958) obtained comparable results in an experiment in which two conditioned stimuli were used. Either a red or a green chamber light was aperiodically paired with the free presentation of food. Food was never presented in the presence of the alternate color. Following these pairings pigeons were conditioned to peck at a key for food reinforcement. Both the key and the chamber were illuminated by white light. During the final stage of the experiment, no responses were reinforced and the chamber light was alternately red or green for equal periods of time. All four subjects responded more in the presence of the color that had previously been paired with food. In a similar experiment using rats, Bower and Grusec (1964) showed that Pavlovian discrimination training could facilitate operant discrimination learning if S+ and S— had previously signaled the occurrence and non-occurrence of food. Operant discrimination learning was slower if CS+ became S— and CS— became S+.

One of the first studies that followed the second paradigm of using two different responses in studying the pre-differentiation of a stimulus was performed by Walker (1942). This experiment showed that a discriminative stimulus, developed in connection with one operant (a running response), had a facilitative effect upon a second operant (lever pressing). In a later, more comprehensive series of studies on the "acquired distinctiveness of cues," Lawrence (1949; 1950) distinguished between learning based on the "acquisition of the correct instrumental responses in a discrimination situation and . . . the learning involved in modifying the initial order of distinctiveness among the cues" (Lawrence, 1949, p. 770). To satisfy this requirement, Lawrence first trained rats on a simultaneous discrimination that was based on one of three possible sets of stimulus dimensions: brightness, width of goal compartment, and texture or roughness of the floor. They were then shifted to a successive discrimination in a different apparatus which required a different response. Positive transfer was only obtained from those rats for which the relevant dimensions were the same in both discrimination tasks. The performance of those rats for which a previously irrelevant cue was made positive, or for which the previously positive cue was made negative, was decidedly poorer. Thus, we again see that the effects of differential reinforcement with respect to a particular stimulus element will transfer to other situations. Differential reinforcement may, therefore, be considered to be a sufficient condition for some element of a complex stimulus to gain control over a particular response. Whether or not it is a necessary condition is not presently known. It seems quite probable that, in many situations, innate factors may determine the "distinctiveness" of a particular stimulus element without the benefit of differential reinforcement with respect to that element.

THE SHARPENING OF STIMULUS CONTROL

Traditional Theoretical Formulations and Methodology

In our discussion of the initial acquisition of stimulus control, we concluded that differential reinforcement with respect to S+ is necessary to establish control over a given response along one of the dimensions on which the stimulus can be specified. It is usually the case, however, that the amount of control that is obtained does not approach the discriminative capacity of the organism. This is illustrated in Figure 9 which shows three hypothetical generalization gradients. Gradient I indicates no stimulus control. Gradient II indicates the maximum possible degree of stimulus control: the difference threshold at S+ for this particular continuum. Gradient

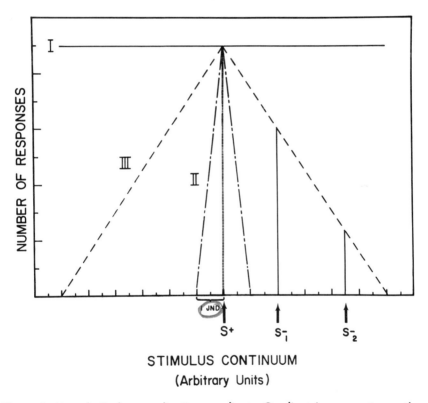

Figure 9. Hypothetical generalization gradients. Gradient I represents no stimulus control. Gradient II represents the maximum possible stimulus control. Gradient III represents an intermediate amount of stimulus control.

III indicates an intermediate degree of stimulus control that is typically obtained following differential reinforcement with respect to the presence and absence of S+.

How gradient II (the differential threshold) is obtained is, of course, one of the traditional problems of psychophysics. A general discussion of threshold measurements, especially in organisms to which no verbal instructions can be given, may be found in Blough's Chapter 8 in this volume on animal psychophysics. Our main concern in this section will be methods for sharpening stimulus control to the degree indicated by a gradient that would fall between gradients II and III. Stated in more traditional terms, our problem is the nature of the acquisition of a discrimination between two stimuli from a given continuum.

It has been generally accepted that a necessary condition for the sharpening of stimulus control is a differential reinforcement procedure in which S— assumes some value between the points at which gradients II and III intersect the abscissa. The sharpening of stimulus control has been generally described in terms of the interaction of gradients of excitation and inhibition or gradients of reinforcement and extinction centered about S+ and S— respectively (e.g., Spence, 1936; Hull, 1950; Keller & Schoenfeld, 1950, pp. 118-120; Kimble, 1961, pp. 364-374). An account of how a discrimination is formed would run as follows: the reinforcement of a response in the presence of S+ adds a large increment of response strength at S+ and, via the process of generalization of excitation, a smaller increment of response strength is added at S—. Non-reinforcement of responding at S— results in a large increment of inhibition at S— and a smaller increment of inhibition at S+. As this process is repeated, in conjunction with the repeated alternation of S+ and S—, the strengths of responding to the two discriminative stimuli draw apart and a discrimination is formed. This description of the formation of a discrimination as an interaction of the processes of reinforcement and extinction was supported by the results of a number of early studies on the acquisition of a discrimination, notably Skinner's data on discrimination learning in the rat (1938). Skinner (1938, Chapter 5) showed that the gradual extinction of responding in the presence of S— initially had the effect of lowering the rate of responding to S+. As training progressed, the rates of responding to S+ and to S— slowly pulled apart. Similar data were obtained by Verplanck (1942) who showed that the latencies and running times of a running response to S+ and S— in a Graham-Gagné runway gradually draw apart at the start of discrimination training.

In another experiment on the acquisition of a discrimination, Skinner (1938, pp. 203-206) demonstrated that the strength of responding to S+ affects the size of the extinction curve in S—. A brightness discrimination was acquired by rats with virtually no responses to S— if discrimination training began immediately after the response to S+ had been conditioned.

Other rats, who received more reinforcements for responding to S+, on either a continuous or an intermittent schedule of reinforcement, made many more responses to S— in acquiring the same discrimination. Thus, the strengthening of responding to S+ seemed to generalize to S—, which resulted in a larger extinction curve of responding to S—. A varied assortment of more recent experiments has, however, shown that the acquisition of a discrimination cannot be adequately described in terms of interacting generalization gradients of reinforcement and extinction.

The generality of induction between responding to S+ and to S— during the formation of a discrimination was sharply questioned by extensive data on the manner in which the rate or latency of responding to S+ changes during the formation of a discrimination. Reynolds (1961a; 1961b) demonstrated that, under a large variety of conditions, the rate of responding to S+ increases as the rate of responding to S— decreases. Jenkins (1961) has similarly shown that the latency of the response to S+ decreased during the acquisition of a discrimination. Any theory of discrimination learning based upon an algebraic interaction of gradients of reinforcement and extinction would have to predict that the rate of responding to S+ would *decrease* during discrimination training as a result of induction from extinction in the presence of S—. Since the change in the rate of responding to S+ is opposite in direction, Reynolds, following Skinner's earlier suggestion (1938), named this phenomenon *behavioral contrast*.

The development of contrast, as observed in an experiment performed by Reynolds (1961), is shown in Figure 10. In this experiment pigeons were trained to discriminate between a red light that was correlated with a VI 3′ schedule of reinforcement and a green light that was correlated with extinction. Prior to mult VI 3′ ext training the pigeons were trained on a mult VI 3′ VI 3′ schedule in which the red and green lights were also correlated with the first and second components. The solid function in Figure 10 shows the rate of responding to the red light; the dotted function shows the rate of responding to the green light. The vertical lines mark the transition from mult VI 3′ VI 3′ to mult VI 3′ ext training and a return to mult VI 3′ VI 3′. At the start of differential reinforcement in the presence of the red and green stimuli, the rate of responding in red increases and remains high while the rate of responding in green declines to a near zero rate.

Similar data obtained from a "trial procedure" (Jenkins, 1961) is shown in Figure 11. A trial was defined as the period of time during which a stimulus appeared on the response key. All trials were terminated by a response or by a failure to respond within 5 sec. of the onset of the trial. Thus, only one response could occur during a trial. A response made during an S+ trial was immediately reinforced. Between trials the houselight remained on but the key was dark. The duration of the intertrial interval was randomly selected from a series of intervals with a range of 5 to 30 sec. and a mean of 15 sec. The latency of responding to S+ (solid function) that

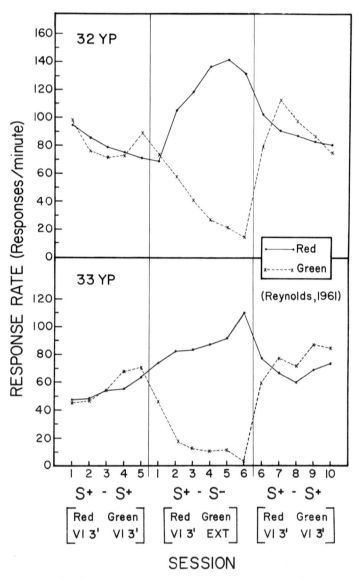

Figure 10. The development of behavioral contrast in individual subjects. The rate of responding to each of two alternating discriminative stimuli are shown during the VI 3′ VI 3′ and VI 3′ ext training. (Adapted from Reynolds, 1961a.)

was obtained from a subject who learned a discrimination between a vertical (S+) and a horizontal (S—) line, should be compared with the latencies of responding under two procedures in which only S+ appeared. In one of these procedures (regular reinforcement) all responses to S+ were reinforced. In the other procedure (intermittent reinforcement) certain responses to S+ were not reinforced. The trials on which reinforcement was omitted were determined by matching an intermittent reinforcement bird with a differential reinforcement bird and noting on which S— trials the bird from the differential reinforcement group responded. By omitting reinforcement from the comparable S+ trial the differential and intermittent reinforcement groups were matched with respect to the distribution of reinforcements.

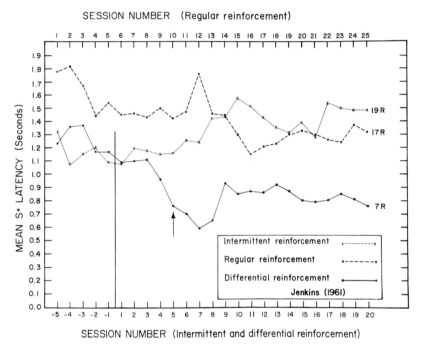

Figure 11. The latency of responding to S+ of individual pigeons under three experimental conditions. See text for explanation of conditions. The arrow represents the first session for the differential reinforcement group in which the probability of responding to S— was less than 0.5. (Adapted from Jenkins, 1961.)

In the sessions plotted to the left of the vertical line of Figure 11 all of the groups were shown only S+ and all responses to S+ were reinforced. Differential and intermittent reinforcement begin to the right of the vertical line. Each point in Figure 11 represents the mean latency of responding to S+ for the session indicated. The arrow under the differential reinforcement latency function indicates the first session in which the probability of responding to S— fell below 0.5. It can clearly be seen in Figure 11 that the differential reinforcement procedure resulted in a sharp decrease in latency of responding to S+ that was correlated with the decline of responding to S—.

It should be emphasized that the effects shown in the group functions plotted in Figures 10 and 11 are extremely reliable and are representative of individual subjects. In similar experiments performed in the author's laboratory contrast was *always* obtained in over 100 cases in which a free-operant discrimination procedure was used, and in over 40 cases in which a "trial procedure" was used.

Strongly related to the assumption that discrimination learning can be described in terms of interacting gradients of reinforcement and extinction, is the widely held assumption that generalization and discrimination are inverse processes. One of the consequences of this assumption is that the shape of a generalization gradient has been used to make predictions concerning the relative difficulty of a given discrimination. This assumption was also initially shown to be qualitatively valid in many situations. More recent studies on discrimination learning have, however, presented numerous exceptions which raise serious questions concerning its validity.

Predicting the relative difficulty of a discrimination from a generalization gradient is a straightforward matter. Suppose, for example, we wanted to compare the formation of a discrimination between S+ and S—$_1$ and S+ and S—$_2$ as illustrated in Figure 9. Since the ordinate at S—$_1$ is higher than the ordinate at S—$_2$ we would predict that a discrimination between S+ and S—$_1$ would be more difficult than a discrimination between S+ and S—$_2$. In general, the difficulty of the discrimination should be inversely related to the difference between S+ and S—. This prediction has been confirmed by Frick (1948) who showed that the number of errors made by rats in the acquisition of an intensity discrimination was inversely related to the S+-S— difference in intensity. Frick's results are shown in Figure 12. In a runway apparatus similar to the Graham-Gagné runway used by Verplanck (1942), Raben (1949) also obtained data on the acquisition of an intensity discrimination that were similar to those from Frick's experiment.

The generality of the finding that discrimination difficulty varies inversely with the S+-S— difference was shown to be somewhat limited by the results of an experiment performed by Hanson (1959). This experiment showed that beyond a rather small S+-S— difference, further increments in the S+-S— difference did not add to the number of responses needed to acquire a discrimination. Hanson's discrimination data are shown in the dashed function of Figure 13. Hanson's "discrimination" gradient shows that the amount of time needed to train a discrimination for differences between S+ and S— larger than 10 mμ remained constant. The generalization gradient (solid function) obtained in the same apparatus with the same stimuli, did not asymptotically approach the abscissa until the difference between S+ and S— exceeded 50 mμ. Thus, the "discrimination" gradient was steeper than the equivalent generalization gradient which indicates that, in this situa-

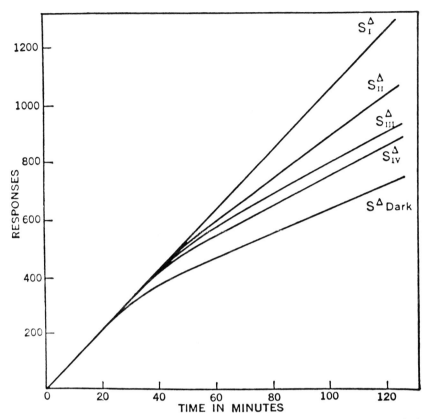

Figure 12. The acquisition of a discrimination in the rat as a function of the S+-S— interval. Shown are average cumulative curves of responding to S— for different S+-S— intervals. S+ for all groups was 20-ft. candles. The intensity of S— for Groups I, II, III, IV, and V was 10-, 7.5-, 5-, .02-, and 0-ft. candles respectively (from Frick, 1948).

tion, the generalization gradient was a relatively poor predictor of the difficulty of a discrimination. This finding has since been confirmed in the author's laboratory by D. Moody who found that different groups of pigeons made the same number of responses to S— during the acquisition of a discrimination between an S+ whose value was 550 mμ and S—s whose values were 530, 570, and 580 mμ.

Another source of trouble for the inverse hypothesis emerged when the original set of gradients of wavelength generalization obtained by Guttman and Kalish (1956) were compared with the wavelength discriminability function. These functions are shown in the lower portion of Figure 1. If the steepness of the generalization gradient reflects the difficulty of a discrimination, one would expect a direct relationship to hold between the slope of the

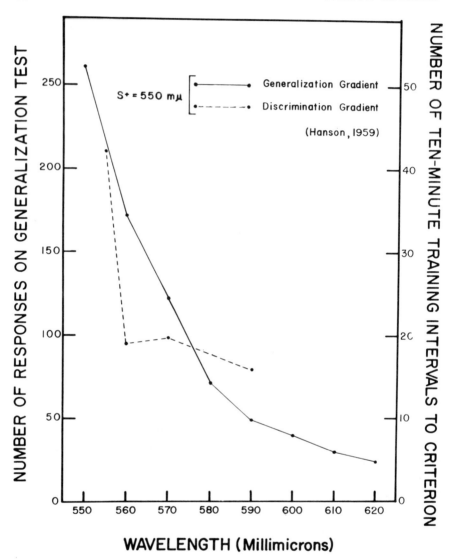

Figure 13. Generalization and discrimination gradients of wavelengths obtained from pigeons. See text for details. (Adapted from Hanson, 1959.)

generalization gradient at a given wavelength and the $\Delta\lambda$ function at that wavelength. At 580 mμ, for example, where the value of $\Delta\lambda$ is low, one would expect the generalization function to be steep. No relationship was, however, shown to exist between the shapes of the generalization and wavelength discriminability functions.

The failure to find a relationship between the slope of a generalization gradient and a discriminability function diminishes in importance when one considers the basis for assuming that generalization and discrimination are inverse processes. If, as Brown has pointed out (1965), one uses generalization to describe some mechanism or process for the transfer of excitation from S+ to other stimuli, and discrimination to mean the perception of differences between two or more stimuli, one could, on a verbal level, conclude that discrimination and generalization are inverse processes. On the other hand, Brown's empirical definitions of generalization and discrimination, which are very similar to the definition of stimulus control offered in this chapter, would suggest that the operations used to obtain a generalization gradient and a discriminability function are but one of numerous ways in which stimulus value and response strength could be related. It should therefore come as no surprise that a particular pair of functions are not well correlated. It would indeed seem more sensible to ask why one would expect two different measures of stimulus control, obtained under different training conditions, to produce similar functions. In Guttman and Kalish's experiment, for example, generalization gradients were obtained following a training procedure in which there was no explicit differential reinforcement with respect to S+, and the jnd function they referred to was obtained after a long history of rigorous differential reinforcement.

Up to this point all of the experiments we have considered have maintained a constant difference between S+ and S− throughout discrimination training. Many studies, however, have started training with a large S+-S− difference that was progressively reduced to the final smaller S+-S− difference. This procedure has typically resulted in the acquisition of a discrimination with fewer responses to S− than does a procedure in which the S+-S− difference was kept constant throughout training.

William James (1890, pp. 505-515), in a discussion of discrimination and psychophysics, was among the first to recognize the value of slowly reducing the interval between two discriminative stimuli. James noted that much smaller two-point limens could be obtained if training began with a widely separated pair of points, after which the distance between the two points was progressively reduced. In this manner "smaller differences affect us as if they were large ones" (James, 1890, p. 515).

In a discussion of training a respondent discrimination, Anrep noted that:

It is common knowledge that in conditioned reflexes, in order to develop a differentiation between two stimuli, the stimuli should be chosen as far apart from each other as possible. Only after such a rough differentiation is established should one pass to finer differentiations and use stimuli more and more close to each other. If one starts with stimuli which are not widely apart, it is found that differentiation develops either with extreme difficulty or not at all (Anrep, 1923, p. 420).

In his studies on conditioned salivation in the dog, Pavlov (1927, p. 117) also noted that respondent discriminations between stimuli whose difference is progressively reduced are learned faster than discriminations between stimuli that were presented at a constant difference. Lawrence (1952), using rats, showed that a simultaneous discrimination between two narrowly separated grays is learned with fewer errors when training begins with two widely separated grays, than when only the narrowly separated grays are presented throughout training.

Again we must conclude that in all of these experiments it would be difficult to explain the superiority of a progressive training procedure in training a discrimination by appealing to an underlying generalization gradient. The assumption of an underlying generalization gradient could explain the fact that little responding to S— occurs at the *start* of a progressive training procedure. Once the final S+-S— value has been reached, however, responding to S— should occur to an extent that is proportional to the height of the gradient at S—, independently of whether or not progressive or constant training was used.

We have seen that various types of experiments strongly suggest that the use of either theoretical or empirical generalization gradients have often proved not to be helpful in the description of discrimination learning. The most relevant aspect of the generalization gradient turns out to be the abscissa; in other words, the stimulus difference between S+ and S— is often the most important independent variable in discrimination learning. This, however, hardly justifies the practice of analyzing discrimination learning in terms of generalization gradients. Gradients of reinforcement and extinction have not been able to predict the phenomenon of behavioral contrast, the relative difficulty of different discriminations drawn from the same continuum, and the superiority of a training method that progressively approaches the final S+-S— difference over a method which maintains the S+-S— difference at a constant value during discrimination training.

The shortcomings of the traditional practice of studying discrimination learning by exposing an organism to an S+ and an S—, separated by a constant physical difference, becomes especially apparent when one attempts to *control* the acquisition of the discrimination. A similar situation can be seen in the development of techniques for conditioning an operant. Taking it for granted that a criterion level of performance will ultimately be achieved is analogous to leaving a cat in a puzzle box and waiting for it to learn to escape on its own, or placing a rat in an experimental chamber containing a bar-operated feeding device and waiting for the rat to learn to press the bar on its own. The effectiveness of the method of successive approximation of responses, as compared with the traditional "constant" methods of conditioning, has been demonstrated in a wide variety of situations among many species. One obvious advantage of the method of successive approximations is that it allows the experimenter to mold the desired response from responses of grossly different topographies. The experimenter is able to produce at will the changes in behavior he desires, instead of having to wait until they occur adventitiously. The application of this approach to the training of a discrimination has yielded surprisingly successful results, even to the point of allowing the experimenter to train certain "difficult" discriminations without the occurrence of any responses to S— (Terrace, 1963b). It has also been shown that performance following discrimination learning without responses to S— (errors) differs in many respects from performance following learning with errors, notably with respect to "emotional" behavior in the presence of S— (Terrace, 1963a; 1963c; 1964a).

Errorless Discrimination Learning

The method used to train a discrimination without errors was based on procedures that have previously proved effective in minimizing the occurrence of errors. Skinner (1938, pp. 203-206) has demonstrated that a brightness discrimination can be acquired by rats with virtually no responses to S— if discrimination training begins immediately after the bar-pressing response has been conditioned. Schlosberg and Solomon (1943) reported that rats could learn a simultaneous discrimination between two narrowly separated grays with *no* errors if the discriminative stimuli were gradually changed from a pair of white and black cards to the final pair of gray cards.

The critical variables in these earlier studies seem to be the time and manner of the introduction of S—. In the author's first experiment on errorless discrimination learning (Terrace, 1963a) two values within each of these variables were studied. Either S— was introduced early during the first conditioning session or after a number of weeks of training in the presence of S+. These conditions will be referred to as *early* and *late* respectively. Under both the early and the late conditions, S— was introduced by one of two procedures. Either S— was initially of the same brightness and duration as S+ and differed only with respect to wavelength, or, in addition to the wavelength difference, S— initially had lower brightness and shorter duration values which were progressively increased until the brightness and duration of S+ was reached. These two conditions will be referred to as *constant* and *progressive,* respectively. The combination of the two sets of independent variables yielded four experimental groups: early-progressive, early-constant, late-progressive, and late-constant introduction of S—.

Discrimination training began for the subjects of the early-progressive group during the first experimental session, immediately following the conditioning of the key peck to S+. S+ was a red key light which was correlated during the first session with a VI 30″ schedule of reinforcement and during all subsequent sessions with a VI 1′ schedule of reinforcement. During the first session, the duration of S+ was held constant at 30 sec.

The progressive introduction of S— was carried out in three stages.

During the first stage S— was a dark key whose duration was initially 5 sec. Over successive presentations of S— its duration was progressively increased in 5 sec. increments to 30 sec. During the second stage the duration of S— was kept constant at 5 sec. and the intensity of S— was gradually increased by reducing the value of a resistor which was in series with the bulb producing the light for S—. During the final stage S— was a fully bright green key whose duration was increased from 5 sec. to 30 sec. During the second and third experimental sessions the duration of S+ was kept constant at 3 min. and the duration of S— was progressively increased from 30 sec. to 3 min.

Late discrimination training was started in both the late-progressive and the late-constant conditions following 14 sessions in which only S+ appeared. During these non-discrimination sessions S+ was correlated with a VI 1′ schedule of reinforcement. Late-progressive training followed the same progressive procedure that was described for the early-progressive group.

The duration of S+ was 3 min. throughout all discrimination sessions for the late-progressive, late-constant, and early-constant groups. In the early-constant group S— was introduced during the first session in which the animal was placed in the experimental chamber. For both the early- and the late-constant S— introduction groups S— was initially presented at full intensity and at full duration (3 min.).

The number of responses emitted in the presence of S— during the first three and during all discrimination sessions are shown in Figure 14. The manner in which S— was introduced clearly affected the number of responses that occurred to S— during the acquisition of the discrimination. Late-constant training resulted in the most errors. Early-constant and late-progressive training resulted in an intermediate number of errors. In all three cases the birds of the early-progressive group learned the discrimination with virtually no responses to S— (range: two to eight responses to S—). Since later variations of the training procedure reliably produced completely errorless acquisitions, and since the performance of these subjects did not differ from the performance of the birds who learned with a few errors, the acquisition of a discrimination with a small number of errors will also be referred to as "errorless." It might also be noted that the few errors made by the early-progressive group could be qualitatively distinguished from those made by the other groups. The few errors obtained under the early-progressive procedure never occurred in bursts. They would either occur at the very end of an S— interval, e.g. between 2′ 55″ and 2′ 59″ of a 3′ S— component, or as a carry-over from responding in S+ at the start of an S— component.

In a second experiment (Terrace, 1963b) it was shown that the progressive procedure for training a discrimination of color could be carried one step further to produce the errorless acquisition of a more difficult discrimination: the orientation of two perpendicular white lines. The proce-

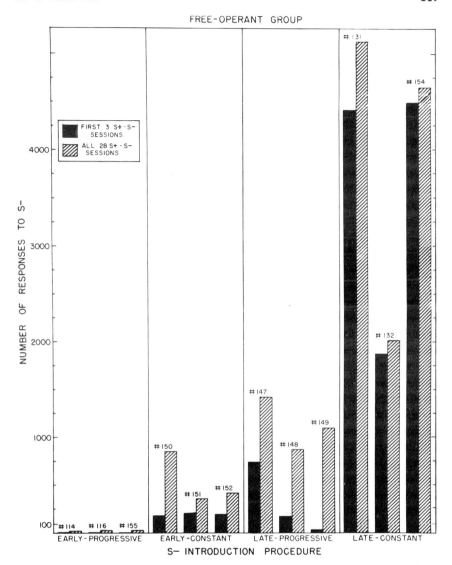

Figure 14. The acquisition of a discrimination under different training procedures. Shown are the number of responses made to S— by individual pigeons during the first three, and during all 28 S+-S— sessions. See text for explanation of groups (from Terrace, 1963a).

dures used to study the acquisition of this discrimination are shown in Figure 15. The subjects in the first three groups were originally trained to acquire a red-green discrimination without any errors by a procedure similar to the one previously described. They were then shifted to the vertical-

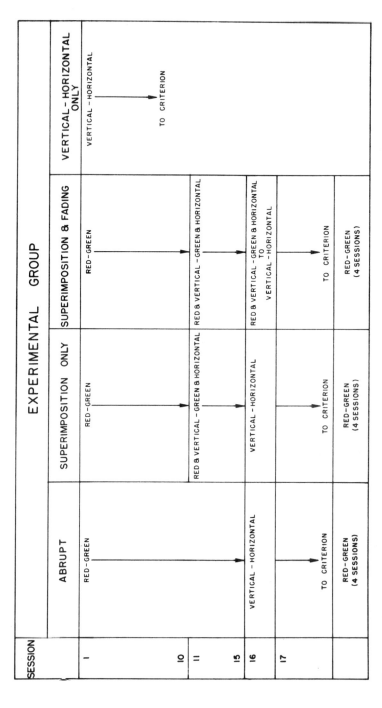

Figure 15. Sequences of training procedures for four experimental groups in the study of transfer between a red-green and a vertical-horizontal discrimination in the pigeon (from Terrace, 1963b).

horizontal discrimination in one of three manners. For the "abrupt" group there was an abrupt shift from the red-green to the vertical-horizontal discrimination following the fifteenth red-green discrimination session. For two additional groups a vertical line was superimposed on a red background and a horizontal line was superimposed on a green background during sessions 11-15. For the "superimposition-only" group the vertical and horizontal stimuli appeared without any colored backgrounds from the start of the sixteenth session. For the "superimposition-and-fading" group, however, the sixteenth session began with the discriminative stimuli superimposed as they were at the end of the fifteenth session. During the course of the sixteenth session the red and green backgrounds were slowly faded out. A fourth group was only trained on the vertical-horizontal discrimination. All four experimental groups were trained to a criterion of four successive sessions in which no responses to S— occurred. Once the criterion was satisfied, the first three groups were each abruptly returned to the red-green discrimination for four sessions. The results of this experiment are shown in Figure 16. The open bars show the number of errors made in satisfying the vertical-horizontal discrimination. The black bars show the number of errors made during the four subsequent red-green discrimination sessions. The birds who had superimposition-and-fading training acquired the horizontal-vertical discrimination with no errors while the superimposition-only, the abrupt, and the vertical-horizontal-only groups made many more errors. Those birds who learned the vertical-horizontal discrimination with errors all made errors upon returning to the red-green discrimination. The birds of the superimposition-and-fading group, who learned the vertical-horizontal discrimination without any errors, performed perfectly upon being returned to the red-green discrimination. In evaluating these data it should be remembered that *all* three of the transfer groups learned the red-green discrimination without *any* errors. Making errors on a different discrimination, trained in the same apparatus, resulted in a disruption of the originally perfect performance on the red-green discrimination. We will return to this point during a discussion of other differences in performance following discrimination learning with and without errors. We must first, however, attempt to account for the different amounts of responding to S— that occurred under the different methods of introducing S— in both experiments on errorless discrimination training.

To begin our analysis it will be important to distinguish between responses to S— emitted during the early and the later portions of discrimination training. Classical generalization theory (e.g., Spence, 1936; 1937; Hull, 1943) can predict the initial amount of responding to S—. In the first experiment, for example, the early-progressive S— introduction procedure would be expected to result in the least amount of generalization because fewer than a dozen responses to S+ were reinforced before discrimination training began, and also because S+ and S— differed with respect to bright-

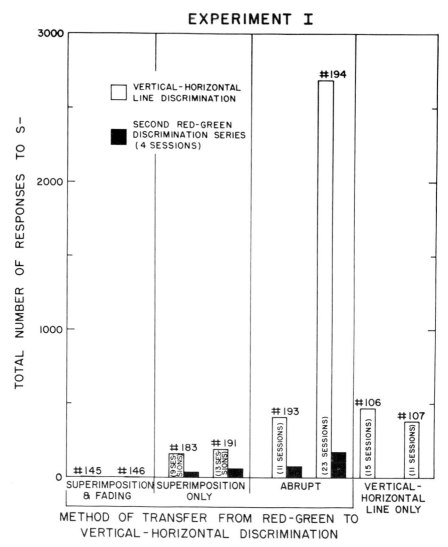

Figure 16. The number of errors made by each subject in acquiring a vertical-horizontal discrimination by each of the groups shown in Fig. 15. Also shown are the number of errors made by each subject during the second series of red-green discrimination sessions (from Terrace, 1963b).

ness and duration as well as with respect to wavelength. At the other extreme, a maximal amount of generalization should result from the late-constant S— introduction procedure because the response to S+ had a long history of reinforcement, and also because S+ and S— differed only with respect to wavelength. The early-constant and the late-progressive S— introduction procedures would result in intermediate amounts of generalization between S+ and S—. The early-constant procedure started discrimination training with two closely spaced stimuli on a relatively low gradient. The late-progressive procedure started discrimination training with two or more widely spaced stimuli on a relatively high gradient.

Discrimination performance *following* the initial S+ and S— sessions *cannot,* however, be predicted from the known properties of generalization gradients. After the third discrimination session, the physical difference between S+ and S— was the same for each experimental group. Furthermore, each of the two early and the two late S— introduction procedures ultimately provided the same number of reinforcements for responding to S+. Thus, according to classical generalization theory, the strength of the response to S— at the end of all of the training procedures should be the same. From this information alone one might, for example, predict that the early-progressive groups would start emitting responses to S— after they had received as many reinforcements in S+ as did the late-progressive group, or after the S+-S— difference had been reduced to its final value.

Similar considerations would apply to the acquisition of the vertical-horizontal discrimination. As a result of superimposing the vertical and the horizontal white lines on the red and green backgrounds respectively, response strength should develop to both line stimuli. More response strength should, of course, develop to the vertical line since this stimulus is correlated with reinforcement. Thus, once the colored backgrounds were removed, classical generalization theory would predict that some responding to S— should occur. It should also be noted that the acquisition of both the red-green and the horizontal-vertical discriminations without the occurrence of any responses to S— presents a second basic problem for classical generalization theory because in these instances inhibitory gradients cannot be used to explain the absence of responding to S—.

In both experiments the absence of responding to S— as training progressed suggests that certain features of the progressive S— introduction procedure produced a permanent "short-circuiting" of the S— extinction process. This is also true, to a lesser extent, of the early-constant and the late-progressive groups in the first experiment and the superimposition-only group in the second experiment. These data and the results of other discrimination experiments (e.g., Lawrence, 1952) also suggest a short-circuiting of the extinction process.

The short-circuiting of the extinction process in the presence of S—, by the progressive discrimination training procedure, seems to result from a number of different factors and events. The most important of these seems to be what a pigeon did following the first presentation of S—. In all of the training procedures used so far, S— has initially been a dark key. The initial response, typically, is jerking back the head. Since the duration of the first S— is short (2-5 sec.), S+ appeared soon after the pigeon abruptly pulled away from the key. The reappearance of S+ could have served as a conditioned reinforcer for the movement away from the key during S—.

One factor responsible for the initial sequence of behavior in the presence of S+ and S— might have been earlier differential reinforcement that occurred during the everyday environment of the pigeon. The presentation of food, for example, has been a cue for movements which resulted in its ingestion. During the absence of food such movements have not been reinforced. In other similar situations the presence of a stimulus served as a cue for responding and the removal of a stimulus as a cue for not responding. These tendencies, acquired in earlier differential reinforcement situations, probably transferred to the presence or absence of an experimental S+. The tendency not to respond to the removal of S+ was kept intact by the gradual prolongation of S—. Thus, as Guthrie (1935) has pointed out, what the pigeon does in the presence of an S— of duration t is a good predictor of what he will do in the presence of a slightly longer S—. Once S— has become a cue for responding, the pigeon will continue to respond until he learns to make a response incompatible with key pecking in the presence of S—.

Experimental evidence which supports this account of responding or lack of responding to S— comes mainly from situations in which a progressive discrimination procedure failed to produce errorless discrimination learning. Some of the examples that will be discussed were obtained from informal observations of a pigeon's gross behavior over a closed-circuit TV system. These admittedly anecdotal bits of evidence occurred with sufficient regularity, however, to warrant a strong belief that they would reliably appear in more rigorous observational procedures.

The most commonly observed cause of responding to S— is too large a change in the value of S—. In increasing the duration of S—, for example, many birds seemed "ready" to respond to the key at approximately the point at which the previous S— had ended. Seeming "ready" means approaching or turning toward the key, pulling the head back, and bringing it toward the key. In certain cases this behavior adapts out and no actual key pecking occurs. In other instances key pecking will occur, in which case future presentations of S—, independently of its duration, will evoke responding to S—. Once responding to S— begins, it is usually impossible to stop, no matter how S— is changed. One possible explanation of this recurrent finding is that the proprioceptive feedback of responding to S— becomes a strong cue for further responses because similar feedback that results from responding to S+ has been paired with reinforcement.

Another factor which will disrupt errorless performance is a sudden reduction of reinforcement density in S+. In changing from a continuous reinforcement schedule (crf) to a VI 1' schedule, with the duration of each presentation of S+ held constant at 1 min., a point will be reached in which reinforcement will not be available in certain S+ components. In many cases, responses to S— will occur immediately following an S+ component in which no responses were reinforced. Here again responses to S— are obtained following completely errorless performance without any change in the values of the discriminative stimuli. It is interesting to note Pavlov's similar observation concerning the development of a respondent discrimination:

> It was noticed that when, after a conditioned reflex to a definite stimulus (e.g. a definite musical tone) had been firmly established, the effect of another closely allied stimulus (a neighbouring musical tone) was tried for the first time, the conditioned reflex which resulted from the new stimulus was frequently much weaker than that obtained with the original conditioned stimulus. On repetition of the stimulus of the neighbouring tone, always, of course, without reinforcement, the secretory effect increased until it became equal to that given by the originally established stimulus, but subsequently on further repetition began to diminish, falling finally to a permanent zero. Thus it appeared that at first the two closely allied stimuli were discriminated straight away, but that later this discrimination for some reason disappeared, only gradually to reestablish itself and finally to become absolute (Pavlov, 1927, p. 118).

Another kind of failure of the errorless training procedure has been observed in the transfer from a discrimination of color to a discrimination of the orientation of a line. In many instances it was observed that the final few steps in which the colored backgrounds of line stimuli were faded out had to be very small. Otherwise discrimination performance that is perfect up to these final steps abruptly disintegrates. In these instances the lines apparently acquired little or no control over responding. Responding to S— seemed to begin when the colored backgrounds which controlled the occurrence or non-occurrence of responding were no longer visible.

A similar situation was encountered when an attempt was made to train a different group of pigeons on a vertical-horizontal discrimination without fading from a previous discrimination of color (Terrace, unpublished data). In this case, the intensity of S— was progressively increased just as it was in the original errorless training of a wavelength discrimination. Here again the discrimination performance was perfect until the last few increments in intensity, at which point discrimination performance disintegrated. The intensity difference, rather than the difference in the orientation of the lines, appeared to have been the controlling factor in the acquisition of this discrimination.

We have seen that a wide range of variables, such as an abrupt reduction of reinforcement density in S+, large steps in the progressive change of S—, and the use of an inappropriate dimension along which the values of S+ and S— are changed, will disrupt a previously errorless performance. Following a large increase in the duration of S—, for example, responses to S— start occurring at the end of a given S— interval at a point at which

S+ had previously been presented. These observations should again remind us that the discriminative stimuli varied by the experimenter often provide an incomplete picture of the controlling stimuli.

The efficacy of the progressive training procedure seems to be based on its ability to insure that control of responding does not pass from the exteroceptive experimentally manipulated stimuli to proprioceptive stimuli generated by responding to S— and to other factors beyond the experimenter's control. By reinforcing not responding to the absence of S+ with the almost immediate reappearance of S+, the progressive training procedure insures that a stimulus differing from S+ becomes an occasion for not responding. Once this tendency is interrupted, however, it is almost always the case that responding to S— cannot be stopped even when the values of the discriminative stimuli are radically changed.

Differences in Performance Following Discrimination Learning With and Without Errors

Observations of a pigeon's gross behavior in the presence of S—, following discrimination learning with and without errors, indicated that "not responding" took a different form in each case. Photographs of a bird's gross reaction to S— in each case are shown in Figure 17. It has been regularly observed that following discrimination learning with errors, S— evokes various emotional responses such as wing flapping (Figure 17 a, b) and turning away from the key (Figure 17 b, c). Following errorless discrimination learning, however, the usual response to S— is a slow settling down under the response key (Figure 17 d). In these instances the pigeon quietly waits for the next appearance of S+.

The patterns of emotional responses that were observed in the presence of S— following discrimination learning with errors appear to be similar to those reported by Azrin and his colleagues (Azrin, 1965; Azrin, Hutchinson, & McLaughlin, 1965) at the start of extinction. Of special interest to us is Azrin's observation that the removal of a positive reinforcer resulted in aggressive behavior that was strikingly similar to aggressive behavior that resulted from the presentation of an aversive stimulus. Azrin also demonstrated that both the removal of a positive reinforcer and the presentation of a negative reinforcer established the opportunity to attack another organism, or even an inanimate object, as a strong reinforcer. We shall return to the similarity between the presentation of a positive reinforcer and the removal of a negative reinforcer in the discussion of inhibition that appears at the end of this section. We must first, however, consider some of the differences in performance that are obtained following discrimination learning with and without errors.

The occurrence of emotional responses in the presence of S—, possibly of aggressive nature, is but one line of evidence that suggests that S— functions differently following discrimination learning with and without errors. This difference seems to be reliably reflected by numerous differences in the rate or latency of responding to S+, the accuracy of long-term discrimination performance, the effects of drugs on responding to S—, and the location of the peak of a post-discrimination generalization gradient.

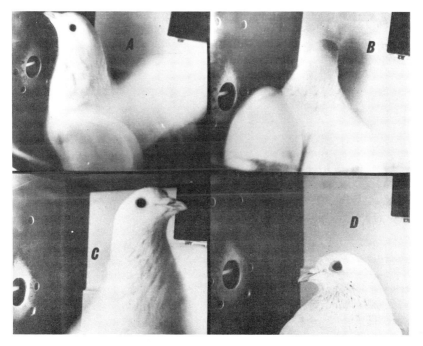

Figure 17 (A, B, & C). Photographs of a pigeon, at the onset of S—, who learned a horizontal-vertical discrimination with errors. (D). Photograph of a pigeon, at the onset of S—, who learned the same discrimination without errors.

Behavioral Contrast

We have previously noted that one of the consequences of training a discrimination was an increase in the rate (Reynolds, 1961a) or a decrease in the latency (Jenkins, 1961) of responding to S+. Reynolds called these changes behavioral contrast because in each case the rate and latency of responding to S+ *contrasted* with the rate and latency of responding to S— during the formation of a discrimination.

The discriminations that were studied by Reynolds' and by Jenkins' experiments were both acquired with many errors. If a similar discrimination is trained without errors, no contrast is obtained (Terrace, 1963a; 1963b). Typical results from a more recent unpublished experiment are shown in

Figure 18. The data shown are individual rate functions obtained following discrimination training between an S+ of 580 mμ and an S— of 540 mμ.

In interpreting the data shown in Figure 18 it should be remembered that, in training a discrimination without any errors, discrimination training begins during the first conditioning session. It is, therefore, impossible in these instances to obtain a preliminary baseline rate of responding to S+

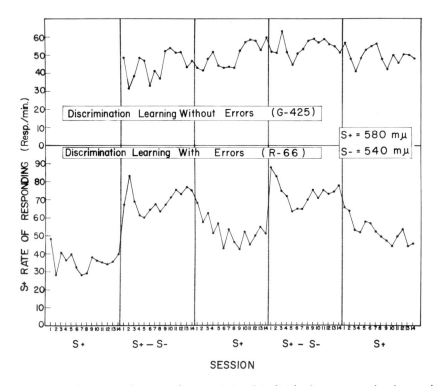

Figure 18. The rate of responding to S+ of individual pigeons who learned discrimination between 580 and 540 mμ (R-66 with errors; G-425 without errors). In each case 14 sessions of S+-S— training are alternated with 14 sessions of S+ training (Terrace, unpublished data).

against which contrast effects can be assessed. In order to determine whether contrast is obtained following errorless discrimination training it is necessary to make use of another property of contrast. This is shown by the lower function of Figure 18 which was obtained from a pigeon who learned the 580-540 mμ discrimination *with* errors. The first two panels are similar to Reynolds' functions shown in Figure 10. The rate of responding to S+ increased following the onset of discrimination training. The next three panels show the rate of responding to S+ during a series of sessions in which (1)

S+ was presented alone, (2) S+ was again alternated with S—, and (3) S+ was again presented alone. The effect of presenting S | alone was a reduction in the rate of responding to S+. When S— is reintroduced and is again alternated with S+, the rate of responding to S+ increases. It should be noted that when S— is reintroduced little or no responding to S— occurs. Thus, once a discrimination has been trained with errors, the rate of responding to S+ may be manipulated by presenting or removing S— in a given session.

To ascertain whether or not contrast occurs during discrimination learning without errors, it is only necessary to remove or to reintroduce S—. A typical function obtained from a pigeon who learned the 580-540 mμ discrimination without any errors is shown in the upper function of Figure 18. No changes in the rate of responding to S+ were obtained as a result of alternating or not alternating S— with S+. Similar results were obtained in an experiment in which a red-green discrimination was trained with and without errors both in a free-operant and in a trial situation (Terrace, 1963a). In both situations the acquisition of a discrimination did not affect the rate or the latency of responding to S+.

The changes in rate of responding to S+ obtained by alternating between a differential and a non-differential reinforcement procedure suggest that within a differential reinforcement session the magnitude of the contrast effect might depend on the temporal proximity of a given S+ to the previous appearance of an S—. In a random series of alternating S+ and S— presentations, for example, some S+ presentations are preceded by S— whereas others are preceded by S+. A comparison of the rates of responding to S+ in these instances (S+ preceded by S— and S+ preceded by another S+) is shown in Figure 19. It should be noted that both sets of individual functions are typical of the performance of the groups from which they have been selected. These data were obtained from an experiment (Terrace, unpublished data) in which S+ was correlated with a VI 1′ schedule of reinforcement. The discriminative stimuli (S+ = 580 mμ; S— = 540 mμ) were presented for 1-min. periods which were each followed by a 2-sec. TO period. Following each TO the probability that the next stimulus would be S+ or S— was 0.5. The functions shown in the lower left hand portion of Figure 19 were obtained from a subject who learned this discrimination with errors (pigeon G-356). Throughout the 20 discrimination sessions that were studied, the rate of responding to S+ following an S— component was reliably higher than the rate of responding following an S+ component. Similar results have been reported by Boneau and Axelrod (1962) and by Catania and Gill (1964). In the Boneau and Axelrod experiment, pigeons were trained on a successive discrimination in which 8 min. of S+ were alternated with 1 min. of S—. The rate of responding to S+ was highest during the first minute of each S+ period (with the exception of the first S+ presentation of a session) and subsequently de-

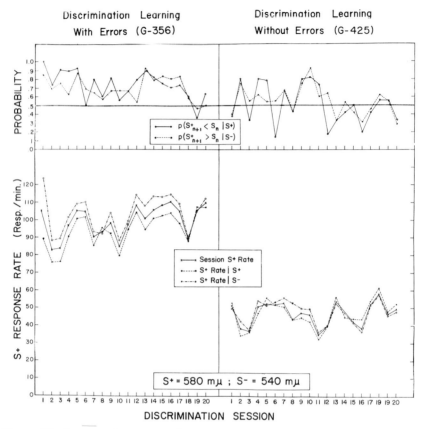

Figure 19. Sequential contrast effects. Lower portion: The rate of responding to S+ of individual pigeons who learned a discrimination between 580 and 540 mμ (G-356 with errors; G-452 without errors). In addition to the overall S+ session rate, the rates of responding to those S+ components which were preceded by S— and those S+ components which were preceded by S+ are also shown. Upper portion: Individual probability functions corresponding to two of the four conditional probabilities shown in Table 1. See text for additional details (Terrace, unpublished data).

clined during the remaining seven minutes prior to the appearance of S—. In the Catania and Gill experiment S+ and S— alternated successively. The duration of S+ was always 5 min.; the duration of S— was either 1 or 3 min. The rate of responding during the first minute of each S+ presentation was twice the value of the rate during the next four minutes.

The lower right-hand portion of Figure 19 shows the measures of the rate of responding to S+ of a subject who learned the same discrimination without errors (G-425). Following discrimination learning without errors there is no difference between the rates of responding to S+ following S— and an S+ component.

It should also be noted that G-356's higher overall rate of responding to S+ is consistent with our previous observation that contrast does not occur following discrimination learning without errors. The pre-discrimination rate of responding to S— of G-356 (not shown) was approximately 45 responses per minute. As a result of his acquiring a discrimination with errors, his rate of responding to S+ doubled. G-356's separate rate functions indicate, however, that the value of the preceding stimulus is not sufficient to account for the whole contrast effect. Thus, there seem to be at least two factors which contribute to the increase in the rate of responding to S+. One is the value of the preceding stimulus and the other is the fact that the organism has been confronted with a differential reinforcement procedure. In this particular situation the differential reinforcement procedure seems to be the more important factor.

The relatively small increase in rate following the presentation of an S— should not be allowed to obscure the reliability of these increases. A further analysis of the data revealed that when a discrimination was learned with errors, the effect of the preceding stimulus on the rate of responding to the next S+ could be reliably detected in almost all S+ presentations. In this analysis successive pairs of S+ presentations were compared and the direction of the change in rate was tallied as a function of whether or not an S— intervened. Thus, $S+_n$ was compared with $S+_{n+1}$ to derive the probabilities shown in Table 1.

Table 1

Conditional Probabilities Based on Comparisons of the Rates of Responding to S+ During Two Successive S+ Components

The term entered into the upper left hand portion of the table is read "the probability that the rate of responding to S+ was higher in S+ component$_{n+1}$ than in S+ component$_n$, given that no S— components intervened." The sums of the probabilities in each row is 1.0 (Terrace, 1965a).

	Previous Stimulus	
Increases	$P(S+_{n+1} > S+_n \mid S+)$	$P(S+_{n+1} > S+_n \mid S-)$
Decreases	$P(S+_{n+1} < S+_n \mid S+)$	$P(S+_{n+1} < S+_n \mid S-)$

It should be noted that the entries in Table 1 represent *instances* of an increase or a decrease in the rate of responding to S+. Thus, an increase of 20 responses per minute carries the same weight as an increase of two responses per minute. Despite the weakness of these comparisons it was observed that the probability of an increase in the rate of responding to S+, given that the preceding stimulus was S—, was typically 0.70. Conversely, the probability of a decrease in the rate of responding to S+, given that the preceding stimulus was another S+, was also of at least the same magnitude. The results of a similar analysis following discrimination learning without errors revealed that the rate of responding to S+ was found to be unaffected by whether or not a given S+ was preceded by the presentation of S—. A session-by-session plot of two of the four probabilities entered in Table 1 for G-356 and G-425 is shown in the upper portion of Figure 19. The remaining two unplotted probabilities are the complements of the probabilities that have been plotted.

At the beginning of our discussion of contrast it was suggested that contrast might be a manifestation of "emotional" responses generated by the aversiveness of receiving no reinforcements for responding to S—. If this were true, one would expect that after prolonged exposure to S+ and S— in a differential reinforcement procedure contrast would disappear. The results of a pilot study indicate that the rate of responding to S+ decreases to its pre-discrimination level after approximately two to three months of training on a 580 (S+)-540 (S—) mμ discrimination. The data obtained from a group of three pigeons are shown in Figure 20.

Another interesting line of evidence relating contrast effects to aversive stimuli which are known to produce emotional effects comes from a study performed by Brethower and Reynolds (1962). A red and a green light were correlated with independent VI 3' schedules of reinforcement. Each response to the green light resulted in the brief presentation of an unavoidable electric shock. This resulted in a decrease in the rate of responding to the green light and an increase in the rate of responding to the red light. One especially interesting implication of this finding is related to the previously noted similarity between the effects of non-reinforced responding during the acquisition of a discrimination and the effects of presenting a response-produced negative reinforcer, i.e., punishment. It should also be noted that in the Brethower and Reynolds experiment some of the subjects responded to the green light at a rate that was sufficient to insure that none of the reinforcements programmed by the VI 3' schedule were missed. Thus the suppression of the rate of responding, rather than a reduction in reinforcement density per se, in the presence of two alternating stimuli seems to be a sufficient condition to produce contrast. Other examples of this principle will be discussed in the treatment of post-discrimination generalization gradients below.

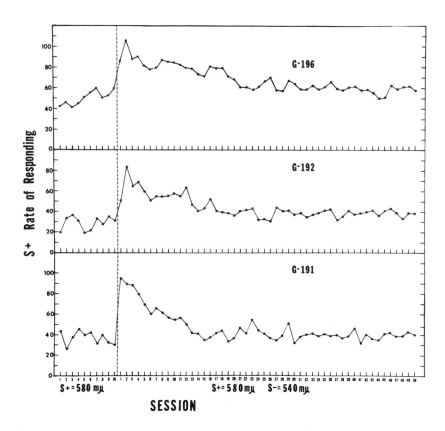

Figure 20. The decline of contrast. The rates of responding to S— for three subjects following discrimination training (S+ = 580 mμ; S— = 540 mμ) during
a two-month period (Terrace, unpublished data).

Quality of Discrimination Performance

Discrimination performance following discrimination learning with
errors is occasionally disrupted by bursts of responding to S— long after a
stable near-zero rate of responding has been achieved. These occasional
disruptions of discrimination performance have been observed in both the
free-operant and trial procedures (Terrace, 1963a). Following discrimination learning without errors, disruptions of performance were never observed. A related finding was mentioned earlier in the context of a discussion of the experiment on errorless transfer from a discrimination of color
to a discrimination of the orientation of a line (Terrace, 1963b). In this

experiment the occurrence of errors on the vertical-horizontal discrimination resulted in the disruption of performance on a red-green discrimination that had previously been learned without errors. Anrep made similar observations in a discussion of the acquisition of various types of discriminations:

> If an untrained brain is presented with a problem beyond its capacity, and its solution insisted upon, the brain will not only not solve the problem, but will lose the power to solve problems with which it was previously capable of dealing. For instance, a child who, having mastered addition, is taught multiplication, will make mistakes when he first returns to addition (Anrep, 1923, p. 420).

The relatively poor performance of the subjects who learned with many errors may be partially attributed to early intermittent reinforcement resulting from responding to S—. This may have had the effect of retarding the subsequent extinction of responding to S—. Occasional bursts of responding to S— may in turn generate a further intermittent effect which could, under appropriate conditions, result in permanently faulty performance. This interpretation is supported by the results of Jenkins' (1961) previously described experiment on discrimination learning in which a trial procedure was used. Jenkins showed that intermittent reinforcement generated by responding to S— during the acquisition of a discrimination (differential reinforcement) resulted in the same resistance to extinction of the response to S+ as did the same schedule of intermittent reinforcement that was entirely correlated with S+ (intermittent reinforcement). The resistance to extinction, however, of a group of pigeons who had been continuously reinforced in the presence of S+ (regular reinforcement) was lower than the resistance to extinction of the pigeons of both the differentially and the intermittently reinforced groups.

Effects of Drugs

It has been generally observed that certain drugs will disrupt discrimination performance by inducing responding to S— (e.g., Dews, 1955; Dews & Skinner, 1956). In a follow-up of the errorless transfer study it was shown that two drugs, chlorpromazine and imipramine, would disrupt performance only if the discrimination was learned with errors (Terrace, 1963c). In this experiment, one group of pigeons learned a discrimination between a vertical and a horizontal line without any errors by the transfer procedure previously described. A second group learned the same discrimination with many errors. As shown in Table 2, neither imipramine nor chlorpromazine have any effect on responding to S— following discrimination learning without errors. Both of these drugs, however, seriously disrupted previously perfect discrimination performance in the group that learned the same discrimination with errors.

Table 2

Number of Responses to S— During Vertical (S+)-Horizontal (S—)
Discrimination Training Following Injections of Chlorpromazine
or Imipramine (Terrace, 1963c)

RESPONSES

Dose (mg)	Bird No. 75	Bird No. 100	Bird No. 334	Bird No. 217
Chlorpromazine				
1	0	0	5	76
	0	0	18	86
3	0	0	409	149
	0	0	421	235
10	0	0	496	272
	0	0	521	315
17	0	0	1325	862
	0	0	1514	1655
Imipramine				
1	0	0	137	324
	0	0	161	207
3	0	0	544	522
	0	0	415	254
10	0	0	987	904
	0	0	2084	1186
17	0	0	3655	2651
	0	0	1872	2764

The lack of any effect of either drug on discrimination performance after learning without errors demonstrates that the disruption that was obtained following learning with errors could not be explained in terms of a sensory deficit. An alternative explanation would take into account the emotional effects of non-reinforced responding to S— which may have been temporarily reduced by chlorpromazine and imipramine. According to this point of view, responding to S— became aversive because of the extinction of responses which occurred in its presence. No such effect would be obtained when a discrimination is learned without errors. Following discrimination learning with errors, chlorpromazine and imipramine presumably reduce the aversiveness of responding to S—.

Post-Discrimination Generalization Gradients

Another situation which suggests that S— becomes an aversive stimulus as a result of discrimination learning with errors emerged from Hanson's (1959) study of post-discrimination generalization gradients. Hanson showed that following discrimination training in which errors occurred, the peak of the gradient was displaced away from S+ in a direction which also moved it further away from S—. If, as shown in Figure 21, a discrimination is trained between an S+ of 550 mμ and an S— of either 555, 560, 570, or 590 mμ, the peak of the gradient occurs at 540 mμ, instead of at 550 mμ.

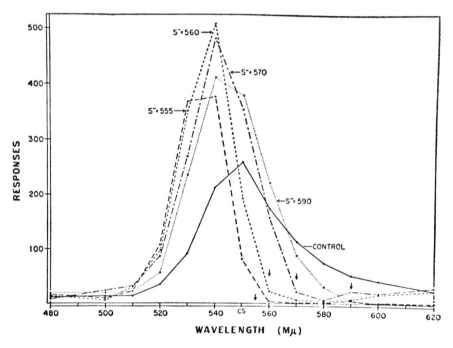

Figure 21. The effect of discrimination training upon wavelength generalization in the pigeon. Different groups of pigeons were trained to respond to an S+ of 550 mμ and S—s of 555, 560, 570, or 590mμ. The control group was also trained to respond to 550 mμ but received no discrimination training (from Hanson, 1959).

A replication of Hanson's experiment in which a discrimination between 580 (S+) and 540 (S—) mμ was trained with and without errors demonstrated that a peak shift was obtained only if the discrimination was learned with errors (Terrace, 1964a). Figure 22 shows that the peaks of all but one of the gradients obtained from groups 1 and 2 (S+ training only, and discrimination learning without errors) occurred at 580 mμ (S+). Another important feature of the gradients obtained from groups 1 and 2

is the asymmetrical distribution of the area above and below S+. In each
case there is more area below than above S+.

The gradients obtained from group 3 (discrimination learning with
errors) clearly differ from the group 1 and group 2 gradients with respect
to both the distribution of the area above and below S+ and the location
of the peak. In all of the group 3 gradients there is more area above than
below S+, and in two out of three cases the peak of the gradient is displaced away from S—. In both of these cases the peak occurred at 590 mμ
instead of at 580 mμ (S+).

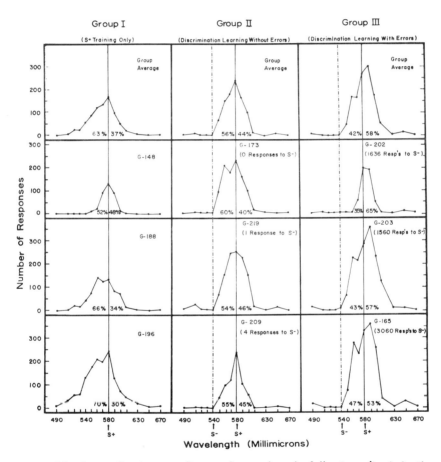

Figure 22. Generalization gradients of wavelength following discrimination
learning with and without errors and following S+ training only. The numbers
to the right and to the left of the solid vertical lines represent the percentage of
total area under the gradient that lies above and below S+, respectively (from
Terrace, 1964a).

The gradients shown in Figure 22 also show that the distribution of area above and below S+ may prove to be more sensitive than the location of the peak as a measure of the effects of discrimination training. A peak shift was obtained in two out of three of the individual gradients of group 3, whereas a shift in the distribution of area above and below S+ appeared in all three gradients. Hanson's (1959) data on a 40 mμ discrimination (S+ = 550 mμ; S— = 590 mμ) also showed that "area-shifts" occurred within gradients which did not show a peak shift. Only four out of eight gradients showed a peak shift but, in each case, there was more area on the side of S+ that was away from S—, despite the fact that an asymmetry in the opposite direction was obtained from a non-differential reinforcement control group.

The differences between the generalization gradients obtained after discrimination learning with errors and without errors appear to be related to the other differences in performance that were found in experiments on errorless discrimination learning. These findings and the demonstration that the peak of a post-discrimination gradient is displaced away from S— only if the discrimination is learned with errors, suggest that S— functions differently in a discrimination trained without errors. If no (or few) responses to S— occur during the formation of a discrimination, S— may function as a neutral stimulus. If, however, responses to S— are extinguished during discrimination training, S— may function as an aversive stimulus. According to this hypothesis a shift of the peak, or of the area, of a generalization gradient away from S— would be described as a shift away from an aversive stimulus.

The change in function of S— as a result of extinction that has occurred in its presence can be strikingly demonstrated in an individual organism. We have previously seen that the occurrence of responses to a new S— resulted in the disruption of performance on discriminations that had previously been learned without errors. In the generalization test, a pigeon who has learned a discrimination without errors is confronted with stimuli other than S+ to which he does respond. The gradients shown in the left hand portion of Figure 22 show that a pigeon who has learned the 580 mμ (S+)-540 mμ (S—) discrimination without errors did not respond to 540 mμ during the generalization test. They did, however, respond to test stimuli other than S+. Following the generalization test both subjects were returned to the 580-540 mμ discrimination. Quite unexpectedly they responded many times to S—. Following eight sessions of 580-540 mμ discrimination training a second generalization test was given. The results are shown in the right hand portion of Figure 23. This time the peaks of the gradients were shifted away from S—, indicating that the cause of the peak shift was the occurrence of non-reinforced responses to S—.

As was the case for behavioral contrast, the peak shift also eventually

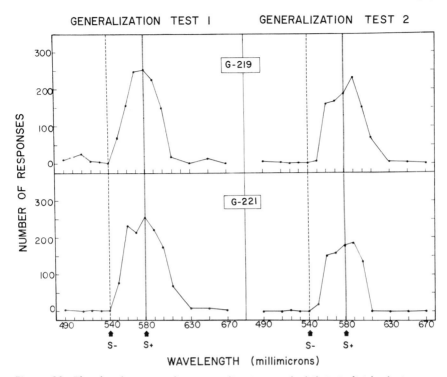

Figure 23. The development of a generalization peak shift in individual pigeons. Prior to the first generalization test no response to S— had occurred in errorless discrimination training. During the discrimination sessions between generalization test 1 and generalization test 2 responses to S— did occur (Terrace, unpublished data).

disappears with extended discrimination training. Figure 24 shows successive generalization gradients, each separated by 12 sessions of mult VI 1′ (580 mμ) ext (550 mμ) training. This discrimination was acquired with errors. In each case the peak of the gradient was shifted away from S— on the first generalization test. By the fourth generalization test, however, all of the peaks were located at S+. Similar results have been reported by Pierrel and Sherman (1960). In this experiment rats were trained to discriminate between different auditory intensities. Initially the highest rate of responding occurred at the extreme of the intensity continuum farthest removed from S—. Following prolonged training, however, the peak of the gradient shifted back to S+.

The fact that the effects of non-reinforced responding in the presence of S— were not permanent is consistent with our view that behavioral contrast and the peak shift are emotional effects that are generated by the non-reinforcement of responding in the presence of S—. Once responding to S— has ceased, one would expect the aversive effects of S— to gradually disappear, as they have been shown to do in Figures 20 and 24.

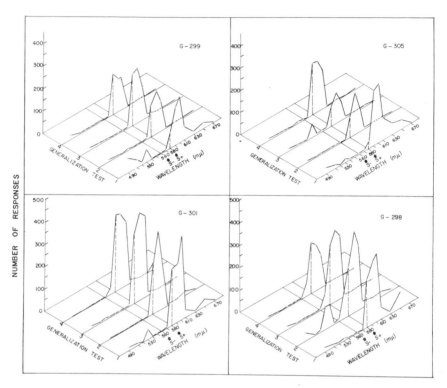

Figure 24. The non-permanence of the peak shift. Successive generalization gradients of wavelength for individual pigeons are shown following wavelength discrimination training (S+ = 580 mμ; S— = 540 mμ). Twelve training sessions occurred between tests. (Terrace, unpublished data).

Another interesting procedure which results in a peak shift has been developed by Guttman (1959). Instead of training a discrimination in which the discriminative stimuli were correlated with a VI schedule and extinction, Guttman trained a discrimination in which the discriminative stimuli were correlated with two different VI schedules of reinforcement: VI 1′ and VI 5′. The VI 1′ schedule of reinforcement was correlated with 550 mμ while the VI 5′ schedule of reinforcement was correlated with 570 mμ. A generalization test was given following 12 sessions of discrimination training. The results are shown by the solid function of Figure 25. The peak of the gradient was shifted away from the stimulus correlated with the VI 5′ schedule of reinforcement. This gradient is similar in form to the gradient shown by the dotted function of Figure 25 that was obtained following VI 1′ ext training (S+ = 550 mμ; S— = 570 mμ) in Hanson's (1959) study.

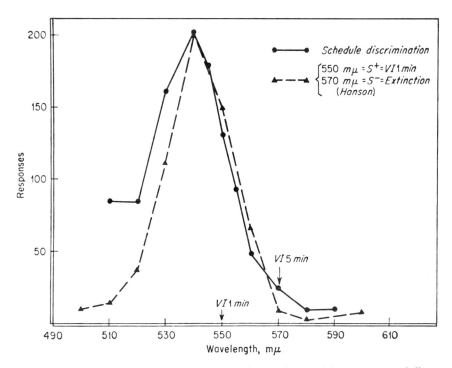

Figure 25. Wavelength generalization gradients obtained from pigeons following schedule discrimination training (solid function) and successive discrimination training (dashed function) to a criterion of extinction (from Guttman, 1959).

The results of Guttman's experiment demonstrated that a peak shift could be obtained following discrimination training in which one of the discriminative stimuli was correlated with a relatively poor schedule of reinforcement instead of with extinction. In a replication of Guttman's experiment we set out to determine more specifically the factors responsible for the peak shift following mult VI 1′ VI 5′ training. In this experiment two groups of pigeons were given 12 sessions of discrimination training in which a VI 1′ schedule of reinforcement was correlated with 579 mμ and a VI 5′ schedule was correlated with 559 mμ. Prior to this training one group of pigeons was trained on a multiple schedule in which both discriminative stimuli, 579 and 559 mμ, were correlated with identical but independent VI 1′ schedules of reinforcement. The second group of pigeons had five prior sessions in which the discriminative stimuli were correlated with identical but independent VI 5′ schedules of reinforcement. It should be noted that for the first group there was a reduction in the reinforcement density correlated with 559 mμ. For the second group, however, the reinforcement density in the presence of 559 mμ was kept constant. The results are shown in Figure 26. The peaks of the gradients shifted away from 559 mμ for each of the subjects who underwent the transition from VI 1′ to VI 5′ in the presence of 559 mμ. No peak shifts were obtained from the group which had VI 5′ VI 5′ training prior to their exposure to VI 1′ VI 5′ training.

These findings suggest two possible explanations for the occurrence of a peak shift: the reduction of reinforcement density in the presence of one of the discriminative stimuli, and the reduction of response rate in the presence of one of the discriminative stimuli. Normally these events occur simultaneously. As shown in Brethower and Reynolds' (1962) previously cited experiment it is possible, however, to separate these factors by using operations which lower response rate but which can also maintain a high density of reinforcement.

One method of reducing response rate without necessarily lowering reinforcement density is a drl schedule of reinforcement. By adjusting the value of the drl schedule one could maintain a relatively high reinforcement density while at the same time reducing the rate of responding. In a pilot experiment involving three subjects, wavelength generalization gradients were obtained following training on a mult VI 1′ drl 7″ schedule of reinforcement where the VI 1′ schedule was correlated with 580 mμ and the drl 7″ schedule was correlated with 550 mμ. In each case more reinforcements were obtained in the presence of 550 mμ than were obtained in the presence of 580 mμ. In each instance a peak shift was obtained away from 550 mμ, the schedule correlated with the drl 7″ schedule of reinforcement.

On the basis of the data that have thus far been obtained it would seem reasonable to conclude that the reduction of rate of responding in the presence of one discriminative stimulus (S_2) relative to the rate of responding as maintained in the presence of another discriminative stimulus (S_1) is a sufficient condition to make the stimulus correlated with the reduction of response rate an aversive one. This conclusion seems to hold for the data obtained from experiments on errorless discrimination learning and on the peak shift. In the case of discrimination learning without errors there is no reduction of response rate in the presence of S_2 since responding to S_2 never occurred. The opposite, of course, is true in the case of discrimination learning with errors. In experiments in which S_2 was correlated with a schedule of reinforcement other than extinction, e.g., VI 5′ or drl 7″, peak shifts were obtained in those instances in which there was a reduction of response rate in S_2.

Another principle that has emerged from these experiments is the fact that contrast and the peak shift seem to be produced by the same condi-

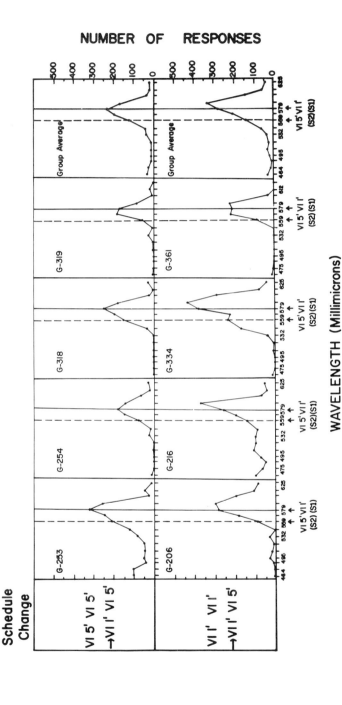

Figure 26. Wavelength generalization gradients obtained from pigeons following a schedule discrimination (579 mμ correlated with a VI 1' schedule and 559 mμ correlated with a VI 5' schedule). The two groups differed with respect to the type of training they had prior to discrimination training. See text for further details (Terrace, unpublished data).

tions. In all of the experiments in which a post-discrimination peak shift was obtained, contrast also occurred. Conversely, peak shifts were not obtained in those instances in which contrast did not occur. An interesting illustration of this generalization comes from an experiment performed by Honig, Thomas, and Guttman (1959) in which responding was reinforced in the presence of 550 mμ and extinguished in the presence of 570 mμ. S+ and S— were not successively alternated in this experiment. Following *one* presentation of S+ that was followed by *one* presentation of S—, a generalization test was given. The usual peak shift was not obtained. It should be noted, however, that contrast could not have developed in this situation because the discriminative stimuli were only alternated once. It may turn out that a peak shift cannot be obtained unless contrast has previously occurred. This, of course, does not detract from the generalization that peak shifts are usually obtained in those situations which produce contrast and that both contrast and the peak shift result from a relative reduction of rate in the presence of one of a pair of successively alternated discriminative stimuli.

A different but not incompatible account of the conditions that are necessary for the occurrence of contrast has been suggested by Reynolds, who stated that ". . . a change in the relative frequency of reinforcement associated with one of several successive stimuli changes the rate of responding during that stimulus; an increase in relative frequency produces an increase in the rate of responding" (Reynolds, 1961b, p. 70). This account of contrast does not take into account the changes in response rate resulting from changes in reinforcement density. In each of Reynolds' experiments there was a reduction of response rate with a reduction in reinforcement density.[2] Thus, Reynolds' data could be easily incorporated into the present formulation which holds that the crucial condition for the occurrence of contrast is the reduction of rate in the presence of one of two alternating discriminative stimuli.

Stability of Performance Following Discrimination Learning With and Without Errors

The numerous examples of emotional responses following discrimination learning may be erroneously construed as evidence that it would be

---

[2] One possible exception to this generalization was the observation that no contrast was observed under a mult VI 3′ dro 50″ condition. Dro refers to the differential reinforcement of not responding. Under this schedule, reinforcement occurs at regular intervals if no responses occur for t sec. The fact that the subjects who were placed on the mult VI dro schedule had had a history of discrimination training on other schedules makes the failure to obtain contrast under this schedule difficult to interpret. It is very likely that few responses occurred during the dro component because the stimulus that was correlated with the dro schedule was previously correlated with extinction. Thus, Reynolds' failure to obtain contrast under the VI dro procedure could be attributed either to an equal reinforcement density in S_1 and S_2 or to the absence of an extinction curve in the presence of S_2.

generally desirable to train all discriminations without errors. It may at first glance actually seem desirable to minimize the possibility of emotional upset in a discrimination. It is quite probable, for example, that the difference in emotional responses following discrimination learning with and without errors may be relevant to various "emotional blocks" which are generated by various learning situations. A child who undergoes too much frustration during his first attempts at mathematical problems may later find it difficult to master other areas of mathematics. The experimental neuroses produced by Pavlov (1927) and Masserman (1943) may be considered as extreme examples of the effects of prolonged non-reinforcement in S—. It should be noted, however, that numerous factors would detract from the wisdom of trying to train all discriminations without errors. Perhaps the most important of these is the lack of frustration tolerance that would result from a steady diet of errorless discrimination learning.

An example of the unstable nature of discrimination performance following training without errors was unexpectedly obtained during the extinction of the response of S+ (Terrace, 1961). In this experiment it was demonstrated that, under certain conditions, discriminations learned without errors are more susceptible to disruption than discriminations learned with errors. Following 14 sessions of errorless performance on the red-green discrimination, trained under a trial procedure in which the probability of reinforcement for a response on an S+ trial was 1.0, the response to S+ was extinguished by correlating *both* discriminative stimuli with extinction. The results are shown in the left-hand panel of Figure 27. In each case, as the response to S+ extinguished, responding to S— equalled or exceeded the number that occurred during a "normal" training procedure in which errors were allowed to occur. The extinction of responding to S+ following discrimination learning with errors produced no disruption of discrimination performance. Typical data are shown in the right-hand panel of Figure 27.

In attempting to account for the disruptive effects of the extinction of responding to S+ following discrimination learning without errors, it should be noted that the transition from discrimination training to extinction involved a change in reinforcement probability, with respect to S+, from 1.0 to 0.0. The disruption of performance, shown in the left-hand panel of Figure 27, does not occur following errorless training on the same discrimination when a mult VI ext schedule of reinforcement was used. It is important to note that on this schedule responses to S+ are not continuously reinforced. This suggests that one of the factors which led to the disruption of performance might have been the abrupt change of reinforcement probability correlated with S+. This prompted a second experiment in which the probability of reinforcement in S+ was gradually reduced during discrimination training in small decrements. The probability of reinforcement during the first five sessions was 1.0. The probability was then gradually reduced to a probability of 0.25 over the next 15 sessions. The frequency of responding

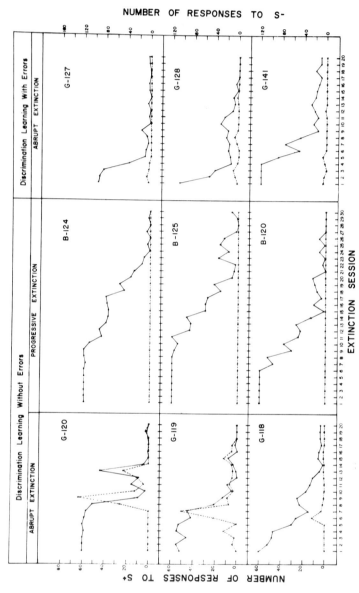

Figure 27. The number of responses to S+ and S- emitted in extinction following discrimination training by pigeons who learned the discrimination with and without errors. See text for further details (Terrace, unpublished data).

in extinction to S+ and to S— is shown in the middle panel of Figure 27. In no instance was discrimination performance disrupted.

The results of this experiment are similar to the effects of changing from a crf to a VI schedule of reinforcement in training an errorless discrimination in a free-operant situation. Both experiments demonstrate the importance of progressively developing a tolerance for non-reinforcement. If this precaution is taken, the available evidence indicates that performance following discrimination learning without errors is remarkably stable.

The Concept of Inhibition in the Sharpening of Stimulus Control

The concept of inhibition has recently shown promise of serving a useful function in the analysis of discrimination learning. Skinner's observation that Pavlov's definition of inhibition was based on the absence of an excitatory effect (Skinner, 1938, pp. 17-18) was in large part responsible for the disrepute that the concept of inhibition suffered during the last 30 years. During the past few years, however, new conceptual and experimental analyses of inhibition have suggested how inhibition might be demonstrated independently of excitatory effects. In an incisive discussion of this problem Jenkins points to Pavlov's concept of differential inhibition as the basis for distinguishing "the absence of an inhibitory effect from the absence or reduction of an excitatory effect . . ." (Jenkins, 1965, p. 56).

> The bare fact that an animal has learned a "go/no-go" discrimination with, say, S_1+ and S_2-, does not in itself [however] provide evidence of inhibitory control. One can equally well assume the animal to be operating by any one of the following rules: 1. Respond if S_1; otherwise do not respond. 2. Do not respond if S_2; otherwise respond. 3. Respond if S_1, and do not respond if S_2. The first rule entails only excitatory control, the second, only inhibitory control, the third, a combination of the two (Jenkins, 1965, p. 56).

Jenkins concerned himself mainly with Rules 1 and 3. ("The rejection of Rule 2 will come as a surprise to no one familiar with discriminative operant conditioning" pp. 56-57.) To determine whether, under Rule 3, an organism has learned not to respond to S—, it is necessary to vary the value of S— along some dimension and to observe whether or not this affects the tendency not to respond. S—'s control over not responding is clearest in a situation in which S— and S+ are from different and independent continua. This allows the value of S— to be changed without moving closer to, or farther from, S+. Two experiments which have satisfied this condition have both yielded evidence of inhibitory control. Jenkins and Harrison (1962) trained pigeons to discriminate between an S+ which was either white noise or the absence of any auditory stimulus and an S— which was a pure tone. During a subsequent generalization test, changes in the value of S— resulted in an *increasing* tendency to respond. It should be noted, however, that these gradients of inhibition were rather shallow when compared with the gradients of excitation that were obtained by presenting stimuli from the continuum on which S+ is located. Similar results have been obtained by Honig, Boneau, Burstein, and Pennypacker (1963) in which, for half the subjects, S+ was a white key and S— was a black vertical line on a white background. For the remaining subjects S+ was a vertical line and S— was the white key. Changing the tilt of the black line for the first group resulted in a pronounced inhibitory gradient while changes in tilt for the second group produced a symmetrical excitatory gradient. Both sets of gradients are shown in Figure 28.

In both of the experiments by Jenkins and Harrison and by Honig *et al.*, the discriminations were learned with errors. At this writing no com-

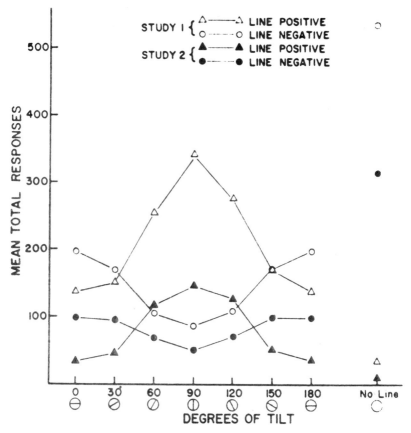

Figure 28. Generalization gradients of responding ("excitation") and not responding ("inhibition") to a vertical line obtained from pigeons. For different subjects the vertical line served as S+ and S— respectively in a discrimination between the vertical line and a blank key (from Honig *et al.*, 1963).

parable experiments have been performed in which similar discriminations were learned without errors. Various considerations, however, strongly suggest that no inhibitory gradients would have been obtained and that discrimination learning in these situations is in accordance with Jenkins' Rule 1 and not with Rule 3. As described in the previous section on errorless discrimination learning, the removal of S+ seemed to be a signal not to respond, independently of what value of S— represented the removal of S+. Thus, the control over not responding to S— seemed to mainly depend upon the absence of S+ and not on a particular value of S—.

Of the syndrome of performance characteristics which are peculiar to errorless discrimination learning, the absence of a peak shift most specifically suggests the absence of an inhibitory gradient centered around S—. Since the occurrence of the peak shift is highly correlated with behavioral contrast, with the differential effects of drugs and with gross patterns of emotional behavior, the speculative leap that these features of performance are also specifically correlated with inhibitory control does not appear to be very tenuous.

SUMMARY AND CONCLUSIONS

The most significant conclusion to be drawn from the experiments that have been discussed in this chapter is that non-differential reinforcement does not necessarily result in stimulus control. It is primarily for this reason that I have preferred the concept of stimulus control over its traditional counterpart, the concept of stimulus generalization. Contrary to various theoretical assertions, response strength does not "spread" around a stimulus that is correlated with reinforcement. A differential reinforcement procedure is necessary for the typical generalization gradient to emerge. Once the gradient with non-zero slope is obtained, however, we are still left with the unanswered question of why response probability varies directly with the distance between S+ and a test stimulus. Information regarding just how much differential reinforcement along a given continuum is necessary for the typical generalization gradient to emerge is not yet available. We know, for example, from Peterson's (1962) study that a generalization gradient of wavelength that is obtained from a duckling who has been reared in monochromatic light is flat, whereas a gradient that is obtained from a duckling who has been reared in white light will have a greater-than-zero slope. But these results do not tell us how many colors must be discriminated before a steep gradient is obtained. It may turn out that a discrimination between two wavelengths will suffice, in which case one would have to assume an innate sensory mechanism which results in the ordering typically obtained among colors (cf., Guttman, 1963).

Our discussion of the problem of attention revealed yet another unanswered problem. Differential reinforcement will establish control along one stimulus dimension, but in many cases one cannot predict what that dimension will be. Here again more knowledge is needed concerning the development of control along the numerous dimensions by which a stimulus can be specified. It would seem, in certain instances, that innate factors would initially dictate the distinctiveness of a particular dimension, e.g., brightness or movement.

The sharpening of stimulus control within a particular dimension was shown to require differential reinforcement with respect to two stimuli on that dimension. The use of a progressive training method in which the final S+-S— difference is progressively approached from a larger S+-S— difference was shown to be an efficient procedure for sharpening control. The superiority of the progressive method over the traditional method, which maintains the S+-S— difference at a constant value throughout discrimination training, could not be accounted for by a generalization theory which postulated the spread of response strength around S+ and of inhibition around S—.

In certain instances the progressive training procedure was shown to result in the acquisition of a discrimination without any responses to S— (errors). Various performance measures indicated that S— functions differently following discrimination learning with and without errors. Emotional responses following the onset of S—, behavioral contrast, the disruption of discrimination performance by drugs, and the peak shift were only obtained following discrimination learning with errors. These differences in performance led to the conclusion that S— functions as an aversive or inhibitory stimulus following discrimination learning with errors and as a neutral stimulus following discrimination learning without errors.

REFERENCES

ANREP, G. V. (1923) The irradiation of conditioned reflexes. In *Proceedings of the Royal Society of London,* Series B, Vol. 94. London. Pp. 404-425.
AZRIN, N. (1965) Extinction-induced aggression. Paper presented at meetings of the Amer. Psychol. Ass., Chicago.
AZRIN, N., HUTCHINSON, R. R., and MCLAUGHLIN, R. (1965) The opportunity for aggression as an operant reinforcer during aversive stimulation. *J. exp. Anal. Behav., 8,* 171-180.
BARON, M. R. (1965) The stimulus, stimulus control, and stimulus generalization. In D. I. Mostofsky (Ed.), *Stimulus generalization.* Stanford: Stanford Univ. Press. Pp. 62-71.
BLOUGH, D. S. (1963) Interresponse time as a function of continuous variables: A new method and some data. *J. exp. Anal. Behav., 6,* 237-246.
BLOUGH, D. S. (1965) Definitions and measurement in generalization research. In D. I. Mostofsky (Ed.), *Stimulus generalization.* Stanford: Stanford Univ. Press. Pp. 30-37.
BLUM, R. A., and BLUM, J. S. (1949) Factual issues in the "continuity controversy." *Psychol. Rev., 56,* 33-50.

BONEAU, C. A., and AXELROD, S. (1962) Work decrement and reminiscence in pigeon operant responding. *J. exp. Psychol., 64,* 352-354.

BOWER, G., and GRUSEC, T. (1964) Effect of prior Pavlovian discrimination training upon learning an operant discrimination. *J. exp. Anal. Behav., 7,* 401-404.

BRETHOWER, D. M., and REYNOLDS, G. S. (1962) A facilitative effect of punishment on unpunished behavior. *J. exp. Anal. Behav., 5,* 191-199.

BROWN, J. S. (1965) Generalization and discrimination. In D. I. Mostofsky (Ed.), *Stimulus generalization.* Stanford: Stanford Univ. Press. Pp. 7-23.

BUTTER, C. M. (1963) Stimulus generalization along one and two dimensions in pigeons. *J. exp. Psychol., 65,* 339-346.

CATANIA, A. C., and GILL, C. A. (1964) Inhibition and behavioral contrast. *Psychonomic Science, 1,* 257-258.

DEWS, P. B. (1955) Studies on behavior: II. The effects of pentobarbital, methamphetamine and scopolamine on performances in pigeons involving discriminations. *J. Pharmacol. exp. Therap., 115,* 380-389.

DEWS, P. B., and SKINNER, B. F. (Eds.) (1956) Techniques for the study of behavioral effects of drugs. *Ann. N. Y. Acad. Sci., 65,* 247-356.

ESTES, W. K. (1943) Discriminative conditioning: I. A discriminative property of conditioned anticipation. *J. exp. Psychol., 32,* 150-155.

ESTES, W. K. (1948) Discriminative conditioning: II. Effects of a Pavlovian conditioned stimulus upon a subsequently established operant response. *J. exp. Psychol., 38,* 173-177.

FINK, J. B., and PATTON, R. M. (1953) Decrement of a learned drinking response accompanying changes in several stimulus characteristics. *J. comp. physiol. Psychol., 46,* 23-27.

FRICK, F. C. (1948) An analysis of an operant discrimination. *J. Psychol., 26,* 93-123.

GANZ, L., and RIESEN, A. H. (1962) Stimulus generalization to hue in the dark-reared macaque. *J. comp. physiol. Psychol., 55,* 92-99.

GUTHRIE, E. R. (1935) *The psychology of learning.* New York: Harper & Row.

GUTHRIE, E. R. (1959) Association by contiguity. In S. Koch (Ed.), *Psychology: A study of a science.* Vol. 2. New York: McGraw-Hill. Pp. 158-195.

GUTTMAN, N. (1959) Generalization gradients around stimuli associated with different reinforcement schedules. *J. exp. Psychol., 58,* 335-340.

GUTTMAN, N. (1963) Laws of behavior and facts of perception. In S. Koch (Ed), *Psychology: A study of a science.* Vol. 4. New York: McGraw-Hill. Pp. 114-178.

GUTTMAN, N., and KALISH, H. I. (1956) Discriminability and stimulus generalization. *J. exp. Psychol., 51,* 79-88.

HABER, A., and KALISH, H. I. (1963) Prediction of discrimination from generalization after variations in schedule of reinforcement. *Science, 142,* 412-413.

HANSON, H. M. (1959) Effects of discrimination training on stimulus generalization. *J. exp. Psychol., 58,* 321-334.

HEARST, E. (1960) Simultaneous generalization gradients for appetitive and aversive behavior. *Science, 132,* 1769-1770.

HEARST, E. (1962) Concurrent generalization gradients for food-controlled and shock-controlled behavior. *J. exp. Anal. Behav., 5,* 19-31.

HEARST, E., KORESKO, M. B., and POPPEN, R. (1964) Stimulus generalization and the response-reinforcement contingency. *J. exp. Anal. Behav., 7,* 369-380.

HEINEMANN, E. G., and RUDOLPH, R. L. (1963) The effect of discriminative training on the gradient of stimulus-generalization. *Amer. J. Psychol.*, *76*, 653-658.

HONIG, W. K. (1965) The effects of irrelevant discrimination training on the slope of a generalization gradient. Paper presented at meetings of the Eastern Psychol. Ass., Atlantic City, April.

HONIG, W. K., BONEAU, C. A., BURSTEIN, K. R., and PENNYPACKER, H. S. (1963) Positive and negative generalization gradients obtained after equivalent training conditions. *J. comp. physiol. Psychol.*, *56*, 111-116.

HONIG, W. K., THOMAS, D. R., and GUTTMAN, N. (1959) Differential effects of continuous extinction and discrimination training on the generalization gradient. *J. exp. Psychol.*, *58*, 145-152.

HULL, C. L. (1929) A functional interpretation of the conditioned reflex. *Psychol. Rev.*, 36, 498-511.

HULL, C. L. (1943) *Principles of behavior.* New York: Appleton-Century-Crofts.

HULL, C. L. (1950) Simple qualitative discrimination learning. *Psychol. Rev.*, *57*, 303-313.

JAMES, W. (1890) *Principles of psychology.* New York: Holt, Rinehart & Winston. 2 vols.

JENKINS, H. M. (1961) The effect of discrimination training on extinction. *J. exp. Psychol.*, *61*, 111-121.

JENKINS, H. M. (1965) Generalization gradients and the concept of inhibition. In D. I. Mostofsky (Ed.), *Stimulus generalization.* Stanford: Stanford Univ. Press. Pp. 55-61.

JENKINS, H. M., and HARRISON, R. H. (1960) Effect of discrimination training on auditory generalization. *J. exp. Psychol.*, *59*, 246-253.

JENKINS, H. M., and HARRISON, R. H. (1962) Generalization gradients of inhibition following auditory discrimination learning. *J. exp. Anal. Behav.*, *5*, 435-441.

KELLEHER, R. T. (1958) Stimulus-producing responses in chimpanzees. *J. exp. Anal. Behav.*, *1*, 87-102.

KELLER, F. S., and SCHOENFELD, W. N. (1950) *Principles of psychology.* New York: Appleton-Century-Crofts.

KIMBLE, G. A. (1961) *Hilgard and Marquis' conditioning and learning.* New York: Appleton-Century-Crofts.

KÖHLER, W. (1929) *Gestalt psychology.* New York: Liveright.

LASHLEY, K. S. (1938) The mechanism of vision: XV. Preliminary studies of the rat's capacity for detail vision. *J. gen. Psychol.*, *18*, 123-293.

LASHLEY, K. S. (1942) An examination of the "continuity theory" as applied to discriminative learning. *J. gen. Psychol.*, *26*, 241-265.

LASHLEY, K. S., and WADE, M. (1946) The Pavlovian theory of generalization. *Psychol. Rev.*, *53*, 72-87.

LAWRENCE, D. H. (1949) Acquired distinctiveness of cues: I. Transfer between discriminations on the basis of familiarity with the stimulus. *J. exp. Psychol.*, *39*, 770-784.

LAWRENCE, D. H. (1950) Acquired distinctiveness of cues: II. Selective association in a constant stimulus situation. *J. exp. Psychol.*, *40*, 175-188.

LAWRENCE, D. H. (1952) The transfer of a discrimination along a continuum. *J. comp. physiol. Psychol.*, *45*, 511-516.

MASSERMAN, J. H. (1943) *Behavior and neurosis.* Chicago: Univ. of Chicago Press.

MORSE, W. H., and SKINNER, B. F. (1958) Some factors involved in the stimulus control of operant behavior. *J. exp. Anal. Behav., 1,* 103-107.

MUENZINGER, K. F. (1956) On the origin and early use of the term vicarious trial and error (VTE). *Psychol. Bull., 53,* 493-494.

PAVLOV, I. P. (1927) *Conditioned reflexes.* Trans. by G. V. Anrep. London: Oxford Univ. Press.

PETERSON, N. (1962) Effect of monochromatic rearing on the control of responding by wavelength. *Science, 136,* 774-775.

PIERREL, R., and SHERMAN, J. G. (1960) Generalization of auditory intensity following discrimination training. *J. exp. Anal. Behav., 3,* 313-322.

PROKASY, W. F., and HALL, J. F. (1963) Primary stimulus generalization. *Psychol. Rev., 70,* 310-322.

RABEN, M. W. (1949) The white rat's discrimination of differences in intensity of illumination measured by a running response. *J. comp. physiol. Psychol., 42,* 254-272.

RAZRAN, G. (1949) Stimulus generalization of conditioned responses. *Psychol. Bull., 46,* 337-365.

REYNOLDS, G. S. (1961) Behavioral contrast. *J. exp. Anal. Behav., 4,* 57-71. (a)

REYNOLDS, G. S. (1961) Relativity of response rate and reinforcement in a multiple schedule. *J. exp. Anal. Behav., 4,* 179-184. (b)

REYNOLDS, G. S. (1961) Attention in the pigeon. *J. exp. Anal. Behav., 4,* 203-208. (c)

SCHLOSBERG, H., and SOLOMON, R. L. (1943) Latency of response in a choice discrimination. *J. exp. Psychol., 33,* 22-39.

SIDMAN, M. (1953) Two temporal parameters of the maintenance of avoidance behavior by the white rat. *J. comp. physiol. Psychol., 46,* 253-261.

SKINNER, B. F. (1935) Two types of conditioned reflex and a pseudo-type. *J. gen. Psychol., 12,* 66-77.

SKINNER, B. F. (1938) *The behavior of organisms.* New York: Appleton-Century-Crofts.

SKINNER, B. F. (1950) Are theories of learning necessary? *Psychol. Rev., 57,* 193-216.

SKINNER, B. F. (1953) *Science and human behavior.* New York: Macmillan.

SPENCE, K. W. (1936) The nature of discrimination learning in animals. *Psychol. Rev., 43,* 427-449.

SPENCE, K. W. (1937) The differential response in animals to stimuli varying within a single dimension. *Psychol. Rev., 44,* 430-444.

SPENCE, K. W. (1956) *Behavior theory and conditioning.* New Haven: Yale Univ. Press.

TERRACE, H. S. (1961) Discrimination learning with and without "errors." Unpublished doctoral dissertation, Harvard University.

TERRACE, H. S. (1963) Discrimination learning with and without "errors." *J. exp. Anal. Behav., 6,* 1-27. (a)

TERRACE, H. S. (1963) Errorless transfer of a discrimination across two continua. *J. exp. Anal. Behav., 6,* 223-232. (b)

TERRACE, H. S. (1963) Errorless discrimination learning in the pigeon: Effects of chlorpromazine and imipramine. *Science, 140,* 318-319. (c)

TERRACE, H. S. (1964) Wavelength generalization after discrimination learning with and without errors. *Science, 144,* 78-80. (a)

TERRACE, H. S. (1964) Wavelength generalization of stimuli correlated with different schedules of reinforcement. Paper presented at meetings of the Psychonomic Society, Niagara Falls, October. (b)

TOLMAN, E. C. (1939) Prediction of vicarious trial and error by means of the schematic sowbug. *Psychol. Rev., 46,* 318-336.

VERPLANCK, W. S. (1942) The development of discrimination in a simple locomotor habit. *J. exp. Psychol., 31,* 441-464.

WALKER, K. C. (1942) Effect of a discriminative stimulus transferred to a previously unassociated response. *J. exp. Psychol., 31,* 312-321.

WARREN, J. M. (1953) Additivity of cues in a visual pattern discrimination by monkeys. *J. comp. physiol. Psychol., 46,* 484-486.

WYCKOFF, L. B., JR. (1954) The role of observing responses in discrimination learning. Part I. *Psychol. Rev., 61,* 89-97.

ZEIGLER, H., and WYCKOFF, L. B. (1961) Observing responses and discrimination learning. *Quart. J. exp. Psychol., 13,* 129-140.

8

The Study of
Animal Sensory Processes
by Operant Methods [1]

Donald S. Blough

INTRODUCTION

This chapter concerns some methods that have recently been used to study the sensory processes of animals, and some of the problems that arise in this sort of work. The discussion concentrates on modern operant techniques and makes little mention of past work that has provided the background for present practices. Since Yerkes' classic work (1907), ingenious men with discrimination boxes, jumping stands, runways, and mazes have produced a large amount of information about animal sensory capacities. These workers faced methodological questions that are with us still: the placement of stimuli, the choice of response measures, the control of extraneous stimuli, and many others. Also contributing to the foundation upon which recent work has built are the related fields of animal discrimination learning and human psychophysics. Some knowledge of all these is of value to the investigator who is setting up an experiment in animal psychophysics.

Though it might be said that animal psychophysics asks what an animal "sees" (or "hears," etc.), the behavior of the animal provides, of course, the data from which psychophysical functions are constructed. Since a whole animal does the behaving, it is appropriate to ask in what ways *sensory* research differs from other animal work such as that in *learning, discrimination,* or *stimulus control*. The distinctions are fuzzy, but, roughly speaking, the sensory field is defined by its concentration upon one particular sort of independent variable: changes in a relatively simple stimulus

[1] Preparation of this chapter and the author's work reported therein were partially supported by USPHS grant MY-2456.

situation along a relatively simple stimulus dimension. Typical stimulus dimensions are the intensity of a light, the frequency of a tone, the concentration of an odorous substance. Functions that relate such stimulus changes to changes in behavior are sensory functions. In sensory experiments, other variables that might affect the behavioral measure are, by and large, held constant. Such things as the nature of the reinforcement, amount of training, or hours of deprivation are not of direct interest; rather, they constitute the context within which the stimulus variable reveals its effect. The more directly a stimulus change seems to control behavior in a given situation, the more comfortable we become in saying that we deal with a sensory process. For example, despite procedural differences and many other important variables, the threshold for a tone depends on the frequency of the tone, visual acuity depends on the part of the retina that is stimulated, and so on. Other variables may shift these curves up or down, but there remains a clear relationship between the behavioral measure and a relatively simple stimulus continuum.

Sensory problems, as just defined, fall roughly into two categories, which we might call the *differential* type and the *non-differential* type. These names are intended to suggest general differences in experimental procedure, rather than differing underlying processes. In the differential type of experiment, stimulus differences are emphasized: the animal is required to vary its behavior in response to small stimulus changes. Such studies include the determination of absolute thresholds and of difference thresholds or resolving power. The critical stimuli are usually restricted to a narrow range and responses often fall into two categories. For example, in a threshold experiment the stimulus may vary up and down over a rather small range of intensities while the human subject responds "yes" or "no." The animal subject may press one lever for intensities below the threshold and another lever for intensities above the threshold.

The non-differential type of experiment places less emphasis on the detection of stimulus differences; loosely speaking, it tends to stress "similarity." Studies of stimulus generalization, intensity "dynamism," and magnitude scaling, among others, fall in this category. Such research involves a relatively wide range of stimuli and often uses a graded response rather than two or three response categories. For example, in a generalization experiment the stimulus might vary up and down over a very wide range of intensities, while the response takes on many values that are ordered with respect to one another. A human subject might assign numbers to the different intensities; an animal might respond at different rates.

It may seem strange to speak of generalization as a sensory problem. This strangeness arises perhaps from the historic attachment of generalization research to learning and behavior theory. Non-stimulus variables have commanded much attention, and theoretical issues such as the relationship between excitation and inhibition have evoked a good deal of discussion.

Yet, when stress is laid on the stimulus, generalization and other non-differential researches are as much "sensory" problems as are threshold experiments; and all merit our consideration in this chapter.

Between them, the differential and the non-differential types of research include a lot of territory only a small section of which can be covered in these pages. Methods, rather than results, receive stress here; among the methods singled out are those that involve a brief, repeatable response of the sort usually used in free-operant experiments. Furthermore, techniques that use positive reinforcement are discussed at the expense of methods that involve aversive control, classical conditioning, or unconditioned behavior. For clarity, much of the discussion is couched in terms appropriate to the study of a single modality—vision—rather than in generalities. For example, the discussion of observing behavior mentions "looking at" a stimulus, when "sniffing" might be appropriate for olfaction.

Some Definitions and Assumptions

In the course of the chapter, we shall have occasion to discuss a number of factors that affect stimulus control. Certain definitions and principles are, however, taken for granted from the start. These include the following definitions: A *stimulus* is some aspect of an animal's environment that can be shown to control the animal's behavior under some circumstances. A stimulus is said to *control* some aspect of behavior if a change in this behavior regularly follows a change in the stimulus. The controlled behavior may include attending or observing responses. (A controlling stimulus is sometimes said to be "attended to.")

The following principles are accepted: (1) A stimulus must control some behavior in order to acquire further control over behavior. (2) When reinforcement immediately follows a response, that response becomes more probable in the presence of the stimuli (*discriminative stimuli*) controlling behavior at or slightly before the moment of reinforcement. (3) When reinforcement fails to follow a response as just stated, that response becomes less probable in the presence of the stimuli. (4) The probability of a response at any moment is ordinarily determined by more than one stimulus, the animal's own behavior providing an important source of the stimuli.

These definitions and principles have practical value in constructing an effective psychophysical experiment. For other purposes they are loosely stated and incomplete, and these flaws become progressively more serious as one departs from simple operant situations and animals, like the pigeon, that are dominated by external stimuli.

A SURVEY OF SOME METHODS

Anyone who plans an experiment in animal psychophysics may choose from the bewildering variety of methods that have been used in the past, or he may easily invent a new one. To produce a new method, he need only pick an unused combination of the many parameters that go into such an experiment, as, for example, the manner of stimulus presentation (continuous or discrete stimuli, simultaneous or successive presentation, etc.), the response measures (rate, percentage correct, latency, etc.), and scheme of reinforcement (frequency, schedule, contingency with regard to stimuli and responses, etc.). With ingenuity, he can probably contribute new approaches that do not arise simply from such recombinations. But, he may well ask, which *should* he use; which is *best?* The answer to these questions clearly depends upon the particular circumstances of his research. Among these are the problem under study, the species of subject, and the aspects of the data that the experimenter wishes to emphasize (for example, efficiency or precision). In addition, the answer depends upon behavioral principles that are not yet fully understood (for example, the role of non-reinforcement in discrimination training). Because clearcut answers are lacking, the remainder of this chapter simply surveys some successful operant procedures and then outlines what seem to be the more important characteristics and difficulties of these procedures.

Non-differential Studies

The series of stimulus generalization studies begun by Guttman and Kalish (1956) constitutes the most extensive available treatment of a non-differential type of problem. These studies are marked by the two most important characteristics of non-differential research: a wide range of stimuli and a graded response measure. The following procedure is typical. Pigeons are trained in a standard single-key box for a number of hours. They receive reinforcement on a random schedule, commonly a short VI, for striking a plastic disc upon which the stimulus is projected. The stimulus light remains constant during training. For a generalization test, reinforcement ceases, and one aspect of the stimulus changes periodically, assuming in random sequence a number of pre-set values. These values lie along some stimulus dimension: wavelength, intensity, angular tilt of a line, and the like. Counters record the number of times the bird strikes the key during the presentation of each of the stimulus values, and these data yield a generalization function.

We have already noted that much of this stimulus generalization work has concentrated on problems that are not sensory—like effects of deprivation—and reference to these studies and their associated theoretical issues can be found elsewhere in this book (see Chapter 7). However, the answers to certain questions may turn out to be relatively dependent on stimulus variables, and these sensory questions deserve mention here, although we cannot treat them in detail. (1) Are gradients over a given stimulus continuum discontinuous; i.e., do they come to a sharp point at the training stimulus? At the moment, existing pigeon data suggest that they are discontinuous on the auditory frequency continuum (Jenkins & Harrison, 1960), but perhaps not on the visual intensity or spectral continuum (Blough, 1959b; 1961). (2) Is the gradient flatter over certain parts of the continuum than over certain other parts of that continuum? This may be generally true of the pigeon's spectral gradient, although interpretations conflict (Guttman, 1956; Blough, 1961a). These and other studies agree, however, that the pigeon's gradient following training at 550 mμ is relatively flat toward longer wavelengths. (3) Are such variations in data collected by the generalization procedure related to data on discriminability or resolving power over the same continuum? Existing data on wavelength suggest that they are not (Guttman & Kalish, 1956) although complete data on discriminability are not yet available in the pigeon. (4) Can the generalization gradient be assigned any universal "shape": concave (Hull, 1943), convex (Spence, 1937), linear (Schlosberg & Solomon, 1943)? The new data have not resolved this question either. It is very important to remember that all of these "shape" questions are answerable only for a given set of coordinates. A logarithmic ordinate can change an apparently linear or concave gradient into a convex one, although a true discontinuity will survive this change. Since response rate—the ordinate in this work—has thus far acquired no absolute significance, no particular ordinate scale can be presupposed. A rescaled abscissa (from "frequency" to "wavelength," for example) can steepen a gradient here and flatten it there. The question of a universal "shape" usually is argued in terms of an abscissa scaled in units of discriminability, for no one suggests that arbitrary physical scales should be comparable across different sensory dimensions.

A number of researchers have modified the "pure" generalization procedure by introducing extinction at one or more stimulus values (e.g., Hanson, 1959; Honig, 1961; Jenkins & Harrison, 1960; Pierrel & Sherman, 1960). In certain respects these studies are of the differential variety, but they retain a graded response measure (rate) and wide stimulus range. Whether such experiments deserve the label *sensory* is a moot question for the time being. Further research is necessary before we will know whether an effect such as Hanson's "peak shift" (1959) varies in characteristic ways with simple stimulus changes, or whether it can be predicted almost entirely from the length and type of training and similar non-stimulus factors.

Stimulus generalization has dominated animal work of the non-differential variety to the neglect of other interesting problems. Herrnstein and van Sommers (1962) have recently made a start on the problem of stimulus magnitude estimation. They trained birds to respond at different rates to a number of different stimulus intensities and then measured their response rate at intermediate intensities. An "estimation of magnitude" given by the rate at the intermediate stimuli was predicted by a power function relating intensity and magnitude, an interesting result in view of recent arguments and data in human psychophysics (Stevens, 1957).

In a related study, Honig and Shaw (1962) began work on the problem of bisection of stimulus intervals. They used pigeons in a two-key box. Both keys were illuminated by the same wavelength, but this wavelength could be varied across the visual spectrum. At two training wavelengths, the birds were reinforced on a VI schedule for pecking the left key; at two other wavelengths, they were reinforced for pecking the right. Wavelengths between the training values were then presented to determine at what point the birds would respond equally to the two keys—the point of "bisection." The results were somewhat ambiguous, but, as in the case of the generalization results of Guttman and Kalish (1956), they were not clearly predictable from the presently available discriminability data on the wavelength continuum.

To readers familiar with human psychophysics, the names "scaling" and "bisection" may imply responding controlled by abstract relations among stimuli. This is not necessarily the case in the studies just mentioned; there, the pigeons' pecking may be controlled, as in threshold experiments, by the "confusability" of test stimuli with training stimuli. Another new and very promising procedure appears to require a more abstract sort of control. This is the method, used by Honig (1965) and his associates, that establishes "stimulus difference" as a stimulus dimension. Pigeons are trained, for example, to pick the right one of two keys if the keys are illuminated by identical wavelengths, and to peck the left key if the wavelengths differ. Since a given wavelength appears equally often on both keys and is paired equally often with itself or a different wavelength, the birds cannot base their discrimination upon any absolute wavelength discrimination. They must either learn a sizable series of conditional discriminations (e.g., 500 mμ right + 500 mμ left, peck right; 500 mμ right + 540 mμ left, peck left; 540 mμ right + 500 mμ left, peck left; etc., through the various wavelengths being used); or they must learn to peck "right if same, left if different." Results so far indicate that the birds do the latter; for example, combinations of new wavelengths are responded to appropriately.

Honig presents very regular generalization gradients along the difference dimension, and he suggests that the method opens new possibilities for the study of animal perception and scaling, both within and between modalities. The method would be especially fruitful if animals that were trained to respond to differences on one dimension responded systematically to differences among stimuli on a different dimension, perhaps in a new modality. If this did not work with pigeons, it might with other animals, perhaps monkeys. Even if such transfer did not occur, the method seems well worth pursuing for the information it can yield about stimulus relations within a given stimulus dimension.

Threshold Studies with a Single Manipulandum

Differential research usually requires only two identifiably different response categories rather than a response continuum. These two categories may be identified with two different manipulanda, but they may equally well be two distinguishable patterns of response to the same manipulandum. Lever presses of differing force, latency, or rate would serve, for example. A simple example of this is the "go, no-go" situation. Heise (1953) used this to determine auditory thresholds; the pigeon's rate of pecking on a single key served as the response measure. Tones were presented to the pigeon at intervals, and the bird was reinforced only if it pecked ten times within the 15-sec. duration of the tone. Discrimination of the tone was indicated by a higher rate during the tone than in silent periods. Heise had a good deal of trouble suppressing responses during silence. This plight is not uncommon where a difficult discrimination is involved, and it suggests that where precise control by a small stimulus change is required, it may be better to go to a two-manipulandum situation (see below).

Moving one step from Heise's simple discrimination situation, one may retain a single manipulandum, but reinforce two behaviors with respect to this manipulandum. One may, for example, reinforce responses in the presence of a "positive" stimulus and also reinforce if no responses are given during an exposure of the "negative" stimulus. Mishkin and Weiskrantz (1959) did this in an experiment on critical flicker frequency (CFF) in monkeys. In that experiment, the monkey could press a single response panel above a translucent stimulus disc. If the light on the disc was flickering, a panel press was reinforced; if the light was steady, reinforcement followed when the panel was not pressed for 5 sec. An effective discrimination developed that yielded reliable CFFs—although the monkeys kept getting better (giving higher CFFs) as the experiment progressed.

The experiment of Mishkin and Weiskrantz calls our attention to the fact that free-operant methods do not constitute a group apart from the more classical, more restrictive techniques. The brief, repeatable response is present here, and the unrestrained animal. On the other hand, the stimulus occurred in discrete trials, single responses were reinforced, and the response measure was percent correct.

Reinforcement of "responding" to a positive stimulus and "not responding" to a negative stimulus may differ only superficially from procedures that involve two manipulanda. In a study of wavelength discrimination in pigeons (as yet unpublished), the author has found that the reinforcement of "no response" for one stimulus and key pecking for another might as well be called a two-response situation. Observations of birds that are "not responding" to the negative stimulus revealed that they were actually responding with vigor; they performed some superstitious behavior that ended with reinforcement. For example, one bird pecked at the wall below the response key in the presence of the negative stimulus, while another spent the "no response" period waving its head in front of the key. These behaviors are very typical of the pigeon in situations involving reinforcement following periods of no response (Skinner, 1948; Blough, 1959a). The response chosen by the animal is a chance matter, and its varying topography yields individual differences in performance. For the sake of stable, uniform data, it may be better to provide for two explicit responses, each reinforced in the presence of its respective stimulus. We turn now to experiments in which two such manipulanda are used.

Threshold Studies with Two or More Manipulanda

Two choices and discrete trials mark the classic technique of animal psychophysics described by Yerkes over 50 years ago (Yerkes, 1907; Yerkes & Watson, 1911). Recent applications of this technique use the Y box, the WGTA, or the Lashley jumping stand (for example, Gunter, 1951; Miles, 1958; Feldman, et al., 1959). These retain essential ingredients of Yerkes' procedure; they also incorporate improvements, for they make the animal respond to the stimulus rather than looking one way and going another, and they provide immediate reinforcement for correct responses. These methods have proven their worth; the interested reader may find out more about them by way of a general reference such as Warden, Jenkins, and Warner (1935), or Hess (1960).

Some recent operant experiments are first cousins of these older two-choice procedures, and we shall look at three of these next. The experiments illustrate a distinction of long standing between *successive* and *simultaneous* presentation of discriminative stimuli. It is best to take this distinction at face value, as simply describing different procedures. Though some researchers believe that the two procedures involve different discriminative processes, this has not been clearly demonstrated. The first two sample experiments exemplify a successive discrimination. Only one of two stimuli is present at any time; which one it is determines the animal's response. The third experiment involves a simultaneous discrimination; both stimuli are available, and the animal responds to one or the other.

The first experiment by Michelsen (1959) concerns olfactory discrimination in pigeons. The bird faced a panel diagrammed in Figure 1. It put its head through a hole (A) into a cylinder through which passed a stream of air that sometimes carried an odor; it pecked key 1 if an odor was present and key 2 if there was no odor. Reinforcement was scheduled on a ratio; a trial terminated with reinforcement after seven correct pecks or without reinforcement after four incorrect pecks. This meant that responding not based on an odor discrimination brought reinforcement on fewer than half of the trials, for random pecking would tend to run up four pecks on whichever key was incorrect before reaching seven on the other key. As in other experiments of this sort, perseveration on one key from trial to trial was prevented by a correction procedure: the same stimulus conditions were presented again and again until a correct response sequence was emitted.

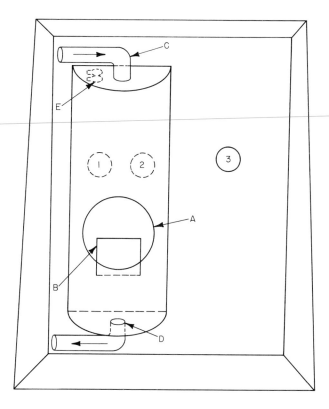

Figure 1. Front wall of the experimental chamber in Michelsen's olfactory experiment. Pecking key 3 started the air flowing through the cylinder, and nine seconds later another peck turned off the lights outside the cylinder and turned on the light inside. Then the bird pecked key 1 if an odor was present, key 2 if not. (From Michelsen, 1959.)

The presentation of trials in this experiment exemplifies the flexibility that free-operant techniques can bring to a classical situation. A trial began with the illumination of a house light in the outer chamber and the illumination of a third key (3) outside the odor-filled cylinder. When the pigeon pecked this third key, the airstream began to flow into the cylinder. Nine seconds later, when air bearing the odorous stimulus had filled the cylinder, another peck on key 3 turned off the lights outside the cylinder and turned on lights inside the cylinder. The appearance of the lights within the cylinder was the signal for the bird to put in its head and peck key 1 or key 2. Thus, the bird provided itself with a controlled, stable stimulus before it was required to make the discrimination.

Michelsen made no attempt in this study to determine thresholds for olfactory stimuli. He was content to show that the pigeons could discriminate odors, for the ability of birds to do this has been in doubt. With two odorous substances, sec-butyl acetate (a strong, irritating stimulus) and iso-octane (a substance with minimal irritating effects), the birds performed above 80 percent correct trials. On control days, when the stimulus air was passed through distilled water rather than through an odorous substance, performance fell to chance levels.

The next experiment illustrates the use of operant procedures to obtain detailed psychophysical functions and to measure, as well as detect, a perceptual phenomenon. This study, by Scott and Powell (1963), measured a visual motion aftereffect in a rhesus monkey. Some months of training were required. First, the monkey learned to watch a bright circle and to press a left lever if the circle expanded and a right lever if it contracted. The monkey was reinforced with food for correct presses, shocked for incorrect presses. Then the monkey was trained to fixate a spot of light during a pre-discrimination period; the reinforcement for doing this was the appearance of the circle. Finally, a stationary spiral pattern was placed around the fixation point during the pre-discrimination period. After the monkey's performance became good enough, tests were conducted as follows. Sometimes, during the pre-discrimination period, the spiral was slowly rotated, producing, for a human observer, the familiar expansion or contraction effect, depending on the direction of rotation. Then, as before, the bright circle replaced the spiral. On any one trial, the circle objectively expanded or contracted at one of a number of rates, or remained stationary. As before, the monkey pressed its levers, reporting the "apparent" expansion or contraction of the circle.

Scott and Powell constructed for each pre-exposure condition (spiral expanding, contracting, or stationary) a psychophysical function relating the proportion of left lever presses to the objective rate of change of the test circle (Figure 2). As expected from human data, the functions obtained following exposure to the rotating spiral were shifted up or down, depending on the direction of rotation. For example, following exposure to the expanding spiral (clockwise rotation), the monkey judged stationary circles to be contracting (about 80 percent left lever presses). As will be seen from Figure 2 the data are sufficiently regular to permit a quantitative estimate of the motion aftereffect, which, the authors report, is not as great as the average human effect, but well within the range of individual human results.

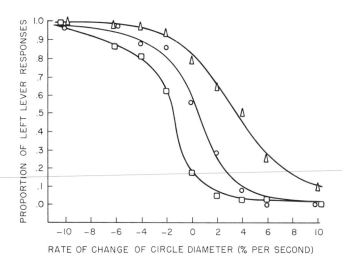

Figure 2. Proportion of left lever ("contracting") responses as a function of rate of change of circle diameter, following pre-exposure to three spiral conditions: stationary—open circles; counterclockwise rotation ("contracting")—squares; clockwise rotation ("expanding")—triangles. (From Scott & Powell, 1963.)

A third experiment, concerned this time with taste thresholds in the rat, took another step toward the control of the stimulus by the animal's behavior (Koh & Teitelbaum, 1961). It involved two stimulus conditions and two manipulanda, and this time the stimuli were presented simultaneously, one at each manipulandum. These two stimuli were water and a taste solution, available at the end of drinking tubes. If the rats showed any preference for water or for the solution, the preferred stimulus was chosen as correct. (Thus, sugar was correct versus water, and water was correct versus quinine.) The rat received a pellet of food if it licked the correct solution on any trial ten times before it had licked the incorrect solution eight times. If the rat licked the incorrect solution eight times before it gave ten correct licks, the trial terminated without food reinforcement. Drinking tubes were mounted in pairs around a large disk, so that rotating the disk in a stepwise fashion brought tubes containing various concentrations of the test solutions within reach of the rat.

This experiment introduced a simple version of the *tracking* method of determining thresholds. Consider an experiment with sugar, for example.

Each time the rat chose the correct drinking tube, the concentration of sugar in the taste solution was decreased by one step. Each time the rat made a mistake and chose the "tasteless" water, the concentration of sugar increased by two steps. A recorder, following these steps up and down, yielded a graphic record of the threshold (Figure 3). The steps between the concentrations were chosen in such a way that there was a concentration that was almost always chosen correctly and just below this a concentration that was usually missed. In analyzing the data, the solution between these concentrations was the one taken to be the threshold solution. This threshold was approached several times during each session; after the animal caused the stimulus to fluctuate up and down around the threshold for a while, it was returned to the strong end of the series to start again.

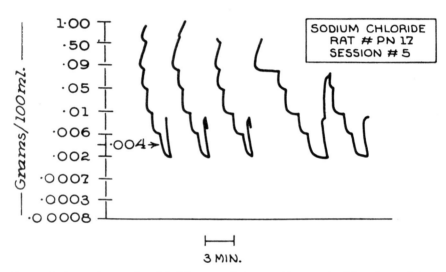

Figure 3. Typical record yielded by a trialwise tracking method for determining the absolute taste threshold. Each downward step in concentration came after a correct choice (ten licks) of solution; each incorrect choice increased concentration two steps. After a threshold determination, the concentration returned to the "strong" end of the series. (From Koh & Teitelbaum, 1961.)

Tracking, to which we shall return, is only one of several research methods that bridge the gap between animal psychophysics and modern developments in human psychophysics; the scaling and bisection studies mentioned earlier also illustrate this trend. Two threshold studies, which we shall now briefly describe, are further cases in point. The first (Mentzer, 1963) compared "forced-choice" with "yes-no" methods for determining intensity difference limens. In this work Mentzer simulated paradigms of human research, using single responses and discrete trials. In the forced-choice experiments, the pigeon was trained to peck the one key from among two or four available keys on which a small spot of white light appeared, superimposed on a background of white light. In the yes-no experiments, the bird was reinforced for pecks at the right key when a spot appeared on it and at the left key when no spot was present. The intensity of the spot varied over ten values covering a range of two log units. Following an incorrect response, identical trials were repeated until a correct response occurred. Mentzer obtained psychophysical ogives comparable in form to those yielded by human subjects, although the results from the different methods did not yield significantly different curves. The thresholds were relatively high, and it was clear that non-stimulus factors such as position habits exerted strong control.

Hack (1963) applied the powerful apparatus of signal detection theory to auditory thresholds in the rat. As in Michelsen's odor experiment, responses to one lever presented the discriminative stimulus, as follows. Presses on lever R (FI 7 sec.) turned on a small signal lamp for 1 sec. For 2 sec. after this visual signal, a tone of fixed intensity was presented with a probability ranging from .75 to .14. That is, the lamp signalled a 2-sec. interval during which the tone might be presented. If the tone was presented, and the rat pressed a second lever (lever L) during the 2-sec. interval, the animal was reinforced with water. There were no consequences for false responses. A new sequence started when the rat broke a light beam above lever R.

A regimen of discrimination training to the tone preceded the testing procedure just described. Despite this, one rat always pressed lever L after the signal light appeared, regardless of the tone. This behavior is typical of procedures where false responses have no consequence; see p. 375 below for a discussion of punishment contingencies for incorrect responding.

From data obtained in this way, Hack calculated the conditional probabilities of a lever L ("yes") response in the presence of the auditory signal and in the absence of the auditory signal. From these he computed response-conditional operating characteristics and detectability indices. Detectability was found to increase with signal intensity over the three signal intensities that Hack used. Such signal detection analysis holds great promise for animal work, for the measure of sensitivity is unaffected by changes in the animal's response criterion, resulting from deprivation, reinforcement patterns, or other variables.

Threshold Studies with Tracking Procedures

The author has used a tracking method that does not use the trialwise stimulus presentation of the experiment just described. Because the method is relatively new and rather complex, we shall look at it in some detail (for a complete description, see Blough, 1958a). It was suggested by Békésy's technique for tracking the human auditory threshold (Békésy, 1947). Békésy's subjects listened to a soft tone that was on continuously. When the tone was audible, the subject pressed a key. This caused an automatic mechanism to diminish the intensity of the tone gradually. When the tone was no longer heard, the subject released the key, whereupon the tone increased in intensity until it was again audible. This process continued, and the tone oscillated up and down across the subject's threshold. A continuous chart of the tone's intensity gave a graphic record of the threshold through time.

A series of experiments on the pigeon's absolute visual threshold used essentially the procedure just described (Blough, 1956; 1957a; 1957b; 1958b). The bird was reinforced for pecking one response key (key A) when the stimulus patch was visible and another (key B) when the patch was dark. These pecks controlled the intensity of the patch. Pecks on key A reduced the intensity of the patch; pecks on key B increased it. As a result, the intensity oscillated up and down across the pigeon's threshold, and a continuous record of the stimulus intensity pictured the threshold changes through time. Figure 4 is a schematic picture of the apparatus.

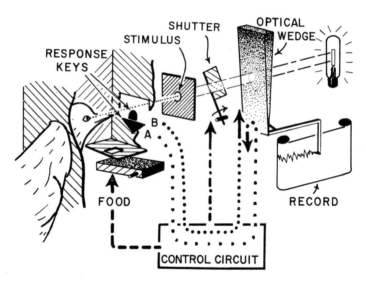

Figure 4. A schematic picture of the threshold tracking apparatus used with the pigeon. (From Blough, 1958a.)

The reinforcement contingencies that we used here are a good deal more complex than those used in the animal sensory experiments described so far. However, the discrimination itself is not complex; it is the same as that which a human subject makes in a standard visual threshold experiment. In both cases, the subject's responses are limited to two classes. Each gives one response (peck key A, "yes") when he can see the stimulus, and another (peck key B, "no") when he cannot see the stimulus. With humans, verbal instructions given at the beginning of the session usually suffice to maintain stimulus control. With pigeons, reinforcement is used throughout each session in order to establish and maintain stimulus control. Thus, it is necessary to superimpose a reinforcement procedure upon the essentially simple psychophysical paradigm.

How are the two responses maintained? Essentially, the object is to reinforce pecks on key A when the stimulus spot is visible and pecks on key B when it is not. But the experimenter does not know when the stimulus is visible; indeed, this information is the goal of the experiment. However, the stimulus is certainly invisible when the light is turned off, so pecks on key B are reinforced only when a shutter in the path of the light beam is closed.

The response to key A might be maintained in the same fashion, that is, by reinforcing it with food in the presence of a single intensity known to be visible to the bird. This procedure runs the risk that the birds will discriminate any such "visible" light from test stimuli of lower intensities. This difficulty is resolved by the use of a reinforcer that is ineffective when the stimulus is below threshold, but which becomes effective when the stimulus is above threshold. This reinforcer is the disappearance of the stimulus light. The onset of darkness acquires reinforcing properties here, because reinforcement with food occurs only when the stimulus is off. Responding to key A is maintained, therefore, by having key A responses turn off the stimulus. The bird pecks key A "to turn out the light" and key B "to get food."

This reinforcement procedure (key A pecks turning the stimulus light off, then key B pecks bringing food) is inserted into the sequence of events often enough to keep the bird responding, but not often enough to prevent tracking from continuing during most of an experimental session. Figure 5 shows this sequence of events in schematic form—how tracking goes on with an occasional interruption by the reinforcement sequence. Several sample threshold curves appear in Figure 6. The scheduling of reinforcement allows time for tracking, and it is also done in such a way as to minimize other factors that may interfere with stimulus control. Because the problems involved are not peculiar to the tracking method, we shall take them up in detail with other problems in a later section.

The tracking method just outlined has successfully yielded visual thresholds with monkeys (Blough & Schrier, 1963) as well as pigeons. Other investigators have used it to determine visual and auditory thresholds in other species (Adler & Dalland, 1959; Gourevitch, Hack, & Hawkins, 1960; Elliott, Frazier, & Riach, 1962; Symmes, 1962). At least two major difficulties have appeared in attempts to apply the tracking technique as

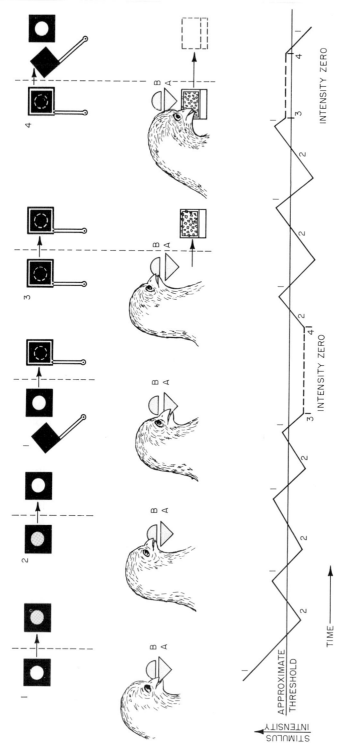

Figure 5. Series of events during tracking runs. The bird pecks key A when it can see the light, key B when it cannot. Most of the time key A pecks (1) drive the intensity down and key B pecks raise it (2). Occasionally, at random intervals, a reinforcement sequence is introduced: as the bird pecks A (1) a shutter closes (3), and pecks on key B bring access to food (4). Then shutter reopens and tracking resumes. (From Blough, 1961b.)

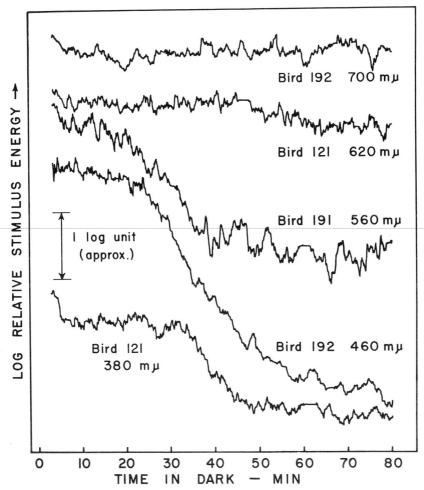

Figure 6. Threshold tracking during dark adaptation, with different stimulus wavelengths. Samples from three birds are shown. The shape of the curve is a function of wavelength. (From Blough, 1957a.)

described. First, training often takes a relatively long time and may not be justified if only a brief series of observations is desired, or if it is not necessary to follow continuous threshold changes. Second, the method probably does not provide for maximal stimulus control under difficult circumstances. This may be at least partly due to the asymmetrical reinforcement of responses to the two manipulanda, only one of which brings food. Meyerson and Michael (1960) tackled the latter problem in auditory research with retarded children by giving primary reinforcement on a random schedule for appropriate responses on either manipulandum. Such responses also occasionally turned the stimulus on or off, as in the original procedure. The subject switched keys in response to such stimulus changes and this provided the measure from which the threshold was determined. Elliott *et al.* (1962) also suggest employing some primary reinforcement on both manipulanda.

We shall conclude our survey by considering an application of the tracking technique to a problem involving the equation of stimulus intensities—just one of many non-threshold differential problems that have scarcely been touched in recent animal psychophysics. The aim of this experiment was to measure brightness contrast effects in the pigeon (Blough, 1961b). The birds were required to match the brightness of two spots of light. The two spots appeared on a black field during training, but in the testing procedure a white surround was put around one of the spots. Human subjects report that the spot with the white surround looks darker than an equally intense spot with a black surround and achieve a brightness match by adjusting the spots' intensities away from objective equality. In the training situation, the birds were reinforced for pecking at the brighter of two spots. Such pecks, operating through an electro-optical system, made that spot

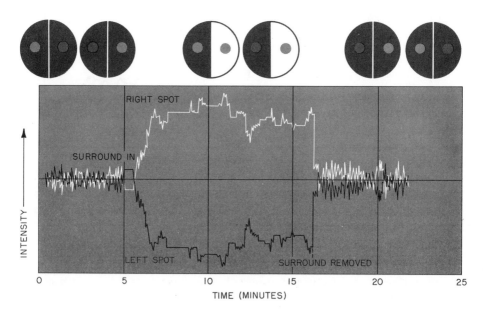

Figure 7. Data from a run in the brightness contrast experiment. The bird is trained to peck the brighter spot; the pecked spot gets dimmer, the other brighter. When the backgrounds are the same, the bird keeps the intensities of the two spots about equal; when the right spot has a bright surround, the bird raises its intensity considerably (by pecking the left key), presumably producing a new match of apparent brightness. (From Blough, 1961b.)

dimmer and the other spot brighter. The trained bird switched back and forth between the two spots and a record of the intensity of either of the spots tracked the bird's point of subjective equality. In the testing situation, reinforcement had to cease for fear of biasing the bird's choice of keys; but, while they did not respond very rapidly, the birds almost always chose the spot with the dark surround as the "brighter" and drove it dimmer until a new point of subjective equality was reached (Figure 7). We shall touch later on some difficulties with this procedure (p. 368) and the interpretation of the results.

PROBLEMS OF STIMULUS CONTROL

The preceding survey of recent experiments gives some idea of the ways that operant techniques can be applied to animal psychophysics, but little has been said about the pitfalls and problems that are met in research of this kind. The following pages take up these general matters common to most sensory experiments. The discussion centers around one task of all experimenters: to control some convenient behavior by a chosen stimulus change or stimulus dimension, while minimizing control by other variables.

Sources of Behavioral Control

Unconditioned Control: Preferences

Animals may bring with them to the experimental situation tendencies to respond more readily to certain stimuli than to others. We usually do not know whether this happens because the stimuli have unconditioned eliciting or reinforcing properties, or whether the stimuli gained their effectiveness through experience prior to the experiment. In any case, the preferences may be very strong, as with taste or pain stimuli, or weak, as they usually are with lights and tones. Strong response predispositions are the basis for some methods of measuring sensory capacity (Warden, Jenkins, & Warner, 1935, p. 184); but even weak ones can cause trouble in operant work. The problem is acute, for example, in stimulus generalization experiments. Animals may tend to respond more readily to some test stimuli than to others, quite apart from their experimental training. Perhaps a higher response rate goes with a more intense stimulus, as some authors suggest, although recent operant data indicate that this may not generally be correct (e.g., Blough, 1959b; Pierrel, 1958). There are also indications (e.g., Reid, 1958) that pigeons peck more readily at certain colors than at others. If this is true, making sense out of the birds' wavelength generalization gradients will be even more difficult than it now appears.

To measure a stimulus preference, or to be reasonably sure of its absence, one must stalk it with care. To start with, one might measure the operant level of responding in the presence of the various test stimuli. Hess

(1956) allowed chicks and ducklings to peck at panels of different colors. Fortunately, these birds peck for the joy of it, and Hess found that the chicks preferred orange and blue, while the ducklings pecked most at yellowish green. If such operant responding is insufficient, preference must be measured after some training procedure. Artifactual "preferences" then become a problem. To continue with the wavelength example, one might attempt to build up response strength by training with a "neutral" stimulus, say a white light. But what is "white" to a pigeon? And is white "neutral"? Human observers report that spectral yellow looks unsaturated and thus relatively similar to white. Abandoning the neutral stimulus, one might try exposing all test stimuli during training, and reinforce responses equally to each. In this case, "superstitious preferences" may develop. Morse and Skinner (1957) show that different response rates appear in the presence of different stimuli, even if the different stimuli are associated with the same reinforcement conditions. However, Honig (1961) employed the technique with some success on the wavelength continuum, as did Blough (1959b) with intensity.

If a preference is identified or suspected, one may try to eliminate it at the source. This may be impossible, if the preference is built into the animal —such as a liking for sweet things. If the preference is learned, controlling the experience of the animal may solve the problem; birds might be raised solely on black food in a dim box to eliminate a color preference based on experience with yellow grain, for example.

As yet there is no entirely satisfactory solution to the preference problem. Fortunately, preference probably plays little part in experiments that involve discriminations between slightly different stimuli. It seems improbable, for example, that a preference for bright lights would seriously affect an experiment on differential sensitivity to intensity. If a preferential bias were suspected, appropriate procedures might balance its effects; the brighter stimulus might be made sometimes S^D and sometimes S^Δ, for example.

The Role of Differential Reinforcement

We have just seen that stimulus control may antedate experimental manipulations. Usually, however, the experimenter gains the control he wants by associating different reinforcement conditions with two or more different stimulus situations. Just what is the importance of such differential reinforcement? Is it necessary for experimental control? The generalization studies mentioned earlier provide some answer to these questions. They attempted to exclude differential reinforcement, and they have generated stimulus control on at least two stimulus dimensions: the wavelength and the intensity of the light illuminating a pigeon's response key (cf. Guttman & Kalish, 1956; Blough, 1959b). The training procedure involved no explicit differential reinforcement; the birds simply pecked at one stimulus for a number of hours and received reinforcement on a variable interval schedule. The generalization functions that emerged after this training were regular and reproducible, and there is no question that they represent a close relationship between the stimulus and the behavior of the individual bird. As Guttman (1956) remarked, the changing response rate as the stimulus moves away from its training value "is very impressive to see—it is like turning off a running faucet."

In other cases, generalization tests not preceded by some sort of discrimination training have yielded flat gradients; that is, changes along the prescribed stimulus dimension do not control the response rate. When an interrupted tone ("beep-beep-beep. . . .") was on continuously throughout a pigeon's key-pecking career, the rate of pecking did not change in any regular way when the frequency of the tone departed from its training value (Figure 8). Jenkins and Harrison (1960) achieved stimulus control in this

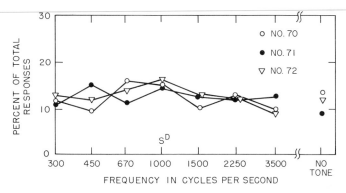

Figure 8. Generalization gradients after non-differential training with 1000-cps tone as S^D. The gradients are from three birds and are based on the means of several generalization tests. (From Jenkins & Harrison, 1960.)

situation by training the birds to peck only when the tone was on and not when it was off—a discrimination presumably irrelevant to the frequency dimension. After this, tests revealed a precise control of response rate by tone frequency (Figure 9).

Why does training that omits differential reinforcement sometimes produce stimulus control and sometimes fail? In the failures, the animal did not *attend* to the stimulus (by definition); we shall return to the matter of attention and observing later on. In cases where non-differential training seems to work, the animal is attending, but in these cases, it seems possible that undetected discrimination training lurks in the procedure or in the past history of the animal. In the wavelength generalization experiments, for example, the pigeon is reinforced only for pecking at the bright key and not for possible occasional pecks on the dark surrounding wall; learning to respond *to* the stimulus may thus involve unreinforced responses to a negative

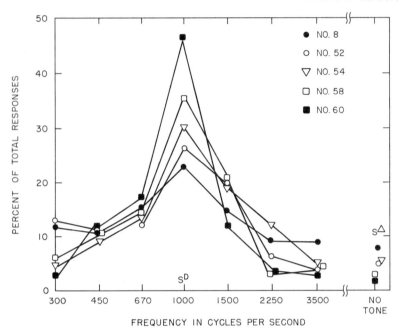

Figure 9. Generalization gradients after training with 1000-cps tone as S^D, no tone as S^Δ. Compare with Figure 7. (From Jenkins & Harrison, 1960.)

stimulus. Heinemann and Rudolph (1963) report that when the visual stimulus covers a wide area, luminance has far less control in the generalization test than when the stimulus is limited to an area immediately around the response key. The periodic blackouts that usually occur at some point in generalization training may likewise foster discriminative control by functioning as unreinforced stimuli. Another possibility is that birds respond differentially to wavelength because they learned to discriminate color earlier in life; ducks raised in monochromatic light have flat wavelength gradients (Peterson, 1962).

These arguments carry weight, but, to be sure, demonstrating that control is achieved without *any* differential reinforcement is like demonstrating the null hypothesis. At least as a practical matter, stimulus control can be "shaped" with little or no unreinforced responding to negative stimuli. This received a clearcut demonstration recently by Terrace (1963), who trained pigeons to make a difficult discrimination without error by starting with a stimulus difference so large that it controlled behavior from the beginning, and then gradually reducing the stimulus difference. The basic idea of the procedure—the gradual approach to a difficult discrimination—has great utility. Though receiving little attention in the learning literature (but cf. Lawrence, 1952), it has been employed for years in animal psychophysics;

Pavlov (1927) provides a classic example in his studies of the "analysers." Recent applications in psychophysical studies are exemplified by some work mentioned earlier. Elliot *et al.* (1962) found that turning a light on over the correct bar speeded up cats' discrimination of a steady from a warbling tone; the lights were gradually dimmed out over a period of several sessions. Meyerson and Michael (1960) used an analogous method of training children to discriminate tones.

Shifting stimulus control from either a pre-existing discrimination or from one easily acquired may be efficient for several reasons. The learning involves relatively few (or no) "errors" or S^Δ responses, so the animal is less likely to stop work altogether or exhibit the other emotional behaviors typical of extinction. It can also pick up various response techniques required by the discrimination, such as efficient lever-pressing and response-switching behavior. The easy discrimination may teach the animal where to look and what to look for; Wyckoff's experiments (1952) indicate that a good discrimination effectively maintains observing behavior, and recent work on the acquired distinctiveness of cues points in the same direction. Unfortunately, the fascinating theoretical issues raised by comparing the differential reinforcement and the gradual-shaping procedures for attaining stimulus control cannot receive further attention here. (See Chapter 7 for a fuller treatment.)

Selective Attention

Just as some stimuli are preferred to others, or otherwise control behavior prior to experimental training, certain stimuli quickly gain control over behavior in an experiment, while others are slow to acquire any effect (Jones, 1954). For example, in the pigeon, a visual stimulus projected on a response key is highly effective; visual stimuli at other locations are usually less so, as are auditory stimuli. In psychophysics, the experimenter usually plans to maximize the likelihood that the particular stimulus in which he is most interested will gain control. We have just seen that he may start with an effective stimulus and gradually shift to a less effective one. He also builds his apparatus to favor control. It is accepted that best results are obtained when the stimulus is presented in close association with the manipulandum. Similar stimuli are removed from the environment, and other distractions are eliminated. The same sort of thing is done in an experiment with human subjects, but ordinarily the most important step is to tell the human subject to "pay attention" to a restricted aspect of the stimulus.

As we have seen, we ordinarily tell the animal to "pay attention" by differentially reinforcing two or more values of the controlling stimulus. Any aspect of the stimulus that is differentially related to reinforcement may then come to control the animal's behavior. Usually more than one aspect is differentially reinforced, and the question arises which one or several of these aspects actually controls the behavior. The experimenter may have one aspect in mind, the animal another. An experiment by Reynolds (1961) demonstrated this in a clear-cut way. Two birds learned a discrimination in which a triangle on a red ground was S^D and a circle on a green ground was S^Δ. In a subsequent test, one bird responded correctly to the triangle but was indifferent to color; the other responded correctly to red but was indifferent to shape.

The critical nature of this selective attention for animal psychophysics may become clearer from two examples. In preliminary experiments on brightness contrast (Ratliff & Blough, 1954; Blough, 1961a; cf. p. 363) birds learned to peck at the brighter of two spots, each projected on an otherwise dark response key. That is, we hoped that they learned to peck at the brighter spot, for they were also being reinforced for other possible discriminations. Among these, for example, was this: "Peck the left key if the amount of light from the whole surface of that key exceeds a certain amount; otherwise peck the right key." Or this: "Peck the right key if the intensity of the spot there exceeds the background intensity by so and so much." Either of these discriminations would depend on the observation of a single key and have nothing to do with the spot comparison that was intended. Only an analysis of the discrimination based on the independent variation of the possible stimulus aspects would assure us that such stimuli were not controlling the birds' behavior.

Perhaps the discriminations suggested in the preceding example seem unlikely. Let us look at another psychophysical experiment conducted by the author (unpublished). Here, a bird pecked a key on which were projected two monochromatic spots. The bird was to peck the key when the spots were of the same wavelength and refrain when the spots were different. Again, this seems to involve a comparison of the two spots. A subsequent test showed, however, that the bird was controlled by the wavelength of a single spot. The bird distinguished, on successive trials, between the wavelength of this spot in the "same" condition and its wavelength in the "different" condition; its behavior was unaffected by the wavelength of the second spot. This absolute wavelength discrimination seems much more difficult to the human observer than the comparison that was intended. It seems characteristic of the pigeon (perhaps it is true of other stimulus-bound animals as well) to depend if possible on a single restricted aspect of a stimulus pattern, rather than on any sort of relation.

Varying the stimulus in many dimensions in *test trials* will show which dimensions control behavior; varying the stimulus in all non-essential dimensions during *training* may eliminate in advance a dependence on undesired stimulus aspects, for such variation prevents particular stimulus values from becoming correlated with reinforcement. The absolute wavelength discrimination mentioned in the preceding paragraph was wiped out by varying the wavelength of both spots along the continuum in such a way that the only dependable discriminative stimulus was the wavelength difference between the two. Similarly in the brightness contrast experiment, the two unwanted discriminations suggested could be eliminated by varying the background brightness around the spots over a wide range during training.

Fewer measures of this sort will be needed if the experiment is simplified as much as possible to start with, by reducing the number of discriminable dimensions. Thus, brightness can be eliminated as a factor in a color discrimination problem by equating the stimuli for brightness at the start, instead of varying brightness randomly during training. Unfortunately, eliminating a dimension in this way is not always easy to do, because one must know in advance what the animal can discriminate. This is one reason that the brightness problem has plagued experiments on animal color vision for decades.

Limitations on Pre-arranged Stimulus Control

We have just seen that the careful use of differential reinforcement is the primary means of restricting control to a predetermined aspect of the stimulus. In other words, the experiment builds into the subject a tendency to respond in certain ways to certain stimuli. However, the data that emerge from psychophysical experiments are also relationships between stimuli and responses; if these are to tell anything new, they cannot be completely predetermined by the experimenter. Roughly restated, this means that the testing situation which demonstrates stimulus control must differ from the training situation which establishes control.

The success of a procedure may depend on the extent of the difference between training and testing conditions. In most differential types of work, the two conditions differ but little; the animal is pushed to a limit, reaching a point at which it "cannot see the difference" between specified stimuli. Here the prearranged stimulus control fails, and the point of failure is a critical datum. In tracking the absolute visual threshold, animals do not discriminate "stimulus off," when they are reinforced, from "stimulus below threshold," when they are not. Reinforcement in the former condition thus maintains responding in the latter, and this is the core of the method.

Training and testing often differ substantially in non-differential experiments, and this can cause a great deal of trouble. Stimulus generalization is ordinarily studied in extinction, because continued reinforcement might introduce stimulus control that would confound the generalization effects. Similarly, in the brightness contrast experiment already cited, birds were reinforced for pecking the brighter of two spots on a dark field, but reinforcement had to cease when a bright surround was placed around one spot (the test situation) for fear of generating unwanted control. Such tests in extinction mean not only that the animal soon quits working, but also that the test is done in an unstable transition state that unquestionably increases variability and probably introduces other confusing effects. In addition, the novelty of the test situation may cause a substantial and immediate decline in responding. In the brightness contrast experiment, the birds were evidently taken aback by the bright surround; they responded little after it appeared, and soon stopped responding altogether.

Various measures can be taken to reduce the novelty of a test situation; that is, to increase generalization between test and training situations. Anything that reduces the difference between the reinforced training situation and the unreinforced test should help, so long as that essential difference remains which is the point of the experiment. Generalization data may be improved, for example, by training the subject on a long VI schedule (cf. Blough, 1961a) so that extinction is felt only slowly. In the brightness contrast experiment, training with a variety of symmetrical surrounds should reduce the novelty of the test situation without destroying the meaning of the test, which depends on having the surround around one spot differ from that around the other.

Control by Extraneous Stimuli, including Reinforcement

The "stimulus" in a psychophysical experiment supplies but one set of events that control the subject's behavior; many other things happen constantly, any of which may qualify as a discriminative stimulus if given the chance. The most obvious are incidental events like the click of a shutter, the sound of a footstep, the vibration of a motor, the momentary dimming of lights as electrical loads change. The experimenter attempts to eliminate as many of these as possible by sound insulation, masking noise, mechanical and electrical isolation, and the like. In scrutinizing the set-up for such possible cues, it helps sometimes to assume the animal's point of view: "Can I (as subject) use any sound, smell, light, or vibration to get more reinforcement for less work?" If the experimenter answers this in the affirmative, the animal probably will, too. For example, animals are notoriously sensitive to very faint auditory stimuli that are closely correlated with the opportunity for reinforcement—the closure of a programmer microswitch, for example. Still more classic is the animal's ability to respond to serial cues (". . . third, go left; fourth, go right; . . ." or ". . . reinforced left this time, go right next time . . ."). When all possible precautions have been taken, the method should be submitted to the animal as the final authority. One test is to remove the intended stimulus; there is nothing quite like seeing a pigeon continue to make a difficult "visual" discrimination after the stimulus lamp has been turned off.

An almost inescapable source of unwanted discriminative control is the reinforcement itself. If reinforcement is available at certain periods, but not at others, one reinforcement often means that more are on the way. An experimenter may produce a beautiful "stimulus discrimination," in the absence of stimuli, simply by mixing randomly periods of extinction with periods in which food is available on a short variable ratio. Responses dribble out slowly until a reinforcement occurs, and then pour with a rush until reinforcements stop coming. If the experimenter does happen to have a stimulus, say a light, associated with the periods of reinforcement, he may think that stimulus controls the behavior. Trying to guard against this unhappy state of affairs, the researcher may see to it that a reinforcement is never programmed following another reinforcement. In that case, of course, a subject will soon learn to retire after each reinforcement, disregarding any light or sound that may tell it to respond. A correlation such as this occurred at an early stage in the pigeon threshold tracking experiments (cf. Blough, 1958a). With the stimulus shutter closed, responses to key B brought reinforcement. After each reinforcement, the shutter opened, so that only key A responses were effective. Thus, reinforcement became a discriminative stimulus for key A responses and the stimulus light was disregarded at this time. The situation was remedied by leaving the shutter closed after about one-fifth of the reinforcements. Similarly, in procedures that involve the presentation of stimuli for discrete intervals, it is well to terminate the stimulus presentation after a reinforcement. In any case, if stimulus control is to be maintained following a reinforcement, the probability of reinforcement of the various response alternatives should remain unchanged by the occurrence of reinforcement.

Reinforcement or other events may also cause trouble at a distance. If reinforcement becomes available a certain period of time after a previous reinforcement or after some other distinctive stimulus, the animal subject may discriminate this fact and respond "by the clock" rather than following the desired stimulus. The *response latency* or *reaction time* experiment presents a good example of this. Suppose an animal receives food for responding as soon as possible after a light comes on. If the light comes on regularly five seconds after the preceding reinforcement, the stimulus is apt to lose control, for the animal may respond on the basis of elapsed time, anticipating the stimulus or giving impossibly short "reaction times." One way to minimize this problem is to use intertrial intervals of somewhat varying length. It is likely that discrimination based on time is often mediated by some sort of response chain, in pigeons at least. The next section discusses such response aspects of stimulus control.

The Role of Response in Stimulus Control

Single or Multiple Manipulanda

Many psychophysical experiments of the differential variety can be set up equally well with one or with two manipulanda. For example, an animal can indicate "yes" or "no" by generating different response rates on a single manipulandum or by choosing between a "yes" manipulandum and a "no" manipulandum. Something may be said for both possibilities. A relative response measure like the preponderance of lever A responses over lever B responses may suffer relatively little from extraneous variables that affect overall rate (such things as deprivation, emotional behavior, and disturbing stimuli). There is considerable evidence (cf. Heise's experiment, p. 351) that it is harder to make an animal stop responding to one of two stimuli successively presented than to make it redirect responses in the presence of this stimulus to a second manipulandum. On the other hand, a second manipulandum complicates the procedure. Not only the two responses but also the behavior of "switching" between them may have to be taken into account. The two responses may become chained together, though Herrnstein (1961) and Catania (1962) have found that a brief delay of reinforcement after switching seems effectively to separate the two. If a stimulus patch is associated with each manipulandum, the animal has two things to look at instead of one, but if a single stimulus is retained it must usually be a bit distant from the manipulanda. The relative importance of these factors varies with the particulars of the individual experiment, but they are worth considering.

Chaining and Observing

In previous sections, we have considered the response as a dependent variable under the control of other events. However, the response may itself control later behavior. The terms *chaining* and *observing* suggest two ways in which this happens. In chaining, one response directly produces the discriminative stimulus for another. In observing, the first response controls more indirectly; it exposes the animal to an external stimulus that in turn governs subsequent responses. Rather than dealing with these two kinds of control as separate entities, it is more appropriate to consider them as different points on a continuum. At one extreme, a given response brings on the next without fail. At the other extreme, preceding behavior is irrelevant to subsequent responding. In between, preceding behavior and exteroceptive stimuli function together in varying degrees. If there need be little reference to external stimuli, we have the *proprioceptive chain* (cf. Keller & Schoenfeld, 1950, p. 210). The rapid response runs that occur under ratio schedules are probably chains of this sort. Farther along the continuum, the controlled response may be regularly predicted from the first response, but only because the first response regularly causes the reception of particular external stimuli (the *exteroceptive chain*). Demonstrations of animal tricks are often of this sort ("turn around, stretch the neck, peck the key, go to the food magazine"). Response alternation on two keys can probably be placed in this category. *Observing* falls still farther down the continuum. Here, the first response prepares the animal to receive the discriminative stimuli, but these stimuli vary, and until they are specified, the controlled behavior cannot be predicted. Wyckoff (1952) recorded explicit observing responses in pigeons. Red and green key lights indicated which of two reinforcement contingencies was in effect. However, the appropriate color appeared only if the bird stepped on a treadle. Otherwise, the key remained white, and there was no indication which reinforcement condition was in effect. The treadle press was, then, an observing response, maintained because it produced the discriminative stimuli. Wyckoff found that when red and green were no longer differently reinforced, treadle pressing decreased markedly.

Behavior is hard to deal with as a source of control, because the experimenter does not manipulate it directly in the same sense that he turns on a light. Instead, he works through stimuli that he can control directly. If this indirect control is uncertain or neglected, behavior chains and observing responses develop willy-nilly, and the animal may control its own behavior to the detriment of external control. Will a chain of alternating responses on two manipulanda bring reinforcement? If it will, alternation is likely to appear regardless of all the lights that may be flashed at the animal. Will alternation of short bursts of responses pay off? The animal can produce these, too.

Such behavior patterns as response alternation are conveniently treated as response chains in which each response is the principal controlling stimulus for the next. In alternation, response A is a discriminative stimulus for response B. When responses on a single key are reinforced on a ratio schedule, each response is a discriminative stimulus for the next, so bursts of responses result. In each case, the occurrence of the first response means that the next has a relatively good chance of being reinforced. Unfortunately, such correlations between response patterns and reinforcement are almost inevitable. Even procedures that seek to eliminate all correlations between reinforcement and other events generate superstitious patterns of behavior (Skinner, 1948) because responses reinforced by chance become more frequent and thereby are followed by reinforcement progressively more often.

It is still more difficult to avoid patterned responding when reinforcement, instead of appearing randomly, must be correlated with stimulus conditions, as it is in the psychophysical experiment. Correlating reinforcement with a stimulus usually means that certain patterns of behavior are also more likely to be reinforced than others. For example, suppose a pigeon is to peck on the left key if a stimulus is red and on the right one if it is green. The bird is to be reinforced for responding on the basis of color and, ideally, should not receive reinforcement for any responding that color does not control. Is there any way to prevent a color-blind bird from getting reinforcement? Suppose the bird is fed on a VI schedule on this contingency. Even though incorrect responses yield no reinforcement, the bird can collect all its reinforcements simply by alternating responses between the two keys. If one stipulates that no response will be reinforced if it follows a response on the other key, the bird can simply peck two or three times on each key before switching. If a fairly long run of responses on the correct key is required for reinforcement, and the colors change frequently, it is less likely that a random burst of responses will yield reinforcement. Delaying reinforcement on the correct key after each response on the incorrect key also helps to reduce the chances that any particular pattern of responses will be associated with reinforcement. The threshold tracking procedure described earlier provides examples of these techniques in a psychophysical context.

Clearly, these restrictive procedures do not make reinforcement impossible in the absence of stimulus control, but they may make it very unlikely. Thus, as we have already seen (p. 366 f), it is usually advisable to approach an ultimately difficult discrimination through easier stages. In these, the stimuli may be highly discriminable and the controls upon response patterning less stringent.

Methods that discourage response chaining usually tend to reinforce observing behavior; they improve the animal's chance of reinforcement if it looks at the stimulus, relative to its chance of reinforcement if it fails to look. Nevertheless, a more explicit concern with observing behavior may be the key to a successful experiment. Behavior that interferes with observing must be eliminated. This behavior may be superstitious and can be minimized by careful shaping. A pigeon sometimes fails to discriminate stimuli projected on its response key because it scarcely sees the stimuli; it stands out of view and quickly reaches over to peck the key, or it hugs the panel and pecks down through its feathers. Strong chains may preclude observing: when birds first learned the threshold tracking task, they tended to peck rapidly on key A and then switch to key B without stopping to look at the stimulus. Stimulus control was regained when a delay circuit cut off reinforcement unless the birds paused momentarily while switching keys; this presumably gave the birds time to look. It may be of great help to condition explicit observing behavior, as did Michelsen (1959), whose birds pecked to turn on an odorous airstream. Where responses are made at a location any distance from the stimulus, a preliminary response to the stimulus may be necessary for effective control. This technique is common in matching experiments (e.g., Cumming & Berryman, 1961), where a response to the sample stimulus turns on comparison stimuli to which the animal then responds.

Some Remarks about Reinforcement

The experimenter concerned with animal sensory processes can scarcely help thinking of reinforcement as a necessary evil, an evil that must be tolerated despite the fact that it introduces stimuli grossly extraneous to the task at hand. However, the primary positive reinforcers (food pellets, etc.) that he grudgingly dispenses are not the only source of reinforcement in most experiments. We now consider briefly some other reinforcing consequences of responding.

Discriminative Stimuli as Conditioned Reinforcers

While the relation between discriminative stimuli and conditioned reinforcers is not yet clear (Myers, 1958), there is no escaping the fact that
the appearance of a discriminative stimulus strengthens the behavior that
it immediately follows. Psychophysical experiments provide endless examples of this principle; observing behavior depends on it, for example. The
explicit use of conditioned reinforcers can be very helpful, as in the threshold tracking technique, in which responses to key A are reinforced when
they produce the stimulus appropriate for responses to key B. Future psychophysical procedures will surely specify increasing use of conditioned
reinforcers.

On the other hand, the reinforcing properties of discriminative stimuli
cause trouble in some experiments. Such stimuli may either keep the animal
responding when it is not supposed to, or they may maintain some superstitious jump or dance that interferes with the experiment. Sidman (1960,
pp. 352ff.) suggests that since the presentation of a discriminative stimulus
will inevitably have a reinforcing effect, we may as well make explicit the
contingency between the stimulus and the animal's behavior. We will then
be in a better position to predict and control the effect of the stimulus. This
may be done by requiring that a response produce the stimulus, requiring a
period of no responding before the stimulus is to appear, or scheduling the
appearance of the stimulus in some other way just as we might schedule the
presentation of food. The *delay for false responses* is one of the most useful
contingencies. The chance appearance of S^D following a response often
maintains unwanted responses in S^Δ. If each response in S^Δ is "punished"
by delaying the appearance of S^D, so that the response and S^D never occur
in swift sequence, the S^Δ responding often disappears.

Punishment and Effort

Researchers have generally felt (see Warden, Jenkins, & Warner, 1935,
p. 177) that the way to get the best discrimination in animal work is to
combine reinforcement for correct responses with punishment for incorrect
responses. Punishment has usually meant the presentation of an aversive
stimulus, like shock, but operant procedures typically substitute a period of
extinction for the aversive stimulus. Thus, as we have just seen, behavior
that prolongs a period of non-reinforcement is sometimes said to be
punished.

A link between the effects of aversive stimuli and the effects of extinction is suggested by the term *effort*. Effort and punishment have often been
linked (cf. Solomon, 1948), and it seems likely that they operate in similar
ways to improve stimulus control. Indeed, the argument is growing that
extinction and aversive stimulation may play identical roles in discrimination learning. In any case, most workers feel that, in the absence of shock or

a similar stimulus, animals discriminate best if they have to "work hard" at their task. Almost all of the methods that we surveyed earlier call for multiple responses rather than single responses; Heise (1953) had birds peck ten times in 15 seconds, the rats of Koh and Teitelbaum (1961) licked their chosen tube ten times in succession, and the various tracking animals responded on intervals and ratios. Jenkins (personal communication, 1962) found that requiring multiple responses improved performance on a difficult discrimination; the animals got worse when returned to a single response procedure. We shall not try to account for this apparent "work effect," other than to point out that, in addition to more direct action, effort may alter observing behavior. It has been found that when shock may await them, rats look before they run; equally, if work is involved, animals may look before they respond.

In the Future

In this chapter we have taken a look at new developments in a classic area that has developed rapidly in the past half-dozen years. Looking ahead, we can hope for progress in two directions. First, we can expect an increasing flow of information about the sensory processes of all kinds of animals, based upon the continued refinement of apparatus and upon modern techniques of behavioral control. Second, we can predict a gradual convergence, at the conceptual level, of animal psychophysics, human psychophysics, and discrimination learning. The essential identity of human and animal psychophysics is pointed up by the use, with animals, of tracking, scaling, and signal detection methods. Such procedures are basically refinements in our ability to relate measured behavior to measured stimuli. These refinements are sure to have an important impact upon studies of animal learning, where the need for potent measures has been all too evident for several decades.

REFERENCES

ADLER, H. E., and DALLAND, J. I. (1959) Spectral thresholds in the starling. *J. comp. physiol. Psychol., 52,* 438-445.

BÉKÉSY, G. VON (1947) A new audiometer. *Acta Oto-laryn., 35,* 411-422.

BLOUGH, D. S. (1955) Method for tracing dark adaptation in the pigeon. *Science, 121,* 703-704.

BLOUGH, D. S. (1956) Dark adaptation in the pigeon. *J. comp. physiol. Psychol., 49,* 425-430.

BLOUGH, D. S. (1957) Spectral sensitivity in the pigeon. *J. opt. Soc. Amer., 47,* 827-833. (a)

BLOUGH, D. S. (1957) Effect of lysergic acid diethylamide on absolute visual threshold of the pigeon. *Science, 126,* 304-305. (b)

BLOUGH, D. S. (1958) A method for obtaining psychophysical thresholds from the pigeon. *J. exp. Anal. Behav., 1,* 31-43. (a)

BLOUGH, D. S. (1958) Rise in the pigeon's threshold with a red test stimulus during dark adaptation. *J. opt. Soc. Amer., 48*, 274. (b)

BLOUGH, D. S. (1959) Delayed matching in the pigeon. *J. exp. Anal. Behav., 2*, 151-160. (a)

BLOUGH, D. S. (1959) Generalization and preference on a stimulus intensity continuum. *J. exp. Anal. Behav., 2*, 307-317. (b)

BLOUGH, D. S. (1961) The shape of some wavelength generalization gradients. *J. exp. Anal. Behav., 4*, 31-40. (a)

BLOUGH, D. S. (1961) Animal psychophysics. *Scient. Amer., 205*, 113-122. (b)

BLOUGH, D. S., and SCHRIER, A. M. (1963) Scotopic spectral sensitivity in the rhesus monkey. *Science, 139*, 493-494.

CATANIA, A. C. (1962) Independence of concurrent responding maintained by interval schedules of reinforcement. *J. exp. Anal. Behav., 5*, 175-184.

CUMMING, W. W., and BERRYMAN, R. (1961) Some data on matching behavior in the pigeon. *J. exp. Anal. Behav., 4*, 281-284.

ELLIOTT, D. N., FRAZIER, L., and RIACH, W. (1962) A tracking procedure for determining the cat's frequency discrimination. *J. exp. Anal. Behav., 5*, 323-328.

FELDMAN, R. S., ELLEN, P., LIBERSON, W. T., and ROBINS, J. (1959) The effect of chlorpromazine on the brightness discrimination of rats with habits and fixations. *J. comp. physiol. Psychol., 52*, 322-326.

GOUREVITCH, G., HACK, M. H., and HAWKINS, J. E., JR. (1960) Auditory thresholds in the rat measured by an operant technique. *Science, 131*, 1046-1047.

GUNTER, R. (1951) The absolute threshold for vision in the cat. *J. Physiol., 114*, 8-15.

GUTTMAN, N. (1956) The pigeon and the spectrum and other perplexities. *Psychol. Rep., 2*, 449-460.

GUTTMAN, N., and KALISH, H. I. (1956) Discriminability and stimulus generalization. *J. exp. Psychol., 51*, 79-88.

HACK, M. H. (1963) Signal detection in the rat. *Science, 139*, 758-759.

HANSON, H. M. (1959) Effects of discrimination training on stimulus generalization. *J. exp. Psychol., 58*, 321-334.

HEINEMAN, E. G., and RUDOLPH, R. L. (1963) The effect of discriminative training on the gradient of stimulus-generalization. *Amer. J. Psychol., 76*, 653-658.

HEISE, G. A. (1953) Auditory thresholds in the pigeon. *Amer. J. Psychol., 66*, 1-19.

HERRNSTEIN, R. J. (1961) Relative and absolute strength of response as a function of frequency of reinforcement. *J. exp. Anal. Behav., 4*, 267-272.

HERRNSTEIN, R. J., and VAN SOMMERS, P. (1962) Method for sensory scaling with animals. *Science, 135*, 40-41.

HESS, E. H. (1956) Natural preferences of chicks and ducklings for objects of different colors. *Psychol. Rep., 2*, 477-483.

HESS, E. H. (1960) Sensory processes. In R. A. Warden, D. A. Rethlingshafer, and W. E. Caldwell (Eds.), *Principles of comparative psychology*. New York: McGraw-Hill. Pp. 74-101.

HONIG, W. K. (1961) Generalization of extinction on the spectral continuum. *Psychol. Rec., 11*, 269-278.

HONIG, W. K. (1965) Discrimination, generalization, and transfer on the basis of stimulus differences. In D. I. Mostofsky (Ed.), *Stimulus generalization*. Stanford: Stanford Univ. Press. Pp. 218-254.

HONIG, W. K., and SHAW, JOYCE. (1962) The bisection of spectral intervals by pigeons: A first attempt. Paper read at Eastern Psychol. Ass., April.

HULL, C. L. (1943) *Principles of behavior.* New York: Appleton-Century-Crofts.

JENKINS, H. M., and HARRISON, R. H. (1960) Effect of discrimination training on auditory generalization. *J. exp. Psychol., 59,* 246-253.

JONES, L. V. (1954) Distinctiveness of color, form and position cues for pigeons. *J. comp. physiol. Psychol., 47,* 253-257.

KELLER, F. S., and SCHOENFELD, W. N. (1950) *Principles of psychology.* New York: Appleton-Century-Crofts.

KOH, S. D., and TEITELBAUM, P. (1961) Absolute behavioral taste thresholds in the rat. *J. comp. physiol. Psychol., 54,* 223-229.

LAWRENCE, D. H. (1952) The transfer of a discrimination along a continuum. *J. comp. physiol. Psychol., 45,* 511-516.

MENTZER, T. L. (1963) A comparison of methods for obtaining psychophysical thresholds from the pigeon. Unpublished doctoral dissertation, Brown University.

MEYERSON, L., and MICHAEL, J. L. (1960) The measurement of sensory thresholds in exceptional children. *Monogr. in Somatopsychology,* No. 4, Coop. Res. Proj. #418, Univ. of Houston.

MICHELSEN, W. J. (1959) Procedure for studying olfactory discrimination in pigeons. *Science, 130,* 630-631.

MILES, R. C. (1958) Color vision in the marmoset. *J. comp. physiol. Psychol., 51,* 152-154.

MISHKIN, M., and WEISKRANTZ, L. (1959) Effects of cortical lesions in monkeys on critical flicker frequency. *J. comp. physiol. Psychol., 52,* 660-666.

MORSE, W. H., and SKINNER, B. F. (1957) A second type of superstition in the pigeon. *Amer. J. Psychol., 70,* 308-311.

MORSE, W. H., and SKINNER, B. F. (1958) Some factors involved in the stimulus control of operant behavior. *J. exp. Anal. Behav., 1,* 103-107.

MYERS, J. L. (1958) Secondary reinforcement: A review of recent experimentation. *Psychol. Bull., 55,* 284-301.

PAVLOV, I. P. (1927) *Conditioned reflexes.* Trans. by G. V. Anrep. London: Oxford Univ. Press.

PETERSON, N. (1962) Effect of monochromatic rearing on the control of responding by wavelength. *Science, 136,* 774-775.

PIERREL, ROSEMARY (1958) A generalization gradient for auditory intensity in the rat. *J. exp. Anal. Behav., 1,* 303-313.

PIERREL, ROSEMARY, and SHERMAN, J. G. Generalization of auditory intensity following discrimination training. *J. exp. Anal. Behav., 3,* 313-322.

RATLIFF, F., and BLOUGH, D. S. Behavioral studies of visual processes in the pigeon. USN, ONR, Tech. Rep., 1954, Contract N5 ori-07663, Proj. NR 140-072.

REID, R. L. (1958) Discrimination-reversal learning in pigeons. *J. comp. physiol. Psychol., 51,* 716-720.

REYNOLDS, G. S. (1961) Attention in the pigeon. *J. exp. Anal. Behav., 4,* 203-208.

SCHLOSBERG, H., and SOLOMON, R. L. (1943) Latency of response in a choice discrimination. *J. exp. Psychol., 33,* 22-39, 361-372.

SCOTT, T. R., and POWELL, D. A. (1963) Measurement of a visual motion aftereffect in the rhesus monkey. *Science, 140,* 57-59.

SIDMAN, M. (1960) *Tactics of scientific research.* New York: Basic Books.

SKINNER, B. F. (1938) *The behavior of organisms.* New York: Appleton-Century-Crofts.

SKINNER, B. F. (1948) "Superstition" in the pigeon. *J. exp. Psychol., 38*, 168-172.

SOLOMON, R. L. (1948) The influence of work on behavior. *Psychol. Bull., 45*, 1-31.

SPENCE, K. W. (1937) The differential response of animals to stimuli varying within a single dimension. *Psychol. Rev., 44*, 430-444.

STEVENS, S. S. (1957) On the psychophysical law. *Psychol. Rev., 64*, 153-181.

SYMMES, D. (1962) Self-determination of critical flicker frequencies in monkeys. *Science, 136*, 714-715.

TERRACE, H. S. (1963) Discrimination learning with and without "errors." *J. exp. Anal. Behav., 6*, 1-27.

WARDEN, C. J., JENKINS, T. N., and WARNER, L. H. (1935) *Comparative psychology.* Vol. I. *Principles and methods.* New York: Ronald.

WYCKOFF, L. B. (1952) The role of observing responses in discrimination learning, Part I. *Psychol. Rev., 59*, 431-442.

YERKES, R. M. (1907) *The dancing mouse.* New York: Macmillan.

YERKES, R. M., and WATSON, J. B. (1911) Methods of studying vision in animals. *Behavioral Monogr., 1*, No. 2.

9

Punishment[1]

N. H. Azrin and W. C. Holz

INTRODUCTION

Few of us, whether psychologists or laymen, are likely to approach the topic of punishment in neutral terms. Rather, our reaction to the use of punishment often seems to be determined by prescientific opinions. At one time, the use of punishment was widely approved. Our educational system and penal practices, for example, relied heavily on the elimination of behavior by punishment. Currently, the climate of opinion appears to be such that the use of punishment is held in disfavor. Many types of evaluative questions have been raised regarding punishment, such as "Should punishment be used? Is punishment effective? Does punishment produce changes in behavior that are only temporary? Is punishment less effective than reinforcement?" Scientific neutralism demands that we withhold judgment until the experimental evidence is fairly definitive. It is in this spirit that we address the subject of punishment: What does punishment do to behavior?

We shall first examine the methodology upon which punishment experiments have been based since the validity of experimental data cannot exceed the adequacy of the procedures used to obtain the data. Our examination of methodology will not consist of a simple enumeration of the different procedures used; rather, the procedures will be critically evaluated in terms of their probable adequacy in isolating the effects of the punishment process. A primary purpose of this methodological treatment is to provide direction and incentive to further the development of improved methodology. We shall then examine a number of variables related to the administration of punishment, such as punishment intensity, and to other variables related to matters, such as the motivational state of the subject, that determine the effectiveness of a particular punishing stimulus. Our attention will

[1] A major part of the original research reported herein was supported by the State of Illinois Mental Health Fund, NIMH Grants 4925 and 4926, and NSF Grant G16357R. Grateful acknowledgement is given to Drs. D. F. Hake, K. Miller, R. R. Hutchinson, and T. Ayllon for their careful reading of the manuscript.

then shift to a detailed examination of the types of behavioral changes that have been found to emerge from the use of punishment, such as recovery during punishment and post-punishment increases of responding. Only after this examination of the specific experimental findings concerning the determinants and outcomes of punishment, will we attempt to answer such general questions as "Is punishment effective?" Finally, we shall deal with the question of whether punishment is desirable. Our answer to this question will require us to consider findings from several areas which employ aversive stimulation.

METHODOLOGY

Definition of Punishment

Informal definitions of punishment are not lacking. At one extreme is the subjective type of definition whereby punishment refers to an unpleasant subjective state, as in the "annoying after effect" of Thorndike (1911). The difficulty in measuring the subjective states, however, forces us to look elsewhere. A second type of definition of punishment is implied in designating punishment as a drive variable, as in Dollard and Miller (1950). Since this type of definition is based on inferences about behavior, it would be preferable as an initial step to look at the behavior itself for our minimal definition. An unequivocal aspect of punishment seems to be that punishment reduces a behavior when the punishment is arranged as a consequence of that behavior. Hence, our minimal definition will be *a consequence of behavior that reduces the future probability of that behavior.* Stated more fully, *punishment is a reduction of the future probability of a specific response as a result of the immediate delivery of a stimulus for that response.* The stimulus is designated as a *punishing stimulus;* the entire process is designated as *punishment.*

Several aspects of this definition require comment. First, the definition is not in terms of a subjective feeling or a state of being. Therefore, it will be incorrect to designate a stimulus as a punishing stimulus simply because that stimulus leads to a statement of unhappiness or to an emotional state. Secondly, a specific event must be produced by a specific response in order to be considered a punishing stimulus. A simple decrease in responding is not a sufficient reason for classifying a procedure as punishment. Satiation, extinction, drugs, disease, stimulus change, etc. also may reduce responding. These procedures are clearly distinguished from punishment in that they do not produce a response reduction that is attributable to the production of a specific stimulus (the punisher) by the response. Only when a reduction of responses results because the responses produce a specific stimulus do we designate the process as punishment. A corollary to this definition is that it is contradictory to speak of punishment for not responding since no specifiable response produces the punishing stimulus. Such a procedure is best designated as escape or avoidance (Sidman, 1953). A third critical aspect of this definition is that it specifies the future probability of a response. The reduction in responding during the actual presentation of a stimulus is not indicative of punishment. If intense foot-shock is delivered after a response, the shock may well produce reactions such as jumping that are physically incompatible with the response; but this is not sufficient to categorize the shock as a punishing stimulus. Similarly, the delivery of food results in consummatory behavior that is usually incompatible with the response. The change in response frequency *subsequent* to a stimulus defines the reinforcing or punishing properties of that stimulus. For this reason, our definition of punishment is in terms of a reduction in the future probability of the punished response.

The present definition of punishment differs in several respects from previous definitions of punishment. One definition (Dinsmoor, 1954; Keller & Schoenfeld, 1950; Skinner, 1953) defines punishment in procedural terms as the delivery of an aversive stimulus following a response. An aversive stimulus is then defined as a stimulus that increases the probability of the responses that terminate that stimulus. This definition of aversiveness requires a demonstration that the termination of the stimulus can be used to reinforce escape behavior. Any reduction that results from the punishment procedure is attributed to the existence of escape responses that interfere or compete in some way with the punished response (Dinsmoor, 1954; Skinner, 1953). Under this definition, punishment is a secondary process in terms of the procedure since the designation requires that prior escape conditioning be possible. Similarly, the behavioral effect of punishment is viewed as a secondary or indirect result of competing escape responses. The present definition considers punishment as a primary process in that (1) no independent evidence is required that the stimulus will maintain escape behavior, and (2) the defining characteristic of punishment is directly measurable in terms of the existence of response reduction.

This definition appears to have several advantages. Virtually none of the studies of punishment have determined initially that the termination of the punishing stimulus reinforced escape behavior. In the absence of this determination, the stimulus could not be considered aversive and the procedural definition of punishment could not be applied to most studies that have involved this designation. The present definition requires only that a response reduction be obtained when the response produces the stimulus. A second advantage of defining punishment in terms of a response reduction is that no recording or observation is required of the hypothesized—but thus far unrecorded—escape responses that are presumed to produce the response reduction. A third advantage of this definition is that it focuses the investigator's attention on the independent variables rather than on an intervening set of "competing" behaviors that are often given "explanatory" status.

The present definition of a punishing stimulus is identical to the definition of a reinforcing stimulus in that it requires a change in the future probability of a response resulting from the production of that stimulus by the response. The definitions differ only with respect to the direction of change of the response probability: an increase of probability for positive reinforcement, a decrease for punishment. Neither process is secondary to the other.

Development of Prerequisite Reinforcement Technology

According to our definition, a reduction of response rate characterizes the punishment process. It follows that there must be a pre-existing level of responding before a study of punishment can be initiated. The usual procedure has been to use positive reinforcement to condition and to maintain the response at a frequency that is high enough to permit observation of response reduction by the punishment procedure. Only rarely has the operant level of a response been used (Baron & Antonitis, 1961). The stability and orderliness of the reinforced response rate will determine the extent to which any changes in responding can be definitively attributed to the punishment. If the response measure is variable or unpredictable prior to punishment, few conclusions are possible when the punishment is added.

Not until recently (Ferster & Skinner, 1957) has a reinforcement technology been so highly developed that we can specify the moment-to-moment occurrence of conditioned operant responses of an individual organism. Historically, "orderliness" of the response data has been obtained through group averages and through discrete-trial procedures (Muenzinger, 1934). The early free operant work of Skinner (1938) made it possible for Estes (1944) to use group averages involving as few as four subjects and to dispense completely with a restricted trials procedure that constantly interrupted the flow of behavior with an intertrial interval. The reinforcement procedures of Ferster and Skinner (1957) now make it possible to dispense with response averages both within and between subjects and to deal directly with the moment-to-moment occurrence of the responses. This development makes possible a more accurate appraisal of the effects of punishment and allows us to view the lawfulness of behavioral changes without statistical devices or large groups of subjects.

Punishing Stimulus

Requirements of the "Ideal" Punishing Stimulus

Ideally, a punishing stimulus should have properties that will permit an appraisal of the punishment process without allowing extraneous factors to enter into the procedure. First, the punishing stimulus should have precise physical specification. Unless the relevant dimensions of the stimulus can be measured accurately and in physical units, we have imposed limits on studies from the outset in terms of replicability and reliability.

A second desirable feature of a punishing stimulus is the constancy of the stimulus in terms of the actual contact it makes with the subject. A stimulus may be specified precisely at its source, yet be quite variable in its impact on the subject. For example, foot-shock delivered through a grid may be specified accurately in terms of the potential difference at the stimulator, but variations in humidity of the air will result in great variability of the intensity that actually impinges on the organism.

A third characteristic of the ideal punishing stimulus concerns the ability of the subject to escape or minimize the stimulation by means of some unauthorized behavior. Here, we are not concerned with the physical uniformity of the punishing stimulus except insofar as the subject is able to control it. The uniformity of foot-shock, for example, depends on the degree of contact of the skin with the floor grid. This contact is always under control of the subject's behavior. Even if the response bar, walls, ceiling, and floor grid are electrified, a rat can and does alter his posture, jump, run, dance about, attempt to stand on one bar, and use hairy portions of the body in responding. All of these behaviors will alter the effective intensity of stimulation in spite of the constancy of the shock as measured at the floor grid. The problems engendered by this unauthorized control go far beyond any puristic concern for physical constancy. Presumably, punishment achieves its effect on behavior primarily by an increase in the amount of stimulation impinging on the organism. If the subject can decrease this stimulation by an unauthorized or undetected means, then our response counts will be meaningless, as was noted in a study by Dinsmoor and Campbell (1956). On the one hand, no reduction of responses may be apparent as evidenced by the extreme instance depicted in Figure 1, "Breakfast in Bed," in which a rat learned to press a response lever with its foot while lying on its back, thereby eliminating the possibility of shock while still producing the food pellets. Similarly, a response reduction may result from an awkward, but shock-reducing, posture such as putting only one foot on the grid. The awkwardness may produce a reduction of responses that is only an indirect consequence of the punishing stimulus. In one study by Azrin, Hake, Holz, and Hutchinson (1965) this problem was studied by experimentally providing a specific escape response. It was found that the overall reductive effects of punishment were nullified by the availability of the escape response.

A fourth characteristic of the ideal punishing stimulus is that there be few skeletal reactions to that stimulus. In studying punishment, we are concerned with the reduction in the future likelihood of a response. If the punishing stimulus elicits strong and enduring skeletal reactions, then the elicitation of these reactions per se may well decrease the response frequency. In such a case, the response reductions will occur because of simple incompatibility of the elicited reactions with the punished response, and not necessarily because of the aversiveness of the punishing stimulus. Illustration of this problem may be obtained from studies using foot-shock, where gross observation reveals that partial immobilization of the subject often results from high intensities of foot-shock, physically interfering with the emission of the measured response.

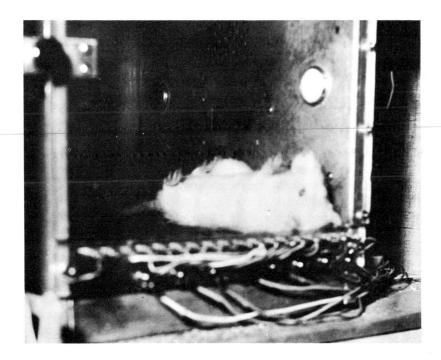

Figure 1. "Breakfast in Bed." A rat that has learned to avoid grid shock by lying on its back while pressing the response lever with its hind foot to produce food pellets. (From Azrin & Holz, unpublished data.)

A fifth characteristic of the ideal punishing stimulus is that it can be varied over a very wide range of values and provide degrees of response reduction that vary from no effect at the lower values to complete response reduction at the higher values. In the absence of such variation, the full range of effectiveness of punishment cannot be ascertained.

Having viewed some of the criteria for desirability of a punishing stimulus, let us evaluate some of the stimuli used. Foot-shock has been by far the most extensively used stimulus. The major advantage of shock is that it can be varied over the full range of effectiveness in reducing the response. A second advantage to using shock might appear to be that the shock can be specified precisely in physical (i.e., electrical) units of measurement. This apparent specifiability is illusory, however, as seen from the above examples which considered foot-shock in terms of its actual contact with the subject. Several devices have been developed to minimize the variability of foot-shock. Dinsmoor (1958) has used large tubular grids to minimize shorting between them and to maximize contact of the subject with the grids. Skinner and Campbell (1947) have developed a scrambler for alternating the polarity of the individual grids to avoid straddling of grids of like polarity. Dinsmoor (1961) has devised a stimulator to minimize variations in current flow through the subject. Hoffman and Fleshler (1962) have improved the scrambling technique so as to permit more rapid and more reliable alternations of polarity. In spite of these substantial improvements, foot-shock suffers from the disadvantages of (1) allowing unauthorized escape, as well as (2) allowing variability in the actual stimulation reaching the subject. The production of enduring skeletal reactions has been somewhat reduced by the use of very brief durations of stimulation; Estes (1944), for example, made use of a brief capacitor discharge.

We may well question at this point the necessity for such precise control of shock as a punishing stimulus. Certainly, studies of avoidance conditioning (Boren, Sidman, & Herrnstein, 1959) have found little change of avoidance responding over a wide range of intensities of foot-shock. A minimal intensity appears to be required to maintain the avoidance responses, but beyond that point, an increase of intensity produced little or no change in the rate of avoidance responses. Punished responses, on the other hand, have been found to be very sensitive to changes in the intensity of the punishing stimulus. In one study (Hake & Azrin, 1963), an increase of intensity from 50 to 60 volts (20 percent change) produced an instantaneous reduction of about 50 percent in the rate of punished responses.

The sensitivity of punished responses to shock intensity, as compared with the insensitivity of avoidance responses, can be accounted for by comparing the punishment and avoidance procedures in terms of the frequency of contact between the subject and the aversive stimulus. Under shock-avoidance conditioning, the responses soon occur at a rate that is sufficient to eliminate virtually all of the shock deliveries. The end result is that a large number of responses are emitted; but the shocks are so infrequent that a long period of time is required before the absence of shocks can be detected. As a result, we find that avoidance behavior persists for long periods (Sidman, 1955). Under punishment by means of shock, the situation is different since every response is typically followed by the shock. Thus, the subject is continuously making contact with the shock, unless complete suppression of the punished response has occurred. Under partial suppression, no problem exists in discriminating the precise moment at which the shock is discontinued. Consequently, the termination of the shock contingency during punishment usually results in an immediate change in the punished behavior (Azrin, 1960b). By the very nature of the processes involved, precise control appears essential in studies of punishment, whereas studies of avoidance conditioning may not require more than a minimally effective stimulus for many purposes. The continuing contact between the subject and the aversive stimulus also accounts for the sensitivity of escape responses to changes in the intensity of the aversive stimulus (Barry & Harrison, 1957; Dinsmoor & Winograd, 1958; Harrison, Abelson, & Fisher, 1960; Kaplan, 1952).

Different Kinds of Aversive Stimuli

Several types of punishing stimuli have been found effective. Masserman (1946) has used a blast of air with cats as well as a toy snake with monkeys. Skinner (1938) has used a bar-slap with rats. Noise has been effective with humans (Azrin, 1958; Flanagan, Goldiamond, & Azrin, 1958, Herman & Azrin, 1964) and pigeons (Holz & Azrin, 1962a). By far the most extensively used punishing stimulus has been electric shock delivered through a floor grid.

It has already been seen that foot-shock has the disadvantage of allowing variation in the intensity actually received, of allowing control of the intensity and duration by unauthorized escape responses, and also of producing extreme skeletal disruption. Punishing shock has also been delivered through implanted electrodes (Azrin, 1959a) and surface electrodes (Hake & Azrin, 1963), thereby minimizing physical variations in the intensity of the shock, and preventing control of the intensity by unauthorized escape behavior. The problem of extreme skeletal reactions still remains but is minimized by the usual brevity of shock presentation. These disruptive reactions were minimized further by locating the electrodes on the tails of squirrel monkeys that were restrained in a seated position (Hake & Azrin, 1963). This procedure eliminated the gross postural imbalance that usually results from foot-shock. Noise appears similarly desirable in that the stimulus intensity received by the subject has been capable of precise specification and control through the use of earphones (Flanagan, Goldiamond, & Azrin, 1958) or by speaker systems that produce a fairly uniform sound field (Holz & Azrin, 1962a). Noise appears to have many advantages for use in studies of punishment. The principal disadvantage is the absence of a wide range of effectiveness. Even at high intensities, noise has not resulted in complete response reduction. Other aversive stimuli, such as bar-slaps, snakes, air blasts, etc., have not been subjected to the test of extensive use but appear to offer no major advantage over electric foot-shock or noise.

Conditioned Aversive Stimulation as Punishment

The punishing stimuli that we have described thus far are defined in terms of their primary aversive properties. Theoretically, it should be possible to use a punishing stimulus that is effective because of its association with a primary aversive stimulus, rather than through any aversive properties of its own. This type of punishment appears to be used very often in many ordinary types of control over human behavior. For example, when we punish a child, physical assault is used only infrequently. The more frequent procedure is to frown, shout, or express statements that are presumed to have some association with more natural aversive events. Several studies have attempted to achieve this "conditioned punishment," as we shall call it (Barlow, 1952; Evans, 1962; Mowrer & Aiken, 1954; Mowrer & Solomon, 1954). The procedures used in these studies can be described in general terms as follows: a neutral stimulus, CS, is associated with an electric shock, UCS, prior to any conditioning of the animal's behavior. After several such pairings of the CS and the UCS, the animal is conditioned to respond for food but with no CS or UCS present. Once the response has been conditioned, the CS is then made to follow the responses. The resulting reduction in the frequency of these responses is attributed to the conditioned punishing effects of the CS by virtue of its previous association with the UCS shock. Unfortunately, this basic paradigm does not permit long-term investigation of conditioned punishment, since the CS loses its effectiveness after it is no longer paired with the UCS.

Recent experiments (Hake & Azrin, 1965) attempted to overcome the problem of maintaining conditioned punishment. Figure 2 depicts the general experimental situation as well as the control procedure. A pigeon was reinforced by food for responding on a key. The lower cumulative record on the left shows the typical VI schedule performance obtained. In the second segment from the left, each response produced a 5-sec. stimulus change consisting of a change of illumination as well as a change of the ambient noise level. It can be seen that the neutral stimulus produced little change in behavior. In the third segment, the same neutral stimulus was presented at irregular intervals of time averaging 6 min. apart. Again, the neutral stimulus did not affect the response rate. A brief electric shock was then delivered through electrodes implanted in the tail region of the pigeon. This shock was delivered at the end of the 15-sec. stimulus presentation, as indicated in the fourth segment of the cumulative record. This procedure is similar to the conditioned suppression procedure developed by Estes and Skinner (1941). It can be seen that the suppression of responses resulted during the stimulus (CS) but did not appreciably affect behavior in the absence of the CS. The segment of the cumulative record on the right depicts the results obtained under the conditioned punishment procedure during which every response produced the CS for 5 sec. It can be seen that the rate of responding was reduced from its previous level of about 80 responses per minute to a level of almost complete suppression. Gradually the response rate recovered during the conditioned punishment but still did not exceed 20 responses per minute. A crucial feature of this procedure is that the pairings of the CS and UCS were continued. The response-pro-

PROCEDURE

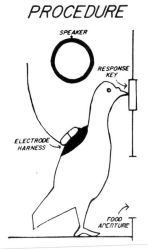

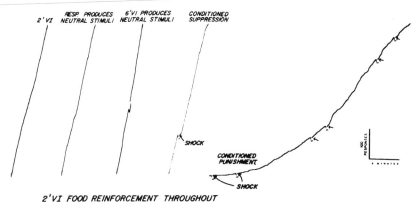

Figure 2. A method for producing conditioned punishment. See text for explanation. (From Azrin & Holz, unpublished data.)

duced CS therefore retained its conditioned aversive properties and could be effective in suppressing the punished behavior for as long as the procedure remained in effect. It appears that conditioned punishment need not be a transitory phenomenon; a previously neutral stimulus will continue to suppress the responses which it follows if that neutral stimulus is occasionally associated with the unconditioned stimulus.

Time-out from Positive Reinforcement as a Punishing Stimulus

Another example of a conditioned punishing stimulus is the time-out period. In the well known Law of Extinction, it is found that when the reinforcer is discontinued, the previously reinforced response will decrease in frequency. If we alternately reinforce a response in the presence of one stimulus but do not reinforce it in the presence of another stimulus, then the latter stimulus may be designated as a time-out stimulus; that is, time-out from positive reinforcement (Ferster & Skinner, 1957). Historically, time-out from positive reinforcement has been considered in a static sense; that is, simply as a period of time that separates the opportunities to respond. Such is the case, for example, in restricted trial procedures, such as runways, alleys, choice procedures, etc. in which the time-out is designated as an intertrial interval. Although the restricted trial methods have necessarily utilized time-out periods, the possible dynamic properties of this time-out had not been realized. Only recently has it been discovered that a time-out stimulus may possess reinforcing or aversive properties and may, therefore, control the frequency of responses by arranging that stimulus as a consequence of the responses.

The earliest realization of the possible reinforcing or aversive properties of time-out appears to be a study by Herrnstein (1955) in which response frequency was altered by arranging for time-out periods of varying durations to follow responses. The means whereby a time-out stimulus acts as a punishing stimulus is not completely clear at the present time. If we examine the simple situation in which a pigeon is responding for food under a VI schedule of reinforcement, we may arrange a punishment paradigm by allowing, say, every fiftieth response to produce a time-out period. If the time-out period is a punishing stimulus, then we might expect the overall rate of responding for food to decrease. In our own experience no decrease has been noted, as can be seen in Figure 3 (unpublished data) where a 60-sec. time-out was delivered for the first response after 1 min. Indeed, an increase of the overall rate has been noted previously when time-out periods are introduced independently of responses (Ferster & Skinner, 1957). If we apply our definition of a punishing stimulus, it would appear that a time-out period does not qualify as a punishing stimulus since the occurrence of a time-out period following the pecking response did not reduce the future probability of that response.

Punishing effects of a time-out stimulus have been seen in a number of studies, however, in which some alternative mode of behavior was available to the subject. For example, Ferster (1958) found that time-out would suppress behavior if a pre-time-out stimulus was available. Only those responses that occurred during the pre-time-out stimulus were punished by the onset of the time-out. If the subject did not emit a response during this brief pre-time-out stimulus, then the time-out period was not presented. An alternative mode of behavior was available to the subject to prevent time-out periods, in the sense that the punishing stimulus could be eliminated by responding at different times rather than by ceasing to respond. Ferster extended the use of time-out as a punishing stimulus still further in demonstrating that a time-out period could selectively eliminate punished interresponse times (IRTs) while leaving the unpunished IRTs unaffected.

Ferster programmed the time-out periods so that they followed long IRTs but not short IRTs. As a result, the relative frequency of the long IRTs declined. Again, the effect of time-out as a punishing stimulus was obtained by providing the subject with an alternative mode of responding (short IRTs) that eliminated the punishing stimulus without requiring a complete cessation of the responses.

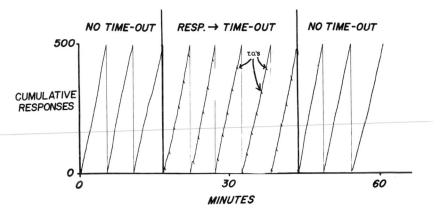

Figure 3. Cumulative response record of a pigeon under a VI schedule of food reinforcement. The food deliveries are not indicated on the record. The short pips of the recorder pen (see examples at the arrows) indicate the delivery of a time-out period of one minute during which time illumination in the experimental chamber was eliminated, thereby preventing the occurrence of any responses and any reinforcements. The recorder paper did not feed during the time-out period. The time-out was delivered immediately following the first response after an interval of one minute since the previous time-out. (From Azrin & Holz, unpublished data.)

A later study by Holz, Azrin, and Ayllon (1963a) shed further light on the possible means whereby a time-out period could act as a punishing stimulus. In this study, humans were conditioned to respond for cigarette reinforcements on a VI schedule. In one part of the experiment, one response manipulandum was available to the subjects. A time-out period was then programmed to occur for every tenth response on that manipulandum. The results of this procedure were in accord with the general rule mentioned above. That is, where no alternative response was available, the time-out period produced at most only partial suppression of the punished responses. In a second part of the procedure, two responses were available, either of which would result in reinforcement. Time-out was then scheduled in the same way as before to occur after every tenth response on one of the manipulanda. Under this alternative response procedure, almost immediate and virtually complete suppression was produced on this manipulandum by the time-out period. Responding was displaced to the manipulandum for which no time-out period was being programmed as a punishing stimulus. It appears, then, that a period associated with extinction, that is a time-out period, can serve as a punishing stimulus, but that it is not very effective compared with other types of punishing stimuli such as noise or electric shock or even conditioned aversive stimuli. Nevertheless, time-out can be a very effective punishing stimulus if the organism has available an alternative response that is unpunished and that will produce the reinforcement. The effectiveness of time-out as a punishing stimulus has been found to be a function of the duration of the time-out and has been used effectively to eliminate "incorrect" responses in a matching-to-sample procedure (Ferster & Appel, 1961; Zimmerman & Baydan, 1963; Zimmerman & Ferster, 1963).

Punishment by Means of "Response Cost"

A third type of conditioned punishment is *response cost* which Weiner (1962) has used on human subjects who were working for points on a counter. After behavior had become fairly stable, he arranged to have each response subtract one point from the counter. This subtraction of counter points as a consequence of a response was designated as *response cost*. The effect of this procedure was greater than that usually seen when a time-out period (signaling the absence of reinforcement) has been used as the punishing stimulus. Weiner found a reduction of responses that was immediate and in some instances almost complete. For every subject, the response cost contingency reduced the number of responses to a small fraction of the unpunished level. It would appear, then, that response cost is similar to intense electric shock in terms of the extent of the response reduction achieved. Another point of similarity to intense electric shock was that the response cost contingency did not allow recovery of the punished responses during the period of punishment. Two considerations seem necessary in creating a situation in which response cost can be used. First, some level of positive reinforcement must be made available in order to provide the opportunity for experimentally withdrawing that reinforcement. Secondly, a conditioned reinforcer must be made available since it does not seem possible to arrange a situation in which one could remove a primary reinforcer that the animal has already obtained. Despite these limitations, response cost appears to be a punishing stimulus that has a great effect on human responses. The response cost procedure is particularly interesting because of its similarity to the use of monetary exchange. In addition, the response cost procedure provides an elegant illustration of how positive and negative reinforcement may be considered to lie along a single continuum. In Weiner's procedure, the addition of a point to the response counter constituted a reinforcement. Conversely, the subtraction of a point from the response counter constituted a punishing stimulus. Presumably, no change in the response counter would constitute a neutral state of affairs. Weiner's procedure appears to provide excellent opportunity for studying concurrent reinforcement and punishment using a single stimulus dimension to program both the reinforcing and the punishing consequences.

VARIABLES RELATED TO THE ADMINISTRATION OF PUNISHMENT

Once the punishing stimulus has been specified, its effect depends greatly on the manner in which the stimulus is administered. The punishing stimulus may be introduced gradually or suddenly, immediately following a response or after a delay. It may be mild or severe; all of the responses may be punished or only some may be punished. It may be arranged to occur continuously or a vacation or "break" may be allowed. Since these considerations have been found to affect the degree of reduction obtained, each of them will be examined in detail.

Manner of Introduction

The manner in which punishment is first introduced is critical. The sudden introduction of punishment appears to produce a much larger reduction of the punished responses than if the punishment intensity is increased gradually. Masserman (1946) reports that cats would continue to respond under severe punishment if the punishing stimulus had been introduced at a low intensity and gradually increased over a period of time. Similarly, it has been noted (Azrin, Holz, & Hake, 1963) that

> Great care was necessary when introducing punishment to the subject for the first time. Previous study of continuous punishment had shown that if a high intensity (80 volts or more) was used initially, the responses were likely to be completely and usually irreversibly suppressed. If the initial introduction to punishment involved lower intensities (60 volts or less), performance was easily maintained even when the punishment was later increased to intensities as great as 130 volts.

Brethower and Reynolds (1962) noted that the initial introduction of high intensity punishment produced a great reduction of responses for one subject. In a direct experimental study of this problem, Miller (1960) found that less response reduction resulted from punishment if the intensity of the punishing stimulus was increased gradually over successive days. It appears then that the suppression of responses that is induced by punishment is accentuated by suddenly introducing the punishment stimulus at full intensity. This phenomenon is not restricted to the introduction of punishment. It has been found that a sudden and substantial increase of the prevailing intensity of the punishing stimulus will also accentuate the degree of suppression produced (Azrin, 1959a; 1960b; Holz & Azrin, 1963).

The basis for this accentuated effectiveness of punishment is not completely clear. It may very well be that the initial appearance of punishment is especially effective not only because of its aversive properties but also because it constitutes such a dramatic stimulus change. It is well known that the sudden introduction of a novel stimulus per se will reduce responding. This novelty may combine with the aversiveness of the punishing stimulus to produce a profound initial reduction of the punished responses.

Somewhat the same situation appears to exist with respect to positive reinforcement by means of food delivery. When food is delivered to a pigeon by means of a loud solenoid-operated magazine, the initial activation of the solenoid often causes a disruption in the animal's behavior. Paradoxically, then, it seems that the delivery of food reinforcements has actually reduced behavior. The usual procedure adopted under such circumstances is to adapt the animals to the sound of the solenoid before attempting to evaluate the effectiveness of the food reinforcement. By analogy, then, it would appear that punishment might well be similarly studied by first adapting the animal to the sheer novelty of the punishing stimulus rather than by presenting the punishing stimulus at a high intensity upon its initial presentation. In the absence of such precautions, it may well be that the extreme suppression induced by the initial occurrence of high intensity punishment may constitute a confounding of the aversive properties of the punishing stimulus with its properties as a novel stimulus. This explanation does not appear to account entirely for the sensitivity of the punished responses to a sudden increase in punishment. Chung (1965) has noted this same effect when the force requirement of a response was suddenly increased.

Immediacy of Punishment

In defining punishment we stated that the punishing stimulus should be delivered after the response that was to be punished. By implication, we were stating that such delivery should be immediate for maximum effectiveness. Estes (1944) raised the question of whether the immediacy of punishment was necessary. He performed a control experiment in which the punishing stimulus was not delivered immediately following the response but rather some time after a response occurred. The results of this non-immediate punishment procedure were compared with the results of an immediate punishment procedure. They indicated that the punishing stimulus was just as effective in reducing responses when it was non-immediate as when it was immediate. A study by Hunt and Brady (1955) obtained similar results. In both studies the administration of punishment was restricted to a period of less than one hour. Later studies (Azrin, 1956) obtained similar results in that immediate punishment was no more effective than non-immediate punishment during the first hour. After that time, however, the responses recovered substantially and often completely during non-immediate punishment, whereas the responses were reduced indefinitely and often completely during immediate punishment. For enduring effectiveness, the punishing stimulus should be delivered immediately.

When one wishes to deliver punishment immediately after a response, the technical procedure is straightforward. The study of non-immediate punishment, however, presents some methodological problems. Technically, four methods have been used to program non-immediate punishment. In one of these methods, the aversive stimulus is delivered by a timing device without regard to the subject's behavior (Azrin, 1956). The apparent disadvantage with this method is that the aversive stimulus may occasionally follow immediately after a response. To prevent this occasional pairing of the aversive stimulus with the response, a second method has been used wherein the experimenter observes the subject and delivers the shock only when the subject is not responding. Some investigators (Estes, 1944; Hunt & Brady, 1955) have used a combination of these two methods to avoid accidental coincidences of the responses and the punishing stimulus. A third method has been to deliver a punishing stimulus automatically whenever a fixed period of time has elapsed without a response. It would appear that this third procedure should be foolproof in eliminating any coincidences of the response and the punishing stimulus. Yet this is precisely the method which has been used extensively by Sidman (1953) to maintain rather than to eliminate behavior. When this method is used concurrently with positive reinforcement for a response (Azrin, 1958; Kelleher & Cook, 1959), the responses are found to increase rather than decrease as should be the case in punishment.

A fourth method of preventing the response from being followed by the onset of a punishing stimulus is to abandon the use of a discrete punishing stimulus. In this simplest of all methods of non-contingent stimulation, the punishing stimulus is presented continuously rather than as a discrete event. If the stimulus is presented without interruption, no possibility exists for either the onset or the termination of the stimulus to coincide with the occurrence of a particular response. This method of programming non-immediate punishment avoids the disadvantages of the previous three methods. Yet electric shock cannot be used easily in comparing this method of non-immediate punishment with immediate punishment since continuous electric shock generates skeletal reactions that may interfere with the emission of responses. Noise is a more appropriate punishing stimulus to use for continuous presentation since continuous noise does not appear to produce interfering skeletal reactions. In one study which used noise as an immediate punishment, a comparison was made with the effects of continuous noise (Azrin, 1958). Noise was programmed with human subjects in two ways: in the immediate punishment procedure a burst of noise followed each response immediately, whereas in the second procedure the noise was delivered continuously. It was found that the responses were reduced for as long as the punishing contingency was present in the procedure where the noise was delivered immediately following the responses. When the noise was delivered on a continuous rather than on a response-contingent basis, no enduring reduction resulted. It appears, then, that the immediacy of punishment is a critical determinant of the degree of response reduction obtained. Under all four methods, it is only during the initial stages of punishment that non-immediate punishment has an appreciable effect in reducing responding.

Intensity of Punishment

The intensity of punishment has been found to be a major determinant of the degree of response reduction by punishment. All studies of the intensity of punishment have found that the greater the intensity of the punishing stimulus, the greater is the reduction of the punished responses (Appel, 1963; Azrin, 1959b; 1960a; Azrin, Holz, & Hake, 1963; Brethower & Reynolds, 1962; Dinsmoor, 1952; Estes, 1944). When electric shock has been used, as in the above studies, suppression has been virtually complete at high intensities (Appel, 1961; Azrin, 1959a). As indicated previously, the wide range of effectiveness of electric shock constitutes its principal advantage. The severity of electric shock can be manipulated over a range wide enough to produce whatever degree of suppression is desired. Not all aversive stimuli have been found to possess the degree of effectiveness of electric shock. As was seen previously in Figure 3, time-out punishment produced little suppression even when the time-out duration was quite extended. Similarly, punishment by means of intense noise does not seem to be capable of completely eliminating responding within the practicable range of intensities that has been employed. Using humans as subjects, Azrin (1958) found relatively little suppression when the intensity of noise punishment was 105 decibels or less. Intensities as great as 135 decibels reduced the responses by approximately 50 percent. When pigeons were used as subjects, Holz and Azrin (1962a) found that noise punishment reduced the responses by no more than 80 percent even though the intensity of the noise was 138 decibels. When a bar-slap is used as a punishing stimulus, the degree of suppression seems to have been similarly mild (Skinner, 1938) although no experimental manipulation was made of the intensity of the bar-slap to determine whether the degree of suppression could be increased. Air blasts appear to be quite effective. Masserman (1946) reported complete suppression when responses were punished by air blast. Again, no study was made of changes in the degree of suppression as a function of the intensity of the air blast. The ability of electric shock to produce whatever degree of suppression is desired probably accounts in part for the widespread use of electric shock as a punishing stimulus.

Schedule of Punishment

Fixed Ratio

In the simplest instance, a punishing stimulus is delivered for every response. This punishment schedule may be designated as continuous punishment by analogy with positive reinforcement. Alternatively, a punishing stimulus may be delivered for every nth response (FR punishment). The initial introduction of FR punishment produced positive acceleration during the period between successive deliveries of the punishing stimulus (Azrin, Holz, & Hake, 1963). Under continued exposure, a uniform rate of response emerged with no acceleration or deceleration of the punished responses between successive deliveries of the punishing stimulus. The uniformity of the response rate prevailed when the ratio of unpunished to punished responses was increased from 1:1 to 1000:1, the uniformity of the response pattern was not altered by changes in the intensity of punishment or the level of food deprivation, although each of these operations did change the absolute rate of response. The frequency of the punished responses was a direct function of the fixed ratio: the greater the proportion of punished responses, the greater was the response reduction. Thus, continuous punishment (FR1) produced the greatest suppression. The same superiority of continuous punishment over intermittent punishment was obtained by Zimmerman and Ferster (1963) using a period of time-out as the punishing stimulus. Hendry and Van-Toler (1964) have found negative acceleration of responses under fixed ratio punishment when the responses were maintained by continuous reinforcement rather than by the variable interval schedule of reinforcement used by Azrin, Holz, and Hake (1963).

Fixed Interval

Under FI punishment, the punishing stimulus is delivered for the first response that is emitted after a fixed duration since the previous punishment. This schedule has been used with some modification by Hunt and Brady (1955) and Azrin (1956). In both studies, a general reduction of responses was produced by the first few deliveries of punishing stimulus. After extended exposure to the FI schedule, it was found (Azrin, 1956) that the response rate dropped to zero as the moment approached for the scheduled punisher to be delivered. The existence of this "anticipatory" suppression demonstrates how the effect of punishment can be specifically restricted to the moment at which the punishment is scheduled. This temporal patterning of responses appears to be analogous to the temporal patterning observed under FI food reinforcement (Skinner, 1938) except that negative rather than positive acceleration of the response results.

Other types of punishment schedules have not been extensively studied. In comparing continuous punishment with an intermittent punishment schedule, Estes (1944) found that continuous punishment was more effective than the intermittent punishment for as long as the punishment was in effect. This finding is in agreement with the finding concerning fixed ratio punishment which is also an intermittent schedule. One study compared the VI with the FI schedule of punishment and found that the former produced more suppression (Azrin, 1956). Another example of a schedule of punishment is the differential punishment of high response rates by Ferster (1958).

Vacation from Punishment

It might appear that a "vacation" or time-out from a period of punishment would allow the punished response to gain strength. The results obtained indicate that this is not the case. One method of providing a vacation is to prevent the response from occurring (no response, no reinforcements, no punishment) for a period of time between sessions. The results indicate that reintroduction into the punishment situation suppresses the responses as much (Masserman, 1946) and often more (Azrin, 1959b; 1960b) than before the vacation. This high level of suppression also resulted when a single session was briefly interrupted (Azrin, 1960b). A dramatic example is provided by Masserman (1946) who gave a rest of 20 months to a cat whose responses had been completely suppressed. When the subject was reintroduced into the experimental situation, the responses remained completely suppressed even though the punishing stimulus had been discontinued.

A second type of vacation allows the response to be reinforced but the punishment is temporarily discontinued. It might appear that the response would be strengthened by the additional reinforcements and resist the effects of any later punishment. Again, the findings indicate that if anything, the withdrawal of punishment results in as great (Brethower & Reynolds, 1962) or greater (Azrin, 1960b; Masserman, 1946) suppression when the punishment is later reintroduced. The lapse of time per se does not reduce the suppressive effects of punishment.

We have seen that the effectiveness of a punishing stimulus is influenced by the intensity, frequency, scheduling, and temporal distribution of the stimulus. Each of these factors has also been found to be important as a determinant of the effectiveness of a reinforcing stimulus. For example, delayed reinforcement has been found to be less effective (but not ineffective) in maintaining response by food reinforcement (Skinner, 1938). Similarly, we have seen that delayed punishment was less effective (but by no means ineffective) in suppressing responses. And a rest period or time-out period has been found to increase the effectiveness of a positive reinforcer (Ferster & Skinner, 1957; Reynolds, 1961) just as we have seen that a rest period or vacation has increased the effectiveness of punishment. Positive reinforcement and punishment appear to be comparable in many other respects as we shall see again in later sections.

As a rough rule of thumb, it appears appropriate to describe punishment as a process similar to positive reinforcement in terms of its determinants, but opposite in terms of the direction of behavioral change. For example, frequency is an important determinant of food-reinforced responses (Skinner, 1938) as well as of punished responses. An increased frequency of food delivery will increase the food-reinforced responses, but an increased frequency of delivery of punishment will decrease the punished responses. Additional research is certainly necessary to elucidate the generality of this theoretical comparison of reinforcement and punishment. At a descriptive level, however, punishment and reinforcement are inextricably intertwined: the very existence of the punishment process demands that there be some concurrent reinforcement procedures, as we shall see in the next section.

REINFORCEMENT VARIABLES INFLUENCING PUNISHMENT EFFECTS

If a response is punished but not reinforced in some manner, it will extinguish through the absence of reinforcement, and the use of punishment will only expedite the elimination of the response. Dinsmoor (1952) has made this same point regarding the necessary existence of reinforcement.

> In order that a person may learn to make a certain response in the first place, some type of reinforcement is presumably necessary. If the reinforcement follows as a simple physical consequence of the act, there seems to be no reason to assume that reinforcement should cease whenever punishment begins. Indeed, if the reinforcement is long withheld, extinction sets in, and there may no longer be a response to be punished (p. 27).

An enduring punishment situation must include reinforcement as well as punishment for the responses. Let us examine several aspects of the reinforcement procedure that have been found to be relevant to the effectiveness of punishment.

Schedules of Reinforcement

Since the punished response is also reinforced, the choice of a particular reinforcement schedule should be relevant in determining the effect of a punishing stimulus. In the simplest case, every response is reinforced as well as punished. A schedule of continuous reinforcement creates a special situation in that the punishment is delivered at the very moment that the organism is approaching the reinforcement as in Masserman's study (1946). As a result, the punishing air blast eliminated the feeding behavior as well as the operant response. This problem is minimized by using an intermittent schedule of reinforcement where the punishing stimulus is not paired exclusively with the food reinforcement since the non-reinforced responses are also punished.

The type of response reduction that is induced by punishment has been found to depend on the type of schedule of reinforcement that is maintaining the punished responses. When a VI schedule of reinforcement is used alone, the responses occur at a fairly uniform rate (Ferster & Skinner, 1957). Punishment for every response reduces the rate but does not change this basic uniformity (Azrin, 1960a; 1960b; Brethower & Reynolds, 1962; Dinsmoor, 1952; Holz & Azrin, 1961).

When an FI schedule of reinforcement is used, a positive acceleration of responses normally results between reinforcements (Ferster & Skinner, 1957). The degree of this response acceleration can be considered to be a type of "temporal discrimination" or patterning. Two measures have been developed (Fry, Kelleher, & Cook, 1960; Herrnstein & Morse, 1957b) for quantifying the degree of response acceleration. When punishment is delivered for every response, the number of FI responses may be reduced considerably (Azrin, 1958; Estes, 1944; Skinner, 1938) but the degree of temporal discrimination remains unchanged (Azrin & Holz, 1961).

Under FR reinforcement, the response rate is usually bivalued: a period of zero responding occurs immediately after reinforcement followed by an abrupt change to a "ratio-run" at a very high response rate (Skinner, 1938). When punishment is delivered for every response during FR reinforcement, the post-reinforcement pause is lengthened but the high response rate is reduced only slightly (Azrin, 1959b). Dardano and Sauerbrunn (1964a) found the same result when a single punishment was given for the first response of the fixed ratio. The initial part of the ratio run appears to be very sensitive to the effects of punishment. This can be seen in a second experiment by Dardano and Sauerbrunn (1964b) in which a long pause preceded the ratio-run when intense shock was delivered during the initial part of the ratio. The pause was shorter when the intense shock was delivered during the later part of the ratio. In a third experiment, Dardano and Sauerbrunn (1964c) found that their subjects preferred a high ratio requirement that was not punished to a low ratio requirement that was punished. The use of punishment during FR reinforcement does not manifest itself in a lower rate as would be expected from the basic definition of punishment. The terminal rate of response remains fairly constant; it is the overall rate of response that is reduced.

A reinforcement procedure may also be arranged in such a way that there is differential reinforcement of low rates. This drl schedule ordinarily produces a low rate of responding in which the interresponse times usually approximate the minimum interresponse time required for reinforcement (Anger, 1956). Occasional response bursts are obtained; this is seen in a high frequency of very short interresponse times in the interresponse time distribution. When every response is punished during drl reinforcement, these short interresponse times are eliminated, even at the low punishment intensities that do not change the rest of the interresponse time distribution (Holz, Azrin, & Ulrich, 1963). At the higher punishment intensities, the modal interresponse time is lengthened.

We have seen that the choice of a particular reinforcement schedule to maintain the punished response will determine the temporal patterning of the responses during punishment. In order to specify the nature of the response reduction by punishment, it is necessary to specify the schedule of reinforcement that is maintaining the responses. The simple statement that punishment reduces the punished responses is inadequate and occasionally inaccurate.

Reinforcement Frequency

Two studies (Azrin & Holz, 1961; Estes, 1944) have compared the degree of response reduction when punishment was applied during extinction with the degree of reduction when punishment was applied during reinforcement. Both studies found that the punishment produced a lower response rate when applied during the periods of extinction. Similarly, both studies showed that as long as the punishment was maintained for the duration of the extinction period, the extinction process could be considerably shortened, both with respect to the number of responses as well as with respect to the time to extinction (see Figure 4). It appears, then, that a reduced frequency of reinforcement and an increased intensity of punishment both operate in the same direction; both procedures reduce the rate of the response. Thus, when both are used simultaneously, the elimination of the behavior is more rapid than when either punishment or extinction is used alone.

We have seen that the presence or absence of reinforcement of the punished response determines the effectiveness of the punishment. It is also true that the addition of punishment alters the frequency of the reinforcement for the punished response. As stated earlier, punishment is usually used to counteract a concurrent reinforcement. Since the delivery of reinforcement depends on the emission of responses, the reduction of responses by punishment usually leads to a reduction of the reinforcement frequency as well. If an FR schedule of reinforcement is used, an inverse interrelationship exists between the intensity of punishment and the reinforcement frequency (Azrin, 1959b), since the frequency of reinforcement is reduced in direct proportion to the effectiveness of the punishment. Under interval schedules, the number of responses emitted is usually much greater than the number needed to obtain the maximum frequency of reinforcement. Reduction of the response frequency by punishment, therefore, leads to

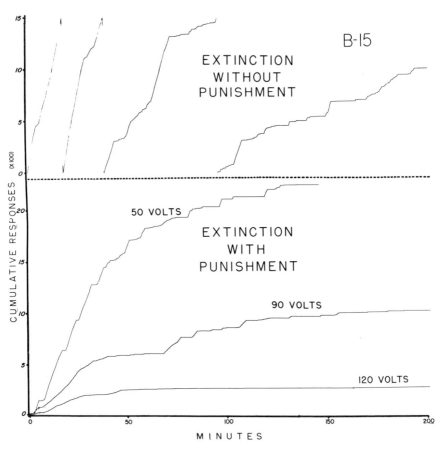

Figure 4. The effects of extinction of fixed interval responding at various intensities of maintained punishment. No food reinforcement was available after the first reinforcement at the start of the session. Punishment was delivered after every response. (From Azrin & Holz, 1961.)

little or no reduction of the frequency of reinforcement except when the responses are almost completely suppressed (Azrin & Holz, 1961; Holz, Azrin, & Ulrich, 1963). It is likely that the interval schedules of reinforcement have been used by many investigators because of this high degree of independence between the punishment and the frequency of reinforcement.

The drl schedule of reinforcement is especially useful as a method of studying punishment. Since punishment produces longer pauses between responses, the result is that the frequency of reinforcement often increases during punishment (Holz, Azrin, & Ulrich, 1963). Punishment of drl responses may be considered to be "in the best interests" of the punished subject (increased frequency of positive reinforcement). In summary, the punishment process leads indirectly to a decreased reinforcement frequency under ratio reinforcement schedules, an increased reinforcement frequency under drl reinforcement, and little change under interval reinforcement.

A common view of punishment is that it interferes with desirable or productive performance. The use of drl reinforcement is an instance in which punishment of a response actually increases the efficiency of that response. Thus, it is inaccurate to consider the concurrent use of punishment and reinforcement as necessarily constituting a "conflict" situation regarding the receipt of reinforcement. Indeed, it is only during the ratio schedules of reinforcement that the reductive effects of punishment lead to a consistent decrease of reinforcement.

Motivation to Respond

The extent to which a food-reinforced response resists the effects of punishment depends on the degree of food deprivation. Dinsmoor (1952) found that responses were reduced by punishment whether the subject was deprived of food to a large or a slight degree. However, under severe food deprivation, the responses were reduced by a smaller proportion. When a long history of VI food reinforcement has been in effect, it has been found that the response rate does not change appreciably as a function of the degree of food deprivation (Ferster & Skinner, 1957). Yet, when punishment is added after this long history, the punished response rate appears to be unusually sensitive to even slight changes in food deprivation (Azrin, 1960b; Azrin, Holz, & Hake, 1963). In one instance, punishment was rendered almost ineffective by increasing the degree of motivation for emitting the punished responses (Azrin, Holz, & Hake, 1963). If the responses have been completely suppressed under low food motivation, however, an increase in motivation does not appear to be effective in restoring the responses (Masserman, 1946; Storms, Boroczi, & Broen, 1962).

Number of Responses Available

In most studies of punishment, a single response is made available to the subject for obtaining the reinforcement. When this response is also punished, the subject has no alternative means available for obtaining the food reinforcement. If the punishment causes the subject to cease responding entirely, no reinforcement results. Let us now consider the situation in which the subject does have some alternative response available that is unpunished and that can produce the reinforcement. We have seen examples of this previously in the experiment by Holz, Azrin, and Ayllon (1963) in a preceding section on the effects of time-out. We may question at this point whether the results of this experiment are applicable to punishing situations in general or whether they are restricted to situations that utilize the unique properties of a time-out period as a punishing stimulus.

An experiment was conducted by Herman and Azrin (1964) in which the essential features of the Holz procedure were repeated. However, instead of using time-out as the punishing stimulus, noise was used. The results otained with noise, as seen in Figure 5, were essentially the same as those obtained with the time-out. The response rate in a single response situation was affected only slightly at a given intensity of noise punishment, whereas the punished response rate on the same manipulandum in an alternative response situation was reduced completely and almost immediately. It appears that the alternative response situation will lead to a greater suppression of the punished response than a single response situation.

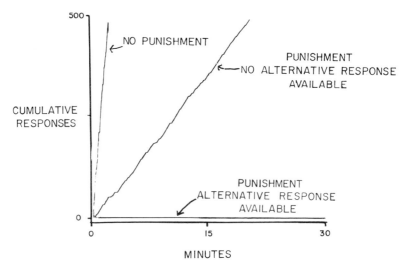

Figure 5. Cumulative response records of the punished responses of human subjects under a VI schedule of reinforcement. The reinforcement deliveries are not indicated. The punishment was an annoying buzzing sound that was delivered for each response. (Based on data from Herman & Azrin, 1964.)

In an additional experiment (Azrin, unpublished data), pigeons were used as subjects and electrode shock was used as the punishing stimulus to study the effects of an alternative response situation as compared with a single response situation. Two circular response keys were used as the manipulanda. Pecks on either key were reinforced according to an FR 25 schedule of food reinforcement. When only one key was made available to the subject by covering the second key, all 25 responses in the fixed ratio requirement had to be emitted on the available manipulandum. When both keys were available, the subject could distribute the 25 responses in any manner; all, part, or none of the 25 responses could be made on a given manipulandum. Punishment via tail-shock was administered for each response on one of the keys. When only one manipulandum was available (single response situation), a punishment was recorded for each response. When both manipulanda were available in the alternative response situation, only the responses on one manipulandum (the preferred manipulandum) were punished.

Part of the results of this experiment are summarized in Figure 6 which shows the response rate on the punished manipulandum at various intensities of shock. It can be seen that the rate of responding on the punished manipulandum was an inverse function of the shock intensity, as shown above in the section on the intensity of punishment. No reduction of responding could be seen up to about 40 volts in the single response situation; at 50 volts, the rate was reduced by only 10 percent. Even at 60 volts, the re-

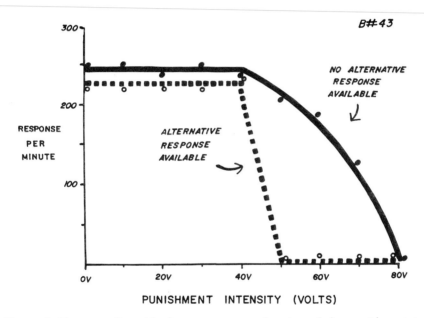

Figure 6. The rate of punished responses as a function of the punishment intensity. The data are from a pigeon that had been reinforced under an FR 25 schedule. Two response keys were available; responses on both keys were effective in fulfilling the FR requirement. Punishment was delivered for all responses on the preferred key concurrently with the FR food schedule. The intensity of the punishing shock was increased in steps of ten volts, allowing at least five days at each intensity. This procedure was carried out with the non-preferred key covered (no alternative response available) as well as with both response keys uncovered (alternative response available). (From Azrin & Holz, unpublished data.)

sponse rate was still about 70 percent of the unpunished rate. In the alternative response situation, the punishment had a more profound effect. At 50 volts, the responses on the punished manipulandum were completely suppressed even though the same intensity of punishment produced very little reduction in the single response situation. We may conclude, therefore, that the alternative response situation leads to greater suppression by a given intensity of punishment than does a single response situation, whether the aversive stimulus is a period of time-out, an annoying noise, electrode shock, or whether the subjects are human or pigeon.

Escape from a Punishing Stimulus

We have just considered the situation in which an alternative unpunished response is concurrently available to the subject while a different response is being punished. Let us now consider the situation in which the subject has available a means of escaping from the situation in which the response is punished to a situation in which the response is unpunished. In the usual punishment procedure, the subject has the choice of responding and receiving the punishment as well as the reinforcement, or else the subject may not respond, in which case he receives neither. The alternative response procedure differs from the usual procedure in that a second response is available providing the same frequency of reinforcement but no punishment. In the third procedure that we are now considering, the subject is given the opportunity to escape entirely from the situation involving punishment.

The procedure is as follows: A pigeon is reinforced according to a fixed ratio schedule of food reinforcement in order to build up a high frequency of responses. Punishment is then delivered in the form of an electric shock following each response, thereby providing the usual procedure of concurrent punishment and food reinforcement. A second response key is then made available. A response on this second response key produces neither reinforcement nor punishment. Rather, it produces a stimulus change consisting of a change of illumination as well as a change in the ambient noise level. During this changed stimulus, the subject can respond on the usual response key and obtain food reinforcement but without any deliveries of punishment. The function of the escape response on the second response key, then, is to provide a period of escape during which the response may be emitted without being punished. Once having made an escape response, the period of safety lasts until the delivery of the reinforcement. Immediately following the food reinforcement, the subject must emit another escape response in order to reinstate the escape period.

Figure 7, based on data from Azrin, Hake, Holz, and Hutchinson (1965), shows the results of this procedure. When no punishment, or very mild punishment, was delivered, very few escape responses were made.

When the intensity reached 40 volts, the subject was emitting sufficient escape responses to remain in the safe situation for almost the entire experimental session. The same figure shows that the responses were displaced from the stimulus situation involving punishment to the stimulus situation in which punishment was absent. Under this procedure, the punishment not only led to a reduction of the punished responses, but it drove the subject out of the stimulus situation in which the punishment had been programmed.

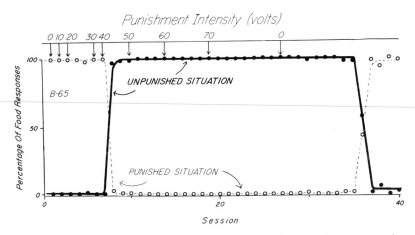

Figure 7. Responses of a typical pigeon for FR 25 food reinforcement. The responses were concurrently punished (solid curve) unless the subject emitted an escape response on a second response key, thereby producing a period during which the responses could be emitted without the punishment (dotted curve). (From Azrin, Hake, Holz, & Hutchinson, 1965.)

The above investigation experimentally compared this escape procedure with the usual punishment procedure in which no escape was possible. The results of this comparison are shown in Figure 8, taken from Azrin, Hake, Holz, and Hutchinson (1965). The punishment-escape procedure resulted in greater suppression of the punished responses than did the nonescape procedure. The solid line of Figure 8 shows the progressive reduction in responses as a function of punishment intensity without opportunity to escape. It can be seen from this figure that complete suppression was not obtained until an intensity of 70 volts was reached. At 30 volts, little or no suppression was observed when no escape was possible. Under the punishment-escape procedure (dotted line), however, 30 volts produced almost complete elimination of the punished responses. At the fairly mild intensity of 40 volts, the punished response was reduced to a zero level. Thus, an intensity of punishment which produced little or no suppression in the procedure in which there was no opportunity to escape produced complete

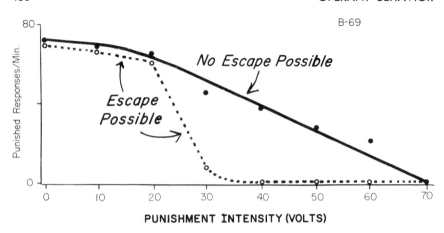

Figure 8. Rate of punished responses when no escape was possible compared with rate of punished responses when escape was possible. A single response on an "escape" key eliminated the punishment for a period of time that was terminated by the next reinforcement. The food responses were being maintained on an FR 25 schedule. (From Azrin, Hake, Holz, & Hutchinson, 1965.)

suppression in the punishment-escape procedure. In order to evaluate the strength of this escape behavior, a third part of the procedure required the subject to emit more than one response in order to produce the escape period. It was found (see Figure 9) that fixed ratio requirements up to about 100 responses could be maintained, using the escape period as the reinforcing event. Similarly, when the escape response was scheduled according to an FI schedule, the usual FI pattern of responses emerged. Thus, it seems clear that the tendency to escape from a severely punishing situation was sufficiently great to maintain substantial levels of escape responding. These results show that a major effect of punishing a response is to generate a strong tendency on the part of the subject to escape from the punishing situation entirely. This tendency to escape from the punished situation is seen even at intensities of punishment that are not severe enough to suppress the punished response itself.

We have seen that the reinforcement procedure that is used to maintain a response is a critical determinant of the effectiveness of punishment on that response. The same punishment intensity that completely eliminates responses under one set of reinforcement procedures may not affect the response at all under a different set of reinforcement procedures. It is not sufficient to specify the variables related to the administration of punishment, such as intensity, immediacy, and gradualness. Equally important are the frequency and schedule of reinforcement, the motivation to respond, as well as the opportunity to obtain the reinforcement by means of an unpunished response or in an unpunished situation. The contribution of these be-

FR Escape From Punishment

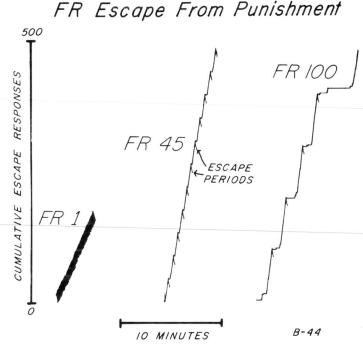

Figure 9. Fixed ratio reinforcement of escape responses by a period of escape from punishment. The escape periods are indicated by the short oblique line on the response record. The recording paper did not move during the escape periods. The three escape response records were taken from the start of the experimental sessions for one subject. During the escape period, responses on a different response key were being reinforced. (From Azrin, Hake, Holz, & Hutchinson, 1965.)

havioral variables is considerable. Failure to observe any reductive effects of a stimulus that is presumably punishing may be attributable to the reinforcement situation used and not to its ineffectiveness as a punishing stimulus.

CHARACTERISTICS OF THE PUNISHMENT PROCESS

We have examined in some detail various factors that determine the effectiveness of punishment. Let us now view some of the changes in behavior that appear to be a characteristic result of the use of punishment. First, we shall consider the results of punishment studies in terms of the permanence, rapidity, and degree of suppression during continued punishment. Then, we shall go on to examine some distinctive changes in behavior upon the termination of punishment. Next, we will deal with the discriminative aspects of punishment, which have received relatively little recognition in spite of their considerable importance. The discriminative aspect of punishment is concerned with the relation of a punishing stimulus to other events. These other events may concern the presence or absence of punishment itself as in a situation involving intermittent punishment or alternating periods of punishment. The punishment may be discriminatively associated with a reinforcing stimulus or a period of reinforcement, or even with a stimulus associated with reinforcement. We shall see that there are characteristic changes in behavior that result from punishment; but some of these changes derive from the unique association that the punishment has with other events, rather than from the strictly aversive properties of the punishing stimulus.

Permanence of Suppression

One of the most dramatic characteristics of punishment is the virtual irreversibility or permanence of the response reduction once the behavior has become completely suppressed. Investigators have noted that the punished response does not recover for a long period of time even after the punishment contingency has been removed (Appel, 1961; Azrin, 1960b; Masserman, 1946; Storms, Boroczi, & Broen, 1962). For example, in one study (Azrin, 1960b) that used very intense shock as the punishing stimulus, it was found that the responses were reduced to zero and did not recover for a period of six days even though the punishment was no longer present. In that study, it was found that the likelihood of obtaining such enduring suppression was a function of the punishment intensity. At lower intensities of punishment, this enduring and partly irreversible effect of punishment did not occur. An explanation of these enduring effects of punishment may be attempted by taking into account the absoluteness of the degree of suppression. Intense punishment did not merely reduce responses to the unconditioned or operant level, but reduced them to an absolute level of zero. Since punishment is delivered only after a response occurs, there is no opportunity for the subject to detect the absence of punishment unless he responds. If punishment is so severe as to completely eliminate the responses, then the opportunity for detecting the absence of punishment no longer exists.

The same type of reasoning was previously used in analyzing the persistence of avoidance behavior when the shock contingency was eliminated. In both the punishment and avoidance procedures, the animal's behavior may be altered in such a way as to eliminate virtually all contact between himself and the shock presentations. For purpose of comparison, we may compare punishment with extinction of food reinforcement in terms of the degree of reduction of responding obtained. Extinction leads to a reduction of responses; long term extinction reduces the behavior to the unconditioned or operant level (Skinner, 1938), especially if spontaneous recovery is being observed. The continued existence of responses during extinction, albeit at a low operant level, ensures that the animal will adjust his behavior in accord with any experimental change of the extinction procedure. In contrast with extinction, punishment can produce a complete and enduring reduction of responses that will prevent a return of the punished responses even after the punishment is removed.

Rapidity of the Effects of Punishment

How quickly does punishment reduce behavior? Virtually all studies of punishment have been in complete agreement that the reduction of responses by punishment is immediate if the punishment is at all effective. When the data have been presented in terms of the number of responses per day, the responses have been drastically reduced or eliminated on the very first day in which punishment was administered. When the data have been presented in terms of moment-to-moment changes, the reduction of responses has resulted within the first few deliveries of punishment (Azrin, 1956; 1959a; 1959b; 1960b; Dinsmoor, 1952) or within a few minutes (Estes, 1944). The extent (Estes, 1944) and duration (Azrin, 1960b) of this initial suppression is, of course, a direct function of the intensity of punishment. A minor variation on this rule regarding the immediacy of the effect was a short-lived response burst following the introduction of the bar-slap as a punishing stimulus (Skinner, 1938).

Recovery During Punishment

Just as intense punishment has been found to produce a characteristic completeness and irreversibility of suppression, so has mild punishment been found to allow a characteristic recovery from punishment. Figure 10, from Azrin (1960a), shows the performance of a pigeon which was being reinforced by food deliveries. When punishment was introduced for the first time in the form of a brief electric shock after each response, the response rate decreased substantially to about 50 percent of the unpunished rate during the first 30 minutes of punishment. On subsequent days, however, the response rate climbed gradually until almost complete recovery had occurred by the tenth hour. Recovery of responses also occurred within each session while punishment was still in effect. In the same series of studies, it was found that the degree of recovery was only partial at higher intensities of punishment. When the intensity of punishment was very high (about 100 volts or so), no recovery resulted. Thus, the degree of recovery during punishment is a function of the intensity of punishment. This recovery process has been found to characterize many punishment situations. Recovery has been observed when using a bar-slap with rats (Skinner, 1938), noise with

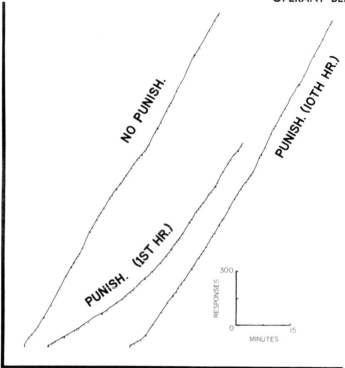

Figure 10. Complete recovery of responding during maintained mild punishment. Each curve is the cumulative record of the responses during a one-hour daily session. A VI 1 schedule of food reinforcement was in effect at all times. The small oblique lines on the record indicate delivery of the reinforcement. The punishment was delivered after each response during the punishment session. (From Azrin, 1960b.)

pigeons (Holz & Azrin, 1962a), foot-shock with pigeons (Azrin, 1956), shock with monkeys (Hake & Azrin, 1963), and conditioned punishment with pigeons (Hake & Azrin, 1965). Not all studies have shown this recovery process, however, as evident when time-out was used (Holz, Azrin, & Ulrich, 1963). Thus, it appears that the recovery phenomenon depends not only on the intensity of the punishing stimulus, but also on other variables, such as the nature of the punishing stimulus.

Recovery Following Punishment

Punishment Contrast Effect

Another general characteristic of behavior arising from the punishment process is an increase in behavior following the termination of the punishment. Figure 11 shows that when punishment was no longer delivered, the responses occurred at a rate that exceeded the unpunished level. This unusually high rate of responding is maintained only temporarily, of course, and the responses eventually returned to the usual unpunished baseline. It has been found that the compensatory increase occurred after use of shock intensities up to the point of complete suppression (Azrin, 1960b). But, as was previously noted, when complete suppression of responses oc-

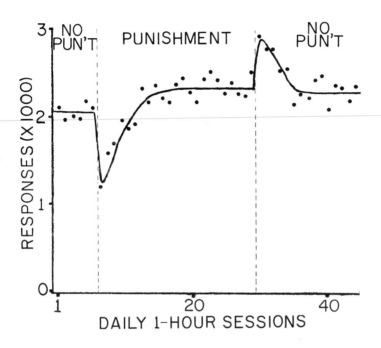

Figure 11. Effect of the addition and removal of punishment upon the food-reinforced responses of one subject. The punishment was a brief electric shock which followed every response on the days between those represented by the vertical dashed lines. Food reinforcement was obtained on a VI 1 schedule on all days. (From Azrin, 1960a.)

curs, termination of the punishment contingency may not lead to recovery of the responses, much less any compensatory increase. Figure 11 also shows that the compensatory increase occurs following extended punishment even when the response rate during punishment has recovered to its pre-punishment level. One interpretation of this post-punishment increase in responses (Estes, 1944) has been that the increased rate was "making up for" the decrease of responses that had been produced by the punishment. But as Figure 11 shows, this increase resulted even when the rate of punished responses recovered completely and there is nothing to be "made up." It may be more appropriate, therefore, to describe this effect as a *punishment contrast* effect rather than a compensatory effect. Along these same lines, it has been discovered that severe or extended punishment reduces the response to such an extent that the extra responses in the contrast phenomenon do not equal or make up for the reduction of responses during the period of punishment (Azrin, 1960b; Estes, 1944).

The explanation of this punishment contrast effect is not altogether clear. We have already seen that its existence cannot be accounted for on the basis of a compensatory increase that makes up for responses lost during punishment. Another explanation is possible. It is known (Ferster & Skinner, 1957) that if a period of extinction or time-out is introduced in the middle of a session, then the post-extinction responding may be increased. Stated otherwise, it appears that an increased rate of responding follows a reduced frequency of reinforcement. This general principle has been elaborated in some detail by the work of Reynolds (1961). It will be recalled that some punishment procedures simultaneously reduce the frequency of reinforcement to some extent. When one eliminates the punishment contingency, one is simultaneously allowing an increased frequency of reinforcement. It might very well be that the increased level of responding that is seen upon the discontinuation of punishment (post-punishment increase) is really a product of the change in reinforcement frequency rather than the change in punishment.

If one uses a ratio schedule of reinforcement to maintain the behavior (Azrin, 1959b), the post-punishment increase can be accounted for in these terms since any decrease in the rate of responding necessarily leads to a corresponding decrease in the rate of reinforcement. When using an interval schedule of reinforcement to maintain the responses, however, the degree of reduction of the reinforcement is usually very slight unless the responses are completely suppressed. It is unlikely that this decrease could account for the post-punishment increase of responses. Furthermore, the results of experiments using a drl schedule of food reinforcement make it quite clear that the altered reinforcement frequency cannot explain the post-punishment increase in responding. As stated above, Holz, Azrin, & Ulrich (1963) found that punishment actually increased the frequency of drl reinforcement during the period of punishment. Yet the results showed that the post-punishment increase still occurred upon the discontinuation of punishment of the drl responses. In this case, the punishment contrast effect followed an increased rather than a decreased frequency of reinforcement. It would appear, then, that there are two types of contrast phenomena; one that occurs upon the transition from a lower to a higher frequency of reinforcement (reinforcement contrast) and the second upon the transition from a high frequency of punishment to a lowered frequency of punishment (punishment contrast). The two types of contrast phenomena have been experimentally analyzed and compared by Holz and Azrin (1962a) and found to be separate processes.

Gradual Recovery Following Punishment

It was seen above that when the punishment procedure was discontinued, an unusually high level of responding resulted almost immediately. This immediate return of the responses has been observed only after continuous punishment. Intermittent punishment leads to a gradual recovery of the responses after the punishment has been terminated (Azrin, Holz, & Hake, 1963; Estes, 1944). We had seen previously that intermittent punishment produced less suppression during the period of punishment than did continuous punishment. We can summarize the comparison between continuous and intermittent punishment as follows: Continuous punishment produces more suppression than does intermittent punishment for as long as the punishment contingency is maintained. However, after the punishment contingency has been discontinued, continuous punishment allows more rapid recovery of the responses, possibly because the absence of punishment can be more rapidly discriminated.

At very high intensities of punishment, the relationship is probably more complicated. Continuous punishment would be expected to produce complete suppression whereas intermittent punishment would produce only partial suppression. Since recovery is delayed or absent after complete suppression, it appears that at very high intensities continuous punishment would be more effective than intermittent punishment, in terms of permanence as well as the extent of suppression.

Discrimination and Generalization via Punishment

Discrimination of Punishment Conditions

One especially informative procedure for studying punishment is to present two stimuli alternately, punishing the responses during one stimulus (warning) while allowing the responses to go unpunished during the other stimulus (safe period). This procedure results in a reduction of responses during the warning stimulus but little or no lasting reduction during the safe stimulus (Azrin, 1956; Brethower & Reynolds, 1962; Dinsmoor, 1952; Hunt & Brady, 1955). Thus, punishment can be used to produce a discrimination between two stimulus situations. When the punishing stimulus is delivered only intermittently during the warning stimulus, we find that the warning stimulus itself controls a low rate of responding (Azrin, 1956; Hunt & Brady, 1955). In one study, for example, the responses were punished on an average of once every two minutes during the warning stimulus (Azrin, 1956). After a while, the response rate abruptly dropped to zero as soon as the warning stimulus appeared, even though a punishing stimulus had not yet been delivered during that particular presentation of the warning stimulus.

Generalization of Punishment

When we punish responses in the presence of one stimulus and not in the presence of another stimulus, it is found that suppression is fairly restricted to the former. Let us examine now what punishment does to responses in the presence of the other stimulus. The findings are that some suppression of the responses generalizes to the safe period initially; but after continued exposure, the responses during the safe stimulus recover substantially, usually to the unpunished level (Azrin, 1956; Dinsmoor, 1952; Honig & Slivka, 1964). Indeed, the responses during the safe period eventually reach a level exceeding the level present before the punishment was introduced in the other stimulus (Brethower & Reynolds, 1962). This increase during the unpunished stimulus is the same punishment contrast effect that has been described previously.

Figure 12, representing unpublished work conducted in our laboratory, shows the typical results obtained when punishment is delivered for responses in one stimulus but not another. Although this figure is included primarily to portray the phenomenon of generalization of suppression, the results also depict the phenomenon of the immediacy of effect of punishment, the establishment of a discrimination based on punishment, and the usual recovery during punishment, as well as the punishment contrast effect. Two stimuli alternate every ten minutes; the moment of change-over is indicated by the vertical reset line of the pen. In the top segment no punishment is present, and the rate of response is approximately equal in both stimuli. Food reinforcements are programmed for the responses but are not indicated on the record. In the second segment from the top, a brief shock consisting of an intensity of about 60 volts is delivered after each response in the presence of one stimulus (as indicated by the shading in the figure). It can be seen that responses were suppressed during both of the stimuli. This generalization of suppression endures for ten days. Not until the eleventh day do responses return, and then primarily during the safe stimulus. By the twelfth day many responses are also being made during the stimulus in which the responses are being punished. By the fifteenth day responding is occurring at a high rate during both stimuli, but at a slightly reduced level during punishment.

The initial effects of punishment, then, are to reduce responses not only during the stimulus in which the responses are being punished, but also in the presence of the stimulus in which the responses are not being punished. This generalization of suppression eventually disappears and the responses return to their unpunished level during the safe stimulus. Actually the rate of responding during the safe stimulus (twelfth to fifteenth day) is greater than the rate of responding that had been obtained prior to the introduction of punishment, showing a contrast effect. These results not only show the recovery phenomenon during punishment but also the effect of a "vacation from punishment." The insertion of the safe period or "vacation" alternating with punishment results in a greater degree of response suppression after the vacation is over.

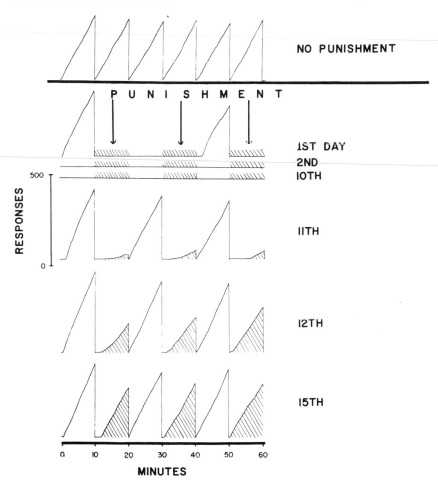

Figure 12. Cumulative response records for one pigeon. The vertical line represents the moment of change-over from one stimulus color to a second stimulus color of the transilluminated response key. The responses were being reinforced on a VI schedule of food reinforcement; the food deliveries are not indicated on the record. The two stimulus lights alternated every ten minutes. The top record (no punishment) is for the condition in which no shocks were delivered. The cross-hatched marks designate the stimulus condition in which each response was punished by a brief (100 msec.) shock of 60 volts. (From Azrin & Holz, unpublished data.)

Punishment as a Discriminative Stimulus

The principal effect of punishment is to decrease the response which is being punished. In addition, the punishing stimulus may acquire discriminative properties. That is to say, the punishing stimulus may come to serve as a signal for some other event. The discriminative or signaling properties of a punishing stimulus are not specific to that stimulus as a punishing stimulus but rather may be acquired by any stimulus. The discriminative properties of punishment have not been generally realized in past studies of punishment. Traditionally, the effects of a punishment procedure have been interpreted in terms of the reductive effects of the punishing stimulus. Yet, as we shall see, the discriminative properties may enhance, conceal, or even override the usual suppressive properties of the punishing stimulus and thereby produce what seems to be a paradoxical effect of punishment.

Punishment as a discriminative stimulus for another punishing stimulus. A punishing stimulus may become a discriminative stimulus for many different types of events. Let us consider first the situation in which a punishing stimulus becomes a discriminative stimulus for another punishing stimulus. Dinsmoor (1952) alternated fixed periods of time during which punishment was programmed with fixed periods of time during which no punishment was programmed. No external stimulus was used to indicate the change-over from one period to the next. Under such circumstances, the only means that the subject had available for predicting whether punishment would occur was whether or not the last response had been punished. In Dinsmoor's experiment, the subject soon learned that delivery of the punishing stimulus meant that the next response would also be punished. This could be seen from the fact that shortly after a response was punished, there was an immediate lowering of the probability of the succeeding responses. Conversely, once one or two responses went unpunished, there was a very rapid recovery of the response rate to its unpunished level. Under this procedure, the subjects used the occurrence of a punishing stimulus as a signal for the occurrence of subsequent punishment.

Punishment can also be arranged so that the delivery of punishment is a discriminative stimulus for the absence rather than the presence of additional punishing stimuli. In one experiment (Azrin, Holz, & Hake, 1963), FR punishment was programmed. When the FR punishment was first introduced, the responses were completely suppressed following each delivery of the punishing stimulus. Soon the subject learned that a response was never punished immediately after the delivery of a punishing stimulus. Consequently, the period of complete suppression after punishment gradually disappeared. In the stable state, subjects soon resumed responding immediately following delivery of each punishing stimulus.

Punishment as a discriminative stimulus for the absence of food reinforcement. The punishing stimulus may also be arranged in such a way that the punishing stimulus becomes a discriminative stimulus for the absence of the food reinforcement that had been maintaining the response. Several methods exist for producing such discriminative properties of the punishing stimulus. In most of the studies where the punishing stimulus could become a discriminative stimulus for food reinforcement, the experimenters did not view the problem in the way that we are viewing it here. Let us, therefore, view these other studies after we have first examined one experiment (Holz & Azrin, 1961) which explicitly associated the punishing stimulus and the reinforcement in such a way as to study the discriminative properties directly. In this experiment, periods of intermittent food reinforcement were alternated with periods of extinction. No external stimulus was present. Under these circumstances, the subject had no way of discriminating reinforcement from extinction conditions. The procedure was then arranged so that all responses were punished during the period of extinction but none of the responses were punished during the period of reinforcement. This differential punishment procedure provided the subject with a discriminative stimulus for the presence or absence of potential reinforcements. The result of this selective association of punishment with extinction was that the punishing stimulus produced large reductions in responding. These reductions in responding could not be attributed to the punishing stimulus since the intensity of this stimulus produced little or no suppression ordinarily. Thus, we see that very mild and otherwise ineffective intensities of punishment will produce a substantial reduction of responding if the mild punishment is differentially associated with a period of no reinforcement.

Punishment as discriminative stimulus for the presence of reinforcement. Punishment may also be arranged in such a way that the delivery of the punishment is a discriminative stimulus for the presence of food reinforcement. In a second portion of the experiment by Holz and Azrin (1961), all responses were punished only during the period of reinforcement. This procedure again allowed the subject to use the occurrence of the punishing stimulus as a means of detecting whether reinforcement was available. The result of this procedure was to reverse completely the usual effects of punishment. The rate of responding actually increased in the period during which punishment was programmed and decreased in the period during which there was no punishment. This increased level of responding during punishment existed at an intensity of punishment that had produced response suppression under the more usual circumstances when there were no discriminative properties of the stimulus. The apparently paradoxical phenomenon existed in which the initiation of punishment caused an increase of the responses rather than the usual decrease. This use of a punishing stimulus as a discriminative stimulus for food reinforcement is comparable to the use of a neutral stimulus as a discriminative stimulus for food reinforcement. When a neutral stimulus, such as the click of a food magazine, has been specifically associated with the delivery of food, the neutral stimulus has been found to increase the response rate during extinction. This increased response rate has been considered to arise from the conditioned reinforcement provided by the magazine click (Skinner, 1938). The procedure used by Holz and Azrin (1961) substituted a punishing stimulus for the neutral stimulus. Therefore, we may consider the punishing stimulus as having acquired conditioned reinforcing properties.

Aversive versus discriminative properties of punishment. We noted above that many procedures that were designed to study the effects of punishment may have inadvertently allowed the discriminative properties of the punishing stimulus to become dominant. In the results cited above, it was seen that the effects of punishment could be considerably modified by explicitly associating the punishment with the presence or absence of the reinforcing stimulus. The results were interpreted in terms of the discriminative properties of the punishing stimulus rather than the aversive properties. Yet, discriminative control is usually studied with continuous presence of a neutral stimulus (Ferster & Skinner, 1957). Consideration of a punishing stimulus as a discriminative stimulus is somewhat unusual in that the punishing stimulus is necessarily response-produced rather than continuous. Holz and Azrin (1962b) experimentally analyzed the discriminative properties of punishment by using a control procedure in which a neutral stimulus was delivered in the manner of a brief electric shock. It was found that the response-produced neutral stimulus could acquire discriminative properties if that stimulus were differentially associated with the presence or absence of food deliveries. In many instances, it was not necessary to appeal to the aversive properties of the shock since essentially the same results could be obtained by using a neutral stimulus, such as a flash of light, rather than the electric shock.

Let us now examine the results of a procedure that has been used in the past to study punishment (Estes, 1944; Skinner, 1938). In this procedure, a rat is first reinforced with pellets of food on an intermittent schedule of reinforcement in order to build up a substantial level of responding. After the level of food-reinforced responding has become stable, extinction is introduced. Simultaneously, brief electric shocks or bar-slaps are delivered for each response. The question that has been asked in using this procedure is whether the concurrent use of punishment will facilitate the reduction of responding that is found during extinction. Under this procedure, the punishment and extinction are allowed to endure until the level of responding is quite low. Then the punishment contingency is discontinued and the animal is allowed to continue responding but still without food reinforcement. The rationale behind terminating the punishment period is to see whether the reduction of responses persists during the extinction period even after the punishment is no longer there. The characteristic result of this procedure is that the concurrent use of punishment and extinction leads to a greater reduction of responding than does the use of extinction alone. Also, it has been found that when the punishment has been discontinued, the responses show a sudden increase in frequency even though the extinction period is still in force. This sudden increase in responding after the termination of punishment has been put forward as evidence that punishing stimuli did not really weaken the responses but only "suppressed" them. (This position will be considered in detail in a later section.)

Although the above results were originally interpreted in terms of the aversive properties of the shock, we can see from our preceding analysis that the shock may also have acquired discriminative properties. It will be recalled that in the original part of the procedure, the responses were reinforced and no punishment was programmed. Thus, the availability of food reinforcements could potentially be associated with the absence of punishment. In the second part of the procedure, extinction was introduced together with punishment. This procedure now produces a differential association between punishment and extinction, as well as a differential association between no punishment and reinforcement. The punishing stimulus could have become a signal that no food was available. If this line of reasoning is correct, the termination of the punishment period should lead to an increase of responding since termination of the punishment reinstates the discriminative stimuli for the availability of reinforcement. At a theoretical level, then, it appears possible to account for the changes in behavior on the basis of the discriminative properties of the shock rather than the aversive properties.

This theoretical analysis was evaluated in our laboratory by arranging the same procedure described above but substituting a neutral flash of light for the use of electric shock. First, a pigeon was reinforced for responding on a key by means of a VI 2 schedule of food reinforcement. This schedule was in effect for approximately one month. During that time, the key was transilluminated by a white light. No other light was ever present during the experimental sessions. The procedure used by Estes was then duplicated in its essential details, but no punishment was used. Instead, each response produced a 400 msec. change of illumination on the key from the usual white light to a green light. Concurrently, the food reinforcements were discontinued. The effect of this procedure can be seen in Figure 13 (unpublished data) which shows that the concurrent use of the "pseudo-punishment," that is the green light and the extinction period, produced a rapid decrease of responding to a level near zero. In the second part of the procedure, the "pseudo-punishment" was discontinued: the brief green light no longer followed each response. The period of extinction was continued. It

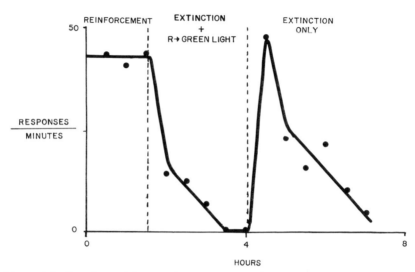

Figure 13. Pseudo-punishment. Response rate of a pigeon on a VI 2 schedule of food reinforcement during an uninterrupted seven-hour session. During the period designated as "extinction only," the reinforcement was not delivered. During the period designated as "R→green light," each response changed the illumination of the response key from white to green for 400 msec. (From Azrin & Holz, unpublished data.)

can be seen that the discontinuation of the green light produced an immediate and rapid increase of responding. Indeed, the response level slightly exceeded the level that had been seen earlier during reinforcement. The response level then very gradually decreased once again to a level near zero. The large number of extinction responses that occurred when the responses did not produce the green light, shows that extinction was considerably hastened by arranging for the green light to follow the responses.

This is the same result that was obtained in the experiments using electric shock; that is, the addition of an electric shock following a response considerably hastened the extinction process. Similarly, the present procedure produced an immediate increase of responding when the green light was discontinued, just as the procedure using shock resulted in an immediate increase of responding when the shock was discontinued. In accord with our theoretical analysis, the same results were obtained in this procedure using a neutral stimulus rather than an aversive stimulus. These changes in behavior need not, therefore, be attributed to the punishing properties of the shock. The result of this experiment makes it clear that close attention must be paid to the discriminative properties that may possibly be acquired by the presentation of the shocks.

This discriminative control by punishing stimuli should not be considered unique to punishing stimuli. Discriminative control is also commonly found with positively reinforcing stimuli. A familiar example is the fixed interval schedule of food reinforcement wherein the delivery of food becomes a discriminative stimulus for the absence of food, thereby producing a decreased level of responding following each food delivery (Skinner, 1938). Conversely, when we use a mixed crf extinction schedule of food reinforcement, the food delivery becomes a discriminative stimulus for the possibility of further food deliveries. In such a schedule, every response is reinforced for, say, 20 responses. Then, with no warning, the responses go unreinforced for, say, ten minutes. The results of such a procedure conducted in our laboratory may be seen in Figure 14 (unpublished data). On the first day of extinction after 20 food reinforcements, a large number of extinction responses were emitted. By the fourth day, however, it can be seen that only two or three responses were emitted during extinction. The subject had learned that if a single response was not followed by food delivery, then additional responses would not be followed by food delivery either. The food delivery, or its absence, had taken on a discriminative control. The repeated reinforcement and extinction periods established a discriminative control which decreased the number of extinction responses, thereby reversing the usual relationship in which the number of extinction

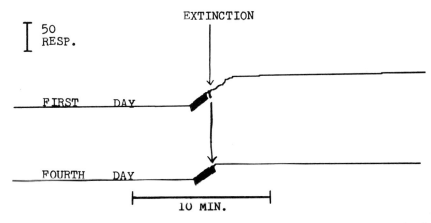

Figure 14. Cumulative response record for a pigeon for alternating periods of continuous reinforcement and extinction. The availability of the first reinforcement is signaled by a response buzz; thereafter, no discriminative stimulus is available to the subject for discriminating between the extinction period and the reinforcement period. Each food reinforcement produced a short downward deflection of the recorder pen, thereby giving the record the appearance of a solid bar when the food deliveries followed in rapid succession. (From Azrin & Holz, unpublished data.)

responses increases as a function of number of reinforcements (Perin, 1942). The effects of a behavioral consequence must be analyzed in terms of its discriminative properties as well as its reinforcing or punishing properties.

Correct versus incorrect responses. Consideration of the possible discriminative properties of the punishing stimulus helps to clarify many other types of punishment procedures in which apparently paradoxical results were obtained. In the past, a frequent procedure for studying punishment was the choice situation involving two responses, one of which was designated as correct and the other as incorrect. This type of procedure has been used by Thorndike (1932), Muenzinger (1934), and Tolman, Hall, and Bretnall (1932). Operationally, the designation of "correct" and "incorrect" have no meaning other than that the correct response is the one that is followed by positive reinforcement and the incorrect one is not. When the procedure is arranged so that the correct response is punished, we are saying in effect that one response is punished as well as reinforced whereas the other response is unpunished as well as unreinforced. Under these circumstances, the punishment and the reinforcements are associated with each other. The absence of punishment can easily then become the signal or discriminative stimulus for the absence of reinforcement. Similarly, the presence of punishment can become the discriminative stimulus for the presence of reinforcement. From our theoretical analysis, we could expect that punishment of a "correct" response might very well cause an increase in the likelihood of that response in contrast to the situation in which no punishment was programmed. Essentially, these very results have been obtained in the above-mentioned experiments; that is, the addition of punishment to the correct response was found to have no great effect in reducing the response in question. These results appear and have been presented as paradoxical in view of the presumed aversive properties of the electric shock. However, these results follow reasonably from the discriminative properties that undoubtedly were acquired by the shock. According to our theoretical analysis, it would not matter whether the punishment was delivered for the correct response or the incorrect response, so long as the procedure was consistent. Punishment of either the correct or incorrect response might be expected to result in faster learning than no punishment, since either of the punishment procedures provides discriminative stimuli.

Punishment during avoidance conditioning. The discriminative properties of a punishing stimulus seem to be effective in the situation in which a response is punished by the same stimulus that had previously been used to maintain avoidance behavior. Under the Sidman (1953) avoidance procedure, a response postpones the delivery of shock for a fixed period of time. In the absence of responses, shocks follow each other at a predetermined frequency. Results from this procedure have generally indicated that the electric shock assumed discriminative properties in that the delivery of shock becomes the occasion for emitting a response in order to postpone additional deliveries of shock. This discriminative property of shock during shock-avoidance conditioning can also be seen from studies in which a high level of responding was maintained by programming unavoidable shocks (Sidman, Herrnstein, & Conrad, 1957) since shock presumably constituted the occasion for emitting responses.

This somewhat speculative analysis of the avoidance conditioning situation provides an understanding of some results obtained by Black and Morse in their study of shock avoidance with dogs (1961). In their procedures, dogs were trained to avoid electric shock by emitting a jumping response. From our theoretical analysis, we might expect the shock to assume discriminative properties; that is, the delivery of shock would be the occasion upon which a jumping response would terminate or avoid the shock. After providing the subject with a history of shock-avoidance conditioning, Black and Morse delivered the shock as a punisher for the jumping response. The result was a temporary increase of these punished responses, as might be expected from the discriminative properties acquired by the shock. Eventually, of course, the responses were suppressed by the additional deliveries of the punishing stimulus. A similar increase of responding was obtained by Migler (1963) when shocks were delivered as punishing stimuli for responses that were concurrently being reinforced by shock-escape. Appel (1960) found this same increase in responding when punishment for responses alternated with shock avoidance in a mixed schedule. Again, we see that the reductive effect of punishment can be reversed by a previous history or by a concurrent procedure which allows the shock to acquire discriminative properties.

We have seen several characteristic changes in behavior as a consequence of punishment. Some of the changes are a function of the aversiveness of the punishing stimulus, such as immediacy of effect, potentially complete response reduction, the punishment contrast effect, generalization of suppression, and recovery during punishment. Other effects of punishment are a function of the discriminative properties that the punishment acquires, such as an increased suppression or a paradoxical facilitation.

Furthermore, we have seen that punishment is a complex process in that its effectiveness depends not only on the administration of the punishing stimulus but also on the characteristics of the reinforcement procedure that is maintaining the punished response. Moreover, the reinforcement procedure may well interact with the punishment procedure in such a way that the primary effect of a punishment procedure is a consequence of the discriminative properties of the punishing stimulus and not a necessary consequence of punishment per se. In light of the large, and usually unsuspected, number of interactions between punishment and reinforcement procedures, it is not surprising that contradictory conclusions have been reached concerning punishment. On the one hand we may be urged to abandon the use of punishment because of its ineffectiveness; on the other hand, punishment is held to be largely responsible for chronic mental disorder. Now that we have reviewed some of the basic experimental findings, let us examine some of these general issues.

GENERAL ISSUES: EFFECTIVENESS OF PUNISHMENT

Is Punishment Effective in Eliminating Behavior?

It has often been suggested that punishment should not be used. One of the presumed reasons for making this statement is that punishment is supposedly not very effective in eliminating behavior. Yet, there is little evidence for this statement. As a descriptive generalization, we can say that punishment can be quite effective; many studies have produced complete suppression of responding. Indeed, the suppression of responding has often persisted for long periods of time even after the punishment contingency was eliminated. Although it is certainly true that many studies have produced only partial suppression, we would be in error to conclude that greater reduction was not possible. It will be recalled that most investigations deliberately strengthened a response with positive reinforcement so that a stable behavioral baseline would be available against which to evaluate reductive effects of punishment. Thus, it is probably safe to state that investigators have deliberately not utilized intensities of punishment severe enough to cause complete suppression since the existence of complete suppression prevents quantitative evaluation of the extent of the reduction. The question of whether punishment is effective cannot be answered simply, since the effectiveness is known to depend on all of the factors discussed thus far. A definitely affirmative answer may be given if the question is rephrased as "Can punishment reduce behavior?" Indeed, the extent to which it does eliminate behavior may constitute a problem.

How Should Punishment Be Arranged for Maximum Effectiveness?

We have seen above that punishment can be quite effective in eliminating behavior. Let us imagine that we are given an assignment to eliminate behavior by punishment. Let us summarize briefly some of the circumstances which have been found to maximize its effectiveness: (1) The punishing stimulus should be arranged in such a manner that no unauthorized escape is possible. (2) The punishing stimulus should be as intense as possible. (3) The frequency of punishment should be as high as possible; ideally the punishing stimulus should be given for every response. (4) The punishing stimulus should be delivered immediately after the response. (5) The punishing stimulus should not be increased gradually but introduced at maximum intensity. (6) Extended periods of punishment should be avoided, especially where low intensities of punishment are concerned, since the recovery effect may thereby occur. Where mild intensities of punishment are used, it is best to use them for only a brief period of time. (7) Great care should be taken to see that the delivery of the punishing stimulus is not differentially associated with the delivery of reinforcement. Otherwise the punishing stimulus may acquire conditioned reinforcing properties. (8) The delivery of the punishing stimulus should be made a signal or discriminative stimulus that a period of extinction is in progress. (9) The degree of motivation to emit the punished response should be reduced. (10) The frequency of positive reinforcement for the punished response should similarly be reduced. (11) An alternative response should be available which will not be punished but which will produce the same or greater reinforcement as the punished response. For example, punishment of criminal behavior can be expected to be more effective if non-criminal behavior which will result in the same advantages as the criminal behavior is available. (12) If no alternative response is available, the subject should have access to a different situation in which he obtains the same reinforcement without being punished. (13) If it is not possible to deliver the punishing stimulus itself after a response, then an effective method of punishment is still available. A conditioned stimulus may be associated with the aversive stimulus, and this conditioned stimulus may be delivered following a response to achieve conditioned punishment. (14) A reduction of positive reinforcement may be used as punishment when the use of physical punishment is not possible for practical, legal, or moral reasons. Punishment by withdrawal of positive reinforcement may be accomplished in such situations by arranging a period of reduced reinforcement frequency (time-out) or by arranging a decrease of conditioned reinforcement (response cost). Both methods require that the subject have a high level of reinforcement to begin with; otherwise, no withdrawal of reinforcement is possible. If non-physical punishment is to be used, it appears desirable to provide the subject with a substantial history of reinforcement in order to provide the opportunity for withdrawing the reinforcement as punishment for the undesired responses.

How Can a Stimulus Be Ineffective and Still Be Called a Punishing Stimulus?

Let us re-examine our previous definition of a punishing stimulus as a *consequence of a response that reduces the future probability of that response*. A problem arises as to the designation of a stimulus that reduces a response at one time but does not reduce it at another time. For example, if the punished response is being maintained by a schedule of frequent reinforcement and a strong state of deprivation exists, then even high intensities of punishment may be ineffective. A dilemma exists therefore in defining a stimulus of a given intensity as a punishing stimulus when no decrease in the probability of the punished response is detectable. The critical point is that the effectiveness of punishment depends greatly upon the reinforcement variables that are maintaining the response. If one fails to obtain a reduction of responses by an event that is known to be punishing, these results serve to indicate only that the variables maintaining the punished response are overriding the reductive effect of the punishment.

How Is It That a Subject May Seem To Be Enjoying Punishment?

In some instances, it appears that the subject may be enjoying punishment. This type of observation has been related to the general question of whether punishment is effective and whether punishment should be used. We have already seen how a response can continue to occur without reduction in frequency in spite of the use of a punishment procedure. The reinforcement variables may easily eliminate the reductive effects. What we are considering now is the phenomenon in which the use of a punishment procedure has actually increased the frequency of the response above the frequency that existed prior to punishment. This type of observation has been made frequently in clinical psychology under the designation of masochism, in criminology under the designation of self-punitiveness, and in child psychology as attention-getting. An example of this phenomenon is the child who appears to be deliberately misbehaving until the mother drops what she is doing and administers a scolding or a spanking. An explanation of this effect of punishment may be obtained from the findings concerning the discriminative properties of punishment wherein it was seen that punishment would increase the frequency of a response if positive reinforcement were selectively associated with the punishing stimulus.

Consider the example of pathological masochism. It is very common for medical assistance and sympathy to be administered to a person on whom an injury has been inflicted. Assuming that the assistance and sympathy are positive reinforcers, these reinforcers are being selectively associated with an aversive stimulus which is the injury. In the case of masochism, the response of self-abuse produces the reinforcement (sympathy) as well as the aversive stimulus (injury). If sympathy and assistance are absent when there is no injury, then the basic paradigm for establishing the discriminative properties of punishment has been fulfilled since the presence of pain is selectively associated with reinforcement whereas the absence of pain is associated with the absence of reinforcement. It follows that masochistic behavior may be eliminated by (1) withdrawing any excess attention or sympathy when injury is inflicted and (2) providing sympathy and attention to the individual for behavior other than self-injury. The same line of reasoning follows for the elimination of criminal behavior in adults as well as the elimination of undesired behavior in children. The parent who pays attention to a child only when he misbehaves (and is consequently punished) has unwittingly transformed the punishing stimulus into a conditioned reinforcing stimulus. The end result may well be such that the individual appears to be "seeking out" the punishment. This phenomenon is not to be construed as a contradiction of the effectiveness of punishment but rather as a confirmation of the effectiveness of conditioned reinforcement.

COMPARISON OF PUNISHMENT WITH OTHER PROCEDURES

Comparison of Punishment with Other Methods of Aversive Stimulation

Thus far, we have been considering punishment as a fairly isolated process. It is possible, however, to compare punishment with other types of schedules of aversive control both in terms of the procedure used as well as the results obtained. Sidman has provided a simple and useful means of depicting avoidance schedules (1953). The designation of R-S is used to describe the duration of time between the response and the aversive stimulus. The designation of S-S is used to describe the duration of time between the aversive stimuli in the absence of a response. Punishment can be similarly described in terms of R-S and S-S intervals. In the punishment paradigm, the response produces the aversive stimulus immediately; thus we can designate the R-S interval in punishment as equal to zero. On the other hand, the S-S interval in punishment is infinitely great since no aversive stimulus will be delivered unless a response occurs. So we would assign a value of infinity to the S-S interval. While punishment can be described as a procedure where the R-S interval equals zero and the S-S interval is infinitely long, avoidance or escape conditioning has an R-S interval greater than zero and an S-S interval less than infinity. Punishment differs from both escape and avoidance conditioning in terms of whether the response results in an increase or a decrease in aversive stimulation. This basic difference between punishment on the one hand and escape and avoidance conditioning on the other concerns the relationship between the response and the direction of change of aversive stimulation impinging on the subject. We see that in analyzing the effects of aversive stimulation on behavior it is necessary to specify the temporal relationship that exists between the aversive stimulation and the ongoing behavior.

A comparison may also be made between the punishment procedure and the conditioned suppression procedure developed by Estes and Skinner (1941). Like the punishment procedure, the conditioned suppression procedure serves to reduce responding. The conditioned suppression procedure differs from punishment, escape, and avoidance in that the relationship between the aversive stimulus and a specific response is left unspecified. Rather, what is specified is the relationship between the aversive stimulus and some neutral stimulus. This essential procedural difference between conditioned suppression and the other three procedures is reflected in the results obtained. Under punishment, escape, and avoidance conditioning, the direction of change in responding can be determined by analyzing the direction of change of aversive stimulation that results from the emission of the responses. Under conditioned suppression, the aversive stimulus has no fixed relationship to responses but rather to a previously neutral stimulus. It is not clear why the conditioned suppression procedure should lead to a reduction rather than an increase of the ongoing responses since the aversive stimulus has no fixed relationship to those responses. Since both the conditioned suppression procedure and the punishment procedure do reduce responses, we may well ask which of the two procedures is more effective in eliminating ongoing responses. In one study where the two procedures were experimentally compared, it was found that punishment produced far greater suppression of responding than did the conditioned suppression procedure (Azrin, 1956). The great suppression of responses by punishment indicates that the relationship between the response and the aversive stimulus is still a critical factor. The effects of aversive stimuli follow in a fairly straightforward manner from the relationship between the responses and the aversive stimuli. If the responses produce the aversive stimulus, a decreased rate of responses results. If the responses produce no change in the aversive stimulus, then little or no change in the responding results. If the responses eliminate the aversive stimulus, an increased rate results. An apparent exception to the general rule is the conditioned suppression procedure. Even under this procedure, however, it has been found that a specification of the relationship between the response and the shock enhances the degree of suppression obtained.

Which Produces Faster Learning: Reward or Punishment?

The question has often been raised whether punishment is more or less effective than reward in teaching new behavior. This question has no meaning if we abide by the technical definition of punishment since punishment is a method of eliminating behavior whereas reinforcement is a method of producing or maintaining behavior. A special type of experimental situation has conveyed the spurious impression that punishment does increase or teach new behavior. This is the choice situation in which the subject is forced to choose one out of several alternatives on each trial. In this choice situation, a decrease in the proportion of the punished response necessarily results in an increased proportion of the unpunished response. Thus, the results may be misinterpreted to mean that punishment of one response generally leads to an increase of other responses. As we have seen in the studies utilizing an alternative unpunished response, an increase did occur if the unpunished responses were also being reinforced. However, the elimination of a response by punishment is not known to result in an increase of unpunished responses unless those responses are concurrently under the control of some reinforcement procedure. Only when the subject is forced to choose between two responses on each trial, do we see an increase of the unpunished response without any obvious reinforcement for that response. Thus, it is inappropriate to consider punishment as a method for teaching new behavior. Punishment is a method of eliminating behavior. One can rephrase the question in terms of the relative effectiveness of escape or avoidance compared with reinforcement, since escape, avoidance, and reinforcement are all methods for teaching new behavior. Punishment and reward, however, are antagonistic processes.

Comparison of Punishment with Other Methods of Eliminating Behavior

Punishment is one method of eliminating behavior; conditioned suppression is another method. As seen above, a comparison between the two methods revealed that punishment was more effective than conditioned suppression in terms of reducing responses. Similarly, it is possible for us to compare punishment to some of the other methods that are commonly used to eliminate behavior. Although it is hazardous to compare general procedures with each other, we believe that it is still possible to compare procedures when parameters are selected that have been found to be maximally effective for each procedure. For example, extinction is a general procedure for eliminating responses. Yet the speed with which extinction eliminates responses depends greatly on several factors, especially the intermittency of the schedule of reinforcement that is used prior to the extinction (Skinner, 1938). Extinction appears to be maximally effective following continuous reinforcement. It is possible to compare the degree of response reduction that occurs during extinction after continuous reinforcement with the degree of reduction seen in studies of punishment when maximally effective parameters of the punishment procedure have been used. In this way, it is possible for us to compare these two procedures at the parameter values at which each procedure approximates maximum effectiveness.

In one experiment (Holz & Azrin, 1963), a comparison was made between stimulus change, extinction, satiation, and punishment in terms of the effectiveness of these four procedures in reducing responses that had been maintained according to a drl schedule of food reinforcement. One of the differences in the effect of these procedures was the pattern of responding. In analyzing the interresponse time distribution of the responses, Holz and Azrin found that "the extinction, satiation, and punishment procedures led to different IRT (interresponse time) distributions when the overall rates of response were equated. The distributions that occurred during satiation and extinction were considerably flatter than the distributions resulting during punishment" (p. 403).

The three different procedures, as well as the effect of stimulus change, also differed in terms of the overall reductive effect. They were analyzed in terms of the degree to which responding was eliminated. The criteria were whether a procedure: (1) reduces the response rate immediately upon the introduction of that procedure, (2) reduces the responses for as long as the procedure is in effect, (3) reduces the response rate to zero while the procedure is in effect, and (4) maintains the response reduction after the procedure is discontinued.

The overall conclusions are summarized in Table 1 which describes each of five reductive procedures in terms of the immediacy, duration, extent, and degree of irreversibility of the response reduction. A fifth procedure, physical restraint, is also included. Figure 15 is a schematic representation of the response changes commonly observed during and subsequent to the use of punishment, satiation, extinction, and stimulus change.

It appears that punishment can be at least as effective as extinction, satiation, stimulus change, and physical removal in terms of the degree, extent, duration, and irreversibility of the response reduction. It should be remembered that the above comparison between procedures is based upon a set of parameters at which each procedure is close to maximum

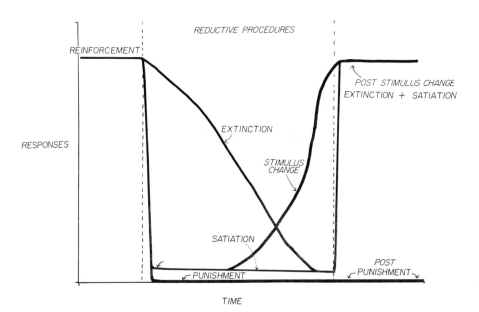

Figure 15. A schematic representation of the temporal course of response reduction by extinction, stimulus change, satiation, and punishment. (From Azrin & Holz, unpublished data.)

effectiveness. If other parameters are chosen that are less effective, such as partial satiation, extinction after intermittent reinforcement, mild punishment, etc., then the rank order of superiority of these methods could easily be altered.

Table 1
A Comparison of Several Procedures which Reduce Response Rate

Procedure	Immediate Effect	Enduring Effect	Complete Suppression	Irreversible Effect
Stimulus change	Yes	No	No	No
Extinction	No	Yes	No	No
Satiation	Yes	Yes	No	No
Physical Restraint	Yes	Yes	Yes	No
Punishment	Yes	Yes	Yes	Yes

Source: Holz and Azrin (1963b).

'One might insist that extinction could be made more effective than punishment by instituting complete extinction. If one never reinforced a response, then punishment would scarcely be possible since the response would rarely occur. For a large class of behavior, however, this complete absence of reinforcement is impossible. The physical world often provides reinforcement contingencies that cannot be eliminated easily. The faster we move through space, the quicker we get to where we are going, whether the movement be walking or driving an auto. Hence, running and speeding will inevitably be reinforced. Extinction of running and speeding could be accomplished only by the impossible procedure of eliminating all reinforcing events that result from movement through space. Some other reductive method, such as punishment, must be used.

Is Punishment General in Its Effect Whereas Reinforcement Is Specific?

Our previous discussion concerned a comparison between punishment and other methods of reducing behavior. Punishment has also been compared with positive reinforcement, which is a method of increasing behavior. One of the common statements is that punishment is more general in its action on the punished response than reinforcement is on the reinforced response. We have already seen that when punishment was first introduced, there was a general disruption of behavior during the stimulus in which the responses were unpunished as well as during the stimulus in which responses were punished. Gross observation of a rat that is being shocked often reveals that the animal "freezes" after receiving a punished stimulus. Thus, it does appear that the initial introduction of punishment produces a general alteration of behavior. Yet the experimental findings reviewed here do not support the statement that this general effect is peculiar to punishment and not to reinforcement. For example, under positive reinforcement, Sidman (1958) found that when one response was reinforced or extinguished in a multiple response situation, generalization occurred and the other responses were similarly affected in the same direction. Likewise, gross observation of the conditioning process shows that during response acquisition, a rat often receives its first reinforcement after "accidentally" pressing a lever. A general increase in activity usually arises in the vicinity of the lever. In conditioning pigeons to peck a key for food reinforcement, the same general increase in activity is seen following the first few reinforcing stimuli. After several reinforcements are delivered, the increase in general activity is commonly seen to give way to a selective increase in the frequency of the lever press (Skinner, 1938).

Similarly, gross observation of a punished subject reveals that the punishing stimulus initially produces a reduction in general activity; but again this gives way to a selective reduction of the punished response if the punishing stimulus is delivered immediately after that response.

We noted previously (Azrin, 1956) that a temporary reduction of responses resulted when shocks were not delivered immediately. Since the responses were reinforced and were occurring at a moderate rate, occasional coincidences between the shock and a response were possible. The reduction of responses by non-immediate shock cannot, therefore, be interpreted to mean that punishment has a general effect since the occasional coincidences between the shock and the response may account for the reduction. The same type of consideration seems to be involved in positive reinforcement. Skinner (1948) has noted an increase in general activity when food reinforcement was delivered at random (superstitious behavior). Also, Skinner (1938) reported an enduring maintenance of an existing response when food reinforcement was delivered at random. Thus, reinforcement as well as punishment has general effects on behavior if care is not taken to arrange that the reinforcer or the punishing stimulus occurs immediately after the measured response. On the other hand, the specificity of the effects of punishment was seen clearly when the unpunished response in one stimulus was unaffected by having the same response punished during another stimulus. We may summarize these results by stating that food reinforcement and punishment appear to be quite similar in that both procedures initially affect behavior in general, but after extended exposure, the effect is largely restricted to the particular response being manipulated. Punishment does not appear to be more general in its effect than reinforcement.

THEORETICAL BASIS OF PUNISHMENT

Several discussions of the punishment process have attempted to formulate a theory as to why punishment reduces the frequency of the punished response. It was mentioned that punishment had been considered to achieve its effect because of its annoying aftereffects. This explanation did not appear to be too useful since at the animal level, a subjective report of the degree of annoyance is impossible. Even at the human level, this type of explanation is inadequate because of the necessarily subjective aspect of the verbal report of the subject.

Competing Response Theory

A more recent theoretical account has been given of why punishment is effective (Dinsmoor, 1954; 1955). This explanation states that the punished response decreases in frequency because of the increase in frequency of responses that compete with the punished response. An example of this would be the emergence of withdrawal responses in a rat that has been punished for pressing a bar. Our position in this review has been neutral with respect to the adequacy of the competing response theory in accounting for the effects of punishment. Only recently have there been attempts to arrange "competing" responses experimentally and to study the effects of punishment on these competing responses. Until such time as these competing responses have been more fully and directly measured, it seems preferable to postpone judgment on this explanation of the effects of punishment.

At present, the best indication of these competing responses is the absence of the punished response; this measure is operationally identical to a direct measure of the extent of reduction of the punished response. Somewhat the same situation has existed with respect to positive reinforcement. Current theory regarding the determinants of the reinforcing properties of a reinforcing stimulus is on a fairly descriptive level. If a stimulus is found to increase the response when delivered immediately following that response, then it is classified as a reinforcing stimulus. An explanation of why a stimulus should be reinforcing was offered by Thorndike in terms of the satisfying consequences; but as in the case of punishment, this type of explanation has not been generally acceptable to those who wish to accomplish a behavioral analysis of the reinforcement process. Similarly, a competing response theory has been offered to account for the changes observed during positive reinforcement and extinction. On the one hand, the observed increase in the frequency of the reinforced response is explained on the basis of the extinction of inferred competing responses. On the other hand, the observed decrease in the frequency of an extinguished response has been accounted for on the basis of an increase in the frequency of these inferred competing responses. As Marx (1963) has pointed out in a recent comment on the competing response theory of positive reinforcement, very few investigators currently are making use of this theory. At the present time, it appears more parsimonious to consider punishment at the same descriptive level at which positive reinforcement has been considered, without appeal to changes in behavior that thus far have been inferred rather than directly measured.

The present treatment has not attempted to present an "explanation" of the effects of punishment except insofar as identification of the independent variables constitutes an explanation. Rather, the response reduction by punishment has been considered as a primary process that follows directly from the definition of punishment. At the present time, it appears more useful to describe the nature and extent of the behavioral changes during punishment and to identify the independent variables responsible for these changes. Past punishment research has too often been concerned with the implications of a given behavioral change for some theory that is stated in terms of fear reduction, anxiety, emotional suppression, competing responses, proprioceptive responses, increased drives, decreased drives, conditioned drives, neurosis, etc. Until such time as the above terms refer to directly measurable events, their use will do little to increase our understanding of punishment. Rather, the use of these terms prevents the investigator from focusing attention on the observable response reduction as a phenomenon that is of interest in its own right and not as an "index" of some underlying process that defies direct measurement.

Does Punishment Weaken Behavior or Just Suppress It?

Another theoretical approach to the punishment process has been concerned with the question of whether punishment really weakens behavior. By implication, it is inferred that positive reinforcement really strengthens behavior. The suggestion is that the effects of positive reinforcement are genuine whereas the changes induced by punishment are only apparent. It is difficult to know exactly why the decrease in behavior induced by punishment should be considered only apparent. But one interpretation that we may offer is that the effect of punishment has often been found to be reversible. Except at high intensities of punishment, the removal of the punishment contingency results in a return of the previously punished behavior. In this sense, there can be no doubt about the temporary effect of punishment. Yet, most other procedures for eliminating behavior must also be considered temporary by this criterion when applied to extinction, satiation, stimulus change, physical removal, and conditioned suppression. We must conclude, therefore, that punishment really does "weaken" a response in the same sense that other procedures for reducing behavior "weaken" behavior as we have already seen. (Cf. Figure 15 and Table 1). Indeed, punishment appears to be potentially more effective than other procedures for weakening a response.

A second interpretation may be given for the common belief that punishment really does not weaken behavior. This interpretation derives from the theoretical formulations that utilize the concept of "strength" of response. Hull (1943), for example, used the concept of habit strength, and Skinner (1938) at one time used the concept of reflex reserve. According to this concept of response strength, several measures of response strength are available, including the frequency of response and the number of responses during extinction. If the notion of strength of response is to have any utility, then presumably the several measures of response strength should be found to covary. The failure of these measures to covary has been a source of embarrassment. Considering only positive reinforcement for the moment, it is known that the rate of responding is a function of the frequency of reinforcement (Skinner, 1938). Maximum rate of responding occurs under continuous reinforcement when we exclude the actual time necessary for the delivery and consumption of the reinforcement. If rate of response and resistance to extinction are two equivalent measures of response strength, then we should expect that continuous reinforcement should lead to the greatest resistance to extinction. Of course, just the opposite has been found to be the case: continuous reinforcement results in little resistance to extinction. If resistance to extinction is taken as the real measure of strength, then the high response rate during continuous reinforcement must be designated as being weak.

This same notion of response strength appears to be responsible for the statement that punishment does not weaken behavior in spite of experimental evidence that shows an extreme reduction of the behavior during punishment. According to the notion of response strength, any reduction of the rate of response during punishment should be accompanied by a decrease in the resistance to extinction since the two measures should covary. If strength of response is best measured by the rate of the response, then punishment would have to be considered genuinely to weaken behavior. On the other hand, if the strength of response is best measured by resistance to extinction, then punishment would have to be considered ineffective in weakening behavior. At the present time, it appears to be more fruitful to abandon the notion of response strength and to consider rate of response on the one hand and resistance to extinction on the other as two separate entities.

The conclusion that punishment does not weaken a response is based on the recovery of previously punished responses during extinction (Estes, 1944). Yet the results obtained in various punishment studies do not support the statement that punishment produces only an apparent weakening of the response, so long as we take precautions to avoid discriminative or conditioned reinforcing properties from accruing to the punishing stimulus. It will be recalled that resistance to extinction was decreased by punishment so long as the punishing contingency was maintained for the duration of the extinction period. Recovery of the responses during extinction has been found in other studies to result upon the termination of punishment. Yet we have seen (Figure 13) that this recovery during extinction is probably not a function of the punishment process, but rather a function of the discriminative properties acquired by the "punishing" stimulus. The empirical basis for the alleged ineffectiveness of punishment appears subject to reinterpretation.

UNDESIRABLE ASPECTS OF PUNISHMENT

Can We Eliminate Punishment as a Method of Behavioral Control?

We have seen that several methods other than punishment are available for eliminating behavior. For whatever the reasons, we may wish to use methods other than punishment. To what extent is this objective practicable? At the institutional level, it would seem to be quite possible to eliminate the use of physical punishment. Conceivably, administrative regulations could be altered such that public punishment in the form of flogging, spankings, or other physical abuse would be excluded. At the level of individual behavior, it seems somewhat more difficult but still not impossible to eliminate the use of physical punishment. One type of punishment, however, seems to be virtually impossible to eliminate, and that is the punishing contingencies that are arranged by the physical world. Whenever we interact with the physical world, there are many punishing contingencies awaiting us. A good example of this would be any behavior that moves us through space such as walking, running, or reaching. It is only necessary to shut one's eyes while running to realize the extent to which punishing contingencies surround our movement. The degree to which these punishing contingencies are actually applied can be seen in the initial efforts of the young child in learning to walk and to run. So powerful are these potential punishing contingencies that they exist even when we sleep. The response of rolling off a bed is punished immediately and severely by collision with the floor below. Elimination of punishing contingencies by the physical world would appear to require elimination of all behavior that involves interaction with the physical world.

It appears, then, that it is possible to eliminate physical punishment as an institutional procedure; it even seems possible, though not very likely, that punishment might be eliminated as an individual activity. But there seems to be little or no likelihood that punishment by the physical world will be eliminated in the foreseeable future. Even where the punishment is delivered by a person or institution, it would not seem very likely that time-out or response cost would be easily eliminated as methods of punishment. Time-out punishment appears to be far more frequently used in human behavior than is physical punishment. To eliminate time-out as a punishing contingency would mean to eliminate fines, imprisonment, dismissal from a job, denial of favors, or withdrawal of privileges. It appears accurate to state at this time that punishment is a frequent method of behavioral control and that its elimination in the foreseeable future appears extremely unlikely. Punishment appears to be here to stay.

Emotional Concomitants

A frequent reason for attempting to eliminate punishment is that aversive stimuli in general, and punishment in particular, produce disruptive and undesirable emotional states. We shall be concerned with these emotional states only if they result in chronic behavioral disruption. Yet, it does not seem completely clear that we can attribute such an emotional state specifically to the use of aversive stimuli. For example, in the Sidman avoidance procedure, aversive stimuli are scheduled at a high frequency. Yet gross observation of an animal during Sidman avoidance usually shows no outward signs of distress after the initial period of acquisition. Instead, subjects under Sidman avoidance have been found to distribute their responses in a well-defined temporal pattern that is well adapted to meeting the avoidance contingencies. Similarly, gross observation of a pigeon that is being punished reveals no greater outward signs of distress or behavioral vacillation than are observed during alternative procedures, such as extinction. Experimental evidence regarding the non-disruptive effects of punishment has been obtained by Hunt and Brady (1955) who found little emotional effect, as measured by defecation of rats, when shock was used as a punishment as compared with non-contingent shock. Similarly, Hearst (1965) has found that although non-contingent shock produced an enduring disruption of an established discrimination, shock used as a punishment produced only a temporary disruption. At the human level, gross observation similarly indicates no chronic emotional maladjustment engendered by a child's having been burned in the past by touching a hot radiator. Rather, the experience seems to simply lower the likelihood of the child touching the radiator again. In spite of the severity of the burn that might have been inflicted, there is little evidence in such cases that chronic behavioral disruption was caused by the experience. Since it is unlikely that punishment by the physical world will ever be eliminated, it is rather fortunate that such punishment does not appear to generate emotional duress of a chronic nature.

Social Disruption

It is in the area of social disruption that punishment does appear to be capable of producing behavioral changes that are far-reaching in terms of producing an incapacity for an effective life. When we punish a response, we usually desire to obtain a decrease of that specific response while desiring other aspects of the individual's behavior to remain relatively unchanged. For example, a teacher may punish a child for talking in class, in which case it is desired that the unauthorized vocalization of the child be eliminated but his other behaviors remain intact. We have seen previously, however, that one side-effect of the punishment process was that it reinforced tendencies on the part of the individual to escape from the punishment situation itself. In terms of the example we are using, this means that punishment of the vocalization would not only be expected to decrease the vocalization, but also increase the likelihood of the child leaving the classroom situation. Behavior such as tardiness, truancy, and dropping out of school would be strengthened. The end result would be termination of the social relationship, which would make any further social control of the individual's behavior impossible. This side-effect of punishment appears to be one of the most undesirable aspects of having punishment delivered by one individual against another individual since the socialization process must necessarily depend upon continued interaction with other individuals.

Operant Aggression

When physical punishment is administered by another organism, social aggression appears to result. Two types of social aggression seem possible. The first type we shall call *operant aggression*. We have already seen that when a response is being punished, the individual may eliminate the punishment contingency by leaving the situation. A second way of eliminating the punishment contingency would be to destroy or immobilize the individual who is delivering the punishing stimulus (Delgado, 1963). Aggressive behavior toward the punishing stimulus appears to have the function of serving just such a purpose. Although experimental evidence regarding the importance of the consequences of aggression are not definitive, successful aggression against the source of a punishing stimulus will presumably result in the elimination of the punishing stimuli. The designation of operant aggression indicates that this type of aggression is maintained by the potentially favorable consequences of the aggression.

Elicited Aggression

A second type of aggression we shall call *elicited aggression* (Ulrich & Azrin, 1962). This type of aggression has been found to occur when painful stimuli are delivered to an organism when in the company of another organism, even though the organism being attacked did not deliver the painful stimulus. This type of aggression does not appear to depend on any favorable operant consequence for its existence. The study by Ulrich and Azrin (1962) illustrates some of the characteristics of this elicited aggression. In that experiment, two rats were placed in a chamber containing a floor grid. In the absence of foot-shock, the animals showed no signs of aggression. Upon the delivery of foot-shock by the experimenter, however, the rats turned and attacked each other. This elicited aggression has been found to exist in several species and to be elicited by different types of painful stimulation (Azrin, 1964; Azrin, Hake, & Hutchinson, 1965; Azrin, Hutchinson, & Hake, 1963; Azrin, Hutchinson, & Sallery, 1964; Hutchinson, Ulrich, & Azrin, 1965; Ulrich, Wolff, & Azrin, 1964).

For our purposes, the important thing about this reflexive fighting is that it appears to be a general response to aversive stimulation. Since physical punishment requires the delivery of aversive stimulation, this social aggression would be expected as an elicited reaction to physical punishment. Unlike operant aggression, this elicited aggression cannot serve the function of reducing aversive stimulation since neither of the combatants is in any way responsible for the aversive stimulation. Rather, it appears that when intense painful stimulation is delivered to an organism, then aggression or attack against nearby organisms results. Our main objective of eliminating a response by punishing that response may have the completely unexpected effect of producing aggression by the punished organism. Further, under this elicited aggression, the punished individual can be expected to attack any other nearby individuals, even those who have had nothing to do with delivering the punishing stimulus.

The principal disadvantages of using punishment seem to be that when the punishment is administered by an individual, (1) the punished individual is driven away from the punishing agent, thereby destroying the social relationship; (2) the punished individual may engage in operant aggression directed toward the punishing agent; and (3) even when the punishment is delivered by physical means rather than by another organism, elicited aggression can be expected against nearby individuals who were not responsible for the punishment. These three disadvantages seem to be especially critical for human behavior since survival of the human organism appears to be so completely dependent upon the maintenance of harmonious social relations.

SUMMARY AND CONCLUSIONS

At the level of a definition, punishment simply reduces the frequency of the punished response. As a reductive procedure, punishment appears to be at least as effective as most other procedures for eliminating responses. Unconditioned stimuli, such as shock and noise, are the stimuli used most frequently in experimental investigations; but other types of punishing stimuli, such as time-out, response cost, and conditioned punishment appear to be used more often as punishment in the social control of behavior. Several aspects of the punishing stimulus have been found to be critical, such as the intensity, frequency, scheduling and immediacy of punishment. At least as important are the reinforcement variables that are maintaining the punished response, such as the frequency and schedule of reinforcement as well as the opportunity of the subject to engage in alternative modes of behavior. The role of these reinforcement variables in determining the effectiveness of punishment has not received sufficient attention.

Several characteristic behavioral changes have been identified during punishment, such as an immediacy of response reduction, a gradual recovery during punishment, a punishment contrast effect, generalization, and discrimination. Perhaps the most paradoxical and confusing aspect of punishment has been the ability of a punishing stimulus to become a discriminative or conditioned reinforcing stimulus. This confusion arises when we fail to remember that a punishing stimulus is still a stimulus; as such, it can be inadvertently associated with reinforcing stimuli, with periods of reinforcement, with periods of extinction, and with other punishing stimuli. The result of such selective temporal association may be to strengthen, to neutralize, or even to reverse the aversive aspect of the punishing stimulus.

When we punish a response, our primary concern is to reduce the frequency of that response. If we have not overlooked the effects of the reinforcement variables or the discriminative variables, there is every reason to believe that our punishment procedure will be completely effective in eliminating the undesired response. The emotional state or enduring behavioral disruption of the punished subject are not necessarily undesirable outcomes of punishment; nor are the severity of the response reduction or the behavioral generalization of the punishing effects undesirable. In fact, all of these effects are probably quite useful where a physical punishment is concerned, from the evolutionary point of view, in reducing the future likelihood of painful and possibly destructive events. Since physical punishment is an inevitable and continuing part of our interaction with the physical world, these extensive behavioral changes that are produced by punishment will continue to be a useful part of the behavioral repertoire.

The primary disadvantage of punishment for humans may well be the social disruption that results and not the severity or generality of response reduction or even the existence of an emotional state. The existence of the human animal is completely dependent upon the assistance of other humans during the first few years of life. Even in the most primitive societies, this dependence continues for the life of the person. To the extent to which punishment eliminates or disrupts social interaction, it can be expected to make the individual incapable of existing in human society. Three sources of disruption have been found to result from punishment: (1) escape from a situation in which punishment is delivered, (2) operant aggression, and (3) elicited aggression. The first two phenomena are somewhat adaptive from a short-range view in that the behavioral reaction of the subject does decrease the future likelihood of punishment. Yet escape from a social situation in which punishment is delivered has the unfortunate side effect of preventing any future social interaction in that situation. This behavior would not appear to be too unfortunate as long as social interactions in other unpunished situations were maintained. Operant aggression seems similarly unfortunate in that social aggression would disrupt the particular social relation; but, again, the aggressive behavior would be expected to occur only in the situation in which the aggression reduced the punishment.

Elicited aggression, on the other hand, appears to be non-functional in that the aggression is displayed even toward individuals who are in no way concerned with the punishment. Thus, this aggression is non-adaptive as a specific means of reducing future aversive stimulation, since non-punitive as well as punitive individuals are attacked. The indiscriminate nature of this aggression can be expected to disrupt or terminate social relations that are in no way punitive.

We may conclude, therefore, that the disruption of social behavior constitutes the primary disadvantage to the use of punishment. The changes in the punished response per se appear to be distinctly secondary in importance to the social products of the use of punishment.

REFERENCES

ANGER, D. (1956) The dependence of interresponse times upon the relative reinforcement of different interresponse times. *J. exp. Psychol., 52,* 145-161.

APPEL, J. B. (1960) Some schedules involving aversive control. *J. exp. Anal. Behav., 3,* 349-359.

APPEL, J. B. (1961) Punishment in the squirrel monkey *saimiri sciurea. Science, 133,* 36.

APPEL, J. B. (1963) Punishment and shock intensity. *Science, 141,* 528-529.

AZRIN, N. H. (1956) Effects of two intermittent schedules of immediate and nonimmediate punishment. *J. Psychol., 42,* 3-21.

AZRIN, N. H. (1958) Some effects of noise on human behavior. *J. exp. Anal. Behav., 1,* 183-200.

AZRIN, N. H. (1959) A technique for delivering shock to pigeons. *J. exp. Anal. Behav., 2,* 161-163. (a)

AZRIN, N. H. (1959) Punishment and recovery during fixed-ratio performance. *J. exp. Anal. Behav., 2,* 301-305. (b)

AZRIN, N. H. (1960) Sequential effects of punishment. *Science, 131,* 605-606. (a)

AZRIN, N. H. (1960) Effects of punishment intensity during variable-interval reinforcement. *J. exp. Anal. Behav., 3,* 123-142. (b)

AZRIN, N. H. (1964) Aggressive responses of paired animals. Paper read at Symposium on Medical Aspects of Stress. Walter Reed Institute of Research, Washington, April.

AZRIN, N. H., HAKE, D. F., HOLZ, W. C., and HUTCHINSON, R. R. (1965) Motivational aspects of escape from punishment. *J. exp. Anal. Behav., 8,* 31-44.

AZRIN, N. H., HAKE, D. F., and HUTCHINSON, R. R. (1965) Elicitation of aggression by a physical blow. *J. exp. Anal. Behav., 8,* 55-57.

AZRIN, N. H., and HOLZ, W. C. (1961) Punishment during fixed-interval reinforcement. *J. exp. Anal. Behav., 4,* 343-347.

AZRIN, N. H., HOLZ, W. C., and HAKE, D. (1963) Fixed-ratio punishment. *J. exp. Anal. Behav., 6,* 141-148.

AZRIN, N. H., HUTCHINSON, R. R., and HAKE, D. F. (1963) Pain-induced fighting in the squirrel monkey. *J. exp. Anal. Behav., 6,* 620.

AZRIN, N. H., HUTCHINSON, R. R., and SALLERY, R. D. (1964) Pain-aggression toward inanimate objects. *J. exp. Anal. Behav., 7,* 223-228.

BARLOW, J. A. (1952) Secondary motivation through classical conditioning: One trial nonmotor learning in the white rat. *Amer. Psychologist, 7,* 273.

BARON, A., and ANTONITIS, J. J. (1961) Punishment and preshock as determinants of bar-pressing behavior. *J. comp. physiol. Psychol., 54,* 716-720.

BARRY, J. J., JR., and HARRISON, J. M. (1957) Relation between stimulus intensity and strength of escape responding. *Psychol. Rep., 3,* 3-8.

BLACK, A. H., and MORSE, P. (1961) Avoidance learning in dogs without a warning stimulus. *J. exp. Anal. Behav., 4,* 17-23.

BOREN, J. J., SIDMAN, M., and HERRNSTEIN, R. J. (1959) Avoidance, escape and extinction as functions of shock intensity. *J. comp. physiol. Psychol., 52,* 420-425.

BRETHOWER, D. M., and REYNOLDS, G. S. (1962) A facilitative effect of punishment on unpunished behavior. *J. exp. Anal. Behav., 5,* 191-199.

CHUNG, S. H. (1965) Effects of effort on response rate. *J. exp. Anal. Behav., 8,* 1-7.

DARDANO, J. F., and SAUERBRUNN, D. (1964) Selective punishment of fixed-ratio performance. *J. exp. Anal. Behav., 7,* 255-260. (a)

DARDANO, J. F., and SAUERBRUNN, D. (1964) An aversive stimulus as a correlated block counter in FR performance. *J. exp. Anal. Behav., 7,* 37-43. (b)

DARDANO, J. F., and SAUERBRUNN, D. (1964) Selective punishment of concurrent progressive ratio behavior. *J. exp. Anal. Behav., 7,* 51-65. (c)

DELGADO, J. M. R. (1963) Cerebral heterostimulation in a monkey colony. *Science, 141,* 161-163.

DINSMOOR, J. A. (1952) A discrimination based on punishment. *Quart. J. exp. Psychol., 4,* 27-45.

DINSMOOR, J. A. (1954) Punishment: I. The avoidance hypothesis. *Psychol. Rev., 61,* 34-46.

DINSMOOR, J. A. (1955) Punishment: II. An interpretation of empirical findings. *Psychol. Rev., 62,* 96-105.

DINSMOOR, J. A. (1958) A new shock grid for rats. *J. exp. Anal. Behav., 1,* 182.

DINSMOOR, J. A. (1961) A wide range constant current shock stimulator. *J. exp. Anal. Behav., 4,* 273-274.

DINSMOOR, J. A., and CAMPBELL, S. L. (1956) Escape-from-shock training following exposure to inescapable shock. *Psychol. Rep., 2,* 43-49.

DINSMOOR, J. A., and WINOGRAD, E. (1958) Shock intensity in variable-interval escape schedules. *J. exp. Anal. Behav. 1,* 145-148.

DOLLARD, J., and MILLER, N. E. (1950) *Personality and psychotherapy: An analysis in terms of learning, thinking, and culture.* New York: McGraw-Hill.

ESTES, W. K. (1944) An experimental study of punishment. *Psychol. Monogr., 57* (Whole No. 263).

ESTES, W. K., and SKINNER, B. F. (1941) Some quantitative properties of anxiety. *J. exp. Psychol., 29*, 390-400.

EVANS, W. D. (1962) Producing either positive or negative tendencies to a stimulus associated with shock. *J. exp. Anal. Behav., 5*, 335-337.

FERSTER, C. B. (1958) Control of behavior in chimpanzees and pigeons by time-out from positive reinforcement. *Psychol. Monogr., 72* (Whole No. 461).

FERSTER, C. B., and APPEL, J. B. (1961) Punishment of S^Δ responding in matching-to-sample by time-out from positive reinforcement. *J. exp. Anal. Behav., 4*, 45-56.

FERSTER, C. B., and SKINNER, B. F. (1957) *Schedules of reinforcement.* New York: Appleton-Century-Crofts.

FLANAGAN, B., GOLDIAMOND, I., and AZRIN, N. H. (1958) Operant stuttering: The control of stuttering behavior through response-contingent consequences. *J. exp. Anal. Behav., 1*, 173-177.

FRY, W., KELLEHER, R. T., and COOK, L. (1960) A mathematical index of performance on fixed-interval schedules of reinforcement. *J. exp. Anal. Behav., 3*, 193-199.

HAKE, D. F., and AZRIN, N. H. (1963) An apparatus for delivering pain-shock to monkeys. *J. exp. Anal. Behav., 6*, 297-298.

HAKE, D. F., and AZRIN, N. H. (1965) Conditioned punishment. *J. exp. Anal. Behav., 8*, 279-293.

HARRISON, J. M., ABELSON, R. M., and FISHER, G. L. Some relations between the auditory system of the medulla and auditory stimulus functions. *J. exp. Anal. Behav., 3*, 207-220.

HEARST, E. (1965) Stress-induced breakdown of an appetitive discrimination. *J. exp. Anal. Behav., 8*, 135-146.

HENDRY, D. P., and VAN-TOLER, C. (1964) Performance on a fixed-ratio schedule with correlated amount of reward. *J. exp. Anal. Behav., 7*, 207-209.

HERMAN, R. L., and AZRIN, N. H. (1964) Punishment by noise in an alternative response situation. *J. exp. Anal. Behav., 7*, 185-188.

HERRNSTEIN, R. J. (1955) Behavioral consequences of the removal of a discriminative stimulus associated with variable-interval reinforcement. Unpublished doctoral dissertation, Harvard University.

HERRNSTEIN, R. J., and MORSE, W. H. (1957) Effects of pentobarbital on intermittently reinforced behavior. *Science, 125*, 929-931.

HOFFMAN, H. S., and FLESHLER, M. (1962) A relay sequencing device for scrambling grid shock. *J. exp. Anal. Behav., 5*, 329-330.

HOLZ, W. C., and AZRIN, N. H. (1961) Discriminative properties of punishment. *J. exp. Anal. Behav., 4*, 225-232.

HOLZ, W. C., and AZRIN, N. H. (1962) Recovery during punishment by intense noise. *Psychol. Rep., 11*, 655-657. (a)

HOLZ, W. C., and AZRIN, N. H. (1962) Interactions between the discriminative and aversive properties of punishment. *J. exp. Anal. Behav., 5*, 229-234. (b)

HOLZ, W. C., AZRIN, N. H., and AYLLON, T. (1963) Elimination of behavior of mental patients by response-produced extinction. *J. exp. Anal. Behav., 6*, 407-412. (a)

HOLZ, W. C., AZRIN, N. H., and AYLLON, T. (1963) A comparison of several procedures for eliminating behavior. *J. exp. Anal. Behav., 6*, 399-406. (b)

HOLZ, W. C., AZRIN, N. H., and ULRICH, R. E. (1963) Punishment of temporally spaced responding. *J. exp. Anal. Behav., 6*, 115-122.

HONIG, W. K., and SLIVKA, R. M. (1964) Stimulus generalization of the effects of punishment. *J. exp. Anal. Behav., 7*, 21-25.

HULL, C. L. (1943) *Principles of behavior.* New York: Appleton-Century-Crofts.

HUNT, H. F., and BRADY, J. V. (1955) Some effects of punishment and intercurrent anxiety on a simple operant. *J. comp. physiol. Psychol., 48*, 305-310.

HUTCHINSON, R. R., ULRICH, R. E., and AZRIN, N. H. (1965) Effects of age and related factors on the pain-aggression reaction. *J. comp. physiol. Psychol., 59*, 365-369.

KAPLAN, M. (1952) The effect of noxious stimulus intensity and duration during intermittent reinforcement of escape behavior, *J. comp. physiol. Psychol., 45*, 538-549.

KELLEHER, R. T., and COOK, L. (1959) An analysis of the behavior of rats and monkeys on concurrent fixed-ratio avoidance schedules. *J. exp. Anal. Behav., 2*, 203-211.

KELLER, F. S., and SCHOENFELD, W. N. (1950) *Principles of psychology.* New York: Appleton-Century-Crofts.

MARX, M. H. (1963) The need for more specific formulation of the competing response interpretation of extinction. *Psychol. Rep., 12*, 729-730.

MASSERMAN, J. H. (1946) *Principles of dynamic psychiatry.* Philadelphia: Saunders.

MIGLER, B. (1963) Experimental self-punishment and superstitious escape behavior. *J. exp. Anal. Behav., 6*, 371-385.

MILLER, N. E. (1960) Learning resistance to pain and fear effects over learning, exposure, and rewarded exposure in context. *J. exp. Psychol., 60*, 137-145.

MOWRER, O. H., and AIKEN, E. G. (1954) Contiguity *vs* drive-reduction in conditioned fear: Temporal variations in conditioned and unconditioned stimulus. *Amer. J. Psychol., 67*, 626-638.

MOWRER, O. H., and SOLOMON, L. N. (1954) Contiguity *vs* drive-reduction in conditioned fear: The proximity and abruptness of drive-reduction. *Amer. J. Psychol., 67*, 15-25.

MUENZINGER, K. F. (1934) Motivation in learning: I. Electric shock for correct responses in the visual discrimination habit. *J. comp. Psychol., 17*, 439-448.

PERIN, C. T. (1942) Behavior potentiality as a joint function of the amount of training and the degree of hunger at the time of extinction. *J. exp. Psychol., 30*, 93-113.

REYNOLDS, G. S. (1961) Behavioral contrast. *J. exp. Anal. Behav., 4*, 57-71.

SIDMAN, M. (1953) Avoidance conditioning with brief shock and no exteroceptive warning signal. *Science, 118*, 157-158.

SIDMAN, M. (1955) On the persistence of avoidance behavior. *J. abnorm. soc. Psychol., 50*, 217-220.

SIDMAN, M. (1958) By-products of aversive control. *J. exp. Anal. Behav., 1*, 265-280.

SIDMAN, M., HERRNSTEIN, R. J., and CONRAD, D. G. (1957) Maintenance of avoidance behavior by unavoidable shock. *J. comp. physiol. Psychol., 50*, 553-557.

SKINNER, B. F. (1938) *The behavior of organisms.* New York: Appleton-Century-Crofts.

SKINNER, B. F. (1948) "Superstition" in the pigeon. *J. exp. Psychol., 38*, 168-172.

SKINNER, B. F. (1953) *Science and human behavior.* New York: Macmillan.

SKINNER, B. F., and CAMPBELL, S. L. (1947) An automatic shocking grid apparatus for continuous use. *J. comp. physiol. Psychol., 40,* 305-307.

STORMS, L. H., BOROCZI, G., and BROEN, W. E. (1962) Punishment inhibits an instrumental response in hooded rats. *Science, 135,* 1133-1134.

THORNDIKE, E. L. (1911) *Animal intelligence: Experimental studies.* New York: Macmillan.

THORNDIKE, E. L. (1932) *The fundamentals of learning.* New York: Teachers College.

TOLMAN, E. C., HALL, C. S., and BRETNALL, E. P. (1932) A disproof of the law of effect and a substitution of the laws of emphasis, motivation, and disruption. *J. exp. Psychol. 15,* 601-614.

ULRICH, R. E., and AZRIN, N. H. (1962) Reflexive fighting in response to aversive stimulation. *J. exp. Anal. Behav., 5,* 511-520.

ULRICH, R. E., WOLFF, P. C., and AZRIN, N. H. (1964) Shock as an elicitor of intra- and inter-species fighting behavior. *Anim. Behav., 12,* 14-15.

WEINER, H. (1962) Some effects of response cost upon human operant behavior. *J. exp. Anal. Behav., 5,* 201-208.

ZIMMERMAN, J., and BAYDAN, N. T. (1963) Punishment of S$^\Delta$ responding of humans in conditional matching-to-sample by time-out. *J. exp. Anal. Behav., 6,* 589-597.

ZIMMERMAN, J., and FERSTER, C. B. (1963) Intermittent punishment of S$^\Delta$ responding in matching-to-sample. *J. exp. Anal. Behav., 6,* 349-356.

10

Avoidance Behavior [1]

Murray Sidman

INTRODUCTION

The literature on avoidance behavior consists largely of a series of variations on a single theme: The subject is first made anxious through a process of Pavlovian conditioning; his avoidance behavior is reinforced when it terminates or reduces the conditioned anxiety state.

In one guise or another, this formula can encompass all the known data on avoidance behavior. There are no exceptions. Whenever a challenge does arise, the properties of anxiety are simply revised to fit the new facts. For example, if the subject's rate of avoidance responding is highest immediately *after* it has been shocked, it is because anxiety is most intense at that time; if, in another experiment, the probability of avoidance behavior is highest just *before* the subject is due to be shocked, this is when anxiety reaches its peak (Mowrer & Keehn, 1958). If surgical damage to the peripheral nervous system causes animals to learn a new avoidance response more slowly, but has no effect on a response they have learned before the operation, this may mean that ". . . peripheral components of anxiety reactions are important during early phases of the avoidance learning process, but they are not important during later phases . . ." (Solomon & Brush, 1956). If the generalization gradient is steep when exteroceptive stimuli warn the subject of impending shocks, but is flat when the experimental procedure does not provide the subject with a warning signal, it is because anxiety produced by internal stimuli generalizes more widely than externally generated anxiety (Miller, 1959).

Instead of invoking anxiety, some theorists appeal to operationally defined aversive functions of warning stimuli (e.g., Schoenfeld, 1950; Dinsmoor, 1954). But the conditioning processes are the same (Pavlovian and operant), and when there is no exteroceptive warning stimulus for the organism to terminate, the subject's own behavior is postulated to perform

[1] The preparation of this paper was supported in part by PHS research grant MH–05408 from the National Institute of Mental Health, Public Health Service.

this function (Hefferline, 1950; Sidman, 1953), or some unknown temporal process within the subject takes the place of anxiety (Anger, 1963).

It is likely that all of these mechanisms are involved; but my own investigations have convinced me that avoidance behavior is considerably more intricate than any single one of these formulations suggests. It has also become apparent to me that the early experiments have disproportionately influenced most current formulations. If we were to take later experiments as our starting point, some of the notions we now cherish might not even occur to us. The data would not require them. In this chapter I shall summarize some of the experiments performed by my colleagues and myself. I shall not attempt to formalize the data but shall simply present a few of the problems they raise.

FREE-OPERANT AVOIDANCE[2]

The experimenter places a white rat in a small metal chamber, of which detailed descriptions may be found in the references listed at the end of the chapter. Projecting through one end of the chamber is a lever which the animal may depress; a grid of stainless steel rods forms the floor of the chamber.

By means of automatically programmed electrical or electronic equipment the experimenter then gives the animal a series of intense but brief electric shocks through the grid floor. Two recycling timers program the shocks. When the animal does not press the lever, the time interval between shocks, called the *shock-shock interval,* is specified by the first timer. The animal can postpone the shock by pressing the lever. The amount of time the animal postpones a shock by pressing the lever is called the *response-shock interval,* and is programmed by the second timer. The two timers never operate simultaneously. Each shock starts the shock-shock interval anew; the first time the animal depresses the lever after being shocked, it ends the shock-shock interval and starts the response-shock timer. The response-shock interval begins anew each time the animal presses the lever. By pressing the lever, the animal ensures that the second timer cannot deliver a shock before the response-shock interval has elapsed.

No exteroceptive stimulus warns the animal that a shock is impending. The duration of the shock is fixed at a fraction of a second, so that the animal does not terminate the shock. The animal postpones a shock *every* time it presses the lever.

Figure 1 is a diagrammatic representation of the procedure. If the animal does not press the lever, the shock-shock timer determines the base

[2] The basic technique has been given several names, e.g., nondiscriminated avoidance, the method of temporal pacing, continuous avoidance, and Sidman avoidance. The term *free-operant avoidance,* if not self-explanatory, is more accurate descriptively than the first of these, is not as theoretically committed as the second and third, and gives a more appropriate historical credit than the last.

rate, or density, of shock. The extent to which the animal can reduce the base shock density is limited only by the rate and temporal pattern of its responses on the lever.

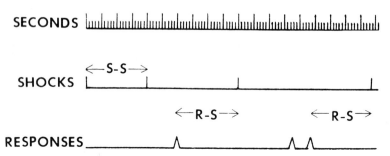

Figure 1. A diagrammatic representation of the free-operant avoidance procedure. S-S indicates the shock-shock interval; R-S indicates the response-shock interval.

Equal Shock-shock and Response-shock Intervals in Acquisition

Subjects differ widely in their acquisition of free-operant avoidance behavior. Such variability should neither surprise nor impress us. When we simply place a subject in an unfamiliar environment, set a task for it, and wait for reinforcement contingencies to take hold, we leave to chance the operation of variables that may either facilitate or obstruct the learning process.

Hively (1962) has suggested that the procedure of successive approximations is effective in teaching stimulus discriminations because the procedure directs the subject's attention to relevant stimulus dimensions. This is probably true also in the shaping of responses; the subject learns to attend to relevant aspects of its own behavior, as well as to other variables. When we do not arrange contingencies optimally during learning, subjects will differ from each other in the kind of variables they observe. They will also follow different temporal sequences in establishing contact with relevant aspects of both their own behavior and environmental stimuli.

In learning an avoidance response, animals have considerable opportunity to display such variability, perhaps more so than in other learning situations because the reinforcement for avoidance is less immediate. This makes it more difficult for them to differentiate those particular aspects of their own behavior which are responsible for the avoidance of the shock. Furthermore, there are a number of possible sources of reinforcement for the avoidance response; not all animals will be reinforced by the same events, and control may shift from one source of reinforcement to another during different stages of learning.

Keeping in mind these nonquantitative considerations, let us look at some data that illustrate several varieties of behavior during the animal's first conditioning session. What features strike us in the cumulative record of Figure 2?

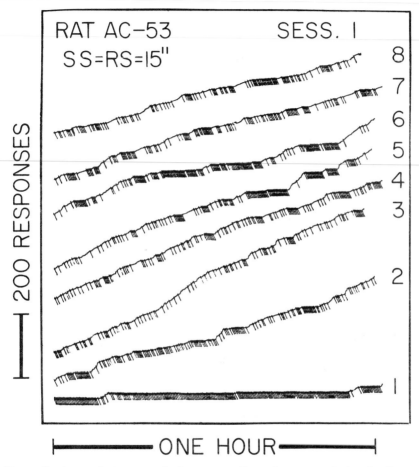

Figure 2. A cumulative record of an animal's performance during its first exposure to the free-operant avoidance procedure. To condense the figure, the record has been cut into segments of approximately one hour each; the segments are numbered in their temporal order. The oblique "pips" on the record indicate shocks.

Perhaps the first observation is that the animal did learn to press the lever and avoid shocks; it responded more than 2000 times in the eight-hour session. A second feature of the record is the decline in response rate as the session progressed; the animal pressed the lever more frequently during the second and third hours than during the final hours. But in spite of its lower rate of lever pressing, Rat AC-53 received only 17 more shocks during the final hour than during the third hour. Third, we note that the animal often stopped pressing the lever and received an uninterrupted series of shocks before pressing again. The longest of these unbroken series of shocks occurred in the first hour, but shorter ones continued to appear at irregular times throughout the session. Finally, although the rat unquestionably learned to press the lever, it never went very long without receiving at least one shock. The longest time the animal was able to keep completely free of shocks was a four-minute period near the end of the sixth hour.

Rat AD-14 (Figure 3) pressed the lever only 253 times in approximately eight hours, and avoided few of the scheduled shocks. It would be difficult to prove that this animal learned anything. Not until the end of its fourth session did Rat AD-14 press the lever at a substantial rate.

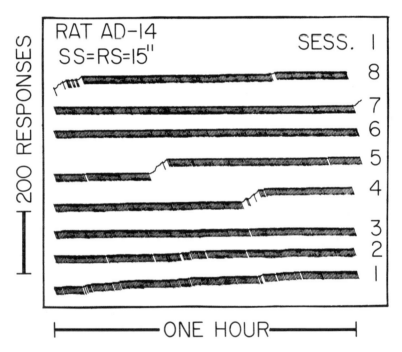

Figure 3. See legend for Figure 2.

Rat CQ-35 (Figure 4) differs from Rats AD-14 and AC-53. Rat CQ-35 began pressing the lever relatively early in its first session; it gradually increased its response rate and by the end of the session was avoiding shocks quite effectively. Few animals perform as well after only six hours of conditioning.

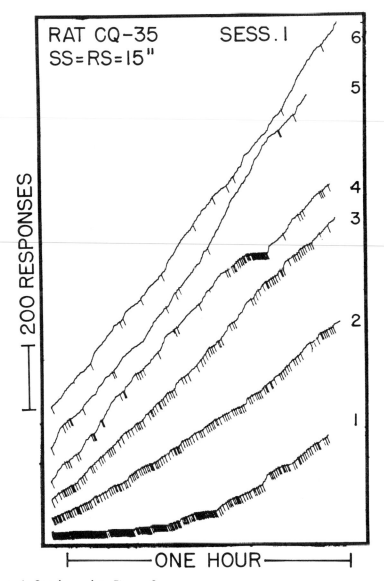

Figure 4. See legend to Figure 2.

The different rates of acquisition are not the data of prime interest here. Other species of subjects (e.g., Ader & Tatum, 1961; Black & Morse, 1961) or rats in other types of experimental situations (e.g., Mowrer & Keehn, 1958) may learn much more quickly to avoid shocks than these records suggest. The cumulative curves in Figures 2-4 derive their interest from the inconsistencies they reveal in the acquisition process itself. For example, noteworthy features of Rat AD-14's record (Figure 3) are those isolated instances in the fourth, fifth, seventh, and eighth hours in which the animal pressed the lever at a high rate and markedly reduced the frequency of shocks it received. Unlike Rat CQ-35 (Figure 4), which gradually increased the frequency and duration of such periods of successful avoidance responding, Rat AD-14's success seemed to have no lasting effect. The record suggests that successful avoidance, while perhaps necessary, is far from a sufficient condition for the learning of avoidance.

It is probably incorrect to say that Rat AD-14 learned nothing during its brief periods of successful avoidance. A more likely conclusion would be that it learned the wrong things. Rat AD-14 probably was not attending to the downward movement of the lever as the critical element of the avoidance response, but rather to some other aspect of its behavior that was imperfectly correlated with lever pressing. We might expect more rapid avoidance conditioning and less intersubject variability if we specified an avoidance response that is a component of all possible patterns of the subject's behavior; if the subject could avoid shock with *any* movement, it might learn successfully and rapidly without ever differentiating reality from superstition.

Or we might teach the subject to attend to the critical response in situations similar to avoidance. For example, if animals can both escape and avoid shock with the same response, they learn the avoidance response more rapidly than animals that cannot themselves terminate the shock, or that have to use different responses for escape and avoidance (Mowrer & Lamoreaux, 1946; Kamin, Campbell, Judd, Ryan, & Walker, 1959). The facilitative transfer from escape to avoidance has been attributed to mediation by a drive state, e.g., anxiety, that is common to both escape and avoidance (Solomon & Wynne, 1953). The transfer may take place, instead, along perceptual channels. The more easily learned escape response, with its immediate reinforcement, may facilitate the animal's observation of the part of its behavior which is critical for avoidance.

Although Rat AD-14's record indicates that the animal's occasional interruption of the steady series of shocks was not a sufficient condition for avoidance learning, Figure 2 (Rat AC-53) suggests that frequent reexposure to the shocks does serve an important function. It would not be difficult to conclude from this record, which is probably the most typical of all those I have observed, that termination of the shock series per se is an important source of reinforcement for the animal in learning to avoid. It is, perhaps, equally likely that the repeated occurrence of several shocks in succession is not a necessary part of the acquisition process, but that it is simply a by-product of the animal's imperfect differentiation of the critical response. Rat CQ-35 (Figure 4) experienced relatively few sustained periods of shocks after the first hour. Either such periods are actually not necessary, or some kind of transition takes place, more quickly in some animals than others, in which control of the reinforcement process shifts from a series of shocks to a single one.

The decline in response rate as the session proceeds (Figure 2) is a consistent phenomenon but is not necessarily compressed into the initial conditioning session. The animal may actually increase its rate of lever pressing for several consecutive sessions before it begins to slow down; this is illustrated in Figure 5. It is not clear whether the decline in the animal's

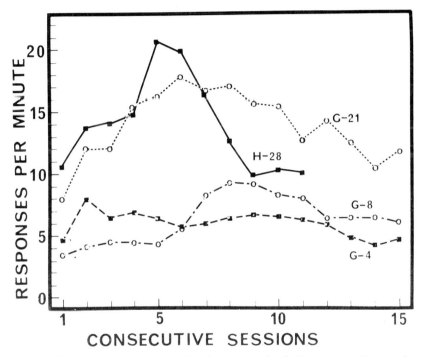

Figure 5. Average response rates for four animals during consecutive sessions of exposure to the free-operant avoidance procedure.

rate of lever pressing during the first session reflects the same processes as the long-term decline shown in Figure 5. The latter is correlated with a change in the way the animal spaces its responses temporally, a change to be described more fully in the section on temporal discrimination.

Unequal Shock-shock and Response-shock Intervals in Acquisition

When the shock-shock interval is considerably shorter than the response-shock interval, animals generally learn more quickly to avoid than when the two intervals are equal. Figure 6 shows an animal's first-session

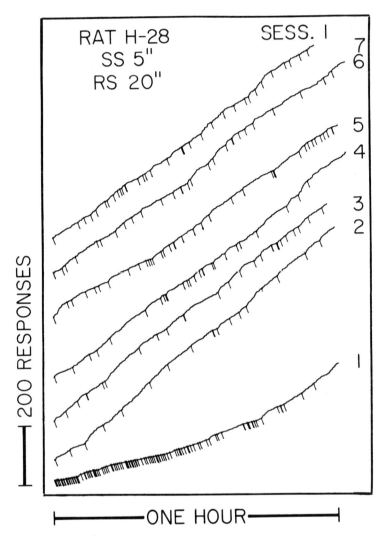

Figure 6. See legend for Figure 2.

performance with a shock-shock interval of five seconds and a response-shock interval of 20 seconds. Although this combination of intervals does not always produce such effective behavior during the first session, few animals fail to show a substantial rate of avoidance responding within the first hour. Black and Morse (1961) have also demonstrated more rapid avoidance conditioning with shorter shock-shock intervals.

Figure 7 demonstrates the effectiveness of short shock-shock intervals in yet another way. Rat GF-11 had shock-shock and response-shock intervals each equal to 20 seconds during most of the first two hours of conditioning, and failed to learn the avoidance response during that time. Rats which respond so infrequently during the first two hours rarely learn to avoid later in the same session unless the conditions change in some way. One method of improving the poor prognosis is to reduce the shock-shock interval. Rat GF-11 took slightly more than 45 minutes to react to this change with a substantial increase in its rate of lever pressing.

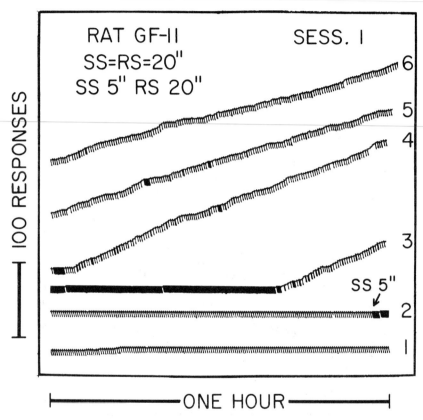

Figure 7. See legend for Figure 2. At the arrow, the shock-shock interval was reduced from 20 to 5 seconds.

In examining Figure 2, we noted that the interruption of a series of shocks was a possible source of reinforcement for the animal's avoidance behavior. The efficacy of short shock-shock intervals in facilitating avoidance learning reemphasizes this possibility. In Figure 7, the animal rarely experienced the shock-shock interval during the last part of the session; it almost always pressed the lever at least once between shocks. Rat GF-11's prevailing pattern of behavior was to terminate the five-second shock-shock interval by pressing the lever soon after receiving a shock, and then to wait out the 20-second response-shock interval. This response pattern, frequently observed in both rats and monkeys, is illustrated again in Figure 8. It is a phase through which most animals pass before they achieve a more effective mode of avoiding shocks, and its duration may range from a few minutes to several sessions; some animals may even progress no further unless the experimenter takes special measures. Dinsmoor (1962) has shown that the reinforcement during this stage is powerful enough to keep the animals responding even when they can only occasionally terminate the series of shocks.

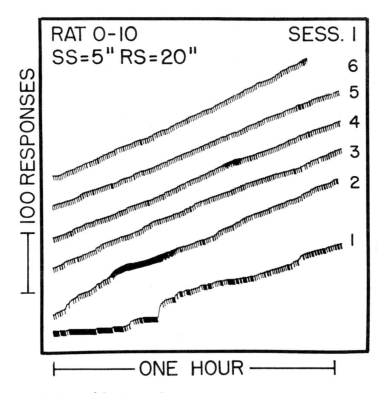

Figure 8. See legend for Figure 2.

Temporal Parameters and the Maintenance of Free-operant Avoidance

After the animal learned to press the lever and avoid shocks, and had preliminary experience with several values of shock-shock and response-shock intervals, the experimenter set the shock-shock interval at a fixed value and determined the animal's rate of avoidance responding for a series of response-shock intervals, in mixed order. He then changed the shock-

shock interval and recorded the animal's response rates again at several response-shock intervals. The procedure was repeated until the animal had generated a family of curves that related its rate of avoidance responding to the length of the response-shock interval, the set of response-shock intervals being combined with a series of different shock-shock intervals. Figure 9 shows a sample of the data from this experiment (Sidman, 1953).

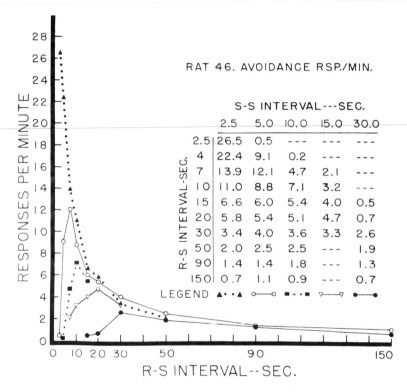

Figure 9. The table gives the average response rates for one animal at each combination of shock-shock and response-shock intervals. The response rates are partially plotted in the curves. (After Sidman, 1953.)

As the response-shock interval decreases from its highest values, the animal presses the lever more rapidly until it reaches a maximum rate for a given shock-shock interval. With continued decreases in the response-shock interval, the animal's rate of avoidance responding drops sharply from its maximum value. The two segments of the curves intersect at a response-shock interval whose value is determined by the shock-shock interval; with briefer shock-shock intervals we can use shorter response-shock intervals and still maintain the animal's behavior.

In a preliminary analysis, Anger (personal communication) examined how the shock-shock and response-shock timers may interact with the animal's behavior to alter the number of shocks it receives. His analysis helps to clarify at least one feature of curves like those of Figure 9: namely, the response-shock interval at which the animal ceases to press the lever (the points at the extreme left of Figure 9). When the shock-shock interval is longer than the response-shock interval, the animal can actually produce more frequent shocks by pressing the lever. For example, with the shock-shock timer set at 20 seconds, the animal would receive a shock every 20 seconds if it did not press the lever. But with the response-shock timer set at ten seconds, if the animal presses the lever once within the first half of the shock-shock interval, it would receive the next shock ten seconds after that response—earlier than if it had allowed the shock-shock timer to deliver the shock.

Assuming that the animal responds randomly in time, we reach a critical point when the response-shock interval becomes less than half of the shock-shock interval. At this value, the probability that the animal will increase the frequency of shocks by pressing the lever at certain rates becomes higher than 0.5—higher than the probability of postponing the shock. Anger replotted the data of Figure 9, using not the response-shock interval on the abscissa but, instead, the ratio of response-shock to shock-shock intervals. He found, indeed, that the animals almost always ceased pressing the lever whenever the ratio of response-shock to shock-shock intervals was within the range of 0.40 to 0.55.

The location of the maxima in curves like those of Figure 9 also reflects the critical ratio of 0.5. When the shock-shock interval is zero, the curve shows no indication of passing through a maximum, even with a response-shock interval as low as 1.7 seconds (Sidman, 1953). In most other instances the animal's rate of lever pressing continues to rise with shorter response-shock intervals but drops off sharply as the critical ratio approaches. This sharp drop in response rate may be regarded in principle as a discontinuous change, so that the maximum also is determined by the critical ratio. Those curves in which the positive wing appears to be a gradual rather than a discontinuous function, probably indicate that our assumption of random responding in time is inadequate. The probability that the animal could increase the frequency of shocks by responding would depend both on the rate at which it was pressing the lever and the way it spaced its responses.

Shock frequency, then, directly controlled by the shock-shock interval, may determine the positive slopes and the location of the maxima in the curves of Figure 9. But what of the more extensive negative slopes of these curves? The shape of the gradients to the right of the maxima bears no consistent relation to the shock-shock interval (Sidman, 1953). It would be pointless for me to recapitulate here my many hours of futile endeavor to derive these functions quantitatively. I have not even been able to appeal successfully to the "common-sense" observation that the animals must respond more rapidly at shorter response-shock intervals if they are to continue to avoid shocks. The data reveal a number of instances in which the animals actually received more shocks than they would have received if they had maintained an unchanged rate of lever pressing at shorter response-shock intervals.[3] A quantitatively verifiable answer to the question of why the animals increased their rate of avoidance responding with shorter response-shock intervals remains to be found.

Temporal Discrimination

The free-operant avoidance technique ensures that the subject will receive a shock whenever it fails to press the lever within the response-shock or the shock-shock interval. The fixed temporal relations between shocks and lever-pressing responses suggest that some form of temporal conditioning may be involved when the subject learns to avoid. Evidence bearing on this possibility is presented in Figures 10-13; these data were obtained with shock-shock and response-shock intervals of 20 seconds.

One method of demonstrating the presence or absence of temporal discrimination is to record the amount of time the animal allows to elapse between each of its successive lever-pressing responses. These *interresponse times* may then be classified into a frequency distribution. If the animal has indeed formed a precise temporal discrimination, we should expect to find that it usually presses the lever and then allows almost the entire response-shock interval to go by before pressing again.

The histogram of Figure 10, recorded during the animal's twenty-ninth 7.5-hour session of avoidance conditioning, is almost the mirror image of what we would expect if Rat D-4 had formed a temporal discrimination. For contrast, see the histogram of Figure 11.

Anger (1956) has pointed out, however, that the frequency distribution of interresponse times may be a relatively insensitive indicator of temporal processes and may even blind us to their existence. Short interresponse times may predominate simply because there are not so many opportunities for long interresponse times. The dotted curve of Figure 10 illustrates this. I have replotted the data of the histogram to show, in percentages, how many of the animal's interresponse times were greater than each particular interresponse time. For example, 100 percent of the interresponse times had to be longer than zero seconds; but after 33 percent of its responses the animal pressed the lever again within two seconds, leaving

[3] This conclusion was based on the assumption that the animals spaced their responses randomly in time (see, for example, Mueller, 1950). The data do not completely justify this assumption, but there are indications that deviations from it are the result of special processes (see below; also Sidman, 1954; 1955).

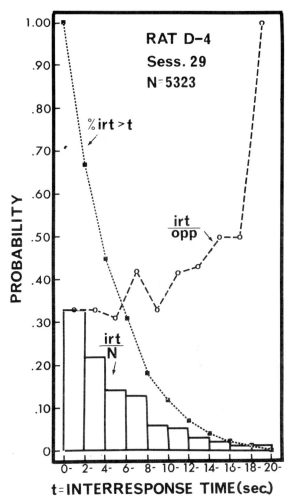

Figure 10. Free-operant avoidance. Three methods of depicting the probability of interresponse times. The histogram shows the number of interresponse times (IRTs) in each class, divided by the total number (N) of interresponse times during the session; the dotted curve shows the percentage of the total IRTs that was greater than the lower limit of each IRT class (t); the dashed curve shows the number of IRTs in each class, divided by the total number of opportunities (OPP) for IRTs in that class.

only 67 percent of the interresponse times available for the rest of the frequency distribution. Similarly, an additional 22 percent of the animal's responses came within two to four seconds of the preceding one, leaving only 45 percent of the total available for interresponse times greater than four seconds. The population of interresponse intervals from which to calculate

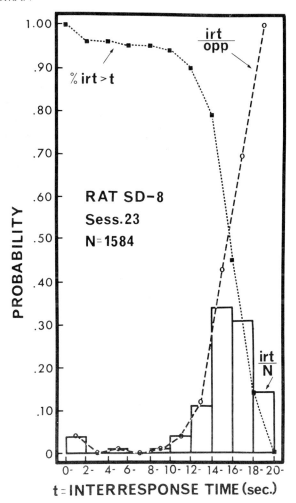

Figure 11. See legend for Figure 10.

our probabilities must decline as we move out along the abscissa of our graph.

The histogram, then, is derived from the number of interresponse times in each class. The cumulative distribution (broken line) shows how the number of opportunities for longer interresponse times declines. By dividing the height of each bar of the histogram by the corresponding value on the cumulative distribution we take account of the declining opportunities and obtain the probabilities shown in the dashed curve of Figure 10. Anger (1956; 1963) has called this a curve of "interresponse times per opportunity" (IRT/OPP), and has argued persuasively that it provides the most sensitive indicator of interresponse-time probabilities.

An imperfect temporal discrimination is indeed shown in the IRT/ OPP curve of Figure 10 even though the corresponding histogram obscures the discrimination. But there are several grounds on which we may question how relevant the temporal processes are while the animal is learning to avoid shocks. First, the magnitude of the discrimination is relatively small, with response probabilities ranging only from .31 in the 4-6-second class to .50 in the 16-18-second class.[4] Second, the discrimination is relatively imprecise; the likelihood that the animal will press the lever begins to rise early in the response-shock interval and increases only gradually as the interval passes. Rat D-4 evinced such a small and inaccurate temporal discrimination after 217.5 hours of training. Again, for comparison, see Figure 11.

Third, we may ask about the total amount of avoidance behavior the temporal discrimination accounts for. As the shock became more imminent, Rat D-4 did indeed accept an increasing percentage of its available opportunities to press the lever. But the actual number of opportunities was small. We may select ten seconds—halfway into the response-shock interval—as an arbitrary dividing point; only 12 percent of the animal's interresponse times were longer than ten seconds. Again, by comparison, Rat SD-8 (Figure 11) spaced its responses so that 94 percent of its opportunities to respond came in the last half of the response-shock interval.

The question, then, is not whether temporal discrimination is involved in avoidance behavior; Figures 10, 11, and others give clear evidence that it is. But the small magnitude of Rat D-4's discrimination, its relative imprecision, and the small proportion of the animal's responses involved in the discrimination, all suggest that temporal processes of the sort illustrated in Figure 10 are secondary in the acquisition of avoidance behavior. As Figure 11 may lead us to suspect, these temporal processes can play an important role in maintaining the behavior once the animal has learned to avoid.

Even when the temporal discrimination appears earlier and more clearly than it did with Rat D-4, we may question its primacy in acquisition. Figure 12 illustrates a much more advanced discrimination as early as Session 5. Again, however, comparison with Figure 11 indicates that the temporal processes do not yet exert full control. We may note, further, that Rats D-4 and G-18 received 24 and 40 shocks, respectively, in the sessions illustrated—a favorable comparison with Rat SD-8, which received 83 shocks. Efficient avoidance behavior, in terms of the number of shocks the animal avoids successfully, may develop long before the temporal dis-

---

[4] Because of the relatively small number of opportunities for the animal to respond after long pauses, the final points on the curve are subject to extreme fluctuations with only small changes in the number of long pauses. Therefore, the final jump to a probability of 1.00 must be interpreted conservatively.

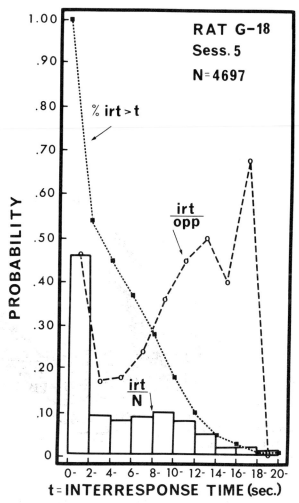

Figure 12. See legend for Figure 10.

crimination involves a substantial amount of the animal's total avoidance behavior.

Up to now, we have been examining interresponse times; we may also look at shock-response times, i.e., the time interval between each shock and the animal's *subsequent* avoidance response. Figures 13A and 13B give the probability functions for each of these time intervals separately. This animal received enough shocks to yield reliable probabilities for the shock-response times. We see two distinct temporal patterns existing "side by side" during the same session. For time intervals that begin with shocks (Figure 13A), Rat G-38 shows a relatively advanced temporal discrimination; in Figure

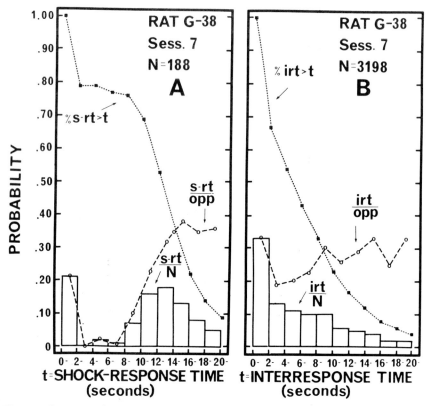

Figure 13. A. Similar to Figures 10-12, except that the intervals are between each shock and the next response (shock-response times, or S-RT) instead of between responses. B. See legend for Figure 10.

13B, the response-response intervals (interresponse times) indicate only a poorly developed temporal discrimination. Figure 13A includes only approximately 5 percent of all the animal's avoidance responses, indicating again that temporal discrimination may be considered a product of, rather than a causative factor in, avoidance conditioning. It is not clear whether the temporal discrimination based on shocks always develops earlier than the one based on responses, or whether the two discriminations are dependent on each other in any way.

Why do animals develop a temporal discrimination? One consequence of a longer interresponse time is that the animal postpones the shock for a longer period. (This refers, of course, to interresponse times that are not so long as to bring on the shock.) The animal will gain more time free of shock with two well-spaced responses than by spacing two responses close together. Although it is possible that an animal may, by chance, distribute its first lever-pressing responses efficiently and thereby be reinforced from the beginning for a temporal discrimination, this is not likely. It is more probable that the temporal discrimination is a second-order process, with temporally spaced responses emerging through differential reinforcement from a higher, less efficient response rate. We may check this by means of two additional procedures for conditioning avoidance behavior, *adjusting avoidance* and *fixed cycle avoidance*.

ADJUSTING AVOIDANCE

The rat receives a shock every five seconds as long as it does not press the lever. Each time it presses the lever, however, it adds five seconds to the time that must elapse before the next shock. For example, if the animal were to press the lever two seconds before a shock was due, that shock would not come until seven (two plus five) seconds had elapsed; if the animal pressed again after one more second had gone by, it would have lost one of the seven seconds it had accumulated, and the next shock would come eleven (six plus five) seconds later. At any point, then, the time remaining before the rat can receive a shock will depend jointly on how often it has pressed the lever and how much time has elapsed since it was shocked last. Within limits, therefore, the animal can adjust the duration of the response-shock interval.

A feature of the adjusting procedure is that the amount of safe time the animal gains each time it presses the lever is independent of the interval that has elapsed since its preceding response. Every time it presses the lever, regardless of when it responded previously, the animal receives an additional five seconds free from the possibility of shock. There is no differential reinforcement for long interresponse times.

Figure 14 summarizes one animal's temporal pattern of lever pressing during its first conditioning session with the adjusting procedure. There is no evidence here to suggest that temporal conditioning was involved. Even after several hundred hours of exposure to the adjusting procedure, animals show no consistent evidence of temporal discrimination (Sidman, 1962a). This is in marked contrast to the free-operant procedure, in which the animal avoids shocks most effectively by spacing its responses widely apart in time. The adjusting procedure gives each avoidance response equal weight, and this may help explain the failure of a temporal discrimination to emerge.

The adjusting procedure does provide some opportunity for the selective punishment of responses that are spaced more than five seconds apart. If the animal spaces several successive responses less than five seconds from each other, the next shock can come only after a relatively long time interval, depending on the number of responses in the "burst." After an interresponse time greater than five seconds, shock may come sooner than after

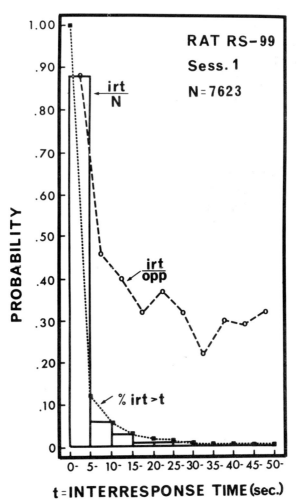

Figure 14. Like Figure 10, except that the procedure was adjusting avoidance.

a burst, depending on the length of the interresponse time and the animal's temporal location with respect to shock. If the animal could make this distinction as early as its first conditioning session, it might account for the fact that 88 percent of the responses in Figure 14 were separated by less than five seconds. However, bursts of rapid responses are also common in the early sessions of the free-operant procedure where they have no advantage with respect to delay of punishment. A more likely assumption is that response bursts have the same origin in both procedures but that they tend to diminish in the free-operant procedure where they are a relatively inefficient way for the animal to avoid shocks.

FIXED CYCLE AVOIDANCE

The experimental session is divided into successive 15-second cycles. Shocks are scheduled to be delivered to the rat at the end of each cycle, i.e., every 15 seconds. The animal has only to press the lever once during any cycle to prevent shock at the end of that cycle; additional responses during that particular cycle have no programmed effect. A new cycle always begins every 15 seconds, at the point where the animal is shocked or would have been shocked if it had not successfully avoided. This is different from the free-operant avoidance procedure in which the subject initiates a new cycle each time it presses the lever.

With the fixed cycle procedure, we can examine the behavior for evidence of temporal discrimination by recording the number of times the animal presses the lever in successive 1.5-second segments of each 15-second cycle. If the subject distributed its responses evenly throughout the ten subintervals of the cycle, each interval would contain 10 percent of the total. Figure 15 illustrates the temporal distribution of lever-pressing responses

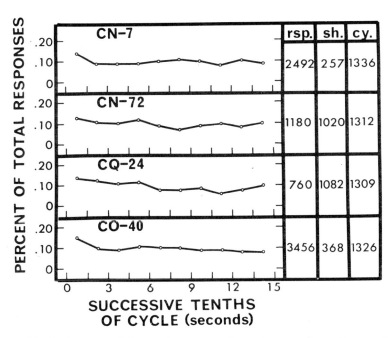

Figure 15. Percentage of the total responses in each successive 1.5-second segment of the 15-second cycle for four animals during this first session on the fixed cycle avoidance procedure. The numbers at the right give the total responses (RSP.), total shocks (SH.), and total cycles (CY.) during the session.

for four rats during their first conditioning session. All responses during each cycle were counted.

The probabilities depart little from .10; if there is any trend at all, it is toward lower response probabilities in the last part of the cycle. These animals apparently learned to press the lever without assistance from a temporal discrimination. Two of the animals, CN-7 and CO-40, learned to avoid much more effectively than the others, but all of them showed the same even distribution of responses throughout the cycle.

Up to this point the data indicate that temporal discrimination is not critical for animals to learn to avoid shocks. Temporal factors enter the picture later and eventually may exert considerable control over the animal's avoidance behavior. Whatever these temporal factors are, there seems to be no immediate necessity to consider the nature of their control to be different from any other events which serve the animal as cues. The critical question is: How do the temporal processes acquire and maintain discriminative control over an animal's behavior? The animal must be able to use the temporal processes to enhance the effectiveness of its avoidance behavior; like any discriminative stimuli, temporal factors must lead to reinforcing consequences if they are to assume control over behavior.

The fixed cycle procedure has a consistent shock-shock interval. Yet even Rats CN-72 and CQ-24, each of which received more than 1000 shocks during its first conditioning sessions, gave no evidence of a temporal discrimination based on shocks. After 15 6.5-hour sessions, there was still no evidence of temporal discrimination (Sidman, 1962b). During the later sessions, when the animals received only a few shocks, temporal discrimination based on shock could not have been relevant to the animals' avoidance behavior. But if the number of shocks an animal receives is high enough to control a substantial segment of its avoidance responses, and if the animal can use the temporal relation to avoid shock more effectively, it will demonstrate a temporal discrimination. These conditions produced the data of Figure 13A. Even if the animal gains no actual benefit from a temporal discrimination, the consistent spacing of shocks in time provides an opportunity for temporal processes to be correlated adventitiously with reinforcement.

The following variations in the fixed cycle procedure illustrate additional temporal discriminations.

LIMITED INTERVAL AVOIDANCE

The animal is first exposed to the fixed cycle avoidance procedure as described above. It can press the lever at any time during a cycle and avoid the shock that would otherwise come at the end of the cycle. The avoidance interval therefore equals the total cycle length, 15 seconds.

We then reduce the avoidance interval to three seconds. Only by pressing the lever during this limited interval can the animal avoid the shock that is due at the end of the cycle. The interval can be located in different parts of the cycle, but we shall describe only two instances here. In one, the avoidance interval constitutes the last three seconds of the cycle. The animal can prevent the shock by pressing the lever 12 to 15 seconds after the beginning of the cycle; responses earlier in the cycle have no programmed effect. In the other variation, the avoidance interval is located between 7.5 and 10.5 seconds. The animal cannot prevent the shock by responding during the first 7.5 seconds or the last 4.5 seconds of the cycle; it can keep itself from being shocked at the end of the cycle only by pressing the lever at least once between 7.5 and 10.5 seconds.

Figure 16 illustrates the animals' temporal discriminations after we re-

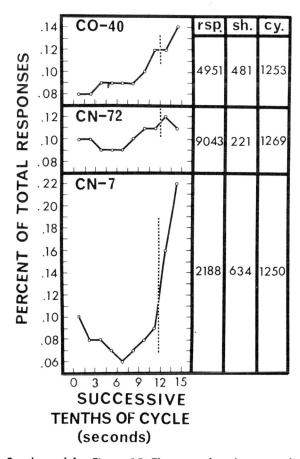

Figure 16. See legend for Figure 15. The procedure here was limited interval avoidance. A response served to avoid the shock only in the 12- to 15-second interval. (After Sidman, 1962b.)

stricted the avoidance interval to the final three seconds of the cycle. Enough cycles began with a shock to give the animals a substantial number of reference points from which to locate themselves within the cycle. Furthermore, the animals were differentially reinforced for responding near the end of the cycle. Both conditions were satisfied for the establishment and maintenance of a temporal discrimination based on shock.

When the avoidance interval was located close to the center of the cycle, from 7.5 to 10.5 seconds, the animals avoided much less effectively and received large numbers of shocks. Figure 17 shows five consecutive sessions for one animal. Although Rat CN-72's response rate was high during two of these sessions, it was low during the others, and eventually the avoidance behavior all but disappeared. Temporal discrimination, however, was prominent, even though it represented a "wrong" discrimination.

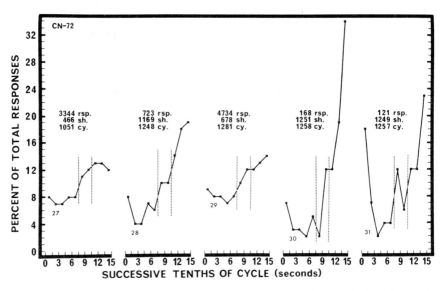

Figure 17. See legend for Figure 15. Five consecutive sessions of limited interval avoidance, with the avoidance interval between 7.5 and 10.5 seconds. (After Sidman, 1962b.)

When the avoidance interval comes at the end of the cycle the animal has little difficulty, for successful avoidance behavior is closely positively correlated with the temporal cycle generated by the periodic shocks. But when the avoidance interval comes near the middle of the cycle, this correlation breaks down. Successful avoidance responses must be out of phase with the shocks. It should be possible to help the animal avoid shock successfully no matter where in the cycle we locate the avoidance interval. For example, stimulus A might be on at all times unless the animal pressed the lever during the avoidance interval. An effective response would terminate stimulus A and turn on stimulus B which would remain on till the beginning of the next avoidance interval. All shocks would then occur in the presence of stimulus A; the animal would never be shocked when stimulus B was on. Stimulus B would be out of phase with the shocks. Which temporal cycle would predominate in controlling the animal's behavior?

Let us now look at a procedure, related to limited interval avoidance, in which temporal discrimination permits the animal to avoid shocks under conditions that normally cause it to stop responding.

FIXED INTERVAL AVOIDANCE

The animal learns to press the lever and avoid shocks under the free-operant procedure. The avoidance procedure, itself, is then programmed according to a fixed interval schedule. Figure 18 is a diagrammatic repre-

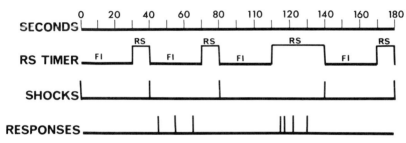

Figure 18. A diagrammatic representation of the fixed interval avoidance procedure. Responses during the fixed interval period (FI) have no effect on the shock; responses during the response-shock period (RS) postpone the shock.

sentation of the schedule. Nothing happens during the fixed interval (FI) after each shock; if the animal presses the lever during this period, it accomplishes nothing. At the end of the fixed interval, the response-shock timer (RS) begins to operate. At the end of the response-shock interval, the animal receives a shock. If the animal presses the lever during the response-shock interval, it postpones the shock. In the illustration, the fixed interval is 30 seconds and the response-shock interval is ten seconds. If the animal never pressed the lever, it would receive a shock every 40 seconds; the shock-shock interval, then, equals the sum of the fixed interval and the response-shock interval.

In discussing the free-operant avoidance procedure, we noted that when the response-shock interval was briefer than the shock-shock interval, the animal could increase the shock density by pressing the lever at certain rates. In fixed interval avoidance, however, the animal cannot increase the shock density by responding, no matter how much the shock-shock interval exceeds the response-shock interval. Because of this property of the fixed interval procedure, it has been possible to maintain the animals' avoidance behavior with a fixed interval of four minutes and a response-shock interval of 15 seconds, i.e., a shock-shock interval of 255 seconds.

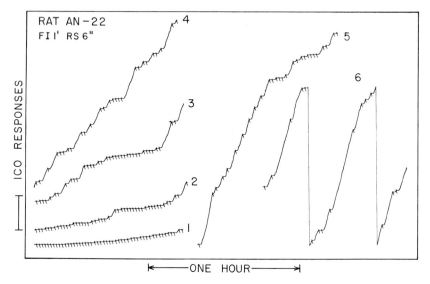

Figure 19. Cumulative record of an animal's performance on the fixed interval avoidance procedure. Segments of the record are numbered consecutively.

Figure 19 shows one animal's performance with a fixed interval of 60 seconds, a response-shock interval of only six seconds, and a shock-shock interval, therefore, of 66 seconds. The schedule generates a high response rate even with a response-shock interval less than one-tenth of the shock-shock interval. The record also illustrates the temporal discrimination that is typical of the fixed interval procedure. After each shock, the animal pauses for an appreciable length of time before beginning to press the lever.

In explaining the positive slopes in the curves of Figure 9, we noted that the ratio 0.5 of response-shock to shock-shock interval is critical if the animal distributes its responses randomly in time. However, if the animal forms a temporal discrimination, the critical ratio can be considerably less than 0.5. For example, if the animal presses the lever only in the last half of the response-shock interval it can continue to decrease the shock density by responding even when the shock-shock interval is more than twice as long as the response-shock interval. The temporal discrimination illustrated in Figure 19 also makes it possible for the animal to maintain successful avoidance behavior under normally unfavorable conditions. An example appears in Figure 20. After considerable experience with a fixed interval of two minutes and a response-shock interval of 30 seconds, the animal was returned to free-operant avoidance with the same temporal parameters. Because of the long pause after each shock, the animal rarely caused shocks to occur closer together than the shock-shock interval (ex-

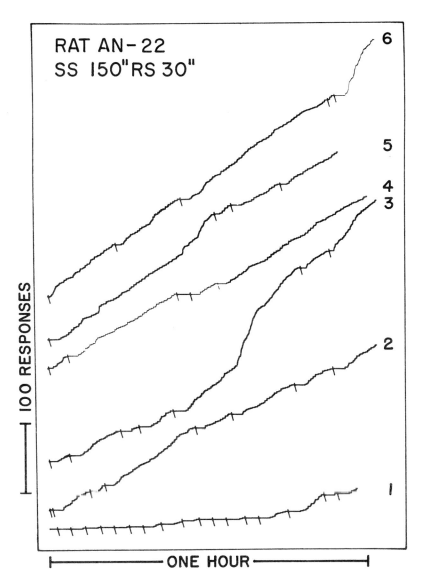

Figure 20. Performance of an animal on free-operant avoidance after exposure to fixed interval avoidance with the same temporal parameters.

amples may be seen at the start of the second hour and the end of the sixth hour), and it continued to press the lever at a respectable rate. Temporal discrimination, then, may play an important role either to help or to hinder an animal in avoiding shocks.

VARIABLE RESPONSE-SHOCK INTERVALS

In the adjusting avoidance procedure, each time the animal presses the lever it adds five seconds to the time remaining before a shock can be delivered. Inevitably, then, the response-shock interval varies. The experimenter, however, cannot specify the variations in advance, since they depend on the rate and temporal distribution of the animals' responses.

In the experiments to be described now, variations in the response-shock interval were *shock contingent*. A given response-shock interval remained in effect until the animal permitted the shock to occur. The interval changed after each shock. This procedure permits us to specify in advance the sequence of response-shock intervals that will actually make contact with the behavior, for the animal must receive a shock at a given response-shock interval before a new interval can be programmed.

Five animals were first trained to press the lever and avoid shock with the free-operant avoidance procedure, using a response-shock interval of 20 seconds. They were then changed to the variable procedure, in which the response-shock intervals were 4, 10, 15, and 20 seconds, changing after each shock. In later phases of the experiment a fifth interval was added: 25 seconds, 40 seconds, or 80 seconds. In addition, several animals were also conditioned from the beginning on the variable response-shock interval procedure.

The detailed data of this experiment need not be presented here (Sidman & Boren, 1957b). The major finding was that the animals successfully learned and maintained their avoidance behavior with variable response-shock intervals.

Those animals that had formed a temporal discrimination during the initial free-operant procedure maintained the discrimination even with variable response-shock intervals. Anger (1963) pointed out that although shocks are programmed equally often after short and long pauses in the variable procedure, there are necessarily many more short pauses. The number of shocks per opportunity, therefore, is lowest soon after the animal responds and increases as the animal goes longer without pressing the lever. The temporal discrimination may be a reflection of this gradually increasing shock probability as time passes without a response.

The variable procedure may also be viewed as one in which the schedule of shocks is intermittent for each response-shock interval. The animal receives a shock every time it pauses for a duration equal to the longest response-shock interval, but shocks follow briefer pauses only when shorter response-shock intervals are being programmed. The following procedure is a simpler and more explicit method of programming intermittent shocks.

INTERMITTENT SHOCKS

The procedure is a variant of free-operant avoidance in which the animal does not receive a certain proportion of the shocks that come due when it fails to press the lever within the shock-shock or response-shock interval.

The animals were first conditioned to press the lever and avoid shock under the basic free-operant procedure, with shock-shock and response-shock intervals both equal to 20 seconds. The intermittent shock procedure was then introduced.

In the 100 percent shock procedure the animals received a shock every time 20 seconds elapsed without their pressing the lever. In the intermittent shock procedures, the animals received a shock only on a predetermined percentage of the occasions on which they waited 20 seconds without responding. For example, in the 50 percent shock procedure a shock became due each time the animal waited 20 seconds without pressing the lever, but only 50 percent of the due shocks were actually delivered. The shock percentages used were 100, 50, 30, 20, 10, 5, and 2.5.

The major results of this procedure appear in Figure 21 (Boren & Sidman, 1957b). These data demonstrate that at least 70 percent of the shocks normally administered when the animals fail to respond may be omitted without appreciably lowering the animals' response rates.

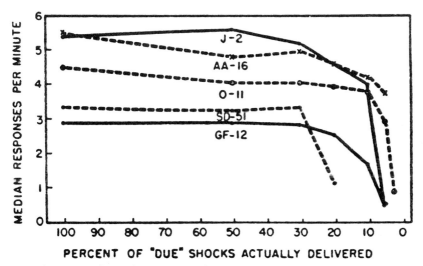

Figure 21. Rate of avoidance responding by each of five animals as a function of the percentage of shocks delivered. (From Boren & Sidman, 1957b.)

As indicated above, the variable response-shock interval procedure and the intermittent procedure are related. Whenever a due shock is not delivered, the animal has an opportunity to experience a response-shock interval considerably longer than 20 seconds. Each shock not delivered increases the potential interval another 20 seconds. However, an analysis of the animals' interresponse times indicated that they rarely paused long enough to experience the longer response-shock intervals until the shock percentage dropped below 30 percent. The demonstration that we can maintain the animals' avoidance behavior even with a considerable economy of shocks leads to the suggestion that we examine the role played by the shocks. But before doing this in any detail, let us first examine two some-what more complex procedures.

CONCURRENT FREE-OPERANT AVOIDANCE

In this procedure the rat has two levers it can press. Two independent recycling timers program the shocks. Each timer delivers a shock every 20 seconds, but since the timers are slightly variable they are out of phase with each other and the rat receives shocks at irregular intervals; if the animal does not press either lever, the average rate of shocks is one every ten seconds. The shocks delivered by both timers are identical.

If the rat presses Lever A it resets Timer A back to the beginning of its timing cycle and postpones the shock that Timer A would otherwise have delivered. Similarly, by pressing Lever B, the animal can reset Timer B and postpone its shock. The contingencies on each lever are independent. If the animal pressed only Lever A, it would postpone the shocks that Timer A was to deliver, but Timer B would be unaffected and would continue to deliver a shock to the animal every 20 seconds. Likewise, if the animal pressed only Lever B, Timer A would continue to deliver a shock every 20 seconds. The animal can avoid all shocks only by alternating sufficiently often between the two levers.

In this experiment, each timer individually programs a shock-shock interval of 20 seconds. The response-shock interval controlled by each lever and its associated timer is also 20 seconds. By pressing either lever, the animal ensures that one of the timers cannot deliver a shock before 20 seconds have elapsed; during that 20-second period, however, the other timer may deliver a shock if the animal has not pressed the other lever.

Acquisition

Several animals failed to alternate between the two levers and confined their responses almost exclusively to one. This proved to be an instructive development and Figure 22 illustrates an example. Rat CO-41 rarely pressed Lever A and received a shock from Timer A nearly every 20 seconds. In spite of the frequent shocks, it pressed Lever B more than 500 times during its first session.

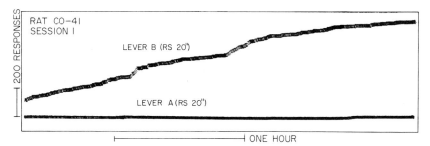

Figure 22. Cumulative records of an animal's responses on each lever during its first session of the concurrent free-operant procedure. All shocks, regardless of which timer delivered them, are recorded on both curves. (From Sidman, 1962d.)

What were the observable consequences of Rat CO-41's behavior? If the animal did not press either lever, it would have received a shock every ten seconds, on the average; if it pressed one of the levers often enough, it could have reduced the shock rate to one every 20 seconds. Rat CO-41 tended toward the latter type of adjustment to the situation. Although its solution was not optimal, it did succeed in decreasing the overall number of shocks it received.

Shock-shock and Response-shock Intervals

Figure 23A is a record of an animal which, after several sessions, settled almost exclusively on Lever B. It pressed Lever A only 66 times in six hours and pressed Lever B more than 11,000 times, a rate of approximately 30 responses per minute. Rat CL-8's performance was quite remarkable. Even with a shock every 20 seconds the animal's rate of lever pressing was not only relatively stable but was one of the highest we had ever seen in conjunction with free-operant avoidance procedures with rats. By pressing lever B at such a high rate the animal ensured that it would be shocked soon after it responded. A powerful reinforcement must have been operating in this situation to keep the animal pressing continuously in the face of such frequent punishments.

After Session 21, the shock-shock and response-shock intervals programmed on Timer B were increased from 20 to 40 seconds. Timer A still delivered a shock whenever the animal did not press Lever A within 20 seconds, but Timer B delivered its shock only when the animal failed to press Lever B for 40 seconds.

During Session 23 Rat CL-8 changed its behavior radically (Figure

23B). Its response rate on Lever B declined, but even though the response-shock interval on Lever A had not been altered, the animal pressed Lever A much more frequently than it ever had before.

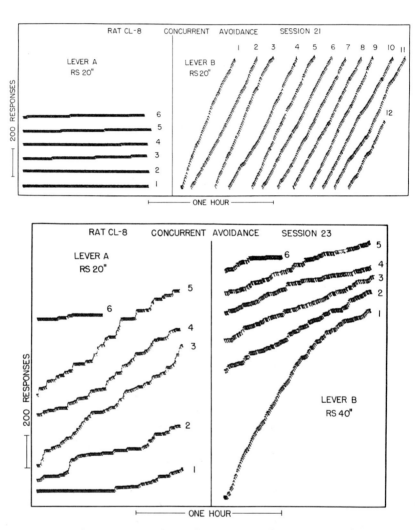

Figure 23 (A and B). An animal's performance on the concurrent free-operant procedure before (Session 21) and after (Session 23) a change on Lever B's response-shock interval. (From Sidman, 1962d.)

A close examination of Figure 24 may help clarify the results of this experiment. With the intervals on both timers set for 20 seconds, line *a* of Figure 24 shows that the rate of shocks (shocks per second) is .100 if the animal never presses either lever. If the animal presses Lever B often enough (line *b*), it will cut the shock rate in half, to .050; this is analogous. to Rat CL-8's performance in Figure 23A.

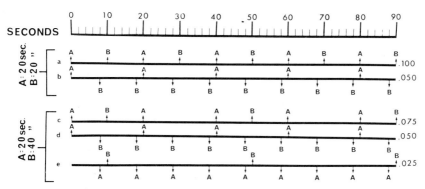

Figure 24. A schematic representation of the effects of various response patterns on shock density. The arrows pointing upward indicate shocks, delivered by Timer A or Timer B. The arrows pointing downward indicate responses, on Lever A or Lever B. The numbers at the right of each line give the average shock density (shocks per second) for each type of response pattern. The numbers outside the brackets on the left side give the response-shock intervals on Levers A and B.

When we maintain the interval of 20 seconds on Timer A and increase Timer B to 40 seconds, the shock rate becomes .075 if the animal never responds at all (line *c*). If the animal continues to press Lever B exclusively (line *d*), it will maintain the same rate of shocks as before, .050. But whereas this performance originally reduced the base rate by 50 percent, from .100 to .050, the same behavior now reduces the shock density by only one-third, from .075 to .050. The animal can achieve a reduction of two-thirds (.075 to .025) by switching its preference to the other lever (line *e*). Rat CL-8 tended toward this type of adjustment to the changed conditions, decreasing its response rate on Lever B and increasing its preference for Lever A; this became the more effective method of lowering the frequency of shocks after the response-shock interval on Lever B had changed to 40 seconds.

Additional results from this concurrent procedure may be found elsewhere (Sidman, 1962c), but the analysis presented here suggests several elegant ways to obtain a more complete picture. For example, we might keep the two timers, each with its own shock-shock interval, but give the rat only one lever to press. By pressing the lever, the animal could reset one of the timers and postpone its shock, but the other timer could continue to cycle uninterruptedly and would set the lowest shock rate the animal could achieve. A series of different shock-shock intervals on the fixed timer, correlated with various response-shock intervals on the other, would show quantitatively how the base rate of shocks and the level to which the animal can reduce the base rate combine to influence the animal's avoidance responding.

We have seen that animals which have only one lever available press it more rapidly when we decrease the response-shock interval. We might interpret the results of the concurrent procedure as indicating simply that the animal responds more rapidly on the lever associated with the shorter response-shock interval. The experiment to be described next demonstrates that animals may also behave in the opposite way. They will select the lever associated with the longer response-shock interval if that is the more efficient method of reducing the frequency of shocks.

MIXED FREE-OPERANT AVOIDANCE

As in the concurrent procedure, the animal has two levers available. Unlike the concurrent procedure, shock may be programmed by any one of three timers, and these timers are not independent of each other. Whenever the animal receives a shock, the shock-shock timer begins to operate and continues to deliver a shock every ten seconds as long as the animal fails to press either lever. When the animal presses either lever, the shock-shock timer stops operating and Timer C or V begins, depending on which lever was pressed. At any given moment only one of the three timers is operating: the shock-shock timer if the animal has not pressed a lever since last receiving a shock, Timer C if the animal has pressed Lever C last, or Timer V if the animal has pressed Lever V last.

Timer C has a constant setting of 20 seconds; each time the rat presses Lever C it resets Timer C back to the beginning of its cycle, but if the animal then allows 20 seconds to elapse without pressing either lever, Timer C delivers a shock and the shock-shock timer begins to operate. The setting on Timer V varies, its response-shock intervals ranging from 5 to 150 seconds in different phases of the experiment. Each time the rat presses Lever V it resets Timer V back to the beginning of its cycle; but if it allows the cycle to elapse without pressing either lever, Timer V delivers a shock to the animal and the shock-shock timer begins to operate.

The shock-shock timer determines the base shock rate; as long as the animal never presses either lever, it will receive a shock every ten seconds. It can reduce the shock rate by pressing either lever, but it can achieve a greater reduction by pressing the lever associated with the longer response-shock interval. This is unlike the concurrent procedure in which the lever associated with the shorter interval was more efficient.

Figure 25 illustrates one animal's data from this experiment (Sidman, 1954a). The response-shock intervals on the abscissa refer only to Lever V, since the interval associated with Lever C was always 20 seconds. The

arrow shows where the interval was the same on both levers. We see that
the animal responds more on the lever with the longer response-shock interval. It is not inevitable, therefore, that the shorter response-shock interval
generates the higher rate of lever pressing; to do so, it must also allow for
a greater reduction in shock rate.

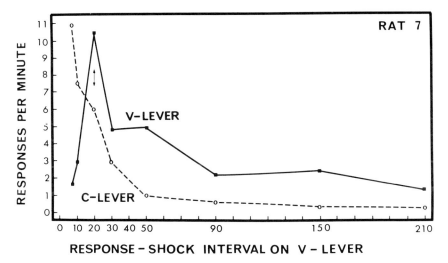

Figure 25. An animal's response rates on the two bars (V-bar and C-bar) as a
function of the response-shock interval associated with the V-bar. The response-
shock interval on the C-bar was always 20 seconds. (After Sidman, 1954a.)

It is not easy, however, to specify how changes in shock rate make
contact with the animal. Are we, for example, to regard the animal as a
computer, capable of integrating shocks over time and calculating their
density? Unlikely as this may seem, particularly when there are long intervals between shocks, the possibility cannot be ruled out. To evaluate it
properly, one would have to devise a method that would allow the animal
to react to shock density per se without more direct environmental cues.

The somewhat idealized situations depicted in Figure 24 suggest a
second possibility. To simplify the discussion Figure 24 was constructed as
though the timers did not vary, so that the shocks in line *a* come regularly
every ten seconds. By pressing Lever B the animal interrupts this steady
series, producing "holes" in it (line *b*). A single such interruption is the
smallest change that can occur in the base rate. Can the omission of one or
more shocks from such a regular sequence be a source of reinforcement for
the animal? Conversely, can the insertion of one or more extra shocks in
the series be an avenue through which the animal reacts to increased shock
rates?

Anger (1957) has presented evidence that rats can use the omission of one event from a regular series as a discriminative stimulus, but we have yet to determine the temporal course and quantitative limits of this process. The problem is even more complex when the series of events is irregular. For example, in line *c* of Figure 24 the base pattern of shocks varies, albeit in a predictable way. If we make the temporal sequence even less predictable, it should become more difficult for the animal to react to the omission of one shock. Again, the limits have yet to be worked out (see Dinsmoor, 1962). Temporal discrimination is a third avenue by which changes in shock rate may make contact with the animal. Anger (1963) has argued at some length that a conditioned temporal gradient of aversiveness permits the animal to discriminate "safe" periods (low shock rate immediately after it presses the lever) from "danger" periods (higher shock rates at longer intervals after the response). But the argument may also be turned about; changes in shock rate reinforce the animal for the temporal discrimination. Shock rate and temporal discrimination are both dependent variables. Of the two, which is the chicken and which the egg?

A fourth possible connection between shock frequency and the animal's avoidance behavior will emerge from the following experiments. It was already noted, in the discussion of initial avoidance learning, that behavioral control may transfer from a series of shocks to a single shock. If this does indeed happen, the low frequency of shocks which the well-trained animal receives may not be a bar to the explanatory power of shock rate.

EXTINCTION

Animals learn to avoid shocks only if they have already been shocked. Once we shock an animal, we create a potential for reinforcement. If we allow the animal to press a lever and thereby to postpone or prevent a shock that it would otherwise have received, we observe that lever pressing becomes a prominent feature of the animal's behavior. The more frequently we shock the animal for failing to press the lever, the more frequently it presses the lever. Once the animal has learned to avoid shock we can return the behavior to its original low level by disconnecting the shock. The animal will eventually stop pressing the lever; the behavior is extinguished.

Shocks are necessary, then, if the animal is both to learn and to maintain its avoidance behavior. This "motivating" function of the shock is perhaps its most obvious characteristic, and is probably responsible, at least in part, for the effects of such variables as shock density (Sidman, 1962d) and shock intensity (Boren, Sidman, & Herrnstein, 1959). But the shock also performs other functions. For example, we have already seen that it may form a reference point in time and thereby permit the animal to develop an efficient temporal discrimination (e.g., Figure 13A).

The shock may also assume another type of discriminative control over the animal's behavior. It may become an important aspect of the total experimental situation, similar to the illumination or to the spatial and geographic aspects of the experimental space. In a manner of speaking, shocks, like the walls of the experimental chamber, tell the animal that it is in an avoidance situation. When the animal has been avoiding successfully for a while, and has received no shocks, the situation has, in effect, changed. Successful avoidance creates a situation like one in which avoidance is not necessary. Eventually, therefore, the animal will stop pressing the lever long enough to receive another shock. This discriminative function of the shock is possibly responsible for the fact that it may take only a single shock to reinstate the animal's avoidance behavior.

If we condition an animal to press a lever and avoid shocks, then extinguish the lever-pressing response by disconnecting the shock, then recondition the lever-pressing response, extinguish it again, and continue to expose the animal to alternate periods of conditioning and extinction, we may place the extinction operation more explicitly under the control of the shocks. An experiment was performed in which rats were first trained to press a lever with the free-operant avoidance procedure. Then, each consecutive experimental session was divided into two parts. During the first part of each session, the shock was connected and the animal had to press the lever if it was to avoid shock. During the second part of each experimental session, the shock was disconnected.

A sample of the data from this experiment (Boren & Sidman, 1957a) may be seen in Figure 26. In the first extinction period for Rat M-14, in Session 1, there was little evidence of extinction. However, by the eighteenth session of alternate conditioning and extinction, the animal's rate of lever pressing dropped to a low level soon after the shock was disconnected. The animal had learned to discriminate that shocks were no longer forthcoming.

There are at least two ways in which the animal might have used the shock to discriminate the extinction periods. One possibility is that the animal used the time intervals between shocks. Upon the lapse of an interval which was outside the range of intershock times to which the animal had become accustomed during its avoidance periods, the animal might then slow down or stop its lever-pressing activity. An experiment in which such periods were deliberately introduced at various times during an avoidance session suggests that other factors are more critical (Sidman, 1955a).

A second possibility involves a more local type of discrimination based on response-shock intervals rather than intershock times. The animal may learn that once it goes beyond the response-shock interval without receiving a shock, it will not be shocked again during that session. We have already seen that animals can discriminate the response-shock interval quite pre-

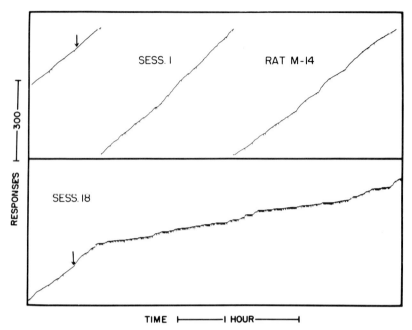

Figure 26. Cumulative records of an animal's performance during the first and the eighteenth sessions of alternate free-operant avoidance conditioning and extinction. The arrows show where the shock was disconnected; after this point, the "pips" on the curves occurred whenever the animals went 20 seconds without pressing the lever. (From Boren & Sidman, 1957a.)

cisely (e.g., Figure 11). The following additional experiment indicates that the animals can also learn to adapt quickly when we change the response-shock interval.

ADAPTATION OF THE TEMPORAL DISCRIMINATION

Rat G-4 had had extensive experience with the free-operant procedure at shock-shock and response-shock intervals of 20 and 40 seconds. The dashed curves with open circles in Figures 27A and 27B indicate excellent temporal discriminations based on these two intervals. Figure 27A shows what happened to the temporal discrimination when the response-shock interval was changed from 20 to 40 seconds while the shock-shock interval was maintained throughout at 20 seconds. Figure 27B shows what happened when the response-shock interval was changed in the other direction, from 40 seconds to 20 seconds, while the shock-shock interval was maintained at 40 seconds. In both instances the animal adjusted its temporal discrimination to the new intervals, and the adjustment was almost complete within the first hour. Because the shock-shock interval was kept constant, the animal had to respond and experience the response-shock interval before it had any basis for adjusting its behavior. These data, particularly Figure 27A in which the animal received only eight shocks in the first hour at the new interval, indicate that the animal is capable of a rapid and precise adjustment to the occurrence or non-occurrence of shock at a particular time following a response. It is not unreasonable to suppose that a similar mechanism is responsible for the animal's well-developed discrimination of the extinction procedure demonstrated above.

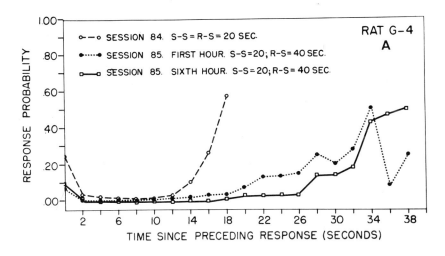

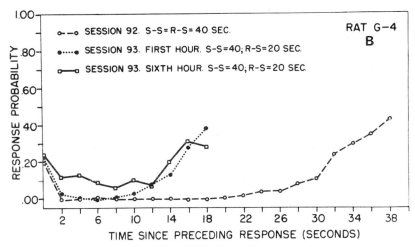

Figure 27 (A and B). An animal's temporal discrimination before and after the response-shock interval was changed. Response probability was calculated as interresponse times per opportunity.

If this discrimination, or the discrimination based on intershock times, or both, are responsible for the speed at which the animal's avoidance behavior extinguishes, we may still wonder about an additional phenomenon of extinction. As we noted before (e.g., Figure 4), progressively longer periods of time without shock occur as the animal learns the avoidance response. A well-trained monkey may press the lever at a high rate for hundreds of hours without ever receiving a shock. If, as implied above, successful avoidance generates the conditions for its own extinction, what is responsible for the animal's progressively increasing persistence?

We have considered the role of the shock as a discriminative event that the animal may use as a cue either to continue or to stop pressing the lever. It is possible to consider the animal's lever-pressing behavior itself in a similar way. Like the shock and the environmental stimuli, the animal's own lever-pressing activity informs it that it is in an avoidance situation. As the animal's own behavior develops this discriminative function, its responses becoming self-generating. Whenever it presses the lever, it reinstates a part of the stimulus complex that marks the situation as one requiring avoidance behavior, and this in turn generates additional responses.

FREE SHOCK

In an experiment on the intermittent shock procedure, in which the animal was scheduled to receive only every fifth shock that became due, we noticed one day that the rat began to press the lever much more rapidly than usual. On checking the apparatus we discovered that a component had failed and the animal was unable to postpone every fifth shock no matter whether it pressed the lever or not. Our interest was captured by the implication that the rate of avoidance responding could be increased by occasionally shocking the animal *in spite of* its avoidance response. We then carried out a series of experiments to see what would happen when we deliberately gave the animal occasional unavoidable shocks (free shocks). Our original observation was confirmed many times over. When we delivered free shocks to an animal which was avoiding shock, or which had learned to avoid shocks, the animal always increased its rate of lever pressing. (See also, Kelleher, Riddle, & Cook, 1963; Waller & Waller, 1963).

In one experiment, with monkeys as subjects, we trained the animals to avoid shocks with shock-shock and response-shock intervals of 20 seconds on the free-operant procedure. We then gave the animals a free shock every ten minutes. During the five minutes immediately preceding each free shock we turned on a clicking noise. Thus, the animal had alternating five-minute periods of silence and clicking noise, and the free shock always came at the end of the clicking noise. In this way we were able to compare the animal's avoidance behavior in a situation without free shock (during the silent periods) with its behavior in a situation in which it received free shocks (the clicking noise periods). Figure 28 shows that the free shock produced approximately a threefold increase in the animal's rate of lever pressing both in the presence and absence of the clicking noise.

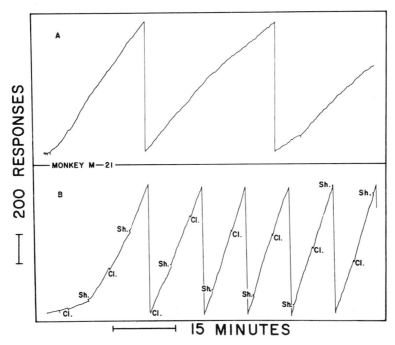

Figure 28. Increase in response rate (from record A to record B) when the animal was given free shocks. "Cl" marks the beginning of the clicking noise; "Sh" marks the shock and the end of the clicking noise. The curve is displaced downward slightly while the clicking noise is on. (From Sidman, Herrnstein, & Conrad, 1957.)

The effect of the free shock was not permanent. The animal's rate of lever pressing began to decrease, first in the silent periods and then in the clicking noise as well. Because the decline in the animal's rate of lever pressing followed a different time course in the presence and absence of the stimulus, there was a period of several hours during which the animal pressed the lever more rapidly during the stimulus than during its absence. By changing the procedure slightly we were able to accentuate this difference. We eliminated the shock that had usually come when the animal failed to press the lever and thereby placed the avoidance behavior on an extinction procedure. But we continued to deliver the free shock at the end of each five-minute period of clicking noise. Eventually, the animal almost completely stopped pressing the lever during the silent periods. It continued its low rate of responding during the first part of the clicking noise, but as the time for the free shock approached, the animal pressed the lever more rapidly. Figure 29 shows an example of a two-hour session in which the monkey pressed the lever rapidly during the clicker and rarely pressed the lever at other times. The free shock alone was sufficient to maintain a high rate of response. Although the animal continued this pattern of behavior for many hours, it eventually stopped pressing the lever altogether, both in the presence and in the absence of the stimulus.

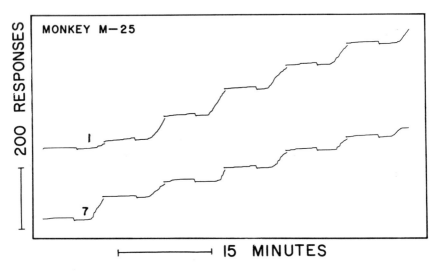

Figure 29. Cumulative response curve illustrating the nearly complete extinction between stimuli and the positive acceleration during stimuli. The two-hour record is divided into one-hour segments, with the initial clicker presentation of the first hour indicated by 1 and the first clicker of the second hour by 7. (From Sidman, Herrnstein, & Conrad, 1957.)

Giving the animal occasional free shocks is another way to program a variable response-shock interval. The animal will sometimes press the lever and receive a shock sooner than the customary response-shock interval. If the free shocks do not come too often, the animal cannot possibly learn that they are, in fact, unavoidable. Since the interval between lever-pressing responses and subsequent unavoidable shocks will usually be shorter than the programmed response-shock interval, the animal's increased rate of lever pressing may be a reaction to the seemingly shorter intervals. I have some incomplete data suggesting that the effect of free shocks disappears sooner the more frequently they are given to the animal. The more frequently the free shocks come, the more quickly the animal can discriminate that they are unavoidable.

In some experiments, with rats as subjects, I have observed that the facilitating effect of free shocks not only lasts for a shorter time than with monkeys, but that the free shocks eventually come to depress the animal's rate of avoidance responding. Figure 30 shows this effect clearly. The first part of this figure shows the animal's rate of responding when a free shock came every two and a half minutes; when the free shock was removed, there was approximately a threefold increase in the animal's rate of lever pressing; when the free shock was reintroduced, the animal's rate of lever pressing dropped again, increased again when the free shock was removed, decreased again when the free shock was reintroduced every two and a half minutes, and then increased slightly when the free shocks were delivered only half as often.

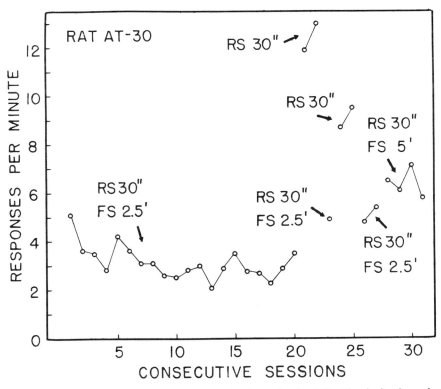

Figure 30. Depression of response rates by free shocks (FS). Shock-shock and response-shock intervals were 30 seconds during all sessions. From left to right, the segments represent the following conditions: twenty consecutive sessions with free shock every 2.5 minutes; two sessions without free shock; one session with free shock every 2.5 minutes; two sessions without free shock; two sessions with free shock every 2.5 minutes; and four sessions with free shock every 5 minutes.

The effect of the free shock in keeping the animal pressing the lever even after it is no longer possible to avoid shock may be attributed to the function of the free shock in creating a spurious response-shock interval. It may also be attributed to the role of the shock as a discriminative stimulus. Until the animal learns that the shocks are actually unavoidable, the shocks continue to serve as stimuli which "tell" the animal that it is in an avoidance situation. As long as the shock continues to serve either or both of these functions, the animal will continue to press the lever as if avoidance were still possible. When the animal does learn that the shocks are in fact unavoidable, the shocks take on the opposite function; they then indicate to the animal that the situation is one in which avoidance is impossible. Once the shock has acquired this type of discriminative function, it may be extremely difficult, if not impossible, to recondition the animal's avoidance response (Sidman, Mason, Brady, & Thach, 1962).

A third, less well-defined function of the shock, will be indicated in the next section.

STIMULUS CONTROL

We shall not go deeply into the special problems that arise when we explicitly introduce exteroceptive stimuli into the avoidance situation. Perhaps the most general statement we can make is that any of the procedures which have been described may be placed under stimulus control. For example, we may program the free-operant avoidance procedure whenever a clicking noise is on; whenever the noise is off, the animal receives no shocks and does not have to press the lever. The animal will eventually learn to press the lever only when the clicking noise is on. Because a well-trained animal rarely pauses longer than the response-shock interval, and therefore receives few shocks, it may be difficult to teach it that avoidance is unnecessary when the stimulus is off. The learning process may be hastened in two ways. If we begin discrimination training early in conditioning, before the animal has learned to avoid efficiently, there will be greater opportunity for it to learn that shocks do not come when it pauses longer than the response-shock interval in the absence of the stimulus. Also, if we leave the stimulus off for long periods of time, thereby giving the avoidance behavior opportunity to extinguish, the animal will have more opportunity to learn that shocks come only if it pauses too long while the stimulus is on, and not while the stimulus is off.

In a discrimination procedure, with a monkey as subject, the shock was turned off and the monkey did not have to press the lever when clicks came at a rate of six per second; when the clicks came at a rate of two per second, shock-shock and response-shock intervals of 20 seconds were in effect. During the first nine sessions the two stimuli alternated every 15 minutes. In later sessions, the stimulus durations were gradually reduced to one minute. In the first session, the animal pressed the lever almost equally often during both stimuli, but in successive sessions it pressed the lever more frequently during the positive stimulus (2/sec.) and decreased its response rate during the negative stimulus (6/sec.). Eventually, the animal came to maintain an effective rate of lever pressing during the positive stimulus and pressed only rarely during the negative stimulus.

Figure 31 shows selected portions of cumulative records in which the stimulus duration decreased from nine to three minutes. All shocks which

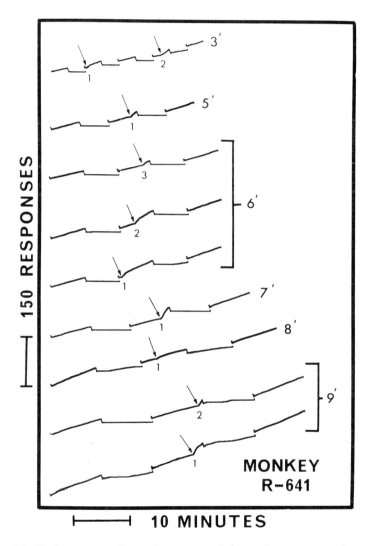

Figure 31. Each segment of cumulative record shows three presentations of the positive stimulus and two of the negative stimulus. The curves were displaced downward slightly when the negative stimulus was on. Stimulus durations are indicated at the right of each segment. Arrows indicate shocks, and shocks are numbered in consecutive order within each session.

the animal received during these sessions are shown in the figure. The records were selected to illustrate a common effect of the shocks. In almost all instances the animal increased its rate of lever pressing immediately after it received a shock. Of particular interest are those instances in which the animal continued to respond rapidly up to the point where the negative stimulus came on. If the monkey increased its response rate after the shock simply because the shock re-established the avoidance contingency, we would expect the negative stimulus to have no effect upon the rate at which the animal resumed lever pressing the next time the positive stimulus reappeared. We note, however, that when the positive stimulus came on again, the animal did not resume the high rate of lever pressing that was interrupted by the negative stimulus. The effect of the shock seems to have dissipated while the negative stimulus was on and the animal was not pressing the lever. This suggests that the shock has another effect in addition to establishing and maintaining the avoidance contingency or to its function as a discriminative event. The observation has not been pursued.

STIMULUS GENERALIZATION

In the experiment described above, the monkey at first pressed the lever equally often when clicks were coming at a rate of two or six per second. This suggests that free-operant avoidance behavior generalizes widely, a suggestion that has been confirmed by Hearst (1960). However, after the animal has learned to discriminate the two click frequencies, it shows a classical generalization gradient. Figure 32 shows a set of such generalization gradients for a monkey which was exposed not only to click frequencies of two and six per second but also to frequencies between these extremes. Although the monkey increased its overall rate of lever pressing with shorter response-shock intervals, it changed its rate proportionately during each stimulus, and the percentage gradients are almost identical at each response-shock interval. Hearst (1960; 1962) has extended these findings in a number of provocative directions. For example, he has found that the generalization gradients are considerably steeper when the animal is reinforced with food than when shock avoidance is used. This finding led Hearst to suggest that avoidance behavior is partly controlled by stimuli other than the exteroceptive ones which he used to obtain the generalization gradients.

ESCAPE FROM AN AVOIDANCE SITUATION

In this experiment monkeys could either postpone shock by pressing a lever or pull a chain to produce a period of time-out from the avoidance procedure. When a light was on, the animal received a brief shock every 20 seconds unless it pressed the lever; each time it pressed the lever it post-

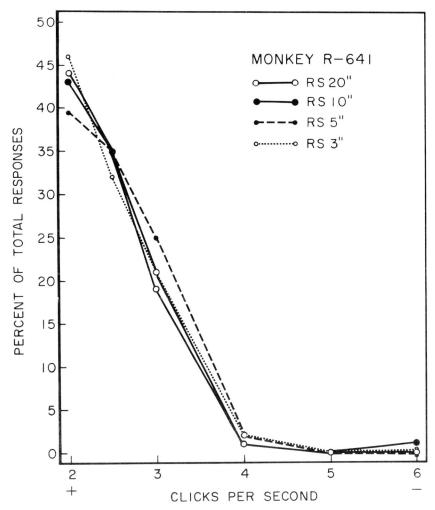

Figure 32. Relative generalization gradients at four response-shock intervals. (From Sidman, 1961.)

poned the next shock for 20 seconds (free-operant avoidance). When the light was off, there were no shocks whether or not the animal pressed the lever (time-out from avoidance). The monkey could turn off the light by pulling the chain a fixed number of times (fixed ratio schedule), and thereby produce a five-minute period of time-out from avoidance.

Figure 33 shows concurrent records of the animal's lever-pressing and chain-pulling responses. The animal pressed the lever at a fairly steady rate and avoided shocks, while at the same time it pulled the chain and terminated the avoidance situation with every one hundredth chain-pulling re-

sponse. It is evident that termination of the light associated with the avoidance procedure was a powerful reinforcement for the animal. The light not
only functioned as a discriminative stimulus to govern the animal's avoidance behavior, but also constituted a situation from which the animal would
go to great lengths to escape (Sidman, 1962; Verhave, 1962).

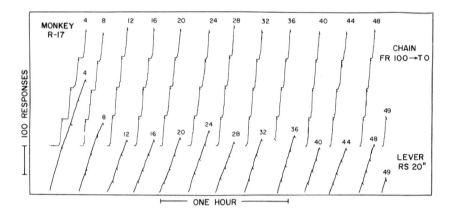

Figure 33. Concurrent records of lever pressing and chain pulling. The two sets
of curves are superimposed on a single time axis. The diagonal marks indicate
periods of time-out; during these periods the recorders did not run. Every
fourth time-out period, as well as the final one, is numbered.

It is highly likely that the same factors which govern the animal's rate
of avoidance responding also determine how effectively the animal will be
reinforced by escaping from the avoidance situation. I believe that a simple
formulation of this sort can probably encompass the classical data from
avoidance conditioning procedures that involve warning stimuli. Experimental techniques that permit us to measure the animal's rate of avoidance
responding in the presence of the warning stimulus provide sensitive tools
for assessing the state of the animal's avoidance behavior from moment to
moment in both the presence and absence of the warning stimulus (e.g.,
Sidman & Boren, 1957a).

REFERENCES

ADER, R., and TATUM, R. (1961) Free-operant avoidance conditioning in
    human subjects. *J. exp. Anal. Behav., 4,* 275-276.
ANGER, D. (1956) The dependence of interresponse times upon the relative
    reinforcement of different interresponse times. *J. exp. Psychol., 52,* 145-
    161.
ANGER, D. (1957) Discrimination of the omission of members of a periodic
    sequence. Paper read at convention of Eastern Psychol. Ass., Philadelphia.

ANGER, D. (1963) The role of temporal discriminations in the reinforcement of Sidman avoidance behavior. *J. exp. Anal. Behav.*, 6, 477-506.

BLACK, A. H., and MORSE, P. (1961) Avoidance learning in dogs without a warning stimulus. *J. exp. Anal. Behav.*, 4, 17-23.

BOREN, J. J., and SIDMAN, M. (1957) A discrimination based upon repeated conditioning and extinction of avoidance behavior. *J. comp. physiol. Psychol.*, 50, 18-22. (a)

BOREN, J. J., and SIDMAN, M. (1957) Maintenance of avoidance behavior with intermittent shocks. *Canad. J. Psychol.*, 11, 185-192. (b)

BOREN, J. J., SIDMAN, M., and HERRNSTEIN, R. J. (1959) Avoidance, escape, and extinction as functions of shock intensity. *J. comp. physiol. Psychol.*, 52, 420-425.

DINSMOOR, J. A. (1954) Punishment: I. The avoidance hypothesis. *Psychol. Rev.*, 61, 34-46.

DINSMOOR, J. A. (1962) Variable-interval escape from stimuli accompanied by shocks. *J. exp. Anal. Behav.*, 5, 41-47.

HEARST, E. (1960) Simultaneous generalization gradients for appetitive and aversive behavior. *Science, 132,* 1769-1770.

HEARST, E. (1962) Concurrent generalization gradients for food-controlled and shock-controlled behavior. *J. exp. Anal. Behav.*, 5, 19-31.

HEFFERLINE, R. F. (1950) An experimental study of avoidance. *Genet. Psychol. Monogr., 42,* 231-334.

HIVELY, W. (1962) Programming stimuli in matching to sample. *J. exp. Anal. Behav., 5,* 279-298.

KAMIN, L., CAMPBELL, D., JUDD, R., RYAN, T., and WALKER, J. (1959) Two determinants of the emergence of anticipatory avoidance. *J. comp. physiol. Psychol.*, 52, 202-205.

KELLEHER, R. T., RIDDLE, W. C., and COOK, L. (1963) Persistent behavior maintained by unavoidable shocks. *J. exp. Anal. Behav.*, 6, 507-517.

MILLER, N. E. (1959) Liberalization of basic SR concepts: Extensions to conflict behavior, motivation, and serial learning. In S. Koch (Ed.), *Psychology: A study of a science.* Vol. 2. New York: McGraw-Hill.

MOWRER, O. H., and KEEHN, J. D. (1958) How are intertrial "avoidance" responses reinforced? *Psychol. Rev.*, 65, 209-221.

MOWRER, O. H., and LAMOREAUX, R. R. (1946) Fear as an intervening variable in avoidance conditioning. *J. comp. Psychol.*, 39, 29-50.

MUELLER, C. G. (1950) Theoretical relationships among some measures of conditioning. *Proc. nat. Acad. Sci.*, 36, 123-130.

SCHOENFELD, W. N. (1950) An experimental approach to anxiety, escape, and avoidance behavior. In P. H. Hoch and J. Zubin (Eds.), *Anxiety.* New York: Grune & Stratton. Pp. 70-99.

SIDMAN, M. (1953) Two temporal parameters of the maintenance of avoidance behavior by the white rat. *J. comp. physiol. Psychol.*, 46, 253-261.

SIDMAN, M. (1954) Delayed-punishment effects mediated by competing behavior. *J. comp. physiol. Psychol.*, 47, 145-147. (a)

SIDMAN, M. (1954) The temporal distribution of avoidance responses. *J. comp. physiol. Psychol.*, 47, 399-402. (b)

SIDMAN, M. (1955) On the persistence of avoidance behavior. *J. abnorm. soc. Psychol.*, 50, 217-220. (a)

SIDMAN, M. (1955) Some properties of the warning stimulus in avoidance behavior. *J. comp. physiol. Psychol.*, 48, 444-450. (b)

SIDMAN, M. (1961) Stimulus generalization in an avoidance situation. *J. exp. Anal. Behav.*, 4, 157-169.

SIDMAN, M. (1962) An adjusting avoidance schedule. *J. exp. Anal. Behav.,* *5,* 271-277. (a)

SIDMAN, M. (1962) Classical avoidance without a warning stimulus. *J. exp. Anal. Behav., 5,* 97-104. (b)

SIDMAN, M. (1962) Reduction of shock frequency as reinforcement for avoidance behavior. *J. exp. Anal. Behav., 5,* 247-257. (c)

SIDMAN, M. (1962) Time out from avoidance as a reinforcer: A study of response interaction. *J. exp. Anal. Behav., 5,* 423-434. (d)

SIDMAN, M., and BOREN, J. J. (1957) The relative aversiveness of warning signal and shock in an avoidance situation. *J. abnorm. soc. Psychol., 55,* 339-344. (a)

SIDMAN, M., and BOREN, J. J. (1957) The use of shock-contingent variations in response-shock intervals for the maintenance of avoidance behavior. *J. comp. physiol. Psychol., 50,* 558-562. (b)

SIDMAN, M., HERRNSTEIN, R. J., and CONRAD, D. G. (1957) Maintenance of avoidance behavior by unavoidable shocks. *J. comp. physiol. Psychol., 50,* 553-557.

SIDMAN, M., MASON, J. W., BRADY, J. V., and THACH, J. (1962) Quantitative relations between avoidance behavior and pituitary-adrenal cortical activity. *J. exp. Anal. Behav., 5,* 353-362.

SOLOMON, R. L., and BRUSH, E. S. (1956) Experimentally derived conceptions of anxiety and aversion. In M. R. Jones (Ed.), *Nebraska symposium on motivation.* Lincoln: Univ. of Nebraska Press. Pp. 212-305.

SOLOMON, R. L., and WYNNE, L. C. (1953) Traumatic avoidance learning: Acquisition in normal dogs. *Psychol. Monogr., 67* (Whole No. 354), 19 pp.

VERHAVE, T. (1962) The functional properties of a time out from an avoidance schedule. *J. exp. Anal. Behav., 5,* 391-422.

WALLER, M. B., and WALLER, P. F. (1963) The effects of unavoidable shocks on a multiple schedule having an avoidance component. *J. exp. Anal. Behav., 6,* 29-37.

11

The Analysis of
Discriminated Avoidance [1]

Howard S. Hoffman

INTRODUCTION

The strategy that is employed in the analysis of discriminated avoidance is basically simple. A neutral stimulus is scheduled to precede, and in this sense serve as a warning for, each occurrence of a noxious event. If the S emits an appropriate operant during the warning period, the noxious event fails to occur. Under these conditions, discriminated avoidance represents a performance in which the S consistently prevents the noxious event, but seldom emits the operant in the absence of the warning signal. The behavior is said to be discriminated in the sense that it is under the control of the exteroceptive stimulus.

In certain respects, the methods which are involved in the analysis of this behavior represent a departure from the usual operant conditioning approach. For example, in most operant conditioning experiments, attention is focused on the steady-state behavior that emerges after extended exposure to a given set of conditions. In studies of discriminated avoidance, on the other hand, attention is usually focused on the acquisition process itself. In most operant conditioning experiments, the techniques of data analysis are particularly suited to the examination of trends in a continuous record of what is, generally, a freely emitted behavior. In work on discriminated avoidance, the analysis of the data customarily proceeds on a trial by trial basis, despite the fact that, in general, the response can be emitted at any time. Perhaps for this reason more than any other, work on discriminated avoidance represents a merging of operant conditioning techniques with the methods of the classical conditioning laboratory. Indeed, the paradigm for the analysis of discriminated avoidance may be said to represent a transla-

[1] This chapter was written in the course of a research project supported by NIMH grant MH 02433-C4.

tion of the classical avoidance experiment (Bechterev, 1932) to variables which are compatible with the equipment and methods of the operant conditioning laboratory.

At the outset, it is important to recognize that although it may appear natural for Ss to learn to avoid, one frequently encounters failures under conditions which, on the surface at least, seem ideal for rapid learning. The occurrence of such failures is, of course, instructive to the investigator; but as pointed out by Solomon and Brush (1956), one seldom encounters them in the literature. An exception is a paper by Meyer, Cho, and Wesemann (1960) which describes a long sequence of unsuccessful attempts to develop efficient avoidance behavior in their Ss. Coons, Anderson, and Myers (1960) highlight a similar problem by reporting a study in which, after learning to avoid, the Ss gradually lost the behavior and did so with no change in the conditions which initially were responsible for the development of the response. In a similar vein, Hoffman, Fleshler, and Chorny (1961) described an experiment in which a number of Ss failed to meet a criterion for efficient avoidance despite the fact that they had been subjected to 50 sessions of training. Recently, Nakamura and Anderson (1962) have reported large differences in avoidance behavior between strains of rats. In general, females were markedly superior to males and Long-Evans hooded rats were superior to Sprague-Dawley albinos. Moreover, large differences were found between rats of the same strain (Long-Evans) when supplied by different vendors.

In most of the experiments cited above, the avoidance response consisted of a lever press, and it has been suggested (Meyer *et al.,* 1960) that this factor in itself may be largely responsible for the failures. It is noteworthy, however, that even with the more commonly used shuttlebox (Mowrer & Miller, 1942) failures to develop efficient avoidance are occasionally reported. For example, Levine and Soliday (1962) report a study in which the control Ss only achieved 60 percent avoidance after 90 trials. Moreover, there is evidence that under certain circumstances, well-developed discriminated lever-press avoidance *can* be rapidly produced in the laboratory. For example, Hoffman and Fleshler (1962a) report an experiment in which 12 out of 12 Ss achieved almost perfect avoidance in less than 100 trials, and more recently Feldman and Bremner (1963) have described procedures which consistently yielded efficient avoidance behavior.

EXPERIMENTAL TECHNIQUES

The Basic Program

Figure 1 provides a schematic representation of the stimulus-response relationships that hold in the typical experiment. Ordinarily, the program is such that a response during the warning period terminates the warning signal and prevents the noxious event. When the S fails to avoid, however, both the warning signal and the noxious event remain on until an escape response occurs, whereupon both are terminated. The intertrial interval is usually varied from trial to trial so as to minimize the chances that cues associated with the passage of time will gain control over the response. Responses during the interval between trials do not ordinarily affect the program, but they are customarily recorded since this information is needed to evaluate the degree of discriminative control acquired by the warning signal.

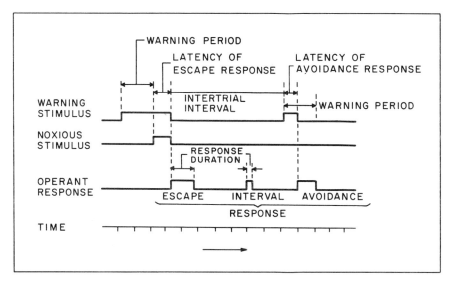

Figure 1. Schematic representation of the stimulus-response relationships in a typical discriminated avoidance experiment.

The Avoidance Chamber

There have been a wide variety of approaches to the analysis of avoidance (for example, the use of dogs, rats, man, in combination with the shuttlebox, the activity wheel, the leg flexion device, etc.), but the S which is most widely used is the rat, and the apparatus which is generally most compatible with the equipment and methods of the operant conditioning laboratory is the Skinner box. The typical arrangement consists of a source of noxious stimulation (generally electric shock delivered through a stainless steel grid floor), a source of exteroceptive stimulation to serve as a warning signal, and a manipulandum.

The construction of the chamber itself has been found to be quite critical. For example, in a well-arranged chamber designed for the rat, the bars of the grid floor are spaced approximately 7/8 in. apart. Experience has shown that if they are much closer together, they will hold fecal boluses and these will short out the shock system. If they are spaced much wider than ⅞ in., the S may be able to escape by wriggling between them.

The manipulandum is, ideally, constructed of stainless steel or some other very hard material to protect it from the rat's teeth. In work on avoidance, it is not uncommon to observe bars constructed of aluminum or plastic gnawed completely in half. At least one wall of the chamber should be constructed of plexiglass or some other transparent material so as to permit observation of the S, and the door to the chamber must be arranged in such a way that it is impossible for the S to force it open from the inside. Finally, the device, if properly designed, will be assembled in such a fashion that all of its components are easily accessible for repair, and, what is equally important, for frequent cleaning. In this respect it is helpful if the chamber is constructed so that the grid bars pass beneath the walls to external supporting members. This will insure that debris which might collect on the walls will not become a part of the shock circuit.

The Control of Shock

When delivering shock through a grid floor, special precautions must be taken to prevent the S from locating and straddling bars of similar polarity, for by doing so the S would escape all shock stimulation. The problem is typically resolved by providing that the polarity of the bars is rapidly switched so that during the shock, each bar is at an opposite polarity to every other bar for some part of the time. Commercial devices for this purpose generally involve a commutator arrangement or a series of motor-driven cam-operated switches. Several papers have appeared which describe the construction details of such instruments (Skinner & Campbell, 1947; Wyckoff & Page, 1954). As an alternative, a recently developed arrangement (Hoffman & Fleshler, 1962b) can be constructed which provides high speed scrambling, but uses only relays.

Even when grid shock is effectively scrambled, however, the control of shock is not necessarily complete. There remains the problem of manipulating the physical characteristics of the shock itself. Most investigators subscribe to the position that the magnitude of the sensation produced by an electrical shock is primarily a function of the current (or current density) which passes through the tissue of the organism. From Ohm's law, it follows that at any given moment the current (generally in milliamperes) will be directly proportional to the applied voltage and inversely proportional to the resistance (in ohms) offered by the load (tissue). When using a transformer to supply shock, the E fixes the voltage. Since, however, the electrical resistance of the S changes from moment to moment, special steps must be taken to prevent the current from varying also. One approach has been to place a large resistor (about 200,000 ohms) in series with the S and to use relatively high voltages (up to about 600 volts). Under such circumstances, variations in the S's resistance will usually be small compared to the total resistance of the system, and hence, at a constant voltage, variations in the current will also be small. A second approach has been to use electronic devices which automatically regulate the supply voltage so as to maintain a constant current output despite wide variations in load resistance. These instruments are available on the market, and a recent paper by Dinsmoor (1961) describes the construction details of one such device.

Many shock stimulators employ alternating current or half-wave rectified alternating current to generate shock. Since alternating current will effectively pass through a capacitor and since the connecting lines and other components of the experimental chamber possess a certain amount of capacitance, a part of the output of the stimulator will bypass the S. Fortunately, however, the effect is generally small and is comparable to that which would occur if a large resistor were parallel with the S. Capacitor leakage can, to some extent, be reduced by using short connections between the stimulator and the grid bars of the chamber and by shielding these connecting lines. Even so, however, if it is necessary to measure accurately the amount of current passing through the S, it is important to take measurements at the grid bars, rather than to rely on the meter which is a built-in component of most constant current stimulators. Finally, it is sound experimental procedure to check the resistance of the bars (with no S in the chamber) prior to each experimental run and to clean the chamber thoroughly whenever this resistance begins to fall appreciably.

The question of shock intensity is at present essentially pragmatic. Obviously in work on avoidance the shock must have sufficient intensity to be aversive. In general, a shock of about 0.5 milliamperes will consistently elicit an observable response in most rats. It is also obvious that the shock must not be so intense as to tetanize or otherwise harm the S (about 5 milliamperes is the upper limit for the rat). The effect of variations in shock intensity within these limits is at present not clearly understood. For example, Stone (1960) reports no difference between a 0.5 milliampere shock and a 1 milliampere shock in the development of avoidance, and Hoffman, Fleshler, and Chorny (1961) report that increasing shock intensity for Ss which performed poorly on discriminated avoidance did not facilitate their performance. Certainly one would expect variations in shock intensity to have some effect and it is anticipated that with technological advances in the control of shock, these effects will be isolated.

The Problem of Lever Holding

One of the most persistent phenomena observed in work on avoidance is the tendency for Ss to hold the lever during the interval between trials. In general, such behavior is considered undesirable and special precautions are usually instituted to prevent, or at least reduce, its frequency. Attempts to eliminate holding by arranging the circuit so that only the initial depression of the lever (or the initial release of the lever) will affect the program have not been successful. Holding persists despite these arrangements. In an experiment involving escape behavior, Campbell (1962) compared holding under programming arrangements in which (1) shock was terminated with the release of the lever, and (2) shock was terminated with the initial press of the lever. He found that although there were differences in behavior under the two arrangements, both procedures yielded relatively large amounts of holding. One technique which seems to reduce holding is to put shock on the manipulandum at the same time that it appears on the grid floor (Myers, 1959). A second effective technique is to make the manipulandum relatively inaccessible to the S so that it would be physically difficult to maintain a holding response (Sidman, 1953). A third technique is to employ a form of manipulandum which itself discourages holding. One such manipulandum is the wheel. But even when a wheel is used, Ss tend to hover nearby and rapidly turn the wheel, especially in the period which immediately follows the termination of the aversive stimulus (Myers, 1959).

Perhaps the most effective way to reduce the probability of holding is to arrange the program so that momentary grid shock is delivered whenever the S fails to release the manipulandum within a few seconds of either escape or avoidance responses. (Feldman & Bremner, 1963). It should be noted, however, that this procedure involves the introduction of grid shocks during the intertrial interval, and these shocks may have a variety of secondary effects which would tend to complicate efforts at interpretation.

Finally, it is important to recognize that although the problem of holding might be obviated by retracting the manipulandum between trials, the procedure would also remove the opportunity for the S to emit responses in the intertrial interval and hence make it impossible to determine the degree of discriminative control exercised by the warning signal. It is of interest that in many experiments which employ the shuttlebox, responses are deliberately prevented in the intertrial interval. Either the Ss are removed from the apparatus between trials or, more commonly, a barrier is raised during the intertrial interval. Obviously, both procedures preclude the determination of whether or not the avoidance response is in fact under the control of the warning signal.

Apparently, there is no simple solution to the problem of holding. Perhaps the best that can be done at present is to be alert to its existence and to seek clues to the behavioral mechanisms which control it.

The Problem of Freezing

Freezing, like bar holding, tends to interfere with the performance of the avoidance response. Even when avoidance is well developed, Ss frequently appear to freeze in their tracks with the onset of the warning signal, and when they execute the avoidance response, they do so in a most tentative fashion. On other occasions the *S* may approach the manipulandum with the onset of the warning signal but then hover over it and fail to execute the response until the noxious event finally occurs (Myers, 1959; Stone, 1960; Hoffman et al., 1961; Hoffman & Fleshler, 1962a; Hearst & Whalen, 1963).

While very little is known about the mechanisms which produce this kind of behavior, its overt properties suggest that the *S* is under the control of conflicting response tendencies. Sources of such conflict can be readily located in the avoidance paradigm. If, for example, the *S* begins to execute the avoidance response but fails to complete it prior to the delivery of the noxious event, the *S* is, in effect, punished for the same behavior that ordinarily permits avoidance. It is conceivable that if punishment of this sort occurs, it might generate sufficient conflict to partially inhibit subsequent avoidance behavior and hence make additional punishment more likely. A mechanism like this could, in principle, explain the loss of avoidance reported by Coons, Anderson, and Myers (1960), and it may also be partly responsible for the other failures at avoidance learning that have been reported.

Although further work will obviously be necessary before freezing is understood, it is of interest that Feldman and Bremner (1963) recently described a procedure which appears to reduce drastically the probability of freezing. The technique involves the use of a relatively long warning signal (30 seconds) and requires that the experimenter observe the *S* and initiate a sequence of shocks whenever the *S* exhibits freezing during the warning period. The shocks are maintained for as long as the *S* maintains a fixed posture and are only terminated when a clear-cut movement is detected. In essence, the procedure consists of punishing freezing (by introducing shock) and reinforcing movement (by terminating shock).

As with the previously described technique of punishing holding responses, the punishment of freezing behavior also involves the presentation of extra shocks, and these may complicate efforts at interpretation.

THE ACQUISITION OF DISCRIMINATED AVOIDANCE

The Acquisition Process

The results of a study mentioned earlier (Hoffman & Fleshler, 1962a) provide a fairly detailed illustration of the way in which discriminated avoidance behavior develops. In that study, attention was focused upon the relationship between emotional responses and the avoidance response. Previous work by a number of investigators (e.g., Estes & Skinner, 1941; Brady & Hunt, 1955; Hoffman & Fleshler, 1961) had revealed that when a neutral stimulus typically precedes an *unavoidable* noxious event, subsequent presentations of the stimulus will cause a reduction in the rate of ongoing positively reinforced responses. By numerically evaluating this reduction, or suppression, of response rate, a quantitative index of the emotional reaction that is evoked by the warning signal can be obtained. The plan was to assess the role of emotionality in avoidance by developing the avoidance response while the Ss were concurrently engaged in positively reinforced behavior. In essence, the work sought to delineate emotional responses during avoidance learning by determining the level of conditioned suppression at various stages in the acquisition process. The method was as follows:

A group of rats was first taught to press a lever to terminate shock. Then the use of electric shock was temporarily discontinued and the Ss were taught to press a plate to obtain positive reinforcement. Throughout the rest of the experiment, plate pressing was maintained on a VI schedule of reinforcement. When the rate of plate pressing had stabilized, tones (1000 cps at 88 db. spl) which lasted 60 seconds were periodically presented (once every ten minutes on the average) with conditions arranged so that if the S pressed the lever during a tone, that tone would be terminated. Since there were no changes in the VI schedule of food reinforcement during this and during all subsequent operations, a plate press at any time (i.e., during tone or in later stages during tone plus shock) might yield reinforcement. The purpose of presenting tones without an accompanying shock was to determine whether, prior to its pairing with shock, the tone would exhibit control over the lever press. Sessions were run every other day, and on each session 20 tones were presented. After two sessions of tone "adaptation," shock was introduced at the end of tone. Under this condition, the Ss could terminate the tone and prevent shock by pressing the lever during the tone. If, however, they failed to avoid shock, both shock and tone remained on until a lever press occurred.

The top section of Figure 2 shows the percentage of avoidance responses per session along with the median latency of response in each session. It also shows the percentage of one-minute intervals just prior to the onset of each tone that contained one or more lever presses. It can be seen in the top section of this figure that, prior to its pairing with shock, the tone exhibited little, if any, tendency to control the lever press. During subsequent sessions, however, the percentage of avoidance responses increased, the latency of the avoidance response decreased, and the percentage of interval responses increased initially, and then gradually declined. Taken together, the three functions in this section of Figure 2 illustrate the development of a well-discriminated avoidance behavior.

The bottom section of Figure 2 shows several indices of emotionality that were derived from the measures of concurrent plate pressing. The index of emotionality was computed by forming a ratio (called a *suppression*

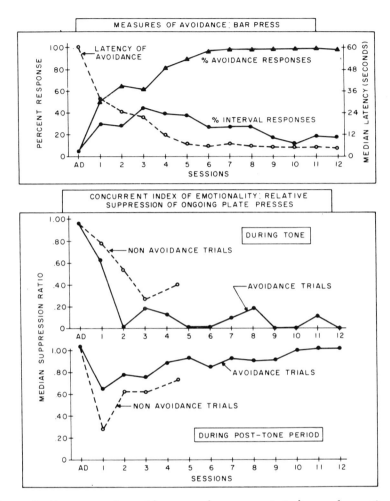

Figure 2. Measures of avoidance and concurrent indices of emotionality throughout the acquisition of discriminated avoidance behavior (see text). AD refers to the final session of tone adaptation when tones were presented without an accompanying shock. (From Hoffman & Fleshler, 1962a.)

ratio) which consists of the *rate* of plate pressing during a given tone divided by the *rate* during the one-minute period which immediately preceded the onset of the tone. With this index, ratios with values near 1.00 indicate little or no emotionality during the tone, whereas ratios with values at or near zero indicate that the rate during the tone was greatly suppressed, which reflects the existence of a high degree of emotionality. The middle section of Figure 2 shows the suppression ratios during tone for avoidance trials and for trials on which the animals failed to avoid. The bottom section of this figure shows the suppression ratios that were derived by comparing the rate during the 60 seconds following the termination of the tone to the rate during the 60 seconds which preceded the onset of the tone (i.e., the suppression ratio during the post-tone period) for trials on which the animals avoided and also for trials in which the Ss failed to avoid.

The development of the avoidance response involved gross changes in the several indices of concurrent emotionality. Prior to its pairing with shock, the tone exhibited no tendency to suppress ongoing behavior. However, when shock began to occur at the end of tone (from Session 1 on), the tone rapidly acquired the capacity to suppress ongoing plate presses. Further examination of Figure 2 also reveals that although the tone caused complete suppression by Session 2, performance on avoidance was nowhere near optimal for several additional sessions.

Statistical analysis of the data revealed that during the early sessions (1-5), suppression during tone on avoidance trials was significantly higher than the suppression during the tone on trials where the S failed to avoid. This finding is predicted by those theoretical treatments of avoidance (Hull, 1943; Mowrer, 1950; Miller, 1951; Spence, 1956) which assert that the motivation for the avoidance response is provided by an emotional reaction to the warning signal.

Statistical analysis also revealed that from Session 2 on, suppression during the post-tone period on avoidance trials was significantly less than suppression during the tone on these trials. This result supports an auxiliary hypothesis that has been proposed by the above theorists; namely, that in discriminated avoidance, reinforcement consists of a reduction in emotionality, which occurs when the warning signal is terminated. It is noteworthy that during Session 1, suppression during the post-tone period on avoidance trials was not significantly different from suppression during the tone on these trials. Apparently some process other than reinforcement with tone offset must be invoked to explain the avoidance behavior during Session 1. A reasonable possibility is that these responses reflect the action of the conditioned emotional response to the tone. Prior to the initiation of avoidance procedures, the Ss received considerable training on the escape response. During escape training, each shock was followed by a lever press, and undoubtedly each shock also led to a more or less severe emotional reaction. If one assumes that the internal stimulation resulting from these emotional reactions could acquire the capacity to act as discriminative cues for the lever press, then on later occasions, any source of similar emotional responses would act as an indirect source of discriminative stimuli for the lever press. During the early trials of the avoidance procedure, the pairing of tone and shock led to a condition in which the tone came to evoke an emotional reaction; and it seems possible that this reaction provided stimulation which was responsible for the avoidance responses observed in the first session.

In addition to the gross behavioral effects discussed above, the acquisition process was characterized by consistent performance changes within and between sessions. These are illustrated in Figure 3, which shows the percentage of avoidance responses per block of five trials. The within-session changes in emotionality are not shown because when based on samples of only five trials, the random fluctuations of the several indices were of such magnitude as to obscure any underlying trends.

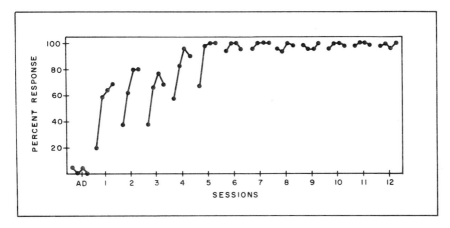

Figure 3. Percentages of avoidance responses per block of five trials throughout the course of acquisition of discriminated avoidance behavior. AD refers to the final session of tone adaptation when tones were presented without an accompanying shock.

As seen in Figure 3, during the final session of tone adaptation there were no systematic changes in the tendency to press the bar during the tone. With the introduction of shock at the end of tone, however, a performance emerged in which, during the initial five sessions, the tendency to avoid increased markedly within each session and decreased (to a lesser extent) in the 48-hour interval between sessions. After Session 5, the performance had reached a stage in which very few shocks were received and such changes as occurred within and between sessions were small and unreliable. This rather striking within-session improvement and between-session decrement is often seen during avoidance training. It is described by the term *warm-up*.

The Phenomenon of Warm-Up

One sometimes encounters warm-up even after Ss have been exposed to considerable training. Figure 4 shows the percentage of responses per block of ten trials on each of three consecutive sessions for a group of Ss

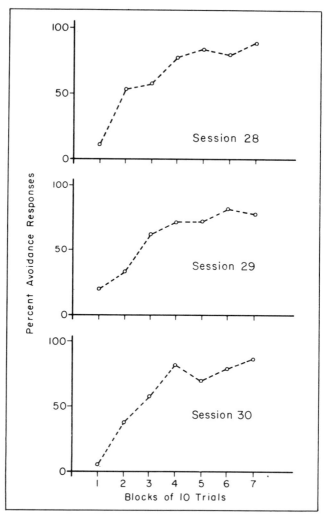

Figure 4. Warm-up after extended training on discriminated avoidance. These functions show the percent avoidance responses during sessions 28, 29, and 30. (From Hoffman, Fleshler, & Chorny, 1961.)

which previously had received 27 sessions of avoidance conditioning (Hoffman, Fleshler, & Chorny, 1961). In that experiment, the intertrial interval was approximately 30 seconds. The interstimulus interval was four seconds. The warning signal was a 3500 cps tone, the noxious event was shock, and the operant which avoided shock was a lever press. At first glance, it might appear that these Ss have somehow lost the response in the interval between sessions and must therefore relearn it during each session. That this explanation is incorrect is illustrated in the top section of Figure 5, which

shows the effects of making the lever inaccessible and removing the warning signal during the first 40 trials of the fifty-eighth session. For these
trials, the duration of the shock was fixed at .79 seconds, the mean latency
of the escape response during the prior sections of the experiment. Clearly,
the effect of 40 unsignaled and inescapable shocks was to eliminate the

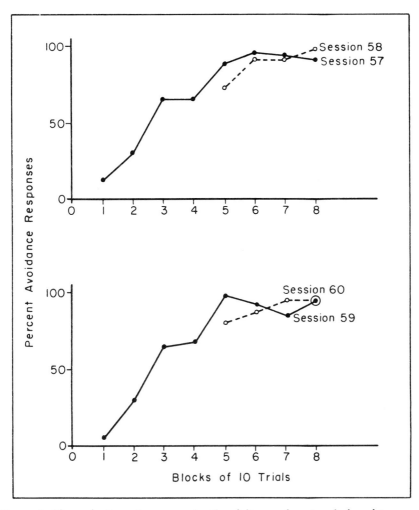

Figure 5. The reduction of warm-up by the delivery of unsignaled and inescapable shocks. The dashed functions show percentage avoidance responses during treatment sessions (58 and 60) when the tone was disconnected and the
lever was inaccessible for the first 40 trials. The solid functions show the percentage avoidance response during control sessions (57 and 59) when tones
were presented on all trials and the lever was continually accessible. (From Hoffman, Fleshler, & Chorny, 1961.)

decrement in performance when avoidance was finally possible. That the effects of these shocks were limited to the session in which they were applied is illustrated in the bottom section of this figure, which shows an additional session in which the shock was avoidable from the very beginning, followed by another session in which the first 40 trials consisted of unsignaled and inescapable shocks. This study led to the conclusion that the decrement in performance at the start of each session represented a motivational phenomenon; apparently as shocks occur, their motivational aftereffects persist and summate to create an emotional state which somehow facilitates avoidance. When, however, the S was removed from the apparatus, this motivational state dissipated and was not reinstated until the S again made contact with aversive stimulation on subsequent sessions. It is of interest that recently Nakamura and Anderson (1962) have reported comparable warm-up data, and that they too suggest that in avoidance, warm-up probably reflects the action of motivational variables.

VARIABLES WHICH AFFECT DISCRIMINATED AVOIDANCE

Temporal Variables

The Interstimulus Interval

Solomon and Brush (1956) have summarized a number of studies concerned with the temporal relationships in avoidance. In general, these studies suggest that the acquisition of avoidance proceeds more slowly as the interval between the onset of the warning signal and the onset of the noxious event is increased beyond five seconds. Most of the studies, however, employed the shuttlebox and there is some question as to whether this conclusion can be generalized to lever press experiments. The bulk of the experiments involving lever press have employed a warning interval of about five seconds, but whether or not this is an optimal value is not yet clear. There is, in fact, some indication that the acquisition of the avoidance response can proceed at a rapid pace even though relatively long warning intervals are employed. In the study on which Figure 2 was based, a warning interval of 60 seconds was used, and as was seen in that figure, the avoidance had reached very nearly 100 percent by the end of 100 trials. Moreover, Feldman and Bremner (1963) reported that avoidance developed rapidly when the warning period lasted for 30 seconds.

The Intertrial Interval

The effects of variations in the intertrial interval have been examined in several experiments which employed the shuttlebox (Murphy & Miller, 1956; Levine & England, 1960; Brush, 1962). Brush's results corroborate and extend the earlier work. He found that variations in the intertrial interval from 60 seconds to 20 minutes led to variations in the speed of avoidance learning with the fastest acquisition occurring when the intertrial interval was approximately five minutes. Brush suggested that the explanation may lie in the action of two motivational processes. One of these is a conditioned emotional response to the warning signal, and the other is a conditioned emotional response to apparatus cues. Presumably, the overall level of motivation during a given warning period is determined by a summation of these two emotional responses. If reinforcement for avoidance is a decrease in the overall level of emotionality with the offset of the warning signal, then maximum reinforcement would occur when emotionality controlled by apparatus cues is low, while emotionality controlled by the warning signal is high. By assuming that the emotional response to apparatus cues extinguishes in the interval between trials, one is led to the conclusion that a certain degree of spacing between trials would enhance reinforcement and hence be conducive to the rapid development of avoidance. If, however, trials are too widely spaced (for example, 20 minutes), too much extinction of apparatus-controlled emotionality would occur, and the overall motivational level, during a given warning period, might not be high enough to support the response.

Intersession Interval

Kamin (1963) has examined the effects of the intersession interval during acquisition in a sequence of experiments involving the shuttlebox. He found that any non-zero interval led to reduced performance at the beginning of subsequent sessions and that the effect increased as the intersession interval was increased. He also found that relative to intersession intervals of 24 and 192 hours, a one-hour interval yielded reduced within-session improvement. Figure 6 provides a schematic illustration of these features of Kamin's data.

As seen in Figure 6, the decrement between the end of one session and the beginning of the next was smallest when sessions were separated by one hour, but the improvement within sessions was also smaller for this group. The combination of these two effects yielded an overall performance in which the one-hour group was markedly inferior to the other groups during the early sessions but not during later sessions. Kamin also found that the reduced within-session improvement was relatively specific to the one-hour intersession interval. Thus intersession intervals of less than or greater than one hour did not usually produce a reduction in the rate of improvement within the session. The fact that variations in the interval between sessions affect both the decrement between sessions and the improvement within sessions, and that these effects are to some extent independent, suggests the action of two mechanisms. Further research, however, will be necessary before these mechanisms can be clearly delineated.

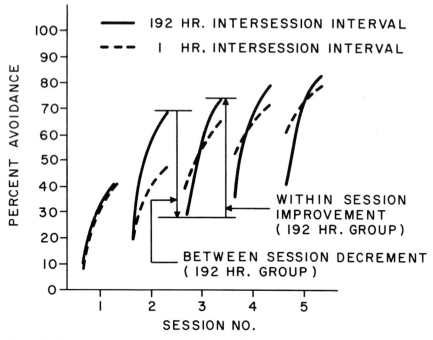

Figure 6. Schematic representation of the effects of intersession interval on the development of avoidance. (After Kamin, 1963.)

Stimulus Variables

The stimulus which precedes the noxious event plays a complex role in the development and maintenance of avoidance. It has already been shown that this stimulus can evoke a conditioned emotional response. In addition, it serves in a discriminative capacity in that it sets the occasion for the occurrence of the operant which prevents shock. When working with discriminated avoidance, however, one must take care that the warning signal acquire these properties because of its relationship to shock, and specifically because it precedes and in this sense serves as a warning for shock. The importance of such precautions is illustrated in a study by Myers (1959) which showed that when a buzzer was used as the warning signal, a large proportion of the avoidance responses could be attributed to pseudo-conditioning. Specifically, Myers found that rats will learn to press a lever which terminates a buzzer under conditions in which the buzzer and shock occur independently. Moreover, he found that the degree of pseudo-conditioning could be increased by increasing the intensity of the buzzer. On this basis, it seems obvious that it would be inadvisable to use a buzzer as the warning signal in discriminated avoidance. But the use of a tone as the warning signal is not likely to lead to unwanted effects, since Myers also

found that a pure tone even at intensities as high as 100 db. spl did not lead
to pseudo-conditioning.

It has been shown above that when *S*s were trained on avoidance while
concurrently engaged in ongoing positively reinforced behavior, the tendency to avoid was directly related to the capacity of the warning signal to
suppress the ongoing behavior (Hoffman & Fleshler, 1962). For this reason, studies of conditioned suppression per se can be expected to provide information which is relevant to the understanding of discriminated
avoidance.

Figure 7 shows a portion of the results of a sequence of studies on the
stimulus generalization of conditioned suppression (Fleshler & Hoffman,
1961; Hoffman & Fleshler, 1961; Hoffman, Fleshler, & Jensen, 1963). In
this work, pigeons were taught to peck a key for food on a VI schedule.
Then a 1000-cycle tone which lasted 48 seconds and which ended with eight
seconds of unavoidable shock was presented at irregular intervals until the

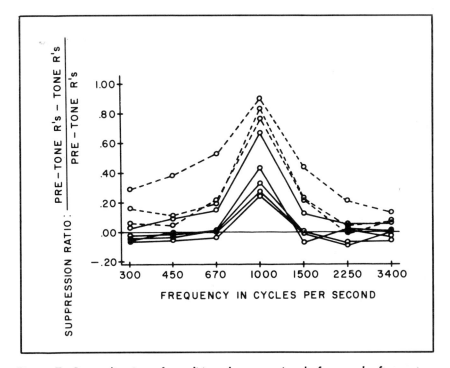

Figure 7. Generalization of conditioned suppression before and after a two-
and-one-half year interruption. The solid lines show results of a recent sequence
of tests, whereas the dashed lines show the terminal gradients obtained two-
and-one-half years earlier. Each gradient represents data averaged across
four successive sessions for five birds, and the sequence of gradients shows successive blocks of sessions in descending order. (From Hoffman, Fleshler, & Jensen,
1963.)

tone exhibited a strong tendency to suppress all pecking. Finally the use of shock was discontinued, and tones of various frequencies, including 1000 cycles, were presented sequentially and in random order (without shock) for a large number of sessions.

The gradients in Figure 7 show the average suppression ratios computed on blocks of four presentations of each tone, with the top gradient representing the first block, and lower gradients representing subsequent blocks. The suppression ratios for this figure were computed as follows: Suppression ratio equals the number of responses in the 40-second period before tone onset, minus the number of responses during the initial 40 seconds of tone, divided by the number of responses in the 40-second period before tone onset. Observe that this index has a value of 1.00 when the tone causes complete suppression and that it has a value of zero when the rate of responding during the tone is the same as the rate just prior to tone onset.

In Figure 7 the dotted gradients were obtained in a sequence of test sessions run shortly after the completion of suppression training. Initially all tones tended to cause some suppression, but as testing proceeded (without shock) the gradient of generalization narrowed severely. The solid gradients in this figure show the results of continued testing after a two-and-one-half-year interruption. During this time, the Ss were returned to their home loft and were maintained under normal conditions with no exposure to any experimental treatments. When testing was finally resumed, they were placed in the experimental chamber with neither tone nor shock, and run for several sessions until their key-pecking rate had stabilized. Then the several tones were again presented without shock and the capacity of the tones to suppress key pecking was once more evaluated.

As can be seen in Figure 7, the behavioral consequences of the aversive training administered almost three years previously were extremely inert. Not only did the birds continue to suppress, but the gradient of generalization of suppression was almost exactly where it would be expected had testing been administered without interruption. In general, these results suggest that the emotional response to a given warning signal is largely unaffected by the passage of time.

Figure 8 shows the results of a sequence of operations on the same birds which were designed to determine how the level and the generalization of conditioned suppression were affected by an increase in the level of ongoing emotionality (Hoffman *et al.,* 1963). The dotted line shows the last gradient from the sequence of tests after the two-and-one-half-year interruption. The solid and dashed lines show the gradients that were obtained in subsequent sessions in which shocks of short duration were periodically administered in the course of continued tests. These shocks were presented during periods of darkness which occurred in the ten-minute interval between presentations of tone. The periods of darkness lasted two minutes and occurred approximately six minutes before each tone. Since these pigeons never pecked the key during periods of darkness, the operation of administering shocks in darkness enabled us to supply noxious stimulation throughout testing under conditions which would minimize its association both with the tones and with the pecking behavior itself.

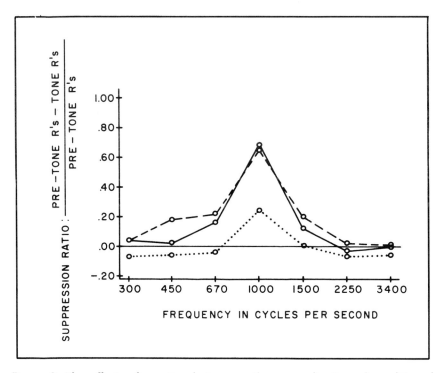

Figure 8. The effects of emotional stress on the generalization of conditioned suppression. The dotted line shows the final gradient from the most recent previous sequence of tests (Figure 7). The solid and dashed lines show the gradients obtained during subsequent stress conditions when electrical shocks were delivered between presentations of tones. (From Hoffman, Fleshler, & Jensen, 1963.)

It was found that the introduction of shocks during the periods of darkness did not cause a disruption of the base rate of pecking but that, as seen in Figure 8, it produced a marked elevation in the capacity of the tones to cause suppression of pecking. This finding is of special interest to the student of avoidance, because it suggests that in avoidance the level of the emotional response to the warning signal is only partly determined by conditioning that occurs during the *pairings* of that signal with the noxious event. Apparently the noxious events which occur during a given session also leave a lingering aftereffect which contributes to subsequent emotional reactions. As suggested earlier, if the aftereffect of these noxious events disappears in the interval between sessions, the mechanism can provide an explanation of the warm-up in discriminated avoidance which can be eliminated with the administration of free shocks.

DISCRIMINATED AVOIDANCE COMPARED TO OTHER OPERANT BEHAVIORS

Non-discriminated Avoidance versus Discriminated Avoidance

While the paradigm for discriminated avoidance shares features of the paradigm of non-discriminated avoidance, the similarities in the two procedures are maximized in those arrangements which, at one stage or another, employ an exteroceptive warning signal (Sidman & Boren, 1957). It differs from such paradigms, however, in certain important respects. First, in studies of discriminated avoidance, responses in the absence of the warning signal typically have no effect on the program. In studies of non-discriminated avoidance, such responses usually postpone the noxious event, and in some cases, they may also postpone the onset of the warning signal. Secondly, in most studies of discriminated avoidance, the initial response during a given warning period terminates the signal and prevents the associated noxious event. In non-discriminated procedures which employ an exteroceptive stimulus, responses during a given warning period ordinarily serve to postpone the occurrence of the noxious event, but they do not, typically, terminate either the warning signal or the danger period. Thirdly, in most studies of discriminated avoidance, the initial opportunity to avoid occurs when the warning signal is introduced for the first time. In non-discriminated procedures that employ a warning signal, the signal is typically introduced well after the *S* has already learned the response which postpones the noxious event. Finally, in non-discriminated procedures the noxious event is ordinarily of very short duration (i.e., a 500 millisecond pulse of shock) and, more important, its duration (once delivered) is independent of the behavior of the *S*. In the typical discriminated avoidance procedure, on the other hand, the noxious event is of variable duration since it is terminated by the *S*. Because these differences are of relatively large magnitude, it is difficult to form meaningful comparisons between the behaviors which emerge from discriminated versus non-discriminated procedures. Obviously, both behaviors are based upon aversive control, but the question of whether or not the nature of this control involves identical mechanisms must remain open for the present.

Positively Reinforced Behavior versus Discriminated Avoidance

In certain respects, discriminated avoidance has a counterpart in positively reinforced behavior that has been brought under stimulus control.

The similarities and differences in the two forms of behavior are illustrated in a study (Hoffman & Fleshler, 1962a) which compared discriminated lever-press avoidance to a similar behavior (plate press) that was brought under stimulus control using positive reinforcement. In that study, one group of rats (the avoidance group) was taught to avoid shock, the signal for which was a five-second tone with a frequency of 3500 cps. For these Ss, tone-shock combinations were programmed to occur every 35 seconds (on the average), and responses which occurred during a tone but prior to the shock terminated that tone and prevented the occurrence of the shock. A second group of rats (which will be called the approach group) was taught to perform a similar operant (plate press), but in this case, the animals were deprived of food, and the first response in the presence of a 3500 cps tone of five-seconds duration produced a pellet of laboratory chow. When the Ss in both groups exhibited a performance in which responses tended to occur consistently in the presence of the 3500-cps tone, but seldom in its absence, discrimination training was instituted. In this phase of the work, the 3500-cps tone as well as tones having lower frequencies were presented in random order at intervals of approximately 35 seconds. The program was arranged so that the appropriate shock and food contingencies were in effect for each group only with the 3500-cps tone.

Figure 9 shows the probability of response to each stimulus for each group during the first, the fifth, and the tenth session of this program. As can be seen, at first all tones exhibited some control over the response (i.e., stimulus generalization occurred), but with continued differential reinforcement, responses to stimuli on the wing of the gradient gradually ceased. One curious aspect of the data seen in Figure 9 is that despite the initial broader generalization of approach than of avoidance, the discrimination was learned more rapidly in the approach group than in the avoidance group. Figure 10 permits a more careful examination of this process. It shows for each stimulus (other than the 3500-cps tone) the total number of responses emitted during the development of the discrimination and plots them as a function of the probability of response to that stimulus in the initial session. The number of unreinforced responses to a given stimulus on the wing of the gradient is seen to be an increasing function of the probability of response to that stimulus during Session 1. Moreover, at a given probability, there were many more responses for the avoidance group than for the approach group.

These findings are consistent with the observations of Solomon and Wynne (1953) among others, which indicate that avoidance is extremely resistant to extinction. It extends them, however, by revealing that even when its initial response strength is low (in terms of probability of response), avoidance extinguishes more slowly than comparable behavior that has been maintained by positive reinforcement. These results also explain why the sole use of aversive controls is likely to prove inefficient in

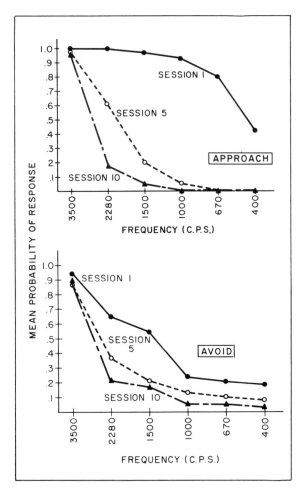

Figure 9. The development of discrimination among tones for approach and for avoidance responses. These functions show the mean probability of response to an S^D, 3500 cps, and to five test frequencies during the first, fifth, and tenth session of training. During these sessions, food reinforcement was programmed to occur with the S^D only for the approach Ss, and shock was programmed for the S^D only for the avoidance Ss. (From Hoffman & Fleshler, 1963.)

training discrimination. Apparently, aversive control can create a condition whereby any generalized response tendencies extinguish very slowly.

THEORETICAL CONSIDERATIONS

In the past, theoretical treatments of avoidance have taken several forms. The classical explanation of the avoidance phenomenon is exempli-

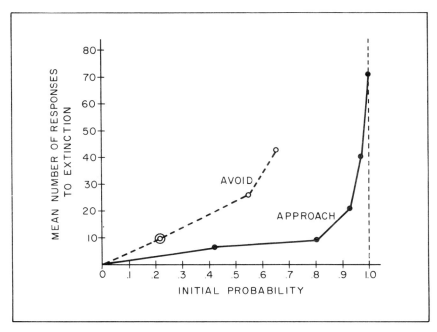

Figure 10. The extinction of generalized approach vs. avoidance responses in the course of tone discrimination training. The coordinates for each point represent the probability of response to a given stimulus other than the S^D during the first session of discrimination training—initial probability—and the total number of responses to that stimulus throughout the course of discrimination training—responses to extinction. For example, during the training on approach, the 670-cps tone produced an initial probability of .8 and, on the average, yielded nine responses throughout discrimination training. The circled points represent averages for those stimuli which yielded similar initial probabilities. (From Hoffman & Fleshler, 1963.)

fied by dual process theory (Hull, 1943; Mowrer, 1950; Miller, 1951; Spence, 1956). According to a dual process interpretation, the avoidance response is motivated by a conditioned emotional reaction which develops on trials where the S fails to avoid. Reinforcement, according to the dual process position, occurs when the avoidance response terminates the warning signal and leads to a reduction in emotionality. As suggested earlier, the basic assumptions of this approach appear to be consistent with the results of the Hoffman and Fleshler study (1962a), and it is noteworthy that they are also largely compatible with the results of a similar but more recent study by Kamin, Brimer and Black (1963).

An alternative explanation of avoidance (e.g., Schoenfeld, 1950; Sidman, 1953; Dinsmoor, 1954) assigns the growth of the response to processes which result from the punishment of non-avoidance behavior. According to this position, the avoidance paradigm is such that all behavior other than the avoidance response itself is likely to be followed by the onset of the aversive stimulus. Presumably, these conditions lead to a situation in which the avoidance response acts to terminate behavior which is aversive (by virtue of its association with the noxious event). The result is a reduction in the probability of non-avoidance behavior and a corresponding increase in the probability of the avoidance response. In general, this approach seems well suited to handling the data derived from studies of non-discriminated avoidance. The theory would, however, have to be greatly expanded in order to account for the several emotional processes which are found to covary with discriminated avoidance.

A third approach is represented by the expectancy theory of Tolman and his associates (Tolman, 1932). According to their view, the S learns to anticipate the noxious event, and the avoidance response represents a reaction which exemplifies foresight. Despite its obvious simplicity, this account has had little impact upon the efforts of workers in the area. Perhaps the reason is that the problems introduced by the concept of foresight have seemed just as difficult as the problem of accounting for avoidance.

Another point of view is represented by contiguity theory (Sheffield, 1948). According to a contiguity interpretation, avoidance responses become associated with and controlled by the stimuli which prevail at the time of their occurrence. The basic mechanism involved is the temporal juxtaposition of stimulus and response. Although a contiguity interpretation of avoidance has considerable intuitive appeal, like most other theories it provides no account of the emotional behaviors that covary with avoidance.

A more recent approach to the conceptualization of discriminated avoidance is represented by the work of the mathematical theorists (Bush & Mosteller, 1955; 1959; Bush, Galanter, & Luce, 1959; Theios, 1963). The general position of these theorists is exemplified by the two-operator linear model proposed by Bush and Mosteller. The model makes no formal assertions about mechanisms which presumably underlie avoidance; instead, it assumes only that during avoidance training the events on each trial lead to progressive changes in the probability of the avoidance response. These changes are represented by the action of linear operators. Thus the acquisition process is conceptualized as an increase in the probability of the avoidance response (P) that results when P is transformed by the successive application of an avoidance operator Q_1 (for trials on which the S avoids) and an escape operator Q_2 (for trials on which the S fails to avoid).

The operators Q_1 and Q_2 have the form

$$Q_iP = \alpha_iP + (1 - \alpha_i) \lambda_i.$$

where the parameter λ_i represents the limit (fixed point) for repeated application of the operator, and the parameter α_i is a reflection of the effectiveness of the event in question. For example, if P_n equals the probability of avoidance on trial n, and an avoidance response occurs on trial n, then

$$P_{n+1} = \alpha_1 P_n + (1 - \alpha_1)\, \lambda_1.$$

If, however, the S fails to avoid on trial n, then

$$P_{n+1} = \alpha_2 P_n + (1 - \alpha_2)\, \lambda_2.$$

In applying the model to a given set of data, either of two methods can be used to derive the theoretical learning curve. The first involves estimating the constants P_0, α_1, α_2, λ_1, and λ_2 and solving a series of general equations. The second, though less mathematically elegant, is in certain respects more interesting. It involves estimating the parameters of the operators (as in the first method) and running a group of stat animals using Monte Carlo computations. The technique is quite straightforward and is comparable to deriving an approximation to a theoretical probability distribution by throwing dice.

A given stat S is assigned an initial probability of avoidance on the first trial. Then a die (with the appropriate probability built in) is thrown to determine whether or not the S makes an avoidance response. If the fall of the die says that the S avoids, the avoidance operator is applied to the probability that existed on trial 1, thus transforming it to a new probability. If the fall of the die says that the S fails to avoid, the escape operator is applied. Trial 2 for this S is simulated in the same way except that the die which is thrown is arranged to represent the transformed probability. When enough stat Ss have been run for enough trials, their data are summarized and analyzed in the same fashion as the data derived in an actual experiment.

In order to test their model, Bush and Mosteller (1955) employed Monte Carlo computations to simulate an avoidance experiment that was conducted earlier by Solomon and Wynne (1953). The resulting theoretical functions bore an almost point for point correspondence to the data produced by the living Ss. In a subsequent paper, Bush and Mosteller (1959) performed a kind of mathematical experiment in which they compared their model to several others by applying each to the Solomon and Wynne data. They concluded that although all of the models exhibited one deficiency or another, their original two-operator linear model provided the best overall approximation of the data.

In view of these initial successes, it might have been expected that the interpretation of avoidance suggested by the mathematical theorists would have had an immediate influence upon the practices of laboratory workers in the area. To date, it has not. Only two avoidance experiments have been treated in terms of mathematical theory (Solomon & Wynne, 1953; Theios, 1963), and of these one was carried out prior to the development of the theory.

Apparently, the gulf between theory and practice in the area of discriminated avoidance is difficult to bridge. As was seen in earlier discussions, much of the research to date suggests that discriminated avoidance represents a complex interaction of operant and respondent processes. But theories which seek to deal with these interactions (for example, dual process theory) have never been fully articulated. The reason is clear enough. The formal quantification of such theory would require a set of extremely complex mathematical derivations. And most experimentalists have neither the time nor the inclination to engage in such endeavors.

Fortunately, there now appears to be a way out of the dilemma. In exploring the quantitative implications of their model, Bush and Mosteller employed a high speed computer to simulate the behavior generated by their assumptions, and recently, my co-workers and I (Hoffman, 1965) employed a computer to explore a quantitative approach which might encompass the behavioral interactions seen in discriminated avoidance. To do so we turned to dual process theory.

The basic procedure was to write a simplified version of the theory in formal terms and then to program a computer to derive its implications by performing Monte Carlo calculations. It was felt that by this procedure we might bypass the sophisticated mathematics that had for so long prevented precise analysis.

As indicated earlier, dual process theory holds that the avoidance response is motivated by emotional reactions to the warning signal and that reinforcement occurs when the avoidance response terminates the warning signal. In our quantitative version of dual process theory, it was assumed that on the nth trial, the probability of avoidance (P_n) was determined by three factors: (1) the strength of the discriminative control exercised by the warning signal on that trial ($_sH_{rn}$); (2) the strength of the conditioned emotional reaction to the warning signal CER_n; and (3) the level of arousal (AR_n) at the time the warning signal occurred.

In the terminology of Hull (1943) and Spence (1956) we were assuming that $P_n = {_sH_{rn}} (CER_n + AR_n)$.

Each time the S fails to avoid, the noxious event occurs. As a result, (1) the level of AR increases, and (2) through respondent conditioning the warning signal acquires an increased tendency to evoke a CER. On trials where the S avoids, on the other hand, $_sH_r$ increases. Finally, in order that the model might account for warm-up, we also assumed that AR would dissipate as a function of time and that in the interval between sessions it would be reduced to zero.

We instructed the computer to proceed on a trial-by-trial basis by calculating P_n on a given trial and then dipping into a random numbers table and deciding whether or not the trial was to be scored as avoidance. If the trial yielded an avoidance response, the computer was to increase $_sH_r$ by a specified amount and then calculate the value of P for the next trial (P_{n+1}). If the trial was scored as escape, the value of $_sH_r$ was to remain fixed while the computer increased CER and AR before calculating the value of P_{n+1}. Having calculated P_{n+1}, the computer was to dip again into the random numbers table, score the trial, and, in the above fashion, proceed to trial $n + 2$. When enough trials had been run to simulate a given S's performance in a given session, AR was to be reset to zero before calculating the P for the first trial of the next session. When a given stat rat had been run for enough sessions, the computer was to start over again, and duplicate these procedures with a second stat rat. Eventually, when data had been accumulated for a number of stat rats, the results were to be summarized in the same fashion as in experiments with living Ss.

In order to test the adequacy of the model, we programmed the computer to simulate one of the experiments that was reported earlier in this chapter (Hoffman & Fleshler, 1962a).

Figure 11 shows the percentage of avoidance response per session in the Hoffman-Fleshler experiment and also shows the comparable data generated by the computer. The overlap is striking and it is apparent that on a gross level, the model provides a very good approximation to the behavior of the living subjects.

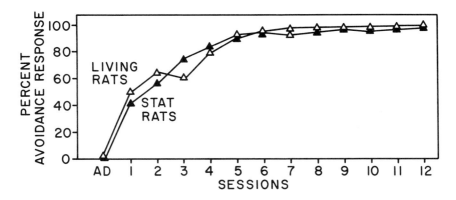

Figure 11. Computer simulation of discriminated avoidance. Percentage avoidance responses per session for living Ss and for stat rats. AD refers to a pretraining session with the living rats in which the warning signal was presented without an accompanying electrical shock. (From Hoffman, 1965.)

Figure 12 shows the percentage of avoidance response per block of five trials for the stat rats and for the living rats. The two sets of curves show similar trends, but during the early sessions, the living rats exhibited much more warm-up than the stat rats.

Figure 13 shows one of the indices of emotionality throughout acquisition in the Hoffman-Fleshler study and also shows a comparable measure on

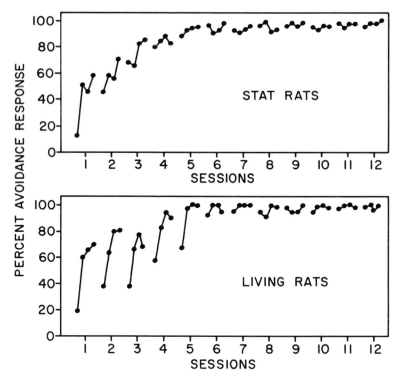

Figure 12. Warm-up during computer simulation of discriminated avoidance. The two sets of functions show the percentage of avoidance responses per block of five trials through the course of acquisition. (From Hoffman, 1965.)

the stat rats. It will be recalled that on each trial and for each rat in the Hoffman-Fleshler study we measured the rate of plate pressing (for food) during the warning signal and during a period of comparable duration which ended with the onset of the signal. For the present purpose these rates were employed to compute a modified suppression ratio that was numerically equal to 1.00 minus the suppression ratio that was used in Figure 2. This modified ratio was employed in the present context so that it could serve as a direct index of the CER evoked by the warning signal. Thus the present suppression ratio was numerically equivalent to the one used in Figures 7 and 8. It has values near 1.00 when suppression is nearly complete and it has values near 0.00 when there is little slowdown in rate. The top half of Figure 13 shows the median suppression ratio per session (across all Ss) for those trials on which the Ss avoided the noxious event. The second curve in the top section of Figure 13 shows the median CER value per session (across all stat rats) for those trials on which an avoidance response occurred. In general, the model exhibits the trends in the data yielded by living Ss, but the data from the stat rats is less variable than the data from living rats.

The bottom section of Figure 13 shows the suppression ratios from living Ss and CERs from stat Ss on those trials during which the Ss failed to produce an avoidance response. As suggested in the earlier discussion of the Hoffman-Fleshler experiment, only the first few sessions are included in the curves because of the scarcity of escape trials in the late sessions. The same trends can be seen in both sets of data, but the function derived from the stat rats is consistently higher than the function obtained from living rats.

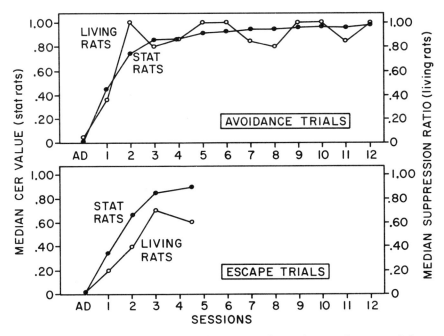

Figure 13. Computer simulation of discriminated avoidance. The several functions show indices of emotionality throughout the course of acquisition for living rats and CER values during the same periods for stat rats. AD refers to a pre-training session with the living rats in which the warning signal was presented without an accompanying electrical shock. (From Hoffman, 1965.)

From these comparisons it seems apparent that even in its present simplified version the model can provide a reasonably accurate reproduction of discriminated avoidance and of its emotional correlates. What is more important, however, is that the techniques employed in the articulation of the model could easily be adapted to any of a variety of other modes of interpreting avoidance. Experimentalists have long been accustomed to interpreting the behavior of their *S*s in terms of loosely formulated theories. It now appears that through the use of computers it will be possible to place these theories on a sound, quantitative basis. Perhaps the theories will perform as expected, but there may be some surprises in store; and in either event it will be important to know.

A word of caution is, however, in order. It has become clear that discriminated avoidance is a complicated phenomenon which involves a variety of interactions between operant and respondent processes. Presumably, a fully articulated theory will help us to gain insight into these interactions by permitting us to conceptualize them in quantitative terms. But whether it does or not, it must be borne in mind that laboratory examples of discriminated avoidance seldom represent the kind of pure phenomenon that theory describes. For example, a theory of avoidance might be concerned with relationships between avoidance and emotional behavior, but it would not ordinarily concern itself with secondary behavioral processes such as lever holding and freezing. Since, however, both holding behavior and freezing interact with and affect the performance of the avoidance response, their existence in a given experiment might make the application of theory tenuous. There is, of course, a straightforward solution to this problem. We need to learn more about the confounding behaviors and then include factors which describe them in our theories.

Apparently, we are now at a point where our understanding of discriminated avoidance can begin to undergo rapid expansion. Up to now there have been many experiments, but very little formal theorizing, and, as a result, our conceptions are still quite fragmentary. Hopefully, future work of both an experimental and a theoretical nature will rectify this state of affairs.

REFERENCES

BECHTEREV, V. M. (1932) *General principles of human reflexology*. New York: International.

BRADY, J. V., and HUNT, H. (1955) An experimental approach to the analysis of emotional behavior. *J. Psychol., 40,* 313-325.

BRUSH, R. R. (1962) The effects of intertrial interval on avoidance learning in the rat. *J. comp. physiol. Psychol., 55,* 888-892.

BUSH, R. R., GALANTER, E., and LUCE, R. D. (1959) Tests of the "Beta Model." In R. R. Bush and W. K. Estes (Eds.), *Studies in mathematical learning theory*. Stanford: Stanford Univ. Press.

BUSH, R. R., and MOSTELLER, F. (1955) *Stochastic models for learning*. New York: Wiley.

BUSH, R. R., and MOSTELLER, F. (1959) A comparison of eight models. In R. R. Bush and W. K. Estes (Eds.), *Studies in mathematical learning theory*. Stanford: Stanford Univ. Press.

CAMPBELL, S. L. (1962) Lever holding and behavior sequences in shock escape. *J. comp. physiol. Psychol., 55,* 1047-1053.

COONS, E. E., ANDERSON, N. H., and MYERS, A. K. (1960) Disappearance of avoidance responding during continued training. *J. comp. physiol. Psychol.,* *53,* 290-292.

DINSMOOR, J. A. (1961) A wide-range constant current shock stimulator. *J. exp. Anal. Behav., 4,* 273-274.

DINSMOOR, J. S. (1954) Punishment: I. The avoidance hypothesis. *Psychol. Rev., 61,* 34-46.

ESTES, W. K., and SKINNER, B. F. (1941) Some quantitative properties of anxiety. *J. exp. Psychol., 29,* 390-400.

FELDMAN, R. S., and BREMNER, F. J. (1963) A method for rapid conditioning of stable avoidance bar pressing behavior. *J. exp. Anal. Behav., 6,* 393-394.

FLESHLER, M., and HOFFMAN, H. S. (1961) Stimulus generalization of conditioned suppression. *Science, 133,* 753-755.

HEARST, E., and WHALEN, R. E. (1963) Facilitation effects of d-amphetamine on discriminated avoidance performance. *J. comp. physiol. Psychol., 56,* 124-128.

HOFFMAN, H. S. (1965) Theory construction through computer simulation. In W. F. Prokasy (Ed.), *Classical conditioning: A symposium.* New York: Appleton-Century-Crofts. Pp. 107-117.

HOFFMAN, H. S., and FLESHLER, M. (1961) Stimulus factors in aversive controls: The generalization of conditioned suppression. *J. exp. Anal. Behav., 4,* 371-378.

HOFFMAN, H. S., and FLESHLER, M. (1962) The course of emotionality in the development of avoidance. *J. exp. Psychol., 64,* 288-294. (a)

HOFFMAN, H. S., and FLESHLER, M. (1962) A relay sequencing device for scrambling grid shock. *J. exp. Anal. Behav., 5,* 329-330. (b)

HOFFMAN, H. S., FLESHLER, M., and CHORNY, H. (1961) Discriminated bar press avoidance. *J. exp. Anal. Behav., 4,* 309-316.

HOFFMAN, H. S., FLESHLER, M., and JENSEN, P. (1963) Stimulus aspects of aversive controls: The retention of conditioned suppression. *J. exp. Anal. Behav., 6,* 575-583.

HULL, C. L. (1943) *Principles of behavior.* New York: Appleton-Century-Crofts.

KAMIN, L. J. (1963) Retention of an incompletely learned avoidance response: Some further analyses. *J. comp. physiol. Psychol., 56,* 713-718.

KAMIN, L. J., BRIMER, C. J., and BLACK, A. H. (1963) Conditioned suppression as a monitor of fear of the CS in the course of avoidance training. *J. comp. physiol. Psychol., 56,* 497-501.

LEVINE, S., and ENGLAND, S. J. (1960) Temporal factors in avoidance learning. *J. comp. physiol. Psychol., 53,* 282-283.

LEVINE, S., and SOLIDAY, S. (1962) An effect of adrenal demedullation on the acquisition of a conditioned avoidance response. *J. comp. physiol. Psychol., 55,* 214-216.

MEYER, D. R., CHO, C., and WESEMANN, A. F. (1960) On problems of conditioning discriminated lever-press avoidance responses. *Psychol. Rev., 67,* 224-228.

MILLER, N. E. (1951) Learnable drives and rewards. In S. S. Stevens (Ed.), *Handbook of experimental psychology.* New York: Wiley. Pp. 435-472.

MOWRER, O. H. (1950) *Learning theory and personality dynamics.* New York: Ronald.

MOWRER, O. H., and MILLER, N. E. (1942) A multipurpose learning-demonstration apparatus. *J. exp. Psychol., 31,* 163-170.

MURPHY, J. V., and MILLER, R. E. (1956) Spaced and massed practice in the methodological consideration of avoidance learning. *J. exp. Psychol., 52,* 77-81.

MYERS, A. K. (1959) Avoidance learning as a function of several training conditions and strain differences in rats. *J. comp. physiol. Psychol., 52,* 381-386.

NAKAMURA, C. Y., and ANDERSON, N. H. (1962) Avoidance behavior differences within and between strains of rats. *J. comp. physiol. Psychol., 55,* 740-747.

SCHOENFELD, W. N. (1950) An experimental approach to anxiety, escape, and avoidance behavior. In P. S. Hoch and J. Zubin (Eds.), *Anxiety.* New York: Grune & Stratton. Pp. 70-99.

SHEFFIELD, F. D. (1948) Avoidance training and contiguity principle. *J. comp. physiol. Psychol., 41,* 165-177.

SIDMAN, M. (1953) Avoidance conditioning with brief shock and no exteroceptive warning signal. *Science, 118,* 157-158.

SIDMAN, M., and BOREN, J. J. (1957) The relative aversiveness of warning signal and shock in an avoidance situation. *J. abnorm. soc. Psychol., 55,* 339-344.

SKINNER, B. F., and CAMPBELL, S. L. (1947) An automatic shocking-grid apparatus for continuous use. *J. comp. physiol. Psychol., 40,* 305-307.

SOLOMON, R. L., and BRUSH, E. S. (1956) Experimentally derived conceptions of anxiety and aversion. In M. R. Jones (Ed.), *Nebraska symposium on motivation,* Lincoln: Univ. of Nebraska Press. Pp. 212-305.

SOLOMON, R. L., and WYNNE, L. L. (1954) Traumatic avoidance learning: The principle of anxiety conservation and partial irreversibility. *Psychol. Rev., 61,* 353-385.

SPENCE, K. W. (1956) *Behavior theory and conditioning.* New Haven: Yale Univ. Press.

STONE, G. C. (1960) Effects of some centrally acting drugs upon learning of escape and avoidance habits. *J. comp. physiol. Psychol., 53,* 33-37.

THEIOS, J. (1963) Simple conditioning as two stage all-or-none learning. *Psychol. Rev., 70,* 403-417.

TOLMAN, E. C. (1932) *Purposive behavior in animals and men.* New York: Appleton-Century-Crofts.

WYCKOFF, L. B., and PAGE, H. A. (1954) A grid for administering shock. *Amer. J. Psychol., 67,* 154.

12

The Study of Drugs
with Operant Techniques

John J. Boren

INTRODUCTION

In the early 1950's chlorpromazine and reserpine, the first tranquilizers, were found to be useful in the treatment of psychiatric patients. This finding was made in the clinic and came more as a surprise than as the logical outcome of planned laboratory research. However, due in large part to this important medical advance, interest in laboratory research in behavioral pharmacology took a sharp upswing. The first interest centered upon two problems: (1) How can one discover new drugs with a useful application in the psychiatric field? (2) How can the behavioral actions of these drugs be better understood through a laboratory analysis? Later the interest broadened to include the most general problems of the action of drugs upon behavior.

In the analysis of drug-behavior relationships, operant conditioning techniques have been applied quite usefully. The purpose of this chapter is to describe this application, to provide representative drug-behavior data, and to discuss some of the experimental problems and their solutions. The emphasis will be upon experimental design and the evaluation of the results. The chapter may be of interest either to those who wish to perform drug-behavior experiments or to those who wish to evaluate the experimental literature.

A common feature of the operant approach involves the intensive study of individual subjects. Typically, a small number of subjects are used for an experiment. The emphasis is upon close observation and firm experimental control of the individual subject. If the experimenter is successful, each subject will behave predictably from session to session and even from minute to minute. Thus, when an effective drug is injected in the middle of a session, a change from the dependable baseline behavior should be read-

531

ily apparent in an individual subject. Furthermore, on different sessions a range of drug dosages can be studied in the same subject with a sound basis for comparison.

Representative data for well-known drugs have been selected to illustrate certain facts and to elucidate particular problems. Although no attempt has been made to cover the literature of behavioral pharmacology, the interested reader may refer to the excellent reviews by Brady (1959), Sidman (1959), Dews and Morse (1961), Cook and Kelleher (1963), and Gollub and Brady (1965).

WHY EXPERIMENT WITH DRUGS?

The reasons for selecting a drug for an experimental study are no less complicated than the reasons for investigating any variable which affects behavior. However, at least a few of the more common reasons can be indicated:

1. *Curiosity about the behavioral effects of drugs.* How will atropine affect conditioned avoidance behavior? Is behavior maintained by a fixed interval schedule more sensitive to drugs than behavior maintained by a fixed ratio schedule? Such questions are typical of those which a behavioral pharmacologist might find interesting. Drugs can be powerful variables; they can eliminate behavior altogether or increase its output tenfold. Any drug might have an interesting or unusual action in a behavioral situation, and the fact that such a situation occasionally arises may be quite enough to support the research behavior of a scientist.

2. *Practical utility of drugs in human affairs.* The use of drugs in treating human ills probably represents the most socially valuable application of pharmacological science. As a result, a great deal of research is directed toward potential applications of drugs. For example, scientists in government and industrial laboratories study thousands of newly synthesized organic chemicals every year in the expectation that they will discover a novel and medically useful drug.

3. *Analysis and verification of clinical findings.* A drug which is useful in the clinic is interesting to the research worker for several reasons. He may wish to understand the clinical effect and the mechanism of action more fully than can be done conveniently and without danger in human patients. In the laboratory with animal subjects, he can readily perform surgery, administer toxic doses, or implant electrodes in an effort to understand the drug's action. In another case he may use the drug as a test to see if his laboratory procedures are relevant to a clinical problem. For example, suppose a researcher has found a way to disrupt the complex conditioned behavior of guinea pigs by injecting a toxin isolated from the blood of psy-

chotic patients, and he wants to know if his experimental situation is related to the psychoses of human patients. Now, if Drug A is known to affect psychotic patients favorably, and if Drug A also reduces the toxin-induced disruption of his guinea pigs, then the researcher has reason to believe that his behavioral technique might be useful in studying anti-psychotic agents, such as drugs. However, he may be incorrect. Drug A may reduce the disrupted behavior of the guinea pigs for entirely different reasons from those responsible for relieving patients, and the laboratory situation may bear only a superficial resemblance to clinical psychosis. If he were certain of the basic cause of psychosis in humans, he might then make sure he produced psychosis in his animals the same way. Unfortunately, this knowledge is not available. However, to increase his confidence, the researcher might continue his investigation of other anti-psychotic agents. If he found that not only Drug A but also Drug B, Surgery C, and Therapy D affected his guinea pig preparation the same way that they affected human psychosis, then his confidence that his preparation is related to clinical psychosis, while never complete, would be increased a great deal.

4. *Examining generalizations, explanations, or hypotheses.* A drug can occasionally be found which either has a specific effect or at least has a main effect that is not seriously disrupted by secondary effects. This drug can then be used as an analytical tool. For example, Dews (1955) showed that behavior maintained by a fixed interval (FI) schedule of reinforcement was much more sensitive to pentobarbital than was behavior maintained by a fixed ratio (FR) schedule. In a related study, Herrnstein and Morse (1956) examined the effect of the same drug with similar values of a tandem FI FR schedule, where the behaviors generated by the two components of the schedule were joined in a single performance and could not be easily disentangled. However, when pentobarbital was given in a high dosage, the post-reinforcement pause characteristic of fixed ratio behavior remained. Thus, the drug experimentally separated the two behaviors and gave the experimenters additional evidence that the complex tandem performance could indeed be properly analyzed into the simple components. As another example, Carlton (1963) was interested in the general proposition that cholinergic mechanisms in the brain selectively antagonize the activation of non-reinforced behavior. He examined this proposition by administering atropine, an anticholinergic drug, and found that behavior normally absent due to non-reinforcement was emitted under atropine. He further tested the hypothesis that the cholinergic mechanisms of interest were located in the brain by administering methyl atropine, a peripheral anticholinergic drug which does not act centrally. In accordance with his hypothesis, Carleton found that methyl atropine was almost ineffective in mimicking the effects of atropine, thus providing evidence that the cholinergic system of interest was located in the brain.

A TYPICAL EXPERIMENT

In order to explain more specifically how drugs can be studied with operant techniques, I will describe a typical experiment. I have selected one of my own experiments (Boren & Navarro, 1959), not because it is better or "more typical" than others (it is not), but rather because I am familiar with the details, and because the experiment illustrates many of the common problems of drug-behavior research.

The research originated with an interest in benactyzine, which was considered at that time a promising new psychotherapeutic agent. The drug was known to have peripheral anticholinergic effects (such as pupillary dilation) and to produce CNS effects (such as slowing of EEG waves) which were presumed to be anticholinergic. Therefore, two classical anticholinergic drugs, atropine and scopolamine, were selected for study as standard comparison agents. In terms of the reasons for studying drugs described above, the experimental study was based upon (1) simple curiosity (How would benactyzine change fixed interval behavior?), and (2) an interest in a generalization (Would drugs sharing anticholinergic effects also share behavioral effects?).

The Experimental Design and the Procedure

The first aim of the experimental design was to establish a stable behavioral performance or baseline. This performance could then be modified by the injection of drugs. In the preparation of the baseline performance, two albino rats were conditioned to press a lever for a water reinforcement. Then the rats were well-trained on a multiple schedule with fixed ratio (FR) and fixed interval (FI) components. More specifically, in the presence of a clicking noise the water reinforcement was delivered when the rat had pressed the lever 26 times (FR 26); in the presence of a tone the reinforcement was delivered for the first lever press after four minutes (FI 4). The value of the multiple schedule was to permit the drug effects on both schedules to be closely compared in an individual animal during the same session.

The drug phase of the experiment was planned so that each subject served as his own control and received each drug in a range of doses. For example, one rat was injected intraperitoneally with atropine in doses of 1, 2, and 4 mg/kg; with benactyzine in doses of 0.1, 0.5, 4, and 8 mg/kg; and with scopolamine in doses of 0.1, 0.4, 0.8, 1.6, and 3.2 mg/kg. A complete experimental session was devoted to the study of each dosage.

The various doses of the various drugs might have been given in a random order. However, to facilitate the comparison among the dosage levels of a given drug, all doses of a drug were studied during a block of sessions. Atropine was studied first, next benactyzine, then scopolamine; but during the block of sessions, the dosage levels were administered in a mixed order. At least one control session (usually with no injection but sometimes with a saline injection) was run between drug sessions. Thus, the subject's baseline performance was examined often to assess any long-term drifts in the baseline. The wide spacing of the drug sessions (four to six days) also reduced the possibility of tolerance, summation of two doses, or other carryover effects from drug session to drug session.

The Analysis of the Results

The data for the individual subjects were treated separately since in fact a separate experiment was performed on each subject. Two important aspects of the results received attention: (1) changes in the characteristic temporal pattern of the fixed interval and the fixed ratio performance; and (2) changes in the baseline response rates for the two schedules of reinforcement. The cumulative records were carefully inspected to assess the changes in temporal pattern. Many control records were examined in order to determine the subject's typical pattern of behavior; then this typical pattern was compared with the behavior under the drug. The main features of these data for atropine may be seen in Figure 1 and are described in the legend. One mg/kg produced relatively little change in this rat's performance, but 2 mg/kg clearly modified the temporal pattern of the FI behavior. By the end of the session the post-reinforcement pause had shortened drastically, and the gradual positive acceleration in rate (the scallop on the record) had been replaced by a more or less steady rate of responding. Since similar changes had not been observed in over 50 control sessions, there was good reason to believe that the changes were due to the drug and not to uncontrolled fluctuation of the baseline. In contrast to the FI behavior, the FR behavior was hardly altered by 2 mg/kg.

With a dose of 4 mg/kg, however, the effects were greater and less specific. The onset of drug action occurred earlier in the session, and the temporal patterns of both the FI and the FR performances were disrupted.

The second approach to the analysis of the results was more quantitative. The basic aim was to analyze the drug-induced changes in terms of response rate. The average response rates for the two components of the multiple schedule were computed separately, so that any specific effects on the FI and the FR performances could be assessed. The basic comparison was between the rate during the drug session and the rate during pre- and post-control sessions for the individual subject. The comparison which is possible with one subject is considerably easier than is sometimes realized. For example, consider the following series of numbers which represent one rat's FI response rate during the second half of each session: 49.2, 56.4, 52.1, 46.3, 11.1, 46.4, 49.6, 54.1, 47.5. Since the underlined value occurred after scopolamine had been injected, it is easy to see that the drug produced

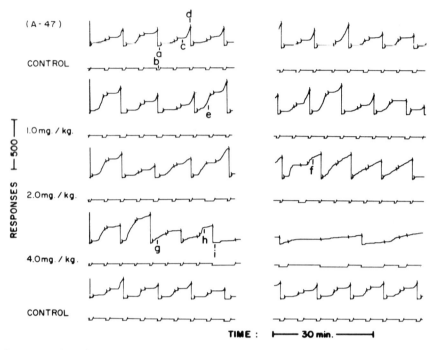

Figure 1. Cumulative records for Rat A-47 illustrating the effects of atropine upon temporal patterning of the FR and the FI peformances. The event pen record below each cumulative record marks the duration of the FR portion of the procedure. The top and bottom records illustrate the non-drugged control performance of this subject. On the left the panel of records shows the first 45 minutes of the 2.5-hour session, and on the right the panel shows the last 45 minutes. Significant aspects of the recording are indicated by the lower case letters. For example, at a the rat had entered the FR portion of the schedule (also shown by the pen offset at b) and paused briefly before breaking abruptly into a typical high rate FR run. At c, the FI schedule was in force, and the rat paused at length before lever pressing at a gradually accelerating rate. The reinforcement was delivered at d, and the pen reset to the starting point. The effects of atropine are shown at e, where 1 mg/kg slightly increased the usual number of FI responses; at f, where 2 mg/kg disrupted the normal temporal pattern of the FI behavior; at g, where a similar effect was produced by 4 mg/kg; at h, where an FR-like run occurred during the FI schedule; and at i, where the temporal pattern of the FR behavior was severely disrupted. (From Boren & Navarro, 1959.)

a substantial rate decrease, because the rate under drug was considerably below the limits of normal variability. A number of statistical analyses of such data can be applied if desired.

A convenient way to derive a single number showing the relation between the drug data and the control data is a drug/control ratio. For example, the control value might be the average FI rate for three sessions before and three sessions after the drug session. Thus, the drug/control ratio for the values shown above would be $11.1/50.8 = 0.22$. Ratios substantially greater than 1.0 represent drug-induced rate increases while ratios substantially less than 1.0 represent rate decreases.

The interpretation of these numerical analyses of response rate required frequent checking with the cumulative records as shown in Figure 1. Higher doses of the drugs often lowered the FR rate, but always at the point where the temporal patterning had been disrupted. In the case of the FI, the changes in temporal pattern were not necessarily accompanied by changes in response rate. Although the drug might change the typical FI scallop into steady responding (as at f in Figure 1), the overall average rate did not necessarily change. In many cases a decrease in the terminal rate was offset by an increase in post-reinforcement responding. Further detail concerning the effects of the drugs is not essential at this point, but in this experiment, as in most experiments, a thorough consideration of the relations among the various measures of the behavior is quite informative.

While certain differences among the drugs were observed (e.g., benactyzine had a shorter duration of action, scopolamine was active at about 1/10 the dose of atropine, etc.), the three drugs shared a main effect in common: at appropriate dosage levels each drug disturbed the temporal patterns of both the FI and the FR performances, and the response rate changed to low steady responding. How should one interpret this finding? Although it might be attractive, would it be correct to believe that disruption of the FI FR pattern is a general action of anticholinergic compounds? The answer is a tentative "not yet." One reason is that other classes of drugs which are not anticholinergic will also disrupt the FI scallop. Another reason is that the behavioral changes might not be due to the anticholinergic action of the three drugs; some other common action might be responsible. Thus, the fact that the three different drugs had a common effect is not entirely compelling although it is suggestive. One experimental approach to this problem might be the study of additional anticholinergic agents (which, as a group, share only the ability to antagonize acetylcholine) to see if they, too, disrupted the FI FR patterns.

The following features of this experimental design are often found in drug studies with operant techniques: (1) The subjects were trained on a behavioral performance to the final stable state. This performance formed a baseline from which to compare drug-induced changes. (2) Each subject served as his own control and under every drug condition of the experiment. Thus, a complete experiment was performed with each individual subject. (3) The drugs were administered to each subject in a wide range of doses so that the various actions at various dosage levels could be observed. (4) The data of each subject were analyzed separately.

THE DOSE-EFFECT CURVE

Pharmacology is a science of an independent variable—the administration of a chemical agent. The dependent variable may be any biological effect, ranging from alterations of cellular structure, to changes in blood pressure, to modifications of behavior. Because the formal emphasis is upon the independent variable, it is not surprising to find that most pharmacological experiments are intimately concerned with the quantity of chemical (the dose) administered. The object is to give graded doses of the drug and then to observe the graded effect on the biological system under study. When a graph is plotted from the data of such experiments, with the dosage indicated on the abscissa and the biological effect indicated on the ordinate, we have the familiar dose-effect curve. An example is shown in Figure 2. The

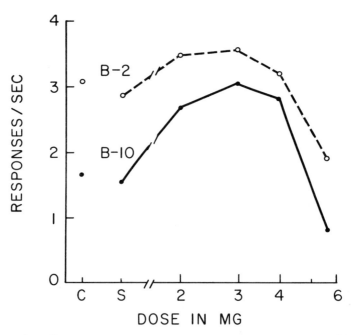

Figure 2. The effects of pentobarbital on rate of responding on FR 30. The dose is plotted on a log scale while the rate is plotted on a linear scale. The dose-effect curves of two individual pigeons (B-2 and B-10) are shown. The points above "S" show the rate after saline injections (mean of two observations). The points above "C" show the non-injection control rates (mean of six to eight observations). The points for each dosage are the mean of two observations. The dosage is given in terms of number of mg injected. Since the birds weighed slightly more than 400 g, the dosage in mg/kg can be readily calculated. (From Waller & Morse, 1963.)

data are from an experiment by Waller and Morse (1963) and show how pentobarbital affects two pigeons' key-pecking rates. The pecking response was maintained by reinforcement on an FR 30 schedule (i.e., the thirtieth peck produced grain). The dose-effect curves for both birds show an orderly increase in the response rate as a result of the intramuscular injection of 2 and 3 mg (total dose per pigeon). Three mg seemed to produce the maximum rate while the largest dose (5.6 mg) substantially decreased the response output. The dose-effect curve, taken as a whole, shows how pentobarbital over an effective dosage range quantitatively affects the FR 30 response rate.

Selecting the Dose Range

Once the drug has been decided upon, the next step is the selection of the dose range. According to a common notion, every drug has a "just right" dose which is standard, appropriate, and physiologically active. This notion may have some justification where a specific effect of a drug is desired. For example, when a physician must treat a patient for an acute bacterial infection, he will probably administer a "standard" dose of an antibacterial drug. On the basis of extensive experience he has probably selected this dose as being large enough to have a therapeutic effect on most patients and small enough to avoid unfortunate side effects. Even in this restricted situation, however, the notion of the "just right" dose may be inappropriate where the dose happens to be too low for a particular infection or too large for a particular patient who is sensitive to the toxic side effects.

In a more general sense, the concept of the "just right" dose is quite misleading. It overlooks the fact that drugs, like most variables, can be applied at different levels to produce different effects. At the extreme ends of the dose range, every drug has a dose which is so low that it is ineffective and one which is so high that it is lethal. Between these two extremes are dose levels which are generally appropriate for a pharmacological study.

An estimate of the lethal dose is usually quite important so that it can be avoided. Not only is the behavior of a dead animal of no interest but also the loss of a well-trained animal can be quite unfortunate. Information on the LD_{50} (the dose that is lethal to 50 percent of the animals treated) can often be found in published sources. As an approximate rule of thumb, a dose of 1/10 the LD_{50} is likely to be safe for experimental use with animal subjects. Another alternative is simply to inject untrained animals with substantially higher doses than are planned for the trained animals. If these animals survive the higher doses without great difficulty, it is usually safe to attempt lower doses with the trained animals.

For drugs used in clinical practice, another source of dosage information is the human dose, calculated in mg/kg. While this dose is likely to be a conservative estimate of a minimally effective dose in animals, it can provide a starting point from which larger doses may be tried.

Knowledge of the minimally effective dose is sometimes difficult to obtain but is usually an interesting datum. For an estimate of this dose, information from the literature or from a nearby pharmacologist can be useful. It must be kept in mind, however, that such dose estimates may not be appropriate to the species, to the route of administration, or to other conditions of an experiment. The only sure way is to try a range of doses and to see what effects are produced.

The spacing of doses, particularly in advance, is something of an art. However, a geometric series is often useful. For example, a twofold dosage increment (such as 10, 20, 40, 80 . . . mg/kg) is applicable to many drugs. The range of doses might well extend from the minimally effective dose to the maximally tolerable dose (i.e., the dose which approaches but does not produce adverse side effects or serious toxicity) with perhaps three or four intermediate doses. In this way the experimenter can determine a full dose-effect curve.

The Use of Dose-effect Curves

Why is it important to determine a dose-effect curve for a drug? Perhaps the major reason is that drugs often have different effects at different doses. Therefore, one can have full knowledge of a drug's effects only if one studies a full dosage range. In the data shown in Figure 2, pentobarbital both increased and decreased the response rate—depending on the dose. As a general rule, any drug which will increase behavioral output at some intermediate dose will surely decrease output at some higher dose. The decrease will occur, if for no other reason, because a toxic effect can always be produced by excessively high dosages. The selection of one particular dose does not permit a valid statement of what the drug does. To return to the example of Figure 2, if one selected 3 mg of pentobarbital to study, one would be convinced that the drug was a *stimulant* which increased response output. If one chose 6 mg, one would be equally sure that the drug was a *depressant* which decreased response output. If one picked .01 mg, the drug would be classed *inactive,* and if one picked 100 mg, it would appear to be a deadly toxin.

Even if two dosage levels were studied, the conclusion might be misleading. For example, one might choose two dosages, one on each side of a maximal level, and then find that they had almost the same effect. A logical but erroneous conclusion might be that increased dosage levels of this drug cause little additional effect and that the dose-effect curve is relatively flat. Furthermore, it would be easy to select two doses from the left or the right side of the maximum. Thus, one might conclude that larger doses either increase the behavioral output or decrease it. One can guard against such conclusions only by studying a number of doses distributed over the effective dosage range of the drug.

Another general reason for determining a dose-effect curve is to replicate and confirm the effects of higher and lower dosage levels. Thus, the reliability of the experimental effects can often be estimated from the dose-effect curve. Two reasonable assumptions are involved: (1) similar dosages should cause similar effects; (2) increasing dosages should cause orderly quantitative changes. If adjacent data points are scattered widely or if the curve is disorderly, the experimenter should look for uncontrolled variables.

As another example of confirmation by other doses, suppose that the results from a low dose suggested ambiguously that the subject's ability to discriminate between a steady light and a flashing light had deteriorated slightly. To clarify this matter, the investigator might consider two alternative procedures. One is to study the low dose again to see if the small effect on the discrimination could be observed. If so, he would have greater confidence in the effect. In all probability, however, the effect will be as ambiguous as before (within the range of extreme control effects), so that a definite conclusion may still be difficult. A second alternative is to increase the dose (as one would normally do in determining a dose-effect relationship) to see if the effect on the discrimination is increased. If the effect now emerges as large and clear, the investigator's confidence in the effect increases a great deal. This principle of experimental design is not limited to drug-behavior experiments. In the study of any independent variable where the effects are small, it is often more efficient to enlarge the effect by intensifying the variable than simply by replicating the small effect.

A further use of the dose-effect curve is in the quantitative comparison of two or more drugs. The pharmacologist will frequently want to know which of two drugs is the more *potent,* or synonymously, which is the more *active.* In other words, he wants to know which drug produces a given effect at the smaller dosage. The first step is to determine a dose-effect curve for each drug. Figure 3 illustrates several possible outcomes (assumed values) for Drugs A, B, and C. The figure might, for example, represent the decreases in the rate of avoidance responding produced by three depressant drugs. Comparison of Drugs A and B is easy. Drug A is clearly more potent than Drug B in the sense that equivalent effects are produced at lower doses by Drug A. The comparison is easy partly because the effective dosage ranges overlap very little but largely because the dose-effect curves are parallel. The parallel feature permits one to reach the same conclusion about potency regardless of the size of the effect. In Figure 3, Drug A is about eight times more potent than Drug B, regardless of whether the comparison is based on a 50 percent effect, a 25 percent effect, etc. Furthermore, because of the parallel curves, it is possible to calculate a single number for each drug which represents its potency. Conventionally, the number would represent the dose which causes a 50 percent reduction in responding

—the ED_{50} (for Effective Dose 50). In group studies, the ED_{50} represents the dose which causes a given effect in 50 percent of the animals tested. This usage is to be contrasted with the individual subject approach where ED_{50} refers to a 50 percent change in some measure of the individual's baseline behavior.

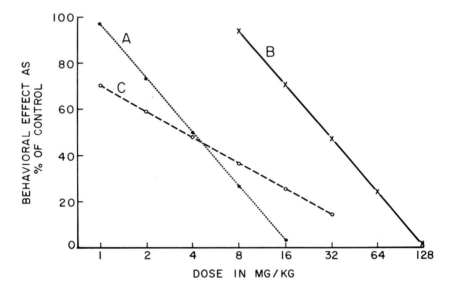

Figure 3. Three possible dose-effect curves illustrating the comparison of potency.

The comparison of Drugs A and C is considerably more difficult. The dose-effect curves are *not* parallel, and the effective dose ranges overlap. To be more specific, Drug C appears to be more potent at 1 and 2 mg/kg and less potent at 8 and 16 mg/kg. In such cases the use of an ED_{50} to compare the potency of the two drugs is arbitrary and misleading. Statistical or computational devices do not help since the ambiguity is inherent in the data. The most convenient solution is to end the search for a single number which relates the potency of each drug and simply to recognize the characteristics of the two dose-effect curves.

Note the likelihood of error if Drugs A and C were to be compared at a single dose of each instead of the full dose range. If 1 mg/kg were used, one would definitely conclude that Drug C was more potent; if 16 mg/kg were used, one would conclude equally definitely that Drug A was more potent. To gain complete and accurate information about a drug there is no substitute for a study which determines a full dose-effect curve.

A Shortcut Approach to a Dose-effect Curve

An experiment in which six dosage levels are studied three times each in four individual animals is indeed a valuable and informative study. It is also extremely time-consuming. Some investigators have sought shorter techniques, particularly where a number of drugs are to be compared and where the precise quantitative details of dosage are not important.

One approach is cumulative dosing. I am indebted to Harley M. Hanson for bringing this approach to my attention. A typical experiment might go as follows: A monkey is trained to press a lever to avoid an electric shock. The procedure is such that the animal can perform his task without important change for many hours. Then, in a single experimental session of seven hours, multiple doses can be given, with each successive dose being larger than the preceding one. The first hour may be used as a control or for a saline injection (although the entire preceding or following sessions may also serve as controls). At the beginning of the second hour, a dose of perhaps 1 mg/kg is given. At the third hour, a dose of 2 mg/kg is given. If the drug is extremely long acting, the effect on the avoidance behavior during the third hour might be similar to that produced by a single injection of 3 mg/kg. Additional and larger doses are given at hourly intervals, so that the graded effects of the drug, from small, to moderate, to large may be seen in a single session. The saving in time is great, and one has an opportunity to observe the full range of drug effects.

One may have to pay a price for this type of efficiency. For example, there is the risk of tolerance due to the repeated doses. In practice, however, this risk appars to be small with most drugs. The following problem is more common and must be kept in mind. How much drug is acting at any given time? Or, to phrase the question differently, what dose should be given in a single injection to produce a similar effect? The answer depends upon the rapidity of onset and the duration of action. Consider two drugs with different time courses. If the onset of Drug A is rapid (five minutes) and the duration is long (12 hours), the acting dosage level toward the middle of any hour in the experiment described above would approximate the sum of all previous doses. On the other hand, if the onset of Drug B is equally rapid (five minutes), but the duration is short (40 minutes), the acting dose level in the middle of any hour would result primarily from the dose given at beginning of the hour. Drugs of these two types present little difficulty. However, the type of drug and the dosing schedule must be coordinated to make the cumulative dosing technique useful. As a more difficult example, suppose that a drug has a two-hour delay in onset, lasts for one hour, but that the doses are given every 15 minutes. By the time the first dose has an effect, the second and third doses are already intermingling, so that conclusions about the acting dosage level are exceedingly difficult. Before the experimenter can terminate the dosing schedule, his experimental animals may even suffer from the toxicity of doses which were given two hours earlier.

The cumulative dosing technique is most useful where one is interested simply in determining the variety of effects from a range of drug dosages. In this case, which is a common one, it is of no great consequence to know the acting dose exactly or to label the abscissa of the dose-effect curve precisely. It may be quite enough to know that each successive dose is larger than the last and to observe in a short period of time the range of effects which can be expected from the drug. Furthermore, the experimenter can always give single injections in later sessions to determine the one-dose equivalent of selected parts of the cumulative dosing session.

THE BEHAVIORAL BASELINE

What types of behavior are appropriate for the study of drugs? To such a general question the answer is, "All types." It is difficult to exclude any behavior on the grounds that a drug could not change it, that the results would hold no interest, etc. On the other hand, as soon as the question is made more specific, certain behaviors become quite appropriate and others inappropriate. For example, what behaviors will be *sensitive* to Drug X? The question limits the choice to behaviors which can be easily changed by relatively small doses of Drug X. Or, if the question is asked, "What *stable* behaviors can be studied with drugs?" only those behaviors which occur dependably with little variability can be considered. This section will be concerned with the considerations of selecting, using, and interpreting a behavioral baseline for the study of drugs. It will be assumed that the experimental design is appropriate to the study of the individual organism whose behavior has stabilized on a given procedure and who will serve under all conditions (e.g., drug doses) of the experiment.

Baseline Stability

The ideal behavioral baseline should be stable. *Stable* means that the behavior remains about the same from one observation period to another (i.e., from session to session or from hour to hour). For example, if an animal's lever-pressing rate to avoid a shock remained between 9.5 and 10.5 responses per minute over 20 sessions, then the behavior would surely be regarded as stable because of the low variability. One would have considerable confidence that the response rate in the next session would remain between 9.5 and 10.5 responses per minute. If a drug were given prior to this session and the response rate went up as little as 20 percent (to 12 responses/minute), one would still conclude that the drug had increased the rate because of the clear departure from the usual variability of the baseline.

Note the relation between the degree of stability and the magnitude of effect with which the experimenter can work. The greater the stability, the smaller the effect which can be reliably studied. For example, if the mean of 20 control values is 10.0 responses/minute and the range is $\pm$ .1 response/minute (a very stable baseline), then a 10 percent increase to 11 responses/minute following a drug injection would be considered a reliable effect. On the other hand, with the same mean and a range of $\pm$ 5 responses/minute (a less stable baseline), a 10 percent increase above the mean would be well within normal variation. Thus, a drug dose which was injected before the session would be considered ineffective. Statistical tests of significance can be used for a more formal analysis of this issue. By any analysis, however, greater baseline stability makes for easier evaluation of small drug effects.

Extreme baseline stability can be a mixed blessing. It is sometimes a hallmark of powerful control by determining variables which may make it hard to produce any departure from it. Simple escape behavior to an intense electric shock (e.g., the rat presses a lever to turn off a shock) is a case in point. This behavior is quite stable and typically occurs less than a second from the shock onset. However, a drug must produce a massive effect, such as making the rat severely ataxic or prostrate, before the escape responding is reduced.

Another case where stability assumes secondary importance involves behavior which is interesting partly because it is inappropriate to or fails to meet the current environmental contingencies. Such behaviors are not likely to remain stable. However, a drug study of individual subjects in such situations is not necessarily difficult since the behavior frequently is temporarily stable or undergoes slow, systematic change. A drug which rapidly brings the behavior under the control of the current contingencies (a "therapy" effect) provides an interesting outcome. Morse and Herrnstein (1956) described a pigeon which was required to peck a key 160 times (FR 160) for a food reinforcement. For the conditions of the experiment the number of responses required was overly large, so that the bird sometimes paused half an hour or more before working for a reinforcement (a "strained" fixed ratio performance). Methamphetamine not only greatly increased the bird's pecking rate immediately but the rate remained high in the next session when the drug was no longer present. The high rate in the next session was presumably due to the unusually large number of reinforcements made possible by the drug's action on the previous day. Another attractive type of semi-stable procedures involves behavior which is maintained because of past or spurious contingencies. The free-shock avoidance procedure (Sidman, Herrnstein, & Conrad, 1957) is an example. In this experiment monkeys were first trained on an avoidance procedure where each lever press postponed a shock. Then the avoidance contingency was dropped, and a free unavoidable shock was given after five minutes of a clicking noise.

Since the animal's lever pressing had no effect on the shock, any behavior due to the free shock was maintained spuriously and superstitiously. Nevertheless, the monkey's response rate increased several fold, occurred mainly during the clicker, and was maintained for a number of sessions. For this effect to occur, a past history of avoidance conditioning was essential. While the procedure has not yet received pharmacological attention, a drug which diminished the behavioral control of the free shock and increased the control of current contingencies would be of interest. This type of experiment is somewhat analogous to the behavioral situation in which some psychiatric patients find themselves, so the study of drugs is appealing. Baseline stability, while it makes drug work more convenient and exact, need not be a critical consideration. Semi-stable procedures may permit useful observations which are not possible with the more conventional techniques.

Baseline Sensitivity

Sensitivity to drugs is usually considered a baseline virtue. Sensitivity means that a relatively low dose of a drug can cause substantial changes in the baseline behavior. The dose is "relatively low" in the sense that it is lower than is required to affect other behavior, physiological systems, or even human clinical syndromes. For example, if the behavioral baseline showed an effect only at dosages which approached a lethal dose or at the same dosages which affected other behaviors, the baseline would not be considered selectively sensitive. On the other hand, if 2 mg/kg of Drug X produced changes in baseline behavior maintained by an FI schedule of positive reinforcement while 10 mg/kg was required to change avoidance behavior and 100 mg/kg was required to cause death, then the FI baseline would be considered relatively sensitive.

Sensitivity may be selectively related to a particular drug or drug class. Thus, Behavior A may be sensitive to Drug X but insensitive to Drug Y. As an experimental example, the discriminative performance on a complex conditional discrimination is sensitive to pentobarbital but relatively insensitive to scopolamine. Dews (1955b) trained pigeons to peck a disc on a VI schedule for a food reinforcement in the presence of certain combinations of stimuli (such as a red light alone or a blue light plus the house light). In the presence of other combinations of stimuli (such as the red light plus the house light or the blue light alone) the pigeon was never reinforced. After thorough training, the birds learned to peck only when the S^D (positive reinforced) stimuli were present; they pecked very little during the S^Δ (negative non-reinforced) stimuli. Doses of pentobarbital from 3.0 mg to 5.2 mg disrupted this discrimination by increasing the rate of pecking in S^Δ. S^Δ responding was elevated even by doses that decreased S^D responding. Typical data from one pigeon are shown in Figure 4. On the other hand, scopolamine did not disturb the discrimination (elevate S^Δ responding) at

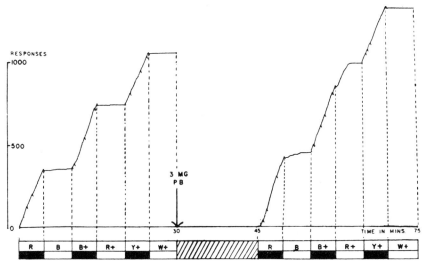

Figure 4. The effect of pentobarbital on a complex discrimination. The sequence of stimuli is shown in the lower diagram. R, B, Y, and W indicate red, blue, yellow, and white lights behind the pigeon's translucent key while + shows that the house lights were also on. During the time periods indicated by the filled blocks, reinforcements were programmed on a one-minute variable interval schedule. The cumulative record on the left illustrates the pigeon's normal performance while the record on the right shows the effects of 3 mg of pentobarbital. (From Dews, 1955b.)

doses ranging from inactive to those that almost eliminated S^D responding. These results illustrate the point that a behavioral baseline can be selectively sensitive to some drugs and selectively insensitive to others. Note that the judgment of selective baseline sensitivity is not based upon the absolute dosage levels of the two drugs. Pentobarbital was effective on the S^D rate at 3-5.2 mg while the equivalent range for scopolamine was about .01-0.1 mg. Yet the discrimination baseline was considered relatively sensitive to pentobarbital, because even doses that barely changed the S^D rate elevated the S^Δ rate, and, of course, large doses increased the effect. The baseline was considered insensitive to scopolamine because doses ranging from ineffective to those that sharply curtailed S^D responding did not increase the S^Δ rate.

SELECTED PROBLEMS OF EXPERIMENTAL DESIGN WITH DRUGS AS THE INDEPENDENT VARIABLE

The final paragraph of the third section ("A Typical Experiment") summarizes a basic approach to experimental design with operant techniques using drugs as the independent variable. However, this basic approach will not take care of all problems of design which may arise in the course of studying specific drugs. In this section, some of the more common technical issues will be discussed.

The Time Course of Drug Action

Many behavioral variables can be applied and removed almost instantaneously. A light can be turned on and off; a shock can be delivered and removed. Such events are public and easily observed so the experimenter knows when the variable is present, at what intensity, and when it is absent. The situation is not so simple with a drug. Although the experimenter knows he has injected an animal with drug, he does not know in advance when the drug will take effect, the current drug concentration at the site of action, or how long the effect will last. For this sort of information concerning the drug's time course, the basic source is an experiment where the magnitude of the drug effect is followed over time.

Every drug has its own time course. After administration, there is a delay in onset of action, an increasing effect up to a peak, and finally a decreasing effect until the pre-drug state is again reached. In Figure 5 (Stein, 1964) d-amphetamine illustrates a rather common time course. For example, after the rat was injected with 1 mg/kg IP, the onset of action was delayed less than five minutes, the response rate was increased up to a peak at about 30 minutes, and finally the effect slowly declined for approximately two hours. Note that with larger doses the onset of action was more rapid and the duration of action was longer. An illustration of an unusual time course is provided by iproniazid (see Figure 6). This drug is a monoamine oxidase inhibitor which has been used clinically in the treatment of depressed psychiatric patients. Heise and Boff (1960) performed a tetrabenazine-blocking experiment with rats conditioned by a Sidman avoidance procedure. Although iproniazid itself had negligible effects, pre-treatment with this drug blocked the marked decrease in avoidance behavior caused by tetrabenazine. The time course is shown in Figure 6. Following a single dose of iproniazid (40 mg/kg), individual rats were tested repeatedly over a 40-day period with a standard dose of tetrabenazine. The results showed that pre-treatment with iproniazid blocked the depressant action of tetrabenazine for the extraordinary time of 30 days or more.

A knowledge of time course is vital when two or more drugs are to be compared. If one arbitrarily selects a time after administration, there is no guarantee that this time will be appropriate for the drugs under study. For example, suppose the relative potency of d-amphetamine and iproniazid are to be determined in a tetrabenazine-blocking test (as in the Heise and Boff experiment). After pre-treatment with either d-amphetamine or iproniazid, when shall the test dose of tetrabenazine be given? If ten min-

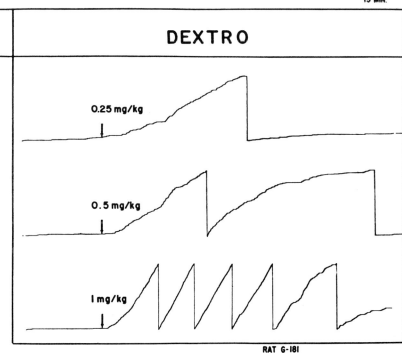

RAT G-181

Figure 5. Cumulative records showing the time course of dextroamphetamine on lever pressing for threshold brain stimulation. The control performance, which occurred at a very low rate because of the threshold stimulation, is shown on the left of each record. The injections, indicated by the arrows, were intraperitoneal. (From Stein, 1964.)

utes is selected, then d-amphetamine will appear to be more potent, since amphetamine will be near its peak and since iproniazid has not yet begun to act. If 24 hours is selected, iproniazid will appear to be more potent, since iproniazid will be near its peak and the effects of d-amphetamine will have disappeared many hours before. One solution to this problem is clear and is often used by pharmacologists. Each drug should be tested at its own peak time of action. This approach avoids arbitrary time periods which might favor one drug or the other, and it permits each drug to be examined in its most favorable light.

As an added complication, the time course of a drug is not a fixed value but rather it is a function of several variables. As shown in Figure 5, the dose level affects the time course, with larger doses having a faster onset of action and a longer duration. The route of administration is important,

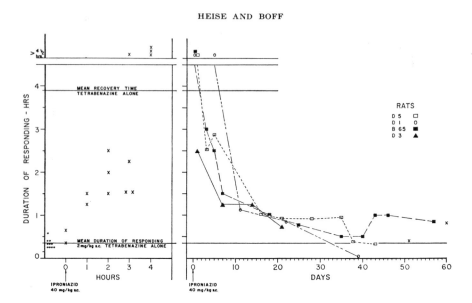

TIME SINCE IPRONIAZID

Figure 6. Time-effect curves for 40 mg/kg s.c. iproniazid in a tetrabenazine-blocking test. The curve on the left shows the gradual onset of action of iproniazid. The ordinate represents the duration of responding after tetrabenazine was given (i.e., the amount of time the rat successfully avoided the shock over the approximately four-hour period when the tetrabenazine nomally would eliminate avoidance behavior). The solid circles show the brief duration of responding from ten animals who received tetrabenazine alone. The mean duration under this condition is shown by the lower hoizontal line. The upper line shows the mean length of the tetrabenazine effect. Each point indicated by an x at the left was obtained from a different animal given a standard dose of 2 mg/kg tetrabenazine at various times after pre-treatment with iproniazid. The curves on the right show the duration of responding as a function of days since iproniazid administration. Separate curves are drawn for each of four rats that were tested repeatedly with tetrabenazine after a single dose of iproniazid. (From Heise & Boss, 1960.)

with intravenous injection usually providing a rapid onset and oral administration a delayed onset. Other variables include the vehicle, presence of other drugs, the behavioral baseline, and the species of animal being tested.

How Many Subjects?

The intensive study of the individual subject has been emphasized in this chapter and in other discussions of operant techniques. This might be labeled the "N of One" approach, and has sometimes been misunderstood. The approach is *not* simply to use a small number of subjects for its own sake. For example, one might attempt a drug-behavior experiment with three subjects stabilized on a behavioral baseline. The first subject is given dose Number 1, the second subject is given dose Number 2, and the third subject is given dose Number 3. From such an experiment, one can do little more than estimate crudely the nature of the dose-effect curve. Differences among subjects will be confounded with differences produced by the drug dosage so that one cannot tell which is which. A more informative use of three subjects would be to administer each dose on separate sessions to each of the subjects. Then with each individual, one could determine how the different doses modified this subject's behavior.

Would a single, carefully-studied subject suffice? One subject serving as his own control and receiving all drug doses can provide a great deal of useful information. Indeed, under some circumstances and for some purposes, the information gained from a single subject may be quite sufficient. However, the analysis of individual behavior and the intensive study of the individual subject need not stop with only one subject. In my own drug work, I have occasionally had difficulty with such problems as a drifting baseline performance or an intended intraperitoneal injection which actually went into the intestine; therefore, I generally use at least two subjects, and three to four may be desirable. In my experience three to four subjects have permitted a reasonable judgment as to the adequacy of experimental control. For example, if all subjects show similar changes in performance, many experimenters have found by experience that additional subjects add little new information. In case the subjects show dissimilar changes, there are two options. First, one might add more subjects (or replicate with the previous subjects) and hope for the best. Perhaps, for example, the baseline will not drift and the intraperitoneal injection will not go astray the second time. While this option may provide a way out where the problems are not serious or where they are known and cannot be easily controlled, it cannot be recommended. A second option is to ferret out the source of the uncontrolled variables. For example, one might establish a more stable baseline performance by changing the schedule of reinforcement, or one might perfect intraperitoneal injections by injecting dye into untrained animals. This approach is a more positive way to solve the problem directly and at the source.

There is no simple rule of thumb for deciding on the number of subjects. The critical question is whether the experiment can be replicated, and the most straightforward answer comes from successful replications. If unknown and/or uncontrolled variables are operating in the experiment, replication will be difficult, and the experimenter will be aware of trouble with his technique. Thus, when the experimenter has reason to suspect uncontrolled variables, he is wise to use more than one subject.

There *are* circumstances where a single subject is adequate. Opinions differ on this matter, but as I see it, the circumstances are as follows: (1) The experimenter is working in a well-controlled experimental situation with a thorough knowledge of his techniques and his subjects. Thus, the experimenter probably has the problem of uncontrolled variables well in hand. (2) The results from the single subject are in accord with previous data and fit plausibly into a well-understood body of knowledge. (3) The experimenter has studied other subjects with related procedures, and the results are consistent. Sidman's (1960) more extensive discussion of this matter under the topic of "systematic replication" is recommended to the interested reader.

Under these circumstances the probability of successful replication is high, so that additional subjects are not required. The same amount of experimental time might be better spent in studying variations on the experiment rather than replicating. By the same token, if these circumstances do not hold, the use of additional subjects is indicated.

Tolerance

The repeated administration of some drugs results in a diminution of the effect. Schuster and Zimmerman (1961) found that the increase in response rates generated by .75 — 1.5 mg/kg of dl-amphetamine was considerably smaller after repeated doses. This phenomenon is referred to as *tolerance*. As an interesting complication, they also found that the elevation of locomotor activity, measured separately in the same rats, did not decrease with repeated doses. Thus, the development of tolerance seems to be more than a physiological affair; an interaction with behavioral parameters is also involved. If an experiment is aimed at determining a dose-effect curve, tolerance can be a pesky problem. Other things being equal, the first dose administered is likely to have a larger effect than later doses. Fortunately, if the experimenter has sufficient time, he can usually avoid the problem by spacing the drug injections far enough apart. The spacing prevents the development of the tolerance effect so that each administration is relatively independent of previous administrations.

Classification of Drugs and Drug Effects

With operant techniques a common measure of behavior is response rate. In drug-behavior studies the data are often described in terms of how many times per minute the monkey pressed a lever or how many times per second the pigeon pecked a key. While the exact nature of the behavioral effect may differ, certain drugs share the ability to increase the response rate while other drugs share the ability to decrease the rate. Following common pharmacological practice, the rate-increasing drugs can be called *stim-*

ulants, and the rate-decreasing drugs can be called *depressants.* By the same token, drug-produced increases or decreases in rate can be referred to as *stimulant* or *depressant effects.* A third class of drugs and effects involves performances which are inappropriate to the environmental contingencies. For example, a drugged rat may respond excessively in the first minute of a fixed interval schedule even though reinforcements have never been delivered at this time; or a pigeon may put out a fixed ratio performance in a red light and a fixed interval performance in a blue light when the reverse is actually correct. Drugs which produce such effects can be called *disruptants* and the changes can be referred to as *disruptant effects.*

The use of such classification terms as stimulant, depressant, and disruptant can be convenient. If, for example, a number of phenothiazine compounds decrease both fixed interval and avoidance behavior, it is convenient to describe the group of compounds as depressant. Or suppose a given drug elevates avoidance rates, fixed ratio rates for food, variable interval rates for water, etc. When someone asks, "What type of effects does this drug produce?" it is convenient to answer, "The drug produces stimulant effects." The problem with such terms is that the drug effect is not usually that simple. Pentobarbital can increase fixed ratio response rates at low doses and decrease rates at high doses (Waller & Morse, 1963). Is pentobarbital to be classed a stimulant or a depressant? In the Boren and Navarro (1959) study described above, atropine increased the rate in the initial part of the fixed interval, and decreased the rate in the terminal part. Should the effect on the initial section be classed stimulant and the effect on the terminal section depressant? Or should the entire effect be called disruptant? I once injected trained rats intraperitoneally with a weak solution of HCl. The rats sucked in their sides and showed the usual signs of being injected with an irritant. At the same time the lever-pressing rate was reduced in much the same way that chlorpromazine might have reduced it. Should a solution of HCl be put in the same depressant class as chlorpromazine? From such considerations, one must conclude that grouping drugs and their effects into such classes as stimulant, depressant, and disruptant must be done cautiously and is likely to overlook important facets of the drug and its effects.

Table 1 lists a number of drugs which affect behavior. The drugs are grouped into classical pharmacological categories—categories which are subject to the advantages and disadvantages discussed above. The table was designed to serve two purposes: (1) to describe representative drugs and drug classes which are in pharmacological use; and (2) to illustrate pharmacological classification schemes. While the chemical structure can sometimes form a useful category (e.g., barbiturates or phenothiazine derivatives), the categories are usually based upon an effect which the drugs produce (e.g. muscle relaxation or reduction of psychotic depression). Unfortunately, the formal classification may be based upon an effect which is secondary to the main effect of interest. For example, in terms of clinical importance, meprobamate and chlordiazepoxide fall into the same class because they are useful in treating neurotic complaints rather than because they are muscle relaxants.

Table 1

A Partial List of Representative Behavioral Drugs[1]

I. Stimulants
    d-amphetamine (Dexedrine)
    methamphetamine (Methedrine and others)
    methylphenidate (Ritalin)
    pipradrol (Meratran)
II. Antidepressants
    A. Monoamine oxidase inhibitors
        iproniazid (Marsilid)
        isocarboxazid (Marplan)
        nialimid (Niamid)
        phenelzine (Nardil)
    B. Other antidepressants
        amitryptaline (Elavil)
        imipramine (Tofrãnil)
III. Depressants
    A. Tranquilizers
        1. Phenothiazine derivatives
            chlorpromazine (Thorazine)
            fluphenazine (Permatil or Prolixin)
            perphenazine (Trilafon)
            prochlorperazine (Compazine)
            thioridazine (Mellaril)
            trifluoperazine (Stelazine)
        2. Rauwolfia alkaloids
            reserpine
        3. Muscle relaxants
            meprobamate (Miltown or Equanil)
            chlordiazepoxide (Librium)
    B. Barbiturate hypnotics
        pentobarbital (Nembutal)
        phenobarbital (Luminal)
        secobarbital (Seconal)
        thiopental (Pentathal)
IV. Anticholinergics
    atropine
    benactyzine (Suavitil)
    benztropine (Cogentin)
    methantheline (Banthine)
    scopolamine
V. Hallucinogens
    lysergic acid diethylamide (LSD)
    mescaline
VI. Analgesics
    meperidine (Demerol)
    morphine

Selecting Drugs for Comparison

A great deal of useful information can come from comparative studies of several drugs. For example, suppose one is interested in a new analgesic agent which, however, is known to have depressant and anticholinergic side effects (i.e., the drug makes mice less active and dilates their pupils). In order to evaluate both the new drug and the appropriateness of the behavioral techniques, the following classes of drugs might be compared:

1. *Standard drugs which exhibit the main effect.* Morphine and meperidine as standard analgesic agents might be studied. Hopefully, the standard

---

[1] The generic name of the drug is given first, and the trade name appears second in parenthesis.

analgesics and the new analgesic will share significant behavioral effects which might be expected of a drug which attenuates pain.

2. *Standard drugs which exhibit the side effects.* A barbiturate and a phenothiazine might be selected as representative depressants. Atropine or scopolamine could be studied as typical anticholinergics. Since none of these drugs are known to produce analgesia, they should not share the significant analgesic effect with morphine, meperidine, and the new drug of interest. Otherwise, one might suspect that the side effect of the new drug is actually responsible for the alleged main effect. For example, perhaps the analgesic action was claimed because animal subjects would tolerate a higher shock intensity before pressing a lever to terminate the shock. If the shock were given through a grid floor, the increased tolerance might be due to the anticholinergic effect of reducing perspiration. With less sweat, the foot resistance might go up and permit the animal to tolerate higher voltage shock.

3. *Standard drugs which have similar chemical structures.* Similarities or differences in structure may be related to similarities or differences in behavioral action. A better understanding of structure-activity relationships can emerge from such studies.

The Route of Administration

For general experimental work, there are five practical routes of administration: (1) intravenous (2) intraperitoneal, (3) intramuscular, (4) subcutaneous, and (5) oral. With a given drug, certain considerations may dictate a specific route or avoidance of certain other routes. For example, if a drug degrades into an inactive compound within ten minutes after injection, the intravenous route should be used since it usually permits the most rapid absorption and distribution. Or, some drugs when given orally are not absorbed from the gastrointestinal tract and thus should be given parenterally. A number of considerations regarding the various routes are presented in Table 2.

Multiple Behavioral Actions of Drugs

Most drugs produce multiple effects. A well-studied drug such as chlorpromazine provides an instructive example. In the physiological and biochemical sphere, chlorpromazine has anti-emetic, CNS depressive, adrenolytic, hypotensive, antispasmodic, hypothermic, and antihistaminic effects. In the behavioral sphere, chlorpromazine is known to affect (among other things) spontaneous motor activity, avoidance behavior, intake of food and water, brain self-stimulation, and performance on various schedules of positive reinforcement. While some effects are small or occur at relatively high doses, multiple effects do occur over much of the useful dosage

Table 2
Routes of Drug Administration

Route and Abbreviation	Speed of Onset	Special Considerations
Intravenous (I.V.)	rapid	Requires considerable skill. May be dangerous if drug is given too fast or if drug precipitates out in the blood. Soluble compounds only.
Intraperitoneal (I.P.)	intermediate	Easily done. Care must be taken to avoid an injection into the large intestine. Insoluble drugs may be given. Irritants cause difficulty.
Intramuscular (I.M.)	intermediate	Easily done. Irritants cause difficulty as do insoluble compounds which encapsulate.
Subcutaneous (S.C.)	intermediate	Similar to I.M. Care must be taken to ensure that the drug does not leak out through the injection site.
Oral (P.O.)	slow	Some compounds are not absorbed orally. This route is frequently used for insoluble compounds and for irritants. When application to human medical practice is involved, the oral route is preferred since most drugs are given to humans by this route.

range. In producing a multiplicity of effects, chlorpromazine is by no means an atypical drug. Thus, the experimenter must keep the likelihood of multiple actions in mind when interpreting his data on a particular behavioral baseline. The chances that a randomly picked drug will act specifically upon the behavior under study are small. The drug will probably affect other behavioral baselines and several physiological systems as well. For a more complex example, the fact that chlorpromazine is useful in treating psychiatric patients (assumed to be strongly influenced by aversive control) and that chlorpromazine also decreases avoidance behavior (known to involve aversive control) might lead one to believe that chlorpromazine has a specific anti-aversive property. An experiment by Cook and Kelleher (1962) bears on this issue. They trained squirrel monkeys on a concurrent avoidance fixed ratio procedure which involved both aversive and appetitive control. When the monkey pressed the lever, he both avoided a shock (aversive control) and added a response toward the number required for a food reinforcement (appetitive control). The performances relevant to the two concurrent procedures could be readily distinguished, because the fixed ratio performance was characterized by a quickly accelerating high rate while the avoidance performance was characterized by a steady, low rate (see the upper panel in Figure 7). When chlorpromazine was administered at oral doses of 0.5 and 1.0 mg/kg, behavior controlled by the appetitive fixed ratio schedule was more strongly affected than was the behavior controlled by the aversive avoidance procedure. Typical results are shown in the lower panel of Figure 7. Thus, the results ran counter to the theory that chlorpromazine specifically alters behavior under aversive control.

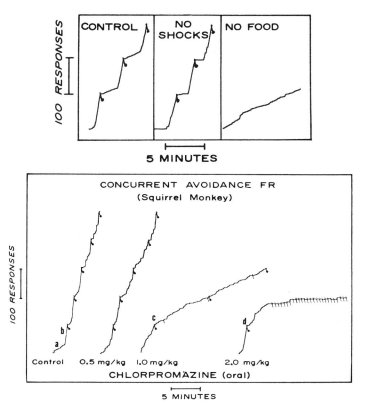

Figure 7. Control performance on concurrent avoidance FR 100 (upper section) and the effects of chlorpromazine (lower section). The middle panel of the upper section shows the monkey's perfomance when only the FR schedule for food was programmed; the right panel shows the performance when only shock avoidance was programmed; and the left panel shows the combined performance when both procedures were progammed concurrently. The lower section illustrates the effects of chlorpromazine at oral doses of 0.5, 1.0 and 2.0 mg/kg. (From Cook & Kelleher, 1962.)

Because chlorpromazine affected appetitively controlled behavior, one can reasonably discard the blanket generalization that chlorpromazine has specific anti-aversive effects. However, one should not draw the opposite conclusion that chlorpromazine specifically affects the appetitive behavior. As Cook and Kelleher point out, we do not know the relative strength of control exerted by avoidance versus the fixed ratio procedure. For example, if the monkeys were food-deprived longer, or if the size of the fixed ratio were reduced, or if the amount of food reinforcement were increased, the fixed ratio behavior might be made more resistant to the drug. If at the same time the shock intensity were reduced, the percentage of shocks decreased, or the response-shock interval increased, the avoidance behavior might be made more sensitive to the drug. By such procedural changes, one might even find a set of conditions where chlorpromazine affected the aversive behavior more than the appetitive behavior. The point is that the conclusions must take into account the fact that a single set of conditions have been studied and that other sets might change the drug results.

Specific Behavioral Effects of Drugs

Many experimenters have searched for specific behavioral effects of a drug. They were interested in determining whether a drug can specifically change one behavior and not another. In other words, can Drug X affect Behavior A but not Behavior B? When such an observation is made, what interpretations are warranted? What experiments can extend the generality of the observations?

A well-known experimental example can be found in the behavioral work on chlorpromazine (e.g., Cook & Weidley, 1957; Verhave, Owen, & Robbins, 1958). The baseline was composed of two components, avoidance behavior and escape behavior. According to Verhave's arrangement, the rat was placed in a box containing a grid floor which could be electrified and a wheel which the animal could turn to avoid or escape the shock. A buzzer was sounded seven seconds before the shock was scheduled. If the rat turned the wheel during the buzzer, the shock was not delivered. However, if the animal failed to respond, the shock followed and was terminated only when the animal did turn the wheel. A response to the buzzer is referred to as avoidance behavior while a response to the electric shock is considered escape behavior. Once the animals were trained to avoid the shock on better than 95 percent of the buzzer trials, Verhave and co-workers administered chlorpromazine in a range of doses. He found that the avoidance was much more sensitive to the drug than was the escape behavior. For example, a dose of chlorpromazine which caused an avoidance loss of more than 80 percent (i.e., the rat responded to the buzzer on less than 30 percent of the trials) caused an escape loss of less than 5 percent. These results can be interpreted in several ways: (1) Under the conditions of the experiment (with the stated procedure, response, shock intensity, etc.) chlorpromazine selectively inhibited avoidance behavior while affecting escape behavior relatively little. Such a qualified interpretation is justified. (2) An extended interpretation is that, in general, avoidance behavior is more sensitive to chlorpromazine than escape behavior. But this interpretation ignores the possible role of the many variables which maintain the two behaviors. For example, suppose the experimenter were to strengthen the variables maintaining avoidance and to weaken the variables maintaining escape. He might make the buzzer louder, make the avoidance wheel turn more easily, etc. At the same time he might make the escape behavior more difficult by applying heavy friction to the wheel during the shock, by requiring 40 wheel turns to shut off the shock instead of 1, or by turning off the shock after a delay rather than immediately. Under such circumstances, would chlorpromazine still affect avoidance more strongly than escape behavior? If so, the generality of the original observation would have been extended a great deal. With only the information at hand, however, a general interpretation that chlorpromazine selectively affects avoidance behavior rather than escape behavior is unwarranted because only a single set of conditions maintaining the behaviors were studied. The generality of the finding can be investigated by studying other sets of conditions, preferably in a parametric fashion.

Another example of specificity of drug action was discovered in an experiment by Dews (1955). Dews trained pigeons to peck a plastic key for a reinforcement of grain. Each bird worked on FR 50 and FI 15 schedules of reinforcement and was given a number of doses of pentobarbital while working on each schedule. After 1 or 2 mg of pentobarbital, the response rate on the FI schedule was sharply reduced even though visual inspection of the bird revealed no apparent effect. At the same dosages the FR rate was hardly changed. It did not drop below control baseline until much higher doses were used.

The critical issue concerns what conclusions may be drawn from these data. A particularly attractive interpretation is that behavior controlled by fixed interval schedules is more sensitive to drugs than behavior controlled by fixed ratio schedules. In point of fact, however, the data show only that a fixed ratio of 50 is relatively insensitive in comparison to a fixed interval of 15 minutes. The critical element making for differential sensitivity may not be the schedule of reinforcement. It might just as logically be the frequency of reinforcement (the birds were reinforced far more often on an FR 50 than on an FI 15), or responses per reinforcement (on the FI 15 the bird made many more than 50 responses per reinforcement), or the response rate (FR rates were much higher than FI rates). In order to extend the generality of the finding and to relate the differential sensitivity to the schedules of reinforcement per se, a more complicated set of experiments would be required. The basic plan would be to manipulate parametrically the important conditions controlling the two schedules; then, for each set of conditions, the drug should be administered in a range of doses. For example, fixed ratios of 10, 40, 160, and 640 might be compared with fixed intervals of .5, 2, 8, and 32 minutes. One possible finding might be that behavior maintained by a short fixed interval is more sensitive to the drug than behavior maintained by a large fixed ratio. Such an outcome would indicate that fixed ratio behavior is not always less sensitive than fixed interval behavior, but that it depends on a more complex set of conditions.

Methods of Extending the Generality of Drug Effects
Beyond a Single Set of Conditions

Unfortunately, experiments of the above type require a prodigious amount of work. Since relatively few investigators have the time to do the parametric study, and at the same time to investigate a full dose-effect curve, shortcut methods of attacking the same problem are quite appealing.

One approach is a large multiple schedule. In order to study the fixed interval-fixed ratio variable, individual animals could be trained on several fixed intervals and several fixed ratios with specific stimuli associated with each. For example, FR 10 is programmed in the presence of a red light, FR 30 is programmed in an orange light, FR 90 in a yellow light, etc. Then, the same animal might be trained on an FI .5 during a 500-cycle tone, on FI 2 during a 1,000-cycle tone, etc. While the original training might require considerable time, the dose-effect curve with the drug could be accomplished with great efficiency. When a given dose is administered prior to a session, the effects of this dose can be observed on all the various FI and FR components of the multiple schedule. As the dose increases, the sensitivity of the schedules and of particular values of each schedule should be apparent within the individual subject.

The large multiple schedule can work best where the drug under study is long-acting in comparison with the time required to program the many components. A short-acting drug which reaches its time of peak action and then decays before all the components can be programmed could not be studied efficiently by this approach.

Another approach requires an adjusting or a progressive procedure. The basic ingredient of an adjusting procedure is that the magnitude of a controlling variable is manipulated depending upon the performance of the subject. The titration escape procedure of Weiss and Laties (1961) provides an experimental example. According to their procedure, animals were trained to press a lever to reduce an electric shock applied through a grid floor. The intensity of the shock was increased one step every x seconds. When the rat pressed a lever, however, the intensity was reduced one step. Additional lever pressing further reduced the shock in steps until finally the intensity was so low that the animal stopped responding. At this point another cycle began whereby the intensity was stepped up until once again the animal started responding to reduce the shock. When Weiss and Laties gave sodium salicylate and aspirin to animals working on this titration procedure, the amount of shock current the animal would tolerate was substantially increased. Unfortunately, the interpretation of this result was complicated by the additional finding that the same doses also produced decreases in behavior reinforced by drl and VI schedules of water reinforcement. From these results one is able to avoid the erroneous conclusion that the drugs caused a specific elevation in shock tolerance (a specific analgesic effect). One can be aware that the increase in shock tolerance may be related to general behavioral depression.

The Weiss and Laties experiment illustrates the use of an adjusting procedure which modifies a controlling variable (the shock) depending on the behavioral performance. As the drug decreased escape behavior at shock intensities which formerly produced it, the procedure automatically increased the intensity. Thus, a wide range of intensities was automatically explored. The usefulness of the adjusting procedure may be more easily appreciated by contrasting it with the multiple procedures which would be necessary if a set of fixed shock intensities were used. The experimental question is: Under the effect of a drug, what is the minimal intensity required to produce escape behavior? One might design the experiment so that the animals are first trained at shock intensity one and then are given a range of drug doses which will yield a dose-effect curve. Then the animals could be retrained at shock intensity two and again administered the range of doses—and so on for other shock intensities. In comparison, the adjusting procedure is clearly more efficient in yielding the desired information.

DRUG SCREENING

The major application of pharmocology has been in discovering new drugs which are medically useful. A team of organic chemists can synthesize hundreds of compounds a year. Yet it is not possible to predict from the chemical structure which, if any, of these compounds will have clinical utility. The compounds must be studied in laboratory animals to determine if any useful activity is present. How does one go about designing behavioral techniques which can select the few drugs with clinical promise from the multitude of compounds? There are two classical approaches: (1) constructing a laboratory model of the clinical problem and (2) finding a laboratory technique which empirically selects the known, useful drugs. In building a laboratory model it is useful to analyze the clinical problem and to extract its important characteristics. For example, if one is interested in a drug to treat hypertension, one can induce high blood pressure in laboratory animals and then screen compounds to find one which reduces the elevated pressure. In the behavioral area, if one is interested in an "anti-appetite" drug, the reduction of eating behavior might be the target. Thus, one could set up a model where the amount of food eaten by obese white rats provides the data. Then organic compounds could be tested in the expectation that a compound which reduced the eating behavior of obese rats would also reduce the eating behavior of obese humans.

The second approach is to find a laboratory technique which empirically selects out a model drug (or drugs) known to be useful in the clinic. Using any convenient laboratory technique (often developed for some other purpose), the model drug and a number of other drugs are studied. If the model produces a distinctive effect which can be distinguished from the effects of the other drugs, then the technique can be used to screen compounds in an effort to find one that mimics the model. The laboratory techniques need not relate in any way to the clinical problem. For example, if a useful drug makes mice flick their tails and other drugs do not, then the tail-flick test might be used for screening. The risk of this kind of screening test is that it may reflect a trivial side effect of the model drug. As a more practical example, a technique involving avoidance and escape behavior has been widely used in the drug industry for screening antipsychotic, chlorpromazine-like, tranquilizers. Few would contend that avoidance is an exact model of the agitated psychotic patient. However, the technique is appealing because chlorpromazine, known to be useful in treating agitated psychotics, selectively affects avoidance behavior in preference to escape behavior. Barbiturates, which are not useful in treating psychotics, do not show such selectivity. For such reasons, the avoidance-escape technique has been widely used for screening.

Occasionally a drug-behavior paper in the literature concludes with the suggestion that the technique described might be useful for screening. Unfortunately, the fact that a technique can be used for studying drugs does not make it a good screening test. A major requirement of a screening test is that a large number of drugs can be studied efficiently and rapidly. In most drug and chemical companies where screening is done, literally thousands of organic compounds are available for study; but relatively few of them will prove to be useful. The general consensus among those experienced in screening is that the more compounds studied, the greater are the chances of finding a useful new drug.

Here are some of the technical criteria for a rapid screening technique:

1. The behavioral baseline should show the main effect of interest as clearly and specifically as possible. There is little time to be misled by ambiguous effects. If a random assortment of irritants, anticholinergics, or other unwanted agents affect the behavior, too much time is spent in following up false leads.

2. The screening test ideally should provide some measure of an expected side effect or behavioral toxicity. The drug of choice must not only have a main effect of interst but it must also be relatively free of adverse side effects. Multiple schedules are useful for this purpose.

3. The behavioral baseline must be stable. Variability is troublesome since it masks drug effects.

4. The behavioral system should be poised so that drugs can drive the behavior up or down. One does not always find what one is looking for. Even if the screening test is oriented toward depressants, the discovery of a new stimulant would hardly be disappointing.

5. The training time for new subjects should not be long. Animals sometimes die from overdoses or repeated injection of nearly toxic compounds, so the resources of the screening program should not be overloaded with training replacement animals.

6. Differences among animals which complicate the analysis should not be great. There is little time to manipulate the experimental parameters for each animal in the screening program.

7. Data analysis should be simple, fast, and should not require complex interpretation. If a large number of compounds must be processed, the data analysis should be within the scope of a well-trained technician. Perhaps in the future it will be sufficient to say that the data analysis should be within the scope of a well-programmed computer.

Once the screening test (or battery of tests) has indicated a promising drug, the job has only begun. The evaluation by a variety of other techniques and in other species is essential before confidence can be placed in the drug. However, the screening test will have done its job if it reduces the large number of possible compounds to a few compounds with promise.

A Final Comment

This chapter has been oriented toward an analysis of drug-behavior relationships with operant techniques. Problems of experimental design and the interpretation of the results were emphasized. Not all the possible problems have arisen, nor have ideal solutions been found. On the contrary, in a field which is growing as rapidly as behavioral pharmacology, an unexpected problem can sometimes arise with each new study. Nevertheless, past solutions to past problems are always informative and may well form the basis for a solution to a future problem. This chapter has been written in the hope that the solutions of the recent past will have some relevance to the problems of the future.

REFERENCES

Boren, J. J., and Navarro, A. P. (1959) The action of atropine, benactyzine, and scopolamine upon fixed interval and fixed ratio behavior. *J. exp. Anal. Behav., 2*, 107-115.

Brady, J. V. (1959) Comparative psychopharmacology: Animal experimental studies on the effects of drugs on behavior. In J. Cole and R. Gerard (Eds.), *Psychopharmacology: Problems in evaluation.* Publication 583, National Academy of Sciences, National Research Council.

Carlton, P. L. (1963) Cholinergic mechanisms in the control of behavior by the brain. *Psychol. Rev., 70*, 19-39.

COOK, L., and KELLEHER, R. T. (1962) Drug effects on the behavior of animals. *Ann. N.Y. Acad. Sci., 96,* 315-335.

COOK, L., and KELLEHER, R. T. (1963) Effects of drugs on behavior. *Annu. Rev. Pharmacol., 3,* 205-222.

COOK, L., and WEIDLEY, E. (1957) Behavioral effects of some psychopharmacological agents. *Ann. N.Y. Acad. Sci., 66,* 740-752.

DEWS, P. B. (1955) Studies on behavior: I. Differential sensitivity to pentobarbital of pecking performance in pigeons depending on the schedule of reward. *J. Pharmacol. exp. Therap., 113,* 343-401. (a)

DEWS, P. B. (1955) Studies on behavior: II. The effects of pentobarbital, metamphetamine, and scopolamine on performances in pigeons involving discriminations. *J. Pharmacol. exp. Therap., 115,* 380-389. (b)

DEWS, P. B., and MORSE, W. H. (1961) Behavioral pharmacology. *Annu. Rev. Pharmacol., 1,* 145-174.

GOLLUB, L. R., and BRADY, J. V. (1965) Behavioral pharmacology. *Annu. Rev. Pharmacol., 5,* 235-262.

HEISE, G. A., and BOFF, E. (1960) Behavioral determination of time and dose parameters of monoamine oxidase inhibitors. *J. Pharmacol. exp. Therap., 129,* 155-162.

HERRNSTEIN, R. J., and MORSE, W. H. (1956) Selective action of pentobarbital on component behaviors of a reinforcement schedule. *Science, 124,* 367-368.

MORSE, W. H., and HERRNSTEIN, R. J. (1956) Effects of drugs on characteristics of behavior maintained by complex schedules of intermittent positive reinforcement. *Ann. N.Y. Acad. Sci., 65,* 303-317.

SCHUSTER, C. R., and ZIMMERMAN, J. (1961) Timing behavior during prolonged treatment with dl-amphetamine. *J. exp. Anal. Behav., 4,* 327-330.

SIDMAN, M. (1959) Behavioral pharmacology. *Psychopharmacol., 1,* 1-19.

SIDMAN, M. (1960) *Tactics of scientific research.* New York: Basic Books.

SIDMAN, M., HERRNSTEIN, R. J., and CONRAD, D. G. (1957) Maintenance of avoidance behavior by unavoidable shocks. *J. comp. physiol. Psychol., 50,* 553-557.

STEIN, L. (1964) Self-stimulation of the brain and the central stimulant action of amphetamine. *Fed. Proc., 23,* 836-849.

VERHAVE, T., OWEN, J. E., JR., and ROBBINS, E. B. (1958) Effects of chlorpromazine and secobarbital on avoidance and escape behavior. *Arch. intern. Pharmacodynamie, 116,* 45-53.

WALLER, M. B., and MORSE, W. H. (1963) Effects of pentobarbital on fixed-ratio reinforcement. *J. exp. Anal. Behav., 6,* 125-130.

WEISS, B., and LATIES, V. G. (1961) Changes in pain tolerance and other behavior produced by salicylates. *J. Pharmacol. exp. Therap., 131,* 120-129.

13

The Use of Operant Methods in the Assessment and Control of Motivational States [1]

Philip Teitelbaum

INTRODUCTION

The Operant as a Criterion of Motivation

When we observe an animal's behavior, we are often struck by its apparent purposiveness. A pinprick to the sole of the foot elicits a vigorous leg withdrawal, an act that immediately terminates a painful stimulus. A greylag goose, sitting on its nest of eggs, will, if one of the eggs rolls out of the nest, reach out with its head, tuck the egg under its bill, and roll it back into the nest. A young herring gull chick, having been without food for several hours, will peck at the bill of the parent gull, thereby stimulating the parent bird to regurgitate food. A hungry rat, after having been trained, will press a lever many times to obtain a pellet of food.

All these acts produce an apparently desirable outcome: pain is terminated, the egg is back in the nest, or food is obtained. In trying to explain such behavior, it is tempting to anthropomorphize—to project what we would feel and do in the same situation as a valid description and explanation of the animal's behavior. This is easy to do, but it may be attributing more complexity to the behavior than is necessary. For example, the pinprick will elicit the same leg-withdrawal response in an anesthetized animal, or in an animal whose spinal cord has been completely cut so that no pain impulses from the foot can proceed to the brain. The leg-withdrawal is a

[1] This paper was written with the support of funds from National Science Foundation Grant NSF G-24386. The author wishes particularly to thank Drs. Alan N. Epstein, Francis W. Irwin, R. Duncan Luce, and David R. Williams for their helpful criticism of the manuscript.

spinal reflex—a built-in fixed response to a particular kind of stimulus (one which stimulates nerve endings mediating pain). There are no alternatives here. The reflex response is a stereotyped automatic consequence of the stimulus. The greylag goose will respond to any egg-shaped object, even a gigantic artificial one. If the egg should happen to slip out from under its bill while being rolled back to the nest, the bird cannot correct its movement but must carry out the egg-retrieving response to completion, even without the egg (Tinbergen, 1951). The herring gull chick will peck at any stimulus object when it is hungry, preferably one which is long and narrow with a red spot near its tip, like that of the parent's beak. The chick will continue to peck at such an object though no food is obtained from it, and will do so just after being hatched, even before it has had the experience of being fed by the parent (Tinbergen & Perdeck, 1950). Egg retrieving and pecking at the bill therefore should not be classed as purposive acts; they are fixed instinctive movement patterns, which, particularly in lower animals, seem to be elicited only under specific hormonal states and in response to particular configurations of stimulus elements (sign stimuli). Such instinctive acts are often not subject to correction and control by the animal. Once elicited, they must be completed, even if they fail to produce their normal outcome.

When we speak of purposive acts, we mean behavior that is directed toward a goal and is accompanied by a corresponding motivation to obtain that goal. The essential quality is the motivational state—the physiological state of events that corresponds to the urge to perform a particular act, to obtain a certain object, or to produce a desired outcome. If we could be sure that such a state exists during a given act, we could justifiably call that act motivated behavior.

Clearly, if the response is a completely automatic consequence of the stimulus, we cannot speak of motivation. As long as a fixed built-in relation exists between a stimulus and a response, we have no justification for inferring the additional existence of a motivational state underlying that response to the stimulus. Such a state may exist, but we can have no positive proof of it. Only if we can be sure that a central motivated state exists apart from the stimulus and the response, should we speak of motivated behavior.

To infer motivation, we must break the fixed connection between stimulus and response. The learning process involved in operant conditioning enables us to do so. Let us consider the last example of apparently purposive behavior mentioned above: the rat pressing a bar to obtain food. How do we train an animal to perform such an act? We arbitrarily choose almost any act from the animal's repertoire and reinforce it with food, water, or whatever else the animal will work to obtain. Although typically we teach a rat to press a bar or a pigeon to peck a key to obtain a pellet of food, we can readily train either to dance around the cage if we so choose. We usually use a light to signal the delivery of a pellet but we can use a tone or a buzzer or any other stimulus the animal can detect. The animal can also exert a good measure of control over the occurrence of its response or whether it will respond at all. These characteristics of an operant (the arbitrary, essentially interchangeable nature of the act and of the stimulus that elicits it, as well as the measure of control the animal exerts over the response) distinguish it as a voluntary act. This voluntary act, once learned, can be used to obtain any kind of reinforcement. In training, we ordinarily make the animal hungry and reinforce it with food, but we can use water for thirsty animals, or the termination or avoidance of painful electric shock to reward an animal for performing the appropriate act. The same act can be used for any reinforcement. Therefore, unlike many instinctive responses, the bar press can be separated from the animal's internal state. In effect, in any operant situation, the stimulus, the response, and the reinforcement are completely arbitrary and interchangeable. No one of them bears any biologically built-in fixed connection to the others. We arrange the experimental situation so that the response produces the reward and the animal learns the connection between them. Once having learned this relationship, the animal reveals its motivation by the fact that it works to obtain the reinforcement. This is what all operant conditioning situations have in common: the animal's motivation to obtain the reinforcement. By taking advantage of the animal's capacity to learn, and by training it to respond with an arbitrary, voluntary act to obtain a given reinforcement we can be sure the animal is motivated. If an operant occurs, motivation exists.

This is important when we wish to decide whether the behavior of lower animals is motivated. In an insect, such as the blowfly, quantitative variations in the amount of a sugar solution it will eat, and in the concentrations that it will accept, are directly related to how long it has been without food (Dethier & Rhoades, 1954). But we cannot infer from this anything about the animal's hunger motivation. The act of eating in the blowfly is a stereotyped automatic extension of its proboscis in response to chemical stimulation by sugar of the taste receptors on its mouth or legs. Whether or not the response occurs depends upon the state of sensory adaptation of the taste receptors and upon signals transmitted from the foregut via the recurrent nerve to the brain. When the sensory threshold is low the response occurs unless inhibited by signals from the foregut. Eating is a fixed automatic response over which the fly apparently has no control. This we can conclude because if the recurrent nerve is sectioned, inhibition no longer occurs, and feeding is continued until the fly dies (Dethier & Bodenstein, 1958.) Therefore, we cannot assert anything about the psychological state of hunger in the fly. But higher animals, such as rats, can be trained by operant methods to make arbitrary voluntary acts to obtain food. However, as Dethier (1964) points out, by using insects like the honey bee which are clearly capable of learning, it may be possible to demonstrate the existence of various motivations in insects. Like rats, they may be trained by operant methods to make arbitrary, voluntary acts to obtain food. These acts can serve as an indication of the animal's hunger for food, independent of the consummatory acts normally used in eating.

The Operant as a Measure of Motivation

Much of the success of operant methods as a technique of training results from the use of automatic equipment for the accurate detection of an appropriate response and the instantaneous follow-up with a reinforcement. The sensing instrument, such as a microswitch on a bar or the grid circuit of a drinkometer (Stellar & Hill, 1952), requires a certain degree of uniformity in the act that triggers it. The bar press must always be firm enough to close the switch and the tongue lap must make contact with the fluid to operate the drinkometer. This eliminates much of the variability in an animal's trained behavior that results when we rely on our own judgment as to whether or not it has performed the appropriate act, and thereby earned its reward. Moreover, the automatic equipment has infinite patience. It constantly delivers the reinforcement, merely awaiting the animal's act, thousands and thousands of times, day in and day out—a task beyond the ordinary limits of human energy and endurance. This results in astonishingly powerful control over the animal's behavior. We can train it to perform extremely complex acts, to make very fine discriminations, and to keep working hour after hour; feats of skill we would not have believed possible for animals become commonplace tasks. The techniques of automation have therefore combined with the principles of operant conditioning to increase the power of the operant method.

An added and unexpected dividend of these automatic techniques is their appropriateness for the assessment and control of physiological and behavioral regulations. Regulations go on at all times, and many are long-term phenomena manifesting themselves only over days and weeks. Until recently, it has not been practical to study regulatory behavior continuously over very long periods. Even a straightforward study of how animals eat their food (the number of meals, the size of each meal, and the way they eat each meal) was not really feasible until automatic control equipment was applied to the problem.

Automation can be coupled to any process that can be made to generate an electrical signal, even a very slight one. Sensitive devices are available to detect not only behavioral acts but even internal physiological events, such as changes in body temperature, gastric contractions, and heart rate (Holter, 1961; Mackay, 1961). The electrical signals they generate can be amplified sufficiently to be recorded and used to operate automatic control equipment, thereby making the internal environment as well as overt behavior available for study and possible control by operant techniques.

Most of the effort to date in applying operant techniques has been in the study of behavior controlled by schedules of reinforcement (Ferster &

Skinner, 1957; see also Chapter 3 by W. H. Morse). The schedule on which we reward an animal for his work generates a characteristic pattern of work output. Reinforce a hungry animal only for the first response that occurs after a fixed interval following his previous reinforced response, and he learns to wait for much of that time before he begins to work. Once he starts, he responds faster and faster until he receives the pellet of food. This is the so-called *fixed interval scallop* in the rate of response. Deliver food to an animal for responses following variable intervals of time after each reinforcement, interspersing very short intervals and longer ones at random, and he learns to work at a remarkably steady rate which varies with the mean of the intervals in the schedule. Such schedules generate an enormous amount of work for relatively few reinforcements. The number of responses is considerably greater than when the animal is reinforced for each response, thereby increasing the range over which a given environmental or physiological variable can operate, and hence increasing the ease of observing the effect of that variable (Skinner, 1938). The small effect on each response is magnified into a total effect on many. A schedule of this type acts as a microscope that enables us to see in the record the cumulative effect of the variable on the behavior.

Schedules also instill a remarkable element of stereotypy into the behavior (Herrnstein, 1961). For each schedule, a characteristic pattern of responding exists that is uniform throughout an experimental session. This provides a stable, well-defined behavioral baseline for the normal animal, which serves as a comparison to assess the effect of physiological or environmental variables that influence motivation.

We can measure changes in the strength of the animal's motivation by observing the rate at which he works for reinforcement. On a given schedule of reinforcement, once the animal has been very well trained, the greater the amount of deprivation, the more vigorously will he work for a given reinforcement. Different schedules of reinforcement reveal this increased motivation in different aspects of the animal's performance. On a temporal schedule, such as a variable interval schedule, the animal increases his rate of bar pressing as he becomes more deprived. A work-output schedule, such as a fixed ratio schedule, in which the animal must perform a fixed number of responses before he receives his reward, is less sensitive in revealing changes in the rate of bar pressing, because all well-trained animals press rapidly on such a schedule. However, other aspects of his performance, such as the length of the pause after reinforcement and the size of the ratio the animal will tolerate before quitting (Hodos, 1961), will vary in relation to the amount of his deprivation. Therefore, the way the animal works in an operant conditioning situation can serve as a measure of the strength of his motivation for a reinforcement.

These elements (the use of a voluntary act to ascertain motivation, the sensitivity and power of automation, the huge output of work with its characteristic stable baseline for each schedule of reinforcement, and the sensitivity of these baselines to changes in deprivation states) make the operant method very useful for the assessment and control of motivational states. In the discussion that follows, we examine how it has been used to study normal and disturbed physiological and behavioral regulations.

REGULATORY BEHAVIOR

Normal Hunger and Thirst

The Nature of the Regulation

The basic difficulty in the analysis of homeostatic regulations, such as hunger or thirst, is that a number of feedback control systems combine to give the overall regulation. Because these regulations are essential to an animal's survival, nature has provided a large safety factor by developing multiple controls. Any one of these controls, and perhaps more than one, may be damaged without destroying or too seriously impairing the overall regulation, and for this reason it is difficult to interfere experimentally with the regulation of food or water intake. Interruption of a single control loop, be it denervation of taste by surgery (Bellows & Van Wagenen, 1939), denervation of the stomach by removal of vagus and splanchnic nerves (Bash, 1939; Morgan & Morgan, 1940), or even removal of the entire stomach (Ingelfinger, 1944), does not seriously impair the overall regulation of feeding. When one control is removed, the others compensate to the extent that no effect is seen using present techniques. This is also why it is difficult to defend or believe any single-factor theory of the regulation of food intake. Some years ago, Cannon (1929) stated that stomach contractions were responsible for the feeling of hunger and the regulation of food intake. More recently, Brobeck (1948; 1960) has postulated a *thermostatic* theory that states in essence that animals eat to keep warm. Mayer (1952; 1955) developed a *glucostatic* theory that says that hunger is regulated by the detection of glucose utilization in the body. And Kennedy (1953) proposed a *lipostatic* control of feeding that asserts that long term regulation of feeding is controlled by the state of the animal's fat reserve. Each of these theories accounts for some of the phenomena in the regulation of food intake, but none accounts for all of them. It will not be possible to evaluate the relative importance of these factors, or others, in the control of food intake until we have a stable, objective picture not merely of the total amount of food an animal eats in a day, but also of its patterns of ingestion (the number of meals, the size of each, and the way meals are distributed throughout the day and night). Once we have this as a baseline, we can damage the different control systems, singly and in combination, and see how the disturbance in regulation is reflected in the pattern of feeding and perhaps even in the total daily food intake.

Ingestion Patterns in Normal Animals

Operant techniques have been used to study the feeding patterns of normal animals. In rats, the number and size of liquid meals and the rate of ingestion during a meal were recorded (Teitelbaum & Campbell, 1958) by a drinkometer which detects each lick of the fluid (Stellar & Hill, 1952). By teaching rats to press a bar once for each pellet of food, it was possible to record their meal patterns on a solid diet (see Figure 1). The methods agree in showing that normal rats tend to eat 50 to 60 large calories (kilocalories) each day in about ten distinct meals. Normal mice, pressing a bar for food, also show definite 24-hour feeding rhythms (Anliker & Mayer, 1956; Larsson & Strom, 1957).

Goldfish have been trained to press a lever to get pellets of food (Rozin

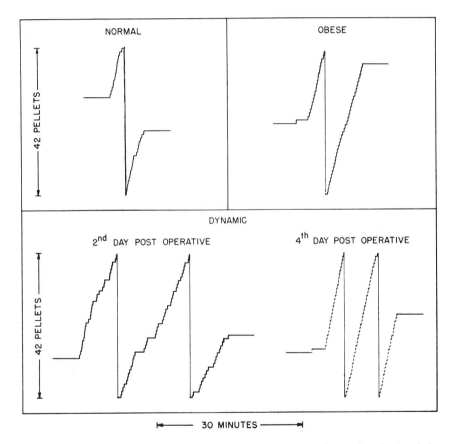

Figure 1. Cumulative response records showing typical meals obtained by pressing a lever once for each pellet of food. Each discrete step upward represents a single pellet. (From Teitelbaum & Campbell, 1958.)

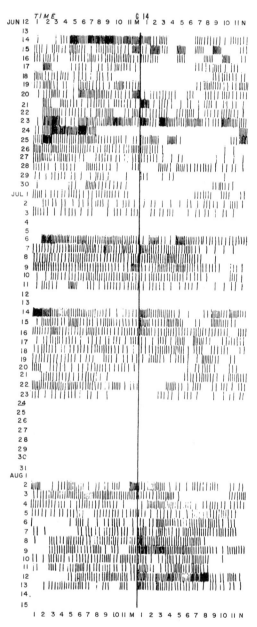

Figure 2. Typical transcription of Esterline-Angus records. Each line represents one lever-pressing response. Continuous dark line divides transcription into daylight on left and moonlight on right. Each row equals one day. Blank rows equal days of deprivation. (From Rozin & Mayer, 1961a.)

& Mayer, 1961a), and, as shown in Figure 2, they maintain regular patterns of food intake which, unlike the rat, do not appear as "meals." Within the limits set by their light cycle the fish seemed to distribute their feeding fairly evenly over time. Thus goldfish, whose feeding behavior ordinarily consists mainly of stereotyped instinctive activities, reveal by pressing a lever for food that their feeding is accompanied by hunger motivation.

Removal of the Physiological Signals Involved in the Regulation of Food and Water Intake

Any homeostatic control system involved in regulating feeding must detect the physiological state of hunger, counteract it by the initiation of feeding, and then stop this behavior when sufficient food is ingested. The signals that control the amount of food eaten in a meal can arise from the act of eating, from the distention of the stomach by food, and from any of the events that occur in the subsequent digestion and utilization of food in the body. The same is true of water intake. The sensory signals that arise from these events must cooperate to regulate the total amount ingested. For example, in a single sitting a thirsty dog with an esophageal fistula drinks an amount of water proportional to its water deficit (Towbin, 1949). Because the water fails to reach the stomach, more is drunk than is actually needed; but the amount is always related to the deficit. This indicates that a form of pharyngeal or mouth metering occurs (Adolph, 1950). When sufficient water to relieve the deficit is placed in a dog's stomach an hour before he is allowed to sham drink, he drinks nothing, which indicates that gastric or other post-ingestional factors cooperate with mouth metering to produce satiety and to regulate the amount ingested. Similarly, Janowitz and Grossman (1949), in comparable experiments on sham feeding in esophagostomized dogs, found that both oral and gastric factors operate and cooperate to regulate food intake during a meal.

How essential is mouth metering for normal day-to-day control of food and water intake? Can an animal regulate intake normally without the oral sensations arising from the act of eating or drinking? This question has been answered for rats using an ingenious operant technique. Epstein (1960a) devised a gastric tube that can be permanently implanted in a rat, that does not require gastrointestinal surgery with its ever-present risk of infection, and that does not interfere with the animal's normal feeding and drinking. The implanted stomach tube is shown in Figure 3. It consists of a small-diameter (PE-50) polyethylene tube (D in Figure 3) that is passed into the rat's nostril, through the nasal and oral pharynx, into the esophagus, and down into the stomach. The external end is attached to a sharply curved metal tube (C), which in turn is connected to a polyvinyl tube that is brought under the skin of the snout and scalp (B), to the top of the skull where it is attached to a metal inlet tube (A), and fixed permanently by

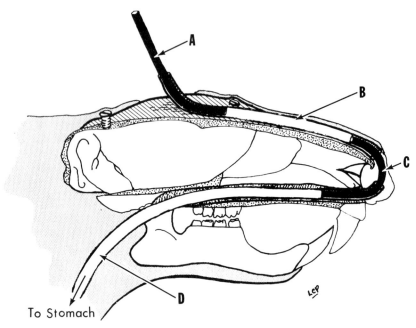

Figure 3. The course of the nasopharyngeal gastric tube shown in a schematic drawing of a midsaggital section of the rat's head. (From Epstein & Teitelbaum, 1962b.)

screws and cement. The size of the gastric tube is exaggerated in the figure so that it can be seen clearly. It is actually so small relative to the diameter of the esophagus that the animal can eat and drink normally by mouth with the tube in place. Water or liquid food can also be pumped directly into the animal's stomach. If such a rat is taught to operate the pump by pressing a bar, it can feed or water itself intragastrically. It is first taught to press a bar in order to have a fluid delivered into a cup in its cage. This is ingested by mouth. The pump is then connected to the animal's gastric tube so that food or water is delivered directly into its stomach when it presses the bar. The arrangement is shown in Figure 4. A swivel joint (Epstein & Teitelbaum, 1962a), placed between the delivery tube and the inlet to the gastric tube, allows the animal freedom to turn without kinking the delivery tube. The rat can now feed or water itself day and night for months at a time without tasting, smelling, or feeling food or water in its mouth—indeed, without even the act of swallowing (Epstein & Teitelbaum, 1962b).

Such rats regulate their daily water intake normally, and they even compensate for the increased water loss of diabetes insipidus by voluntarily pressing a bar for the direct injection of water into the stomach (Epstein, 1960a). For as long as a month and a half, rats have also regulated their caloric intake in this way holding their body weight at normal levels (Epstein & Teitelbaum, 1962b). Metering by mouth is not necessary for regulation of food or water intake in normal rats.

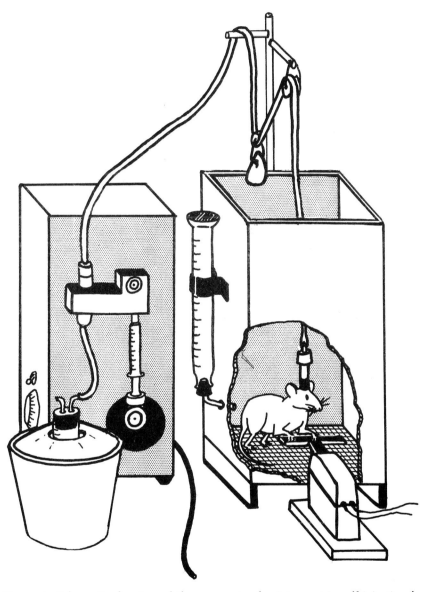

Figure 4. Schematic drawing of the apparatus for intragastric self-injection by the rat. The rat presses the bar in order to activate the pipetting machine (center) thus delivering a liquid diet from the reservoir (left foreground) through the chronic gastric tube directly into its own stomach. (From Epstein & Teitelbaum, 1962b.)

Rats also display strong motivation for food or water delivered intra-gastrically. They pressed the bar as many as 36 times for each injection into the stomach. This corroborates the work of Miller and Kessen (1952) that showed gastric injection to be a reinforcing stimulus for rats.

The same method with minor modifications can be used to inject fluids, nutrients, or drugs directly into the blood stream. Again the animal can be given control of the process. Clark, Schuster, and Brady (1961) implanted catheters in the jugular veins of monkeys and showed that they will press a bar to water themselves intravenously with saline when thirsty. Again, because monkeys will press a bar many times to receive a single injection, it is clear that intravenous injection is a potent reinforcing stimulus. Similarly, Coppock and Chambers (1954) showed that glucose administered intravenously in rats can be used to train them to keep their heads in particular positions. Headlee, Coppock, and Nichols (1955) taught rats to move their heads far enough to interrupt a light beam in order to get an intraperitoneal injection of morphine. More recently, Weeks (1962) showed that rats can become sufficiently addicted to morphine to press a lever for intravenous morphine injections.

Such experiments are important not only because they give some information about the regulation of food, water, and drug ingestion, but because they illustrate the phenomenon of voluntary controls in homeostatic mechanisms. Some years ago, Richter (1942) emphasized the importance of behavioral regulation of homeostasis by pointing out how appetites for special substances are strongly increased in animals and people who suffer from deficiencies in those substances. An adrenalectomized rat ingests more sodium chloride and prefers it at lower concentrations than normal animals. By increasing its intake, an adrenalectomized animal is able to compensate for its excessive renal loss of sodium. Now we are able to divorce the regulation of internal physiological states from the natural, often fixed, instinctive acts of ingestion that normally achieve homeostasis. We can bypass the normal routes whereby food, water, and other substances enter the body, and we are thus able to analyze the separate elements of the regulatory process. Because we can train animals to use voluntary acts, we can also evaluate the motivation that accompanies normal and disturbed physiological regulations.

The Assessment of Disturbed Physiological Regulations

Hypothalamic Hyperphagia

For many years, it has been known that many people with tumors of the pituitary gland become very obese (Frohlich, 1904). Today we know how to produce the phenomenon experimentally in animals; but although a number of facts have become clear, we still do not really understand the nature of the disturbance. It is not the pituitary that must be damaged, but rather the region of the ventromedial nuclei of the hypothalamus at the base of the brain just above the pituitary (Hetherington & Ranson, 1939). No metabolic disturbance causes the obesity. The animals become obese simply because they eat too much (Brobeck, Tepperman, & Long, 1943; Brooks, 1946), and no one really knows why they do. All species investigated thus far (rats, rabbits, cats, dogs, monkeys, and mice) become tremendously fat after hypothalamic damage, because for a period they eat two to three times

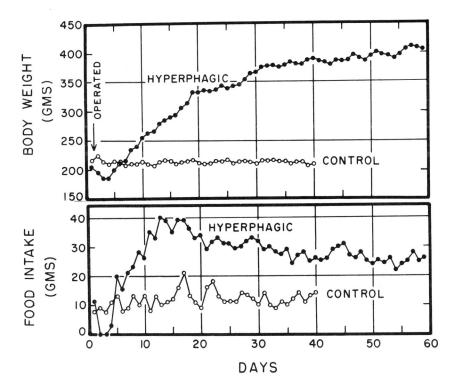

Figure 5. Post-operative body weight and daily food intake of a typical operated animal compared to that of an unoperated normal control animal. (From Teitelbaum, 1955.)

as much as normal. Figure 5 shows the typical course of hypothalamic hyperphagia in rats. After the operation, such an animal overeats and gains weight rapidly for a month or two. This is the dynamic phase of hypothalamic hyperphagia. Once the rat is obese, its food intake decreases practically to normal and its weight remains static, but at an abnormally high level (Brobeck, Tepperman, & Long, 1943).

In recent years, operant techniques have been used to answer a number of questions about this disturbance in feeding. Is there anything about the way these animals overeat that reveals more about the nature of the disturbance? Perhaps they eat more frequently, which would presumably mean they get hungry sooner than normal animals. Or perhaps they eat more at each meal, which might mean that they are not as readily satisfied as normal animals. In either case, maybe they gulp their food more quickly, in which case we would suspect a ravenous quality in their feeding. Figure 6 shows the typical meals of a normal, of a dynamic hyperphagic, and of an obese hyperphagic animal. In this experiment (Teitelbaum & Campbell, 1958),

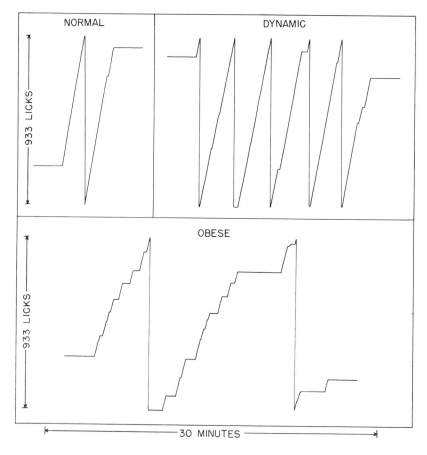

Figure 6. Bursts of licking as recorded directly on a cumulative recorder. The pen moves upward with each lick and toward the right as time elapses. Each burst represents a typical meal on the third day for the median animal In each group. (From Teitelbaum & Campbell, 1958.)

the animals were fed a liquid diet and the patterns of ingestion were measured by a drinkometer which recorded each lick on a cumulative recorder. It is clear that hyperphagic animals overeat by eating larger meals than normals. They neither ate more often nor more quickly. Their overeating was due to eating twice as much as normal at each meal. This may mean that a satiety mechanism is disturbed in such a way that they are not as sensitive as normals to the short-term satiety induced by eating a normal meal.

When the animals were taught to press a bar for solid pellets of food, hyperphagic animals again ate larger meals (Figure 1). But because the solid pellets were bulky, they did not get as many calories in each meal as they had gotten on the liquid diet, and so they ate more often as well. This can be interpreted to mean that when the diet is calorically less concentrated, the animals also become hungry sooner.

Dynamic hyperphagic rats tend to abandon the normal nocturnal feeding pattern, and they eat as much during the day as during the night (Brooks, Lockwood, & Wiggins, 1946). A similar result was obtained by Anliker and Mayer (1956), who studied hyperphagic mice with lesions in the hypothalamus resulting from the systemic injection of goldthioglucose. These mice, trained to press a bar for pellets of food, also overate by distributing their food intake uniformly over 24 hours.

A long-term regulation of feeding exists which is associated not with the amount of food eaten during a meal or in a day, but with how fat the animal is. This is suggested by the fact that after becoming obese, hyperphagic animals reduce their food intake to normal and maintain a steady overweight. But if the weight is dropped by several days of starvation, overeating occurs until the former level of obesity is reached. This could mean that hyperphagic animals overeat because they are not obese. Once fat, they no longer overeat (Teitelbaum, 1961). It follows, then, that a sufficiently fat animal should not overeat when his hypothalamus is damaged.

Hoebel and Teitelbaum (cited in Teitelbaum, 1961) injected protamine zinc insulin twice daily to induce normal animals to overeat and become obese. Animal Number 3 in Figure 7 went from a normal weight of 250 grams to an obese weight of 460 grams. After the hypothalamic operation, it gained only 66 grams in 36 days, leveling off at an obese weight of 526 grams. Animal Number 4 whose hypothalamus was damaged at a normal weight of 302 grams, gained 292 grams at a very fast rate, leveling off at a weight of 594 grams. Since there was the danger that animal Number 3 gained so little weight because the damage to its hypothalamus was ineffective, we starved it down to a normal weight of 300 grams, and then allowed it free access to food. It overate and gained back at a very fast rate all of the lost weight. Therefore, hyperphagic rats do not overeat if they are already fat.

The use of insulin to produce obesity has the serious difficulty of the

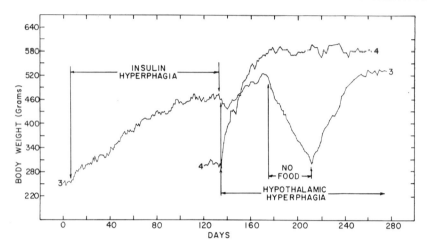

Figure 7. Rate of weight gain in hypothalamic hyperphagia if the animal (No. 3) is previously made to overeat and become obese by protamine zinc insulin injections. This is compared with the rate of weight gain in animal No. 4, which starts from a normal weight; and with its own weight gain after it has been starved back to its normal weight level. (From Hoebel & Teitelbaum, unpublished data.)

animals needing so much hypoglycemia to keep them consistently overeating and gaining weight that they are likely to become comatose and die. Therefore, Teitelbaum & Epstein (1962b) turned to the implanted intragastric tube to produce obese but otherwise normal rats by having hyperphagic rats overfeed them while feeding themselves. The hyperphagic rat was trained to feed itself orally by pressing a bar to pump a small amount of liquid food into a cup in its cage. Simultaneously, the same amount of food was delivered through a nasopharyngeal gastric tube to the stomach of a normal rat in a nearby cage. The normal rat also had food available for oral ingestion. The two animals grew fat together. As might be expected, the normal rats voluntarily ate little or no food while being overfed by the hyperphagics. After two weeks, when both animals had gained nearly 100 grams of excess weight, the overfeeding of the normal animals was stopped. For as long as the next two weeks, the normal animals ate very little food, practically none initially and then more as they lost weight. Only after their weight had returned to nearly its previous level did the overfed normal animals eat their ordinary daily ration. This corroborates Hoebel and Teitelbaum's earlier results with insulin and the more recent results of Cohn and Joseph with force feeding (1962), and it suggests that obesity exerts a long-term braking control over food intake.

Since overfed normal animals voluntarily diet to lose excess weight, they must somehow detect body weight and use it to regulate long-term feeding. How can they do this? Clearly, both normal animals and those with ventromedial hypothalamic damage regulate their weight levels; but the two levels are very different. A hyperphagic animal must be much fatter before its food intake is curbed. The simplest assumption is that the cells of the ventromedial hypothalamus are sensitive to some correlate of obesity. It may be humoral or thermal, but it must be related to obesity, not simply to some short-term aspect of daily feeding (Teitelbaum, 1961).

Is the overeating of hyperphagic animals accompanied by increased hunger? If so, such animals should be willing to work more than normally to get a pellet of food. Miller, Bailey, and Stevenson (1950) tested this hypothesis by requiring hyperphagic animals to lift a weighted lid on their food cup, to pull against a spring as they ran down an alley to food, or to press a bar on a fixed interval schedule for food. In an experiment designed to answer a similar question, the number of times a bar had to be pressed to obtain each pellet of food was varied, and the behavior of obese and non-obese hyperphagics with that of normal animals was compared (Teitelbaum, 1957). The results are shown in Figure 8. They agree with the findings of Miller, Bailey, and Stevenson in showing that hyperphagic rats do not work harder to get food. When few bar presses are required for each pellet, hyperphagics press the bar more and get more food, but this is so little work that it is practically the same as the act of eating, and hyperphagic animals do eat more. But when many bar presses are required for each pellet, hyperphagic rats stop working long before normals. This is especially true when they are obese. Obese animals starve rather than work hard for food. So, even though they do overeat, hyperphagic rats do not seem to display an increased hunger drive.

These techniques, then, establish the rather puzzling picture of animals that overeat but fail to display the normal powerful motivation for food. The results seem reconcilable, however, if we view hypothalamic hyperphagia as a disturbance in satiety rather than hunger. But we must always be wary of the methods used, for a result may depend largely on the method. For example, a reinforcement schedule other than the fixed ratio one might prove to be more sensitive to changes in hunger. It should also be remembered that ventromedial hypothalamic lesions do a number of other things as well as increasing food intake. They increase the animal's emotional irritability and viciousness, interrupt its sexual behavior, and decrease its general level of activity. Obese hyperphagic animals, and maybe even dynamic hyperphagics, are probably physically weaker than normal. Perhaps a schedule that requires an animal to wait rather than work hard for food might reveal an increase in hunger. This is suggested by Falk's recent finding that when hyperphagic animals work for food on a variable interval schedule, they press at a higher rate than do normals (Falk, 1961a). Although hyperphagic rats do not work harder than normals for food, apparently they are more impatient to receive it.

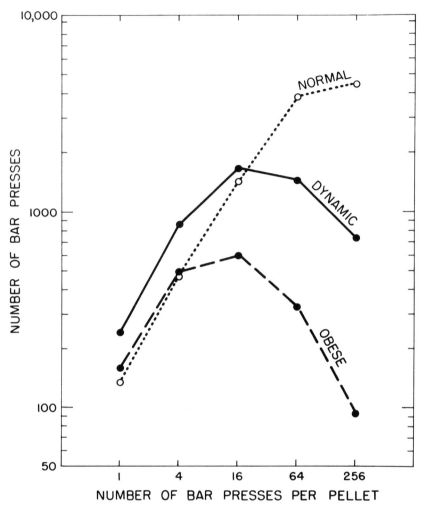

Figure 8. Mean number of bar presses (per 12-hr. period) of normal, obese hyperphagic, and dynamic (non-obese) hyperphagic animals, as a function of the number of bar presses required to obtain each pellet. (From Teitelbaum, 1957.)

The Lateral Hypothalamic Syndrome

Following hypothalamic damage located just lateral to the ventrome-dial nuclei, animals stop eating and die of starvation (Anand & Brobeck, 1951). Not only do they starve, but they also refuse to drink (Teitelbaum & Stellar, 1954). An animal that neither eats nor drinks is difficult to study; even in the brief time it remains alive, there is little one can do to influence its behavior as it grows steadily weaker. However, when such rats were kept alive by tube feeding, we were able to show that eventually they recover both feeding and drinking (Teitelbaum & Stellar, 1954). The recovery exhibited the following regular sequence: at first the animals accepted only very palatable foods such as sweet chocolate or milk but not water; later they drank water and ate dry food again. Because eating and drinking are closely interdependent, especially in the rat, it is a problem to determine the extent to which the refusal to eat results from the refusal to drink, and vice versa. That is why the lateral hypothalamic syndrome is so complicated. But the gradual recovery provides an opportunity to study these defects that disappear by degrees. By using powerful and sensitive operant techniques, it has been possible to learn a great deal about the way the lateral hypothalamus controls feeding and drinking behavior.

We first chose to analyze the stage of recovery in which the lateral hypothalamic animal accepts a liquid diet and maintains its weight on it, but refuses to drink water or eat dry Purina chow. When the caloric content of the liquid diet was varied, lateral hypothalamic animals adjusted the amount they ate to maintain a constant caloric intake. Yet, despite this evidence of their capacity to regulate feeding normally, when offered only water and dry food the animals refused to drink or eat, and they died (Williams & Teitelbaum, 1959).

Since the act of licking the liquid diet from a tube is the same as drinking water from it, clearly they could have drunk water if they wished to do so. Could they be forced to drink the water sooner, and if so, would this accelerate their recovery of normal food and water intake? To answer this specific question about the lateral hypothalamic rat, we developed an operant conditioning technique to force rats to drink (Williams & Teitelbaum, 1956; see also p. 585 f of this chapter). Each rat was trained to lick at a tube to escape and postpone shock. For three or more licks in a second, shock was postponed 15 seconds. For only one or two licks, it was postponed only one second. Normal rats learn quickly to avoid shock, licking steadily for hours. Figure 9 shows a cumulative record of this performance. The normal rat licked water several times for each 15-second postponement (detail A in the top part of Figure 9), but when the fluid was made highly aversive by mixing quinine in it, or when the rat was too full to drink much more, he refused to lick in bursts even though the isolated licks resulted in many more shocks. This pattern of reluctant licking is similar to that shown in detail B in the bottom half of Figure 9. In addition, detail B in Figure 9 shows that lateral hypothalamic rats can also be forced to drink water if they are trained before the operation. But they drink with extreme reluctance in single licks, as if water is highly aversive. Though forced to drink a little water for an hour each day, they did not drink any extra water voluntarily, and within a week to ten days they died. Being forced to drink evidently does not speed their recovery (Williams & Teitelbaum, 1959).

Recently we have shown that refusal to drink water actually causes

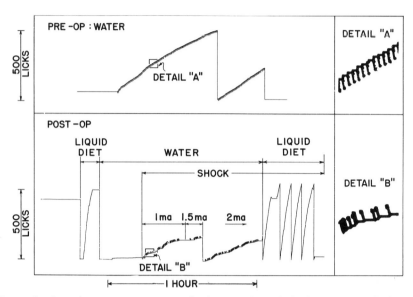

Figure 9. Cumulative response records showing forced drinking to avoid electric shock. The pen moves upward with each lick and toward the right as time elapses. Each shock period is indicated by a small downward displacement of the pen. Pre-op: Normal forced drinking of water, showing several licks after each shock and then the wait for the next shock. Post-op: The lateral hypothalmic animal drinks the liquid diet freely but shows great reluctance to drink water even when forced. (From Williams & Teitelbaum, 1959.)

starvation in this stage of recovery in the sense that the dehydration prevents the rat from eating dry food (Teitelbaum & Epstein, 1962a). If such a rat is hydrated intragastrically with sufficient water, he eats dry food and survives.

In summary, then, lateral hypothalamic lesions produce a combination of deficits in both feeding and drinking from which the rat recovers at different rates. There are four distinct stages in this recovery process. First, there is aphagia and adipsia, in which animals refuse to eat or drink anything, and they die unless kept alive artificially. Then they pass into a stage of anorexia and adipsia, in which palatable foods are accepted but not in sufficient quantity to keep body weight up. They still refuse to drink water. In the third stage, the rats regulate their food intake and weight on wet palatable foods, so that they no longer have to be tube-fed, but still refuse to drink water and die if offered only water and dry food. It was this stage of adipsia with secondary dehydration aphagia that Williams and Teitelbaum saw. Ultimately, most of these animals accept water again and therefore survive on water and dry food.

Operant Control Over Ingestion

It is worth examining the method of forced drinking in more detail, because this shows how reinforcement can be used to manipulate feeding and drinking. Suppose a rat is to be trained to escape electric shock by drinking (Williams & Teitelbaum, 1956). To induce a high operant rate of drinking, we deprive it of all food and water except for a tube of 10 percent sucrose solution. This satisfies both hunger and thirst, but to obtain enough calories to maintain its weight the animal must drink about 150 ml. per day, which means that it drinks frequently. At the same time, it is shocked through its feet from the grid floor of the cage by a series of weak electrical pulses that are just strong enough to motivate the animal to avoid them, but not so intense as to prevent it from licking the sucrose. Each time it drinks, the shock is turned off and postponed for a minute or so. Therefore, in addition to drinking to satisfy hunger and thirst, it is also reinforced by the cessation and avoidance of the painful electric shock. The next day, the shock is increased in intensity, and because of his experience in having the shock turned off when it drinks, the rat now drinks to turn off the shock even when it is not thirsty. By introducing a schedule that requires several licks for each postponement and by shortening the postponement interval, it is possible to induce rats to drink large volumes of fluid. Also, by offering the choice of a long postponement for many licks or a very brief postponment for a single lick, we can determine how reluctant a rat is to drink. If it is very full of water, or if the fluid has a very bitter taste, the rat refuses to lick several times, thus choosing short postponements despite the fact that it is shocked more frequently.

This method introduces several variations into standard operant procedures. First, it detects and reinforces a consummatory act, thus exerting operant control over the act of ingestion. Just as a microswitch detects a rat's bar press or a pigeon's peck on a key, a drinkometer detects a lick. Fortunately, a lick by a rat is as good as a swallow, since they do not seem able to spit out a fluid after having licked it. We therefore detect and reinforce the act of ingestion when we detect and reinforce each lick. Second, instead of "shaping up" a complex instrumental act by systematically reinforcing a series of rudimentary acts that tend to approximate the desired one, we "shape down" from consummatory behavior. We select the lick from the ongoing act of feeding or drinking and follow it immediately by an appropriate, but extraneous reinforcement. "Shaping down" is essential because rats normally will not lick the fluid except in the act of ingestion, and approximation techniques do not elicit it. Third, it uses one kind of motivation to elicit and maintain an act that is usually controlled by other motivations. Escape from shock is used to elicit drinking. The effectiveness of the technique illustrates the power of reinforcement in controlling regulatory behavior. The old adage is no longer true: you can lead a horse to water but now you *can* make him drink.

Reinforcement principles of this sort suggest possible explanations for some aberrations in normal feeding and drinking. For example, since we can induce rats to become obese by licking a liquid diet to escape shock (Williams & Teitelbaum, 1956), perhaps a similar reinforcement history underlies the obesity produced in people who assuage the gnawing of anxiety by eating (Bruch, 1957).

Like electric shock, hunger can be used to induce drinking. Hungry rats can be trained to drink enormous quantities of water simply by feeding them only after they have drunk a little water (Koh & Teitelbaum, 1961). The principle and the schedule used are exactly the same as when an animal drinks to escape shock, except that the hungry animal learns that it receives food only after it drinks fluid. It is easier to train the rat to drink for food than to avoid shock. It is as though an animal works willingly to satisfy the urge (hunger) that comes from within, but would stubbornly rather do anything except what is required of it when working to escape pain. When aversive control is used to maintain behavior, the trick is to prevent the animal from learning how to escape the shock by some other response; the experimenter continually has to foil each new method that the animal discovers to avoid the shock without giving the appropriate response. For example, it is necessary to scramble the pattern of shock on the grid floor because the animal soon learns to straddle fixed shock grids and to stand on those of the same polarity; the walls and even the roof of the cage must be electrified to prevent the animal from avoiding shock by standing on one foot and leaning on the cage wall; and when the response is licking a fluid in a tube, the animal learns to nuzzle the tube with its nose, to swipe it with its paws, to bite it with its teeth, or even to lick around the edge of the tube without touching the fluid—in short, anything that closes the circuit except licking the fluid. Unless the aperture in the cage wall in front of the tube is made so small that the only way to avoid the shock is actually to lick the fluid with its tongue, the rat will successfully avoid shock with little or no fluid consumption.

However, these troubles disappear as if by magic when the animal must drink to get solid pellets of food. Once he has learned that food is delivered for drinking, a rat will drink without the stubborn resistance so often seen when he works to avoid shock. These behavioral differences seem to me to support Skinner's view that positive reinforcement is more effective than aversive control in controlling behavior (Skinner, 1953, p. 190f).

Koh and Teitelbaum used these forced drinking techniques in studying behavioral taste thresholds in the rat (Koh & Teitelbaum, 1961). They motivated rats to lick at tubes of fluid either to get food or to avoid shock. They then offered them two tubes, one containing a strong taste solution and the other water. The rats were reinforced only when they chose the taste solution. When they did this perfectly, Koh and Teitelbaum began to decrease the difference between the solutions until they made a mistake, at which point the difference was increased until they were correct again. When the rats were well-trained, they "zeroed in" within two or three minutes on a concentration that represented their actual taste threshold. This is shown in Figure 10 which represents a version of the "staircase" psychophysical method developed by von Békésy for measurements of human hear-

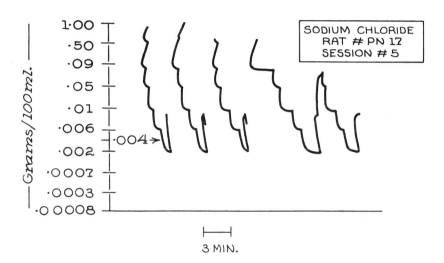

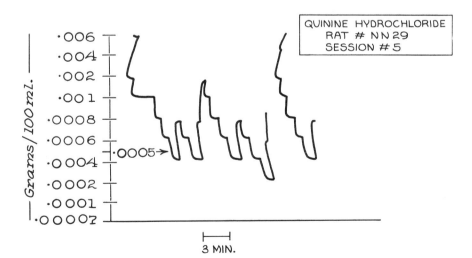

Figure 10. Typical records obtained during a taste threshold determination session. Top: rat tasting NaCl to get food. Bottom: rat tasting quinine to avoid shock.

ing sensitivity (1947), and used by Blough to measure visual sensitivity in pigeons (1958). As shown in Figure 11, the behavioral measures obtained in this way are as good as the best electrophysiological measures presently available. Figure 11 also shows that taste thresholds obtained with positive reinforcements are always somewhat lower and less variable than those obtained with electric shock.

Still another kind of excessive drinking, psychogenic hyperdipsia, has

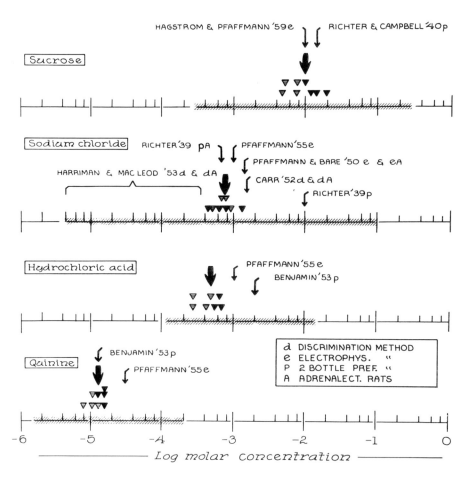

Figure 11. Comparison of taste thresholds for the rat obtained by different methods. The hatched triangles show mean thresholds obtained for each rat using positive reinforcement (food), and the solid triangles show thresholds obtained using negative reinforcement (electric shock). The heavy arrows indicate the mean thresholds obtained for each substance. The light arrows represent thresholds obtained for that substance by other workers using methods described in the legend. (From Koh & Teitelbaum, 1959.)

been seen in operant conditioning situations in which rats press a bar for food on a VI 1 schedule (Falk, 1961b). Under such treatment, animals drink three or four times their normal daily requirements during the course of a three- or four-hour session. One might think that this is actually another instance of training rats to drink to get food. For example, suppose the rat drinks while pausing in his work for food. If a very short interval in the schedule has just been programmed, the very next bar press after drinking will be reinforced. Such accidental reinforcement could cause superstitious drinking to become a part of a chain of response used in working for food under a VI schedule. This, however, does not appear to be correct for the following reasons.

If psychogenic hyperdipsia were really superstitious, then drinking should usually occur before eating since it is reinforced by food. But Falk pointed out that the animal drinks *after* each pellet. On a VI schedule, it is sometimes difficult to judge whether drinking occurs before or after reinforcement, because often the intervals are very short and the behavior is quite continuous. Stein eliminated this ambiguity by switching such hyperdipsic animals to an FI schedule after training them on a VI schedule. He found, as Falk did, that they drink immediately *after* eating each pellet and that they allow a long time to elapse before starting to work again for food (Stein, 1962).

Because they drink after eating, this is not superstitious drinking. Why, then, do they drink excessively? The answer is still not known. Perhaps it is due to the spaced character of feeding induced by the operant schedule. Since feeding causes dehydration by pulling water into the stomach from the tissues, this should produce a state of thirst accompanied by a dry mouth. Chewing and swallowing a dry pellet may be difficult for a thirsty animal, so he drinks to help wash each pellet down. This is, of course, highly speculative, but it does suggest that this form of psychogenic hyperdipsia should disappear if either a liquid reinforcement is substituted for the dry pellet, or if the animal is hydrated with water immediately before the experiment. Stein (1962) has recently shown the first of these suggestions to be correct.

A similar type of prandial drinking has been observed in many recovered lateral hypothalamic rats who drink only while they eat (Teitelbaum & Epstein, 1962a). They seem to have lost the ability to detect or to respond to a state of true thirst since they never drink unless eating, no matter how long they have been without water. It may be that the spaced character of eating imposed by the operant schedule increases dryness of the mouth which in turn exaggerates prandial drinking in normal rats.

Psychogenic hyperdipsia also occurs in human beings (Carter & Robbins, 1947). For unknown reasons, some people drink so much more water than they need that they become water intoxicated (Goodman & Gilman, 1955, p. 769). Because they can influence fluid intake, operant methods may prove to be valuable laboratory tools in the study of abnormal states of excessive overhydration in otherwise normal animals.

The Regulation of Body Temperature

Let us next turn to other regulatory systems which may be influenced by voluntary behavior. In the same way that the voluntary bar press has been used as an index of regulation and motivation of feeding and drinking behavior, Weiss and Laties (1961) used an operant method to study the behavioral regulation of body temperature. They kept rats, without food and shaved of their fur, at a temperature of two degrees centigrade. Under these conditions, a rat cannot maintain its body temperature indefinitely, and eventually it freezes to death. But when it is given the opportunity to press a bar to obtain a burst of heat from an infrared lamp, the rat learns to press the bar and keeps itself warm by vigorous and steady bar pressing, as shown in Figure 12. Weiss and Laties found that the temperature under the skin is a sensitive measure which is directly related to the time at which an animal begins to press the bar. The sooner its temperature dropped, the sooner it pressed for heat. The longer the burst of heat furnished by each bar press, the longer the animal stayed warm; and the animal pressed the bar correspondingly less often. With the thyroid gland removed, the rats were unable to increase their metabolic rate and so they grew cold faster. As might be anticipated, they pressed the bar much sooner and more frequently than normal animals, and thereby succeeded in keeping warm (Laties & Weiss, 1959). The experiment shows, as Richter (1942) had pointed out earlier, that even when one of the body's homeostatic temperature controls is impaired, behavioral thermoregulation can compensate for it. Hypophysectomized rats build better nests than normals in a cold environment (Stone & King, 1954). We would anticipate that like thyroidectomized animals, they would press a bar for heat more often than normals and so manage to keep warm.

Another instance of behavioral thermoregulation (this time with goldfish) was provided by Rozin and Mayer (1961b). The fish were kept in an overheated tank, and they were taught to press a lever to obtain a brief flow of cold water. The fish pressed the lever vigorously, thereby dropping the temperature of the water to a cooler, presumably more comfortable level. Even though fish are normally poikilothermic, they appear to be motivated to maintain a comfortable body temperature. This is an instance of purely behavioral homeostasis, since fish, as poikilotherms, possess no physiological mechanisms for temperature regulation.

Normally, the body makes reflex adjustments by means of the nervous system and endocrine organs which compensate for being cold. It decreases blood flow in the skin to cut down heat loss and it raises the metabolic rate and initiates shivering to generate more heat. Complex instinctive activities like nest building are also aroused. In higher animals, accompanying all these integrated reflex and instinctive activities, there is always the corresponding motivation.

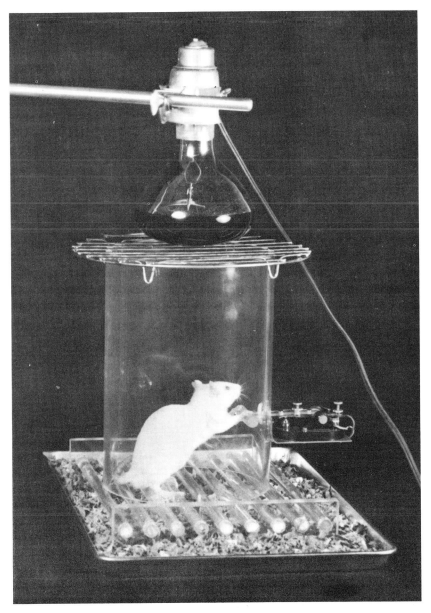

Figure 12. The heat reinforcement apparatus. Depessing the lever closes a switch that activates the heat lamp. (From Weiss & Laties, 1961.)

The best evidence available suggests that, just as with hunger and thirst, the hypothalamus serves to integrate the reflexive, instinctive, and behavioral acts that maintain body temperature. Cooling the preoptic area (which is in the anterior part of the hypothalamus) elicits shivering in the goat (Andersson, Gale, & Sundsten, 1962) and in the dog (Hammel, Hardy, & Fusco, 1960). Heating this region elicits panting and vasodilation (Fusco, Hardy, & Hammel, 1961). Using a microelectrode to record the activity of single neurons, Nakayama, Eisenman, and Hardy (1961) and Hellon, Hardy, and Sutherland (1963) have shown that some cells in the preoptic area are directly activated by local heating, while others are excited by local cooling. These cells are therefore receptors for temperature change, i.e., thermoreceptors.

Is an animal actually aware of stimulation of its hypothalamic thermoreceptors? Does cooling of these cells arouse the urge to keep warm as well as the reflex changes in blood flow, metabolic rate, and shivering that compensate for feeling cold? Satinoff (1963) has recently answered these questions using the method of Weiss and Laties (1961) to train rats to press a bar for heat when they are in a cold environment. She implanted a very small thermode in the hypothalamus of several rats so that the preoptic

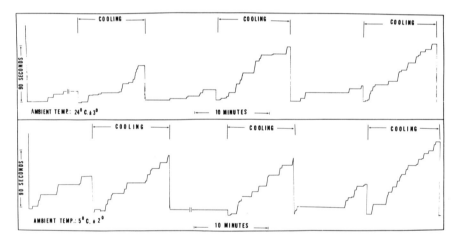

Figure 13. A rat presses a bar to turn on a heat lamp when its brain is cooled. The cumulative recorder pen moves upward when the bar is held depressed and moves to the right with time. (From Satinoff, 1964.)

area of the hypothalamus could be cooled by running a very cold fluid through the thermode. She found that rats, just like dogs and goats, shiver when their hypothalamus is cooled. But, in addition, as shown in Figure 13, if they had previously been trained to press a bar for heat in the cold, then when their hypothalamus was cooled they pressed the bar to get bursts of infrared heat. Even in a neutral environmental temperature in which they would ordinarily hardly work at all for heat, they did so when their brains were cooled. Indeed, they heated themselves so much that rectal temperatures increased as much as 5°F above the normal temperature of about 100°F. Unless they were responding to their reflexive shivering, they must have been able to discriminate the feeling of cold in the brain because they used an operant to counteract it. Therefore, in addition to the reflex response of shivering, cooling the hypothalamus aroused the sensation of cold and the motivation to keep warm.

Interrelation of Homeostatic Control Systems

We eat because we are hungry, but we may be hungry because we are cold. Conversely, we may be cold because we have not eaten for a long time. Rats and other animals eat much more in cold than in warm environments (Brobeck, 1960). This is one reason why Brobeck (1948) says that we eat to keep warm. When food is broken down, part of its chemical energy is liberated as heat. This is the *specific dynamic action* of food. So, as Weiss (1957a; 1957b), Hamilton (1959), and Hamilton and Sheriff (1959) have shown, hungry rats in the cold press a bar for more heat than when they have just been fed. Weiss (1957a) has also shown that a specific nutritional deficiency, such as a lack of pantothenic acid, makes rats work harder to keep warm.

The running activity of rats is a good indicator of their nutritional state (Wald & Jackson, 1944). But since we have seen that hungry rats press a bar for more heat, it may be that the running of hungry rats also serves to keep them warm (Stevenson & Rixon, 1957). Since thiamin deficiency produces marked running activity (Wald & Jackson, 1944), it would be interesting to know whether thiamin deficiency also increases bar pressing for heat. Perhaps whenever a rat responds to a nutritional deficiency by running, it would also work for more heat in the cold.

Bar pressing, like running, is a form of exercise that is very effective in raising an animal's body temperature. Heat production and its effect on body temperature during bar pressing must therefore be considered as a variable in every bar-pressing experiment. Hamilton (1963) has made this point very effectively in a study of the way hyperphagic animals work for food. As described earlier, hyperphagic animals eat a great deal, but they do not seem to be willing to work for food. Hamilton reasoned that because of excess weight, obese hyperphagics become warmer more quickly than normal and, to prevent hyperthermia, must stop working sooner when many bar presses are required for each pellet. They therefore should be able to work more easily in a cold environment. Figure 14 shows the results of Hamilton's experiment. In a normal environment at 27°C, Hamilton found,

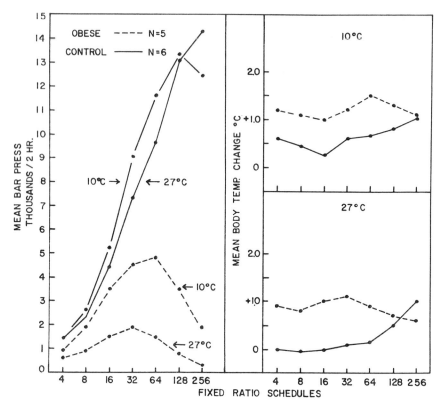

Figure 14. Bar-press rates and body temperature changes in obese and normal rats as a function of fixed ratio schedules. (From Hamilton, 1963.)

as did Teitelbaum (see Figure 8), that obese hyperphagics stop working at ratios higher than 32:1. By measuring their body temperature before and after each session, Hamilton found that they became hyperthermic while bar pressing at those high ratios, whereas normals did not. Normal rats could continue working at ratios up to as much as 256:1 before they became excessively warm. As shown in Figure 14, when the temperature was reduced to 10°C, the hyperphagic animals did not become hyperthermic as soon, and they worked much harder for food. Apparently, at room temperature, fever prevented these obese animals from working hard, either by forcing them to reduce their energy output or actually by decreasing their motivation for food.

Hyperthermia prevents an animal from feeding itself as well as bar pressing for food. Rats do not eat at all if the environmental temperature is so warm (94°F) that they run a fever when they eat (Brobeck, 1948). Direct heating of the hypothalamus inhibits feeding in a hungry goat whereas cooling of the hypothalamus causes a satiated animal to eat more than normal (Andersson & Larsson, 1961). These observations agree with our everyday experience of loss of appetite when the weather is very warm, and they provide strong evidence for thermostatic regulation of food intake. Animals also eat little if they are dehydrated. Particularly in the desert, dehydration produces hyperthermia and decreased food intake. This might be why lateral hypothalamic rats do not eat when they do not drink (Teitelbaum & Epstein, 1962).

Clearly, many regulatory systems are interrelated, and behavior is often controlled by a complex interaction of them. Feeding is related to environmental temperature, and temperature regulation depends on the state of nutrition. Similarly, motivation parallels regulation. Bar pressing for food depends on the environmental temperature, and bar pressing for heat in the cold varies with the state of nutrition. So we may learn about the interaction of homeostatic physiological controls by studying the way an animal works for various kinds of reinforcement during different states of bodily need.

Control of Autonomic Events

In much the same way that we use reinforcement to gain control over the consummatory act of drinking, it may be possible to gain voluntary control of physiological processes now considered to be involuntary and automatic. There are many reports of remarkable control over bodily functions that normally are considered to be reflexive or involuntary. Indian fakirs are reported to be able to speed up or to slow down their heart rate, to prevent bleeding in specific areas of the body when a pin or a knife is passed through the tissue, and to control breathing or even metabolic rate so that they may be buried alive for long periods of time (Yeats-Brown, 1930). Some of these remarkable powers, such as voluntary control over gastrointestinal activities, are well documented by Behanan (1937).

If we can reliably detect these autonomic events and pair an external signal and a reinforcement with them, we have the conditions necessary for operant control. Spurred by the need to send back information from rockets, miniaturization and telemetric techniques have been developed for physiological and psychological experiments. Tiny sensing devices can be surgically implanted, swallowed, or merely carried around (Mackay, 1961). For example, microphones can detect heart rate, thermistors can detect whole body temperature or local temperature that reflects local blood flow, straingauges can detect smooth muscle contractions, etc. When these sensing devices detect a desired response, they can be made to activate an easily discriminated signal which can help the person or animal to discriminate the presence of that action. And if a reinforcement follows the act, we may be able to motivate the animal to control it. If operant conditioning is not possible with such responses, it should at least be possible to study many instances of classical conditioning (in which control over the response or even its occurrence may not be necessary). The work of several Russian investigators provides many instances of such types of autonomic conditioning (Bykov, 1957; Razran, 1961). In addition, Shearn (1962) has shown that heart rate may be slowed or accelerated by human subjects who are reinforced for an appropriate change in rate. Perez-Cruet (1962) has induced extra-systoles by operant conditioning. Not only autonomic responses, but also subtle skeletal movements may be studied. Thumb twitches so slight as to be undetectable without the aid of an electromyograph can be conditioned successfully by standard operant procedures (Hefferline & Keenan, 1961). Indeed, when the electrical activity of the muscle is heard through a loud speaker and displayed on an oscilloscope, subjects soon learn to achieve such amazing control over their muscles that they can play drum rolls and beat out all sorts of rhythms with muscular contractions which are otherwise completely undetectable (Basmajian, 1963). After such learning, some subjects retain this exquisite muscular control even without the sound provided by electronic detection. Although it is doubtful that all the above examples represent true operant conditioning, this type of research may prove valuable in the study of psychosomatic changes, and it might be a powerful technique for teaching people to gain voluntary control over muscles and bodily organs that ordinarily seem completely involuntary and automatic in their action.

INSTINCTIVE MOTIVATED BEHAVIOR

Electrical Stimulation of the Brain

Neurophysiologists have used electrical stimulation very fruitfully to study the function of different parts of the brain. At first, it was necessary to study anesthetized animals, and, consequently, most acts that were elicited were reflexes and fragmentary parts of instinctive motor patterns. With the development of the implanted electrode technique (Hess, 1932), stimulation of the brain of awake animals has become possible, and instinctive behavior patterns of great complexity have been observed. The hypothalamus and parts of the brain intimately connected with it have been shown to be involved in such instinctive behaviors as feeding, aggression, and mating. Operant techniques are proving extremely useful in evaluating the motivation that underlies the behavior produced by brain stimulation in these areas.

Stimulation in the lateral hypothalamus elicits feeding in satiated animals (Brugger, 1943; Larsson, 1954). In the medial hypothalamus, it inhibits feeding in hungry animals (Wyrwicka & Dobrzecka, 1960). This supports the idea that there are two centers in the hypothalamus that control feeding: a medial "satiety" center and a lateral "feeding" center

(Anand & Brobeck, 1951). Stimulation of the hypothalamus in the region rostral and medial to the lateral feeding centers elicits drinking behavior in the goat (Andersson & McCann, 1955). Drinking also occurs in rats during lateral hypothalamic stimulation at the level of the lower dorso-medial nucleus (Greer, 1955). Brain stimulation not only elicits the con-summatory act, but also the motivation that accompanies it: rats stimulated in the lateral "feeding" center press a panel (Miller, 1958) or cross an electrically charged grid (Morgane, 1961) to obtain food; and goats stimu-lated in the "drinking" center perform the learned instrumental act of climb-ing a staircase to obtain water (Andersson & Wyrwicka, 1957).

Implanted cannulae have made possible the study of direct chemical stimulation and local anesthetization of the brains of awake animals. Minute amounts of hypertonic saline injected into the rostral hypothalamus stimu-late goats to drink as much as nine liters of water, to the point of extreme gastric distension (Andersson, 1953). This evidence supports the view that osmoreceptors in the drinking areas control thirst. Procaine injected into the medial "satiety centers" of the hypothalamus anesthetizes the tissue and causes feeding, whereas in the lateral "feeding centers," it inhibits food in-take (Epstein, 1960b). Grossman (1960; 1962) showed that the drinking and feeding systems are activated by different neuro-humors. At the same locus in the lateral hypothalamus, noradrenaline produces feeding, and car-bachol (a drug that acts like acetylcholine) elicits drinking. These chemi-cals act selectively to produce the appropriate motivation as well. Satiated rats press a bar for food rather than water if they are stimulated by nor-adrenaline, and they work for water rather than food when carbachol is de-posited in the same place in the lateral hypothalamus. This agrees with the work on lesions in this area (Teitelbaum & Epstein, 1962a), and it sug-gests that tissues concerned with both feeding and drinking lie in the lateral hypothalamus of the rat.

Instinctive behavior patterns other than feeding and drinking have been observed after chemical stimulation of the hypothalamus. Estrogen pellets implanted in the posterior hypothalamus produce full-blown sexual behavior in ovariectomized cats (Harris, Michael, & Scott, 1958). Minute quantities of testosterone injected into the hypothalami of male rats yield the rather amazing sight of vigorous maternal behavior (Fisher, 1956). Such a male retrieves young pups and returns them to the nest just as a nursing mother would do. This shows that at least some of the brain struc-tures controlling both male and female behavior are present in every animal, but they are not active unless stimulated by hormones. These tissues must be sensitive to sex hormones. Quantities so small as to be ineffective if in-jected systemically produce vigorous instinctive behavior when deposited directly into the hypothalamus (Harris, Michael, & Scott, 1958).

Because many other kinds of instinctive behavior patterns that are elicited directly by chemical or electrical stimulation of the hypothalamus are also accompanied by corresponding motivational states, one might expect that sexual or maternal behavior elicited in this way would also be appropriately motivated. But how can we determine this? Clearly, if an animal will work to receive the opportunity to engage in sexual behavior, it is sexually motivated. This has been shown in a number of studies on male rats (Beach, 1956). Recently, Bermant (1961) used an operant technique to study sexual motivation in female rats. He brought them into heat by systemic injections of estrogen and progesterone, and he taught each to press a bar to allow a male to enter its cage. Copulation, of course, resulted. By interrupting the sexual act before completion, he was able to show that the female's desire for her sexual partner was greater after incomplete sexual activity than before. She pressed the bar sooner to allow a male to re-enter the cage and complete the sexual act. After the male had ejaculated, the motivation of the female apparently dropped to a low ebb, since she waited a long time before pressing the bar again for a male. By giving the female the opportunity to escape from the male, Pierce and Nuttall (1961) showed that the male's ejaculation may even produce in the female a temporary aversion toward further mating.

These techniques serve as a measure of how the various appetitive acts leading to sexual consummation are accompanied by, and in turn may produce, changes in the sex drive. As the ethologists have pointed out (Tinbergen, 1951), instinctive behavior consists of chains of acts leading eventually to the final consummatory instinctive act. For example, as an animal becomes hungry, it initially engages in various exploratory and hunting activities which generally lead it to encounter food or prey, at which point the more stereotyped consummatory acts of killing and eating food are initiated by the sight or smell of the prey. Similarly, in sexual behavior, the stereotyped consummatory act of copulation is preceded by more loosely organized appetitive acts involved in setting up a mating territory and engaging in courtship activities which are initiated when a potential partner is encountered.

It is quite probable that all instinctive behavior is accompanied by a corresponding drive. When each sign stimulus elicits the next act in the instinctive behavior chain, and when these responses are triggered in a very stereotyped way by sign stimuli, it is difficult to determine the degree of motivation that accompanies the act unless a voluntary response such as pressing a bar can be interpolated between the members of the chain. When that is possible, we have a definition and a measure of the motivation accompanying the act. If, for instance, a male fish can be taught to press a bar to obtain the opportunity of mating with a female, we have proof that, even though its mating behavior is quite stereotyped, the male fish wants to mate with the female. And if its rate of bar pressing increases as the final act of copulation approaches, we interpret this as evidence that the fish is more strongly motivated to mate as the sexual act nears completion. Such an assessment of the motivation accompanying stereotyped reflexive and instinctive behavior is beginning to be accomplished. For example, rats will press a lever to avoid high carbon dioxide concentrations in the air they breathe (Van Sommers, 1963a). Turtles kept underwater will press a lever to gain access to air (Van Sommers, 1963b), and goldfish will swim to interrupt a light beam to obtain air in their water (Van Sommers, 1962). Thompson (1963) has shown that the sight of a male Siamese fighting fish, which elicits an attack and fighting behavior from another male, is reinforcing for that male. He will press a bar just for a glimpse of the other male. In a similar manner, Peterson (1960) has shown that a duckling will press a bar insatiably for the sight of a moving object with which he had been presented (imprinted on) during a presumably critical period in the first two days of his life.

The same methods can be used to study the motivation that accompanies all instinctive behavior that is elicited by stimulation of various levels of the nervous system, such as the medulla, hypothalamus, rhinencephalon, and neocortex. Wherever they have been studied, the results of both stimulation and ablation of the hypothalamus show that hypothalamic activity produces motivated instinctive behavior. But the functions of lower levels of the brain, such as the midbrain and the medulla, when separated from the integrating action of the hypothalamus, have been shown to be fragmentary and uncoordinated. Cats which are decerebrated below the hypothalamus show isolated fragments of emotional or sexual behavior, but never their integrated expression (Bard, 1939). Similarly, the polyphagia seen by Larsson (1954) in the goat during stimulation of the dorsal motor nucleus of the vagus in the medulla may very well be different from the feeding evoked by hypothalamic stimulation, in that merely a fragment of the instinctive act of feeding is elicited. If so, such goats should not work for food during medullary stimulation, whereas they will do so when receiving lateral hypothalamic stimulation.

These methods introduce a new dimension into the study of brain and behavior. Where we used to study reflexes in anesthetized animals and in isolated portions of the nervous system, such as the spinal cord, we now study instinctive and conditioned behavior in awake animals. Where we used to speak of the integrative action of the nervous system mainly in terms of the integration of automatic reflexes (Sherrington, 1906), we must now speak of the integration of complex behavioral, instinctive, and voluntary activities. Where the hypothalamus was thought to integrate primarily the homeostatic reflexes, we must now use concepts of motivation, such as the hunger drive, and speak of the urge to eat when we describe the regulation of food intake. We now believe that regulation does not exist without adequate motivation (Teitelbaum & Epstein, 1962a). Many studies of the regulation of food intake assume that regulation is an automatic homeostatic process which is not subject to very much voluntary influence. But all of these studies used normal animals which possess a very strong motivation for food. Where the urge to eat is impaired, as in animals with hypothalamic damage, then very slight changes in the taste or texture of the food cause animals to refuse to eat and even to starve to death. Regulation is much more easily disturbed, and it can only be seen to operate when the food is very palatable.

The hypothalamus integrates the series of instinctive acts from appetitive to consummatory behavior. It may do this by producing the appropriate drive state. In other words, the hypothalamus is necessary for the existence of a drive state which welds together appetitive and consummatory behavior into integrated instinctive activities. Therefore, when damage to the hypothalamus impairs instinctive activities such as eating, drinking, or mating, this may not occur as a result of primary damage to the nervous structures responsible for the individual components of these acts, such as chewing, swallowing, mounting, etc., but rather to the motivational processes which must energize them sufficiently for them to be elicited in response to the stimuli that normally release them. Therefore, increasing the level of motivation, either by using supernormal stimuli or by changing the internal environment, may be sufficient to elicit the behavior once again, though under normal circumstances it would appear to be permanently abolished.

Affective Correlates of Instinctive Behavior

Not only does brain stimulation elicit motivated instinctive behavior patterns, but it can also be used to provide immediate positive or negative reinforcement. Rats, cats, and monkeys will bar press many thousands of times for hour after hour to obtain electrical stimulation of the brain. People, when stimulated in specific subcortical regions, reported pleasure or pain (Heath & Mickle, 1960). Olds and Sinclair showed that rats crossed an electrified grid more willingly for brain stimulation than for food, even when they were very hungry (cited in Olds, 1960). Stimulation maintained bar pressing on various schedules, just as did other reinforcers such as food and water (Olds, 1955). Neutral stimuli, when paired with self-stimulation, acquired secondary reinforcing properties (Stein, 1958). Therefore, stimulation of the brain in the right places can duplicate the effects of many of the more traditional reinforcing stimuli.

Olds, Travis, and Schwing (1960) have shown that the system of brain structures for which stimulation is reinforcing seems to follow the course of the medial forebrain bundle. This runs from the olfactory bulbs through the septal area and the lateral hypothalamus into the midbrain, making connections with and receiving fibers from many of the structures that it passes along the way. In the more medial periventricular system that runs through the ventromedial areas of the hypothalamus into the midbrain, stimulation is aversive: rats pressed a bar to escape stimulation in this medial system (Olds, 1960).

The tissue of the lateral hypothalamus that excites feeding lies within the system in which stimulation is reinforcing (Margules & Olds, 1962; Hoebel & Teitelbaum, 1962), whereas the inhibitory "satiety center" lies within the aversive region. To explore the interactions between these reinforcing and feeding systems, Hoebel and Teitelbaum (1962) implanted simultaneously four hollow electrodes in the hypothalamic areas that control feeding in rats. By injecting chemicals through the cannulae or by stimulating them electrically, we were able at will to excite or to depress the medial and lateral hypothalamus both bilaterally and simultaneously in awake rats. In brief, we found that whenever feeding was elicited or increased, so was lateral hypothalamic self-stimulation. When feeding was inhibited, self-stimulation was also inhibited. As shown in Figure 15, either stimulation of the ventromedial area or satiety induced by excessive feeding inhibits lateral hypothalamic self-stimulation; ventromedial destruction disinhibits it. It appears as if the feeding systems control self-stimulation in a manner that is analogous to their control of feeding. Lateral hypothalamic self-stimulation is more reinforcing when an animal is hungry than when it is satiated. This suggests that the feeding centers are involved not only in the regulation of food intake, but also in the urge to eat and in the pleasure that results from eating.

The technique of self-stimulation may reveal the affective correlates of motivated behavior (Teitelbaum, 1962). Just as the rate of bar pressing for food or water is a sensitive measure of the hunger and thirst drive, so too the rate of bar pressing for brain stimulation in the feeding systems is indicative of changes in hunger or satiety. Perhaps self-stimulation of the brain will prove ultimately to be an even more sensitive measure of motivation than is bar pressing which is reinforced in the usual way. It has, of course, the added advantage of identifying which parts of the brain are involved in each type of motivation.

Just as with ordinary reinforcement, the amount of brain stimulation strongly determines the resulting rate of bar pressing (Olds, 1955). By allowing the magnitude as well as the rate of stimulation to be manipulated by the animal, information about stimulation preferences and thresholds may be obtained and stable baselines established. Stein and Ray (1959) allowed rats to regulate the amount of brain-stimulating current delivered as a reinforcement. This permitted a continuous determination of the preferred intensity as well as the rate of stimulation. By allowing each succeeding response at the brain stimulation lever to decrease the intensity of the next brain stimulation reward, a continuous record was obtained of the weakest current levels that stimulate positive cell groups sufficiently to produce a rewarding effect (Stein & Ray, 1960). An animal pressed the stimulation lever repeatedly for brain stimulation until the intensity of the cur-

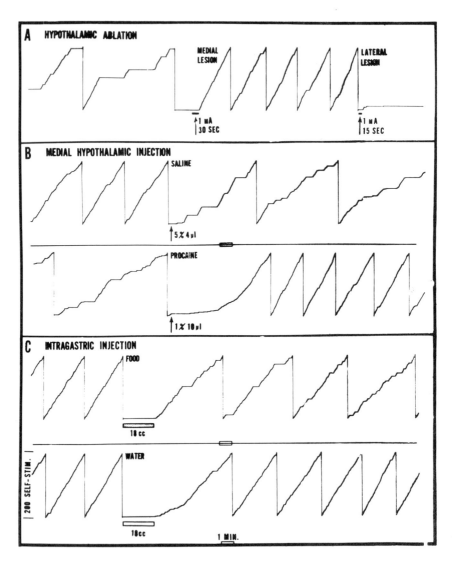

Figure 15. Representative cumulative recorder records showing the changes in lateral self-stimulation rate produced by experimental influence of the hypothalamus or by feeding. (A) Acceleration of self-stimulation caused by destuction of both ventromedial regions. (B) Inhibition of self-stimulation by chemical excitation of both ventromedial regions, and subsequent disinhibition of self-stimulation by their anesthetization. (C) Prolonged inhibition of self-stimulation by tube feeding a liquid diet but only transient inhibition by tube feeding an equal volume of water. (From Hoebel & Teitelbaum, 1962.)

rent was driven down to a point at which it was presumably no longer sufficiently reinforcing. It then pressed another lever to reset the current to the highest intensity and returned to the stimulation lever to start the next cycle. In a sense, the animal told the experimenter exactly how strong a brain stimulation was required for him to continue working.

Such a method should be extremely sensitive to changes in activity in those areas of the brain that are reinforcing. As an area becomes more active, less stimulation should be needed to excite it, and as it becomes inactive, more should be required. This technique shows clearly that tranquillizing or energizing drugs change the activity of reward systems in the brain (Stein, 1962). In the same way, variations in activity of brain areas controlling each kind of instinctive act may reflect changes in the urge to perform that act. Therefore, the rate (Hoebel & Teitelbaum, 1962; Margules & Olds, 1962) and the threshold (Stein & Ray, 1960) of self-stimulation may be sensitive indicators of variations in the affective components of motivated behavior. By studying how willingly an animal presses a bar to stimulate the areas of the brain controlling a particular instinctive act, we may be able to measure the magnitude of the pleasure that accompanies feeding, sexual activity, and all other instinctive behavior.

REFERENCES

ADOLPH, E. F. (1950) Thirst and its inhibition in the stomach. *Amer. J. Physiol., 161,* 374-386.

ANAND, B. K., and BROBECK, J. R. (1951) Hypothalamic control of food intake. *Yale J. Biol. Med., 24,* 123-140.

ANDERSSON, B. (1953) The effect of injections of hypertonic NaCl solutions into different parts of the hypothalamus of goats. *Acta physiol. Scand., 28,* 188-201.

ANDERSSON, B., GALE, C. C., and SUNDSTEN, J. W. (1962) Effects of chronic central cooling on alimentation and thermoregulation. *Acta physiol. Scand., 55,* 177-188.

ANDERSSON, B., and LARSSON, B. (1961) Influence of local temperature changes in the preoptic area and rostral hypothalamus on the regulation of food and water intake. *Acta physiol. Scand., 52,* 75-89.

ANDERSSON, B., and McCANN, S. M. (1955-1956) Drinking, antidiuresis and milk ejection from electrical stimulation within the hypothalamus of the goat. *Acta physiol. Scand., 35,* 191-201.

ANDERSSON, B., and WYRWICKA, W. (1957) The elicitation of a drinking motor-conditioned reaction by electrical stimulation of the hypothalamic "drinking area in the goat." *Acta physiol. Scand., 41,* 194-198.

ANLIKER, J., and MAYER, J. (1956) An operant conditioning technique for studying feeding-fasting patterns in normal and obese mice. *J. appl. Physiol., 8,* 667-670.

BARD, P. (1939) Central nervous mechanisms for emotional behavior patterns in animals. *Res. Publ. Ass. nerv. ment. Dis., 19,* 190-218.

BASH, K. W. (1939) An investigation into a possible organic basis for the hunger drive. *J. comp. Psychol., 28,* 109-134.

604 OPERANT BEHAVIOR

BASMAJIAN, J. V. (1963) Control and training of individual motor units. *Science, 141,* 440-441.

BEACH, F. A. (1956) Characteristics of masculine "sex drive." In M. R. Jones (Ed.), *Nebraska symposium on motivation.* Lincoln: Univ. of Nebraska Press. Pp. 1-32.

BEHANAN, K. T. (1937) *Yoga: A scientific evaluation.* New York: Macmillan.

BÉKÉSY, G. VON. (1947) A new audiometer. *Acta otolaryng. Stockh., 35,* 411-422.

BELLOWS, R. T., and VAN WAGENEN, W. P. (1939) The effect of resection of the olfactory, gustatory, and trigeminal nerves on water drinking in dogs with diabetes insipidus. *Amer. J. Physiol., 126,* 13-19.

BERMANT, G. (1961) Response latencies of female rats during sexual intercourse. *Science, 133,* 1771-1773.

BLOUGH, D. S. (1958) A method for obtaining psychophysical thresholds from the pigeon. *J. exp. Anal. Behav., 1,* 31-43.

BROBECK, J. R. (1948) Food intake as a mechanism of temperature regulation. *Yale. J. Biol. Med., 20,* 545-552.

BROBECK, J. R. (1960) Food and temperature. *Recent progress in hormone research, 16,* 439-466.

BROBECK, J. R., TEPPERMAN, J., and LONG, C. N. H. (1943) Experimental hypothalamic hyperphagia in the albino rat. *Yale J. Biol. Med., 15,* 831-853.

BROOKS, C. McC. (1946) A study of the respiratory quotient in experimental hypothalamic obesity. *Amer. J. Physiol., 147,* 727-734.

BROOKS, C. McC., LOCKWOOD, R. A., and WIGGINS, M. L. (1946) A study of the effect of hypothalamic lesions on the eating habits of the albino rat. *Amer. J. Physiol., 147,* 735-741.

BRUCH, H. (1957) *The importance of overweight.* New York: Norton.

BRUGGER, M. (1943) Fresstrieb als hypothalamisches Symptom. *Helv. Physiol. Acta, 1,* 183-198.

BYKOV, K. M. (1957) *The cerebral cortex and the internal organs.* Ed. & trans. by W. H. Gantt. New York: Chemical Publishing.

CANNON, W. B. (1929) *Bodily changes in pain, hunger, fear and rage.* New York: Appleton-Century-Crofts.

CARTER, A. C., and ROBBINS, J. (1947) The use of hypertonic saline infusions in the differential diagnosis of diabetes insipidus and psychogenic polydipsia. *J. clin. Endocrinol., 7,* 753-766.

CLARK, R., SCHUSTER, C. R., and BRADY, J. V. (1961) Instrumental conditioning of jugular self-infusion in the rhesus monkey. *Science, 133,* 1829-1830.

COHN, C., and JOSEPH, D. (1962) Influence of body weight and body fat on appetite of "normal" lean and obese rats. *Yale J. Biol. Med., 34,* 598-607.

COPPOCK, H. W., and CHAMBERS, R. M. (1954) Reinforcement of position preference by automatic intravenous injections of glucose. *J. comp. physiol. Psychol., 47,* 355-357.

DETHIER, V. G. (1964) Microscopic brains. *Science, 143,* 1138-1145.

DETHIER, V. G., and BODENSTEIN, D. (1958) Hunger in the blowfly. *Z. Tierpsychol., 15,* 129-140.

DETHIER, V. G., and RHOADES, M. V. (1954) Sugar preference-aversion functions for the blowfly. *J. exp. Zool., 126,* 177-204.

EPSTEIN, A. N. (1960) Water intake without the act of drinking. *Science, 131,* 497-498. (a)

EPSTEIN, A. N. (1960) Reciprocal changes in feeding behavior produced by intrahypothalamic chemical injection. *Amer. J. Physiol., 199,* 969-974. (b)

EPSTEIN, A. N., and TEITELBAUM, P. (1962) A watertight swivel joint permitting chronic injection into moving animals. *J. appl. Physiol., 17,* 171-172. (a)

EPSTEIN, A. N., and TEITELBAUM, P. (1962) Regulation of food intake in the absence of taste, smell and other oro-pharyngeal sensations. *J. comp. physiol. Psychol., 55,* 753-759. (b)

FALK, J. L. (1961) Comments on Dr. Teitelbaum's paper. In M. R. Jones (Ed.), *Nebraska symposium on motivation.* Lincoln: Univ. of Nebraska Press. Pp. 65-68. (a)

FALK, J. L. (1961) Production of polydipsia in normal rats by an intermittent food schedule. *Science, 133,* 195-196. (b)

FERSTER, C. B., and SKINNER, B. F. (1957) *Schedules of reinforcement.* New York: Appleton-Century-Crofts.

FISHER, A. E. (1956) Maternal and sexual behavior induced by intracranial chemical stimulation. *Science, 124,* 228-229.

FROHLICH, A. (1904) Ein Fall von Tumor der Hypophysis Cerebri ohne Akromegalie. Trans. by Hilde Bruch. (1940) *Res. Publ. Ass. nerv. ment. Dis., 20,* xvi-xxviii.

FUSCO, M. M., HARDY, J. D., and HAMMEL, H. T. (1961) Interaction of central and peripheral factors in physiological temperature regulation. *Amer. J. Physiol., 200,* 572-580.

GOODMAN, L. S., and GILMAN, A. (1955) *The pharmacological basis of therapeutics.* (2nd. ed.) New York: Macmillan.

GREER, M. A. (1955) Suggestive evidence of a primary "drinking center" in the hypothalamus of the rat. *Proc. Soc. exp. Biol., N.Y., 89,* 59-62.

GROSSMAN, S. P. (1960) Eating or drinking elicited by direct adrenergic or cholinergic stimulation of the hypothalamus. *Science, 132,* 301-302.

GROSSMAN, S. P. (1962) Direct adrenergic and cholinergic stimulation of hypothalamic mechanisms. *Amer. J. Physiol., 202,* 872-882.

HAMILTON, C. L. (1959) Effect of food deprivation on thermal behavior of the rat. *Proc. Soc. exp. Biol., N.Y., 100,* 354-356.

HAMILTON, C. L. (1963) Interactions of food intake and temperature regulation in the rat. *J. comp. physiol. Psychol., 56,* 476-488.

HAMILTON, C. L., and SHERIFF, W., JR. (1959) Thermal behavior of the rat before and after feeding. *Proc. Soc. exp. Biol., N.Y., 102,* 746-748.

HAMMEL, H. T., HARDY, J. D., and FUSCO, M. M. (1960) Thermoregulatory responses to hypothalamic cooling in unanesthetized dogs. *Amer. J. Physiol., 198,* 481-486.

HARRIS, G. W., MICHAEL, R. P., and SCOTT, P. P. (1960) Neurological site of action of stilbesterol in eliciting sexual behavior. *Ciba Found. symposium on the neurological basis of behavior.* Boston: Little, Brown. Pp. 236-254.

HEADLEE, C. P., COPPOCK, H. W., and NICHOLS, J. R. (1955) Apparatus and technique involved in a laboratory method of detecting the addictiveness of drugs. *J. Amer. pharm. Ass.,* scient. ed., *44,* 229-231.

HEATH, R. G., and MICKLE, W. A. (1960) Evaluation of seven years' experience with depth electrode studies in human patients. In E. R. Ramey and D. S. O'Doherty (Eds.), *Electrical studies on the unanesthetized brain.* New York: Hoeber-Harper. Pp. 214-247.

HEFFERLINE, R. F., and KEENAN, B. (1961) Amplitude-induction gradient of a small human operant in an escape-avoidance situation. *J. exp. Anal. Behav., 4,* 41-43.

HELLON, R. F., HARDY, J. D., and SUTHERLAND, K. (1963) Temperature sensitive neurons in the dog's hypothalamus. *The Physiologist, 6,* 199.

HERRNSTEIN, R. J. (1961) Stereotypy and intermittent reinforcement. *Science, 133,* 2067-2069.

HESS, W. R. (1932) *Beiträge z. Physiologie des Hirnstammes I. Die Methodik der lokalisierten Reizung und Ausschaltung subkortikaler Hirnabschnitte.* Leipzig: Georg Thieme.

HETHERINGTON, A. W., and RANSON, S. W. (1939) Experimental hypothalamico-hypophysial obesity in the rat. *Proc. Soc. exp. Biol., N.Y., 41,* 465-466.

HODOS, W. (1961) Progressive ratio as a measure of reward strength. *Science, 134,* 943-944.

HOEBEL, B. G., and TEITELBAUM, P. (1962) Hypothalamic control of feeding and self-stimulation. *Science, 135,* 375-377.

HOLTER, N. J. (1961) New methods for heart studies. *Science, 134,* 1214-1220.

INGELFINGER, F. J. (1944) Late effects of total and subtotal gastrectomy. *New Eng. J. Med., 231,* 321-327.

JANOWITZ, H. D., and GROSSMAN, M. I. (1949) Some factors affecting food intake of normal dogs and dogs with esophagostomy and gastric fistula. *Amer. J. Physiol., 159,* 143-148.

KENNEDY, G. C. (1953) The role of depot fat in the hypothalamic control of food intake in the rat. *Proc. Roy. Soc., Ser. B., 140,* 578-592.

KOH, S. D., and TEITELBAUM, P. (1961) Absolute behavioral taste thresholds in the rat. *J. comp. physiol. Psychol., 54,* 223-229.

LARSSON, S. (1954) On the hypothalamic organization of the nervous mechanism regulating food intake. *Acta physiol. Scand., 32,* Suppl. 115, 7-40.

LARSSON, S., and STROM, L. (1957) Some characteristics of goldthioglucose obesity in the mouse. *Acta physiol. Scand., 38,* 298-308.

LATIES, V. G., and WEISS, B. (1959) Thyroid state and working for heat in the cold. *Amer. J. Physiol., 197,* 1028-1034.

MACKAY, R. S. (1961) Radio telemetering from within the body. *Science, 134,* 1196-1202.

MARGULES, D. L., and OLDS, J. (1962) Identical "feeding" and "rewarding" systems in the lateral hypothalamus of the rat. *Science, 135,* 374-375.

MAYER, J. (1952) The glucostatic theory of regulation of food intake and the problem of obesity. *Bull. N.E. Med. Cen., 14,* 43-49.

MAYER, J. (1955) Regulation of energy intake and body weight: The glucostatic theory and the lipostatic hypothesis. *Ann. N.Y. Acad. Sci., 63,* 15-43.

MILLER, N. E. (1958) Central stimulation and other new approaches to motivation and reward. *Amer. Psychol., 13,* 100-108.

MILLER, N. E., BAILEY, C. J., and STEVENSON, J. A. F. (1950) Decreased "hunger" but increased food intake resulting from hypothalamic lesions. *Science, 112,* 256-259.

MILLER, N. E., and KESSEN, M. L. (1952) Reward effects of food via stomach fistula compared with those via mouth. *J. comp. physiol. Psychol., 45,* 555-564.

MORGAN, C. T., and MORGAN, J. D. (1940) Studies in hunger: II. The relation of gastric denervation and dietary sugar to the effect of insulin upon food intake in the rat. *J. genet. Psychol., 57,* 153-163.

MORGANE, P. J. (1961) Distinct "feeding" and "hunger motivating" systems in the lateral hypothalamus of the rat. *Science, 133,* 887-888.

NAKAYAMA, T., EISENMAN, J. S., and HARDY, J. D. (1961) Single unit activity of anterior hypothalamus during local heating. *Science, 134,* 560-561.

OLDS, J. (1955) Physiological mechanisms of reward. In M. R. Jones (Ed.), *Nebraska symposium on motivation.* Lincoln: Univ. of Nebraska Press. Pp. 73-139.

OLDS, J. (1960) Approach-avoidance dissociations in the rat brain. *Amer. J. Physiol., 199,* 965-968. (a)

OLDS, J. (1960) Differentiation of reward systems in the brain by self-stimulation techniques. In E. R. Ramey and D. S. O'Doherty (Eds.), *Electrical studies on the unanesthetized brain.* New York: Hoeber-Harper. Pp. 17-51. (b)

OLDS, J., TRAVIS, R. P., and SCHWING, R. C. (1960) Topographic organization of hypothalamic self-stimulation function. *J. comp. physiol. Psychol., 53,* 23-32.

PEREZ-CRUET, J. (1962) Conditioning of extrasystoles in humans with respiratory maneuvers as unconditional stimulus. *Science, 137,* 1060-1061.

PETERSON, N. (1960) Control of behavior by presentation of an imprinted stimulus. *Science, 132,* 1395-1396.

PIERCE, J. T., and NUTTAL, R. L. (1961) Self-paced sexual behavior in the female rat. *J. comp. physiol. Psychol., 54,* 310-313.

RAZRAN, G. (1961) The observable unconscious and the inferable conscious in current Soviet psychophysiology: Interoceptive conditioning, semantic conditioning, and the orienting reflex. *Psychol. Rev., 68,* 81-147.

RICHTER, C. P. (1942-1943) Total self-regulatory functions in animals and human beings. *Harvey Lect., 38,* 63-103.

ROZIN, P., and MAYER, J. (1961) Regulation of food intake in the goldfish. *Amer. J. Physiol., 201,* 968-974. (a)

ROZIN, P., and MAYER, J. (1961) Thermal reinforcement and thermoregulatory behavior in the goldfish, carassius auratus. *Science, 134,* 942-943. (b)

SATINOFF, E. (1964) Behavioral thermoregulation in response to local cooling of the rat brain. *Amer. J. Physiol., 206,* 1389-1394.

SHEARN, D. (1962) Operant conditioning of heart rate. *Science, 137,* 530-531.

SHERRINGTON, C. S. (1906) *The integrative action of the nervous system.* Forge Village, Mass.: Murray Printing Company. Issued as a Yale Paperbound, Yale Univ. Press, 1961.

SKINNER, B. F. (1938) *The behavior of organisms.* New York: Appleton-Century-Crofts.

SKINNER, B. F. (1953) *Science and human behavior.* New York: Macmillan. Pp. 190-191.

STEIN, L. (1958) Secondary reinforcement established with subcortical stimulation. *Science, 127,* 466-467.

STEIN, L. (1962) Effects and interactions of imipramine, chlorpromazine, reserpine, and amphetamine on self-stimulation: Possible neurophysiological basis of depression. In J. Wortis (Ed.), *Recent advances in biological psychiatry.* Vol. 4. New York: Plenum Press. Pp. 288-307.

STEIN, L., and RAY, O. S. (1959) Self-regulation of brain-stimulating current intensity in the rat. *Science, 130,* 570-572.

STEIN, L., and RAY, O. S. (1960) Brain stimulation reward "thresholds" self-determined in the rat. *Psychopharmacologia, 1,* 251-256.

STELLAR, E., and HILL, J. H. (1952) The rat's rate of drinking as a function of water deprivation. *J. comp. physiol. Psychol., 45,* 96-102.

STEVENSON, J. A. F., and RIXON, R. H. (1957) Environmental temperature and deprivation of food and water on the spontaneous activity of rats. *Yale J. Biol. Med., 29,* 575-584.

STONE, C. P., and KING, F. A. (1954) Effects of hypophysectomy on behavior in rats: I. Preliminary survey. *J. comp. physiol. Psychol., 47,* 213-219.

TEITELBAUM, P. (1955) Sensory control of hypothalamic hyperphagia. *J. comp. physiol. Psychol., 48,* 156-163.

TEITELBAUM, P. (1957) Random and food-directed activity in hyperphagic and normal rats. *J. comp. physiol. Psychol., 50,* 486-490.

TEITELBAUM, P. (1961) Disturbances in feeding and drinking behavior after hypothalamic lesions. In M. R. Jones (Ed.), *Nebraska symposium on motivation.* Lincoln: Univ. of Nebraska Press. Pp. 39-68.

TEITELBAUM, P. (1962) Motivational correlates of hypothalamic activity. *XXII International Congress of Physiological Sciences.* Leiden, Netherlands.

TEITELBAUM, P., and CAMPBELL, B. A. (1958) Ingestion patterns in hyperphagic and normal rats. *J. comp. physiol. Psychol., 51,* 135-141.

TEITELBAUM, P., and EPSTEIN, A. N. (1962) The lateral hypothalamic syndrome: Recovery of feeding and drinking after lateral hypothalamic lesions. *Psychol. Rev., 69,* 74-90. (a)

TEITELBAUM, P., and EPSTEIN, A. N. (1962) Production of obesity in the normal rat. Film presented at meeting of Eastern Psychol. Ass., Atlantic City. (b)

TEITELBAUM, P., and EPSTEIN, A. N. (1963) The role of taste and smell in the regulation of food and water intake. In Y. Zotterman (Ed.), *Olfaction and taste.* Oxford: Pergamon Press.

TEITELBAUM, P., and STELLAR, E. (1954) Recovery from the failure to eat produced by hypothalamic lesions. *Science, 120,* 894-895.

THOMPSON, T. I. (1963) Visual reinforcement in Siamese fighting fish. *Science, 141,* 55-57.

TINBERGEN, N. (1951) *The study of instinct.* London: Oxford.

TINBERGEN, N., and PERDECK, A. C. (1950) On the stimulus situation releasing the begging response in the newly hatched herring gull chick (Larus a. argentatus Pont.). *Behavior, 3,* 1-38.

TOWBIN, E. J. (1949) Gastric distension as a factor in the satiation of thirst in esophagostomized dogs. *Amer. J. Physiol., 159,* 533-541.

VAN SOMMERS, P. (1962) Oxygen-motivated behavior in the goldfish, carassius auratus. *Science, 137,* 678-679.

VAN SOMMERS, P. (1963) Carbon dioxide escape and avoidance behavior in the brown rat. *J. comp. physiol. Psychol., 56,* 584-589. (a)

VAN SOMMERS, P. (1963) Air-motivated behavior in the turtle. *J. comp. physiol. Psychol., 56,* 590-596. (b)

WALD, G., and JACKSON, B. (1944) Activity and nutritional deprivation. *Proc. nat. Acad. Sci., Wash., 30,* 255-263.

WEEKS, J. R. (1962) Experimental morphine addiction: Method for automatic intravenous injections in unrestrained rats. *Science, 138,* 143-144.

WEISS, B. (1957) Pantothenic acid deprivation and the thermal behavior of the rat. *Amer. J. clin. Nutrition, 5,* 125-128. (a)

WEISS, B. (1957) Thermal behavior of the subnourished and pantothenic-acid-deprived rat. *J. comp. physiol. Psychol., 50,* 481-485. (b)

WEISS, B., and LATIES, V. G. (1961) Behavioral thermoregulation. *Science, 133,* 1338-1344.

WILLIAMS, D. R., and TEITELBAUM, P. (1956) Control of drinking behavior by means of an operant-conditioning technique. *Science, 124,* 1294-1296.

WILLIAMS, D. R., and TEITELBAUM, P. (1959) Some observations on the starvation resulting from lateral hypothalamic lesions. *J. comp. physiol. Psychol., 52,* 458-465.

WYRWICKA, W., and DOBRZECKA, C. (1960) Relationship between feeding and satiation centers of the hypothalamus. *Science, 132,* 805-806.

YEATS-BROWN, F. (1930) *The lives of a Bengal Lancer.* New York: Viking.

14

Operant Methodology and the Experimental Production of Altered Physiological States

Joseph V. Brady

INTRODUCTION

Among the many areas of psychological inquiry upon which the technological developments of operant methodology have been brought to bear, few have had a shorter laboratory history than that with which this chapter is concerned. Although it has long been recognized in so-called "psychosomatic" circles that the behavior of an organism can profoundly influence its physiological status, experimental laboratory models encompassing the many critical and complex aspects of such "psychophysiological" relationships have been slow to emerge. For the most part, laboratory research in this area has focused almost exclusively upon respondent conditioning situations and their physiological correlates, with little or no attention to the role of instrumental behavior in the development of such bodily changes. As early as 1879, for example, I. P. Pavlov reported changes in cardiovascular function related to behavioral conditioning involving his classical procedures with dogs; and a host of subsequent studies with both animals and humans have continued to focus upon respondent methodology for such experimental analyses (Cannon, 1929; Gantt, 1944; 1960; Lacey, 1956; Liddel, 1956; Mahl, 1949; 1952; Malmo, 1950; Pavlov, 1879). The methodological contribution of these important studies has been well documented and will not be elaborated further in the present treatment of operant procedures.

During the past decade experimental interest in the application of instrumental procedures to the analysis of psychophysiological relationships has been developing at an accelerated pace. To a rather obvious extent, this development has paralleled the emergence of technological advances in operant methodology, but experimental efforts in this general area of instrumental conditioning and the production of altered physiological states have not been the exclusive domain of devoted operant research workers. For the most part, relatively transient respiratory and cardiovascular changes have provided a major focus for such psychophysiological studies. Recently, however, more durable physiological alterations involving the endocrine systems have been related to instrumental performance requirements, and a final group of studies to be reviewed in the chapter will deal with chronic gastrointestinal changes and infectious disease processes.

TRANSIENT PHYSIOLOGICAL CHANGES

Respiratory and Cardiovascular Effects

Scattered research reports over the past ten years have called attention to somewhat transient physiological changes related to performance in instrumental conditioning experiments. For the most part, the respiratory and cardiovascular effects described tend to be confined to experimental periods during which performance is required, and appear to represent physiological responses conditioned to stimuli produced by the instrumental behavior. Eldridge (1954), for example, reported changes in respiratory rate associated with instrumental avoidance responding in rats. The animals were confined on a small perch and a head movement was required to lift a panel and avoid illumination of an aversive bright light directly before their eyes. Respiration was recorded continuously and the rate was measured in temporal relationship to the panel-lifting avoidance response. In all cases, respiration rate increased during conditioning and decreased during extinction of such avoidance behavior. But the extent to which these physiological changes can be reliably attributed to the avoidance performance requirement per se, as distinguished from unconditioned responses to the bright light, is far from clear.

Blood pressure and plasma pepsinogen changes have also been reported by Shapiro and Horn (1955) to be associated which intermittent punishment of an instrumental feeding response in cats. The behavioral procedure used in these experiments followed closely the instrumental methods developed by Masserman (1943) involving discriminated response chains with both lever-pressing and lid-lifting components. Shapiro and Horn reported slight elevations in blood pressure and mild declines in plasma pepsinogen levels in animals subjected to intermittent punishment (air blast or electric shock) of the terminal lid-lifting member of the response chain. The precise temporal relationship between exposure to this conditioning procedure and determination of the physiological changes, however, represents but one of the procedural areas which fails to receive adequate coverage in this early report.

Wenzel (1961) has reported changes in heart rate associated with the instrumental performance of cats in a two-lever operant response situation. The animals were trained on a stimulus and response discrimination problem which required pressing on one lever in the presence of one auditory stimulus to produce food, and pressing on a second lever in the presence of a different auditory stimulus to avoid shock. Performance on the food lever in the presence of the appropriate auditory stimulus was associated with acceleration of heart rate, while responding on the avoidance lever in the presence of the second auditory stimulus was correlated with a marked deceleration of the heart rate. There is no indication in this report, however, that the effects described were any more than transient physiological alterations with a rapid reversal to normal levels upon termination of the specific situational requirements of the experiment. In fact, the author clearly indicates that such changes could not even be elicited when the same two auditory stimuli were presented to trained animals outside the experimental apparatus. It is at least clear in this experiment, however, that lever responding per se (as distinguished from the conditions under which the responses were emitted) could not account for the alterations in heart rate, since the same lever-pressing behavior produced acceleration of heart rate under conditions of food reinforcement and deceleration of heart rate during shock avoidance.

More recently, two additional experimental reports have described heart rate changes related to the instrumental performance of rats in an operant setting (Bélanger & Feldman, 1962; Hahn, Stern, & McDonald, 1962). In both instances, the primary focus of the research efforts appears to have been upon the effects of systematically varied levels of water deprivation upon the heart rate, but the results described clearly implicate the instrumental bar-pressing performance as a most significant factor in producing elevations in heart rate. The Bélanger and Feldman (1962) experiment involved ten-minute exposures to continuous water reinforcement in a more or less conventional operant behavior box, during which time heart rate was recorded via wire electrodes implanted above each shoulder. Data reported from experimental sessions following 12, 24, 36, 48, 60, and 72 hours of water deprivation show a clear increase in heart rate with increasing durations of deprivation. Changes in the lever-pressing response rate under these same conditions, however, are described by an inverted U-shaped function, with intervals of deprivation up to 48 hours producing an increase in lever pressing and intervals of 60 and 72 hours producing lowered response frequencies. An essentially similar U-shaped function was described by Hahn, Stern, and McDonald (1962) for experiments involving levels of water deprivation up to 96 hours, when heart rate was recorded in a comparable manner during ten-minute sessions on continuous reinforcement in an instrumental lever-pressing situation. When heart rate was recorded following these same extended periods of deprivation, but without the lever-pressing requirement for access to water during the ten-minute experimental sessions, no such progressive increases in heart rate with increasing levels of deprivation could be demonstrated. Clearly, these results implicate the instrumental performance as an essential factor in production of the heart rate changes, although both reports confirm the transient nature of these cardiovascular effects.

Two reports by Malmo (1961) and Perez-Cruet, Black, and Brady (1963) describing heart rate changes in rats during electrical self-stimulation of the brain bear at least some indirect relevance to the application of operant methodology in the analysis of altered physiological states. In both experiments, rats with chronically implanted electrodes maintained stable lever-pressing rates for brief electric shocks in the brain while heart rate was recorded concurrently. The operant performance appeared to produce differential effects upon the heart rate as a function of the specific electrode location in the brain, suggesting only an incidental and obviously arbitrary relationship between the lever-pressing behavior per se and the cardiovascular changes. Interestingly, however, when the lever-pressing response produced electrical stimulation of the septal region of the brain, deceleration of the heart rate was observed (Malmo, 1961; Perez-Cruet, Black, & Brady, 1963), and when hypothalamic stimulation reinforced the lever response, acceleration of heart rate occurred (Perez-Cruet, Black, and Brady, 1963).

Methodologically, a recent report by Perez-Cruet, Tolliver, Dunn, Marvin, and Brady (1963) would seem to represent a significant contribution to the experimental analysis of psychophysiological relationships involving operant behavior and cardiovascular changes. The report describes a method for concurrent measurement of heartbeats and lever responses utilizing cumulative recorder techniques for developing graphic representations of both rates. The EKG signal activates a fixed trigger circuit and relay driver through a DC amplifier and effectively steps a standard cumulative recorder. Illustrative data presented in their report show the effects of instrumental avoidance behavior in producing heart rate changes in the rhesus monkey. The EKG was obtained through chronically implanted tantalum electrodes placed on the right and left arms and brought out subcutaneously to a fixed pedestal secured to the animal's skull. The three monkeys used in these experiments were restrained in primate chairs (Mason, 1958) and trained on an avoidance procedure which provided for the delivery of brief electric shocks to the monkey's feet every 20 seconds unless a lever response during that interval delayed the shock another 20 seconds (Sidman, 1953). Concurrent cumulative heart rate and avoidance response rate recording obtained during experimental sessions of several hours' duration clearly show the effects of instrumental avoidance performance in producing consistent heart rate increases even during periods when no shocks were programmed (avoidance extinction). Increases in heart rate of the greatest magnitude, however, were obtained in experiments in which shocks were programmed aperiodically and independently of the animal's lever-pressing performance (free shock), and produced maximal increases in the avoidance response rate. The reliability of the method for recording cardiovascular changes described in this report was verified by means of simultaneous records taken on three channels of a Grass polygraph which confirmed activation of the cumulative recorder by every R-wave deflection of the EKG and a mean heart rate increase of 39 beats/min. from the control (138 beats/min.) to avoidance (177 beats/min.) periods. As with previous reports reflecting such cardiovascular changes produced by instrumental performance, however, the heart rate was observed to revert to normal levels upon termination of the experimental avoidance sessions.

Neurophysiological Changes

The search for neurophysiological correlates of behavioral processes has traditionally focused upon the effects of brain lesions and, more recently, upon the electrical activity of the nervous system as reflected in the electroencephalogram. Only within the past few years, however, has attention been directed toward the experimental analysis of such brain wave changes in relation to instrumental performance. In 1959, three reports appeared describing electroencephalographic changes related to instrumental conditioning procedures. Operant methodology contributed significantly to at least two of these experiments. Anliker (1959), for example, described a procedure for analyzing the alpha-frequency data of the brain waves in the form of cumulative records and comparing such electroencephalographic activity with operant response data. Surface potentials from transoccipital electrodes were recorded in human subjects required to press a modified telegraph key at regular intervals in an escape-avoidance situation involving bursts of white noise of increasing intensity. Cumulative recordings of the operant response showed an orderly and progressive increase in interresponse times preceding onset of the auditory stimulus, while concurrent brain wave records showed a corresponding fall in alpha activity during the pause between responses. Significantly, however, emission of the lever-pressing response was associated with an increase in alpha activity, suggesting a possible contributory role of the instrumental performance in the production of at least these transient neurophysiological alterations.

Somewhat less direct effects of operant performance upon brain wave activity were reported by Porter, Conrad, and Brady (1959) in an experiment involving electrical self-stimulation of the brain with laboratory primates. Nine rhesus monkeys restrained in primate chairs (Mason, 1958) and implanted with electrode arrays in deep limbic system structures of the brain were reinforced with brain stimulation (100 cycles/sec., 5-20 ma, 0.2 ms pulse duration, 0.5 sec. train duration) for every lever press on a modified telegraph key. Some 29 electrode placements in various limbic-system structures of the nine monkeys were found to yield positively rewarding effects in response to electrical self-stimulation and 15 of these placements consistently showed electroencephalographic patterns which could be correlated in systematic ways with characteristics of the self-stimulation lever-pressing behavior. Of particular interest in this regard would seem to be the findings relating the appearance of specific electrical patterns to changes in the lever-pressing response rate, suggesting that these response-produced electrical changes may actually play some role in maintaining the operant behavior. With electrode placements in the medial forebrain bundle at the pre-optic level, for example, manifestations of spike and slow-wave activity appeared to be positively correlated with the lever-pressing rate. And in the case of several hippocampal placements, bursts of lever-pressing responses frequently produced relatively long seizure discharge patterns followed by the maintenance of lever responding at consistently high rates. Repetition of the response-produced seizures with only brief time intervals between their reappearances resulted in markedly decreased durations for the seizure discharge patterns and ultimately in their complete disappearance for extended periods. During these refractory intervals when lever pressing did not produce the seizure pattern, the response rate dropped to near zero values. With recovery from this refractory period (usually within 30 minutes from the time of the last seizure discharge) lever pressing again produced hippocampal seizure activity and high rates of responding reappeared, suggesting that the high lever-pressing rates were being maintained by production of the seizures. With electrode placements in the amygdala, however, response-produced seizure activity had the effect of suppressing the lever-pressing rate completely for prolonged periods. Clearly, the operant performance utilized in these experiments can be seen to play only a very indirect role in the production of these somewhat transient neurophysiological alterations because of the rather arbitrary link between lever responding and the passage of electrical current through the brain. The application of operant methodology to the experimental analysis of such psychophysiological relationships,. however, provides a degree of control over the behavioral processes involved in such studies which has frequently been absent in traditional neurophysiological investigations.

John and Killam (1959) also reported changes in electrical activity recorded from deep brain structures in the cat related to acquisition of an instrumental avoidance performance in a two-compartment hurdle box. Although it is difficult to arrive at a firm conclusion about the performance-produced nature of the electrophysiological changes they describe, increases in the frequency of the instrumentally conditioned hurdle-jumping response were accompanied by definite shifts in the electrical response patterns recorded from specific limbic-reticular brain sites during the actual behavioral tests. The most marked changes observed were increases in the activity of the amygdala (which displayed characteristic bursts of brain waves) and decreases in electrical responses recorded from the reticular formation during experimental sessions involving avoidance performances without any errors. Many additional methodological and theoretical contributions are to be gleaned from this excellent experimental report, but there is unfortunately little more to be found of direct relevance to the topic of primary interest in the present volume.

In a similar but somewhat more directly relevant effort, Hearst, Beer, Sheatz, and Galambos (1960) recorded electrical activity from chronically implanted deep-brain electrodes in monkeys during performance under several different conditioning procedures, including instrumental lever pressing for both sugar pellets and shock avoidance. The animals were restrained in primate chairs and the evoked electrical responses to auditory click stimuli were recorded from electrodes in the caudate nucleus, hippocampus, medial geniculate body, and cochlear nucleus. In addition to changes in the amplitude of the evoked responses from these electrode placements recorded during a series of "Pavlovian" conditioning experiments (pairing the click stimuli with the delivery of food or electric shock), Hearst *et al.* report effects of operant discrimination performance upon the click-evoked EEG activity. When the animals were trained to obtain sugar pellets for lever pressing on an FI 1 schedule with the clicks as an S^D, performance of the instrumental lever-pressing behavior was reported to suppress the amplitude of the click-evoked EEG responses. Similarly, performance on a Sidman avoidance procedure (five-second response-shock interval) with clicks as an S^D produced marked suppression of the click-evoked EEG responses, although a particular EEG pattern was consistently noted in hippocampal records taken during avoidance performance. Interestingly, this characteristic hippocampal rhythm appeared to be closely correlated with rapid bursts of lever pressing although similar effects could not be found in any of the other deep-brain areas monitored.

Most recently, Ross, Hodos, and Brady (1962) reported an experiment in which EEG activity recorded from several chronically implanted deep-brain electrodes was analyzed in relation to the operant performance of rhesus monkeys on a multiple schedule. The animals were restrained in primate chairs and performed during 15-minute alternating periods (separated by 15-minute "time-outs") on a Sidman shock-avoidance schedule (20-second response-shock and shock-shock intervals) and a spaced responding (drl) schedule for food pellets which required that a lever response follow the preceding response by at least 21 seconds in order to be reinforced. A small but consistent increase in the frequency of the EEG waves was observed to develop during performance on the drl and avoidance components of the schedule as compared with the lack of such a change during the "time-out" periods when no lever pressing occurred. Despite these frequency changes, however, the EEG as recorded from the several brain loci in this study did not reflect the gross differences in performance required by the drl and avoidance schedules. Clearly, the most parsimonious explanation of these changes would seem to be in terms of nonspecific "alerting" patterns frequently observed in the EEG, a conclusion which is supported by the results of several drug studies reported in this same paper.

DURABLE PHYSIOLOGICAL ALTERATIONS

Alimentary Functions

Perhaps the first published reference to the direct application of operant methodology in experimental production of more durable physiological alterations is to be found in the paper by Williams and Teitelbaum (1956) on the "Control of drinking behavior by means of an operant-conditioning technique." In these experiments, rats were trained to lick fluid from the end of a tube in order to avoid electric shocks to the feet. Each lick postponed the shock for 15 seconds and the rats could effectively avoid all shocks by licking from the end of the tube at least once every 15 seconds. Animals exposed to this forced drinking procedure on an alternating one hour "on," one hour "off" schedule, 24 hours a day for 20 days, were observed to consume almost twice their normal daily volume of a liquid nutrient and virtually to double their body weights over this brief period. In addition to the production of marked obesity in normal rats using this operant conditioning technique, the authors reported that they also succeeded in forcing ingestion of liquids normally refused by their experimental animals (quinine) and in controlling and altering the pattern and volume of fluid ingestion in normal satiated rats. Subsequent experiments investigated the effects of amphetamine administration on forced drinking maintained with this technique, and demonstrated greatly increased fluid intake levels following drug administration, even though amphetamine normally depresses thirst-induced water consumption (Teitelbaum & Derks, 1958).

A related series of observations was reported by Clark and Polish (1960) in experiments with rhesus monkeys given access to alcohol during instrumental performance on a Sidman shock-avoidance schedule. Measures of water intake and intake of a 20 percent alcohol solution in water were obtained from the animals restrained in primate chairs before, during, and after exposure to the avoidance procedure. Under several different testing conditions involving the availability of alcohol alone, water alone, and both water and alcohol simultaneously, the monkeys consistently drank more alcohol when pressing the lever to avoid shock on an alternating one-hour work, one-hour rest schedule (one-second R-S and S-S) than during the pre-avoidance baseline period. Although appropriate controls for the effects of shock alone in the absence of an avoidance requirement were not included in this study, the increased alcohol intake level remained elevated during a prolonged post-avoidance period of several weeks after the lever-pressing performance was no longer required to avoid shocks. And this increased alcohol intake level was not accompanied by an increase in the water intake level during either phase of the study. Clark and Polish also report that this instrumental response-produced alteration in alcohol intake was also reflected in a changed intake pattern both during and after the avoidance phase of the experiment. Before avoidance conditioning, the monkeys drank alcohol at a fairly uniform rate throughout the day, but during the avoidance and post-avoidance periods, they drank the major portion of their daily alcohol intake within two or three hours after exposure to the refilled bottle. Furthermore, when alcohol and water were simultaneously available during the pre-avoidance phase, the animals invariably drank 20 to 30 ml of water before taking any alcohol. During the avoidance and post-avoidance phases of the experiment, the monkeys consumed large amounts of alcohol before drinking any water.

Neuroendocrinological Effects

Unlike most of the behaviorally produced respiratory and cardiovascular alterations which reportedly endure only as long as the instrumental performance is maintained, endocrinological effects associated with such behavioral conditioning procedures are apparently somewhat less transient. A programmatic effort involving a systematic analysis of operant procedures in relation to such physiological processes is described in a series of reports from the laboratories of the Walter Reed Army Institute of Research. The first of these (Mason, Brady, & Sidman, 1957) described experiments in which pituitary-adrenocortical activity in rhesus monkeys was related to behavioral performance on several different schedules of reinforcement. Plasma 17-hydroxycorticosteroid (17-OH-CS) levels provided the index of ACTH secretion (Harwood & Mason, 1956) and behavioral performances were generated and maintained using both appetitive and aversive control procedures. In these initial experiments, monkeys reinforced with food on either a continuous or an FR schedule displayed no elevations in plasma 17-OH-CS levels during the course of an experimental session. Nor was there any evidence of an adrenocortical response in the monkeys when the reinforcement schedules were abruptly shifted from low to high fixed ratios and even to extinction. Two of the behavioral procedures reported in this study, however, did produce near-maximal rates of elevation in plasma 17-OH-CS levels.

One of the effective procedures was a modification of the Estes-Skinner conditioned suppression technique (Estes & Skinner, 1941). While lever pressing for food on a VI schedule, monkeys were given occasional unavoidable shocks, each shock preceded by a warning stimulus. The animals typically ceased pressing the lever when the warning stimuli were presented, and all five animals in this part of the study consistently showed marked increases in plasma 17-OH-CS levels during the experimental sessions. Significantly, this increased adrenocortical activity occurred even though shock was never administered during experimental sessions in which hormone measurements were made. Within one hour after termination of such a "conditioned anxiety" session, however, plasma 17-OH-CS levels had returned to pre-experimental baseline values in virtually all cases. A further analysis of this relationship between conditioned suppression and steroid elevations showed that repeated doses of reserpine (0.75 mg/kg) administered 20 to 22 hours before the experimental sessions markedly attenuated the "anxiety" response and eliminated the steroid elevation (Mason & Brady, 1956).

The second effective procedure reported in these experiments was conditioned avoidance without an exteroceptive warning stimulus and with an R-S interval of 20 seconds (Sidman, 1953). Performance on such an avoidance schedule for a period of two hours was invariably associated with two- to four-fold rises in corticosteroid levels for all four animals in this part of the study as illustrated in Figure 1, even in those experiments where the monkey successfully avoided all shocks. Although plasma 17-OH-CS levels were again observed to return to pre-experimental baseline values within a few hours after termination of the avoidance session, repeated exposures with two of the animals during seven consecutive weekly sessions clearly demonstrated the persistence of this pituitary-adrenocortical response to the avoidance requirement. And a recent report from the same Walter Reed laboratories (Sidman, Mason, Brady, & Thach, 1962) has focused upon a more quantitative clarification of the relations between the instrumental avoidance behavior and pituitary-adrenocortical activity.

In the first of a series of five experiments reported in this paper, the effects of varying the R-S interval of the avoidance requirement were evaluated in relation to changes in steroid levels. The general picture suggested that the higher rates of lever pressing produced by shorter R-S intervals were accompanied by higher steroid levels. Some striking discrepancies were observed to occur, however, in the detailed relationship between the magnitude of the behavioral and hormonal changes, and it was not clear whether these transient alterations in the physiological status of the two monkeys in the experiment could be accounted for in terms of changes in the R-S interval, shock frequency, or rate of avoidance responding. The second experiment involving a comparison between discriminated and non-discriminated avoidance in relation to steroid changes, however, succeeded in holding the R-S interval constant while demonstrating covariation of the lever-pressing rate and steroid level. Shock frequency again appeared to play a strong determining role in both the steroid and lever-pressing rate increases, a relationship which was readily corroborated in the following experiment. Three monkeys were maintained on an R-S interval of two seconds for several sessions in this third experiment during which moderate

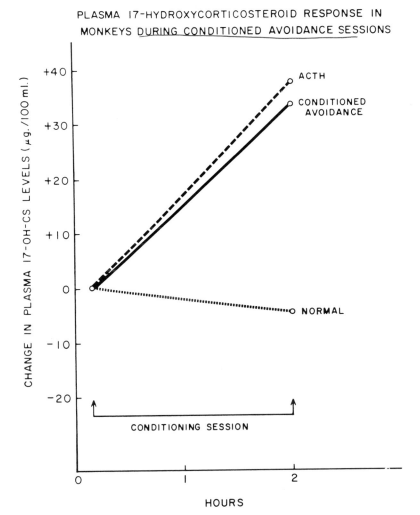

PLASMA 17-HYDROXYCORTICOSTEROID RESPONSE IN
MONKEYS <u>DURING CONDITIONED AVOIDANCE</u> SESSIONS

Figure 1. Plasma 17-hydroxycorticosteroid response in monkeys during two-hour performance on Sidman avoidance. The heavy dotted line labeled "ACTH" shows the rate of steroid rise over a two-hour period following only an I.V. injection of 16 mg/kg ACTH. The heavy solid line labeled "conditioned avoidance" compares this with the rate of steroid elevation during a two-hour exposure to the shock avoidance contingency. The "normal" levels for a similar two-hour control period are represented by the smaller dotted line in the lower portion of the figure (from Mason, Brady, & Sidman, 1957).

elevations in steroid levels were observed. In subsequent sessions, "free" or unavoidable shocks were administered to the animals at a rate of one every five minutes, even though the animals were successfully postponing most of the avoidable shocks. In all cases both lever-pressing rates and steroid levels showed marked elevations in response to the free-shock procedure. Removal of the free shocks brought both the response rates and steroid changes back to their former levels in the one monkey with which this reversal procedure was carried out.

The final two experiments in this series represent a heroic, if somewhat unsuccessful, attempt to disentangle the independent effects of lever-pressing rate and shock frequency upon the steroid response. The fourth experiment evaluated changes in steroid level in a situation where shock frequency was kept constant while the rate of lever pressing declined. This was accomplished by means of an extended avoidance-extinction procedure with accompanying brief, unavoidable shocks superimposed every two minutes. When the lever-pressing rate had declined to almost zero, despite the maintenance of a relatively high shock frequency by administration of the free shocks, steroid elevations were virtually absent during the experimental sessions, clearly implicating the animal's lever-pressing rate as at least one determinant of the steroid change. This same experiment, however, further demonstrated that shock frequency could not be ruled out as a second determinant of the steroid output, since an increase in shock frequency following reinstatement of the avoidance procedure did produce a steroid response. After extended exposure to extinction, a single two-hour avoidance session (20-second R-S and S-S), during which no lever responses were emitted, produced a shock rate six times greater than the free-shock procedure and a near maximal rise in steroid levels. Finally, in the fifth experiment, the avoidance response rate was manipulated by a stimulus control procedure involving a warning stimulus in a well-established discriminated avoidance performance. This reaffirmed the finding that the lever-pressing behavior per se could activate the pituitary-adrenocortical system, independently of the shocks. Frequent presentation of the warning stimulus generated a relatively high response rate without changing the shock frequency, and a substantial steroid elevation was elicited even though not a single shock was received during the two-hour experimental sessions.

Several more recent research reports from the Walter Reed group have been concerned with the problem of behaviorally induced endocrine effects, emphasizing pattern changes which involve multiple hormone measurements. Patterns of corticosteroid and pepsinogen levels in rhesus monkeys have been analyzed in relation to performance on the Sidman avoidance procedure during continuous experimental sessions of 72 hours' duration (Mason, Brady, Polish, Bauer, Robinson, Rose, & Taylor, 1961). Although the plasma 17-hydroxycorticosteroid levels showed the expected substantial rate of elevation throughout the 72-hour avoidance session, plasma pepsinogen levels were consistently depressed below baseline values during this same period. Significantly, however, the post-avoidance recovery period for all of the animals in this study was characterized by a marked and pro-

longed elevation of pepsinogen levels which endured for several days beyond the 48-hour post-avoidance interval required for recovery of the pre-
avoidance corticosteroid baseline. Concurrent biochemical measurements of
plasma 17-hydroxycorticosteroids, nor-epinephrine, and epinephrine levels
during performance on several different operant conditioning procedures
were also described in a recent paper by Mason, Mangan, Brady, Conrad,
and Rioch (1961). Under conditions similar to those studied in earlier experiments (Mason, Brady, & Sidman, 1957), both the Estes-Skinner conditioned suppression technique and Sidman avoidance during sessions of
only 30 minutes' duration were observed to produce consistent elevations in   /\/β
both 17-hydroxycorticosteroid and nor-epinephrine levels, with little or no
change in plasma epinephrine levels. Marked epinephrine elevations were
apparent, however, in studies which measured hormone changes in monkeys during relatively brief ten-minute intervals preceding the start of an
experimental session in which the peformance requirements were varied and
unpredictable. The animals in these latter experiments had been trained on
a series of multiple-schedule procedures with conditioned suppression, Sidman avoidance, discriminated punishment, VI food reinforcement alone,
and S^Δ or "time-out" components, all under the control of different stimulus
conditions (colored lights, clicks, etc.). Sessions on such multiple schedules
were initiated by different components presented in random order on different days, and dramatic alterations in the hormone pattern were observed
during the ten-minute interval immediately preceding these sessions. The
withdrawal of blood from the monkey's vein obviously served as a warning
signal that the performance session would begin ten minutes hence. Significantly, such epinephrine elevations could not be observed when the experimental session began immediately following withdrawal of the blood sample,
regardless of the multiple-schedule component which initiated the performance. Even in those experiments involving large epinephrine elevations
during the ten-minute pre-session "waiting" periods, blood samples taken   /\/β
within one and a half minutes following presentation of the stimulus signaling the first multiple-schedule component revealed precipitous drops in the
epinephrine levels which consistently remained low throughout the rest of
the session.

Most recently, this "endocrine pattern" approach has been extended to
include a broader spectrum of hormonal changes in relation to instrumental
performance requirements in the rhesus monkey (Mason, Brady, Robinson,
Taylor, Tolson, & Mougey, 1961). Alterations in thyroid, gonadal, and
adrenal hormone secretion patterns were produced by continuous 72-hour
experimental sessions on Sidman avoidance, and the biochemical consequences of exposure to this behavioral stress were detectable for prolonged
periods following its termination. The 17-hydroxycorticosteroid, epinephrine,
and nor-epinephrine levels were at least twice the baseline value during the
avoidance session, but returned to normal within two to six days. Andro-

sterone and estrone levels dropped to below half the baseline value during avoidance but showed substantial rebound changes above baseline from three to six days following completion of the session. There was little change in the thyroid levels during the initial portions of the avoidance performance period, but a gradual elevation throughout the session produced a peak value early in the post-avoidance recovery period which did not return to baseline for a full three weeks following termination of the three-day session.

The operant avoidance technique, reliably producing alterations in hormone levels, has also been used to advantage in studies involving neurological mechanisms controlling endocrine balance. Mason, Nauta, Brady, Robinson, and Sachar (1961) have reported that the increase in 17-hydroxy-corticosteroid levels, which invariably accompanies Sidman avoidance performance during sessions of two hours in length, fails to appear in monkeys following bilateral removal of the amygdaloid nuclei. Although this suppressing effect of amygdalectomy on the steroid response to avoidance develops only four to six weeks post-operatively, elevations in the hormone levels cannot be observed as long as one year after surgery during performance on the standard Sidman schedule. When a free-shock procedure is superimposed upon the avoidance baseline, however, a marked elevation of the 17-hydroxycorticosteroids does appear, indicating that the system is capable of responding under somewhat extreme conditions even in the absence of the presumed modulation or facilitation normally provided by the limbic amygdala structures.

This rather extensive series of endocrinological-behavioral studies would seem to represent one of the more systematic applications of operant methodology to the experimental analysis of psychophysiological relationships. The emphasis upon neuroendocrinological processes in such an analysis reflects the obvious importance of these critical physiological systems in the mediation of many basic psychosomatic relationships. And the studies summarized in this section provide at least the basis for a more operational definition of the behavioral interactions which produce specified alterations in this critical mediating system. Certainly, continuing attempts to define more precisely the nature of these mediating processes in the production of altered physiological states and pathological somatic conditions must build upon these somewhat preliminary applications of behavioral analysis techniques to the study of neuroendocrine processes.

SOMATIC PATHOLOGY

The experimental analysis of controlling relations between the behavioral interactions of an organism with its external environment and the production of chronic somatic changes presents many difficult problems. The research literature on this topic, particularly as it relates to the application of operant conditioning methods, is sparse indeed. One obvious limitation on laboratory investigations in this area is imposed by the generally irreversible character of the behaviorally produced somatic changes and the consequent restriction on experimental manipulations of the type which are so appealing to workers using operant methods. This stricture further presents elaborate and cumbersome experimental design problems involving numerous control groups to provide assurances that the presumably relevant behavioral condition is in fact responsible for the observed changes. In a series of experiments first reported in 1956, for example, Sawrey and Weisz described an instrumental "conflict" procedure for producing gastric ulcers in rats. The animals in these experiments lived for a period of 30 days in an experimental chamber which required the crossing of electrically charged grids in order for the rats to obtain food or water. Although exposure to this "conflict" was reported by these authors to produce a significantly higher incidence of gastric lesions than exposure to comparable periods of food and water deprivation without "conflict," subsequent studies have suggested that interactions involving hunger, fear, shock, weight loss, and even social experience play a significant role in the production of altered physiological states under such conditions (Conger, Sawrey, & Turrell, 1958; Sawrey, 1961; Sawrey, Conger, & Turrell, 1956; Weisz, 1957).

More recently, Rasmussen, Marsh, and Brill (1957) have reported a series of experiments with mice involving the effects of avoidance learning on susceptibility to infectious agents. The animals were exposed to six-hour experimental sessions in a shuttlebox which required them to cross a barrier from one section of a grid floor to another upon presentation of a warning signal in order to avoid shock. Daily six-hour sessions on this procedure, with avoidance trials every five minutes, continued for up to 28 days after which the animals, along with appropriate controls, were inoculated with herpes simplex virus. The results indicated an increased susceptibility to infection with the virus (in terms both of survival time and of mortality) in those mice subjected to prior avoidance training as compared with control animals not exposed to the behavioral stress. In a similar recent report on mice repeatedly exposed to shock escape and avoidance, extensive adrenocortical changes, as well as marked vascular engorgement of the spleens in the experimental animals, were described (Simson, 1958). Unfortunately, however, the possible influence of physical trauma associated with electric shock and forced activity were not independently assessed in either of these studies.

The initial applications of operant conditioning methodology in the experimental production of such pathological conditions appear to have emerged somewhat fortuitously in the course of studies concerned with the analysis of less permanent behaviorally induced physiological alterations. In 1958, Porter, Brady, Conrad, Mason, Galambos, and Rioch reported a "high incidence of gastrointestinal disease in a group of monkeys undergoing psychological conditioning studies . . . ," and a detailed analysis of this unusual occurrence in the rhesus monkey was pursued with great vigor. Eleven of 19 monkeys involved in various "emotional" conditioning experiments (including conditioned suppression, Sidman avoidance, discriminated punishment, and various combinations of these procedures as components of multiple schedules) either died or had to be sacrificed in a moribund condition in the course of these studies. Five of these animals were found to have well-developed duodenal ulcers, four showed extensive hemorrhages and/or erosive lesions of the stomach, and two were found with chronic colitis. Despite a careful "post-hoc" analysis of the antecedent conditions presumably related to these pathological findings, it proved difficult to isolate the critical behavioral process responsible for these somatic changes. Indeed, two factors did emerge from this analysis which ultimately proved to be of considerable value in the experiments following up these initial observations. First, the Sidman avoidance procedure was found to be a common element in the performance programs for most of the animals, and second, the schedule requirements for these animals were such as to impose rather severe work-rest cycles which frequently involved long night sessions (Porter, Brady, Conrad, Mason, Galambos, & Rioch, 1958).

A subsequent series of experiments represented a somewhat more systematic attempt to identify the critical behavioral factors related to the development of such gastrointestinal pathology (Brady, Porter, Conrad, & Mason, 1958). Eight rhesus monkeys, restrained in chairs as illustrated in Figure 2, were divided into pairs and conditioned according to a "yoked-chair" avoidance procedure. Each pair of monkeys received brief electric shocks (5 ma, 60 cycle AC, for 0.5 sec.) to the feet from a common source every 20 seconds unless the experimental animal of the pair pressed a lever which delayed the shock another 20 seconds for both animals. Inactivation of the lever available to the control animal insured an equal number and temporal distribution of shocks to both monkeys ("physical trauma"), while providing the avoidance contingency for only the experimental animal. Each pair of monkeys received six-hour sessions on this procedure, alternating with six-hour "off-periods" (no shocks) 24 hours each day for periods up to six and seven weeks. A red light was illuminated in plain view of both animals during the six-hour avoidance periods, and was turned out during the six-hour off-periods. Throughout the entire experiment, urine was collected continuously from all animals in 24- or 48-hour samples for 17-hydroxycorticosteroid determinations.

The stable performance developed on this procedure by the experimental animal of each pair is illustrated in Figure 3 and showed little change throughout the experiment. The lever-pressing rates for the experimental animals during the six-hour avoidance periods approximated 15 to 20 responses per minute, dropping to far less than one response per hour during the six-hour off-periods in the absence of the red light. The control animals

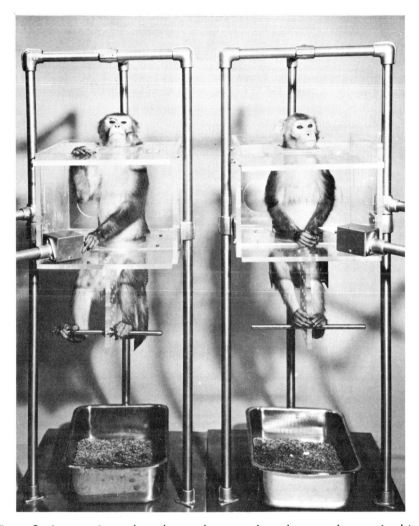

Figure 2. An experimental monkey and a control monkey, gently restrained in primate chairs, illustrate the "yoked-chair" avoidance procedure. The lever available to each animal is shown within easy reach, although only the experimental "avoidance" monkey on the left is observed to press the lever.

of each pair maintained a similarly low "operant level" at far less than one response per hour throughout all phases of the study. The shock rates for all animals never exceeded two per hour during the six-hour avoidance periods and typically averaged less than one per hour. As might be expected, urinary 17-hydroxycorticosteroids showed an elevation during the initial phases of the recurrent performance program but levels appeared to be within the normal range during subsequent phases. Within three to four

MONKEY M−67
(DAY ≠ 18)

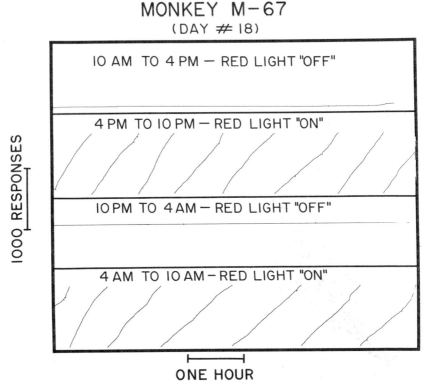

1000 RESPONSES

10 AM TO 4 PM − RED LIGHT "OFF"

4 PM TO 10 PM − RED LIGHT "ON"

10 PM TO 4 AM − RED LIGHT "OFF"

4 AM TO 10 AM − RED LIGHT "ON"

ONE HOUR

Figure 3. Sample cumulative response curve showing one 24-hour session (six-hour "on," six-hour "off" cycles) for an experimental "avoidance" monkey on day 18 of the experiment. The oblique pips on the record indicate shocks.

weeks after initiation of the six-hour "on," six hour "off" avoidance require-ment, however, all four of the experimental animals had developed exten-sive gastrointestinal lesions with ulceration as a prominent feature of the pathological picture. None of the control animals, which were sacrificed with their experimental partners and subjected to complete post-mortem exami-nation, showed any indications of such gastrointestinal complications.

Like most such investigative efforts, these initial applications of oper-ant methodology in the experimental production of somatic pathology raised many more questions than they answered. On the behavioral side, interest has focused upon the characteristics of the avoidance performance in rela-tion to the development of such somatic changes, particularly as these in-volve variations in the work-rest cycles. Follow-up studies have indicated, for example, that experimental manipulations of this variable, even in the direction of imposing apparently more demanding avoidance performance requirements (18 hours avoidance, 6 hours rest in each 24-hour cycle; alternating 30-minute avoidance, 30-minute rest throughout the 24-hour cycle; reduction of the R-S interval to two seconds during avoidance; introducing a "punishment" contingency for responding during the rest period), may actually reduce the incidence of ulcers when compared with the original six-hour "on," six-hour "off" procedure (Brady, 1958). Typically, for example, monkeys would show performances of the type illustrated in Figure 4 on a schedule requiring alternating 30-minute periods of avoidance (two-

MONKEY M—74

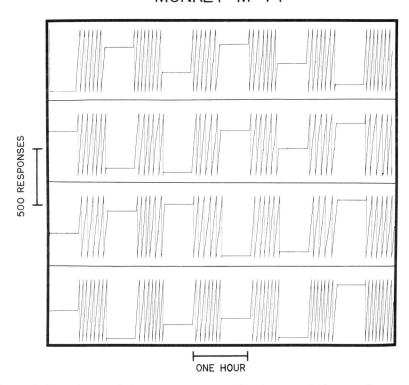

500 RESPONSES

ONE HOUR

Figure 4. Sample cumulative response curve showing one 24-hour peformance for a monkey on a schedule requiring alternating 30-minute periods of avoidance (two-second R-S interval) and "rest" (with "shock punishment" of lever responses) with no exteroceptive stimulus indicating the beginning or end of the 30-minute intervals. The oblique pips on the record indicate shocks.

second R-S interval) and rest (with "shock punishment" of lever responses) with no exteroceptive stimulus indicating when the respective 30-minute intervals began and ended, for periods of several months without any indication of somatic disturbance. Only when the original six-hour "on," six-hour "off" schedule was again utilized with a new group of animals did the gastrointestinal disturbances reappear.

Significantly, a recent report using rats on this same basic avoidance procedure confirms the critical nature of the work-rest relationship in the production of gastric ulcers (Rice, 1963). The experiments described in this paper involved 13 groups of animals performing on a wheel-turning avoidance procedure for a period of 21 days. Each of the 13 groups performed on a different work-rest schedule, ranging from an alternating one-hour "on," one-hour "off" schedule to an alternating 12-hour "on," 12-hour "off." A control group with no avoidance training was included as well as groups covering each of the alternating hourly cycles between 1 and 12 (2/2, 3/3 . . . 11/11). The incidence of ulcers in the 1/1 and 12/12 groups was extremely low and did not differ significantly from the control group. The intermediate groups showed progressively higher incidences of ulcers with the peak frequencies occurring in the alternating five-hour "on," five-hour "off" and six-hour "on," six-hour "off" groups.

Subsequent studies in this area have focused upon an analysis of avoidance behavior and gastrointestinal processes presumed to bear some critical relationship to ulcer formation. A technique has been developed for the

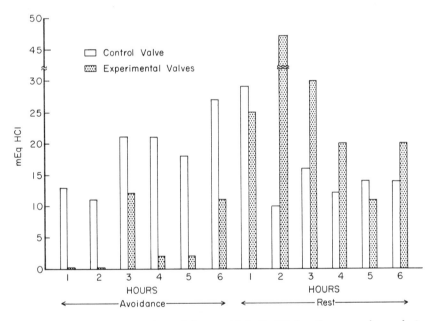

Figure 5. Mean concentration of free acid (mEq/1) for three monkeys during 12 hourly samples on a control day (no avoidance session) and an experimental day (six hours of avoidance followed by six hours of rest). Stippled bars represent the experimental day samples and unstippled bars represent the control day samples.

sampling of gastric contents with the rhesus monkey through a cannula in the stomach wall, and changes in acid levels have been analyzed in relationship to the avoidance schedule and ulcer development (Polish, Brady, Mason, Thach, & Niemeck, 1962). Initial observations in experiments involving 12 hourly samples taken throughout six-hour avoidance sessions followed by six-hour rest periods as shown in Figure 5 revealed a marked suppression of the total gastric acid during the six-hour avoidance as compared to pre-avoidance baseline levels. During the six-hour post-avoidance rest period, however, as Figure 5 shows, dramatic elevations in gastric acid, significantly above basal levels, were recorded.

These observations have been verified in several acute experiments with monkeys and extended by the analysis of gastric secretory changes in a series of nine monkeys exposed to the more chronic six-hour "on," six-hour "off" avoidance procedure for a period of 28 days (Polish *et al.*, 1962). The gastric secretory samples for this 28-day period were taken during both avoidance and rest cycles and combined to reflect 24-hour concentration levels. In all cases, as illustrated in Figure 6, the average daily concentration of free acid showed a consistent increase during the first ten days to two weeks of the experiment, with some animals maintaining elevated levels throughout the entire 28-day exposure and others showing a

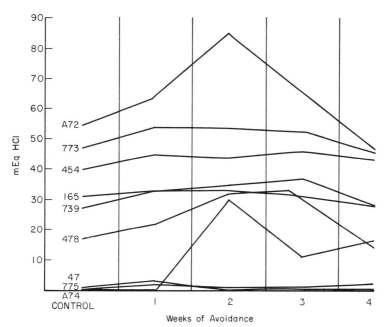

Figure 6. Average daily concentation of free HCl during the control period and during each week of a 28-day avoidance experiment (six hours "on," six hours "off") for nine monkeys.

decline during the terminal two weeks. Marked differences in initial control levels of free acid were also observed for the nine monkeys in this series. It may be significant that the two animals (A72 and 773) found to have developed peptic ulcers by the end of this 28-day period had the highest initial levels, showed a general increase in these levels during the first two weeks of avoidance, and maintained generally high levels throughout the entire four weeks of the experiment. These same two monkeys showed a progressive increase in their avoidance response rates throughout the four-week experiment, although none of the remaining seven animals in this series could be observed to show similar consistent changes in response rate throughout the 28-day period(Brady & Polish, 1960).

The general relationships between gastrointestinal activity and operant avoidance performance suggested by these studies with rhesus monkeys have been extended recently to the human experimental laboratory at Indiana University (Davis & Berry, 1963). Twenty-four pairs of human volunteers reclining on adjoining cots in a partially darkened experimental room were conditioned according to a "yoked-cot" avoidance procedure similar to that described above for the monkeys. Each pair of subjects received a strong auditory stimulus (800 cps at 90 db) every 30 seconds, unless the experimental subject of the pair pressed a button during a five-second interval preceding onset of the noise. The control subject in each pair did not have access to the avoidance button, was unaware of the nature of the task, but received the same auditory stimulation when the experimental subject failed to meet the avoidance requirement. Recordings of the electrical output of gastrointestinal movement (gastric motility) were obtained from electrodes on the upper right and left abdominal quadrants during relatively brief experimental sessions consisting of a 15-minute pre-avoidance rest period, a ten-minute "avoidance" period, and a final seven-minute post-avoidance rest period. Although there were no differences between the motility patterns for the experimental and control subjects during the pre-avoidance rest periods, the experimental subjects showed a consistent and significant elevation in the amplitude of the gastrointestinal movements during the avoidance performance both in contrast with their own pre-avoidance baselines and with the recordings obtained from the control subjects during the avoidance periods. During the post-avoidance rest period, motility patterns for the experimental subjects returned to baseline levels within five minutes after termination of the avoidance requirement.

The contrast between the Davis and Berry finding of *increased* gastrointestinal motility during avoidance performance and the Polish *et al.* report of consistent *decreases* in acid concentration during avoidance is of some considerable interest (Brady, 1963). There are, of course, many critical differences between these two experiments, but under relatively "normal" physiological conditions (and at least in some "pathological" states) gastric acidity and motility can be expected to covary in similar directions. The suggestion that this relationship may not obtain under conditions of behavioral avoidance stress raises provocative questions about the involvement of selective neuroendocrine and autonomic control mechanisms which are known to have effects upon acid secretion without comparable influence upon motility. The continued application of operant methodology to the experimental analysis of such psychophysiological relationships promises to provide new insights into the contributory role of behavioral processes in the development of many common forms of somatic pathology.

REFERENCES

ANLIKER, J. (1959) Brain waves and operant behavior. *J. exp. Anal. Behav., 2,* 252.

BÉLANGER, D., and FELDMAN, S. (1962) Effects of water deprivation upon heart rate and instrumental activity in the rat. *J. comp. physiol. Psychol., 55,* 220-225.

BRADY, J. V. (1958) Ulcers in "executive" monkeys. *Scient. Amer., 199,* 95-100.

BRADY, J. V. (1963) Further comments on the gastrointestinal system and avoidance behavior. *Psychol. Rep., 12,* 742.

BRADY, J. V., and POLISH, E. (1960) Performance changes during prolonged avoidance. *Psychol. Rep., 7,* 554.

BRADY, J. V., PORTER, R. W., CONRAD, D. G., and MASON, J. W. (1958) Avoidance behavior and the development of gastroduodenal ulcers. *J. exp. Anal. Behav., 1,* 69-72.

CANNON, W. B. (1929) *Bodily changes in pain, hunger, fear and rage.* Newton Center, Mass.: Branford.

CLARK, R., and POLISH, E. (1960) Avoidance conditioning and alcohol consumption in rhesus monkeys. *Science, 132,* 223-224.

CONGER, J. J., SAWREY, W. L., and TURRELL, E. S. (1958) The role of social experience in the production of gastric ulcers in hooded rats placed in a conflict situation. *J. comp. physiol. Psychol., 51,* 214-220.

DAVIS, R. C., and BERRY, F. (1963) Gastrointestinal reactions during a noise avoidance task. *Psychol. Rep., 12,* 135-137.

ELDRIDGE, L. (1954) Respiration rate change and its relation to avoidance behavior. Unpublished doctoral dissertation, Columbia University.

ESTES, W. K., and SKINNER, B. F. (1941) Some quantitative properties of anxiety. *J. exp. Psychol., 29,* 390-400.

GANTT, W. H. (1944) *Experimental basis of neurotic behavior.* New York: Hoeber-Harper.

GANTT, W. H. (1960) Cardiovascular component of the conditional reflex to pain, food and other stimuli. *Physiol. Rev., 40,* 266-291.

HAHN, W. W., STERN, J. A., and MCDONALD, D. G. (1962) Effects of water deprivation and bar pressing activity on heart rate of the male albino rat. *J. comp. physiol. Psychol., 55,* 786-790.

HARWOOD, C. T., and MASON, J. W. (1956) A systematic evaluation of the Nelson-Samuels plasma 17-hydroxycortico-steroid method. *J. clin. Endocrinol., 16,* 790-800.

HEARST, E., BEER, B., SHEATZ, G., and GALAMBOS, R. (1960) Some electrophysiological correlates of conditioning in the monkey. *EEG & Clin. Neurophysiol. J., 12,* 137-162.

JOHN, E. R., and KILLAM, K. F. (1959) Electrophysiological correlates of avoidance conditioning in the cat. *J. Pharm. exp. Therapeut., 125,* 252-274.

LACEY, J. I. (1956) The evaluation of autonomic responses: Toward a general solution. *Ann. N.Y. Acad. Sci., 67,* 123-164.

LIDDEL, H. S. (1956) *Emotional hazard in animals and man.* Springfield, Ill.: Charles C Thomas.

MAHL, G. F. (1949) Effect of chronic fear on gastric secretion of HCL in dogs. *Psychosomat. Med., 11,* 30.

MAHL, G. F. (1952) Relationship between acute and chronic fear and the gastric acidity and blood sugar levels in macaca mulatta monkeys. *Psychosomat. Med., 14,* 182-210.

MALMO, R. B. (1950) Experimental studies of mental patients under stress. In M. L. Reymert (Ed.), *Feelings and emotions.* New York: McGraw-Hill. Pp. 169-180.

MALMO, R. B. (1961) Slowing of heart rate after septal self-stimulation in rats. *Science, 133,* 1129.

MASON, J. (1958) Restraining chair for the experimental study of primates. *J. appl. Physiol., 12,* 130-133.

MASON, J., and BRADY, J. V. (1956) Plasma 17-hydroxycorticosteroid changes related to reserpine effects on emotional behavior. *Science, 124,* 983-984.

MASON, J., BRADY, J. V., POLISH, E., BAUER, J. A., ROBINSON, J. A., ROSE, R. M., and TAYLOR, E. D. (1961) Patterns of corticosteroid and pepsinogen change related to emotional stress in the monkey. *Science, 133,* 1596-1598.

MASON, J. W., BRADY, J. V., ROBINSON, J. A., TAYLOR, E. D., TOLSON, W. W., and MOUGEY, E. H. (1961) Patterns of thyroid, gonadal and adrenal hormone secretion related to psychological stress in the monkey. *Psychosomat. Med., 23,* 446.

MASON, J. W., BRADY, J. V., and SIDMAN, M. (1957) Plasma 17-hydroxycorticosteroid levels and conditioned behavior in the rhesus monkey. *Endocrinology, 60,* 741-752.

MASON, J. W., MANGAN, G., BRADY, J. V., CONRAD, D., and RIOCH, D. McK. (1961) Concurrent plasma epinephrine, norepinephrine and 17-hydroxycorticosteroid levels during conditioned emotional disturbances in monkeys. *Psychosomat. Med., 23,* 344-353.

MASON, J. W., NAUTA, W. J. H., BRADY, J. V., ROBINSON, J. A., and SACHAR, E. J. (1961) The role of limbic system structures in regulation of ACTH secretion. *Acta Neurovegetativa, 23,* 4-14.

MASSERMAN, J. H. (1943) *Behavior and neurosis.* Chicago, Ill.: Univ. of Chicago Press.

PAVLOV, I. P. (1879) Über die normalen Blutdrukschwankungen beim Hunde. *Arch. Gesamte Physiol., 20,* 215.

PEREZ-CRUET, J., BLACK, W. C., and BRADY, J. V. (1963) Heart rate: Differential effects of hypothalamic and septal self-stimulation. *Science, 140,* 1235-1236.

PEREZ-CRUET, J., TOLLIVER, G., DUNN, G., MARVIN, S., and BRADY, J. V. (1963) Concurrent measurement of heart rate and instrumental avoidance behavior in the rhesus monkey. *J. exp. Anal. Behav., 6,* 61-64.

POLISH, E., BRADY, J. V., MASON, J. W., THACH, J. S., and NIEMECK, W. (1962) Gastric contents and the occurrence of duodenal lesions in the rhesus monkey during avoidance behavior. *Gastroenterology, 43,* 193-201.

PORTER, R. W., BRADY, J. V., CONRAD, D., MASON, J. W., GALAMBOS, R., and RIOCH, D. McK. (1958) Some experimental observations on gastrointestinal lesions in behaviorally conditioned monkeys. *Psychosomat. Med.*, *20*, 379-394.

PORTER, R. W., CONRAD, D. G., and BRADY, J. V. (1959) Some neural and behavioral correlates of electrical self-stimulation of the limbic system. *J. exp. Anal. Behav.*, *2*, 43-55.

RASMUSSEN, A. J., MARSH, J. T., and BRILL, N. Q. (1957) Increased susceptibility to herpes simplex in mice subjected to avoidance-learning stress or restraint. *Proc. Soc. exper. Biol. Med.*, *96*, 183-189.

RICE, H. K. (1963) The responding-rest ratio in the production of gastric ulcers in the rat. *Psychol. Rep.*, *13*, 11-14.

ROSS, G. S., HODOS, W., and BRADY, J. V. (1962) Electroencephalographic correlates of temporally spaced responding and avoidance behavior. *J. exp. Anal. Behav.*, *5*, 467-472.

SAWREY, W. L. (1961) Conditioned responses of fear in relationship to ulceration. *J. comp. physiol. Psychol.*, *54*, 347-348.

SAWREY, W. L., CONGER, J. J., and TURRELL, E. S. (1956) An experimental investigation of the role of psychological factors in the production of gastric ulcers in rats. *J. comp. physiol. Psychol.*, *49*, 457-461.

SAWREY, W. L., and WEISZ, J. D. (1956) An experimental method of producing gastric ulcers. *J. comp. physiol. Psychol.*, *49*, 269-270.

SHAPIRO, A. P., and HORN, P. W. (1955) Blood pressure, plasma pepsinogen and behavior in cats subjected to experimental production of anxiety. *J. nerv. ment. Dis.*, *122*, 222-231.

SIDMAN, M. (1953) Avoidance conditioning with brief shock and no exteroceptive warning signal. *Science*, *118*, 157-158.

SIDMAN, M., MASON, J. W., BRADY, J. V., and THACH, J. (1962) Quantitative relations between avoidance behavior and pituitary-adrenal cortical activity. *J. exp. Anal. Behav.*, *5*, 353-362.

SIMSON, L. R. (1958) Some physiological correlates of psychological stress in the adrenal organs of the white mouse. *J. Scient. Labs, Denison Univ.*, *44*, 135-150.

TEITELBAUM, P., and DERKS, P. (1958) The effect of amphetamine on forced drinking in the rat. *J. comp. physiol. Psychol.*, *51*, 801-810.

WEISZ, J. D. (1957) The etiology of experimental gastric ulceration. *Psychosomat. Med.*, *19*, 61-73.

WENZEL, B. M. (1961) Changes in heart rate associated with responses based on positive and negative reinforcement. *J. comp. physiol. Psychol.*, *42*, 638-644.

WILLIAMS, D. R., and TEITELBAUM, P. (1956) Control of drinking behavior by means of an operant-conditioning technique. *Science*, *124*, 1294-1296.

WOLFF, H. G. (1950) Life situations, emotions and bodily disease. In M. L. Reymert (Ed.), *Feelings and emotions*. New York: McGraw-Hill. Pp. 284-324.

15

Synthesizing the Components of Arithmetic Behavior [1]

C. B. Ferster and Clifford E. Hammer, Jr.

INTRODUCTION

A simple response, such as pressing a lever, has been useful in research on many dynamic variables, such as delay and amount of reinforcement, schedules of reinforcement, punishment, etc. There remain, however, experiments where the behavior which is maintained is more complex than a simple bar press, as in matching to sample and counting (Doehring & Ferster, 1962; Ferster, 1960; Findley, 1962). In such cases, the frequency of the response in the complex unit is measured as it would be with a simple free operant, but the appropriateness of the animal's behavior provides an additional important measure. For example, we may ask not only how frequently, but also how accurately, a sample is matched.

Skinner's extension of the principles of behavioral control derived from simple experimental situations to verbal behavior represents the same kind of transition from an analysis of simple responses to larger units under the control of a complex environment. Skinner (1957) analyzed verbal behavior as an example of complex and multi-determined systems of responses which are analyzed by noting their relation to the simpler, general processes of behavioral control. The defining property of verbal behavior lies in the relation between the speaker and the listener. There remains, however, the laboratory synthesis of the component repertoires out of the simpler processes which are the constituent elements. In the present experiments, we attempted to synthesize experimentally a complex behavioral repertoire (binary arithmetic) by establishing the component performances in turn. When we have established the kinds of stimulus control characteristic of a verbal

[1] This research was carried out with support of grant NSFG 25122 from the National Science Foundation, grant MHK3-5744 from the National Institute of Mental Health, and grant NSG 450 from the National Aeronautics and Space Administration.

repertoire, we will be in a position to arrange additional contingencies of reinforcement to interrelate the repertoires of two animals, each having the common repertoire defining "the language." In the sense that we speak of the "language of mathematics," arithmetic shares many of the important properties of a verbal system.

The kinds of analyses Skinner has made in *Verbal Behavior* point up the controlling variables of arithmetic behavior and provide a starting point for a laboratory analysis. Other kinds of behavior might have been used as a laboratory model of a complex verbal repertoire. Arithmetic had the advantages that it is already a well-developed system with mnemonic values for the experimenters, that the behavioral repertoire can be exactly specified, since all of the contingencies of reinforcement can be specified, and that there is a point-to-point correspondence with the physical environment as in numerosity and counting. The kinds of experimental procedures that will effectively synthesize an arithmetic repertoire will provide information about the complex repertoire. In addition, after substantial components of an arithmetic repertoire have been established, it will be possible to investigate with arithmetic many of the variables which have proved important in the study of the simple operant, such as punishment, the effect of conditioned aversive stimuli, schedules of reinforcement, conditioned reinforcement in extended chains, or changes in quality of reinforcement.

Analysis of the Contingencies of Reinforcement in Binary and Decimal Arithmetic

Any one instance of the component behaviors of an arithmetic repertoire involves essentially quite simple discriminations. For example, $X \cdot X = X^2$ or $2 + 2 = 4$ specify very elementary discriminations of which any organism would be capable, given the ability to make the response. The animal could respond to the specific spatial patterns of the stimuli. The complexities of arithmetic arise, however, in terms of the rules of usage and syntax, and the methods of translation from one term to the next. The number of symbols which are used is quite small, compared with the complex ways in which they may be arranged, and the additional stimuli, such as the position of digits, critically determine which of several responses may be reinforced. Thus, in decimal arithmetic, 2 is an appropriate response for $1 + 1$, $0 + 2$, or $4 - 2$; or, given the numbers 4 and 4, the correct response is 16, 0, or 8, depending upon whether an "X," a "—," or a "+" appears between them. 1, 2, 3 . . . is the S^D for "4," but 123 (one hundred and twenty-three) is the appropriate occasion for a whole system of different responses: $10 \times 10 + 23$, $1 \times 10^2 + 2 \times 10^1 + 3 \times 10^0$, $200 - 77$, etc. All of these stimuli bear a relation to each other in a way which is analogous to thematic, metaphorical, and autoclitic properties of verbal stimuli as analyzed by Skinner. Thus, 123, 147, and 133 are all numbers "over 100 and under 200," contain the term 1×10^2, are not divisible by 2, etc.

Binary arithmetic as the specification of a verbal system has the advantage of consisting of only two elements, 0 and 1, as compared to the ten numbers of the decimal system. This means that the numbers can be presented to the animal by a series of lights, one for each digit of the number. A "1" is represented by a lamp which is illuminated, and "0" by one which is not. Representing binary stimuli by lights which are either on or off makes it possible for the animal to write numbers without the extensive fine-grain repertoire, as in handwriting or speaking. The animal can turn the lights on or off, or alter the pattern of a row of other lights by operating simple pushbuttons under each light.

Table 1

A Comparison of Addition in Binary and Decimal Arithmetic

Binary	*Decimal*
0000	0
+1	+1
0001	1
+1	+1
0010	2
+1	+1
0011	3
+1	+1
0100	4
+1	+1
0101	5
+1	+1
0110	6
+1	+1
0111	7
+1	+1
1000	8
+1	+1
1001	9
+1	+1
1010 $(1\times2^3 + 0\times2^2 + 1\times2^1 + 0\times2^0)$	10 $(1 \times 10^1 + 0 \times 10^0)$

Binary arithmetic has the further advantage that the reiterative, abstract aspects of the system appear early in the development of the repertoire. Table 1 and Table 2 illustrate the simplicity of binary addition and its relation to decimal arithmetic.

The first ten numbers are illustrated in Table 1 by adding 1s progressively in both the binary and decimal systems. Note that the carry operation occurs in every alternate addition in the binary system, while in the decimal system it occurs only after the tenth addition. In Table 2, the corresponding addition tables emphasize the discriminative nature of the repertoires. All of the operations of binary addition are contained in four discriminations in the binary system. The total addition table in binary arithmetic may be analyzed as four chains of responses as follows: Given the stimulus $1 + 0$, any response which produces a "binary 1" is the occasion upon which some terminal response may be reinforced. $1 + 1$ is a little more complicated because of the carry operation. On the occasion of $1 + 1$, the required behavior is any response which produces a 0 and indication of the carry operation. The completion of the carry operation is, in turn, the occasion for repeating the first discriminative repertoire in the next column. The reader can construct the contingencies associated with $0 + 1$ and $0 + 0$. If the four discriminations described above can be augmented by the carry operation, then one additional discrimination would make possible the addition of two numbers of any size. Once the carry operation is established on the occasion

Table 2

A Comparison of Addition Tables in Binary and Decimal Arithmetic

	0	1	2	3	4	5
0	0	1	2	3	4	5
1	1	2	3	4	5	
2	2	3	4	5	6	
3	3	4	5	6	7	
4						
5						

	1	0
1	10	1
0	1	0

$S^D\ 1 + 1 \cdot R_{10} \longrightarrow S^2$

$S^D\ 1 + 0 \cdot R_1 \longrightarrow S^2$

$S^D\ 0 + 1 \cdot R_1 \longrightarrow S^2$

$S^D\ 0 + 0 \cdot R_0 \longrightarrow S^2$

of 1 by putting a 1 over the next column, the rest of the performance is defined by four discriminations of the addition table.

The Notation of Verbal Chains

The chaining of verbal responses differs from the simple chains of
response that are usually described in animal experiments. We describe a
chain of responses in an animal experiment by saying, "The peck changed
the light from red to green." The verbal (especially vocal) response is a
complex unit, however, consisting of movements of the mouth, tongue,
larynx, and diaphragm. We ordinarily do not specify these behaviors and
describe instead the verbal response by its effect upon the environment—
the patterns of sound waves it generates, and the effect upon the listener.
This is convenient, since the measurement of the actual behaviors leading
to the auditory stimulus is extremely difficult. In binary arithmetic, however, where all of the component behaviors involve the operation of
switches, it is possible to indicate the actual performances, as well as their
effect upon the visual environment. Such a refinement of the notation of
these chains becomes necessary when we actually attempt to synthesize
these repertoires. It is convenient to describe the behavior of an animal
who "writes" the binary number 10 as R_{10}, just as we specify verbal responses by their effect on another speaker or writer. Nevertheless, the
actual sequence of behaviors is more accurately written as:

S^D (1+1) $\cdot$ R

$$\begin{array}{l} \text{(Turn off left light)} \\ \text{(Turn on right light)} \end{array} \longrightarrow S^D\ 10 \cdot R \longrightarrow S^r$$

On the occasion of $1 + 1$, push the button on the left lamp which turns
it off, and push the button on the right lamp which turns it on. These responses produce the binary stimulus 10 which reinforces the behavior. We
will follow the convention here, as with vocal behavior, of indicating responses by the nature of the stimulus change they produce. The chain
above is more simply written as S^D $(1 + 1)$ $\cdot$ $R_{10} \longrightarrow S^r$, where
R_{10} designates a performance whose effect is to produce that pattern of
two lights.

The addition of two three-digit numbers is carried out step-by-step
below to show that this complex addition is the serial application of the
four discriminations of the addition table.

	1	1		
A. 111	B. 111	C. 101	D. 1001	E. 1001
111	111	111	111	111
	0	10	110	1110

In (A) looking at column 1, we have

$$\begin{array}{ccccc} & & & & 1 \\ S^D\,1\cdot R & \longrightarrow & S^D\,1\cdot R & \longrightarrow & 11 \\ 1 & & 1 & & 11 \\ \rule{1em}{0.4pt} & & \rule{1em}{0.4pt} & & \rule{1em}{0.4pt} \\ & & 0 & & 0 \end{array}$$

In (B), looking at the two 1s in the second column, the same responses under the control of the same stimuli are repeated, except that the zero is written in the place of the two 1s. When there are no longer numbers which can be carried, the remaining discriminations are applied.

Arithmetic and Communication

Ordinarily, we think of verbal systems as involving the interpersonal control between a speaker and a listener. The speaker provides stimuli which strengthen behavior in the listener. The resulting behavior in the listener is the reinforcement for the speaker's behavior. The speaker then, in turn, provides a consequence which reinforces the behavior of the listener. The social nature of the performance makes possible the development of a generalized reinforcer, an essential process for human verbal behavior (Skinner, 1957). In the present experiment, relay programming equipment provides the functions of the listener and the verbal community, and food provides the function of the generalized reinforcer. Thus, the experimental program does not emphasize the communicative or social aspects of the verbal system. The relation of the repertoire of the present experiment to verbal behavior lies in the complex interrelation between the binary stimuli and the parts of the environment they "describe" by means of the contingencies of reinforcements supplied by the programming system. This aspect of the arithmetic repertoire is analogous to the relation between verbal stimuli in the English language, and those parts of the environment which they "describe" as a result of the reinforcement contingencies which the social community applies. Arithmetic becomes more completely verbal in the sense of a spoken language when there is a listener who can potentially emit the same behaviors on the occasion of the same stimuli. The chimpanzee who counts the number of triangles in a window by writing a binary number is engaging in behavior which is functionally equivalent to the sentinel who counts the number of approaching troops. The major difference between the two repertoires occurs when the sentinel strengthens behavior in his commanding officer who has the same repertoire in respect to these stimuli, as opposed to the chimpanzee, who receives food when he counts correctly. While a verbal repertoire could probably not emerge in the speaker in a normal ecology in the first instance without a listener, it should be possible to study many of its important properties in the laboratory in a single individual by maintaining the required behavior directly with a controlled reinforcer, such as food.

EXPERIMENTAL PROCEDURES

Subjects

The subjects of the experiment were a male (Dennis) and a female (Elizabeth) chimpanzee, approximately three and one-half years old at the start of the experiment and weighing 16.3 and 15.2 kilograms, respectively. We chose chimpanzees as experimental subjects on the assumption that they would be capable of the simultaneous development of many forms of stimulus control. Single elements of the arithmetic repertoire could undoubtedly be studied in an animal such as a pigeon. The cumulative synthesis of the larger repertoire justified the use of a higher animal. The animals were purchased from a commercial supplier who obtained them from Africa. The female was discarded from the experiment after 11 months, when the slowness with which the discriminative control could be developed in her repertoire, and the lability and erratic maintenance of existing discriminations, suggested that there was some brain damage or other physiological pathology which prevented the normal development of a behavioral repertoire. She was replaced by a female (Margie), approximately three years old, weighing 12.8 kilograms.

Matching to Sample

Matching to sample was one of the major procedures used to develop some of the component kinds of discriminative control required in the arithmetic repertoire. Figure 1 illustrates the major kinds of matching-to-sample procedures which we used. The arrangement in *A* of Figure 1 is the simplest procedure. Each group of three circles represents a three-bit (digit) binary number. The open circle denotes a light which is on, and the closed circle, a light which is off. Thus, the center number is 010, or 2 in the decimal system. When the chimpanzee presses the key under the center number, he lights the numbers on either side. When he presses the number which corresponds to that in the center, he produces a conditioned reinforcer (a brief tone). When he presses a non-corresponding stimulus (the left one in this case), he produces a brief time-out. Every response is reinforced by a conditioned reinforcer or punished by a time-out, but food is delivered only after a fixed number of correct responses. In the experiment where the binary stimuli are matched identically, it was necessary to study all combinations of all of the binary stimuli which were to be used, varying the pattern of left-right reinforcement.

In the experiments with the paradigm indicated in *B*, the side-key

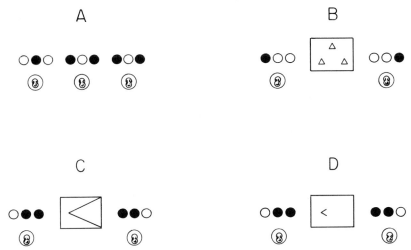

Figure 1. Diagrams of the various paradigms used in matching to sample. A: Matching identical stimuli. B: Matching a binary sample to a numerosity stimulus. C & D: The sample consists of an instruction which determines which of the binary stimuli is to be reinforced. A response to the larger or smaller binary stimulus is reinforced depending upon whether the symbol in the center window is large or small.

responses are reinforced when the chimpanzee indicates a binary stimulus which corresponds to the number of objects in the center window. Otherwise, the procedure is identical to that described in *A*. In the example shown, the chimpanzee first observes the numerosity by touching the center window, thereby increasing the likelihood of his attending to it and illuminating the two numbers to the left and right. In the example shown in *B*, a response on the left key (binary stimulus 011) would be followed by a brief tone, indicating that it was correct, while a response on the right key (binary stimulus 110) would be punished with a short time-out. The procedure indicated in *B* is not matching in the sense of the geometric or physical identity of the sample and choice stimuli, but rather correspondence, in terms of an arbitrary relation specified by the reinforcement contingencies. We are essentially establishing a language with which the chimpanzees can indicate special features of their environment in a way that would permit an observer (listener), who had the same repertoire, to have access to the stimulus controlling the behavior of the chimp (speaker) by observing only his response. In a limited sense, we are giving the chimp a language for describing a feature of the physical environment, numerosity. Each binary stimulus corresponds to a numerosity property of the physical (non-verbal) environment. It would have been possible to use simpler stimuli, such as colors correlated with the numerosities, but the binary stimuli were used because of their consistent relation to other properties of arithmetic.

The experimental program to date has not reached the stage where relationships between stimuli such as "larger than" and "smaller than" have been established, but these are no different in quality from the numerosity discrimination in *B*. In *C,* a response to the key under the larger of the two binary numbers is reinforced and in *D* a response to the smaller.

The actual devices which were used in the matching-to-sample experiments are shown in Figure 2. With the device on the left, the stimuli are presented on a continuous paper tape behind the translucent windows. The window itself is a response key which operates a switch when pushed. Holes punched on one side of the tape (not shown) index it and set up the conditions for reinforcement, recording, and time-out. The initial matching-to-sample procedures and the numerosity experiments were carried out with this device. The panel on the right side of the experiment was used during most of the later matching-to-sample experiments (the procedure indicated in *A* of Figure 1). A key was added under the center

Figure 2. A photograph of two of the actual matching-to-sample devices used in the experiment. The door into the experimental chamber is held in the open position and the photograph of the intelligence panel is taken through the door aperture. Pellets are delivered through the small square window in the lower center part of the panel.

sample binary stimulus, however, to encourage the subjects to observe it. Three-digit numbers are the largest used to date. The left-hand light was not used and was removed during the later stages of the experiment.

Intermediate procedures using colored stimuli behind the windows of the left-hand device were used to establish the basic matching-to-sample performance. At first, the animal simply pressed the window in which a colored stimulus was present. Then a chain was required in which pressing the center window produced a color in one of the side windows. Finally, one side window contained the matching color, while the other presented a non-matching color. The transition from colors to open and closed circles was accomplished in a manner somewhat similar to the procedures reported by Terrace (1963), in which open and closed colored circles provided an intermediate transition from the previous discriminations based on color.

Textual Responses

The functional equivalent of writing was arranged by giving the chimpanzee a key which altered the patterns of lights in a binary number. Figure 3 illustrates the procedure. A binary sample is presented to the animal, as in the matching-to-sample procedure. In the procedure described in the left part of the figure, every response on Key 1 alters the pattern of

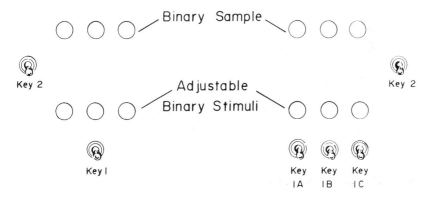

Figure 3. Diagram of the adjustment procedures. Binary stimuli are presented to the animal with the three lights in the binary sample. In the left procedure, every time the animal presses Key 1, he alters the pattern of lights of the adjustable binary stimulus, either in order or at random. Operating Key 2 produces a reinforcer if the adjustable binary stimulus corresponds to the binary sample, and a time-out if the stimuli do not correspond. The procedure in the right part of the figure is similar, except that each light of the adjustable binary stimulus is controlled by its own key.

the lights immediately above it (the adjustable binary stimulus). The response on Key 2 is reinforced when the adjustable binary stimulus has been made to correspond with the binary sample. This experiment was designed to build a repertoire of adjustment. We judged that the development of this repertoire depends upon the discriminations established in the matching-to-sample experiments. The right-hand part of Figure 3 illustrates the procedures which were used to achieve fine-grain control over the textual response. The procedure is identical with the one described for the left part, except that the digits (lights) of the adjustable binary stimulus have to be changed one at a time by operating each of the three keys appropriately. All of the procedures of matching-to-sample experiments can be carried out using a performance which produces a binary stimulus instead of a choice of two binary stimuli, one of which corresponds with the sample. For example, the animal could adjust a binary stimulus to correspond with a numerosity sample.

The adjusting procedures described above were used as a first step in the development of a "counting repertoire" in the sense of an intraverbal chain. While the experimental program has not reached the stage of the final synthesis of the component repertoires into counting, the following descriptions will clarify the long-term goals of the procedures which were actually used. The kind of behavioral control in the intraverbal chain is to be contrasted with those procedures (e.g., Ferster, 1958; Mechner, 1958) where a response is reinforced on lever 2 if a certain number of responses are made on lever 1, and a probability distribution is recorded, giving the frequency of counting "1," "2," and "3," when "2," for example, is the required count. On the other hand, in counting with an intraverbal chain, the stimulus control is precise and the accuracy of the counting does not decrease at large numbers, so long as the intraverbal chain is of sufficient length. The experiments where the chimpanzees write a number, digit by digit, are the prior conditions for developing such an intraverbal chain and bringing it under the control of a numerosity sample. The plan is to synthesize the intraverbal chain in the same way as other chains are constructed.

Overall Design of the Experimental Space

The experimental space was a 9' x 10' x 8' chamber, inside of which were three interconnecting cubicles housing the experimental apparatus. Figure 4 is a diagram of the overall features of the chamber, and Figure 5 is a photograph which shows some of the details of construction and the actual appearance of the chamber. The animals lived in the chamber continuously and entered the experiment proper through the doors leading to the experimental cubicles. The arrangements shown in Figure 4 evolved continuously during the experiment, and represent one of the outcomes of

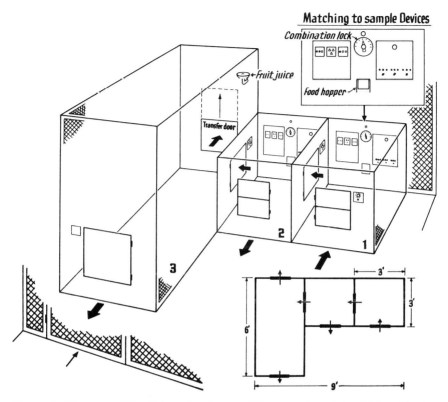

Figure 4. Diagram of the living chamber and the experimental cubicles. The insert in the upper right-hand corner represents the experimental arrangement on the intelligence panel in the first cubicle.

the experiment. The following considerations led to this particular arrangement and construction of the experimental space:

1. *It was not necessary to handle the animals during any phase of the experiment.* The animals entered the work cubicles because they received all of their food inside. When an animal received the specified number of reinforcements or remained in the cubicle for a specified period of time, the stimuli correlated with that chamber's experimental procedures were turned off and the exit door opened. The animals quickly learned to proceed through the work chambers serially, under the control of the relevant stimuli. The beginning of an experimental period was defined by the entering of a chamber and locking of the door, and the end by the termination of the relevant stimuli. The transfer of the animal from cubicle to cubicle and from one experimental procedure to the next was accomplished by the reinforcement contingencies inherent in the experimental procedures.

2. *Repair and modification of the equipment.* We had continuous access to any portion of the experimental space for repair and modification. To make changes in the experimental cubicles, the entrance doors to cubicles 1 and 2, and the exit doors to cubicle 3 were locked. When it was necessary to enter the living area for cleaning or repairs, door 3 was locked, so that as each animal went through cubicles 1 and 2 and entered cubicle 3, he was prevented from entering the main chamber or going backward through the cubicles.

3. *Transfer of the animals out of the experimental space.* On the rare occasions when it was necessary to remove the animals entirely from the experimental space, they were locked in the third work cubicle and a transfer cage was fastened against the transfer door. The performance (entering the transfer cage) was successively approximated, using food. Initially, the animals were reluctant to enter the transfer cage; but after several occasions when the experiment was terminated for several days without food, the presence of the transfer cage provided the only occasion for reinforceable behavior. Food was at first given when the animal entered the transfer cage, but later only after the door was locked behind him.

4. *Serial arrangement of the experimental panels.* Because the plan of the experiment required the simultaneous development of several repertoires, several arrangements of stimulus displays and response keys were required, each of which took considerable space. Each experimental chamber, therefore, was used for one or more individual experiments. To date, four individual experiments have been programmed simultaneously, two in each chamber. It was intended also that the spatial separation of the intelligence panels for each experiment would help emphasize the different performances required in each experiment and minimize inductive effects between them. The serial arrangement of the experimental chambers was also intended to provide cumulative reinforcement for the serial experiments. Reinforcers delivered in the third experimental chamber would help maintain the behavior in chambers 1 and 2, and similarly, the reinforcers delivered in chamber 2 would have some effect in maintaining performance in the first chamber. The serial arrangement of the performances also made it possible, during the course of the experiment, to simplify the instrumentation of food delivery by moving the delivery of food toward the end of the chain. The reinforcement for the performance in one experiment became the discriminative stimuli controlling the performance in the next.

5. *Management of urine and feces.* The floor of the experimental chamber was covered with a three-inch layer of wood shavings which rapidly absorbed moisture from feces and urine. Because of the large area of the experimental chamber relative to the amount of fecal material de-

posited, the feces decomposed rapidly to a fine powder or a small residue which had little odor, and which did not adhere to the animals or the cage. The shavings were replaced approximately every two weeks, and from time to time the cage was washed with carbolic acid, particularly early in the experiment, to kill parasitic ova. The chimpanzees rub their fur and

Figure 5. A photograph taken from inside the living area. Both animals are in cubicle 3, and the experimental chamber shown is numbered 2 in the diagram of Figure 4.

skin with the sawdust, and we judge that the generally dry state of the floor contributed to the absence of dysentery.

Individual Recording and Programming

Even though both animals had continuous access to the experimental chambers, the performances were recorded and programmed individually, with automatic locks on the entrance and exit doors and a combination lock. The system we used was similar in principle to that reported by Reynolds, Catania, and Skinner (1963) in which two separate responses not ordinarily occurring in the repertoire of the animal are successively approximated separately in each animal. The design of the combination lock may be seen in the upper right part of Figure 4. It consists of a pointer which can be rotated to any one of 16 positions indicated by the 16 lamps which describe the circumference of the pointer. The pointer rotates a two-pole, 32-point switch behind the panel. One pole of the switch connects the lights to the panel, so that each lamp lights in turn as the pointer is rotated. The color of the lamps varied. On the second pole, one position was selected for each animal, and the animals were trained individually to turn the pointer to the assigned position and hold it there for six seconds. The effective position for each animal was defined by an arc of approximately 11°. Each animal was trained separately for approximately 1000 reinforcements, until its responses came narrowly under the control of its particular position on the selector switch.

The effective positions on the switch were 180° apart, to minimize the likelihood of one animal accidentally adjusting the pointer to the second animal's position. The requirement of holding the pointer at the effective light for six seconds made it unlikely that any random movement of the pointer would activate an effective circuit. We never observed an instance of one animal adjusting the pointer to another animal's position. In the final procedure the door, the combination lock, and the experimental performances were chained together: closing the entrance door activated the combination lock, setting the combination lock to an effective position turned on the experiment. The large single lamp at the top of the combination lock indicated when it could be used to turn on the experiment. The entrance door to an experimental space opened again when the animal entered the second cubicle and locked the door behind him with the beginning of the next experimental procedure. We were able to sense electrically whether a door was open or closed by a switch built into the door frame.

At the early stages of the experiment, two animals occasionally entered the experimental chamber together. When this occurred, however, the dominant animal which set the combination performed in the experimental procedures and received the food pellets.

Order of the Experiments

The serial arrangement of the experimental chamber, as well as the possibility of several intelligence panels in each cubicle, allowed us to schedule several experiments simultaneously. The order of development of the experiments reported here is roughly as follows, although some of the experiments overlap because they were run concurrently: (1) matching to sample with the binary stimuli as open and closed black and white circles drawn on a paper tape; (2) matching to sample with a numerosity as the sample stimulus and binary stimuli as the choices; (3) matching to sample with three lights in a row as the binary sample, and similar lights as the binary choices; (4) the development of a textual repertoire with adjusting procedures by which the animal could adjust the binary stimulus.

Reinforcers

Conditions of reinforcement changed progressively during the experiment as the animals were able to sustain longer chains of behavior. Initially, performances in the first chamber were reinforced by one-gram banana pellets (CIBA).[2] After ten reinforcements or several minutes, the discriminative stimuli controlling the behavior in the first work chamber went out, and the door leading to the second work chamber was operative. The discriminative stimuli controlling the performances in chamber 2 came on whenever the animal closed the door behind him, and the first response in chamber 2 locked the door. A universal feeder in chamber 2 delivered fresh and dried fruit and large crackers. After one reinforcement in chamber 2, the door to the third work chamber opened, and when it was closed a light above the key controlling a valve on a juice dispenser came on. The animal could then drink approximately 10 cc of fresh fruit juice. A water fountain in the first cubicle could be operated only after the chimpanzee locked the door behind him. In this chamber, a continuous supply of fresh water was available. During the phase when more than one experiment was carried out in each experimental chamber, the discriminative stimuli controlling the second performance became the reinforcement for the first performance. During the later stages of the experiment, we installed a dispenser in the third cubicle which delivered 13-gram whole wheat biscuits, and eliminated food pellets altogether in the first two chambers. The fixed ratio schedules previously in effect were continued, however, by substituting a conditioned reinforcer (a tone of different frequency from the time-out or the conditioned reinforcer which occurred as a consequence of each correct response).

[2] We are indebted to Dr. Dom Finnochio of the CIBA Pharmaceutical Company for donating the food pellets used in the experiment.

Schedules of Reinforcement

Fixed ratio schedules of reinforcement were used in all of the procedures as one of the major methods of bringing the behavior under the
control of the stimuli and for generating larger amounts of performance
(Ferster, 1960). Each reinforced response produced a brief tone and each
S^Δ response produced a time-out consisting of a disappearance of all of
the stimuli and a correlated tone of a different frequency from the conditioned reinforcer. In general, the schedules of reinforcement and time-out
punishment were systematically changed, depending upon how closely the
animal's performance was controlled by the binary stimuli. The general
principle was to arrange contingencies so that the frequency of food reinforcement was markedly decreased by S^Δ responses. During the final
stages of the development of control by a particular set of stimuli, a typical
schedule of reinforcement might be FR 15 with a time-out of ten seconds
for S^Δ responses, and a contingency which extended the entire fixed ratio
on S^Δ responses. For example, if an S^Δ response occurred on the thirteenth
response in a particular fixed ratio, the counter which programmed the
fixed ratio reset to 0, and reinforcement then occurred when 15 additional
S^D responses were made consecutively.

Such a requirement would have been much too stringent during the
initial stages, and the contingencies of reinforcement, punishment, and
ratio resetting were adjusted continuously with the animal's performance.
Table 3 contains the criteria for the adjustment at one stage of the experiment. For most of the schedules, the fixed ratio was programmed in two

Table 3
Criteria for Adjustment of Schedule Values

Error Level (Percent)	Initial FR	Tandem FR (Reset)	Time-Out (Seconds)
First Exposure	15	—	1
35	15	—	1
25	13	2	1
20	11	4	1
15	9	6	1
10	7	8	1
8	5	10	1
6	3	12	1
4	0	15	5
2	0	15	10

parts. After completing the first part of the ratio, the second part (tandem)
was completed only when the required number of matches occurred without any intervening errors. Each S^Δ response reset the tandem counter.

Thus, under tandem FR 13 FR 2, the second of two successive correct matches delivered a pellet after the chimp completed, with or without errors, 13 correct matches. As the chimp's behavior came under the control of the stimuli, the size of the tandem ratio was increased, e.g., tandem FR 11 FR 4, tandem FR 9 FR 6. . . . The rationale for the size of the tandem ratio was the total number of responses (correct and incorrect) per reinforcement. The size of the tandem fixed ratio was adjusted so that on the one hand, the overall ratio of responses to reinforcement did not get so high as to weaken the behavior, and, on the other hand, a low frequency of S^Δ responses produced a markedly higher rate of reinforcement than high S^Δ rates. Thus, as the experiment progressed from one set of discriminations to the next, the overall ratio of responses ($S^D + S^\Delta$) to reinforcement remained approximately constant, if the chimpanzee's behavior came under the control of the relevant stimuli at the prescribed rate. Simultaneously with the fall in error level, the duration of the time-out for incorrect responses was increased, reaching 15 seconds or more when the error level was .02. The adjustment of the frequency of time-outs is in accord with the finding (Ferster & Appel, 1962; Zimmerman & Ferster, 1963) that a high frequency of long time-outs tends to disrupt whatever stimulus control is present.

Maintaining the Animals' Behavior in a Continuous Experiment

During the first weeks of the experiment, while the experimental chambers, locking doors, combination locks, and other special features of the experimental environment were being designed, both animals were adapted to the new environment with an experiment in which a single key, continuously available to both animals, operated a one-gram pellet dispenser on FR 50. Figure 6 is a continuous record of an FR 75 performance over a 48-hour period, illustrating the distribution of the animals' behavior over two days. Since the combination lock had not yet been installed, the cumulative curve is a composite record of the performance of both animals. Either one or the other of the two animals was continuously engaged in pressing the key from 6:30 A.M. until approximately 6:30 P.M. The 400-800 pellets received daily by the two animals were more than sufficient to maintain their body weights. In spite of the free-feeding body weights and absence of a history of starvation, the performances were sustained and characteristic of those normally generated by fixed ratio schedules. The insert illustrates typical performances taken from the bracketed portions of the overall curve. It was relatively easy to identify each animal's performance, even though there was no differential recording for the two animals. The portion of the record to *a* is the performance of the female; from *a* to *b*, that of the male; *c* to *d*, the female; and *d* to *e*, the male. A similar temporal pattern of performance and level of activity and food

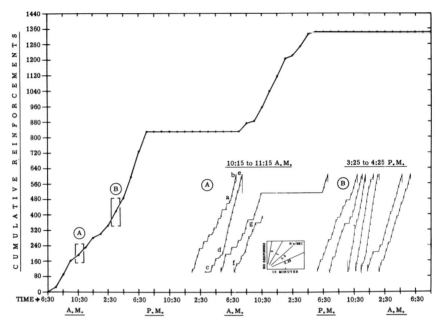

Figure 6. A reduced cumulative response curve taken over 48 hours, combining the performances of Dennis and Elizabeth. The inserts show details of the fixed ratio performances.

intake continued through the remainder of the binary arithmetic procedures.

Both animals continued to grow during the 24-month period of the experiments reported here, and we judged that at all stages of the experiment, they were close to free-feeding body weights. Figure 7 shows the cumulative eating curve for both animals, and body weights taken early and late in the experiment. The total amount of food eaten is, in general, a function of the overall experimental conditions. During the first 140 sessions of the experiment, the conditions of reinforcement were favorable, and the food intake was quite high. The next experimental procedures involved the numerosity experiments, and the high S^Δ rates occurring due to the difficulty of discriminations were probably responsible for the lowered food intake. The experiment was resumed after a two-month interruption around the four hundred and thirtieth session, and the overall ratio of the amount of food delivered to the number of responses required was kept quite low compared with the previous values. It appears, then, in general, that the total amount of food eaten is some function of the size of the fixed ratio. This appears true even though at the highest fixed ratios there was still ample time during the day when the animal could work for

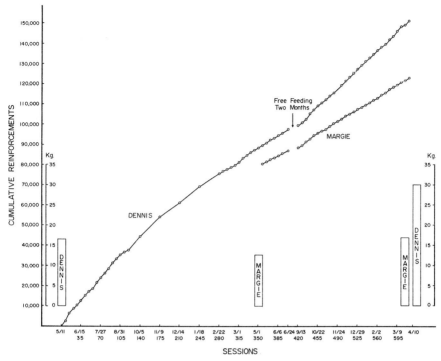

Figure 7. Cumulative eating curve taken over the first two years of the experiment. Reinforcements may be roughly translated as grams of food. The bars give the body weights at the indicated times.

additional food. Both animals show normal growth, in spite of the fact that all of their food is delivered during the experiment on intermittent schedules of reinforcement.

EXPERIMENTS IN MATCHING IDENTICAL STIMULI

First Development of the Matching-to-Sample
Performance with Binary Stimuli

Different procedures were used with the two animals whose results are reported here. Dennis' performance was developed with the fading procedure mentioned above, as was that of Elizabeth, the animal who was discarded from the experiment. Figure 8 illustrates the first performances for Dennis and Elizabeth when the stimuli were two circles, both either open or closed. The combination lock had not yet been installed, so that the recorders operated continuously and contained performances of both animals. Nevertheless, it was possible, at this stage, to distinguish between the animals as indicated on the record. Record *A* shows an intermediate stage of development after the first exposure with a combined error rate of approximately 30 percent for both animals. By Record *B*, the fifteenth session, Dennis' performance was under complete control of the stimuli.

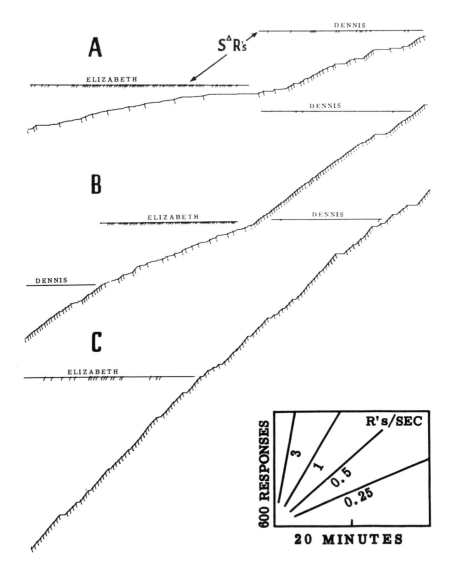

Figure 8. Cumulative curves of the matching-to-sample performances early in the experiment when the stimuli were restricted samples of the binary stimuli. The distinctive performances of each animal allowed us to indicate which was performing. The signal marks on the cumulative record indicate reinforcements and the baseline marks indicate time-outs (see text).

By Record *C,* Dennis' performance is virtually perfectly controlled by several two-digit numbers. The female, Elizabeth, came under control of the same stimuli much more slowly. Her error level reached 3 percent only after 35 sessions and 150,000 trials.

When the binary stimuli were changed to three-digit numbers, (001, 010, and 100), Dennis' performance came under control of the new stimuli in three sessions, with error levels of less than 5 percent. The female, however, failed to develop the required control. During approximately 100 sessions, we varied the schedules of reinforcement, time-outs, and levels of food deprivation. Probes of discriminations developed in the earlier experiments showed that these were intact, and attempts at successively approximating the stimulus control confirmed the fact that this animal was not capable of acquiring stimulus control of this complexity. While there was no way of estimating the possibility of organic deficits, the oscillation in the error rate was reminiscent of some of the performance changes sometimes observed clinically with brain damage. From time to time, error rates of less than 5 percent were sustained for several hundred trials, suggesting that the difficulty lay in maintaining the animal's attention. Because of the suspicion of a defective animal, Elizabeth was replaced by a new animal, Margie.

We attempted to develop the matching-to-sample performance directly with binary stimuli with Margie, rather than using the intermediate procedures, using colors which were faded to black or white circles on lighted or unlighted lamps. Without the transitional procedures, the discriminative control by the binary stimuli developed much more slowly. Fifty-three sessions, comprising 114,400 trials and involving many transitional procedures were required before Margie achieved error rates of approximately 5 percent with the binary stimuli 001, 111, and 011.

Survey of Matching to Sample with All of the Three-digit Binary Numbers

After both animals were matching several binary stimuli accurately (Dennis—001, 010, 011 and 110; Margie—001, 111, and 011), we surveyed control by all the three-digit binary numbers, each serving in turn as the sample of one of the choices. The experiment was designed to determine to what extent the animal was matching particular stimuli, or under the control of "identity of the sample to the choices." On successive days, each animal was presented a different pair of binary stimuli in the matching-to-sample procedure, until each binary stimulus had been paired with every other. The order of the stimuli and the results of the experiments are shown in Figure 9. The data were recorded differentially for the two binary stimuli of each experimental session. The numbers at the top and bottom of the graph indicate the two binary stimuli which were programmed on that particular session, and each of the two S$^\Delta$ values recorded in that session. Thus, in Dennis' first session, the binary stimuli were 111 and 001; for those trials when 111 was the S^D, and 001 the S$^\Delta$, the accuracy level was .004.

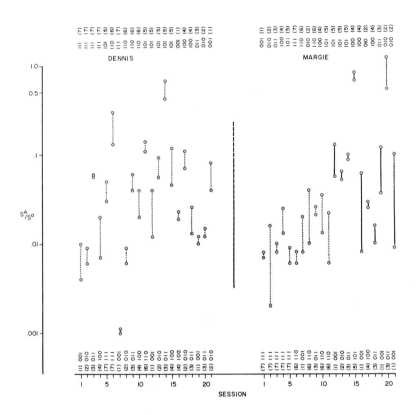

Figure 9. A survey of S$^\Delta$ levels as each animal was exposed to each pair of binary stimuli for one session. The two points on each session represent the error level for those trials where the indicated binary stimulus was the S^D. The numbers above the binary numbers represent the decimal equivalent of the binary stimuli.

The level of errors varies widely between stimulus pairs in both animals. Dennis, in Session 7, makes one error per 1000 correct responses when the binary stimuli are 111 and 001, and over 500 errors per 1000 correct responses when the binary stimuli are 101 and 011. Margie's error level varies from two errors per 1000 correct responses on Session 2, when the binary stimuli were 111 and 010, to over 1000 errors per 1000 correct responses on Session 20, when the binary stimuli were 010 and 011. The error level from one stimulus pair to the next in Dennis' performance is partly a function of the physical similarity of the binary stimuli. In general, those stimulus pairs in which either 111 or 001 occurred, and those stimuli which differed by two digits, such as 111 and 011, showed lower error rates. The result is not completely general, however. The differential recording of the performance according to which stimulus was the S^D showed a difference in error level frequently reaching 0.3 to 0.5 log units. For example, on Session 12, when the binary stimuli were 001 and 101, the error level was .015 when 001 was the reinforced binary stimulus and 101 the unreinforced stimulus, and .04 when 101 was the reinforced stimulus and 001 the unreinforced stimulus. Margie showed a wider range of performances with the same program and there is a suggestion of a trend of increasing error levels. The difference between the error levels, depending upon whether a binary stimulus is S^D or S^Δ, is even more marked with Margie than with Dennis, reaching a whole log unit on Session 21.

The extreme variations in error level of matching identical binary stimuli indicate that the criterion performances acquired during the previous exposure to matching-to-sample experiments were not general, but limited to the specific stimuli that had been programmed. All the cases in which Dennis' error level exceeded .05 involved binary stimuli which had not been presented before. The controlling relation in the performance, therefore, is not simply the identity of the sample and a choice stimulus, but the identity of particular combinations of the binary digits. This was borne out by the next experiment (see below). Rather than learning to match "stimuli in general," both animals are acquiring discrete discriminations.

Probes of the Matching-to-Sample Performances with a Range of Binary Stimuli, Using a Baseline Discrimination as a Reference

In the previous experiment, there was a daily shift from one set of discriminations to the next, regardless of the level of S^Δ responding or the inductive effects of one discrimination on the next. In the present experiment, we established a baseline performance, using the binary stimuli 101 and 110, to see how much single-session probes with other binary stimuli would interfere with the prevailing low error rate, and to observe whether the error level of the probe itself would change from the levels that were recorded in the previous experiment.

Figure 10 shows the results of the experiment with Dennis. The binary stimuli 101 and 110 are those which produced a high error level during the survey of the previous experiment, and the first session of Figure 10 confirms the previous error level. The discriminations develop slowly. The criterion performance (now two sessions at .03 or less) does not occur until Session 31. The first probe on Session 34 disrupts the baseline slightly by increasing the error rate to .07, but thereafter the rest of the probes have no effect. The S^Δ level of the probes is of the same magnitude as the S^Δ levels recorded during the survey of the previous experiment. Thus, there was no evidence of interference, from session to session, of one probe with another.

These results suggest that the control by the binary stimuli develops discretely, with little interference or facilitation from one stimulus to the next.

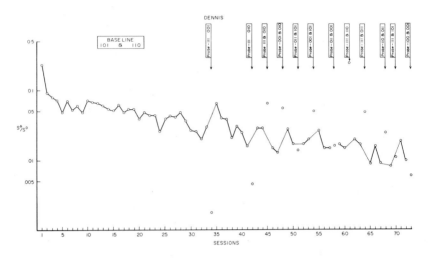

Figure 10. Denis: Matching-to-sample performances with the binary stimuli 101 and 110 serve as a baseline for single-session probes of other pairs of binary stimuli, as indicated in the figure.

Figure 11 shows the analogous experiment with Margie. The initial discrimination with the stimuli 101 and 110 develops much more rapidly than with Dennis, but the probes on single sessions neither disrupt the baseline nor result in higher error levels than were recorded in the previous survey. In the second part of the graph, the experiment is repeated, using 011 and 010 as the baseline. These discriminations are more difficult than the earlier ones, but again the probes do not interfere with the baseline. The new baseline, however, increases the error level of the probes somewhat, although the error level is already low. (The probes are the same with the second baseline as with the first.) As with Dennis, the performances from session to session are relatively independent.

Both animals confirm the finding of the previous experiment that the discriminative control by each binary sample stimulus is relatively independent of the others, and that rather than learning to match spatially similar patterns, the animals are coming under control of discrete pairs of stimuli.

Developing Criterion Performances with All of the Binary Numbers

In order to test the independence of the various pairs of binary stimuli, we then continued reinforcement on *each* of the 21 pairs of binary stimuli until the S^Δ/S^D levels fell below .05. The first evidence of interaction among

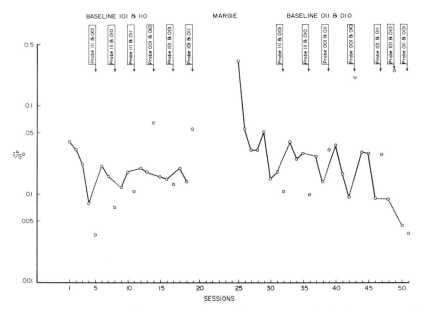

Figure 11. Margie: Matching-to-sample performances with the binary stimuli 101 and 110 serve as a baseline for single-session probes with pairs of binary stimuli, as indicated in the legend. After the twenty-fifth session, the baseline was altered to 011 and 010, and the probes continued as indicated in the legend.

the performances with the various stimulus pairs came with Margie when reinforcement was continued with each pair of binary stimuli individually until a criterion performance was reached. Initial error levels increased to levels of approximately 0.10, as compared with levels generally less than .05 during the previous probes. Presumably, the development of criterion performances with the more difficult discriminations, such as 101 and 110, was responsible for the new induction effects.

Having achieved criterion performance on each discrimination in turn, we could then determine whether programming a group of these stimuli simultaneously would weaken the discriminative control. The test of induction among the discriminations was carried out by the random presentation of seven pairs of binary stimuli (one-third of the total possible combinations which could occur with a three-digit number) within each experimental session. Even less independence among the component discriminations of three-digit stimuli was demonstrated under these conditions. Figures 12 and 13 show the results of the combined stimuli alternating randomly during the experimental session. The graphs give the mean and range of error levels among the pairs of binary stimuli. The error level increased markedly, in spite of the criterion performances (less than 5 percent errors) that had just previously been developed when each of these pairs of stimuli had

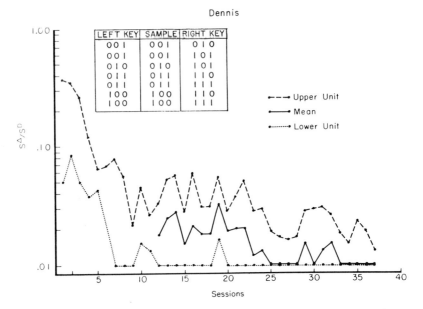

Figure 12. Dennis: Development of matching-to-sample performances with seven pairs of binary stimuli, progammed concurrently. The dashed curve gives the S^Δ levels for the least accurate stimuli, and the dotted curves for the most accurate. Values less than .01 are indicated as .01. The mean value is not recorded for the first 12 sessions.

been programmed in turn for the number of sessions required to produce the required accuracy. Accurate performances with all of these stimuli programmed together apparently required differential reinforcements in close temporal proximity, so that induction could occur and the required extinction of induction effects take place. It would be profitable to speculate whether a fading procedure (Terrace, 1963) could be devised with stimuli of the complexity of these seven pairs of binary numbers to produce stimulus control without S^Δ responding.

CONTROL BY BINARY STIMULI ON THE BASIS OF NUMEROSITY

Establishing Control by Binary Stimuli

Data in the experiment are available only for Dennis, since the second animal began the experiment later. The numerosity control eventually developed in this experiment involved conditional discriminations, in which stimuli controlling a response by reinforcement at one time are occasions for non-reinforcement another time. Thus, the binary stimulus, 001, is the

Margie

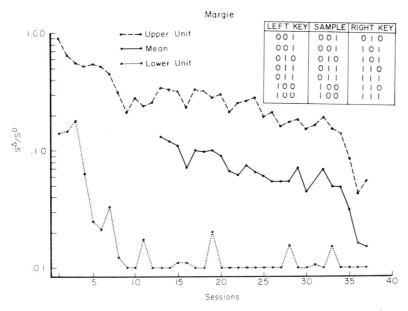

LEFT KEY	SAMPLE	RIGHT KEY
0 0 1	0 0 1	0 1 0
0 0 1	0 0 1	1 0 1
0 1 0	0 1 0	1 0 1
0 1 1	0 1 1	1 1 0
0 1 1	0 1 1	1 1 1
1 0 0	1 0 0	1 1 0
1 0 0	1 0 0	1 1 1

Figure 13. Margie: Development of matching-to-sample performances with seven pairs of binary stimuli, programmed concurrently. The dashed curve gives the $S^\triangle$ levels for the least accurate stimuli, and the dotted curves for the most accurate. Values less than .01 are indicated as .01. The mean value is not recorded for the first 12 sessions.

occasion for a reinforced response when the sample window contains one triangle, but the same binary stimulus is the occasion for an unreinforced response on the next trial when the sample stimulus contains two triangles. The conditional nature of these discriminations suggested a simple transitional procedure for reducing the level of difficulty. Some of the stimuli which provided the occasion when a response was not reinforced *never* corresponded with the numerosities in the sample window and hence were never occasions for reinforcement. Thus with one, two, or three triangles in the sample window, the binary stimuli programmed in the side windows included 000(0), 101(5), 110(6), and 111(7), stimuli which never occasioned reinforcement at this stage of the numerosity experiment. These "extraneous" stimuli provided a supplementary basis for the control of a reinforced response either by a reduced tendency to respond on the occasion of the $S^\triangle$ stimulus, strong control by the S^D, or both. The results of these experiments provide information as to the nature of stimulus control in these complex discriminations. The same problem was alluded to by Nissen (1953) when he discussed whether an animal in performing a discrimination is avoiding the negative stimulus or going to the positive.

In the first numerosity experiment, therefore, the sample window contained one, two, three triangles, the stimulus which was the occasion for reinforcement was the corresponding binary number, and the non-reinforced stimuli were occasionally 001(1), 010(2), or 011(3) but predominantly 000(0), 101(5), 110(6), and 111(7).

The first record of Figure 14 shows the rate of decline of errors for Dennis. After six sessions (approximately 35,000 trials), the rate of S$^\Delta$ responses to S^D responses reaches .05. This performance was an intermediate stage of development, however, since we could be sure the reinforced response was under the control of the numerosity sample in only three out of the 15 stimulus settings. In the remaining settings, the chimp's performance could simply have been under the negative control of the binary stimuli 000, 101, 110, and 111 which were never the occasion for reinforcement, without any reference to the numerosity sample.

The performance recorded in the second experiment confirmed the hypothesis that most of the control was by the S$^\Delta$ stimulus, rather than the numerosity sample. In the experiment shown in the record on the right of the Figure 14, the numerosity stimuli in the sample remained the same (one, two, or three triangles) and, of necessity, so did the reinforced binary stimuli. The S$^\Delta$ stimulus was now, however, always one of the numbers corresponding with the numerosity samples in use. Thus, if the sample contained two crosses, the reinforced binary stimulus would be 010(2) and the S$^\Delta$ stimulus, either 001(1) or 011(3), stimuli which might be reinforced on the next trial when the numerosity stimulus might be one or three crosses. The new S$^\Delta$ stimuli bring the performance to nearly chance levels. The control of the binary stimuli by the numerosity sample develops more slowly than before, but by the tenth session (about 60,000 trials), the error rate is below 5 percent again.

Abstracting the Control by the Binary Stimuli

To be certain that the controlling relation between the animal's behavior and the two stimuli is *numerosity,* rather than specific features of the stimuli, it is necessary to vary the numerosity sample in all details except the essential property of *number of objects.* Thus, the form, size, and spatial arrangement of the sample stimuli vary from trial to trial, still preserving the number relations and thereby reducing the control of the chimp's behavior only to those aspects of the stimulus defined by the reinforcement contingency. We did not vary the numerosity stimulus in every detail, but the final performance which was developed did not depend on the specific form or spatial arrangement of the numerosity sample. The results confirm the general proposition that abstraction is a property of the reinforcement contingencies rather than the stimuli. As with the other kinds of stimulus control developed in these experiments, a reinforcement contingency was necessary which "forced" stimulus control.

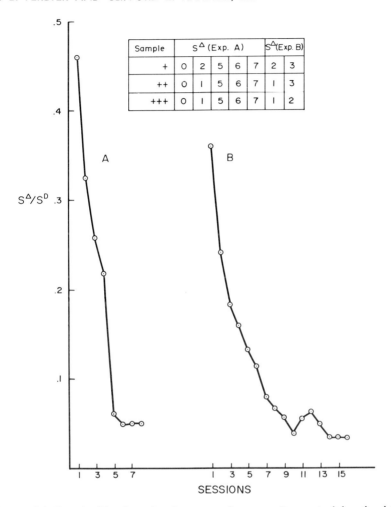

Figure 14. Dennis: The first development of numerosity control by the binary stimuli. In the left curve, the S^Δ binary stimuli include 5, 6, and 7, which do not correspond with any of the numerosity samples. In the right curve, all of the binary stimuli correspond with the numerosity samples.

Figure 15 shows the result of changing the form of the stimuli of the numerosity sample after criterion performance had developed with numerosities 1, 2, and 3. The form of the stimuli was altered from triangles alone, to triangles, squares, stars, slant marks, and crosses. The new forms of the numerosity sample increased the error level to near chance level, and 17 sessions were required to redevelop the previous level of the stimulus control. The result is partially confounded by the new sequence of left-right reinforcement sequences, but the sequence control is minor because

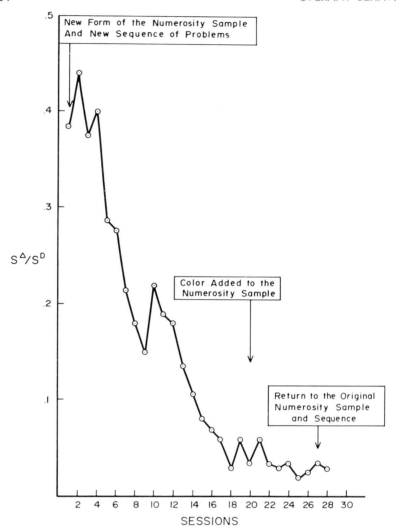

Figure 15. Dennis: Disruption of the matching-to-sample performance with numerosities 1, 2, and 3, when the spatial arrangement of the numerosity sample is altered.

it had been changed frequently during the preceding experiments until its control was weakened. The abstraction of the control by the numerosity sample was carried out further in a later experiment (see Figure 18).

While we have not attempted to abstract the essential properties of the binary stimuli, it is probable that the animals are under the control of the specific features of the lights which serve as the binary stimuli, rather than the "on-off pattern." To bring the animals' behavior under the control of the essential property of the binary stimulus, we would probably have to vary the intensity, size, and color of the lights. Experiments in which the animals match binary numbers, for example, might have a sample consisting of small green lights, all illuminated, while the reinforced binary stimulus would be large red lights all illuminated, and the unreinforced binary stimulus small green lights, not illuminated. The sample shows more properties in common with the unreinforced than with the reinforced binary stimulus, but the reinforcement contingency would force the control to the essential stimulus property.

Adding "Numerosity 4" to the Set of Discriminations

We next attempted to extend the relation between the number of triangles in the sample and the corresponding binary stimuli, by adding a sample containing four triangles and the corresponding binary stimulus 100(4). The reinforcement contingencies associated with the new stimuli were maximized by presenting the new binary stimulus, 100, in every discrimination, either as the S^D, when the numerosity sample contained four triangles, or as the S^Δ when the numerosity sample contained one, two, or three triangles. Thus, in three out of four trials, the required discrimination was the same as in the previous problem, except that the S^Δ stimulus was new. The performance with these stimuli (the first record of Figure 16) showed almost no carry-over from the previous discriminations. If the animal's performance had remained under the control of the numerosities 1, 2, or 3, as in the previous experiment, we would expect an *initial* error level of approximately .15, assuming a random choice on that quarter of the trials when the numerosity sample was four triangles (.50) and the prevailing low error level on the remaining trials when it was one, two, or three triangles (.025). The error level that in fact occurred in the experiment is approximately what we would expect by chance (.50), however, and it takes 11 sessions and 21,730 trials before the error level falls below .15 (one error to approximately six correct responses).

The disruption of the performance by the new numerosity stimulus led us to redetermine whether the stimulus control established in the previous experiment with numerosities 1, 2, and 3 was still intact. This performance is shown in Record B, obtained with the identical stimuli and procedure of the previous experiment; stimulus control was lost, and five additional sessions of differential reinforcement were required before the error level again fell to the criterion level.

The disruption which occurred when we added numerosity 4, suggested that the loss of discriminative control came from the use of the binary stimulus 4 as an S^Δ for the performances with numerosities 1, 2, and 3, rather than from the new numerosity stimulus. The next procedure bore out the importance of the S^Δ stimulus in the matching-to-sample perform-

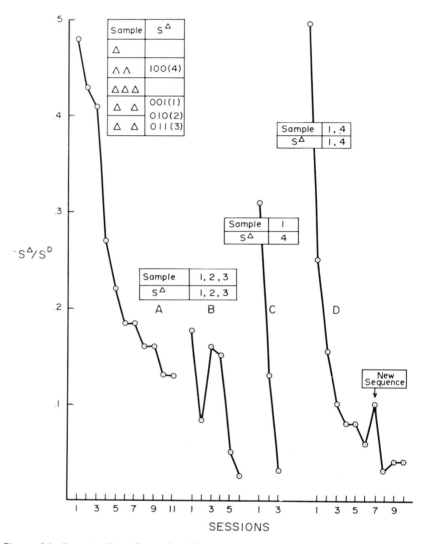

Figure 16. Dennis: The effect of adding numerosity 4 after control had already developed with numerosities 1, 2, and 3.

ance. With numerosities 4 and 1 as the sample, error levels reached chance values in spite of the fact that these stimuli had controlled the animal's behavior accurately during thousands of trials previously (Figure 16, Record A). The development of the discriminations with numerosities 4 and 1, and binary stimuli 4 and 1 are shown in the Records C and D of Figure 16. Control by the new numerosity sample 4 develops to the 5-percent criterion level only after eight sessions. A new sequence of left-right reinforcement patterns on the eighth session produces only a slight and temporary increase in S^Δ responding, indicating that the stimuli, rather than the alternation series, are controlling the performance.

We then developed discriminative control of the binary stimuli 001, 010, 011, and 100 by the numerosity stimuli 1, 2, 3, and 4 in stages, by programming components of the total program in turn. Approximately 100 experimental sessions and 268,717 trials were required to develop control by a numerosity sample over a binary response with the full range of possible S^Δ responses. Figure 17 shows an intermediate stage of development of control of numerosities 1, 2, and 4 by the corresponding binary stimuli. The first development of 4 and 2 (Record A) takes considerably longer than was needed for 4 and 1, but the performance developed progressively. Thereafter, there is no interference between the two sets of discriminations (Records B and D) until the program was changed to

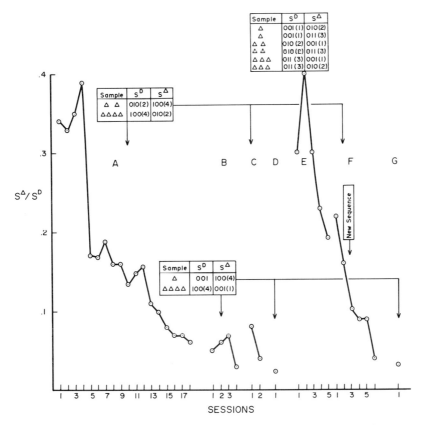

Figure 17. Dennis: The development of the control by numerosity 4, in combination with 1 and 2, and the subsequent disruption of the control by numerosities 1, 2, and 3.

numerosities 1, 2, and 3. This increased the error level to near chance levels on numerosities 1, 2, and 3 and in addition disrupted the performances with numerosities 4 and 2 (Record F). Six sessions were required to reinstate a criterion performance with numerosities 4 and 2 (Record F), but once this was achieved, the shift to 4 and 1 (Record G) produced a criterion performance immediately. The experimental procedures of Figure 17 confirm again the major importance of the specific form of the S^Δ con-

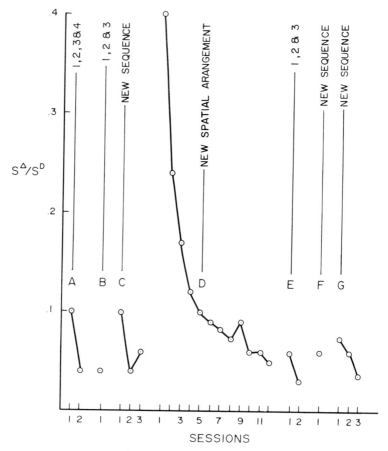

Figure 18. Dennis: Final development of control by all four binary stimuli together. The indicated sessions occurred successively. Record A is the performance with all four numerosities. Record B was taken with only numerosities 1, 2, and 3. Record C contains numerosities 1 to 4, but with a different sequential arrangement than in Record A. The contingencies programmed in Record D were the same as in C, except that the spatial arrangement of the numerosity sample was altered. Record E was taken with numerosities 1, 2, and 3, and Records F and G were taken with numerosities 1 to 4, but in different sequences.

ditions. The sets of discriminations which interfered with each other were the ones with $S^\triangle$ stimuli in new relations to the numerosities.

This property of the $S^\triangle$ stimulus becomes more important in the numerosity experiments, where the sample is not topographically the same as the stimulus controlling the reinforcement, than in matching-to-sample experiments, where the stimuli are identical. In the simple matching to sample it is possible for the performance to come entirely under the control of the sample, with no control being exerted by the non-reinforced stimulus.

During the additional experimental sessions required to bring the chimpanzee's behavior under the control of a full range of numerosities and binary stimuli, alternating exposure to sets of stimuli containing parts of the total produced a progressive decline in the amount of interference from one set of discriminations to the next. Figure 18 shows the error levels during the final stages, when error levels do not exceed 0.1, and reach criterion levels in one session thereafter. The high error level in Record D shows the result of shifting the control of the numerosity sample to a second level of abstraction, beyond the variations in shapes of stimuli that were introduced in Figure 15. The geometric forms were now arranged irregularly in the sample window instead of a row. The first effect is a complete disruption of the performance ($S^\triangle/S^D = 0.4$), but control by the new numerosity stimuli is rapidly redeveloped on the new abstract level.

DEVELOPMENT OF TEXTUAL BEHAVIOR

This experiment is the first to work in the direction of a fine-grain repertoire functionally equivalent to textual behavior. The performance involves the development of a point-to-point correspondence with a controlling, visual stimulus (the sample) and actually results in a stimulus having the same properties as the sample. It will not be possible to use repertoires controlled by binary numbers and numerosities in a truly "verbal" experiment involving control of a speaker and listener (writer and reader) until the animals can "write."

The general procedures are described in the preceding section on "Textual Responses" (p. 643 f) and the apparatus is illustrated in Figure 3. Chance error levels were considerably higher in the experiments where the chimp adjusted a stimulus digit by digit under the control of a sample than in the matching-to-sample experiments. With all seven three-digit numbers we would expect $S^\triangle/S^D = 6.0$ in contrast to .5 with matching to sample.

Figures 19 and 20 report the first development of textual behavior for both Dennis and Margie, using the devices displayed in Figure 3. In the first procedure, the sample alternated between 001 and 010 from trial to trial. The adjustable lights under the sample also alternated between 001 and 010 with each press of the adjustment key (Key 1, Figure 3). The ordinate records the ratio S^Δ/S^D of register-key responses (Key 2, Figure 3). An S^Δ register-key response occurred when the adjustable stimulus did not match the sample and an S^D register-key response occurred when it did. Both Dennis and Margie begin at higher than chance levels ($S^\Delta/S^D = 1.0$). In Dennis' first session, the S^Δ level is over 2.0 (two incorrect responses for every correct one), but the S^Δ responses fall sharply, reaching 0.3-0.4 with four sessions, while Margie begins at a similar level, but reaches a less accurate performance than Dennis' in 11 sessions.

We then continued to add additional numbers to the sample sequence, so that there were additional possibilities of S^Δ adjustment responses. With each additional binary sample stimulus, the chance error level increases. Thus, for 1, 2, and 3, a random performance gives two errors for every correct response ($S^\Delta/S^D = 2.0$); for 1, 2, 3, and 4, $S^\Delta/S^D = 3.0$, etc.

Dennis was exposed to the full set of binary stimuli more quickly than Margie, but both animals reached criterion performances in approximately the same number of sessions. In Dennis' third experiment (Record C), randomizing the order of occurrence of the binary sample stimuli only partially disrupts the performance, indicating that the binary stimuli carry the major part of the behavioral control as opposed to the regular se-

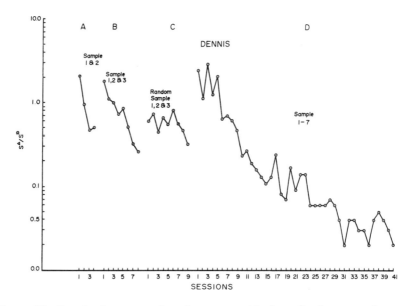

Figure 19. Dennis: Accuracy of performance with the adjusting procedures, as the number of binary stimuli in the sample and the range of possible binary stimuli in the adjustable stimulus is increased.

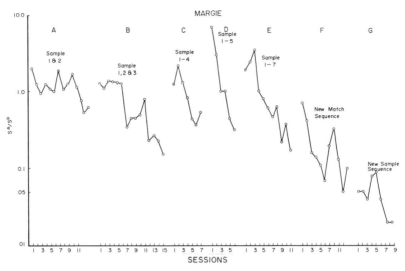

Figure 20. Margie: Accuracy of performance with the adjusting procedures, as the number of binary stimuli in the sample and the range of possible binary stimuli in the adjustable stimulus is increased.

quence of "counts" that is required as the sample numbers are regularly changed from 1–7. When Dennis was exposed to the entire set of binary stimuli, the initial error level begins considerably above chance. An initial error level of $S^\Delta/S^D = 2.0$ is approximately what we would expect if he were under the control of 1, 2, and 3, and at chance levels with 4, 5, 6, and 7.

Margie's initial error levels in the successive problems are all approximately what we would expect from chance, but the error rate falls more sharply with each increase in the number of binary stimuli. In the fourth curve, for example, S^Δ/S^D changes from approximately 4.0 to 0.25 in six sessions. When the remaining two binary stimuli are added, as shown in the fifth curve, the decline in error rate is almost as rapid as in the preceding curve. The sixth curve, where the sequence by which the adjusting key produces the binary stimuli is randomized, and the seventh curve, where the sequence of presentation of sample stimuli is randomized, show that the performance is largely controlled by the correspondence between the adjustable binary stimulus and the sample binary stimulus.

The remainder of the experiment was concerned with further development of the control by the stimuli to a low level of S^Δ responses which is required for the later development of an intraverbal chain. For Dennis, systematic changes in the random sequence of both the sample and the adjustable stimulus were required. Under these conditions, the only possible basis for an accurate performance would be the control by

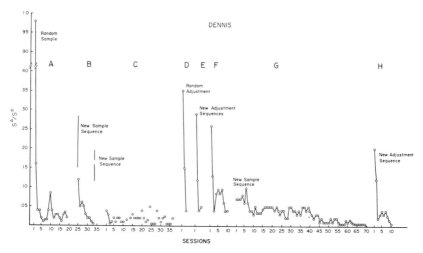

Figure 21. Dennis: Final development of the adjustment repertoire, with changes in the order of presentation of the binary sample as well as the adjustable stimulus.

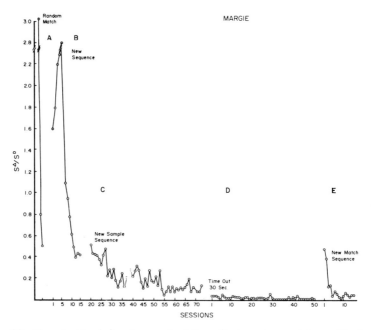

Figure 22. Margie: Final development of the adjustment repertoire, with changes in the order of presentation of the binary sample as well as the adjustable stimulus.

the binary stimuli, rather than the sequence. Figure 21 shows that each sequence change produces temporary disruption in the performance, but these disruptions decrease in magnitude each time the sequence is altered.

Similar procedures were carried out with Margie, and S^Δ/S^D values fell below 0.1 with the same schedules of reinforcement as were used with Dennis (Figure 22). When the time-out was increased to 30 seconds, the S^Δ level fell even further. Both animals made many more responses on the adjustment key than were required to produce the match between the adjustable stimulus and the sample stimulus, particularly with time-out. Frequently, they cycled the count from 1–7 several times before stopping at the correct binary stimulus and operating the register key.

DISCUSSION

An experimental paradigm different from the usual operant experiment has emerged from the present experimental program. An animal is conventionally isolated in an environment carefully restricted by use of a sound-resistant chamber in which he lives alone, influenced only by those events programmed by the experimenter. We did not isolate the animals, either visually or auditorily, from the non-experimental environment. Even when an animal was operating the experimental devices, he had visual access to the other animals in the cage and observers looking in, and could hear noises made in the laboratory or by the other animals in the experiment. Eventually, the animals "sorted out" the stimuli in their environment in the manner of a multiple schedule. With a long history of experience in the experimental environment, the differential reinforcement, which occurs day in and day out with respect to the various kinds of stimulation, eventually brings the animals' behavior narrowly under the control of those stimuli related to the important reinforcers. The situation which finally evolves is similar to the normal environment in which a host of stimuli in a given situation exert no control over the individual's behavior because the important contingencies occur in respect to other events.

In general, the schedules and amount of reinforcement were arranged so that the animals maintained normal body weights and growth curves during the experiment without a regime of food deprivation or restriction in terms of body weights. Despite the limited deprivation conditions, it still proved possible to maintain substantial amounts of behavior and arrange contingencies as might be done under more stringent deprivation conditions. The cumulative development of successive repertoires was one of the reasons for designing a special environment for the animals different from the usual isolated experiment. Each successive experiment in the program depended upon a repertoire developed in an earlier experiment, so that it became essential that the animals be maintained under optimal conditions and in good health over a period of several years and possibly longer.

Because most of the individual experiments require a basic repertoire common to many experiments, a cumulative redevelopment of all of the prior procedures in each experiment would be required in a new experiment. For example, control of the animal's behavior by details of the binary stimulus is a prerequisite for all of the adjusting procedures or the construction of intraverbal chains. All those experiments in which the response to the binary stimulus is controlled by a numerosity sample require a disposition to attend to the details of two-dimensional objects on the screen. In addition to the results inherent in the investigation, the numerosity control of binary stimuli in matching-to-sample experiments prepares the animals for experiments with textual behavior under the control of numerosity stimuli.

In general, we found that it was necessary at each stage of the experiment, to "force" discriminative control by imposing widely differing rates of reinforcement, depending upon how much S^Δ responding was occurring, and by punishing S^Δ responding with time-out. At most stages of the development of discriminative control by a given set of stimuli and the related reinforcement contingencies, we judged that the overall schedules of reinforcement would continue to maintain the animal's behavior, even with high frequencies of S^Δ responses. In most cases, fixed ratio schedules, time-out punishment of S^Δ responses, and increases in the size of the required fixed ratio as a result of S^Δ responses, are necessary to force the animal's behavior under the control of the relevant stimuli. We confirmed the observations by Kelleher (1958) and Rohles, Belleville, and Grunzke (1963) that the chimpanzee's behavior can come under the control of long sequential patterns of left-right responses. In the present experiment we had to change the sequence of left-right reinforcement patterns in matching-to-sample and other procedures in order to bring the behavior under the control of the sample stimuli rather than the sequence. In the adjusting experiments, the sequence of counts also controlled the performance instead of the stimulus changes produced by the adjustment key. Only when the sequences were randomized (Figures 22 and 23) could we be sure that the stimuli, rather than the sequence, controlled the performance. It was necessary, therefore, to introduce new variations of the sequence patterns at each stage of the experiment.

All of the controlling stimuli also need to be varied in details that are not related to the reinforcement contingencies. Each stimulus has, of course, many properties, each of which can control the chimpanzee's behavior in varying degrees. "Three triangles" is an abstraction involving the control of the experimenter's behavior, rather than a specification of the controlling property of the stimulus. The color of the stimuli, their spatial arrangement, the specific form of the elements, and the general surroundings in which they are placed, can all potentially control the animal's behavior. Only by differential reinforcement in respect to each of the properties of the stimulus complex can we ascertain which aspects of the stimulus are controlling the chimpanzee's behavior. The two experiments in which "incidental" properties of the stimulus were altered confirm this analysis. The large numbers of stimuli that controlled the animal's behavior in the present experiments produce induction effects that are not present in experiments of stimulus control by limited sets of stimuli. Each new procedure in which similar stimuli enter into new relations with new reinforcement contingencies makes for possible additional inductive effects among the stimuli. New inductions will occur among a group of stimuli when they are programmed in the same experiment with a related group of stimuli. For example, in matching a binary stimulus with a binary sample, disruption occurred when seven pairs of stimuli were programmed concurrently in a single experimental session, even though performances were at criterion levels with each of the stimulus pairs presented separately during the preceding experiments.

The major datum in the present experiment is the change in the frequency of S^Δ responses, and the error curves describe the course of development of the discriminative control in a manner resembling traditional learning curves. But they differ from these in several respects. The curves are a complex function of the various schedules of reinforcement that were continuously manipulated. Without these special conditions, the differential reinforcement would not in most cases have produced the required stimulus control, and the behavior would have been maintained on some intermittent schedule of reinforcement defined by the frequency of S^Δ responses. The major form of the curve, therefore, is determined by the size of the FR schedules, the tandem FR which reset when an S^Δ response occurred, and the punishment of S^Δ responses. Further, many of these factors determining the S^Δ level had an autocatalytic influence. As the frequency of S^Δ responses fell it became possible to arrange more effective contingencies by allowing larger fixed ratios, longer time-outs, and a larger tandem FR.

The success which we met in adapting the new animal to the same procedures as Dennis confirms our hypothesis of some organic deficiency in the female which was discarded from the experiment. It is not likely that we would have noticed any difficulty with this animal except for the increase in the complexity of the stimuli and the associated reinforcement contingencies. The performances of both animals appeared comparable until the stimuli took the form of the binary numbers. It is likely that procedures such as those reported above will have special usefulness in examining new effects of experimental manipulation of the central nervous system.

The present experiments are not about verbal behavior in the sense of a relation between a speaker and a listener. Yet the techniques and performances resulting from it have a relevance to the experimental analysis of verbal behavior beyond single-key, single-stimulus experiments. Although the crucial dimension of verbal behavior lies in the relation between the speaker and the listener (Skinner, 1957, p. 224), the discriminative control by verbal stimuli has properties which require special experiments. Discriminative control by verbal stimuli is highly abstracted, responses are controlled by multiple stimuli, and single stimuli control multiple responses through multiple reinforcement contingencies. All of these processes may be duplicated in the laboratory in their essential form but the development of a repertoire which may be arranged verbally depends upon procedures for developing the simpler processes of stimulus control in the direction of the interrelated stimuli and contingencies out of which a communication system is built.

REFERENCES

DOEHRING, D. G., and FERSTER, C. B. (1962) Psychophysiological responses in a human operant situation. *Psychol. Rec., 12*, 251-261.

FERSTER, C. B. (1960) Intermittent reinforcement of matching to sample in the pigeon. *J. exp. Anal. Behav., 3*, 259-272.

FERSTER, C. B. (1958) Intermittent reinforcement of a complex response in a chimpanzee. *J. exp. Anal. Behav., 1*, 163-165.

FERSTER, C. B., and APPEL, J. B. (1961) Punishment of S^{Δ} responding in matching to sample by time out from positive reinforcement, *J. exp. Anal. Behav., 4*, 45-56.

FINDLEY, J. D. (1962) An experimental outline for building and exploring multi-operant behavior repertoires. *J. exp. Anal. Behav., 5*, 113-166.

KELLEHER, R. T. (1958) Concept formation in chimpanzees. *Science, 128*, 777-778.

MECHNER, F. (1958) Probability relations within response sequences under ratio reinforcement. *J. exp. Anal. Behav., 1*, 109-121.

NISSEN, H. W. (1953) Sensory patterning versus central organization. *J. Psychol., 36*, 271-287.

REYNOLDS, G. S., CATANIA, A. C., and SKINNER, B. F. (1963) Conditioned and unconditioned aggression in pigeons. *J. exp. Anal. Behav., 6*, 73-74.

ROHLES, F. H., BELLEVILLE, R. E., and GRUNZKE, M. E. (1961) Measurement of higher intellectual functioning in the chimpanzee. *Aerospace Med., 32*, 121-125.

SKINNER, B. F. (1957) *Verbal behavior.* New York: Appleton-Century-Crofts.

ZIMMERMAN, J., and FERSTER, C. B. (1963) Intermittent punishment of S^{Δ} resonding in matching to sample. *J. exp. Anal. Behav., 6*, 349-356.

16

Operant Methods in Space Technology [1]

Frederick H. Rohles, Jr.

INTRODUCTION: PROBLEMS AND METHODS FOR SPACE RESEARCH

It is generally agreed that there are two basic questions that can be answered by animal participants in flights beyond our atmosphere. The first is concerned with physiological functioning: we need to know whether, after being subjected to excessive noise and accelerative forces, an organism can survive in an environment devoid of gravity and containing cosmic radiation. Consequently, we are concerned with the functional adequacy of the various body systems in the presence of these environments. This is also important when the space vehicle re-enters the earth's atmosphere, because it is during this phase of the flight that the animal is subjected to temperature extremes, buffeting and vibration, and negative acceleration. The aftereffects of space flight in terms of long-term genetic implications are likewise related to survival.

But these factors are related to the physiological state of the organism. More subtle, but equally important in a complete appraisal of the effects of space flights on an animal, is the second area of concern: the behavioral effectiveness of the animal during and following exposure to these environments (Banghart, 1958). Here we are concerned with the ability of the animal to perform a task in space that has been learned on the ground. This suggests specific questions about the visual and auditory processes of the animal during space flight and how they affect perception and cognition. An additional factor related to effectiveness is whether the adaptive processes of the organism are still functional under conditions of prolonged space flight. Finally, the ability of the organism to maintain

[1] The author is grateful to M. E. Grunzke and H. H. Reynolds for their help, suggestions, and comments.

vigilance for extended periods of time, coupled with speed and accuracy of responding, is also related to the effectiveness of the animal once it is in orbit. These are the questions that comprise the basis for research in comparative aerospace psychology.

However, the behavioral questions are not as readily answered as those concerned with physiological functioning. Paramount in this regard is the fact that the measures of the psychological state of the organism are not as well standardized and universally employed as the physiological measures of heart rate, respiration, and body temperature. Not only is this important in terrestrial psychology, but it is magnified when we attempt to assess any type of behavior in an animal that is circling the earth every 90 minutes at an altitude of 400 miles. In fact, several considerations which are irrelevant to normal laboratory experimentation must be taken into account when measuring animal behavior during space flight (Rohles, 1960).

The first consideration is based on the engineering aspects of the space vehicle which specify the maximum weight and volume of the animal and accompanying equipment for measuring its behavior. In addition, the available electrical power must be considered as well as the number of telemetry channels which can be used for recording performance information. Of major importance from a behavioral viewpoint is the type of flight (a ballistic flight or probe of short duration, or an orbital flight of longer duration) which will have a bearing on the type of performance selected for measurement.

Operant conditioning techniques are the most readily adaptable to the animal satellite. The reasons for this are quite apparent. First, the single-subject approach to the study of animal behavior is important since, at the beginning of space exploration with animals, only one subject was employed. Second, the reliability of behavioral information obtained from the single subject with operant procedures points to their use during space flight. Third, the operant chamber itself is not unlike the biosatellite: the subject is placed in a sound-attenuated chamber and further isolated from his environment by a masking noise. Here the animal performs almost independently of the experimenter. A fourth, and equally important reason, is the extent to which operant conditioning has progressed in the use of automatic programming and recording equipment. This means that programming apparatus can be miniaturized by the use of transistors, thereby reducing the space and weight required aboard the vehicle; and the recording methods can be made compatible with telemetry procedures. A fifth factor which points to the selection of the free operant as a method for measuring animal behavior during space flight is the success enjoyed by the field of psychopharmacology in using operant techniques to determine the effects of drugs on learned behavior. Thus, if exposure to the space environments of acceleration, temperature, radiation, etc. is comparable to the procedures involved in the evaluation of behavior under drug conditions, then it is reasonable to assume that the experimental designs employed by our colleagues in psychopharmacology would also apply to the study of behavior in space environments.

These are the reasons that dictate the use of operant conditioning procedures for measuring animal performance during space flight; the implementation of these procedures falls into four major categories.

The first task involves the adaptation of standard laboratory equipment for use in the space vehicle; the second is concerned with adapting conventional reinforcement schedules and developing new ones for measuring behavior during the flight; the third is to determine the effects on performance of the various environments which can be reproduced on the ground; and the fourth is the development of what we have chosen to call laboratory models, and consists of acquiring normative data in the laboratory setting under simulated conditions of space flight. It is toward these objectives that most of the efforts in comparative aerospace psychology are directed.

IMPLEMENTATION OF OPERANT PROCEDURES

Equipment Adaptation

One of the first modifications of an operant chamber was accomplished by R. M. Herrick in 1957 (personal communication) at the Naval Aeromedical Acceleration Laboratory, Johnsville, Pennsylvania. This chamber, for use with a rat, consisted of a half-cylinder of lucite with a grid floor, contained a light and a lever, and was designed for measuring shock-avoidance behavior. Another chamber designed for performance on a shock-avoidance program was developed by W. L. Brown (1959) of the University of Texas for the Aerospace Medical Division, Brooks Air Force Base, Texas. Designed for a monkey, it consisted of two parts. The subject was restrained in a nylon mesh suit in one-half of the unit, and the lever and programming units were in the other half. The complete chamber was approximately 12 inches long, 30 inches high, and 12 inches wide, and was modified for use in the ballistic flights of Little Joe No. 2 and No. 1-B that carried SAM and Miss SAM.

An operant chamber for a mouse was designed by Rohles and Coy (1959) and is shown in Figure 1. This unit was mechanically driven by an eight-day clock and was programmed for the subject to press a lever on an FR 25 reinforcement schedule for 20 minutes out of every six hours. Performance was rewarded with specially designed hard-coated pellets which were held by two small plastic fingers until removed by the animal. This design, which was necessitated by the weightless environment in which a pellet could not drop from a hopper to the subject, was also used in developing a feeding device for a chimpanzee. Shown in Figure 2, it

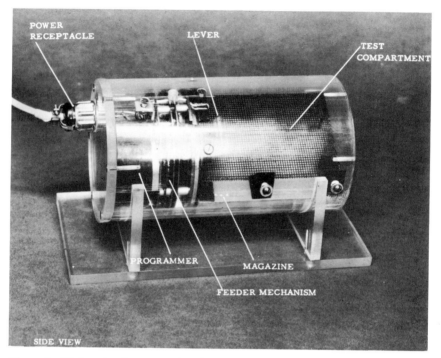

Figure 1. Miniaturized operant chamber for a mouse.

consisted of a tube or magazine for holding a supply of pellets and a sole-noid-operated plunger that was mounted perpendicular to the magazine. When the solenoid was activated, it forced a pellet out of the magazine into the chamber where it was held until removed by the animal (Grunzke, 1961a; Rohles, 1962).

Another pellet feeder, which is capable of holding more food pellets and is readily adaptable to the weightless environment, is described by Grunzke (1963). It is operated very much like a cigarette or candy machine in that the power for its operation is supplied by the animal. The cue that food is available is the illumination of the small light over the plunger, and when the subject pulls the plunger a food pellet is delivered. Obviously, the advantage of this device is that it makes no demand on the electrical power supply of the vehicle.

A zero gravity feeder which was built by Inventive Engineers for the Air Force is described in a paper by Gilbert (1964). In this feeder, special food pellets, developed by Ciba Pharmaceuticals, are glued to spools of MYLAR tape and are delivered to the animal when a lever press is made. Eight of these spools are mounted side by side to permit a maximum capacity of 2400 pellets.

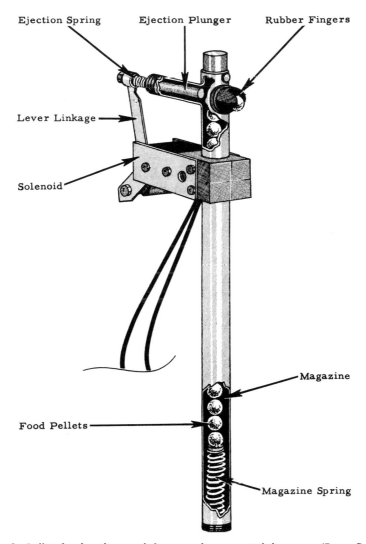

Figure 2. Pellet feeder designed for use during weightlessness. (From Rohles 1962.)

Special water reinforcement devices have also been designed for use during space flight. In this regard it should be pointed out that most engineers favor pressurization of the space capsule at 5 psi (pounds per square inch), the atmospheric pressure at an altitude of approximately 27,000 feet. Under this reduced atmospheric pressure and weightlessness, the impracticality of conventional watering devices immediately becomes apparent. To cope with these variables, a special dispenser was developed (Grunzke, 1961a) which consists of a lip-lever drinking tube, a solenoid

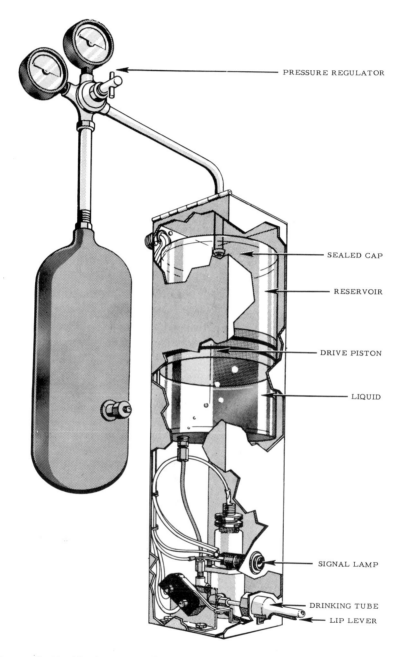

PRESSURE REGULATOR

SEALED CAP

RESERVOIR

DRIVE PISTON

LIQUID

SIGNAL LAMP

DRINKING TUBE
LIP LEVER

Figure 3. Liquid dispenser designed for use during weightlessness. (From Grunzke, 1961c.)

valve, and a column of water that is kept under pressure by a bottle of compressed air. When the subject bites on the drinking tube, the lip-lever activates a switch which opens the valve for a period of time sufficient for delivering water to the subject. This device is shown in Figure 3 and can be used for training and general laboratory work without the compressed air (Grunzke, 1961c).

Several additional modifications have been made in standard laboratory equipment. One of these was in the operant lever itself since, during launch, less force would be required to press the lever than during weightlessness. A novel solution to this problem has been suggested by Herrick (1961a), who designed a constant torque lever that moves through an arc containing nine contacts. The subject is required to press the lever to Position 5. Failure to press the lever as far as Position 5 and presses beyond Position 5 are unrewarded. Results obtained with this lever show a normal distribution of responses about the fifth contact point. In fact, his findings show that under increased acceleration there are fewer responses but the distribution of responses about the Number 5 contact is essentially the same as under normal gravitational conditions (Herrick, 1961b).

Another device which has been adapted for measuring animal behavior under conditions of space flight and which has enjoyed wide acceptance in other fields of operant research, is the In-line Digital Display (IDD). This is a projection device that is capable of presenting one of 12 symbols or colors on a ground glass screen. When combined with a lucite response key as shown in Figure 4, it can be used in matching, oddity, or similar problems. This device, referred to as a Stimulus-Response Key (SRK), has been used successfully with both monkeys and chimpanzees (Rohles & Grunzke, 1961a).

Reinforcement Schedules and Performance Tasks

For assessing the effects of the various environments of space flight on learned behavior, several unique schedules of reinforcement have been developed and have been used individually or have been incorporated with the more standard or conventional schedules.

One of the basic schedules that has been employed in much of the animal research in space environments is the response-shock (RS) or free operant, avoidance schedule (Sidman, 1953; see also Chapter 10 in this book). However, a discrete avoidance task has been added to this by incorporating another stimulus and lever. The combined tasks, described by Belleville, Rohles, and Grunzke (1960) as continuous avoidance (CA, for the Sidman schedule) and discrete avoidance (DA), involve two lights and two levers. In the presence of a red light, the subject performs on an avoidance schedule with a response-shock interval of 15 seconds (RS-15) and a shock-shock interval of three seconds (SS-3). At the

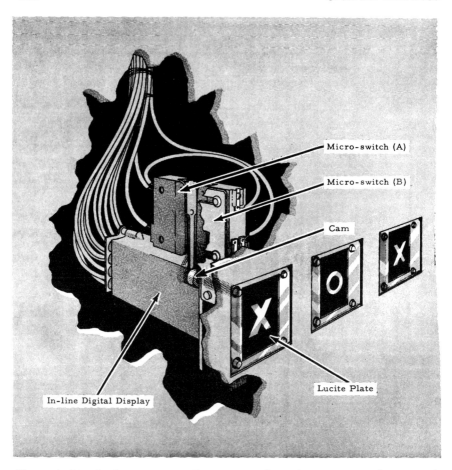

Figure 4. Stimulus-Response Key (SRK) using a lucite key over an In-line Digital Display.

same time, as the subject is performing on this schedule, a blue light is turned on over the left lever. When the blue light comes on, the subject has five seconds (interstimulus interval, ISI-5) to press the left lever in order to avoid shock. The combined schedules are designated as $CA_{RS-15,SS-3}/DA_{ISI-5}$.

A second schedule which has been developed builds on these two tasks by adding a drl 20 schedule for water, an FR 50 schedule for food, and 18 three-stimulus oddity problems. In this schedule, three IDDs are used and a lever is mounted below each display. The cues for the CA/DA tasks are the same as before; the red light is presented on the right IDD for CA and the blue light is presented on the left IDD for DA. The S^D for this component is ten minutes. Following an S^Δ of six minutes, a green light is presented on the right IDD as a cue for the drl 20 schedule. If the subject waits the required length of time, i.e., 20 seconds or longer, and then presses the light lever, a light is turned on above the lip-lever drinking tube of the watering device (Grunzke, 1961c) to cue the subject that water is available. When the subject bites on the lip-lever drinking tube, the water reward is delivered. This component is in effect for ten minutes and is followed by a six-minute S^Δ. Next, a yellow light is presented on the middle IDD to cue the subject that the FR 50 schedule is in effect. Like the other components, this schedule is in effect for ten minutes and is followed by a six-minute time-out. The last component of the schedule utilizes all three IDDs for presenting 18 three-stimulus oddity problems. Three stimuli are used, a circle, triangle, and square; and both positive and negative reinforcement have been employed. When positive reward is used, either the correct response to each problem is rewarded or a ratio reinforcement schedule may be used in which a fixed number of correct discriminations are required for a single reward. When the oddity component is used with negative reinforcement, an electric shock is presented following an incorrect discrimination or if there is no response within 15 seconds following the presentation of the problem. This complete schedule with the oddity problem used with negative reinforcement, designated as mult $CA_{RS-15,SS-3}/DA_{ISI-5}$, $S^\Delta 6$, drl 20, $S^\Delta 6$, FR 50, $S^\Delta 6$, 3S Oddity (avoid), is described in detail by Belleville, Rohles, Grunzke, and Clark (1963).

An extension of the 18 three-stimulus oddity problem has been used for studying the instrumental skill sequence (Rohles, 1961a; Rohles, Belleville, & Grunzke, 1961). In these studies a chimpanzee was rewarded for each correct discrimination. When the accuracy of discriminations reached 90 percent, every nineteenth correct discrimination was rewarded. This resulted in an increase of both the response rate and level of accuracy; in fact, under this procedure the animal worked so fast that it was obvious that the response order or sequence had been learned since the response rate was too great to allow for the subject to attend the oddity problem and make the discrimination.

Related to the FR 19 reinforcement of the 18 oddity problems is a variation reported by Rohles (1961b), who studied performance on a four-stimulus oddity problem with an FI 1 reinforcement schedule. In this problem a monkey had to press the lever under the odd stimulus, but regardless of the number of discriminations, reward was presented only on the first correct discrimination after a one-minute period. Performance was then analyzed both in terms of the accuracy of the discriminations and the number of reinforcements for a given test period. This provided an extension of the types of behavior usually studied with the conventional FI I schedule, and suggested that the response order was not learned with an FI schedule whereas it was with an FR schedule.

While tracking ability in humans has been studied extensively, it has received little attention from comparative psychologists and would not fall under the usual definition of operant behavior. However, in developing different tasks for sampling behavior during space flight, a tracking device was developed (Grunzke, Rohles, Belleville, & Wilson, 1962) which readily lends itself to operant reinforcement schedules; this device is shown in Figure 5. As in the Complex Coordination Test that was used during World

Figure 5. Two-dimensional discrete tracking device for a chimpanzee.

War II for selecting aircrew personnel (Melton, 1947), the subject had to match a red light on the vertical row with a green light that moves by pressing the left lever either forward or backward; then the red light on the horizontal row is matched with a green light by pressing the right lever either left or right. When the two rows of lights are matched, the subject presses a third lever, which presents a new pattern. When a fixed number of patterns are matched, the pressing of the third lever not only presents a new pattern but also delivers a reward. In brief, the subject is on an FR reinforcement in that one reward is given for a fixed number of matches. High and steady rates of performance have been obtained from a chimpanzee on an FR 7 schedule.

Another performance task designed to study performance during extended space flight has been suggested by Rohles, Reynolds, Grunzke, and Farrer (1962). The performance test panel is shown in Figure 6, and consists of eight Stimulus-Response Keys (SRK), two one-inch diameter lights, and three levers. A 1024-cps tone at 60 db is presented through a speaker mounted behind the top SRK on the panel. The tone is presented aperiodically for five seconds, and when this occurs the subject has to press the SRK within five seconds in order to avoid shock. A blue light is mounted behind each of SRKs A through E (see Figure 7). These lights come on aperiodically in random order and the subject has five seconds in which to push the SRK having the lighted cue. Failure to make this response within five seconds results in the delivery of electric shock.

Both of these tasks, referred to as auditory and visual monitoring (AM and VM) tasks were superimposed on conventional operant schedules. The red light served to cue the subject to perform on a continuous avoidance ($CA_{RS-20,SS-3}$) task by pressing Lever 3 at least once every 20 seconds to avoid shock. At the same time that this task is in effect, the blue light comes on every two minutes for five seconds for the discrete avoidance (DA_{ISI-5}) task. When this light comes on, the subject has to press Lever 1 within five seconds to avoid shock. This combined task, CA and DA, is performed for 7.5 minutes and is followed by a three-minute S^Δ. After this rest period, a light is turned on over Lever 2 to cue the subject to press this lever on an FR 50 reinforcement schedule. When the subject makes 50 responses, the light above Lever 2 is turned out and the two SRKs above the cue light come on. If the subject desires food, he presses the yellow SRK and is rewarded with a one-gram food pellet. If, however, water is desired, the subject presses the green SRK; this response causes a light to come on at the water feeder to cue the subject that water is available and will be delivered when the lip-lever drinking tube is bitten. This program is in effect for nine minutes and is followed by a three-minute S^Δ.

This schedule, designed for measuring behavior during extended space flight, has been modified for studying the behavioral effects of exposure to exotic rocket fuels (Reynolds, Rohles, Prine, Carter, & Brunson, 1963).

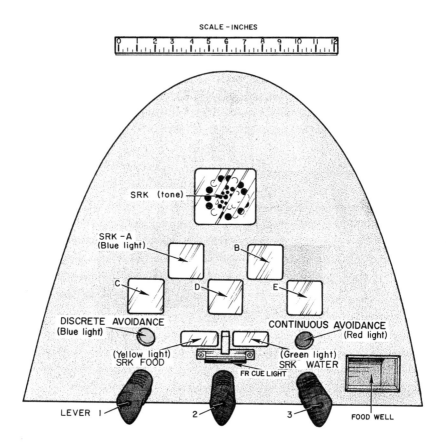

Figure 6. Test panel for a task designed to measure chimpanzee performance during extended orbital flight.

In this modification, the FR component was omitted and behavior was studied with only the avoidance components using different R-S intervals. By using IDDs, oddity or matching problems can also be introduced into the schedule.

Another schedule described by Reynolds, Bogo, and Rohles (1963) incorporates three avoidance tasks. The apparatus contains three IDDs, a small signal lamp, and three levers, one under each IDD. In the first component, a green light is presented on the right IDD and, at the same time, the signal light flashes to cue the subject that time has begun. The subject can avoid shock by responding 15 seconds after these cues are presented. Responses before 15 seconds or after 30 seconds result in the delivery of a shock. After a five-minute S^Δ, a red light is presented on the middle IDD. When this light comes on, the subject must make 20 responses on the center lever within 20 seconds to avoid a shock. Between 20 and 30 seconds after the red light comes on, a blue light is presented on the left IDD as a cue for a discrete avoidance (DA) task with an ISI of two seconds.

THE EFFECTS OF SPACE ENVIRONMENTS ON BEHAVIOR

When an animal participates in actual space flight it is subjected to several environmental stresses. As stated previously, these are acceleration, noise, and vibration during launch, altered composition of the gas that is breathed, reduced atmospheric pressure, confinement, isolation, weightlessness, cosmic radiation, heating, buffeting, deceleration, and impact. Since several of these environmental stresses are imposed simultaneously, it is difficult to determine which single aspect of the environment affects performance. Where one of these factors alone may not produce any decrement in performance, it is possible that two or more in combination may produce a performance change.

At the outset, therefore, it immediately becomes apparent that to study the effects of all of these environments in a systematic manner is a monumental task which not only requires considerable time, but demands much in the way of specialized equipment to simulate the specific environments under study. Steps have been taken, however, to study the effects of these factors on behavior, and most noteworthy has been the work in the area of acceleration.

Acceleration and Deceleration, Noise, and Vibration

Prior to the Little Joe flights, in which monkeys SAM and Miss SAM were placed through a ballistic trajectory, monkeys were exposed to simulated launch accelerations on the Navy centrifuge at Johnsville, Pennsylvania (Brown, 1959). Likewise, before the Mercury-Redstone flight, chimpanzees were subjected to simulated Redstone launch profiles on the centrifuge at the Aerospace Medical Laboratory, Dayton, Ohio, and performed the CA/DA tasks described previously. The results showed a decrement in response rate on the CA task when the subject was exposed to six Gs, but reaction times as measured by the DA task were unchanged (Belleville, 1959).

Before the Mercury-Atlas flights, chimpanzees were exposed to simulated Atlas launch accelerations on the centrifuge at the University of Southern California (Reynolds, Grunzke, & Rohles, 1963). Three tests were conducted with five chimpanzees. In the first, the effects of launch acceleration were studied. From the twentieth minute to the fourteenth minute before the simulated launch, and from 1.5 minutes before launch until 10.5 minutes after launch, the subject performed the CA task. Peak acceleration of 9.9 Gs occurred two minutes and 19 seconds following launch. This subsided quickly to 3.2 Gs and was followed by a secondary acceleration of 6 Gs which occurred 1.5 minutes later. This same procedure was used in the second and third series of tests. However, in the second series the subject was vibrated both in the lateral and longitudinal planes at 6.75 cps from one minute before launch until 4.25 minutes after launch, and was exposed to 110 db white noise from 30 seconds before launch until 4.25 minutes after launch. During the next 270 minutes, which were designed to simulate three 90-minute orbits, the subject performed on the Multiple $CA_{RS-15,SS-3}/DA_{ISI-5}$, drl 20 (water), FR 50 (food), 3S Oddity (avoid) schedule, in a one G environment without noise and vibration; then the subjects were exposed to simulated re-entry accelerations, while again performing the CA task. The re-entry period lasted 3.5 minutes, and a peak acceleration of 7.7 Gs occurred 1.5 minutes after the start of the re-entry period. Performance on the CA task was assessed during two consecutive periods; from 1.5 minutes before re-entry to 4.5 minutes after re-entry, and from 4.5 minutes after re-entry to 10.5 minutes after re-entry.

In addition to being exposed to the launch acceleration, noise, and vibration in the third series of tests, the subject was fitted with two catheters, one for collecting urine, and a second for measuring blood pressure. Performance during these tests are presented in Figure 7. The conclusions were:

> When noise and vibration of the sort expected in the actual launch are introduced, behavior is not additionally affected (beyond that evolving from launch alone); nor is behavior additionally affected when blood pressure and urine catheterization are "added" to noise and vibration.
>
> Performance during the three launches and two re-entries differed from the Launch −20′ to Launch −14′ baseline performance period at the .01 level of statistical significance. However, performance following launch and re-entry indicates that the subjects experienced a normal recovery.
>
> During the third and fourth minutes of launch acceleration (peak G of 9.9 reached at Launch +2′ 19″) animals showed greater impairment in performance than at any other time. Approximately 58 percent of all the shocks the five chimanzees received during the 15 centrifuge runs came about during this two-minute period, but a total of 80 percent occurred during launch or immediately thereafter. By the end of four minutes following peak launch G, animals are back "in stride" although not up to their baseline performance previous to launch.
>
> During the second, third, and fourth minutes of re-entry (peak G of 7.7 reached at Re-entry +1′ 30″) animals showed an impairment in performance, but not of the magnitude experienced during launch. It is pertinent to reiterate at this time that normal earth gravity existed during

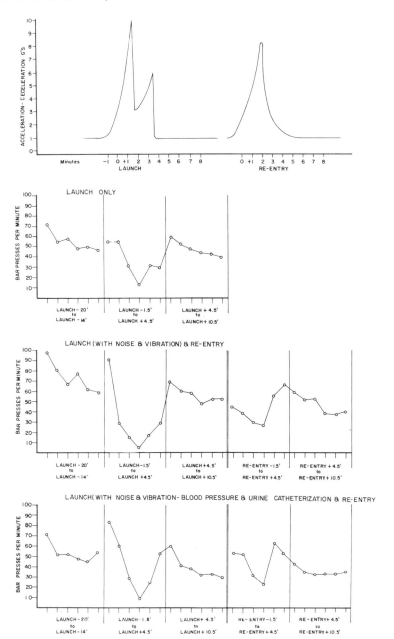

Figure 7. Chimpanzee performance on the CA task under simulated launch condition alone, with noise and vibration, and with noise, vibration, and catheteriza-
tion. The response records are lined up underneath the record indicating acceleration and deceleration. The first record under each condition represents a
pre-launch control period.

the "weightlessness" phase of these profile runs. Re-entry from an actual state of weightlessness may very well bring about behavior different from these findings. In any event, the data from this investigation show that the animals only took some 20 percent of the total shocks during re-entry as compared with 80 percent during launch (Reynolds, Grunzke, & Rohles, 1963, p. 200).

The foregoing studies were designed specifically as applied efforts to determine the effects of acceleration on performance for the three booster vehicles involved: the Little Joe, the Redstone, and the Atlas. In a more basic study (Farrer, Grunzke, Gilbert, Barnhart, & Jacobs, 1963) the effects of acceleration on the CA task were investigated on the centrifuge at the White Sands Missile Range, New Mexico. Four chimpanzees were used and performance was sampled during 15 four-minute test sessions with a one-minute S^Δ between every two sessions. Two of the subjects performed the CA task for five sessions at 1 G, then continued for five sessions at 4 G; this was followed by five post-test sessions at 1 G. The other two subjects performed the task for the same number of sessions at 1 G, 2 G, and 1 G. During the second phase of testing, the subjects who had received the 1 G, 4 G, 1 G, exposure were tested during a 1 G, 2 G, 1 G exposure and the subjects who had been exposed to these accelerations on the original test were exposed to 1 G, 4 G, 1 G. From this study the authors concluded that a performance decrement occurred when the subjects were exposed to 4 G transverse (the force operating from chest to back) for 30 minutes; however, no significant reduction in response rate was observed in the subjects receiving 2 G.

Similar findings were observed in a replication of the study (Farrer, Warrell, & Gilbert, 1964). It confirmed the 4 G decrement which was previously obtained, but the consistent performance increment occurring during the 2 G exposure in the first study was not found in the second study.

Atmospheric Conditions

Another environmental variable of space flight which has received study by behavioral scientists is the atmospheric pressure and oxygen composition of the inspired air. Using six chimpanzees, Farrer and Reynolds (1962) studied the effects upon performance of breathing pure oxygen at 14.7 psi (sea-level pressure). Each subject was tested both in a 100 percent O_2 environment and a 20 percent O_2 environment (normal oxygen composition of air at sea level) for 15 hours, and performance on the $CA_{RS-15,SS-3}/DA_{ISI-5}$ tasks was measured during five 15-minute test sessions which were equally distributed during the 15-hour period. In the 100 percent O_2 environment, one subject exhibited a decrement in response rate on the CA task and two subjects showed an increase in reaction time as measured by the DA task.

In a similar study with two chimpanzees, Farrer and Bogo (1962) studied performance during a simulated environmental flight profile (social isolation, restraint, and 100 percent oxygen) of 97 hours duration which involved a pre-launch vehicle environment (100 percent oxygen, 14.7 psi) time for 15 hours, followed by the flight environment (100 percent oxygen, 5 psi) time of 82 hours. Using a test-retest counterbalanced design, the subject received the two treatment conditions in reverse order; four weeks were allowed between tests. Performance was measured with the mult $CA_{RS-15,SS-3}/DA_{ISI-5}$, drl 20 (water), FR 50 (food), 3S Oddity (food) schedule.

The results showed that one of the subjects exhibited a response rate during exposure to the pure oxygen environment which was significantly less than under normal conditions; the performance by the other subject was essentially the same under both conditions.

Evidence for diurnal cycle maintenance was found in the CA response rate data. The mean performance rate during the day sessions was as much as 41.28 bar presses per minute higher than the mean performance rate during the night sessions for one subject. Both subjects performed at lower rates during the night sessions than during day sessions on all tests.

DA performance reflected individual differences between the two subjects. Both subjects had slightly faster reactions to the DA stimulus light during the 100 percent oxygen condition, and the analysis of variance for the combined data reflected this difference ($P<.01$). However, the individual analysis of variance showed that only one subject reacted more rapidly during the 100 percent oxygen condition.

Exotic Rocket Fuels

The techniques of operant conditioning have also been employed in evaluating the effects upon behavior of exposure to the exotic rocket fuels. In one study in which java monkeys were exposed to 1-1 dimethylhydrazine (UDMH), a dosage of 30 mg/kg did not produce a significant decrement in response rate when compared to the non-UDMH performance (Reynolds, Rohles, Fineg, Back, & Thomas, 1962). In a second study (Reynolds, *et al.*, 1963), monkeys were trained on the $CA_{RS-15,SS-3}/DA_{ISI-3}$ $VM_{ISI-2} + AM_{ISI-2}$ schedule described previously. After performance became stabilized the subjects were administered a 30 mg/kg dose of UDMH and performance was assessed during six 13-minute test sessions with a 45-minute rest between each session. On the first replication one of the four subjects exhibited significant performance decrements after three and one-half hours. On the second replication three of the four subjects exhibited significant performance decrements after three and one-half hours. Of the nine instances of performance decrement occurring during the two replications, seven are attributable to two subjects. Only two instances of a significant increment in performance occurred, one in one subject who showed no decrement at anytime during testing, and the other in one of the two subjects responsible for the majority of decrements. At the same time as decrements on continuous and discrete avoidance occurred at the .01 level of statistical significance, the increment on auditory monitoring was taking place. Seven of the nine instances of performance decrement occurred during the second replication, and the other two instances which occurred in the first replication involved the same subject. All subjects exhibiting a decrement in performance or exhibiting clinical illness recovered within the day of the experiment.

It was upwards of 11 days, however, before performance returned to pre-drug levels in a similar study designed to determine the performance effects following exposure to the high energy fuel, decaborane (Reynolds, Brunson, Back, & Thomas, 1964). In this study, eight monkeys were trained on a $CA_{RS-15,SS-3}/DA_{ISI-2} + AM_{ISI-2}$ reinforcement schedule. When their performance was stabilized, the subjects were divided into two groups and were administered 2 mg and 4 mg/kg body weight, respectively. Following this, performance was measured for eight 15-minute sessions per day. The results showed that dosage of 2 mg and 4 mg/kg body weight produced decrements in continuous motor behavior in all eight subjects, and three-fourths of the subjects exhibited a decrement on the discrete tasks. In over half the subjects a performance decrement preceded clinical symptoms by a distinct time period, suggesting the importance of performance measures in any assessment of organismic functioning.

Circadian Rhythms

The free operant has also been a valuable tool in the study of behavior as it is affected by circadian rhythms. Ordinarily, rhythmicity would not be considered as a subject for study under the general heading of space environments; however, because it is known that the light-dark cycle affects the circadian rhythm and, since during prolonged orbital flight the normal day-night cycle will be absent, it would be reasonable to assume that a change in the circadian rhythm will result and organismic functioning might be affected.

Two classical methods for demonstrating circadian rhythms use gross motor activity and body temperature. Since changes in motor activity are unlikely in a restrained animal participating in space flight, changes in body temperature appear as the logical approach to the study of rhythms. Because of the interest in this area, a study was conducted by Bush, Rohles, Reynolds, & Koestler (1962) to determine if there were a relationship between response rate and skin temperature. Four java monkeys were trained on a CA task to a stabilized response rate and placed into isolation. Each subject performed the task for 12 hours per day during three work periods of four hours each, and the work periods were scheduled so that two of the animals were working while the other two rested for the three days of the test. By partialling out the effects of ambient temperature and comparing the response rate with skin temperature, 8 of the 12 correlations were significant beyond the .05 percent level of confidence. The correlations are shown in Table 1.

Table 1

Correlations Between Bar-Pressing Rate and Skin Temperatures of Individual Subjects

(When the effect of cubicle temperature is partialled out)

Subject	Day 1	Day 2	Day 3
1	.670**	−.176	.572*
2	.364	.875**	.272
3	.507*	.518*	.490*
4	.636**	.145	.646**

** p<.01
* p<.05

LABORATORY MODELS

The development of the laboratory model of a space flight is an applied effort designed to answer specific questions about animal physiology and behavior under the simulated conditions of isolation and confinement. In this respect, it could be considered as a special case in the study of space environments. However, the laboratory model yields considerably more information than studies designed to determine specific environmental effects.

The primary value of models lies in the acquisition of normative data under ground conditions which can be compared with flight results. These models define performance characteristics on specific schedules and yield average response rates and their variability, as well as establishing ranges for selected physiological measures. But perhaps most important, they permit the experimenter to determine for the engineer the daily food and water required, the volume of urine and feces produced, and the specific gravity of the metabolic waste. Thus, information from the laboratory model serves many disciplines—psychology, physiology, and engineering.

One such model for an orbital flight with a mouse was developed by Rohles and Grunzke (1961b). In this model the subject was a C-57 BL mouse of the Roscoe B. Jackson Laboratory strain. The subject was selected for two reasons: (1) its black hair turns white when exposed to radiation; and (2) the strain is not susceptible to audiogenic seizures. In fact, no behavioral effects were observed in this species when it was exposed to 120 db of wide-band noise for three minutes, an important factor when considering the noise that accompanies launch of a rocket booster. Standard deprivation procedures were used, and the subject was placed in an operant chamber and given magazine training. As soon as the subject was responding in the continuous reinforcement schedule the ratio of responses to rewards was increased and discrimination training was begun. When this was completed it provided a six-hour cycle for the animal, a 20-minute work period in which the FR 100 schedule was in effect under S^D, followed by a five-hour 40-minute rest period under S^Δ.

After the subject was discriminating on this schedule, it was tested for eight days. During the first four days, performance during the 20-minute work periods was reinforced; however, it was not reinforced during the last four days. Response rates were high and steady during reinforcement. During extinction, bursts of responding alternated with zero response rate during each session. As the latter became increasingly prevalent, response totals during the 20-minute work periods were correspondingly reduced.

In another laboratory model, a chimpanzee was restrained in a training couch and isolated from the usual laboratory distractions for 14 days. The subject performed on the mult $CA_{RS-15,SS-3}/DA_{ISI-3}$, drl 20, FR 50, 3S Oddity (avoid) schedule for the times shown in Table 2. Pulse and respira-

Table 2
Daily Work-Rest Schedules by Orbit* for a Chimpanzee
On a Simulated 14-Day Space Flight

		Time (Min)	
Orbit	Performance	Work	Rest
1	All components	66	24
2	All components	66	24
3, 4, 5	None	0	270
6	All components	66	24
7	CA-DA only	15	75
8	All components	66	24
9	CA-DA only	15	75
10	All components	66	24
11, 12	None	0	180
13	CA-DA only	15	75
14	CA-DA only	15	75
15	All components	66	24
16	All components	66	24
		522	918
		8 hr.	15 hr.
		42 min.	18 min.

* There are 16 90-min. orbits every 24 hrs.

tion rates were determined for one minute every 15 minutes throughout the 14-day period and skin temperature was recorded at the end of each 15-minute period. In addition, the urine volume and feces weight were determined for each four-hour period and food pellet and water consumption were measured for each work session.

Aside from the behavioral and physiological data acquired in this 14-

day laboratory model, several important factors were discovered in the area of equipment design. On three separate occasions the cubicle had to be opened—to repair the feeder, to replace a burned-out bulb, and to connect a wire which had become loose. In addition, it was found that every other day it was necessary to add electrolytes to the water used for reward on the drl schedule.

It was concluded that a chimpanzee could withstand social isolation and restraint for 14 days without serious physical damage or behavioral impairment. The number of equipment malfunctions, while few, confirmed the necessity for redundancy in all electrical and mechanical systems. The results also provided parameters of food and water consumption, waste production, skin temperature, pulse, and respiration. The performance schedule provided the subject with sufficient food and water, since the animal did not lose any weight for the 14-day period. Improvement in the performance of some of the behavioral tasks occurred during the study. And while the subject was weak when removed from the couch, his recovery was rapid (Rohles, Reynolds, Grunzke, & Farrer, 1961).

In another study (Rohles, Reynolds, & Grunzke, 1963), three chimpanzees were individually isolated from the usual laboratory distractions for 30 days after having been trained on what the investigators termed a self-paced FR 50 schedule for food or water. The apparatus consisted of a lever which was mounted below two SRKs. On the fiftieth lever press a yellow light came on behind one SRK and a green light came on behind the other. If the subject desired food, he pressed the yellow SRK, but if water was desired the green SRK was pushed. The "self-paced" aspect of

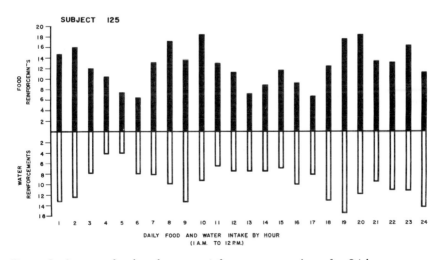

Figure 8. Average food and water reinforcements per hour for 24 hours over a 30-day period for a chimpanzee on a self-paced FR 50 (food or water) reinforcement schedule.

the schedule was that the subject could work on this schedule at any time of the day he was so motivated. The daily food and water intake for a representative subject is shown in Figure 8.

The results of this study are useful in several ways. Their greatest importance is that they serve as a guideline for determining the orbits during which work should be scheduled. Next, they demonstrate that the chimpanzee can readily withstand social isolation for 30 days. Finally, the results indicate that the chimpanzee can, with only a slight weight loss, be sustained for 30 days on a pellet and water diet.

FLIGHT PERFORMANCE

In March, 1959, the National Aeronautics and Space Administration (NASA) announced its plans for Project Mercury, the United States man-in-space program. Part of this program involved the testing of the space capsule with animals, and specified that both physiological and psychological measures would be made. As a result of this announcement, the USAF School of Aerospace Medicine, Brooks Air Force Base, Texas, was given the responsibility of testing the escape system; the testing of the capsule itself was assigned to the Aeromedical Research Laboratory, Holloman Air Force Base, New Mexico.

Mercury—Little Joe

The testing of the escape system in which animal performance was measured was accomplished in two flights of the Little Joe booster. The first flight, designated as Little Joe No. 2, occurred on December 4, 1959, and reached an altitude of 280,000 feet. Little Joe No. 1-B, as the second flight was called, was launched on January 21, 1960; its maximum altitude was 49,000 feet.

A rhesus monkey served as the subject in each of the flights and the apparatus consisted of a panel containing a light and a lever. When the light came on, the subject had two seconds in which to press the lever in order to avoid shock. This response turned off the light for two seconds. If the subject did not respond within two seconds after the light came on, or held the lever down for longer than two seconds, the animal received one shock every two seconds. Training on this program was begun in October, 1958, approximately 14 months before the actual flight. This consisted of five ten-minute work periods per day for the six animals involved in the program. The average number of lever presses per work period was between 500 and 800. All animals except SAM (*S*chool of *A*erospace *M*edicine), who participated in the first flight, were exposed to simulated launch accelerations of the Little Joe booster on the centrifuge at the Naval Air Development Center, Johnsville, Pennsylvania.

On the first flight the subject was placed in the life support cell, and loaded into the capsule approximately 14 hours before launch. At launch the subject was exposed to a maximum G of 5.9, and the firing of the escape rockets created a maximum acceleration of 14.76 Gs. The subject was weightless for 3.2 minutes.

The behavioral apparatus was turned on 60 seconds before launch, and the subject began to respond, continuing this performance until 1.3 seconds before launch when failure to respond to the stimulus light resulted in the delivery of shock. However, the subject responded in 0.76 seconds and pressed the lever again at lift-off.

Two seconds after launch the cue light came on, but the animal failed to respond and was shocked; however, he did respond in 0.5 seconds. On the third appearance of the light, he did not respond and was shocked every 2 seconds for 14 seconds. Then he began responding and continued at a high rate for the next 34 seconds. The subject pressed the lever at the exact instant of the firing of the escape rockets and four times afterward, but from 63 seconds after launch until the end of the flight, he failed to perform. The capsule was recovered from the Atlantic Ocean.

In the second flight, the subject was a female rhesus monkey, Miss SAM. The behavioral task was the same as for the Little Joe No. 2 flight. The subject was sealed in the life support cell and placed in the Mercury capsule approximately 19 hours before launch. The animal was subjected to 6 Gs upon launch and 11.3 Gs during the firing of the escape rockets. The duration of the flight was 514.7 seconds.

The performance apparatus was turned on two minutes before launch for ten seconds, and during this period the subject received one shock for failing to press the lever. Sixty seconds before launch the apparatus was turned on again. The stimulus light came on twelve times and the subject was shocked ten times. During the 20 seconds before launch, however, the response rate increased and only three shocks were received.

For the first 30 seconds following launch, performance was impaired. During the first period, the subject was shocked eight times for holding down the lever, which was attributed to the Gs experienced during the launch phase of the flight. When the escape rockets fired, the cue light was on, and the subject received one shock for failing to respond and another for holding down the lever. The subject also failed to perform from 35.5 seconds after launch until 65 seconds after launch. At 66 seconds the subject began responding again and received only eight shocks from them until the end of the flight.

There is little information on the pre-flight performance of these animals available, and this makes a comparison with inflight performance difficult. These flights do represent the first attempts at measuring performance of this type during space flight. The training was accomplished by W. Lynn Brown and H. C. Blodgett of the Radiobiological Laboratory at the University of Texas through contract with the School of Aviation Medicine. Complete details of these flights are reported by Green, Welch, Brown, Lamb, Tang, Gisler, and Blodgett (1961).

Mercury—Redstone

Following the Little Joe series, the USAF Aeromedical Research Laboratory, Holloman Air Force Base, New Mexico, prepared animals for two additional flights which took place at Cape Canaveral, Florida. In the first of these, which occurred January 31, 1961, and was designated as Mercury-Redstone 2 (MR-2), a chimpanzee was placed into a ballistic

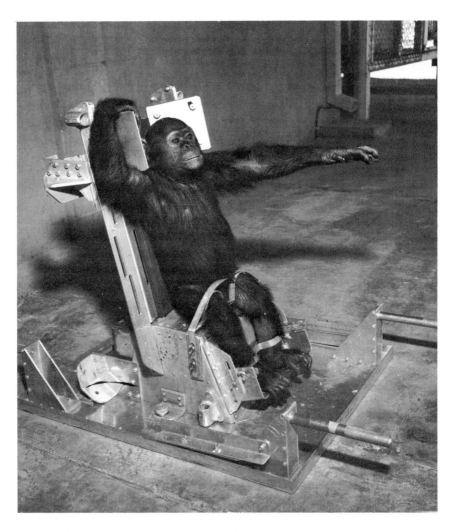

Figure 9. Restraint chair for laboratory training of the chimpanzee.

trajectory to an altitude of 136.2 nautical miles and was recovered 363 nautical miles from the point of launch.

Prior to this flight, the training proceeded through several stages. In the first stage the training was conducted with standard equipment in a chair (developed by Grunzke, 1961b) like the one shown in Figure 9. Restraint is accomplished by a neck yoke and by bars that fit over the knees and ankles; shock may be delivered through brass plates which are hinged and in constant contact with the subject's feet. After the subject was responding well under these conditions, it was moved from the chair to the training couch. This was made of molded plastic and fit the body contours of the animal; restraint was accomplished by lacing the animal's nylon mesh suit to the back of the couch. The training couch was a laboratory model of the actual couch that was used in flight with two exceptions: (1) it could not be pressurized, and (2) it used standard laboratory programming equipment. However, the performance requirements in the training couch are the same as in the chair, with the exception of the position of the subject and his relationship to the stimuli and levers. The third and final stage of training involved measurement of behavior in the flight couch. Here performance data were recorded in the same form as they were during the space flight. This permitted testing of the miniaturized programming equipment which was an integral part of the flight couch. When this final stage of training was completed the subjects were kept at peak proficiency until the flight. This procedure required 15 months for eight chimpanzees which were used in this flight.

In the MR-2 flight, four major pieces of equipment were used: the rocket booster, the Mercury capsule (including the escape tower and accompanying rockets), the animal couch, and the performance test panel. The relative physical locations of these four items are shown in Figure 10. At launch, the Mercury capsule was mounted on the booster; however, it separated from the booster shortly after launch and its escape tower was jettisoned. The flight couch was rigidly mounted inside the Mercury capsule. The performance test panel, which was 17 inches long and 5.5 inches wide, was located level with the subject's waist and was perpendicular to the long axis of his body.

The subject, HAM (Holloman AeroMedical Laboratory), was a male chimpanzee weighing 37 pounds whose age at the time of the flight was estimated to be 44 months. He had been trained on the performance task for over 15 months and prior to the flight had been exposed to simulated Redstone launch acceleration profiles on the centrifuge at the Aerospace Medical Laboratory, Dayton, Ohio. Performance consisted of the $CA_{RS-15, SS-3}/DR_{ISI-5}$ task.

The task was programmed with transistorized units and shock was delivered through brass plates which were taped to the soles of the subject's feet. The shock was 160 volts AC, 400 cycles at ten milliamperes.

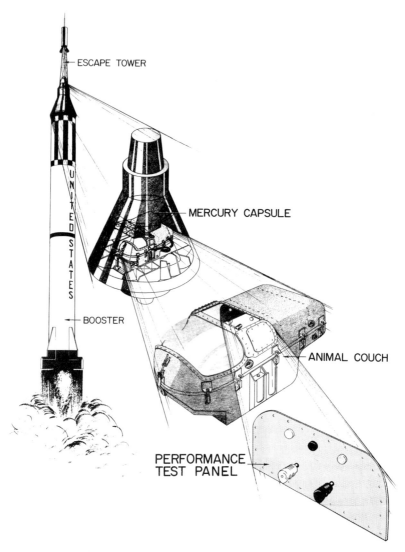

Figure 10. Diagram showing the locations of the Mercury capsule, animal couch, and performance test panel relative to the rocket booster.

At approximately 5:30 A.M., EST, on 31 January, 1961, the couch containing the subject was placed inside the capsule and connected to the capsule life support and electrical systems. After countdown procedures, which were interrupted by a delay of approximately four hours because of inverter heating, the launch occurred at 11:55 A.M. During launch, the main booster imposed a 6 G accelerative force on the subject; this was followed by a momentary exposure of 17 Gs when the rockets on the escape system fired. The subject experienced 7.5 minutes of weightlessness. When the capsule started on its downward course its flight attitude was reversed so that during re-entry the deceleration again imposed a transverse gravitational force from the front to the back of the subject. While the magnitude of the force at this time was not as great as it was during launch, it was of longer duration. The atmosphere inside the couch was maintained at 5 psi by adding 100 percent oxygen throughout the flight.

The G forces experienced by the subject during the flight, together with his performance on the CA/DA tasks, are presented in Figure 11. The sharp reduction in response rate on the CA task following launch was expected on the basis of performance following a 6 G exposure of the subject on the Aerospace Medical Laboratory centrifuge. Immediately following launch the subject received a shock; however, it is believed that this was due to a malfunction in the timing apparatus since careful analysis of the telemetry recording shows the time between responses during this period was less than 15 seconds. Performance was not affected during weightlessness; however, during re-entry a continuous decrement in response rate occurred and the subject received a second shock.

Reaction time, as measured by the discrete avoidance task, remained stable throughout the flight. For nine presentations of the blue light, the mean reaction time was 0.82 second, which was essentially the same as the pre-flight mean of 0.80 second.

Mercury—Atlas

In the second flight of this series, designated as Mercury-Atlas 5 (MA-5), the subject was a 42-pound male chimpanzee, Enos, whose age, at the time of this flight, was estimated to be 65 months. Prior to the flight he had been exposed to simulated launch accelerations on the centrifuge at the University of Southern California. He had received approximately 1263 hours of training over a 16-month period; 343 hours of this training was accomplished under restraint conditions in a laboratory model of the actual couch used during the flight.

The performance task was the mult $CA_{RS-15,SS-3}/DA_{ISI-5}$, drl 20, FR 50, 3S Oddity (Avoid). The major pieces of equipment were the same as in the MR-2 flight, however, a pellet feeder was also incorporated into the MA-5 performance panel. The pellets were loaded into the tube on the left side of the panel, curved behind the panel, and terminated at the plastic fingers.

For water reinforcement, a lip-lever drinking tube was mounted in the couch to the right of the subject's head. A small green lamp was mounted both above and below this tube and, when illuminated, served to cue the subject that water was available when he bit the lever. Water for this device was kept under pressure against a valve on the lip-lever by a bottle of com-

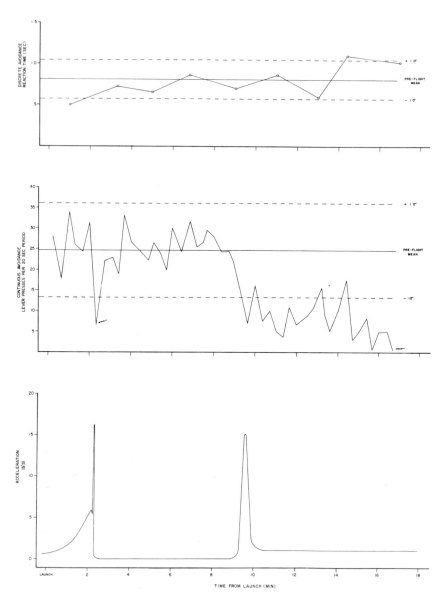

Figure 11. MR-2 Flight: Performance on the CA/DA task and acceleration-profile. Arrows indicate administration of shock.

pressed air. Both the liquid and pellet feeders were modifications of the feeders developed by Grunzke.

The method for programming the tasks, the procedure for delivering the electrical shock, and the shock level were the same as in the MR-2 flight. The task programmer units were transistorized and housed behind the performance test panel.

The subject and couch were loaded into the capsule at 3:30 A.M., EST on 29 November, 1961, and launch occurred at 10:07 A.M. During the launch phase of the flight the subject experienced two peak accelerations. The magnitude of the first peak was 6.5 Gs, and occurred approximately two minutes after lift-off; the second acceleration peak of 7.2 Gs occurred three minutes later. This was followed by approximately 183 minutes of weightlessness. During this time the capsule orbited the earth twice with a perigee of 99 miles and an apogee of 146 miles. The atmosphere of the couch was the same as for the MR-2 flight, namely, 5 psi maintained by 100 percent oxygen. When the capsule re-entered the earth's atmosphere, the subject experienced six minutes of deceleration with a peak of 7.8 Gs. Impact occurred at 1:28 P.M. in the Atlantic Ocean.

The CA/DA task was turned on two minutes before launch and performance was measured from then until ten minutes after impact. The time during the flight that each component task was in effect is presented in Table 3.

Table 3

Temporal Sequence of Performance Components During the MA-5 Flight

Component (Session)	Time from Launch (Min.)	Time Component in Effect (Min.)	Total Accumulated Time (Min.)
CA-DA (1)	−2 to +17	19	19
REST	18–23	6	25
DRL-20 (1)	24–33	10	35
REST	34–39	6	41
FR-50 (1)	40–49	10	51
REST	50–55	6	57
ODDITY (1)	56–65	10	67
CA-DA (2)	66–80	15	82
REST	81–86	6	88
DRL-20 (2)	87–96*	10	98
REST	97–102	6	104
FR-50 (2)	103–112	10	114
REST	113–118	6	120
ODDITY (2)	119–128	10	130
CA-DA (3)	129–143	15	145
REST	144–149	6	151
DRL-20 (3)	150–159	10	161
REST	160 165	6	167
FR-50 (3)	166–175	10	177
REST	176–181**	6	183
ODDITY (3)	182–191	10	193
CA-DA (4)	192–206***	15	208

° Completed first orbit at Launch + 88.5 min.
°° Completed second orbit at Launch + 177 min.; retro-rockets fired at Launch + 181 min.
°°° Impact at sea occurred at Launch + 201 min.

Performance on the CA/DA task is presented in three figures: Figure 12 shows the performance during the first session together with the launch accelerations; Figure 13 shows the performance during Sessions 2 and 3 when the subject was weightless; and Figure 14 depicts the performance during re-entry with the accompanying deceleration profile. While performing the CA/DA task, the subject received only two shocks—one on the CA component during the first session and one on the DA task during the

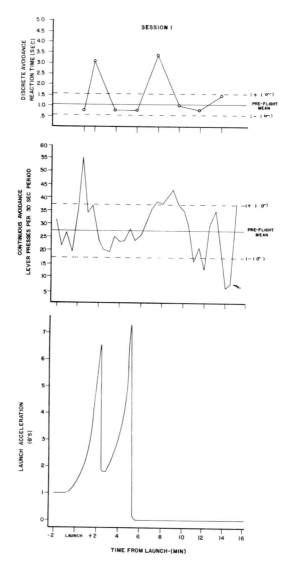

Figure 12. MA-5 Flight: Performance on the CA/DA task (Session 1) and launch accelerations. Arrow indicates administration of shock.

fourth session. While performance on the CA component was variable during and immediately following launch (Session 1) the subsequent sessions show a stable response rate within the range of the pre-flight mean, plus or minus one standard deviation. The blue light was presented eight times during Session 1 and seven times each during Sessions 2, 3, and 4; the mean

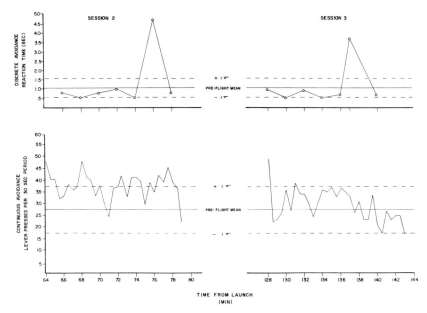

Figure 13. MA-5 Flight: Performance on the CA/DA task (Sessions 2 and 3) during weightlessness.

response time for these 29 presentations of the blue light was 1.49 seconds. While this was somewhat higher than the pre-flight mean, 23 of the 29 reaction times were within the range of plus and minus one standard deviation from the pre-flight mean.

Performance on the three sessions of the drl task is presented in Figure 15. On this task, the interresponse times were somewhat higher than those established during the pre-flight conditions but were well within the predicted limits. Each response on the drl task is represented during each of the three ten-minute periods that the task was in effect, e.g., during Session 1 the first response occurred 20.3 seconds after the drl cue light came on; however, this response was unrewarded apparently due to a programmer malfunction; the second response occurred 33 seconds after the first response, etc. During Session 1 the subject made 14 responses and earned 13 water reinforcements (7 cc of water for each reinforcement); during Session 2, 16 responses were made and 16 reinforcements received, and during Session 3, 20 responses were made and 18 of these were rewarded.

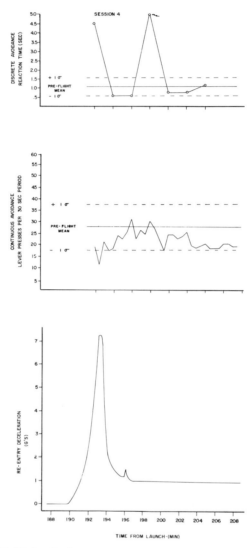

Figure 14. MA-5 Flight: Performance on the CA/DA task (Session 4) and re-entry decelerations. Arrow indicates administration of shock.

In the FR task, as shown in Figure 16, the subject received 12 pellets during the first FR session and exhibited an extremely stable response rate which closely approximated his pre-flight average. While the second session of the FR component was in effect, a malfunction occurred in the switch of Lever 2. This prohibited an accurate measurement of performance on Sessions 2 and 3 of the FR task, as well as the performance on the two subsequent oddity components.

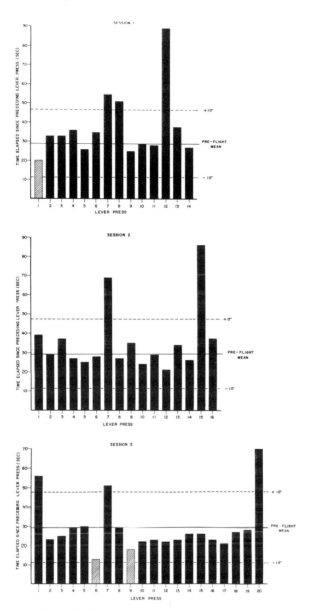

Figure 15. MA-5 Flight: Performance on the drl task for Sessions 1, 2, and 3. Solid bars indicate rewarded lever presses; crosshatched bars indicate unrewarded presses.

During the first session of the oddity problem the subject performed at 64.2 percent efficiency which was essentially the same as his pre-flight mean of 66 percent; ten shocks were delivered because of errors. Due to the malfunctioning of Lever 2, the efficiency of discrimination is virtually meaningless for Sessions 2 and 3.

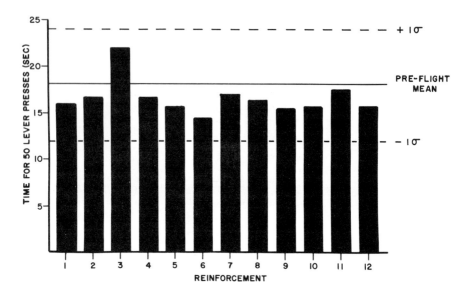

Figure 16. MA-5 Flight: Performance on the FR task (Session 1).

An indication of the subject's discriminatory ability can be derived from the fact that no lever presses were recorded during the nine six-minute rest periods.

CONCLUSIONS BASED ON FLIGHT DATA

Following the MR-2 flight, several factors that occurred immediately prior to the flight were studied. These were the awakening of the subject after only five hours of sleep, the suturing of the physiological sensors, and the nearly nine hours of restraint prior to launch. These gave rise to questions concerning the general physical condition of the subject at the time of launch and suggest that the subject may have been fatigued. If this were true, then one might expect a reduced response rate on the CA task and an increased reaction time on the DA task. However, because neither of these was observed, and because the novelty and uniqueness of the flight itself could possibly compensate for subject fatigue, these insults were again imposed upon the subject two weeks after the flight was made. The subject was kept awake on the thirteenth day after launch, was awakened at 1 A.M. on the fourteenth day and subjected to the same activities as he was during the countdown. He was then given a 17-minute trial in which both tasks were performed. This test indicated that the physical condition of the subject resulting from pre-flight activities did not affect subsequent performance on these tasks.

In addition to the factors just mentioned, there were also certain environmental variables occurring before launch. The first of these was the composition of the gas that was breathed by the subject. Five hours before launch the couch was filled with 100 percent oxygen at ambient atmospheric pressure (14.7 psi). After launch a bleed-off valve permitted the pressure to drop to 5 psi where it stabilized until re-entry; when the capsule descended, a vent was opened at an altitude of approximately 10,000 feet. Thus, it was conceivable that the breathing of 100 percent oxygen might have counteracted the fatigue associated with the conditions noted above. To test these effects upon performance, the pressurization and breathing of oxygen encountered in the actual flight, together with the variables associated with the insults noted above, were duplicated four weeks after the flight. It should be mentioned that whereas ambient pressure at Cape Canaveral, Florida, is 14.7 psi, it is 12.6 psi at Holloman Air Force Base, New Mexico; but since the subject was at Cape Canaveral for four weeks before the flight and was at Holloman Air Force Base for four weeks before this test, adaptation probably occurred in both instances and 12.6 psi was used as the ambient pressure during this test. While the investigators were unable to duplicate completely the period of pressurization of the flight due to mechanical malfunction on this simulated test, indications were that these two aspects of the flight did not affect performance. It should be pointed out that these conditions (the composition of the gas breathed by the subject and the atmospheric pressure, as well as the other insults already noted) were essentially the same in the MA-5 flight; however, these two studies were not repeated following that flight.

The next two environmental variables peculiar to the flight were the noise and vibration that accompanied launch. However, both of these were ruled out as deterrents to performance since, during ten separate exposures to vibrations of 6.75 cps (0.25 inch amplitude) and 110 db wide band noise, performance on the CA/DA tasks was not affected.

Thus, the environmental factors associated with the remainder of both flights can be summarized in terms of the physical forces acting upon the subject during the periods of launch, free flight, and re-entry into the earth's atmosphere. The magnitude, duration, and time of occurrence of these forces have been presented in Figure 11 for the ballistic flight and Figures 12 and 14 for the orbital flight. As it happened, fortunately, both subjects were performing the CA/DA tasks during the launch and re-entry periods. Concerning performance on the CA component, the variability in response rate following launch was expected on the basis of exposure to simulated launch accelerations on the centrifuge. During the MR-2 flight, there was a sharp decline in rate and, immediately following launch, the subject received his first shock; however, it is believed that this was due to a malfunction in the timing apparatus as indicated above. In contrast, this decrement was not observed in the MA-5 flight. Therefore, it is believed that the reduction in response rate of the subject in the MR-2 flight was a function of the 17 Gs experienced during the launch as compared with the two smaller accelerations (6.7 and 7.4 Gs) for MA-5. However, in the MA-5 flight the performance immediately following launch was more variable than performance during this period of the MR-2 flight, and it was during this time that the subject received his first shock. As predicted, performance was not affected during the weightless portion of either flight (Rohles, 1958).

During the re-entry period of the MR-2 flight a gradual decrement in the response rate was observed. This was not the case in the MA-flight. During the MR-2 flight the animal was subjected to 14 Gs for five seconds and 10 Gs for ten seconds during re-entry, whereas a deceleration of only 7.4 Gs was experienced during the orbital re-entry.

Therefore, it was concluded that launch and re-entry accelerations of the magnitude and duration of the MR-2 flight affected subsequent performance rate on the CA task. However, this statement is not without qualification. While it is true that a reduction in rate occurred, the number of responses for any 20-second period was never more than two standard deviations from the pre-flight mean. This fact becomes more striking in the MA-5 flight. Here performance on the CA component was essentially the same as during pre-flight with little variability. Von Beckh (1959) has shown that human subjects who were flown through the Zero-G trajectory and then exposed to increased longitudinal G forces "blacked out" at only 3.5 to 4 Gs whereas, without prior exposure to weightlessness, they could withstand 5 Gs before "blackout." In the MR-2 flight, in which transverse G occurred, the decrement in response rate following re-entry might be related to von Beckh's findings. However, since a decrement was not observed during the MA-5 flight, another explanation is offered. It is believed that the short duration of time involved in the MR-2 flight between launch and re-entry did not permit adequate recovery from the launch phase. In this flight the subject was weightless for only 7.5 minutes, whereas the weightless portion of the MA-5 flight was 183 minutes and permitted adequate recovery from the G stress of the launch. Thus, the accelerative forces accompanying re-entry in the MR-2 flight probably were not instrumental in bringing about a performance decrement.

An increase in the variability on the performance of the DA task was observed in the MA-5 flight. This was not true of the ballistic flight. The subject received one shock for failing to respond to the fourth presentation of the blue light on the fourth DA session. However, in comparing the pre-flight and in-flight means, it was concluded that visual reaction time was unaffected.

The performance on the drl component was also unaffected. In this regard, it is interesting to note that the malfunctioning of Lever 2, which resulted in the subject receiving 35 shocks on the second session of the oddity problem, did not disrupt his subsequent performance on either the third drl session nor the third session of the CA/DA component. And likewise, the 41 shocks received during the third oddity session did not affect performance during the subsequent fourth session of the CA/DA task. Certainly, following a malfunction of this nature, it would be expected that behavior would be disrupted; but this was not at all in evidence.

Performance on the first FR session was extremely stable and the discrimination accuracy for the first oddity session was also close to the preflight mean. Unfortunately, the malfunctioning of Lever 2 during the two subsequent sessions made the measurement on both tasks meaningless.

From a behavioral standpoint it can be concluded that, with the exception of the difficulty encountered with the middle lever during the orbital flight, both flights were successful. The tasks selected proved to be adequate, but more important, the telemetry afforded continuous recording of the behavioral data. The MA-5 flight also provided the weightless environment necessary for testing both pellet feeder and water dispenser; neither of these showed any evidence of malfunction.

In comparing the two flights of the Little Joe series with MR-2 and MA-5, a possible interpretation could arise that the performance during the Redstone and Atlas flights was far superior to the flights of the Little Joe booster. However, the nature of the two tasks must be considered. In the CA task of the MR-2 and MA-5 flights, the subject had to press the lever only once every 15 seconds to avoid shock, whereas during the Little Joe flights this response was required at least once every two seconds. Had the chimpanzee subjects been required to perform at this rate, the results might have been different. The value of exposing the subjects to simulated launch accelerations is also apparent. Three of the four subjects, Miss SAM, HAM, and Enos, had received such exposures prior to flight; SAM had not. The performance of the three subjects who had experienced simulated launch was superior to the one who had not.

The question of species differences must also be considered. The results of the MR-2 and MA-5 flights suggest that the chimpanzee is superior to other sub-human species for space flight involving behavioral experimentation. However, future experiments will be required to confirm this hypothesis.

The inclusion of performance measures also facilitated the interpretation of the effects of space flight on the subjects. This was clearly demonstrated in the case of the MA-5 flight where the subject exhibited a considerable number of premature ventricular heart contractions. By comparing contractions with performance, it was found that they correlated neither with any particular task component nor the delivery of shocks.

On the basis of these space flights, it was concluded that: (1) Behavioral measurements must be made along with physiological measurements if a complete appraisal of the animal subject is to be made. (2) The insults of prolonged periods without sleep, the suturing of the physiological sensors, and the long period of restraint before launch, did not affect performance during flight; this also appeared true of the prolonged breathing of 100 percent oxygen under reduced atmospheric pressures for the time periods of these flights. (3) The noise and vibration accompanying launch did not affect performance during flight. (4) Accelerations accompanying launch and re-entry in excess of 7 Gs had an immediate effect upon performance; however, recovery to a prelaunch level appeared to be rapid. (5) Performance decrements did not occur during weightlessness. (6) Adaptation to weightlessness apparently took place during the long exposures to the weightless state, and re-entry accelerations did not have as severe effect upon performance as during the shorter flight. (7) Eating and drinking were accomplished during weightlessness without difficulty. (8) The visual processes, as measured, were unaffected by the rigors of space flight; this was also true of temporal response processes as well as continuous and discrete motor behavior. (9) The pellet and water dispensers functioned properly during weightlessness. (10) The chimpanzee appears to be a highly reliable subject for future space flights. (11) The effects of cosmic radiation on performance, which were not measured during the two flights reported in this paper, should be determined in additional flights of higher altitude before man is exposed to this hazard (Rohles, Grunzke, & Reynolds, 1962; 1963).

FUTURE EFFORTS

Although the MR-2 and MA-5 flights were most successful, two major unknowns of space flight still remain: prolonged weightlessness and cosmic radiation. A systematic approach to the psychophysiological effects of these environments has been suggested by Rohles and Reynolds (1962). For example, in one flight, during an equatorial orbit, weightlessness would be studied for a prolonged period, e.g., 30 days. If this flight were successful, a flight of comparable duration would be launched on a polar orbit to study both weightlessness and radiation.

A series of studies for an orbiting laboratory has been suggested by Reynolds and Rohles (1963). Many types of behavior are recommended for study in this orbiting laboratory in which scientists would actually conduct their research in the weightless environment.

But much research is needed before such an undertaking as the manned space laboratory. Continued work is underway for improved reinforcement devices. Transistorization of present programming equipment is being developed and tested. New schedules of reinforcement as well as the extension of present ones must be made. Of the environments, prolonged low-level acceleration must be studied since an artificial gravitational field is being considered for a manned space station. Noise and vibration have been only superficially studied. Radiation has been studied by behavioral scientists but the usefulness of radiation prophylaxis has not. This is an area which is closely allied to psychopharmacology. As more exotic fuels are developed, additional work will be required in this area. And the study of relationships of circadian rhythms and performance has only begun.

Thus, there are many areas of space research where meaningful contributions can be made by the behavioral scientists. And within this framework, operant conditioning is certain to be an important tool.

REFERENCES

BANGHART, F. W. (Ed.) (1958) Biological payloads in space flight. *Air Research and Development Command report 58-58*. Charlottesville, Va.: Division of Educational Research, Univ. of Virginia.

BELLEVILLE, R. E., ROHLES, F. H., and GRUNZKE, M. E. (1960) Complex avoidance behavior in the chimpanzee and its applicability to the study of space environments. *USAF MDC TR 60-27,* Holloman AFB, New Mexico.

BELLEVILLE, R. E., ROHLES, F. H., and GRUNZKE, M. E. (1961) Behavior of the chimpanzee on a complex multiple schedule. *USAF MDC TR 61-27,* Holloman AFB, New Mexico.

BELLEVILLE, R. E., ROHLES, F. H., GRUNZKE, M. E., and CLARK, F. C. (1963) Development of a complex multiple schedule in the chimpanzee. *J. exp. Anal. Behav., 6,* 549-556.

BROWN, W. L. (1959) Primates in space. Bioastronautics: Advances in research. *USAF School of Aviation Medicine special report,* Brooks AFB, Texas.

BUSH, R. D., ROHLES, F. H., REYNOLDS, H. H., and KOESTLER, F. (1962) The relationship between skin temperature and performance in the java monkey. *USAF ARL-TDR 62-21,* Holloman AFB, New Mexico.

FARRER, D. N., and BOGO, V. (1962) Champanzee performance during a simulated three-day space flight. *USAF ARL-TDR 62-25,* Holloman AFB, New Mexico.

FARRER, D. N., GRUNZKE, M. E., GILBERT, G. A., BARNHART, G. T., and JACOBS, P. D. (1963) Chimpanzee performance on a continuous avoidance task during acceleration at sustained low levels. *USAF ARL-TDR 63-6,* Holloman AFB, New Mexico.

FARRER, D. N., and REYNOLDS, H. H. (1962) Chimpanzee performance during exposure to 100% oxygen at 14.7 psi. *USAF ARL-TDR 62-8,* Holloman AFB, New Mexico.

FARRER, D. N., WARRELL, J. E., and GILBERT, G. A. (1964) A replication of chimpanzee performance during acceleration at sustained low levels. *USAF ARL-TR 64-8,* Holloman AFB, New Mexico.

GILBERT, G. A. (1964) A zero gravity pellet dispenser for use with primates in long term space flights. *USAF ARL-TR 64-15,* Holloman AFB, New Mexico.

GREEN, C. D., WELCH, B. E., BROWN, W. L., LAMB, L. E., TANG, P. C., GISLER,

D. B., and BLODGETT, H. C. (1961) Studies of escape from ballistic space vehicles: I. Biomedical evaluation. *USAF School of Aviation Medicine report 61-29*, Brooks AFB, Texas.

GRUNZKE, M. E. (1961) Feeding devices for use with primates in space flight. *USAF MDC-TDR 61-35*, Holloman AFB, New Mexico. (a)

GRUNZKE, M. E. (1961) A restraint device for behavioral research with the chimpanzee. *USAF MDC-TDR 61-37*, Holloman AFB, New Mexico. (b)

GRUNZKE, M. E. (1961) A liquid dispenser for primates. *J. exp. Anal. Behav., 4*, 326. (c)

GRUNZKE, M. E. (1963) A manually operated pellet dispenser for primates. *USAF ARL-TDR 63-12*, Holloman AFB, New Mexico.

GRUNZKE, M. E., ROHLES, F. H., BELLEVILLE, R. E., and WILSON, G. L. (1962) Two-dimensional discrete pursuit performance by the chimpanzee. *USAF ARL-TDR 62-16*, Holloman AFB, New Mexico.

HERRICK, R. M. (1961) A displacement-sensing constant-torque response lever designed for use in satellites. *U.S.N. Air Development Center report NADC-MA-6105*, Johnsville, Pennsylvania. (a)

HERRICK, R. M. (1961) Accuracy of lever-displacement behavior of rats following exposure to positive accelerations. *U.S.N. Air Development Center report NADC-MA-6111*, Johnsville, Pennsylvania. (b)

MELTON, A. W. (Ed.) (1947) Apparatus tests. *Army Air Force Aviation Psychology Program research reports*. Washington: U.S. Government Printing Office.

REYNOLDS, H. H., BOGO, V., and ROHLES, F. H. (1963) A multiple avoidance schedule for measuring temporal processes in the chimpanzee. *USAF ARL-TDR 63-8*, Holloman AFB, New Mexico.

REYNOLDS, H. H., BRUNSON, H. W., BACK, K. C., and THOMAS, A. A. (1964) The effect of decaborane injection on macaca mulatta and macaca vius operant behavior. *USAF TDR 64-74*, Wright-Patterson AFB, Ohio.

REYNOLDS, H. H., GRUNZKE, M. E., and ROHLES, F. H. (1963) The effects of exposure to simulated launch and reentry profiles on chimpanzee performance. *Aerospace Med. 34*, 196-200.

REYNOLDS, H. H., and ROHLES, F. H. (1963) Behavioral research with animals in the manned space laboratory. Paper read at American Institute of Astronautics and Aeronutronics, Los Angeles, June.

REYNOLDS, H. H., ROHLES, F. H., FINEG, J., BACK, K. C., and THOMAS, A. A. (1962) The effect of UDMH injection on learned behavior in the java monkey. *USAF MRL-TDR 62-64*, Wright-Patterson AFB, Ohio.

REYNOLDS, H. H., ROHLES, F. H., PRINE, J. R., CARTER, V. L., and BRUNSON, H. W. (1963) The effect of UDMH injection on complex avoidance behavior in the java monkey. *USAF ARL-TDR 63-14*, Holloman AFB, New Mexico.

ROHLES, F. H. (1958) Psychology's role in space research. Paper read at Central Ohio Psychological Association.

ROHLES, F. H. (1960) Behavioral measurements on animals participating in space flight. *Amer. Psychologist, 15*, 668-669.

ROHLES, F. H. (1961) The development of an instrumental skill sequence in the chimpanzee. *J. exp. Anal. Behav., 4*, 323-325. (a)

ROHLES, F. H. (1961) Performance by a rhesus monkey on a temporally reinforced oddity problem. *USAF MDC TDR 61-31*, Holloman AFB, New Mexico. (b)

ROHLES, F. H. (1962) Comparative aerospace psychology. *Aerospace Med., 33*, 826-830.

ROHLES, F. H., BELLEVILLE, R. E., and GRUNZKE, M. E. (1961) The measurement of higher intellectual functioning in the champanzee: Its relevance to the study of behavior in space environments. *Aerospace Med., 32,* 121-125.

ROHLES, F. H., and COY, R. E. (1959) A miniaturized operant conditioning chamber for behavioral research in the upper atmosphere. *USAF WADC-TR 59-261,* Wright-Patterson AFB, Ohio.

ROHLES, F. H., and GRUNZKE, M. E. (1961) A spatially continguous stimulus-response apparatus for primates. *USAF MDC-TDR 61-32,* Holloman AFB, New Mexico. (a)

ROHLES, F. H., and GRUNKZE, M. E. (1961) A model for behavioral research with mice in biosatellites. *Aerospace Med., 32,* 755. (b)

ROHLES, F. H., GRUNZKE, M. E., and REYNOLDS, H. H. (1962) A detailed account of chimpanzee performance during the ballistic and orbital Project Mercury flights. *USAF ARL-TDR 62-15,* Holloman AFB, New Mexico.

ROHLES, F. H., GRUNZKE, M. E., and REYNOLDS, H. H. (1963) Chimpanzee performance during the ballistic and orbital Project Mercury flights. *J. comp. physiol. Psychol., 56,* 2-10.

ROHLES, F. H., and REYNOLDS, H. H. (1962) A proposed approach toward determining the psychophysiological effects of prolonged manned space flight. *USAF ARL-TDR 62-28,* Holloman AFB, New Mexico.

ROHLES, F. H., REYNOLDS, H. H., and GRUNZKE, M. E. (1963) A thirty-day study of chimpanzee performance on a self-paced task for food and water. *USAF ARL-TDR 63-15,* Holloman AFB, New Mexico.

ROHLES, F. H., REYNOLDS, H. H., GRUNZKE, M. E., and FARRER, D. N. (1961) A laboratory model for a 14-day orbital flight with a chimpanzee. *USAF MDC-TR 61-33,* Holloman AFB, New Mexico.

ROHLES, F. H., REYNOLDS, H. H., GRUNZKE, M. E., and FARRER, D. N. (1962) A performance schedule for extended space flight with the chimpanzee. *USAF ARL-TDR 62-14,* Holloman AFB, New Mexico.

SIDMAN, M. (1953) Avoidance conditioning with no exteroceptive warning stimulus. *Science, 118,* 157-158.

VON BECKH, H. J. (1959) Human reactions during flight to acceleration preceded by or following weightlessness. *Aerospace Med., 30,* 391-409.

17

Operant Methods in Child
Behavior and Development [1]

Sidney W. Bijou and Donald M. Baer

INTRODUCTION

It is appropriate to begin with a quotation from a brief and prophetic paper by Keller (1950), in which he considered the future role of reinforcement theory in the analysis of child behavior and development:

> Its future will depend upon the ease with which it handles questions of social and verbal interaction. The experimental investigation of infant and child behavior presents itself as an alluring approach to this goal. It will be a pity if outmoded objections and extrascientific considerations stand in the way of its attainment (p. 12).

The future Keller spoke of in 1950 is now, in part, the present. Current research seems to be contributing three functions of operant principles and methods to developmental psychology: (1) It offers a basis for a positivistic approach to a developmental analysis of behavior. (2) It constitutes a segment of a theory of description and explanation of the development of child behavior, especially of social behaviors and "personality." (3) It provides techniques for measurement and experimentation relevant to general theories of the behavior of organisms young and old, human and infra-human.

The bulk of this chapter will deal with the third contribution—techniques of measurement and experimentation. However, the first and second contributions, a basis for a positivistic approach and a theory of behavior development, will constitute the essence of the initial discussion. These topics have obvious systematic significance and are thus appropriate as an

[1] Many of the studies by the authors cited in this chapter and the preparation of the chapter per se, were supported in large measure from two grants (M-2208 and M-2232) from the National Institute of Mental Health, Public Health Service.

introduction to the application of operant techniques to developmental problems.

A Basis for a Positivistic Approach

Those who follow a positivistic approach may be said to be devoted to the development of concepts which either are frankly tautological or else have operational definitions. Furthermore, they attempt to arrange their concepts into explanations of behavior which are testable at least in principle. A vivid description of this type of investigator is made by Stevens (1939). His account and ours suggest that the application of concepts of operant and respondent behavior developed by Skinner (1938; 1953) and by Keller and Schoenfeld (1950) to an analysis of the complex social behavior of humans will have the requisite appeal to many.

The positivistic approach is usually functional: an area of behavior is defined and then procedures are established to discover those variables which control it. As discoveries are made, responses are described as functions of certain experimental manipulations, usually of stimulus events in the past and present environments, and a set of empirical laws evolves. Concepts arise, not because of their imaginative, logical, or global characteristics, but only as they serve to describe and summarize the experimental stimulus operations which control behavior. Hence, such concepts are functional in that they pertain only to those procedures demonstrated to influence the behaviors in question.

The subject matter of child development has often been treated by virtually the reverse approach. Its concepts have had functional value mainly for the behavior of the theorist, not for the behavior of the child. This situation is probably related to the fact that, for the most part, these concepts have not been founded on experimental procedures. Instead, they have remained comfortably located in areas where no experimenter had the competence to manipulate processes: in the child's genes, for example, or in his state of neuro-muscular development, or in his intelligence, or in his ego.

Confronted with this tradition, a functionally-oriented investigator entering this area should find the concepts of operant and respondent behaviors and their controlling conditions appealing to him. These concepts emphasize the variety of environmental factors that may control a behavior through a sequence of development; they suggest the possibility of a response having an initial resemblance to a respondent, but with development showing operant characteristics; they tend to be free of non-operational definitions; and they tend to remain open to additions and revisions, since they contain no commitment to their own completeness.

A Segment of Theory

The concepts of operant and respondent conditioning can be more than mere operational handles on which to hang environmentally controlled behavior. Owing to their number and scope, they can yield an account of the development of the human child's motor, perceptual, linguistic, intellectual, emotional, social, and motivational repertoires. Indeed, these concepts suggest that the foregoing list of traits is vague and overlapping. All of these presumed "faculties" can be described in their ontogenesis by combinations of the principles of operant and respondent behavior.

Such a theory, which has been presented by the authors elsewhere (Bijou & Baer, 1961), proceeds by the following chain of propositions:

1. The developing child is conceptualized as a source of responses and stimuli.

2. The responses are divided into two functional classes: *respondents,* which are controlled primarily by preceding stimulation and are largely insensitive to consequent stimulation; and *operants,* which are controlled primarily by consequent stimulation, their attachment to preceding (discriminative) stimuli being dependent upon the stimulus consequences of behavior made in the presence of these discriminative stimuli. Some responses may share attributes of both respondents and operants. Some responses may initially have only respondent properties, but with development may gain operant characteristics (and possibly lose their respondent features).

3. The stimuli are described as the child's environment (including the part within the body wall). Stated another way, the child's environment is conceptualized as a source of stimuli interacting with and controlling his respondent and operant responses. Some of these stimuli are identified as setting events (conditions that are identified as influencing specific stimulus-response relationships), such as satiation, deprivation, and level of biological maturity. Catalogues of classes of stimuli and setting events are required.

4. Subsequent analysis of the child's development proceeds by listing the ways in which respondents are attached to new stimuli and detached from old ones, through respondent conditioning and extinction. Similarly, a listing is made of the ways in which operants are strengthened or weakened through reinforcement contingencies, and discriminated to stimuli which mark occasions on which these contingencies hold. Many of these respondents are included in the category called *emotional;* some of their conditioned stimuli are provided by people, and hence are *social.* Some of the operants strengthened are manipulatory, and some of their S^Ds (discriminative stimuli) are the size, distance, weight, and motion of objects; hence this development may be described as *perceptual-motor.* Some of

the operants are vocal, as are some of the respondents, and their discriminative stimuli, reinforcing stimuli, and conditioned stimuli typically are both objects and the behavior of people; hence this development is both *cultural* and *linguistic*.

5. Through discrimination and generalization the child's operants and respondents become attached to classes of eliciting and discriminative stimuli. These classes may vary in breadth, depending upon the history of conditioning and extinction procedures applied. Consequently, the child's manipulatory and verbal behaviors seem to deal in classes. This phenomenon, coupled with the complexity of S^Ds possible in discriminating operants, and the use of verbal behavior to provide S^Ds for self-control, gives the label *intellectual* to many of these behaviors.

6. The equation of discriminative stimuli to conditioned reinforcers (Keller & Schoenfeld, 1950, p. 236) suggests that many S^Ds play a significant role in strengthening and weakening operants as the child develops. Some of these S^Ds consist of the behavior of people (typically parents), and thus give rise to *social* reinforcers: attention, affection, approval, achievement, pride, status, and the like. Again, the preceding principles are applied, but now to social reinforcement for social behaviors, under social S^Ds. Hence, the development described is social behavior or *personality*.

7. In all of these steps, the scheduling of eliciting, discriminative, and reinforcing stimuli has important consequences. The principles involved give some explanation of the characteristic modes of response which may distinguish children: typical rates, the use of steady responding or bursts of activity, resistance to extinction, likelihood of pausing after reinforcement, etc.

8. Setting events such as deprivation and satiation cycles would have similar application, especially in areas said to be *motivational*.

Even from this sketchy outline, it should be clear that, in number and range of application, the basic principles are adequate to describe much of the development discussed in child psychology. Indeed, it seems at this stage that enough conceptual equipment is available to raise programmatic questions such as: Is there any aspect of child development which might not be analyzed by these concepts? Is there any range of individual differences exhibited by children which cannot be covered by an appropriate combination of the degrees of freedom possible in these procedures?

A different question arises as well. Even if child development can be described in terms of operant and respondent conditioning principles, is it necessarily stated *correctly* in those terms? That is, of course, a matter to be decided only after completion of a large number of experiments. Unfortunately, many of these experiments will be extremely difficult or impossible to perform due to practical, legal, and moral considerations. However, the use of operant and respondent principles to construct a theory of human development is no more susceptible to such limitations than is the use of the principles of Hull, Freud, Lewin, Piaget, or Rogers. And in those instances in which practical, legal, or moral restraints do not apply or can be overcome, an operant-respondent theory of development will generate empirical laws and directly testable hypotheses.

LABORATORIES AND PROCEDURES FOR FREE-OPERANT STUDIES OF CHILDREN

Except for a few studies published in the twenties and thirties on young infants (for example, those on sensory equipment and respondent conditioning in the neonate), experimental investigations with children have not been characterized by careful control over physical and social stimuli. This state of affairs continues despite general acceptance of the dictum that what is observed is, in part, a function of the procedures and circumstances of observation, and despite general recognition that the laboratory method has advantages because it permits direct control of behavior.

Many recent studies have been performed under makeshift conditions in the home, clinic, hospital, school, residential home, and recreational hall. Even in those conducted in specially designed laboratories, adequate control is not always exercised over non-experimental stimuli. Most often the interaction of investigator and S (subject) is not adequately evaluated, controlled, or eliminated.

The question of social reinforcement of child behavior can often prove to be a fundamental one in the design or evaluation of research on child behavior. It is, of course, an important area in its own right and will be discussed as such later in this section. At this point, however, it is important to discuss the role of social reinforcers in situations where they are not the stimulus of primary interest to the experimenter (E). Since children represent a species highly sensitive to social reinforcement, and indeed represent an age in which their parents and other members of society typically are striving to implant and develop this sensitivity, it is clear that unrecognized social reinforcement contingencies may abound in almost any experimental situation. For example, instructions that tell the child what he *may* do are sometimes responded to as if he had been told what he *must* do. Children are observed to give thousands of extinction responses after only modest reinforcement programs. (One child sat and responded with tears rolling down his cheeks. When asked what the trouble was, he replied, "I don't want to do this any more." When asked why he didn't stop, he said, "You didn't tell me I could stop!" While it is not wise to give complete credence to the verbal behavior of children as indicators of controlling variables, it is likely that a process like this has played a part in many experimental contingencies.)

No doubt because of distinctive past histories of reinforcement, some children respond to reinforcement contingencies themselves as a kind of instruction, which, for example, could make discrimination reversal difficult once the discrimination is established. Others respond to reinforcement as if it is aversive, and do not want to take anything from E. When offered a tray of toys from which they are to pick the one they want, they choose the smallest and least attractive, and if asked, "Is *that* the one you want?" may say, "I shouldn't take the best." Where E uses demonstration methods, the demonstration may act as a command, and S may not modify his behavior from imitation of the demonstration, even in the face of protracted changes in the discriminative stimulus or reinforcement schedule. Yet a simple re-demonstration of the new behavior pattern by E may produce an immediate (and appropriate) change in the behavior. Merely the statement by E, "You're not doing it right" or "You do not have to press the button all the time," may bring about a prompt change to the appropriate behavior, although thousands of inappropriate responses have been emitted previously.

Extensive work with the experimentally manipulated stimulus usually demonstrates to E when he does not in fact have control of the child's behavior, and may lead him to investigate what social reinforcers unwittingly have been dispensed (if any). In this instance, although the experiment will not have proceeded as planned, at least no erroneous conclusions will be drawn. However, in studies where stimulus operations are not used extensively to show the responsiveness of the child's behavior to them, it is easier to attribute a behavior pattern actually controlled by unsuspected social reinforcement to the experimentally manipulated stimulus, which may, in fact, have been ineffective.

An example of methods to show the role of uninvited social reinforcement in operant studies with children may be given in the context of the Robinsons' study (1961), which was designed to show the role of negative reinforcers in supporting avoidance behavior in preschool children. A stimulus consisting of a 50-db tone pitched at 2300 cycles per second was used as the negative reinforcer; it was introduced to the child as an interruption in an ongoing tape recording of children's music, stories, and songs. A plunger-pulling response terminated the sound or avoided its next presentation. A signal light was presented 1.5 seconds before the sound. The child received the following instructions: "A very loud, bad noise is going to come out of here; it's really a very bad noise, a terrible noise; it may even hurt your ears a little. I don't like to hear it and I'm sure you won't either. But you can turn off the noise, or keep it from ever coming on. First the lights will come on, and then the noise. You will have time to turn it off before it ever comes on. The way you do it is to pull this (demonstrating). Let's see you do it. Let it go back each time as soon as you pull it out, or else your hand will get tired." During the early trials, if the child did not respond by turning off or avoiding the sound, E said, "Oh, that awful, nasty noise," "Turn that awful noise off," or "You can keep that bad noise from ever coming on" (p. 21).

As the authors point out (pp. 22-23), there is considerable room in the procedure for social reinforcement to exert more control than the noise which is of primary interest. The following possibilities arise:

1. The noise does, indeed, act as a negative reinforcer, or as a loss of the positive reinforcers on the tape recording, and the rest of the procedure is perhaps helpful to prompt development of the avoidance behavior, but is not essential. Elimination of the instructions would constitute a condition, then, in which avoidance learning would still take place, perhaps more slowly. (But the authors say, ". . . it would soon become obvious that such comments were required by the children . . ." [p. 22].)

2. It is possible that neither the tone nor the interruption of the tape recording is negatively reinforcing, but that the child responds to prevent E from receiving negative reinforcement. E says, "I don't like to hear it." Many children have a history of reinforcement for "consideration" for the comfort of others. The instructions might be pared down to include only such statements from E, or they might be purged of such comments; E might be removed from the situation entirely; a neutral tone might be substituted for the loud one; or any combination of these might be employed.

3. It is possible that the child responds simply to gain E's approval and maintain it. E has said that the noise is "bad" and "terrible." Again, instructions might be reduced to this kind of statement; this kind of statement might be eliminated from the instructions; a neutral tone might be substituted; or E might be removed.

4. Perhaps the child responds on the basis of implied commands. E says, "I don't like to hear it, and I'm sure you won't either" (speaking of the tone). This may constitute a command for some children. Or, E's demonstration of how and when to respond may constitute a command for a child possibly unresponsive to what E does not like to hear. Finally, there is the explicit command, "Turn that awful noise off." Each statement or demonstration might be tried alone or eliminated, in conjunction with E's presence or absence, and tones known to be neutral or negatively reinforcing might be used in order to determine the controlling factors.

5. The most realistic possibility is that every one of the above processes (and others as well) will be exemplified in the behavior of *some* of the children. The logic of single-subject analysis which pervades operant conditioning with animal Ss has at least equally compelling application in studies with children. This is clear when considering how variable are children's histories of social conditioning, and how many stimuli serve as S^Ds for these social reinforcers, as the previous example shows. It is extremely difficult to guarantee that an experimental situation does not exemplify S^Ds for social reinforcement for some children. E must either turn his at-

tention explicitly to these social reinforcers and their cues, or engage in sufficient manipulation of the other stimuli of greater interest to show that they do indeed control the experimental behavior of some of his Ss.

Laboratories for the Study of Infants

Let us consider a laboratory situation for the free-operant study of infants. Because of the infrequent use of free-operant methods with neonates and young babies, it is difficult to cite a reference which contains a description of a laboratory entirely adequate for presenting stimuli, recording stimulus and response events, and controlling other extrinsic conditions for this age of development. It might, however, be of value to point out that enclosures and laboratory cribs designed for infant respondent conditioning have potential for free-operant studies. For example, the stabilimeter used in neonatal studies (e.g., Dockery & Valentine, 1939) could be appropriately modified. Also, fruitful suggestions might be found in the work of Crowell, Peterson, and Safely (1960), and especially Lipsitt and De-Lucia (1960), who devised cribs with associated control units for presenting stimuli such as shock, lights, and tones and for recording foot and leg responses and general bodily activity.

A laboratory or a method for studying infants from about three to six months has been developed by Rheingold, Stanley, and Cooley (1962). A diagram of the apparatus is given in Figure 1. The investigators describe the device in these words:

> An apparatus designed for use in studying the beginning of this behavior [exploratory behavior], especially in relation to feedback from the external environment, is also adaptable to the study of other kinds of early behavior, both human and animal. The apparatus holds the infant in a suitable position, permits measurement of certain behavior, and provides for sensory feedback from that behavior (1962, p. 1054).

A study situation for infants about eight months of age was built around a discrimination apparatus by Lipsitt (1960), and used in a discrimination study by Simmons and Lipsitt (1961). (The device and data obtained from it are described in the section on convenient responses studied in children.) The authors state that if the infant is placed in a steady seat, one that gives him ample support, and is situated so that he can reach and touch the two panels in front of him, he will sustain attention long enough to establish reasonably stable discriminations.

Laboratories for the Study of Early and Middle Childhood Subjects

There have been several descriptions of free-operant laboratories and procedures for youngsters from two to five years. Bijou gives an ac-

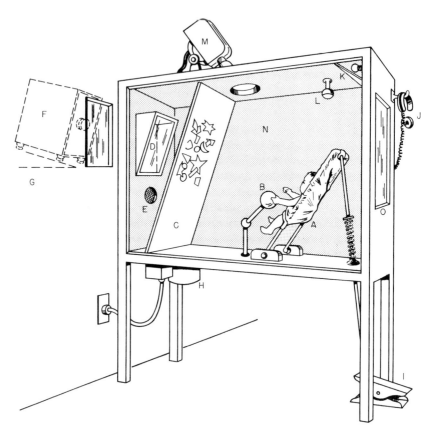

Figure 1. An experimental crib: seat (A), operandum (B), screen (C), projection opening (D), sound source (E), projector (F), control room (G), ventilator (H), rocker (I), intercom (J), crib lights (K), microphone (L), television camera (M), doors of crib (N), window (O). (From Rheingold, Stanley, & Cooley, 1962.)

count of one in a child development institute (1957a) and another in a mobile unit (1958b). Both are designed to produce a playroom atmosphere, to handle a wide variety of free-operant problems, to utilize automated devices for presenting stimuli and recording responses, and to control extraneous stimulations. One aspect of the procedure used in each is that the young lady who escorts the child to and from the laboratory remains behind an opaque screen while *E* monitors the equipment in the control room and observes through a one-way screen. Figure 2 shows the mobile-laboratory floor plan, which is similar to the laboratory at the university.

A laboratory and methodology for children from about four to ten

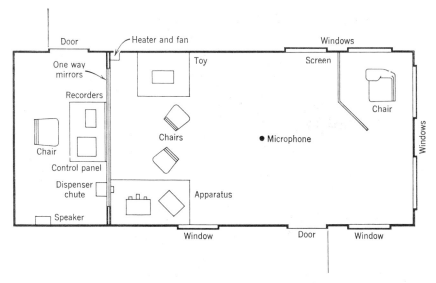

Figure 2. Floor plan of a mobile child-study laboratory. (From Bijou, 1958b.)

years of age has been described by Long, Hammack, May, and Campbell (1958b), and Long (1959a) (see Figure 3). Regarding the procedures, Long says:

> . . . a child sits at a console in a relatively isolated experimental cubicle. Before him [on the face of the console] are a manipulandum (an enclosed telegraph key), colored lights used as discriminative stimuli, a translucent screen on which pictures or other stimuli are projected, and a tray into which reinforcers are delivered. . . . Inside is a Gerbrands universal feeder for delivering reinforcers, an automatic projector, a buzzer, and additional lights (1959a, pp. 113-114).

Several free-operant laboratories for children with deviant behaviors are in operation. Some are for retarded *Ss* in residential institutions (Ellis, Barnett, & Pryer, 1960; House, Zeaman, Orlando, & Fischer, unpublished progress report, 1957; Orlando, Bijou, Tyler, & Marshall, 1961); others, for severely disturbed youngsters (Ferster & DeMyer, 1961; Lindsley, 1956). In all of these laboratories, *S* is alone in the experimental chamber, stimuli are manipulated and responses are recorded by switching circuits, the operanda are sturdy and harmless, extraneous conditions are controlled, and observing and communication devices are utilized. Figure 4 is a photograph of the experimental room devised by Ferster and DeMyer for autistic children. Coins may be deposited for candy, food, milk, motion pictures, and color-wheel movement in the vending machines shown.

It is apparent that advances have been made in preparing experimental situations for normal children between three and ten, and for retarded and

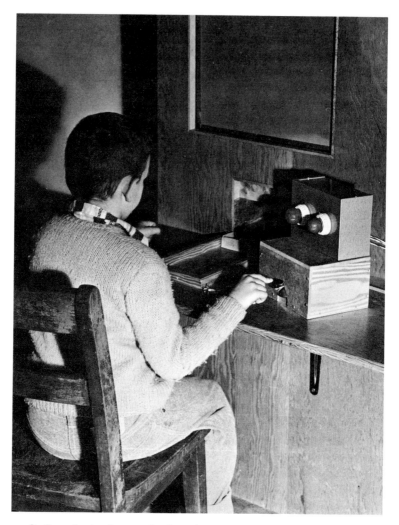

Figure 3. Experimental console for elementary school children. (From Long, 1959a.)

severely disturbed children in residential institutions. Exploratory work on the physical setting, equipment, and procedures for infants and for adolescents, normal and deviant, is yet to be accomplished in corresponding detail.

PROCURING AND PREPARING SUBJECTS FOR PARTICIPATION IN STUDIES

In addition to sampling problems, the laboratory study of children poses problems of procuring and preparing children for participation in

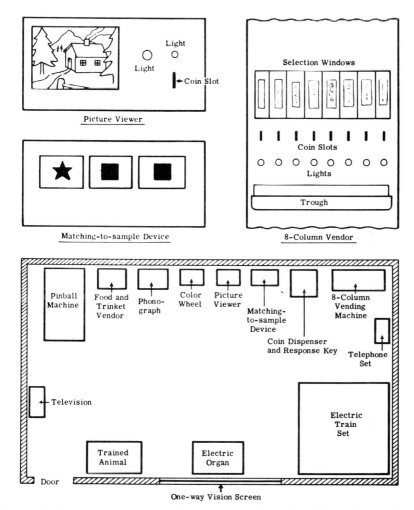

Figure 4. An experimental room for the study of autistic children. Operation of the coin dispenser produced coins, which could be inserted in the other machines pictured to produce other reinforcers. (From Ferster & De Meyer, 1961.)

studies. A corollary consideration relates to basic social and ethical practices naturally involved in working with children. Each topic will be discussed briefly with the view of orienting investigators new to the field.

Procurement of Subjects

Infants

Babies have been procured from practically all the agencies and institutions involved in child care. For example, out-patient research clinics with psychological laboratories are usually part of a medical school and frequently operate in conjunction with a child-care or a well-baby clinic in which mothers and infants are seen at regular intervals. Often mothers and babies receive professional services in exchange for their cooperation. The advantage of such a setting is the possibility of making repeated observations over weeks, months, or even years.

Most neonate and young-infant studies have been conducted in psychological laboratories attached to maternity wards. Procuring young Ss in this way presents problems such as finding and retaining adequate working space, establishing cooperative operating procedures with the medical and nursing staffs, and coordinating laboratory sessions with hospital routines. Also, investigations in maternity wards or hospital laboratories must necessarily be limited to the time from birth until mothers are discharged, a period which is continually shrinking, and which now seems to average four days.

Experimental studies in foundling homes, children's homes, and orphanages have been conducted with and without the advantages of a psychological laboratory. Establishing and operating a laboratory in a children's institution poses problems similar to those associated with working in a maternity ward. One major limitation is the possibility of loss of Ss at any time through adoption. Another limitation is the small probability of finding laboratory space within such institutions. One advantage of institutional laboratories is the opportunity to study infants at the different stages of development and for longer periods. Another is that many studies can be carried out with little disruption of living routines. Since the current practice is to place infants at the earliest age possible, infants and babies of this source are becoming scarce.

Infants might also be studied in a mobile laboratory which could be moved to an institution or even a private home and remain for the duration of the study. Under these conditions, it would be possible to conduct research under the constant conditions of a laboratory in a child center, without using institutional space. Studies conducted in a movable laboratory would probably be more disruptive to the baby's routines than those conducted in an institution laboratory, however.

Young Children

Much of the research on young children has been made possible by the availability of Ss in nursery schools. An additional impetus was given by the establishment, in about 1920, of laboratory nursery schools in colleges or universities (Moustakas & Berson, 1955). One advantage of the laboratory nursery school is the interest of the staff in research; another is the stimulation that research derives from training college students in child behavior and development. On the other hand, a frequent disadvantage is the limited number of Ss, apparent particularly when teaching and research needs are heavy. Nevertheless, even then a sufficient number are usually available for pilot studies and intensive individual analyses. In most laboratory schools it is expected that the investigator give occasional talks to parents and teachers on the research and its implications.

Probably the second largest number of Ss have come from private nursery schools and from private and public day-care centers. Day-care centers (all-day schools for youngsters of working mothers) often pose the problem of finding adequate working space and conditions. When space limitations make it impractical to control experimental conditions adequately, children have been taken from school to a nearby research center or to a mobile laboratory. In this setting, too, the investigator is expected to discuss his research with parents and teachers.

Ss have also been procured through direct contacts with parents. Lists of parents with children of the required age have been obtained from pediatricians, teachers, clinic waiting lists, mothers' clubs, and students from university housing groups. In all instances, personal and written contacts are usually made, and in many situations, transportation is provided to a research center.

Residential institutions—orphanages or schools for exceptional children such as the retarded, blind, disturbed, and dependent—provide further opportunities for laboratory research. Some (especially those for the retarded and emotionally disturbed) already have research laboratories (as has been pointed out in the section on laboratory considerations). Many are more than willing to provide space and basic facilities on request.

Older Children and Preadolescents

As would be expected, most Ss between six and twelve have been procured through public and private schools. The procedure for obtaining permission to work with elementary school children varies but basically consists of personal or written contact with the principal or superintendent, describing the nature, method, and implications of the investigation, the time required of each child, and the time needed for the entire study. Frequently, time problems arise, such as adjusting the time of experimental sessions so that it does not conflict with class schedules. When a study requires the children to return for a sequence of sessions, arrangements may have to be worked out for the children to compensate for lost time. It is a foregone conclusion that an adequate laboratory cannot at present be constructed in the schools. This means that studies have to be conducted in a mobile laboratory parked near the school, or in a nearby research center. The latter arrangement involves problems associated with transporting children.

Some investigators have obtained elementary school Ss through parent contacts. Long, for example, wrote a letter telling parents that he had received their child's name and address through the school office and asked permission to have their child serve in his research. He described the study and pointed out that it was part of a university project, indicating also what was not included. ("Lest you be concerned, let me assure you that the situation involves no competition between children, no psychological tests, or anything else that might be disturbing.") Finally, he gave basic information on appointments and transportation arrangements. Long's approach has particular merit for obtaining Ss during the summer.

Ss have also been obtained through organizations such as boys' clubs, community centers, Boy Scouts, and Campfire Girls. For example, a settlement house was the setting for a study by Azrin and Lindsley (1956) on cooperative behavior in pairs of children. Permission to conduct a study ordinarily is obtained from both the person in charge and the parents.

Finally, large numbers of elementary-school-age children living in schools and hospitals for the retarded and emotionally disturbed have been studied in laboratories in the institutions.

Preparation for Participation

Most experimental child psychologists would agree that it is essential to prepare children for a study. Thus far, however, little attention has been given to this aspect of experimental procedure, and consequently practices vary from carefully planned and rigidly maintained routines to no explicit preparation at all.

A case might be made that a pre-experimental preparation procedure is even more essential in work with children than in work with infra-humans. A child, at the beginning of a study, is exposed not only to mild emotional stimuli (being separated from his group and accompanying a relative stranger to a new room with unusual furnishings) but also to stimuli which may have conditioned aversive influence. (This does not apply, of course, to certain groups such neonates, young infants, and children who are grossly disturbed or injured.) For example, it is commonplace to find a school child who believes he is going to the laboratory to take a test which will determine his class placement, or a preschool child who likes to "play the games" but who is reluctant to accept "gifts" from a stranger. Our discussion on the special problems of operant level in the next section also bears on the need for adequate preparation of Ss.

Without going into the details required for a specific study, the following general suggestions are offered for consideration. First, the child should be given an opportunity to become acquainted with the person who will take him to and from the laboratory. With nursery school children one practice is to have the young lady serving as research assistant spend several days in the classrooms and yards, taking the role of a teacher or observer. Second, when it is a child's turn to go to the laboratory, he should be told where he will go, what he will do ("play games," perhaps), and how long he will stay. Third, when he enters the laboratory he should be shown around the room and given an opportunity to explore and examine the situation. He should then be given instructions—the fewer, the better.

Social and Ethical Practices in Research with Children

Throughout the discussions on procuring Ss and preparing them for participation, practices were advocated which bear on safeguarding the children, their parents, and others responsible for their care. Psychologists (field observers as well as laboratory workers) have long been aware of and have devoted much thought to the problem of doing reliable and meaningful research with children, and at the same time, preserving and promoting the welfare of all involved (e.g., Shakow, 1959). When E establishes appropriate working relationships with Ss and orients their caretakers to the nature and purpose of the study, the specific findings, and their ultimate implications, he not only helps to dispel misconceptions about psychological research, but also makes a positive contribution as a community teacher.

OPERANT RESPONSES STUDIED IN CHILDREN

The operant resonses of the child studied thus far may be grouped into two classes: (1) The first includes those that are unremarkable in themselves but are taken as typical of the class of operants. These are selected because they are easy to emit, observe, record, and integrate with stimulus operations. They include bar pressing, button pushing, knob pulling, window pressing, and box opening. (2) The second includes those that are studied because they are intrinsically interesting. Examples are thumb-sucking, verbal and vocal behavior, hesitant speech, and smiling. Often studies involving such responses are concerned with the implicit question, "Is this an operant response?" An occasional study deals with one response which is intrinsically interesting and chains it to another response chosen for its convenience for study, e.g., chaining verbal behavior to bar-pressing behavior, as in the studies by Lovaas (1961a; 1961c).

Whatever the reasons dictating the choice of response, the response selected must have certain characteristics to be practical for free-operant techniques. These have been discussed by Ferster (1953), who points out that the optimal free operant is a response which results in a minimal displacement of the organism in both space and time, requires little muscular exertion, and can display a wide range of rates. Adherence to these criteria results in a measuring technique which can give accounts of behavior changes with slight environmental manipulations.

In studies with children, other characteristics of the response require attention as well. One is the stability of the operant level of the response. Some children are likely to respond to any response device as if it were a new toy. Performance is likely to be characterized by initial bursts of responding, which may be followed quickly by a zero level if they are free to explore other parts of the laboratory. Returns to the operandum are likely but may result in successively smaller bursts of output. The overall picture is reminiscent of the course of satiation, which very likely it is. The reinforcers supporting the initial response rate presumably are implicit in the action of the operandum and accompanying clicks, thuds, or bangs which are produced.

There is also the probability of extensive generalization from the child's own toys to the operandum. Indeed, a common technique in child studies is to paint the operandum and its housing unit so as to emphasize its toylike appearance. These additional stimuli are also subject to quick satiation effects (as most parents and baby sitters will testify). Hence, experimental reinforcement of responses to such devices may produce effects which are confounded with the satiation phenomenon. If the experimental reinforcers are of low value, or if the child is slow to respond to the operandum ("warm-up" is descriptive, not explanatory), erroneous conclusions may be drawn about the experimental reinforcer. Attention to these possibilities in pilot work can save considerable embarrassment. In general, a two-minute operant level, unsupported by pilot work on the course of the operant level over time, is not likely to produce easily interpreted data.

An opposite effect may result from the adaptation of some children to the laboratory, within the first session or over several sessions. As was pointed out in the discussion on preparing a child for participation, almost any new situation is aversive for some children. The salient condition may be the strange adult (E), the physical setting, or the discriminative function of the particular reinforcing stimulus. Many children have heard their parent repeat, "Never take candy from strangers." Many have also been told about the devastating effect of candy on their teeth. (One of the authors was once reproached by an S on receiving the first candy reinforcement, "I have 11 cavities.") In instances such as these, the child's continued experience with the laboratory situation may eventually produce a weakening of avoidance behaviors, resulting possibly in increasing responding which would appear to be related to the experimental reinforcer. A judiciously inserted extinction period may show that the experimental reinforcer is not the controlling stimulus. Valuable information on this possibility would also be provided by fairly extensive observations of the operant level.

Unfortunately, it seems that the responses which qualify as representative of operant behavior in general, with the characteristics just described, are those most subject to satiation and adaptation effects. Since it has not as yet been demonstrated that a response situation can be engineered which has all of the characteristics important to a study of free operants, most Es accept the possibilities of satiation and adaptation effects, control for them, and design operanda in terms of the other criteria.

The following discussion deals with: (1) responses and response situations in which the aim is to develop a sensitive and convenient response measure, and (2) responses interesting in themselves. Sacrifices in technical advantages often required in studying the latter will also be noted.

Convenient Responses

Bijou has designed a simple bar-pressing operandum suitable for Ss of preschool age and above. This is a modification of a sponge-mop assembly which holds and squeezes the sponge (O'Cedar Mop). With the sponge and mop handle removed, the bright, chromed handle becomes a bar (see Figure 5), and its spring loading provides satisfactory tension for a small child to press against. The part of the assembly to which the sponge is ordinarily

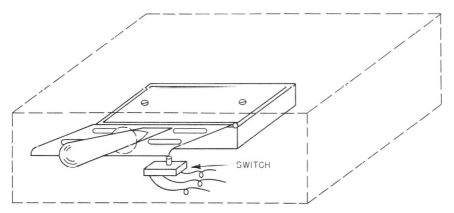

Figure 5. A simple bar-pressing operandum adapted from a sponge-mop assembly. (From Bijou, 1957a.)

attached may be screwed to a horizontal surface within a box housing all but the handle. The rest of the assembly offers a wealth of flat area moving with the bar which can operate several switches of various designs. The assembly is of heavy-gauge chromed metal and has so far resisted determined onslaughts from Ss of various ages (Baer, 1960; 1961; Bijou, 1957a; 1958a; 1961; Bijou & Orlando, 1961; Lovaas, 1961a; 1961b; 1961c).

This type of bar defines a response which is easily emitted, even by very young Ss. Added springs may be employed to lighten or stiffen the action. The response requires very little time to emit, and it can be shaped readily by defining the lifting of the bar after depression as the response to be reinforced. Alternatively, the E may define the maintenance of bar depression as the response, keeping positive reinforcement (like movies or music) present as long as the bar is held down. In either event, the response is simple to record. The child is not displaced while responding; the movement of the bar may be made as little as 1/16 inch, or as much as five inches.

Typically, the bar is worked by one hand; occasionally, response is accomplished with a finger, chin, forehead, foot, or fist. Rate is continuously flexible through a wide range. Satiation and adaptation phenomena are often seen, but typically they disappear by the second session.

Another response device largely sharing these characteristics is the Lindsley operandum. With this device, the response consists of pulling a plunger out from a panel. The plunger is a one-half-inch metal rod with a one-inch metal ball welded to its end as a handle. The spring tension and travel of the plunger are adjustable. Two notable advantages of the operandum are its ruggedness and the limited range of responses which can be used to pull the plunger. The second characteristic eliminates the variance in response rate apparent with other operanda when the child turns to using chin, forehead, or feet to effect the response. (However, in many such eventualities, it is not likely that much experimental control over the child's behavior has been achieved. A change in reinforcers or schedules may be more helpful than a change in response device.) The Lindsley operandum was designed to survive occasional attacks from psychotic adults or aggressive primates; thus, it has seen useful application in the study of developmentally retarded as well as normal children (Ellis, Barnett, & Pryer, 1960; Long, Hammack, May, & Campbell, 1958; Orlando, 1961a; 1961b; Orlando, Bijou, Tyler, & Marshall, 1961).

In his earlier work, Bijou (1955; 1957b; Bijou & Oblinger, 1960) made use of a response device which may be classified as a free operant, although the response did require more time than the bar and plunger described above. The child sat before a panel in which two holes appeared, one above the other. The response consisted of dropping a handball in the top hole; the ball returned out the bottom hole 3.3 seconds later, and could be picked up and dropped again. In its travels through the apparatus, the ball triggered switches which recorded the response and activated a reinforcement dispenser. Gewirtz and Baer (1958a; 1958b) used a somewhat similar technique which partially removed the restriction on response rate. In their situation, S sat before a small toy. The toy had two holes in its top surface (allowing for response descrimination) and another hole near the base of its front surface. Directly below this was a tray holding marbles. The response was to take a marble from the tray and drop it down either of the two top holes. The child did not have to wait for the marble to return to the tray; he could immediately pick up another of the marbles in the tray and drop it down a hole (see Figure 6).

Again, internal switches tripped by the marble rolling through the apparatus allowed for recording the response, and could have been used to operate reinforcer dispensers as well. Similar techniques involving marble dropping in one or several holes have been used by Stevenson and his associates and others (Stevenson, 1961; Stevenson & Cruse, 1961; Stevenson & Fahel, 1961; Walters & Ray, 1960). Where more than one hole is used, response measures may include rate over time for each hole, the proportion of responses for each hole per unit of time, or the proportion of responses for each hole per block of total responses.

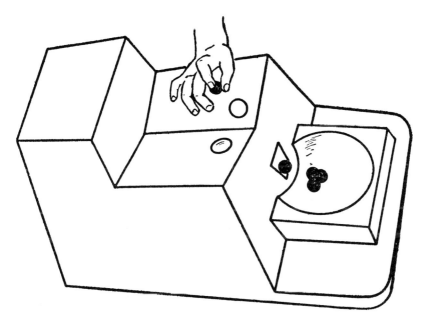

Figure 6. "Marble game" used as a free-operant response situation. (From Gewirtz & Baer, 1958b.)

A response device which is an anlogue to a pigeon apparatus has been developed by Ferster (1962) for a study of complex discrimination processes in children: matching to sample. The child sits or stands facing a panel on which appear three milk-glass screens. The central screen is stationary, but the screens on each side are attached to switch arms and may be pushed back a fraction of an inch. The child presses the center window to bring on the next set of stimuli. In a typical problem, stimulus A is projected on the middle screen, stimulus A on one side screen, and stimulus B on the other side screen. In some conditions the child is reinforced for pressing the screen matching the center screen (stimulus A); in other conditions, he is reinforced for pushing the screen differing from the center screen (stimulus B). The practice of presenting the next three stimuli as an immediate consequence of a correct response allows for a high rate and yields data in terms of both speed of pressing and accuracy of matching. The close integration of the response to the stimuli being discriminated and the fact that the response may be shaped without instruction (for example, by displaying stimulus A on the center and one side screen and leaving the other side screen blank during early trials) are important features of the method.

Variations on Ferster's device were developed by Hively (1962) and J. G. Holland (1963) for discrimination studies with elementary school children and retardates. Both involve a slide projector to present stimuli on windows in the front panel. The sample stimulus is projected on a window above the choice windows. Hively, in his studies on stimuli which differed systematically in shape, size, and color, limited his S to two choices, although it was possible to use as many as four. Holland, working with Long, programmed material on inductive reasoning, coin discrimination, and conceptualization. Their Ss made selections from five stimuli. In Hively's situation the correct response automatically presented the next problem, and an incorrect response did not produce a change, thereby permitting the S to respond again immediately. In Holland's procedure a correct response produced the sample for the next match, and a window-pressing response to the sample presented the five stimuli. An incorrect response blacked out the choices, and another press on the sample window was required to re-present them. A correct response after an incorrect response automatically backed up the slide magazine so that the previous slide was presented again. In other words, progress through the stimulus material was uninterrupted as long as the first response on each match was correct. The same apparatus and procedure was used by Bijou (Bijou & Baer, 1964) to study mirror-image concepts in young normal and retarded children.

A response device developed by Solomon, suitable for problems emphasizing work output, has been described by Lambert, Lambert, and Watson (1953). The response consists of turning a crank on the side of a vending machine which dispenses tokens and candy, and potentially, almost any other tangible reinforcer of reasonable size (see Figure 7). The response may be defined as any number of turns (or any fraction of a turn), and the crank may be made easy or difficult to turn. The device usually needs a ratchet arrangement so that the crank can be turned only in one direction. Even when the crank is easy to turn, the response is not as minimal a movement as bar pressing or plunger pulling. Screven (1954) has also reported data concerning the role of the effort required in a crank-turning response with preschool children.

Azrin and Lindsley (1956) have devised a response situation notable for the discriminability of the response to an onlooker who must cooperate to obtain reinforcers. In this situation, two children sit at opposite sides of a table, with a wire screen between them so that each may observe the other. In front of each child is a row of three small holes. Each child holds a metal stylus connected to a wire from the experimental programmer. The response which is reinforced requires that the children place their styli in corresponding holes within .04 seconds of each other. The wired metal styli are parts of the programmer circuit, as are the bottoms of the holes. (Naturally, low voltages are employed.)

When S is an infant, the design of a suitable response device must be

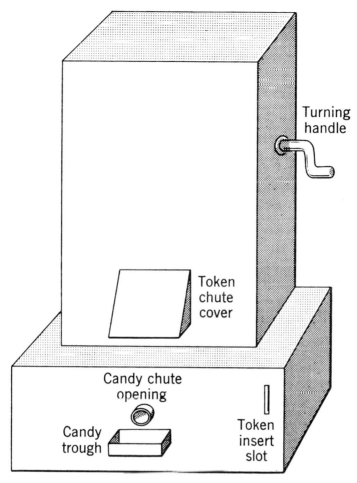

Figure 7. The Solomon token-reward vendor. (From Lambert, Lambert, & Watson, 1953.)

a compromise between the desirable characteristics of the free operant technique and the limited motor capabilities of the infant. Lipsitt (1960) has developed a practical solution for infants 8 to 12 months of age, and possibly younger.

A black box with two white panels is placed in a playpen. The two panels are hinged and each activates a microswitch when depressed. . . . In the middle of each panel is a stimulus aperture in which it is possible to produce any one of four different colored lights. . . . Inside the black box is a set of door chimes, which can be activated by either of the panels, under any present condition. Our procedure involves showing one color in one of the panels and another color in the other. Only one of the colors is associated with chimes. When the child pushes the panel of the appropriate color he hears (and presumably is reinforced by) chimes.

With this technique, Simmons and Lipsitt (1961) have shown color discrimination (red vs. pink) in their Ss.

Rheingold, Stanley, and Cooley (1962) have used an even more minimal response for studies of the reinforcement of hypothesized operant behavior in six-month-old infants. In their situation, the infant is seated in a special chair, half reclining, half sitting, as seen in Figure 1. He faces a screen on which can be projected brightly colored moving images for a brief period as reinforcement of the response. The response consists of the infant's merely touching a ball mounted in front of him near his hands. Responses may be scored by an observer, visually, or the ball may be made the antenna of an oscillator circuit serving as a capacity-sensitive relay, yielding automatic recording and programming. This device allows for shaping the desired response, since the circuit can be set to respond to the approach of the infant's hand in varying degrees of proximity, as well as to his touch. Since Rheingold has approached this as part of a study of the development of exploratory behavior in the human infant, it might well be included in the next section.

Interesting Responses

The compromise with optimal design of the operandum involved in the study of infants and children is more apparent when the investigator wishes to study a response because of its intrinsic interest. Most of the preceding descriptions of response devices have come from studies concerned with stimulus operations that can be integrated with response operations. Hence, the response is engineered for the ease of such integration, because such responses can be readily shaped into a baseline. Given such a stable rate, the stimulus operations of interest can be evaluated by their effect on the baseline.

In the studies to be discussed here, the response in each is deemed to be significant in itself. The significance of a response may derive from the fact that it may be considered as an early behavior in social development, like smiling or vocalizing. Or it may seem to be the prototype of a class of behaviors which later will constitute certain personality characteristics. Sucking, for example, may be thought to be an initial behavior in the learning of "dependency." Again, a response class may be of interest because it is so pervasive, such as verbal behavior, and may come to coordinate still larger classes of behavior. Other behaviors are interesting because they constitute a "problem" in children, like stuttering or thumb-sucking.

Whatever the context from which such responses arise, their identification as operant behavior may have significance. Positive findings would relate the behavior to the known (and suspected) laws describing the acquisition, control, maintenance, and weakening of the behavior and thereby give the investigator specific and pointed hypotheses about the development of the behavior in the history of any child: what reinforcers have followed this response, on what schedules, under what S^Ds, how often, with what delay, and under what deprivation states. Similarly, a reliable failure to identify a behavior as an operant suggests the irrelevance of all such questions, and points instead to an examination of the child's environment in terms of responses controlled by antecedent stimuli.

In general, it should be emphasized that contributions from studies of this category do not lie in the identification of another response, somewhat "cuter" than bar pressing, to be used for studying scheduling procedures. Instead, studies in this area represent a first step in the developmental analysis of the behavior in either a particular or a typical individual's history.

Sucking

The youngest Ss to be involved in what might be considered operant conditioning studies are probably those of Jensen (1932). These were newborn infants in some cases, and not more than three weeks old in others. His study incorporates a sensitive method of recording the natural sucking responses of the infants in feeding (and other) situations, and shows the control over this response exercised by the taste and temperature of the fluid ingested. Since these are stimulus consequences of the response, the control may testify to the reinforcing qualities of taste and temperature. However, stimuli are also close antecedents of the *next* response, given the usual rate of sucking. The control produced therefore may be related to their eliciting qualities in a respondent paradigm. These distinctions are absent from Jensen's report, and would not be easy to establish in any event. However, the close stimulus control achieved is intriguing, be it eliciting, discriminative, or reinforcing. Furthermore, sucking is a response which often excites the interest of the psychologist, in that it is a well-coordinated and differentiated response apparent in the first hours after birth. Hence, it is tempting to analyze sucking behavior for fundamental principles since it is uncomplicated by much prior experience. In addition, it is viewed by some as the infant's route to his first dependency relationships.

The method of recording sucking involved insertion of a tube into the nursing bottle. Pressure changes within the bottle resulting from sucking were transmitted through the tube to a series of manometers driving a pressure-sensitive metal bellows, which activated a pen writing on a moving tape of paper. (The apparatus is obviously a refined piece of engineering, incorporating solutions to a number of plumbing problems inherent in such recording, and Jensen's detailed description of his apparatus is recommended to the interested reader.) The recording system allowed graphic and instantaneous accounts of rate, magnitude, interresponse times, and the often increasing pressure differential built up during an unbroken chain of sucking.

Jensen's procedure was to establish a baseline of sucking behavior, using milk at 40°C for ten seconds. (This is a short operant level, but one collected at repeated intervals. Data indicated that the response was sufficiently stable for this purpose.) The bottle would be removed for 20 seconds and replaced for 20 seconds by another bottle holding the experimental mixture (which might be milk or formula, sterile water, or various concentrations of salt or glucose), at the same or different temperatures. After another 20-second delay, the baseline was remeasured, sometimes for 20 seconds. Procedure continued in this sequence of baseline-delay-experimental mixture-delay-baseline until six baseline periods had been established, which constituted a session for S. The method was adequate to show differential sucking to variations in the temperature and taste of the experimental mixtures, as is evident in Figure 8.

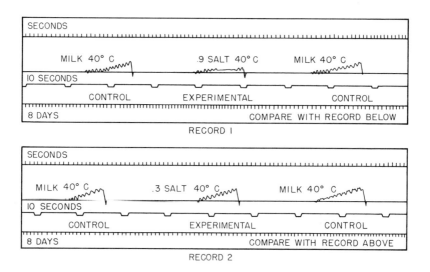

Figure 8. A typical record from Jensen's (1932) study of sucking in newborns. Curves show individual responses (non-cumulative) under various conditions of temperature and taste of the ingested formula, as indicated. (From Jensen, 1932.)

Smiling

Brackbill's study of smiling (1958) in infants four months of age was generated by her interest in the response in relation to its presumed social nature and its early role in social learning. The infants were chosen as old enough to remain awake throughout the experimental sessions, young enough not to respond differentially to "mother" versus "others," placid enough not to cry too often during sessions and to lie on their backs for at least five minutes without struggling, and responsive enough to show an operant level of at least two smiles per five-minute session. Brackbill offers no verbal description of smiling, but reports that prior to the main study, she and another judge observed some 970 occasions of smiling or non-smiling in infants, and agreed in 97.5 percent of their judgments.

Clearly, smiling (like vocalization) can be a lingering response in infants, and for this reason can detract from the flexibility of its rate. Another factor in this study was the duration of the social reinforcement offered as a consequence of smiling: "Five seconds were required for picking S up; 30 seconds for reinforcement; five seconds for putting S down; and five seconds for recording. Therefore, no more than six responses could occur and be reinforced during any five-minute interval" (p. 117).

Despite these limitations, differences emerged between experimental conditions. These consisted of an operant level period, a conditioning period of either continuous or intermittent reinforcement, and an extinction period. The operant level was taken as the rate observed through at least eight separate five-minute intervals, during which E stood motionless over the infant (who lay on his back in his crib), maintaining an expressionless face about 15 inches from the infant's. During conditioning sessions (consisting of 10 to 12 five-minute intervals), E reinforced smiling by smiling and cuddling the infant, using continuous reinforcement (crf) with one group and working steadily from crf to variable ratios of 1, 2, 3, and 4 with another group. Extinction was similar to the operant level condition, and was observed over 15 or more five-minute intervals. The conditioning rate was reliably higher than operant level. During extinction, the intermittently reinforced group extinguished less rapidly; both groups fell in rate of smiling to below their previous operant level and displayed "protest" behavior to the unsmiling E, crying or turning away from her.

All Ss were studied immediately after a meal following a nap. The mother phoned Brackbill when her infant awoke, and Brackbill would arrive at the infant's home in time for a freshly diapered infant just satiated with food. The mother cooperated to the extent of subjecting her infant to a period of social "deprivation," involving only minimal contact between her and the infant, prior to an experimental session. The study took place in the infant's own home and crib.

Vocal and Verbal Behavior

Among the youngest children whose vocal behavior has been studied are the three-month-olds of Rheingold, Gewirtz, and Ross (1959). These investigators were interested in showing that the vocalizations of young infants have operant properties. Because of their belief that vocalizations seem to provide an index of the whole social response, they used social reinforcement which "an attentive adult might naturally make when a child vocalizes" (p. 68). Clearly, the response had to be judged as such by *E* doing the reinforcing. On those occasions when the response was ambiguous or otherwise difficult to judge, a reinforcement was probably delayed (and at times incorrectly administered). This disadvantage is probably unavoidable, considering the definition of the response employed:

> Every *discrete,* voiced sound produced by *S* was counted as a *vocalization.* A number of other sounds characteristically made by very young infants, e.g., straining sounds and coughs, and the whistles, squeaks, and snorts of noisy breathing, were not counted as vocalizations. Sounds falling under the categories of protests, fusses, and cries . . . were recorded separately. No attempt was made to record any of the phonetic characteristics of any of the sounds or their duration (p. 69).

Their definition of the response clearly precludes any effective use of an electronic voice key, apart from other disadvantages implicit in that device. A voice key, of course, allows for objective recording and instantaneous programming. However, it also records, programs, and reinforces any stray sounds of sufficient intensity to be picked up, like chair squeaks, passing autos, dropped reinforcers, footsteps, or apparatus pounding. Some of the extraneous pickup can be reduced by using a throat microphone in those *S*s that will both tolerate and ignore it. A less useful method is to have older *S*s wear space helmets, in a spirit of "This is all part of the game (i.e., experiment)." The limitations of these methods are clear.

A second observer checked the reliability of *E*'s judgments, and *E* and the observer traded roles for half the *S*s as a further check on their mutual reliability. Their percentage of agreement ranged from 67 to 100, with a median of 96, over some 27 three-minute periods involving 13 *S*s. The infants were observed lying on their backs in their cribs. The unit of observation was a three-minute period, usually grouped in blocks of three, separated by two-minute rest periods during which the *E*s moved away from the crib. An attempt was made to have three such blocks of observation every day: early morning, late morning, and post-lunch. The first two days of study constituted an operant level or baseline period, during which *E* stood by the baby's crib looking down at him for three-minute periods with "an expressionless face," while the observer (out of the baby's sight) tallied vocalizations. During the second two days of study, vocalizations were reinforced by a smile, the sounds "tsk, tsk, tsk," and a light touch to the baby's abdomen. If the rate of vocalization increased sufficiently, reinforcement was then given successively on FR 2 and FR 3 schedules (but this was rare). The third two days of the study were an extinction period, identical in procedure to the first two days of baseline.

The two days of reinforcement significantly increased the rate to nearly double the baseline rate; two days of extinction returned the rate to very nearly the baseline level. This pattern is shown in Figure 9. The experiment was duplicated with minor changes and the results were similar in both sets of observations.

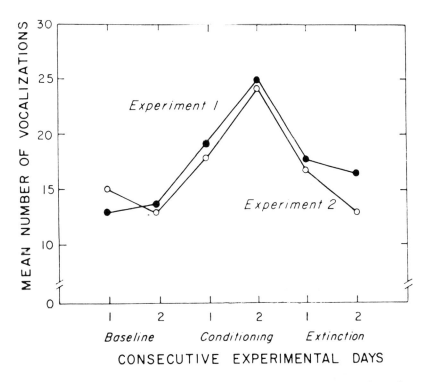

Figure 9. Vocalizations of three-month-old children as a function of reinforcement and extinction procedures. (From Rheingold, Gewirtz & Ross, 1959.)

The authors suggest, consequently, that infants' vocal behavior can be brought under experimental control and that a social event composed of ordinary acts performed by a relatively strange adult can function rather quickly as a reinforcer. They carefully point out, however, that identification of vocalization as an operant response requires observation of a condition in which the reinforcer is delivered as frequently but not contingent upon the response. Results obtained under this condition, when compared with the results reported, would indicate whether the social stimuli presented to the infant served to reinforce the preceding response or elicit the following one.

Weisberg (1963) extended the work of Rheingold, Gewirtz, and Ross along these lines by seeking the answer to two questions: Does the presence of a human adult elicit vocalizations? Can the infant's vocal behavior be controlled by social as well as nonsocial consequences? Thirty-three three-month-old institutionalized infants, divided into six groups, were studied over a period of eight consecutive days.

> Group I. No E present. During days 1-8 the E was hidden from S's view, keeping social stimulation to a minimum.
>
> Group II. E was present. On days 1-2, no E present; on days 3-8, E was seated before S but his behavior did not depend upon S's vocal behavior; he did not smile, frown, or make rapid jerky movements of his head.

As in the preceding group, the remaining four groups had no E present on days 1 and 2 and had E present on days 3 and 4.

> Group III. Noncontingent social stimulation. On days 5-8, S received stimulation on a prearranged random schedule from E who was seated before S. This consisted of tactual contact with S's chin, an open-mouthed smile and an aspirated "yeah" sound that we presented independently of S's vocal behavior.
>
> Group IV. Noncontingent nonsocial stimulation. On days 5-8, a door chime sounded on the same schedule as that of Group III while E was seated before S.
>
> Group V. Contingent social stimulation. Conditioning was attempted on days 5 and 6 by presenting the social stimulus only after each vocalization; on days 7 and 8, social reinforcement was omitted.
>
> Group VI. Contingent nonsocial stimulation. On days 5 and 6, the chime, in E's presence was given as a possible reinforcer and was omitted on days 7 and 8.

Weisberg's findings indicated that the infant's rate of vocalizing: (1) increased when reinforced by the social consequences used in the study; (2) decreased under extinction after social reinforcement, but not to the level of baseline performance; and (3) did not increase when an unresponding adult was incorporated into the environment, when the social stimulus was noncontingent upon vocalization, or when the auditory stimulus was presented either independently of, or contingent upon, vocalization.

Lovaas (1961c) used a combination of differential reinforcement and instructions to achieve control of preschool children's speech. The children were shown two dolls seated on the top of a "talk-box" which contained a microphone. The box was placed beside a tray for receiving trinkets. One doll was clean and new; the other was badly soiled and old; otherwise they were identical. The child was instructed as follows:

> This is a talk-box; when you talk to this box, it will give you toys right here (points to reinforcement tray). Now see here are two dolls. This (pointing) is the good doll; this (pointing) is the bad doll. Say "good doll" (if necessary coaches S to say, "good doll"; this response is rein-

forced). See what you got; this is your toy; you can keep it. Now say, "bad doll" (coaching if necessary; this response is also reinforced). See what the box gave you; this is your toy to keep. Now you sit here and tell the box all about the dolls; tell the box what is going to happen to the dolls (1961c, p. 331).

E then withdrew to a screened corner of the room, but coached *S* again in a similar way if necessary. All *S*s were reinforced for selected verbal responses (words, phrases, or sentences) until a rate of at least 12 verbal responses within a two-minute period was achieved. Half of the *S*s were then reinforced for aggressive verbal behavior, and half for non-aggressive verbal behavior. The only aggressive verbal behavior this sample emitted consisted of the phrases "bad doll," "dirty doll," and "doll should be spanked." Non-aggressive verbal responses included all other statements or words; however, if an *S* restricted his behavior to "friendly" behavior (e.g., "good doll" exclusively), then this was extinguished by non-reinforcement until other verbal responses, neither friendly nor aggressive, were produced (and reinforced). This was to ensure that the contrast between the groups could be fairly labeled *aggressive* and *non-aggressive* rather than *aggressive* and *friendly*. Conditioning was largely successful, as seen in Figure 10. Subsequent to the conditioning (and prior to it, as well) *S*s were confronted with a two-bar situation. One bar operated an innocuous ball-toy. The other bar activated a pair of mechanized puppets, one of which

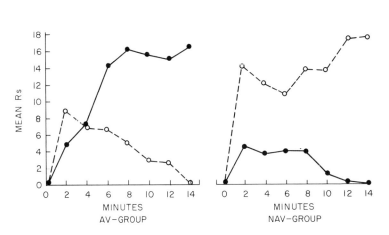

Figure 10. Mean number of aggressive and non-aggressive verbal responses during a verbal conditioning period, for Ss being reinforced for aggressive verbalizations (AV) and non-aggresive verbalizations (NAV) separately. (From Lovaas, 1961c.)

struck the other with a stick when the bar was pressed, exemplifying an aggressive stimulus consequence of the response. Ss conditioned to give aggressive verbal responses showed a shift in behavior to this latter toy from pre- to post-sessions; the other Ss did not.

A use of social reinforcement has been developed by Baer (1962b) to study both verbal and non-verbal behavior. An animated cowboy puppet speaks to the child (E's voice is piped through the puppet while the jaw is worked in correlation with the words), attends to or ignores the child, and can press a puppet-sized bar much like the regular-sized one beside the child. In addition to giving social reinforcers, he can deliver trinkets from a built-in dispenser. A preliminary application of this technique to verbal behavior indicates that the inherent flexibility of the puppet has real advantages in studies of this sort. The puppet can tailor the stimulus consequences of the child's verbal behavior (or non-verbal behavior) to the particular child. That is, consequences can be "drawn out" by the puppet's taking the brunt of the conversation, answering his own questions, dispensing a good deal of approval, awarding an occasional trinket, and the like.

Bijou and Zylstra (unpublished data) have employed trinkets and visual feedback to strengthen verbal behavior in young children. In their situation the child sits facing a small box in which is mounted a microphone and either an oscilloscope or an "electric eye" tube. (The "electric eye" tube is of the sort commonly used in radio receivers to indicate the precision of tuning. It is more technically referred to as an electron-ray tube. Useful examples are identified by manufacturers as types 6E5, 6G5, and 6AD6G.) As the child speaks, he is reinforced both by the correlated changes in the pattern on the oscilloscope or eye tube and by scheduled trinkets. The use of a decibel meter as a measure of response strength offers an easy way of programming reinforcement for increasingly louder speech; E relies upon his ear for selective reinforcement of content.

A record of both the verbal behavior and various stimulus events correlated with it is easily obtained by a tape recorder. Stimulus events not audible to S can be recorded by E if the shield on the microphone lead is broken and the leads from it brought out to a hand switch (normally closed). E, by flicking the switch, records a correspondingly short 60-cycle buzz on the tape. A code is readily devised for a small number of stimulus events (e.g., one buzz for a reinforcement, two for an S^D change, etc.). The tape can be played back later and E can transcribe the responses (and stimulus events) to a cumulative record by listening and pulsing the cumulative recorder appropriately. This procedure is more reliable than attempting to record the experimental behavior directly onto a cumulative recorder as it occurs.

Erickson (1963) used a technique which is suitable for children who can read, but departed somewhat from the flexibility of the free operant. She had fifth-grade Ss pronounce one of two nouns appearing on a display. One was an animate, the other an inanimate noun. Reinforcement was given for animate nouns after a baseline period to establish the operant level, and was either social ("good") or material (a marble). Immediately after reinforcement, the next pair of words was shown, allowing for a fairly good approximation to a free operant situation, much as in matching to sample. Some Ss experienced prior social deprivation (isolation for 15 minutes); and some, satiation for E's approval (30 instances of approval during 15 minutes of playing with a puzzle). Those Ss who had undergone social deprivation and were socially reinforced formed the verbal differentiation most clearly, saying the animate rather than inanimate noun increasingly often. Since none of the nouns was used twice during reinforcement, this amounted to a verbal concept of "animate" formed under selective reinforcement.

Hesitant Speech

Two studies by Flanagan, Goldiamond, and Azrin (1958; 1959) have demonstrated experimental control of stuttering or hesitant speech through reinforcement procedures. Using a 6000-cycle tone at 105 db delivered to S through earphones in contingency with the stuttering response, they showed that presentation of the tone as a consequence of stuttering weakened stuttering (relative to speech rate), and that cessation of the tone as a consequence of stuttering strengthened the behavior. Their youngest S was 15.

Felty (1959) extended their procedure to children as young as 12 with known speech difficulties. He used both escape and aversive schedules, as in the Flanagan et al. studies. In the escape condition, the tone was continuously present and a five-second termination of it was contingent upon stuttering; in the aversive condition, a one-second blast of tone was presented following the response. The S read from material considered easy and interesting for his age level to supply an ongoing operant level of speech and stuttering.

A typical session involved three 25-minute periods: operant level, escape or aversive schedule of reinforcement, and recovery. Each S had two sessions on consecutive days, one with an aversive and one with an escape schedule. As in the Flanagan et al. study, the schedules produced the expected strengthening or weakening of the behavior, independently of overall reading rate. Figure 11 shows the response curves for one of Felty's Ss.

The definition of the response was accomplished by E listening to the speech from a control room. A stuttering response was considered to be "any hesitation, stoppage, repetition, or prolongation in the rhythmic flow of vocal behavior" (Flanagan et al., 1958, adopted by Felty). Obviously, this criterion requires a judgment by E who is recording the behavior as hesitant or stuttering and is programming reinforcement. Such judgments may be late or inaccurate, of course—a source of error which apparently must be ac-

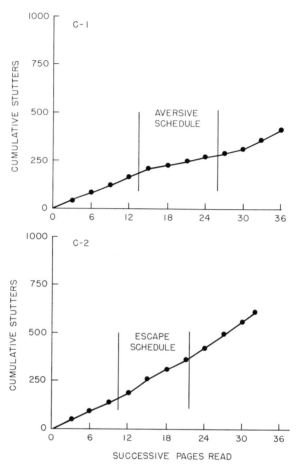

Figure 11. The course of stuttering behavior through aversive and escape schedules involving loud noise. (From Felty, 1959.)

cepted as a limitation on good technique when studying this kind of behavior.

After-the-fact assessments of the reliability of E in judging and reinforcing the response can be made in a variety of ways: by having two listeners independently rate a session of speech and/or a tape recording of the session, comparing ratings to produce a percentage of agreement (Felty's procedure); or by having two Es run cumulative recorders simultaneously as they listen to the speech, subsequently comparing the records visually for agreement, not in number of responses, but in changes of slope from moment to moment (Goldiamond, 1962); or by having S run a cumulative recorder, pulsing it every time *he* thinks he has stuttered and so producing a record which is compared to E's (Flanagan *et al.*, 1959). These techniques are adequate to show only the reliability of E in the past session. Probably they best function as reinforcements to E to improve and/or maintain his future performance.

Thumb-sucking

In the course of studies dealing with the withdrawal of positive reinforcement, Baer noted an S who watched movie cartoons and sucked his thumb almost continuously. The decision to apply withdrawal of reinforcement techniques to this response started a tangential study of thumb-sucking as a potential operant (Baer, 1962a). The technique which was developed involved giving S a long (42-minute) session of cartoons which was broken into alternating periods of operant level and punishment of the thumb-sucking response. Punishment was accomplished by turning off the sight and sound of the cartoons as soon as S put his thumb in his mouth, and re-presenting the films as the thumb was removed. This double-barrelled procedure (which punishes thumb-sucking and positively reinforces thumb removal) yielded increasingly greater depression of thumb-sucking during three consecutive sessions spaced a few days apart. During the interspersed operant level periods, however, the response quickly returned to its usual high rate, suggesting that the response was quickly discriminated to its own consequences rather than generally weakened. This is shown in Figure 12.

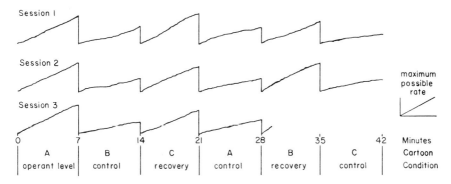

Figure 12. Cumulative thumbsucking rates of a young boy under alternating conditions of reinforcement-withdrawal ("control" in the figure) and recovery. The letters A, B, and C refer to three different cartoons shown in the sequence indicated (see text). (From Baer, 1962a.)

Two other Ss with similarly high operant levels of thumb-sucking were run in a yoked situation: one experienced contingent withdrawal and re-presentation of the cartoons as a function of thumb-sucking as described above, while the other, watching the same movie screen, experienced the same withdrawals and re-presentations, but not contingent upon thumb-sucking. During the next session, their roles were reversed. Contingent withdrawal and re-presentation procedures yielded control of the response, but random, yoked withdrawal and re-presentation did not, indicating the importance of the contingency between the response and these withdrawal and presentation techniques.

The response was recorded as a cumulative response by using a programmer which pulsed the recorder for every three seconds of thumb-sucking. *E* watched *S* through a one-way mirror and activated a switch on the programmer as long as *S* had his thumb in his mouth. The thumb-sucking response is a simple one to judge and shows nearly perfect reliability, as shown by having two judges simultaneously make cumulative records of the same performance. (It is necessary to isolate the recorders from the judges, since the clicking of one judge's recorder may serve as an S^D to the other judge, if it is audible. A visual comparison of the records usually shows thorough agreement.)

REINFORCERS AND CONTINGENCIES

Operant research with children has a distinctive aspect to its procedures, which sometimes seem divorced from the simplicities of the animal compartment. Probably this is due to the nature of the reinforcing stimuli in child studies. Typically, they are weak. This may be because they are in themselves low-order reinforcers with only a slight biological or learning basis, because they are subject to quick satiation, or because it is impractical to institute proper deprivation conditions for them. Any combinations of these reasons may hold. In any event, operant research with children has had to develop highly specialized techniques to make available powerful and lasting reinforcing stimuli, or has had to be restricted to short segments of behavior over only a few occasions.

Of course, these comments pertain only to the average child. Almost every *E* working with children has come upon *S*s who give large quantities of behavior for a dozen plastic trinkets, or who will continue to behave under tight stimulus control for tokens despite the fact that they have acquired a large pile. An example in the University of Washington laboratory was a five-year-old boy who performed repeatedly and consistently for trinkets, finally on an FR 600, and showed great resistance to extinction. Such a performance is unusual in *S*s who have been to the laboratory long and often and have acquired a large number of trinkets. Investigation showed that at the end of each session, this child would gather up his trinkets and rush back to his play group, where he would show them to the other children and boast at length about the number he was building up, comparing this to the much smaller number of trinkets the other children had acquired in the laboratory. It is likely that the reinforcer dispensed was an acquired reinforcer, ultimately supported by social reinforcers on the playground on a sort of percentage schedule.

For the researcher interested in determining what stimuli have reinforcing strength for individual children, such Ss are a delight and a challenge. But for the investigator (e.g., Witryol & Fischer, 1960) who wants a typically effective, durable reinforcer, to support the behavior of most children over long or repeated sessions while studying other variables (like discrimination or scheduling), there is no simple, satisfactory answer. Obviously, the deprivation procedures of animal experimentation cannot be applied, and strong aversive stimulation such as electric shock is inappropriate. Hence, two aspects of child operant research deserve discussion: the development of distinctive procedures yielding reinforcing stimuli adequate for protracted study, and specific reinforcers used in typical studies to date.

The Development of Durable Reinforcers

In Ss old enough to have an adequate reinforcement history for it, money in adequate denominations is probably the most durable reinforcer for experimental use. However, young children are inclined to respond to money essentially as to tokens. For dealing with children of all ages, however, it would seem that candy is probably the most available, universal, and durable reinforcer. Modern business technology has even supplied brightly colored M & Ms which will not melt in S's hand but in his mouth. Hersheyettes and other common candies are also useful. However, there are two serious drawbacks. One is the growing concern of parents and school administrators over the effects of candy on tooth decay, which in some children results in the development of a history of conditioning to refuse candy. A second drawback is that although it is generally known that children will eat candy when they will not eat other food, candy is not insensitive to satiation. This occurs more quickly in children than in adults, due in part to the frequent feeding of children. It is difficult to find a child who is more than two hours away from his last feeding; it is virtually impossible to find a nursery school child who is.

One solution to the problem of satiation for candy (and for other reinforcers suitable for children) is the use of what Ferster and Skinner call "percentage" reinforcement (1957, p. 67). In this procedure some kind of conditioned reinforcer is introduced between primary reinforcers on an increasing VR schedule. Practically all experimental setups contain a certain number of cues on reinforcement occasions in addition to the reinforcer itself, such as the dispenser noise or deliberately added lights, buzzers, or tone (momentary room darkening is a favorite).

Percentage reinforcement involves the continued use of these cues *without the reinforcer* on an increasing percentage of response occasions ordinarily scheduled for reinforcement. Clearly, this involves a use of secondary reinforcers built up within the the experimental situation and kept from extinguishing by a certain percentage of reinforcement by the ultimate reinforcing stimulus.

In addition, the technique makes increasingly sparing use of the ultimate reinforcer, thus decreasing the rate of satiation. A procedure of this kind was mentioned by Keller and Schoenfeld (1950, p. 246), who described the general procedures as a "tempting" possibility but could find no data to support it at the time of their writing. Bijou (1958a) has since applied this technique to children, using trinkets as the ultimate reinforcer, but eventually presenting the trinket on about one third of the scheduled reinforcement occasions. On the other occasions (as well as on trinket occasions) the child receives only the motor noise of the reinforcement dispenser (which, in itself, has slight if any reinforcement value for most children). If the reduction in percentage of reinforcement occasions which produces a trinket is gradual, the method produces more behavior for the reinforcer than does dispensing it on every reinforcement occasion and more than a similar schedule of trinkets without the additional motor noises.

A variation of this technique, used by Bijou (unpublished data) and by Lovaas (1961a), allows the child to choose one toy from an array of attractive items. The selected toy is locked in a transparent box which can be seen throughout the experiment. The child is told that the toy will be his when he opens the box. He is shown that the box may be opened by dropping tokens in a tube projecting from the box. The number of tokens required to open the plastic box may be varied. Preliminary shaping of the routine is helpful in ensuring that the child can respond to the contingency and in establishing a VR schedule of token insertion for box opening. With this arrangement the tokens can support a considerable amount of nonverbal behavior such as bar pressing, or verbal behavior of a given class.

Ferster and DeMyer (1961) report another variation of percentage reinforcement which also requires shaping. In their experimental situation the child obtains coins or tokens by operating a switch or performing on a matching-to-sample task. The coins may have little intrinsic reinforcement value for some children but are used to obtain candy and other reinforcers from coin-operated dispensers. The machines work, however, only when signal lights are on; hence, coins inserted when the lights are off are wasted. This discrimination must be established first; then by keeping the signal lights off for an increasing percentage of the time, the child, in effect, is put on a percentage schedule. Thus, the reinforcer dispensed by the machine is used more sparingly, and increasingly long segments of behavior uninterrupted by reinforcer-consumption result.

Ferster and DeMyer also describe a "generalized reinforcer" which sustains substantial amounts of behavior over long periods. This was achieved by having a large number of reinforcement-dispensing devices in the room, all of which were operated by the coin given as reinforcement. Included were a vending machine with eight kinds of food, candy, toys, or trinkets to be chosen by coin insertion; a pigeon in a transparent box who performed for 30 seconds; a pinball machine simulating a baseball game and giving two balls to play; a phonograph playing children's music for 30 seconds; a color-wheel giving a kaleidoscopic display for 30 seconds; a portable electric organ which the child could play for 30 seconds; and a vending machine dispensing a one-ounce container of milk or juice.

> Such a conditioned generalized reinforcer has the advantage that it derives its reinforcing effect from other reinforcers which are effective under various kinds of deprivation. Should the level of deprivation in respect to several of the specific reinforcements used in the experiments be low, the generalized reinforcer would continue to maintain behavior through the remaining devices which might be relevant to current deprivations. If the number of reinforcing devices were large enough so that at least some of these would be reinforcing for each subject, the same experimental room could be used for a number of subjects. There is also the possibility that the generalized reinforcer may have its effect by the sum of the specific reinforcers (pp. 315-316).

Some of the studies with normal and retarded children at the University of Washington Developmental Psychology Laboratory have combined percentage and generalized reinforcement in experiments requiring long sessions. The technique involves dispensing two kinds of tokens, white and red. At first the red tokens are dispensed exclusively. Later they are dispensed less frequently with white tokens filling the time gaps. The child can "cash in" the red tokens at the end of the session for any of a variety of reinforcers offered to him then: toys, candies, trinkets, mechanical and electrical games, etc. Hence, the red token is a generalized reinforcer given on a percentage basis, and the white token is a tangible conditioned reinforcer. The white token cannot be traded for other reinforcers, but serves to inform the child that his behavior is of the reinforcible kind; and as such the white token acts as a stabilizing stimulus. One advantage of this procedure is that the session is not interrupted with reinforcer-consumption; the red tokens serve as reinforcement until the end of the session.

Other approaches to the development of a durable reinforcing stimulus have concentrated upon enhancing the "game" or "toy" aspects of the stimulus situation. In addition to decorated operanda, complex toys have been modified for experimental control and offered as reinforcers: animated dolls, electric trains, mechanical animals, movies, tape recordings of music or stories, etc. Some of these will be discussed later in this section.

Specific Examples of Reinforcers Developed for Children

The following examples will illustrate a number of the stimuli which have been developed for experimental use as reinforcers for children and some of their possible contingencies. The discussion will follow this order:

1. Positive reinforcers produced by a response
2. Positive reinforcers lost or withdrawn by a response
3. Negative reinforcers produced by a response
4. Negative reinforcers escaped or avoided by a response

Positive Reinforcers Produced by a Response

The most common experimental situation with children involves the presentation of positive reinforcers. Consequently, there exists a relative wealth of such studies in the literature. Such popularity probably stems from the fact that sensitivity to stimulus consequences is one basic criterion for establishing a response as an operant and that presentation of positive reinforcers is the most acceptable reinforcement operation to apply to children.

Bijou and Sturges (1959) classify these stimuli as consumable and/or manipulable. Consumables include candy (M & M's, gumdrops, "Little Gems," mints, small Hershey bars, jelly beans, corn candy, sour balls, Tootsie Rolls); other foods (raisins, currants, peanuts, cookies, and honey); and liquids (milk and fruit juices), which are, naturally, dispensed in sanitary, water-tight containers. (One way to accomplish percentage reinforcement is to schedule a certain number of empty containers on reinforcement occasions.)

Manipulable objects, which are typically less powerful as reinforcers, include dime-store toys; plastic trinkets or "charms" (of the sort dispensed by gumball machines); stuffed animals (teddy bears, etc.); pictures or "stickers" of animals, birds, and toys. Also included are mechanized toys with interesting routines, made available for watching rather than given as gifts. The use of action toys allows an increasing wealth of choice, as toy shops currently stock a great variety of mechanized toys, many of which are electrical and can be run on the rectified voltage from filament transformers with minimal filtering. Remote experimental control is readily accomplished.

Bijou and Sturges offer the following practical recommendations: (1) Before dispensing reinforcers to children, it is expedient to check with parents and/or custodians on their acceptability. E should not be surprised to enocunter vehement opposition, on occasion, to candy, electrical devices, toys that seem "aggressive," trinkets, religious symbols, and devices of somewhat ribald humor. Occasionally a parent will respond to the sanitary properties of experimentally dispensed consumable reinforcers. (2) It is often efficient to investigate the suitability of the intended experimental reinforcers for the age and economic class of the Ss prior to conducting the main study. (3) Precise control over the delivering of reinforcers should be attempted. (4) A complete description of the method of delivery and the nature of the reinforcers should be given. Commercially available reinforcers are preferred over homemade ones, as they facilitate replication.

Now we turn to studies involving social reinforcement. This requires more exploration than was given to toys and edibles, since these procedures and stimuli require more engineering. An excellent analysis of the problems involved in social reinforcement is given by Gewirtz (1961).

A technique of social reinforcement applicable to three-month-old Ss will be recalled from studies by Rheingold, Gewirtz, and Ross (1959) and Weisberg (1963). Brackbill's (1958) reinforcement of smiling in four-month-old infants is relevant here, and has been described previously (p. 742 ff). As soon as the infant smiled, E smiled in return, and began to speak softly to the infant, and picked it up. The baby was then held, jostled, patted, and "talked to" for 30 seconds before being replaced in the crib. The reinforcement procedure was recorded on 12 feet of color film and filed with the American Documentation Institute (Washington, D.C.).

Gewirtz and Baer have published two studies in which social stimuli served as reinforcers (1958a; 1958b). The child sat before a toy containing two holes in which marbles could be dropped. One of these responses was chosen for reinforcement.

> The reinforcer, designed to appeal primarily to the concept of approval, consisted most frequently of the word "Good!" and less frequently of such phrases as "Hm-hmm," "Good one!" "That's a good one!" and "Fine!" These reinforcers were delivered by E in a casual manner, according to a schedule incorporating four successive fixed ratios. . . (1958a, p. 50).

The schedule began with continuous reinforcement and progressed through FR 2 and FR 3 to FR 5, unless S made as many as five consecutive incorrect responses, in which case a retreat was made briefly to a lower ratio. Since the reinforcing stimulus was produced by an adult cognizant of the meaning of possible results, the adult was observed throughout the experiment and judged as properly standardized in his or her behavior by observers behind a one-way mirror. Similar use of social reinforcement has been made by Walters and Ray (1960), and Zigler, Hodgden, and Stevenson (1958).

Baer (1962b) studied social reinforcement in children by using a mechanized talking puppet. The puppet had an articulated jaw which could move in correlation with his "talking." It could also attend to (look at) the child or ignore the child, press a miniature bar, and deliver trinket or candy reinforcers (see Figure 13). E watched from behind a one-way mirror, spoke through the puppet, and programmed various contingencies. Preliminary work indicated that some of the stimuli produced by the puppet, such as his attention and verbal approval, functioned as social reinforcers for the children in that situation. The findings correlated well with judgments about the effectiveness of similar stimuli in other situations, such as nursery school.

There are at least two advantages of a talking puppet over a talking adult. One is the ease of standardizing the stimulus output of the puppet. Considering the variety and subtlety of stimuli which may function as social

Figure 13. An animated, talking puppet for studies of social reinforcement with young children. (From Baer, 1962b.)

reinforcers (nods, smiles, raised eyebrows, winces, and other facial expressions), it is important to ensure that only controlled delivery of such stimuli takes place. An adult may require considerable practice before achieving satisfactory uniformity in the output of social stimuli. The other advantage lies in the less forbidding aspect of an interaction with a puppet, as opposed to one with a relatively strange adult. Response to the puppet's social reinforcement develops more rapidly. However, it remains to be seen how fully these two advantages can be realized.

We close our discussion of this topic, positive reinforcers produced by a response, with a description of a series of studies in which social reinforcement was made contingent upon certain desirable responses of normal preschool children. All of these investigations were conducted in the natural setting of a university nursery school. Basically the procedures consisted of: (1) obtaining a baseline over several days; (2) observing changes in behavior under conditions of administering social reinforcement contingent upon the desired behavior, and withholding social reinforcement following the undesired behavior; and (3) reversing the contingencies once or perhaps twice. The data were gathered by a trained observer, with a second observer added from time to time to check on reliability. The reinforcers (social nearness, praise, support, encouragement, and the like) were administered by a trained teacher assigned to the task. In one study, a three-year-old girl, who persisted in crawling despite the fact that she had developed walking behavior in the usual manner, was reinforced for standing, walking, and running (Harris, Johnston, Kelley, & Wolf, 1964). After she had engaged in behaviors in upright positions for one week, the baseline conditions were reinstituted. Crawling behavior reappeared in high strength. "On-feet" behavior was again systematically reinforced while "off-feet" behavior was not. Again activities involving upright behavior occurred in high frequency. These contingencies were reversed again with the same results. The last phase of the study involved reinforcing on-feet behavior on a continuous and then an intermittent schedule. The same procedures were employed to weaken isolate play and strengthen group play in a four-year-old girl (Allen, Hart, Buell, Harris, & Wolf, 1964). They were also used to decrease the frequency of operant crying and to increase the occurrences of more acceptable verbal behavior in two four-year-old boys (Hart, Allen, Buell, Harris, & Wolf, 1964). These studies, together with three others involving another case of strengthening group play behavior in a three-year-old boy, heightening vigorous play behavior in a three-year-old boy, and increasing the verbal output of a four-year-old girl, were reported and analyzed by Baer, Harris, and Wolf (1963).

Positive Reinforcers Lost or Withdrawn by a Response

The removal of a positive reinforcer from the possession of a child, contingent upon his response, has received little attention, probably because of the reluctance of many investigators to take candy from a near-baby. Nevertheless, the process deserves study.

Baer (1961) used movie cartoons as an ongoing state of positive reinforcement which could be terminated or withdrawn, contingent upon a response. Previous work had shown that these cartoons were excellent reinforcers for the great majority of young children (Baer, 1960), in that Ss would consistently press a bar to return them when withdrawn. The cartoons were of the Woody Woodpecker sort, and were shown on a Busch Cinesalesman, a 16 mm movie projector with built-in screen and sound system. This apparatus is particularly suitable as it never requires rewinding and can use "endless" reels of film which can be run over and over again indefinitely without pause. Withdrawal of the cartoons was accomplished by automatically flipping a shield over the lens and opening loudspeaker circuit. (It proved impractical to stop the film cleanly and repeatedly.) Ss were first taught a bar-pressing response for peanut reinforcement. After such training one group was extinguished and punished by the withdrawal of the cartoons for two seconds, contingent upon every bar-pressing response. Subsequent sessions with and without cartoons (but without peanuts or punishment) showed maintenance of the response-weakening effect in the punished group and the usual spontaneous recoveries in the other group. This is shown in Figure 14.

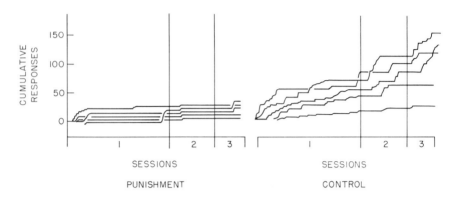

Figure 14. Individual response curves of Ss undergoing punishment in Session 1 (withdrawal of positive reinforcement) during extinction of a bar-pressing response, compared to Ss not being punishing. (From Baer, 1961.)

A similar application of cartoon withdrawal was made to the thumb-sucking response of three preschool boys (Baer, 1962a). It was shown that thumb-sucking was weakened by withdrawing the cartoons as long as S had his thumb in his mouth, but the response recovered quickly during periods of no withdrawal or withdrawal not contingent upon thumb-sucking (see p. 751 f).

Cartoons are not convenient for reinforcing behavior for a few seconds at a time, contingent upon responding. Unless a continuous schedule of reinforcement is used, only scattered and disjointed bits of the cartoons are seen, since the projector continues to run film even if the picture is not projected. Such discontinuity detracts somewhat from its reinforcing value. (Some of this difficulty might be avoided by the use of taped music developed by Jeffrey [1955]. Children listen to the music through earphones, which probably enhances its reinforcing value. There is the problem, however, of rapid satiation.) An alternative to continuous reinforcement would be percentage reinforcement, where the reinforcer may be tokens which, at the end of the session, would be used by the child to run the projector continuously through one or more cartoons.

Negative Reinforcers Produced by a Response

As would be expected, there is a scarcity of research dealing with punishment in children through the presentation of a negative reinforcer. The major emphasis has been an auditory stimuli. As mentioned previously, Flanagan, Goldiamond, and Azrin (1958; 1959) used a 6000-cycle tone at 105 db, delivered through earphones, contingent upon stuttering in Ss 15 years of age and older. It is probably the hesitancy of Es to use intense stimuli, rather than the suitability of the technique, which will determine the lower age limits to which this method will be extended.

Tyler (1960) utilized a pair of heavy-duty relays in a flip-flop circuit which produced a loud and rapid clatter. Ss were taught a discrimination, some with the relay clatter used as a consequence of S^Δ responding, some with a mild tone used in the same role, and some with no added stimulus consequences of S^Δ responding. For some Ss, the relay clatter served as a punishing stimulus in the acquisition of the discrimination, and in the maintenance of the discrimination under extinction procedures with both relay and positive reinforcement absent. Other Ss responded to the clatter as a positive reinforcer.

Young (unpublished data) has done some preliminary work on the presentation of negative social reinforcement contingent upon preferences for colors. The Ss were preschoolers; the response was filling in outlined patterns with chips of colored wood. The task was much like putting together a picture puzzle, except that there were many identical pieces in piles of four different colors. Young obtained baselines of color preference over several blocks of responses, and then negatively reinforced a preferred color by saying, "No," "No no," "Uh-uhh," whenever the child picked up a piece of that color. Without exception, the first delivery of negative reinforcement stopped ongoing behavior. Subsequently, the further use of the disapproved color markedly decreased in most Ss. There were a few children who were less sensitive to disapproval as trials progressed. No doubt, children could be found who would respond to this stimulus as positive reinforcement.

Negative Reinforcers Escaped or Avoided by a Response

Most avoidance situations present S with a negative reinforcer which he must endure until the "correct" response is made. For this reason it is, again, a difficult technique to engineer with children. Two compromises are possible: (1) the use of sufficiently mild stimuli or limited durations of more intense stimuli, and (2) the use of withdrawal of positive reinforcement as the punishing event which can be avoided.

The Robinsons (1961) exemplify the first procedure in their use of a 50 db, 2300-cycle tone lasting up to ten seconds and programmed as an interruption of an ongoing tape recording of music and stories. Light cues were given 1.5 seconds prior to the onset of the noise, and a plunger-pulling response would avoid the noise (or, if late, would turn it off). However, the Robinsons point out that the noise alone would not support avoidance behavior in nursery school children. Complex instructions were required. It is quite possible that they added negative social reinforcement value to the noise.

Baer (1960) has used the withdrawal of movie cartoons as a negatively reinforcing event which could be escaped and/or avoided by a bar-pressing response. The movies were withdrawn after a three-second (or five- or ten-second) interval, and could be re-presented only by a bar press. In one schedule, any bar press served to delay the next withdrawal for three (or five or ten) seconds. S could never be more than three (or five or ten) seconds away from the next withdrawal. In another schedule any response served to add three seconds to the interval between that response and the next scheduled withdrawal, so that time could be "saved up" by responding and S could be several minutes away from the next withdrawal. (This is a minor variation on Sidman's "escalator" schedule. See Chapter 10 in this book.)

Under the first schedule practically all children showed highly consistent, precise, and durable "escape" responding, escaping from the withdrawal condition by reacting immediately as the cartoons went off. A few showed some tendency to develop additional responses which would avoid the next withdrawal for some time, but these patterns were not consistent and tended to disappear in the course of a dozen sessions. Using the escalator schedule, however, many children of preschool age showed response patterns which maintained the cartoons uninterruptedly for increasingly long periods; a few children developed quite efficient rates of response which prevented all but a few of the scheduled interruptions during a half-hour session.

In an extension of this technique to social reinforcement, Baer (1962b) made the attention of a mechanized talking puppet contingent upon bar pressing which avoided its withdrawal (see Figure 13). Again, the escalator schedule was used, with a three-second interval. (That is, any response added three seconds to the interval between the response and the next scheduled withdrawal of attention.) The quickness with which preschool Ss learned to avoid the withdrawal of the puppet's attention, and their efficiency in maintaining the attention, correlated well with ratings of attention-seeking tendencies in the nursery school setting.

DISCRIMINATION PROCEDURES, DISCRIMINATIVE STIMULI, AND SECONDARY REINFORCEMENT

Operant discrimination serves as an organizing section in this chapter because it is conceived of as a basic process in children's behavior, and because of its role in general behavior theory. The study of discriminative processes in children has generated a number of distinctive procedures. Occasionally it is simply the choice of the discriminative stimulus itself, rather than the discrimination process in which it functions, which deserves attention. And since an equation is usually made between discriminative stimuli and secondary reinforcers, the few studies of secondary reinforcement in children involve discrimination procedures as an essential ingredient. Hence the tripartite nature of this section.

Discrimination Procedures

Most studies of the discriminative process in children use ordinary discriminative stimuli and focus attention on reinforcement and extinction contingencies. Many of these arrangements are an almost literal translation of animal discrimination procedures. Indeed, a great number of studies employ techniques which reflect common Y- and T-maze situations, which are in effect variations on restricted operant procedures. (See Spiker, 1960, for a review of literature involving such techniques.) The restricted operant multiple-choice situations have many advantages such as simplicity, ease of instrumentation, economy of operation, and little or no preliminary training. Furthermore, these devices are often thought to resemble common learning situations in school and other aspects of everyday life.

The restricted operant multiple-choice techniques have a number of disadvantages, when compared to a free operant situation. One is the lack of sensitivity to slight changes in the controlling variables (probably due to the spaced and inflexible response rate involved). Another is the difficulty of examining the strength of one of the responses except as relative to the others. That is, the child can respond to either of, say, two stimuli, S^D or S^Δ. He makes either an S^D or S^Δ response on discrete occasions, and his score is the relative proportion of S^D responses to S^Δ responses over a block of responses. As soon as S^D responding has increased in strength sufficiently, S^Δ responses disappear; but it is possible that S^Δ responses have not extinguished completely. There may still be responses to S^Δ, but stronger responses to S^D are prepotent. Furthermore, since the child now does not respond further to S^Δ, thorough extinction may be prevented by the adequate power of S^D to control responding.

It is, of course, possible to examine the strength of S^D and S^Δ responding separately in a two-choice situation, for example, by presenting only S^Δ on some trials, with the S^D position empty or blank. However, this is a new stimulus situation in the child's training history, and results obtained by such a procedure are confounded by the novelty and/or ambiguity of the procedure.

Still another limitation of restricted operant multiple-choice discrimination techniques is the impression they produce (often unintentionally) that discrimination is a response in itself, which is strengthened or weakened as a unitary organization of behavior. Since responses to the two stimuli in a two-choice situation are typically not independently examined, the simpler processes underlying a discrimination cannot be brought out.

Some of these difficulties may be overcome by eliminating the restricted character of this operant situation, so as to allow a rapid and flexible response rate to both S^D and S^Δ. This was done by Gewirtz and Baer (1958a; 1958b) and Stevenson and Fahel (1961), in a situation in which the child dropped marbles down either of two holes (one S^D, the other S^Δ) at a high rate. However, such methods merely allow for greater sensitivity in showing the rate at which S^D responses increase in strength until they successfully compete with S^Δ responses. They do not reveal the strength of S^D responding independently of S^Δ responding.

The combination of a free-operant and a multiple schedule has its virtues. In a multiple schedule there are two or more component schedules of reinforcement, each with its distinctive S^D. For the study of discrimination processes, it may be advantageous to use extinction as one of the schedule components (its S^D thereby being properly labeled as S^Δ), and any convenient reinforcement schedule (e.g., VI or VR) as another. S^D and S^Δ periods are programmed in either regular or irregular alternations, and the response rate of a free operant can then serve as a measure of the ability of both S^D and S^Δ to control the response. These measures are independent of each other, if taken as absolute rates; alternatively, rate under S^Δ can be expressed as a proportion of rate under S^D if a relative measure is desired.

Bijou (1961) made a direct application of multiple scheduling to discrimination problems in young children. The multiple schedule consisted of two components, one a VR 50 schedule of reinforcement, with the illumination of an amber light on the left side of the response device as S^D; the other, extinction, with the illumination of a blue pilot light on the right side of the response device as S^Δ. Stable discrimination developed in six or seven 20-minute sessions, spaced about a week apart. This is shown in Figure 15, curve A.

Also apparent in Figure 15 (curves B, C, and D) is the effect on the discrimination of a change in the experimental situation in which two switches were added that could be used by the child to turn off the S^D and S^Δ lights. Turning off a light did not alter the contingencies associated with it; they remained in force for the time called for by the program. Responding during S^D periods was greatly disrupted at first (curve B), but response during S^Δ remained virtually zero, testifying to the effectiveness of the extinction procedures inherent in this type of discrimination training. In the second session following the change (curve C), response during S^D periods recovered its smoothness; in the third session (curve D), S^D rate was even higher than at the beginning of stable discrimination (curve A). Bijou argued that such discrimination performance, with its distinctive pattern of response to S^D and S^Δ, is highly appropriate to the individual analysis of children, "since a clear functional relationship has been shown between a stable baseline performance and the introduction of a special stimulus condition" (p. 170).

The establishing of the discrimination, in this study as in others, was accomplished by an initial shaping and strengthening of the response in the continuous presence of the S^D. Subsequently S^D was removed and S^Δ was presented, with extinction programmed. After a fixed time of extinction

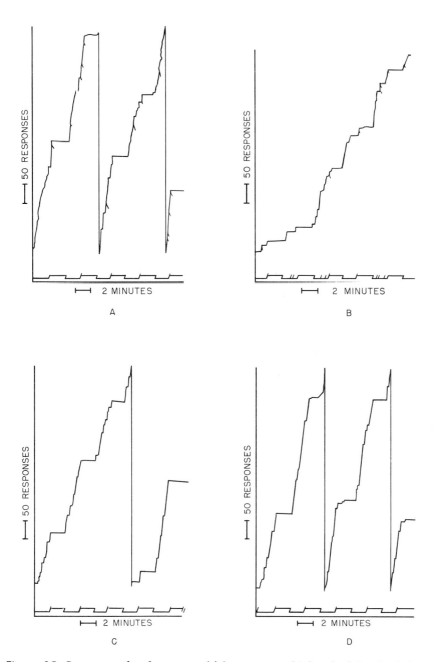

Figure 15. Response of a four-year-old boy to a multiple-schedule discrimination training procedure. Periods of VR 50 alternate regularly with extinction periods. In B, C, and D the effects of a new variable are shown. (From Bijou, 1961.)

under S$^\Delta$, the S^D was re-presented and the response was again reinforced according to schedule. Thus, S^D and S$^\Delta$ periods of standard lengths were alternated, the response being strengthened under S^D and extinguished under S$^\Delta$. The discrimination was considered to have been acquired when response rate under S^D exceeded a certain value, and/or response rate under S$^\Delta$ fell below a certain value, and/or S^D rates exceeded S$^\Delta$ rates by a certain proportion.

With this technique many Ss achieved the discrimination criterion only after considerable training, probably because the initial shaping and strengthening of the response gave it considerable resistance to extinction, which the relatively short periods of S$^\Delta$ extinction did not diminish sufficiently to produce discriminated behavior. Through generalization, the frequently interspersed S^D periods of reinforcement probably contribute too often and too much to response rates under S$^\Delta$, sometimes directly reinforcing these rates.

Bijou and Orlando, in a series of papers (Orlando & Bijou, 1960a; unpublished manuscript; Bijou & Orlando, 1961), have described a procedure which produced a rapid acquisition of multiple-schedule discrimination performance in retarded children. The technique involved manipulation of the relative lengths and distribution of S^D and S$^\Delta$ periods, and considerable care to the specific steps in the initial shaping and strengthening of the response. Basically it consisted of a drl contingency between response during S$^\Delta$ and the presentation of the next S^D period. That is, during S$^\Delta$, not only were all responses extinguished, but in addition any response served to delay the next presentation of S^D for a certain number of seconds. Hence, the S$^\Delta$ extinction schedule remained in effect until the response was extinguished sufficiently to produce an interresponse interval, or pause, exceeding a certain time limit. Then S^D was re-presented, and responding during the S^D period was reinforced. With the next presentation of S$^\Delta$, the pattern was repeated. As S's behavior began to shape to the reinforcement contingencies, the length of pauses during S$^\Delta$ required for presentation of the S^D was increased according to objective criteria, and the length of S^D periods was also increased. (Initial S^D periods terminated with the first response, which was always reinforced. Subsequently, S^D periods were lengthened to half-minute, minute, and two-minute intervals, with FR, VR, FI, or VI schedules of reinforcement, which also were increased as the discrimination stabilized.)

An additional technique in the training program was an initial *rate evaluation* phase with a one-minute period of FI 15-second reinforcement in the presence of the stimulus to be established as the S^D. If S made fewer than 20 responses during this first minute, an additional minute was programmed. If no acceleration in rate was observed, use was made of ratio scheduling to increase rate, prior to any discrimination training. However, if S made 20 responses or more, S^D was replaced by S$^\Delta$, the drl ("pause-building") contingency was put into effect, and discrimination training began. The authors state that

. . . if training on low rates of responding [to S$^\Delta$] is undertaken when the initial rate is low . . . extinction may develop. Hence, this stage includes operations designed to strengthen rate when required. On the other hand, if pause training is attempted when the initial rate is very high, pausing may require an excessive amount of time to develop and stabilize. The second function of the evaluation procedure, therefore, is to detect high rates as early as possible to avoid dispensing any more reinforcers than necessary (Bijou & Orlando, 1961, p. 10).

Figure 16 shows the results of this procedure on the performance of three retarded children. S^D presentations are shown as offset portions of the lower timeline. Reasonably stable discriminations are shown by the second session.

From these curves it is possible to inspect in detail the simultaneous

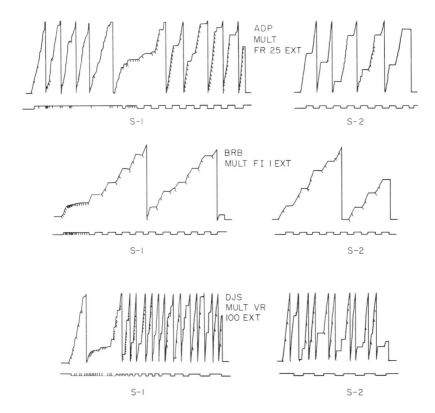

Figure 16. The rapid development of a multiple-schedule discrimination through the use of drl contingencies during extinction responding, as seen in three subjects. S^D times correspond to offset portions of the lower timeline. Blips in the cumulative curves mark reinforcement occasions. Sessions are labeled S-1 or S-2 to indicate their sequence. (From Bijou & Orlando, 1961.)

strengthening of response to S^D and weakening of response to S^Δ; the strength of S^D and S^Δ responses is seen independently *and* relatively; and an emphasis is achieved which defines discrimination as the result of several simpler concurrent response processes, rather than as a unitary process or unique response. Furthermore, this procedure focuses on the formation of the discriminated behavior, rather than concentrating on previously formed discriminations in the way that much of formal education does.

Orlando (1961a) analyzes the classical response pattern to fixed interval scheduling as a complex discrimination. The usual pattern of response after extensive fixed interval schedules of reinforcement is a low rate of responding, restricted mainly to moments just prior to the regularly spaced times when a response will be reinforced. Orlando suggests that there are, in fact, two component discriminations involved. "The first is the use of temporal interval as a discriminative stimulus and the second is withholding from responding in the presence of stimuli associated with non-reinforcement" (p. 615). A test of this hypothesis involved three discriminations, each considered simpler than, but relevant to, optimal fixed interval response: (1) The simplest discrimination was a two-choice situation in which S had to discriminate the position of a stimulus light alternating between two locales. The alternations occurred randomly but on the average every 30 seconds. At each locale was a Lindsley operandum. Response to the plunger located by the light was reinforced (VI 10 seconds), and response to the other plunger was extinguished. This procedure was used as a screening device to eliminate Ss lacking the behaviors which the discrimination involved. Two of 12 Ss were eliminated. (2) The second problem was a simplification of fixed interval scheduling, involving a "crutch" which consisted of a buzzer-produced tone to mark the time when the response would be reinforced. Technically, this was a single-response, multiple crf extinction schedule, the extinction component having a 40-second duration. That is, every 40 seconds a buzzer would sound, whereupon the next response would be reinforced, and the buzzer would terminate. No responses would be reinforced until 40 seconds later, when the buzzer would sound again. Stable discrimination of this pattern of reinforcement indicated that S could withhold responding when appropriate, apart from any discrimination of temporal stimuli. Eight of the ten Ss screened made this discrimination. (3) The third problem was a standard FI 40-second schedule, identical to the second "crutch" problem except that there was no stimulus except for the passage of time to mark occasions when a response would be reinforced. This task involved not only the withholding of response, but the discrimination of temporal stimuli as well. The four Ss who showed appropriate behavior under this fixed interval schedule were drawn at random from the eight who had solved the "crutch" problem.

Orlando analyzed discrimination behavior into simpler components in another study (1961b) involving a two-response situation. In this experimental situation, there were two Lindsley response devices, each on its own panel, and each with its own pair of red and blue S^D lights. The program consisted of alternating two-minute periods, during which one panel would have a red light illuminated and the other, a blue. S was reinforced for responding to the panel with the red light and extinguished for responding to the panel with the blue. The reinforcement schedule was developed to VR 100, and the discrimination was made so stable that a two-minute period of correct responding without reinforcement did not disturb the pattern of response. Then, after demonstration of the stability of the discrimination to periods of non-reinforcement, either the S^D cue from the correct panel, or the S^Δ cue from the incorrect panel was eliminated for a two-minute period of non-reinforcement. E was interested in seeing whether S was responding to the panel *with* a red light, or to the panel *without* a blue light. Results indicated that one S stably showed one pattern and two the other; none of the three Ss tested showed both. "The method avoids the confounding effects of novelty in a restricted-operant ambiguous-cue technique and permits repeated measures on the same Ss" (pp. 160-161). Furthermore, it re-emphasizes one of the more basic corollaries of operant-respondent conditioning: the multiplicity of learning histories which can produce behaviors similar in appearance, and the consequent need for the experimental analysis of complex behaviors into the varieties of simpler components.

Long (1959b; 1962) has shown techniques for establishing multiple-schedule control in young children through the use of different kinds of reinforcers under two schedules. The experimental situation involved is described on p. 727. The behavior of his Ss became discriminated to the schedule components, not only to the S^Ds programmed with these schedule components, but also to the different reinforcements associated with each schedule.

The two-component schedules were FI and FR ranging between FI 1.5 FR 10, and FI 3 FR 10. Some children were reinforced with a penny plus a "highly valued trinket" under FR schedules, but with a "less valued trinket" alone under FI schedules. For other children, the reverse was true. Within two to four sessions the two procedures, which, incidentally, proved to be equally serviceable, produced consistent multiple control in ten Ss. Eight previous sessions using the same reinforcers (pennies and trinkets) uniformly under both schedules failed to produce stable multiple-schedule effects. In other words, the nature of the reinforcer seems to have been a cue to the next phase of the multiple schedule.

Long followed up this work with an extensive exploratory study of chained and tandem schedules on school children between four and seven years of age (1963). Trinkets and pennies served as reinforcers on chain drl FR, chain dro FR, chain FI FR, tand FI FR, and tand dro FR. (The dro schedule is one in which reinforcers are delivered for any behaviors *other* than the one reinforced during the other components of the schedule.

The initials stand for *differential reinforcement of other responses*. This schedule allows reinforcers to be delivered at the usual rate to the subject, but not contingent on previously reinforced behavior; thus it constitutes an extinction condition minimally different from the reinforcement conditions of the schedule.)

> Chain drl FR and chain dro FR schedules almost always produced strong schedule and stimulus control, but chain FI FR schedules rarely did if additional techniques were not used. Strong control was produced with chain FI FR schedules, however, if: (a) the FR component was increased in size; (b) schedule and stimulus control was first established with chain drl FR or chain dro FR schedules before shifting to the chain FI FR; or (c) an external clock was attached to the FI. Tand FI FR schedules never produced regular or repeatable patterns of responding when additional procedures were not used. Rate patterns resembling those of chain FI FR schedules were produced by tand FI FR schedules, however, if: (a) an external clock was attached to the FI component or (b) control was established by means of tand dro FR schedules before the tand FI FR was used. Stimulus control was found to be exercised by specific signal stimuli, change in stimuli, and schedule order (Long, 1963, p. 459).

Stoddard (1962) studied timing behavior per se in children two to ten years of age by means of drl schedules. The Ss were required to wait at least 10 (or 20) seconds between responses; otherwise responses went unreinforced. Ss who attended a median of 20 sessions were also observed under conditions of VI and multiple schedules. All Ss learned to make appropriately spaced responses under the drl contingency. Stoddard concluded: "The processes by which children discriminate time intervals, such as the mediating function of collateral behavior patterns, can be studied systematically" (p. 143).

Discriminative Stimuli

In most studies of discrimination, the stimuli serving as S^D or S^Δ are of the types convenient for laboratory work: pilot lights, illuminated panels, room lights, buzzers, relay clicks, tones from audio-oscillators, pictures, or projected slides, etc. (see, for example, Lane & Curran, 1963; Risley, 1964). Ordinarily the choice of the stimuli follows from considerations of simplicity and economy, coupled with the importance of presenting a stimulus display as obvious as possible. (Exceptions to this are the situations in which S's current ability to respond to minimal stimulation is of interest, as in threshold determinations.) Although important from a systematic point of view, there is little in the work of this sort which requires discussion here. There are, however, a few problems which merit discussion because they pose technical or procedural difficulties or because they deal with particularly interesting or unusual S^Ds.

Technical Procedures

A common problem in the programming of discriminative stimuli is the discovery that unwanted stimuli are systematically presented on S^D or S^Δ occasions. This may be especially common in child research, where the physical limitations of the usual laboratory make it difficult to insulate the child completely from the controlling apparatus. A frequent discovery is that the child is responding not to a visual S^D but rather to an audible relay click from the programmer which also marks stimulus changes. Techniques to counter this possibility range from better sound insulation of the child and/or the relay to the introduction of masking noises in the child's room. A simple method for accomplishing the latter is to set aside an interval programmer with a short interval VI tape running a relay. This device programs a random series of clicks for the child, which are indiscriminable from the other relay clicks emanating from the control apparatus, and thus may rob all such noises of their discriminative possibilities.

Occasionally an E who wishes to use visual stimuli will find it necessary to ensure that S attends to the stimuli, especially when weak reinforcing stimuli are used. Two simple options are available. One is to make the visual display extremely obvious—for example, by using changes in the room illumination as the S^D or by using so large an illuminated panel that changes can be seen from most angles of visual regard. Another method is to use an auditory stimulus to mark visual stimulus changes. If the child is not looking at the visual display at the moment of change, a click or buzz serves as an additional S^D marking stimulus changes and often will cause the child to look back immediately at the stimulus display. This procedure, however, can establish the auditory stimulus as functional in place of the visual stimulus. To avoid this the auditory "warning" stimulus can be programmed occasionally during S^D periods as well as whenever S^Ds change.

Several devices are available commercially which simplify the devising and presentation of complex discriminative stimuli. One of these, distributed by Grason-Stadler and Foringer, and used by Ferster, Levitt, Zimmerman, and Brady (1961), is the Miniature Display unit which contains 12 different stimuli, any one of which can be selected for display on the screen of the unit. Selection and change are immediately accomplished through proper switching. There are a great variety of stimulus patterns (letters, numbers, geometric figures, etc.) available for it, and any special stimuli can be made to order by the manufacturer. Another device, and one more flexible, is the projector-programmer, a 35 mm slide projector which accomplishes both S^D presentation and programming through holes punched on the slides which control photo-electric sensing units (Hively, 1962; Holland, 1963).

Interesting Discriminative Stimuli

A stimulus may be "interesting," in this context, for one of several reasons. It may represent a stimulus of systematic significance in behavior theory (e.g., frustration); it may be a stimulus that, at first glance, would seem difficult to translate in the laboratory (e.g., social stimuli); it may be a stimulus frequently encountered in real-life situations (e.g., aggression); or it may be a stimulus, varied over a wide dimension, that has potential significance for a technology of education (e.g., conceptual stimuli, such as "mirror images"). The studies which follow exemplify responses with one or more of these possibilities.

Lovaas (1961b) found that certain movie cartoons could serve as a device for presenting aggressive stimulus events of a wide variety and at a high rate to children. He used the Official Films' cartoon "Rassling Match," which "was cut to give an almost continual display of aggression (hitting, biting, etc.) inflicted by one human-like cartoon figure upon another" (p. 38). (The slight amount of cutting required is a comment on what is considered a suitable cartoon for children by film makers.) As a control condition, a non-aggressive film (Castle Films: "Bear Facts") was found and also edited to depict "three bear cubs and a mommy bear engaging in pleasant human-like play" (p. 38). These five-minute stimulus presentations were used between pre- and post-measures of aggressive responding, i.e., responding to make one animated doll strike another. Lovaas found an increase in responding in those Ss exposed to symbolic aggressive stimuli.

In a similar study, Larder (1962) used the animated puppet developed by Baer (1962b; see also p. 757 f above) to tell either an aggressive or non-aggressive story to the child, again using the hitting dolls as a pre- and post-measure. The story was taped and played "through" the puppet, whose jaw was worked in coordination with the words so that he appeared to be telling the story. Her findings were that the group given the aggressive story tended to increase in aggressive responding to the dolls, while those children given the non-aggressive story tended to decrease or increase only slightly.

Baer (1962b) has made some preliminary use of the same puppet to provide social discriminative stimuli to preschool children. In one case, S had been shown to be insensitive to the puppet's attention, which was designed to serve as a positive reinforcer. However, S was brought to stable performance after the puppet, through conversation and demonstration, had made his attention discriminative for trinket-reinforcements which were effective for the child. In another case, the puppet pressed a miniature bar-pressing apparatus while giving social reinforcement to the child talking with him. On some occasions, especially when receiving positive social reinforcers from the puppet, the child developed a similar bar-pressing response, even though no reinforcement was programmed for it. Here the puppet's bar-pressing behavior provided a discriminative stimulus to the child.

Baer and Sherman (1964) made a study of such imitative responding by reinforcing children who imitated other responses by the puppet, such as head nodding, mouthing, and verbal nonsense-syllable chains. Children reinforced by approval from the puppet for such imitation also typically began imitating his bar-pressing behavior, although this response was never reinforced by the puppet. This generalized imitative bar pressing was sensitive to time-out or extinction procedures applied to the child's other behavior emitted in imitation of the puppet's responses.

Other studies of social discriminative stimulation are found in the work of Azrin and Lindsley (1956; see above, p. 738) and Cohen (1962). The latter provides a more elaborate use of social stimuli as discriminative for reinforcement contingencies. This study used two Ss working in adjoining rooms connected by a clear plexiglass window through which each could view the other under certain conditions (See Figure 17).

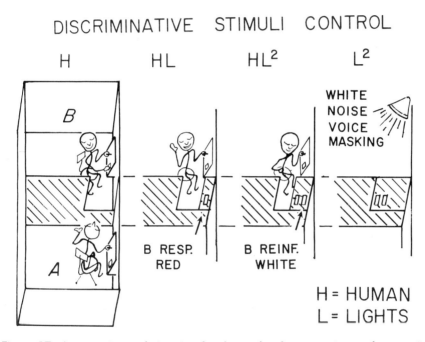

DISCRIMINATIVE STIMULI CONTROL

H   HL   HL²   L²

Figure 17. An experimental situation for the study of cooperative and competitive responding, using the behavior of another subject as discriminative stimuli. In the H condition, the discriminative stimuli are "human" only, produced by subject B; in the HL condition, a red light marks B's responses as well; in the HL² condition, a white light is added to mark B's reinforcement occasions; and in the L² condition, only the lights remain as discriminative stimuli. (From Cohen, 1962.)

An opaque sliding panel could be closed in several stages to block the plexiglass window. Mounted on each side of the panel were two lights which acted as mechanical stimuli. One light (red) flashed on when the person in the other room pulled his plunger; the other light (white) flashed on when he was reinforced. By successively sliding the panel it was possible to have only human stimuli (H), human stimuli and the response light (HL), human stimuli and both lights (HL^2), or the response and reinforcement lights alone (L^2) (pp. 699-700).

Cohen devised reinforcement contingencies which required discrimination by each S of the other's responding, and he collected data in terms of individual and team responses. The latter required the participation of both Ss. As individual A pulled his plunger, the movement was converted into a brief electric impulse. Similarly, B's response was converted into an electric impulse. Responses were divided into four groups: A followed by B (AB); B followed by A (BA); A followed by A (AA); B followed by B (BB). AB and BA were team responses; AA and BB were individual responses.

In order to facilitate the study of socially defined or team behavior the individual responses were mildly punished. The punishment for an AA consisted of A's room being darkened for two and one-half seconds during which a pure tone (500 cycles) was sounded through his speaker (see Ferster & Skinner, 1957, p. 35). When either A or B was being blacked out, no responses entered the sequence analyzer.

Cooperation was operationally defined as behavior in which both Ss were involved and in which both were reinforced on a given trial. Competition was defined as behavior in which both Ss were involved and only one was reinforced. That is, cooperation and competition were team responses differentiated on the basis of the reinforcement, or "pay-off" contingency.

One of the two Ss was always Justin, a 13-year-old boy. The other was, from occasion to occasion, his mother, his brother (age 16), his sister (age 14), a close friend (age 13), or a stranger (age 14). Cohen's findings led him to conclude that "the close similarity between the experimentally measured patterns and the extra-experimental relationships as determined by questionnaires and interviews demonstrates that these experimental measures have high validity" (p. 717). The experimentally measured patterns referred to are findings that for a given pair of subjects, cooperation was more likely than competition, or that cooperation was frequent only when A led and B followed his lead, while for another pair (Justin and someone else), different relationships held.

Recently a series of studies have been concerned with programming complex auditory and visual stimuli for normal and deviant children. They might be viewed as interesting in that they deal with perceptual, conceptual, and "cognitive" processes and have implications for training, remediation, and psychotherapy. For example, Audrey L. Holland and Mathews (1963) evaluated the effectiveness of three programs for teaching discrimination of the "s" phoneme to children with defective "s" articulation in order to develop a machine suitable for presenting the programs. Their Ss, normal children ranging in age from 8 to 11, were required to listen to tape recordings. Every time they heard an "s" they pushed a blue button, and every time they heard any other sound, they pressed a red button. In Program I they were required to discriminate isolated sounds spaced five seconds apart, then to discriminate the sound in words, then to identify the position of the sound within a word, and finally to discriminate correctly articulated from misarticulated sounds within a word. In Program II they were required to differentiate only between the "s" sound and other speech sounds when they were not embedded in phonetic context; and in Program III they were given training similar to that in Program I, except that the last phase—identifying the position of "s" within a word—was extended. They found Program I to be adequate in improving scores on the "s" discrimination test and concluded that techniques for the improving of "s" discrimination in children who misarticulate "s" are amenable to teaching-machine programming.

Another example is the work of Hively (1962). He studied concept formation in five- and six-year-old children by means of a two-choice, matching-to-sample technique (decribed on p. 770), employing visual material that differed systematically in shape, size, and color. On the basis of an analysis of errors he concluded that: (1) the difference between consecutive discriminations, and (2) the amount of training at each level of discrimination play a part in facilitating or retarding progress through the sequence. Still another illustration is the investigation by J. G. Holland (1963). Working with Long, he explored "inductive reasoning" by presenting a picture of a series of objects, uniform in size and shape, that differed in color and/or horizontal or vertical position. S's task was to select from five alternatives the pictures of the object which continued the series; in other words, the task was a variation of a non-verbal analogies test. The material was presented to children between the ages of six and nine and to institutionalized retarded Ss, by means of an automated matching-to-sample apparatus (see p. 770). The last example is the study by Bijou (Bijou & Baer, 1964), who used the apparatus and procedures of Holland and Long to program nonsense forms (all with right angles, straight lines, and identical areas). The forms were systematically modified and arranged to train young normals (three to six years of age) and institutionalized retarded children to discriminate patterns despite rotations in the vertical and horizontal planes.

Instructions to Ss, as a class of operations, might be considered discriminative stimuli. Ordinarily, it could be argued, instructions provide a complex set of stimuli which are discriminative for a correspondingly complex series of responses by the child. The details of these discriminated operants lie presumably in his history of conditioning to verbal stimuli and to the various social reinforcers implicit in most instructions. However, primarily because there are so few experiments which manipulate instructions as such (as is done with most discriminative stimuli) instructions will not be considered in this section but in the section on setting events.

Secondary Reinforcement

Findings from the meager literature on secondary reinforcement processes in children largely mirror those from the more extensive literature on the same problem in animal behavior: the results are inconsistent in general, and the procedures show varying degrees of commitment to making the potential secondary reinforcer truly discriminative for reinforcement. The most frequent practice is to present the reinforcer-to-be on reinforcement occasions, with the hope that S will discriminate it. If E places any confidence in the equation of secondary reinforcers to stimuli having prior discriminative value, then it would seem reasonable that he present data showing that a stimulus did indeed have a discriminative function before testing it to determine its secondary reinforcing value.

Such guarantees are readily possible in the laboratory. In the usual paradigm, there is a dispenser for reinforcers (candy, money, etc.), and a hopefully neutral stimulus, the reinforcer-to-be, which can be presented on reinforcement occasions. (Elementary precautions will ascertain that the reinforcers, rather than E's instructions, are effective for each S, and that the "neutral" stimulus is initially neutral for each S and not either positively or negatively reinforcing.) A series of trials is instituted in which the stimulus is presented on some schedule in conjunction with, or briefly preceding, the reinforcer. This allows E to observe S's dispenser-approaching responses, and to note when they have become discriminated to stimulus occasions and extinguished to all other occasions. Given such observations, it may be concluded that the stimulus has a discriminative function, and that it is meaningful to test its reinforcing properties.

Since in this procedure it is essential to note some response coming under the discriminative control, the response should be one which is easily observable by E and which does not occur all the time. Approach to the reinforcer-dispenser tray is usually convenient. The aspect of the approach response selected as the dependent variable should be other than mere looking at the chute, or standing by it, since such responses may occur continuously and may thus not become discriminated. It may be necessary to arrange the situation so that countable responses are highly probable. For example, one solution is to place a panel, which must be opened by S, over the tray; this has the advantage of being suitable for mechanical recording. Rate of door opening in the presence of the reinforcer-to-be, compared to rate of door opening in its absence, permits quantitative judgment of the discriminative function of the stimulus in question. Furthermore, it should be clearly demonstrated that it is the reinforcer-to-be which fills this discriminative function, and not some other stimulus like the hum of the dispenser or the rattle of the reinforcer falling down the chute.

Finally, much confusion can be avoided if the prospective secondary reinforcer is tested by making it a consequence of some new response, one having minimal resemblance to the dispenser-approaching response for which it is discriminative. If the new response is strengthened, it is more likely that the effect is due to the reinforcing function of the stimulus than to its discriminative function. That is, it is more likely that the stimulus strengthened the response that produced it than that it set the occasion for the response that followed it.

A study by Lambert, Lambert, and Watson (1953) on nursery school children is an example of an elaborate experimental situation within which both the discriminative and the reinforcing properties of the same stimulus may have operated on the dependent variable. The experiment employed the Solomon token-reward vendor (see Figure 7), a box with a crank which can be turned repeatedly, a chute from which tokens fall, a slot for the insertion of the tokens, and a second chute which deposits candy in a trough. One of the more complex procedures was as follows: The child turned the crank nine times, which produced a click followed by a red token; the red token was inserted in the slot, whereupon the handle was turned nine times again, producing a second click followed by a white token; the white token, when inserted in the slot, produced a different sound, and a piece of candy was dropped into the trough. During extinction of this sequence, the chain was broken in the following four places for four groups: (1) after the first nine turns (no red token was produced); (2) after the insertion of the red token (repeated turning produced another red token); (3) after the second nine turns (no white token was produced); and (4) after the insertion of the white token (no candy). It was found that the first and second groups resisted extinction longer than the third and fourth groups. The results might be attributed to the various secondarily reinforcing values of the stimuli in this chain, or to their varying resemblance to the training situation, since the response is the same in both cases (crank turning), or to the work involved in crank turning.

This experimental situation contains many possibilities for further investigation of discrimination and secondary reinforcement processes. However, it might be enhanced by adding two other features: (1) A door might be fitted over the reinforcer trough, which would have to be opened to obtain the reinforcers. This operandum would bring the final approach response under the discriminative control of preceding stimuli. (2) *Two* slots might be provided for token insertion, one for red and one for white. This situation would establish response differentiation to the tokens on the basis of color.

Myers (1960) performed a study with apparatus functionally similar to that of Lambert *et al.* It consisted of a clown face with red jewel-light eyes, a push-button nose and a slot-tray mouth.

When the nose of the clown was pressed, a token was delivered from the clown's mouth. The token was inserted in the ear of the clown, and the nose pressed again. This time a candy fell from the mouth. . . . Each child received either 10 or 20 conditioning trials, with either 50% or 100% token reinforcement, and 50% or 100% candy reinforcement, followed by 40 5-sec. extinction trials. . . . Groups receiving the token during extinction showed considerably greater resistance to extinction than did groups receiving no token. Furthermore, these token-in-extinction groups differed significantly in the number of responses in extinction from a control group which received tokens for nose-presses, but which had never received candy conditioning (pp. 178-179).

Thus Myers, like Lambert *et al.,* has shown that the token was discriminative (for an ear-insertion response which produced reinforcement), and in addition has controlled for the reinforcing value of the tokens per se. However, as in the work of Lambert *et al.,* the same response was used in training and extinction; hence, results may be attributed to the reinforcing and/or discriminative value of the tokens.

A more recent study by Myers, Craig, and Myers (1961) employed the same situation, with the addition of another push-button to the clown's face. Pushing one button produced a token; after token insertion, pushing the other button produced candy. During extinction more candy-button responses were made by groups receiving tokens; more token-button responses were made by the groups receiving nothing (extinction). Again, the discriminative function of the stimulus is confounded with its possible reinforcing function.

SETTING FACTORS OR EVENTS

"Setting factors or events" is a term from Kantor's writings which serves to describe a large class of stimulus operations pertinent to both operant and respondent behavior.

Such setting factors as the hungry or satiated condition of the organism, its age, hygienic or toxic condition, as well as the presence or absence of certain environing objects, clearly influence the occurrence or non-occurrence of interbehavior or facilitate the occurrence of the activities in question in varying degrees (Kantor, 1959, p. 95).

These are the operations to which the term *motivation* has been so widely, loosely, and variously applied as to rob it of any consistent meaning. The concept of setting events helps to avoid most of this ambiguous connotation. Another advantage is that it encourages an initial description of operant behavior in terms of the reinforcement contingencies that control it. Setting events subsequently can account for variance in the effectiveness of reinforcing stimuli resulting from other stimulus operations, such as deprivation. Hence, most of the studies reviewed have been cited under concepts such as response, reinforcer, contingency, and discrimination. There remain only a few researches which need mentioning in this section: the major concern will be with the concept of deprivation; the rest of the section will deal briefly with instructions. This plan of treatment does not imply that the effect of instructions is slight. Very likely the opposite is true. Unfortunately, however, there exists little literature dealing with demonstrated effects of instruction.

Deprivation, Satiation, and Sex-Membership

In an attempt to apply the concept of deprivation to the behavior of children for social reinforcers, Gewirtz and Baer (1958a) argued that

> . . . relevant stimuli (e.g., food, water) acquire maximal reinforcing value for an organism only subsequent to its recent deprivation of them. Other reinforcers of no apparent biological importance, like that provided by the opportunity to make a brief observation response, appear also to be raised in effectiveness following preceding periods of deprivation. In this context, it is a provocative question whether *social* reinforcers (those dispensed by people), postulated to possess reinforcing value through a history of conditioning, respond in a similar manner to deprivation (p. 49).

The method used to study this question involved a two-response marble game (previously described) and adult approval, contingent upon dropping marbles down one of two holes to accomplish response (hole) differentiation. The degree to which such differentiation took place (relative to operant level) was taken as a measure of the reinforcing strength of the adult's approval for the S on that occasion. For each S, there were two critical conditions. One, labeled a *non-deprivation* session, consisted of reinforcing the correct response for ten minutes, after establishment of the operant levels of the two responses, with no previous deprivation of S (at least, not by E). The other, designated a *social deprivation* condition, involved isolation accomplished as follows:

> On this occasion, when S (escorted by E) arrived at the experimental room, a familiar adult would appear to announce that the toy was "broken" and was "being fixed." S was given plausible assurance that the toy would be repaired "in a few minutes," and that since E wanted him not to miss his turn with the game, he might as well wait in the experimental room, since the adjoining "repair" room was clearly crowded. S was then left to wait alone without playthings in the experimental room with the door closed (or slightly ajar if he was more comfortable that way), while both adults retired to "repair" the toy. (During this process, occasional appropriate noises were emitted to indicate that repairs were progressing.) This procedure was carefully structured so as not to imply sanctions and appeared adequate to guard against the possibility that S might feel rejected. If S

poked his head out and asked to leave during the 20-minute isolation period, he was warmly reassured that the toy was "almost fixed," and he returned to the room. (This rarely occurred.) After 20 minutes, E returned
with the "repaired" toy, and the game was played in the usual fashion
(Gewirtz & Baer, 1958a, p. 50).

Under the non-deprivational condition, S began the game immediately upon
his arrival at the experimental room from his nursery group.

This study has given rise to a rather large number of replications and
elaborations. Some of these clearly were intended to reproduce the phenomena sensitive to this operation and analyze it further. Others were apparently
aimed at demonstrating that the isolation procedures of Gewirtz and Baer
were not essentially deprivation procedures but instead presented the child
with discriminative stimuli, for punishment perhaps, or for especially powerful reinforcement of subsequent obedience or affiliation. (Thus, any increase
in later behaviors by the child for social approval might be attributed to
causes other than deprivation *per se,* according to such arguments.) At any
rate, some of the replications did reproduce the same effects as Gewirtz and
Baer had demonstrated; other failed to do so. It would seem likely that the
operations for accomplishing the deprivation or satiation of social reinforcers for a child could hardly be so straightforward as those accomplishing the same operations for a lower organism with reinforcers like food or
water. Consequently, we have reproduced the authors' description of these
procedures in detail (and will do the same later in the case of their satiation
procedures); it is likely in such research that differences in results will
parallel rather detailed differences in procedures.

The effect of *this* deprivation operation was to accomplish a significantly greater strengthening of the approved marble-dropping response than
was possible when S was not deprived. However, the effect was qualified by
a significant relationship which also may be characterized as a setting event:
an interaction between the condition of deprivation and cross-sex relationship of the child and E. Deprivation had consequences only with boys reinforced by a female E, and with girls reinforced by a male E. (Indeed, a
male E appeared to lose effectiveness with boys after deprivation.)

A similar cross-sex pattern was found in a study by Gewirtz (1954) in
which children's attention-seeking behavior to E was related to the sex of
the child, the sex of E, and the availability of E. "High availability" meant
that an adult was sitting near the child (who was engaged in easel painting)
and attending to him continually. By contrast, "low availability" meant that
an adult was maintaining some distance between himself and the child, i.e.,
busily engaged in paperwork and attending to the child only when ad-
dressed. As in the deprivation study, low availability of the adult showed
its greatest effect in the increased attention-seeking behavior of the child
when the unavailable adult was of the opposite sex. The similarity of the
results in the two studies is seen in Figure 18.

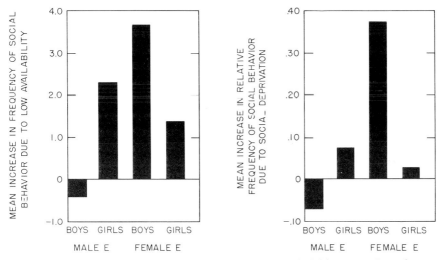

Figure 18. The effect of sex of experimenter and sex of child on social-reinforcer effectiveness in two studies by Gewirtz (1954) and Gewirtz and Baer (1958a). (From Gewirtz, Baer, & Roth, 1958.)

Reviewing the similarity of findings on cross-sex interaction, Gewirtz, Baer, and Roth (1958) argued that both social deprivation and low availability are experimental procedures which involve a simple dimension of the relative supply of social reinforcers. Hence availability of reinforcers might as well be labeled as a satiation-deprivation concept.

A second study by Gewirtz and Baer (1958b) replicated the deprivation and non-deprivation conditions, adding a satiation operation.

. . . each of these Ss was introduced to E in the classroom by the teacher, but during the walk to the experimental room, E maintained a very pleasant and interested attitude toward S, responding to all details of his comments and questions, asking questions to draw out more of S's conversation, and generally approving of anything about S which might reasonably be praised or admired. Upon reaching the experimental room, E showed S around the room, seated him, told him that the game was in use elsewhere and that she would go fetch it in a little while when it would be free. She suggested that meanwhile S might like to draw pictures or cut out designs, and proferred the essential materials. Then for 20 minutes S drew or cut out designs, while E maintained a stream of friendly conversation with him, inducing him to talk about himself if he did not do so naturally. The E alternated her praise and admiration of whatever S did with whatever he said about himself, all in an appropriate fashion, and attempted to dispense 30 such reinforcers during the 20-minute satiation period at an approximate rate of three every two minutes (p. 166).

The game was played in the usual manner. E's ability to accomplish response differentiation within the game, with her approval as a reinforcer, was minimal following satiation, intermediate following nondeprivation, and maximal following deprivation. Only a female *E* was used. Half the *S*s were boys; half were girls. No pattern involving the sex-membership of *E* or the *S*s emerged as statistically significant; however, satiation seemed to have appreciably more effect on girls than on boys.

A different approach to the concept of deprivation as a setting event is exemplified in the work of Stevenson and Fahel (1961) and Zigler, Hodgden, and Stevenson (1958). In these studies deprivation is considered as a long-term operation, or as a complex series of operations over a long period. Procedures are more or less similar to those of Gewirtz and Baer in testing the effectiveness of social stimuli as reinforcers, and the patterns of results generally agree (not always, see Stevenson & Fahel, 1963) in showing that institutionalized children are more sensitive to social reinforcement than non-institutionalized children. Subsequently, Zigler (1961) has argued that histories of institutionalization may be considered not simply as long-term deprivational conditions, but rather as histories establishing behaviors discriminated to the presence or absence of adults.

Still another study relevant to a deprivation-satiation dimension is by Stevenson and Odom (1961). They show that children with a pre-session of playing with tops differ from controls, on a bar-pressing response reinforced by pictures of animals. Here the similarity between the stimuli of the pre-session and of the test are rather different. The generalization of the effects of satiation has not been explored.

Instructions

Only one study will be cited in which instructions were manipulated in a free-operant situation. This is the one by Walters and Ray (1960), in which two sets of preliminary instructions were administered, prior to a marble-game test of the effectiveness of adult approval as a reinforcer (similar to the Gewirtz and Baer method). In one procedure,

> The assistant knocked on the classroom door and unless the teacher answered, asked for the teacher by name. By prior arrangement the teacher called *S* to the door and said, "I want you to go with this man." The assistant then said to *S*: "Come with me into the next building." He did not introduce himself or explain why *S* was being taken out of the class. He initiated no conversation, answered *S*'s questions in a brief, aloof manner, and deliberately avoided giving any information about the nature of the experiment. . . . *S* was brought to the outer of two adjoining rooms and told:
>
> > "We have something for you to do, but we are not ready yet. You wait in this room until we fix the machine. You sit here (indicating an adult-size chair), and I shall be back for you in a little while when the machine

is ready. Do not touch anything in the room and do not leave the room until I come for you" (p. 360).

In the other procedure, the school secretary brought S to the experimental room, in a friendly and relaxed manner, and introduced him to the E, saying:

> This is a friend of mine, Mr. Ray. I want you to play a game with him, but I'm afraid the game is broken right now. I do not want you to miss your turn, so why don't you wait in this room (indicating the adjoining room) while we fix it. It won't take long. You can sit here (indicating a child-size chair), and Mr. Ray will call you as soon as the game is ready. Be a good boy and don't come out until you are called (p. 360).

After these instructions were given, some children experienced a 20-minute period of isolation. Others were handled in the same two ways, but with the instructions tailored to avoid any reference to a delay while the machine was being "fixed," and played the game immediately.

The first set of instructions produced a greater sensitivity to E's approval than the second, whether followed by deprivation (isolation) or not. (However, deprivation is probably not critical in this study, because one of the setting events is the similarity of sex-membership of E and Ss. This is the sex-by-sex condition which Gewirtz and Baer found to be insensitive to the effects of deprivation.)

It seems clear that if differences in instructions such as these can produce significant statistical differences, then many of the instructions in child studies are probably at least equally effective in contributing to differences in performances. One program of research awaiting intensive investigation concerns the role of instructions in providing social reinforcement to individual Ss in a manner which differs from that intended by E.

Some examples of instructions which seem likely to contain surplus social reinforcement for the behavior observed are listed here:

1. Each S was told to push the button-nose, insert the token, and push again to see what happens. When another token appeared, E exclaimed, "*Another penny!* What do you do now?" When S replied that he put it in the ear, E answered, "That's right, now do you understand how to play this game? Go ahead."

2. "Something funny happens when you press his nose. Let's see what happens."

3. "See? Here's candy for you. Now you do it. You get candy."

4. "Go ahead and get some candy. I'll be back when it is time for you to go."

5. "We're going to play a game today. I think it will be fun."

6. "I'll tell you when to stop."

In these instructions, as well as in many others, it is a question of whether a particular S is performing under the control of the experimental reinforcer (candy, penny, token, etc.) or under the control of E's remarks. Is the reinforcer the penny or E's delight over the penny? Is it the candy or E's command to get more of it? When E says, "Let's see what happens," is it the experimental reinforcer or the child's history of reinforcement for what constitutes an adequate demonstration of "what happens" that determines "resistance to extinction?" If E says, "The game is fun," does the child perform under the control of the reinforcer contained in the game or under the control of his history of reinforcement for doing what strange adults in authority say? When E says, "I'll tell you when to stop," how does he separate the child's sensitivity to the experimental reinforcer from his history of training in obedience to adults? Also, when the words, "I'll tell you when to stop" are followed by experimental social reinforcement, it is possible that approval of the experimental response may serve to terminate responding. The response of approval may be responded to as: "I am now telling you to stop."

Three recommendations evolve from this discussion on instructions. The first is to study systematic variations of instructions and other statements by E to determine the nature and range of their effects on individual children. The second is to eliminate them when their effects in a given experimental situation are not separately evaluated. Perhaps it is undesirable for E to emulate a deaf-mute when dealing with child Ss; however, a close approximation to such a practice would seem to be the safest and most economical alternative to an extensive study of the effect of E's statements. The third is to exploit the advantages of individual experimental analysis. Since the effect of instructions will never be uniform for all children, or even nearly so, verbal instructions and demonstrations may be evaluated and separated from the effects of other experimental stimuli more readily for individuals than for groups of children.

A future chapter of operant methods in child research would be expected to have a large section on setting events. Variables such as social-class membership, histories of institutional deprivation, education, socialization, injury, medication, etc. will probably have been studied in relation to operant techniques. This section may be closed, then, with the characterization of such variables as one of the promising and interesting areas for future investigation.

REFERENCES

ALLEN, K. EILEEN, HART, BETTY, BUELL, JOAN S., HARRIS, FLORENCE R., and WOLF, M. M. (1964) Effects of social reinforcement on isolate behavior of a nursery school child. *Child Develpm., 35,* 511-519.

AZRIN, N. H., and LINDSLEY, O. R. (1956) The reinforcement of cooperation between children. *J. abnorm. soc. Psychol., 52,* 100-102.

BAER, D. M. (1960) Escape and avoidance response of pre-school children to two schedules of reinforcement withdrawal. *J. exp. Anal. Behav., 3,* 155 159.

BAER, D. M. (1961) Effect of withdrawal of positive reinforcement on an extinguishing response in young children. *Child Develpm., 32,* 67-74.

BAER, D. M. (1962) Laboratory control of thumbsucking through the withdrawal and re-presentation of positive reinforcement. *J. exp. Anal. Behav., 5,* 525-528. (a)

BAER, D. M. (1962) A technique for the study of social reinforcement in young children: Behavior avoiding reinforcement withdrawal. *Child Develpm., 33,* 847-858. (b)

BAER, D. M., HARRIS, FLORENCE R., and WOLF, M. M. (1963) Control of nursery school children's behavior by programming social reinforcement from their teachers. Paper read at Amer. Psychol. Ass., Philadelphia, Pa., September.

BAER, D. M., and SHERMAN, J. A. (1964) Reinforcement control of generalized imitation, *J. exp. child Psychol., 1,* 37-49.

BIJOU, S. W. (1955) A systematic approach to an experimental analysis of young children. *Child Develpm., 26,* 161-168.

BIJOU, S. W. (1957) Methodology for an experimental analysis of child behavior. *Psychol. Rep., 3,* 243-250. (a)

BIJOU, S. W. (1957) Patterns of reinforcement and extinction in young children. *Child Develpm., 28,* 47-54. (b)

BIJOU, S. W. (1958) Operant extinction after fixed-interval schedules with young children. *J. exp. Anal. Behav., 1,* 25-29. (a)

BIJOU, S. W. (1958) A child-study laboratory on wheels. *Child Develpm., 29,* 425-427. (b)

BIJOU, S. W. (1961) Discrimination performance as a baseline for individual analysis of young children. *Child Develpm., 32,* 163-170.

BIJOU, S. W., and BAER, D. M. (1961) *Child development: A systematic and empirical theory.* New York: Appleton-Century-Crofts.

BIJOU, S. W., and BAER, D. M. (1964) Some methodological contributions from a functional analysis of child development. In L. P. Lipsitt and C. C. Spiker (Eds.), *Advances in child behavior and development.* New York: Academic.

BIJOU, S. W., and OBLINGER, BARBARA. (1960) Responses of normal and retarded children as a function of the experimental situation. *Psychol. Rep., 6,* 447-454.

BIJOU, S. W., and ORLANDO, R. (1961) Rapid development of multiple schedule performances with retarded children. *J. exp. Anal. Behav., 4,* 7-16.

BIJOU, S. W., and STURGES, PERSIS T. (1959) Positive reinforcers for experimental studies with children—consumables and manipulatables. *Child Develpm., 30,* 151-170.

BRACKBILL, YVONNE. (1958) Extinction of the smiling response in infants as a function of reinforcement schedule. *Child Develpm., 29,* 115-124.

COHEN, D. J. (1962) Justin and his peers: An experimental analysis of a child's social world. *Child Develpm., 33,* 697-717.

CROWELL, D. H., PETERSON, J., and SAFELY, MARY ANNE. (1960) An apparatus for infant conditioning research. *Child Develpm., 31,* 47-51.

DOCKERY, F. C., and VALENTINE, W. L. (1939) A new isolation cabinet for infant research. *J. exp. Psychol., 24,* 211-214.

ELLIS, N. R., BARNETT, D. C., and PRYER, MARGARET W. (1960) Operant behavior in mental defectives: Exploratory studies. *J. exp. Anal. Behav., 3,* 63-69.

ERICKSON, MARILYN T. (1962) Effects of social deprivation and satiation on verbal conditioning in children. *J. comp. physiol. Psychol., 56,* 953-957.

FELTY, J. (1959) The operant nature of stuttering behavior of adolescent boys. Unpublished Master's thesis, University of Washington.

FERSTER, C. B. (1953) The use of the free operant in the analysis of behavior. *Psychol. Bull., 50,* 263-274.

FERSTER, C. B., and DEMYER, MARIAN K. (1961) The development of performances in autistic children in an automatically controlled environment. *J. chron. Dis., 13,* 312-345.

FERSTER, C. B., and DEMYER, MARIAN K. (1962) A method for the experimental analysis of the behavior of autistic children. *Amer. J. Orthopsychiat., 32,* 89-98.

FERSTER, C. B., LEVITT, E. E., ZIMMERMAN, J., and BRADY, J. P. (1961) The measurement of hypnotic effects by operant-reinforcement techniques. *Psychol. Rec.,* 11, 427-430.

FERSTER, C. B., and SKINNER, B. F. (1957) *Schedules of reinforcement.* New York: Appleton-Century-Crofts.

FLANAGAN, B., GOLDIAMOND, I., and AZRIN, N. (1958) Operant stuttering: The control of stuttering behavior through response-contingent consequences. *J. exp. Anal. Behav., 2,* 173-177.

FLANAGAN, B., GOLDIAMOND, I., and AZRIN, N. (1959) Instatement of stuttering in normally fluent individuals through operant procedures. *Science, 130,* 979-981.

GEWIRTZ, J. L. (1954) Three determinants of attention-seeking in young children. *Monogr. Soc. Res. child Develpm., 19,* No. 2.

GEWIRTZ, J. L. (1961) A learning analysis of the effects of normal stimulation, privation and deprivation on the acquisition of social motivation and attachment. In B. M. Moss (Ed.), *Determinants of infant behavior.* New York: Wiley.

GEWIRTZ, J. L., and BAER, D. M. (1958) The effect of brief social deprivation on behaviors for a social reinforcer. *J. abnorm. soc. Psychol., 56,* 49-56. (a)

GEWIRTZ, J. L., and BAER, D. M. (1958) Deprivation and satiation of social reinforcers as drive conditioners. *J. abnorm. soc. Psychol., 57,* 165-172. (b)

GEWIRTZ, J. L., BAER, D. M., and ROTH, CHOYA L. (1958) A note on the similar effects of low social availability of an adult and brief social deprivation on young children's behavior. *Child Developm., 29,* 149-152.

GOLDIAMOND, I. (1962) The maintenance of ongoing fluent behavior and stuttering. *J. Mathetics, 1,* 57-95.

HARRIS, FLORENCE R., JOHNSTON, MARGARET K., KELLEY, C. SUSAN, and WOLF, M. M. (1964) Effects of positive social reinforcement on regressed crawling of a nursery school child. *J. ed. Psychol., 55,* 35-41.

HART, BETTY M., ALLEN, K. EILEEN, BUELL, JOAN S., HARRIS, FLORENCE R., and WOLF, M. M. (1964) Effects of social reinforcement on operant crying. *J. exp. child Psychol., 1,* 145-153.

HIVELY, W. (1962) Programming stimuli in matching to sample. *J. exp. anal. Behav., 5,* 279-298.

HOLLAND, AUDREY, and MATTHEWS, J. (1963) Application of teaching machine concepts to speech pathology and audiology. *Asha, 5,* 474-482.

HOLLAND, J. G. (1963) New directions in teaching-machine research. In J. Coulson (Ed.), *Proceedings of the conference on applications of digital computers to automated instruction.* New York: Wiley.

JEFFREY, W. E. (1955) New technique for motivating and reinforcing children. *Science, 121,* 371.

JENSEN, K. (1932) Differential reactions to taste and temperature stimuli in newborn infants. *Genet. Psychol. Monogr., 12,* 361-479.

KANTOR, J. R. (1959) *Interbehavioral psychology.* (Rev. ed.) Bloomington, Ind.: Principia Press.

KELLER, F. S. (1950) Animals and children. *Child Develpm., 21,* 7-12.

KELLER, F. S., and SCHOENFELD, W. N. (1950) *Principles of psychology.* New York: Appleton-Century-Crofts.

LAMBERT, W. W., LAMBERT, ELIZABETH C., and WATSON, P. D. (1953) Acquisition and extinction of an instrumental response sequence in the token-reward situation. *J. exp. Psychol., 45,* 321-326.

LANE, H., and CURRAN, C. (1963) Auditory generalization gradients of blind retarded children. *J. exp. Anal. Behav., 6,* 585-588.

LARDER, DIANE L. (1962) Effect of aggressive story content on non-verbal play behavior. *Psychol. Rep., 11,* 14.

LINDSLEY, O. R. (1956) Operant conditioning methods applied to research in chronic schizophrenia. *Psychiat. res. Rep., 5,* 118-139.

LIPSITT, L. P. (1960) Conditioning in the human infant. Paper read at Amer. Psychol. Ass. meeting, Chicago, September.

LIPSITT, L. P., and DE LUCIA, C. A. (1960) An apparatus for the measurement of specific response and general activity of the human neonate. *Amer. J. Psychol., 73,* 630-632.

LONG, E. R. (1959) The use of operant conditioning techniques in children. In S. Fisher (Ed.), *Child research in psychopharmacology.* Springfield, Ill.: Charles C Thomas. (a)

LONG, E. R. (1959) Multiple scheduling in children. *J. exp. Anal. Behav., 2,* 268. (b)

LONG, E. R. (1962) Additional techniques for producing multiple schedule control in children. *J. exp. Anal. Behav., 5,* 443-462.

LONG, E. R. (1963) Chained and tandem scheduling with children. *J. exp. Anal. Behav., 6,* 459-472.

LONG, E. R., HAMMACK, J. T., MAY, F., and CAMPBELL, B. J. (1958) Intermittent reinforcement of operant behavior in children. *J. exp. Anal. Behav., 4,* 315-339.

LOVAAS, O. I. (1961) The control of operant responding by rate and content of verbal operants. Paper read at Western Psychol. Ass. meeting, Seattle, June. (a)

LOVAAS, O. I. (1961) Effect of exposure to symbolic aggression on aggressive behavior. *Child Develpm., 32,* 37-44. (b)

LOVAAS, O. I. (1961) Interaction between verbal and nonverbal behavior. *Child Develpm., 32,* 329-336. (c)

MOUSTAKAS, C. E., and BERSON, MINNIE P. (1955) *The nursery school and childcare center.* New York: Morrow.

MYERS, NANCY A. (1960) Extinction following partial and continuous primary and secondary reinforcement. *J. exp. Psychol., 60,* 172-179.

MYERS, NANCY A., CRAIG, GRACE J., and MYERS, J. L. (1961) Secondary reinforcement as a function of the number of reinforced trials. *Child Develpm., 32,* 765-772.

ORLANDO, R. (1961) Component behaviors in free temporal discrimination. *Amer. J. ment. Defic., 65,* 615-619. (a)

ORLANDO, R. (1961) The functional role of discriminative stimuli in free operant performance of developmentally retarded children. *Psychol. Rec., 11,* 153-161. (b)

ORLANDO, R., and BIJOU, S. W. (1960) Single and multiple schedules of reinforcement in developmentally retarded children. *J. exp. Anal. Behav., 3,* 339-348.

ORLANDO, R., BIJOU, S. W., TYLER, R. M., and MARSHALL, D. A. (1961) A laboratory for the experimental analysis of developmentally retarded children. *Psychol. Rep., 7,* 261-267.

RHEINGOLD, HARRIET L., GEWIRTZ, J. L., and ROSS, HELEN W. (1959) Social conditioning of vocalizations in the infant. *J. comp. physiol. Psychol., 52,* 68-73.

RHEINGOLD, HARRIET L., STANLEY, W. C., and COOLEY, J. A. (1962) A crib for the study of exploratory behavior in infants. *Science, 136,* 1054-1055.

RISLEY, T. (1964) Generalization gradients following two-response discrimination training. *J. exp. Anal. Behav., 7,* 199-204.

ROBINSON, NANCY M., and ROBINSON, H. R. (1961) A method for the study of instrumental avoidance conditioning with young children. *J. comp. physiol. Psychol., 54,* 20-23.

SCREVEN, C. G. (1954) The effects of interference on response strength. *J. comp. physiol. Psychol., 47,* 140-144.

SHAKOW, D. (1959) Research in child development: A case illustration of the psychologist's dilemma. *Amer. J. Orthopsychiat., 29,* 45-59.

SIMMONS, MAE W., and LIPSITT, L. P. (1961) An operant discrimination apparatus for infants. *J. exp. Anal. Behav., 4,* 233-235.

SKINNER, B. F. (1938) *The behavior of organisms.* New York: Appleton-Century-Crofts.

SKINNER, B. F. (1953) *Science and human behavior.* New York: Macmillan.

SPIKER, C. C. (1960) Research methods in children's learning. In P. H. Mussen (Ed.), *Handbook of research methods in child development.* New York: Wiley.

STEVENS, S. S. (1939) Psychology and the science of science. *Psychol. Bull., 36,* 221-263.

STEVENSON, H. W. (1961) Social reinforcement with children as a function of CA, sex of E, and sex of S. *J. abnorm. soc. Psychol., 63,* 147-154.

STEVENSON, H. W., and CRUSE, D. B. (1961) The effectiveness of social reinforcement with normal and feeble-minded children. *J. Pers., 29,* 124-135.

STEVENSON, H. W., and FAHEL, LEILA S. (1961) The effect of social reinforcement on the performance of institutionalized and noninstitutionalized normal and feebleminded children. *J. Pers., 29,* 136-147.

STEVENSON, H. W., and ODOM, R. D. (1961) Effects of pretraining on the reinforcing value of visual stimuli. *Child Develpm., 32,* 739-744.

STODDARD, L. T. (1962) Operant conditioning of timing behavior in children. Unpublished doctoral dissertation, Columbia University.

TYLER, R. M. (1960) Discriminative behavior of developmental retardates under conditions of discriminative and negatively reinforcing stimulation. Unpublished Master's thesis, University of Washington.

WALTERS, R. H., and RAY, E. (1960) Anxiety, social isolation, and reinforcer effectiveness. *J. Pers., 28,* 358-367.

WEISBERG, P. (1963) Social and nonsocial conditioning of infant vocalization. *Child Develpm., 34,* 377-388.

WITRYOL, S. L., and FISCHER, W. F. (1960) Scaling children's incentives by the method of paired comparisons. *Psychol. Rep., 7,* 471-474.

ZIGLER, E. F. (1961) Recent findings on social reinforcement. Paper used at meeting of Soc. for Res. in Child Develpm., Pennsylvania State University.

ZIGLER, E. F., HODGDEN, L., and STEVENSON, H. W. (1958) The effect of support on the performance of normal and feeble-minded children. *J. Pers., 26,* 106-122.

ZYLSTRA, J. (1961) The interaction of extinction of simultaneously occurring verbal and manual operants. Unpublished Master's thesis, University of Washington.

18

Conditioning Human Verbal Behavior [1]

W. C. Holz and N. H. Azrin

INTRODUCTION: AN HISTORICAL OVERVIEW

Mentalistic Conceptions

Of all behavior, verbal behavior enjoys a peculiar status. Verbal behavior is taken as the index of mental life of which all behavior is a manifestation. To know a man's thoughts we need only to ask him. To study prejudice toward the Negro, it is not often deemed necessary to observe how an individual actually behaves toward Negroes. Rather, if he merely states that he is not prejudiced, then it matters not that he engaged in anti-integration activities the night before. Even when verbal behavior is not accepted at face value, verbal report is still the primary datum. The psychoanalyst interprets the report of his patient's dreams in order to reveal their true meaning. In such cases, verbal behavior remains the major avenue to an individual's psychic life. It is this intimate relationship to mental processes that gives verbal behavior a very special significance.

Mental processes, in turn, have been considered the critical determinant of motor behavior from the very beginning of psychology. In the early reaction time experiments (Woodworth, 1938, pp. 298-310) it was considered insufficient simply to relate the speed of reaction to the circumstances that modified this speed. Instead, the time measurements were considered to reflect central processes of "choice," "cognition," and the like. The ultimate explanation of reaction time was not sought in the physical specification of the stimulus conditions, but rather in the accompanying mental processes. Although early psychoanalysis (Zilboorg & Henry, 1941, pp.

[1] The preparation of this chapter was supported in part by Grant M-4926 from the National Institute of Mental Health, by grants from the Illinois Department of Mental Health, and by a grant from the Carnegie Corporation to the Harvard University Committee on Programmed Instruction.

790

486-489) rejected the importance of conscious determinants of behavior, it substituted instead unconscious motivation. Today the mentalistic entities of psychoanalysis, such as the "ego" and the "id," continue to assume explanatory powers. Modern clinical psychology uses such concepts as "personal constructs" (Kelly, 1955), and "plans" (Miller, Galanter, & Pribram, 1960) to explain observed behavior patterns. The mental test movement has resulted in numerous objective mathematical measures. Yet, here too, the measurements refer to "attitudes," "opinions" or the like, which are taken as the inner causes. Such mentalistic causes are sometimes called intervening variables or hypothetical constructs rather than entities; however, the addition of philosophical sophistication does not modify the attempt to ascribe explanatory properties to the concepts.

For a large part of psychology, then, our feelings, our desires, our interests, our wants have been and continue to be considered the prime determinants of our behavior. Insofar as verbal statements are the overt expression of inner mental states, they would seem to be the key to a proper understanding of behavior.

The Behavioristic Influence

The impossibility of directly measuring inner mental states was the protest voiced by the early behaviorists (e.g., Watson, 1913). But the initial protest could point only to limited grounds for an alternative approach. Only gradually have advances been made in discovering the relationships between environmental variables and behavior that make mentalistic concepts unnecessary. Loeb's (1918) work with tropisms and Sherrington's (1906) work with reflexes showed that such behavior could be accounted for in largely mechanistic terms. Yet, not all behavior is reflexive. An organism learns to respond to new situations. Pavlov (1928) derived the principles which could account for behavior occurring under new circumstances. His principles of classical conditioning avoided the need for mentalistic terms. But even Pavlov's principles, one might argue, applied only to involuntary behavior. In the 1930's Skinner (1938) provided the system of generalizations about voluntary behavior that made it possible to bypass mentalistic explanations. The basic principle in Skinner's work was the Law of Reinforcement which states that when certain types of specifiable consequences follow a response, that response will increase in frequency. A corollary is the Law of Extinction which states that when such consequences no longer follow the response, it will decrease in frequency.

Let us examine an instance in which these simple laws of reinforcement and extinction provide an alternative to a mentalistic conception of behavior. A rat has been deprived of food. In the past he has received food immediately after depressing a lever while a distinctive tone was present. Lever presses in the absence of this tone were not followed by food. The end result of the rat's history is that the behavior is controlled by specifiable conditions. When the tone is presented, the animal presses the lever. When the tone is discontinued, the animal ceases pressing the lever. The factors which govern this behavior (the deprivation of food, the tone, and the presentation of food) can all be observed and manipulated directly. The simplicity of these relationships does not minimize the complexity of the behavior. Even the most elemental coordinated movement is vastly complex in terms of neural innervation, light rays impinging on the retina, etc. No statement is made concerning the origin of the sensory or motor capabilities of the animal, which are obviously important to the behavior. Nor is it implied that all of the minute movements which make up the activity are individually established by reinforcement. Rather, the laws relate aspects of behavior to environmental events. These laws have broad generality and can be demonstrated to apply to a variety of species, environmental conditions, and behaviors.

An alternative account of this situation is a description of mental processes that might be considered to cause the observed performance. We have a *hungry* rat who is *aware* that when the tone is present he can use the lever as an instrument for satisfying his *needs*. Because he is *hungry* and *expects* the food to result, he *chooses* to press the lever when the *signal* occurs. We might even say that he was following certain *rules* in coordinating his movements (e.g., when walking, his left forepaw step follows his right). Although these terms allow us to describe the events in much the same way that we have learned to describe our own behavior, none of the concepts can be manipulated directly. The rat's condition of *hunger,* his *awareness,* his *expectations,* or his *choice* cannot be modified without altering some aspect of his environment or history. Whether or not the terms are descriptive is beside the point, when the task is to determine objective relationships. The artist may vividly portray the majesty of a mountain; but the miner should still consult a geologist. It is Occam's razor which denies importance to the mentalistic concepts for a science of behavior.

Nor are objective accounts of behavior restricted to animals. Classical conditioning principles were soon extended to human motor performance as, for example, in the work of Bechterev (1932). Similarly, the work of Fuller (1949), Azrin and Lindsley (1956), and Holland (1958) showed that the principles of operant conditioning could be applied to the voluntary performance of humans. Thus far, we have seen that mentalistic causations can be dispensed with as superfluous for a major portion of animal behavior as well as for motor behavior of humans. To the extent that mental processes are unnecessary, verbal behavior loses importance as the method for explicating them. But what about verbal behavior? Can this too be accounted for in terms other than the subjective processes of thoughts and ideas?

The attempt to analyze verbal behavior experimentally is, of course, not new. One of the earliest investigations was that of Ebbinghaus (1913), who utilized nonsense syllables to study memory. In his work he applied the experimental method in an ingenious manner, relating the learning of verbal material to numerous parameters of the learning situation. Yet memory itself was taken as an internal state designed to account for changes in the likelihood that the subject would say the words as a function of the passage of time. The results were interpreted as the fading of a memory trace. Similar work by later investigators (McGeoch & Irion, 1952) continued to use mentalistic concepts as an explanation of verbal learning. Terms like "reminiscence," "transfer," and "inhibition" imply internal mechanisms. Other studies such as those with the semantic differential (Osgood, Suci, & Tannenbaum, 1957) are even more explicit in invoking mentalistic states. The sequence in which words are used is attributed to their meaning or to grammatical rules, the dimensions of which are to be found only in the mind. Perhaps the most explicit method of studying verbal behavior from the mentalistic point of view is seen in the use of projective techniques, such as the Rorschach (Rorschach, 1949), which are designed to reveal the inner thoughts and feelings of the subject. The deliberate ambiguity of the stimulus situation precludes any statement of control of the verbal statement by the characteristics of the stimulus. Whatever the subject states verbally is presumed to arise from inner motives.

The merit of the objective findings from studies such as these is independent of the objectivity or subjectivity of their formulation. However, in all of these instances an appeal is made to unobservable inner processes to account for the results. A large number of these experiments have been directed only toward proving or disproving hypotheses concerning inner events. Where this has dominated, the quest for objective determinants has suffered.

Objective Treatments

Can verbal behavior be handled in terms that do not require these mentalistic conceptions? At the level of animal vocalization, the answer appears to be affirmative. Warner (1932) and Schlosberg (1934) found that the vocal response of squealing could consistently be elicited from the rat in response to an aversive stimulus. Cowles and Pennington (1943) discovered that vocal responses in these animals could be classically conditioned. They paired a tone with a shock that was delivered to rats and found that the rat squealed upon the presentation of the tone alone. At the animal level then, vocal responses were capable of control by the objective procedures of classical conditioning. Early attempts to condition vocal responses through operant procedures were not too successful (Mowrer, Palmer, & Sanger, 1948); however, more recent attempts (Ginsburg, 1960; Grosslight, Harrison, & Weiser, 1962; Lane, 1960b; 1961; Molliver, 1963;

Salzinger & Waller, 1962) have clearly demonstrated such conditioning.

These experiments have not only shown that the frequency of vocal responses can be influenced by reinforcement, but also that the vocal response can be controlled by specific aspects of the environment (discriminative stimuli) and that the vocal response is affected by schedules of reinforcement in much the same way as are motor responses. Communication among animals, studied in their natural environment, is also an active area of investigation (Lanyon & Tavolga, 1960). From the direction-giving dance of bees (Lindauer, 1961; Von Frisch, 1950) to the warning cries of birds (Tinbergen, 1953) objective determinants of this type of behavior have been identified.

At the human level, Thorndike (1933) experimented with the effect of saying "right" and "wrong" after a subject's verbal response. His data indicated that he could, in this way, influence the subsequent emission of verbal responses. Unfortunately, this important discovery was overshadowed by the tradition which required the results to be interpreted in terms of mentalistic causes. What was required was a theoretical basis for considering verbal behavior in purely objective terms. Such an analysis was provided by Skinner in his William James Lectures on verbal behavior in 1947, later published as *Verbal Behavior* (1957). In this work, Skinner asserted that the verbal response can be studied just as any other response and that the verbal response is probably subject to the same kinds of variables that were seen previously in his operant conditioning studies. Mentalistic notions such as meanings, attitudes, and ideas were avoided. The emphasis was on the external, measurable events that determined verbal behavior. As might be expected, this revolution in thinking about verbal behavior aroused a storm of indignation at this assault upon the citadel of the mind (Chomsky, 1959). The verbal behavior of humans is the last stronghold from which one can defend the necessity of mentalistic conceptions. The importance of this completely behavioristic analysis of verbal behavior cannot be overestimated. Investigators began utilizing Skinner's formulation by attempting to manipulate verbal behavior of humans in a wide variety of situations to determine whether the law of effect could provide an effective substitute for the mentalistic conceptions.

Greenspoon's Experiment

The pioneering study of Greenspoon (1955) was among the first to demonstrate Skinner's formulation capable of experimental application. Because of the special importance of this experiment in influencing the course of research on verbal conditioning, let us examine its procedure and findings in some detail. A subject (S) was seated in a small, isolated room. After a brief, casual conversation, the experimenter (E) seated himself behind and out of view of the subject. He presented standardized instructions: "What

I want you to do is to say all the words that you can think of. Say them individually. Do not use any sentences or phrases. Do not count. Please continue until I say stop. Go ahead."

Two response classes were specified by *E*. One class consisted of plural nouns; the second consisted of all other words. *E* classified the words as *S* spoke them and took common grammatical usage as his criterion. In the aspect of the experiment which is most important to us, *E* uttered the sound "mmm-hmm" immediately after words he classified as plural nouns. This procedure continued for 25 minutes. Then, *S* continued to speak words for another 25 minutes, but without comment from *E*. The words emitted by other *S*s were studied over 50-minute sessions, during all of which *E* remained silent. Tape recordings were taken, and the frequency of words in the two response classes was counted after the experiment.

Thus, the experiment was designed to assess the effect of the utterance "mmm-hmm" following a particular classification of verbal responses. If "mmm-hmm" acted as a reinforcer, we would expect that more words in the plural noun classification would be emitted during the period in which "mmm-hmm" was contingent upon these words. The results, as seen in Figure 1, indicate that this is exactly what occurred. When "mmm-hmm" followed plural nouns, the number of plural nouns averaged approximately 22 per five minutes. This contrasts with an average of 11 per five minutes during the equivalent time period for the *S*s who did not receive that stimulus. Similarly, when the plural nouns were no longer reinforced in the second half of the session, the number of responses declined to approximately the level of the control *S*s. It should be pointed out, however, that the control exerted by reinforcement was not complete. Plural nouns constituted only about 30 percent of the total words emitted. Furthermore, the intersubject variability was rather large. Although the effect was found to be statistically significant, its magnitude was small.

Many studies of verbal conditioning soon appeared. The majority of them used the same basic procedure or a variant of the procedure used by Greenspoon. However, the results of these studies were not in complete agreement. Krasner (1958a), in his review of studies of verbal conditioning, found that about one quarter of the studies failed to find any increase of verbal responses as a consequence of the reinforcement procedure used. Similarly, many studies reported difficulties in achieving conditioning. Unexpected procedural difficulties arose. These failures to replicate the reinforcement effect, as well as the difficulties encountered, appeared to question whether the Law of Reinforcement could adequately account for changes in verbal responding.

It is not the intent of this report to describe in detail the results obtained in the many studies that have been conducted. Several such reviews have been published (Greenspoon, 1962; Krasner, 1958a; Salzinger, 1959). Instead, we shall be concerned here primarily with an examination of meth-

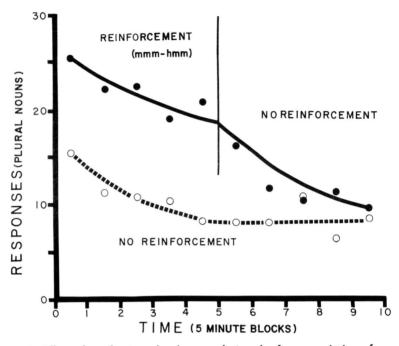

Figure 1. Effect of reinforcing plural nouns during the free association of words. Data points represent the average number of responses during successive five-minute periods. In the upper curve, to the left of the vertical line, all plural nouns were reinforced; at the vertical line, reinforcement was discontinued. The lower curve shows the performance of a control group which did not receive reinforcement at any time. (Data from Greenspoon, 1955.)

odological issues involved in the reinforcement of verbal behavior. In this way, we hope to clarify some of the reasons why the results of verbal conditioning experiments have not been more substantial and more consistent as well as to suggest, by example, the direction in which current research is moving. We shall be concerned primarily with those experiments which attempt to clarify the conditioning of free-operant verbal responses with individual subjects.

The Definition of Verbal Behavior

Verbal behavior has been defined as ". . . behavior reinforced through the mediation of other persons . . ." (Skinner, 1957, p. 2). The implications of this definition have been discussed by several authors (Chomsky, 1959; Dulany, 1959). Although the definition allows different interpretations, it provides an orientation toward the type of activities being considered and formulates the problem in a way that an experimental analysis can be related to the general principles of behavior. Since behavior cannot be specified independently of the conditions under which it occurs, refinement of the definition must come from the experiments themselves.

Behaviors generally conceded to be verbal, such as talking, writing, and the like, are the starting point for experiments. All considerations of why these behaviors occur form the independent variables of the analysis. Thus, we shall see that the experiments may actually isolate the subject from a social environment with other types of stimuli being substituted for the role naturally played by other persons. Similarly, the traditional concept of "meaningfulness" may not play an important part in the experiments. The role of "meaning" in verbal behavior has been discussed at length by Skinner (1957). In a behavioral analysis "meaning" is not a property of the behavior alone. "Technically, meanings are to be found among the independent variables in a functional account, rather than as properties of the dependent variables. When someone says that he can see the meaning of a response, he means that he can infer some of the variables of which the response is usually a function" (Skinner, 1957, p. 14).

METHODOLOGICAL PROBLEMS

Delimitation of the Response Class

One of the problems encountered in verbal conditioning experiments centers upon the accurate assignment of words to appropriate response classes. Following the lead of Greenspoon, many studies attempted to manipulate the category of plural nouns (Dulany, 1961; Mandler & Kaplan, 1956; Matarazzo, Saslow, & Pareis, 1960; Sidowski, 1954; Spielberger & DeNike, 1962; Wilson & Verplanck, 1956). Related studies used other grammatical classifications, such as verbs or adverbs (Craddick & Campitell, 1963; Craddick & Leipold, 1962; Kanfer, 1958; Wilson & Verplanck, 1956). Still other studies established classes of words based upon the content or referents of the words, such as "travel" words or "emotional" words (Krasner, 1958b; Krasner, Weiss, & Ullmann, 1961; Simkins, 1962; Weiss, Krasner, & Ullmann, 1960). Superficially, it would seem that an experimenter would experience little difficulty in distinguishing between words in these classifications. Yet, difficulties have been reported:

> There are many factors which make difficult E's scoring of Ss' responses in studies such as those reported here. Some of these are: the rapidity with which some Ss give their serial verbal responses; the low voice level and other verbal characteristics of some Ss, forcing Es to "guess" whether, for example, a word ended with "s" and was thus a plural; rapid judgments by E as to whether a word he is hearing for the first time falls in the response class, e.g., "astronaut" . . . (Matarazzo et al., 1960, p. 195).

Another investigator indicated that his survey of the literature suggested that a ". . . source of variability might lie in the delineation of a verbal class and *E*'s subsequent identification of class-members" (Kanfer, 1958, p. 443). Although the classes are distinct as defined by grammatical usage, many disturbing cases arise when words are removed from their natural context of connected discourse. Some plural nouns lack the phonetic cues typically associated with plural nouns. "Dice" and "data" could easily be overlooked if the observer was hurried. Some words may be either singular or plural nouns and yet retain the same form, e.g., "deer" or "sheep." A very large number of words may be either singular verbs or plural nouns. The word "sēz" may be either "sees," "seize," or "seas." "Runs" may refer to the act of running or to a number of events, such as "runs" in a baseball game. One experimenter reported, for example, that problems arose, ". . . when *E* said 'Mmm-hmm' after two words that could have been either singular or plural ['rows' ('rose') and 'sheep']" (Spielberger & De-Nike, 1963, p. 103). Thus, the classification *plural noun* vs. *non-plural noun* involves several complexities. Since the problem is basically one of validity, the fact that interobserver reliability coefficients may be high does not eliminate it. If two observers are listening to the same ambiguous words, they may be influenced in exactly the same way by the textural cues that surround the words. Many words simply do not permit a single valid statement of plurality or singularity without bringing in extraneous factors. A similar analysis would show ambiguities in the other types of word classifications which have been studied.

Without consistency in definition of the response there cannot be consistency in application of the reinforcer. Some responses would necessarily go unreinforced, while other words of a different classification would be accidentally reinforced. As a result, we would at least expect the conditioning process to be retarded.

Several types of solutions have been offered for this problem of ambiguity in the response. Electronic amplifiers have been used to increase the intelligibility of the subjects' utterances (Matarazzo *et al.*, 1960). Auxiliary criteria have been introduced to provide greater specificity to the response class. An example of this is the insistence by Matarazzo *et al.* (1960) that only words ending with the letter "s" be included in the plural nouns category. Similarly, Verplanck (1955), using opinion statements, specified that in order to meet the criteria, the statement must include the phrase, "I think," "I believe," "It seems to me," etc. Perhaps the most positive solution to the problem of establishing consistency in the response class has been to eliminate the necessity for the human interpreter. This type of solution involves the use of a voice-operated relay instead (Lane, 1960a; Lane & Shinkman, 1963).

Thematic Control

Verbal responses do not necessarily exist in their natural state as isolated units or neatly separated into grammatical classes. Rather, they would appear to be related in a highly complex manner so that an attempt to manipulate one word may result in manipulation of an entire sequence of words. Skinner (1957) describes such sequences as responses under common thematic control. Wilson and Verplanck (1956) noted that reinforcement strengthened a response property other than the one they intended. These experimenters were reinforcing words that had some human characteristic and observed that one of their subjects began emitting only the names of Indian tribes. Since these names constituted a consistent subclass of the designated category, no difficulty was encountered. However, in our experience, this same phenomenon has produced difficulties. As in Greenspoon's study, we were reinforcing plural nouns. A subject soon emitted the sequence of words: "tables," "chairs," "desks," "lamps," "windows," "walls." These words were reinforced because all were plural nouns. But the words which followed were "door," "ceiling," "ash tray," "carpet." All of these words were under common thematic control as objects commonly found in a room. By reinforcing words that referred to some of these objects, the reinforcement apparently strengthened all words referring to objects in the room, and not specifically plural nouns.

The problem here is that one is not dealing with a differentiated response. The experimenter is attempting to impose his units upon words which have entered into complex interrelationships long before the subject enters the experiment. The inability of some investigations to obtain conditioning of a specific word classification may well arise from the existence of strong control exerted by such thematic classes.

One solution would be to continue the conditioning process long enough that the response class would be narrowed by the reinforcement contingency. This solution is the one customarily used in conditioning experiments. The bar press with rats does not originally exist as an isolated unit, but rather it arises as a part of a natural behavioral chain. When this response is consistently reinforced and other behavior is not, the bar press becomes differentiated as a response unit. Such a solution in verbal conditioning might require longer experimental durations than the typical one-hour session. An example of this solution is the research reported by Goldiamond (1962) in which verbal behavior was studied in daily sessions over periods of several months. A second solution would be to avoid verbal responses which are a part of the established language pattern. Such a solution was used by Lane (1960a) in instructing his subjects to use only one word. A third solution is to define the verbal response according to its physical characteristics, rather than in terms of its content. Studies by Lane and Shinkman (1963) achieve this solution. Any utterance that reached a specified intensity, frequency, and duration was recorded as a response by a voice-operated relay.

Response Units

Another problem intimately related to those of delimiting the response class and thematic control, depends upon the selection of appropriate response units. Salzinger (1959) refers to groups of words related by a common thematic thread as *natural response classes.* He suggests that conditioning can be expedited by using such classes, because their differentiation has already been accomplished. Verplanck (1955) in defining his response class as statements beginning with "I think" or "I believe" attempted to capitalize upon such an already existing response class. The words "think" and "believe" may have greater natural unity than, say, words related on the basis of grammatical characteristics. Other investigations (Buss & Durkee, 1958; Matarazzo *et al.,* 1960; Portnoy & Salzinger, 1964) have also been concerned with identifying word classifications with a natural cohesiveness. These investigations have suggested that some classifications (e.g., human content as opposed to plural nouns—Matarazzo *et al.,* 1960) are more readily conditioned than others, but the differences demonstrated thus far have not been great. Goldiamond has pointed out the danger of assuming universality of such classes: ". . . the words, *sweet, nice,* or *good* are in the same response class for drug store cowboys, but are not synonymous in an English class" (Goldiamond, 1962, p. 92).

A further problem involves the lack of correspondence between physical and grammatical characteristics of speech. Shearn, Sprague, and Rosenzweig (1961) studied the number of responses recorded by their voice-operated relay as a subject read a particular passage aloud at different speeds. They found that as the subject read faster, fewer responses were recorded. Changes in articulation apparently resulted as reading speed increased and consequently, the sound pressure patterns differed. This produced the anomaly that reading rate (as defined by words per minute) increased, but that response rate (defined by the voice-operated relay) decreased. Other investigators (Starkweather, 1960) have also noted a lack of direct equivalence between the traditional units, "words," and the units defined by voice-operated relays. It may be found necessary to abandon the traditional units in such experiments, at least until more complex equipment is developed.

Operant Level

Another problem area which has been reported in verbal conditioning experiments concerns the operant level of the response being studied. Greenspoon (1955), for example, found that reinforcement had less effect upon the response class *non-plural nouns* than upon the response class *plural nouns*. Greenspoon suggested the possible explanation for this was that the initial level of the response of non-plural nouns was so high that there was little room for increase. Since the effect of conditioning can only be assessed with respect to a change in response level, a low operant level would seem desirable. However, difficulties have also been reported when the operant level of the response is low. Wilson and Verplanck (1956) report that 9 out of their 16 subjects gave no responses (adverbs) during the operant level period. In the absence of any responses, the reinforcement contingency could not be effective. Others (e.g., Goldiamond, 1962) have also called attention to difficulties encountered in attempting to condition responses with low operant level. Such difficulties led Salzinger and Pisoni (1958; 1960; 1961) and Salzinger *et al.,* (1962) to suggest that on the basis of their experience a verbal response must be reinforced eight to ten times before conditioning will reliably occur.

These problems related to the operant level of the response are not peculiar to verbal conditioning experiments but are common to many studies of operant conditioning. If the difficulty is that of a high operant level, there seems little alternative to selecting another response with a low operant level. The thousand-fold differences found when the pecking response of pigeons is conditioned would be impossible if the operant level of this response was not near zero. The distinctive patterns of response associated with various schedules of reinforcement would not be apparent if the response occurred with a high frequency independently of conditioning. Thus, a low operant level is essential for the study of conditioning, and several procedures have been described (Ferster, 1953) for dealing with the problems arising from this requirement: (1) to shape the response from the existing repertoire of the subject; (2) to elicit the response initially by some artificial means, such as "baiting the bar"; and (3) to allow extended periods of time for the response to occur.

Each of these methods has been suggested in verbal conditioning studies as a solution to the problem of a low operant level. Isaacs, Thomas, and Goldiamond (1960) and Sherman (1963), for example, attempted to shape verbal responses in mute mental hospital patients by reinforcing successive approximations to talking. Other experiments (Lane, 1960a; Lane & Shinkman, 1963) have elicited the response by means of instructions. This method makes determination of the operant level difficult; but since extinction of a response typically results in its rate returning to the operant level, the rate of the verbal response in the terminal stages of extinction may be used as an estimate (Lane & Shinkman, 1963). More subtly, Shearn *et al.* (1961) used the presence of a microphone in the experimental room to occasion the initial verbal responses. Finally, Goldiamond (1962) and Lindsley (1963) allowed long periods of time for the conditioning of responses which initially occurred only infrequently.

Duration of Experimental Sessions

Several experimenters have questioned the advisability of using the short, fixed time periods which are typical of many verbal conditioning experiments. Matarazzo *et al.* (1960), for example, point out that the first reinforced response frequently did not occur until some time after the start of the period designated for reinforcement. They considered it inappropriate to include this time in the reinforcement period. As a solution, they analyzed their data with the reinforcement periods beginning with the first reinforced response. Goldiamond (1962), commenting upon the same problem, adopted the solution of basing the duration of his experimental periods upon the behavior of his subjects. The contingencies changed only after the conditions had been in effect an extended period of time and the behavior had reached an asymptotic level. This latter procedure is common to most experiments in operant conditioning and seems well advised in the case of verbal conditioning. Longer introductory periods, during which emotional reactions to the novel situation might adapt, has also been suggested as important to secure conditioning (Salzinger & Pisoni, 1958). Greenspoon (1955) and Mandler and Kaplan (1956) observed that the operant level of plural nouns decreases as a function of time. If the experimental period does not first allow the response to reach an asymptotic level, it is hazardous to compare the reinforced or extinguished rate with the initial operant level. Mandler and Kaplan found in one instance that continued reinforcement eventually led to a rate of verbalization that was below the previously measured operant level for that response.

Adequacy of the Reinforcing Stimulus

A critical issue in the reinforcement of verbal responses is whether the stimulus used is indeed a reinforcer. Mandler and Kaplan (1956), for example, raise the question of whether it is justifiable to consider the stimulus "mmm-hmm" a universal reinforcer. In analyzing the responses of individual subjects they found that "mmm-hmm" was reinforcing for some subjects but punishing for others. Hildum and Brown (1956), Sullivan and Calvin (1959), and Ulrich (1962) also question the effectiveness of such verbal reinforcers. In Ulrich's study 80 percent of the subjects walked out of the situation when the experimenter did not react in any way except to agree with their statements of opinion. In general, it appears unwise to assume on an intuitive basis that certain verbal phrases will be reinforcing for subjects being studied under the conditions of the experiment. Some studies (Cohen, Greenbaum, & Mansson, 1963; Gewirtz & Baer, 1958) have suggested that social deprivation may increase the effectiveness of such social reinforcers. Other investigators, in attempting to solve the problem of an effective reinforcer, are turning to other consequences as well as social reinforcers. Staats, Staats, Schutz, and Wolf (1962), for example, have demonstrated the effectiveness of trinkets as reinforcers for maintaining verbal behavior of children. Other experiments have used money as the reinforcer (Kapostins, 1963; Lane, 1964).

Consistency of the Reinforcing Stimulus

The effectiveness of a reinforcer may depend upon the consistency of its application. Failure to obtain conditioning may be due to a failure to maintain the essential property of the reinforcer throughout the procedure. Several investigators have pointed to difficulties in specifying the stimulus used as a reinforcer. Hildum and Brown (1956), observing that "mmm-hmm" was ineffective in their experiment, suggested that the intonation of this utterance may be critical in determining its effectiveness. Greenspoon (1955) noted that care was taken to assure that the word, "mmm-hmm" was spoken in a consistent tone of voice. Verplanck (1955) restricted the reinforcing statements by specifying in advance that they should be restricted to phrases, such as "That's right," "I agree," etc. Thus, some investigators have attempted to solve the problem by standardizing the tone of voice and/or facial expression of the person administering the reinforcing sounds. Other types of reinforcers, especially those which require the person reinforcing to engage in a complex set of behaviors—smiles, nods, forward movements, etc. (Rheingold, Gewirtz, & Ross, 1959; Weiss *et al.,* 1960)— would seem to be less capable of simple standardization. The problem of specifying and assuring the consistency of the reinforcing stimulus, of course, can also be solved by using reinforcers that do not involve human activity, such as points on a counter, money, or the flash of a signal light.

Immediacy of Reinforcement

Another problem posed by the use of the human observer to supply the reinforcer concerns the possibility of a delay in its delivery. Matarazzo *et al.* (1960), for example, have pointed out that the experimenter often needs some time to decide whether a particular word falls into the response class that is to be reinforced. Even where no difficulty is encountered, it is clear that some time is required by the experimenter to categorize the response and to emit the reinforcing sounds. If the delay is great, there is a risk that the reinforcer will follow some other verbalization subsequent to the response (Salzinger, 1959). On the basis of other conditioning experiments, we could expect both of these factors (delayed and inconsistent reinforcement) to retard the conditioning process. In order to minimize the delay, some experimenters have turned to the voice-operated relay and automatic delivery of the reinforcer (e.g., Lane & Shinkman, 1963; Shearn *et al.,* 1961).

Influence of the Observer

As we have seen, the reports of investigators in the area of verbal conditioning indicate several difficulties which appear to be directly attributable to the use of the human observer. These include difficulties in classifying responses and consistently delivering reinforcement. Yet another problem related to the use of the human observer has been reported, and its effect is even more difficult to evaluate. This is the problem of the subtle biases in the experiments which may be introduced by the observer. Matarazzo *et al.* (1960), for example, state that one of their observers who believed strongly in conditioning was found to score ambiguous words as positive when they occurred in the period designated for reinforcement, but as negative during operant level and extinction periods. Similarly, Ulrich (1962) attributes the lack of conditioning in his experiment to the absence of any expectation on the part of his observers of the results that should occur. Azrin, Holz, Ulrich, and Goldiamond, (1961) reversed the effect of reinforcement by their instructions to the observers, some of whom were told that disagreement with the subject's statement of opinions would produce more opinions than would agreement. These observers reported such results, while others, given opposite instructions, reported diametrically opposite results.

In other cases the biasing factors have not been so blatant. Kanfer (1958) found that one of the largest differences in his study was between experimenters rather than between experimental conditions. This occurred in spite of precautions to limit the interaction between the experimenters and the subjects. He relates:

> Several studies have shown the effects of *E*'s status, attitudes, or physical appearance on the behavior of respondents, *S*s, or clients. In the present study the obvious gross diffrences between *E*s were minimal. Both were male, and both were trained to treat *S*s in the same manner during the initial contact. Differences between *E*s rested only on a clear-cut decision, namely the assignment of a word to a fairly objectively defined response class. Thus, the apparent major sources of variability on which other studies have capitalized seem to have been minimized here. Nevertheless, the far-reaching consequences of these seemingly minimal differences between *E*s are clearly shown by the data (p. 451).

Other investigators have also observed that subtle differences between experimenters appear to influence the data of verbal conditioning studies (Hildum & Brown, 1956; Salzinger & Pisoni, 1958; Verplanck, 1955).

Among the influences that may result from the observer's presence in the experimental situation are those which Skinner included under the heading of "audience" control. This term refers to the discriminative stimulus function of the listener who can mediate the reinforcement of vast groups of responses. Because of the distinctive histories of the subjects with various audiences, such an influence of the observer in the experimental situation is difficult to predict. However, Weiss *et al.* (1960) report that generally fewer responses occurred when the examiner acted as a critical and aloof audience than when he was warm and sympathetic. Similarly, Reece and Whitman (1962) report that the warmth of the experimenter acted to increase the general output of verbalizations on the part of their subjects. In both cases "warmth" was defined on the basis of prescribed actions the experimental assistant was to perform.

The effect of the audience is implicit in the problem that arose in an experiment that attempted to study statements of opinions in a "casual" conversation (Azrin *et al.*, 1961). These investigators found that a conversation could not be maintained if the observer completely refrained from participating:

> . . . the procedure requires that the *E* restrict himself to agreement (or disagreement) of opinions, and stipulates no questions, statements, nods, smiles, or other types of interaction. The reason for forbidding such behavior proved to be obvious: *E*'s reaction, however subtle, could often be seen to exert profound but uncontrolled effects upon the conversation of the subject. In the absence of any reaction by the four *E*s, however, all of the twelve *S*s terminated the conversation within 10 minutes by leaving the room . . ." (p. 29).

This effect of the audience proved to be the overriding consideration in this experiment.

Partial solutions to these problems have included the physical separation of the experimenter and the subject (e.g., Goldiamond, 1962; Greenspoon, 1955; Kapostins, 1963), the use of multiple observers in order to gain greater reliability (Matarazzo *et al.*, 1960), the employment of automatic recording devices (Lane, 1960a; Lane & Shinkman, 1963), and the use of nonsocial reinforcers, such as points on a counter, or the flash of a lightbulb. Wherever possible, it would appear best to minimize the role of the experimenter. Complete elimination of the experimenter as either observer or reinforcer has been achieved in some instances (Lane & Shinkman, 1963; Lindsley, 1963; Shearn *et al.*, 1961). Investigation of audience control seems to be an important area for further research; however, it would appear advisable to treat the audience as an explicit experimental variable separate from other experimental events. The tasks of recording and reinforcing, as well as programming his own behavior, would seem too demanding for the observer in the experimental situation.

Mental Causes

The problems we have considered thus far concern procedural aspects of the experiments themselves. However, there would seem to be additional difficulties of a more subtle nature. As earlier investigators of verbal learning found it necessary to explain their results according to inner mental events, so current investigators of verbal conditioning are similarly influenced. Although the dictates of objective psychology prevail, vestiges of mentalism tend to determine the types of problems considered and the approach to analyzing the objective data. It has been difficult to treat verbal behavior itself as the subject of the experiments and not merely the result of some more fundamental inner cause. The issue of "awareness" seems representative of this problem.

In the initial study by Greenspoon (1955) subjects were asked several questions about their experience after they had completed the experiment. The subjects who correctly described the relationship between the contingent stimulus and the response were omitted from further analysis of the data. This procedure of eliminating subjects who could state the contingencies after some interrogation set the stage for a major inquiry into the role of awareness in verbal conditioning. Interest in awareness during human learning, of course, was not new with the study of verbal conditioning. We witness interest in this since the time of Thorndike and Rock (1934). But this issue, unresolved in earlier work (Irwin, 1935; Thorndike & Rock, 1935) came to dominate the more recent experiments on verbal conditioning. Perhaps three-fourths of the experiments have dealt with this issue in one form or another, and even today the dispute over the role of awareness in conditioning continues unabated (Eriksen, 1962).

Greenspoon found that less than 15 percent of his subjects were aware of the essential experimental contingencies. But later experimenters reported a higher incidence of awareness accompanying conditioning. As the experimenters became concerned with appropriate methods for assessing awareness, more extensive questioning procdures evolved. The subject was initially asked very innocuous, non-leading questions; but later experiments added questions more directly related to the contingencies. As the questions became more elaborate, a higher proportion of the subjects were declared to possess awareness (Levin, 1961). We reach the extreme opposite from Greenspoon in the experiment by Dulany (1961), who found that all of the subjects who showed conditioning were aware of the experimental contingencies. All of Dulany's subjects who failed to report them also failed to condition. Spielberger and DeNike (1962) failed to find either conditioning or awareness with their subjects.

Throughout the course of this development, in which the awareness accompanying conditioning rose from 15 percent to 100 percent, a number of investigators asked whether this might not be a futile problem. Greenspoon (1963), for example, has suggested that the questions themselves may gradually lead the subject to awareness: "It is conceivable that all Ss in the verbal conditioning paradigm would verbalize the contingency if enough questions are asked in the interview. Each question may provide S with some information about the contingency" (p. 29). Others have suggested that the answers to the interrogation are themselves verbal behavior and hence, under the control of consequences (Krasner & Ullmann, 1963). Verplanck (1962) has suggested that awareness itself would appear to function as operant behavior. That is, correlated subjective events may arise because they have been reinforced for occurring in the past.

As a simple descriptive statement of correlated subjective events, awareness poses no particular problem. Only when awareness is provided a causative role in determining verbal behavior does it create trouble. To explain the occurrence of an utterance by saying that the subject was aware of why he produced that utterance, we have come full circle to the notion of control by inner events. As Greenspoon has indicated, even though we determine that all subjects who condition are in some sense aware, it is not logically defensible to say that the subject conditioned because he was aware. According to Greenspoon (1963), ". . . even if S verbalizes the contingency, we do not know if he is aware because he showed a change of rate of emission of critical responses, or he showed a change of rate of emission because he was aware" (p. 29).

The problem is not far removed from our earlier example of the rat pressing a lever. We saw that there was a beguiling simplicity in saying that the rat pressed the lever because he was aware that by so doing he would produce a food pellet. It would be no more feasible to attempt to show that such inner processes were not functioning with the rat as it is to show that they are not necessary for the analysis of human behavior. Such inner events are plausible in *both* cases, but the question posed by the behaviorist remains: Can external events be identified which control the behavior? An appeal to hypothetical constructs which intervene between the controlling environment and the behavior is no resolution. It simply changes the form of the questions posed. If awareness is postulated, we must then ask what are the conditions which produce awareness and what conditions cause the response to occur or not occur once awareness exists? If these questions can be answered, the law of parsimony may again be exercised to eliminate the intervening constructs.

Insofar as there is some matter for concern involved in this issue of awareness, it would seem to be a question of whether the results demonstrated thus far are merely experimental artifacts. Other factors in the situation may be responsible for the control over the verbal response rather than the consequences provided in the experiment. This, of course, is an important question, but it would seem answerable only by experimental investigations of the attendant conditions. A few experiments have considered such conditions. Letchworth and Wishner (1963), for example, indicate that the nature of the initial instructions may be critical in experiments using social reinforcers. Their data suggest that instructions which emphasized the problematic aspects of the subjects' task led to greater conditioning. Other experiments (Ekman, Krasner, & Ullmann, 1963; Weinstein & Lawson,

1963) have introduced instructions explicitly related to the contingencies as an experimental variable. Investigations of the control exerted by instructions and the attendant conditions seem ultimately more capable of leading to greater clarification of the factors controlling verbal behavior than an endless repetition of the question, "Are they really unaware?" The repeated asking of this question seems to have served only to delay investigation of objective determinants.

Summary of Methodological Considerations

We may summarize the methodological considerations in the following way. The initial experiments on verbal conditioning preponderantly suggested that verbal responses could be increased by arranging certain types of consequences for them. However, the observed effects were neither large nor entirely consistent. Some of the methodological problems that arose during the course of the experiments might be responsible for this limited control. But on the other hand, there were other methodological considerations that might account for the success when it occurred.

Some of the problems concerned the adequacy of the stimuli used as reinforcers and the uniformity of their application. Other difficulties arose in attempts to define the verbal response so that it could be recorded and treated consistently. The complex history of the subject's verbal behavior appeared influential in many cases and may have exerted strong control over the responses in the experiment. Numerous problems seemed attributable to the observer who frequently appeared as an integral part of the experimental situation. His biases and human limitations in performing the tasks of recorder, reinforcer, and programmer could easily account for discrepancies in the experiments. The magnitude of these methodological problems seemed to leave open to question the extent to which the results of the experiment could be attributed to conditioning.

Certainly not all of the problems are an inevitable part of verbal conditioning experiments. Throughout the past decade of research many of the methodological problems have been greatly clarified and solutions for them have been proposed. Let us examine now some of the results of experiments which have succeeded in overcoming many of the pitfalls. The investigations to be considered are not an inclusive list of these experiments, but they provide illustrations of the direction of current research as well as the types of findings that have emerged.

RECENT EXPERIMENTS

Arbitrary Responses

The majority of the experiments on the conditioning of verbal behavior deal with arbitrary responses. The response units are arbitrary in the sense that they are chosen for their experimental convenience and not their content, which has no intrinsic interest. The conditionability of plural nouns, for example, is of little importance in its own right. Only insofar as this classification is an example of verbal behavior in general does it provide us with useful information. From an experimental standpoint, the arbitrary response has several advantages over a response which is specific to a particular set of circumstances. These have been noted in the context of other conditioning experiments (Ferster, 1953; Sidman, 1960). Of special importance is that arbitrary responses may be selected to minimize the effect of their prior history on the experiment. We might expect previous experiences to have less influence on the emission of plural nouns than, for example, the expression of opinions. It is reasonable to assume that statements of opinions have occurred in a variety of circumstances and have resulted in unknown consequences of considerable importance, while plural nouns as a class have probably received less attention.

A second important point is that arbitrary responses of short duration can be selected; this allows the experimenter to observe numerous instances in a short period of time. When the arbitrary response is studied as a free operant, the response is released from the restrictions on frequency which a discrete-trial procedure imposes. This allows the experimenter to study the distribution of the response in time and the changes in absolute rate of response (Ferster, 1953). Studies of arbitrary responses are also important because they allow direct comparisons between the conditioning of verbal responses and the conditioning of arbitrary motor responses in similar experimental situations.

Effects of Schedules of Reinforcement

In an experiment by Lane (1960a), subjects were instructed to speak the sound "u" (as in boot) into a microphone. The "u" sound was simply a convenient one for the subject; the response class was actually defined by a voice-operated relay. Electromagnetic switching circuits recorded the responses and programmed the contingencies. After the subject had received the standardized instruction, he was isolated during the session which lasted from 30 minutes to two hours. The consequence of the verbal response was to display a screen upon which signals were occasionally presented. In this respect, the experimental procedure utilized the findings from Holland's (1958) study of observing behavior. Holland had found the presentation of signals an effective reinforcing stimulus for the observing response and Lane made use of this function to reinforce verbal behavior. In one part of the experiment the signals occurred only if the preceding verbal responses were spaced by a specified duration (drl schedule). With the drl schedule in effect, responses came to be emitted at low steady rates which closely approximated the rate which would yield maximum reinforcement. The signals were next scheduled for every response regardless of their spacing (crf).

When this schedule was introduced, responding accelerated smoothly as the control exerted by the previous schedule was eliminated. Neither the intensity nor the duration of the vocal responses was found to vary in any appreciable way with either the reinforcement schedule or time in the experimental sessions.

In another experiment (Lane & Shinkman, 1963) the vocal response "u" was studied with other reinforcement schedules. The subjects served individually under experimental conditions similar to those in the experiments just described. However, instead of reporting visual signals, they wrote down numbers they heard over a loud speaker. Presentation of the pre-recorded numbers constituted the reinforcing stimulus. Thus the situation is similar to Holland's observing response paradigm, but used auditory signals. Verbalizations activated a voice-operated relay, and the output of this relay automatically controlled the presentation of the reinforcer when appropriate.

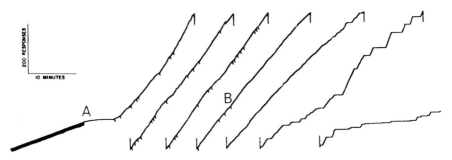

Figure 2. Effect of schedules of reinforcement on a verbal response. Responses were recorded cumulatively during: (1) continuous reinforcement (up to A); (2) VI reinforcement (A to B); and (3) extinction (after B). Diagonal lines on record indicate the occurrence of reinforcement. (From Lane & Shinkman, 1963.)

Figure 2 shows an example of the resulting performance during continuous reinforcement, variable interval (VI) reinforcement, and extinction. The response was instated initially by the instructions, and then each response was reinforced until a stable performance resulted. A VI schedule (geometric VI 1.5) was then instituted (at A in the figure) and a high steady rate of response resulted. A consistent effect, which is apparent in Figure 2, was a higher rate of response with VI reinforcement than with crf. The basis for this difference in rate is unclear, but may simply be a result of the time required for writing down the numbers which were presented as signals. This activity was necessary after every response during continuous reinforcement and hence may have taken a significant amount of the time.

After 40 reinforcements on the VI schedule, reinforcement was discontinued and the response was allowed to extinguish (starting at B in Figure 2). The verbal response continued to occur at the rate appropriate to the VI schedule for approximately 45 minutes. Then, after some cyclical changes, the response level dropped to a low value. Extinction was found to progress much more slowly after intermittent reinforcement than after continuous reinforcement. At A in the figure we see a brief period of extinction before the first reinforcement was received. In less than ten minutes the response rate virtually reached *zero,* which is in contrast to the extended extinction period following VI reinforcement.

The results obtained with the several reinforcement schedules (drl, crf, VI, extinction) seem comparable in their major respects to the results found with motor responses under similar circumstances (Ferster & Skinner, 1957; Holland, 1958). This control exerted by the schedule of reinforcement lends credence to the notion that the consequence is indeed controlling the response.

Modification of Topographical Features of the Response

The intensity, pitch, and duration of the vocal response were also measured during the experiment by Lane and Shinkman (1963). Only small differences were observed in these variables and, unfortunately, continuous reinforcement was not reinstated after extinction to assure that the observed changes were not correlated in some way with the length of time that the subject responded. However, differences were consistent and suggested to the experimenters that both the mean and variance for each tended to increase from continuous reinforcement to VI reinforcement and from VI reinforcement to extinction.

Although these changes in intensity, pitch, and duration of the vocal response may not be entirely clear, at least one of these characteristics seemed to be capable of direct manipulation by reinforcement. An experiment (Lane, 1964) using the "u" response attempted to modify the duration of the utterance by differential reinforcement. In this case, money was the reinforcer. The duration of each response was measured initially, and the mean of a sample of these durations was calculated. A fixed increment was added to the mean value, and this new value was taken as the minimum duration to be reinforced in the next phase of the experiment. A discrete-trial procedure was adopted to allow the experimenter time to read the durations from a Hewlett-Packard counter. Each phase lasted until ten successive responses met the durational criterion and then a different criterion was adopted. In this way, the vocal response was shaped to longer durations by differential reinforcement.

In another aspect of this experiment, control of response duration was demonstrated by reversing the direction of the shaping procedure. After the response duration had been lengthened by reinforcing only those responses

above a particular criterion, it was then shortened by reinforcing only responses of a duration below a criterion. Figure 3 illustrates the results of
both procedures. The abscissa on this figure indicates the duration required
for reinforcement. For the left half of the figure, the abscissa values represent minimum durations; for the right half of the figure they represent the
maximum durations when the direction of the shaping was reversed. The
inverted open triangles show the mean duration of all responses which failed
to meet the criterion; the upright open triangles show the mean duration of
responses meeting the criterion before stable performance was achieved; and
the filled triangles show the mean durations after performance stabilized. In
this figure we see that the duration of the verbal response increased above
the initial level (about 200 milliseconds) as the minimum duration for reinforcement increased. Then the duration of the verbal response decreased as
the maximum duration for reinforcement was reduced. Durations both
longer and shorter than the initial level were thereby achieved.

    The conditionability of response duration is of particular importance,

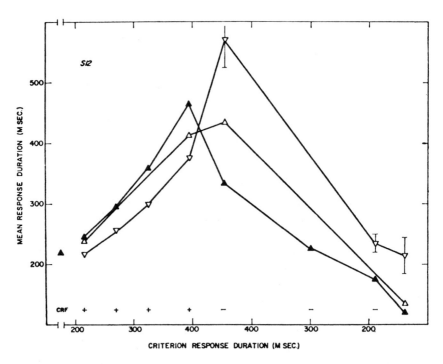

Figure 3. Effect of shaping the duration of a verbal response. Duration of response (ordinate) is plotted as a function of duration required for reinforcement
(abscissa). Filled triangles represent values of the stable performance. See text
for further explanation. (From Lane, 1964.)

because duration along with pitch and intensity comprise the major physical dimensions of speech. If these dimensions can be modified by conditioning, then it is plausible that words, phrases, and the like, which are the more traditional units, are derived as differentiated operants. This is not to imply that such units are necessarily a concatenation of smaller ones, as sometimes has been suggested, but rather that these aspects of the flow of speech can be shaped into various patterns by their consequences. From a practical standpoint, procedures effective in shaping these aspects of vocal behavior will find utility in teaching speech to the deaf and correct pronunciation in the language laboratory. Another experiment (Cross & Lane, 1962) reports some success in conditioning the pitch of utterances using differential reinforcement. However, the procedures produced less consistent results and were sucessful with only about half of the subjects studied.

"Words" as a Response Unit

An experiment by Kapostins (1963) used words as the verbal unit, but in a manner somewhat different than they were used by Greenspoon. In this experiment, college students were instructed to say words individually with repetitions permissible. Each subject was isolated during the several experimental sessions. Monetary payment was proportional to the number of times a bell sounded in the experimental room. A tape recorder and a voice-operated relay recorded all of the subject's verbal utterances. After a brief period of adaptation to the experimental situation, one of the spoken words was selected as the response to be studied. The experimenter monitoring the session recorded each instance of this response and scheduled reinforcement according to preselected drl schedules.

This experiment showed that the drl schedules exerted extremely precise control over the selected response. Figure 4 shows the interresponse time distributions for the stable performance of several subjects on several of the schedules. The modal value of these distributions closely approximates the minimum time required for reinforcement by the schedule. The variance of these distributions is quite small. Another noteworthy aspect of these data is that after schedule control was established, a different word could be readily substituted as the verbal response. The solid lines in the figure indicate the distributions for the first selected verbal response, the dashed lines represent the distribution for the second, and the dotted lines for the third. The author concludes that:

> . . . the analysis of the slight changes in the distributions of the relative frequencies of IRTs with changes in the SVR [selected verbal response] under the same *drl* schedule did not seem to indicate any disruption of the pattern of responding. At the most, it revealed changes associated with a continued development of some kind of "timing behavior" (Kapostins, 1963, p. 284).

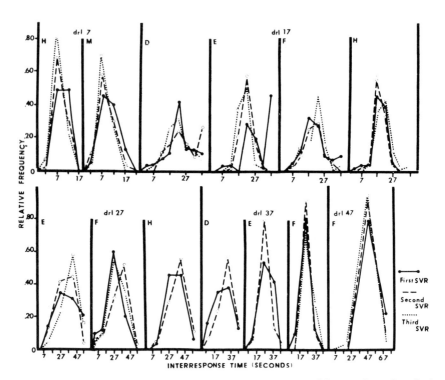

Figure 4. Effect of differential reinforcement of low rate (drl) on selected verbal responses (SVR). The relative frequency distributions show the proportion of responses occurring at the interresponse times indicated on the abscissa. Letters identify individual subjects and the drl values are specified in seconds. (From Kapostins, 1963.)

As reinforcement of the selected verbal response progressed, the extraneous verbal behavior instated by the instructions tended to drop out. Two of the subjects vocalized only the selected response at spaced intervals. Other subjects continued to fill the interresponse times with other words. In general, the overall rate of saying words was not found to be correlated in any obvious way with the drl performance. But in a number of instances recurrent sequences of particular words intervened between the responses. These sequences appeared to be loosely organized "collateral chains" and served to space responses appropriate to the schedule requirement. These chains, prominent with the shorter drl schedules, but less obvious with the longer ones, may have been maintained by adventitious reinforcement.

In these experiments with arbitrary verbal responses we see the emergence of greater experimental control over the verbal response. Schedules of reinforcement appear to exert their characteristic effects. The duration of response and the use of particular words, as well as response frequency, appear to be manipulable by reinforcement. All of the experiments have been concerned with the aspect of verbal behavior Skinner (1957) has referred to as *mands*—verbal responses characteristically followed by certain specific consequences. Other classes of verbal behavior, such as *tacts, intraverbal behavior,* and *autoclitic,* have not been considered thus far in experiments with arbitrary verbal responses. Perhaps, because of the polemic regarding the conditionability of verbal response, the experiments have been forced into strict parallels of basic motor conditioning experiments. As a result, no distinctly "verbal" characteristics or effects seem to have emerged from these experiments.

Nonarbitrary Verbal Responses

An experimental analysis isolates circumscribed aspects of behavior in order to relate them to environmental events. The selection of arbitrary responses and arbitrary reinforcers frees the experiment from "natural" and implicit attendant factors which might otherwise constrain the investigation. Arbitrary responses clearly simplify the analysis by allowing the experimenter to manipulate explicitly the critical consequences and antecedents, measure the response unambiguously, and hold factors of unknown effect constant. However, we may then desire to fit the generalizations discovered in the experimental analysis to a specific situation of greater intrinsic interest. Such an application requires us now to take into account the effect of the factors inherent in the natural situation that we initially sought to avoid. The influence of such factors is difficult to assess, both because of our limited knowledge of the variables that do affect verbal behavior, and because the known factors may occur in distorted form. These considerations have prompted some investigators to study specific types of verbal behavior that possess important practical implications under highly controlled conditions.

These investigations would seem to have special importance for verbal conditioning. Not only may they illuminate the particular behavior being studied, but they may also uncover factors of general importance. Perhaps only in such experiments can the distinctively social aspects of verbal behavior emerge. The danger involved in these experiments is that of unduly sacrificing experimental control. This problem was emphasized in one report:

> Operant-conditioning procedures have generally been characterized by a high degree of control. In order to avoid unreliability, the response is usually defined very simply and precisely. In order to ensure proper programming of the procedure, automatic apparatus is used. Printed records of the responses are also obtained by automatic means to eliminate bias from the *E*'s expectations. These and other precautions have been used, not because of any inherent fascination with "artificial" situations or with complex equipment, but because empirical considerations have demanded such

control. The importance of extending the procedures of operant conditioning to "real-life" situations should not be allowed to override the elementary
considerations of experimental control (Azrin *et al.,* 1961, p. 29).

The following experiments exemplify the study of specific types of verbal
behavior under highly controlled experimental conditions.

Stuttering

Recent investigations of stuttering (Flanagan, Goldiamond, & Azrin,
1958; 1959; Goldiamond, 1959; 1962) offer an interesting extension of
operant conditioning procedures to a response of intrinsic importance. These
studies have shown that stuttering, which traditionally has been considered
respondent behavior stemming from emotional causes, can be controlled by
its consequences. The experimental situation entailed instructing the subject
to read aloud from standardized material in a sound-isolated room. Since
automatic recording of the response was not feasible, an observer in a separate room monitored the tape recording as the subject read and recorded
each nonfluency by activating an electrical switch. This method of measuring
the response was found to be reliable by comparing the observer's definition
with the subject's own definiton of nonfluencies and by the definition of
independent observers. The electrical impulse, which resulted from the observer's switch activation, in turn controlled the standard electric recording
and programming devices.

Figure 5 illustrates the effect of punishing the nonfluencies of a stut-
terer by making intense noise contingent upon every such response (Flanagan *et al.,* 1958). Up to the first vertical line in this figure, no consequences
were arranged for the response. The cumulative recording of nonfluencies
shows that a stable rate occurred. Between the two vertical lines, each response was punished and the rate of nonfluencies was reduced. When the
contingency was removed, responding returned to its original level. Although an explanation of stuttering in terms of emotion would suggest that
aversive stimuli should increase the frequency of stuttering, the response-
contingent aversive stimulus reduced it.

Even more unexpected results emerged in further analyses. It has been
known that when a delay is interposed between the speaking of an utterance
and the normal auditory feedback from that utterance, severe disruption
of speech results (Black, 1951). In one experiment, Goldiamond (1962)
attempted to use the aversive nature of delayed feedback (delayed sidetone)
to condition nonfluencies. An avoidance schedule was arranged whereby a
nonfluency removed a delay of the sidetone for ten seconds. Insofar as delayed sidetone is an aversive event, one would expect the response which
removed it to increase in frequency. Such an increase was indeed the initial
effect of this procedure. However, continued observation showed that it was
not a stable effect. Under the conditions of delayed sidetone, changes began
to occur in the topography of the reading response. Words were read slowly

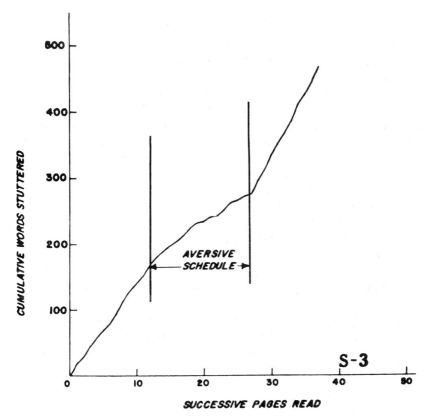

Figure 5. Effect of punishment upon stuttering. Cumulative response recording for an individual subject in a session where punishment (between vertical lines) was introduced and then discontinued. Number of responses are shown in relation to the amount of material the subject read (abscissa). (From Flanagan, Goldiamond, and Azrin, 1958.)

and were markedly prolonged. Thereby, the disruption typically produced by the delayed sensory return was minimized. With this new response topography, stuttering did *not* occur. Stuttering was virtually eliminated, and the new topography tended to persist even after delayed feedback was eliminated from the experiment.

Although the latter experiment began as a conventional investigation of operant control of stuttering, the unexpected findings assumed major importance. The topography of the vocal response is clearly an important dimension of stuttering. Furthermore, the normal auditory stimuli produced by vocal behavior were shown to exert powerful control over oral reading. Investigation of these factors is continuing (Goldiamond, Atkinson, & Bilger, 1962) and may reveal additional parameters of verbal behavior.

Educational Technology (Teaching Machines)

An area closely related to verbal conditioning is the developing area of educational technology. This technology takes as its basic task the production of behaviors which constitute skills and knowledge. Since such behaviors are largely verbal, verbal conditioning is implicit. Superficially at least, the experimental procedures used in this area differ from those employed in verbal conditioning. Yet insofar as both have the aim of manipulating verbal behavior, rapprochement of the two areas would seem to offer mutual benefit. The experimental research on programmed instruction has been reviewed recently (Holland, 1964); but one study merits special mention here, because it is so directly related to the study of vocal conditioning.

In this experiment Holland and Matthews (1963) studied discrimination of the "s" sound when it was included in the context of highly similar sounds. The subjects were children with measured deficits in both discrimination and articulation of this sound. A tape-recorded sequence presented the "s" sound in juxtaposition to similar sounds in the context of otherwise similar words. The subject responded differentially to the "s" by pressing one of several buttons. The experimenters arranged the stimulus sequence so that initially the sounds to be discriminated were grossly different. Gradually the difference between stimulus pairs was reduced. Eventually, the discrimination required was between the "s" sound and distorted forms of that sound which had been reported by speech pathologists. The result was that the subjects progressed through the carefully prepared sequence with virtually errorless performance. Post-tests revealed that not only was the discrimination of "s" improved, but also *articulation* of this sound improved somewhat.

Such improvement in articulation, without explicit training, was carefully interpreted by the authors but certainly deserves further analysis. It suggests another role of specific consequences in determining verbal behavior. Since the speaker is in one sense his own audience, the auditory stimuli arising from vocalizations act to control speech. Investigation of physical parameters of feedback (see, for example, Black, 1951) have pointed to such factors as the intensity of sensory return as influential in determining the forcefulness (loudness) of speech. Furthermore, the delayed feedback experiments also point to the regulative effect of these response-produced stimuli. The experiment by Holland and Matthews (1963), however, would seem to have implications reaching even further, pointing to factors important for the very emergence of echoic responses. Apparently, discrimination of the proper sound is necessary for the response-produced sounds to reinforce proper articulation.

Current experiments in this area are also delving into the problems of experimentally producing and explicating the process of *concept formation*. Experiments (Moore & Goldiamond, 1964) have shown, for example, that transfer of stimulus control from one stimulus to another may require several repetitions of a shaping procedure. By such repetition, control could be transferred while a single sequence proved ineffective. Other investigations have been concerned with the precision with which a stimulus sequence can be developed to transfer these controlling properties of verbal behavior (Goldiamond, 1964). Although these experiments are not directly encompassed by the verbal conditioning paradigm, they demonstrate ways in which consequences mold particular patterns and groups of verbal behavior.

Psychotherapy

The obvious implications of the control of verbal behavior for psychotherapy has led to the study of this activity directly (Ayllon & Michael, 1959; Lindsley, 1959; 1963; Slechta, Gwynn, & Peoples, 1963). Such investigations obviously place a great burden on the experimenter to maintain adequate control. Yet the beginnings have been made and they suggest that order can be obtained from such data.

Figure 6 illustrates one attempt to modify psychotic verbal behavior by conditioning procedures. In this experiment (Ayllon & Michael, 1959) psychotic patients were studied in a special treatment ward. This ward provided a highly regulated environmental setting for the experiments. Attendants were carefully trained to observe the patients' behavior at frequent, predetermined intervals. One category of behavior that they recorded was

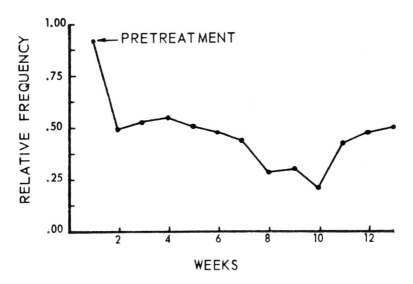

Figure 6. Effect of extinction and concurrent reinforcement of an alternative response on psychotic verbalizations. Relative frequency is based upon approximately 24 observations a day. The experimental contingencies were in effect continuously after the first week. (From Ayllon & Michael, 1959.)

psychotic talk, defined by particular types of bizarre statements one of the patients made. The first point in Figure 6 shows that with this patient the behavior occurred in 90 percent of the observation periods. Beginning the second week, the attendants ignored the patient if she was engaged in such verbalization but were attentive to her if she talked about anything else. Thus, the behavior psychotic talk was extinguished, while social reinforcement was provided for an alternative response. As seen in Figure 6 the frequency of the psychotic verbalizations was reduced to approximately 50 percent.

The use of a natural but controlled environment, such as that used by Ayllon and Michael, offers a potential resolution of several of the problems encountered in verbal conditioning. One problem, it will be recalled, involved effective reinforcers, while another concerned the particular history of the response. The controlled environment provides opportunity for extended and detailed observation of behavior. It allows the experimenter to select reinforcers which form an integral part of the subject's existence and to utilize the extensive natural history of the response.

These factors are perhaps better exemplified in some of Ayllon's later work. Another experiment with mental hospital patients (Ayllon & Azrin, 1964) demonstrated the complementary effects of instruction and reinforcement in determining a social response. The social response in this case was that of picking up tableware before meals. Reinforcement alone proved ineffective in producing the response. Direct instruction of the response without consequent reinforcement produced the response only partially and temporarily. Instructions and reinforcement of the response were necessary in combination to produce consistent and sustained responding.

In commenting upon the role of instructions as discriminative stimuli based upon the prior history of the subjects, the authors point out:

> The use of instructions is in accord with the theory and practice of operant conditioning. Behavioral changes should proceed from the existing behavior repertoire of the organism (Ferster, 1953). For example, the exploratory behavior of rats often is utilized to initiate a bar-pressing. Similarly, the existing behavior of discrete pecks by pigeons has led experimenters to select the response of key-pecking. In the present study, the existing verbal behavior of patients was used to achieve the desired response of obtaining cutlery. Failure to utilize the existing verbal repertoire of humans places great constraints on any attempt at behavioral modification (Ayllon & Azrin, 1964, p. 330).

Another important aspect of this experiment was that it demonstrated the control that could be exerted by manipulation of slight delays in serving the subjects their meals. Reinforcement consisted of immediate serving, while otherwise a short delay was interposed. Such a reinforcer, seemingly small in magnitude, but intimately related to the subject's daily life, proved very effective.

This experiment provides a somewhat different approach to the experimental study of human behavior. It utilizes the obvious procedures which influence behavior under conditions of experimental control that allow an analysis of their effects. The use of this approach in studies of verbal conditioning may prove equally effective.

CONCLUSION

Verbal behavior has held a special place in psychology because of its apparent relation to inner mental processes. As external determinants of motor behavior have emerged, the importance of mental processes as causes of behavior has diminished. It is in the realm of verbal behavior itself, where similar determinants have been more difficult to identify, that mental processes continue to hold basic explanatory roles. "Thoughts," "ideas," "meanings," "rules," and the like are still taken to be the necessary antecedents of manifest behavior. Only recently has an alternative account appeared possible.

The theoretical framework for dealing with verbal behavior objectively was provided by Skinner's analysis which extended operant conditioning principles to incorporate these phenomena. Greenspoon's experiment was one of the first successful attempts to apply this analysis. The initial success led to many other experiments on verbal conditioning; but numerous methodological problems arose during their course. These later investigations have tended to clarify the problems and to suggest solutions for them. However as a result of the difficulties, our understanding of the factors governing verbal behavior is still rudimentary. Recent experimentation suggests that further advances may arise through the experimental analysis of "natural" types of verbal behavior as well as through continued analysis of arbitrary verbal responses. Even though the experiments have emphasized objective methods, mentalistic explanations still occasionally creep into the studies themselves. We appear to experience great difficulty in studying verbal behavior in its own right and not as a reflection of some inner life.

REFERENCES

AYLLON, T., and AZRIN, N. H. (1964) Reinforcement and instructions with mental patients. *J. exp. Anal. Behav.*, 7, 327-331.

AYLLON, T., and MICHAEL, J. (1959) The psychiatric nurse as a behavioral engineer. *J. exp. Anal. Behav.*, 2, 323-334.

AZRIN, N. H., HOLZ, W. C., ULRICH, R., and GOLDIAMOND, I. (1961) The control of the content of conversation through reinforcement. *J. exp. Anal. Behav.*, 4, 25-30.

AZRIN, N. H., and LINDSLEY, O. R. (1956) The reinforcement of cooperation between children. *J. abnorm. soc. Psychol.*, 52, 100-102.

BECHTEREV, V. M. (1932) *General principles of human reflexology*. New York: International Publishers.

BLACK, J. W. (1951) The effect of delayed sidetone upon vocal rate and intensity. *J. speech hear. Disord.*, *16*, 56-60.

BUSS, A. H., and DURKEE, ANN. (1958) Conditioning of hostile verbalizations in a situation resembling a clinical interview. *J. consult. Psychol.*, *22*, 415-418.

CHOMSKY, N. (1959) Review of *Verbal behavior* by B. F. Skinner. *Language*, *35*, 26-58.

COHEN, A. R., GREENBAUM, C. W., and Mansson, H. H. (1963) Commitment to social deprivation and verbal conditioning. *J. abnorm. soc. Psychol.*, *67*, 410-421.

COWLES, J. T., and PENNINGTON, L. A. (1943) An improved conditioning technique for determining auditory acuity of the rat. *J. Psychol.*, *15*, 41-47.

CRADDICK, R. A., and CAMPITELL, J. (1963) Verbal conditioning: Resistance to extinction using one or two reinforcements under partial versus continuous scheduling. *Psychol. Rep.*, *12*, 210.

CRADDICK, R. A., and LEIPOLD, W. D. (1962) Verbal conditioning: Experimental extinction as a function of the position of a single reinforcement. *Psychol. Rep.*, *10*, 427-436.

CROSS, D. V., and LANE, H. L. (1962) On the discriminative control of concurrent responses: The relations among response frequency, latency, and topography in auditory generalization. *J. exp. Anal. Behav.*, *5*, 487-496.

DULANY, D. E. (1959) Review of *Verbal behavior* by B. F. Skinner. *Science*, *129*, 143-144.

DULANY, D. E. (1961) Hypotheses and habits in verbal "Operant conditioning." *J. abnorm. soc. Psychol.*, *63*, 251-263.

EBBINGHAUS, H. (1913) *Memory*. New York: Teachers College.

EKMAN, P., KRASNER, L., and ULLMANN, L. P. (1963) The interaction of set and awareness as determinants of response to verbal conditioning. *J. abnorm. soc. Psychol.*, *66*, 387-389.

ERIKSEN, C. W. (Ed.) (1962) *Behavior and awareness: A symposium of research and interpretation.* Supplement to *J. Pers.*, *30*, pp. 1-158.

FERSTER, C. B. (1953) The use of the free operant in the analysis of behavior. *Psychol. Bull.*, *50*, 263-274.

FERSTER, C. B., and SKINNER, B. F. (1957) *Schedules of reinforcement.* New York: Appleton-Century-Crofts.

FLANAGAN, B., GOLDIAMOND, I., and AZRIN, N. H. (1958) Operant stuttering: The control of stuttering behavior through response-contingent consequences. *J. exp. Anal. Behav.*, *1*, 173-178.

FLANAGAN, B., GOLDIAMOND, I., and AZRIN, N. H. (1959) Instatement of stuttering in normally fluent individuals through operant procedures. *Science*, *130*, 979-981.

FULLER, P. R. (1949) Operant conditioning of a vegetative human organism. *Amer. J. Psychol.*, *62*, 587-590.

GEWIRTZ, J. L., and BAER, D. M. (1958) Deprivation and satiation of social reinforcers as drive conditions. *J. abnorm. soc. Psychol.*, *57*, 165-172.

GINSBURG, N. (1960) Conditioned vocalization in the Budgerigar. *J. comp. physiol. Psychol.*, *53*, 183-186.

GOLDIAMOND, I. (1959) Instatement of laboratory stuttering in normally fluent individuals through operant procedures. *J. exp. Anal. Behav.*, *2*, 269.

GOLDIAMOND, I. (1962) The maintenance of ongoing fluent verbal behavior and stuttering. *Mathetics*, *1*, 57-95.

GOLDIAMOND, I. (1964) A research and demonstration procedure in stimulus control, abstraction and environmental programming. *J. exp. Anal. Behav.*, 7, 216.

GOLDIAMOND, I., ATKINSON, C. J., and BILGER, R. C. (1962) Stabilization of behavior and prolonged exposure to delayed auditory feedback. *Science*, 135, 437-438.

GREENSPOON, J. (1955) The reinforcing effect of two spoken sounds on the frequency of two responses. *Amer. J. Psychol.*, 68, 409-416.

GREENSPOON, J. (1962) Verbal conditioning and clinical psychology. In A. J. Bachrach (Ed.), *Experimental foundations of clinical psychology*. New York: Basic Books. Pp. 510-553.

GREENSPOON, J. (1963) Reply to Spielberger and DeNike: Operant conditioning of plural nouns: A failure to replicate the Greenspoon effect. *Psychol. Rep.*, 12, 29-30.

GROSSLIGHT, J. H., HARRISON, P. C., and WEISER, C. M. (1962) Reinforcement control of vocal responses in the Mynah Bird. *Psychol. Rec.*, 12, 193-201.

HILDUM, D. C., and BROWN, R. W. (1956) Verbal reinforcement and interview bias. *J. abnorm. soc. Psychol.*, 53, 108-111.

HOLLAND, AUDREY L., and MATTHEWS, J. (1963) Application of teaching-machine concepts to speech pathology and audiology. *Asha*, 5, 474-482.

HOLLAND, J. G. (1958) Human vigilance. *Science*, 128, 61-67.

HOLLAND, J. G. (1964) Research on programming variables. In R. Glaser and J. H. Reynolds (Eds.), *Teaching machines and programmed learning: II. Data and directions*. Washington: National Educ. Ass.

IRWIN, F. W. (1935) A rejoinder. *J. exp. Psychol.*, 18, 389.

ISAACS, W., THOMAS, J., and GOLDIAMOND, I. (1960) Application of operant conditioning to reinstate verbal behavior in psychotics. *J. speech hear. Disord.*, 25, 8-12.

KANFER, F. H. (1958) Verbal conditioning: Reinforcement schedules and experimenter influence. *Psychol. Rep.*, 4, 443-452.

KAPOSTINS, E. E. (1963) The effects of drl schedules on some characteristics of word utterance. *J. exp. Anal. Behav.*, 6, 281-290.

KELLY, G. A. (1955) *The psychology of personal constructs*. New York: Norton.

KRASNER, L. (1958) Studies of the conditioning of verbal behavior. *Psychol. Bull.*, 55, 148-171. (a)

KRASNER, L. (1958) A technique for investigating the relationship between the behavior cues of the examiner and the verbal behavior of the patient. *J. consult. Psychol.*, 22, 364-366. (b)

KRASNER, L., and ULLMANN, L. P. (1963) Variables affecting report of awareness in verbal conditioning. *J. Psychol.*, 56, 193-202.

KRASNER, L., WEISS, R. L., and ULLMANN, L. P. (1961) Responsivity to verbal conditioning as a function of "awareness." *Psychol. Rep.*, 8, 523-538.

LANE, H. L. (1960) Temporal and intensive properties of human vocal responding under a schedule of reinforcement. *J. exp. Anal. Behav.*, 3, 183-192. (a)

LANE, H. L. (1960) Control of vocal responding in chickens. *Science*, 132, 37-38. (b)

LANE, H. L. (1961) Operant control of vocalizing in the chicken. *J. exp. Anal. Behav.*, 4, 171-177.

LANE, H. L. (1964) Differential reinforcement of vocal duration. *J. exp. Anal. Behav.*, 7, 107-115.

LANE, H. L., and SHINKMAN, P. G. (1963) Methods and findings in an analysis of a vocal operant. *J. exp. Anal. Behav.*, 6, 179-188.

LANYON, W. E., and TAVOLGA, W. N. (Eds.) (1960) *Animal sounds and communication.* Washington: Amer. Inst. Biol. Sci.

LETCHWORTH, G. E., and WISHNER, J. (1963) Studies in efficiency: Verbal conditioning as a function of degree of task centering: A replication. *J. abnorm. soc. Psychol., 67,* 282-286.

LEVIN, S. M. (1961) The effects of awareness on verbal conditioning. *J. exp. Psychol., 61,* 67-75.

LINDAUER, M. (1961) *Communication among social bees.* Cambridge, Mass.: Harvard Univ. Press.

LINDSLEY, O. R. (1959) Reduction in rate of vocal psychotic symptoms by differential positive reinforcement. *J. exp. Anal. Behav., 2,* 269.

LINDSLEY, O. R. (1963) Direct measurement and functional definition of vocal hallucinatory symptoms. *J. nerv. ment. Dis., 136,* 293-297.

LOEB, J. (1918) *Forced movements, tropisms and animal conduct.* Philadelphia: Lippincott.

MANDLER, G., and KAPLAN, W. K. (1956) Subjective evaluation and reinforcing effect of a verbal stimulus. *Science, 124,* 582-583.

MATARAZZO, J. D., SASLOW, G., and PAREIS, E. N. (1960) Verbal conditioning of two response classes: Some methodological considerations. *J. abnorm. soc. Psychol., 61,* 190-206.

McGEOCH, J. A., and IRION, A. L. (1952) *The psychology of human learning.* New York: David McKay.

MILLER, G. A., GALANTER, E., and PRIBRAM, K. H. (1960) *Plans and the structure of behavior.* New York: Holt, Rinehart and Winston.

MOLLIVER, M. E. (1963) Operant control of vocal behavior in the cat. *J. exp. Anal. Behav., 6,* 197-202.

MOORE, R., and GOLDIAMOND, I. (1964) Errorless establishment of visual discrimination using fading procedures. *J. exp. Anal. Behav., 7,* 269-272.

MOWRER, O. H., PALMER, F., and SANGER, M. (1948) Individual learning and "racial experience" in the rat, with special reference to vocalization. *J. genet. Psychol., 73,* 29-43.

OSGOOD, C. E., SUCI, G. J., and TANNENBAUM, P. H. (1957) *The measurement of meaning.* Urbana, Ill.: Univ. of Illinois Press.

PAVLOV, I. P. (1928) *Lectures on conditioned reflexes.* Trans. by W. H. Gantt. New York: International Publishers.

PORTNOY, STEPHANIE, and SALZINGER, K. (1964) The conditionability of different verbal response classes: Positive, negative and nonaffect statements. *J. gen. Psychol., 70,* 311-323.

REECE, M. M., and WHITMAN, R. N. (1962) Expressive movements, warmth, and verbal reinforcement. *J. abnorm. soc. Psychol., 64,* 234-236.

RHEINGOLD, HARRIET L., GEWIRTZ, J. L., and ROSS, H. W. (1959) Social conditioning of vocalizations in the infant. *J. comp. physiol. Psychol., 52,* 68-73.

RORSCHACH, H. (1949) *Psychodiagnostics.* New York: Grune & Stratton.

SALZINGER, K. (1959) Experimental manipulation of verbal behavior: A review. *J. genet. Psychol., 61,* 65-95.

SALZINGER, K., and PISONI, S. (1958) Reinforcement of affect responses of schizophrenics during clinical interview. *J. abnorm. soc. Psychol., 57,* 84-90.

SALZINGER, K., and PISONI, S. (1960) Reinforcement of verbal affect responses of normal subjects during the interview. *J. abnorm. soc. Psychol., 60,* 127-130.

SALZINGER, K., and PISONI, S. (1961) Some parameters of the conditioning of verbal affect responses in schizophrenic subjects. *J. abnorm. soc. Psychol.,* *63,* 511-516.

SALZINGER, SUZANNE, SALZINGER, K., PORTNOY, STEPHANIE, ECKMAN, JUDITH, BACON, PAULINE, DEUTSCH, M., and ZUBIN, J. (1962) Operant conditioning of continuous speech in young children. *Child Develpm., 33,* 683-695.

SALZINGER, K., and WALLER, M. B. (1962) The operant control of vocalization in the dog. *J. exp. Anal. Behav., 5,* 383-389.

SCHLOSBERG, H. (1934) Conditioned responses in the white rat. *J. genet. Psychol., 45,* 303-335.

SHEARN, D., SPRAGUE, R., and ROSENZWEIG, S. (1961) A method for the analysis and control of speech rate. *J. exp. Anal. Behav., 4,* 197-201.

SHERMAN, J. A. (1963) Reinstatement of verbal behavior in a psychotic by reinforcement methods. *J. speech hear. Disord., 28,* 398-401.

SHERRINGTON, C. S. (1906) *The integrative action of the nervous system.* New York: Scribner.

SIDMAN, M. (1960) *Tactics of scientific research.* New York: Basic Books.

SIDOWSKI, J. B. (1954) Influence of awareness of reinforcement on verbal conditioning. *J. exp. Psychol., 48,* 355-360.

SIMKINS, L. (1962) Scheduling effects of punishment and nonreinforcement on verbal conditioning and extinction. *J. verbal Learn. verbal Behav., 1,* 208-213.

SKINNER, B. F. (1938) *The behavior of organisms.* New York: Appleton-Century-Crofts.

SKINNER, B. F. (1957) *Verbal behavior.* New York: Appleton-Century-Crofts.

SLECHTA, JOAN, GWYNN, W., and PEOPLES, C. (1963) Verbal conditioning of schizophrenics and normals in a situation resembling psychotherapy. *J. consult. Psychol., 27,* 223-227.

SPIELBERGER, C. D., and DeNIKE, L. D. (1962) Operant conditioning of plural nouns: A failure to replicate the Greenspoon effect. *Psychol. Rep., 11,* 355-366.

SPIELBERGER, C. D., and DeNIKE, L. D. (1963) Implicit epistemological bias and the problem of awareness in verbal conditioning: A reply to Greenspoon. *Psychol. Rep., 12,* 103-106.

STAATS, A. W., STAATS, CAROLYN K., SCHUTZ, R. E., and WOLF, M. (1962) The conditioning of textual responses using "extrinsic" reinforcers. *J. exp. Anal. Behav., 5,* 33-40.

STARKWEATHER, J. A. (1960) A speech rate meter for vocal behavior analysis. *J. exp. Anal. Behav., 3,* 111-114.

SULLIVAN, M. W., and CALVIN, A. D. (1959) Further investigation of verbal conditioning. *Psychol. Rep., 5,* 79-82.

THORNDIKE, E. L. (1933) An experimental study of rewards. *Teach. Coll. Contr. Educ.,* No. 580. New York: Teachers College.

THORNDIKE, E. L., and ROCK, R. T. (1934) Learning without awareness of what is being learned or intent to learn it. *J. exp. Psychol., 17,* 1-19.

THORNDIKE, E. L., and ROCK, R. T. (1935) A further note on learning without awareness of what is being learned. *J. exp. Psychol., 18,* 388-389.

TINBERGEN, N. (1953) *Social behavior in animals.* New York: Wiley.

ULRICH, R. (1962) Conversation control. *Psychol. Rec., 12,* 327-330.

VERPLANCK, W. S. (1955) The control of the content of conversation: Reinforcement of statements of opinion. *J. abnorm. soc. Psychol., 51,* 668-676.

VERPLANCK, W. S. (1962) Unaware of where's awareness. *J. Pers., 30,* 130-158.

VON FRISCH, K. (1950) *Bees.* Ithaca, N.Y.: Cornell Univ. Press.

WARNER, L. H. (1932) An experimental search for the "conditioned response."
    J. genet. Psychol., 41, 91-115.

WATSON, J. B. (1913) Psychology as the behaviorist views it. *Psychol. Rev.,
    20,* 158-177.

WEINSTEIN, W. K., and LAWSON, R. (1963) The effect of experimentally-
    induced "awareness" upon performance in free-operant verbal condition-
    ing and on subsequent tests of "awareness." *J. Psychol., 56,* 203-211.

WEISS, R. L., KRASNER, L., and ULLMANN, L. P. (1960) Responsivity to verbal
    conditioning as a function of emotional atmosphere and pattern of rein-
    forcement. *Psychol. Rep., 6,* 415-426.

WILSON, W. C., and VERPLANCK, W. S. (1956) Some observations on the re-
    inforcement of verbal operants. *Amer. J. Psychol., 69,* 448-451.

WOODWORTH, R. S. (1938) *Experimental psychology.* New York: Holt, Rine-
    hart and Winston.

ZILBOORG, G., and HENRY, G. (1941) *A history of medical psychology.* New
    York: Norton.

19

Programmed Environments for the Experimental Analysis of Human Behavior

Jack D. Findley

INTRODUCTION AND RATIONALE

Although a behavioral determinism would seem to be widely accepted in principle, its full expression is not readily found in laboratory research with humans. Indeed, experimental work with humans aimed at a basic behavioral analysis has long been constrained. Unfortunately, determinism as a system, and its resultant body of information, is severely limited without the support of good laboratory operations. Furthermore, a laboratory in which known relevant variables cannot be freely manipulated is not very likely to yield powerful information or uncover important new principles. All such constraints unduly impede the progress of a behavioral science. I would like to suggest that there is currently only a very limited experimental analysis of basic human behavior, and, furthermore, that its progress is unduly slow in view of the knowledge and technology at hand. Although the slow pace is no doubt due to several factors, I think they reduce in large measure to a new kind of entrenched secularism which overemphasizes an understanding of man in the world as we now know it. For example, in studying sleep behavior, it is usually assumed implicitly that man must function in an environment with 24-hour days. Not only is such an assumption erroneous, but it is not even drawn from information suggesting 24-hour days to be most desirable. In studying motivations, as another example, the concern is usually with the existing and familiar, rather than with an effort to devise experimental conditions which would establish new and quite different motivations for orderly dissection. Likewise, in studying marital relations, economic behaviors, and social interaction, the orientation is always toward the existing system and never toward an experimental one.

The lack of extensive experimental studies of human behavior, in the light of existing knowledge and technology, suggests the thought of an outdated alchemist, who, seeking gold, would not employ the techniques of metallurgy because of the "violation of natural substances." In short, experimental analysis of human behavior lacks a real laboratory providing direct manipulation, objective recording, and experimental control for those human behaviors which we know to be most malleable.

Aside from a view which does not permit the behavioral scientist to forget even momentarily the existing order, much fear surrounds the experimental control of human behavior. Although the continuously changing structure of the natural world brings destruction and deprivation upon man, the purposeful management of human behavior under laboratory conditions where such aversive agents may be substantially reduced is usually met with suspicion. Certainly the degradation of individuals, which sometimes results from the total institutional management of their affairs as a result of illness or asocial behavior, is to be feared and avoided. However, such instances of control are not necessarily comparable to a total laboratory study of human behavior. It will be argued in this paper that the full and continuous laboratory control of human behavior need not be aversive or at variance with an individual's long-range best interests. Unfortunately, some human engineering and sensory deprivation experiments have perhaps added to the prejudice against laboratory control of humans. These studies, however, emphasize either negative aspects of our natural environment or examine behavior under an impoverished one. They therefore provide a poor basis for speculations about studies aimed at the discovery of the most favorable environmental conditions.

Recent work by several investigators, engrossed in a rigorous experimental analysis of behavior, suggests a more encouraging view of the future. Investigators such as Ayllon and Michael (1959), Azrin (1958), Bijou (1958), Ferster (1961), Goldiamond (1964), Lindsley (1960), and others, have all extended the laboratory analysis of behavior to actual human situations. Their work, in most cases, is characterized by a degree of experimental control and objective measurement uncommon to the traditional study of human behavior. This control and measurement is achieved by placing human subjects within a structured experimental environment composed of realistic contingencies and adequate reinforcement. In this type of human research, emphasis is placed upon the variables controlling individual performance. Differences between individuals are reduced either by having the subject serve as his own control or by the manipulation of variables sufficient to overcome individual differences. The success of this work demonstrates the potential of the underlying technology and provides a more proper basis for generalization as to what might be the nature of a full and continuous laboratory analysis of human behavior.

Basically, then, the study of man and human behavior has been far too worldy in its outlook and has been held back by unreasonable fears and by the lack of an extensive experimental approach. Since the work of several investigators has been judged as quite promising, where then do the difficulties lie at present? They rest with both the scope of current experimental analysis and the specific behaviors under investigation. Throughout the history of philosophy and recorded verbal discourse, every conceivable aspect of man's behavior has been scrutinized, observed, analyzed, and reanalyzed. Moreover, in everyday experience all individuals observe and manipulate the conditions which profoundly affect the affairs of others as well as their own. In the laboratory, however, man's behavior is observed usually for very brief periods of time and is subject only to the most modest of manipulations. Then too, the particular behaviors observed are traditionally physiological reactions, simple motor responses, or extremely complex intellectual functions as evidenced by pencil and paper tests. The behaviors of eating, working on arduous tasks, making love, winning friends, playing games, crying, washing clothes, training a child, or writing a paper, are almost never investigated experimentally. Although each of these behaviors could be brought under good experimental control, and perhaps should be, the argument here is not that the study of these particular behaviors will generate a more fundamental analysis of behavior, but rather than a science of behavior which will effectively generalize to the richness of human behavior should be based upon laboratory behaviors more closely approximating those ultimately to be controlled. The suggestion, then, is for more total and richer laboratory studies of human behavior. How can this be accomplished? One approach would be the design and establishment of continuous laboratory environments which place demands, offer rewards, and generally support a full range of human behaviors. Such environments would be structured not only to support such behavior, but to provide for extensive objective measurement and manipulation of relevant conditions.

In the following section a summary is presented of the study by Findley, Migler, and Brady (1963), which is designed to explore the feasibility of the general approach suggested here. This new approach is not offered as a replacement for current experimental efforts, but rather as a supplementary method which could open new dimensions of human research. The final section of this paper is devoted to a brief discussion of suggested research possibilities and to some of the technical difficulties likely to be encountered.

A PROGRAMMED ENVIRONMENT FOR AN ISOLATED INDIVIDUAL

The study summarized here consisted essentially of the design of a special behavioral environment for an isolated individual and the testing of the individual's performance in that environment for an extended period of time. In designing this environment the aims were to maintain the individual subject in good health, to insure a high level of performance, and to provide for extensive measurement and control of his behavior. It was assumed that these aims could be best accomplished by the proper organization of numerous contingencies or requirements between the performance of the subject

MAIN CONTROL PANEL

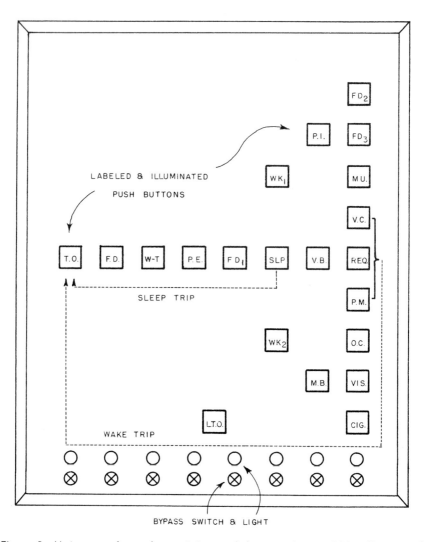

Figure 1. Main control panel containing push buttons that could be illuminated red or green. Each button is labeled with the abbreviations of the activity represented. "Wake Trips" and "Sleep Trips" are indicated by arrows.

and the changes in his environment of a rewarding or aversive nature. The experiment, therefore, was centered around the testing of a behavioral program, rather than a special outward physical environment, since the latter was chosen out of convenience simply to implement the former. The behavioral program provided for use of toilet facilities, eating, sleeping, exercise, several kinds of work, and various other activities of a more desirable sort. Each specific activity was allowed to occur only under specific conditions, and once it was in process, the specific requirements surrounding that activity had to be met before it was possible to proceed to other activities.

Presented in Figure 1 is an outline of the behavioral program as presented to the subject. Each activity was initiated by the subject pressing an appropriate button once it became illuminated. Table 1 provides a brief description of these activities and their abbreviations. Completing the requirements associated with a given activity illuminated the switch for the next. As illustrated in Figure 1, the early part of the program provided for the sequential arrangement of the following activities: T.O., allowing full use of the toilet facilities and access to fresh clothes; F.D., requiring an indication of desire either to extend or reduce the duration of the experiment; W-T, requiring the automatic recording of weight and oral temperature; P.E., a physical exercise activity requiring the location of random light and running about the chamber, plus the pulling of weights; and FD_1, permitting a light snack from an automated food vendor. Following FD_1, the subject was permitted a choice between three activities: WK_1, a complex tracking task; WK_2, requiring the solution of various verbal and mechanical problems presented in a box; and SLP, the sleep activity. If the subject selected SLP, the bunk became unlocked from the wall, the room temperature began to drop, the lights were extinguished, and an outlet for a heating blanket was activated. The subject was allowed to sleep for an unlimited period. When the bed was re-locked, normal conditions were reinstated but the program was reset to the beginning. The activities from T.O. to SLP, therefore, constituted a minimum program recycling in nature which would sustain the subject if ill or not motivated to complete the full program. If the subject selected one of the work tasks, WK_1 or WK_2, the completion of requirements allowed a choice from among the three next activities: P.I., which required use of a reading machine; V.B., which required use of a teletype transmitter; and M.B., which allowed free access to hobby material from a normally locked drawer. Completion of any one of these three activities presented the final part of the program, in which the subject was required to make selections in any order from among eight activities. Each activity had to be completed before selection of the next. These activities included: the selection of a complete meal; the selection of a dessert item; the selection of music which could be played along with other activities; the selection of a limited number of cigarettes; the selection of a work task on a heavy foot switch which avoided a darkened interruption of the entire

Table 1
Programmed Activities Available to the Subject

Abbreviation of Activity	Full Name of Activity	Brief Description of Activity
L.T.O.	Limited Toilet Operations	Use of commode in toilet at any time
1. T.O.	Toilet Operations	Use of all facilities in toilet and T.O. drawer
2. F.D.	Flight Duration	Select flight-extend or flight-reduce
3. W-T	Weight-Temperature	Use of ceiling bar then mouth temperature probe
4. P.E.	Physical Exercise	Press buttons on lighted boxes, then pull weights
5. FD_1	Food One (Light Snack)	Two selections from food dispenser
6. Activity Group		
WK_1	Work Task One	Tracking task in work room
SLP	Sleep	Bunk unlocks from wall
WK_2	Work Task Two	Problem box
7. Activity Group		
P.I.	Programmed Instruction	Use of reading machine in work room
V.B.	Verbal Behavior	Use of teletype machine in work room
M.B.	Manual Behavior	Use of art supplies, M.B. drawer
8. Activity Group		
FD_2	Food Two (Dessert)	One selection from food dispenser
FD_3	Food Three (Major Meal)	Three selections from food dispenser
MU.	Music	Earn record selections
V.C.	Variable Consequence	Earn delayed delivery of variable consequence
REQ.	Requisitions	Earn delayed delivery of requisitions
P.M.	Power Maintenance	Operate heavy foot switch
O.C.	Oral Communication	Earn delayed delivery of intercom conversation
VIS.	Visitors	Not in program
CIG.	Cigarettes	Earn cigarettes from dispenser

program; and finally, the selection of three different activities in which delayed rewards could be earned. By means of V.C. the subject could earn the right to an unknown and variable reward which might be favorable or unfavorable. By means of O.C. the subject could earn the right to a limited conversation via an intercom system; and by means of REQ. the subject could earn various sorts of supplies and documentary movies. All of the activities with delayed rewards, once earned by the subject, were honored at the onset of the last part of the program after an appropriate delay of several completions of the entire program. After the subject had exhausted the number of selections permitted in the final part of the program, a recycle to the beginning activity, T.O., occurred in a manner similar to that following completion of the sleep activity.

Another activity in the program, L.T.O., provided for limited access to the essential toilet facilities and was the one activity which could be selected at any time. Selection of this activity extinguished all lights except in the toilet and suspended the current activity for the duration of the L.T.O.

Although the subject was allowed to proceed through the program at his own pace, the specific requirements of accuracy, the amount of work and the minimum time associated with each activity generally set the minimum time to complete the full program at approximately two hours. In the implementation of all activities, the aim was to provide as self-sufficient an environment as possible, and for that reason the use of radio, commercial television, and the like was excluded.

The general features of the program as well as the specific requirements associated with a given activity were programmed by automatic equipment. This equipment, together with the physical features of the chamber shown in Figure 2, resulted in a highly specified environment which changed only as a consequence of the moment-to-moment behavior of the subject or as a result of manipulations by the experimenters. The integration of the physical aspects of the environment with the behavioral program not only allowed for the design of a structured environment, but also provided for the automatic recording of most aspects of the subject's performance. In addition to measurements of frequency and duration, each activity provided numerous measurements specific to that activity. With regard to T.O., for example, not only were frequency and duration measured, but the use of specific items such a shower, sun lamp, drinking water, basin, shaver, etc. was also indicated. Within P.E. and WK_1, as other examples, performance accuracy was provided. In addition to automatic recording, visual and auditory monitoring was available by means of TV cameras and an intercom system as shown in Figure 2.

Following the completion of the chamber, a preliminary test run was conducted for three days with a 34-year old male subject. The subject was selected on the basis of physical, psychological, and psychiatric examinations, and his willingness to contribute to behavioral science in this particular way. The preliminary test was employed to acquaint the subject further with the manifold conditions of the living environment and to allow the

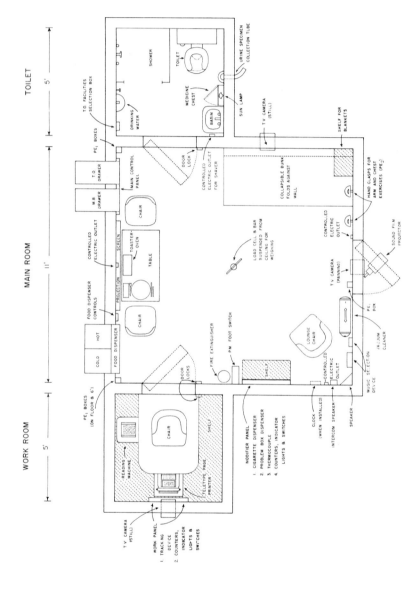

Figure 2. Diagram of experimental chamber showing furnishings and facilities in each room.

experimenters to select various parameters and cost requirements. Following a two-week period of further preparation, the subject entered the chamber for an indefinite period.

After approximately three weeks of the experiment proper, it was clear that the environment was generally livable and that the behavior of the subject was under good experimental control and could be extensively measured. The experiment was then continued for a total duration of 152 days in order to examine possible changes in the subject's performance as related to the duration of the experiment and in order to investigate specific manipulations within the program.

Perhaps the most general result of the experiment was found in the development of behavioral strain or stress after approximately 90 days. Although the subject remained in excellent health throughout the experiment, there were numerous indications of deteriorating performance. An examination of all aspects of the subject's performance, however, showed the effects of the duration of the confinement to be differential and specific to certain activities. An introduction to the kind of performance changes observed is presented in Figure 3, which shows the percent time spent in various activities and groups of activities throughout the course of the experiment. Examination of the percent time spent in sleep (Figure 3-A) reveals very little, if any, systematic change in the percent time measure, indicating that the subject suffered no undue sleep loss nor did he sleep excessively on the average throughout the experiment. However, measures of duration and frequency of sleep showed systematic changes during the experiment. The duration of sleep declined and the frequency increased. These changes are revealed in Figure 4, which presents the period, or what might be called the length of the subject's "day," for the duration of the experiment. The subject's day declined from an approximately 35-hour one, during the early part of the experiment, to considerably less than 24 hours near the end. The introduction of a clock into the subject's environment reduced the variability of the sleep-wake periods, but its limited removal was not sufficient to reverse the trend toward more frequent and shorter periods of sleep. These results suggest that the length of a man's day could be made to depart considerably from the normal 24-hour period provided that there is no loss in net sleep time.

In Figure 3-B is found one of the clearest indications of the build-up of stress. This figure shows an increase in percent time spent in the toilet operations activity from less than 10 percent at the beginning of the experiment to approximately 22 percent during the final stages of the experiment. Other supporting data show that the rise in total time spent in T.O. resulted only from increasing time spent in those T.O. periods followed by an excursion into the full program, and further, that the utilization of this additional time was not concerned with increased maintenance of bodily needs or care of the chamber, but rather with the emergence of time-consuming behaviors

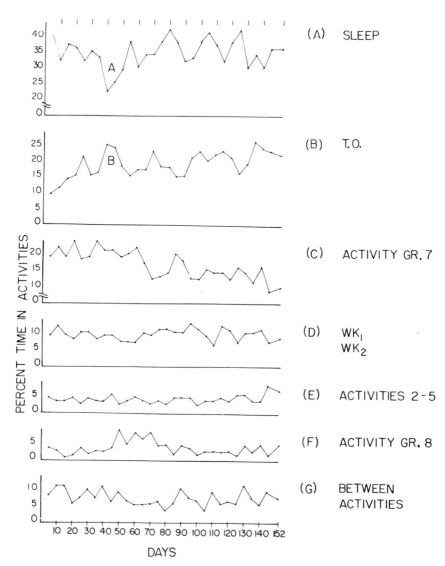

Figure 3. Distribution of percent times the subject spent in some of the activities and groups of activities for the duration of the experiment.

such as excessive sitting, resting, pacing, and general "milling about." The increasing time spent in T.O., therefore, was taken to indicate the lessened rewarding properties of the full program and as a general indicator of stress.

The increasing time spent in T.O. is most notably associated with a decline in the time spent in the group of activities involving intellectual and creative skills, namely programmed reading, use of the teletype, and the

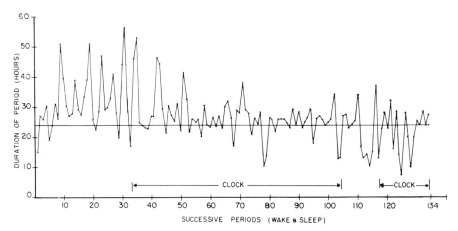

Figure 4. Duration of periods for the entire experiment; a period equals a consecutive wake and sleep period. A 24-hour period is shown by the horizontal line.

hobby activity. This result is shown in Figure 3-C, and in greater detail in Figure 5. The latter figure shows a decline in the cumulative time spent in each of these activities, particularly near the end of the experiment. It is interesting to note that the P.I., or reading activity, suffered least, perhaps because of the input of new material, and that the M.B., or hobby activity in which the subject initially did considerable oil painting, showed perhaps the greatest decline. The weakening of these types of activities, which normally depend upon some degree of social reinforcement, may have been largely responsible for the increasing time spent in T.O.

In Figure 3-D, it can be observed that the percent time spent in WK_1 and WK_2, tracking task and problem box, did not decline substantially until the final stages of the experiment. The time spent in these activities throughout the experiment was only slightly in excess of the minimum requirement; thus, the major effect of the experiment was seen in a declining accuracy of performance during the final stages. The contrast between changes in the work activities of WK_1 and WK_2 and the more creative activities of Group 7 (P.I., V.B., M.B.) is perhaps best accounted for by the differing importance of the exclusion from social reinforcement and by the more exacting requirements placed upon the subject in the two work tasks.

Other changes in the percent time data are shown in Figures 3-E, 3-F, and 3-G. In the first of these, the percent time spent in the activities F.D., W-T, P.E., and FD_1 remained relatively low and constant, except at the end of the experiment where a small but reliable rise was found. This increase, related to the increasing time spent in the snack activity, parallels the change found in T.O. Since the food quantity available in FD_1 was con-

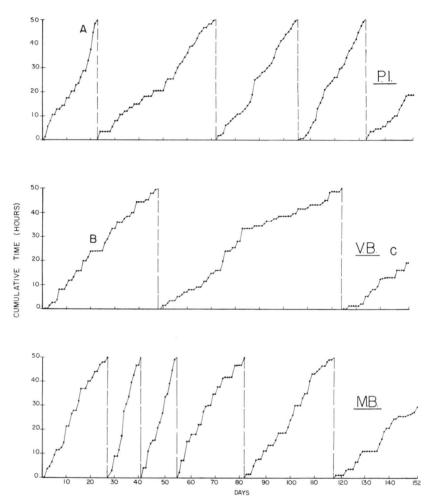

Figure 5. Cumulative time spent in P.I. (reading), V.B. (use of teletype), and M.B. (hobby activities) for each day of the experiment.

stant, the rise in time spent in this activity is taken as another indicator of stress. Presented in Figure 3-F is the percent time spent in all of the activities located in the latter part of the program. These times remained relatively low due to the modest time required to consume or obtain the rewards available within these activities. One exception can be noted, however, from approximately days 50 to 80. During this time a sub-experiment with the cost of cigarettes was in progress and the increase in time spent in the last activity group reflects the increased work requirements imposed.

The final percent time measure shown in Figure 3-G totalizes the time spent between the beginning of availability of a given activity and the exercise of this option by the subject. The lack of any systematic trend in these data generally indicates the high level of stimulus control of the overall behavioral program. In other words, the changes in the behavior of the subject which took place during the course of the experiment were reflected in the specific activities rather than in the pauses before beginning an activity. Other general indications of the degree of experimental control resulting from the behavioral program were found in the very rapid weakening of behaviors for which there were no explicit consequences provided. For example, during T.O. the subject had been trained and specifically requested prior to the beginning of the experiment to make written reports of actometer readings in order to obtain data on general activity. After the first few weeks of the experiment, the subject became so irregular in his reports that they had to be discarded. This irregularity and others of a similar nature presumably resulted from the lack of any programmed consequence.

During the course of the experiment several sub-experiments of limited duration were conducted. One of these sub-experiments came about in an attempt to reverse the growing development of strain. On day 121 of the experiment the subject was informed that the experimenters were instigating a "vacation" during which the subject would be allowed full use of the by-pass switches on the control panel. These switches made it possible for the subject to follow any one activity in the program by itself or any other activity. Once selecting an activity, however, the requirements had to be completed before selecting another. In this way the program was made maximally flexible and the subject was allowed ready access to the more rewarding activities without completing the less desired ones. During this "vacation" which lasted only 24 hours, the subject spent all of his time at first in the final part of the program consuming food, smoking, listening to music, and earning delayed reinforcements. During this period the delay associated

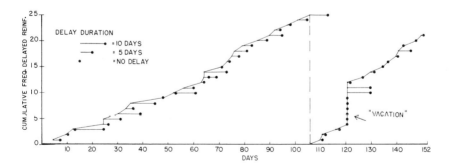

Figure 6. Cumulative frequency of earning all delayed reinfocements (REQ., V.C., and O.C.) combined into one curve. Duration of delay in delivery of reinforcement is shown by circles and horizontal lines. The curve was constructed by connecting the days on which reinforcements were earned.

with delayed reinforcements was set at a minimum. The results are shown in Figure 6. After approximately 12 hours, the supply of delayed rewards was exhausted and the normal delay was reinstated. Shortly thereafter, the subject selected the reading activity as his first selection, exclusive of those in the final part of the program and T.O. Following the reading activity the subject selected sleep and the "vacation" was ended. Although the "vacation" resulted in increased activity and a general state of euphoria in the subject, very few effects could be detected lasting more than one or two days.

In another sub-experiment, the response cost for obtaining cigarettes was increased from the normal value of 25 responses per cigarette to 500 responses per cigarette over approximately a 30-day period. The effect of this manipulation on the frequency of smoking is shown in Figure 7. The

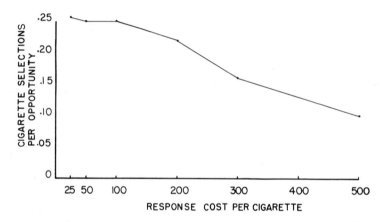

Figure 7. Relationship between selection of cigarette activity (selections/opportunities for selection) and response cost per cigarette.

decline in the frequency of selecting cigarettes reflects a decline in smoking rate from about 25 per 24 hours to 10 per 24 hours. The most interesting results of the cigarette experiment, however, were to be found in the effects this manipulation had on other activities, some of which were remote. One example of this effect can be seen in Figure 8 which shows the general decline in the use of the vacuum cleaner during T.O. The effect noted at point A shows a complete absence of use of the vacuum cleaner during the most stringent requirements of the cigarette experiment. Another example of the effects of the cigarette experiment is shown in Figure 9, which presents a plot of the cumulative frequency with which the subject selected the music activity. A depressive effect is noted from point A to point B, which again corresponds with the most difficult part of the cigarette experiment which was ended on day 78. The overall high and sustained rate with which the

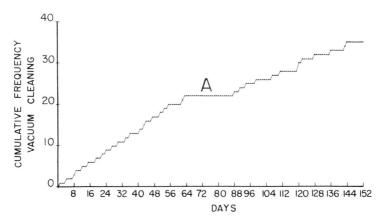

Figure 8. Cumulative frequency of use of the vacuum cleaner for the entire experiment.

subject selected the music activity throughout the experiment can be observed in Figure 9 and generally reflects the rewarding properties of such an activity to one in confinement.

The general build-up of stress indicated in some of the results presented thus far is further amplified by several measures of behavior which were concurrent with all other activities in the formal program. These two sources of data were the verbal behavior of the subject as monitored over the intercom system, and the use of the L.T.O. activity. Regarding the first of these, verbal comments from all sources were analyzed for their general negative content, and the frequency of such occurrences throughout the experiment are presented in Figure 10. It will be observed that the overall frequency of negative comments was quite low corresponding to the general well-being and cooperation of the subject. The frequency of these com-

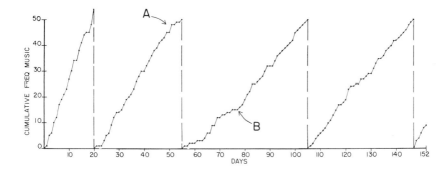

Figure 9. Cumulative frequency of selections of Music activity for each day of the experiment.

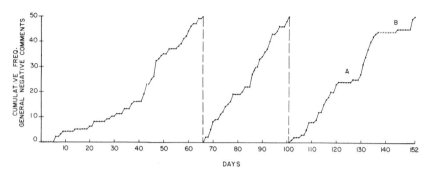

Figure 10. Cumulative frequency of general negative comments, received from intercom system, special reports, and T.O. notes, for each day of the experiment.

ments as well as their judged intensity was found to increase beyond approximately 40 days and to remain reasonably constant thereafter except at the points noted (A and B). At point A one of the few relatively lasting effects of the experimental "vacation" can be observed in the temporary decline in negative comments. At point B the quality of the food, which had been a frequent source of negative comment, was improved, which resulted in a temporary but clear decline in negative comments. The results from general negative complaints is supported in a general way by the data from the L.T.O. activity. These data are presented in Figure 11 showing a cumulative plot of the frequency with which the subject made use of the limited toilet facilities. It is apparent that the frequency with which this activity occurred increased as the experiment progressed and is perhaps best understood by the fact that this activity temporarily terminated and removed the subject from whatever activity in which he was currently engaged. The increasing frequency of L.T.O. was found in both sleep and wake activities and is a further indication of the lessened rewarding properties of the environment and the general behavioral strain of the subject.

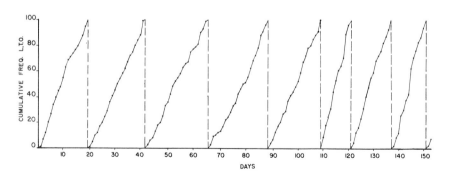

Figure 11. Cumulative frequency of selection of the Limited Toilet Operations activity for each day of the experiment.

In general, the increased frequency of L.T.O.s, the rise in frequency of general negative comments and mild somatic complaints, the increased frequency of entering the sleep activity rather than the full program, the increased duration of T.O., FD_1, and the declining time spent in the creative activities (particularly M.B. and V.B.) all combine to describe a progressive weakening of the subject's behavior during the latter phases of the experiment. The extent of this weakening is shown in the last figure contrasting the rising percent time spent in the T.O. activity with the declining percent time spent in the major work and creative activities (WK_1, WK_2, P.I., V.B., and M.B.). A striking convergence of these curves can be observed. During the last ten days of the experiment, it can be seen that not only had the functions converged, but the subject was actually spending more total time in the T.O. activity than in the work and creative activities combined. It was at this time, interestingly enough, that the experiment was terminated by joint consent of experimenters and subject. At that time neither was aware of this convergence effect.

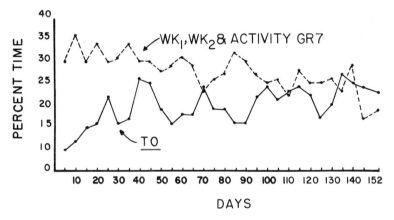

Figure 12. Percent of total time spent in Toilet Operations versus percent of total time spent in the Work Tasks and in Activity Group 7 (reading, writing, and creative activities) for the entire experiment.

During the 152 days of the experiment the subject completed the minimum program 465 times. On only six occasions did the subject select the button indicating a desire to reduce the duration of the experiment. These data, together with the excellent health of the subject and the fact that he could have terminated the experiment at any time, generally suggest that the overall environment was not highly aversive. The accumulative build-up of stress and lessened performance after approximately 90 days, therefore, resulted most likely from the extensive social isolation along with specific shortcomings of the programmed conditions. In general, it was concluded: (1) that it is feasible to maintain human subjects under continuous laboratory conditions for extensive periods of time where programmed environments are employed; (2) that the full use of specific behavioral requirements make possible good experimental control and extensive measurement of human behaviors; (3) that it is possible to make specific manipulations within the type of experimental context employed here, and that their effects may be observed upon a wide range of behaviors; and (4) that social isolation and confinement generally result in a pattern of behavioral strain, but that the specific effects are highly differential with respect to specific behaviors and the nature of the environment.

PROGRAMMED ENVIRONMENTS AS A RESEARCH METHOD

The feasibility of the study summarized above certainly does not answer all questions related to the prospects for continuous laboratory treatment of human behavior. The study does, however, suggest that laboratory confinement and measurement of the full range of human behavior may not be as difficult as first expected. If this is true, the facilitation is most likely due to the difference between the simple confinement and observation of individuals in relatively unstructured environments on the one hand, and the special features of a programmed environment on the other. In the study described, some aspects of the environment deserve particular note: (1) The environment was designed to be as comfortable and livable as possible, approximating ordinary household furnishings in contrast to furnishings of a space chamber or medical laboratory. (2) The subject was not given elaborate instructions nor asked to perform in a given manner, nor even asked to remain within the chamber for a given period. Instead, he was introduced to an environment which placed demands and required certain behaviors, however crude, for the obtaining of life's necessities and other reinforcing conditions for as long as he remained. (3) The specific program provided some degree of flexibility for the subject by way of options and some opportunity for altering the environment by means of the introduction of new materials and the like. Of particular note is the fact that these changes in the environment were, for the most part, a consequence of the subject's behavior. One obvious conclusion, based upon the results of the experiment and these characteristics of the environment, is that the management of the total affairs of an individual need not be aversive; they can in fact be reinforcing, depending upon the specific features of that management.

A final characteristic of the environment that is of critical importance here, was the provision for objective measurement of behavior and alteration of conditions. In this respect the experiment was quite successful, despite the occasional crudeness and omission of many measurements which could have been obtained with further planning. There appears to be almost no limitation or inherent difficulty in the measurement of ordinary human behaviors within a fully programmed environment when the problem is approached by requiring some minor additional behavior from the subject, by making the behavior physically impossible except under specified stimulus conditions, or both. Thus, in the experiment summarized, once an exercise task was decided upon as a required activity and placed under stimulus control, design of a suitable task which would bring the behavior under objective recording became simple. As a general example, should it be desired to measure the frequency with which a subject observed a clock, it could be easily arranged by placing the clock behind a one-way mirror, thus making the clock observable only when the subject pressed a switch illuminating a light. Such structuring of the environment for purposes of experimental control and measurement becomes increasingly easy as more and more of the subject's behavior is brought under control. Refined measurement of sleep, exercise, and food intake, for example, becomes readily obtainable in a structured environment where the subject remains continuously; and having brought these kinds of behaviors under control, a basis is established for the measurement of much more subtle behaviors and their interrelationships. It is in this sense that the development of fully programmed environments promises control and measurement of behaviors that would be extremely difficult or impossible otherwise.

It seems clear, therefore, that by the use of properly designed environments, human behavior could be measured and manipulated experimentally to a degree as yet only imagined. That such environments could be relatively desirable from the subject's point of view, particularly where they provide social interaction and special education, also seems reasonable. But questions regarding the scientific merit, the kinds of experimental problems which could be attacked, and the general usefulness of these procedures, are yet to be answered in full. It has been assumed throughout this paper that true experimental control and manipulation of human behavior will ultimately yield a far richer understanding of behavior than is presently available. The preliminary study described above is perhaps suggestive but not sufficient to validate this assumption. The only further argument that can be offered at this time, therefore, is a speculative view of what might be accomplished.

Extension of the present work could proceed in many directions. One such direction could be the use of individual programmed environments for the study of specific problems currently under study by other means. Specific questions related to sleep behavior, its onset, limitations, and reinforcing properties, would be one example. Another would be the use of programmed environments for the experimental establishment of conditioned reinforcement in humans, and analysis of the variables modifying its effectiveness and interrelationships with more fundamental reinforcement. Individual programmed environments could certainly be used to study motivational aspects of programmed instruction; they provide an ideal setting for questions related to intensive educational possibilities. They could serve as a baseline and setting for experiments in intensive psychotherapy, using conventional methods, or in conjunction with direct manipulation of environment. Also, fully programmed environments for single individuals would seem to hold considerable promise for the description of drug effects upon behavior. In this latter instance, since a wide range of ordinary human behaviors would be under careful measurement, drug action profiles affording increased predictability for clinical usage might result. Further possibilities suggest themselves if, in addition to basic behavioral manipulations, a more interdisciplinary approach were employed in the design and management of the environments. Such an approach might allow for the unraveling of many questions related to the relative importance of constitution, past history, and immediate environmental factors in human personality and individual differences.

Another promising direction for programmed environments is in the design of complexes for two or more individuals. Although the design of an environment for more than one individual poses special problems in measurement and identification, it would make possible a much richer environment for each subject and open up many additional experimental possibilities for the experimenter. A programmed environment which provided for the separate maintenance of two individuals, for example, could also provide for unique experimental control over a wide range of social interactions. By proper design, provisions could be made for each sort of social behavior to serve, in turn, both as dependent and independent variables. In one case, for example, quantitative aspects of the social performance might be the focus of attention with the contingencies governing the individual non-social conditions as the independent variable. In other instances, the opportunities for social behavior and its qualitative aspects might be manipulated to study the effects upon individual non-social performances. Such experiments might result in the clarification of many questions related to the dynamics of social interaction, their relative dependence upon individual past history versus controlling factors in the immediate environment, and the establishment and maintenance of specific social behaviors commonly agreed to be highly desirable. In the investigation of such questions, one unique advantage offered by the use of programmed environments is the prospect for measurement and control of many behaviors which underlie changes in the more obvious social behaviors. For example, in a continuous experimental environment maintaining two individuals, it would not only be possible to measure verbal interchange and performance on cooperative work tasks of a direct nature, but it would also be possible to measure and control less obvious social behaviors such as individual performance in cooking tasks, maintenance of the physical aspects of the environment, and the scheduling of temporal events, each such behavior having consequences for the other individual.

Totally controlled environments, either for individuals or for small groups, would seem to offer, in addition to extensive measurement of behavior at all levels, an opportunity for realism and duration of experimentation not presently available. Realism could be accomplished, in part, by the design of environments which would have a proper degree of isolation from the normal world and would demand considerable self-sufficiency from the subjects. The adequacy of a given design and the overall quality of the environment would seem to be the major factors in the availability of subjects and in the duration of experiments which might be possible. Social environments that included proper educational material and opportunities for personal growth, within a well-planned system, relatively free of aversive control, would probably compete sufficiently with the natural world so that duration of experimentation and subject compensation would present only minor problems for the experimenter.

The general approach to a richer experimental analysis of human behavior suggested here is not without inherent difficulties and special problems. Some of these difficulties, such as the management of data, the selection of subjects, and adequate techniques for the replication of experiments, are not substantially different from those common to most laboratory projects. They will, however, require special consideration due to the scope and demands of total environmental control.

Difficulties of another sort are the philosophical arguments raised against the ultimate usefulness of this approach. For example, it is sometimes argued that even though programmed environments might eventually be quite feasible and answer many formal questions well within the limitations of social customs, no amount of measurement and control of behavior within the walls of an artificial environment would ever supply the guidance needed for the management of human affairs in the natural world. This type of objection generally reflects the excessive practicality of contemporary behavioral science and a very weak faith in laboratory science. Most important, it embraces a limited conception of how science contributes to the natural world. The only adequate answer is that we can not really know until fully programmed environments have been given a proper try. In the meanwhile, however, it is suggested that the increased measurement and experimental control possible with programmed environments could very well result in a new order of dynamic relationships between man's behavior and his environment. Certainly to be expected would be new and improved techniques for controlling specific behaviors, and new ground rules for more effective organizations of the environment. The usefulness of such new knowledge, however, would not be a direct application to the natural world as we know it, since the relationships would apply only under certain stated conditions. What could be expected, on the other hand, is a partial restructuring of the natural world to accommodate the new techniques and to put to work those aspects of the new knowledge that had sufficient power and desirability to command their introduction.

REFERENCES

AYLLON, T., and MICHAEL, J. (1959) The psychiatric nurse as a behavioral engineer. *J. exp. Anal. Behav.*, 2, 323-334.

AZRIN, N. H. (1958) Some effects of noise on human behavior. *J. exp. Anal. Behav.*, 1, 183-200.

BIJOU, S. W. (1958) Operant extinction after fixed-interval reinforcement with young children. *J. exp. Anal. Behav.*, 1, 25-29.

FERSTER, C. B. (1961) The development of performances in autistic children in an automatically controlled environment. *J. chron. Dis.*, 13, 312-345.

FINDLEY, J. D. (1962) An experimental outline for building and exploring multi-operant behavior repertoires. *J. exp. Anal. Behav.*, Supp. vol. 5, 113-166.

FINDLEY, J. D., MIGLER, B. M., and BRADY, J. V. (1963) A long-term study of human performance in a continuously programmed experimental environment. *Technical Report*, Space Research Laboratory, University of Maryland, submitted to the National Aeronautics and Space Administration.

GOLDIAMOND, I. (1964) Stuttering and fluency as manipulable operant response classes. In L. Krasner and L. P. Ullmann (Eds.), *Research in behavior modification*. New York: Holt, Rinehart and Winston.

LINDSLEY, O. R. (1960) Characteristics of the behavior of chronic psychotics as revealed by free-operant conditioning methods. *Dis. nerv. Syst., Monogr. Suppl.*, 21, 66-78.

SKINNER, B. F. (1953) *Science and human behavior*. New York: Macmillan.

Name Index

Numbers appearing in roman type refer to the mention of the name in the regular text; numbers appearing in italics refer to the mention of the name in a list of references. Where the person referred to by an entry is the author of one or more chapters, the page numbers of the chapter(s) are printed in bold face.

Tang, P. C., 700, *715*
Tannenbaum, P. H., 793, *824*
Tatum, R., 453, *496*
Tavolga, W. N., 794, *824*
Taylor, E. D., 620 f, *632*
Teitelbaum, P., 355 f, 376, *378,* **565-608,** *605 ff,* 616, *633*
Tepperman, J., 577 f, *604*
Terrace, H. S., 18, *32,* 56, 57, 83, 91, *108,* 247, 265, *269,* **271-344,** *343,* 366, *379,* 643, *660*
Thach, J., 492, *498,* 618, 629, *632 f*
Theios, J., 522 f, *530*
Thiessen, D. D., *158*
Thomas, A. A., 693, 694, *716*
Thomas, D. G., *158*
Thomas, D. R., 334, *342*
Thomas, J., 801, *823*
Thompson, R. H., 144, *158*
Thompson, T. I., 599, *608*
Thompson, W. R., 139, 147, *152 ff*
Thorndike, E. L., 12 ff, 381, 424, 434, *447,* 794, 806, *825*
Tinbergen, N., 566, 598, *608,* 794, *825*
Tolliver, G., 612, *632*
Tolman, E. C., 290, *344,* 424, 447, 522, *530*
Tolson, W. W., 621, *632*
Towbin, E. J., 573, *608*
Travis, R. P., 600, *607*
Turrell, E. S., 623, *631 ff*
Tyler, D. W., 176, *210*
Tyler, R. M., 727, 736, 761, *788*

Ullmann, L. P., 797, 807, *822 ff*
Ulrich, R. E., 401 f, 412, 414, 440 f, *445 ff,* 802, 804, *821 ff,* 825

Valentine, W. L., 725, *785*
Van Sommers, P., 349, *377, 599, 608*
Van-Toler, C., 397, *445*
Van Wagenen, W. P., 570, *604*
Verhave, T., 227, 235, *269,* 496, 558, *564*
Verplanck, W. S., 52, *108,* 298, 302, *344,* 797, 798 ff, 807, *825 f*
Von Beckh, H. J., 712, *717*
Von Frisch, K., 794, *825*

Wade, M., 275 f, *342*
Wald, G., 593, *608*
Walk, R. D., 141, *158*
Walker, J., 454, *497*
Walker, K. C., 296, *344*

Waller, M. B., 200, *212,* 488, *498,* 539, 553, *564,* 794, *825*
Waller, Patricia, 488, *498*
Walters, R. H., 736, 757, 782, *788*
Warden, C. J., 352, 363, 375, *379*
Warner, L. H., 352, 363, 375, *379,* 793, *826*
Warrell, J. E., 692, *715*
Warren, J. M., 293, *344*
Watson, J. B., 352, *379,* 791, *826*
Watson, P. D., 738, 777, *787*
Wechkin, S., 140, *153, 158*
Weeks, J. R., 576, *608*
Weidley, E., 558, *564*
Weiner, H., 392 f, *447*
Weinstein, W. K., 807, *826*
Weisberg, P., 745 f, *757, 788*
Weiser, C. M., 793, *823*
Weiskrantz, L., 351, *378*
Weiss, B., 225, 239, *268 f,* 560 f, *564,* 590, 592, 593, *606 ff*
Weiss, R. L., 797, *823 ff*
Weisz, J. D., 623, *633*
Welch, B. E., 700, *715*
Welker, W. I., 127, 130, 134, 135, 139, 140, 147 f, *158*
Wenzel, B., 122, *158,* 611, *633*
Werboff, J., 140, *158*
Wesemann, A. F., 500, *529*
Whalen, R. E., *158,* 505, *529*
Whitman, R. N., 805, *824*
Wiggins, M. L., 579, *604*
Wilkes, W. P., *153*
Williams, C. D., 138, 139, *152 ff*
Williams, D. R., 583 ff, *608,* 616, *633*
Wilson, G. L., 686, *716*
Wilson, J. J., *159*
Wilson, M. P., 71, 98, *108*
Wilson, W. A., Jr., 244, *270*
Wilson, W. C., 797, 799 ff, *826*
Winograd, E., 387, *444*
Wishner, J., 807, *824*
Witryol, S. L., 753, *788*
Wohlford, J., *157*
Wolf, M. M., 759, *784 ff,* 803, *825*
Wolfe, J. B., 193, *212*
Wolff, H. G., *633*
Wolff, P. C., 441, *447*
Wood, W. O., 143, *151*
Woods, P. J., 142, *159*
Woodworth, R. S., 790, *826*
Woolpy, J. H., *152*
Wulff, J. J., 122, *157*
Wyckoff, L. B., 176, *212,* 290, *344,* 367, 372 f, *379,* 502, *530*
Wynne, L. C., 454, *498,* 519, 523, *530*
Wyrwicka, W., 596, 597, *603 ff*

Topical Index

The topical index is not a subject index in the usual sense, where every mention of a major subject is listed by page number. Instead, the index is based on the topical headings occurring within chapters, and the mention of a term thus implies a fairly specific discussion of that topic. But in many cases this will not be the only discussion of a particular subject, which may be mentioned elsewhere under other topics. Such discussions will not be listed, and the reader should therefore search for a subject of interest to him under a variety of possible topics under which it may be discussed.

Hunger, ingestion patterns, 571-573
  in hypothalamic hyperphagia, 580-581
  normal hunger, 570-576
  regulation, 570, 573-576
Hypothalamic aphagia and adipsia, 582-584
Hypothalamic hyperphagia, 576-582

Ingestion, operant control over, 585-590
  patterns, 571-573
Instinctive behavior, 596-603
  affective correlates, 600-603
  brain stimulation, 596-600
Instructions, in child research, 782-784
Intensity, of punishment, 396
Intermittent reinforcement, 52-108
  sensory reinforcement, 144-145
  see also Schedules of reinforcement
Intermittent shocks, in avoidance, 477-478
Interresponse time(s) (IRT), analyses of
    schedules in terms of, 67-68
  reinforcement of IRTs in FR, 74-78
  reinforcement of IRTs in VI, 73-74
  selective reinforcement (experiments),
    92-102
  terminal IRT and reinforcement, 68-70

Laboratories, for operant studies with
    children, 722-728
  for studies of early and middle child-
    hood subjects, 725-728
  for studies of infants, 725
Laboratory models, in space research,
    695-698
Light-onset reinforcement, 111-112
Light-reduction (as a reinforcer), 136-137
Limited availability schedules, 97-102

Manipulatory behavior, 114-115
Matching to sample, 640-643, 653-660
  with binary stimuli, 653-660
Mental causes in verbal behavior studies,
    805-808
Mentalistic conceptions, of verbal behav-
    ior, 790-791
Methodology, in study of verbal behavior,
    797-808
Mixed schedules, response sequences in,
    167-171
Motivation (and operant behavior), 565-608
  criteria of, 565-568
  measures of, 568-570

Motivation to respond, in punishment
    studies, 403
Multiple schedules, comparisons with
    chained schedules, 189-190
  in child research, 764-770
  with token reinforcement, 197-199
  see also Discrimination, Stimulus con-
    trol

Neurophysiological changes, 613-616,
    617-622
Noise, effects on behavior, 689-692
Novelty, 133
Number of responses available in punish-
    ment, 403-406

Operant analysis, circumvention of, 22-24
Operant behavior, 12-32
  as criterion of motivation, 565-568
  as measure of motivation, 568-570
  see also 1-11
Operant level, in verbal behavior, 800-802
Operant methods, characteristics, 2-6
  implementation in space research, 679-689
  practical advantages, 14-15

Pathology, somatic, 622-631
Physiological signals, in food and water
    intake, 573-576
Physiological states, alteration of, 609-633
  durable alterations, 616-622
  somatic pathology, 622-631
  transient changes, 610-661
  see also 565-608
Primary reinforcement, see Superstition,
    and primary reinforcement
Probability, of reinforcement in chained
    schedules, 185-187
  probability relations and schedules, 68-72
Probes, of matching-to-sample perform-
    ance, 657-658
Procuring subjects, for child research,
    729-732
Programmed environments, 827-848
  as a research method, 844-847
  for an isolated individual, 829-844
    general results, 835-839
    specific activities, 831-833
    stress, 840-844
    sub-experiments, 839-840
Programming, automatic, 5-6
  in study of arithmetic behavior, 648